# *t* DISTRIBUTION

C. I. for p⊘  **P9-DKD-508**

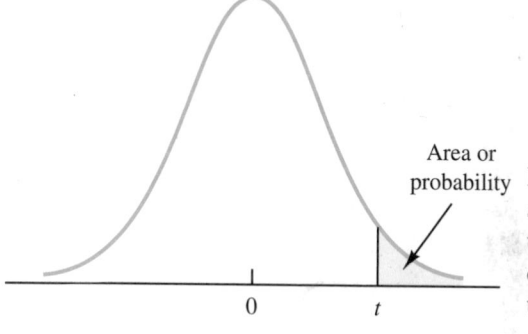

$\mu = np$

$\sigma^2 = np(1-p)$

**Area or probability** Entries in the table give *t* values for an area or probability in the upper tail of the *t* distribution. For example, with 10 degrees of freedom and a .05 area in the upper tail, $t_{.05} = 1.812$.

0    *t*

| Degrees of Freedom | Area in Upper Tail | | | | | |
|---|---|---|---|---|---|---|
| | .20 | .10 | .05 | .025 | .01 | .005 |
| 1 | 1.376 | 3.078 | 6.314 | 12.706 | 31.821 | 63.656 |
| 2 | 1.061 | 1.886 | 2.920 | 4.303 | 6.965 | 9.925 |
| 3 | .978 | 1.638 | 2.353 | 3.182 | 4.541 | 5.841 |
| 4 | .941 | 1.533 | 2.132 | 2.776 | 3.747 | 4.604 |
| 5 | .920 | 1.476 | 2.015 | 2.571 | 3.365 | 4.032 |
| 6 | .906 | 1.440 | 1.943 | 2.447 | 3.143 | 3.707 |
| 7 | .896 | 1.415 | 1.895 | 2.365 | 2.998 | 3.499 |
| 8 | .889 | 1.397 | 1.860 | 2.306 | 2.896 | 3.355 |
| 9 | .883 | 1.383 | 1.833 | 2.262 | 2.821 | 3.250 |
| 10 | .879 | 1.372 | 1.812 | 2.228 | 2.764 | 3.169 |
| 11 | .876 | 1.363 | 1.796 | 2.201 | 2.718 | 3.106 |
| 12 | .873 | 1.356 | 1.782 | 2.179 | 2.681 | 3.055 |
| 13 | .870 | 1.350 | 1.771 | 2.160 | 2.650 | 3.012 |
| 14 | .868 | 1.345 | 1.761 | 2.145 | 2.624 | 2.977 |
| 15 | .866 | 1.341 | 1.753 | 2.131 | 2.602 | 2.947 |
| 16 | .865 | 1.337 | 1.746 | 2.120 | 2.583 | 2.921 |
| 17 | .863 | 1.333 | 1.740 | 2.110 | 2.567 | 2.898 |
| 18 | .862 | 1.330 | 1.734 | 2.101 | 2.552 | 2.878 |
| 19 | .861 | 1.328 | 1.729 | 2.093 | 2.539 | 2.861 |
| 20 | .860 | 1.325 | 1.725 | 2.086 | 2.528 | 2.845 |
| 21 | .859 | 1.323 | 1.721 | 2.080 | 2.518 | 2.831 |
| 22 | .858 | 1.321 | 1.717 | 2.074 | 2.508 | 2.819 |
| 23 | .858 | 1.319 | 1.714 | 2.069 | 2.500 | 2.807 |
| 24 | .857 | 1.318 | 1.711 | 2.064 | 2.492 | 2.797 |
| 25 | .856 | 1.316 | 1.708 | 2.060 | 2.485 | 2.787 |
| 26 | .856 | 1.315 | 1.706 | 2.056 | 2.479 | 2.779 |
| 27 | .855 | 1.314 | 1.703 | 2.052 | 2.473 | 2.771 |
| 28 | .855 | 1.313 | 1.701 | 2.048 | 2.467 | 2.763 |
| 29 | .854 | 1.311 | 1.699 | 2.045 | 2.462 | 2.756 |
| 30 | .854 | 1.310 | 1.697 | 2.042 | 2.457 | 2.750 |
| 40 | .851 | 1.303 | 1.684 | 2.021 | 2.423 | 2.704 |
| 50 | .849 | 1.299 | 1.676 | 2.009 | 2.403 | 2.678 |
| 60 | .848 | 1.296 | 1.671 | 2.000 | 2.390 | 2.660 |
| 80 | .846 | 1.292 | 1.664 | 1.990 | 2.374 | 2.639 |
| 100 | .845 | 1.290 | 1.660 | 1.984 | 2.364 | 2.626 |
| ∞ | .842 | 1.282 | 1.645 | 1.960 | 2.326 | 2.576 |

*Note:* A more extensive table is provided as Table 2 of Appendix B.

# STATISTICS FOR BUSINESS AND ECONOMICS 9e

**David R. Anderson**
University of Cincinnati

**Dennis J. Sweeney**
University of Cincinnati

**Thomas A. Williams**
Rochester Institute of Technology

THOMSON

SOUTH-WESTERN

Australia · Canada · Mexico · Singapore · Spain · United Kingdom · United States

THOMSON
SOUTH-WESTERN

**Statistics for Business and Economics, 9e**

David R. Anderson, Dennis J. Sweeney, Thomas A. Williams

**VP/Editor-in-Chief:**
George Werthman

**Senior Acquisitions Editor:**
Charles E. McCormick, Jr.

**Senior Developmental Editor:**
Alice C. Denny

**Senior Marketing Manager:**
Larry Qualls

**Senior Production Editor:**
Deanna R. Quinn

**Media Technology Editor:**
Jim Rice

**Media Developmental Editor:**
Chris Wittmer

**Media Production Editor:**
Amy Wilson

**Manufacturing Coordinator:**
Diane Lohman

**Internal Design:**
Michael Stratton/Chris Miller

**Cover Design:**
Chris Miller

**Cover Image:**
Getty Images

**Production House and Compositor:**
BookMasters, Inc.

**Printer:**
R. R. Donnelley

**Library of Congress Control Number: 2003112932**

ISBN 0-324-20082-X (package)
ISBN 0-324-20083-8 (book)
ISBN 0-324-20084-6 (CD)

*Dedicated to*
*Marcia, Cherri, and Robbie*

# Brief Contents

# Contents

**Chapter 3**   Descriptive Statistics: Numerical Measures   76

## Chapter 8   Interval Estimation   297

## Chapter 9   Hypothesis Testing   336

# Chapter 13  Analysis of Variance and Experimental Design    490

The purpose of *STATISTICS FOR BUSINESS AND ECONOMICS* is to give students, primarily those in the fields of business administration and economics, a conceptual introduction to the field of statistics and its many applications. The text is applications oriented and written with the needs of the nonmathematician in mind; the mathematical prerequisite is knowledge of algebra.

Applications of data analysis and statistical methodology are an integral part of the organization and presentation of the text material. The discussion and development of each technique is presented in an application setting, with the statistical results providing insights to decisions and solution to problems.

Although the book is applications oriented, we have taken care to provide sound methodological development and to use notation that is generally accepted for the topic being covered. Hence, students will find that this text provides good preparation for the study of more advanced statistical material. A revised and updated bibliography to guide further study is included as an appendix.

# Changes in the Ninth Edition

We appreciate the acceptance and positive response to the previous editions of *STATISTICS FOR BUSINESS AND ECONOMICS*. Accordingly, in making modifications for this new edition, we have maintained the presentation style and readability of those editions. The significant changes in the new edition are summarized here.

## Content Revisions

The following list summarizes selected content revisions for the new edition.

- **New Chapter on Decision Analysis:** We have added a new Chapter 21 on decision analysis. Payoff tables, decision trees, and the development of optimal decision strategies are discussed. The Excel add-in TreePlan is available on the ASW Web site, http://asw.swlearning.com.
- **Interval Estimation:** In past editions, we have followed a large sample/small sample approach for interval estimation of a population mean in Chapter 8. In the new edition, we present interval estimation using the $\sigma$ known and $\sigma$ unknown paradigm. The standard normal distribution is used in all cases where the population standard deviation can be assumed known. The $t$ distribution is used in all cases where the population standard deviation is estimated by the sample standard deviation. This approach simplifies the methodology for the student and is consistent with computer-based procedures provided by Minitab and Excel. In the $\sigma$ unknown case, the new approach provides slightly improved results over the previous large-sample approximation. A $t$ distribution table with up to 100 degrees of freedom is included as Table 2 of Appendix B. This change carries into hypothesis tests about a population mean in Chapter 9 and statistical inferences about the means of two populations in Chapter 10.

- **Hypothesis Testing Using *p*-Values:** Another change in the new edition is the emphasis on the use of *p*-values for hypothesis testing. With more and more use of statistical software packages for data analysis, *p*-values are clearly preferred to the traditional test statistic and rejection region approach. As a result, we now use *p*-values as the primary method for hypothesis testing applications in Chapters 9 to 16.

- **New Procedure for Two Sample Inferences:** We provide new methodology for inferences about the means of two populations when the population standard deviations are unknown. The methodology is based on the *t* distribution and is more general in that it can be applied whether or not the population variances are equal. The student no longer has to consider making the equal population variance assumption and making the pooled variance calculation.

- **Logistic Regression:** We have added a new section on logistic regression in Chapter 15. Logistic regression is used for regression analyses involving a binary dependent variable. Business applications of logistic regression have been increasing in recent years as companies take advantage of large data bases to build response models. For instance, companies often use a logistic regression model to predict individual response to a promotion.

- **Descriptive Statistics:** New sections have been added on the shape of distributions in Chapters 2 and 3. Skewness is introduced as an important measure of the shape of a distribution. In later chapters, we now mention the need for larger sample sizes in interval estimation and hypothesis testing applications involving a skewed population. Crosstabulation material has been expanded to include more discussion of percentage distributions. Simpson's paradox is used to point out a source of potentially erroneous conclusions when working with crosstabulations

- **Probability Distributions:** A discussion of the mean, variance, and standard deviation has been added for the Poisson and hypergeometric distributions in Chapter 5 and the exponential distribution in Chapter 6. Chapter 6 also has a new section on the normal approximation of binomial probabilities.

- **Sampling:** Sampling Survey, Chapter 22, contains an in-depth treatment of stratified simple random sampling, cluster sampling, and systematic random sampling. This chapter is on the CD that accompanies the text.

## New Examples and Exercises Based on Real Data

We have added approximately 150 new examples and exercises based on real data and recent reference sources of statistical information. Using data pulled from sources also used by the *Wall Street Journal, USA Today, Fortune, Barron's,* and a variety of other sources, we have drawn from actual studies to develop explanations and to create exercises that demonstrate many uses of statistics in business and economics. We believe that the use of real data helps generate more student interest in the material and enables the student to learn about both the statistical methodology and its application. The ninth edition of the text contains approximately 350 examples and exercises based on real data.

## New Case Problems

We have added six new case problems to this edition, bringing the total number of case problems in the text to twenty-eight. The new case problems appear in the chapters on descriptive statistics, probability distributions, and regression. These case problems provide students with the opportunity to analyze somewhat larger data sets and prepare managerial reports based on the results of the analysis.

## New Statistics in Practice

Each chapter begins with a Statistics in Practice article that describes an application of the statistical methodology to be covered in the chapter. Statistics in Practice have been provided by practitioners at companies such as Colgate-Palmolive, Citibank, Procter & Gamble, Monsanto, and others. This edition includes three new Statistics in Practice: Food Lion (Chapter 8), John Morrell & Company (Chapter 9) and Alliance Data Systems (Chapter 14).

## New Materials for MINITAB and Microsoft® Excel

MINITAB and Excel appendices appear at the end of most chapters. These appendices provide step-by-step instructions that make it easy for students to use MINITAB or Excel to conduct the statistical analysis presented in the chapter. All appendices have been updated for the latest versions of MINITAB and Excel. Seven new and or revised appendices appear at the end of the chapters on descriptive statistics, interval estimation, hypothesis testing, and regression.

New online resources for students include EASYSTAT: DIGITAL TUTOR FOR MINITAB Release 14 and EASYSTAT: DIGITAL TUTOR FOR MICROSOFT® EXCEL. These focused online tutorials will make it easier for students to learn how to use one of these well-known software products to perform statistical analysis. In each digital video, one of the textbook authors demonstrates how the software can be used to perform a particular statistical procedure.

Students may purchase an online subscription for the MINITAB or the Excel version of EasyStat Digital Tutor at *http://easystat.swlearning.com*.

# Features and Pedagogy

We have continued many of the features that appeared in previous editions. Some of the important ones are noted here.

## Methods Exercises and Applications Exercises

The end-of-section exercises are split into two parts, Methods and Applications. The Methods exercises require students to use the formulas and make the necessary computations. The Applications exercises require students to use the chapter material in real-world situation. Thus, students first focus on the computational "nuts and bolts," then move on to the subtleties of statistical application and interpretation.

## Self-Test Exercises

Certain exercises are identified as self-test exercises. Completely worked-out solutions for those exercises are provided in Appendix D at the back of the book. Students can attempt the self-test exercises and immediately check the solution to evaluate their understanding of the concepts presented in the chapter.

## Notes and Comments

At the end of many sections, we provide Notes and Comments designed to give the student additional insights about the statistical methodology and its application. Notes and Comments include warnings about or limitations of the methodology, recommendations for application, brief descriptions of additional technical considerations, and other matters.

## Data Sets Accompany the Text

Over 200 data sets are now available on the CD-ROM that is packaged with the text. The data sets are available in both MINITAB and Excel formats. Data set logos are used in the text to identify the data sets that are available on the CD. Data sets for all case problems as well as data sets for larger exercises are also included on the CD.

# Ancillary Teaching and Learning Materials

Two print ancillaries are available to students either through their bookstore or for direct purchase through the online catalog at *www.swlearning.com.*

- Prepared by Mohammad Ahmadi of the University of Tennessee-Chattanooga, the **Work Book** (ISBN: 0-324-20086-2) will provide the student with significant supplementary study materials. It contains an outline and review, and list of formulas for each text chapter, sample exercises with step-by-step solutions, exercises with answers, and a series of self-testing questions with answers.
- Another student ancillary is the **Microsoft® Excel Companion for Business Statistics, 3e** (ISBN: 0-324-22253-9) by David Eldredge of Murray State University. This manual provides step-by-step instructions for using Excel to solve many of the problems included in introductory business statistics. Directions for the latest version of Excel are included.
- WebTutor™, an online ancillary, may be ordered as a package with the new edition of *STATISTICS FOR BUSINESS AND ECONOMICS.* WebTutor is used by an entire class under the directions of the instructor. It provides web-based learning resources to students as well as powerful communication and other course management tools including course calendar, chat, online testing, and e-mail for instructors. WebTutor is available with WebCT and Blackboard. See *webtutor.thomsonlearning.com* for more information.

The following instructor support materials are available to adopters from the Thomson Learning™ Academic Resource Center at 800-423-0563 or through **www.swlearning.com.** Some of the materials noted here may also be downloaded from the text's Instructor's Resource page at **asw.swlearning.com.**

**Instructor's Resource CD** (ISBN: 0-324-20087-0)—All instructor ancillaries are provided on a single CD-ROM. Included in this convenient format are:

- **Solutions Manual**—The Solutions Manual, prepared by the authors, includes solutions for all problems in the text.
- **Solutions to Case Problems**—Also prepared by the authors, solutions to all case problems presented in the text are included here.
- **PowerPoint™ Presentation Slides**—Prepared by John Loucks of St. Edward's University, the presentation slides incorporate graphics to help instructors create even more stimulating lectures. New for the ninth edition, the slides include animation. The slides may be adapted using PowerPoint software to facilitate classroom use.
- **Test Bank** and **ExamView Pro™**—Prepared by Mohammad Ahmadi, the Test Bank includes multiple choice questions and problems for each chapter. ExamView computerized testing software allows instructors to create, edit, store, and print exams.

# Acknowledgments

We would like to acknowledge the work of our reviewers who provided comments and suggestions of ways to continue to improve our text. Thanks to:

Philip Boudreaux, University of Louisiana

Richard Claycombe, McDaniel College

Jim Hightower, California State University, Fullerton

David A. Kravitz, George Mason University

John Leschke, University of Virginia

Ronald W. Michener, University of Virginia

Cindy Van Es, Cornell University

Yan Yu, University of Cincinnati

We continue to owe a debt to our many colleagues and friends for their helpful comments and suggestions in the development of this and earlier editions of our text. Among them are:

Mohammad Ahmadi, University of Tennessee at Chattanooga

Lari Arjomand, Clayton College and State University

Robert Balough, Clarion University

Mike Bourke, Houston Baptist University

James Brannon, University of Wisconsin–Oshkosh

John Bryant, University of Pittsburgh

Peter Bryant, University of Colorado

Terri L. Byczkowski, University of Cincinnati

Robert Carver, Stonehill College

Robert Cochran, University of Wyoming

Robert Collins, Marquette University

David W. Cravens, Texas Christian University

Tom Dahlstrom, Eastern College

Gopal Dorai, William Patterson University

Nicholas Farnum, California State University–Fullerton

Donald Gren, Salt Lake Community College

Paul Guy, California State University–Chico

Clifford Hawley, West Virginia University

Alan Humphrey, University of Rhode Island

Ann Hussein, Philadelphia College of Textiles and Science

C. Thomas Innis, University of Cincinnati

Ben Isselhardt, Rochester Institute of Technology

Jeffery Jarrett, University of Rhode Island

Ronald Klimberg, St. Joseph's University

David Krueger, St. Cloud State University

Martin S. Levy, University of Cincinnati

John S. Loucks, St. Edward's University

David Lucking-Reiley, Vanderbilt University

Bala Maniam, Sam Houston State University

Don Marx, University of Alaska, Anchorage

Tom McCullough, University of California–Berkeley

Glenn Milligan, Ohio State University

Mitchell Muesham, Sam Houston State University

Roger Myerson, Northwestern University

Richard O'Connell, Miami University of Ohio

Alan Olinsky, Bryant College

Ceyhun Ozgur, Valparaiso University

Tom Pray, Rochester Institute of Technology

Harold Rahmlow, St. Joseph's University

H. V. Ramakrishna, Penn State University at Great Valley

Tom Ryan, Case Western Reserve University

Bill Seaver, University of Tennessee

Alan Smith, Robert Morris College

Willbann Terpening, Gonzaga University

Ted Tsukahara, St. Mary's College of California

Hroki Tsurumi, Rutgers University

David Tufte, University of New Orleans

Victor Ukpolo, Austin Peay State University

Ebenge Usip, Youngstown State University

Jack Vaughn, University of Texas–El Paso

Andrew Welki, John Carroll University

Ari Wijetunga, Morehead State University

J. E. Willis, Louisiana State University

Mustafa Yilmaz, Northeastern University

Gary Yoshimoto, St. Cloud State University

Charles Zimmerman, Robert Morris College

A special thanks goes to our associates from business and industry that supplied the Statistics in Practice features. We recognize them individually by a credit line in each of the articles. Finally, we are also indebted to our senior acquisitions editor Charles McCormick, Jr., our senior developmental editor Alice Denny, our senior production editor Deanna Quinn, our senior marketing manager Larry Qualls, and others at Thomson/South-Western for their editorial counsel and support during the preparation of this text.

*David R. Anderson*
*Dennis J. Sweeney*
*Thomas A. Williams*

**David R. Anderson.**   David R. Anderson is Professor of Quantitative Analysis in the College of Business Administration at the University of Cincinnati. Born in Grand Forks, North Dakota, he earned his B.S., M.S., and Ph.D. degrees from Purdue University. Professor Anderson has served as Head of the Department of Quantitative Analysis and Operations Management and as Associate Dean of the College of Business Administration. In addition, he was the coordinator of the College's first Executive Program.

At the University of Cincinnati, Professor Anderson has taught introductory statistics for business students as well as graduate-level courses in regression analysis, multivariate analysis, and management science. He has also taught statistical courses at the Department of Labor in Washington, D.C. He has been honored with nominations and awards for excellence in teaching and excellence in service to student organizations.

Professor Anderson has coauthored ten textbooks in the areas of statistics, management science, linear programming, and production and operations management. He is an active consultant in the field of sampling and statistical methods.

**Dennis J. Sweeney.**   Dennis J. Sweeney is Professor of Quantitative Analysis and Founder of the Center for Productivity Improvement at the University of Cincinnati. Born in Des Moines, Iowa, he earned a B.S.B.A. degree from Drake University and his M.B.A. and D.B.A. degrees from Indiana University where he was an NDEA Fellow. During 1978–79, Professor Sweeney worked in the management science group at Procter & Gamble; during 1981–82, he was a visiting professor at Duke University. Professor Sweeney served as Head of the Department of Quantitative Analysis and as Associate Dean of the College of Business Administration at the University of Cincinnati.

Professor Sweeney has published more than thirty articles and monographs in the area of management science and statistics. The National Science Foundation, IBM, Procter & Gamble, Federated Department Stores, Kroger, and Cincinnati Gas & Electric have funded his research, which has been published in *Management Science*, *Operations Research*, *Mathematical Programming*, *Decision Sciences*, and other journals.

Professor Sweeney has coauthored ten textbooks in the areas of statistics, management science, linear programming, and production and operations management.

**Thomas A. Williams.**   Thomas A. Williams is Professor of Management Science in the College of Business at Rochester Institute of Technology. Born in Elmira, New York, he earned his B.S. degree at Clarkson University. He did his graduate work at Rensselaer Polytechnic Institute, where he received his M.S. and Ph.D. degrees.

Before joining the College of Business at RIT, Professor Williams served for seven years as a faculty member in the College of Business Administration at the University of Cincinnati, where he developed the undergraduate program in Information Systems and then served as its coordinator. At RIT he was the first chairman of the Decision Sciences Department. He teaches courses in management science and statistics, as well as graduate courses in regression and decision analysis.

Professor Williams is the coauthor of eleven textbooks in the areas of management science, statistics, production and operations management, and mathematics. He has been a consultant for numerous *Fortune* 500 companies and has worked on projects ranging from the use of data analysis to the development of large-scale regression models.

# CHAPTER 1

# Data and Statistics

**CONTENTS**

## BUSINESS WEEK*
*NEW YORK, NEW YORK*

With a global circulation of more than 1 million, *Business Week* is the most widely read business magazine in the world. More than 200 dedicated reporters and editors in 26 bureaus worldwide deliver a variety of articles of interest to the business and economic community. Along with feature articles on current topics, the magazine contains regular sections on International Business, Economic Analysis, Information Processing, and Science & Technology. Information in the feature articles and the regular sections help readers stay abreast of current developments and assess the impact of those developments on business and economic conditions.

Most issues of *Business Week* provide an in-depth report on a topic of current interest. Often, the in-depth reports contain statistical facts and summaries that help the reader understand the business and economic information. For example, the December 30, 2002, issue reported earnings forecasts and other statistical information for 900 companies; the January 13, 2003, issue contained a report on the best and worst managers in 2002; and the February 3, 2003, issue reported statistics on global outsourcing of white-collar jobs. In addition, the weekly *Business Week Investor* provides statistics about the state of the economy, including production indexes, stock prices, mutual funds, and interest rates.

*Business Week* also uses statistics and statistical information in managing its own business. For example, an annual survey of subscribers helps the company learn about subscriber demographics, reading habits, likely purchases, lifestyles, and so on. *Business Week* managers use the statistical summaries from the survey to provide better services to subscribers and advertisers.

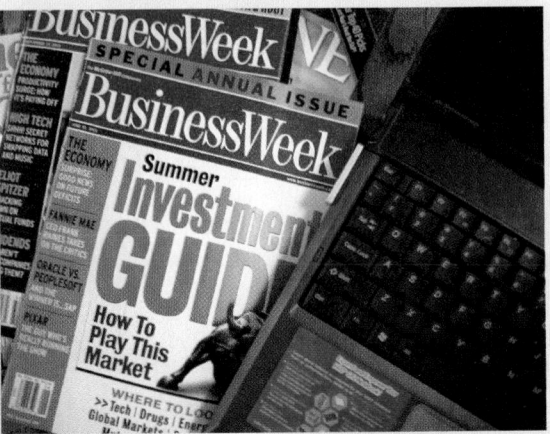

*Business Week* uses statistical facts and summaries in many of its articles. © Terri Miller/E-Visual Communications, Inc.

One recent North American subscriber survey indicated that 90% of *Business Week* subscribers use a personal computer at home and that 64% of *Business Week* subscribers are involved with computer purchases at work. Such statistics alert *Business Week* managers to subscriber interest in articles about new developments in computers. The results of the survey are also made available to potential advertisers. The high percentage of subscribers using personal computers at home and the high percentage of subscribers involved with computer purchases at work would be an incentive for a computer manufacturer to consider advertising in *Business Week*.

In this chapter, we discuss the types of data available for statistical analysis and describe how the data are obtained. We introduce descriptive statistics and statistical inference as ways of converting data into meaningful and easily interpreted statistical information.

*The authors are indebted to Charlene Trentham, Research Manager at *Business Week*, for providing this Statistics in Practice.

Frequently, we see the following kinds of statements in newspaper and magazine articles:

- Of the 16,000 foodmakers, the largest 20 now account for nearly 54% of checkout sales (*Forbes,* April 15, 2002).
- The Consumer Price Index (CPI) declined .3% in April (CNBC, May 16, 2003).
- From a database of 3458 stock funds, only 172 funds earned an A rating (*Business Week,* January 27, 2003).

- At Marriott International, more than 40% of managers worked their way up through the ranks (*Fortune*, January 20, 2003).
- The Dow Jones Industrial Average closed at 9216.79 on July 7 (*The Wall Street Journal*, July 8, 2003).
- Nokia, the world's largest and most profitable mobile phone maker, estimated an annual demand for 405 million phones (*Business Week*, June 25, 2001).

The numerical facts in the preceding statements (16,000, 20, 54%, .3%, 3458, 172, 40%, 9216.79, and 405 million) are called statistics. Thus, in everyday usage, the term *statistics* refers to numerical facts. However, the field, or subject, of statistics involves much more than numerical facts. In a broad sense, **statistics** is the art and science of collecting, analyzing, presenting, and interpreting data. Particularly in business and economics, the information provided by collecting, analyzing, presenting, and interpreting data gives managers and decision makers a better understanding of the business and economic environment and thus enables them to make more informed and better decisions. In this text, we emphasize the use of statistics for business and economic decision making.

Chapter 1 begins with some illustrations of the applications of statistics in business and economics. In Section 1.2 we define the term *data* and introduce the concept of a data set. This section also introduces key terms such as *variables* and *observations,* discusses the difference between quantitative and qualitative data, and illustrates the uses of cross-sectional and time series data. Section 1.3 discusses how data can be obtained from existing sources or through survey and experimental studies designed to obtain new data. The important role that the Internet now plays in obtaining data is also highlighted. The use of data in developing descriptive statistics and in making statistical inferences is described in Sections 1.4 and 1.5.

# 1.1    Applications in Business and Economics

In today's global business and economic environment, anyone can access vast amounts of statistical information. The most successful managers and decision makers understand the information and know how to use it effectively. In this section, we provide examples that illustrate some of the uses of statistics in business and economics.

## Accounting

Public accounting firms use statistical sampling procedures when conducting audits for their clients. For instance, suppose an accounting firm wants to determine whether the amount of accounts receivable shown on a client's balance sheet fairly represents the actual amount of accounts receivable. Usually the large number of individual accounts receivable makes reviewing and validating every account too time-consuming and expensive. As common practice in such situations, the audit staff selects a subset of the accounts called a sample. After reviewing the accuracy of the sampled accounts, the auditors draw a conclusion as to whether the accounts receivable amount shown on the client's balance sheet is acceptable.

## Finance

Financial analysts use a variety of statistical information to guide their investment recommendations. In the case of stocks, the analysts review a variety of financial data including price/earnings ratios and dividend yields. By comparing the information for an individual stock with information about the stock market averages, a financial analyst can begin to draw a conclusion as to whether an individual stock is over- or underpriced. For example, *Barron's* (January 6, 2003) reported that the average price/earnings ratio for the 30 stocks in the Dow Jones Industrial Average was 22.36. General Electric showed a price/earnings ratio of 16. In this case, the statistical information on price/earnings ratios indicated a lower price in comparison to earnings for General Electric than the average for the Dow Jones stocks. Therefore, a financial analyst might conclude that General Electric was underpriced. This and other information about General Electric would help the analyst make a buy, sell, or hold recommendation for the stock.

## Marketing

Electronic scanners at retail checkout counters collect data for a variety of marketing research applications. For example, data suppliers such as ACNielsen and Information Resources, Inc., purchase point-of-sale scanner data from grocery stores, process the data, and then sell statistical summaries of the data to manufacturers. Manufacturers spend hundreds of thousands of dollars per product category to obtain this type of scanner data. Manufacturers also purchase data and statistical summaries on promotional activities such as special pricing and the use of in-store displays. Brand managers can review the scanner statistics and the promotional activity statistics to gain a better understanding of the relationship between promotional activities and sales. Such analyses often prove helpful in establishing future marketing strategies for the various products.

## Production

Today's emphasis on quality makes quality control an important application of statistics in production. A variety of statistical quality control charts are used to monitor the output of a production process. In particular, an $x$-bar chart can be used to monitor the average output. Suppose, for example, that a machine fills containers with 12 ounces of a soft drink. Periodically, a production worker selects a sample of containers and computes the average number of ounces in the sample. This average, or $x$-bar value, is plotted on an $x$-bar chart. A plotted value above the chart's upper control limit indicates overfilling, and a plotted value below the chart's lower control limit indicates underfilling. The process is termed "in control" and allowed to continue as long as the plotted $x$-bar values fall between the chart's upper and lower control limits. Properly interpreted, an $x$-bar chart can help determine when adjustments are necessary to correct a production process.

## Economics

Economists frequently provide forecasts about the future of the economy or some aspect of it. They use a variety of statistical information in making such forecasts. For instance, in forecasting inflation rates, economists use statistical information on such indicators as the Producer Price Index, the unemployment rate, and manufacturing capacity utilization. Often these statistical indicators are entered into computerized forecasting models that predict inflation rates.

Applications of statistics such as those described in this section are an integral part of this text. Such examples provide an overview of the breadth of statistical applications. To supplement these examples, practitioners in the fields of business and economics provided chapter-opening Statistics in Practice articles that introduce the material covered in each chapter. The Statistics in Practice applications show the importance of statistics in a wide variety of business and economic situations.

## 1.2    Data

**Data** are the facts and figures collected, analyzed, and summarized for presentation and interpretation. All the data collected in a particular study are referred to as the **data set** for the study. Table 1.1 shows a data set containing information for 25 of the shadow stocks tracked by the American Association of Individual Investors. Shadow stocks are common stocks of smaller companies that are not closely followed by Wall Street analysts.

### Elements, Variables, and Observations

**Elements** are the entities on which data are collected. For the data set in Table 1.1, each individual company's stock is an element; the element names appear in the first column. With 25 stocks, the data set contains 25 elements.

**TABLE 1.1    DATA SET FOR 25 SHADOW STOCKS**

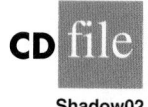

Shadow02

| Company | Exchange | Ticker Symbol | Market Cap ($ millions) | Price/ Earnings Ratio | Gross Profit Margin (%) |
|---|---|---|---|---|---|
| DeWolfe Companies | AMEX | DWL | 36.4 | 8.4 | 36.7 |
| North Coast Energy | OTC | NCEB | 52.5 | 6.2 | 59.3 |
| Hansen Natural Corp. | OTC | HANS | 41.1 | 14.6 | 44.8 |
| MarineMax, Inc. | NYSE | HZO | 111.5 | 7.2 | 23.8 |
| Nanometrics Incorporated | OTC | NANO | 228.6 | 38.0 | 53.3 |
| TeamStaff, Inc. | OTC | TSTF | 92.1 | 33.5 | 4.1 |
| Environmental Tectonics | AMEX | ETC | 51.1 | 35.8 | 35.9 |
| Measurement Specialties | AMEX | MSS | 101.8 | 26.8 | 37.6 |
| SEMCO Energy, Inc. | NYSE | SEN | 193.4 | 18.7 | 23.6 |
| Party City Corporation | OTC | PCTY | 97.2 | 15.9 | 36.4 |
| Embrex, Inc. | OTC | EMBX | 136.5 | 18.9 | 59.5 |
| Tech/Ops Sevcon, Inc. | AMEX | TO | 23.2 | 20.7 | 35.7 |
| ARCADIS NV | OTC | ARCAF | 173.4 | 8.8 | 9.6 |
| Qiao Xing Universal Tele. | OTC | XING | 64.3 | 22.1 | 30.8 |
| Energy West Incorporated | OTC | EWST | 29.1 | 9.7 | 16.3 |
| Barnwell Industries, Inc. | AMEX | BRN | 27.3 | 7.4 | 73.4 |
| Innodata Corporation | OTC | INOD | 66.1 | 11.0 | 29.6 |
| Medical Action Industries | OTC | MDCI | 137.1 | 26.9 | 30.6 |
| Instrumentarium Corp. | OTC | INMRY | 240.9 | 3.6 | 52.1 |
| Petroleum Development | OTC | PETD | 95.9 | 6.1 | 19.4 |
| Drexler Technology Corp. | OTC | DRXR | 233.6 | 45.6 | 53.6 |
| Gerber Childrenswear Inc. | NYSE | GCW | 126.9 | 7.9 | 25.8 |
| Gaiam, Inc. | OTC | GAIA | 295.5 | 68.2 | 60.7 |
| Artesian Resources Corp. | OTC | ARTNA | 62.8 | 20.5 | 45.5 |
| York Water Company | OTC | YORW | 92.2 | 22.9 | 74.2 |

*Source:* American Association of Individual Investors, available at http://www.aaii.com (accessed February 2002).

A **variable** is a characteristic of interest for the elements. The data set in Table 1.1 includes the following five variables:

- *Exchange:* Where the stock is traded—NYSE (New York Stock Exchange), AMEX (American Stock Exchange), and OTC (over-the-counter)
- *Ticker Symbol:* The abbreviation used to identify the stock on the exchange listing
- *Market Cap:* Total value of company (share price multiplied by number of shares outstanding)
- *Price/Earnings Ratio:* Market price per share divided by the most recent 12 months' earnings per share
- *Gross Profit Margin:* Gross profit as a percent of sales

Measurements collected on each variable for every element in a study provide the data. The set of measurements obtained for a particular element is called an **observation**. Referring to Table 1.1, we see that the set of measurements for the first observation (DeWolfe Companies) is AMEX, DWL, 36.4, 8.4, and 36.7. The set of measurements for the second observation (North Coast Energy) is OTC, NCEB, 52.5, 6.2, and 59.3; and so on. A data set with 25 elements contains 25 observations.

## Scales of Measurement

Data collection requires one of the following scales of measurement: nominal, ordinal, interval, or ratio. The scale of measurement determines the amount of information contained in the data and indicates the most appropriate data summarization and statistical analyses.

When the data for a variable consist of labels or names used to identify an attribute of the element, the scale of measurement is considered a **nominal scale**. For example, referring to the data in Table 1.1, we see that the scale of measurement for the exchange variable is nominal because NYSE, AMEX, and OTC are labels used to identify where the company's stock is traded. In cases where the scale of measurement is nominal, a numeric code as well as nonnumeric labels may be used. For example, to facilitate data collection and to prepare the data for entry into a computer database, we might use a numeric code by letting 1 denote the New York Stock Exchange, 2 denote the American Stock Exchange, and 3 denote over-the-counter. In this case the numeric values 1, 2, and 3 provide the labels used to identify where the stock is traded. The scale of measurement is nominal even though the data appear as numeric values.

The scale of measurement for a variable is called an **ordinal scale** if the data exhibit the properties of nominal data and the order or rank of the data is meaningful. For example, Eastside Automotive sends customers a questionnaire designed to obtain data on the quality of its automotive repair service. Each customer provides a repair service rating of excellent, good, or poor. Because the data obtained are the labels—excellent, good, or poor—the data have the properties of nominal data. In addition, the data can be ranked, or ordered, with respect to the service quality. Data recorded as excellent indicate the best service, followed by good and then poor. Thus, the scale of measurement is ordinal. Note that the ordinal data can also be recorded using a numeric code. For example, we could use 1 for excellent, 2 for good, and 3 for poor to maintain the properties of ordinal data. Thus, data for an ordinal scale may be either nonnumeric or numeric.

The scale of measurement for a variable becomes an **interval scale** if the data show the properties of ordinal data and the interval between values is expressed in terms of a fixed unit of measure. Interval data are always numeric. Scholastic Aptitude Test (SAT) scores are an example of interval-scaled data. For example, three students with SAT scores of 1120, 1050, and 970 can be ranked or ordered in terms of best performance to poorest performance. In addition, the differences between the scores are meaningful. For instance, student 1 scored $1120 - 1050 = 70$ points more than student 2, while student 2 scored $1050 - 970 = 80$ points more than student 3.

The scale of measurement for a variable is a **ratio scale** if the data have all the properties of interval data and the ratio of two values is meaningful. Variables such as distance, height, weight, and time use the ratio scale of measurement. This scale requires that a zero value be included to indicate that nothing exists for the variable at the zero point. For example, consider the cost of an automobile. A zero value for the cost would indicate that the automobile has no cost and is free. In addition, if we compare the cost of $30,000 for one automobile to the cost of $15,000 for a second automobile, the ratio property shows that the first automobile is $30,000/$15,000 = 2$ times, or twice, the cost of the second automobile.

## Qualitative and Quantitative Data

*Qualitative data are often referred to as categorical data.*

Data can be further classified as either qualitative or quantitative. **Qualitative data** include labels or names used to identify an attribute of each element. Qualitative data use either the nominal or ordinal scale of measurement and may be nonnumeric or numeric. **Quantitative data** require numeric values that indicate how much or how many. Quantitative data are obtained using either the interval or ratio scale of measurement.

*The statistical method appropriate for summarizing data depends upon whether the data are qualitative or quantitative.*

A **qualitative variable** is a variable with qualitative data, and a **quantitative variable** is a variable with quantitative data. The statistical analysis appropriate for a particular variable depends upon whether the variable is qualitative or quantitative. If the variable is qualitative, the statistical analysis is rather limited. We can summarize qualitative data by counting the number of observations in each qualitative category or by computing the proportion of the observations in each qualitative category. However, even when the qualitative data use a numeric code, arithmetic operations such as addition, subtraction, multiplication, and division do not provide meaningful results. Section 2.1 discusses ways for summarizing qualitative data.

On the other hand, arithmetic operations often provide meaningful results for a quantitative variable. For example, for a quantitative variable, the data may be added and then divided by the number of observations to compute the average value. This average is usually meaningful and easily interpreted. In general, more alternatives for statistical analysis are possible when the data are quantitative. Section 2.2 and Chapter 3 provide ways of summarizing quantitative data.

## Cross-Sectional and Time Series Data

For purposes of statistical analysis, distinguishing between cross-sectional data and time series data is important. **Cross-sectional data** are data collected at the same or approximately the same point in time. The data in Table 1.1 are cross-sectional because they describe the five variables for the 25 shadow stocks at the same point in time. **Time series data** are data collected over several time periods. For example, Figure 1.1 provides a graph of the U.S. city average price per gallon for unleaded regular gasoline. It shows a sharp increase in the average price during March–April 2002, followed by a rather stable average price per gallon in the $1.40 to $1.47 range over the rest of the year. Most of the statistical methods presented in this text apply to cross-sectional rather than time series data.

FIGURE 1.1    U.S. CITY AVERAGE PRICE PER GALLON FOR UNLEADED
REGULAR GASOLINE

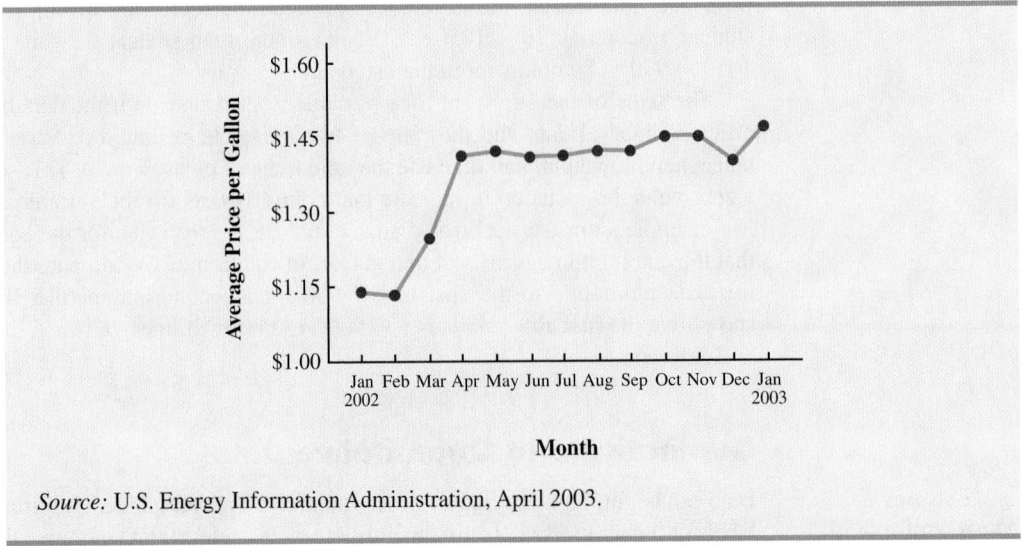

*Source:* U.S. Energy Information Administration, April 2003.

## NOTES AND COMMENTS

1. An observation is the set of measurements obtained for each element in a data set. Hence, the number of observations is always the same as the number of elements. The number of measurements obtained for each element equals the number of variables. Hence, the total number of data items can be determined by multiplying the number of observations by the number of variables.

2. Quantitative data may be discrete or continuous. Quantitative data that measure how many are discrete. Quantitative data that measure how much are continuous because no separation occurs between the possible data values.

 **Data Sources**

Data can be obtained from existing sources or from surveys and experimental studies designed to collect new data.

### Existing Sources

In some cases, data needed for a particular application already exist. Companies maintain a variety of databases about their employees, customers, and business operations. Data on employee salaries, ages, and years of experience can usually be obtained from internal personnel records. Other internal records contain data on sales, advertising expenditures, distribution costs, inventory levels, and production quantities. Most companies also maintain detailed data about their customers. Table 1.2 shows some of the data commonly available from internal company records.

Organizations that specialize in collecting and maintaining data make available substantial amounts of business and economic data. Companies access these external data sources through leasing arrangements or by purchase. Dun & Bradstreet, Bloomberg, and Dow Jones & Company are three firms that provide extensive business database services

**TABLE 1.2    EXAMPLES OF DATA AVAILABLE FROM INTERNAL COMPANY RECORDS**

| Source | Some of the Data Typically Available |
|---|---|
| Employee records | Name, address, social security number, salary, number of vacation days, number of sick days, and bonus |
| Production records | Part or product number, quantity produced, direct labor cost, and materials cost |
| Inventory records | Part or product number, number of units on hand, reorder level, economic order quantity, and discount schedule |
| Sales records | Product number, sales volume, sales volume by region, and sales volume by customer type |
| Credit records | Customer name, address, phone number, credit limit, and accounts receivable balance |
| Customer profile | Age, gender, income level, household size, address, and preferences |

to clients. ACNielsen and Information Resources, Inc., built successful businesses collecting and processing data that they sell to advertisers and product manufacturers.

Data are also available from a variety of industry associations and special interest organizations. The Travel Industry Association of America maintains travel-related information such as the number of tourists and travel expenditures by states. Such data would be of interest to firms and individuals in the travel industry. The Graduate Management Admission Council maintains data on test scores, student characteristics, and graduate management education programs. Most of the data from these types of sources are available to qualified users at a modest cost.

The Internet continues to grow as an important source of data and statistical information. Almost all companies maintain Web sites that provide general information about the company as well as data on sales, number of employees, number of products, product prices, and product specifications. In addition, a number of companies now specialize in making information available over the Internet. As a result, one can obtain access to stock quotes, meal prices at restaurants, salary data, and an almost infinite variety of information.

Government agencies are another important source of existing data. For instance, the U.S. Department of Labor maintains considerable data on employment rates, wage rates, size of the labor force, and union membership. Table 1.3 lists selected governmental agencies and some of the data they provide. Most government agencies that collect and process data also make the results available through a Web site. For instance, the U.S. Census Bureau has a wealth of data at its Web site, www.census.gov. Figure 1.2 shows the homepage for the U.S. Census Bureau.

## Statistical Studies

*The largest experimental statistical study ever conducted is believed to be the 1954 Public Health Service experiment for the Salk polio vaccine. Nearly 2 million children in grades 1, 2, and 3 were selected from throughout the United States.*

Sometimes the data needed for a particular application are not available through existing sources. In such cases, the data can often be obtained by conducting a statistical study. Statistical studies can be classified as either *experimental* or *observational*.

In an experimental study, a variable of interest is first identified. Then one or more other variables are identified and controlled so that data can be obtained about how they influence the variable of interest. For example, a pharmaceutical firm might be interested in conducting an experiment to learn about how a new drug affects blood pressure. Blood pressure is the variable of interest in the study. The dosage level of the new drug is another variable that is hoped to have a causal effect on blood pressure. To obtain data about the effect of the new drug, researchers select a sample of individuals. The dosage level of the new drug

**TABLE 1.3   EXAMPLES OF DATA AVAILABLE FROM SELECTED GOVERNMENT AGENCIES**

| Government Agency | Some of the Data Available |
|---|---|
| Census Bureau<br>*http://www.census.gov* | Population data, number of households, and household income |
| Federal Reserve Board<br>*http://www.federalreserve.gov* | Data on the money supply, installment credit, exchange rates, and discount rates |
| Office of Management and Budget<br>*http://www.whitehouse.gov/omb* | Data on revenue, expenditures, and debt of the federal government |
| Department of Commerce<br>*http://www.doc.gov* | Data on business activity, value of shipments by industry, level of profits by industry, and growing and declining industries |
| Bureau of Labor Statistics<br>*http://www.bls.gov* | Consumer spending, hourly earnings, unemployment rate, safety records, and international statistics |

**FIGURE 1.2   U.S. CENSUS BUREAU HOMEPAGE**

is controlled, as different groups of individuals are given different dosage levels. Before and after data on blood pressure are collected for each group. Statistical analysis of the experimental data can help determine how the new drug affects blood pressure.

*Studies of smokers and nonsmokers are observational studies because researchers do not determine or control who will smoke and who will not smoke.*

Nonexperimental, or observational, statistical studies make no attempt to control the variables of interest. A survey is perhaps the most common type of observational study. For instance, in a personal interview survey, research questions are first identified. Then a questionnaire is designed and administered to a sample of individuals. Some restaurants use observational studies to obtain data about their customers' opinions of the quality of food, service, atmosphere, and so on. A questionnaire used by the Lobster Pot Restaurant in Redington Shores, Florida, is shown in Figure 1.3. Note that the customers completing the questionnaire are asked to provide ratings for five variables: food quality, friendliness of service, promptness of service, cleanliness, and management. The response categories of excellent, good, satisfactory, and unsatisfactory provide ordinal data that enable Lobster Pot's managers to assess the quality of the restaurant's operation.

Managers wanting to use data and statistical analyses as an aid to decision making must be aware of the time and cost required to obtain the data. The use of existing data sources is desirable when data must be obtained in a relatively short period of time. If important data are not readily available from an existing source, the additional time and cost involved in obtaining the data must be taken into account. In all cases, the decision maker should consider the contribution of the statistical analysis to the decision-making process. The cost

**FIGURE 1.3**    CUSTOMER OPINION QUESTIONNAIRE USED BY THE LOBSTER POT RESTAURANT, REDINGTON SHORES, FLORIDA

The
LOBSTER
Pot
RESTAURANT

*W*e are happy you stopped by the Lobster Pot Restaurant and want to make sure you will come back. So, if you have a little time, we will really appreciate it if you will fill out this card. Your comments and suggestions are extremely important to us. Thank you!

Server's Name _____

|  | Excellent | Good | Satisfactory | Unsatisfactory |
|---|---|---|---|---|
| Food Quality | ❑ | ❑ | ❑ | ❑ |
| Friendly Service | ❑ | ❑ | ❑ | ❑ |
| Prompt Service | ❑ | ❑ | ❑ | ❑ |
| Cleanliness | ❑ | ❑ | ❑ | ❑ |
| Management | ❑ | ❑ | ❑ | ❑ |

Comments _____

_____

What prompted your visit to us? _____

_____

Please drop in suggestion box at entrance. Thank you.

of data acquisition and the subsequent statistical analysis should not exceed the savings generated by using the information to make a better decision.

### Data Acquisition Errors

Managers should always be aware of the possibility of data errors in statistical studies. Using erroneous data can be worse than not using any data at all. An error in data acquisition occurs whenever the data value obtained is not equal to the true or actual value that would be obtained with a correct procedure. Such errors can occur in a number of ways. For example, an interviewer might make a recording error, such as a transposition in writing the age of a 24-year-old person as 42, or the person answering an interview question might misinterpret the question and provide an incorrect response.

Experienced data analysts take great care in collecting and recording data to ensure that errors are not made. Special procedures can be used to check for internal consistency of the data. For instance, such procedures would indicate that the analyst should review the accuracy of data for a respondent shown to be 22 years of age but reporting 20 years of work experience. Data analysts also review data with unusually large and small values, called outliers, which are candidates for possible data errors. In Chapter 3 we present some of the methods statisticians use to identify outliers.

Errors often occur during data acquisition. Blindly using any data that happen to be available or using data that were acquired with little care can result in misleading information and bad decisions. Thus, taking steps to acquire accurate data can help ensure reliable and valuable decision-making information.

 ## Descriptive Statistics

Most of the statistical information in newspapers, magazines, company reports, and other publications consists of data that are summarized and presented in a form that is easy for the reader to understand. Such summaries of data, which may be tabular, graphical, or numerical, are referred to as **descriptive statistics**.

Refer again to the data set in Table 1.1 showing data on 25 shadow stocks. Methods of descriptive statistics can be used to provide summaries of the information in this data set. For example, a tabular summary of the data for the qualitative variable Exchange is shown in Table 1.4. A graphical summary of the same data, called a bar graph, is shown in Figure 1.4. These types of tabular and graphical summaries generally make the data easier to interpret. Referring to Table 1.4 and Figure 1.4, we can see easily that the majority of the stocks in the data set are traded over the counter. On a percentage basis, 68% are traded over the counter, 20% are traded on the American Stock Exchange, and 12% are traded on the New York Stock Exchange.

A graphical summary of the data for the quantitative variable Gross Profit Margin for the shadow stocks, called a histogram, is provided in Figure 1.5. The histogram makes it

**TABLE 1.4**   FREQUENCIES AND PERCENT FREQUENCIES FOR THE EXCHANGE VARIABLE

| Exchange | Frequency | Percent Frequency |
|---|---|---|
| New York Stock Exchange (NYSE) | 3 | 12 |
| American Stock Exchange (AMEX) | 5 | 20 |
| Over-the-counter (OTC) | 17 | 68 |
| Totals | 25 | 100 |

FIGURE 1.4    BAR GRAPH FOR THE EXCHANGE VARIABLE

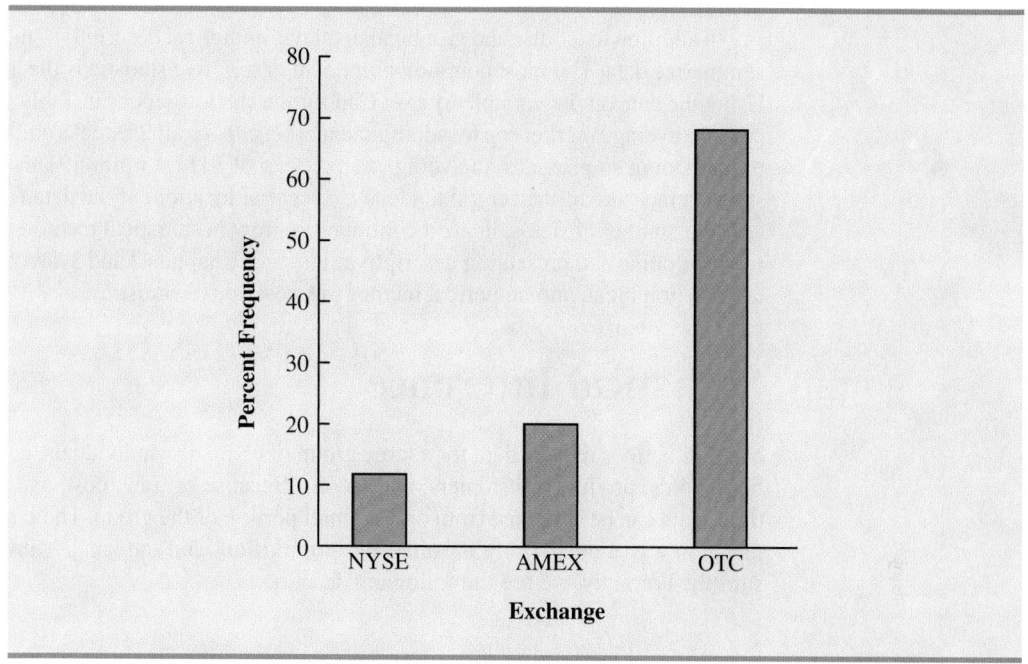

FIGURE 1.5    HISTOGRAM OF GROSS PROFIT MARGIN (%) FOR 25 SHADOW STOCKS

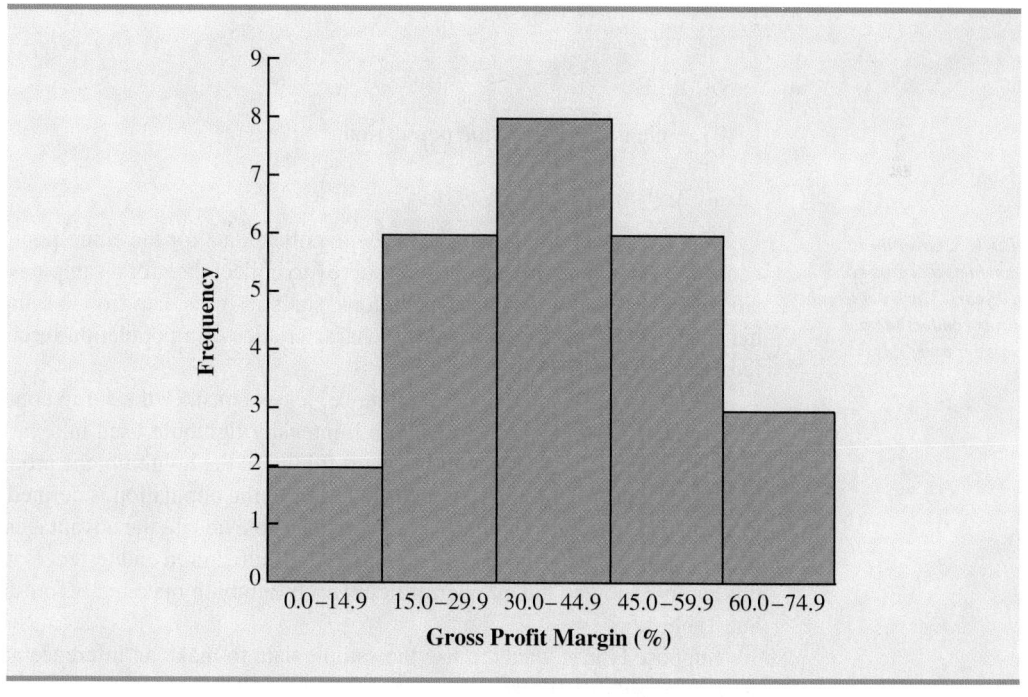

easy to see that the gross profit margins range from 0.0 to 74.9, with the highest concentrations between 30.0 and 44.9.

In addition to tabular and graphical displays, numerical descriptive statistics are used to summarize data. The most common numerical descriptive statistic is the average, or mean. Using the data on the variable Market Cap for the shadow stocks in Table 1.1, we can compute the average market cap by adding the market cap for all 25 stocks and dividing the sum by 25. Doing so provides an average market cap of $112.4 million. This average demonstrates a measure of the central tendency, or central location, of the data for that variable.

In a number of fields, interest continues to grow in statistical methods that can be used for developing and presenting descriptive statistics. Chapters 2 and 3 devote attention to the tabular, graphical, and numerical methods of descriptive statistics.

 # Statistical Inference

Many situations require data for a large group of elements (individuals, companies, voters, households, products, customers, and so on). Because of time, cost, and other considerations, data can be collected from only a small portion of the group. The larger group of elements in a particular study is called the **population**, and the smaller group is called the **sample**. Formally, we use the following definitions.

> **POPULATION**
>
> A *population* is the set of all elements of interest in a particular study.

> **SAMPLE**
>
> A sample is a subset of the population.

*The U.S. government conducts a census every 10 years. Market research firms conduct sample surveys every day.*

The process of conducting a survey to collect data for the entire population is called a **census**. The process of conducting a survey to collect data for a sample is called a **sample survey**. As one of its major contributions, statistics uses data from a sample to make estimates and test hypotheses about the characteristics of a population through a process referred to as **statistical inference**.

As an example of statistical inference, let us consider the study conducted by Norris Electronics. Norris manufactures a high-intensity lightbulb used in a variety of electrical products. In an attempt to increase the useful life of the lightbulb, the product design group developed a new lightbulb filament. In this case, the population is defined as all lightbulbs that could be produced with the new filament. To evaluate the advantages of the new filament, 200 bulbs with the new filament were manufactured and tested. Data collected from this sample showed the number of hours each lightbulb operated before filament burnout. See Table 1.5.

Suppose Norris wants to use the sample data to make an inference about the average hours of useful life for the population of all lightbulbs that could be produced with the new filament. Adding the 200 values in Table 1.5 and dividing the total by 200 provides the sample average lifetime for the lightbulbs: 76 hours. We can use this sample result to estimate that the average lifetime for the lightbulbs in the population is 76 hours. Figure 1.6 provides a graphical summary of the statistical inference process for Norris Electronics.

**TABLE 1.5    HOURS UNTIL BURNOUT FOR A SAMPLE OF 200 LIGHTBULBS FOR THE NORRIS ELECTRONICS EXAMPLE**

| | | | | | | | | | |
|---|---|---|---|---|---|---|---|---|---|
| 107 | 73  | 68 | 97  | 76  | 79 | 94 | 59 | 98 | 57  |
| 54  | 65  | 71 | 70  | 84  | 88 | 62 | 61 | 79 | 98  |
| 66  | 62  | 79 | 86  | 68  | 74 | 61 | 82 | 65 | 98  |
| 62  | 116 | 65 | 88  | 64  | 79 | 78 | 79 | 77 | 86  |
| 74  | 85  | 73 | 80  | 68  | 78 | 89 | 72 | 58 | 69  |
| 92  | 78  | 88 | 77  | 103 | 88 | 63 | 68 | 88 | 81  |
| 75  | 90  | 62 | 89  | 71  | 71 | 74 | 70 | 74 | 70  |
| 65  | 81  | 75 | 62  | 94  | 71 | 85 | 84 | 83 | 63  |
| 81  | 62  | 79 | 83  | 93  | 61 | 65 | 62 | 92 | 65  |
| 83  | 70  | 70 | 81  | 77  | 72 | 84 | 67 | 59 | 58  |
| 78  | 66  | 66 | 94  | 77  | 63 | 66 | 75 | 68 | 76  |
| 90  | 78  | 71 | 101 | 78  | 43 | 59 | 67 | 61 | 71  |
| 96  | 75  | 64 | 76  | 72  | 77 | 74 | 65 | 82 | 86  |
| 66  | 86  | 96 | 89  | 81  | 71 | 85 | 99 | 59 | 92  |
| 68  | 72  | 77 | 60  | 87  | 84 | 75 | 77 | 51 | 45  |
| 85  | 67  | 87 | 80  | 84  | 93 | 69 | 76 | 89 | 75  |
| 83  | 68  | 72 | 67  | 92  | 89 | 82 | 96 | 77 | 102 |
| 74  | 91  | 76 | 83  | 66  | 68 | 61 | 73 | 72 | 76  |
| 73  | 77  | 79 | 94  | 63  | 59 | 62 | 71 | 81 | 65  |
| 73  | 63  | 63 | 89  | 82  | 64 | 85 | 92 | 64 | 73  |

**CD** file

**Norris**

Whenever statisticians use a sample to estimate a population characteristic of interest, they usually provide a statement of the quality, or precision, associated with the estimate. For the Norris example, the statistician might state that the point estimate of the average lifetime for the population of new lightbulbs is 76 hours with a margin of error of ±4 hours. Thus, an interval estimate of the average lifetime for all lightbulbs produced with the new filament is 72 hours to 80 hours. The statistician can also state

**FIGURE 1.6    THE PROCESS OF STATISTICAL INFERENCE FOR THE NORRIS ELECTRONICS EXAMPLE**

how confident he or she is that the interval from 72 hours to 80 hours contains the population average.

 ## Computers and Statistical Analysis

Because statistical analysis typically involves large amounts of data, analysts frequently use computer software for this work. For instance, computing the average lifetime for the 200 lightbulbs in the Norris Electronics example (see Table 1.5) would be quite tedious without a computer. To facilitate computer usage, the larger data sets in this book are available on the CD that accompanies the text. A logo in the left margin of the text (e.g., Norris) identifies each of these data sets. The data files are available in both Minitab and Excel formats. In addition, we provide instructions in chapter appendixes for carrying out many of the statistical procedures using Minitab and Excel.

## Summary

Statistics is the art and science of collecting, analyzing, presenting, and interpreting data. Nearly every college student majoring in business or economics is required to take a course in statistics. We began the chapter by describing typical statistical applications for business and economics.

Data consist of the facts and figures that are collected and analyzed. Four scales of measurement used to obtain data on a particular variable include nominal, ordinal, interval, and ratio. The scale of measurement for a variable is nominal when the data use labels or names to identify an attribute of an element. The scale is ordinal if the data demonstrate the properties of nominal data and the order or rank of the data is meaningful. The scale is interval if the data demonstrate the properties of ordinal data and the interval between values is expressed in terms of a fixed unit of measure. Finally, the scale of measurement is ratio if the data show all the properties of interval data and the ratio of two values is meaningful.

For purposes of statistical analysis, data can be classified as qualitative or quantitative. Qualitative data use labels or names to identify an attribute of each element. Qualitative data use either the nominal or ordinal scale of measurement and may be nonnumeric or numeric. Quantitative data are numeric values that indicate how much or how many. Quantitative data use either the interval or ratio scale of measurement. Ordinary arithmetic operations are meaningful only if the data are quantitative. Therefore, statistical computations used for quantitative data are not always appropriate for qualitative data.

In Sections 1.4 and 1.5 we introduced the topics of descriptive statistics and statistical inference. Descriptive statistics are the tabular, graphical, and numerical methods used to summarize data. The process of statistical inference uses data obtained from a sample to make estimates or test hypotheses about the characteristics of a population. In the last section of the chapter we noted that computers facilitate statistical analysis. The larger data sets contained in Minitab and Excel files can be found on the CD that accompanies the text.

## Glossary

**Statistics** The art and science of collecting, analyzing, presenting, and interpreting data.
**Data** The facts and figures collected, analyzed, and summarized for presentation and interpretation.
**Data set** All the data collected in a particular study.

**Elements** The entities on which data are collected.

**Variable** A characteristic of interest for the elements.

**Observation** The set of measurements obtained for a particular element.

**Nominal scale** The scale of measurement for a variable when the data use labels or names to identify an attribute of an element. Nominal data may be nonnumeric or numeric.

**Ordinal scale** The scale of measurement for a variable if the data exhibit the properties of nominal data and the order or rank of the data is meaningful. Ordinal data may be nonnumeric or numeric.

**Interval scale** The scale of measurement for a variable if the data demonstrate the properties of ordinal data and the interval between values is expressed in terms of a fixed unit of measure. Interval data are always numeric.

**Ratio scale** The scale of measurement for a variable if the data demonstrate all the properties of interval data and the ratio of two values is meaningful. Ratio data are always numeric.

**Qualitative data** Labels or names used to identify an attribute of each element. Qualitative data use either the nominal or ordinal scale of measurement and may be nonnumeric or numeric.

**Quantitative data** Numeric values that indicate how much or how many of something. Quantitative data are obtained using either the interval or ratio scale of measurement.

**Qualitative variable** A variable with qualitative data.

**Quantitative variable** A variable with quantitative data.

**Cross-sectional data** Data collected at the same or approximately the same point in time.

**Time series data** Data collected over several time periods.

**Descriptive statistics** Tabular, graphical, and numerical summaries of data.

**Population** The set of all elements of interest in a particular study.

**Sample** A subset of the population.

**Census** A survey to collect data on the entire population.

**Sample survey** A survey to collect data on a sample.

**Statistical inference** The process of using data obtained from a sample to make estimates or test hypotheses about the characteristics of a population.

## Exercises

1. Discuss the differences between statistics as numerical facts and statistics as a discipline or field of study.

2. Condé Nast Traveler conducts an annual survey of subscribers in order to determine the best places to stay throughout the world. Table 1.6 shows a sample of nine European hotels from one of their surveys. The price of a standard double room during the hotel's high season ranges from \$ (lowest price) to \$\$\$\$ (highest price). The overall score includes subscribers' evaluations of each hotel's rooms, service, restaurants, location/atmosphere, and public areas; a higher overall score corresponds to a higher level of satisfaction.
   a. How many elements are in this data set?
   b. How many variables are in this data set?
   c. Which variables are qualitative and which variables are quantitative?
   d. What type of measurement scale is used for each of the variables?

3. Refer to Table 1.6.
   a. What is the average number of rooms for the nine hotels?
   b. Compute the average overall score.
   c. What is the percentage of hotels located in England?
   d. What is the percentage of hotels with a room rate of \$\$?

TABLE 1.6    RATINGS FOR NINE PLACES TO STAY IN EUROPE

**Hotel**

| Name of Property | Country | Room Rate | Number of Rooms | Overall Score |
|---|---|---|---|---|
| Graveteye Manor | England | $$ | 18 | 83.6 |
| Villa d'Este | Italy | $$$$ | 166 | 86.3 |
| Hotel Prem | Germany | $ | 54 | 77.8 |
| Hotel d'Europe | France | $$ | 47 | 76.8 |
| Palace Luzern | Switzerland | $$ | 326 | 80.9 |
| Royal Crescent Hotel | England | $$$ | 45 | 73.7 |
| Hotel Sacher | Austria | $$$ | 120 | 85.5 |
| Duc de Bourgogne | Belgium | $ | 10 | 76.9 |
| Villa Gallici | France | $$ | 22 | 90.6 |

*Source:* Condé Nast Traveler, January 2000.

4. All-in-one sound systems, called minisystems, typically include an AM/FM tuner, a dual-cassette tape deck, and a CD changer in a book-sized box with two separate speakers. The data in Table 1.7 show the retail price, sound quality, CD capacity, FM tuning sensitivity and selectivity, and the number of tape decks for a sample of 10 minisystems (*Consumer Reports Buying Guide 2002*).
   a. How many elements does this data set contain?
   b. What is the population?
   c. Compute the average price for the sample.
   d. Using the results in part (c), estimate the average price for the population.

5. Consider the data set for the sample of 10 minisystems in Table 1.7.
   a. How many variables are in the data set?
   b. Which of the variables are quantitative and which are qualitative?
   c. What is the average CD capacity for the sample?
   d. What percentage of the minisystems provides an FM tuning rating of very good or excellent?
   e. What percentage of the minisystems includes two tape decks?

6. Columbia House provides CDs to its mail-order club members. A Columbia House Music Survey asked new club members to complete an 11-question survey. Some of the questions asked were:
   a. How many CDs have you bought in the last 12 months?
   b. Are you currently a member of a national mail-order book club? (Yes or No)

TABLE 1.7    A SAMPLE OF 10 MINISYSTEMS

**Minisystems**

| Brand and Model | Price ($) | Sound Quality | CD Capacity | FM Tuning | Tape Decks |
|---|---|---|---|---|---|
| Aiwa NSX-AJ800 | 250 | Good | 3 | Fair | 2 |
| JVC FS-SD1000 | 500 | Good | 1 | Very Good | 0 |
| JVC MX-G50 | 200 | Very Good | 3 | Excellent | 2 |
| Panasonic SC-PM11 | 170 | Fair | 5 | Very Good | 1 |
| RCA RS 1283 | 170 | Good | 3 | Poor | 0 |
| Sharp CD-BA2600 | 150 | Good | 3 | Good | 2 |
| Sony CHC-CL1 | 300 | Very Good | 3 | Very Good | 1 |
| Sony MHC-NX1 | 500 | Good | 5 | Excellent | 2 |
| Yamaha GX-505 | 400 | Very Good | 3 | Excellent | 1 |
| Yamaha MCR-E100 | 500 | Very Good | 1 | Excellent | 0 |

    c.   What is your age?

    d.   Including yourself, how many people (adults and children) are in your household?

    e.   What kind of music are you interested in buying? (15 categories were listed, including hard rock, soft rock, adult contemporary, heavy metal, rap, and country.)

    Comment on whether each question provides qualitative or quantitative data.

7. A *Barron's* subscriber survey (September 15, 2000) asked subscribers to indicate their employment status. The data were recorded with 1 denoting employed full-time, 2 denoting employed part-time, 3 denoting retired, and 4 denoting unemployed (homemaker, student, etc.).

    a.   The variable is employment status. Is it a qualitative or quantitative variable?

    b.   What type of measurement scale is being used for this variable?

8. The Gallup organization conducted a telephone survey with a randomly selected national sample of 1005 adults, 18 years and older. The survey asked the respondents, "How would you describe your own physical health at this time?" (*http://www.gallup.com,* February 7, 2002). Response categories were Excellent, Good, Only Fair, Poor, and No opinion.

    a.   What was the sample size for this survey?

    b.   Are the data qualitative or quantitative?

    c.   Would it make more sense to use averages or percentages as a summary of the data for this question?

    d.   Of the respondents, 29% said their personal health was excellent. How many individuals provided this response?

9. The Commerce Department reported receiving the following applications for the Malcolm Baldrige National Quality Award: 23 from large manufacturing firms, 18 from large service firms, and 30 from small businesses.

    a.   Is type of business a qualitative or quantitative variable?

    b.   What percentage of the applications came from small businesses?

10. State whether each of the following variables is qualitative or quantitative and indicate its measurement scale.

    a.   Age

    b.   Gender

    c.   Class rank

    d.   Make of automobile

    e.   Number of people favoring the death penalty

11. State whether each of the following variables is qualitative or quantitative and indicate its measurement scale.

    a.   Annual sales

    b.   Soft-drink size (small, medium, large)

    c.   Employee classification (GS1 through GS18)

    d.   Earnings per share

    e.   Method of payment (cash, check, credit card)

12. The Hawaii Visitors Bureau collects data on visitors to Hawaii. The following questions were among 16 asked in a questionnaire handed out to passengers during incoming airline flights in June 2001.

    •   This trip to Hawaii is my: 1st, 2nd, 3rd, 4th, etc.

    •   The primary reason for this trip is: (10 categories including vacation, convention, honeymoon)

    •   Where I plan to stay: (11 categories including hotel, apartment, relatives, camping)

    •   Total days in Hawaii

    a.   What is the population being studied?

    b.   Is the use of a questionnaire a good way to reach the population of passengers on incoming airline flights?

    c.   Comment on each of the four questions in terms of whether it will provide qualitative or quantitative data.

FIGURE 1.7    EARNINGS FOR VOLKSWAGEN

13. Figure 1.7 provides a bar graph summarizing the actual and projected earnings for Volkswagen for the years 1997 to 2002 (*Business Week,* July 23, 2001).
   a. Are the data qualitative or quantitative?
   b. Are the data times series or cross-sectional?
   c. What is the variable of interest?
   d. Comment on the trend in Volkswagen's earnings over time. Would you expect to see an increase or decrease in 2003?

14. The Recording Industry of America keeps track of recorded music sales by type of music, format, and age group. The following data show the percentage of music sales by type (*The New York Times 2002 Almanac*).

CD file

**Music**

| Type | 1996 | 1997 | 1998 | 1999 | 2000 |
|------|------|------|------|------|------|
| Rock | 32.6 | 32.5 | 25.7 | 25.2 | 24.8 |
| Country | 12.1 | 11.2 | 12.8 | 10.8 | 10.7 |
| R&B | 12.1 | 11.2 | 12.8 | 10.5 | 9.7 |
| Pop | 9.3 | 9.4 | 10.0 | 10.3 | 11.0 |
| Rap | 8.9 | 10.1 | 9.7 | 10.8 | 12.9 |
| Gospel | 4.3 | 4.5 | 6.3 | 5.1 | 4.8 |
| Classical | 3.4 | 2.8 | 3.3 | 3.5 | 2.7 |
| Jazz | 3.3 | 2.8 | 1.9 | 3.0 | 2.9 |
| Other | 14.0 | 15.5 | 17.5 | 20.8 | 20.5 |

   a. Is the type of music a qualitative or quantitative variable?
   b. Construct a graph of rock music sales over the five-year period; use the horizontal axis to display the year and the vertical axis to display the percentage of music sales. Is this graph based on cross-sectional data or time series data?
   c. Construct a bar graph for type of music sales in 1998. Is this graph based on cross-sectional data or time series data?

15. Refer again to the data in Table 1.7 for the minisystems. Are the data cross-sectional or time series? Why?

16. The marketing group at your company developed a new diet soft drink that it claims will capture a large share of the young adult market.
    a. What data would you want to see before deciding to invest substantial funds in introducing the new product into the marketplace?
    b. How would you expect the data mentioned in part (a) to be obtained?

17. A manager of a large corporation recommends a $10,000 raise be given to keep a valued subordinate from moving to another company. What internal and external sources of data might be used to decide whether such a salary increase is appropriate?

18. In a recent study of causes of death in men 60 years of age and older, a sample of 120 men indicated that 48 died as a result of some form of heart disease.
    a. Develop a descriptive statistic that can be used as an estimate of the percentage of men 60 years of age or older who die from some form of heart disease.
    b. Are the data on cause of death qualitative or quantitative?
    c. Discuss the role of statistical inference in this type of medical research.

19. A *Business Week* North American subscriber study collected data from a sample of 2861 subscribers. Fifty-nine percent of the respondents indicated an annual income of $75,000 or more, and 50% reported having an American Express credit card.
    a. What is the population of interest in this study?
    b. Is annual income a qualitative or quantitative variable?
    c. Is ownership of an American Express card a qualitative or quantitative variable?
    d. Does this study involve cross-sectional or time series data?
    e. Describe any statistical inferences *Business Week* might make on the basis of the survey.

20. A Fall 2002 sample survey of 131 investment managers in *Barron's* Big Money poll revealed the following (*Barron's,* October 28, 2002):
    • 43% of managers classified themselves as bullish or very bullish on the stock market.
    • The average expected return over the next 12 months for equities was 11.2%.
    • 21% selected health care as the sector most likely to lead the market in the next 12 months.
    • When asked to estimate how long it would take for technology and telecom stocks to resume sustainable growth, the managers' average response was 2.5 years.
    a. Cite two descriptive statistics.
    b. Make an inference about the population of all investment managers concerning the average return expected on equities over the next 12 months.
    c. Make an inference about the length of time it will take for technology and telecom stocks to resume sustainable growth.

21. A seven-year medical research study reported that women whose mothers took the drug DES during pregnancy were *twice* as likely to develop tissue abnormalities that might lead to cancer as were women whose mothers did not take the drug.
    a. This study involved the comparison of two populations. What were the populations?
    b. Do you suppose the data were obtained in a survey or an experiment?
    c. For the population of women whose mothers took the drug DES during pregnancy, a sample of 3980 women showed 63 developed tissue abnormalities that might lead to cancer. Provide a descriptive statistic that could be used to estimate the number of women out of 1000 in this population who have tissue abnormalities.
    d. For the population of women whose mothers did not take the drug DES during pregnancy, what is the estimate of the number of women out of 1000 who would be expected to have tissue abnormalities?
    e. Medical studies often use a relatively large sample (in this case, 3980). Why?

22. A firm wants to test the advertising effectiveness of a new television commercial. As part of the test, the commercial is shown on a 6:30 P.M. local news program in Denver, Colorado. Two days later, a market research firm conducts a telephone survey to obtain information on recall rates (percentage of viewers who recall seeing the commercial) and impressions of the commercial.
    a. What is the population for this study?
    b. What is the sample for this study?
    c. Why would a sample be used in this situation? Explain.

23. ACNielsen conducts weekly surveys of television viewing throughout the United States. The ACNielsen statistical ratings indicate the size of the viewing audience for each major network television program. Rankings of the television programs and of the viewing audience market shares for each network are published each week.
    a. What is the ACNielsen organization attempting to measure?
    b. What is the population?
    c. Why would a sample be used for this situation?
    d. What kinds of decisions or actions are based on the ACNielsen studies?

24. A sample of midterm grades for five students showed the following results: 72, 65, 82, 90, 76. Which of the following statements are correct, and which should be challenged as being too generalized?
    a. The average midterm grade for the sample of five students is 77.
    b. The average midterm grade for all students who took the exam is 77.
    c. An estimate of the average midterm grade for all students who took the exam is 77.
    d. More than half of the students who take this exam will score between 70 and 85.
    e. If five other students are included in the sample, their grades will be between 65 and 90.

# CHAPTER 2

# Descriptive Statistics: Tabular and Graphical Presentations

**STATISTICS** *in* PRACTICE

## COLGATE-PALMOLIVE COMPANY*
*NEW YORK, NEW YORK*

The Colgate-Palmolive Company started as a small soap and candle shop in New York City in 1806. Today, Colgate-Palmolive employs more than 40,000 people working in more than 200 countries and territories around the world. Although best known for its brand names of Colgate, Palmolive, Ajax, and Fab, the company also markets Mennen, Hill's Science Diet, and Hill's Prescription Diet products.

The Colgate-Palmolive Company uses statistics in its quality assurance program for home laundry detergent products. One concern is customer satisfaction with the quantity of detergent in a carton. Every carton in each size category is filled with the same amount of detergent by weight, but the volume of detergent is affected by the density of the detergent powder. For instance, if the powder density is on the heavy side, a smaller volume of detergent is needed to reach the carton's specified weight. As a result, the carton may appear to be underfilled when opened by the consumer.

To control the problem of heavy detergent powder, limits are placed on the acceptable range of powder density. Statistical samples are taken periodically, and the density of each powder sample is measured. Data summaries are then provided for operating personnel so that corrective action can be taken if necessary to keep the density within the desired quality specifications.

A frequency distribution for the densities of 150 samples taken over a one-week period and a histogram are shown in the accompanying table and figure. Density levels above .40 are unacceptably high. The frequency distribution and histogram show that the operation is meeting its quality guidelines with all of the densities less than or equal to .40. Managers viewing these statistical summaries would be pleased with the quality of the detergent production process.

In this chapter, you will learn about tabular and graphical methods of descriptive statistics such as frequency distributions, bar graphs, histograms, stem-and-leaf displays, crosstabulations, and others. The goal of these methods is to summarize data so that they can be easily understood and interpreted.

Statistical summaries help maintain the quality of these Colgate-Palmolive products. © Joe Higgins/South-Western.

**Frequency Distribution of Density Data**

| Density | Frequency |
|---------|-----------|
| .29–.30 | 30 |
| .31–.32 | 75 |
| .33–.34 | 32 |
| .35–.36 | 9 |
| .37–.38 | 3 |
| .39–.40 | 1 |
| Total | 150 |

### HISTOGRAM OF DENSITY DATA

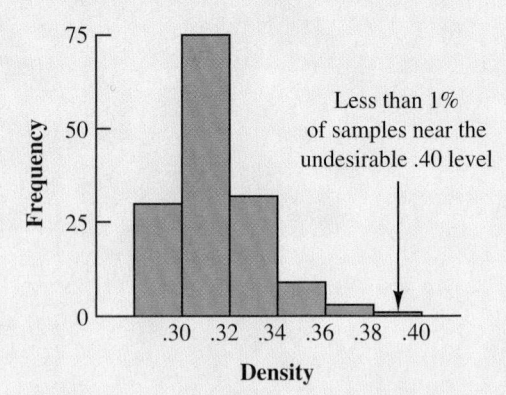

Less than 1% of samples near the undesirable .40 level

*The authors are indebted to William R. Fowle, Manager of Quality Assurance, Colgate-Palmolive Company, for providing this Statistics in Practice.

As indicated in Chapter 1, data can be classified as either qualitative or quantitative. **Quali-tative data** use labels or names to identify categories of like items. **Quantitative data** are numerical values that indicate how much or how many.

This chapter introduces tabular and graphical methods commonly used to summarize both qualitative and quantitative data. Tabular and graphical summaries of data can be found in annual reports, newspaper articles, and research studies. Everyone is exposed to these types of presentations. Hence, it is important to understand how they are prepared and how they should be interpreted. We begin with tabular and graphical methods for summarizing data concerning a single variable. The last section introduces methods for summarizing data when the relationship between two variables is of interest.

Modern statistical software packages provide extensive capabilities for summarizing data and preparing graphical presentations. Minitab and Excel are two packages that are widely available. In the chapter appendixes, we show some of their capabilities.

## 2.1  Summarizing Qualitative Data

### Frequency Distribution

We begin the discussion of how tabular and graphical methods can be used to summarize qualitative data with the definition of a **frequency distribution**.

> FREQUENCY DISTRIBUTION
>
> A frequency distribution is a tabular summary of data showing the number (fre-quency) of items in each of several nonoverlapping classes.

Let us use the following example to demonstrate the construction and interpretation of a frequency distribution for qualitative data. Coke Classic, Diet Coke, Dr. Pepper, Pepsi-Cola, and Sprite are five popular soft drinks. Assume that the data in Table 2.1 show the soft drink selected in a sample of 50 soft drink purchases.

**TABLE 2.1   DATA FROM A SAMPLE OF 50 SOFT DRINK PURCHASES**

**SoftDrink**

| | | |
|---|---|---|
| Coke Classic | Sprite | Pepsi-Cola |
| Diet Coke | Coke Classic | Coke Classic |
| Pepsi-Cola | Diet Coke | Coke Classic |
| Diet Coke | Coke Classic | Coke Classic |
| Coke Classic | Diet Coke | Pepsi-Cola |
| Coke Classic | Coke Classic | Dr. Pepper |
| Dr. Pepper | Sprite | Coke Classic |
| Diet Coke | Pepsi-Cola | Diet Coke |
| Pepsi-Cola | Coke Classic | Pepsi-Cola |
| Pepsi-Cola | Coke Classic | Pepsi-Cola |
| Coke Classic | Coke Classic | Pepsi-Cola |
| Dr. Pepper | Pepsi-Cola | Pepsi-Cola |
| Sprite | Coke Classic | Coke Classic |
| Coke Classic | Sprite | Dr. Pepper |
| Diet Coke | Dr. Pepper | Pepsi-Cola |
| Coke Classic | Pepsi-Cola | Sprite |
| Coke Classic | Diet Coke | |

**TABLE 2.2**

FREQUENCY
DISTRIBUTION OF
SOFT DRINK
PURCHASES

| Soft Drink | Frequency |
|---|---|
| Coke Classic | 19 |
| Diet Coke | 8 |
| Dr. Pepper | 5 |
| Pepsi-Cola | 13 |
| Sprite | 5 |
| Total | 50 |

To develop a frequency distribution for these data, we count the number of times each soft drink appears in Table 2.1. Coke Classic appears 19 times, Diet Coke appears 8 times, Dr. Pepper appears 5 times, Pepsi-Cola appears 13 times, and Sprite appears 5 times. These counts are summarized in the frequency distribution in Table 2.2.

This frequency distribution provides a summary of how the 50 soft drink purchases are distributed across the five soft drinks. This summary offers more insight than the original data shown in Table 2.1. Viewing the frequency distribution, we see that Coke Classic is the leader, Pepsi-Cola is second, Diet Coke is third, and Sprite and Dr. Pepper are tied for fourth. The frequency distribution summarizes information about the popularity of the five best-selling soft drinks.

## Relative Frequency and Percent Frequency Distributions

A frequency distribution shows the number (frequency) of items in each of several nonoverlapping classes. However, we are often interested in the proportion, or percentage, of items in each class. The *relative frequency* of a class equals the fraction or proportion of items belonging to a class. For a data set with $n$ observations, the relative frequency of each class can be determined as follows:

RELATIVE FREQUENCY

$$\text{Relative frequency of a class} = \frac{\text{Frequency of the class}}{n} \qquad (2.1)$$

The *percent frequency* of a class is the relative frequency multiplied by 100.

A **relative frequency distribution** gives a tabular summary of data showing the relative frequency for each class. A **percent frequency distribution** summarizes the percent frequency of the data for each class. Table 2.3 shows a relative frequency distribution and a percent frequency distribution for the soft drink data. In Table 2.3 we see that the relative frequency for Coke Classic is 19/50 = .38, the relative frequency for Diet Coke is 8/50 = .16, and so on. From the percent frequency distribution, we see that 38% of the purchases were Coke Classic, 16% of the purchases were Diet Coke, and so on. We can also note that 38% + 26% + 16% = 80% of the purchases were of the top three soft drinks.

## Bar Graphs and Pie Charts

A **bar graph**, or bar chart, is a graphical device for depicting qualitative data summarized in a frequency, relative frequency, or percent frequency distribution. On one axis of the graph (usually the horizontal axis), we specify the labels that are used for the classes (categories) of data. A frequency, relative frequency, or percent frequency scale can be used for the other

**TABLE 2.3**   RELATIVE AND PERCENT FREQUENCY DISTRIBUTIONS
OF SOFT DRINK PURCHASES

| Soft Drink | Relative Frequency | Percent Frequency |
|---|---|---|
| Coke Classic | .38 | 38 |
| Diet Coke | .16 | 16 |
| Dr. Pepper | .10 | 10 |
| Pepsi-Cola | .26 | 26 |
| Sprite | .10 | 10 |
| Total | 1.00 | 100 |

FIGURE 2.1    BAR GRAPH OF SOFT DRINK PURCHASES

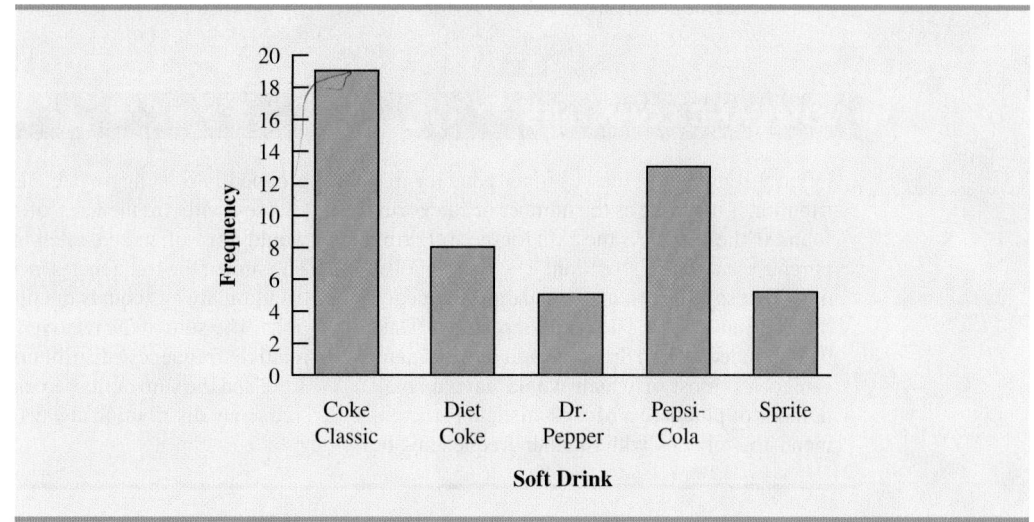

*In quality control applications, bar graphs are used to identify the most important causes of problems. When the bars are arranged in descending order of height from left to right with the most frequently occurring cause appearing first, the bar graph is called a* pareto diagram. *This diagram is named for its founder, Vilfredo Pareto, an Italian economist.*

axis of the graph (usually the vertical axis). Then, using a bar of fixed width drawn above each class label, we extend the length of the bar until we reach the frequency, relative frequency, or percent frequency of the class. For qualitative data, the bars should be separated to emphasize the fact that each class (category) is separate. Figure 2.1 shows a bar graph of the frequency distribution for the 50 soft drink purchases. Note how the graphical presentation shows Coke Classic, Pepsi-Cola, and Diet Coke to be the most preferred brands.

The **pie chart** provides another graphical device for presenting relative frequency and percent frequency distributions for qualitative data. To construct a pie chart, we first draw a circle to represent all of the data. Then we use the relative frequencies to subdivide the circle into sectors, or parts, that correspond to the relative frequency for each class. For example, because a circle contains 360 degrees and Coke Classic shows a relative frequency of .38, the sector of the pie chart labeled Coke Classic consists of .38(360) = 136.8 degrees. The sector of the pie chart labeled Diet Coke consists of .16(360) = 57.6 degrees. Similar calculations for the other classes yield the pie chart in Figure 2.2. The

FIGURE 2.2    PIE CHART OF SOFT DRINK PURCHASES

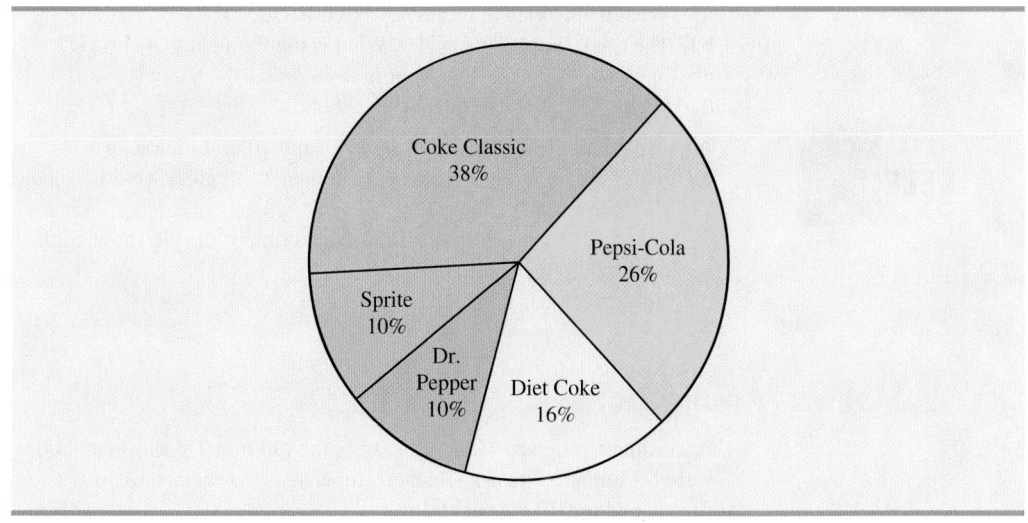

numerical values shown for each sector can be frequencies, relative frequencies, or percent frequencies.

**NOTES AND COMMENTS**

1. Often the number of classes in a frequency distribution is the same as the number of categories found in the data, as is the case for the soft drink purchase data in this section. The data involve only five soft drinks, and a separate frequency distribution class was defined for each one. Data that included all soft drinks would require many categories, most of which would have a small number of purchases. Most statisticians recommend that classes with smaller frequencies be grouped into an aggregate class called "other." Classes with frequencies of 5 percent or less would most often be treated in this fashion.

2. The sum of the frequencies in any frequency distribution always equals the number of observations. The sum of the relative frequencies in any relative frequency distribution always equals 1.00, and the sum of the percentages in a percent frequency distribution always equals 100.

## Exercises

### Methods

1. The response to a question has three alternatives: A, B, and C. A sample of 120 responses provides 60 A, 24 B, and 36 C. Show the frequency and relative frequency distributions.

2. A partial relative frequency distribution is given.

| Class | Relative Frequency |
|-------|--------------------|
| A | .22 |
| B | .18 |
| C | .40 |
| D | |

   a. What is the relative frequency of class D?
   b. The total sample size is 200. What is the frequency of class D?
   c. Show the frequency distribution.
   d. Show the percent frequency distribution.

3. A questionnaire provides 58 Yes, 42 No, and 20 no-opinion answers.
   a. In the construction of a pie chart, how many degrees would be in the section of the pie showing the Yes answers?
   b. How many degrees would be in the section of the pie showing the No answers?
   c. Construct a pie chart.
   d. Construct a bar graph.

### Applications

4. According to Nielsen Media Research, the top four TV shows at 8:00 P.M., April 6, 2000, were Millionaire, Frasier, Chicago Hope, and Charmed (*USA Today*, April 13, 2000). Data for a sample of 50 viewers follow.

**Nielsen**

| | | | | |
|---|---|---|---|---|
| Millionaire | Millionaire | Millionaire | Frasier | Charmed |
| Frasier | Frasier | Millionaire | Millionaire | Frasier |
| Frasier | Millionaire | Millionaire | Chicago Hope | Millionaire |
| Charmed | Millionaire | Frasier | Chicago Hope | Millionaire |
| Chicago Hope | Charmed | Frasier | Frasier | Millionaire |
| Millionaire | Frasier | Millionaire | Millionaire | Chicago Hope |
| Frasier | Millionaire | Millionaire | Charmed | Chicago Hope |
| Chicago Hope | Millionaire | Millionaire | Millionaire | Millionaire |
| Frasier | Frasier | Millionaire | Frasier | Frasier |
| Millionaire | Millionaire | Chicago Hope | Millionaire | Frasier |

a.  Are these qualitative or quantitative data?

b.  Provide frequency and percent frequency distributions.

c.  Construct a bar graph and a pie chart.

d.  On the basis of the sample, which show has the largest market share? Which one is second?

5.  In alphabetical order, the six most common last names in the United States are Brown, Davis, Johnson, Jones, Smith, and Williams (*Time Almanac 2001*). Assume that a sample of 50 individuals with one of these last names provided the following data.

**Names**

| | | | | |
|---|---|---|---|---|
| Brown | Williams | Williams | Williams | Brown |
| Smith | Jones | Smith | Johnson | Smith |
| Davis | Smith | Brown | Williams | Johnson |
| Johnson | Smith | Smith | Johnson | Brown |
| Williams | Davis | Johnson | Williams | Johnson |
| Williams | Johnson | Jones | Smith | Brown |
| Johnson | Smith | Smith | Brown | Jones |
| Jones | Jones | Smith | Smith | Davis |
| Davis | Jones | Williams | Davis | Smith |
| Jones | Johnson | Brown | Johnson | Davis |

Summarize the data by constructing the following:

a.  Relative and percent frequency distributions

b.  A bar graph

c.  A pie chart

d.  Based on these data, what are the three most common last names?

**TABLE 2.4**

**THE EIGHT BEST-SELLING PAPERBACK BUSINESS BOOKS**

- *The 7 Habits of Highly Effective People*
- *Investing for Dummies*
- *The Ernst & Young Tax Guide 2000*
- *The Millionaire Next Door*
- *The Motley Fool Investment Guide*
- *Rich Dad, Poor Dad*
- *The Wall Street Journal Guide to Understanding Money and Investing*
- *What Color Is Your Parachute? 2000*

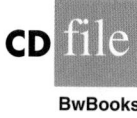

**BwBooks**

6.  The eight best-selling paperback business books in February 2000 are listed in Table 2.4 (*Business Week,* April 3, 2000). Suppose a sample of book purchases in the Denver, Colorado, area provided the following data for these eight books.

| | | | | | |
|---|---|---|---|---|---|
| 7 Habits | Dad | 7 Habits | Millionaire | Millionaire | WSJ Guide |
| Motley | Millionaire | Tax Guide | 7 Habits | Dad | Dummies |
| Millionaire | Motley | Dad | Dad | Parachute | Dad |
| Dad | 7 Habits | WSJ Guide | WSJ Guide | WSJ Guide | 7 Habits |
| Motley | WSJ Guide | Millionaire | 7 Habits | Millionaire | Millionaire |
| Millionaire | 7 Habits | Millionaire | 7 Habits | Motley | Motley |
| Motley | 7 Habits | Dad | Dad | Dad | Dad |
| 7 Habits | WSJ Guide | Tax Guide | Millionaire | Motley | Tax Guide |
| Motley | Motley | Millionaire | Millionaire | Dad | Dummies |
| Millionaire | Millionaire | Millionaire | Dad | Millionaire | Dad |

a.  Construct frequency and percent frequency distributions for the data. Group any books with a frequency of 5% or less in an "other" category.

b.  Rank the best-selling books.

c.  What percentage of the sales are represented by *The Millionaire Next Door* and *Rich Dad, Poor Dad*?

7.  Leverock's Waterfront Steakhouse in Maderia Beach, Florida, uses a questionnaire to ask customers how they rate the server, food quality, cocktails, prices, and atmosphere at the restaurant. Each characteristic is rated on a scale of outstanding (O), very good (V), good (G), average (A), and poor (P). Use descriptive statistics to summarize the following data collected on food quality. What is your feeling about the food quality ratings at the restaurant?

| G | O | V | G | A | O | V | O | V | G | O | V | A |
|---|---|---|---|---|---|---|---|---|---|---|---|---|
| V | O | P | V | O | G | A | O | O | O | G | O | V |
| V | A | G | O | V | P | V | O | O | G | O | O | V |
| O | G | A | O | V | O | O | G | V | A | G |   |   |

8.  Data for a sample of 55 members of the Baseball Hall of Fame in Cooperstown, New York, are shown here. Each observation indicates the primary position played by the Hall of Famers: pitcher (P), catcher (H), 1st base (1), 2nd base (2), 3rd base (3), shortstop (S), left field (L), center field (C), and right field (R).

| L | P | C | H | 2 | P | R | 1 | S | S | 1 | L | P | R | P |
|---|---|---|---|---|---|---|---|---|---|---|---|---|---|---|
| P | P | P | R | C | S | L | R | P | C | C | P | P | R | P |
| 2 | 3 | P | H | L | P | 1 | C | P | P | P | S | 1 | L | R |
| R | 1 | 2 | H | S | 3 | H | 2 | L | P |   |   |   |   |   |

a.  Use frequency and relative frequency distributions to summarize the data.
b.  What position provides the most Hall of Famers?
c.  What position provides the fewest Hall of Famers?
d.  What outfield position (L, C, or R) provides the most Hall of Famers?
e.  Compare infielders (1, 2, 3, and S) to outfielders (L, C, and R).

9.  The flextime system at Electronics Associates allows employees to begin their working day at 7:00, 7:30, 8:00, 8:30, or 9:00 A.M. The following data represent a sample of the starting times selected by the employees.

| 7:00 | 8:30 | 9:00 | 8:00 | 7:30 | 7:30 | 8:30 | 8:30 | 7:30 | 7:00 |
|------|------|------|------|------|------|------|------|------|------|
| 8:30 | 8:30 | 8:00 | 8:00 | 7:30 | 8:30 | 7:00 | 9:00 | 8:30 | 8:00 |

Summarize the data by constructing the following:
a.  A frequency distribution
b.  A percent frequency distribution
c.  A bar graph
d.  A pie chart
e.  What do the summaries tell you about employee preferences in the flextime system?

10. A 2001 Merrill Lynch Client Satisfaction Survey asked clients to indicate how satisfied they were with their financial consultant. Client responses were coded 1 to 7, with 1 indicating "not at all satisfied" and 7 indicating "extremely satisfied." Assume that the following data are from a sample of 60 responses for a particular financial consultant.

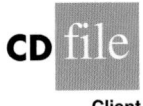

**Client**

| 5 | 7 | 6 | 6 | 7 | 5 | 5 | 7 | 3 | 6 |
|---|---|---|---|---|---|---|---|---|---|
| 7 | 7 | 6 | 6 | 6 | 5 | 5 | 6 | 7 | 7 |
| 6 | 6 | 4 | 4 | 7 | 6 | 7 | 6 | 7 | 6 |
| 5 | 7 | 5 | 7 | 6 | 4 | 7 | 5 | 7 | 6 |
| 6 | 5 | 3 | 7 | 7 | 6 | 6 | 6 | 6 | 5 |
| 5 | 6 | 6 | 7 | 7 | 5 | 6 | 4 | 6 | 6 |

a.  Comment on why these data are qualitative.
b.  Provide a frequency distribution and a relative frequency distribution for the data.
c.  Provide a bar graph.
d.  On the basis of your summaries, comment on the clients' overall evaluation of the financial consultant.

# 2.2 Summarizing Quantitative Data

## Frequency Distribution

**TABLE 2.5**

**YEAR-END AUDIT
TIMES (IN DAYS)**

| 12 | 14 | 19 | 18 |
|----|----|----|----|
| 15 | 15 | 18 | 17 |
| 20 | 27 | 22 | 23 |
| 22 | 21 | 33 | 28 |
| 14 | 18 | 16 | 13 |

As defined in Section 2.1, a frequency distribution is a tabular summary of data showing the number (frequency) of items in each of several nonoverlapping classes. This definition holds for quantitative as well as qualitative data. However, with quantitative data we must be more careful in defining the nonoverlapping classes to be used in the frequency distribution.

For example, consider the quantitative data in Table 2.5. These data show the time in days required to complete year-end audits for a sample of 20 clients of Sanderson and Clifford, a small public accounting firm with the data rounded to the nearest day. The three steps necessary to define the classes for a frequency distribution with quantitative data are:

1.  Determine the number of nonoverlapping classes.
2.  Determine the width of each class.
3.  Determine the class limits.

**Audit**

Let us demonstrate these steps by developing a frequency distribution for the audit time data in Table 2.5.

**Number of classes**  Classes are formed by specifying ranges that will be used to group the data. As a general guideline, we recommend using between 5 and 20 classes. For a small number of data items, as few as five or six classes may be used to summarize the data. For a larger number of data items, a larger number of classes is usually required. The goal is to use enough classes to show the variation in the data, but not so many classes that some contain only a few data items. Because the number of data items in Table 2.5 is relatively small ($n = 20$), we chose to develop a frequency distribution with five classes.

*Making the classes the same width reduces the chance of inappropriate interpretations by the user.*

**Width of the classes**  The second step in constructing a frequency distribution for quantitative data is to choose a width for the classes. As a general guideline, we recommend that the width be the same for each class. Thus the choices of the number of classes and the width of classes are not independent decisions. A larger number of classes means a smaller class width, and vice versa. To determine an approximate class width, we begin by identifying the largest and smallest data values. Then, with the desired number of classes specified, we can use the following expression to determine the approximate class width.

$$\text{Approximate class width} = \frac{\text{Largest data value} - \text{Smallest data value}}{\text{Number of classes}} \quad \text{(2.2)}$$

The approximate class width given by equation (2.2) can be rounded to a more convenient value based on the preference of the person developing the frequency distribution. For example, an approximate class width of 9.28 might be rounded to 10 simply because 10 is a more convenient class width to use in presenting a frequency distribution.

For the data involving the year-end audit times, the largest value is 33 and the smallest value is 12. Because we decided to summarize the data with five classes, using equation (2.2) provides an approximate class width of $(33 - 12)/5 = 4.2$. We therefore decided to round up and use a class width of five days in the frequency distribution.

*No single frequency distribution is best for a data set. Different people may construct different, but equally acceptable, frequency distributions. The goal is to reveal the natural grouping and variation in the data.*

In practice, the number of classes and the appropriate class width are determined by trial and error. Once a possible number of classes is chosen, equation (2.2) is used to find the approximate class width. The process can be repeated for a different number of classes. Ultimately, the analyst uses judgment to determine the combination of the number of classes and class width that provides the best frequency distribution for summarizing the data.

For the audit time data in Table 2.5, after deciding to use five classes, each with a width of five days, the next task is to specify the class limits for each of the classes.

**Class limits**  Class limits must be chosen so that each data item belongs to one and only one class. The *lower class limit* identifies the smallest possible data value assigned to the class. The *upper class limit* identifies the largest possible data value assigned to the class. In developing frequency distributions for qualitative data, we did not need to specify class limits because each data item naturally fell into a separate class (category). But with quantitative data, such as the audit times in Table 2.5, class limits are necessary to determine where each data value belongs.

Using the audit time data in Table 2.5, we selected 10 days as the lower class limit and 14 days as the upper class limit for the first class. This class is denoted 10–14 in Table 2.6. The smallest data value, 12, is included in the 10–14 class. We then selected 15 days as the lower class limit and 19 days as the upper class limit of the next class. We continued defining the lower and upper class limits to obtain a total of five classes: 10–14, 15–19, 20–24, 25–29, and 30–34. The largest data value, 33, is included in the 30–34 class. The difference between the lower class limits of adjacent classes is the class width. Using the first two lower class limits of 10 and 15, we see that the class width is $15 - 10 = 5$.

With the number of classes, class width, and class limits determined, a frequency distribution can be obtained by counting the number of data values belonging to each class. For example, the data in Table 2.5 show that four values—12, 14, 14, and 13—belong to the 10–14 class. Thus, the frequency for the 10–14 class is 4. Continuing this counting process for the 15–19, 20–24, 25–29, and 30–34 classes provides the frequency distribution in Table 2.6. Using this frequency distribution, we can observe that:

1. The most frequently occurring audit times are in the class of 15–19 days. Eight of the 20 audit times belong to this class.
2. Only one audit required 30 or more days.

Other conclusions are possible, depending on the interests of the person viewing the frequency distribution. The value of a frequency distribution is that it provides insights about the data that are not easily obtained by viewing the data in their original unorganized form.

**Class midpoint**  In some applications, we want to know the midpoints of the classes in a frequency distribution for quantitative data. The **class midpoint** is the value halfway between the lower and upper class limits. For the audit time data, the five class midpoints are 12, 17, 22, 27, and 32.

## Relative Frequency and Percent Frequency Distributions

We define the relative frequency and percent frequency distributions for quantitative data in the same manner as for qualitative data. First, recall that the relative frequency is simply the proportion of the observations belonging to a class. With $n$ observations,

$$\text{Relative frequency of class} = \frac{\text{Frequency of the class}}{n}$$

The percent frequency of a class is the relative frequency multiplied by 100.

Based on the class frequencies in Table 2.6 and with $n = 20$, Table 2.7 shows the relative frequency distribution and percent frequency distribution for the audit time data. Note that .40 of the audits, or 40%, required from 15 to 19 days. Only .05 of the audits, or 5%, required 30 or more days. Again, additional interpretations and insights can be obtained by using Table 2.7.

## Dot Plot

One of the simplest graphical summaries of data is a **dot plot**. A horizontal axis shows the range of values for the observations. Each data value is represented by a dot placed above the axis. Figure 2.3 is the dot plot for the audit time data in Table 2.5. The three dots located

**TABLE 2.6**

FREQUENCY DISTRIBUTION FOR THE AUDIT TIME DATA

| Audit Time (days) | Frequency |
|---|---|
| 10–14 | 4 |
| 15–19 | 8 |
| 20–24 | 5 |
| 25–29 | 2 |
| 30–34 | 1 |
| Total | 20 |

**TABLE 2.7    RELATIVE AND PERCENT FREQUENCY DISTRIBUTIONS FOR THE AUDIT TIME DATA**

| Audit Time (days) | Relative Frequency | Percent Frequency |
|---|---|---|
| 10–14 | .20 | 20 |
| 15–19 | .40 | 40 |
| 20–24 | .25 | 25 |
| 25–29 | .10 | 10 |
| 30–34 | .05 | 5 |
| Total | 1.00 | 100 |

above 18 on the horizontal axis indicate that three audit times of 18 days occurred. Dot plots show the details of the data and are useful for comparing the distribution of the data for two or more variables.

## Histogram

A common graphical presentation of quantitative data is a **histogram**. This graphical summary can be prepared for data previously summarized in either a frequency, relative frequency, or percent frequency distribution. A histogram is constructed by placing the variable of interest on the horizontal axis and the frequency, relative frequency, or percent frequency on the vertical axis. The frequency, relative frequency, or percent frequency of each class is shown by drawing a rectangle whose base is determined by the class limits on the horizontal axis and whose height is the corresponding frequency, relative frequency, or percent frequency.

Figure 2.4 is a histogram for the audit time data. Note that the class with the greatest frequency is shown by the rectangle appearing above the class of 15–19 days. The height of the rectangle shows that the frequency of this class is 8. A histogram for the relative or percent frequency distribution of this data would look the same as the histogram in Figure 2.4 with the exception that the vertical axis would be labeled with relative or percent frequency values.

As Figure 2.4 shows, the adjacent rectangles of a histogram touch one another. Unlike a bar graph, a histogram contains no natural separation between the rectangles of adjacent classes. This format is the usual convention for histograms. Because the classes for the audit time data are stated as 10–14, 15–19, 20–24, 25–29, and 30–34, one-unit spaces of 14 to 15, 19 to 20, 24 to 25, and 29 to 30 would seem to be needed between the classes. These spaces are eliminated when constructing a histogram. Eliminating the spaces between classes in a histogram for the audit-time data helps show that, even though the data are rounded to the nearest full day, all values between the lower limit of the first class and the upper limit of the last class are possible.

**FIGURE 2.3    DOT PLOT FOR THE AUDIT-TIME DATA**

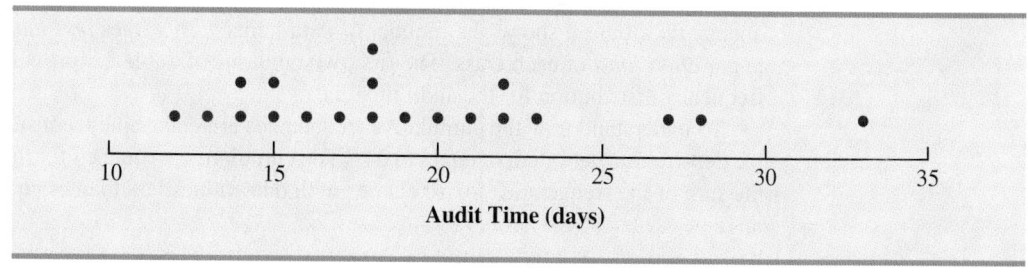

**Audit Time (days)**

FIGURE 2.4    HISTOGRAM FOR THE AUDIT TIME DATA

One of the most important uses of a histogram is to provide information about the shape, or form, of a distribution. Figure 2.5 contains four histograms constructed from relative frequency distributions. Panel A shows the histogram for a set of data moderately skewed to the left. A histogram is said to be skewed to the left if its tail extends farther to the left. This histogram is typical for exam scores. There are no scores above 100%, most of the scores are often above 70%, and only a few really low scores occur. Panel B shows the histogram for a set of data moderately skewed to the right. A histogram is said to be skewed to the right if its tail extends farther to the right. An example of this type of histogram would be for data such as housing values; a few very expensive homes create the skewness in the right tail.

Panel C shows a symmetric histogram. In a symmetric histogram, the left tail mirrors the shape of the right tail. Histograms for data found in applications are never perfectly symmetric, but the histogram for many applications may be roughly symmetric. Data for SAT scores, heights and weights of people, and so on lead to histograms that are roughly symmetric. Panel D shows a histogram highly skewed to the right. This histogram was constructed from data on the amount of customer purchases over one day at a women's apparel store. Data from applications in business and economics often lead to histograms that are skewed to the right. For instance, data on housing values, salaries, purchase amounts, and so on often result in histograms skewed to the right.

## Cumulative Distributions

A variation of the frequency distribution that provides another tabular summary of quantitative data is the **cumulative frequency distribution**. The cumulative frequency distribution uses the number of classes, class widths, and class limits developed for the frequency distribution. However, rather than showing the frequency of each class, the cumulative frequency distribution shows the number of data items with values *less than or equal to the upper class limit* of each class. The first two columns of Table 2.8 provide the cumulative frequency distribution for the audit time data.

To understand how the cumulative frequencies are determined, consider the class with the description "less than or equal to 24." The cumulative frequency for this class is simply the sum of the frequencies for all classes with data values less than or equal to 24. For the

**FIGURE 2.5    HISTOGRAMS SHOWING DIFFERING LEVELS OF SKEWNESS**

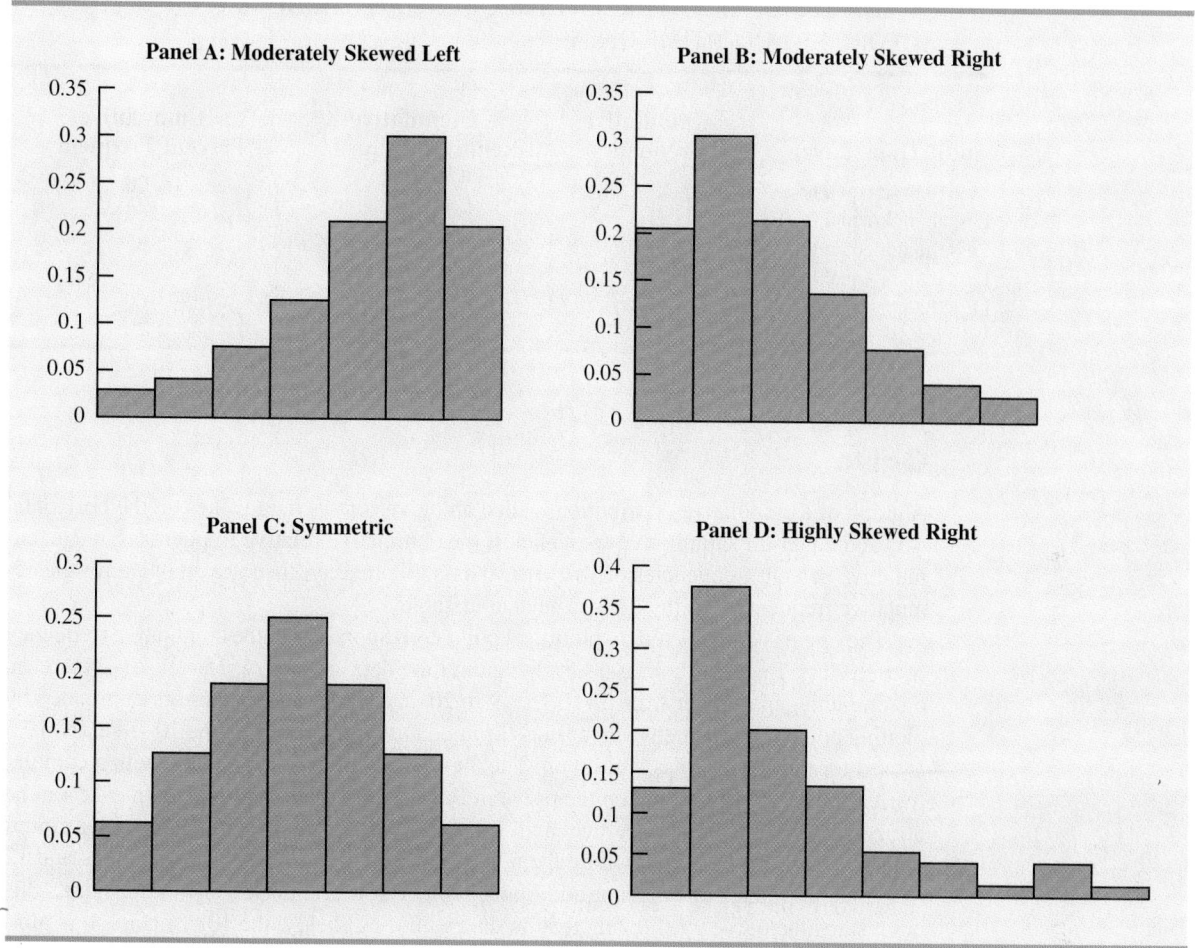

frequency distribution in Table 2.6, the sum of the frequencies for classes 10–14, 15–19, and 20–24 indicates that $4 + 8 + 5 = 17$ data values are less than or equal to 24. Hence, the cumulative frequency for this class is 17. In addition, the cumulative frequency distribution in Table 2.8 shows that four audits were completed in 14 days or less and 19 audits were completed in 29 days or less.

As a final point, we note that a **cumulative relative frequency distribution** shows the proportion of data items, and a **cumulative percent frequency distribution** shows the percentage of data items with values less than or equal to the upper limit of each class. The cumulative relative frequency distribution can be computed either by summing the relative frequencies in the relative frequency distribution or by dividing the cumulative frequencies by the total number of items. Using the latter approach, we found the cumulative relative frequencies in column 3 of Table 2.8 by dividing the cumulative frequencies in column 2 by the total number of items ($n = 20$). The cumulative percent frequencies were again computed by multiplying the relative frequencies by 100. The cumulative relative and percent frequency distributions show that .85 of the audits, or 85%, were completed in 24 days or less, .95 of the audits, or 95%, were completed in 29 days or less, and so on.

**TABLE 2.8**   CUMULATIVE FREQUENCY, CUMULATIVE RELATIVE FREQUENCY, AND CUMULATIVE PERCENT FREQUENCY DISTRIBUTIONS FOR THE AUDIT TIME DATA

| Audit Time (days) | Cumulative Frequency | Cumulative Relative Frequency | Cumulative Percent Frequency |
|---|---|---|---|
| Less than or equal to 14 | 4 | .20 | 20 |
| Less than or equal to 19 | 12 | .60 | 60 |
| Less than or equal to 24 | 17 | .85 | 85 |
| Less than or equal to 29 | 19 | .95 | 95 |
| Less than or equal to 34 | 20 | 1.00 | 100 |

## Ogive

A graph of a cumulative distribution, called an **ogive**, shows data values on the horizontal axis and either the cumulative frequencies, the cumulative relative frequencies, or the cumulative percent frequencies on the vertical axis. Figure 2.6 illustrates an ogive for the cumulative frequencies of the audit time data in Table 2.8.

The ogive is constructed by plotting a point corresponding to the cumulative frequency of each class. Because the classes for the audit time data are 10–14, 15–19, 20–24, and so on, one-unit gaps appear from 14 to 15, 19 to 20, and so on. These gaps are eliminated by plotting points halfway between the class limits. Thus, 14.5 is used for the 10–14 class, 19.5 is used for the 15–19 class, and so on. The "less than or equal to 14" class with a cumulative frequency of 4 is shown on the ogive in Figure 2.6 by the point located at 14.5 on the horizontal axis and 4 on the vertical axis. The "less than or equal to 19" class with a cumulative frequency of 12 is shown by the point located at 19.5 on the horizontal axis and 12 on the vertical axis. Note that one additional point is plotted at the left end of the ogive. This point starts the ogive by showing that no data values fall below the 10–14 class. It is plot-

**FIGURE 2.6**   OGIVE FOR THE AUDIT TIME DATA

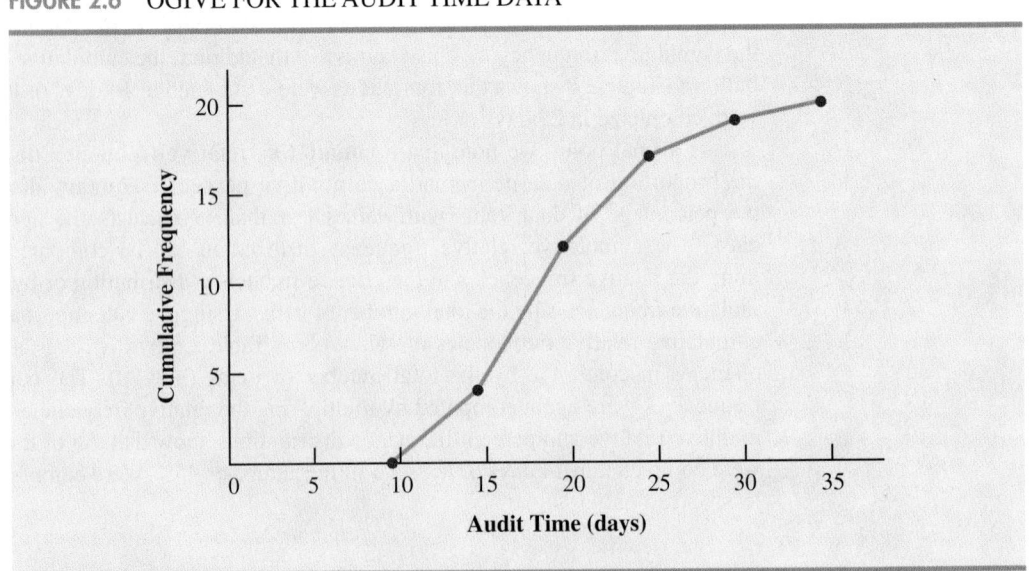

ted at 9.5 on the horizontal axis and 0 on the vertical axis. The plotted points are connected by straight lines to complete the ogive.

## NOTES AND COMMENTS

1. A bar graph and a histogram are essentially the same thing; both are graphical presentations of the data in a frequency distribution. A histogram is just a bar graph with no separation between bars. The separation between bars is appropriate for qualitative data because the data are discrete; no intermediate values are possible. For discrete quantitative data, a separation between bars is also appropriate. Consider, for example, the number of classes in which a college student is enrolled. The data may only assume integer values. Intermediate values such as 1.5, 2.73, and so on are not possible. With continuous quantitative data, however, such as the audit times in Table 2.5, a separation between bars is not appropriate.

2. The appropriate values for the class limits with quantitative data depend on the level of accuracy of the data. For instance, with the audit time data of Table 2.5 the limits used were integer values because the data were rounded to the nearest day. If the data were rounded to the nearest tenth of a day (e.g., 12.3, 14.4, and so on), then the limits would be stated in tenths of days. For instance, the first class would be 10.0–14.9.

If the data were rounded to the nearest hundredth of a day (e.g., 12.34, 14.45, and so on), the limits would be stated in hundredths of days. For instance, the first class would be 10.00–14.99.

3. An *open-end* class requires only a lower class limit or an upper class limit. For example, in the audit time data of Table 2.5, suppose two of the audits had taken 58 and 65 days. Rather than continue with the classes of width 5 with classes 35–39, 40–44, 45–49, and so on, we could simplify the frequency distribution to show an open-end class of "35 or more." This class would have a frequency of 2. Most often the open-end class appears at the upper end of the distribution. Sometimes an open-end class appears at the lower end of the distribution, and occasionally such classes appear at both ends.

4. The last entry in a cumulative frequency distribution always equals the total number of observations. The last entry in a cumulative relative frequency distribution always equals 1.00 and the last entry in a cumulative percent frequency distribution always equals 100.

## Exercises

## Methods

11. Consider the following data.

**Frequency**

| | | | | |
|---|---|---|---|---|
| 14 | 21 | 23 | 21 | 16 |
| 19 | 22 | 25 | 16 | 16 |
| 24 | 24 | 25 | 19 | 16 |
| 19 | 18 | 19 | 21 | 12 |
| 16 | 17 | 18 | 23 | 25 |
| 20 | 23 | 16 | 20 | 19 |
| 24 | 26 | 15 | 22 | 24 |
| 20 | 22 | 24 | 22 | 20 |

a. Develop a frequency distribution using classes of 12–14, 15–17, 18–20, 21–23, and 24–26.

b. Develop a relative frequency distribution and a percent frequency distribution using the classes in part (a).

12. Consider the following frequency distribution.

| Class | Frequency |
|-------|-----------|
| 10–19 | 10 |
| 20–29 | 14 |
| 30–39 | 17 |
| 40–49 | 7 |
| 50–59 | 2 |

Construct a cumulative frequency distribution and a cumulative relative frequency distribution.

13. Construct a histogram and an ogive for the data in exercise 12.

14. Consider the following data.

| 8.9 | 10.2 | 11.5 | 7.8 | 10.0 | 12.2 | 13.5 | 14.1 | 10.0 | 12.2 |
|-----|------|------|-----|------|------|------|------|------|------|
| 6.8 | 9.5 | 11.5 | 11.2 | 14.9 | 7.5 | 10.0 | 6.0 | 15.8 | 11.5 |

a. Construct a dot plot.
b. Construct a frequency distribution.
c. Construct a percent frequency distribution.

## Applications

15. A doctor's office staff studied the waiting times for patients who arrive at the office with a request for emergency service. The following data with waiting times in minutes were collected over a one-month period.

2  5  10  12  4  4  5  17  11  8  9  8  12  21  6  8  7  13  18  3

Use classes of 0–4, 5–9, and so on in the following:
a. Show the frequency distribution.
b. Show the relative frequency distribution.
c. Show the cumulative frequency distribution.
d. Show the cumulative relative frequency distribution.
e. What proportion of patients needing emergency service wait 9 minutes or less?

16. Consider the following two frequency distributions. The first frequency distribution provides an approximation of the annual adjusted gross incomes in the United States (http://www.irs.gov, March 9, 2003). An additional 2.8 million taxpayers report annual adjusted gross income in excess of $200,000 but are not included. The second frequency distribution shows exam scores for students in a college statistics course.

| Income ($1000s) | Frequency (millions) | Exam Score | Frequency |
|-----------------|----------------------|------------|-----------|
| 0–24 | 60 | Below 30 | 2 |
| 25–49 | 33 | 30–39 | 5 |
| 50–74 | 20 | 40–49 | 6 |
| 75–99 | 6 | 50–59 | 13 |
| 100–124 | 4 | 60–69 | 32 |
| 125–149 | 2 | 70–79 | 78 |
| 150–174 | 1 | 80–89 | 43 |
| 175–199 | 1 | 90–99 | 21 |
| Total | 127 | Total | 200 |

a. Develop a histogram for the annual income data. What evidence of skewness does it show? Does this skewness make sense? Explain.

b. Develop a histogram for the exam score data. What evidence of skewness does it show? Explain.

c. Develop a histogram for the data in exercise 11. What evidence of skewness does it show? What is the general shape of the distribution?

**CD** file

Spending

17. Mendelsohn Media Research provided survey data on the annual amount of household purchases by families with an annual income of $75,000 or more (*Money*, 2001). Assume that the following data from a sample of 25 households show the dollars spent in the past year on books and magazines.

| 280 | 496 | 382 | 202 | 287 |
| 266 | 119 | 10 | 385 | 135 |
| 475 | 255 | 379 | 267 | 24 |
| 42 | 25 | 283 | 110 | 423 |
| 160 | 123 | 16 | 243 | 363 |

a. Construct a frequency distribution and relative frequency distribution for the data.

b. Provide a histogram. Comment on the shape of the distribution.

c. Comment on the annual spending on books and magazines for families in the sample.

18. Wageweb conducts surveys of salary data and presents summaries on its Web site. Using salary data as of January 1, 2000, Wageweb reported that salaries of marketing vice presidents ranged from $85,090 to $190,054 (*Wageweb.com*, April 12, 2000). Assume the following data come from a sample of the annual salaries for 50 marketing vice presidents. Data are in thousands of dollars.

**CD** file

Wageweb

| 145 | 95 | 148 | 112 | 132 |
| 140 | 162 | 118 | 170 | 144 |
| 145 | 127 | 148 | 165 | 138 |
| 173 | 113 | 104 | 141 | 142 |
| 116 | 178 | 123 | 141 | 138 |
| 127 | 143 | 134 | 136 | 137 |
| 155 | 93 | 102 | 154 | 142 |
| 134 | 165 | 123 | 124 | 124 |
| 138 | 160 | 157 | 138 | 131 |
| 114 | 135 | 151 | 138 | 157 |

a. What are the lowest and highest salaries?

b. Use a class width of $15,000 and prepare tabular summaries of the annual salary data.

c. What proportion of the annual salaries are $135,000 or less?

d. What percentage of the annual salaries are more than $150,000?

e. Prepare a histogram. Comment on the shape of the distribution.

19. The data for the numbers of units produced by a production employee during the most recent 20 days are shown here.

| 160 | 170 | 181 | 156 | 176 |
| 148 | 198 | 179 | 162 | 150 |
| 162 | 156 | 179 | 178 | 151 |
| 157 | 154 | 179 | 148 | 156 |

Summarize the data by constructing the following:

a. A frequency distribution

b. A relative frequency distribution

c. A cumulative frequency distribution

d. A cumulative relative frequency distribution

e. An ogive

20. The U.S. Census Bureau publishes a variety of information on the U.S. population. Shown here is the percent frequency distribution of the U.S. population by age as of July 1, 2000 (*The World Almanac and Book of Facts 2000*).

| Age | Percent Frequency |
|---|---|
| 0–13 | 20.0 |
| 14–17 | 5.7 |
| 18–24 | 9.6 |
| 25–34 | 13.6 |
| 35–44 | 16.3 |
| 45–54 | 13.5 |
| 55–64 | 8.7 |
| 65 or over | 12.6 |
| | 100.0 |

a. What percentage of the population is 34 years old or younger?
b. What percentage of the population is older than 34 years old?
c. What percentage of the population is between 25 and 54 years old inclusively?
d. The total population is 275 million. How many people are younger than 25 years old?
e. Suppose you believe that half the people in the 55–64 class are retired and that approximately all of the people 65 or older are retired. Estimate the number of retired people in the population.

**Computer**

21. The *Nielsen Home Technology Report* provided information about home technology and its usage by persons aged 12 and older. The following data are the hours of personal computer usage during one week for a sample of 50 persons.

| | | | | | | | | | |
|---|---|---|---|---|---|---|---|---|---|
| 4.1 | 1.5 | 10.4 | 5.9 | 3.4 | 5.7 | 1.6 | 6.1 | 3.0 | 3.7 |
| 3.1 | 4.8 | 2.0 | 14.8 | 5.4 | 4.2 | 3.9 | 4.1 | 11.1 | 3.5 |
| 4.1 | 4.1 | 8.8 | 5.6 | 4.3 | 3.3 | 7.1 | 10.3 | 6.2 | 7.6 |
| 10.8 | 2.8 | 9.5 | 12.9 | 12.1 | 0.7 | 4.0 | 9.2 | 4.4 | 5.7 |
| 7.2 | 6.1 | 5.7 | 5.9 | 4.7 | 3.9 | 3.7 | 3.1 | 6.1 | 3.1 |

Summarize the data by constructing the following:
a. A frequency distribution (use a class width of three hours)
b. A relative frequency distribution
c. A histogram
d. An ogive
e. Comment on what the data indicate about personal computer usage at home.

# 2.3 Exploratory Data Analysis: The Stem-and-Leaf Display

The techniques of **exploratory data analysis** consist of simple arithmetic and easy-to-draw graphs that can be used to summarize data quickly. One technique—referred to as a **stem-and-leaf display**—can be used to show both the rank order and shape of a data set simultaneously.

To illustrate the use of a stem-and-leaf display, consider the data in Table 2.9. These data result from a 150-question aptitude test given to 50 individuals recently interviewed for a position at Haskens Manufacturing. The data indicate the number of questions answered correctly.

To develop a stem-and-leaf display, we first arrange the leading digits of each data value to the left of a vertical line. To the right of the vertical line, we record the last digit for each

**TABLE 2.9    NUMBER OF QUESTIONS ANSWERED CORRECTLY ON AN APTITUDE TEST**

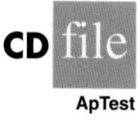

**CD file**

**ApTest**

| 112 | 72 | 69 | 97 | 107 |
|-----|-----|-----|-----|-----|
| 73 | 92 | 76 | 86 | 73 |
| 126 | 128 | 118 | 127 | 124 |
| 82 | 104 | 132 | 134 | 83 |
| 92 | 108 | 96 | 100 | 92 |
| 115 | 76 | 91 | 102 | 81 |
| 95 | 141 | 81 | 80 | 106 |
| 84 | 119 | 113 | 98 | 75 |
| 68 | 98 | 115 | 106 | 95 |
| 100 | 85 | 94 | 106 | 119 |

data value as we pass through the observations in the order they were recorded. The last digit for each data value is placed on the line corresponding to its first digit as follows:

```
 6 | 9  8
 7 | 2  3  6  3  6  5
 8 | 6  2  3  1  1  0  4  5
 9 | 7  2  2  6  2  1  5  8  8  5  4
10 | 7  4  8  0  2  6  6  0  6
11 | 2  8  5  9  3  5  9
12 | 6  8  7  4
13 | 2  4
14 | 1
```

With this organization of the data, sorting the digits on each line into rank order is simple. Doing so leads to the stem-and-leaf display shown here.

```
 6 | 8  9
 7 | 2  3  3  5  6  6
 8 | 0  1  1  2  3  4  5  6
 9 | 1  2  2  2  4  5  5  6  7  8  8
10 | 0  0  2  4  6  6  6  7  8
11 | 2  3  5  5  8  9  9
12 | 4  6  7  8
13 | 2  4
14 | 1
```

The numbers to the left of the vertical line (6, 7, 8, 9, 10, 11, 12, 13, and 14) form the *stem*, and each digit to the right of the vertical line is a *leaf*. For example, consider the first row with a stem value of 6 and leaves of 8 and 9.

$$6 \mid 8 \quad 9$$

It indicates that two data values have a first digit of six. The leaves show that the data values are 68 and 69. Similarly, the second row

$$7 \mid 2 \quad 3 \quad 3 \quad 5 \quad 6 \quad 6$$

indicates that six data values have a first digit of seven. The leaves show that the data values are 72, 73, 73, 75, 76, and 76.

To focus on the shape indicated by the stem-and-leaf display, let us use a rectangle to contain the leaves of each stem. Doing so, we obtain the following.

```
 6 | 8  9
 7 | 2  3  3  5  6  6
 8 | 0  1  1  2  3  4  5  6
 9 | 1  2  2  2  4  5  5  6  7  8  8
10 | 0  0  2  4  6  6  6  7  8
11 | 2  3  5  5  8  9  9
12 | 4  6  7  8
13 | 2  4
14 | 1
```

Rotating this page counterclockwise onto its side provides a picture of the data that is similar to a histogram with classes of 60–69, 70–79, 80–89, and so on.

Although the stem-and-leaf display may appear to offer the same information as a histogram, it has two primary advantages.

1. The stem-and-leaf display is easier to construct by hand.
2. Within a class interval, the stem-and-leaf display provides more information than the histogram because the stem-and-leaf shows the actual data.

*In a stretched stem-and-leaf display, whenever a stem value is stated twice, the first value corresponds to leaf values of 0–4, and the second value corresponds to leaf values of 5–9.*

Just as a frequency distribution or histogram has no absolute number of classes, neither does a stem-and-leaf display have an absolute number of rows or stems. If we believe that our original stem-and-leaf display condensed the data too much, we can easily stretch the display by using two or more stems for each leading digit. For example, to use two stems for each leading digit, we would place all data values ending in 0, 1, 2, 3, and 4 in one row and all values ending in 5, 6, 7, 8, and 9 in a second row. The following stretched stem-and-leaf display illustrates this approach.

```
 6 | 8  9
 7 | 2  3  3
 7 | 5  6  6
 8 | 0  1  1  2  3  4
 8 | 5  6
 9 | 1  2  2  2  4
 9 | 5  5  6  7  8  8
10 | 0  0  2  4
10 | 6  6  6  7  8
11 | 2  3
11 | 5  5  8  9  9
12 | 4
12 | 6  7  8
13 | 2  4
13 |
14 | 1
```

Note that values 72, 73, and 73 have leaves in the 0–4 range and are shown with the first stem value of 7. The values 75, 76, and 76 have leaves in the 5–9 range and are shown with the second stem value of 7. This stretched stem-and-leaf display is similar to a frequency distribution with intervals of 65–69, 70–74, 75–79, and so on.

The preceding example showed a stem-and-leaf display for data with as many as three digits. Stem-and-leaf displays for data with more than three digits are possible. For example, consider the following data on the number of hamburgers sold by a fast-food restaurant for each of 15 weeks.

| 1565 | 1852 | 1644 | 1766 | 1888 | 1912 | 2044 | 1812 |
|------|------|------|------|------|------|------|------|
| 1790 | 1679 | 2008 | 1852 | 1967 | 1954 | 1733 | |

A stem-and-leaf display of these data follows.

Leaf Unit = 10

```
15 | 6
16 | 4  7
17 | 3  6  9
18 | 1  5  5  8
19 | 1  5  6
20 | 0  4
```

*A single digit is used to define each leaf in a stem-and-leaf display. The leaf unit indicates how to multiply the stem-and-leaf numbers in order to approximate the original data. Leaf units may be 100, 10, 1, 0.1, and so on.*

Note that a single digit is used to define each leaf and that only the first three digits of each observation have been used to construct the display. At the top of the display we have specified Leaf Unit = 10. To illustrate how to interpret the values in the display, consider the first stem, 15, and its associated leaf, 6. Combining these numbers, we obtain 156. To reconstruct an approximation of the original data value, we must multiply this number by 10, the value of the *leaf unit*. Thus, $156 \times 10 = 1560$ is an approximation of the original data value used to construct the stem-and-leaf display. Although it is not possible to reconstruct the exact data value from this stem-and-leaf display, the convention of using a single digit for each leaf enables stem-and-leaf displays to be constructed for data having a large number of digits. For stem-and-leaf displays where the leaf unit is not shown, the leaf unit is assumed to equal 1.

## Exercises

### Methods

22. Construct a stem-and-leaf display for the following data.

| 70 | 72 | 75 | 64 | 58 | 83 | 80 | 82 |
|----|----|----|----|----|----|----|----|
| 76 | 75 | 68 | 65 | 57 | 78 | 85 | 72 |

23. Construct a stem-and-leaf display for the following data.

| 11.3 | 9.6 | 10.4 | 7.5 | 8.3 | 10.5 | 10.0 |
|------|-----|------|-----|-----|------|------|
| 9.3 | 8.1 | 7.7 | 7.5 | 8.4 | 6.3 | 8.8 |

24. Construct a stem-and-leaf display for the following data. Use a leaf unit of 10.

| 1161 | 1206 | 1478 | 1300 | 1604 | 1725 | 1361 | 1422 |
|------|------|------|------|------|------|------|------|
| 1221 | 1378 | 1623 | 1426 | 1557 | 1730 | 1706 | 1689 |

## Applications

25. A psychologist developed a new test of adult intelligence. The test was administered to 20 individuals, and the following data were obtained.

| 114 | 99 | 131 | 124 | 117 | 102 | 106 | 127 | 119 | 115 |
| 98 | 104 | 144 | 151 | 132 | 106 | 125 | 122 | 118 | 118 |

Construct a stem-and-leaf display for the data.

26. The *American Association of Individual Investors* conducts an annual survey of discount brokers. The following prices charged are from a sample of 24 discount brokers (*AAII Journal*, January 2003). The two types of trades are a broker-assisted trade of 100 shares at $50 per share and an online trade of 500 shares at $50 per share.

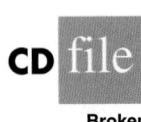

Broker

| Broker | Broker-Assisted 100 Shares at $50/Share | Online 500 Shares at $50/Share | Broker | Broker-Assisted 100 Shares at at $50/Share | Online 500 Shares at $50/Share |
|---|---|---|---|---|---|
| Accutrade | 30.00 | 29.95 | Merrill Lynch Direct | 50.00 | 29.95 |
| Ameritrade | 24.99 | 10.99 | Muriel Siebert | 45.00 | 14.95 |
| Banc of America | 54.00 | 24.95 | NetVest | 24.00 | 14.00 |
| Brown & Co. | 17.00 | 5.00 | Recom Securities | 35.00 | 12.95 |
| Charles Schwab | 55.00 | 29.95 | Scottrade | 17.00 | 7.00 |
| CyberTrader | 12.95 | 9.95 | Sloan Securities | 39.95 | 19.95 |
| E*TRADE Securities | 49.95 | 14.95 | Strong Investments | 55.00 | 24.95 |
| First Discount | 35.00 | 19.75 | TD Waterhouse | 45.00 | 17.95 |
| Freedom Investments | 25.00 | 15.00 | T. Rowe Price | 50.00 | 19.95 |
| Harrisdirect | 40.00 | 20.00 | Vanguard | 48.00 | 20.00 |
| Investors National | 39.00 | 62.50 | Wall Street Discount | 29.95 | 19.95 |
| MB Trading | 9.95 | 10.55 | York Securities | 40.00 | 36.00 |

a. Round the trading prices to the nearest dollar and develop a stem-and-leaf display for 100 shares at $50 per share. Comment on what you learned about trading prices.
b. Round the trading prices to the nearest dollar and develop a stretched stem-and-leaf display for 500 shares online at $50 per share. Comment on what you learned about online trading prices.

27. In a study of job satisfaction, a series of tests was administered to 50 subjects. The following data were obtained; higher scores represent greater dissatisfaction.

JobSat

| 87 | 76 | 67 | 58 | 92 | 59 | 41 | 50 | 90 | 75 | 80 | 81 | 70 |
| 73 | 69 | 61 | 88 | 46 | 85 | 97 | 50 | 47 | 81 | 87 | 75 | 60 |
| 65 | 92 | 77 | 71 | 70 | 74 | 53 | 43 | 61 | 89 | 84 | 83 | 70 |
| 46 | 84 | 76 | 78 | 64 | 69 | 76 | 78 | 67 | 74 | 64 | | |

Construct a stem-and-leaf display for the data.

28. Periodically *Barron's* publishes earnings forecasts for the companies listed in the Dow Jones Industrial Average. The following are the 2000 forecasts of price/earnings (P/E) ratios for these companies implied by *Barron's* earnings forecasts (*Barron's*, February 14, 2000).

PEforecast

| Company | 2000 P/E Forecast | Company | 2000 P/E Forecast |
|---|---|---|---|
| AT&T | 23 | Citigroup | 17 |
| Alcoa | 15 | Coca-Cola | 39 |
| American Express | 25 | Disney | 47 |
| Boeing | 16 | Dupont | 18 |
| Caterpillar | 13 | Eastman Kodak | 11 |

| Company | 2000 P/E Forecast | Company | 2000 P/E Forecast |
|---|---|---|---|
| Exxon/Mobil | 22 | McDonald's | 23 |
| General Electric | 37 | Merck | 25 |
| General Motors | 8 | Microsoft | 60 |
| Hewlett-Packard | 36 | Minnesota Mining | 19 |
| Home Depot | 48 | J. P. Morgan | 11 |
| Honeywell | 13 | Philip Morris | 5 |
| IBM | 28 | Procter & Gamble | 26 |
| Intel | 37 | SBC Comm. | 19 |
| International Paper | 14 | United Technologies | 14 |
| Johnson & Johnson | 23 | Wal-Mart | 40 |

a.  Develop a stem-and-leaf display for the data.
b.  Use the results of the stem-and-leaf display to develop a frequency distribution and percent frequency distribution.

# 2.4    Crosstabulations and Scatter Diagrams

*Crosstabulations and scatter diagrams are used to summarize data in a way that reveals the relationship between two variables.*

Thus far in this chapter, we focused on tabular and graphical methods used to summarize the data for *one variable at a time*. Often a manager or decision maker requires tabular and graphical methods that will assist in the understanding of the *relationship between two variables*. Crosstabulation and scatter diagrams are two such methods.

## Crosstabulation

A **crosstabulation** is a tabular summary of data for two variables. Let us illustrate the use of a crosstabulation by considering the following application based on data from Zagat's Restaurant Review. The quality rating and the meal price data were collected for a sample of 300 restaurants located in the Los Angeles area. Table 2.10 shows the data for the first 10 restaurants. Data on a restaurant's quality rating and typical meal price are reported. Quality rating is a qualitative variable with rating categories of good, very good, and excellent. Meal price is a quantitative variable that ranges from $10 to $49.

**TABLE 2.10**    QUALITY RATING AND MEAL PRICE FOR 300 LOS ANGELES RESTAURANTS

**Restaurant**

| Restaurant | Quality Rating | Meal Price ($) |
|---|---|---|
| 1 | Good | 18 |
| 2 | Very Good | 22 |
| 3 | Good | 28 |
| 4 | Excellent | 38 |
| 5 | Very Good | 33 |
| 6 | Good | 28 |
| 7 | Very Good | 19 |
| 8 | Very Good | 11 |
| 9 | Very Good | 23 |
| 10 | Good | 13 |
| . | . | . |
| . | . | . |
| . | . | . |

A crosstabulation of the data for this application is shown in Table 2.11. The left and top margin labels define the classes for the two variables. In the left margin, the row labels (good, very good, and excellent) correspond to the three classes of the quality rating variable. In the top margin, the column labels ($10–19, $20–29, $30–39, and $40–49) correspond to the four classes of the meal price variable. Each restaurant in the sample provides a quality rating and a meal price. Thus, each restaurant in the sample is associated with a cell appearing in one of the rows and one of the columns of the crosstabulation. For example, restaurant 5 is identified as having a very good quality rating and a meal price of $33. This restaurant belongs to the cell in row 2 and column 3 of Table 2.11. In constructing a crosstabulation, we simply count the number of restaurants that belong to each of the cells in the crosstabulation table.

In reviewing Table 2.11, we see that the greatest number of restaurants in the sample (64) have a very good rating and a meal price in the $20–29 range. Only two restaurants have an excellent rating and a meal price in the $10–19 range. Similar interpretations of the other frequencies can be made. In addition, note that the right and bottom margins of the crosstabulation provide the frequency distributions for quality rating and meal price separately. From the frequency distribution in the right margin, we see that data on quality ratings show 84 good restaurants, 150 very good restaurants, and 66 excellent restaurants. Similarly, the bottom margin shows the frequency distribution for the meal price variable.

Dividing the totals in the right margin of the crosstabulation by the total for that column provides a relative and percent frequency distribution for the quality rating variable.

| Quality Rating | Relative Frequency | Percent Frequency |
|---|---|---|
| Good | .28 | 28 |
| Very Good | .50 | 50 |
| Excellent | .22 | 22 |
| **Total** | 1.00 | 100 |

From the percent frequency distribution we see that 28% of the restaurants were rated good, 50% were rated very good, and 22% were rated excellent.

Dividing the totals in the bottom row of the crosstabulation by the total for that row provides a relative and percent frequency distribution for the meal price variable.

| Meal Price | Relative Frequency | Percent Frequency |
|---|---|---|
| $10–19 | .26 | 26 |
| $20–29 | .39 | 39 |
| $30–39 | .25 | 25 |
| $40–49 | .09 | 9 |
| **Total** | 1.00 | 100 |

Note that the sum of the values in each column do not add exactly to the column total, because the values being summed are rounded. From the percent frequency distribution we quickly see that 26% of the meal prices are in the lowest price class ($10–19), 39% are in the next higher class, and so on.

The frequency and relative frequency distributions constructed from the margins of a crosstabulation provide information about each of the variables individually, but they do not shed any light on the relationship between the variables. The primary value of a

**TABLE 2.11    CROSSTABULATION OF QUALITY RATING AND MEAL PRICE FOR 300 LOS ANGELES RESTAURANTS**

| Quality Rating | Meal Price | | | | Total |
|---|---|---|---|---|---|
| | **$10–19** | **$20–29** | **$30–39** | **$40–49** | **Total** |
| **Good** | 42 | 40 | 2 | 0 | 84 |
| **Very Good** | 34 | 64 | 46 | 6 | 150 |
| **Excellent** | 2 | 14 | 28 | 22 | 66 |
| **Total** | 78 | 118 | 76 | 28 | 300 |

crosstabulation lies in the insight it offers about the relationship between the variables. A review of the crosstabulation in Table 2.11 reveals that higher meal prices are associated with the higher quality restaurants, and the lower meal prices are associated with the lower quality restaurants.

Converting the entries in a crosstabulation into row percentages or column percentages can provide more insight into the relationship between the two variables. For row percentages, the results of dividing each frequency in Table 2.11 by its corresponding row total are shown in Table 2.12. Each row of Table 2.12 is a percent frequency distribution of meal price for one of the quality rating categories. Of the restaurants with the lowest quality rating (good), we see that the greatest percentages are for the less expensive restaurants (50% have $10–19 meal prices and 47.6% have $20–29 meal prices). Of the restaurants with the highest quality rating (excellent), we see that the greatest percentages are for the more expensive restaurants (42.4% have $30–39 meal prices and 33.4% have $40–49 meal prices). Thus, we continue to see that the more expensive meals are associated with the higher quality restaurants.

Crosstabulation is widely used for examining the relationship between two variables. In practice, the final reports for many statistical studies include a large number of crosstabulation tables. In the Los Angeles restaurant survey, the crosstabulation is based on one qualitative variable (quality rating) and one quantitative variable (meal price). Crosstabulations can also be developed when both variables are qualitative and when both variables are quantitative. When quantitative variables are used, however, we must first create classes for the values of the variable. For instance, in the restaurant example we grouped the meal prices into four classes ($10–19, $20–29, $30–39, and $40–49).

## Simpson's Paradox

The data in two or more crosstabulations are often combined or aggregated to produce a summary crosstabulation showing how two variables are related. In such cases, we must be careful in drawing conclusions about the relationship between the two variables in the

**TABLE 2.12    ROW PERCENTAGES FOR EACH QUALITY RATING CATEGORY**

| Quality Rating | Meal Price | | | | Total |
|---|---|---|---|---|---|
| | **$10–19** | **$20–29** | **$30–39** | **$40–49** | **Total** |
| Good | 50.0 | 47.6 | 2.4 | 0.0 | 100 |
| Very Good | 22.7 | 42.7 | 30.6 | 4.0 | 100 |
| Excellent | 3.0 | 21.2 | 42.4 | 33.4 | 100 |

aggregated crosstabulation. In some cases the conclusions based upon the aggregated crosstabulation can be completely reversed if we look at the unaggregated data, an occurrence known as **Simpson's paradox**. To provide an illustration of Simpson's paradox we consider an example involving the analysis of verdicts for two judges in two types of courts.

Judges Ron Luckett and Dennis Kendall presided over cases in Common Pleas Court and Municipal Court during the past three years. Some of the verdicts they rendered were appealed. In most of these cases the appeals court upheld the original verdicts, but in some cases those verdicts were reversed. For each judge a crosstabulation was developed based upon two variables: Verdict (upheld or reversed) and Type of Court (Common Pleas and Municipal). Suppose that the two crosstabulations were then combined by aggregating the type of court data. The resulting aggregated crosstabulation contains two variables: Verdict (upheld or reversed) and Judge (Luckett or Kendall). This crosstabulation shows the number of appeals in which the verdict was upheld and the number in which the verdict was reversed for both judges. The following crosstabulation shows these results along with the column percentages in parentheses next to each value.

| Verdict | Judge | | Total |
| | Luckett | Kendall | |
|---|---|---|---|
| **Upheld** | 129 (86%) | 110 (88%) | 239 |
| **Reversed** | 21 (14%) | 15 (12%) | 36 |
| **Total (%)** | 150 (100%) | 125 (100%) | 275 |

A review of the column percentages shows that 14% of the verdicts were reversed for Judge Luckett, but only 12% of the verdicts were reversed for Judge Kendall. Thus, we might conclude that Judge Kendall is doing a better job because a higher percentage of his verdicts are being upheld. A problem arises with this conclusion, however.

The following crosstabulations show the cases tried by Luckett and Kendall in the two courts; column percentages are also shown in parentheses next to each value.

| Judge Luckett | | | | | Judge Kendall | | | |
| Verdict | Common Pleas | Municipal Court | Total | | Verdict | Common Pleas | Municipal Court | Total |
|---|---|---|---|---|---|---|---|---|
| **Upheld** | 29 (91%) | 100 (85%) | 129 | | **Upheld** | 90 (90%) | 20 (80%) | 110 |
| **Reversed** | 3 (9%) | 18 (15%) | 21 | | **Reversed** | 10 (10%) | 5 (20%) | 15 |
| **Total (%)** | 32 (100%) | 118 (100%) | 150 | | **Total (%)** | 100 (100%) | 25 (100%) | 125 |

From the crosstabulation and column percentages for Luckett, we see that his verdicts were upheld in 91% of the Common Pleas Court cases and in 85% of the Municipal Court cases. From the crosstabulation and column percentages for Kendall, we see that his verdicts were upheld in 90% of the Common Pleas Court cases and in 80% of the Municipal Court cases. Comparing the column percentages for the two judges, we see that Judge Luckett demonstrates a better record than Judge Kendall in both courts. This result contradicts the conclusion we reached when we aggregated the data across both courts for the original crosstabulation. It appeared then that Judge Kendall had the better record. This example illustrates Simpson's paradox.

The original crosstabulation was obtained by aggregating the data in the separate crosstabulations for the two courts. Note that for both judges the percentage of appeals that

TABLE 2.13   SAMPLE DATA FOR THE STEREO AND SOUND EQUIPMENT STORE

| Week | Number of Commercials x | Sales ($100s) y |
|------|-------------------------|------------------|
| 1 | 2 | 50 |
| 2 | 5 | 57 |
| 3 | 1 | 41 |
| 4 | 3 | 54 |
| 5 | 4 | 54 |
| 6 | 1 | 38 |
| 7 | 5 | 63 |
| 8 | 3 | 48 |
| 9 | 4 | 59 |
| 10 | 2 | 46 |

**CD** file

**Stereo**

resulted in reversals was much higher in Municipal Court than in Common Pleas Court. Because Judge Luckett tried a much higher percentage of his cases in Municipal Court, the aggregated data favored Judge Kendall. When we look at the crosstabulations for the two courts separately, however, Judge Luckett clearly shows the better record. Thus, for the original crosstabulation, we see that the *type of court* is a hidden variable that cannot be ignored when evaluating the records of the two judges.

Because of Simpson's paradox, we need to be especially careful when drawing conclusions using aggregated data. Before drawing any conclusions about the relationship between two variables shown for a crosstabulation involving aggregated data, you should investigate whether any hidden variables could affect the results.

## Scatter Diagram and Trendline

A **scatter diagram** is a graphical presentation of the relationship between two quantitative variables, and a **trendline** is a line that provides an approximation of the relationship. As an illustration, consider the advertising/sales relationship for a stereo and sound equipment store in San Francisco. On 10 occasions during the past three months, the store used weekend television commercials to promote sales at its stores. The managers want to investigate whether a relationship exists between the number of commercials shown and sales at the store during the following week. Sample data for the 10 weeks with sales in hundreds of dollars are shown in Table 2.13.

Figure 2.7 shows the scatter diagram and the trendline* for the data in Table 2.13. The number of commercials ($x$) is shown on the horizontal axis and the sales ($y$) are shown on the vertical axis. For week 1, $x = 2$ and $y = 50$. A point with those coordinates is plotted on the scatter diagram. Similar points are plotted for the other nine weeks. Note that during two of the weeks one commercial was shown, during two of the weeks two commercials were shown, and so on.

The completed scatter diagram in Figure 2.7 indicates a positive relationship between the number of commercials and sales. Higher sales are associated with a higher number of commercials. The relationship is not perfect in that all points are not on a straight line. However, the general pattern of the points and the trendline suggest that the overall relationship is positive.

Some general scatter diagram patterns and the types of relationships they suggest are shown in Figure 2.8. The top left panel depicts a positive relationship similar to the one for

---

*The equation of the trendline is $y = 4.95x + 36.15$. The slope of the trendline is 4.95 and the $y$-intercept (the point where the line intersects the $y$ axis) is 36.15. We will discuss in detail the interpretation of the slope and $y$-intercept for a linear trendline in Chapter 14 when we study simple linear regression.

FIGURE 2.7    SCATTER DIAGRAM AND TRENDLINE FOR THE STEREO AND SOUND
              EQUIPMENT STORE

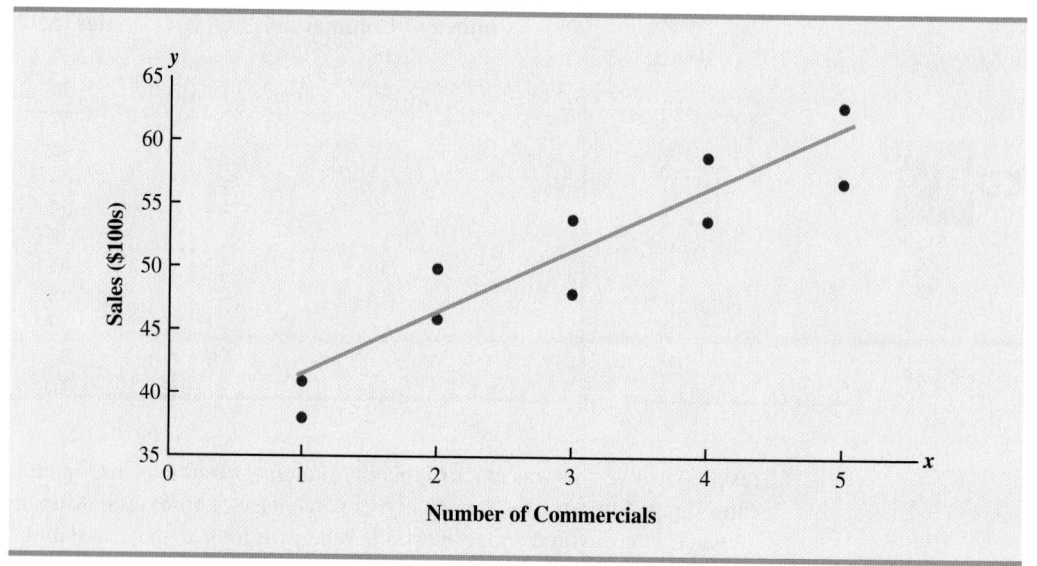

FIGURE 2.8    TYPES OF RELATIONSHIPS DEPICTED BY SCATTER DIAGRAMS

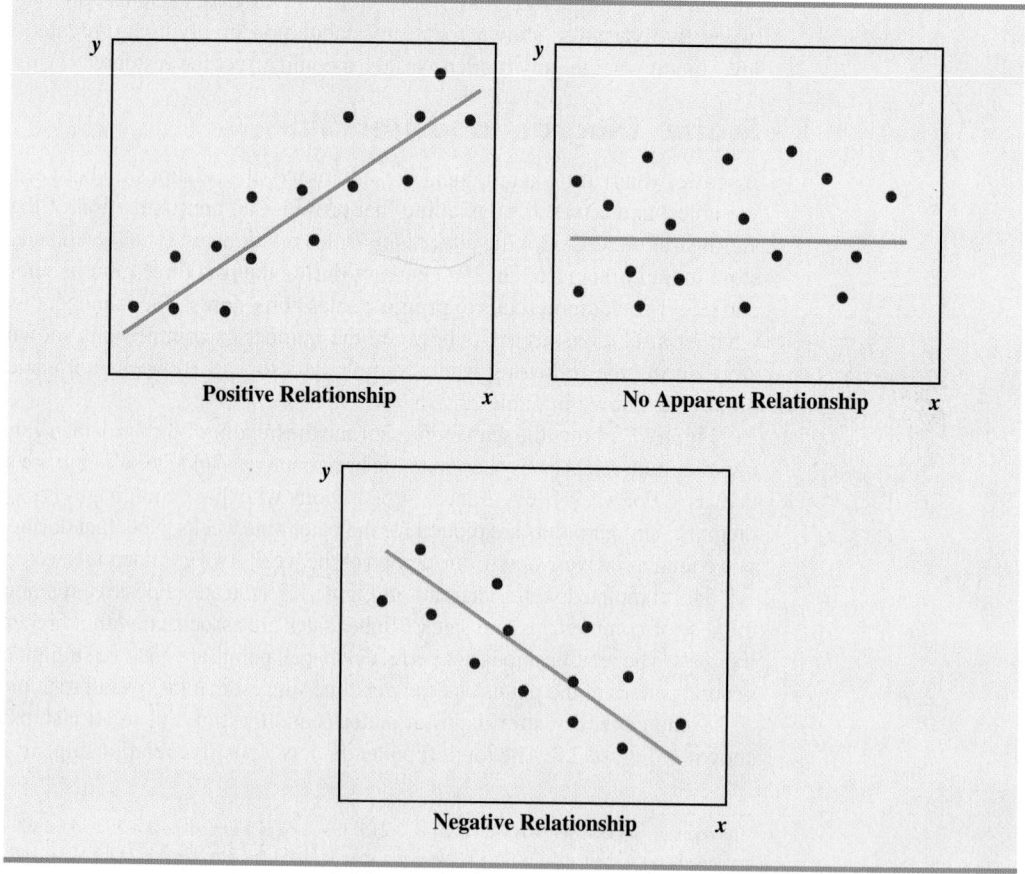

the number of commercials and sales example. In the top right panel, the scatter diagram shows no apparent relationship between the variables. The bottom panel depicts a negative relationship where y tends to decrease as x increases.

## Exercises

## Methods

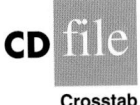

29.  The following data are for 30 observations involving two qualitative variables, x and y. The categories for x are A, B, and C; the categories for y are 1 and 2.

| Observation | x | y | Observation | x | y |
|---|---|---|---|---|---|
| 1 | A | 1 | 16 | B | 2 |
| 2 | B | 1 | 17 | C | 1 |
| 3 | B | 1 | 18 | B | 1 |
| 4 | C | 2 | 19 | C | 1 |
| 5 | B | 1 | 20 | B | 1 |
| 6 | C | 2 | 21 | C | 2 |
| 7 | B | 1 | 22 | B | 1 |
| 8 | C | 2 | 23 | C | 2 |
| 9 | A | 1 | 24 | A | 1 |
| 10 | B | 1 | 25 | B | 1 |
| 11 | A | 1 | 26 | C | 2 |
| 12 | B | 1 | 27 | C | 2 |
| 13 | C | 2 | 28 | A | 1 |
| 14 | C | 2 | 29 | B | 1 |
| 15 | C | 2 | 30 | B | 2 |

a.  Develop a crosstabulation for the data, with x as the row variable and y as the column variable.
b.  Compute the row percentages.
c.  Compute the column percentages.
d.  What is the relationship, if any, between x and y?

30.  The following 20 observations are for two quantitative variables, x and y.

| Observation | x | y | Observation | x | y |
|---|---|---|---|---|---|
| 1 | −22 | 22 | 11 | −37 | 48 |
| 2 | −33 | 49 | 12 | 34 | −29 |
| 3 | 2 | 8 | 13 | 9 | −18 |
| 4 | 29 | −16 | 14 | −33 | 31 |
| 5 | −13 | 10 | 15 | 20 | −16 |
| 6 | 21 | −28 | 16 | −3 | 14 |
| 7 | −13 | 27 | 17 | −15 | 18 |
| 8 | −23 | 35 | 18 | 12 | 17 |
| 9 | 14 | −5 | 19 | −20 | −11 |
| 10 | 3 | −3 | 20 | −7 | −22 |

a.  Develop a scatter diagram for the relationship between x and y.
b.  What is the relationship, if any, between x and y?

# Applications

31. The following crosstabulation shows household income by educational level of the head of household for the year 2000 (*Statistical Abstract of the United States: 2002*).

|  | Household Income ($1000s) | | | | | |
| Educational Level | Under 24.9 | 25.0– 49.9 | 50.0– 74.9 | 75.0– 99.9 | 100 or more | Total |
|---|---|---|---|---|---|---|
| Not H.S. graduate | 9285 | 4093 | 1589 | 541 | 354 | 15862 |
| H.S. graduate | 10150 | 9821 | 6050 | 2737 | 2028 | 30786 |
| Some college | 6011 | 8221 | 5813 | 3215 | 3120 | 26380 |
| Bachelor's degree | 2138 | 3985 | 3952 | 2698 | 4748 | 17521 |
| Beyond bach. deg. | 813 | 1497 | 1815 | 1589 | 3765 | 9479 |
| Total | 28397 | 27617 | 19219 | 10780 | 14015 | 100028 |

a. Compute the row percentages and identify the percent frequency distributions for households in which the head is a high school graduate and in which the head is a bachelor's degree recipient.

b. What percentage of households headed by high school graduates earn $75,000 or more? What percentage of households headed by bachelor's degree recipients earn $75,000 or more?

c. Construct percent frequency histograms of income for households headed by persons with a high school degree and for those headed by persons with a bachelor's degree. Is any relationship evident between household income and educational level?

32. Refer again to the crosstabulation of household income by educational level shown in exercise 31.

a. Compute column percentages and identify the percent frequency distributions displayed. What percent of the heads of households did not graduate from high school?

b. What percent of the households earning $100,000 or more were headed by a person having schooling beyond a bachelor's degree? What percent of the households headed by a person with schooling beyond a bachelor's degree earned over $100,000? Why are these two percentages different?

c. Compare the percent frequency distributions for those households earning "Under 24.9," "100 or more," and for "Total." Comment on the relationship between household income and educational level of the head of household.

33. Recently, management at Oak Tree Golf Course received a few complaints about the condition of the greens. Several players complained that the greens are too fast. Rather than react to the comments of just a few, the Golf Association conducted a survey of 100 male and 100 female golfers. The survey results are summarized here.

**Male Golfers**

| Handicap | Greens Condition | |
| | Too Fast | Fine |
|---|---|---|
| Under 15 | 10 | 40 |
| 15 or more | 25 | 25 |

**Female Golfers**

| Handicap | Greens Condition | |
| | Too Fast | Fine |
|---|---|---|
| Under 15 | 1 | 9 |
| 15 or more | 39 | 51 |

a. Combine these two crosstabulations into one with Male, Female as the row labels and the column labels Too Fast and Fine. Which group shows the highest percentage saying that the greens are too fast?

b.  Refer to the initial crosstabulations. For those players with low handicaps (better players), which group (male or female) shows the highest percentage saying the greens are too fast?

c.  Refer to the initial crosstabulations. For those players with higher handicaps, which group (male or female) shows the highest percentage saying the greens are too fast?

d.  What conclusions can you draw about the preferences of men and women concerning the speed of the greens? Are the conclusions you draw from part (a) as compared with parts (b) and (c) consistent? Explain any apparent inconsistencies.

34.  Table 2.14 provides financial data for a sample of 36 companies whose stock trades on the New York Stock Exchange (*Investor's Business Daily*, April 7, 2000). The data on Sales/Margins/ROE are a composite rating based on a company's sales growth rate, its profit margins, and its return on equity (ROE). EPS Rating is a measure of growth in earnings per share for the company.

**TABLE 2.14    FINANCIAL DATA FOR A SAMPLE OF 36 COMPANIES**

| Company | EPS Rating | Relative Price Strength | Industry Group Relative Strength | Sales/Margins/ ROE |
|---|---|---|---|---|
| Advo | 81 | 74 | B | A |
| Alaska AirGp | 58 | 17 | C | B |
| Alliant Tech | 84 | 22 | B | B |
| Atmos Engy | 21 | 9 | C | E |
| Bank of Am. | 87 | 38 | C | A |
| Bowater PLC | 14 | 46 | C | D |
| Callaway Golf | 46 | 62 | B | E |
| Central Parking | 76 | 18 | B | C |
| Dean Foods | 84 | 7 | B | C |
| Dole Food | 70 | 54 | E | C |
| Elec. Data Sys | 72 | 69 | A | B |
| Fed. Dept. Stor. | 79 | 21 | D | B |
| Gateway | 82 | 68 | A | A |
| Goodyear | 21 | 9 | E | D |
| Hanson PLC | 57 | 32 | B | B |
| ICN Pharm. | 76 | 56 | A | D |
| Jefferson plt | 80 | 38 | D | C |
| Kroger | 84 | 24 | D | A |
| Mattel | 18 | 20 | E | D |
| McDermott | 6 | 6 | A | C |
| Monaco | 97 | 21 | D | A |
| Murphy Oil | 80 | 62 | B | B |
| Nordstrom | 58 | 57 | B | C |
| NYMAGIC | 17 | 45 | D | D |
| Office Depot | 58 | 40 | B | B |
| Payless Shoes | 76 | 59 | B | B |
| Praxair | 62 | 32 | C | B |
| Reebok | 31 | 72 | C | E |
| Safeway | 91 | 61 | D | A |
| Teco Energy | 49 | 48 | D | B |
| Texaco | 80 | 31 | D | C |
| US West | 60 | 65 | B | A |
| United Rental | 98 | 12 | C | A |
| Wachovia | 69 | 36 | E | B |
| Winnebago | 83 | 49 | D | A |
| York Intl. | 28 | 14 | D | B |

*Source: Investor's Business Daily*, April 7, 2000.

   a. Prepare a crosstabulation of the data on Sales/Margins/ROE (rows) and EPS Rating (columns). Use classes of 0–19, 20–39, 40–59, 60–79, and 80–99 for EPS Rating.

   b. Compute row percentages and comment on any relationship between the variables.

35. Refer to the data in Table 2.14.
   a. Prepare a crosstabulation of the data on Sales/Margins/ROE and Industry Group Relative Strength.
   b. Prepare a frequency distribution for the data on Sales/Margins/ROE.
   c. Prepare a frequency distribution for the data on Industry Group Relative Strength.
   d. How has the crosstabulation helped in preparing the frequency distributions in parts (b) and (c)?

36. Refer to the data in Table 2.14.
   a. Prepare a scatter diagram of the data on EPS Rating and Relative Price Strength.
   b. Comment on the relationship, if any, between the variables. (The meaning of the EPS Rating is described in exercise 34. Relative Price Strength is a measure of the change in the stock's price over the past 12 months. Higher values indicate greater strength.)

37. The National Football League rates prospects position by position on a scale that ranges from 5 to 9. The ratings are interpreted as follows: 8–9 should start the first year; 7.0–7.9 should start; 6.0–6.9 will make the team as a backup; and 5.0–5.9 can make the club and contribute. Table 2.15 shows the position, weight, speed (seconds for 40 yards), and ratings for 40 NFL prospects (*USA Today,* April 14, 2000).
   a. Prepare a crosstabulation of the data on Position (rows) and Speed (columns). Use classes of 4.00–4.49, 4.50–4.99, 5.00–5.49, and 5.50–5.99 for speed.
   b. Comment on the relationship between Position and Speed based upon the crosstabulation developed in part (a).
   c. Develop a scatter diagram of the data on Speed and Rating. Use the vertical axis for Rating.
   d. Comment on the relationship, if any, between Speed and Rating.

## Summary

A set of data, even if modest in size, is often difficult to interpret directly in the form in which it is gathered. Tabular and graphical methods provide procedures for organizing and summarizing data so that patterns are revealed and the data are more easily interpreted. Frequency distributions, relative frequency distributions, percent frequency distributions, bar graphs, and pie charts were presented as tabular and graphical procedures for summarizing qualitative data. Frequency distributions, relative frequency distributions, percent frequency distributions, histograms, cumulative frequency distributions, cumulative relative frequency distributions, cumulative percent frequency distributions, and ogives were presented as ways of summarizing quantitative data. A stem-and-leaf display provides an exploratory data analysis technique that can be used to summarize quantitative data. Crosstabulation was presented as a tabular method for summarizing data for two variables. The scatter diagram was introduced as a graphical method for showing the relationship between two quantitative variables. Figure 2.9 shows the tabular and graphical methods presented in this chapter.

With large data sets, computer software packages are essential in constructing tabular and graphical summaries of data. In the two chapter appendixes, we show how Minitab and Excel can be used for this purpose.

TABLE 2.15    NATIONAL FOOTBALL LEAGUE RATINGS FOR 40 DRAFT PROSPECTS

| Observation | Name | Position | Weight | Speed | Rating |
|---|---|---|---|---|---|
| 1 | Peter Warrick | Wide receiver | 194 | 4.53 | 9 |
| 2 | Plaxico Burress | Wide receiver | 231 | 4.52 | 8.8 |
| 3 | Sylvester Morris | Wide receiver | 216 | 4.59 | 8.3 |
| 4 | Travis Taylor | Wide receiver | 199 | 4.36 | 8.1 |
| 5 | Laveranues Coles | Wide receiver | 192 | 4.29 | 8 |
| 6 | Dez White | Wide receiver | 218 | 4.49 | 7.9 |
| 7 | Jerry Porter | Wide receiver | 221 | 4.55 | 7.4 |
| 8 | Ron Dugans | Wide receiver | 206 | 4.47 | 7.1 |
| 9 | Todd Pinkston | Wide receiver | 169 | 4.37 | 7 |
| 10 | Dennis Northcutt | Wide receiver | 175 | 4.43 | 7 |
| 11 | Anthony Lucas | Wide receiver | 194 | 4.51 | 6.9 |
| 12 | Darrell Jackson | Wide receiver | 197 | 4.56 | 6.6 |
| 13 | Danny Farmer | Wide receiver | 217 | 4.6 | 6.5 |
| 14 | Sherrod Gideon | Wide receiver | 173 | 4.57 | 6.4 |
| 15 | Trevor Gaylor | Wide receiver | 199 | 4.57 | 6.2 |
| 16 | Cosey Coleman | Guard | 322 | 5.38 | 7.4 |
| 17 | Travis Claridge | Guard | 303 | 5.18 | 7 |
| 18 | Kaulana Noa | Guard | 317 | 5.34 | 6.8 |
| 19 | Leander Jordan | Guard | 330 | 5.46 | 6.7 |
| 20 | Chad Clifton | Guard | 334 | 5.18 | 6.3 |
| 21 | Manula Savea | Guard | 308 | 5.32 | 6.1 |
| 22 | Ryan Johanningmeir | Guard | 310 | 5.28 | 6 |
| 23 | Mark Tauscher | Guard | 318 | 5.37 | 6 |
| 24 | Blaine Saipaia | Guard | 321 | 5.25 | 6 |
| 25 | Richard Mercier | Guard | 295 | 5.34 | 5.8 |
| 26 | Damion McIntosh | Guard | 328 | 5.31 | 5.3 |
| 27 | Jeno James | Guard | 320 | 5.64 | 5 |
| 28 | Al Jackson | Guard | 304 | 5.2 | 5 |
| 29 | Chris Samuels | Offensive tackle | 325 | 4.95 | 8.5 |
| 30 | Stockar McDougle | Offensive tackle | 361 | 5.5 | 8 |
| 31 | Chris McIngosh | Offensive tackle | 315 | 5.39 | 7.8 |
| 32 | Adrian Klemm | Offensive tackle | 307 | 4.98 | 7.6 |
| 33 | Todd Wade | Offensive tackle | 326 | 5.2 | 7.3 |
| 34 | Marvel Smith | Offensive tackle | 320 | 5.36 | 7.1 |
| 35 | Michael Thompson | Offensive tackle | 287 | 5.05 | 6.8 |
| 36 | Bobby Williams | Offensive tackle | 332 | 5.26 | 6.8 |
| 37 | Darnell Alford | Offensive tackle | 334 | 5.55 | 6.4 |
| 38 | Terrance Beadles | Offensive tackle | 312 | 5.15 | 6.3 |
| 39 | Tutan Reyes | Offensive tackle | 299 | 5.35 | 6.1 |
| 40 | Greg Robinson-Ran | Offensive tackle | 333 | 5.59 | 6 |

FIGURE 2.9   TABULAR AND GRAPHICAL METHODS FOR SUMMARIZING DATA

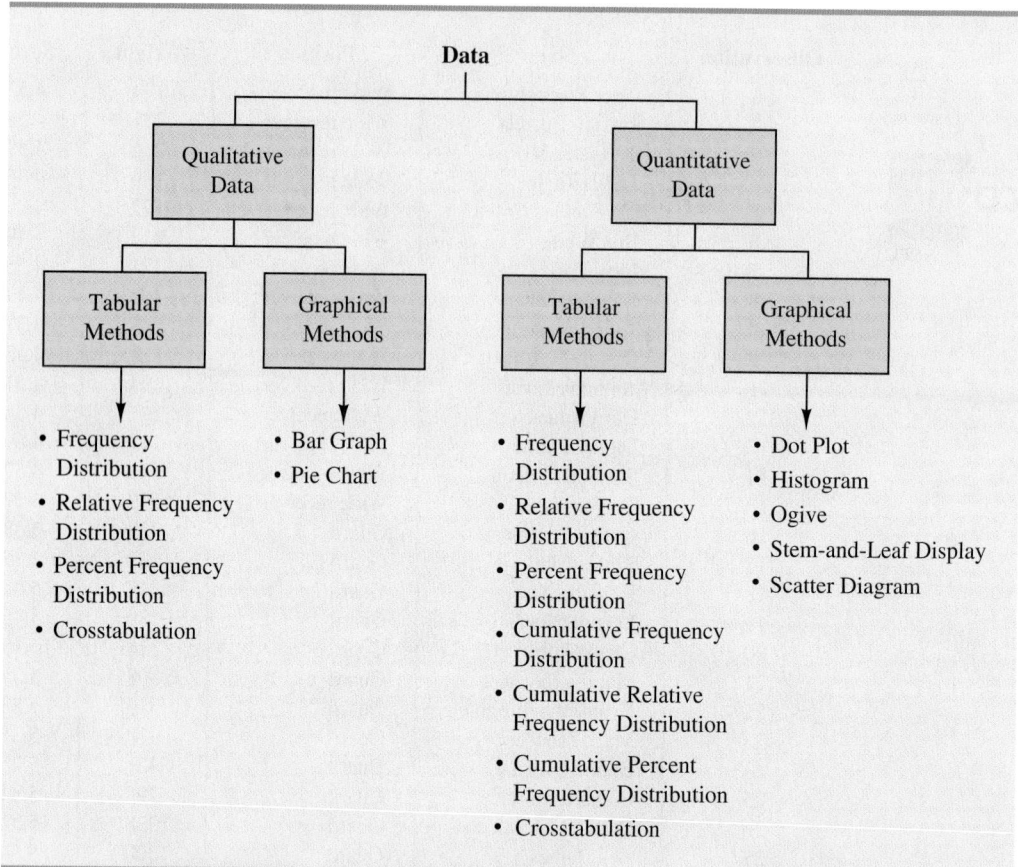

## Glossary

**Qualitative data** Labels or names used to identify categories of like items.

**Quantitative data** Numerical values that indicate how much or how many.

**Frequency distribution** A tabular summary of data showing the number (frequency) of items in each of several nonoverlapping classes.

**Relative frequency distribution** A tabular summary of data showing the fraction or proportion of data items in each of several nonoverlapping classes.

**Percent frequency distribution** A tabular summary of data showing the percentage of items in each of several nonoverlapping classes.

**Bar graph** A graphical device for depicting qualitative data that have been summarized in a frequency, relative frequency, or percent frequency distribution.

**Pie chart** A graphical device for presenting data summaries based on subdivision of a circle into sectors that correspond to the relative frequency for each class.

**Class midpoint** The value halfway between the lower and upper class limits.

**Dot plot** A graphical device that summarizes data by the number of dots above each data value on the horizontal axis.

**Histogram** A graphical presentation of a frequency distribution, relative frequency distribution, or percent frequency distribution of quantitative data constructed by placing the class intervals on the horizontal axis and the frequencies, relative frequencies, or percent frequencies on the vertical axis.

**Cumulative frequency distribution** A tabular summary of quantitative data showing the number of items with values less than or equal to the upper class limit of each class.

**Cumulative relative frequency distribution** A tabular summary of quantitative data showing the fraction or proportion of items with values less than or equal to the upper class limit of each class.

**Cumulative percent frequency distribution** A tabular summary of quantitative data showing the percentage of items with values less than or equal to the upper class limit of each class.

**Ogive** A graph of a cumulative distribution.

**Exploratory data analysis** Methods that use simple arithmetic and easy-to-draw graphs to summarize data quickly.

**Stem-and-leaf display** An exploratory data analysis technique that simultaneously rank orders quantitative data and provides insight about the shape of the distribution.

**Crosstabulation** A tabular summary of data for two variables. The classes for one variable are represented by the rows; the classes for the other variable are represented by the columns.

**Simpson's paradox** Conclusions drawn from two or more separate crosstabulations that can be reversed when the data are aggregated into a single crosstabulation.

**Scatter diagram** A graphical presentation of the relationship between two quantitative variables. One variable is shown on the horizontal axis and the other variable is shown on the vertical axis.

**Trendline** A line that provides an approximation of the relationship between two variables.

## Key Formulas

**Relative Frequency**

$$\frac{\text{Frequency of the class}}{n} \qquad (2.1)$$

**Approximate Class Width**

$$\frac{\text{Largest data value } - \text{ Smallest data value}}{\text{Number of classes}} \qquad (2.2)$$

## Supplementary Exercises

38. *Autodata* and *USA Today* research provided data on the best-selling vehicle models for March 2000 (*USA Today*, April 4, 2000). Among those listed were Chevrolet Silverado/ C/K pickup, Ford F-Series pickup, Ford Taurus, Honda Accord, and Toyota Camry. Data from a sample of 50 vehicle purchases are presented in Table 2.16.

TABLE 2.16   DATA FOR 50 VEHICLE PURCHASES

**Vehicles**

| | | | | |
|---|---|---|---|---|
| Silverado | Taurus | Accord | F-Series | Silverado |
| F-Series | Accord | Silverado | Camry | Taurus |
| Silverado | F-Series | Camry | Silverado | F-Series |
| Taurus | F-Series | Taurus | F-Series | Camry |
| Taurus | F-Series | F-Series | Accord | Camry |
| Silverado | Silverado | Silverado | Silverado | Taurus |
| Camry | Silverado | Accord | F-Series | F-Series |
| Taurus | F-Series | Accord | Camry | Accord |
| F-Series | Silverado | F-Series | F-Series | Taurus |
| Camry | Silverado | F-Series | F-Series | F-Series |

a. Develop a frequency and percent frequency distribution.
b. What are the two top-selling vehicles?
c. Show a pie chart.

39. Each of the *Fortune* 1000 companies belongs to one of several industry classifications (*Fortune,* April 17, 2000). A sample of 20 companies with their corresponding industry classification follows.

| Company | Industry Classification | Company | Industry Classification |
|---------|------------------------|---------|------------------------|
| IBP | Food | Borden | Food |
| Intel | Electronics | McDonnell Douglas | Aerospace |
| Coca-Cola | Beverage | Morton International | Chemicals |
| Union Carbide | Chemicals | Quaker Oats | Food |
| General Electric | Electronics | PepsiCo | Beverage |
| Motorola | Electronics | Maytag | Electronics |
| Kellogg | Food | Textron | Aerospace |
| Dow Chemical | Chemicals | Sara Lee | Food |
| Campbell Soup | Food | Harris | Electronics |
| Ralston Purina | Food | Eaton | Electronics |

a. Provide a frequency distribution showing the number of companies in each industry.
b. Provide a percent frequency distribution.
c. Provide a bar graph for the data.

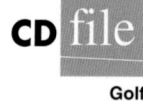
**CD file**

**Golf**

40. *Golf Magazine*'s Top 100 Teachers were asked the question, "What is the most critical area that prevents golfers from reaching their potential?" The possible responses were lack of accuracy, poor approach shots, poor mental approach, lack of power, limited practice, poor putting, poor short game, and poor strategic decisions. The data obtained follow (*Golf Magazine,* February 2002):

| | | | | |
|---|---|---|---|---|
| Mental approach | Mental approach | Short game | Short game | Short game |
| Practice | Accuracy | Mental approach | Accuracy | Putting |
| Power | Approach shots | Accuracy | Short game | Putting |
| Accuracy | Mental approach | Mental approach | Accuracy | Power |
| Accuracy | Accuracy | Short game | Power | Short game |
| Accuracy | Putting | Mental approach | Strategic decisions | Accuracy |
| Short game | Power | Mental approach | Approach shots | Short game |
| Practice | Practice | Mental approach | Power | Power |
| Mental approach | Short game | Mental approach | Short game | Strategic decisions |
| Accuracy | Short game | Accuracy | Mental approach | Short game |
| Mental approach | Putting | Mental approach | Mental approach | Putting |
| Practice | Putting | Practice | Short game | Putting |
| Power | Mental approach | Short game | Practice | Strategic decisions |
| Accuracy | Short game | Accuracy | Practice | Putting |
| Accuracy | Short game | Accuracy | Short game | Putting |
| Accuracy | Approach shots | Short game | Mental approach | Practice |
| Short game | Short game | Strategic decisions | Short game | Short game |
| Practice | Practice | Short game | Practice | Strategic decisions |
| Mental approach | Strategic decisions | Strategic decisions | Power | Short game |
| Accuracy | Practice | Practice | Practice | Accuracy |

a. Develop a frequency and percent frequency distribution.
b. Which four critical areas most often prevent golfers from reaching their potential?

**TABLE 2.17   BOOK VALUE PER SHARE FOR DOW JONES INDUSTRIAL AVERAGE STOCKS**

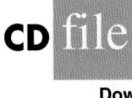

**Dow**

| Company | Book Value per Share | Company | Book Value per Share |
|---|---|---|---|
| AT&T | 14.59 | Home Depot | 7.71 |
| Alcoa | 12.30 | Honeywell | 11.25 |
| Altria Group | 8.96 | IBM | 13.37 |
| Am Express | 9.04 | Intel | 5.39 |
| Boeing | 12.92 | Int'l Paper | 21.37 |
| Caterpillar | 16.18 | Johnson & Johnson | 7.79 |
| Citigroup | 15.09 | JPMorgan Chase | 20.31 |
| Coca-Cola | 4.57 | McDonald's | 7.30 |
| Disney Walt | 11.28 | Merck | 6.89 |
| Du Pont | 14.17 | Microsoft | 8.49 |
| Eastman Kodak | 9.93 | Procter & Gamble | 8.80 |
| ExxonMobil | 10.62 | SBC Comm. | 9.69 |
| Gen Electric | 5.43 | 3M Company | 14.93 |
| GM | 35.15 | United Tech | 17.36 |
| Hewlett-Packard | 7.33 | Wal-Mart | 7.85 |

*Source: Barron's,* March 10, 2003.

41. The data in Table 2.17 show the book value per share for the 30 stocks that compose the Dow Jones Industrial Average (*Barron's,* March 10, 2003).
    a. Construct a frequency distribution to summarize the data. Use a class width of 6.00.
    b. Develop a relative frequency distribution.
    c. Construct a cumulative frequency distribution.
    d. Construct a cumulative relative frequency distribution.
    e. Construct a histogram as a graphical representation of the data. Comment on the shape of the distribution.

42. The closing prices of 40 common stocks follow (*Barron's,* March 10, 2003).

**Comstock**

| | | | | | | | | | |
|---|---|---|---|---|---|---|---|---|---|
| 29.63 | 34.00 | 43.25 | 8.75 | 37.88 | 8.63 | 7.63 | 30.38 | 35.25 | 19.38 |
| 9.25 | 16.50 | 38.00 | 53.38 | 16.63 | 1.25 | 48.38 | 18.00 | 9.38 | 9.25 |
| 10.00 | 25.02 | 18.00 | 8.00 | 28.50 | 24.25 | 21.63 | 18.50 | 33.63 | 31.13 |
| 32.25 | 29.63 | 79.38 | 11.38 | 38.88 | 11.50 | 52.00 | 14.00 | 9.00 | 33.50 |

    a. Construct frequency and relative frequency distributions.
    b. Construct cumulative frequency and cumulative relative frequency distributions.
    c. Construct a histogram.
    d. Using your summaries, make comments and observations about the price of common stock.

43. Ninety-four new shadow stocks were reported by the American Association of Individual Investors (*AAII Journal,* February 1997). The term *shadow* indicates stocks for small to medium-sized firms not followed closely by the major brokerage houses. Information on where the stock was traded—New York Stock Exchange (NYSE), American Stock Exchange (AMEX), and over-the-counter (OTC)—the earnings per share, and the price/ earnings ratio was provided for the following sample of 20 shadow stocks.

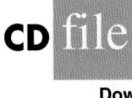

**Shadow**

| Stock | Exchange | Earnings per Share ($) | Price/Earnings Ratio |
|---|---|---|---|
| Chemi-Trol | OTC | .39 | 27.30 |
| Candie's | OTC | .07 | 36.20 |
| TST/Impreso | OTC | .65 | 12.70 |

(*continued*)

| Stock | Exchange | Earnings per Share ($) | Price/Earnings Ratio |
|-------|----------|------------------------|----------------------|
| Unimed Pharm. | OTC | .12 | 59.30 |
| Skyline Chili | AMEX | .34 | 19.30 |
| Cyanotech | OTC | .22 | 29.30 |
| Catalina Light. | NYSE | .15 | 33.20 |
| DDL Elect. | NYSE | .10 | 10.20 |
| Euphonix | OTC | .09 | 49.70 |
| Mesa Labs | OTC | .37 | 14.40 |
| RCM Tech. | OTC | .47 | 18.60 |
| Anuhco | AMEX | .70 | 11.40 |
| Hello Direct | OTC | .23 | 21.10 |
| Hilite Industries | OTC | .61 | 7.80 |
| Alpha Tech. | OTC | .11 | 34.60 |
| Wegener Group | OTC | .16 | 24.50 |
| U.S. Home & Garden | OTC | .24 | 8.70 |
| Chalone Wine | OTC | .27 | 44.40 |
| Eng. Support Sys. | OTC | .89 | 16.70 |
| Int. Remote Imaging | AMEX | .86 | 4.70 |

a. Provide frequency and relative frequency distributions for the exchange data. Where are most shadow stocks listed?

b. Provide frequency and relative frequency distributions for the earnings per share and price/earnings ratio data. Use classes of 0.00–0.19, 0.20–0.39, and so on, for the earnings per share data and classes of 0.0–9.9, 10.0–19.9, and so on for the price/earnings ratio data. What observations and comments can you make about the shadow stocks?

44. A state-by-state listing of per capita personal income for 1998 follows (Bureau of Economic Analysis, *Current Population Survey,* March 2000).

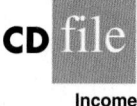

**CD file**

**Income**

| Ala. | 21,500 | Ky. | 21,551 | N.D. | 21,708 |
|------|--------|------|--------|------|--------|
| Alaska | 25,771 | La. | 21,385 | Ohio | 25,239 |
| Ariz. | 23,152 | Maine | 23,002 | Okla. | 21,056 |
| Ark. | 20,393 | Md. | 30,023 | Ore. | 24,775 |
| Calif. | 27,579 | Mass. | 32,902 | Penn. | 26,889 |
| Colo. | 28,821 | Mich. | 25,979 | R.I. | 26,924 |
| Conn. | 37,700 | Minn. | 27,667 | S.C. | 21,387 |
| Del. | 29,932 | Miss. | 18,998 | S.D. | 22,201 |
| D.C. | 37,325 | Mo. | 24,447 | Tenn. | 23,615 |
| Fla. | 25,922 | Mont. | 20,427 | Texas | 25,028 |
| Ga. | 25,106 | Neb. | 24,786 | Utah | 21,096 |
| Hawaii | 26,210 | Nev. | 27,360 | Vt. | 24,217 |
| Idaho | 21,080 | N.H. | 29,219 | Va. | 27,489 |
| Ill. | 28,976 | N.J. | 33,953 | Wash. | 28,066 |
| Ind. | 24,302 | N.M. | 20,008 | W. Va. | 19,373 |
| Iowa | 24,007 | N.Y. | 31,679 | Wis. | 25,184 |
| Kan. | 25,049 | N.C. | 24,122 | Wyo. | 23,225 |

Develop a frequency distribution, a relative frequency distribution, and a histogram.

45. The conclusion from a 40-state poll conducted by the Joint Council on Economic Education is that students do not learn enough economics. The findings were based on test results from 11th- and 12th-grade students who took a 46-question, multiple-choice test on basic economic concepts such as profit and the law of supply and demand. The following table gives sample data on the number of questions answered correctly.

| 12 | 10 | 16 | 24 | 12 | 14 | 18 | 23 |
|----|----|----|----|----|----|----|----|
| 31 | 14 | 15 | 19 | 17 | 9 | 19 | 28 |
| 24 | 16 | 21 | 13 | 20 | 12 | 22 | 18 |
| 22 | 18 | 30 | 16 | 26 | 18 | 16 | 14 |
| 8 | 25 | 22 | 15 | 33 | 24 | 17 | 19 |

Summarize these data using the following:
a.  Stem-and-leaf display
b.  Frequency distribution
c.  Relative frequency distribution
d.  Cumulative frequency distribution
e.  On the basis of these data, do you agree with the claim that students are not learning enough economics? Explain.

46.  The daily high and low temperatures for 20 cities follow (*USA Today*, May 9, 2000).

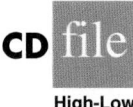

**CD** file

**High-Low**

| City | High | Low | City | High | Low |
|------|------|-----|------|------|-----|
| Athens | 75 | 54 | Melbourne | 66 | 50 |
| Bangkok | 92 | 74 | Montreal | 64 | 52 |
| Cairo | 84 | 57 | Paris | 77 | 55 |
| Copenhagen | 64 | 39 | Rio de Janeiro | 80 | 61 |
| Dublin | 64 | 46 | Rome | 81 | 54 |
| Havana | 86 | 68 | Seoul | 64 | 50 |
| Hong Kong | 81 | 72 | Singapore | 90 | 75 |
| Johannesburg | 61 | 50 | Sydney | 68 | 55 |
| London | 73 | 48 | Tokyo | 79 | 59 |
| Manila | 93 | 75 | Vancouver | 57 | 43 |

a.  Prepare a stem-and-leaf display for the high temperatures.
b.  Prepare a stem-and-leaf display for the low temperatures.
c.  Compare the stem-and-leaf displays from parts (a) and (b), and make some comments about the differences between daily high and low temperatures.
d.  Use the stem-and-leaf display from part (a) to determine the number of cities having a high temperature of 80 degrees or above.
e.  Provide frequency distributions for both high and low temperature data.

47.  Refer to the data set for high and low temperatures for 20 cities in Exercise 46.
a.  Develop a scatter diagram to show the relationship between the two variables, high temperature and low temperature.
b.  Comment on the relationship between high and low temperature.

48.  A study of job satisfaction was conducted for four occupations. Job satisfaction was measured using an 18-item questionnaire with each question receiving a response score of 1 to 5 with higher scores indicating greater satisfaction. The sum of the 18 scores provides the job satisfaction score for each individual in the sample. The data are as follow.

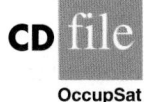

**CD** file

**OccupSat**

| Occupation | Satisfaction Score | Occupation | Satisfaction Score | Occupation | Satisfaction Score |
|------------|-------------------|------------|-------------------|------------|-------------------|
| Lawyer | 42 | Physical Therapist | 78 | Systems Analyst | 60 |
| Physical Therapist | 86 | Systems Analyst | 44 | Physical Therapist | 59 |
| Lawyer | 42 | Systems Analyst | 71 | Cabinetmaker | 78 |
| Systems Analyst | 55 | Lawyer | 50 | Physical Therapist | 60 |

*(continued)*

| Occupation | Satisfaction Score | Occupation | Satisfaction Score | Occupation | Satisfaction Score |
|---|---|---|---|---|---|
| Lawyer | 38 | Lawyer | 48 | Physical Therapist | 50 |
| Cabinetmaker | 79 | Cabinetmaker | 69 | Cabinetmaker | 79 |
| Lawyer | 44 | Physical Therapist | 80 | Systems Analyst | 62 |
| Systems Analyst | 41 | Systems Analyst | 64 | Lawyer | 45 |
| Physical Therapist | 55 | Physical Therapist | 55 | Cabinetmaker | 84 |
| Systems Analyst | 66 | Cabinetmaker | 64 | Physical Therapist | 62 |
| Lawyer | 53 | Cabinetmaker | 59 | Systems Analyst | 73 |
| Cabinetmaker | 65 | Cabinetmaker | 54 | Cabinetmaker | 60 |
| Lawyer | 74 | Systems Analyst | 76 | Lawyer | 64 |
| Physical Therapist | 52 | | | | |

a. Provide a crosstabulation of occupation and job satisfaction score.
b. Compute the row percentages for your crosstabulation in part (a).
c. What observations can you make concerning the level of job satisfaction for these occupations?

49. Do larger companies generate more revenue? The following data show the number of employees and annual revenue for a sample of 20 *Fortune* 1000 companies (*Fortune*, April 17, 2000).

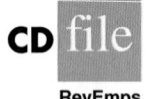

RevEmps

| Company | Employees | Revenue ($ millions) | Company | Employees | Revenue ($ millions) |
|---|---|---|---|---|---|
| Sprint | 77,600 | 19,930 | American Financial | 9,400 | 3,334 |
| Chase Manhattan | 74,801 | 33,710 | Fluor | 53,561 | 12,417 |
| Computer Sciences | 50,000 | 7,660 | Phillips Petroleum | 15,900 | 13,852 |
| Wells Fargo | 89,355 | 21,795 | Cardinal Health | 36,000 | 25,034 |
| Sunbeam | 12,200 | 2,398 | Borders Group | 23,500 | 2,999 |
| CBS | 29,000 | 7,510 | MCI Worldcom | 77,000 | 37,120 |
| Time Warner | 69,722 | 27,333 | Consolidated Edison | 14,269 | 7,491 |
| Steelcase | 16,200 | 2,743 | IBP | 45,000 | 14,075 |
| Georgia-Pacific | 57,000 | 17,796 | Super Value | 50,000 | 17,421 |
| Toro | 1,275 | 4,673 | H&R Block | 4,200 | 1,669 |

a. Prepare a scatter diagram to show the relationship between the variables Revenue and Employees.
b. Comment on any relationship between the variables.

50. A survey of commercial buildings served by the Cincinnati Gas & Electric Company was concluded in 1992 (CG&E Commercial Building Characteristics Survey, November 25, 1992). One question asked what main heating fuel was used and another asked the year the commercial building was constructed. A partial crosstabulation of the findings follows.

| Year Constructed | Fuel Type | | | | |
|---|---|---|---|---|---|
| | Electricity | Natural Gas | Oil | Propane | Other |
| 1973 or before | 40 | 183 | 12 | 5 | 7 — 2⁴⁹ |
| 1974–1979 | 24 | 26 | 2 | 2 | 0 — 54 |
| 1980–1986 | 37 | 38 | 1 | 0 | 6 — 8² |
| 1987–1991 | 48 | 70 | 2 | 0 | 1 — 12¹ |
| | 149 | 317 | 17 | 7 | 14 |

a.   Complete the crosstabulation by showing the row totals and column totals.
b.   Show the frequency distributions for year constructed and for fuel type.
c.   Prepare a crosstabulation showing column percentages.
d.   Prepare a crosstabulation showing row percentages.
e.   Comment on the relationship between year constructed and fuel type.

51.   Table 2.18 contains a portion of the data on the file named Fortune on the CD accompanying the text. It provides data on stockholders' equity, market value, and profits for a sample of 50 *Fortune* 500 companies (*Fortune,* April 26, 1999).

**TABLE 2.18    DATA FOR A SAMPLE OF 50 *FORTUNE 500* COMPANIES**

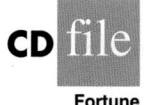

**Fortune**

| Company | Stockholders' Equity ($1000s) | Market Value ($1000s) | Profit ($1000s) |
|---|---|---|---|
| AGCO | 982.1 | 372.1 | 60.6 |
| AMP | 2698.0 | 12017.6 | 2.0 |
| Apple Computer | 1642.0 | 4605.0 | 309.0 |
| Baxter International | 2839.0 | 21743.0 | 315.0 |
| Bergen Brunswick | 629.1 | 2787.5 | 3.1 |
| Best Buy | 557.7 | 10376.5 | 94.5 |
| Charles Schwab | 1429.0 | 35340.6 | 348.5 |
| . | . | . | . |
| . | . | . | . |
| . | . | . | . |
| Walgreen | 2849.0 | 30324.7 | 511.0 |
| Westvaco | 2246.4 | 2225.6 | 132.0 |
| Whirlpool | 2001.0 | 3729.4 | 325.0 |
| Xerox | 5544.0 | 35603.7 | 395.0 |

a.   Prepare a crosstabulation for the variables Stockholders' Equity and Profit. Use classes of 0–200, 200–400, . . . , 1000–1200 for Profit, and classes of 0–1200, 1200–2400, . . . , 4800–6000 for Stockholders' Equity.
b.   Compute the row percentages for your crosstabulation in part (a)
c.   What relationship, if any, do you notice between Profit and Stockholders' Equity?

52.   Refer to the data set in Table 2.18.
a.   Prepare a crosstabulation for the variables Market Value and Profit.
b.   Compute the row percentages for your crosstabulation in part (a).
c.   Comment on any relationship between the variables.

53.   Refer to the data set in Table 2.18.
a.   Prepare a scatter diagram to show the relationship between the variables Profit and Stockholders' Equity.
b.   Comment on any relationship between the variables.

54.   Refer to the data set in Table 2.18.
a.   Prepare a scatter diagram to show the relationship between the variables Market Value and Stockholders' Equity.
b.   Comment on any relationship between the variables.

## Case Problem   Pelican Stores

Pelican Stores is a chain of women's apparel stores operating throughout the country. The chain recently ran a promotion in which discount coupons were sent to customers of related stores. Data collected for a sample of 100 in-store credit card transactions during one day

TABLE 2.19    DATA FOR A SAMPLE OF 100 CREDIT CARD PURCHASES AT PELICAN STORES

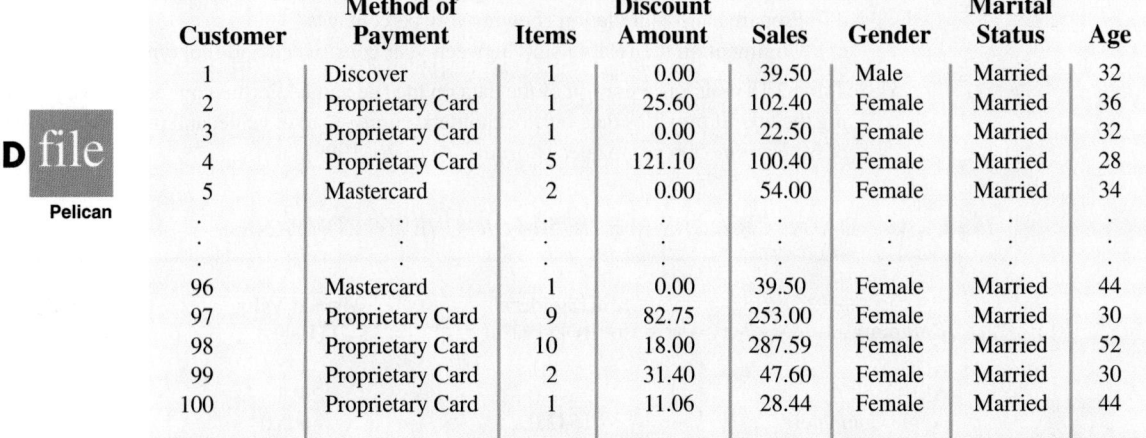

| Customer | Method of Payment | Items | Discount Amount | Sales | Gender | Marital Status | Age |
|---|---|---|---|---|---|---|---|
| 1 | Discover | 1 | 0.00 | 39.50 | Male | Married | 32 |
| 2 | Proprietary Card | 1 | 25.60 | 102.40 | Female | Married | 36 |
| 3 | Proprietary Card | 1 | 0.00 | 22.50 | Female | Married | 32 |
| 4 | Proprietary Card | 5 | 121.10 | 100.40 | Female | Married | 28 |
| 5 | Mastercard | 2 | 0.00 | 54.00 | Female | Married | 34 |
| . | . | . | . | . | . | . | . |
| . | . | . | . | . | . | . | . |
| . | . | . | . | . | . | . | . |
| 96 | Mastercard | 1 | 0.00 | 39.50 | Female | Married | 44 |
| 97 | Proprietary Card | 9 | 82.75 | 253.00 | Female | Married | 30 |
| 98 | Proprietary Card | 10 | 18.00 | 287.59 | Female | Married | 52 |
| 99 | Proprietary Card | 2 | 31.40 | 47.60 | Female | Married | 30 |
| 100 | Proprietary Card | 1 | 11.06 | 28.44 | Female | Married | 44 |

**CD** file

**Pelican**

in November 2002 are contained in the file named Pelican. Table 2.19 shows a portion of the data set. A nonzero amount for the Discount variable indicates that the customer brought in the promotional coupons and used them. For a very few customers, the discount amount is actually greater than the sales amount (see customer 4). The sales amount is net of returns.

Pelican's management would like to use this sample data to learn about its customer base and to evaluate the promotion involving discount coupons.

## Managerial Report

Use the tabular and graphical methods of descriptive statistics to help management develop a customer profile and to evaluate the promotional campaign. At a minimum, your report should include the following.

1. Percent frequency distributions for key variables.
2. A bar graph or pie chart showing the percentage of customer purchases attributable to the promotional campaign.
3. A crosstabulation of type of customer (regular or promotional) versus sales. Comment on any similarities or differences present.
4. A scatter diagram of sales versus discount for only those customers responding to the promotion. Comment on any relationship apparent between sales and discount.
5. A scatter diagram to explore the relationship between sales and customer age.

## Appendix 2.1    Using Minitab for Tabular and Graphical Presentations

Minitab offers extensive capabilities for constructing tabular and graphical summaries of data. In this appendix we show how Minitab can be used to construct several graphical summaries and the tabular summary of a crosstabulation. The graphical methods presented include the dot plot, the histogram, the stem-and-leaf display, and the scatter diagram.

### Dot Plot

**Audit**

We use the audit time data in Table 2.5 to demonstrate. The data are in column C1 of a Minitab worksheet. The following steps will generate a dot plot.

**Step 1.** Select the **Graph** menu and choose **Dotplot**
**Step 2.** Select **One Y, Simple** and click **OK**
**Step 3.** When the Dotplot-One Y, Simple dialog box appears:
      Enter C1 in the **Graph Variables** box
      Click **OK**

### Histogram

**Audit**

We show how to construct a histogram with frequencies on the vertical axis using the audit time data in Table 2.5. The data are in column C1 of a Minitab worksheet. The following steps will generate a histogram for audit times.

**Step 1.** Select the **Graph** menu
**Step 2.** Choose **Histogram**
**Step 3.** Select **Simple** and click **OK**
**Step 4.** When the Histogram-Simple dialog box appears:
      Enter C1 in the **Graph Variables** box
      Click **OK**
**Step 5.** When the Histogram appears:
      Position the mouse pointer over any one of the bars
      **Double Click**
**Step 6.** When the Edit Bars dialog box appears:
      Click on the **Binning** tab
      Select **Midpoint** for Interval Type
      Select **Midpoint/Cutpoint positions** for Interval Definition
      Enter 12:32/5 in the Midpoint/Cutpoint positions box*
      Click **OK**

### Stem-and-Leaf Display

**ApTest**

We use the aptitude test data in Table 2.9 to demonstrate the construction of a stem-and-leaf display. The data are in column C1 of a Minitab worksheet. The following steps will generate the stretched stem-and-leaf display shown in Section 2.3.

**Step 1.** Select the **Graph** menu
**Step 2.** Choose **Stem-and-Leaf**
**Step 3.** When the Stem-and-Leaf dialog box appears:
      Enter C1 in the **Graph Variables** box
      Click **OK**

### Scatter Diagram

**Stereo**

We use the stereo and sound equipment store data in Table 2.13 to demonstrate the construction of a scatter diagram. The weeks are numbered from 1 to 10 in column C1, the data for number of commercials are in column C2, and the data for sales are in column C3 of a Minitab worksheet. The following steps will generate the scatter diagram shown in Figure 2.7.

---

*The entry 12:35/5 indicates that 12 is the midpoint of the first class, 35 is the midpoint of the last class, and 5 is the class width.

**Step 1.** Select the **Graph** menu
**Step 2.** Choose **Scatterplot**
**Step 3.** Select **Simple** and click **OK**
**Step 4.** When the Scatterplot-Simple dialog box appears:
　　　　Enter C3 under **Y variables** and C2 under **X variables**
　　　　Click **OK**

## Crosstabulation

**Restaurant**

We use the data from Zagat's restaurant review, part of which is shown in Table 2.10, to demonstrate. The restaurants are numbered from 1 to 300 in column C1 of the Minitab worksheet. The quality ratings are in column C2, and the meal prices are in column C3.

Minitab can only create a crosstabulation for qualitative variables and meal price is a quantitative variable: So we need to first code the meal price data by specifying the category (class) to which each meal price belongs. The following steps will code the meal price data to create four categories of meal price in column C4: $10–19, $20–29, $30–39, and $40–49.

**Step 1.** Select the **Data** menu
**Step 2.** Choose **Code**
**Step 3.** Choose **Numeric to Text**
**Step 4.** When the Code-Numeric to Text dialog box appears:
　　　　Enter C3 in the **Code data from columns** box
　　　　Enter C4 in the **Into columns** box
　　　　Enter 10:19 in the first **Original values** box and $10–19 in the adjacent **New** box
　　　　Enter 20:29 in the second **Original values** box and $20–29 in the adjacent **New** box
　　　　Enter 30:39 in the third **Original values** box and $30–39 in the adjacent **New** box
　　　　Enter 40:49 in the fourth **Original values** box and $40–49 in the adjacent **New** box
　　　　Click **OK**

For each meal price in column C3 the associated meal price category will now appear in column C4. We can now develop a crosstabulation for quality rating and the meal price categories by using the data in columns C2 and C4. The following steps will create a crosstabulation containing the same information as shown in Table 2.11.

**Step 1.** Select the **Stat** menu
**Step 2.** Choose **Tables**
**Step 3.** Choose **Cross Tabulation and Chi-Square**
**Step 4.** When the Cross Tabulation and Chi-Square dialog box appears:
　　　　Enter C2 in the **For rows** box and C4 in the **For columns** box
　　　　Select **Counts** under Display
　　　　Click **OK**

## Appendix 2.2　Using Excel for Tabular and Graphical Presentations

Excel offers extensive capabilities for constructing tabular and graphical summaries of data. Three of the most powerful tools available are the Insert Function tool, the Chart Wizard, and PivotTable Report.

## Functions and the Insert Function Tool

Excel provides a variety of functions that are useful for statistical analysis. If we know what function we want and how to use it, we can simply enter the function directly into a cell of an Excel worksheet. If not, Excel provides an Insert Function tool to help in identifying the functions available and in using them.

**Insert Function tool**   To access the Insert Function tool, click $f_x$ on the formula bar or select the **Insert** menu and choose $f_x$ **Function.** The **Insert Function** dialog box will then appear (See Figure 2.10). The **Or select a category box** shows a list of the categories of Excel functions; we selected **Statistical** in Figure 2.10. With **Statistical** selected, a list of all the statistical functions available is displayed in the **Select a function** box. Here, we highlight the **COUNTIF** function. Once a function is highlighted, the proper form for the function along with a brief description appears below the **Select a function** box. To obtain assistance in properly using the function, click **OK.**

**SoftDrink**

**Frequency distributions**   We show how the COUNTIF function can be used to construct a frequency distribution for the data on soft drink purchases in Table 2.1. Refer to Figure 2.11 as we describe the tasks involved. The formula worksheet (shows the functions and formulas used) is set in the background and the value worksheet (shows the results obtained using the functions and formulas) appears in the foreground.

The label "Brand Purchased" and the data for the 50 soft drink purchases are in cells A1:A51. We also entered labels in cells C1:D1 and the soft drink names into cells C2:C6. Excel's COUNTIF function can be used to count the number of times each soft drink appears

FIGURE 2.10   EXCEL'S INSERT FUNCTION DIALOG BOX

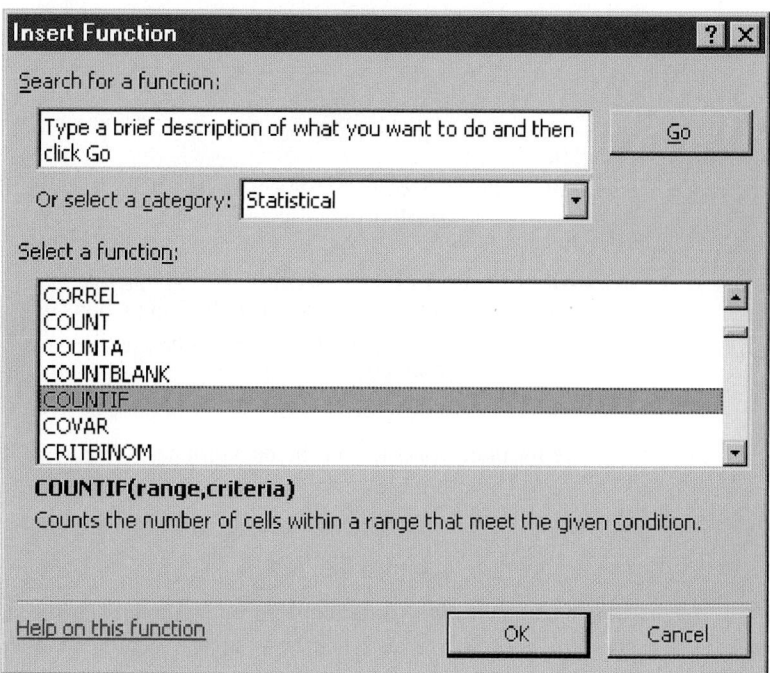

**FIGURE 2.11**    FREQUENCY DISTRIBUTION FOR SOFT DRINK PURCHASES CONSTRUCTED USING EXCEL'S COUNTIF FUNCTION

*Note: Rows 11–44 are hidden.*

| | A | B | C | D | E |
|---|---|---|---|---|---|
| 1 | **Brand Purchased** | | **Soft Drink** | **Frequency** | |
| 2 | Coke Classic | | Coke Classic | =COUNTIF($A$2:$A$51,C2) | |
| 3 | Diet Coke | | Diet Coke | =COUNTIF($A$2:$A$51,C3) | |
| 4 | Pepsi-Cola | | Dr. Pepper | =COUNTIF($A$2:$A$51,C4) | |
| 5 | Diet Coke | | Pepsi-Cola | =COUNTIF($A$2:$A$51,C5) | |
| 6 | Coke Classic | | Sprite | =COUNTIF($A$2:$A$51,C6) | |
| 7 | Coke Classic | | | | |
| 8 | Dr. Pepper | | | | |
| 9 | Diet Coke | | | | |
| 10 | Pepsi-Cola | | | | |
| 45 | Pepsi-Cola | | | | |
| 46 | Pepsi-Cola | | | | |
| 47 | Pepsi-Cola | | | | |
| 48 | Coke Classic | | | | |
| 49 | Dr. Pepper | | | | |
| 50 | Pepsi-Cola | | | | |
| 51 | Sprite | | | | |
| 52 | | | | | |

| | A | B | C | D | E |
|---|---|---|---|---|---|
| 1 | **Brand Purchased** | | **Soft Drink** | **Frequency** | |
| 2 | Coke Classic | | Coke Classic | 19 | |
| 3 | Diet Coke | | Diet Coke | 8 | |
| 4 | Pepsi-Cola | | Dr. Pepper | 5 | |
| 5 | Diet Coke | | Pepsi-Cola | 13 | |
| 6 | Coke Classic | | Sprite | 5 | |
| 7 | Coke Classic | | | | |
| 8 | Dr. Pepper | | | | |
| 9 | Diet Coke | | | | |
| 10 | Pepsi-Cola | | | | |
| 45 | Pepsi-Cola | | | | |
| 46 | Pepsi-Cola | | | | |
| 47 | Pepsi-Cola | | | | |
| 48 | Coke Classic | | | | |
| 49 | Dr. Pepper | | | | |
| 50 | Pepsi-Cola | | | | |
| 51 | Sprite | | | | |
| 52 | | | | | |

in cells A2:A51. The following steps utilize the Insert Function tool to produce the frequency distribution in the foreground of Figure 2.11.

> **Step 1.** Select cell **D2,** access the Insert Function tool, and choose **COUNTIF** from the list of statistical functions
>
> **Step 2.** Click **OK**
>
> **Step 3.** When the Function Arguments dialog box appears:
> > Enter $A$2:$A$51 in the **Range** box
> > Enter C2 in the **Criteria** box
> > Click **OK**
>
> **Step 4.** Copy cell D2 to cells D3:D6

The formula worksheet in the background of Figure 2.11 shows the cell formulas inserted by applying these steps. The value worksheet, in the foreground of Figure 2.11, shows the values computed using these cell formulas; we see that the Excel worksheet shows the same frequency distribution that we developed in Table 2.2.

If you are familiar with the COUNTIF function, and do not need the assistance of the Insert Function tool, you can enter the formulas directly into cells D2:D6. For instance, to count the number of times that Coke Classic appears, enter the following formula into cell D2:

$$=\text{COUNTIF(\$A\$2:\$A\$51,C2)}$$

To count the number of times the other soft drinks appear, copy the formula into cells D3:D6.

Many more of Excel's functions will be demonstrated in future chapter appendixes. Depending on the complexity of the function, we will either enter it directly into the appropriate cell or utilize the Insert Function tool.

## Chart Wizard

Excel's Chart Wizard provides extensive capabilities for developing graphical presentations. This tool allows us to go beyond what can be done with functions and formulas alone. We show how it can be used to construct bar graphs, histograms, and scatter diagrams.

**SoftDrink**

**Bar graphs and histograms**   Here we show how the Chart Wizard can be used to construct bar graphs and histograms. Let us start by developing a bar graph for the soft drink data; we constructed a frequency distribution in Figure 2.11. The chart we are going to develop is an extension of that worksheet. Refer to Figure 2.12 as we describe the tasks involved. The value worksheet from Figure 2.11 is set in the background; the chart developed using the Chart Wizard appears in the foreground.

The following steps describe how to use Excel's Chart Wizard to construct a bar graph for the soft drink data using the frequency distribution appearing in cells C1:D6.

**Step 1.**  Select cells C1:D6
**Step 2.**  Select the **Chart Wizard** button on the Standard toolbar (or select the **Insert** menu and choose the **Chart** option)

**FIGURE 2.12**   BAR GRAPH OF SOFT DRINK PURCHASES CONSTRUCTED USING EXCEL'S CHART WIZARD

| | A | B | C | D | E | F | G | H | I |
|---|---|---|---|---|---|---|---|---|---|
| 1 | Brand Purchased | | Soft Drink | Frequency | | | | | |
| 2 | Coke Classic | | Coke Classic | 19 | | | | | |
| 3 | Diet Coke | | Diet Coke | 8 | | | | | |
| 4 | Pepsi-Cola | | Dr. Pepper | 5 | | | | | |
| 5 | Diet Coke | | Pepsi-Cola | 13 | | | | | |
| 6 | Coke Classic | | Sprite | 5 | | | | | |
| 7 | Coke Classic | | | | | | | | |
| 8 | Dr. Pepper | | | | | | | | |
| 9 | Diet Coke | | | | | | | | |
| 10 | Pepsi-Cola | | | | | | | | |
| 45 | Pepsi-Cola | | | | | | | | |
| 46 | Pepsi-Cola | | | | | | | | |
| 47 | Pepsi-Cola | | | | | | | | |
| 48 | Coke Classic | | | | | | | | |
| 49 | Dr. Pepper | | | | | | | | |
| 50 | Pepsi-Cola | | | | | | | | |
| 51 | Sprite | | | | | | | | |
| 52 | | | | | | | | | |
| 53 | | | | | | | | | |
| 54 | | | | | | | | | |
| 55 | | | | | | | | | |
| 56 | | | | | | | | | |
| 57 | | | | | | | | | |

**Bar Graph of Soft Drink Purchases**

(Frequency on vertical axis, 0 to 20; Soft Drink on horizontal axis: Coke Classic, Diet Coke, Dr. Pepper, Pepsi-Cola, Sprite)

**Step 3.** When the Chart Wizard—Step 1 of 4—Chart Type dialog box appears:

Choose **Column** in the **Chart type** list

Choose **Clustered Column** from the **Chart sub-type** display

Click **Next**

**Step 4.** When the Chart Wizard—Step 2 of 4—Chart Source Data Dialog box appears:

Click **Next**

**Step 5.** When the Chart Wizard—Step 3 of 4—Chart Options dialog box appears:

Select the **Titles** tab

Enter **Bar Graph of Soft Drink Purchases** in the **Chart title** box

Enter **Soft Drink** in the **Category (X) axis** box

Enter **Frequency** in the **Values (Y) axis** box

Select the **Legend** tab and then

Remove the check in the **Show legend** box

Click **Next**

**Step 6.** When the Chart Wizard—Step 4 of 4—Chart Location dialog box appears:

Specify a location for the new chart (We used the current worksheet by selecting **As object in**)

Click **Finish**

The resulting bar graph (chart) is shown in Figure 2.12.*

Excel's Chart Wizard can produce a pie chart for the soft drink data in a similar fashion. To develop a pie chart, choose Pie in the Chart type list in step 3.

As we stated in a note and comment at the end of Section 2.2, a histogram is essentially the same as a bar graph with no separation between the bars. Figure 2.13 shows the audit time data with a frequency distribution in the background and a bar graph developed using the Chart Wizard (using the same steps just described) in the foreground. Because the adjacent bars in a histogram must touch, we need to edit the column chart (the bar graph) in order to eliminate the gap between each of the bars. The following steps accomplish this process.

**Step 1.** Right click on any bar in the column chart to produce a list of options

**Step 2.** Choose **Format Data Series**

**Step 3.** When the Format Data Series dialog box appears:

Select the **Options** tab

Enter **0** in the **Gap width** box

Click **OK**

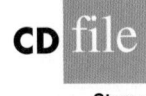

**Stereo**

**Scatter diagram** We use the stereo and sound equipment store data in Table 2.13 to demonstrate the use of Excel's Chart Wizard to construct a scatter diagram. Refer to Figure 2.14 as we describe the tasks involved. The value worksheet is set in the background, and the scatter diagram produced by the Chart Wizard appears in the foreground. The following steps will produce the scatter diagram.

**Step 1.** Select cells B1:C11

**Step 2.** Select the **Chart Wizard** button on the standard toolbar (or select the **Insert** menu and choose the **Chart** option)

**Step 3.** When the Chart Wizard—Step 1 of 4—Chart Type dialog box appears:

Choose **XY (Scatter)** in the **Chart type:** display

Click **Next**

**Step 4.** When the Chart Wizard—Step 2 of 4—Chart Source Data dialog box appears:

Click **Next**

---

*Resizing an Excel chart is not difficult. First, select the chart. Small block squares, called sizing handles, will appear on the chart border. Click on the sizing handles and drag them to resize the figure to your preference.

**FIGURE 2.13** HISTOGRAM CONSTRUCTED USING EXCEL FOR THE AUDIT TIME DATA

**FIGURE 2.14** SCATTER DIAGRAM FOR STEREO AND SOUND EQUIPMENT STORE USING EXCEL'S CHART WIZARD

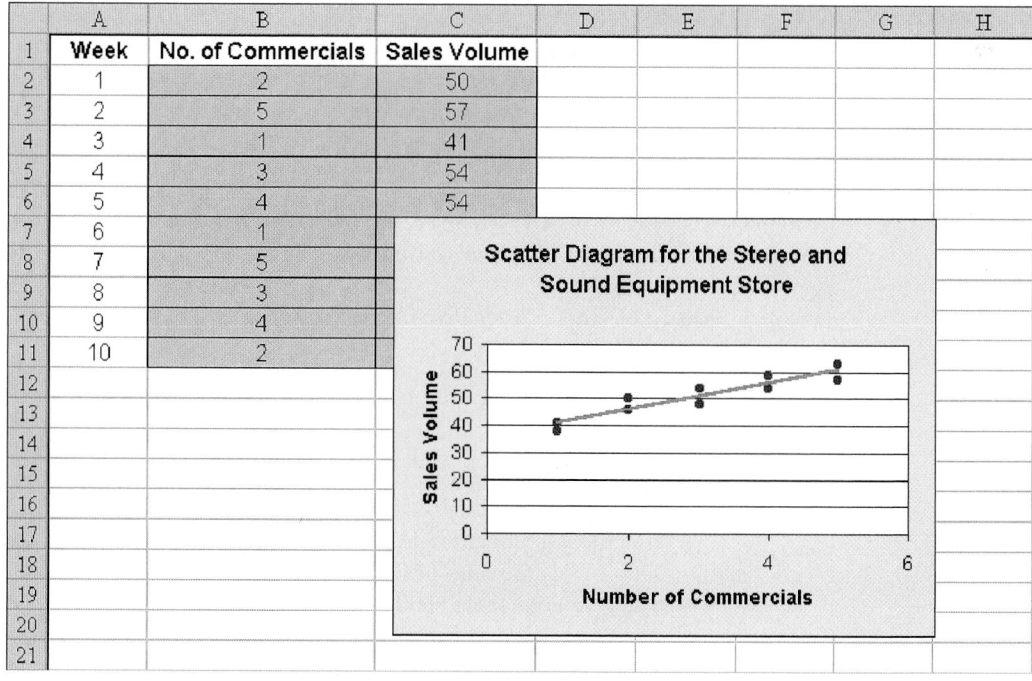

**Step 5.** When the Chart Wizard—Step 3 of 4—Chart Options dialog box appears:

Select the **Titles** tab

Enter **Scatter Diagram for the Stereo and Sound Equipment Store** in the **Chart title** box

Enter **Commercials** in the **Value (X) axis** box

Enter **Sales Volume** in the **Value (Y) axis** box

Select the **Legend** tab

Remove the check in the **Show legend** box

Click **Next**

**Step 6.** When the Chart Wizard—Step 4 of 4—Chart Location dialog box appears:

Specify a location for the new chart (We used the current worksheet by selecting **As object in**)

Click **Finish**

It is easy to now add a trendline to the scatter diagram.

**Step 1.** Position the mouse pointer over any data point in the scatter diagram and right click to display a list of options

**Step 2.** Choose **Add Trendline**

**Step 3.** When the Add Trendline dialog box appears:

Select the **Type** tab

Choose **Linear** from the **Trend/Regression type** display

Click **OK**

## PivotTable Report

Excel's PivotTable Report provides a valuable tool for managing data sets involving more than one variable. We will illustrate its use by showing how to develop a crosstabulation.

**Crosstabulation**  We illustrate the construction of a crosstabulation using the restaurant data in Figure 2.15. Labels are entered in row 1, and the data for each of the 300 restaurants are entered into cells A2:C301.

**Step 1.** Select the **Data** menu

**Step 2.** Choose **PivotTable and PivotChart Report**

**Step 3.** When the PivotTable and PivotChart Wizard—Step 1 of 3—dialog box appears:

Choose **Microsoft Excel list or database**

Choose **PivotTable**

Click **Next**

**Step 4.** When the PivotTable and PivotChart Wizard—Step 2 of 3—dialog box appears:

Enter A1:C301 in the **Range** box

Click **Next**

**Step 5.** When the PivotTable and PivotChart Wizard—Step 3 of 3—dialog box appears:

Select **New Worksheet**

Click **Layout**

**Step 6.** When the PivotTable and PivotChart Wizard—Layout diagram appears (see Figure 2.16):

Drag the **Quality Rating** field button to the **ROW** section of the diagram

Drag the **Meal Price ($)** field button to the **COLUMN** section of the diagram

Drag the **Restaurant** field button to the **Data** section of the diagram

Double click the **Sum of Restaurant** field button in the DATA section

When the PivotTable Field dialog box appears:

Choose **Count** under **Summarize by**

Click **OK** (Figure 2.17 shows the completed layout diagram)

Click **OK**

FIGURE 2.15    EXCEL WORKSHEET CONTAINING RESTAURANT DATA

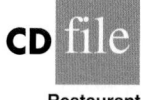

**Restaurant**

*Note: Rows 12–291 are hidden.*

|     | A | B | C | D |
|-----|---|---|---|---|
| 1 | Restaurant | Quality Rating | Meal Price ($) | |
| 2 | 1 | Good | 18 | |
| 3 | 2 | Very Good | 22 | |
| 4 | 3 | Good | 28 | |
| 5 | 4 | Excellent | 38 | |
| 6 | 5 | Very Good | 33 | |
| 7 | 6 | Good | 28 | |
| 8 | 7 | Very Good | 19 | |
| 9 | 8 | Very Good | 11 | |
| 10 | 9 | Very Good | 23 | |
| 11 | 10 | Good | 13 | |
| 292 | 291 | Very Good | 23 | |
| 293 | 292 | Very Good | 24 | |
| 294 | 293 | Excellent | 45 | |
| 295 | 294 | Good | 14 | |
| 296 | 295 | Good | 18 | |
| 297 | 296 | Good | 17 | |
| 298 | 297 | Good | 16 | |
| 299 | 298 | Good | 15 | |
| 300 | 299 | Very Good | 38 | |
| 301 | 300 | Very Good | 31 | |
| 302 | | | | |

FIGURE 2.16    PIVOTTABLE AND PIVOTCHART WIZARD-LAYOUT DIAGRAM

**FIGURE 2.17   COMPLETED LAYOUT DIAGRAM**

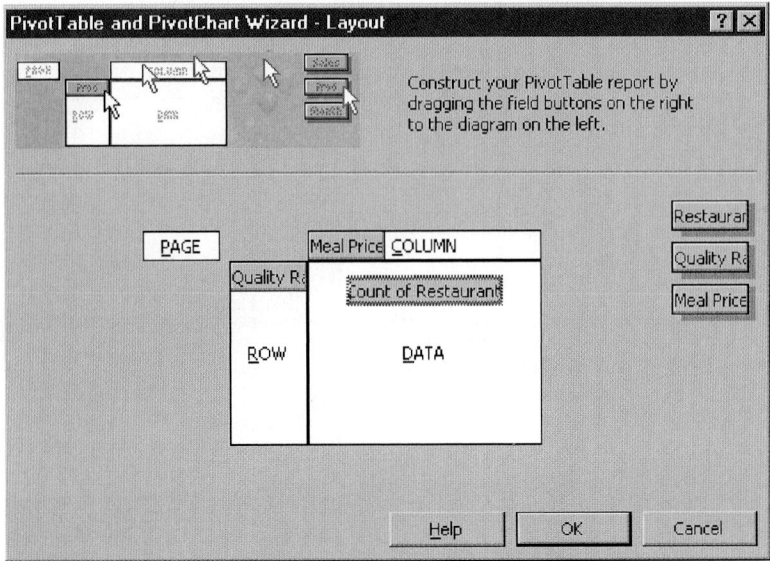

**Step 7.** When the PivotTable and PivotChart Wizard—Step 3 of 3—dialog box reappears:
Click **Finish**

A portion of the output generated by Excel is shown in Figure 2.18. Note that the output that appears in columns D through AK is hidden so the results can be shown in a reasonably sized figure. The row labels (Excellent, Good, and Very Good) and row totals (66, 84, 150, and 300) that appear in Figure 2.18 are the same as the row labels and row totals shown in Table 2.11. But they are in a different order. To put them in the order Good, Very Good, Excellent, follow these steps.

**Step 1.** Right click on Excellent in cell A5
**Step 2.** Choose **Order**
**Step 3.** Select **Move to End**

In Figure 2.18, one column is designated for each possible value of meal price. For example, column B contains a count of restaurants with a $10 meal price, column C contains a count of restaurants with an $11 meal price, and so on. To view the PivotTable Report in a form similar to that shown in Table 2.11, we must group the columns into four price categories: $10–19, $20–29, $30–39, and $40–49. The steps necessary to group the columns for the worksheet shown in Figure 2.18 follow.

**Step 1.** Right click on Meal Price ($) in cell B3 of the PivotTable
**Step 2.** Choose **Group and Show Detail**
          Choose **Group**
**Step 3.** When the **Grouping** dialog box appears
          Enter 10 in the **Starting at** box
          Enter 49 in the **Ending at** box
          Enter 10 in the **By** box
          Click **OK**

The revised PivotTable output is shown in Figure 2.19. It is the final PivotTable. Note that it provides the same information as the crosstabulation shown in Table 2.11.

**FIGURE 2.18   INITIAL PIVOTTABLE REPORT OUTPUT (COLUMNS D:AK ARE HIDDEN.)**

|   | A | B | C | AL | AM | AN | AO |
|---|---|---|---|---|---|---|---|
| 1 | | | | | | | |
| 2 | | | | | | | |
| 3 | Count of Restaurant | Meal Price ($) ↴ | | | | | |
| 4 | Quality Rating      ↴ | 10 | 11 | 47 | 48 | Grand Total | |
| 5 | Excellent | | | 2 | 2 | 66 | |
| 6 | Good | 6 | 4 | | | 84 | |
| 7 | Very Good | 1 | 4 | | 1 | 150 | |
| 8 | Grand Total | 7 | 8 | 2 | 3 | 300 | |
| 9 | | | | | | | |
| 10 | | | | | | | |
| 11 | | | | | | | |
| 12 | | PivotTable        ▾ × | | | | | |
| 13 | | PivotTable ▾ ▦▦ ▔▜ ↕ ▦▦ ▦ | | | | | |
| 14 | | | | | | | |
| 15 | | | | | | | |
| 16 | | | | | | | |
| 17 | | | | | | | |
| 18 | | | | | | | |
| 19 | | | | | | | |
| 20 | | | | | | | |

**FIGURE 2.19   FINAL PIVOTTABLE REPORT FOR RESTAURANT DATA**

|   | A | B | C | D | E | F | G |
|---|---|---|---|---|---|---|---|
| 1 | | | | | | | |
| 2 | | | | | | | |
| 3 | Count of Restaurant | Meal Price ($) ↴ | | | | | |
| 4 | Quality Rating      ↴ | 10-19 | 20-29 | 30-39 | 40-49 | Grand Total | |
| 5 | Good | 42 | 40 | 2 | | 84 | |
| 6 | Very Good | 34 | 64 | 46 | 6 | 150 | |
| 7 | Excellent | 2 | 14 | 28 | 22 | 66 | |
| 8 | Grand Total | 78 | 118 | 76 | 28 | 300 | |
| 9 | | | | | | | |
| 10 | | | | | | | |
| 11 | | | | | | | |
| 12 | | PivotTable        ▾ × | | | | | |
| 13 | | PivotTable ▾ ▦▦ ▔▜ ↕ ▦▦ ▦ | | | | | |
| 14 | | | | | | | |
| 15 | | | | | | | |
| 16 | | | | | | | |
| 17 | | | | | | | |
| 18 | | | | | | | |
| 19 | | | | | | | |
| 20 | | | | | | | |

# Descriptive Statistics: Numerical Measures

**CONTENTS**

## SMALL FRY DESIGN*
*SANTA ANA, CALIFORNIA*

Founded in 1997, Small Fry Design is a toy and accessory company that designs and imports products for infants. The company's product line includes teddy bears, mobiles, musical toys, rattles, and security blankets, and features high-quality soft toy designs with an emphasis on color, texture, and sound. The products are designed in the United States and manufactured in China.

Small Fry Design uses independent representatives to sell the products to infant furnishing retailers, children's accessory and apparel stores, gift shops, upscale department stores, and major catalog companies. Currently, Small Fry Design products are distributed in more than 1000 retail outlets throughout the United States.

Cash flow management is one of the most critical activities in the day-to-day operation of this company. Ensuring sufficient incoming cash to meet both current and ongoing debt obligations can mean the difference between business success and failure. A critical factor in cash flow management is the analysis and control of accounts receivable. By measuring the average age and dollar value of outstanding invoices, management can predict cash availability and monitor changes in the status of accounts receivable. The company set the following goals: the average age for outstanding invoices should not exceed 45 days, and the dollar value of invoices more than 60 days old should not exceed 5% of the dollar value of all accounts receivable.

In a recent summary of accounts receivable status, the following descriptive statistics were provided for the age of outstanding invoices:

| | |
|---|---|
| Mean | 40 days |
| Median | 35 days |
| Mode | 31 days |

*The authors are indebted to John A. McCarthy, president of Small Fry Design, for providing this Statistics in Practice.

Enjoying Small Fry Design products. © Photo courtesy of Small Fry Design, Inc.

Interpretation of these statistics shows that the mean or average age of an invoice is 40 days. The median shows that half of the invoices remain outstanding 35 days or more. The mode of 31 days, the most frequent invoice age, indicates that the most common length of time an invoice is outstanding is 31 days. The statistical summary also showed that only 3% of the dollar value of all accounts receivable was more than 60 days old. Based on the statistical information, management was satisfied that accounts receivable and incoming cash flow were under control.

In this chapter, you will learn how to compute and interpret some of the statistical measures used by Small Fry Design. In addition to the mean, median, and mode, you will learn about other descriptive statistics such as the range, variance, standard deviation, percentiles, and correlation. These numerical measures will assist in the understanding and interpretation of data.

In Chapter 2 we discussed tabular and graphical presentations used to summarize data. In this chapter, we present several numerical measures that provide additional alternatives for summarizing data.

We start by developing numerical summary measures for data sets consisting of a single variable. When a data set contains more than one variable, the same numerical measures can be computed separately for each variable. However, in the two-variable case, we will also develop measures of the relationship between the variables.

Numerical measures of location, dispersion, shape, and association are introduced. If the measures are computed for data from a sample, they are called **sample statistics**. If the measures are computed for data from a population, they are called **population parameters**. In statistical inference, a sample statistic is referred to as the **point estimator** of the corresponding population parameter. In Chapter 7 we will discuss in more detail the process of point estimation.

In the two chapter appendixes we show how Minitab and Excel can be used to compute many of the numerical measures described in the chapter.

 **3.1** ## Measures of Location

### Mean

Perhaps the most important measure of location is the **mean**, or average value, for a variable. The mean provides a measure of central location for the data. If the data are from a sample, the mean is denoted by $\bar{x}$; if the data are from a population, the mean is denoted by the Greek letter $\mu$.

In statistical formulas, it is customary to denote the value of variable $x$ for the first observation by $x_1$, the value of variable $x$ for the second observation by $x_2$, and so on. In general, the value of variable $x$ for the $i$th observation is denoted by $x_i$. For a sample with $n$ observations, the formula for the sample mean is as follows.

*The sample mean $\bar{x}$ is a sample statistic.*

SAMPLE MEAN

$$\bar{x} = \frac{\Sigma x_i}{n} \qquad (3.1)$$

In the preceding formula, the numerator is the sum of the values of the $n$ observations. That is,

$$\Sigma x_i = x_1 + x_2 + \cdots + x_n$$

The Greek letter $\Sigma$ is the summation sign.

To illustrate the computation of a sample mean, let us consider the following class size data for a sample of five college classes.

$$46 \quad 54 \quad 42 \quad 46 \quad 32$$

We use the notation $x_1, x_2, x_3, x_4, x_5$ to represent the number of students in each of the five classes.

$$x_1 = 46 \qquad x_2 = 54 \qquad x_3 = 42 \qquad x_4 = 46 \qquad x_5 = 32$$

Hence, to compute the sample mean, we can write

$$\bar{x} = \frac{\Sigma x_i}{n} = \frac{x_1 + x_2 + x_3 + x_4 + x_5}{5} = \frac{46 + 54 + 42 + 46 + 32}{5} = 44$$

The sample mean class size is 44 students.

Another illustration of the computation of a sample mean is given in the following situation. Suppose that a college placement office sent a questionnaire to a sample of business school graduates requesting information on monthly starting salaries. Table 3.1 shows the

TABLE 3.1    MONTHLY STARTING SALARIES FOR A SAMPLE OF 12 BUSINESS SCHOOL
GRADUATES

**Salary**

| Graduate | Monthly Starting Salary ($) | Graduate | Monthly Starting Salary ($) |
|----------|------------------------------|----------|------------------------------|
| 1 | 2850 | 7 | 2890 |
| 2 | 2950 | 8 | 3130 |
| 3 | 3050 | 9 | 2940 |
| 4 | 2880 | 10 | 3325 |
| 5 | 2755 | 11 | 2920 |
| 6 | 2710 | 12 | 2880 |

collected data. The mean monthly starting salary for the sample of 12 business college
graduates is computed as

$$\bar{x} = \frac{\Sigma x_i}{n} = \frac{x_1 + x_2 + \cdots + x_{12}}{12}$$

$$= \frac{2850 + 2950 + \cdots + 2880}{12}$$

$$= \frac{35{,}280}{12} = 2940$$

Equation (3.1) shows how the mean is computed for a sample with $n$ observations. The
formula for computing the mean of a population remains the same, but we use different notation to indicate that we are working with the entire population. The number of observations in a population is denoted by $N$ and the symbol for a population mean is $\mu$.

*The sample mean $\bar{x}$ is a*
*point estimator of the*
*population mean $\mu$.*

POPULATION MEAN

$$\mu = \frac{\Sigma x_i}{N} \qquad\qquad\qquad \textbf{(3.2)}$$

## Median

The **median** is another measure of central location for a variable. The median is the value
in the middle when the data are arranged in ascending order (smallest value to largest
value). With an odd number of observations, the median is the middle value. An even number of observations has no single middle value. In this case, we follow convention and define the median as the average of the values for the middle two observations. For
convenience the definition of the median is restated as follows.

MEDIAN

Arrange the data in ascending order (smallest value to largest value).

**(a)** For an odd number of observations the median is the middle value.
**(b)** For an even number of observations, the median is the average of the two middle values.

Let us apply this definition to compute the median class size for the sample of five college classes. Arranging the data in ascending order provides the following list.

$$32 \quad 42 \quad 46 \quad 46 \quad 54$$

Because $n = 5$ is odd, the median is the middle value. Thus the median class size is 46 students. Even though this data set contains two observations with values of 46, each observation is treated separately when we arrange the data in ascending order.

Suppose we also compute the median starting salary for the 12 business college graduates in Table 3.1. We first arrange the data in ascending order.

2710   2755   2850   2880   2880   2890   2920   2940   2950   3050   3130   3325

Middle Two Values

Because $n = 12$ is even, we identify the middle two values: 2890 and 2920. The median is the average of these values.

$$\text{Median} = \frac{2890 + 2920}{2} = 2905$$

*The median is the measure of location most often reported for annual income and property value data because a few extremely large incomes or property values can inflate the mean. In such cases, the median offers a better measure of central location, or typical values.*

Although the mean is the more commonly used measure of central location, in some situations the median is preferred. The mean is influenced by extremely small and large data values. For instance, suppose that one of the graduates (see Table 3.1) had a starting salary of $10,000 per month (maybe the individual's family owns the company). If we change the highest monthly starting salary in Table 3.1 from $3325 to $10,000 and recompute the mean, the sample mean changes from $2940 to $3496. The median of $2905, however, is unchanged, because $2890 and $2920 are still the middle two values. With the extremely high starting salary included, the median provides a better measure of central location than the mean. We can generalize to say that whenever a data set contains extreme values, the median is often the preferred measure of central location, or typical values.

## Mode

A third measure of location is the **mode**. The mode is defined as follows.

> MODE
>
> The mode is the value that occurs with greatest frequency.

To illustrate the identification of the mode, consider the sample of five class sizes. The only value that occurs more than once is 46. Because this value, occurring with a frequency of 2, has the greatest frequency, it is the mode. As another illustration, consider the sample of starting salaries for the business school graduates. The only monthly starting salary that occurs more than once is $2880. Because this value has the greatest frequency, it is the mode.

Situations can arise for which the greatest frequency occurs at two or more different values. In these instances more than one mode exists. If the data contain exactly two modes, we say that the data are *bimodal*. If data contain more than two modes, we say that the data are *multimodal*. In multimodal cases the mode is almost never reported because listing three or more modes would not be particularly helpful in describing a location for the data.

The mode is an important measure of location for qualitative data. For example, the qualitative data set in Table 2.2 resulted in the following frequency distribution for soft drink purchases.

| Soft Drink | Frequency |
|------------|-----------|
| Coke Classic | 19 |
| Diet Coke | 8 |
| Dr. Pepper | 5 |
| Pepsi-Cola | 13 |
| Sprite | 5 |
| Total | 50 |

The mode, or most frequently purchased soft drink, is Coke Classic. For this type of data it obviously makes no sense to speak of the mean or median. The mode provides the information of interest, the most frequently purchased soft drink.

## Percentiles

A **percentile** provides information about how the data are spread over the interval from the smallest value to the largest value. For data that do not contain numerous repeated values, the $p$th percentile divides the data into two parts. Approximately $p$ percent of the observations have values less than the $p$th percentile; approximately $(100 - p)$ percent of the observations have values greater than the $p$th percentile. The $p$th percentile is formally defined as follows.

> PERCENTILE
>
> The $p$th percentile is a value such that *at least* $p$ percent of the observations are less than or equal to this value and *at least* $(100 - p)$ percent of the observations are greater than or equal to this value.

Colleges and universities frequently report admission test scores in terms of percentiles. For instance, suppose an applicant obtains a raw score of 54 on the verbal portion of an admission test. How this student performed in relation to other students taking the same test may not be readily apparent. However, if the raw score of 54 corresponds to the 70th percentile, we know that approximately 70% of the students scored lower than this individual and approximately 30% of the students scored higher than this individual.

The following procedure can be used to compute the $p$th percentile.

> CALCULATING THE $p$TH PERCENTILE
>
> **Step 1.** Arrange the data in ascending order (smallest value to largest value).
> **Step 2.** Compute an index $i$
>
> $$i = \left(\frac{p}{100}\right)n$$
>
> where $p$ is the percentile of interest and $n$ is the number of observations.

*Following these steps makes it easy to calculate percentiles.*

> **Step 3.** (a) If $i$ *is not an integer, round up.* The next integer *greater* than $i$ denotes the position of the $p$th percentile.
> (b) If $i$ *is an integer,* the $p$th percentile is the average of the values in positions $i$ and $i + 1$.

As an illustration of this procedure, let us determine the 85th percentile for the starting salary data in Table 3.1.

**Step 1.** Arrange the data in ascending order.

2710   2755   2850   2880   2880   2890   2920   2940   2950   3050   3130   3325

**Step 2.**

$$i = \left(\frac{p}{100}\right)n = \left(\frac{85}{100}\right)12 = 10.2$$

**Step 3.** Because $i$ is not an integer, *round up.* The position of the 85th percentile is the next integer greater than 10.2, the 11th position.

Returning to the data, we see that the 85th percentile is the data value in the 11th position, or 3130.

As another illustration of this procedure, let us consider the calculation of the 50th percentile for the starting salary data. Applying step 2, we obtain

$$i = \left(\frac{50}{100}\right)12 = 6$$

Because $i$ is an integer, step 3(b) states that the 50th percentile is the average of the sixth and seventh data values; thus the 50th percentile is $(2890 + 2920)/2 = 2905$. Note that the *50th percentile is also the median.*

## Quartiles

*Quartiles are just specific percentiles; thus, the steps for computing percentiles can be applied directly in the computation of quartiles.*

It is often desirable to divide data into four parts, with each part containing approximately one-fourth, or 25% of the observations. Figure 3.1 shows a data distribution divided into four parts. The division points are referred to as the **quartiles** and are defined as

$Q_1$ = first quartile, or 25th percentile

$Q_2$ = second quartile, or 50th percentile (also the median)

$Q_3$ = third quartile, or 75th percentile.

The starting salary data are again arranged in ascending order. We already identified $Q_2$, the second quartile (median), as 2905.

2710   2755   2850   2880   2880   2890   2920   2940   2950   3050   3130   3325

The computations of quartiles $Q_1$ and $Q_3$ require the use of the rule for finding the 25th and 75th percentiles. These calculations follow.

For $Q_1$,

$$i = \left(\frac{p}{100}\right)n = \left(\frac{25}{100}\right)12 = 3$$

**FIGURE 3.1    LOCATION OF THE QUARTILES**

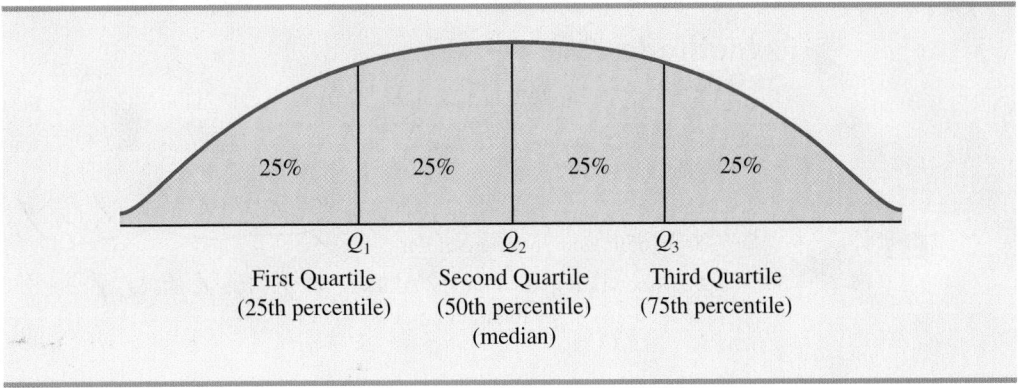

Because $i$ is an integer, step 3(b) indicates that the first quartile, or 25th percentile, is the average of the third and fourth data values; thus, $Q_1 = (2850 + 2880)/2 = 2865$.

For $Q_3$,

$$i = \left(\frac{p}{100}\right)n = \left(\frac{75}{100}\right)12 = 9$$

Again, because $i$ is an integer, step 3(b) indicates that the third quartile, or 75th percentile, is the average of the ninth and tenth data values; thus, $Q_3 = (2950 + 3050)/2 = 3000$.

The quartiles divide the starting salary data into four parts, with each part containing 25% of the observations.

| 2710 | 2755 | 2850 | 2880 | 2880 | 2890 | 2920 | 2940 | 2950 | 3050 | 3130 | 3325 |

$$Q_1 = 2865 \qquad\qquad \underset{\text{(Median)}}{Q_2 = 2905} \qquad\qquad Q_3 = 3000$$

We defined the quartiles as the 25th, 50th, and 75th percentiles. Thus, we computed the quartiles in the same way as percentiles. However, other conventions are sometimes used to compute quartiles, and the actual values reported for quartiles may vary slightly depending on the convention used. Nevertheless, the objective of all procedures for computing quartiles is to divide the data into four equal parts.

## NOTES AND COMMENTS

It is better to use the median than the mean as a measure of central location when a data set contains extreme values. Another measure, sometimes used when extreme values are present, is the *trimmed mean*. It is obtained by deleting a percentage of the smallest and largest values from a data set and then computing the mean of the remaining values. For example, the 5% trimmed mean is ob-tained by removing the smallest 5% and the largest 5% of the data values and then computing the mean of the remaining values. Using the sample with $n = 12$ starting salaries, $0.05(12) = 0.6$. Rounding this value to 1 indicates that the 5% trimmed mean would remove the 1 smallest data value and the 1 largest data value. The 5% trimmed mean using the 10 remaining observations is 2924.50.

## Exercises

## Methods

1. Consider a sample with data values of 10, 20, 12, 17, and 16. Compute the mean and median.

2. Consider a sample with data values of 10, 20, 21, 17, 16, and 12. Compute the mean and median.

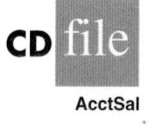

3. Consider a sample with data values of 27, 25, 20, 15, 30, 34, 28, and 25. Compute the 20th, 25th, 65th, and 75th percentiles.

4. Consider a sample with data values of 53, 55, 70, 58, 64, 57, 53, 69, 57, 68, and 53. Compute the mean, median, and mode.

## Applications

5. According to a salary survey conducted by the National Association of Colleges and Employers, bachelor's degree candidates in accounting received starting offers averaging $34,500 per year (Bureau of Labor Statistics, *Occupational Outlook Handbook*, 2000–01 Edition). A sample of 30 students who graduated in 2000 with a bachelor's degree in accounting resulted in the following starting salaries. Data are in thousands of dollars.

AcctSal

| | | | | |
|---|---|---|---|---|
| 36.8 | 34.9 | 35.2 | 37.2 | 36.2 |
| 35.8 | 36.8 | 36.1 | 36.7 | 36.6 |
| 37.3 | 38.2 | 36.3 | 36.4 | 39.0 |
| 38.3 | 36.0 | 35.0 | 36.7 | 37.9 |
| 38.3 | 36.4 | 36.5 | 38.4 | 39.4 |
| 38.8 | 35.4 | 36.4 | 37.0 | 36.4 |

 a. What is the mean starting salary?
 b. What is the median starting salary?
 c. What is the mode?
 d. What is the first quartile?
 e. What is the third quartile?

6. The American Association of Individual Investors conducts an annual survey of discount brokers. The commissions charged by a sample of 24 discount brokers for two types of trades, a broker-assisted trade of 100 shares at $50 per share and an online trade of 500 shares at $50 per share, are shown in Table 3.2.
 a. Compute the mean, median, and mode for the commission charged on a broker-assisted trade of 100 shares at $50 per share.
 b. Compute the mean, median, and mode for the commission charged on an online trade of 500 shares at $50 per share.
 c. Which costs more, a broker-assisted trade of 100 shares at $50 per share or an online trade of 500 shares at $50 per share?
 d. Is the cost of a transaction related to the amount of the transaction?

7. The average person spends 45 minutes a day listening to recorded music (*Des Moines Register*, December 5, 1997). The following data were obtained for the number of minutes spent listening to recorded music for a sample of 30 individuals.

Music

| | | | | |
|---|---|---|---|---|
| 88.3 | 4.3 | 4.6 | 7.0 | 9.2 |
| 0.0 | 99.2 | 34.9 | 81.7 | 0.0 |
| 85.4 | 0.0 | 17.5 | 45.0 | 53.3 |
| 29.1 | 28.8 | 0.0 | 98.9 | 64.5 |
| 4.4 | 67.9 | 94.2 | 7.6 | 56.6 |
| 52.9 | 145.6 | 70.4 | 65.1 | 63.6 |

TABLE 3.2   COMMISSIONS CHARGED BY DISCOUNT BROKERS

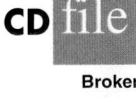

**Broker**

| Broker | Broker-Assisted 100 Shares at $50/Share | Online 500 Shares at $50/Share | Broker | Broker-Assisted 100 Shares at $50/Share | Online 500 Shares at $50/Share |
|---|---|---|---|---|---|
| Accutrade | 30.00 | 29.95 | Merrill Lynch Direct | 50.00 | 29.95 |
| Ameritrade | 24.99 | 10.99 | Muriel Siebert | 45.00 | 14.95 |
| Banc of America | 54.00 | 24.95 | NetVest | 24.00 | 14.00 |
| Brown & Co. | 17.00 | 5.00 | Recom Securities | 35.00 | 12.95 |
| Charles Schwab | 55.00 | 29.95 | Scottrade | 17.00 | 7.00 |
| CyberTrader | 12.95 | 9.95 | Sloan Securities | 39.95 | 19.95 |
| E*TRADE Securities | 49.95 | 14.95 | Strong Investments | 55.00 | 24.95 |
| First Discount | 35.00 | 19.75 | TD Waterhouse | 45.00 | 17.95 |
| Freedom Investments | 25.00 | 15.00 | T. Rowe Price | 50.00 | 19.95 |
| Harrisdirect | 40.00 | 20.00 | Vanguard | 48.00 | 20.00 |
| Investors National | 39.00 | 62.50 | Wall Street Discount | 29.95 | 19.95 |
| MB Trading | 9.95 | 10.55 | York Securities | 40.00 | 36.00 |

*Source: AAII Journal,* January 2003.

a. Compute the mean.
b. Do these data appear to be consistent with the average reported by the newspaper?
c. Compute the median.
d. Compute the first and third quartiles.
e. Compute and interpret the 40th percentile.

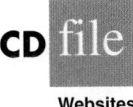

8. Millions of Americans get up each morning and telecommute to work from offices in their home. Following is a sample of age data for individuals working at home.

| 18 | 54 | 20 | 46 | 25 | 48 | 53 | 27 | 26 | 37 |
| 40 | 36 | 42 | 25 | 27 | 33 | 28 | 40 | 45 | 25 |

a. Compute the mean and mode.
b. The median age of the population of all adults is 35.5 years (*The New York Times Almanac*, 2001). Use the median age of the preceding data to comment on whether the at-home workers tend to be younger or older than the population of all adults.
c. Compute the first and third quartiles.
d. Compute and interpret the 32nd percentile.

9. Media Matrix collected data showing the most popular Web sites when browsing at home and at work (*Business 2.0*, January 2000). The following data show the number of unique visitors (thousands) for the top 25 Web sites when browsing at home.

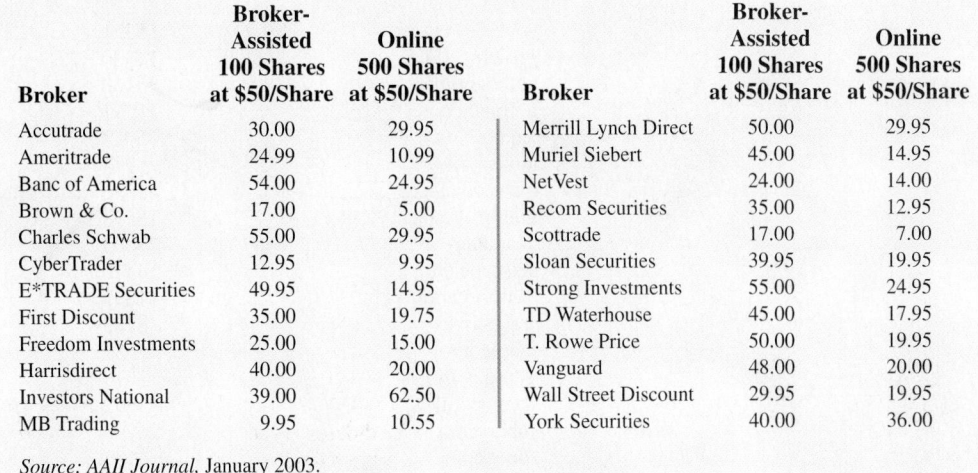

**Websites**

| Web Site | Unique Visitors (1000s) |
|---|---|
| about.com | 5538 |
| altavista.com | 7391 |
| amazon.com | 7986 |
| angelfire.com | 8917 |
| aol.com | 23863 |
| bluemountainarts.com | 6786 |
| ebay.com | 8296 |
| excite.com | 10479 |

(*continued*)

| Web Site | Unique Visitors (1000s) |
|----------|-------------------------|
| geocities.com | 15321 |
| go.com | 14330 |
| hotbot.com | 5760 |
| hotmail.com | 11791 |
| icq.com | 5052 |
| looksmart.com | 5984 |
| lycos.com | 9950 |
| microsoft.com | 15593 |
| msn.com | 23505 |
| netscape.com | 14470 |
| passport.com | 11299 |
| real.com | 6785 |
| snap.com | 5730 |
| tripod.com | 7970 |
| xoom.com | 5652 |
| yahoo.com | 26796 |
| zdnet.com | 5133 |

a. Compute the mean and median.

b. Do you think it would be better to use the mean or the median as the measure of central location for these data? Explain.

c. Compute the first and third quartiles.

d. Compute and interpret the 85th percentile.

10. The *Los Angeles Times* regularly reports the air quality index for various areas of Southern California. Index ratings of 0–50 are considered good, 51–100 moderate, 101–200 unhealthy, 201–275 very unhealthy, and over 275 hazardous. Recent air quality indexes for Pomona were 28, 42, 58, 48, 45, 55, 60, 49, and 50.

a. Compute the mean, median, and mode for the data. Should the Pomona air quality index be considered good?

b. Compute the 25th percentile and 75th percentile for the Pomona air quality data.

11. In automobile mileage and gasoline-consumption testing, 13 automobiles were road tested for 300 miles in both city and highway driving conditions. The following data were recorded for miles-per-gallon performance.

*City:*    16.2  16.7  15.9  14.4  13.2  15.3  16.8  16.0  16.1  15.3  15.2  15.3  16.2
*Highway:* 19.4  20.6  18.3  18.6  19.2  17.4  17.2  18.6  19.0  21.1  19.4  18.5  18.7

Use the mean, median, and mode to make a statement about the difference in performance for city and highway driving.

12. Because of recent technological advances, today's digital cameras produce better-looking pictures than their predecessors did a year ago. The following data show the street price, maximum picture capacity, and battery life (minutes) for 20 of the latest models (*PC World*, January 2000).

| Camera | Price ($) | Maximum Picture Capacity | Battery Life (minutes) |
|--------|-----------|--------------------------|------------------------|
| Agfa Ephoto CL30 | 349 | 36 | 25 |
| Canon PowerShot A50 | 499 | 106 | 75 |
| Canon PowerShot Pro70 | 999 | 96 | 118 |
| Epson PhotoPC 800 | 699 | 120 | 99 |
| Fujifilm DX-10 | 299 | 30 | 229 |

| Camera | Price ($) | Maximum Picture Capacity | Battery Life (minutes) |
|--------|-----------|--------------------------|------------------------|
| Fujifilm MX-2700 | 699 | 141 | 124 |
| Fujifilm MX-2900 Zoom | 899 | 141 | 88 |
| HP PhotoSmart C200 | 299 | 80 | 68 |
| Kodak DC215 Zoom | 399 | 54 | 159 |
| Kodak DC265 Zoom | 899 | 180 | 186 |
| Kodak DC280 Zoom | 799 | 245 | 143 |
| Minolta Dimage EX Zoom 1500 | 549 | 105 | 38 |
| Nikon Coolpix 950 | 999 | 32 | 88 |
| Olympus D-340R | 299 | 122 | 161 |
| Olympus D-450 Zoom | 499 | 122 | 62 |
| Ricoh RDC-500 | 699 | 99 | 56 |
| Sony Cybershot DSC-F55 | 699 | 63 | 69 |
| Sony Mavica MVC-FD73 | 599 | 40 | 186 |
| Sony Mavica MVC-FD88 | 999 | 40 | 88 |
| Toshiba PDR-M4 | 599 | 124 | 142 |

a.  Compute the mean price.
b.  Compute the mean maximum picture capacity.
c.  Compute the mean battery life.
d.  If you had to select one camera from this list, what camera would you choose? Explain.

## 3.2    Measures of Variability

In addition to measures of location, it is often desirable to consider measures of variability, or dispersion. For example, suppose that you are a purchasing agent for a large manufacturing firm and that you regularly place orders with two different suppliers. After several months of operation, you find that the mean number of days required to fill orders is 10 days for both of the suppliers. The histograms summarizing the number of working days required to fill orders from the suppliers are shown in Figure 3.2. Although the mean number of days is 10 for both suppliers, do the two suppliers demonstrate the same degree of reliability in terms of making deliveries on schedule? Note the dispersion, or variability, in delivery times indicated by the histograms. Which supplier would you prefer?

For most firms, receiving materials and supplies on schedule is important. The seven- or eight-day deliveries shown for J.C. Clark Distributors might be viewed favorably; however, a few of the slow 13- to 15-day deliveries could be disastrous in terms of keeping a workforce busy and production on schedule. This example illustrates a situation in which the variability in the delivery times may be an overriding consideration in selecting a supplier. For most purchasing agents, the lower variability shown for Dawson Supply, Inc., would make Dawson the preferred supplier.

We turn now to a discussion of some commonly used measures of variability

### Range

The simplest measure of variability is the **range**.

RANGE

$$\text{Range} = \text{Largest value} - \text{Smallest value}$$

**FIGURE 3.2    HISTORICAL DATA SHOWING THE NUMBER OF DAYS REQUIRED TO FILL ORDERS**

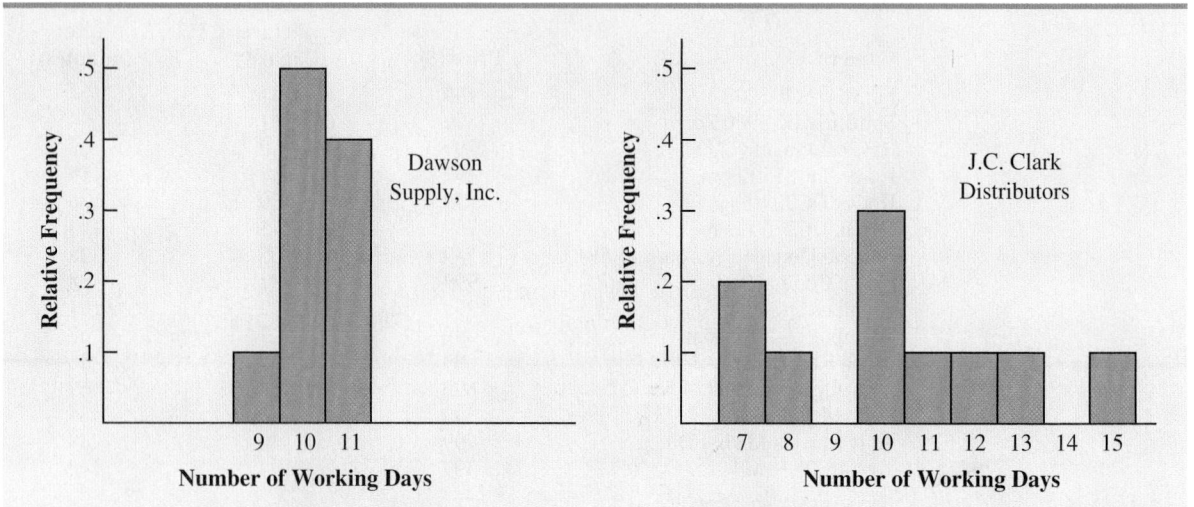

Let us refer to the data on starting salaries for business school graduates in Table 3.1. The largest starting salary is 3325 and the smallest is 2710. The range is $3325 - 2710 = 615$.

Although the range is the easiest of the measures of variability to compute, it is seldom used as the only measure. The reason is that the range is based on only two of the observations and thus is highly influenced by extreme values. Suppose one of the graduates received a starting salary of $10,000 per month. In this case, the range would be $10,000 - 2710 = 7290$ rather than 615. This large value for the range would not be especially descriptive of the variability in the data because 11 of the 12 starting salaries are closely grouped between 2710 and 3130.

## Interquartile Range

A measure of variability that overcomes the dependency on extreme values is the **interquartile range** (IQR). This measure of variability is simply the difference between the third quartile, $Q_3$, and the first quartile, $Q_1$. In other words, the interquartile range is the range for the middle 50% of the data.

> INTERQUARTILE RANGE
>
> $$IQR = Q_3 - Q_1 \qquad (3.3)$$

For the data on monthly starting salaries, the quartiles are $Q_3 = 3000$ and $Q_1 = 2865$. Thus, the interquartile range is $3000 - 2865 = 135$.

## Variance

The **variance** is a measure of variability that utilizes all the data. The variance is based on the difference between the value of each observation ($x_i$) and the mean. The difference between each $x_i$ and the mean ($\bar{x}$ for a sample, $\mu$ for a population) is called a *deviation about the mean*. For a sample, a deviation about the mean is written ($x_i - \bar{x}$); for a population, it is written ($x_i - \mu$). In the computation of the variance, the deviations about the mean are *squared*.

If the data are for a population, the average of the squared deviations is called the *population variance*. The population variance is denoted by the Greek symbol $\sigma^2$. For a population of $N$ observations and with $\mu$ denoting the population mean, the definition of the population variance is as follows.

**POPULATION VARIANCE**

$$\sigma^2 = \frac{\Sigma(x_i - \mu)^2}{N} \qquad (3.4)$$

In most statistical applications, the data being analyzed are for a sample. When we compute a sample variance, we are often interested in using it to estimate the population variance $\sigma^2$. Although a detailed explanation is beyond the scope of this text, it can be shown that if the sum of the squared deviations about the sample mean is divided by $n - 1$, and not $n$, the resulting sample variance provides an unbiased estimate of the population variance. For this reason, the *sample variance,* denoted by $s^2$, is defined as follows.

*The sample variance $s^2$ is the point estimator of the population variance $\sigma^2$.*

**SAMPLE VARIANCE**

$$s^2 = \frac{\Sigma(x_i - \bar{x})^2}{n - 1} \qquad (3.5)$$

To illustrate the computation of the sample variance, we will use the data on class size for the sample of five college classes as presented in Section 3.1. A summary of the data, including the computation of the deviations about the mean and the squared deviations about the mean, is shown in Table 3.3. The sum of squared deviations about the mean is $\Sigma(x_i - \bar{x})^2 = 256$. Hence, with $n - 1 = 4$, the sample variance is

$$s^2 = \frac{\Sigma(x_i - \bar{x})^2}{n - 1} = \frac{256}{4} = 64$$

Before moving on, let us note that the units associated with the sample variance often cause confusion. Because the values being summed in the variance calculation, $(x_i - \bar{x})^2$, are squared, the units associated with the sample variance are also *squared.* For instance, the sample variance for the class size data is $s^2 = 64$ (students)$^2$. The squared units associated with variance make it difficult to obtain an intuitive understanding and interpretation of the

**TABLE 3.3** COMPUTATION OF DEVIATIONS AND SQUARED DEVIATIONS ABOUT THE MEAN FOR THE CLASS SIZE DATA

| Number of Students in Class $(x_i)$ | Mean Class Size $(\bar{x})$ | Deviation About the Mean $(x_i - \bar{x})$ | Squared Deviation About the Mean $(x_i - \bar{x})^2$ |
|---|---|---|---|
| 46 | 44 | 2 | 4 |
| 54 | 44 | 10 | 100 |
| 42 | 44 | −2 | 4 |
| 46 | 44 | 2 | 4 |
| 32 | 44 | −12 | 144 |
| | | 0 | 256 |
| | | $\Sigma(x_i - \bar{x})$ | $\Sigma(x_i - \bar{x})^2$ |

**TABLE 3.4    COMPUTATION OF THE SAMPLE VARIANCE FOR THE STARTING SALARY DATA**

| Monthly Salary ($x_i$) | Sample Mean ($\bar{x}$) | Deviation About the Mean ($x_i - \bar{x}$) | Squared Deviation About the Mean ($(x_i - \bar{x})^2$) |
|---|---|---|---|
| 2850 | 2940 | −90 | 8,100 |
| 2950 | 2940 | 10 | 100 |
| 3050 | 2940 | 110 | 12,100 |
| 2880 | 2940 | −60 | 3,600 |
| 2755 | 2940 | −185 | 34,225 |
| 2710 | 2940 | −230 | 52,900 |
| 2890 | 2940 | −50 | 2,500 |
| 3130 | 2940 | 190 | 36,100 |
| 2940 | 2940 | 0 | 0 |
| 3325 | 2940 | 385 | 148,225 |
| 2920 | 2940 | −20 | 400 |
| 2880 | 2940 | −60 | 3,600 |
| | | 0 | 301,850 |
| | | $\Sigma(x_i - \bar{x})$ | $\Sigma(x_i - \bar{x})^2$ |

Using equation (3.5),

$$s^2 = \frac{\Sigma(x_i - \bar{x})^2}{n - 1} = \frac{301,850}{11} = 27,440.91$$

*The variance is useful in comparing the variability of two or more variables.*

numerical value of the variance. We recommend that you think of the variance as a measure useful in comparing the amount of variability for two or more variables. In a comparison of the variables, the one with the larger variance will show the most variability. Further interpretation of the value of the variance may not be necessary.

As another illustration of computing a sample variance, consider the starting salaries listed in Table 3.1 for the 12 business school graduates. In Section 3.1, we showed that the sample mean starting salary was 2940. The computation of the sample variance ($s^2 = 27,440.91$) is shown in Table 3.4.

In Tables 3.3 and 3.4 we show both the sum of the deviations about the mean and the sum of the squared deviations about the mean. For any data set, the sum of the deviations about the mean will *always equal zero*. Note that in Tables 3.3 and 3.4, $\Sigma(x_i - \bar{x}) = 0$. The positive deviations and negative deviations cancel each other, causing the sum of the deviations about the mean to equal zero.

## Standard Deviation

The **standard deviation** is defined to be the positive square root of the variance. Following the notation we adopted for a sample variance and a population variance, we use $s$ to denote the sample standard deviation and $\sigma$ to denote the population standard deviation. The standard deviation is derived from the variance in the following way.

STANDARD DEVIATION

*The sample standard deviation s is the point estimator of the population standard deviation σ.*

$$\text{Sample standard deviation} = s = \sqrt{s^2} \tag{3.6}$$

$$\text{Population standard deviation} = \sigma = \sqrt{\sigma^2} \tag{3.7}$$

Recall that the sample variance for the sample of class sizes in five college classes is $s^2 = 64$. Thus the sample standard deviation is $s = \sqrt{64} = 8$. For the data on starting salaries, the sample standard deviation is $s = \sqrt{27{,}440.91} = 165.65$.

*The standard deviation is easier to interpret than the variance because the standard deviation is measured in the same units as the data.*

What is gained by converting the variance to its corresponding standard deviation? Recall that the units associated with the variance are squared. For example, the sample variance for the starting salary data of business school graduates is $s^2 = 27{,}440.91$ (dollars)$^2$. Because the standard deviation is the square root of the variance, the units of the variance, dollars squared, are converted to dollars in the standard deviation. Thus, the standard deviation of the starting salary data is $165.65. In other words, the standard deviation is measured in the same units as the original data. For this reason the standard deviation is more easily compared to the mean and other statistics that are measured in the same units as the original data.

## Coefficient of Variation

*The coefficient of variation is a relative measure of variability; it measures the standard deviation relative to the mean.*

In some situations we may be interested in a descriptive statistic that indicates how large the standard deviation is relative to the mean. This measure is called the **coefficient of variation** and is usually expressed as a percent.

COEFFICIENT OF VARIATION

$$\left( \frac{\text{Standard deviation}}{\text{Mean}} \times 100 \right)\% \tag{3.8}$$

For the class size data, we found a sample mean of 44 and a sample standard deviation of 8. The coefficient of variation is $[(8/44) \times 100]\% = 18.2\%$. In words, the coefficient of variation tells us that the sample standard deviation is 18.2% of the value of the sample mean. For the starting salary data with a sample mean of 2940 and a sample standard deviation of 165.65, the coefficient of variation, $[(165.65/2940) \times 100]\% = 5.6\%$, tells us the sample standard deviation is only 5.6% of the value of the sample mean. In general, the coefficient of variation is a useful statistic for comparing the variability of variables that have different standard deviations and different means.

## NOTES AND COMMENTS

1. Statistical software packages and spreadsheets can be used to develop the descriptive statistics presented in this chapter. After the data are entered into a worksheet, a few simple commands can be used to generate the desired output. In Appendixes 3.1 and 3.2, we show how Minitab and Excel can be used to develop descriptive statistics.

2. The standard deviation is a commonly used measure of the risk associated with investing in stock and stock funds (*Business Week*, January 17, 2000). It provides a measure of how monthly returns fluctuate around the long-run average return.

3. Rounding the value of the sample mean $\bar{x}$ and the values of the squared deviations $(x_i - \bar{x})^2$ may introduce errors when a calculator is used in the computation of the variance and standard deviation. To reduce rounding errors, we recommend carrying at least six significant digits during intermediate calculations. The resulting variance or standard deviation can then be rounded to fewer digits.

4. An alternative formula for the computation of the sample variance is

$$s^2 = \frac{\sum x_i^2 - n\bar{x}^2}{n - 1}$$

where $\sum x_i^2 = x_1^2 + x_2^2 + \cdots + x_n^2$.

## Exercises

### Methods

13. Consider a sample with data values of 10, 20, 12, 17, and 16. Compute the range and inter-quartile range.

14. Consider a sample with data values of 10, 20, 12, 17, and 16. Compute the variance and standard deviation.

15. Consider a sample with data values of 27, 25, 20, 15, 30, 34, 28, and 25. Compute the range, interquartile range, variance, and standard deviation.

### Applications

16. A bowler's scores for six games were 182, 168, 184, 190, 170, and 174. Using these data as a sample, compute the following descriptive statistics.
    a. Range           c. Standard deviation
    b. Variance        d. Coefficient of variation

17. *PC World* provided ratings for 15 notebook PCs (*PC World*, February 2000). A 100-point scale was used to provide an overall rating for each notebook. A score in the 90s is exceptional, while one in the 70s is above average. The overall ratings for the 15 notebooks are shown here.

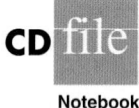

Notebook

| Notebook | Overall Rating |
| --- | --- |
| AMS Tech Roadster 15CTA380 | 67 |
| Compaq Armada M700 | 78 |
| Compaq Prosignia Notebook 150 | 79 |
| Dell Inspiron 3700 C466GT | 80 |
| Dell Inspiron 7500 R500VT | 84 |
| Dell Latitude Cpi A366XT | 76 |
| Enpower ENP-313 Pro | 77 |
| Gateway Solo 9300LS | 92 |
| HP Pavillion Notebook PC | 83 |
| IBM ThinkPad I Series 1480 | 78 |
| Micro Express NP7400 | 77 |
| Micron TransPort NX PII-400 | 78 |
| NEC Versa SX | 78 |
| Sceptre Soundx 5200 | 73 |
| Sony VAIO PCG-F340 | 77 |

Compute the range, interquartile range, variance, and standard deviation for this sample of notebook PCs.

18. The Hawaii Visitors Bureau collects data on the number of visitors to the islands. The following data are a representative sample of visitors (in thousands) for several days in November.

*From the mainland, Canada, and Europe:*
| 108.70 | 112.25 | 94.01 | 144.03 | 162.44 | 161.61 | 76.20 |
| 102.11 | 110.87 | 79.36 | 129.04 | 95.16 | 114.16 | 121.88 |

*From Asia and the Pacific:*
| 29.89 | 41.13 | 40.67 | 40.41 | 43.07 | 24.86 |
| 31.61 | 21.60 | 27.34 | 64.57 | 32.98 | 41.31 |

a. Compute the mean and median number of daily visitors from the two sources.
b. Compute the range, the standard deviation, and the coefficient of variation for the two sources of visitors.
c. What comparisons can you make between the numbers of visitors from the two sources?

19. The *Los Angeles Times* regularly reports the air quality index for various areas of Southern California. A sample of air quality index values for Pomona provided the following data: 28, 42, 58, 48, 45, 55, 60, 49, and 50.
    a.  Compute the range and interquartile range.
    b.  Compute the sample variance and sample standard deviation.
    c.  A sample of air quality index readings for Anaheim provided a sample mean of 48.5, a sample variance of 136, and a sample standard deviation of 11.66. What comparisons can you make between the air quality in Pomona and that in Anaheim on the basis of these descriptive statistics?

20. The following data were used to construct the histograms of the number of days required to fill orders for Dawson Supply, Inc., and J.C. Clark Distributors (see Figure 3.2).

    | *Dawson Supply Days for Delivery:* | 11 | 10 | 9 | 10 | 11 | 11 | 10 | 11 | 10 | 10 |
    |---|---|---|---|---|---|---|---|---|---|---|
    | *Clark Distributors Days for Delivery:* | 8 | 10 | 13 | 7 | 10 | 11 | 10 | 7 | 15 | 12 |

    Use the range and standard deviation to support the previous observation that Dawson Supply provides the more consistent and reliable delivery times.

21. Police records show the following numbers of daily crime reports for a sample of days during the winter months and a sample of days during the summer months.

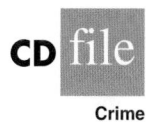

**Crime**

| Winter | Summer |
|---|---|
| 18 | 28 |
| 20 | 18 |
| 15 | 24 |
| 16 | 32 |
| 21 | 18 |
| 20 | 29 |
| 12 | 23 |
| 16 | 38 |
| 19 | 28 |
| 20 | 18 |

    a.  Compute the range and interquartile range for each period.
    b.  Compute the variance and standard deviation for each period.
    c.  Compute the coefficient of variation for each period.
    d.  Compare the variability of the two periods.

**Broker**

22. The American Association of Individual Investors conducts an annual survey of discount brokers (*AAII Journal*, January 2003). The commissions charged by a sample of 24 discount brokers for two types of trades, a broker-assisted trade of 100 shares at $50 per share and an online trade of 500 shares at $50 per share, are shown in Table 3.2.
    a.  Compute the range and interquartile range for each type of trade.
    b.  Compute the variance and standard deviation for each type of trade.
    c.  Compute the coefficient of variation for each type of trade.
    d.  Compare the variability of cost for the two types of trades.

23. A production department uses a sampling procedure to test the quality of newly produced items. The department employs the following decision rule at an inspection station: If a sample of 14 items has a variance of more than .005, the production line must be shut down for repairs. Suppose the following data have just been collected:

    | 3.43 | 3.45 | 3.43 | 3.48 | 3.52 | 3.50 | 3.39 |
    |---|---|---|---|---|---|---|
    | 3.48 | 3.41 | 3.38 | 3.49 | 3.45 | 3.51 | 3.50 |

    Should the production line be shut down? Why or why not?

24. The following times were recorded by the quarter-mile and mile runners of a university track team (times are in minutes).

| Quarter-Mile Times: | .92 | .98 | 1.04 | .90 | .99 |
|---|---|---|---|---|---|
| Mile Times: | 4.52 | 4.35 | 4.60 | 4.70 | 4.50 |

After viewing this sample of running times, one of the coaches commented that the quarter-milers turned in the more consistent times. Use the standard deviation and the coefficient of variation to summarize the variability in the data. Does the use of the coefficient of variation indicate that the coach's statement should be qualified?

##  3.3 Measures of Distribution Shape, Relative Location, and Detecting Outliers

We described several measures of location and variability for data distributions. It is also often important to have a measure of the shape of a distribution. In Chapter 2 we noted that a histogram offers an excellent graphical display showing the shape of a distribution. An important numerical measure of the shape of a distribution is called **skewness**.

### Distribution Shape

Shown in Figure 3.3 are four histograms constructed from relative frequency distributions. The histograms in Panels A and B are moderately skewed. The one in Panel A is skewed to the left; its skewness is −.85. The histogram in Panel B is skewed to the right; its skewness is +.85. The histogram in Panel C is symmetric; its skewness is zero. The histogram in Panel D is highly skewed to the right; its skewness is 1.62. The formula used to compute skewness is somewhat complex.* However, the skewness can be easily computed using statistical software (see Appendixes 3.1 and 3.2). For data skewed to the left, the skewness is negative; for data skewed to the right, the skewness is positive. If the data are symmetric, the skewness is zero.

For a symmetric distribution, the mean and the median are equal. When the data are positively skewed, the mean will usually be greater than the median; when the data are negatively skewed, the mean will usually be less than the median. The data used to construct the histogram in Panel D are customer purchases at a women's apparel store. The mean purchase amount is $77.60 and the median purchase amount is $59.70. The few large purchase amounts pulled up the mean, but the median remains unaffected. The median provides a better measure of typical values when the data are highly skewed.

### $z$-Scores

In addition to measures of location, variability, and shape for a data set, we often are also interested in the relative location of data items within a data set. Such measures can help us determine whether a particular item is close to the center of a data set or far out in one of the tails.

By using both the mean and standard deviation, we can determine the relative location of any observation. Suppose we have a sample of $n$ observations, with the values denoted by $x_1, x_2, \ldots, x_n$. In addition, assume that the sample mean, $\bar{x}$, and the sample standard de-

---

*The formula for the skewness of sample data:

$$\text{Skewness} = \frac{n}{(n-1)(n-2)} \sum \left( \frac{x_i - \bar{x}}{s} \right)^3$$

**FIGURE 3.3**   HISTOGRAMS SHOWING THE SKEWNESS FOR FOUR DISTRIBUTIONS

viation, $s$, are already computed. Associated with each value, $x_i$, is another value called its **z-score**. Equation (3.9) shows how the $z$-score is computed for each $x_i$.

---

Z-SCORE

$$z_i = \frac{x_i - \bar{x}}{s}$$   (3.9)

where

$z_i$ = the $z$-score for $x_i$
$\bar{x}$ = the sample mean
$s$ = the sample standard deviation

---

The $z$-score is often called the *standardized value*. The $z$-score, $z_i$, can be interpreted as the *number of standard deviations $x_i$ is from the mean $\bar{x}$*. For example, $z_1 = 1.2$ would in-dicate that $x_1$ is 1.2 standard deviations greater than the sample mean. Similarly, $z_2 = -.5$

would indicate that $x_2$ is .5, or 1/2, standard deviation less than the sample mean. A $z$-score greater than zero occurs for observations with a value greater than the mean, and a $z$-score less than zero occurs for observations with a value less than the mean. A $z$-score of zero indicates that the value of the observation is equal to the mean.

The $z$-score for any observation can be interpreted as a measure of the relative location of the observation in a data set. Thus, observations in two different data sets with the same $z$-score can be said to have the same relative location in terms of being the same number of standard deviations from the mean.

The $z$-scores for the class size data are computed in Table 3.5. Recall the previously computed sample mean, $\bar{x} = 44$, and sample standard deviation, $s = 8$. The $z$-score of $-1.50$ for the fifth observation shows it is farthest from the mean; it is 1.50 standard deviations below the mean.

## Chebyshev's Theorem

**Chebyshev's theorem** enables us to make statements about the proportion of data values that must be within a specified number of standard deviations of the mean.

> CHEBYSHEV'S THEOREM
>
> At least $(1 - 1/z^2)$ of the data values must be within $z$ standard deviations of the mean, where $z$ is any value greater than 1.

Some of the implications of this theorem, with $z = 2, 3$, and 4 standard deviations, follow.

- At least .75, or 75%, of the data values must be within $z = 2$ standard deviations of the mean.
- At least .89, or 89%, of the data values must be within $z = 3$ standard deviations of the mean.
- At least .94, or 94%, of the data values must be within $z = 4$ standard deviations of the mean.

For an example using Chebyshev's theorem, suppose that the midterm test scores for 100 students in a college business statistics course had a mean of 70 and a standard deviation of 5. How many students had test scores between 60 and 80? How many students had test scores between 58 and 82?

For the test scores between 60 and 80, we note that 60 is two standard deviations below the mean and 80 is two standard deviations above the mean. Using Chebyshev's theo-

**TABLE 3.5    $z$-SCORES FOR THE CLASS SIZE DATA**

| Number of Students in Class ($x_i$) | Deviation About the Mean ($x_i - \bar{x}$) | $z$-score $\left(\dfrac{x_i - \bar{x}}{s}\right)$ |
|:---:|:---:|:---:|
| 46 | 2 | $2/8 = \quad .25$ |
| 54 | 10 | $10/8 = \quad 1.25$ |
| 42 | $-2$ | $-2/8 = \quad -.25$ |
| 46 | 2 | $2/8 = \quad .25$ |
| 32 | $-12$ | $-12/8 = -1.50$ |

rem, we see that at least .75, or at least 75%, of the observations must have values within two standard deviations of the mean. Thus, at least 75% of the students must have scored between 60 and 80.

*Chebyshev's theorem requires z > 1; but z need not be an integer.*

For the test scores between 58 and 82, we see that $(58 - 70)/5 = -2.4$ indicates 58 is 2.4 standard deviations below the mean and that $(82 - 70)/5 = +2.4$ indicates 82 is 2.4 standard deviations above the mean. Applying Chebyshev's theorem with $z = 2.4$, we have

$$\left(1 - \frac{1}{z^2}\right) = \left(1 - \frac{1}{(2.4)^2}\right) = .826$$

At least 82.6% of the students must have test scores between 58 and 82.

## Empirical Rule

*The empirical rule is based on the normal probability distribution, which will be discussed in Chapter 6. The normal distribution is used extensively throughout the text.*

One of the advantages of Chebyshev's theorem is that it applies to any data set regardless of the shape of the distribution of the data. Indeed, it could be used with any of the skewed distributions in Figure 3.3. In many practical applications, however, data sets exhibit a symmetric mound-shaped or bell-shaped distribution like the one shown in Figure 3.4. When the data are believed to approximate this distribution, the **empirical rule** can be used to determine the percentage of data values that must be within a specified number of standard deviations of the mean.

EMPIRICAL RULE

For data having a bell-shaped distribution:

- Approximately 68% of the data values will be within one standard deviation of the mean.
- Approximately 95% of the data values will be within two standard deviations of the mean.
- Almost all of the data values will be within three standard deviations of the mean.

For example, liquid detergent cartons are filled automatically on a production line. Filling weights frequently have a bell-shaped distribution. If the mean filling weight is

**FIGURE 3.4    A SYMMETRIC MOUND-SHAPED OR BELL-SHAPED DISTRIBUTION**

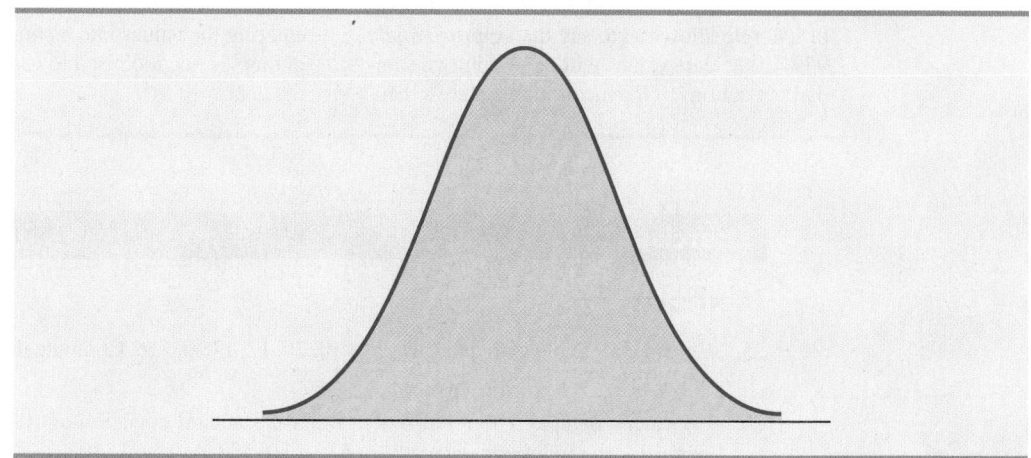

16 ounces and the standard deviation is .25 ounces, we can use the empirical rule to draw the following conclusions.

- Approximately 68% of the filled cartons will have weights between 15.75 and 16.25 ounces (that is, within one standard deviation of the mean).
- Approximately 95% of the filled cartons will have weights between 15.50 and 16.50 ounces (that is, within two standard deviations of the mean).
- Almost all filled cartons will have weights between 15.25 and 16.75 ounces (that is, within three standard deviations of the mean).

## Detecting Outliers

Sometimes a data set will have one or more observations with unusually large or unusually small values. These extreme values are called **outliers**. Experienced statisticians take steps to identify outliers and then review each one carefully. An outlier may be a data value that has been incorrectly recorded. If so, it can be corrected before further analysis. An outlier may also be from an observation that was incorrectly included in the data set; if so, it can be removed. Finally, an outlier may be an unusual data value that has been recorded correctly and belongs in the data set. In such cases it should remain.

*It is a good idea to check for outliers before making decisions based on data analysis. Errors are often made in recording data and entering data into the computer. Outliers should not necessarily be deleted, but their accuracy and appropriateness should be verified.*

Standardized values (z-scores) can be used to identify outliers. Recall that the empirical rule allows us to conclude that for data with a bell-shaped distribution, almost all the data values will be within three standard deviations of the mean. Hence, in using z-scores to identify outliers, we recommend treating any data value with a z-score less than $-3$ or greater than $+3$ as an outlier. Such data values can then be reviewed for accuracy and to determine whether they belong in the data set.

Refer to the z-scores for the class size data in Table 3.5. The z-score of $-1.50$ shows the fifth class size is farthest from the mean. However, this standardized value is well within the $-3$ to $+3$ guideline for outliers. Thus, the z-scores do not indicate that outliers are present in the class size data.

### NOTES AND COMMENTS

1. Chebyshev's theorem is applicable for any data set and can be used to state the minimum number of data values that will be within a certain number of standard deviations of the mean. If the data are known to be approximately bell-shaped, more can be said. For instance, the empirical rule allows us to say that *approximately* 95% of the data values will be within two standard deviations of the mean; Chebyshev's theo-rem allows us to conclude only that at least 75% of the data values will be in that interval.

2. Before analyzing a data set, statisticians usually make a variety of checks to ensure the validity of data. In a large study it is not uncommon for errors to be made in recording data values or in entering the values into a computer. Identifying outliers is one tool used to check the validity of the data.

### Exercises

## Methods

25. Consider a sample with data values of 10, 20, 12, 17, and 16. Compute the z-score for each of the five observations.

26. Consider a sample with a mean of 500 and a standard deviation of 100. What are the z-scores for the following data values: 520, 650, 500, 450, and 280?

27. Consider a sample with a mean of 30 and a standard deviation of 5. Use Chebyshev's theorem to determine the percentage of the data within each of the following ranges.
    a.  20 to 40
    b.  15 to 45
    c.  22 to 38
    d.  18 to 42
    e.  12 to 48

28. Suppose the data have a bell-shaped distribution with a mean of 30 and a standard deviation of 5. Use the empirical rule to determine the percentage of data within each of the following ranges.
    a.  20 to 40
    b.  15 to 45
    c.  25 to 35

## Applications

29. The results of a national survey of 1154 adults showed that on average, adults sleep 6.9 hours per day during the workweek (2000 Omnibus Sleep in America Poll). Suppose that the standard deviation is 1.2 hours.
    a.  Use Chebyshev's theorem to calculate the percentage of individuals who sleep between 4.5 and 9.3 hours per day.
    b.  Use Chebyshev's theorem to calculate the percentage of individuals who sleep between 3.9 and 9.9 hours per day.
    c.  Assume that the number of hours of sleep follows a bell-shaped distribution. Use the empirical rule to calculate the percentage of individuals who sleep between 4.5 and 9.3 hours per day. How does this result compare to the value that you obtained using Chebyshev's theorem in part (a)?

30. According to Nielsen Media Research, kids aged 12 to 17 watched an average of 3 hours of television per day for the broadcast year that ended in August (*Barron's*, November 8, 1999). Suppose that the standard deviation is 1 hour and that the distribution of the time spent watching television has a bell-shaped distribution.
    a.  What percentage of kids aged 12 to 17 watches television between 2 and 3 hours per day?
    b.  What percentage of kids aged 12 to 17 watches television between 1 and 4 hours per day?
    c.  What percentage of kids aged 12 to 17 watches television more than 4 hours per day?

31. Suppose that IQ scores have a bell-shaped distribution with a mean of 100 and a standard deviation of 15.
    a.  What percentage of people should have an IQ score between 85 and 115?
    b.  What percentage of people should have an IQ score between 70 and 130?
    c.  What percentage of people should have an IQ score of more than 130?
    d.  A person with an IQ score greater than 145 is considered a genius. Does the empirical rule support this statement? Explain.

32. The average labor cost for color TV repair in Chicago is $90.06 (*The Wall Street Journal*, January 2, 1998). Suppose the standard deviation is $20.00.
    a.  What is the *z*-score for a repair job with a labor cost of $71.00?
    b.  What is the *z*-score for a repair job with a labor cost of $168.00?
    c.  Interpret the *z*-scores in parts (a) and (b). Comment on whether either should be considered an outlier.

33. Wageweb conducts surveys of salary data and presents summaries on its Web site. Using salary data as of January 1, 2000, Wageweb reported that salaries of benefits managers ranged from $50,935 to $79,577 (Wageweb.com, April 12, 2000). Assume the following

data are a sample of the annual salaries for 30 benefits managers. Data are in thousands of dollars.

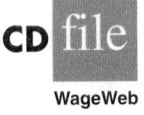

**CD file**

**WageWeb**

| | | | | |
|---|---|---|---|---|
| 57.7 | 64.4 | 62.1 | 59.1 | 71.1 |
| 63.0 | 64.7 | 61.2 | 66.8 | 61.8 |
| 64.2 | 63.3 | 62.2 | 61.2 | 59.4 |
| 63.0 | 66.7 | 60.3 | 74.0 | 62.8 |
| 68.7 | 63.8 | 59.2 | 60.3 | 56.6 |
| 59.3 | 69.5 | 61.7 | 58.9 | 63.1 |

a. Compute the mean and standard deviation for the sample data.
b. Using the mean and standard deviation computed in part (a) as estimates of the mean and standard deviation of salary for the population of benefits managers, use Chebyshev's theorem to determine the percentage of benefits managers with an annual salary between $55,000 and $71,000.
c. Develop a histogram for the sample data. Computer software provides .97 as the measure of skewness. Does it appear reasonable to assume that the distribution of annual salary can be approximated by a bell-shaped distribution?
d. Assume that the distribution of annual salary is bell-shaped. Using the mean and standard deviation computed in part (a) as estimates of the mean and standard deviation of salary for the population of benefits managers, use the empirical rule to determine the percentage of benefits managers with an annual salary between $55,000 and $71,000. Compare your answer with the value computed in part (b).
e. Do the sample data contain any outliers?

34. A sample of 10 National Basketball Association (NBA) scores provided the following data (*USA Today*, April 14, 2000).

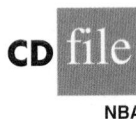

**CD file**

**NBA**

| Winning Team | Points Scored | Losing Team | Points Scored | Winning Margin |
|---|---|---|---|---|
| Philadelphia | 93 | Washington | 84 | 9 |
| Charlotte | 119 | Atlanta | 87 | 32 |
| Milwaukee | 101 | Cleveland | 100 | 1 |
| Indiana | 77 | Toronto | 73 | 4 |
| Seattle | 110 | Minnesota | 83 | 27 |
| Boston | 95 | Orlando | 91 | 4 |
| Detroit | 90 | Miami | 73 | 17 |
| New York | 91 | New Jersey | 89 | 2 |
| Utah | 102 | L.A. Clippers | 93 | 9 |
| Phoenix | 122 | Vancouver | 116 | 6 |

a. Compute the mean and standard deviation for the points scored by the winning teams.
b. Assume that the points scored by the winning teams for all NBA games are bell-shaped. Using the mean and standard deviation computed in part (a) as estimates of the mean and standard deviation of the points scored for the population of all NBA games, estimate the percentage of all NBA games in which the winning team will score 100 or more points. Estimate the percentage of games in which the winning team will score more than 114 points.
c. Compute the mean and standard deviation for the winning margin. Do the winning margin data contain outliers? Explain.

35. *Consumer Review* posts reviews and ratings of a variety of products on the Internet. The following is a sample of 20 speaker systems and the ratings posted on January 2, 1998 (see *http://www.audioreview.com*). The ratings are on a scale of 1 to 5, with 5 being best.

**Speakers**

| Speaker | Rating | Speaker | Rating |
|---|---|---|---|
| Infinity Kappa 6.1 | 4.00 | ACI Sapphire III | 4.67 |
| Allison One | 4.12 | Bose 501 Series | 2.14 |
| Cambridge Ensemble II | 3.82 | DCM KX-212 | 4.09 |
| Dynaudio Contour 1.3 | 4.00 | Eosone RSF1000 | 4.17 |
| Hsu Rsch. HRSW12V | 4.56 | Joseph Audio RM7si | 4.88 |
| Legacy Audio Focus | 4.32 | Martin Logan Aerius | 4.26 |
| Mission 73li | 4.33 | Omni Audio SA 12.3 | 2.32 |
| PSB 400i | 4.50 | Polk Audio RT12 | 4.50 |
| Snell Acoustics D IV | 4.64 | Sunfire True Subwoofer | 4.17 |
| Thiel CS1.5 | 4.20 | Yamaha NS-A636 | 2.17 |

a.  Compute the mean and the median.
b.  Compute the first and third quartiles.
c.  Compute the standard deviation.
d.  The skewness of this data is $-1.67$. Comment on the shape of the distribution.
e.  What are the $z$-scores associated with Allison One and Omni Audio?
f.  Do the data contain any outliers? Explain.

 **3.4**

# Exploratory Data Analysis

In Chapter 2 we introduced the stem-and-leaf display as a technique of exploratory data analysis. Recall that exploratory data analysis enables us to use simple arithmetic and easy-to-draw pictures to summarize data. In this section we continue exploratory data analysis by considering five-number summaries and box plots.

## Five-Number Summary

In a **five-number summary**, the following five numbers are used to summarize the data.

1.  Smallest value
2.  First quartile ($Q_1$)
3.  Median ($Q_2$)
4.  Third quartile ($Q_3$)
5.  Largest value

The easiest way to develop a five-number summary is to first place the data in ascending order. Then it is easy to identify the smallest value, the three quartiles, and the largest value. The monthly starting salaries shown in Table 3.1 for a sample of 12 business school graduates are repeated here in ascending order.

$$2710 \quad 2755 \quad 2850 \mid 2880 \quad 2880 \quad 2890 \mid 2920 \quad 2940 \quad 2950 \mid 3050 \quad 3130 \quad 3325$$

$$Q_1 = 2865 \qquad\qquad Q_2 = 2905 \qquad\qquad Q_3 = 3000$$
$$\text{(Median)}$$

The median of 2905 and the quartiles $Q_1 = 2865$ and $Q_3 = 3000$ were computed in Section 3.1. Reviewing the data shows a smallest value of 2710 and a largest value of 3325. Thus the five-number summary for the salary data is 2710, 2865, 2905, 3000, 3325. Approximately one-fourth, or 25%, of the observations are between adjacent numbers in a five-number summary.

FIGURE 3.5    BOX PLOT OF THE STARTING SALARY DATA WITH LINES SHOWING
THE LOWER AND UPPER LIMITS

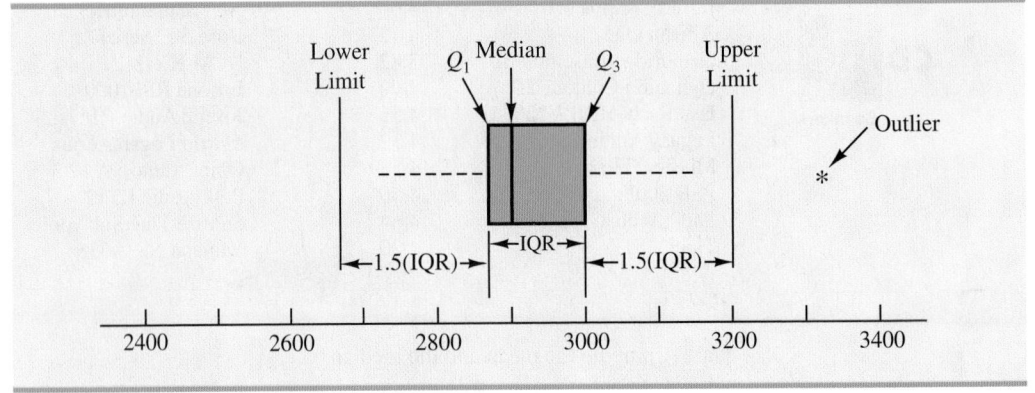

## Box Plot

A **box plot** is a graphical summary of data that is based on a five-number summary. A key to the development of a box plot is the computation of the median and the quartiles, $Q_1$ and $Q_3$. The interquartile range, IQR $= Q_3 - Q_1$, is also used. Figure 3.5 is the box plot for the monthly starting salary data. The steps used to construct the box plot follow.

*Box plots provide another way to identify outliers. But they do not necessarily identify the same values as those with a z-score less than −3 or greater than +3. Either, or both, procedures may be used.*

1. A box is drawn with the ends of the box located at the first and third quartiles. For the salary data, $Q_1 = 2865$ and $Q_3 = 3000$. This box contains the middle 50% of the data.
2. A vertical line is drawn in the box at the location of the median (2905 for the salary data).
3. By using the interquartile range, IQR $= Q_3 - Q_1$, *limits* are located. The limits for the box plot are 1.5(IQR) below $Q_1$ and 1.5(IQR) above $Q_3$. For the salary data, IQR $= Q_3 - Q_1 = 3000 - 2865 = 135$. Thus, the limits are $2865 - 1.5(135) = 2662.5$ and $3000 + 1.5(135) = 3202.5$. Data outside these limits are considered *outliers*.
4. The dashed lines in Figure 3.5 are called *whiskers*. The whiskers are drawn from the ends of the box to the smallest and largest values *inside the limits* computed in step 3. Thus the whiskers end at salary values of 2710 and 3130.
5. Finally, the location of each outlier is shown with the symbol *. In Figure 3.5 we see one outlier, 3325.

In Figure 3.5 we included lines showing the location of the upper and lower limits. These lines were drawn to show how the limits are computed and where they are located for the salary data. Although the limits are always computed, generally they are not drawn on the box plots. Figure 3.6 shows the usual appearance of a box plot for the salary data.

FIGURE 3.6    BOX PLOT OF THE STARTING SALARY DATA

## NOTES AND COMMENTS

1. An advantage of the exploratory data analysis procedures is that they are easy to use; few numerical calculations are necessary. We simply sort the data values into ascending order and identify the five-number summary. The box plot can then be constructed. It is not necessary to compute the mean and the standard deviation for the data.

2. In Appendix 3.1, we show how to construct a box plot for the starting salary data using Minitab. The box plot obtained looks just like the one in Figure 3.6, but turned on its side.

## Exercises

### Methods

36. Consider a sample with data values of 27, 25, 20, 15, 30, 34, 28, and 25. Provide the five-number summary for the data.

37. Show the box plot for the data in exercise 36.

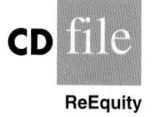

38. Show the five-number summary and the box plot for the following data: 5, 15, 18, 10, 8, 12, 16, 10, 6.

39. A data set has a first quartile of 42 and a third quartile of 50. Compute the lower and upper limits for the corresponding box plot. Should a data value of 65 be considered an outlier?

### Applications

40. A goal of management is to help their company earn as much as possible relative to the capital invested. One measure of success is return on equity—the ratio of net income to stockholders' equity. Shown here are return on equity percentages for 25 companies (*Standard & Poor's Stock Reports*, November 1997).

| 9.0 | 19.6 | 22.9 | 41.6 | 11.4 |
|-----|------|------|------|------|
| 15.8 | 52.7 | 17.3 | 12.3 | 5.1 |
| 17.3 | 31.1 | 9.6 | 8.6 | 11.2 |
| 12.8 | 12.2 | 14.5 | 9.2 | 16.6 |
| 5.0 | 30.3 | 14.7 | 19.2 | 6.2 |

a. Provide a five-number summary.
b. Compute the lower and upper limits.
c. Do the data contain any outliers? How would this information be helpful to a financial analyst?
d. Show a box plot.

41. Annual sales, in millions of dollars, for 21 pharmaceutical companies follow.

| 8408 | 1374 | 1872 | 8879 | 2459 | 11413 |
|------|------|------|------|------|-------|
| 608 | 14138 | 6452 | 1850 | 2818 | 1356 |
| 10498 | 7478 | 4019 | 4341 | 739 | 2127 |
| 3653 | 5794 | 8305 | | | |

a. Provide a five-number summary.
b. Compute the lower and upper limits.
c. Do the data contain any outliers?
d. Johnson & Johnson's sales are the largest on the list at $14,138 million. Suppose a data entry error (a transposition) had been made and the sales had been entered as $41,138 million. Would the method of detecting outliers in part (c) identify this problem and allow for correction of the data entry error?
e. Show a box plot.

42. Corporate share repurchase programs are often touted as a benefit for shareholders. But, Robert Gabele, director of insider research for First Call/Thomson Financial, notes that many companies undertake these programs solely to acquire stock to use for incentive options for top managers. Across all companies, existing stock options in 1998 represented 6.2 percent of all common shares outstanding. The following data show the number of shares covered by option grants and the number of shares outstanding for 15 companies. *Bloomberg* identified these companies as the ones that would need to repurchase the highest percentage of outstanding shares to cover their option grants (*Bloomberg Personal Finance*, January/February 2000).

**CD** file

Options

| Company | Shares Covered by Options Grants (millions) | Common Shares Outstanding (millions) |
|---|---|---|
| Adobe Systems | 20.3 | 61.8 |
| Apple Computer | 52.7 | 160.9 |
| Applied Materials | 109.1 | 375.4 |
| Autodesk | 15.7 | 58.9 |
| Best Buy | 44.2 | 203.8 |
| Cendant | 183.3 | 718.1 |
| Dell Computer | 720.8 | 2540.9 |
| Fruit of the Loom | 14.2 | 66.9 |
| ITT Industries | 18.0 | 87.9 |
| Merrill Lynch | 89.9 | 365.5 |
| Novell | 120.2 | 335.0 |
| Parametric Technology | 78.3 | 269.3 |
| Reebok International | 12.8 | 56.1 |
| Silicon Graphics | 52.6 | 188.8 |
| Toys R Us | 54.8 | 247.6 |

a. What are the mean and median number of shares covered by option grants?
b. What are the first and third quartiles for the number of shares covered by option grants?
c. Do the number of shares covered by option grants show any outliers? Show a box plot.
d. For each company, compute the percentage of shares outstanding that are covered by option grants. How does the mean of this percentage compare to the 1998 percentage of 6.2 reported for all companies?

43. The Highway Loss Data Institute's Injury and Collision Loss Experience report rates car models on the basis of the number of insurance claims filed after accidents. Index ratings near 100 are considered average. Lower ratings are better, indicating a safer car model. Shown are ratings for 20 midsize cars and 20 small cars.

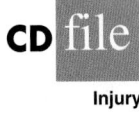

**CD** file

Injury

| *Midsize cars:* | 81 | 91 | 93 | 127 | 68 | 81 | 60 | 51 | 58 | 75 |
|---|---|---|---|---|---|---|---|---|---|---|
| | 100 | 103 | 119 | 82 | 128 | 76 | 68 | 81 | 91 | 82 |
| *Small cars:* | 73 | 100 | 127 | 100 | 124 | 103 | 119 | 108 | 109 | 113 |
| | 108 | 118 | 103 | 120 | 102 | 122 | 96 | 133 | 80 | 140 |

Summarize the data for the midsize and small cars separately.
a. Provide a five-number summary for midsize cars and for small cars.
b. Show the box plots.
c. Make a statement about what your summaries indicate about the safety of midsize cars in comparison to small cars.

TABLE 3.6    PERCENT CHANGE IN VALUE FOR WORLD STOCK MARKETS

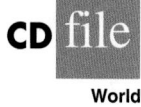

**World**

| Country | Percent Change | Country | Percent Change |
|---------|----------------|---------|----------------|
| Argentina | 24.70 | India | 18.60 |
| Australia | 7.91 | Israel | 27.91 |
| Bahrain | 49.67 | Japan | −21.19 |
| Barbados | 48.29 | Lithuania | 16.82 |
| Bermuda | 51.92 | Mexico | 54.92 |
| Brazil | 44.84 | Namibia | 6.52 |
| Chile | 12.80 | Nigeria | −7.97 |
| Colombia | 69.60 | Panama | 59.40 |
| Croatia | −1.07 | Poland | 2.27 |
| Czech Republic | −3.25 | Russia | 125.89 |
| Ecuador | 5.37 | Slovenia | 18.71 |
| Estonia | 62.34 | Sri Lanka | 15.49 |
| Finland | 32.31 | Taiwan | 18.08 |
| Germany | 47.11 | Turkey | 254.45 |
| Greece | 59.19 | United States | 22.64 |

*Source: The Wall Street Journal*, January 2, 1998.

44.  Birinyi Associates, Inc., conducted a survey of stock markets around the world to assess their performance during 1997. Table 3.6 summarizes the findings for a sample of 30 countries.
    a.  What are the mean and median percentage changes for these countries?
    b.  What are the first and third quartiles?
    c.  Do the data contain any outliers? Show a box plot.
    d.  What percentile would you report for the United States?

## (3.5) Measures of Association Between Two Variables

Thus far we examined numerical methods used to summarize the data for *one variable at a time*. Often a manager or decision maker is interested in the *relationship between two variables*. In this section we present covariance and correlation as descriptive measures of the relationship between two variables.

We begin by reconsidering the application concerning a stereo and sound equipment store in San Francisco as presented in Section 2.4. The store's manager wants to determine the relationship between the number of weekend television commercials shown and the sales at the store during the following week. Sample data with sales expressed in hundreds of dollars are provided in Table 3.7. It shows 10 observations ($n = 10$), one for each week. The scatter diagram in Figure 3.7 shows a positive relationship, with higher sales ($y$) associated with a greater number of commercials ($x$). In fact, the scatter diagram suggests that a straight line could be used as an approximation of the relationship. In the following discussion, we introduce **covariance** as a descriptive measure of the linear association between two variables.

**TABLE 3.7    SAMPLE DATA FOR THE STEREO AND SOUND EQUIPMENT STORE**

**Stereo**

| Week | Number of Commercials $x$ | Sales Volume ($100s) $y$ |
|------|------|------|
| 1 | 2 | 50 |
| 2 | 5 | 57 |
| 3 | 1 | 41 |
| 4 | 3 | 54 |
| 5 | 4 | 54 |
| 6 | 1 | 38 |
| 7 | 5 | 63 |
| 8 | 3 | 48 |
| 9 | 4 | 59 |
| 10 | 2 | 46 |

## Covariance

For a sample of size $n$ with the observations $(x_1, y_1)$, $(x_2, y_2)$, and so on, the sample covariance is defined as follows:

**SAMPLE COVARIANCE**

$$s_{xy} = \frac{\Sigma(x_i - \bar{x})(y_i - \bar{y})}{n - 1} \tag{3.10}$$

This formula pairs each $x_i$ with a $y_i$. We then sum the products obtained by multiplying the deviation of each $x_i$ from its sample mean $\bar{x}$ by the deviation of the corresponding $y_i$ from its sample mean $\bar{y}$; this sum is then divided by $n - 1$.

**FIGURE 3.7    SCATTER DIAGRAM FOR THE STEREO AND SOUND EQUIPMENT STORE**

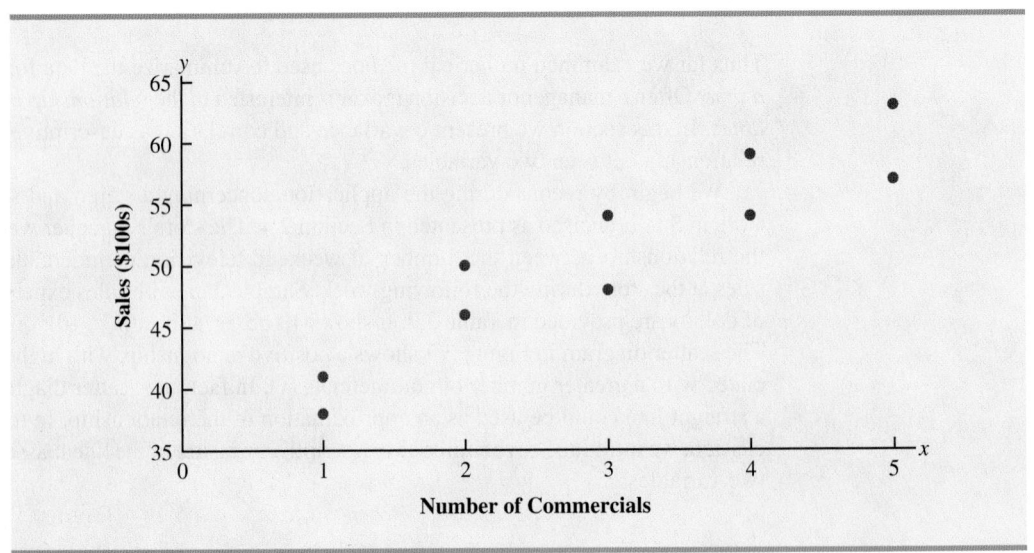

TABLE 3.8   CALCULATIONS FOR THE SAMPLE COVARIANCE

| $x_i$ | $y_i$ | $x_i - \bar{x}$ | $y_i - \bar{y}$ | $(x_i - \bar{x})(y_i - \bar{y})$ |
|---|---|---|---|---|
| 2 | 50 | $-1$ | $-1$ | 1 |
| 5 | 57 | 2 | 6 | 12 |
| 1 | 41 | $-2$ | $-10$ | 20 |
| 3 | 54 | 0 | 3 | 0 |
| 4 | 54 | 1 | 3 | 3 |
| 1 | 38 | $-2$ | $-13$ | 26 |
| 5 | 63 | 2 | 12 | 24 |
| 3 | 48 | 0 | $-3$ | 0 |
| 4 | 59 | 1 | 8 | 8 |
| 2 | 46 | $-1$ | $-5$ | 5 |
| Totals   30 | 510 | 0 | 0 | 99 |

$$s_{xy} = \frac{\Sigma(x_i - \bar{x})(y_i - \bar{y})}{n - 1} = \frac{99}{10 - 1} = 11$$

To measure the strength of the linear relationship between the number of commercials $x$ and the sales volume $y$ in the stereo and sound equipment store problem, we use equation (3.10) to compute the sample covariance. The calculations in Table 3.8 show the computation of $\Sigma(x_i - \bar{x})(y_i - \bar{y})$. Note that $\bar{x} = 30/10 = 3$ and $\bar{y} = 510/10 = 51$. Using equation (3.10), we obtain a sample covariance of

$$s_{xy} = \frac{\Sigma(x_i - \bar{x})(y_i - \bar{y})}{n - 1} = \frac{99}{9} = 11$$

The formula for computing the covariance of a population of size $N$ is similar to equation (3.10), but we use different notation to indicate that we are working with the entire population.

---

POPULATION COVARIANCE

$$\sigma_{xy} = \frac{\Sigma(x_i - \mu_x)(y_i - \mu_y)}{N} \tag{3.11}$$

---

In equation (3.11) we use the notation $\mu_x$ for the population mean of the variable $x$ and $\mu_y$ for the population mean of the variable $y$. The population covariance $\sigma_{xy}$ is defined for a population of size $N$.

## Interpretation of the Covariance

To aid in the interpretation of the sample covariance, consider Figure 3.8. It is the same as the scatter diagram of Figure 3.7 with a vertical dashed line at $\bar{x} = 3$ and a horizontal dashed line at $\bar{y} = 51$. The lines divide the graph into four quadrants. Points in quadrant I correspond to $x_i$ greater than $\bar{x}$ and $y_i$ greater than $\bar{y}$, points in quadrant II correspond to $x_i$ less

FIGURE 3.8    PARTITIONED SCATTER DIAGRAM FOR THE STEREO AND SOUND
EQUIPMENT STORE

*The covariance is a measure of the linear association between two variables.*

than $\bar{x}$ and $y_i$ greater than $\bar{y}$, and so on. Thus, the value of $(x_i - \bar{x})(y_i - \bar{y})$ must be positive for points in quadrant I, negative for points in quadrant II, positive for points in quadrant III, and negative for points in quadrant IV.

If the value of $s_{xy}$ is positive, the points with the greatest influence on $s_{xy}$ must be in quadrants I and III. Hence, a positive value for $s_{xy}$ indicates a positive linear association between $x$ and $y$; that is, as the value of $x$ increases, the value of $y$ increases. If the value of $s_{xy}$ is negative, however, the points with the greatest influence on $s_{xy}$ are in quadrants II and IV. Hence, a negative value for $s_{xy}$ indicates a negative linear association between $x$ and $y$; that is, as the value of $x$ increases, the value of $y$ decreases. Finally, if the points are evenly distributed across all four quadrants, the value of $s_{xy}$ will be close to zero, indicating no linear association between $x$ and $y$. Figure 3.9 shows the values of $s_{xy}$ that can be expected with three different types of scatter diagrams.

Referring again to Figure 3.8, we see that the scatter diagram for the stereo and sound equipment store follows the pattern in the top panel of Figure 3.9. As we should expect, the value of the sample covariance indicates a positive linear relationship with $s_{xy} = 11$.

From the preceding discussion, it might appear that a large positive value for the covariance indicates a strong positive linear relationship and that a large negative value indicates a strong negative linear relationship. However, one problem with using covariance as a measure of the strength of the linear relationship is that the value of the covariance depends on the units of measurement for $x$ and $y$. For example, suppose we are interested in the relationship between height $x$ and weight $y$ for individuals. Clearly the strength of the relationship should be the same whether we measure height in feet or inches. Measuring the height in inches, however, gives us much larger numerical values for $(x_i - \bar{x})$ than when we measure height in feet. Thus, with height measured in inches, we would obtain a larger value for the numerator $\Sigma(x_i - \bar{x})(y_i - \bar{y})$ in equation (3.10)—and hence a larger covariance—when in fact the relationship does not change. A measure of the relationship between two variables that is not affected by the units of measurement for $x$ and $y$ is the **correlation coefficient**.

**FIGURE 3.9    INTERPRETATION OF SAMPLE COVARIANCE**

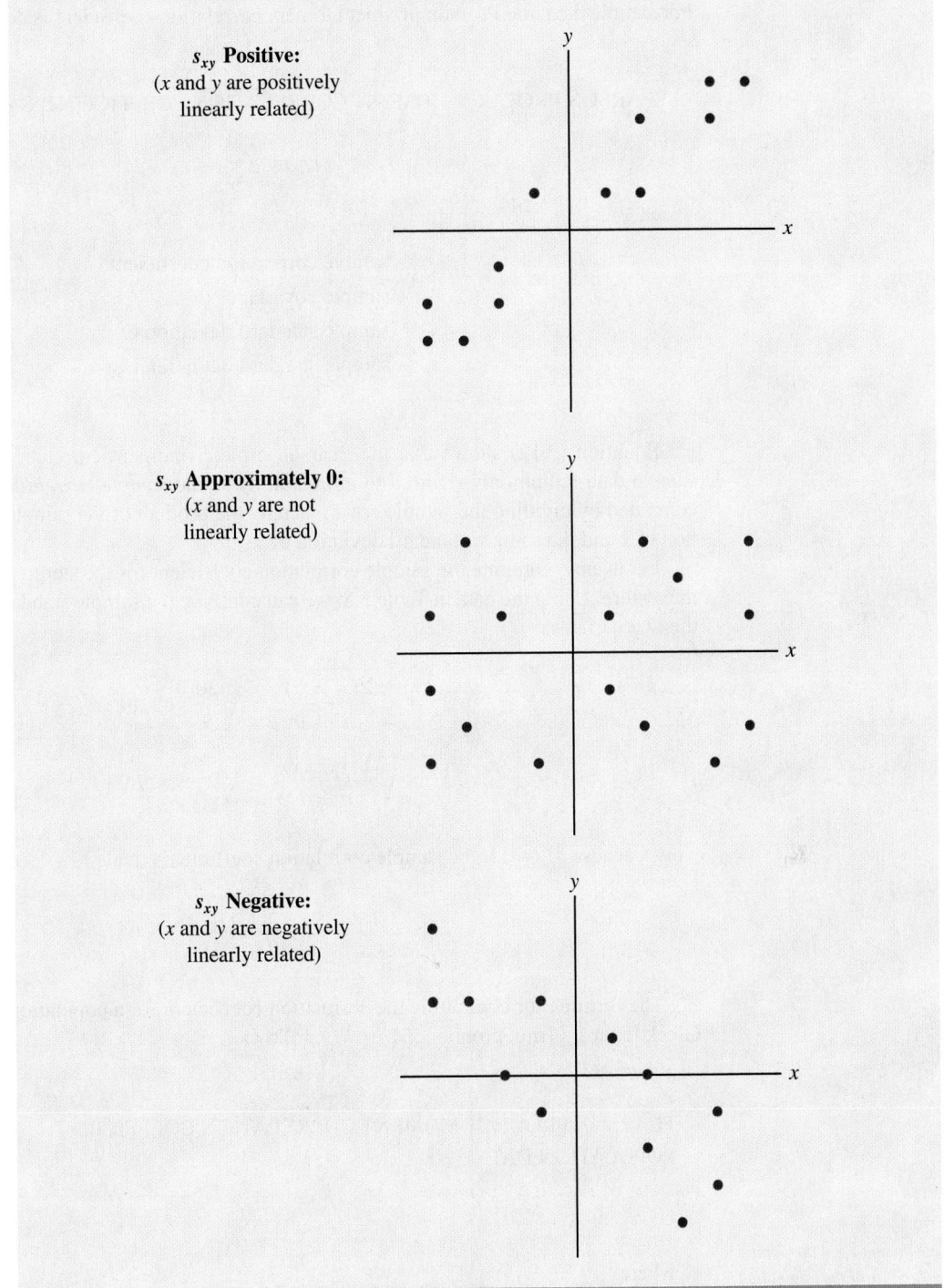

## Correlation Coefficient

For sample data, the Pearson product moment correlation coefficient is defined as follows.

PEARSON PRODUCT MOMENT CORRELATION COEFFICIENT: SAMPLE DATA

$$r_{xy} = \frac{s_{xy}}{s_x s_y}$$    (3.12)

where

$r_{xy}$ = sample correlation coefficient

$s_{xy}$ = sample covariance

$s_x$ = sample standard deviation of $x$

$s_y$ = sample standard deviation of $y$

Equation (3.12) shows that the Pearson product moment correlation coefficient for sample data (commonly referred to more simply as the *sample correlation coefficient*) is computed by dividing the sample covariance by the product of the sample standard deviation of $x$ and the sample standard deviation of $y$.

Let us now compute the sample correlation coefficient for the stereo and sound equipment store. Using the data in Table 3.8, we can compute the sample standard deviations for the two variables.

$$s_x = \sqrt{\frac{\Sigma(x_i - \bar{x})^2}{n - 1}} = \sqrt{\frac{20}{9}} = 1.49$$

$$s_y = \sqrt{\frac{\Sigma(y_i - \bar{y})^2}{n - 1}} = \sqrt{\frac{566}{9}} = 7.93$$

Now, because $s_{xy} = 11$, the sample correlation coefficient equals

$$r_{xy} = \frac{s_{xy}}{s_x s_y} = \frac{11}{(1.49)(7.93)} = +.93$$

The formula for computing the correlation coefficient for a population, denoted by the Greek letter $\rho_{xy}$ (rho, pronounced "row"), follows.

PEARSON PRODUCT MOMENT CORRELATION COEFFICIENT:
POPULATION DATA

*The sample correlation coefficient $r_{xy}$ is the point estimator of the population correlation coefficient $\rho_{xy}$.*

$$\rho_{xy} = \frac{\sigma_{xy}}{\sigma_x \sigma_y}$$    (3.13)

where

$\rho_{xy}$ = population correlation coefficient

$\sigma_{xy}$ = population covariance

$\sigma_x$ = population standard deviation for $x$

$\sigma_y$ = population standard deviation for $y$

The sample correlation coefficient $r_{xy}$ provides an estimate of the population correlation coefficient $\rho_{xy}$.

## Interpretation of the Correlation Coefficient

First let us consider a simple example that illustrates the concept of a perfect positive linear relationship. The scatter diagram in Figure 3.10 depicts the relationship between $x$ and $y$ based on the following sample data.

| $x_i$ | $y_i$ |
|-------|-------|
| 5     | 10    |
| 10    | 30    |
| 15    | 50    |

The straight line drawn through each of the three points shows a perfect linear relationship between $x$ and $y$. In order to apply equation (3.12) to compute the sample correlation we must first compute $s_{xy}$, $s_x$, and $s_y$. Some of the computations are shown in Table 3.9. Using the results in Table 3.9, we find

$$s_{xy} = \frac{\Sigma(x_i - \bar{x})(y_i - \bar{y})}{n - 1} = \frac{200}{2} = 100$$

$$s_x = \sqrt{\frac{\Sigma(x_i - \bar{x})^2}{n - 1}} = \sqrt{\frac{50}{2}} = 5$$

$$s_y = \sqrt{\frac{\Sigma(y_i - \bar{y})^2}{n - 1}} = \sqrt{\frac{800}{2}} = 20$$

$$r_{xy} = \frac{s_{xy}}{s_x s_y} = \frac{100}{5(20)} = 1$$

Thus, we see that the value of the sample correlation coefficient is 1.

**FIGURE 3.10**    SCATTER DIAGRAM DEPICTING A PERFECT POSITIVE LINEAR RELATIONSHIP

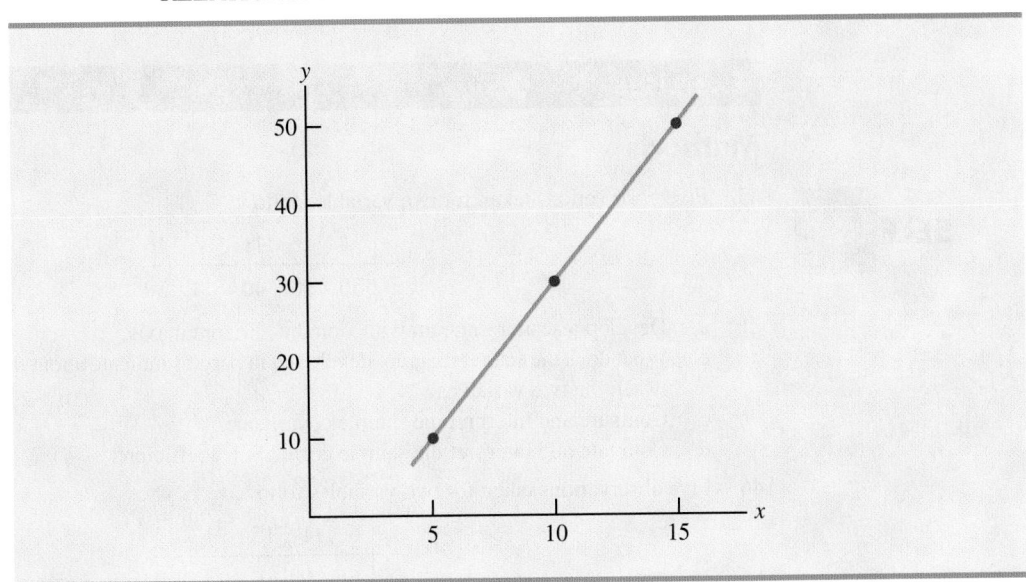

**TABLE 3.9    COMPUTATIONS USED IN CALCULATING THE SAMPLE CORRELATION COEFFICIENT**

| | $x_i$ | $y_i$ | $x_i - \bar{x}$ | $(x_i - \bar{x})^2$ | $y_i - \bar{y}$ | $(y_i - \bar{y})^2$ | $(x_i - \bar{x})(y_i - \bar{y})$ |
|---|---|---|---|---|---|---|---|
| | 5 | 10 | −5 | 25 | −20 | 400 | 100 |
| | 10 | 30 | 0 | 0 | 0 | 0 | 0 |
| | 15 | 50 | 5 | 25 | 20 | 400 | 100 |
| Totals | 30 | 90 | 0 | 50 | 0 | 800 | 200 |

$\bar{x} = 10 \quad \bar{y} = 30$

In general, it can be shown that if all the points in a data set fall on a positively sloped straight line, the value of the sample correlation coefficient is +1; that is, a sample correlation coefficient of +1 corresponds to a perfect positive linear relationship between $x$ and $y$. Moreover, if the points in the data set fall on a straight line having negative slope, the value of the sample correlation coefficient is −1; that is, a sample correlation coefficient of −1 corresponds to a perfect negative linear relationship between $x$ and $y$.

*The correlation coefficient ranges from −1 to +1. Values close to −1 or +1 indicate a strong linear relationship. The closer the correlation is to zero, the weaker the relationship.*

Let us now suppose that a certain data set indicates a positive linear relationship between $x$ and $y$ but that the relationship is not perfect. The value of $r_{xy}$ will be less than 1, indicating that the points in the scatter diagram are not all on a straight line. As the points deviate more and more from a perfect positive linear relationship, the value of $r_{xy}$ becomes smaller and smaller. A value of $r_{xy}$ equal to zero indicates no linear relationship between $x$ and $y$, and values of $r_{xy}$ near zero indicate a weak linear relationship.

For the data involving the stereo and sound equipment store, recall that $r_{xy} = +.93$. Therefore, we conclude that a strong positive linear relationship occurs between the number of commercials and sales. More specifically, an increase in the number of commercials is associated with an increase in sales.

In closing, we note that correlation provides a measure of linear association and not necessarily causation. A high correlation between two variables does not mean that one variable causes the other. For instance, we may find that a restaurant's quality rating and its typical meal price are positively correlated. However, increasing the meal price will not cause quality to increase.

## Exercises

## Methods

45. Five observations taken for two variables follow.

| $x_i$ | 4 | 6 | 11 | 3 | 16 |
|---|---|---|---|---|---|
| $y_i$ | 50 | 50 | 40 | 60 | 30 |

a. Develop a scatter diagram with $x$ on the horizontal axis.
b. What does the scatter diagram developed in part (a) indicate about the relationship between the two variables?
c. Compute and interpret the sample covariance.
d. Compute and interpret the sample correlation coefficient.

46. Five observations taken for two variables follow.

| $x_i$ | 6 | 11 | 15 | 21 | 27 |
|---|---|---|---|---|---|
| $y_i$ | 6 | 9 | 6 | 17 | 12 |

a. Develop a scatter diagram for these data.
b. What does the scatter diagram indicate about a relationship between *x* and *y*?
c. Compute and interpret the sample covariance.
d. Compute and interpret the sample correlation coefficient.

## Applications

47. A high school guidance counselor collected the following data about the grade point averages (GPA) and the SAT mathematics test scores for six seniors.

| GPA | 2.7 | 3.5 | 3.7 | 3.3 | 3.6 | 3.0 |
|-----|-----|-----|-----|-----|-----|-----|
| SAT | 450 | 560 | 700 | 620 | 640 | 570 |

a. Develop a scatter diagram for the data with GPA on the horizontal axis.
b. Is any relationship evident between the GPA and the SAT mathematics test score? Explain.
c. Compute and interpret the sample covariance.
d. Compute the sample correlation coefficient. What does this value tell us about the relationship between the two variables?

48. A department of transportation's study on driving speed and mileage for midsize automobiles resulted in the following data.

| Driving Speed | 30 | 50 | 40 | 55 | 30 | 25 | 60 | 25 | 50 | 55 |
|---------------|----|----|----|----|----|----|----|----|----|----|
| Mileage | 28 | 25 | 25 | 23 | 30 | 32 | 21 | 35 | 26 | 25 |

Compute and interpret the sample correlation coefficient.

49. *PC World* provided ratings for 15 notebook PCs (*PC World*, February 2000). The performance score is a measure of how fast a PC can run a mix of common business applications as compared to a baseline machine. For example, a PC with a performance score of 200 is twice as fast as the baseline machine. A 100-point scale was used to provide an overall rating for each notebook tested in the study. A score in the 90s is exceptional, while one in the 70s is above average. Table 3.10 shows the performance scores and the overall ratings for the 15 notebooks.
a. Compute the sample correlation coefficient.
b. What does the sample correlation coefficient tell about the relationship between the performance score and the overall rating?

TABLE 3.10   PERFORMANCE SCORES AND OVERALL RATINGS FOR 15 NOTEBOOK PCs

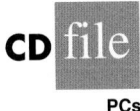

| Notebook | Performance Score | Overall Rating |
|----------|-------------------|----------------|
| AMS Tech Roadster 15CTA380 | 115 | 67 |
| Compaq Armada M700 | 191 | 78 |
| Compaq Prosignia Notebook 150 | 153 | 79 |
| Dell Inspiron 3700 C466GT | 194 | 80 |
| Dell Inspiron 7500 R500VT | 236 | 84 |
| Dell Latitude Cpi A366XT | 184 | 76 |
| Enpower ENP-313 Pro | 184 | 77 |
| Gateway Solo 9300LS | 216 | 92 |
| HP Pavilion Notebook PC | 185 | 83 |
| IBM ThinkPad I Series 1480 | 183 | 78 |
| Micro Express NP7400 | 189 | 77 |
| Micron TransPort NX PII-400 | 202 | 78 |
| NEC Versa SX | 192 | 78 |
| Sceptre Soundx 5200 | 141 | 73 |
| Sony VAIO PCG-F340 | 187 | 77 |

50. The Dow Jones Industrial Average (DJIA) and the Standard & Poor's (S&P) 500 Index are both used as measures of overall movement in the stock market. The DJIA is based on the price movements of 30 large companies; the S&P 500 is an index composed of 500 stocks. Some say the S&P 500 is a better measure of stock market performance because it is broader based. The closing price for the DJIA and the S&P 500 for 10 weeks, beginning with February 11, 2000, are shown (*Barron's*, April 17, 2000).

**DowS&P**

| Date | Dow Jones | S&P 500 |
|------|-----------|---------|
| February 11 | 10425 | 1387 |
| February 18 | 10220 | 1346 |
| February 25 | 9862 | 1333 |
| March 3 | 10367 | 1409 |
| March 10 | 9929 | 1395 |
| March 17 | 10595 | 1464 |
| March 24 | 11113 | 1527 |
| March 31 | 10922 | 1499 |
| April 7 | 11111 | 1516 |
| April 14 | 10306 | 1357 |

a. Compute the sample correlation coefficient for these data.
b. Are they poorly correlated, or do they have a close association?

51. The daily high and low temperatures for 20 cities follow (*USA Today*, May 9, 2000).

**HighLow**

| City | High | Low |
|------|------|-----|
| Athens | 75 | 54 |
| Bangkok | 92 | 74 |
| Cairo | 84 | 57 |
| Copenhagen | 64 | 39 |
| Dublin | 64 | 46 |
| Havana | 86 | 68 |
| Hong Kong | 81 | 72 |
| Johannesburg | 61 | 50 |
| London | 73 | 48 |
| Manila | 93 | 75 |
| Melbourne | 66 | 50 |
| Montreal | 64 | 52 |
| Paris | 77 | 55 |
| Rio de Janeiro | 80 | 61 |
| Rome | 81 | 54 |
| Seoul | 64 | 50 |
| Singapore | 90 | 75 |
| Sydney | 68 | 55 |
| Tokyo | 79 | 59 |
| Vancouver | 57 | 43 |

What is the correlation between the high and low temperatures?

# 3.6  The Weighted Mean and Working with Grouped Data

In Section 3.1, we presented the mean as one of the most important measures of central location. The formula for the mean of a sample with $n$ observations is restated as follows.

$$\bar{x} = \frac{\Sigma x_i}{n} = \frac{x_1 + x_2 + \cdots + x_n}{n} \qquad (3.14)$$

In this formula, each $x_i$ is given equal importance or weight. Although this practice is most common, in some instances, the mean is computed by giving each observation a weight that reflects its importance. A mean computed in this manner is referred to as a **weighted mean**.

## Weighted Mean

The weighted mean is computed as follows:

WEIGHTED MEAN

$$\bar{x} = \frac{\Sigma w_i x_i}{\Sigma w_i} \qquad (3.15)$$

where

$$x_i = \text{value of observation } i$$
$$w_i = \text{weight for observation } i$$

When the data are from a sample, equation (3.15) provides the weighted sample mean. When the data are from a population, $\mu$ replaces $\bar{x}$ and equation (3.15) provides the weighted population mean.

As an example of the need for a weighted mean, consider the following sample of five purchases of a raw material over the past three months.

| Purchase | Cost per Pound ($) | Number of Pounds |
|:---:|:---:|:---:|
| 1 | 3.00 | 1200 |
| 2 | 3.40 | 500 |
| 3 | 2.80 | 2750 |
| 4 | 2.90 | 1000 |
| 5 | 3.25 | 800 |

Note that the cost per pound has varied from $2.80 to $3.40 and the quantity purchased has varied from 500 to 2750 pounds. Suppose that a manager asked for information about the mean cost per pound of the raw material. Because the quantities ordered vary, we must use the formula for a weighted mean. The five cost-per-pound data values are $x_1 = 3.00$, $x_2 = 3.40, x_3 = 2.80, x_4 = 2.90$, and $x_5 = 3.25$. The weighted mean cost per pound is found by weighting each cost by its corresponding quantity. For this example, the weights are $w_1 = 1200, w_2 = 500, w_3 = 2750, w_4 = 1000$, and $w_5 = 800$. Using equation (3.15), the weighted mean is calculated as follows:

$$\bar{x} = \frac{1200(3.00) + 500(3.40) + 2750(2.80) + 1000(2.90) + 800(3.25)}{1200 + 500 + 2750 + 1000 + 800}$$

$$= \frac{18,500}{6250} = 2.96$$

Thus, the weighted mean computation shows that the mean cost per pound for the raw material is \$2.96. Note that using equation (3.14) rather than the weighted mean formula would have provided misleading results. In this case, the mean of the five cost-per-pound values is $(3.00 + 3.40 + 2.80 + 2.90 + 3.25)/5 = 15.35/5 = \$3.07$, which overstates the actual mean cost per pound purchased.

The choice of weights for a particular weighted mean computation depends upon the application. An example that is well known to college students is the computation of a grade point average (GPA). In this computation, the data values generally used are 4 for an A grade, 3 for a B grade, 2 for a C grade, 1 for a D grade, and 0 for an F grade. The weights are the number of credits hours earned for each grade. Exercise 54 at the end of this section provides an example of this weighted mean computation. In other weighted mean computations, quantities such as pounds, dollars, and/or volume are frequently used as weights. In any case, when observations vary in importance, the analyst must choose the weight that best reflects the importance of each observation in the determination of the mean.

*Computing a grade point average is a good example of the use of a weighted mean.*

## Grouped Data

In most cases, measures of location and variability are computed by using the individual data values. Sometimes, however, data are available only in a grouped or frequency distribution form. In the following discussion, we show how the weighted mean formula can be used to obtain approximations of the mean, variance, and standard deviation for **grouped data**.

In Section 2.2 we provided a frequency distribution of the time in days required to complete year-end audits for the public accounting firm of Sanderson and Clifford. The frequency distribution of audit times based on a sample of 20 clients is shown again in Table 3.11. Based on this frequency distribution, what is the sample mean audit time?

To compute the mean using only the grouped data, we treat the midpoint of each class as being representative of the items in the class. Let $M_i$ denote the midpoint for class $i$ and let $f_i$ denote the frequency of class $i$. The weighted mean formula (3.15) is then used with the data values denoted as $M_i$ and the weights given by the frequencies $f_i$. In this case, the denominator of equation (3.15) is the sum of the frequencies, which is the sample size $n$. That is, $\Sigma f_i = n$. Thus, the equation for the sample mean for grouped data is as follows.

SAMPLE MEAN FOR GROUPED DATA

$$\bar{x} = \frac{\Sigma f_i M_i}{n} \qquad (3.16)$$

where

$$M_i = \text{the midpoint for class } i$$
$$f_i = \text{the frequency for class } i$$
$$n = \text{the sample size}$$

With the class midpoints, $M_i$, halfway between the class limits, the first class of 10–14 in Table 3.11 has a midpoint at $(10 + 14)/2 = 12$. The five class midpoints and the weighted

**TABLE 3.11    FREQUENCY DISTRIBUTION OF AUDIT TIMES**

| Audit Time (days) | Frequency |
|---|---|
| 10–14 | 4 |
| 15–19 | 8 |
| 20–24 | 5 |
| 25–29 | 2 |
| 30–34 | 1 |
| Total | 20 |

mean computation for the audit time data are summarized in Table 3.12. As can be seen, the sample mean audit time is 19 days.

To compute the variance for grouped data, we use a slightly altered version of the formula for the variance provided in equation (3.5). In equation (3.5), the squared deviations of the data about the sample mean $\bar{x}$ were written $(x_i - \bar{x})^2$. However, with grouped data, the values are not known. In this case, we treat the class midpoint, $M_i$, as being representative of the $x_i$ values in the corresponding class. Thus the squared deviations about the sample mean, $(x_i - \bar{x})^2$, are replaced by $(M_i - \bar{x})^2$. Then, just as we did with the sample mean calculations for grouped data, we weight each value by the frequency of the class, $f_i$. The sum of the squared deviations about the mean for all the data is approximated by $\sum f_i (M_i - \bar{x})^2$. The term $n - 1$ rather than $n$ appears in the denominator in order to make the sample variance the estimate of the population variance. Thus, the following formula is used to obtain the sample variance for grouped data.

SAMPLE VARIANCE FOR GROUPED DATA

$$s^2 = \frac{\sum f_i (M_i - \bar{x})^2}{n - 1} \qquad (3.17)$$

**TABLE 3.12    COMPUTATION OF THE SAMPLE MEAN AUDIT TIME FOR GROUPED DATA**

| Audit Time (days) | Class Midpoint ($M_i$) | Frequency ($f_i$) | $f_i M_i$ |
|---|---|---|---|
| 10–14 | 12 | 4 | 48 |
| 15–19 | 17 | 8 | 136 |
| 20–24 | 22 | 5 | 110 |
| 25–29 | 27 | 2 | 54 |
| 30–34 | 32 | 1 | 32 |
|  |  | 20 | 380 |

$$\text{Sample mean } \bar{x} = \frac{\sum f_i M_i}{n} = \frac{380}{20} = 19 \text{ days}$$

**TABLE 3.13**  COMPUTATION OF THE SAMPLE VARIANCE OF AUDIT TIMES FOR GROUPED DATA (SAMPLE MEAN $\bar{x} = 19$)

| Audit Time (days) | Class Midpoint ($M_i$) | Frequency ($f_i$) | Deviation ($M_i - \bar{x}$) | Squared Deviation ($M_i - \bar{x})^2$ | $f_i(M_i - \bar{x})^2$ |
|---|---|---|---|---|---|
| 10–14 | 12 | 4 | −7 | 49 | 196 |
| 15–19 | 17 | 8 | −2 | 4 | 32 |
| 20–24 | 22 | 5 | 3 | 9 | 45 |
| 25–29 | 27 | 2 | 8 | 64 | 128 |
| 30–34 | 32 | 1 | 13 | 169 | 169 |
|  |  | 20 |  |  | 570 |
|  |  |  |  |  | $\Sigma f_i(M_i - \bar{x})^2$ |

$$\text{Sample variance } s^2 = \frac{\Sigma f_i(M_i - \bar{x})^2}{n - 1} = \frac{570}{19} = 30$$

The calculation of the sample variance for audit times based on the grouped data from Table 3.11 is shown in Table 3.13. As can be seen, the sample variance is 30.

The standard deviation for grouped data is simply the square root of the variance for grouped data. For the audit time data, the sample standard deviation is $s = \sqrt{30} = 5.48$.

Before closing this section on computing measures of location and dispersion for grouped data, we note that formulas (3.16) and (3.17) are for a sample. Population summary measures are computed similarly. The grouped data formulas for a population mean and variance follow.

---

POPULATION MEAN FOR GROUPED DATA

$$\mu = \frac{\Sigma f_i M_i}{N} \qquad (3.18)$$

---

POPULATION VARIANCE FOR GROUPED DATA

$$\sigma^2 = \frac{\Sigma f_i(M_i - \mu)^2}{N} \qquad (3.19)$$

---

## NOTES AND COMMENTS

In computing descriptive statistics for grouped data, the class midpoints are used to approximate the data values in each class. As a result, the descriptive statistics for grouped data approximate the descriptive statistics that would result from using the original data directly. We therefore recommend computing descriptive statistics from the original data rather than from grouped data whenever possible.

## Exercises

## Methods

52.  Consider the following data and corresponding weights.

| $x_i$ | Weight ($w_i$) |
|-------|----------------|
| 3.2   | 6              |
| 2.0   | 3              |
| 2.5   | 2              |
| 5.0   | 8              |

a.  Compute the weighted mean.
b.  Compute the sample mean of the four data values without weighting. Note the difference in the results provided by the two computations.

53.  Consider the sample data in the following frequency distribution.

| Class | Midpoint | Frequency |
|-------|----------|-----------|
| 3–7   | 5        | 4         |
| 8–12  | 10       | 7         |
| 13–17 | 15       | 9         |
| 18–22 | 20       | 5         |

a.  Compute the sample mean.
b.  Compute the sample variance and sample standard deviation.

## Applications

54.  The grade point average for college students is based on a weighted mean computation. For most colleges, the grades are given the following data values: A (4), B (3), C (2), D (1), and F (0). After 60 credit hours of course work, a student at State University earned 9 credit hours of A, 15 credit hours of B, 33 credit hours of C, and 3 credit hours of D.
a.  Compute the student's grade point average.
b.  Students at State University must maintain a 2.5 grade point average for their first 60 credit hours of course work in order to be admitted to the business college. Will this student be admitted?

55.  *Bloomberg Personal Finance* (July/August 2001) included the following companies in its recommended investment portfolio. For a portfolio value of $25,000, the recommended dollar amounts allocated to each stock are shown.

| Company | Portfolio ($) | Estimated Growth Rate (%) | Dividend Yield (%) |
|---------|---------------|---------------------------|--------------------|
| Citigroup | 3000 | 15 | 1.21 |
| General Electric | 5500 | 14 | 1.48 |
| Kimberly-Clark | 4200 | 12 | 1.72 |
| Oracle | 3000 | 25 | 0.00 |
| Pharmacia | 3000 | 20 | 0.96 |
| SBC Communications | 3800 | 12 | 2.48 |
| WorldCom | 2500 | 35 | 0.00 |

a. Using the portfolio dollar amounts as the weights, what is the weighted average estimated growth rate for the portfolio?
b. What is the weighted average dividend yield for the portfolio?

56. A service station recorded the following frequency distribution for the number of gallons of gasoline sold per car in a sample of 680 cars.

| Gasoline (gallons) | Frequency |
|---|---|
| 0–4 | 74 |
| 5–9 | 192 |
| 10–14 | 280 |
| 15–19 | 105 |
| 20–24 | 23 |
| 25–29 | 6 |
| Total | 680 |

Compute the mean, variance, and standard deviation for these grouped data. If the service station expects to service about 120 cars on a given day, estimate the total number of gallons of gasoline that will be sold.

57. A survey of subscribers to *Fortune* magazine asked the following question: "How many of the last four issues have you read or looked through?" Suppose that the following frequency distribution summarizes 500 responses.

| Number Read | Frequency |
|---|---|
| 0 | 15 |
| 1 | 10 |
| 2 | 40 |
| 3 | 85 |
| 4 | 350 |
| Total | 500 |

a. What is the mean number of issues read by a *Fortune* subscriber?
b. What is the standard deviation of the number of issues read?

## Summary

In this chapter we introduced several descriptive statistics that can be used to summarize the location, variability, and shape of a data distribution. Unlike the tabular and graphical procedures introduced in Chapter 2, the measures introduced in this chapter summarize the data in terms of numerical values. When the numerical values obtained are for a sample, they are called sample statistics. When the numerical values obtained are for a population, they are called population parameters. Some of the notation used for sample statistics and population parameters follow.

*In statistical inference, the sample statistic is referred to as the point estimator of the population parameter.*

| | Sample Statistic | Population Parameter |
|---|---|---|
| Mean | $\bar{x}$ | $\mu$ |
| Variance | $s^2$ | $\sigma^2$ |
| Standard deviation | $s$ | $\sigma$ |
| Covariance | $s_{xy}$ | $\sigma_{xy}$ |
| Correlation | $r_{xy}$ | $\rho_{xy}$ |

As measures of central location, we defined the mean, median, and mode. Then the concept of percentiles was used to describe other locations in the data set. Next, we presented the range, interquartile range, variance, standard deviation, and coefficient of variation as measures of variability or dispersion. Our primary measure of the shape of a data distribution was the skewness. Negative values indicate a data distribution skewed to the left. Positive values indicate a data distribution skewed to the right. We then described how the mean and standard deviation could be used, applying Chebyshev's theorem and the empirical rule, to provide more information about the distribution of data and to identify outliers.

In Section 3.4 we showed how to develop a five-number summary and a box plot to provide simultaneous information about the location, variability, and shape of the distribution. In Section 3.5 we introduced covariance and the correlation coefficient as measures of association between two variables. In the final section, we showed how to compute a weighted mean and how to calculate a mean, variance, and standard deviation for grouped data.

The descriptive statistics we discussed can be developed using statistical software packages and spreadsheets. In Appendix 3.1 we show how to develop most of the descriptive statistics introduced in the chapter using Minitab. In Appendix 3.2, we demonstrate the use of Excel for the same purpose.

## Glossary

**Sample statistic** A numerical value used as a summary measure for a sample (e.g., the sample mean, $\bar{x}$, the sample variance, $s^2$, and the sample standard deviation, $s$).

**Population parameter** A numerical value used as a summary measure for a population (e.g., the population mean, $\mu$, the population variance, $\sigma^2$, and the population standard deviation, $\sigma$).

**Point estimator** The sample statistic, such as $\bar{x}$, $s^2$, and $s$, when used to estimate the corresponding population parameter.

**Mean** A measure of central location computed by summing the data values and dividing by the number of observations.

**Median** A measure of central location provided by the value in the middle when the data are arranged in ascending order.

**Mode** A measure of location, defined as the value that occurs with greatest frequency.

**Percentile** A value such that at least $p$ percent of the observations are less than or equal to this value and at least $(100 - p)$ percent of the observations are greater than or equal to this value. The 50th percentile is the median.

**Quartiles** The 25th, 50th, and 75th percentiles, referred to as the first quartile, the second quartile (median), and third quartile, respectively. The quartiles can be used to divide a data set into four parts, with each part containing approximately 25% of the data.

**Range** A measure of variability, defined to be the largest value minus the smallest value.

**Interquartile range (IQR)** A measure of variability, defined to be the difference between the third and first quartiles.

**Variance** A measure of variability based on the squared deviations of the data values about the mean.

**Standard deviation** A measure of variability computed by taking the positive square root of the variance.

**Coefficient of variation** A measure of relative variability computed by dividing the standard deviation by the mean and multiplying by 100.

**Skewness** A measure of the shape of a data distribution. Data skewed to the left result in negative skewness; a symmetric data distribution results in zero skewness; and data skewed to the right result in positive skewness.

**z-score** A value computed by dividing the deviation about the mean $(x_i - \bar{x})$ by the standard deviation $s$. A $z$-score is referred to as a standardized value and denotes the number of standard deviations $x_i$ is from the mean.

**Chebyshev's theorem** A theorem that can be used to make statements about the proportion of data values that must be within a specified number of standard deviations of the mean.

**Empirical rule** A rule that can be used to compute the percentage of data values that must be within one, two, and three standard deviations of the mean for data that exhibit a bell-shaped distribution.

**Outlier** An unusually small or unusually large data value.

**Five-number summary** An exploratory data analysis technique that uses five numbers to summarize the data: smallest value, first quartile, median, third quartile, and largest value.

**Box plot** A graphical summary of data based on a five-number summary.

**Covariance** A measure of linear association between two variables. Positive values indicate a positive relationship; negative values indicate a negative relationship.

**Correlation coefficient** A measure of linear association between two variables that takes on values between $-1$ and $+1$. Values near $+1$ indicate a strong positive linear relationship, values near $-1$ indicate a strong negative linear relationship; and values near zero indicate the lack of a linear relationship.

**Weighted mean** The mean obtained by assigning each observation a weight that reflects its importance.

**Grouped data** Data available in class intervals as summarized by a frequency distribution. Individual values of the original data are not available.

## Key Formulas

**Sample Mean**

$$\bar{x} = \frac{\Sigma x_i}{n} \tag{3.1}$$

**Population Mean**

$$\mu = \frac{\Sigma x_i}{N} \tag{3.2}$$

**Interquartile Range**

$$\text{IQR} = Q_3 - Q_1 \tag{3.3}$$

**Population Variance**

$$\sigma^2 = \frac{\Sigma(x_i - \mu)^2}{N} \tag{3.4}$$

**Sample Variance**

$$s^2 = \frac{\Sigma(x_i - \bar{x})^2}{n - 1} \tag{3.5}$$

**Standard Deviation**

$$\text{Sample standard deviation} = s = \sqrt{s^2} \tag{3.6}$$

$$\text{Population standard deviation} = \sigma = \sqrt{\sigma^2} \tag{3.7}$$

**Coefficient of Variation**

$$\left(\frac{\text{Standard deviation}}{\text{Mean}} \times 100\right)\%$$    **(3.8)**

$z$-Score

$$z_i = \frac{x_i - \bar{x}}{s}$$    **(3.9)**

**Sample Covariance**

$$s_{xy} = \frac{\Sigma(x_i - \bar{x})(y_i - \bar{y})}{n - 1}$$    **(3.10)**

**Population Covariance**

$$\sigma_{xy} = \frac{\Sigma(x_i - \mu_x)(y_i - \mu_y)}{N}$$    **(3.11)**

**Pearson Product Moment Correlation Coefficient: Sample Data**

$$r_{xy} = \frac{s_{xy}}{s_x s_y}$$    **(3.12)**

**Pearson Product Moment Correlation Coefficient: Population Data**

$$\rho_{xy} = \frac{\sigma_{xy}}{\sigma_x \sigma_y}$$    **(3.13)**

**Weighted Mean**

$$\bar{x} = \frac{\Sigma w_i x_i}{\Sigma w_i}$$    **(3.15)**

**Sample Mean for Grouped Data**

$$\bar{x} = \frac{\Sigma f_i M_i}{n}$$    **(3.16)**

**Sample Variance for Grouped Data**

$$s^2 = \frac{\Sigma f_i (M_i - \bar{x})^2}{n - 1}$$    **(3.17)**

**Population Mean for Grouped Data**

$$\mu = \frac{\Sigma f_i M_i}{N}$$    **(3.18)**

**Population Variance for Grouped Data**

$$\sigma^2 = \frac{\Sigma f_i (M_i - \mu)^2}{N}$$    **(3.19)**

## Supplementary Exercises

58. The average American spends $65.88 per month dining out (*The Des Moines Register*, December 5, 1997). A sample of young adults provided the following dining out expenditures (in dollars) over the past month.

**Eat**

| | | | | | | |
|---|---|---|---|---|---|---|
| 253 | 101 | 245 | 467 | 131 | 0 | 225 |
| 80 | 113 | 69 | 198 | 95 | 129 | 124 |
| 11 | 178 | 104 | 161 | 0 | 118 | 151 |
| 55 | 152 | 134 | 169 | | | |

   a. Compute the mean, median, and mode.
   b. Considering your results in part (a), do these young adults seem to spend about the same as an average American eating out?
   c. Compute the first and third quartiles.
   d. Compute the range and interquartile range.
   e. Compute the variance and standard deviation.
   f. The skewness measure for this data is 1.54. Comment on the shape of this distribution. Is this the shape you would expect? Why or why not?
   g. Do the data contain any outliers?

59. The total annual compensation for a board member at one of the nation's 100 biggest public companies is based in part on the cash retainer, an annual payment for serving on the board. In addition to the cash retainer, a board member may receive a stock retainer, a stock grant, a stock option, and a fee for attending board meetings. The total compensation can easily exceed $100,000 even with an annual retainer as low as $15,000. The following data show the cash retainer (in $1000s) for a sample of 20 of the nation's biggest public companies (*USA Today*, April 17, 2000).

**Retainer**

| Company | Cash Retainer |
|---|---|
| American Express | 64 |
| Bank of America | 36 |
| Boeing | 26 |
| Chevron | 35 |
| Dell Computer | 40 |
| DuPont | 35 |
| ExxonMobil | 40 |
| Ford Motor | 30 |
| General Motors | 60 |
| International Paper | 36 |
| Kroger | 28 |
| Lucent Technologies | 50 |
| Motorola | 20 |
| Procter & Gamble | 55 |
| Raytheon | 40 |
| Sears Roebuck | 30 |
| Texaco | 15 |
| United Parcel Service | 55 |
| Wal-Mart Stores | 25 |
| Xerox | 40 |

Compute the following descriptive statistics.
   a. Mean, median, and mode
   b. The first and third quartiles

    c.   The range and interquartile range

    d.   The variance and the standard deviation

    e.   Coefficient of variation

60.  A survey conducted to assess the ability of computer manufacturers to handle problems quickly obtained the following results (*PC Computing*, November 1997).

| Company | Days to Resolve Problems | Company | Days to Resolve Problems |
|---|---|---|---|
| Compaq | 13 | Gateway | 21 |
| Packard Bell | 27 | Digital | 27 |
| Quantex | 11 | IBM | 12 |
| Dell | 14 | Hewlett-Packard | 14 |
| NEC | 14 | AT&T | 20 |
| AST | 17 | Toshiba | 37 |
| Acer | 16 | Micron | 17 |

    a.   What are the mean and median number of days needed to resolve problems?

    b.   What are the variance and standard deviation?

    c.   Which manufacturer holds the best record?

    d.   What is the *z*-score for Packard Bell?

    e.   What is the *z*-score for IBM?

    f.   Do the data contain any outliers?

61.  According to Forrester Research, Inc., approximately 19% of Internet users play games online. The following data show the number of unique users (in thousands) for the month of March for 10 game sites (*The Wall Street Journal*, April 17, 2000).

| Site | Unique Users |
|---|---|
| aolgames.com | 9416 |
| extremelotto.com | 3955 |
| freelotto.com | 12901 |
| gamesville.com | 4844 |
| iwin.com | 7410 |
| prizecentral.com | 4899 |
| shockwave.com | 5582 |
| speedyclick.com | 6628 |
| uproar.com | 8821 |
| webstakes.com | 7499 |

Using these data, compute the mean, median, variance, and standard deviation.

62.  The typical household income for a sample of 20 cities follow (*Places Rated Almanac*, 2000). Data are in thousands of dollars.

| City | Income |
|---|---|
| Akron, OH | 74.1 |
| Atlanta, GA | 82.4 |
| Birmingham, AL | 71.2 |
| Bismark, ND | 62.8 |

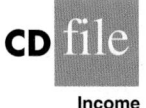

**CD** file

**Income**

(*continued*)

| City | Income |
|------|--------|
| Cleveland, OH | 79.2 |
| Columbia, SC | 66.8 |
| Danbury, CT | 132.3 |
| Denver, CO | 82.6 |
| Detroit, MI | 85.3 |
| Fort Lauderdale, FL | 75.8 |
| Hartford, CT | 89.1 |
| Lancaster, PA | 75.2 |
| Madison, WI | 78.8 |
| Naples, FL | 100.0 |
| Nashville, TN | 77.3 |
| Philadelphia, PA | 87.0 |
| Savannah, GA | 67.8 |
| Toledo, OH | 71.2 |
| Trenton, NJ | 106.4 |
| Washington, DC | 97.4 |

a. Compute the mean and standard deviation for the sample data.

b. Using the mean and standard deviation computed in part (a) as estimates of the mean and standard deviation of household income for the population of all cities, use Chebyshev's theorem to determine the range within which 75% of the household incomes for the population of all cities must fall.

c. Assume that the distribution of household income is bell-shaped. Using the mean and standard deviation computed in part (a) as estimates of the mean and standard deviation of household income for the population of all cities, use the empirical rule to determine the range within which 95% of the household incomes for the population of all cities must fall. Compare your answer with the value in part (b).

d. Do the sample data contain any outliers?

63. Public transportation and the automobile are two methods an employee can use to get to work each day. Samples of times recorded for each method are shown. Times are in minutes.

| Public Transportation: | 28 | 29 | 32 | 37 | 33 | 25 | 29 | 32 | 41 | 34 |
|------|------|------|------|------|------|------|------|------|------|------|
| Automobile: | 29 | 31 | 33 | 32 | 34 | 30 | 31 | 32 | 35 | 33 |

a. Compute the sample mean time to get to work for each method.

b. Compute the sample standard deviation for each method.

c. On the basis of your results from parts (a) and (b), which method of transportation should be preferred? Explain.

d. Develop a box plot for each method. Does a comparison of the box plots support your conclusion in part (c)?

64. The typical household income and typical home price for a sample of 20 cities follow (*Places Rated Almanac*, 2000). Data are in thousands of dollars.

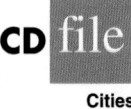

**Cities**

| City | Income | Home Price |
|------|--------|------------|
| Bismark, ND | 62.8 | 92.8 |
| Columbia, SC | 66.8 | 116.7 |
| Savannah, GA | 67.8 | 108.1 |
| Birmingham, AL | 71.2 | 130.9 |
| Toledo, OH | 71.2 | 101.1 |
| Akron, OH | 74.1 | 114.9 |
| Lancaster, PA | 75.2 | 125.9 |

| City | Income | Home Price |
|------|--------|-----------|
| Fort Lauderdale, FL | 75.8 | 145.3 |
| Nashville, TN | 77.3 | 125.9 |
| Madison, WI | 78.8 | 145.2 |
| Cleveland, OH | 79.2 | 135.8 |
| Atlanta, GA | 82.4 | 126.9 |
| Denver, CO | 82.6 | 161.9 |
| Detroit, MI | 85.3 | 145.0 |
| Philadelphia, PA | 87.0 | 151.5 |
| Hartford, CT | 89.1 | 162.1 |
| Washington, DC | 97.4 | 191.9 |
| Naples, FL | 100.0 | 173.6 |
| Trenton, NJ | 106.4 | 168.1 |
| Danbury, CT | 132.3 | 234.1 |

    a. What is the value of the sample covariance? Does it indicate a positive or a negative linear relationship?

    b. What is the sample correlation coefficient?

65. The following data show the media expenditures ($ millions) and shipments in millions of barrels (bbls.) for 10 major brands of beer (*Superbrands '98*, October 20, 1997).

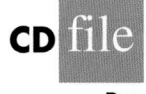

**Beer**

| Brand | Media Expenditures ($ millions) | Shipments in bbls. (millions) |
|-------|--------------------------------|-------------------------------|
| Budweiser | 120.0 | 36.3 |
| Bud Light | 68.7 | 20.7 |
| Miller Lite | 100.1 | 15.9 |
| Coors Light | 76.6 | 13.2 |
| Busch | 8.7 | 8.1 |
| Natural Light | 0.1 | 7.1 |
| Miller Genuine Draft | 21.5 | 5.6 |
| Miller High Lite | 1.4 | 4.4 |
| Busch Lite | 5.3 | 4.3 |
| Milwaukee's Best | 1.7 | 4.3 |

    a. What is the sample covariance? Does it indicate a positive or negative relationship?

    b. What is the sample correlation coefficient?

66. *Road & Track* provided the following sample of the tire ratings and load-carrying capacity of automobiles tires.

| Tire Rating | Load-Carrying Capacity |
|-------------|------------------------|
| 75 | 853 |
| 82 | 1047 |
| 85 | 1135 |
| 87 | 1201 |
| 88 | 1235 |
| 91 | 1356 |
| 92 | 1389 |
| 93 | 1433 |
| 105 | 2039 |

   a. Develop a scatter diagram for the data with tire rating on the *x*-axis.

   b. What is the sample correlation coefficient, and what does it tell you about the relationship between tire rating and load-carrying capacity?

67. The following data show the trailing 52-weeks primary share earnings and book values as reported by 10 companies (*The Wall Street Journal*, March 13, 2000).

| Company | Book Value | Earnings |
|---|---|---|
| Am Elec | 25.21 | 2.69 |
| Columbia En | 23.20 | 3.01 |
| Con Ed | 25.19 | 3.13 |
| Duke Energy | 20.17 | 2.25 |
| Edison Int'l | 13.55 | 1.79 |
| Enron Cp. | 7.44 | 1.27 |
| Peco | 13.61 | 3.15 |
| Pub Sv Ent | 21.86 | 3.29 |
| Southn Co. | 8.77 | 1.86 |
| Unicom | 23.22 | 2.74 |

   a. Develop a scatter diagram for the data with book value on the *x*-axis.

   b. What is the sample correlation coefficient, and what does it tell you about the relationship between the earnings per share and the book value?

68. A forecasting technique referred to as moving averages uses the average or mean of the most recent *n* periods to forecast the next value for time series data. With a three-period moving average, the most recent three periods of data are used in the forecast computation. Consider a product with the following demand for the first three months of the current year: January (800 units), February (750 units), and March (900 units).

   a. What is the three-month moving average forecast for April?

   b. A variation of this forecasting technique is called weighted moving averages. The weighting allows the more recent time series data to receive more weight or more importance in the computation of the forecast. For example, a weighted three-month moving average might give a weight of 3 to data one month old, a weight of 2 to data two months old, and a weight of 1 to data three months old. Use the data given to provide a three-month weighted moving average forecast for April.

69. The days to maturity for a sample of five money market funds are shown here. The dollar amounts invested in the funds are provided. Use the weighted mean to determine the mean number of days to maturity for dollars invested in these five money market funds.

| Days to Maturity | Dollar Value ($ millions) |
|---|---|
| 20 | 20 |
| 12 | 30 |
| 7 | 10 |
| 5 | 15 |
| 6 | 10 |

70. Automobiles traveling on a road with a posted speed limit of 55 miles per hour are checked for speed by a state police radar system. Following is a frequency distribution of speeds.

| Speed (miles per hour) | Frequency |
|---|---|
| 45–49 | 10 |
| 50–54 | 40 |
| 55–59 | 150 |
| 60–64 | 175 |
| 65–69 | 75 |
| 70–74 | 15 |
| 75–79 | 10 |
| Total | 475 |

a.   What is the mean speed of the automobiles traveling on this road?

b.   Compute the variance and the standard deviation.

71.   Dinner check amounts at a French restaurant, La Maison, show the following frequency distribution. Compute the mean, variance, and standard deviation.

| Dinner Check ($) | Frequency |
|---|---|
| 25–34 | 2 |
| 35–44 | 6 |
| 45–54 | 4 |
| 55–64 | 4 |
| 65–74 | 2 |
| 75–84 | 2 |
| Total | 20 |

## Case Problem 1   Pelican Stores

Pelican Stores, a chain of women's apparel stores operating throughout the country, recently ran a promotion in which discount coupons were sent to customers of related stores. Data collected for a sample of 100 in-store credit card transactions during one day in November 2002 are contained in the file named Pelican. Table 3.14 shows a portion of the data set. A

**TABLE 3.14   DATA FOR A SAMPLE OF 100 CREDIT CARD PURCHASES AT PELICAN STORES**

CD file

Pelican

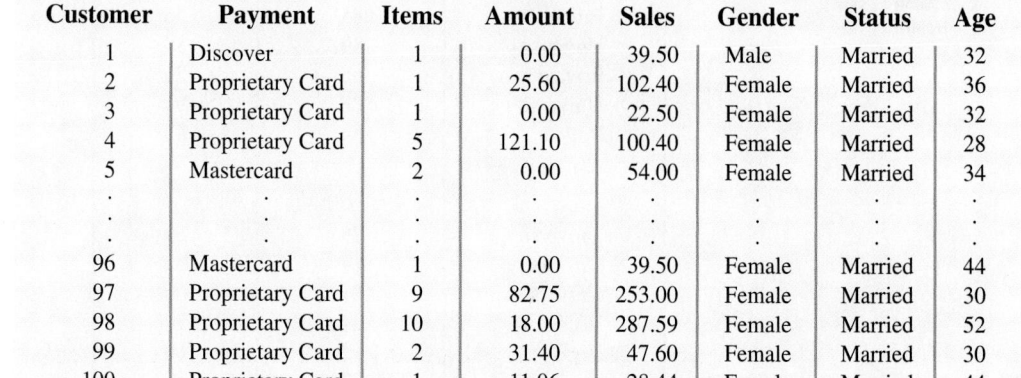

| Customer | Method of Payment | Items | Discount Amount | Sales | Gender | Marital Status | Age |
|---|---|---|---|---|---|---|---|
| 1 | Discover | 1 | 0.00 | 39.50 | Male | Married | 32 |
| 2 | Proprietary Card | 1 | 25.60 | 102.40 | Female | Married | 36 |
| 3 | Proprietary Card | 1 | 0.00 | 22.50 | Female | Married | 32 |
| 4 | Proprietary Card | 5 | 121.10 | 100.40 | Female | Married | 28 |
| 5 | Mastercard | 2 | 0.00 | 54.00 | Female | Married | 34 |
| : | : | : | : | : | : | : | : |
| 96 | Mastercard | 1 | 0.00 | 39.50 | Female | Married | 44 |
| 97 | Proprietary Card | 9 | 82.75 | 253.00 | Female | Married | 30 |
| 98 | Proprietary Card | 10 | 18.00 | 287.59 | Female | Married | 52 |
| 99 | Proprietary Card | 2 | 31.40 | 47.60 | Female | Married | 30 |
| 100 | Proprietary Card | 1 | 11.06 | 28.44 | Female | Married | 44 |

nonzero amount for the Discount variable indicates that the customer brought in the promotional coupons and used them.

Pelican's management wants to use this sample data to learn about its customer base and to evaluate the promotion involving discount coupons.

## Managerial Report

Use the methods of descriptive statistics presented in this chapter to summarize the data and comment on your findings. At a minimum, your report should include the following.

1. Descriptive statistics on sales and descriptive statistics on sales by various classifications of customers.
2. Descriptive statistics on the relationship between discount amount and sales for those customers responding to the promotion.
3. Descriptive statistics concerning the relationship between age and sales.

Comment on any findings that appear interesting and of potential value to management.

**Case Problem 2**    # National Health Care Association

The National Health Care Association is concerned about the shortage of nurses the health care profession is projecting for the future. To learn the current degree of job satisfaction among nurses, the association sponsored a study of hospital nurses throughout the country. As part of this study, 50 nurses in a sample indicated their degree of satisfaction with their work, their pay, and their opportunities for promotion. Each of the three aspects of satisfaction was measured on a scale from 0 to 100, with larger values indicating higher degrees of satisfaction. The data collected also showed the type of hospital employing the nurses. The types of hospitals were Private, Veterans Administration (VA), and University. A portion of the data is shown in Table 3.15. The complete data set can be found on the CD accompanying the text in the file named Health.

**TABLE 3.15    SATISFACTION SCORE DATA FOR A SAMPLE OF 50 NURSES**

**Health**

| Nurse | Hospital | Work | Pay | Promotion |
|-------|----------|------|-----|-----------|
| 1 | Private | 74 | 47 | 63 |
| 2 | VA | 72 | 76 | 37 |
| 3 | University | 75 | 53 | 92 |
| 4 | Private | 89 | 66 | 62 |
| 5 | University | 69 | 47 | 16 |
| 6 | Private | 85 | 56 | 64 |
| 7 | University | 89 | 80 | 64 |
| 8 | Private | 88 | 36 | 47 |
| 9 | University | 88 | 55 | 52 |
| 10 | Private | 84 | 42 | 66 |
| . | . | . | . | . |
| . | . | . | . | . |
| . | . | . | . | . |
| 45 | University | 79 | 59 | 41 |
| 46 | University | 84 | 53 | 63 |
| 47 | University | 87 | 66 | 49 |
| 48 | VA | 84 | 74 | 37 |
| 49 | VA | 95 | 66 | 52 |
| 50 | Private | 72 | 57 | 40 |

## Managerial Report

Use methods of descriptive statistics to summarize the data. Present the summaries that will be beneficial in communicating the results to others. Discuss your findings. Specifically, comment on the following questions.

1. On the basis of the entire data set and the three job satisfaction variables, what aspect of the job is most satisfying for the nurses? What appears to be the least satisfying? In what area(s), if any, do you feel improvements should be made? Discuss.
2. On the basis of descriptive measures of variability, what measure of job satisfaction appears to generate the greatest difference of opinion among the nurses? Explain.
3. What can be learned about the types of hospitals? Does any particular type of hospital seem to have better levels of job satisfaction than the other types? Do your results suggest any recommendations for learning about and improving job satisfaction? Discuss.
4. What additional descriptive statistics and insights can you use to learn about and possibly improve job satisfaction?

## Case Problem 3    Business Schools of Asia-Pacific

**Asian**

The pursuit of a higher education degree in business is now international. A survey shows that more and more Asians choose the Master of Business Administration degree route to corporate success (*Asia, Inc.*, September 1997). The number of applicants for MBA courses at Asia-Pacific schools continues to increase about 30 percent a year. In 1997, the 74 business schools in the Asia-Pacific region reported a record 170,000 applications for the 11,000 full-time MBA degrees to be awarded in 1999. A main reason for the surge in demand is that an MBA can greatly enhance earning power.

Across the region, thousands of Asians show an increasing willingness to temporarily shelve their careers and spend two years in pursuit of a theoretical business qualification. Courses in these schools are notoriously tough and include economics, banking, marketing, behavioral sciences, labor relations, decision making, strategic thinking, business law, and more. *Asia, Inc.* provided the data set in Table 3.16, which shows some of the characteristics of the leading Asia-Pacific business schools.

## Managerial Report

Use the methods of descriptive statistics to summarize the data in Table 3.16. Discuss your findings.

1. Include a summary for each variable in the data set. Make comments and interpretations based on maximums and minimums, as well as the appropriate means and proportions. What new insights do these descriptive statistics provide concerning Asia-Pacific business schools?
2. Summarize the data to compare the following:
   a. Any difference between local and foreign tuition costs.
   b. Any difference between mean starting salaries for schools requiring and not requiring work experience.
   c. Any difference between starting salaries for schools requiring and not requiring English tests.
3. Do starting salaries appear to be related to tuition?
4. Present any additional graphical and numerical summaries that will be beneficial in communicating the data in Table 3.16 to others.

TABLE 3.16  DATA FOR 25 ASIA-PACIFIC BUSINESS SCHOOLS

| Business School | Full-Time Enrollment | Students per Faculty | Local Tuition ($) | Foreign Tuition ($) | Age | % Foreign | GMAT | English Test | Work Experience | Starting Salary ($) |
|---|---|---|---|---|---|---|---|---|---|---|
| Melbourne Business School | 200 | 5 | 24,420 | 29,600 | 28 | 47 | Yes | No | Yes | 71,400 |
| University of New South Wales (Sydney) | 228 | 4 | 19,993 | 32,582 | 29 | 28 | Yes | No | No | 65,200 |
| Indian Institute of Management (Ahmedabad) | 392 | 5 | 4,300 | 4,300 | 22 | 0 | No | No | No | 7,100 |
| Chinese University of Hong Kong | 90 | 5 | 11,140 | 11,140 | 29 | 10 | Yes | No | No | 31,000 |
| International University of Japan (Niigata) | 126 | 4 | 33,060 | 33,060 | 28 | 60 | Yes | Yes | No | 87,000 |
| Asian Institute of Management (Manila) | 389 | 5 | 7,562 | 9,000 | 25 | 50 | Yes | No | Yes | 22,800 |
| Indian Institute of Management (Bangalore) | 380 | 5 | 3,935 | 16,000 | 23 | 1 | Yes | No | No | 7,500 |
| National University of Singapore | 147 | 6 | 6,146 | 7,170 | 29 | 51 | Yes | Yes | Yes | 43,300 |
| Indian Institute of Management (Calcutta) | 463 | 8 | 2,880 | 16,000 | 23 | 0 | No | No | No | 7,400 |
| Australian National University (Canberra) | 42 | 2 | 20,300 | 20,300 | 30 | 80 | Yes | Yes | Yes | 46,600 |
| Nanyang Technological University (Singapore) | 50 | 5 | 8,500 | 8,500 | 32 | 20 | Yes | No | Yes | 49,300 |
| University of Queensland (Brisbane) | 138 | 17 | 16,000 | 22,800 | 32 | 26 | No | No | Yes | 49,600 |
| Hong Kong University of Science and Technology | 60 | 2 | 11,513 | 11,513 | 26 | 37 | Yes | No | Yes | 34,000 |
| Macquarie Graduate School of Management (Sydney) | 12 | 8 | 17,172 | 19,778 | 34 | 27 | No | No | Yes | 60,100 |
| Chulalongkorn University (Bangkok) | 200 | 7 | 17,355 | 17,355 | 25 | 6 | Yes | No | Yes | 17,600 |
| Monash Mt. Eliza Business School (Melbourne) | 350 | 13 | 16,200 | 22,500 | 30 | 30 | No | Yes | Yes | 52,500 |
| Asian Institute of Management (Bangkok) | 300 | 10 | 18,200 | 18,200 | 29 | 90 | No | Yes | Yes | 25,000 |
| University of Adelaide | 20 | 19 | 16,426 | 23,100 | 30 | 10 | No | No | Yes | 66,000 |
| Massey University (Palmerston North, New Zealand) | 30 | 15 | 13,106 | 21,625 | 37 | 35 | No | Yes | Yes | 41,400 |
| Royal Melbourne Institute of Technology Business Graduate School | 30 | 7 | 13,880 | 17,765 | 32 | 30 | No | Yes | Yes | 48,900 |
| Jamnalal Bajaj Institute of Management Studies (Bombay) | 240 | 9 | 1,000 | 1,000 | 24 | 0 | No | No | Yes | 7,000 |
| Curtin Institute of Technology (Perth) | 98 | 15 | 9,475 | 19,097 | 29 | 43 | Yes | No | Yes | 55,000 |
| Lahore University of Management Sciences | 70 | 14 | 11,250 | 26,300 | 23 | 2.5 | No | No | No | 7,500 |
| Universiti Sains Malaysia (Penang) | 30 | 5 | 2,260 | 2,260 | 32 | 15 | No | Yes | Yes | 16,000 |
| De La Salle University (Manila) | 44 | 17 | 3,300 | 3,600 | 28 | 3.5 | Yes | No | Yes | 13,100 |

# Appendix 3.1   Descriptive Statistics Using Minitab

In this appendix, we describe how to use Minitab to develop descriptive statistics. Table 3.1 listed the starting salaries for 12 business school graduates. Panel A of Figure 3.11 shows the descriptive statistics obtained by using Minitab to summarize these data. Definitions of the headings in Panel A follow.

| | |
|---|---|
| N | number of data values |
| Mean | mean |
| SE Mean | standard error of mean |
| StDev | standard deviation |
| Min | minimum data value |
| Q1 | first quartile |
| Median | median |
| Q3 | third quartile |
| Max | maximum data value |

The label SE Mean refers to the *standard error of the mean.* It is computed by dividing the standard deviation by the square root of $N$. The interpretation and use of this measure are discussed in Chapter 7 when we introduce the topics of sampling and sampling distributions.

Although the numerical measures of range, interquartile range, variance, and coefficient of variation do not appear on the Minitab output, these values can be easily computed from the results in Figure 3.11 as follows.

$$\text{Range} = \text{Max} - \text{Min}$$
$$\text{IQR} = Q_3 - Q_1$$
$$\text{Variance} = (\text{StDev})^2$$
$$\text{Coefficient of Variation} = (\text{StDev/Mean}) \times 100$$

Finally, note that Minitab's quartiles $Q_1 = 2857.5$ and $Q_3 = 3025$ are slightly different from the quartiles $Q_1 = 2865$ and $Q_3 = 3000$ computed in Section 3.1. The different conventions* used to identify the quartiles explain this variation. Hence, the values of $Q_1$ and $Q_3$ provided by one convention may not be identical to the values of $Q_1$ and $Q_3$ provided by another convention. Any differences tend to be negligible, however, and the results provided should not mislead the user in making the usual interpretations associated with quartiles.

Let us now see how the statistics in Figure 3.11 are generated. The starting salary data are in column C2 of a Minitab worksheet. The following steps can then be used to generate the descriptive statistics.

**Salary**

**Step 1.** Select the **Stat** menu
**Step 2.** Choose **Basic Statistics**
**Step 3.** Choose **Display Descriptive Statistics**
**Step 4.** When the Display Descriptive Statistics dialog box appears:
Enter C2 in the **Variables** box
Click **OK**

---

*With the $n$ observations arranged in ascending order (smallest value to largest value), Minitab uses the positions given by $(n + 1)/4$ and $3(n + 1)/4$ to locate $Q_1$ and $Q_3$, respectively. When a position is fractional, Minitab interpolates between the two adjacent ordered data values to determine the corresponding quartile.

**FIGURE 3.11    DESCRIPTIVE STATISTICS AND BOX PLOT PROVIDED BY MINITAB**

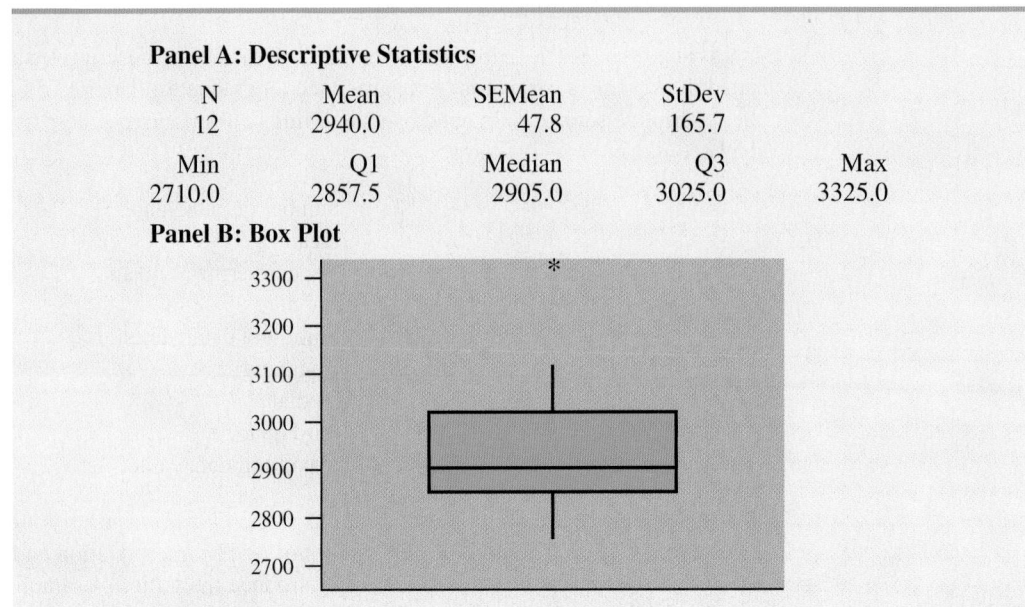

**Panel A: Descriptive Statistics**

| N | Mean | SEMean | StDev | |
|---|---|---|---|---|
| 12 | 2940.0 | 47.8 | 165.7 | |

| Min | Q1 | Median | Q3 | Max |
|---|---|---|---|---|
| 2710.0 | 2857.5 | 2905.0 | 3025.0 | 3325.0 |

**Panel B: Box Plot**

Panel B of Figure 3.11 is a box plot provided by Minitab. The box drawn from the first to third quartiles contains the middle 50% of the data. The line within the box locates the median. The asterisk indicates an outlier at 3325.

The following steps generate the box plot shown in panel B of Figure 3.11.

**Step 1.** Select the **Graph** menu
**Step 2.** Choose **Boxplot**
**Step 3.** Select **Simple** and click **OK**
**Step 4.** When the Boxplot-One Y, Simple dialog box appears:
    Enter C2 in the **Graph variables** box
    Click **OK**

The skewness measure also does not appear as part of Minitab's standard descriptive statistics output. However, we can include it in the descriptive statistics display by following these steps.

**Step 1.** Select the **Stat** menu
**Step 2.** Choose **Basic Statistics**
**Step 3.** Choose **Display Descriptive Statistics**
**Step 4.** When the Display Descriptive Statistics dialog box appears:
    Click **Statistics**
    Select **Skewness**
    Click **OK**
    Click **OK**

The skewness measure of 1.09 will then appear in your worksheet.

Figure 3.12 shows the covariance and correlation output that Minitab provided for the stereo and sound equipment store data in Table 3.7. In the covariance portion of the figure, No. of Comme denotes the number of weekend television commercials and Sales Volume denotes the sales during the following week. The value in column No. of Comme and row Sales Volume, 11, is the sample covariance as computed in Section 3.5. The value in column No. of Comme and row No. of Comme, 2.22222, is the sample variance for the number of

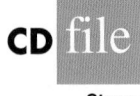

**CD** file

**Stereo**

**FIGURE 3.12**  COVARIANCE AND CORRELATION PROVIDED BY MINITAB
FOR THE NUMBER OF COMMERCIALS AND SALES DATA

```
Covariances: No. of Commercials, Sales Volume

              No. of Comme  Sales Volume
No. of Comme      2.22222
Sales Volume     11.00000       62.88889

Correlations: No. of Commercials, Sales Volume

Pearson correlation of No. of Commercials and Sales Volume = 0.930
P-Value = 0.000
```

commercials, and the value in column Sales Volume and row Sales Volume, 62.88889, is
the sample variance for sales. The sample correlation coefficient, 0.930, is shown in the correlation portion of the output. Note: The interpretation and use of the *p*-value provided in
the output are discussed in Chapter 9.

Let us now describe how to obtain the information in Figure 3.12. We entered the data
for the number of commercials into column C2 and the data for sales volume into column C3 of a Minitab worksheet. The steps necessary to generate the covariance output
in the first three rows of Figure 3.12 follow.

**Step 1.** Select the **Stat** menu
**Step 2.** Choose **Basic Statistics**
**Step 3.** Choose **Covariance**
**Step 4.** When the Covariance dialog box appears:
　　　　　Enter C2 C3 in the **Variables** box
　　　　　Click **OK**

To obtain the correlation output in Figure 3.12, only one change is necessary in the steps
for obtaining the covariance. In step 3, the **Correlation** option is selected.

**Appendix 3.2  Descriptive Statistics Using Excel**

Excel can be used to generate the descriptive statistics discussed in this chapter. We show
how Excel can be used to generate several measures of location and variability for a single
variable and to generate the covariance and correlation coefficient as measures of association between two variables.

### Using Excel Functions

**Salary**

Excel provides functions for computing the mean, median, mode, sample variance, and sample
standard deviation. We illustrate the use of these Excel functions by computing the mean, median,
mode, sample variance, and sample standard deviation for the starting salary data in Table 3.1.
Refer to Figure 3.13 as we describe the steps involved. The data are entered in column B.

Excel's AVERAGE function can be used to compute the mean by entering the following formula into cell E1:

$$=\text{AVERAGE(B2:B13)}$$

Similarly, the formulas =MEDIAN(B2:B13), =MODE(B2:B13), =VAR(B2:B13), and
=STDEV(B2:B13) are entered into cells E2:E5, respectively, to compute the median,

**FIGURE 3.13    USING EXCEL FUNCTIONS FOR COMPUTING THE MEAN, MEDIAN, MODE, VARIANCE, AND STANDARD DEVIATION**

|    | A | B | C | D | E | F |
|----|----------|---------------|---|----------------------|----------------|---|
| 1  | Graduate | Starting Salary | | Mean | =AVERAGE(B2:B13) | |
| 2  | 1 | 2850 | | Median | =MEDIAN(B2:B13) | |
| 3  | 2 | 2950 | | Mode | =MODE(B2:B13) | |
| 4  | 3 | 3050 | | Variance | =VAR(B2:B13) | |
| 5  | 4 | 2880 | | Standard Deviation | =STDEV(B2:B13) | |
| 6  | 5 | 2755 | | | | |
| 7  | 6 | 2710 | | | | |
| 8  | 7 | 2890 | | | | |
| 9  | 8 | 3130 | | | | |
| 10 | 9 | 2940 | | | | |
| 11 | 10 | 3325 | | | | |
| 12 | 11 | 2920 | | | | |
| 13 | 12 | 2880 | | | | |
| 14 | | | | | | |

|    | A | B | C | D | E | F |
|----|----------|----------------|---|--------------------|-----------|---|
| 1  | Graduate | Starting Salary | | Mean | 2940 | |
| 2  | 1 | 2850 | | Median | 2905 | |
| 3  | 2 | 2950 | | Mode | 2880 | |
| 4  | 3 | 3050 | | Variance | 27440.909 | |
| 5  | 4 | 2880 | | Standard Deviation | 165.65 | |
| 6  | 5 | 2755 | | | | |
| 7  | 6 | 2710 | | | | |
| 8  | 7 | 2890 | | | | |
| 9  | 8 | 3130 | | | | |
| 10 | 9 | 2940 | | | | |
| 11 | 10 | 3325 | | | | |
| 12 | 11 | 2920 | | | | |
| 13 | 12 | 2880 | | | | |
| 14 | | | | | | |

mode, variance, and standard deviation. The worksheet in the foreground shows that the values computed using the Excel functions are the same as we computed earlier in the chapter.

Excel also provides functions that can be used to compute the covariance and correlation coefficient. You must be careful when using these functions because the covariance function treats the data as if it were a population and the correlation function treats the data as if it were a sample. Thus, the result obtained using Excel's covariance function must be adjusted to provide the sample covariance. We show here how these functions can be used to compute the sample covariance and the sample correlation coefficient for the stereo and sound equipment store data in Table 3.7. Refer to Figure 3.14 as we present the steps involved.

Excel's covariance function, COVAR, can be used to compute the population covariance by entering the following formula into cell F1:

**CD file**

**Stereo**

$$=COVAR(B2:B11,C2:C11)$$

Similarly, the formula =CORREL(B2:B11,C2:C11) is entered into cell F2 to compute the sample correlation coefficient. The worksheet in the foreground shows the values computed using the Excel functions. Note that the value of the sample correlation coefficient (.93) is the same as computed using equation (3.12). However, the result provided by the Excel COVAR function, 9.9, was obtained by treating the data as if it were a population. Thus, we must adjust the Excel result of 9.9 to obtain the sample covariance. The adjustment is rather simple. First, note that the formula for the population covariance, equation (3.11), requires dividing by the total number of observations in the data set. But the formula for the sample covariance, equation (3.10), requires dividing by the total number of observations minus 1.

**FIGURE 3.14    USING EXCEL FUNCTIONS FOR COMPUTING COVARIANCE AND CORRELATION**

| | A | B | C | D | E | F | G |
|---|---|---|---|---|---|---|---|
| 1 | Week | Commercials | Sales | | Population Covariance | =COVAR(B2:B11,C2:C11) | |
| 2 | 1 | 2 | 50 | | Sample Correlation | =CORREL(B2:B11,C2:C11) | |
| 3 | 2 | 5 | 57 | | | | |
| 4 | 3 | 1 | 41 | | | | |
| 5 | 4 | 3 | 54 | | | | |
| 6 | 5 | 4 | 54 | | | | |
| 7 | 6 | 1 | 38 | | | | |
| 8 | 7 | 5 | 63 | | | | |
| 9 | 8 | 3 | 48 | | | | |
| 10 | 9 | 4 | 59 | | | | |
| 11 | 10 | 2 | 46 | | | | |
| 12 | | | | | | | |

| | A | B | C | D | E | F | G |
|---|---|---|---|---|---|---|---|
| 1 | Week | Commercials | Sales | | Population Covariance | 9.90 | |
| 2 | 1 | 2 | 50 | | Sample Correlation | 0.93 | |
| 3 | 2 | 5 | 57 | | | | |
| 4 | 3 | 1 | 41 | | | | |
| 5 | 4 | 3 | 54 | | | | |
| 6 | 5 | 4 | 54 | | | | |
| 7 | 6 | 1 | 38 | | | | |
| 8 | 7 | 5 | 63 | | | | |
| 9 | 8 | 3 | 48 | | | | |
| 10 | 9 | 4 | 59 | | | | |
| 11 | 10 | 2 | 46 | | | | |
| 12 | | | | | | | |

So, to use the Excel result of 9.9 to compute the sample covariance, we simply multiply 9.9 by $n/(n-1)$. Because $n = 10$, we obtain

$$s_{xy} = \left(\frac{10}{9}\right)9.9 = 11$$

Thus, the sample covariance for the stereo and sound equipment data is 11.

## Using Excel's Descriptive Statistics Tool

As we already demonstrated. Excel provides statistical functions to compute descriptive statistics for a data set. These functions can be used to compute one statistic at a time (e.g., mean, variance, etc.). Excel also provides a variety of Data Analysis Tools. One of these tools, called Descriptive Statistics, allows the user to compute a variety of descriptive statistics at once. We show here how it can be used to compute descriptive statistics for the starting salary data in Table 3.1. Refer to Figure 3.15 as we describe the steps involved.

**CD** file

**Salary**

**Step 1.** Select the **Tools** menu
**Step 2.** Choose **Data Analysis**
**Step 3.** Choose **Descriptive Statistics** from the list of **Analysis Tools**
**Step 4.** When the Descriptive Statistics dialog box appears:
      Enter B1:B13 in the **Input Range** box
      Select **Grouped By Columns**
      Select **Labels in First Row**
      Select **Output Range**
      Enter D1 in the **Output Range** box (to identify the upper left-hand corner
        of the section of the worksheet where the descriptive statistics will appear)
      Select **Summary statistics**
      Click **OK**

Cells D1:E15 of Figure 3.15 show the descriptive statistics provided by Excel. The bold-face entries are the descriptive statistics we covered in this chapter. The descriptive statistics that are not boldface are either covered subsequently in the text or discussed in more advanced texts.

**FIGURE 3.15**　　EXCEL'S DESCRIPTIVE STATISTICS TOOL OUTPUT

| | A | B | C | D | E | F |
|---|---|---|---|---|---|---|
| 1 | Graduate | Starting Salary | | *Starting Salary* | | |
| 2 | 1 | 2850 | | | | |
| 3 | 2 | 2950 | | Mean | 2940 | |
| 4 | 3 | 3050 | | Standard Error | 47.8199 | |
| 5 | 4 | 2880 | | Median | 2905 | |
| 6 | 5 | 2755 | | Mode | 2880 | |
| 7 | 6 | 2710 | | Standard Deviation | 165.653 | |
| 8 | 7 | 2890 | | Sample Variance | 27440.9 | |
| 9 | 8 | 3130 | | Kurtosis | 1.71888 | |
| 10 | 9 | 2940 | | Skewness | 1.09111 | |
| 11 | 10 | 3325 | | Range | 615 | |
| 12 | 11 | 2920 | | Minimum | 2710 | |
| 13 | 12 | 2880 | | Maximum | 3325 | |
| 14 | | | | Sum | 35280 | |
| 15 | | | | Count | 12 | |
| 16 | | | | | | |

# CHAPTER 4

# Introduction to Probability

**CONTENTS**

STATISTICS IN PRACTICE:
MORTON INTERNATIONAL

## MORTON INTERNATIONAL*
*CHICAGO, ILLINOIS*

Morton International is a company with businesses in salt, household products, rocket motors, and specialty chemicals. Carstab Corporation, a subsidiary of Morton International, produces specialty chemicals and offers a variety of chemicals designed to meet the unique specifications of its customers. For one particular customer, Carstab produced an expensive catalyst used in chemical processing. Some, but not all, of the lots produced by Carstab met the customer's specifications for the product.

Carstab's customer agreed to test each lot after receiving it and determine whether the catalyst would perform the desired function. Lots that did not pass the customer's test would be returned to Carstab. Over time, Carstab found that the customer was accepting 60% of the lots and returning 40%. In probability terms, each Carstab shipment to the customer had a .60 probability of being accepted and a .40 probability of being returned.

Neither Carstab nor its customer was pleased with these results. In an effort to improve service, Carstab explored the possibility of duplicating the customer's test prior to shipment. However, the high cost of the special testing equipment made that alternative infeasible. Carstab's chemists then proposed a new, relatively low-cost test designed to indicate whether a lot would pass the customer's test. The probability question of interest was: What is the probability that a lot will pass the customer's test if it has passed the new Carstab test?

Morton Salt: "When It Rains It Pours." © Joe Higgins/South-Western.

A sample of lots was produced and subjected to the new Carstab test. Only lots that passed the new test were sent to the customer. Probability analysis of the data indicated that if a lot passed the Carstab test, it had a .909 probability of passing the customer's test and being accepted. Alternatively, if a lot passed the Carstab test, it had only a .091 probability of being returned. The probability analysis provided key supporting evidence for the adoption and implementation of the new testing procedure at Carstab. The new test resulted in an immediate improvement in customer service and a substantial reduction in shipping and handling costs for returned lots.

The probability of a lot being accepted by the customer after passing the new Carstab test is called a conditional probability. In this chapter, you will learn how to compute this and other probabilities that are helpful in decision making.

---

*The authors are indebted to Michael Haskell of Morton International for providing this Statistics in Practice.

Managers often base their decisions on an analysis of uncertainties such as the following:

1. What are the chances that sales will decrease if we increase prices?
2. What is the likelihood a new assembly method will increase productivity?
3. How likely is it that the project will be finished on time?
4. What is the chance that a new investment will be profitable?

*Some of the earliest work on probability originated in a series of letters between Pierre de Fermat and Blaise Pascal in the 1650s.*

**Probability** is a numerical measure of the likelihood that an event will occur. Thus, probabilities can be used as measures of the degree of uncertainty associated with the four events previously listed. If probabilities are available, we can determine the likelihood of each event occurring.

Probability values are always assigned on a scale from 0 to 1. A probability near zero indicates an event is unlikely to occur; a probability near 1 indicates an event is almost certain to occur. Other probabilities between 0 and 1 represent degrees of likelihood that an event will occur. For example, if we consider the event "rain tomorrow," we understand that when the weather report indicates "a near-zero probability of rain," it means almost no chance of rain. However, if a .90 probability of rain is reported, we know that rain is likely to occur. A .50 probability indicates that rain is just as likely to occur as not. Figure 4.1 depicts the view of probability as a numerical measure of the likelihood of an event occurring.

# 4.1   Experiments, Counting Rules, and Assigning Probabilities

In discussing probability, we define an **experiment** as a process that generates well-defined outcomes. On any single repetition of an experiment, one and only one of the possible experimental outcomes will occur. Several examples of experiments and their associated outcomes follow.

| Experiment | Experimental Outcomes |
| --- | --- |
| Toss a coin | Head, tail |
| Select a part for inspection | Defective, nondefective |
| Conduct a sales call | Purchase, no purchase |
| Roll a die | 1, 2, 3, 4, 5, 6 |
| Play a football game | Win, lose, tie |

By specifying all possible experimental outcomes, we identify the **sample space** for an experiment.

> **SAMPLE SPACE**
>
> The sample space for an experiment is the set of all experimental outcomes.

*Experimental outcomes are also called sample points.*

An experimental outcome is also called a **sample point** to identify it as an element of the sample space.

**FIGURE 4.1**   PROBABILITY AS A NUMERICAL MEASURE OF THE LIKELIHOOD OF AN EVENT OCCURRING

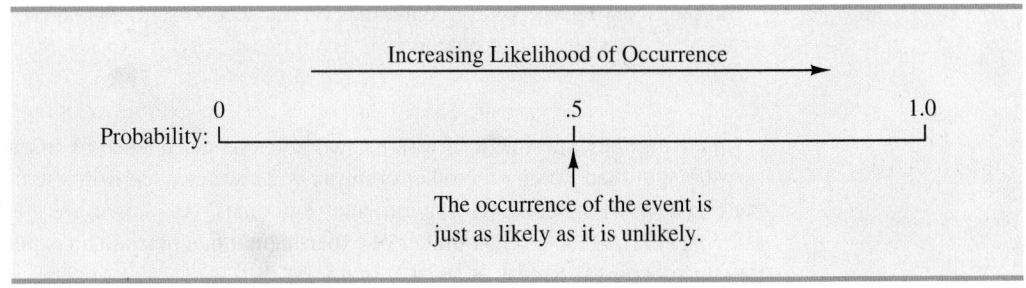

Consider the first experiment in the preceding table—tossing a coin. The upward face of the coin—a head or a tail—determines the experimental outcomes (sample points). If we let S denote the sample space, we can use the following notation to describe the sample space.

$$S = \{Head, Tail\}$$

The sample space for the second experiment in the table—selecting a part for inspection—can be described as follows:

$$S = \{Defective, Nondefective\}$$

Both of the experiments just described have two experimental outcomes (sample points). However, suppose we consider the fourth experiment listed in the table—rolling a die. The possible experimental outcomes, defined as the number of dots appearing on the upward face of the die, are the six points in the sample space for this experiment.

$$S = \{1, 2, 3, 4, 5, 6\}$$

## Counting Rules, Combinations, and Permutations

Being able to identify and count the experimental outcomes is a necessary step in assigning probabilities. We now discuss three useful counting rules.

**Multiple-step experiments** The first counting rule applies to multiple-step experiments. Consider the experiment of tossing two coins. Let the experimental outcomes be defined in terms of the pattern of heads and tails appearing on the upward faces of the two coins. How many experimental outcomes are possible for this experiment? The experiment of tossing two coins can be thought of as a two-step experiment in which step 1 is the tossing of the first coin and step 2 is the tossing of the second coin. If we use $H$ to denote a head and $T$ to denote a tail, $(H, H)$ indicates the experimental outcome with a head on the first coin and a head on the second coin. Continuing this notation, we can describe the sample space ($S$) for this coin-tossing experiment as follows:

$$S = \{(H, H), (H, T), (T, H), (T, T)\}$$

Thus, we see that four experimental outcomes are possible. In this case, we can easily list all of the experimental outcomes.

The counting rule for multiple-step experiments makes it possible to determine the number of experimental outcomes without listing them.

---

A COUNTING RULE FOR MULTIPLE-STEP EXPERIMENTS

If an experiment can be described as a sequence of $k$ steps with $n_1$ possible outcomes on the first step, $n_2$ possible outcomes on the second step, and so on, then the total number of experimental outcomes is given by $(n_1)(n_2) \ldots (n_k)$.

---

Viewing the experiment of tossing two coins as a sequence of first tossing one coin ($n_1 = 2$) and then tossing the other coin ($n_2 = 2$), we can see from the counting rule that there are $(2)(2) = 4$ distinct experimental outcomes. As shown, they are $S = \{(H, H), (H, T), (T, H), (T, T)\}$. The number of experimental outcomes in an experiment involving tossing six coins is $(2)(2)(2)(2)(2)(2) = 64$.

*Without the tree diagram, one might think only three experimental outcomes are possible for two tosses of a coin: 0 heads, 1 head, and 2 heads.*

A **tree diagram** is a graphical representation that helps in visualizing a multiple-step experiment. Figure 4.2 shows a tree diagram for the experiment of tossing two coins. The sequence of steps moves from left to right through the tree. Step 1 corresponds to tossing the first coin, and step 2 corresponds to tossing the second coin. For each step, the two possible outcomes are head or tail. Note that for each possible outcome at step 1 two branches correspond to the two possible outcomes at step 2. Each of the points on the right end of the tree corresponds to an experimental outcome. Each path through the tree from the leftmost node to one of the nodes at the right side of the tree corresponds to a unique sequence of outcomes.

Let us now see how the counting rule for multiple-step experiments can be used in the analysis of a capacity expansion project for the Kentucky Power & Light Company (KP&L). KP&L is starting a project designed to increase the generating capacity of one of its plants in northern Kentucky. The project is divided into two sequential stages or steps: stage 1 (design) and stage 2 (construction). Even though each stage will be scheduled and controlled as closely as possible, management cannot predict beforehand the exact time required to complete each stage of the project. An analysis of similar construction projects revealed possible completion times for the design stage of 2, 3, or 4 months and possible completion times for the construction stage of 6, 7, or 8 months. In addition, because of the critical need for additional electrical power, management set a goal of 10 months for the completion of the entire project.

Because this project has three possible completion times for the design stage (step 1) and three possible completion times for the construction stage (step 2), the counting rule for multiple-step experiments can be applied here to determine a total of $(3)(3) = 9$ experimental outcomes. To describe the experimental outcomes, we use a two-number notation; for instance, (2, 6) indicates that the design stage is completed in 2 months and the construction stage is completed in 6 months. This experimental outcome results in a total of $2 + 6 = 8$ months to complete the entire project. Table 4.1 summarizes the nine experimental outcomes for the KP&L problem. The tree diagram in Figure 4.3 shows how the nine outcomes (sample points) occur.

The counting rule and tree diagram help the project manager identify the experimental outcomes and determine the possible project completion times. From the information in

**FIGURE 4.2　TREE DIAGRAM FOR THE EXPERIMENT OF TOSSING TWO COINS**

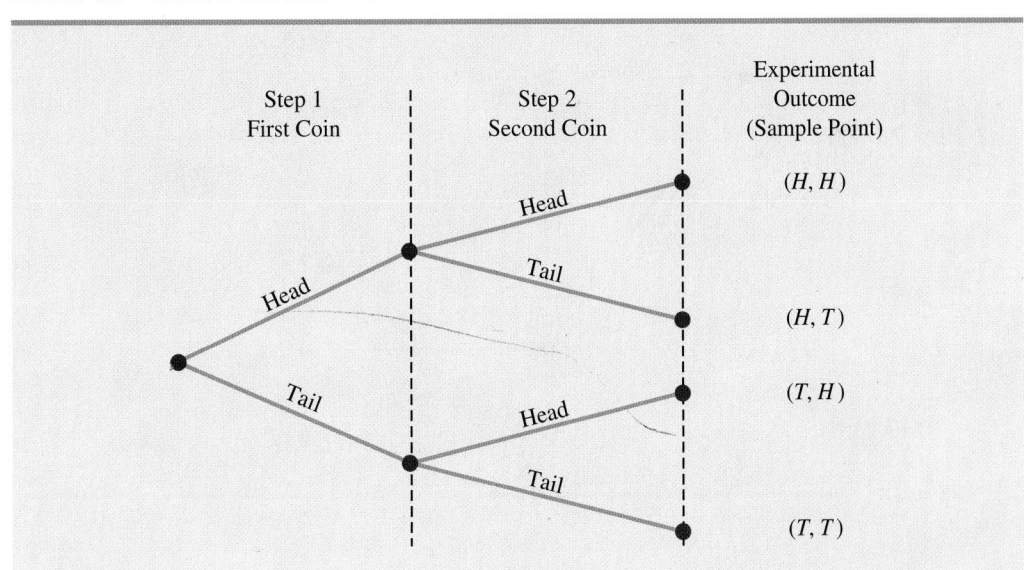

**TABLE 4.1   EXPERIMENTAL OUTCOMES (SAMPLE POINTS) FOR THE KP&L PROJECT**

| Completion Time (months) | | | |
|---|---|---|---|
| **Stage 1 Design** | **Stage 2 Construction** | **Notation for Experimental Outcome** | **Total Project Completion Time (months)** |
| 2 | 6 | (2, 6) | 8 |
| 2 | 7 | (2, 7) | 9 |
| 2 | 8 | (2, 8) | 10 |
| 3 | 6 | (3, 6) | 9 |
| 3 | 7 | (3, 7) | 10 |
| 3 | 8 | (3, 8) | 11 |
| 4 | 6 | (4, 6) | 10 |
| 4 | 7 | (4, 7) | 11 |
| 4 | 8 | (4, 8) | 12 |

**FIGURE 4.3   TREE DIAGRAM FOR THE KP&L PROJECT**

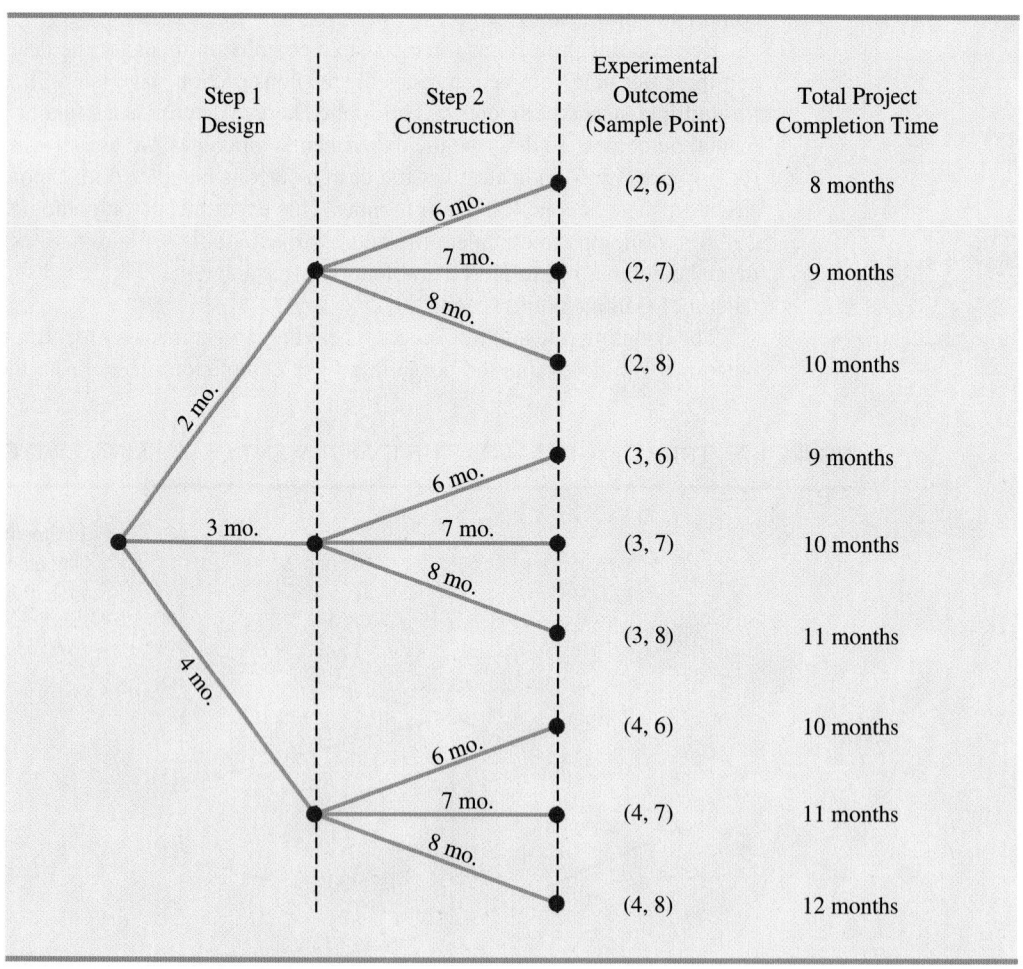

Figure 4.3, we see that the project will be completed in 8 to 12 months, with six of the nine experimental outcomes providing the desired completion time of 10 months or less. Even though identifying the experimental outcomes may be helpful, we need to consider how probability values can be assigned to the experimental outcomes before making an assessment of the probability that the project will be completed within the desired 10 months.

**Combinations** A second useful counting rule allows one to count the number of experimental outcomes when the experiment involves selecting $n$ objects from a (usually larger) set of $N$ objects. It is called the counting rule for combinations.

> **COUNTING RULE FOR COMBINATIONS**
>
> The number of combinations of $N$ objects taken $n$ at a time is
>
> $$C_n^N = \binom{N}{n} = \frac{N!}{n!(N-n)!} \tag{4.1}$$
>
> where
> $$N! = N(N-1)(N-2)\cdots(2)(1)$$
> $$n! = n(n-1)(n-2)\cdots(2)(1)$$
>
> and, by definition,
> $$0! = 1$$

The notation ! means *factorial;* for example, 5 factorial is $5! = (5)(4)(3)(2)(1) = 120$.

*In sampling from a finite population of size N, the counting rule for combinations is used to find the number of different samples of size n that can be selected.*

As an illustration of the counting rule for combinations, consider a quality control procedure in which an inspector randomly selects two of five parts to test for defects. In a group of five parts, how many combinations of two parts can be selected? The counting rule in equation (4.1) shows that with $N = 5$ and $n = 2$, we have

$$C_2^5 = \binom{5}{2} = \frac{5!}{2!(5-2)!} = \frac{(5)(4)(3)(2)(1)}{(2)(1)(3)(2)(1)} = \frac{120}{12} = 10$$

Thus, 10 outcomes are possible for the experiment of randomly selecting two parts from a group of five. If we label the five parts as A, B, C, D, and E, the 10 combinations or experimental outcomes can be identified as AB, AC, AD, AE, BC, BD, BE, CD, CE, and DE.

As another example, consider that the Ohio lottery system uses the random selection of six integers from a group of 47 to determine the weekly lottery winner. The counting rule for combinations, equation (4.1), can be used to determine the number of ways six different integers can be selected from a group of 47.

$$\binom{47}{6} = \frac{47!}{6!(47-6)!} = \frac{47!}{6!41!} = \frac{(47)(46)(45)(44)(43)(42)}{(6)(5)(4)(3)(2)(1)} = 10{,}737{,}573$$

*The counting rule for combinations shows that the chance of winning the lottery is very unlikely.*

The counting rule for combinations tells us that more than 10 million experimental outcomes are possible in the lottery drawing. An individual who buys a lottery ticket has 1 chance in 10,737,573 of winning.

**Permutations** A third counting rule that is sometimes useful is the counting rule for permutations. It allows one to compute the number of experimental outcomes when $n$ objects are to be selected from a set of $N$ objects where the order of selection is important. The same $n$ objects selected in a different order is considered a different experimental outcome.

---

COUNTING RULE FOR PERMUTATIONS

The number of permutations of $N$ objects taken $n$ at a time is given by

$$P_n^N = n! \binom{N}{n} = \frac{N!}{(N-n)!} \qquad (4.2)$$

---

The counting rule for permutations closely relates to the one for combinations; however, an experiment results in more permutations than combinations for the same number of objects because every selection of $n$ objects can be ordered in $n!$ different ways.

As an example, consider again the quality control process in which an inspector selects two of five parts to inspect for defects. How many permutations may be selected? The counting rule in equation (4.2) shows that with $N = 5$ and $n = 2$, we have

$$P_2^5 = \frac{5!}{(5-2)!} = \frac{5!}{3!} = \frac{(5)(4)(3)(2)(1)}{(3)(2)(1)} = \frac{120}{6} = 20$$

Thus, 20 outcomes are possible for the experiment of randomly selecting two parts from a group of five when the order of selection must be taken into account. If we label the parts A, B, C, D, and E, the 20 permutations are AB, BA, AC, CA, AD, DA, AE, EA, BC, CB, BD, DB, BE, EB, CD, DC, CE, EC, DE, and ED.

## Assigning Probabilities

Now let us see how probabilities can be assigned to experimental outcomes. The three approaches most frequently used are the classical, relative frequency, and subjective methods. Regardless of the method used, two **basic requirements for assigning probabilities** must be met.

---

BASIC REQUIREMENTS FOR ASSIGNING PROBABILITIES

1. The probability assigned to each experimental outcome must be between 0 and 1, inclusively. If we let $E_i$ denote the $i$th experimental outcome and $P(E_i)$ its probability, then this requirement can be written as

$$0 \leq P(E_i) \leq 1 \text{ for all } i \qquad (4.3)$$

2. The sum of the probabilities for all the experimental outcomes must equal 1.0. For $n$ experimental outcomes, this requirement can be written as

$$P(E_1) + P(E_2) + \cdots + P(E_n) = 1 \qquad (4.4)$$

---

The **classical method** of assigning probabilities is appropriate when all the experimental outcomes are equally likely. If $n$ experimental outcomes are possible, a probability of $1/n$ is assigned to each experimental outcome. When using this approach, the two basic requirements for assigning probabilities are automatically satisfied.

For an example, consider the experiment of tossing a fair coin; the two experimental outcomes—head and tail—are equally likely. Because one of the two equally likely outcomes is a head, the probability of observing a head is 1/2, or .50. Similarly, the probability of observing a tail is also 1/2, or .50.

As another example, consider the experiment of rolling a die. It would seem reasonable to conclude that the six possible outcomes are equally likely, and hence each outcome is assigned a probability of 1/6. If $P(1)$ denotes the probability that one dot appears on the upward face of the die, then $P(1) = 1/6$. Similarly, $P(2) = 1/6$, $P(3) = 1/6$, $P(4) = 1/6$, $P(5) = 1/6$, and $P(6) = 1/6$. Note that these probabilities satisfy the two basic requirements of equations (4.3) and (4.4) because each of the probabilities is greater than or equal to zero and they sum to 1.0.

The **relative frequency method** of assigning probabilities is appropriate when data are available to estimate the proportion of the time the experimental outcome will occur if the experiment is repeated a large number of times. As an example consider a study of waiting times in the X-ray department for a local hospital. A clerk recorded the number of patients waiting for service at 9:00 A.M. on 20 successive days, and obtained the following results.

| Number Waiting | Number of Days Outcome Occurred |
|:---:|:---:|
| 0 | 2 |
| 1 | 5 |
| 2 | 6 |
| 3 | 4 |
| 4 | 3 |
| Total | 20 |

These data show that on 2 of the 20 days, zero patients were waiting for service; on 5 of the days, one patient was waiting for service; and so on. Using the relative frequency method, we would assign a probability of 2/20 = .10 to the experimental outcome of zero patients waiting for service, 5/20 = .25 to the experimental outcome of one patient waiting, 6/20 = .30 to two patients waiting, 4/20 = .20 to three patients waiting, and 3/20 = .15 to four patients waiting. As with the classical method, using the relative frequency method automatically satisfies the two basic requirements of equations (4.3) and (4.4).

The **subjective method** of assigning probabilities is most appropriate when one cannot realistically assume that the experimental outcomes are equally likely and when little relevant data are available. When the subjective method is used to assign probabilities to the experimental outcomes, we may use any information available, such as our experience or intuition. After considering all available information, a probability value that expresses our *degree of belief* (on a scale from 0 to 1) that the experimental outcome will occur is specified. Because subjective probability expresses a person's degree of belief, it is personal. Using the subjective method, different people can be expected to assign different probabilities to the same experimental outcome.

The subjective method requires extra care to ensure that the two basic requirements of equations (4.3) and (4.4) are satisfied. Regardless of a person's degree of belief, the probability value assigned to each experimental outcome must be between 0 and 1, inclusive, and the sum of all the probabilities for the experimental outcomes must equal 1.0.

Consider the case in which Tom and Judy Elsbernd make an offer to purchase a house. Two outcomes are possible:

$$E_1 = \text{their offer is accepted}$$
$$E_2 = \text{their offer is rejected}$$

Judy believes that the probability their offer will be accepted is .8; thus, Judy would set $P(E_1) = .8$ and $P(E_2) = .2$. Tom, however, believes that the probability that their offer will be accepted is .6; hence, Tom would set $P(E_1) = .6$ and $P(E_2) = .4$. Note that Tom's probability estimate for $E_1$ reflects a greater pessimism that their offer will be accepted.

Both Judy and Tom assigned probabilities that satisfy the two basic requirements. The fact that their probability estimates are different emphasizes the personal nature of the subjective method.

Even in business situations where either the classical or the relative frequency approach can be applied, managers may want to provide subjective probability estimates. In such cases, the best probability estimates often are obtained by combining the estimates from the classical or relative frequency approach with subjective probability estimates.

*Bayes' theorem (see Section 4.5) provides a means for combining subjectively determined prior probabilities with probabilities obtained by other means to obtain revised, or posterior, probabilities.*

## Probabilities for the KP&L Project

To perform further analysis on the KP&L project, we must develop probabilities for each of the nine experimental outcomes listed in Table 4.1. On the basis of experience and judgment, management concluded that the experimental outcomes were not equally likely. Hence, the classical method of assigning probabilities could not be used. Management then decided to conduct a study of the completion times for similar projects undertaken by KP&L over the past three years. The results of a study of 40 similar projects are summarized in Table 4.2.

After reviewing the results of the study, management decided to employ the relative frequency method of assigning probabilities. Management could have provided subjective probability estimates, but felt that the current project was quite similar to the 40 previous projects. Thus, the relative frequency method was judged best.

In using the data in Table 4.2 to compute probabilities, we note that outcome (2, 6)—stage 1 completed in 2 months and stage 2 completed in 6 months—occurred six times in the 40 projects. We can use the relative frequency method to assign a probability of $6/40 = .15$ to this outcome. Similarly, outcome (2, 7) also occurred in six of the 40 projects, providing a $6/40 = .15$ probability. Continuing in this manner, we obtain the probability assignments for the sample points of the KP&L project shown in Table 4.3. Note that $P(2, 6)$ represents the probability of the sample point (2, 6), $P(2, 7)$ represents the probability of the sample point (2, 7), and so on.

**TABLE 4.2      COMPLETION RESULTS FOR 40 KP&L PROJECTS**

| Completion Time (months) | | Sample Point | Number of Past Projects Having These Completion Times |
|---|---|---|---|
| Stage 1 Design | Stage 2 Construction | | |
| 2 | 6 | (2, 6) | 6 |
| 2 | 7 | (2, 7) | 6 |
| 2 | 8 | (2, 8) | 2 |
| 3 | 6 | (3, 6) | 4 |
| 3 | 7 | (3, 7) | 8 |
| 3 | 8 | (3, 8) | 2 |
| 4 | 6 | (4, 6) | 2 |
| 4 | 7 | (4, 7) | 4 |
| 4 | 8 | (4, 8) | 6 |
| | | Total | 40 |

**TABLE 4.3**   PROBABILITY ASSIGNMENTS FOR THE KP&L PROJECT BASED ON THE RELATIVE FREQUENCY METHOD

| Sample Point | Project Completion Time | Probability of Sample Point |
|:---:|:---:|:---:|
| (2, 6) | 8 months | $P(2, 6) = 6/40 = .15$ |
| (2, 7) | 9 months | $P(2, 7) = 6/40 = .15$ |
| (2, 8) | 10 months | $P(2, 8) = 2/40 = .05$ |
| (3, 6) | 9 months | $P(3, 6) = 4/40 = .10$ |
| (3, 7) | 10 months | $P(3, 7) = 8/40 = .20$ |
| (3, 8) | 11 months | $P(3, 8) = 2/40 = .05$ |
| (4, 6) | 10 months | $P(4, 6) = 2/40 = .05$ |
| (4, 7) | 11 months | $P(4, 7) = 4/40 = .10$ |
| (4, 8) | 12 months | $P(4, 8) = 6/40 = .15$ |
| | | Total          1.00 |

## NOTES AND COMMENTS

1. In statistics, the notion of an experiment differs somewhat from the notion of an experiment in the physical sciences. In the physical sciences, researchers usually conduct an experiment in a laboratory or a controlled environment in order to learn about cause and effect. In statistical experiments, probability determines outcomes. Even though the experiment is repeated in exactly the same way, an entirely different outcome may occur. Because of this influence of probability on the outcome, the experiments of statistics are sometimes called *random experiments.*

2. When drawing a random sample without replacement from a population of size $N$, the counting rule for combinations is used to find the number of different samples of size $n$ that can be selected.

## Exercises

## Methods

1. An experiment has three steps with three outcomes possible for the first step, two outcomes possible for the second step, and four outcomes possible for the third step. How many experimental outcomes exist for the entire experiment?

2. How many ways can three items be selected from a group of six items? Use the letters A, B, C, D, E, and F to identify the items, and list each of the different combinations of three items.

3. How many permutations of three items can be selected from a group of six? Use the letters A, B, C, D, E, and F to identify the items, and list each of the permutations of items B, D, and F.

4. Consider the experiment of tossing a coin three times.
   a. Develop a tree diagram for the experiment.
   b. List the experimental outcomes.
   c. What is the probability for each experimental outcome?

5. Suppose an experiment has five equally likely outcomes: $E_1, E_2, E_3, E_4, E_5$. Assign probabilities to each outcome and show that the requirements in equations (4.3) and (4.4) are satisfied. What method did you use?

6. An experiment with three outcomes has been repeated 50 times, and it was learned that $E_1$ occurred 20 times, $E_2$ occurred 13 times, and $E_3$ occurred 17 times. Assign probabilities to the outcomes. What method did you use?

7. A decision maker subjectively assigned the following probabilities to the four outcomes of an experiment: $P(E_1) = .10$, $P(E_2) = .15$, $P(E_3) = .40$, and $P(E_4) = .20$. Are these probability assignments valid? Explain.

## Applications

8. In the city of Milford, applications for zoning changes go through a two-step process: a review by the planning commission and a final decision by the city council. At step 1 the planning commission reviews the zoning change request and makes a positive or negative recommendation concerning the change. At step 2 the city council reviews the planning commission's recommendation and then votes to approve or to disapprove the zoning change. Suppose the developer of an apartment complex submits an application for a zoning change. Consider the application process as an experiment.
   a. How many sample points are there for this experiment? List the sample points.
   b. Construct a tree diagram for the experiment.

9.  Simple random sampling uses a sample of size $n$ from a population of size $N$ to obtain data that can be used to make inferences about the characteristics of a population. Suppose that, from a population of 50 bank accounts, we want to take a random sample of four accounts in order to learn about the population. How many different random samples of four accounts are possible?

10. The availability of venture capital provided a big boost in funds available to companies in recent years. According to Venture Economics (*Investor's Business Daily*, April 28, 2000), 2374 venture capital disbursements were made in 1999. Of these, 1434 were to companies in California, 390 were to companies in Massachusetts, 217 were to companies in New York, and 112 were to companies in Colorado. Twenty-two percent of the companies receiving funds were in the early stages of development and 55% of the companies were in an expansion stage. Suppose you want to randomly choose one of these companies to learn about how they used the funds.
   a. What is the probability the company chosen will be from California?
   b. What is the probability the company chosen will not be from one of the four states mentioned?
   c. What is the probability the company will not be in the early stages of development?
   d. Assuming the companies in the early stages of development were evenly distributed across the country, how many Massachusetts companies receiving venture capital funds were in their early stages of development?
   e. The total amount of funds invested was $32.4 billion. Estimate the amount that went to Colorado.

 11. A company that franchises coffee houses conducted taste tests for a new coffee product. Four blends were prepared, then randomly chosen individuals were asked to taste the blends and state which one they liked best. Results of the taste test for 100 individuals are given.

| Blend | Number Choosing |
|---|---|
| 1 | 20 |
| 2 | 30 |
| 3 | 35 |
| 4 | 15 |

    a.   Define the experiment being conducted. How many times was it repeated?

    b.   Prior to conducting the experiment, it is reasonable to assume preferences for the four blends are equal. What probabilities would you assign to the experimental outcomes prior to conducting the taste test? What method did you use?

    c.   After conducting the taste test, what probabilities would you assign to the experimental outcomes? What method did you use?

12.  The Powerball lottery is played twice each week in 23 states, the Virgin Islands, and the District of Columbia. To play Powerball a participant must purchase a ticket for $1 and then select five numbers from the digits 1 through 53 and a Powerball number from the digits 1 through 42. To determine the winning numbers for each game, lottery officials draw five white balls out of a drum with 53 white balls, and one red ball out of a drum with 42 red balls. To win the jackpot, a participant's numbers must match the numbers on the five white balls in any order and the number on the red Powerball. In August 2001, four winners shared a jackpot of $295 million by matching the numbers 8-17-22-42-47 plus Powerball number 21. In addition to the jackpot, a variety of other prizes are awarded each time the game is played. For instance, a prize of $100,000 is paid if the participant's five numbers match the numbers on the five white balls (www.powerball.com, March 25, 2003).

    a.   Compute the number of ways the first five numbers can be selected.

    b.   What is the probability of winning a prize of $100,000 by matching the numbers on the five white balls?

    c.   What is the probability of winning the Powerball jackpot?

13.  A company that manufactures toothpaste is studying five different package designs. Assuming that one design is just as likely to be selected by a consumer as any other design, what selection probability would you assign to each of the package designs? In an actual experiment, 100 consumers were asked to pick the design they preferred. The following data were obtained. Do the data confirm the belief that one design is just as likely to be selected as another? Explain.

| Design | Number of Times Preferred |
|--------|---------------------------|
| 1 | 5 |
| 2 | 15 |
| 3 | 30 |
| 4 | 40 |
| 5 | 10 |

## 4.2  Events and Their Probabilities

In the introduction to this chapter we used the term *event* much as it would be used in everyday language. Then, in Section 4.1 we introduced the concept of an experiment and its associated experimental outcomes or sample points. Sample points and events provide the foundation for the study of probability. As a result, we must now introduce the formal definition of an **event** as it relates to sample points. Doing so will provide the basis for determining the probability of an event.

EVENT

An event is a collection of sample points.

For an example, let us return to the KP&L project and assume that the project manager is interested in the event that the entire project can be completed in 10 months or less. Referring to Table 4.3, we see that six sample points—(2, 6), (2, 7), (2, 8), (3, 6), (3, 7), and (4, 6)—provide a project completion time of 10 months or less. Let $C$ denote the event that the project is completed in 10 months or less; we write

$$C = \{(2, 6), (2, 7), (2, 8), (3, 6), (3, 7), (4, 6)\}$$

Event $C$ is said to occur if *any one* of these six sample points appears as the experimental outcome.

Other events that might be of interest to KP&L management include the following.

$L$ = The event that the project is completed in *less* than 10 months

$M$ = The event that the project is completed in *more* than 10 months

Using the information in Table 4.3, we see that these events consist of the following sample points.

$$L = \{(2, 6), (2, 7), (3, 6)\}$$
$$M = \{(3, 8), (4, 7), (4, 8)\}$$

A variety of additional events can be defined for the KP&L project, but in each case the event must be identified as a collection of sample points for the experiment.

Given the probabilities of the sample points shown in Table 4.3, we can use the following definition to compute the probability of any event that KP&L management might want to consider.

### PROBABILITY OF AN EVENT

The probability of any event is equal to the sum of the probabilities of the sample points in the event.

Using this definition, we calculate the probability of a particular event by adding the probabilities of the sample points (experimental outcomes) that make up the event. We can now compute the probability that the project will take 10 months or less to complete. Because this event is given by $C = \{(2, 6), (2, 7), (2, 8), (3, 6), (3, 7), (4, 6)\}$, the probability of event $C$, denoted $P(C)$, is given by

$$P(C) = P(2, 6) + P(2, 7) + P(2, 8) + P(3, 6) + P(3, 7) + P(4, 6)$$

Refer to the sample point probabilities in Table 4.3; we have

$$P(C) = .15 + .15 + .05 + .10 + .20 + .05 = .70$$

Similarly, because the event that the project is completed in less than 10 months is given by $L = \{(2, 6), (2, 7), (3, 6)\}$, the probability of this event is given by

$$P(L) = P(2, 6) + P(2, 7) + P(3, 6)$$
$$= .15 + .15 + .10 = .40$$

Finally, for the event that the project is completed in more than 10 months, we have $M = \{(3, 8), (4, 7), (4, 8)\}$ and thus

$$P(M) = P(3, 8) + P(4, 7) + P(4, 8)$$
$$= .05 + .10 + .15 = .30$$

Using these probability results, we can now tell KP&L management that there is a .70 probability that the project will be completed in 10 months or less, a .40 probability that the project will be completed in less than 10 months, and a .30 probability that the project will be completed in more than 10 months. This procedure of computing event probabilities can be repeated for any event of interest to the KP&L management.

Anytime that we can identify all the sample points of an experiment and assign probabilities to each, we can compute the probability of an event using the definition. However, in many experiments the large number of sample points makes the identification of the sample points, as well as the determination of their associated probabilities, extremely cumbersome, if not impossible. In the remaining sections of this chapter, we present some basic probability relationships that can be used to compute the probability of an event without knowledge of all the sample point probabilities.

## NOTES AND COMMENTS

1. The sample space, $S$, is an event. Because it contains all the experimental outcomes, it has a probability of 1; that is, $P(S) = 1$.
2. When the classical method is used to assign probabilities, the assumption is that the experimental outcomes are equally likely. In such cases, the probability of an event can be computed by counting the number of experimental outcomes in the event and dividing the result by the total number of experimental outcomes.

## Exercises

## Methods

14. An experiment has four equally likely outcomes: $E_1$, $E_2$, $E_3$, and $E_4$.
    a. What is the probability that $E_2$ occurs?
    b. What is the probability that any two of the outcomes occur (e.g., $E_1$ or $E_3$)?
    c. What is the probability that any three of the outcomes occur (e.g., $E_1$ or $E_2$ or $E_4$)?

15. Consider the experiment of selecting a playing card from a deck of 52 playing cards. Each card corresponds to a sample point with a 1/52 probability.
    a. List the sample points in the event an ace is selected.
    b. List the sample points in the event a club is selected.
    c. List the sample points in the event a face card (jack, queen, or king) is selected.
    d. Find the probabilities associated with each of the events in parts (a), (b), and (c).

16. Consider the experiment of rolling a pair of dice. Suppose that we are interested in the sum of the face values showing on the dice.
    a. How many sample points are possible? (Hint: Use the counting rule for multiple-step experiments.)
    b. List the sample points.
    c. What is the probability of obtaining a value of 7?
    d. What is the probability of obtaining a value of 9 or greater?
    e. Because each roll has six possible even values (2, 4, 6, 8, 10, and 12) and only five possible odd values (3, 5, 7, 9, and 11), the dice should show even values more often than odd values. Do you agree with this statement? Explain.
    f. What method did you use to assign the probabilities requested?

## Applications

17. Refer to the KP&L sample points and sample point probabilities in Tables 4.2 and 4.3.
    a.  The design stage (stage 1) will run over budget if it takes 4 months to complete. List the sample points in the event the design stage is over budget.
    b.  What is the probability that the design stage is over budget?
    c.  The construction stage (stage 2) will run over budget if it takes 8 months to complete. List the sample points in the event the construction stage is over budget.
    d.  What is the probability that the construction stage is over budget?
    e.  What is the probability that both stages are over budget?

18. Suppose that a manager of a large apartment complex provides the following subjective probability estimates about the number of vacancies that will exist next month.

| Vacancies | Probability |
|-----------|-------------|
| 0         | .05         |
| 1         | .15         |
| 2         | .35         |
| 3         | .25         |
| 4         | .10         |
| 5         | .10         |

Provide the probability of each of the following events.
    a.  No vacancies
    b.  At least four vacancies
    c.  Two or fewer vacancies

19. The National Sporting Goods Association conducted a survey of persons 7 years of age or older about participation in sports activities (*Statistical Abstract of the United States: 2002*). The total population in this age group was reported at 248.5 million, with 120.9 million male and 127.6 million female. The number of participants for the top five sports activities appears here.

|                          | Participants (millions) | |
| Activity                 | Male | Female |
|--------------------------|------|--------|
| **Bicycle riding**       | 22.2 | 21.0   |
| **Camping**              | 25.6 | 24.3   |
| **Exercise walking**     | 28.7 | 57.7   |
| **Exercising with equipment** | 20.4 | 24.4 |
| **Swimming**             | 26.4 | 34.4   |

    a.  For a randomly selected female, estimate the probability of participation in each of the sports activities.
    b.  For a randomly selected male, estimate the probability of participation in each of the sports activities.
    c.  For a randomly selected person, what is the probability the person participates in exercise walking?
    d.  Suppose you just happen to see an exercise walker going by. What is the probability it is a woman? What is the probability it is a man?

20. *Fortune* magazine publishes an annual issue containing information on *Fortune* 500 companies. The following data show the six states with the largest number of *Fortune* 500 companies as well as the number of companies headquartered in those states (*Fortune*, April 17, 2000).

| State | Number of Companies |
|---|---|
| New York | 56 |
| California | 53 |
| Texas | 43 |
| Illinois | 37 |
| Ohio | 28 |
| Pennsylvania | 28 |

Suppose a *Fortune* 500 company is chosen for a follow-up questionnaire. What are the probabilities of the following events?
   a.   Let $N$ be the event the company is headquartered in New York. Find $P(N)$.
   b.   Let $T$ be the event the company is headquartered in Texas. Find $P(T)$.
   c.   Let $B$ be the event the company is headquartered in one of these six states. Find $P(B)$.

21. A survey of 50 students at Tarpon Springs College about the number of extracurricular activities resulted in the data shown.

| Number of Activities | Frequency |
|---|---|
| 0 | 8 |
| 1 | 20 |
| 2 | 12 |
| 3 | 6 |
| 4 | 3 |
| 5 | 1 |

   a.   Let $A$ be the event that a student participates in at least 1 activity. Find $P(A)$.
   b.   Let $B$ be the event that a student participates in 3 or more activities. Find $P(B)$.
   c.   What is the probability that a student participates in exactly 2 activities?

## 4.3 Some Basic Relationships of Probability

### Complement of an Event

Given an event $A$, the **complement of $A$** is defined to be the event consisting of all sample points that are *not* in $A$. The complement of $A$ is denoted by $A^c$. Figure 4.4 is a diagram, known as a **Venn diagram**, which illustrates the concept of a complement. The rectangular area represents the sample space for the experiment and as such contains all possible sample points. The circle represents event $A$ and contains only the sample points that belong to $A$. The shaded region of the rectangle contains all sample points not in event $A$, and is by definition the complement of $A$.

In any probability application, either event $A$ or its complement $A^c$ must occur. Therefore, we have

$$P(A) + P(A^c) = 1$$

FIGURE 4.4    COMPLEMENT OF EVENT A IS SHADED

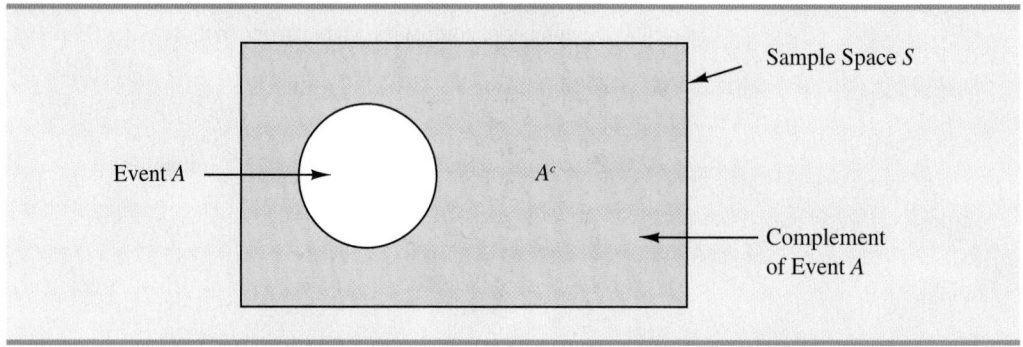

Solving for $P(A)$, we obtain the following result.

COMPUTING PROBABILITY USING THE COMPLEMENT

$$P(A) = 1 - P(A^c) \qquad (4.5)$$

Equation (4.5) shows that the probability of an event $A$ can be computed easily if the probability of its complement, $P(A^c)$, is known.

As an example, consider the case of a sales manager who, after reviewing sales reports, states that 80% of new customer contacts result in no sale. By allowing $A$ to denote the event of a sale and $A^c$ to denote the event of no sale, the manager is stating that $P(A^c) = .80$. Using equation (4.5), we see that

$$P(A) = 1 - P(A^c) = 1 - .80 = .20$$

We can conclude that a new customer contact has a .20 probability of resulting in a sale.

In another example, a purchasing agent states a .90 probability that a supplier will send a shipment that is free of defective parts. Using the complement, we can conclude that there is a $1 - .90 = .10$ probability that the shipment will contain defective parts.

## Addition Law

The addition law is helpful when we are interested in knowing the probability that at least one of two events occurs. That is, with events $A$ and $B$ we are interested in knowing the probability that event $A$ or event $B$ or both occur.

Before we present the addition law, we need to discuss two concepts related to the combination of events: the *union* of events and the *intersection* of events. Given two events $A$ and $B$, the **union of A and B** is defined as follows.

UNION OF TWO EVENTS

The *union* of $A$ and $B$ is the event containing *all* sample points belonging to $A$ *or* $B$ *or both.* The union is denoted by $A \cup B$.

The Venn diagram in Figure 4.5 depicts the union of events $A$ and $B$. Note that the two circles contain all the sample points in event $A$ as well as all the sample points in event $B$.

**FIGURE 4.5    UNION OF EVENTS *A* AND *B* IS SHADED**

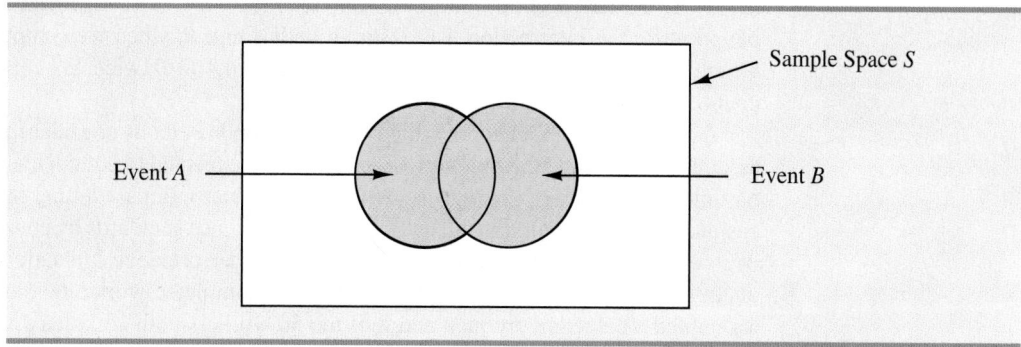

The fact that the circles overlap indicates that some sample points are contained in both *A* and *B*.

The definition of the **intersection of A and B** follows.

---

**INTERSECTION OF TWO EVENTS**

Given two events *A* and *B*, the *intersection* of *A* and *B* is the event containing the sample points belonging to *both A and B*. The intersection is denoted by $A \cap B$.

---

The Venn diagram depicting the intersection of events *A* and *B* is shown in Figure 4.6. The area where the two circles overlap is the intersection; it contains the sample points that are in both *A* and *B*.

Let us now continue with a discussion of the addition law. The **addition law** provides a way to compute the probability that event *A* or event *B* or both occur. In other words, the addition law is used to compute the probability of the union of two events. The addition law is written as follows.

---

**ADDITION LAW**

$$P(A \cup B) = P(A) + P(B) - P(A \cap B) \qquad \textbf{(4.6)}$$

---

**FIGURE 4.6    INTERSECTION OF EVENTS *A* AND *B* IS SHADED**

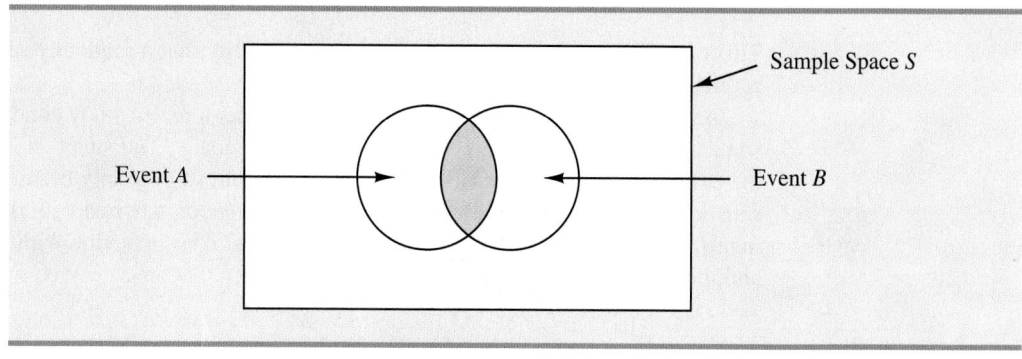

To understand the addition law intuitively, note that the first two terms in the addition law, $P(A) + P(B)$, account for all the sample points in $A \cup B$. However, because the sample points in the intersection $A \cap B$ are in both $A$ and $B$, when we compute $P(A) + P(B)$, we are in effect counting each of the sample points in $A \cap B$ twice. We correct for this overcounting by subtracting $P(A \cap B)$.

As an example of an application of the addition law, let us consider the case of a small assembly plant with 50 employees. Each worker is expected to complete work assignments on time and in such a way that the assembled product will pass a final inspection. On occasion, some of the workers fail to meet the performance standards by completing work late or assembling a defective product. At the end of a performance evaluation period, the production manager found that 5 of the 50 workers completed work late, 6 of the 50 workers assembled a defective product, and 2 of the 50 workers both completed work late *and* assembled a defective product.

Let

$$L = \text{the event that the work is completed late}$$
$$D = \text{the event that the assembled product is defective}$$

The relative frequency information leads to the following probabilities.

$$P(L) = \frac{5}{50} = .10$$

$$P(D) = \frac{6}{50} = .12$$

$$P(L \cap D) = \frac{2}{50} = .04$$

After reviewing the performance data, the production manager decided to assign a poor performance rating to any employee whose work was either late or defective; thus the event of interest is $L \cup D$. What is the probability that the production manager assigned an employee a poor performance rating?

Note that the probability question is about the union of two events. Specifically, we want to know $P(L \cup D)$. Using equation (4.6), we have

$$P(L \cup D) = P(L) + P(D) - P(L \cap D)$$

Knowing values for the three probabilities on the right side of this expression, we can write

$$P(L \cup D) = .10 + .12 - .04 = .18$$

This calculation tells us that there is a .18 probability that a randomly selected employee received a poor performance rating.

As another example of the addition law, consider a recent study conducted by the personnel manager of a major computer software company. The study showed that 30% of the employees who left the firm within two years did so primarily because they were dissatisfied with their salary, 20% left because they were dissatisfied with their work assignments, and 12% of the former employees indicated dissatisfaction with *both* their salary and their work assignments. What is the probability that an employee who leaves within two years does so because of dissatisfaction with salary, dissatisfaction with the work assignment, or both?

Let

$$S = \text{the event that the employee leaves because of salary}$$
$$W = \text{the event that the employee leaves because of work assignment}$$

We have $P(S) = .30$, $P(W) = .20$, and $P(S \cap W) = .12$. Using equation (4.6), the addition law, we have

$$P(S \cup W) = P(S) + P(W) - P(S \cap W) = .30 + .20 - .12 = .38.$$

We find a .38 probability that an employee leaves for salary or work assignment reasons.

Before we conclude our discussion of the addition law, let us consider a special case that arises for **mutually exclusive events**.

---

**MUTUALLY EXCLUSIVE EVENTS**

Two events are said to be mutually exclusive if the events have no sample points in common.

---

Events $A$ and $B$ are mutually exclusive if, when one event occurs, the other cannot occur. Thus, a requirement for $A$ and $B$ to be mutually exclusive is that their intersection must contain no sample points. The Venn diagram depicting two mutually exclusive events $A$ and $B$ is shown in Figure 4.7. In this case $P(A \cap B) = 0$ and the addition law can be written as follows.

---

**ADDITION LAW FOR MUTUALLY EXCLUSIVE EVENTS**

$$P(A \cup B) = P(A) + P(B)$$

---

**FIGURE 4.7   MUTUALLY EXCLUSIVE EVENTS**

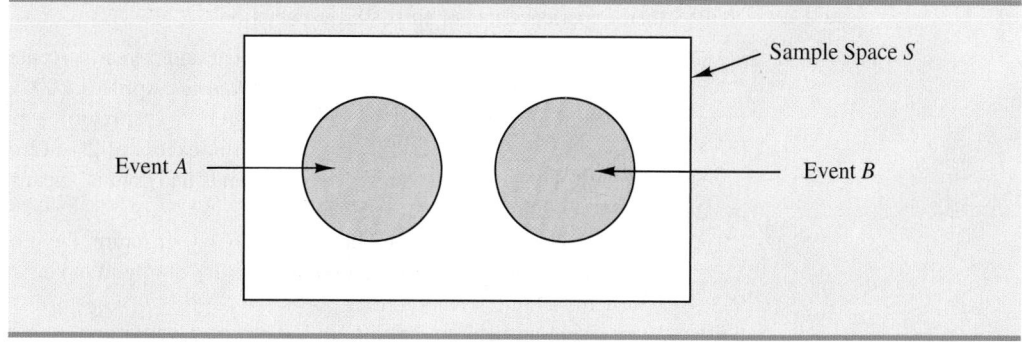

## Exercises

### Methods

22. Suppose that we have a sample space with five equally likely experimental outcomes: $E_1$, $E_2, E_3, E_4, E_5$. Let

$$A = \{E_1, E_2\}$$
$$B = \{E_3, E_4\}$$
$$C = \{E_2, E_3, E_5\}$$

a. Find $P(A)$, $P(B)$, and $P(C)$.
b. Find $P(A \cup B)$. Are $A$ and $B$ mutually exclusive?
c. Find $A^c$, $C^c$, $P(A^c)$, and $P(C^c)$.
d. Find $A \cup B^c$ and $P(A \cup B^c)$.
e. Find $P(B \cup C)$.

23. Suppose that we have a sample space $S = \{E_1, E_2, E_3, E_4, E_5, E_6, E_7\}$, where $E_1, E_2, \ldots,$ $E_7$ denote the sample points. The following probability assignments apply: $P(E_1) = .05$, $P(E_2) = .20$, $P(E_3) = .20$, $P(E_4) = .25$, $P(E_5) = .15$, $P(E_6) = .10$, and $P(E_7) = .05$. Let

$$A = \{E_1, E_4, E_6\}$$
$$B = \{E_2, E_4, E_7\}$$
$$C = \{E_2, E_3, E_5, E_7\}$$

a. Find $P(A)$, $P(B)$, and $P(C)$.
b. Find $A \cup B$ and $P(A \cup B)$.
c. Find $A \cap B$ and $P(A \cap B)$.
d. Are events $A$ and $C$ mutually exclusive?
e. Find $B^c$ and $P(B^c)$.

### Applications

24. Clarkson University surveyed alumni to learn more about what they think of Clarkson. One part of the survey asked respondents to indicate whether their overall experience at Clarkson fell short of expectations, met expectations, or surpassed expectations. The results showed that 4% of the respondents did not provide a response, 26% said that their experience fell short of expectations, and 65% of the respondents said that their experience met expectations (*Clarkson Magazine*, Summer 2001).
a. If we chose an alumnus at random, what is the probability that he or she would say their experience surpassed expectations?
b. If we chose an alumnus at random, what is the probability that he or she would say their experience met or surpassed expectations?

25. Data on the 30 largest bond funds provides 1-year and 5-year percentage returns for the period ending March 31, 2000 (*The Wall Street Journal*, April 10, 2000). Suppose we consider a 1-year return in excess of 2% to be high and a 5-year return in excess of 44% to be high. One-half of the funds had a 1-year return in excess of 2%, 12 of the funds had a 5-year return in excess of 44%, and six of the funds had both a 1-year return in excess of 2% and a 5-year return in excess of 44%.
a. Find the probability of a fund having a high 1-year return, the probability of a fund having a high 5-year return, and the probability of a fund having both a high 1-year return and a high 5-year return.
b. What is the probability that a fund has a high 1-year return or a high 5-year return or both?
c. What is the probability that a fund has neither a high 1-year return nor a high 5-year return?

**SELF** test

26. Data on the 30 largest stock and balanced funds provided 1-year and 5-year percentage returns for the period ending March 31, 2000 (*The Wall Street Journal*, April 10, 2000). Suppose we consider a 1-year return in excess of 50% to be high and a 5-year return in excess of 300% to be high. Nine of the funds had 1-year returns in excess of 50%, seven of the funds had 5-year returns in excess of 300%, and five of the funds had both 1-year returns in excess of 50% and 5-year returns in excess of 300%.

 a. What is the probability of a high 1-year return, and what is the probability of a high 5-year return?
 b. What is the probability of both a high 1-year return and a high 5-year return?
 c. What is the probability of neither a high 1-year return nor a high 5-year return?

27. A 2001 preseason NCAA football poll asked respondents to answer the question, "Will the Big Ten or the Pac-10 have a team in this year's national championship game, the Rose Bowl? Of the 13,429 respondents, 2961 said the Big Ten would, 4494 said the Pac-10 would, and 6823 said neither the Big Ten nor the Pac-10 would have a team in the Rose Bowl (www.yahoo.com, August 30, 2001).

 a. What is the probability that a respondent said neither the Big Ten nor the Pac-10 will have a team in the Rose Bowl?
 b. What is the probability that a respondent said either the Big Ten or the Pac-10 will have a team in the Rose Bowl?
 c. Find the probability that a respondent said both the Big Ten and the Pac-10 would have a team in the Rose Bowl.

28. A survey of magazine subscribers showed that 45.8% rented a car during the past 12 months for business reasons, 54% rented a car during the past 12 months for personal reasons, and 30% rented a car during the past 12 months for both business and personal reasons.

 a. What is the probability that a subscriber rented a car during the past 12 months for business or personal reasons?
 b. What is the probability that a subscriber did not rent a car during the past 12 months for either business or personal reasons?

29. High school seniors with strong academic records apply to the nation's most selective colleges in greater numbers each year. Because the number of slots remains relatively stable, some colleges reject more early applicants. The University of Pennsylvania received 2851 applications for early admission. Of this group, it admitted 1033 students, rejected 854 outright, and deferred 964 to the regular admissions pool. Penn admitted about 18% of the applicants in the regular admissions pool for a total class size (number of early admissions plus number of regular admissions) of 2375 students (*USA Today*, January 24, 2001). Let $E$, $R$, and $D$ represent the events that a student who applies for early admission is admitted, rejected outright, or deferred to the regular admissions pool; and let $A$ represent the event that a student in the regular admissions pool is admitted.

 a. Use the data to estimate $P(E)$, $P(R)$, and $P(D)$.
 b. Are events $E$ and $D$ mutually exclusive? Find $P(E \cap D)$.
 c. For the 2375 students admitted to Penn, what is the probability that a randomly selected student was accepted for early admission?
 d. Suppose a student applies to Penn for early admission. What is the probability the student will be admitted for early admission or be accepted for admission in the regular admissions pool?

## 4.4    Conditional Probability

Often, the probability of an event is influenced by whether a related event already occurred. Suppose we have an event $A$ with probability $P(A)$. If we obtain new information and learn that a related event, denoted by $B$, already occurred, we will want to take advantage of this information by calculating a new probability for event $A$. This new probability of event $A$ is called a **conditional probability** and is written $P(A \mid B)$. We use the notation $\mid$ to indicate that we are considering the probability of event $A$ *given* the condition that event $B$ has occurred. Hence, the notation $P(A \mid B)$ reads "the probability of A given B."

As an illustration of the application of conditional probability, consider the situation of the promotion status of male and female officers of a major metropolitan police force in the eastern United States. The police force consists of 1200 officers, 960 men and 240 women. Over the past two years, 324 officers on the police force received promotions. The specific breakdown of promotions for male and female officers is shown in Table 4.4.

After reviewing the promotion record, a committee of female officers raised a discrimination case on the basis that 288 male officers had received promotions but only 36 female officers had received promotions. The police administration argued that the relatively low number of promotions for female officers was due not to discrimination, but to the fact that relatively few females are members of the police force. Let us show how conditional probability could be used to analyze the discrimination charge.

Let

$$M = \text{event an officer is a man}$$
$$W = \text{event an officer is a woman}$$
$$A = \text{event an officer is promoted}$$
$$A^c = \text{event an officer is not promoted}$$

Dividing the data values in Table 4.4 by the total of 1200 officers enables us to summarize the available information with the following probability values.

$$P(M \cap A) = 288/1200 = .24 = \text{probability that a randomly selected officer is a man \textit{and} is promoted}$$

$$P(M \cap A^c) = 672/1200 = .56 = \text{probability that a randomly selected officer is a man \textit{and} is not promoted}$$

$$P(W \cap A) = 36/1200 = .03 = \text{probability that a randomly selected officer is a woman \textit{and} is promoted}$$

$$P(W \cap A^c) = 204/1200 = .17 = \text{probability that a randomly selected officer is a woman \textit{and} is not promoted}$$

Because each of these values gives the probability of the intersection of two events, the probabilities are called **joint probabilities**. Table 4.5, which provides a summary of the probability information for the police officer promotion situation, is referred to as a *joint probability table.*

The values in the margins of the joint probability table provide the probabilities of each event separately. That is, $P(M) = .80$, $P(W) = .20$, $P(A) = .27$, and $P(A^c) = .73$. These

**TABLE 4.4    PROMOTION STATUS OF POLICE OFFICERS OVER THE PAST TWO YEARS**

|  | Men | Women | Totals |
|---|---|---|---|
| **Promoted** | 288 | 36 | 324 |
| **Not Promoted** | 672 | 204 | 876 |
| **Totals** | 960 | 240 | 1200 |

**TABLE 4.5    JOINT PROBABILITY TABLE FOR PROMOTIONS**

| Joint probabilities appear in the body of the table. | Men ($M$) | Women ($W$) | Totals |
|---|---|---|---|
| **Promoted ($A$)** | .24 | .03 | .27 |
| **Not Promoted ($A^c$)** | .56 | .17 | .73 |
| **Totals** | .80 | .20 | 1.00 |

Marginal probabilities appear in the margins of the table.

probabilities are referred to as **marginal probabilities** because of their location in the margins of the joint probability table. We note that the marginal probabilities are found by summing the joint probabilities in the corresponding row or column of the joint probability table. For instance, the marginal probability of being promoted is $P(A) = P(M \cap A) + P(W \cap A) = .24 + .03 = .27$. From the marginal probabilities, we see that 80% of the force is male, 20% of the force is female, 27% of all officers received promotions, and 73% were not promoted.

Let us begin the conditional probability analysis by computing the probability that an officer is promoted given that the officer is a man. In conditional probability notation, we are attempting to determine $P(A \mid M)$. To calculate $P(A \mid M)$, we first realize that this notation simply means that we are considering the probability of the event $A$ (promotion) given that the condition designated as event $M$ (the officer is a man) is known to exist. Thus $P(A \mid M)$ tells us that we are now concerned only with the promotion status of the 960 male officers. Because 288 of the 960 male officers received promotions, the probability of being promoted given that the officer is a man is 288/960 = .30. In other words, given that an officer is a man, that officer has a 30% chance of receiving a promotion over the past two years.

This procedure was easy to apply because the values in Table 4.4 show the number of officers in each category. We now want to demonstrate how conditional probabilities such as $P(A \mid M)$ can be computed directly from related event probabilities rather than the frequency data of Table 4.4.

We have shown that $P(A \mid M) = 288/960 = .30$. Let us now divide both the numerator and denominator of this fraction by 1200, the total number of officers in the study.

$$P(A \mid M) = \frac{288}{960} = \frac{288/1200}{960/1200} = \frac{.24}{.80} = .30$$

We now see that the conditional probability $P(A \mid M)$ can be computed as .24/.80. Refer to the joint probability table (Table 4.5). Note in particular that .24 is the joint probability of $A$ and $M$; that is, $P(A \cap M) = .24$. Also note that .80 is the marginal probability that a randomly selected officer is a man; that is, $P(M) = .80$. Thus, the conditional probability $P(A \mid M)$ can be computed as the ratio of the joint probability $P(A \cap M)$ to the marginal probability $P(M)$.

$$P(A \mid M) = \frac{P(A \cap M)}{P(M)} = \frac{.24}{.80} = .30$$

The fact that conditional probabilities can be computed as the ratio of a joint probability to a marginal probability provides the following general formula for conditional probability calculations for two events $A$ and $B$.

CONDITIONAL PROBABILITY

$$P(A \mid B) = \frac{P(A \cap B)}{P(B)} \tag{4.7}$$

or

$$P(B \mid A) = \frac{P(A \cap B)}{P(A)} \tag{4.8}$$

The Venn diagram in Figure 4.8 is helpful in obtaining an intuitive understanding of conditional probability. The circle on the right shows that event $B$ has occurred; the portion of the circle that overlaps with event $A$ denotes the event $(A \cap B)$. We know that once event $B$ has occurred, the only way that we can also observe event $A$ is for the event $(A \cap B)$ to occur. Thus, the ratio $P(A \cap B)/P(B)$ provides the conditional probability that we will observe event $A$ given that event $B$ has already occurred.

Let us return to the issue of discrimination against the female officers. The marginal probability in row 1 of Table 4.5 shows that the probability of promotion of an officer is $P(A) = .27$ (regardless of whether that officer is male or female). However, the critical issue in the discrimination case involves the two conditional probabilities $P(A \mid M)$ and $P(A \mid W)$. That is, what is the probability of a promotion *given* that the officer is a man, and what is the probability of a promotion *given* that the officer is a woman? If these two probabilities are equal, a discrimination argument has no basis because the chances of a promotion are the same for male and female officers. However, a difference in the two conditional probabilities will support the position that male and female officers are treated differently in promotion decisions.

We already determined that $P(A \mid M) = .30$. Let us now use the probability values in Table 4.5 and the basic relationship of conditional probability in equation (4.7) to compute

FIGURE 4.8   CONDITIONAL PROBABILITY $P(A \mid B) = P(A \cap B)/P(B)$

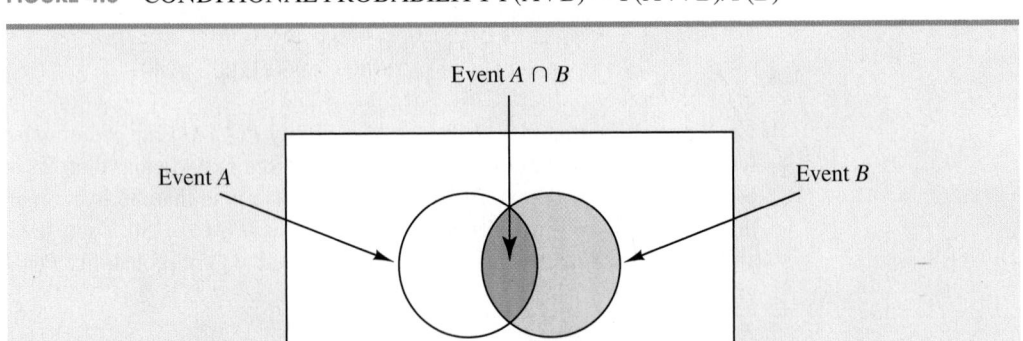

the probability that an officer is promoted given that the officer is a woman; that is, $P(A \mid W)$. Using equation (4.7), with $W$ replacing $B$, we obtain

$$P(A \mid W) = \frac{P(A \cap W)}{P(W)} = \frac{.03}{.20} = .15$$

What conclusion do you draw? The probability of a promotion given that the officer is a man is .30, twice the .15 probability of a promotion given that the officer is a woman. Although the use of conditional probability does not in itself prove that discrimination exists in this case, the conditional probability values support the argument presented by the female officers.

## Independent Events

In the preceding illustration, $P(A) = .27$, $P(A \mid M) = .30$, and $P(A \mid W) = .15$. We see that the probability of a promotion (event $A$) is affected or influenced by whether the officer is a man or a woman. Particularly, because $P(A \mid M) \neq P(A)$, we would say that events $A$ and $M$ are dependent events. That is, the probability of event $A$ (promotion) is altered or affected by knowing that event $M$ (the officer is a man) exists. Similarly, with $P(A \mid W) \neq P(A)$, we would say that events $A$ and $W$ are *dependent events*. However, if the probability of event $A$ is not changed by the existence of event $M$—that is, $P(A \mid M) = P(A)$—we would say that events $A$ and $M$ are **independent events**. This situation leads to the following definition of the independence of two events.

INDEPENDENT EVENTS

Two events $A$ and $B$ are independent if

$$P(A \mid B) = P(A) \tag{4.9}$$

or

$$P(B \mid A) = P(B) \tag{4.10}$$

Otherwise, the events are dependent.

## Multiplication Law

Whereas the addition law of probability is used to compute the probability of a union of two events, the multiplication law is used to compute the probability of the intersection of two events. The multiplication law is based on the definition of conditional probability. Using equations (4.7) and (4.8) and solving for $P(A \cap B)$, we obtain the **multiplication law**.

MULTIPLICATION LAW

$$P(A \cap B) = P(B)P(A \mid B) \tag{4.11}$$

or

$$P(A \cap B) = P(A)P(B \mid A) \tag{4.12}$$

To illustrate the use of the multiplication law, consider a newspaper circulation department where it is known that 84% of the households in a particular neighborhood subscribe to the daily edition of the paper. If we let $D$ denote the event that a household subscribes to the daily edition, $P(D) = .84$. In addition, it is known that the probability that a household that already holds a daily subscription also subscribes to the Sunday edition (event $S$) is .75; that is, $P(S \mid D) = .75$. What is the probability that a household subscribes to both the Sunday and daily editions of the newspaper? Using the multiplication law, we compute the desired $P(S \cap D)$ as

$$P(S \cap D) = P(D)P(S \mid D) = .84(.75) = .63$$

We now know that 63% of the households subscribe to both the Sunday and daily editions.

Before concluding this section, let us consider the special case of the multiplication law when the events involved are independent. Recall that events $A$ and $B$ are independent whenever $P(A \mid B) = P(A)$ or $P(B \mid A) = P(B)$. Hence, using equations (4.11) and (4.12) for the special case of independent events, we obtain the following multiplication law.

MULTIPLICATION LAW FOR INDEPENDENT EVENTS

$$P(A \cap B) = P(A)P(B) \qquad (4.13)$$

To compute the probability of the intersection of two independent events, we simply multiply the corresponding probabilities. Note that the multiplication law for independent events provides another way to determine whether $A$ and $B$ are independent. That is, if $P(A \cap B) = P(A)P(B)$, then $A$ and $B$ are independent; if $P(A \cap B) \neq P(A)P(B)$, then $A$ and $B$ are dependent.

As an application of the multiplication law for independent events, consider the situation of a service station manager who knows from past experience that 80% of the customers use a credit card when they purchase gasoline. What is the probability that the next two customers purchasing gasoline will each use a credit card? If we let

$A$ = the event that the first customer uses a credit card

$B$ = the event that the second customer uses a credit card

then the event of interest is $A \cap B$. Given no other information, we can reasonably assume that $A$ and $B$ are independent events. Thus,

$$P(A \cap B) = P(A)P(B) = (.80)(.80) = .64$$

To summarize this section, we note that our interest in conditional probability is motivated by the fact that events are often related. In such cases, we say the events are dependent and the conditional probability formulas in equations (4.7) and (4.8) must be used to compute the event probabilities. If two events are not related, they are independent; in this case neither event's probability is affected by whether the other event occurred.

## NOTES AND COMMENTS

Do not confuse the notion of mutually exclusive events with that of independent events. Two events with nonzero probabilities cannot be both mutually exclusive and independent. If one mutually exclusive event is known to occur, the other cannot occur; thus, the probability of the other event occurring is reduced to zero. They are therefore dependent.

## Exercises

## Methods

30. Suppose that we have two events, A and B, with $P(A) = .50$, $P(B) = .60$, and $P(A \cap B) = .40$.
    a. Find $P(A \mid B)$.
    b. Find $P(B \mid A)$.
    c. Are A and B independent? Why or why not?

31. Assume that we have two events, A and B, that are mutually exclusive. Assume further that we know $P(A) = .30$ and $P(B) = .40$.
    a. What is $P(A \cap B)$?
    b. What is $P(A \mid B)$?
    c. A student in statistics argues that the concepts of mutually exclusive events and independent events are really the same, and that if events are mutually exclusive they must be independent. Do you agree with this statement? Use the probability information in this problem to justify your answer.
    d. What general conclusion would you make about mutually exclusive and independent events given the results of this problem?

## Applications

32. A Daytona Beach nightclub obtains the following data on the age and marital status of 140 customers.

|       |             | Marital Status | |
|-------|-------------|--------|---------|
|       |             | Single | Married |
| Age   | Under 30    | 77     | 14      |
|       | 30 or Over  | 28     | 21      |

a. Develop a joint probability table for these data.
b. Use the marginal probabilities to comment on the age of customers attending the club.
c. Use the marginal probabilities to comment on the marital status of customers attending the club.
d. What is the probability of finding a customer who is single and under the age of 30?
e. If a customer is under 30, what is the probability that he or she is single?
f. Is marital status independent of age? Explain, using probabilities.

33. In a survey of MBA students, the following data were obtained on "students' first reason for application to the school in which they matriculated."

|                    |           | Reason for Application | | | |
|--------------------|-----------|-------------------|------------------------------|-------|--------|
|                    |           | School Quality | School Cost or Convenience | Other | Totals |
| Enrollment Status  | Full Time | 421               | 393                          | 76    | 890    |
|                    | Part Time | 400               | 593                          | 46    | 1039   |
|                    | Totals    | 821               | 986                          | 122   | 1929   |

a. Develop a joint probability table for these data.
b. Use the marginal probabilities of school quality, school cost or convenience, and other to comment on the most important reason for choosing a school.

c.   If a student goes full time, what is the probability that school quality is the first reason for choosing a school?

d.   If a student goes part time, what is the probability that school quality is the first reason for choosing a school?

e.   Let $A$ denote the event that a student is full time and let $B$ denote the event that the student lists school quality as the first reason for applying. Are events $A$ and $B$ independent? Justify your answer.

34. The following table shows the distribution of blood types in the general population (Hoxworth Blood Center, Cincinnati, Ohio, March 26, 2003).

|       | A   | B  | AB | O   |
|-------|-----|----|----|-----|
| Rh+   | 34% | 9% | 4% | 38% |
| Rh−   | 6%  | 2% | 1% | 6%  |

a.   What is the probability a person will have type O blood?
b.   What is the probability a person will be Rh−?
c.   What is the probability a married couple will both be Rh−?
d.   What is the probability a married couple will both have type AB blood?
e.   What is the probability a person will be Rh− given she or he has type O blood?
f.   What is the probability a person will have type B blood given he or she is Rh+?

35. The U.S. Bureau of Labor Statistics collected data on the occupations of workers 25 to 64 years old. The following table shows the number of male and female workers (in millions) in each occupation category (*Statistical Abstract of the United States: 2002*).

| Occupation | Male | Female |
|------------|------|--------|
| Managerial/Professional | 19079 | 19021 |
| Tech./Sales/Administrative | 11079 | 19315 |
| Service | 4977 | 7947 |
| Precision Production | 11682 | 1138 |
| Operators/Fabricators/Labor | 10576 | 3482 |
| Farming/Forestry/Fishing | 1838 | 514 |

a.   Develop a joint probability table.
b.   What is the probability of a female worker being a manager or professional?
c.   What is the probability of a male worker being in precision production?
d.   Is occupation independent of gender? Justify your answer with a probability calculation.

36. A study of job satisfaction was conducted for four occupations: cabinetmaker, lawyer, physical therapist, and systems analyst. Job satisfaction was measured on a scale of 0–100. The data obtained are summarized in the following crosstabulation.

| Occupation | Satisfaction Score | | | | |
|------------|----------|-------|-------|-------|-------|
|            | Under 50 | 50–59 | 60–69 | 70–79 | 80–89 |
| Cabinetmaker | 0 | 2 | 4 | 3 | 1 |
| Lawyer | 6 | 2 | 1 | 1 | 0 |
| Physical Therapist | 0 | 5 | 2 | 1 | 2 |
| Systems Analyst | 2 | 1 | 4 | 3 | 0 |

a. Develop a joint probability table.

b. What is the probability one of the participants studied received a satisfaction score in the 80s?

c. What is the probability of a satisfaction score in the 80s given the study participant was a physical therapist?

d. What is the probability one of the participants studied was a lawyer?

e. What is the probability one of the participants was a lawyer and received a score under 50?

f. What is the probability of receiving a satisfaction score under 50 given a person is a lawyer?

g. What is the probability of a satisfaction score of 70 or higher?

37. A purchasing agent placed rush orders for a particular raw material with two different suppliers, $A$ and $B$. If neither order arrives in four days, the production process must be shut down until at least one of the orders arrives. The probability that supplier $A$ can deliver the material in four days is .55. The probability that supplier $B$ can deliver the material in four days is .35.

a. What is the probability that both suppliers will deliver the material in four days? Because two separate suppliers are involved, we are willing to assume independence.

b. What is the probability that at least one supplier will deliver the material in four days?

c. What is the probability that the production process will be shut down in four days because of a shortage of raw material (that is, both orders are late)?

38. The Minneapolis Heart Institute Foundation conducted a study to determine the benefit of follow-up care for patients discharged from a hospital after treatment for a heart attack (*The Wall Street Journal,* November 11, 2002). Out of 2060 patients, 1070 did not return for follow-up treatment and 990 did. Within 24 months, 14 of the patients receiving follow-up treatment died, and 29 of the patients not receiving follow-up treatment died. Within 54 months, 20 of the patients receiving follow-up treatment died, and 49 of the patients not receiving follow-up treatment died.

a. What is the probability of a patient dying within 24 months of being discharged after treatment for a heart attack?

b. Using the data for 24 months after discharge, compute the conditional probabilities of dying for patients receiving and not receiving follow-up treatment.

c. Is the probability of dying within 24 months of discharge independent of whether the person receives follow-up treatment? Explain.

d. Using the data for 54 months after discharge, compute the conditional probabilities of dying for patients receiving and not receiving follow-up treatment.

e. Would you recommend enrolling in a follow-up treatment program to a friend?

## 4.5   Bayes' Theorem

In the discussion of conditional probability, we indicated that revising probabilities when new information is obtained is an important phase of probability analysis. Often, we begin the analysis with initial or **prior probability** estimates for specific events of interest. Then, from sources such as a sample, a special report, or a product test, we obtain additional information about the events. Given this new information, we update the prior probability values by calculating revised probabilities, referred to as **posterior probabilities. Bayes' theorem** provides a means for making these probability calculations. The steps in this probability revision process are shown in Figure 4.9.

As an application of Bayes' theorem, consider a manufacturing firm that receives shipments of parts from two different suppliers. Let $A_1$ denote the event that a part is from supplier 1 and $A_2$ denote the event that a part is from supplier 2. Currently, 65% of the parts purchased by the company are from supplier 1 and the remaining 35% are from supplier

**FIGURE 4.9**    PROBABILITY REVISION USING BAYES' THEOREM

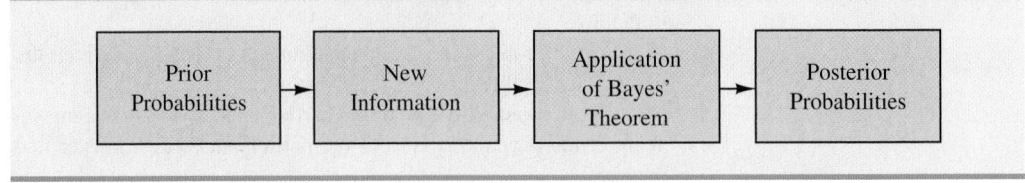

Hence, if a part is selected at random, we would assign the prior probabilities $P(A_1) = .65$ and $P(A_2) = .35$.

The quality of the purchased parts varies with the source of supply. Historical data suggest that the quality ratings of the two suppliers are as shown in Table 4.6. If we let $G$ denote the event that a part is good and $B$ denote the event that a part is bad, the information in Table 4.6 provides the following conditional probability values.

$$P(G \mid A_1) = .98 \quad P(B \mid A_1) = .02$$
$$P(G \mid A_2) = .95 \quad P(B \mid A_2) = .05$$

The tree diagram in Figure 4.10 depicts the process of the firm receiving a part from one of the two suppliers and then discovering that the part is good or bad as a two-step experiment. We see that four experimental outcomes are possible; two correspond to the part being good and two correspond to the part being bad.

Each of the experimental outcomes is the intersection of two events, so we can use the multiplication rule to compute the probabilities. For instance,

$$P(A_1, G) = P(A_1 \cap G) = P(A_1)P(G \mid A_1)$$

The process of computing these joint probabilities can be depicted in what is called a probability tree (see Figure 4.11). From left to right through the tree, the probabilities for each branch at step 1 are prior probabilities and the probabilities for each branch at step 2 are conditional probabilities. To find the probabilities of each experimental outcome, we simply multiply the probabilities on the branches leading to the outcome. Each of these joint probabilities is shown in Figure 4.11 along with the known probabilities for each branch.

Suppose now that the parts from the two suppliers are used in the firm's manufacturing process and that a machine breaks down because it attempts to process a bad part. Given the information that the part is bad, what is the probability that it came from supplier 1 and what is the probability that it came from supplier 2? With the information in the probability tree (Figure 4.11), Bayes' theorem can be used to answer these questions.

**TABLE 4.6**    HISTORICAL QUALITY LEVELS OF TWO SUPPLIERS

|  | Percentage Good Parts | Percentage Bad Parts |
|---|---|---|
| **Supplier 1** | 98 | 2 |
| **Supplier 2** | 95 | 5 |

FIGURE 4.10   TREE DIAGRAM FOR TWO-SUPPLIER EXAMPLE

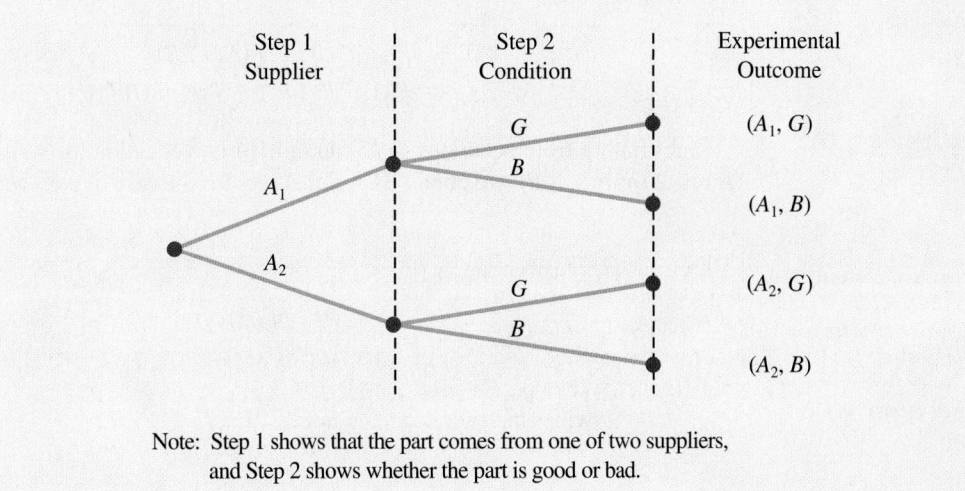

Note:  Step 1 shows that the part comes from one of two suppliers,
       and Step 2 shows whether the part is good or bad.

Letting $B$ denote the event that the part is bad, we are looking for the posterior probabilities $P(A_1 \mid B)$ and $P(A_2 \mid B)$. From the law of conditional probability, we know that

$$P(A_1 \mid B) = \frac{P(A_1 \cap B)}{P(B)} \tag{4.14}$$

Referring to the probability tree, we see that

$$P(A_1 \cap B) = P(A_1)P(B \mid A_1) \tag{4.15}$$

FIGURE 4.11   PROBABILITY TREE FOR TWO-SUPPLIER EXAMPLE

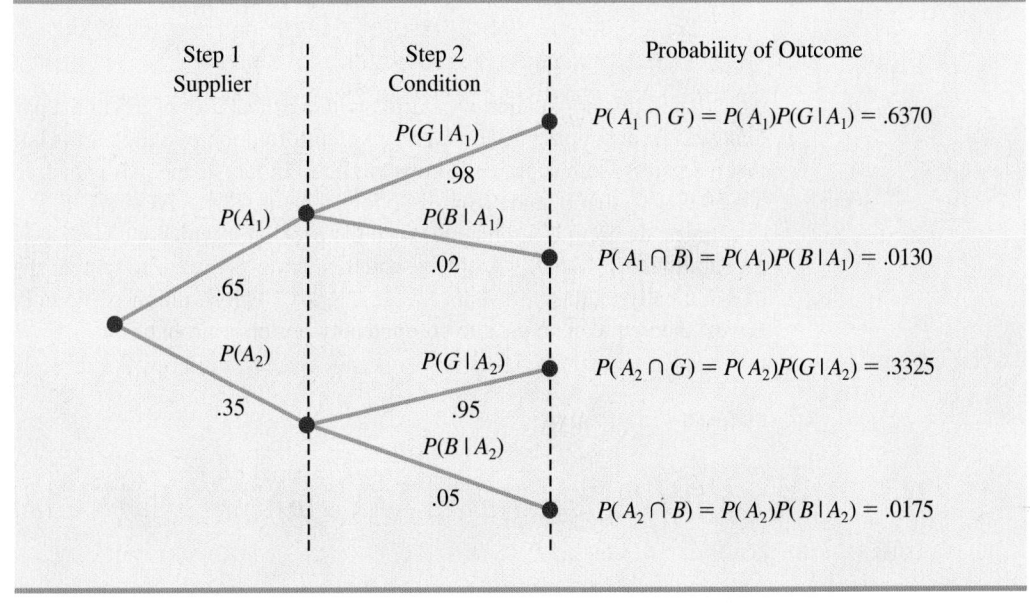

To find $P(B)$, we note that event $B$ can occur in only two ways: $(A_1 \cap B)$ and $(A_2 \cap B)$. Therefore, we have

$$
\begin{aligned}
P(B) &= P(A_1 \cap B) + P(A_2 \cap B) \\
&= P(A_1)P(B \mid A_1) + P(A_2)P(B \mid A_2)
\end{aligned}
\tag{4.16}
$$

Substituting from equations (4.15) and (4.16) into equation (4.14) and writing a similar result for $P(A_2 \mid B)$, we obtain Bayes' theorem for the case of two events.

*The Reverend Thomas Bayes (1702–1761), a Presbyterian minister, is credited with the original work leading to the version of Bayes' theorem in use today.*

**BAYES' THEOREM (TWO-EVENT CASE)**

$$
P(A_1 \mid B) = \frac{P(A_1)P(B \mid A_1)}{P(A_1)P(B \mid A_1) + P(A_2)P(B \mid A_2)}
\tag{4.17}
$$

$$
P(A_2 \mid B) = \frac{P(A_2)P(B \mid A_2)}{P(A_1)P(B \mid A_1) + P(A_2)P(B \mid A_2)}
\tag{4.18}
$$

Using equation (4.17) and the probability values provided in the example, we have

$$
\begin{aligned}
P(A_1 \mid B) &= \frac{P(A_1)P(B \mid A_1)}{P(A_1)P(B \mid A_1) + P(A_2)P(B \mid A_2)} \\
&= \frac{(.65)(.02)}{(.65)(.02) + (.35)(.05)} = \frac{.0130}{.0130 + .0175} \\
&= \frac{.0130}{.0305} = .4262
\end{aligned}
$$

In addition, using equation (4.18), we find $P(A_2 \mid B)$.

$$
\begin{aligned}
P(A_2 \mid B) &= \frac{(.35)(.05)}{(.65)(.02) + (.35)(.05)} \\
&= \frac{.0175}{.0130 + .0175} = \frac{.0175}{.0305} = .5738
\end{aligned}
$$

Note that in this application we started with a probability of .65 that a part selected at random was from supplier 1. However, given information that the part is bad, the probability that the part is from supplier 1 drops to .4262. In fact, if the part is bad, it has better than a 50–50 chance that it came from supplier 2; that is, $P(A_2 \mid B) = .5738$.

Bayes' theorem is applicable when the events for which we want to compute posterior probabilities are mutually exclusive and their union is the entire sample space.* For the case of $n$ mutually exclusive events $A_1, A_2, \ldots, A_n$, whose union is the entire sample space, Bayes' theorem can be used to compute any posterior probability $P(A_i \mid B)$ as shown here.

**BAYES' THEOREM**

$$
P(A_i \mid B) = \frac{P(A_i)P(B \mid A_i)}{P(A_1)P(B \mid A_1) + P(A_2)P(B \mid A_2) + \cdots + P(A_n)P(B \mid A_n)}
\tag{4.19}
$$

---

*If the union of events is the entire sample space, the events are said to be *collectively exhaustive*.

With prior probabilities $P(A_1)$, $P(A_2)$, . . . , $P(A_n)$ and the appropriate conditional probabilities $P(B \mid A_1)$, $P(B \mid A_2)$, . . . , $P(B \mid A_n)$, equation (4.19) can be used to compute the posterior probability of the events $A_1, A_2, \ldots, A_n$.

## Tabular Approach

A tabular approach is helpful in conducting the Bayes' theorem calculations. Such an approach is shown in Table 4.7 for the parts supplier problem. The computations shown there are done in the following steps.

**Step 1.** Prepare the following three columns:

Column 1—The mutually exclusive events $A_i$ for which posterior probabilities are desired.

Column 2—The prior probabilities $P(A_i)$ for the events.

Column 3—The conditional probabilities $P(B \mid A_i)$ of the new information $B$ given each event.

**Step 2.** In column 4, compute the joint probabilities $P(A_i \cap B)$ for each event and the new information $B$ by using the multiplication law. These joint probabilities are found by multiplying the prior probabilities in column 2 by the corresponding conditional probabilities in column 3; that is, $P(A_i \cap B) = P(A_i)P(B \mid A_i)$.

**Step 3.** Sum the joint probabilities in column 4. The sum is the probability of the new information, $P(B)$. Thus we see in Table 4.7 that there is a .0130 probability that the part came from supplier 1 and is bad and a .0175 probability that the part came from supplier 2 and is bad. Because these are the only two ways in which a bad part can be obtained, the sum .0130 + .0175 shows an overall probability of .0305 of finding a bad part from the combined shipments of the two suppliers.

**Step 4.** In column 5, compute the posterior probabilities using the basic relationship of conditional probability.

$$P(A_i \mid B) = \frac{P(A_i \cap B)}{P(B)}$$

Note that the joint probabilities $P(A_i \cap B)$ are in column (4) and the probability $P(B)$ is the sum of column (4).

**TABLE 4.7**   TABULAR APPROACH TO BAYES' THEOREM CALCULATIONS
FOR THE TWO-SUPPLIER PROBLEM

| (1) Events $A_i$ | (2) Prior Probabilities $P(A_i)$ | (3) Conditional Probabilities $P(B \mid A_i)$ | (4) Joint Probabilities $P(A_i \cap B)$ | (5) Posterior Probabilities $P(A_i \mid B)$ |
|---|---|---|---|---|
| $A_1$ | .65 | .02 | .0130 | .0130/.0305 = .4262 |
| $A_2$ | .35 | .05 | .0175 | .0175/.0305 = .5738 |
|  | 1.00 |  | $P(B) = .0305$ | 1.0000 |

> **NOTES AND COMMENTS**
>
> 1. Bayes' theorem is used extensively in decision analysis. The prior probabilities are often subjective estimates provided by a decision maker. Sample information is obtained and posterior probabilities are computed for use in choosing the best decision.
>
> 2. An event and its complement are mutually exclusive, and their union is the entire sample space. Thus, Bayes' theorem is always applicable for computing posterior probabilities of an event and its complement.

## Exercises

### Methods

39. The prior probabilities for events $A_1$ and $A_2$ are $P(A_1) = .40$ and $P(A_2) = .60$. It is also known that $P(A_1 \cap A_2) = 0$. Suppose $P(B \mid A_1) = .20$ and $P(B \mid A_2) = .05$.
    a.  Are $A_1$ and $A_2$ mutually exclusive? Explain.
    b.  Compute $P(A_1 \cap B)$ and $P(A_2 \cap B)$.
    c.  Compute $P(B)$.
    d.  Apply Bayes' theorem to compute $P(A_1 \mid B)$ and $P(A_2 \mid B)$.

40. The prior probabilities for events $A_1, A_2,$ and $A_3$ are $P(A_1) = .20, P(A_2) = .50,$ and $P(A_3) = .30$. The conditional probabilities of event $B$ given $A_1, A_2,$ and $A_3$ are $P(B \mid A_1) = .50, P(B \mid A_2) = .40,$ and $P(B \mid A_3) = .30$.
    a.  Compute $P(B \cap A_1)$, $P(B \cap A_2)$, and $P(B \cap A_3)$.
    b.  Apply Bayes' theorem, equation (4.19), to compute the posterior probability $P(A_2 \mid B)$.
    c.  Use the tabular approach to applying Bayes' theorem to compute $P(A_1 \mid B)$, $P(A_2 \mid B)$, and $P(A_3 \mid B)$.

### Applications

41. A consulting firm submitted a bid for a large research project. The firm's management initially felt they had a 50–50 chance of getting the project. However, the agency to which the bid was submitted subsequently requested additional information on the bid. Past experience indicates that for 75% of the successful bids and 40% of the unsuccessful bids the agency requested additional information.
    a.  What is the prior probability of the bid being successful (that is, prior to the request for additional information)?
    b.  What is the conditional probability of a request for additional information given that the bid will ultimately be successful?
    c.  Compute the posterior probability that the bid will be successful given a request for additional information.

42. A local bank reviewed its credit card policy with the intention of recalling some of its credit cards. In the past approximately 5% of cardholders defaulted, leaving the bank unable to collect the outstanding balance. Hence, management established a prior probability of .05 that any particular cardholder will default. The bank also found that the probability of missing a monthly payment is .20 for customers who do not default. Of course, the probability of missing a monthly payment for those who default is 1.
    a.  Given that a customer missed one or more monthly payments, compute the posterior probability that the customer will default.
    b.  The bank would like to recall its card if the probability that a customer will default is greater than .20. Should the bank recall its card if the customer misses a monthly payment? Why or why not?

43.   Small cars get better gas mileage, but they are not as safe as bigger cars. Small cars accounted for 18% of the vehicles on the road, but accidents involving small cars led to 11,898 fatalities during a recent year (*Reader's Digest*, May 2000). Assume the probability a small car is involved in an accident is .18. The probability of an accident involving a small car leading to a fatality is .128 and the probability of an accident not involving a small car leading to a fatality is .05. Suppose you learn of an accident involving a fatality. What is the probability a small car was involved? Assume that the likelihood of getting into an accident is independent of car size.

44.   A city's professional basketball team plays at home, and its professional hockey team plays away on the same night. A professional basketball team has a .641 probability of winning a home game and a professional hockey team has a .462 probability of winning an away game. Historically, when both teams play on the same night, the chance that the next morning's leading sports story will be about the basketball game is 60% and the chance that it will be about the hockey game is 40%. Suppose that on the morning after these games the newspaper's leading sports story begins with the headline "We Win!!" What is the probability that the story is about the basketball team?

45.   In an article about investment growth, *Money* magazine reported that drug stocks show powerful long-term trends and offer investors unparalleled potential for strong and steady gains. The federal Health Care Financing Administration supports this conclusion through its forecast that annual prescription drug expenditures will reach $366 billion by 2010, up from $117 billion in 2000. Many individuals age 65 and older rely heavily on prescription drugs. For this group, 82% take prescription drugs regularly, 55% take three or more prescriptions regularly, and 40% currently use five or more prescriptions. In contrast, 49% of people under age 65 take prescriptions regularly, with 17% taking three or more prescriptions regularly and 28% using five or more prescriptions (*Money*, September 2001). The U.S. Census Bureau reports that of the 281,421,906 people in the United States, 34,991,753 are age 65 years and older (U.S. Census Bureau, *Census 2000*).
   a.   Compute the probability that a person in the United States is age 65 or older.
   b.   Compute the probability that a person takes prescription drugs regularly.
   c.   Compute the probability that a person is age 65 or older and takes five or more prescriptions.
   d.   Given a person uses five or more prescriptions, compute the probability that the person is age 65 or older.

## Summary

In this chapter we introduced basic probability concepts and illustrated how probability analysis can be used to provide helpful information for decision making. We described how probability can be interpreted as a numerical measure of the likelihood that an event will occur. In addition, we saw that the probability of an event can be computed either by summing the probabilities of the experimental outcomes (sample points) comprising the event or by using the relationships established by the addition, conditional probability, and multiplication laws of probability. For cases in which additional information is available, we showed how Bayes' theorem can be used to obtain revised or posterior probabilities.

## Glossary

**Probability** A numerical measure of the likelihood that an event will occur.
**Experiment** A process that generates well-defined outcomes.
**Sample space** The set of all experimental outcomes.
**Sample point** An element of the sample space. A sample point represents an experimental outcome.

**Tree diagram** A graphical representation that helps in visualizing a multiple-step experiment.

**Basic requirements for assigning probabilities** Two requirements that restrict the manner in which probability assignments can be made: (1) for each experimental outcome $E_i$ we must have $0 \leq P(E_i) \leq 1$; (2) considering all experimental outcomes, we must have $P(E_1) + P(E_2) + \cdots + P(E_n) = 1.0$.

**Classical method** A method of assigning probabilities that is appropriate when all the experimental outcomes are equally likely.

**Relative frequency method** A method of assigning probabilities that is appropriate when data are available to estimate the proportion of the time the experimental outcome will occur if the experiment is repeated a large number of times.

**Subjective method** A method of assigning probabilities on the basis of judgment.

**Event** A collection of sample points.

**Complement of $A$** The event consisting of all sample points that are not in $A$.

**Venn diagram** A graphical representation for showing symbolically the sample space and operations involving events in which the sample space is represented by a rectangle and events are represented as circles within the sample space.

**Union of $A$ and $B$** The event containing all sample points belonging to $A$ or $B$ or both. The union is denoted $A \cup B$.

**Intersection of $A$ and $B$** The event containing the sample points belonging to both $A$ and $B$. The intersection is denoted $A \cap B$.

**Addition law** A probability law used to compute the probability of the union of two events. It is $P(A \cup B) = P(A) + P(B) - P(A \cap B)$. For mutually exclusive events, $P(A \cap B) = 0$; in this case the addition law reduces to $P(A \cup B) = P(A) + P(B)$.

**Mutually exclusive events** Events that have no sample points in common; that is, $A \cap B$ is empty and $P(A \cap B) = 0$.

**Conditional probability** The probability of an event given that another event already occurred. The conditional probability of $A$ given $B$ is $P(A \mid B) = P(A \cap B)/P(B)$.

**Joint probability** The probability of two events both occurring; that is, the probability of the intersection of two events.

**Marginal probability** The values in the margins of a joint probability table that provide the probabilities of each event separately.

**Independent events** Two events $A$ and $B$ where $P(A \mid B) = P(A)$ or $P(B \mid A) = P(B)$; that is, the events have no influence on each other.

**Multiplication law** A probability law used to compute the probability of the intersection of two events. It is $P(A \cap B) = P(B)P(A \mid B)$ or $P(A \cap B) = P(A)P(B \mid A)$. For independent events it reduces to $P(A \cap B) = P(A)P(B)$.

**Prior probabilities** Initial estimates of the probabilities of events.

**Posterior probabilities** Revised probabilities of events based on additional information.

**Bayes' theorem** A method used to compute posterior probabilities.

## Key Formulas

**Counting Rule for Combinations**

$$C_n^N = \binom{N}{n} = \frac{N!}{n!(N-n)!} \tag{4.1}$$

**Counting Rule for Permutations**

$$P_n^N = n!\binom{N}{n} = \frac{N!}{(N-n)!} \tag{4.2}$$

Computing Probability Using the Complement

$$P(A) = 1 - P(A^c)$$
(4.5)

Addition Law

$$P(A \cup B) = P(A) + P(B) - P(A \cap B)$$
(4.6)

Conditional Probability

$$P(A \mid B) = \frac{P(A \cap B)}{P(B)}$$
(4.7)

$$P(B \mid A) = \frac{P(A \cap B)}{P(A)}$$
(4.8)

Multiplication Law

$$P(A \cap B) = P(B)P(A \mid B)$$
(4.11)

$$P(A \cap B) = P(A)P(B \mid A)$$
(4.12)

Multiplication Law for Independent Events

$$P(A \cap B) = P(A)P(B)$$
(4.13)

Bayes' Theorem

$$P(A_i \mid B) = \frac{P(A_i)P(B \mid A_i)}{P(A_1)P(B \mid A_1) + P(A_2)P(B \mid A_2) + \cdots + P(A_n)P(B \mid A_n)}$$
(4.19)

## Supplementary Exercises

46. In a *Business Week*/Harris Poll, 1035 adults were asked about their attitudes toward business (*Business Week*, September 11, 2000). One question asked: "How would you rate large U.S. companies on making good products and competing in a global environment?" The responses were: excellent—18%, pretty good—50%, only fair—26%, poor—5%, and don't know/no answer—1%.
    a. What is the probability that a respondent rated U.S. companies pretty good or excellent?
    b. How many respondents rated U.S. companies poor?
    c. How many respondents did not know or did not answer?

47. A financial manager made two new investments—one in the oil industry and one in municipal bonds. After a one-year period, each of the investments will be classified as either successful or unsuccessful. Consider the making of the two investments as an experiment.
    a. How many sample points exist for this experiment?
    b. Show a tree diagram and list the sample points.
    c. Let $O$ = the event that the oil industry investment is successful and $M$ = the event that the municipal bond investment is successful. List the sample points in $O$ and in $M$.
    d. List the sample points in the union of the events $(O \cup M)$.
    e. List the sample points in the intersection of the events $(O \cap M)$.
    f. Are events $O$ and $M$ mutually exclusive? Explain.

48. In early 2003, President Bush proposed eliminating the taxation of dividends to share-holders on the grounds that it was double taxation. Corporations pay taxes on the earnings that are later paid out in dividends. In a poll of 671 Americans, TechnoMetrica Market Intelligence found that 47% favored the proposal, 44% opposed it, and 9% were not sure (*Investor's Business Daily,* January 13, 2003). In looking at the responses across party lines the poll showed that 29% of Democrats were in favor, 64% of Republicans were in favor, and 48% of Independents were in favor.

    a. How many of those polled favored elimination of the tax on dividends?
    b. What is the conditional probability in favor of the proposal given the person polled is a Democrat?
    c. Is party affiliation independent of whether one is in favor of the proposal?
    d. If we assume people's responses were consistent with their own self-interest, which group do you believe will benefit most from passage of the proposal?

49. A study of 31,000 hospital admissions in New York State found that 4% of the admissions led to treatment-caused injuries. One-seventh of these treatment-caused injuries resulted in death, and one-fourth were caused by negligence. Malpractice claims were filed in one out of 7.5 cases involving negligence, and payments were made in one out of every two claims.

    a. What is the probability a person admitted to the hospital will suffer a treatment-caused injury due to negligence?
    b. What is the probability a person admitted to the hospital will die from a treatment-caused injury?
    c. In the case of a negligent treatment-caused injury, what is the probability a malpractice claim will be paid?

50. A telephone survey to determine viewer response to a new television show obtained the following data.

    | Rating | Frequency |
    |--------|-----------|
    | Poor | 4 |
    | Below average | 8 |
    | Average | 11 |
    | Above average | 14 |
    | Excellent | 13 |

    a. What is the probability that a randomly selected viewer will rate the new show as average or better?
    b. What is the probability that a randomly selected viewer will rate the new show below average or worse?

51. The following crosstabulation shows household income by educational level of the head of household for the year 2000 (*Statistical Abstract of the United States: 2002*).

| Education Level | Household Income ($1000s) | | | | | Total |
|---|---|---|---|---|---|---|
| | Under 24.9 | 25.0– 49.9 | 50.0– 74.9 | 75.0– 99.9 | 100 or more | |
| Not H.S. Graduate | 9,285 | 4,093 | 1,589 | 541 | 354 | 15,862 |
| H.S. Graduate | 10,150 | 9,821 | 6,050 | 2,737 | 2,028 | 30,786 |
| Some College | 6,011 | 8,221 | 5,813 | 3,215 | 3,120 | 26,380 |
| Bachelor's Degree | 2,138 | 3,985 | 3,952 | 2,698 | 4,748 | 17,521 |
| Beyond Bach. Deg. | 813 | 1,497 | 1,815 | 1,589 | 3,765 | 9,479 |
| Total | 28,397 | 27,617 | 19,219 | 10,780 | 14,015 | 100,028 |

a. Develop a joint probability table.
b. What is the probability of a head of household not being a high school graduate?
c. What is the probability of a head of household having a bachelor's degree or more education?
d. What is the probability of a household headed by someone with a bachelor's degree earning $100,000 or more?
e. What is the probability of a household having income below $25,000?
f. What is the probability of a household headed by someone with a bachelor's degree earning less than $25,000?
g. Is household income independent of educational level?

52. A GMAC MBA new-matriculants survey provided the following data for 2018 students.

|  |  | Applied to More Than One School | |
|---|---|---|---|
|  |  | Yes | No |
|  | **23 and under** | 207 | 201 |
|  | **24–26** | 299 | 379 |
| Age | **27–30** | 185 | 268 |
| Group | **31–35** | 66 | 193 |
|  | **36 and over** | 51 | 169 |

a. For a randomly selected MBA student, prepare a joint probability table for the experiment consisting of observing the student's age and whether the student applied to one or more schools.
b. What is the probability that a randomly selected applicant is 23 or under?
c. What is the probability that a randomly selected applicant is older than 26?
d. What is the probability that a randomly selected applicant applied to more than one school?

53. Refer again to the data from the GMAC new-matriculants survey in exercise 52.
a. Given that a person applied to more than one school, what is the probability that the person is 24–26 years old?
b. Given that a person is in the 36-and-over age group, what is the probability that the person applied to more than one school?
c. What is the probability that a person is 24–26 years old or applied to more than one school?
d. Suppose a person is known to have applied to only one school. What is the probability that the person is 31 or more years old?
e. Is the number of schools applied to independent of age? Explain.

54. An IBD/TIPP poll conducted to learn about attitudes toward investment and retirement (*Investor's Business Daily*, May 5, 2000) asked male and female respondents how important they felt level of of risk was in choosing a retirement investment. The following joint probability table was constructed from the data provided. "Important" means the respondent said level of risk was either important or very important.

|  | Male | Female | Total |
|---|---|---|---|
| **Important** | .22 | .27 | .49 |
| **Not Important** | .28 | .23 | .51 |
| Total | .50 | .50 | 1.00 |

a. What is the probability a survey respondent will say level of risk is important?
b. What is the probability a male respondent will say level of risk is important?
c. What is the probability a female respondent will say level of risk is important?
d. Is the level of risk independent of the gender of the respondent? Why or why not?
e. Do male and female attitudes toward risk differ?

55. A large consumer goods company ran a television advertisement for one of its soap products. On the basis of a survey that was conducted, probabilities were assigned to the following events.

$$B = \text{individual purchased the product}$$
$$S = \text{individual recalls seeing the advertisement}$$
$$B \cap S = \text{individual purchased the product and recalls seeing the advertisement}$$

The probabilities assigned were $P(B) = .20$, $P(S) = .40$, and $P(B \cap S) = .12$.
a. What is the probability of an individual's purchasing the product given that the individual recalls seeing the advertisement? Does seeing the advertisement increase the probability that the individual will purchase the product? As a decision maker, would you recommend continuing the advertisement (assuming that the cost is reasonable)?
b. Assume that individuals who do not purchase the company's soap product buy from its competitors. What would be your estimate of the company's market share? Would you expect that continuing the advertisement will increase the company's market share? Why or why not?
c. The company also tested another advertisement and assigned it values of $P(S) = .30$ and $P(B \cap S) = .10$. What is $P(B \mid S)$ for this other advertisement? Which advertisement seems to have had the bigger effect on customer purchases?

56. Cooper Realty is a small real estate company located in Albany, New York, specializing primarily in residential listings. They recently became interested in determining the likelihood of one of their listings being sold within a certain number of days. An analysis of company sales of 800 homes in previous years produced the following data.

|  | | Days Listed Until Sold | | | |
|---|---|---|---|---|---|
|  |  | Under 30 | 31–90 | Over 90 | Total |
| Initial Asking Price | Under $150,000 | 50 | 40 | 10 | 100 |
|  | $150,000–$199,999 | 20 | 150 | 80 | 250 |
|  | $200,000–$250,000 | 20 | 280 | 100 | 400 |
|  | Over $250,000 | 10 | 30 | 10 | 50 |
|  | Total | 100 | 500 | 200 | 800 |

a. If $A$ is defined as the event that a home is listed for more than 90 days before being sold, estimate the probability of $A$.
b. If $B$ is defined as the event that the initial asking price is under $150,000, estimate the probability of $B$.
c. What is the probability of $A \cap B$?
d. Assuming that a contract was just signed to list a home with an initial asking price of less than $150,000, what is the probability that the home will take Cooper Realty more than 90 days to sell?
e. Are events $A$ and $B$ independent?

57.  A company studied the number of lost-time accidents occurring at its Brownsville, Texas, plant. Historical records show that 6% of the employees suffered lost-time accidents last year. Management believes that a special safety program will reduce such accidents to 5% during the current year. In addition, it estimates that 15% of employees who had lost-time accidents last year will experience a lost-time accident during the current year.
   a.  What percentage of the employees will experience lost-time accidents in both years?
   b.  What percentage of the employees will suffer at least one lost-time accident over the two-year period?

58.  The Dallas IRS auditing staff, concerned with identifying potentially fraudulent tax returns, believes that the probability of finding a fraudulent return given that the return contains deductions for contributions exceeding the IRS standard is .20. Given that the deductions for contributions do not exceed the IRS standard, the probability of a fraudulent return decreases to .02. If 8% of all returns exceed the IRS standard for deductions due to contributions, what is the best estimate of the percentage of fraudulent returns?

59.  An oil company purchased an option on land in Alaska. Preliminary geologic studies assigned the following prior probabilities.

$$P(\text{high-quality oil}) = .50$$
$$P(\text{medium-quality oil}) = .20$$
$$P(\text{no oil}) = .30$$

   a.  What is the probability of finding oil?
   b.  After 200 feet of drilling on the first well, a soil test is taken. The probabilities of finding the particular type of soil identified by the test follow.

$$P(\text{soil} \mid \text{high-quality oil}) = .20$$
$$P(\text{soil} \mid \text{medium-quality oil}) = .80$$
$$P(\text{soil} \mid \text{no oil}) = .20$$

   How should the firm interpret the soil test? What are the revised probabilities, and what is the new probability of finding oil?

60.  Companies that do business over the Internet can often obtain probability information about Web site visitors from previous Web sites visited. An article, "Internet Marketing" (*Interfaces*, March–April 2001) described how clickstream data on Web sites visited could be used in conjunction with a Bayesian updating scheme to determine the gender of a Web site visitor. Par Fore created a Web site to market golf equipment and apparel. Management would like a certain offer to appear for female visitors and a different offer to appear for male visitors. From a sample of past Web site visits, management learned that 60% of the visitors to ParFore.com are male and 40% are female.
   a.  What is the prior probability that the next visitor to the Web site will be female?
   b.  Suppose you know that the current visitor previously visited the Dillard's Web site and that women are three times as likely to visit that Web site as men. What is the revised probability that the visitor is female? Should you display the offer that appeals more to female visitors or the one that appeals more to male visitors?

## Case Problem    Hamilton County Judges

Hamilton County judges try thousands of cases per year. In an overwhelming majority of the cases disposed, the verdict stands as rendered. However, some cases are appealed, and of those appealed, some of the cases are reversed. Kristen DelGuzzi of *The Cincinnati Enquirer* conducted a study of cases handled by Hamilton County judges over the years 1994 through 1996 (*The Cincinnati Enquirer*, January 11, 1998). Shown in Table 4.8 are

TABLE 4.8    TOTAL CASES DISPOSED, APPEALED, AND REVERSED IN HAMILTON
COUNTY COURTS DURING 1994 THROUGH 1996

**CD** file

**Judge**

### Common Pleas Court

| Judge | Total Cases Disposed | Appealed Cases | Reversed Cases |
|---|---|---|---|
| Fred Cartolano | 3,037 | 137 | 12 |
| Thomas Crush | 3,372 | 119 | 10 |
| Patrick Dinkelacker | 1,258 | 44 | 8 |
| Timothy Hogan | 1,954 | 60 | 7 |
| Robert Kraft | 3,138 | 127 | 7 |
| William Mathews | 2,264 | 91 | 18 |
| William Morrissey | 3,032 | 121 | 22 |
| Norbert Nadel | 2,959 | 131 | 20 |
| Arthur Ney, Jr. | 3,219 | 125 | 14 |
| Richard Niehaus | 3,353 | 137 | 16 |
| Thomas Nurre | 3,000 | 121 | 6 |
| John O'Connor | 2,969 | 129 | 12 |
| Robert Ruehlman | 3,205 | 145 | 18 |
| J. Howard Sundermann | 955 | 60 | 10 |
| Ann Marie Tracey | 3,141 | 127 | 13 |
| Ralph Winkler | 3,089 | 88 | 6 |
| Total | 43,945 | 1762 | 199 |

### Domestic Relations Court

| Judge | Total Cases Disposed | Appealed Cases | Reversed Cases |
|---|---|---|---|
| Penelope Cunningham | 2,729 | 7 | 1 |
| Patrick Dinkelacker | 6,001 | 19 | 4 |
| Deborah Gaines | 8,799 | 48 | 9 |
| Ronald Panioto | 12,970 | 32 | 3 |
| Total | 30,499 | 106 | 17 |

### Municipal Court

| Judge | Total Cases Disposed | Appealed Cases | Reversed Cases |
|---|---|---|---|
| Mike Allen | 6,149 | 43 | 4 |
| Nadine Allen | 7,812 | 34 | 6 |
| Timothy Black | 7,954 | 41 | 6 |
| David Davis | 7,736 | 43 | 5 |
| Leslie Isaiah Gaines | 5,282 | 35 | 13 |
| Karla Grady | 5,253 | 6 | 0 |
| Deidra Hair | 2,532 | 5 | 0 |
| Dennis Helmick | 7,900 | 29 | 5 |
| Timothy Hogan | 2,308 | 13 | 2 |
| James Patrick Kenney | 2,798 | 6 | 1 |
| Joseph Luebbers | 4,698 | 25 | 8 |
| William Mallory | 8,277 | 38 | 9 |
| Melba Marsh | 8,219 | 34 | 7 |
| Beth Mattingly | 2,971 | 13 | 1 |
| Albert Mestemaker | 4,975 | 28 | 9 |
| Mark Painter | 2,239 | 7 | 3 |
| Jack Rosen | 7,790 | 41 | 13 |
| Mark Schweikert | 5,403 | 33 | 6 |
| David Stockdale | 5,371 | 22 | 4 |
| John A. West | 2,797 | 4 | 2 |
| Total | 108,464 | 500 | 104 |

the results for 182,908 cases handled (disposed) by 38 judges in Common Pleas Court, Domestic Relations Court, and Municipal Court. Two of the judges (Dinkelacker and Hogan) did not serve in the same court for the entire three-year period.

The purpose of the newspaper's study was to evaluate the performance of the judges. Appeals are often the result of mistakes made by judges, and the newspaper wanted to know which judges were doing a good job and which were making too many mistakes. You are called in to assist in the data analysis. Use your knowledge of probability and conditional probability to help with the ranking of the judges. You also may be able to analyze the likelihood of appeal and reversal for cases handled by different courts.

## Managerial Report

Prepare a report with your rankings of the judges. Also, include an analysis of the likelihood of appeal and case reversal in the three courts. At a minimum, your report should include the following:

1. The probability of cases being appealed and reversed in the three different courts.
2. The probability of a case being appealed for each judge.
3. The probability of a case being reversed for each judge.
4. The probability of reversal given an appeal for each judge.
5. Rank the judges within each court. State the criteria you used and provide a rationale for your choice.

# Discrete Probability Distributions

## CONTENTS

STATISTICS IN PRACTICE:
CITIBANK

## CITIBANK*
### LONG ISLAND CITY, NEW YORK

Citibank, a division of Citigroup, makes available a wide range of financial services, including checking and savings accounts, loans and mortgages, insurance, and investment services, within the framework of a unique strategy for delivering those services called Citibanking. Citibanking entails a consistent brand identity all over the world, consistent product offerings, and high-level customer service. Citibanking lets you manage your money anytime, anywhere, anyway you choose. Whether you need to save for the future or borrow for today, you can do it all at Citibank.

Citibanking's state-of-the-art automatic teller machines (ATMs) located in Citicard Banking Centers (CBCs), let customers do all their banking in one place with the touch of a finger, 24 hours a day, 7 days a week. More than 150 different banking functions from deposits to managing investments can be performed with ease. Citibanking ATMs are so much more than just cash machines that customers today use them for 80% of their transactions.

Each Citibank CBC operates as a waiting line system with randomly arriving customers seeking service at one of the ATMs. If all ATMs are busy, the arriving customers wait in line. Periodic CBC capacity studies are used to analyze customer waiting times and to determine whether additional ATMs are needed.

Data collected by Citibank showed that the random customer arrivals followed a probability distribution known as the Poisson distribution. Using the Poisson distribution, Citibank can compute probabilities for the number of customers arriving at a CBC during any time period and make decisions concern-

A Citibank ATM in Manhattan © PhotoDisc/Getty Images.

ing the number of ATMs needed. For example, let $x$ = the number of customers arriving during a one-minute period. Assuming that a particular CBC has a mean arrival rate of two customers per minute, the following table shows the probabilities for the number of customers arriving during a one-minute period.

| x | Probability |
|---|-------------|
| 0 | .1353 |
| 1 | .2707 |
| 2 | .2707 |
| 3 | .1804 |
| 4 | .0902 |
| 5 or more | .0527 |

Discrete probability distributions, such as the one used by Citibank, are the topic of this chapter. In addition to the Poisson distribution, you will learn about the binomial and hypergeometric distributions and how they can be used to provide helpful probability information.

---

*The authors are indebted to Ms. Stacey Karter, Citibank, for providing this Statistics in Practice.

In this chapter we continue the study of probability by introducing the concepts of random variables and probability distributions. The focus of this chapter is discrete probability distributions. Three special discrete probability distributions—the binomial, Poisson, and hypergeometric—are covered.

## 5.1 Random Variables

In Chapter 4 we defined the concept of an experiment and its associated experimental outcomes. A random variable provides a means for describing experimental outcomes using numerical values. Random variables must assume numerical values.

> RANDOM VARIABLE

*Random variables must*
*assume numerical values.*

> A **random variable** is a numerical description of the outcome of an experiment.

In effect, a random variable associates a numerical value with each possible experimental outcome. The particular numerical value of the random variable depends on the outcome of the experiment. A random variable can be classified as being either *discrete* or *continuous* depending on the numerical values it assumes.

## Discrete Random Variables

A random variable that may assume either a finite number of values or an infinite sequence of values such as 0, 1, 2, . . . is referred to as a **discrete random variable**. For example, consider the experiment of an accountant taking the certified public accountant (CPA) examination. The examination has four parts. We can define a random variable as $x$ = the number of parts of the CPA examination passed. It is a discrete random variable because it may assume the finite number of values 0, 1, 2, 3, or 4.

As another example of a discrete random variable, consider the experiment of cars arriving at a tollbooth. The random variable of interest is $x$ = the number of cars arriving during a one-day period. The possible values for $x$ come from the sequence of integers 0, 1, 2, and so on. Hence, $x$ is a discrete random variable assuming one of the values in this infinite sequence.

Although the outcomes of many experiments can naturally be described by numerical values, others cannot. For example, a survey question might ask an individual to recall the message in a recent television commercial. This experiment would have two possible outcomes: the individual cannot recall the message and the individual can recall the message. We can still describe these experimental outcomes numerically by defining the discrete random variable $x$ as follows: let $x$ = 0 if the individual cannot recall the message and $x$ = 1 if the individual can recall the message. The numerical values for this random variable are arbitrary (we could use 5 and 10), but they are acceptable in terms of the definition of a random variable—namely, $x$ is a random variable because it provides a numerical description of the outcome of the experiment.

Table 5.1 provides some additional examples of discrete random variables. Note that in each example the discrete random variable assumes a finite number of values or an infinite sequence of values such as 0, 1, 2, . . . . These types of discrete random variables are discussed in detail in this chapter.

**TABLE 5.1**   EXAMPLES OF DISCRETE RANDOM VARIABLES

| Experiment | Random Variable ($x$) | Possible Values for the Random Variable |
|---|---|---|
| Contact five customers | Number of customers who place an order | 0, 1, 2, 3, 4, 5 |
| Inspect a shipment of 50 radios | Number of defective radios | 0, 1, 2, $\cdots$, 49, 50 |
| Operate a restaurant for one day | Number of customers | 0, 1, 2, 3, $\cdots$ |
| Sell an automobile | Gender of the customer | 0 if male; 1 if female |

## Continuous Random Variables

A random variable that may assume any numerical value in an interval or collection of intervals is called a **continuous random variable**. Experimental outcomes based on measurement scales such as time, weight, distance, and temperature can be described by continuous random variables. For example, consider an experiment of monitoring incoming telephone calls to the claims office of a major insurance company. Suppose the random variable of interest is $x =$ the time between consecutive incoming calls in minutes. This random variable may assume any value in the interval $x \geq 0$. Actually, an infinite number of values are possible for $x$, including values such as 1.26 minutes, 2.751 minutes, 4.3333 minutes, and so on. As another example, consider a 90-mile section of interstate highway I-75 north of Atlanta, Georgia. For an emergency ambulance service located in Atlanta, we might define the random variable as $x =$ number of miles to the location of the next traffic accident along this section of I-75. In this case, $x$ would be a continuous random variable assuming any value in the interval $0 \leq x \leq 90$. Additional examples of continuous random variables are listed in Table 5.2. Note that each example describes a random variable that may assume any value in an interval of values. Continuous random variables and their probability distributions will be the topic of Chapter 6.

**TABLE 5.2   EXAMPLES OF CONTINUOUS RANDOM VARIABLES**

| Experiment | Random Variable ($x$) | Possible Values for the Random Variable |
|---|---|---|
| Operate a bank | Time between customer arrivals in minutes | $x \geq 0$ |
| Fill a soft drink can (max = 12.1 ounces) | Number of ounces | $0 \leq x \leq 12.1$ |
| Construct a new library | Percentage of project complete after six months | $0 \leq x \leq 100$ |
| Test a new chemical process | Temperature when the desired reaction takes place (min 150° F; max 212° F) | $150 \leq x \leq 212$ |

### NOTES AND COMMENTS

One way to determine whether a random variable is discrete or continuous is to think of the values of the random variable as points on a line segment. Choose two points representing values of the random variable. If the entire line segment between the two points also represents possible values for the random variable, then the random variable is continuous.

### Exercises

#### Methods

1. Consider the experiment of tossing a coin twice.
   a. List the experimental outcomes.
   b. Define a random variable that represents the number of heads occurring on the two tosses.
   c. Show what value the random variable would assume for each of the experimental outcomes.
   d. Is this random variable discrete or continuous?

2.  Consider the experiment of a worker assembling a product.
    a.  Define a random variable that represents the time in minutes required to assemble the product.
    b.  What values may the random variable assume?
    c.  Is the random variable discrete or continuous?

## Applications

3.  Three students scheduled interviews for summer employment at the Brookwood Institute. In each case the interview results in either an offer for a position or no offer. Experimental outcomes are defined in terms of the results of the three interviews.
    a.  List the experimental outcomes.
    b.  Define a random variable that represents the number of offers made. Is the random variable continuous?
    c.  Show the value of the random variable for each of the experimental outcomes.

4.  Suppose we know home mortgage rates for 12 Florida lending institutions. Assume that the random variable of interest is the number of lending institutions in this group that offers a 30-year fixed rate of 8.5% or less. What values may this random variable assume?

5.  To perform a certain type of blood analysis, lab technicians must perform two procedures. The first procedure requires either 1 or 2 separate steps, and the second procedure requires either 1, 2, or 3 steps.
    a.  List the experimental outcomes associated with performing the blood analysis.
    b.  If the random variable of interest is the total number of steps required to do the complete analysis (both procedures), show what value the random variable will assume for each of the experimental outcomes.

6.  Listed is a series of experiments and associated random variables. In each case, identify the values that the random variable can assume and state whether the random variable is discrete or continuous.

| **Experiment** | **Random Variable ($x$)** |
| --- | --- |
| a. Take a 20-question examination | Number of questions answered correctly |
| b. Observe cars arriving at a tollbooth for 1 hour | Number of cars arriving at tollbooth |
| c. Audit 50 tax returns | Number of returns containing errors |
| d. Observe an employee's work | Number of nonproductive hours in an 8-hour workday |
| e. Weigh a shipment of goods | Number of pounds |

## 5.2  Discrete Probability Distributions

The **probability distribution** for a random variable describes how probabilities are distributed over the values of the random variable. For a discrete random variable $x$, the probability distribution is defined by a **probability function**, denoted by $f(x)$. The probability function provides the probability for each value of the random variable.

As an illustration of a discrete random variable and its probability distribution, consider the sales of automobiles at DiCarlo Motors in Saratoga, New York. Over the past 300 days of operation, sales data show 54 days with no automobiles sold, 117 days with 1 automobile sold, 72 days with 2 automobiles sold, 42 days with 3 automobiles sold, 12 days with 4 automobiles sold, and 3 days with 5 automobiles sold. Suppose we consider the experiment of selecting a day of operation at DiCarlo Motors and define the random variable of interest as $x$ = the number of automobiles sold during a day. From historical data, we know

$x$ is a discrete random variable that can assume the values 0, 1, 2, 3, 4, or 5. In probability function notation, $f(0)$ provides the probability of 0 automobiles sold, $f(1)$ provides the probability of 1 automobile sold, and so on. Because historical data show 54 of 300 days with 0 automobiles sold, we assign the value $54/300 = .18$ to $f(0)$, indicating that the probability of 0 automobiles being sold during a day is .18. Similarly, because 117 of 300 days had 1 automobile sold, we assign the value $117/300 = .39$ to $f(1)$, indicating that the probability of exactly 1 automobile being sold during a day is .39. Continuing in this way for the other values of the random variable, we compute the values for $f(2), f(3), f(4)$, and $f(5)$ as shown in Table 5.3, the probability distribution for the number of automobiles sold during a day at DiCarlo Motors.

A primary advantage of defining a random variable and its probability distribution is that once the probability distribution is known, it is relatively easy to determine the probability of a variety of events that may be of interest to a decision maker. For example, using the probability distribution for DiCarlo Motors as shown in Table 5.3, we see that the most probable number of automobiles sold during a day is 1 with a probability of $f(1) = .39$. In addition, there is an $f(3) + f(4) + f(5) = .14 + .04 + .01 = .19$ probability of selling 3 or more automobiles during a day. These probabilities, plus others the decision maker may ask about, provide information that can help the decision maker understand the process of selling automobiles at DiCarlo Motors.

In the development of a probability function for any discrete random variable, the following two conditions must be satisfied.

*These conditions are the analogs to the two basic requirements for assigning probabilities to experimental outcomes presented in Chapter 4.*

**REQUIRED CONDITIONS FOR A DISCRETE PROBABILITY FUNCTION**

$$f(x) \geq 0 \tag{5.1}$$
$$\Sigma f(x) = 1 \tag{5.2}$$

Table 5.3 shows that the probabilities for the random variable $x$ satisfy equation (5.1); $f(x)$ is greater than or equal to 0 for all values of $x$. In addition, because the probabilities sum to 1, equation (5.2) is satisfied. Thus, the DiCarlo Motors probability function is a valid discrete probability function.

We can also present probability distributions graphically. In Figure 5.1 the values of the random variable $x$ for DiCarlo Motors are shown on the horizontal axis and the probability associated with these values is shown on the vertical axis.

In addition to tables and graphs, a formula that gives the probability function, $f(x)$, for every value of $x$ is often used to describe probability distributions. The simplest example of

**TABLE 5.3   PROBABILITY DISTRIBUTION FOR THE NUMBER OF AUTOMOBILES SOLD DURING A DAY AT DICARLO MOTORS**

| $x$ | $f(x)$ |
|-----|--------|
| 0 | .18 |
| 1 | .39 |
| 2 | .24 |
| 3 | .14 |
| 4 | .04 |
| 5 | .01 |
| Total | 1.00 |

FIGURE 5.1    GRAPHICAL REPRESENTATION OF THE PROBABILITY DISTRIBUTION
FOR THE NUMBER OF AUTOMOBILES SOLD DURING A DAY AT
DICARLO MOTORS

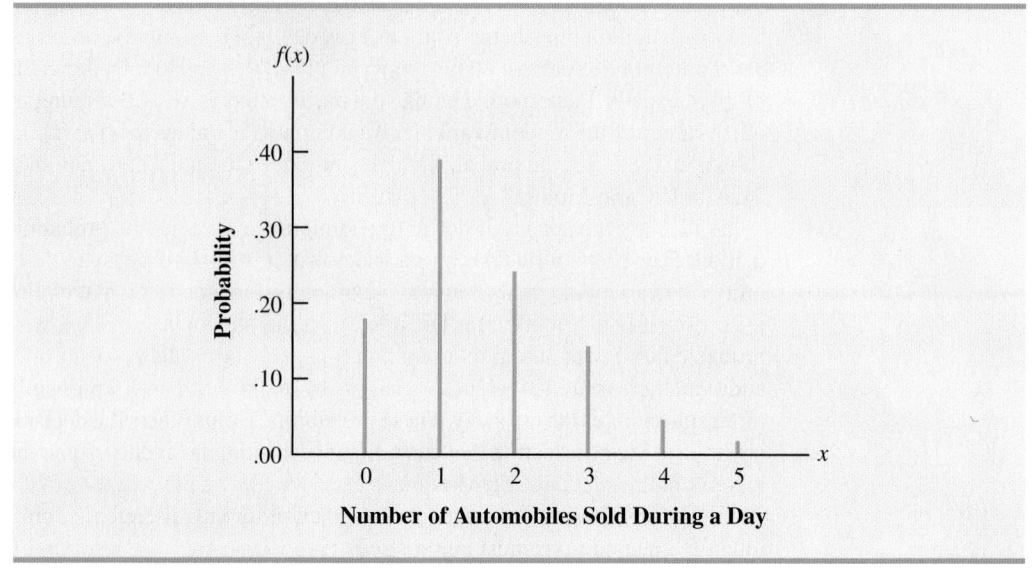

a discrete probability distribution given by a formula is the **discrete uniform probability distribution**. Its probability function is defined by equation (5.3).

DISCRETE UNIFORM PROBABILITY FUNCTION

$$f(x) = 1/n \qquad (5.3)$$

where

$$n = \text{the number of values the random variable may assume}$$

For example, suppose that for the experiment of rolling a die we define the random variable $x$ to be the number of dots on the upward face. There are $n = 6$ possible values for the random variable; $x = 1, 2, 3, 4, 5, 6$. Thus, the probability function for this discrete uniform random variable is

$$f(x) = 1/6 \qquad x = 1, 2, 3, 4, 5, 6$$

The possible values of the random variable and the associated probabilities are shown.

| $x$ | $f(x)$ |
|---|---|
| 1 | 1/6 |
| 2 | 1/6 |
| 3 | 1/6 |
| 4 | 1/6 |
| 5 | 1/6 |
| 6 | 1/6 |

As another example, consider the random variable $x$ with the following discrete probability distribution.

| $x$ | $f(x)$ |
|-----|--------|
| 1   | 1/10   |
| 2   | 2/10   |
| 3   | 3/10   |
| 4   | 4/10   |

This probability distribution can be defined by the formula

$$f(x) = \frac{x}{10} \quad \text{for } x = 1, 2, 3, \text{ or } 4$$

Evaluating $f(x)$ for a given value of the random variable will provide the associated probability. For example, using the preceding probability function, we see that $f(2) = 2/10$ provides the probability that the random variable assumes a value of 2.

The more widely used discrete probability distributions generally are specified by formulas. Three important cases are the binomial, Poisson, and hypergeometric distributions; these are discussed later in the chapter.

## Exercises

### Methods

7.   The probability distribution for the random variable $x$ follows.

| $x$ | $f(x)$ |
|-----|--------|
| 20  | .20    |
| 25  | .15    |
| 30  | .25    |
| 35  | .40    |

   a.   Is this probability distribution valid? Explain.
   b.   What is the probability that $x = 30$?
   c.   What is the probability that $x$ is less than or equal to 25?
   d.   What is the probability that $x$ is greater than 30?

### Applications

8.   The following data were collected by counting the number of operating rooms in use at Tampa General Hospital over a 20-day period: On 3 of the days only 1 operating room was used, on 5 of the days 2 were used, on 8 of the days 3 were used, and on 4 days all 4 of the hospital's operating rooms were used.
   a.   Use the relative frequency approach to construct a probability distribution for the number of operating rooms in use on any given day.
   b.   Draw a graph of the probability distribution.
   c.   Show that your probability distribution satisfies the required conditions for a valid discrete probability distribution.

9. Nationally, 38% of fourth-graders cannot read an age-appropriate book. The following data show the number of children, by age, identified as learning disabled under special education. Most of these children have reading problems that should be identified and corrected before third grade. Current federal law prohibits most children from receiving extra help from special education programs until they fall behind by approximately two years' worth of learning, and that typically means third grade or later (*USA Today*, September 6, 2001).

| Age | Number of Children |
|-----|--------------------|
| 6 | 37,369 |
| 7 | 87,436 |
| 8 | 160,840 |
| 9 | 239,719 |
| 10 | 286,719 |
| 11 | 306,533 |
| 12 | 310,787 |
| 13 | 302,604 |
| 14 | 289,168 |

Suppose that we want to select a sample of children identified as learning disabled under special education for a special program designed to improve reading ability. Let $x$ be a random variable indicating the age of one randomly selected child.

a. Use the data to develop a probability distribution for $x$. Specify the values for the random variable and the corresponding values for the probability function $f(x)$.
b. Draw a graph of the probability distribution.
c. Show that the probability distribution satisfies equations (5.1) and (5.2).

10. Table 5.4 shows the percent frequency distributions of job satisfaction scores for a sample of information systems (IS) senior executives and IS middle managers (*Computerworld*, May 26, 1997). The scores range from a low of 1 (very dissatisfied) to a high of 5 (very satisfied).

TABLE 5.4    PERCENT FREQUENCY DISTRIBUTION OF JOB SATISFACTION SCORES FOR INFORMATION SYSTEMS EXECUTIVES AND MIDDLE MANAGERS

| Job Satisfaction Score | IS Senior Executives (%) | IS Middle Managers (%) |
|---|---|---|
| 1 | 5 | 4 |
| 2 | 9 | 10 |
| 3 | 3 | 12 |
| 4 | 42 | 46 |
| 5 | 41 | 28 |

a. Develop a probability distribution for the job satisfaction score of a senior executive.
b. Develop a probability distribution for the job satisfaction score of a middle manager.
c. What is the probability a senior executive will report a job satisfaction score of 4 or 5?
d. What is the probability a middle manager is very satisfied?
e. Compare the overall job satisfaction of senior executives and middle managers.

11. A technician services mailing machines at companies in the Phoenix area. Depending on the type of malfunction, the service call can take 1, 2, 3, or 4 hours. The different types of malfunctions occur at about the same frequency.

a. Develop a probability distribution for the duration of a service call.
b. Draw a graph of the probability distribution.
c. Show that your probability distribution satisfies the conditions required for a discrete probability function.
d. What is the probability a service call will take 3 hours?
e. A service call has just come in, but the type of malfunction is unknown. It is 3:00 P.M. and service technicians usually get off at 5:00 P.M. What is the probability the service technician will have to work overtime to fix the machine today?

12. The director of admissions at Lakeville Community College subjectively assessed a probability distribution for $x$, the number of entering students, as follows.

| $x$ | $f(x)$ |
|------|--------|
| 1000 | .15 |
| 1100 | .20 |
| 1200 | .30 |
| 1300 | .25 |
| 1400 | .10 |

a. Is this probability distribution valid? Explain.
b. What is the probability of 1200 or fewer entering students?

13. A psychologist determined that the number of sessions required to obtain the trust of a new patient is either 1, 2, or 3. Let $x$ be a random variable indicating the number of sessions required to gain the patient's trust. The following probability function has been proposed.

$$f(x) = \frac{x}{6} \quad \text{for } x = 1, 2, \text{ or } 3$$

a. Is this probability function valid? Explain.
b. What is the probability that it takes exactly 2 sessions to gain the patient's trust?
c. What is the probability that it takes at least 2 sessions to gain the patient's trust?

14. The following table is a partial probability distribution for the MRA Company's projected profits ($x$ = profit in $1000s) for the first year of operation (the negative value denotes a loss).

| $x$ | $f(x)$ |
|------|--------|
| −100 | .10 |
| 0 | .20 |
| 50 | .30 |
| 100 | .25 |
| 150 | .10 |
| 20 | |

a. What is the proper value for $f(200)$? What is your interpretation of this value?
b. What is the probability that MRA will be profitable?
c. What is the probability that MRA will make at least $100,000?

## 5.3 Expected Value and Variance

### Expected Value

The **expected value**, or mean, of a random variable is a measure of the central location for the random variable. The formula for the expected value of a discrete random variable $x$ follows.

*The expected value is a weighted average of the values the random variable may assume. The weights are the probabilities.*

> **EXPECTED VALUE OF A DISCRETE RANDOM VARIABLE**
>
> $$E(x) = \mu = \Sigma x f(x) \tag{5.4}$$

Both the notations $E(x)$ and $\mu$ are used to denote the expected value of a random variable.

Equation (5.4) shows that to compute the expected value of a discrete random variable, we must multiply each value of the random variable by the corresponding probability $f(x)$ and then add the resulting products. Using the DiCarlo Motors automobile sales example from Section 5.2, we show the calculation of the expected value for the number of automobiles sold during a day in Table 5.5. The sum of the entries in the $xf(x)$ column shows that the expected value is 1.50 automobiles per day. We therefore know that although sales of 0, 1, 2, 3, 4, or 5 automobiles are possible on any one day, over time DiCarlo can anticipate selling an average of 1.50 automobiles per day. Assuming 30 days of operation during a month, we can use the expected value of 1.50 to forecast average monthly sales of $30(1.50) = 45$ automobiles.

*The expected value does not have to be a value the random variable can assume.*

### Variance

Even though the expected value provides the mean value for the random variable, we often need a measure of variability, or dispersion. Just as we used the variance in Chapter 3 to summarize the variability in data, we now use **variance** to summarize the variability in the values of a random variable. The formula for the variance of a discrete random variable follows.

*The variance is a weighted average of the squared deviations of a random variable from its mean. The weights are the probabilities.*

> **VARIANCE OF A DISCRETE RANDOM VARIABLE**
>
> $$\text{Var}(x) = \sigma^2 = \Sigma(x - \mu)^2 f(x) \tag{5.5}$$

**TABLE 5.5**  CALCULATION OF THE EXPECTED VALUE FOR THE NUMBER OF AUTOMOBILES SOLD DURING A DAY AT DICARLO MOTORS

| $x$ | $f(x)$ | $xf(x)$ |
|-----|--------|---------|
| 0 | .18 | $0(.18) =$ .00 |
| 1 | .39 | $1(.39) =$ .39 |
| 2 | .24 | $2(.24) =$ .48 |
| 3 | .14 | $3(.14) =$ .42 |
| 4 | .04 | $4(.04) =$ .16 |
| 5 | .01 | $5(.01) =$ .05 |
|   |   | 1.50 |

$$E(x) = \mu = \Sigma x f(x)$$

**TABLE 5.6    CALCULATION OF THE VARIANCE FOR THE NUMBER OF AUTOMOBILES SOLD DURING A DAY AT DICARLO MOTORS**

| $x$ | $x - \mu$ | $(x - \mu)^2$ | $f(x)$ | $(x - \mu)^2 f(x)$ |
|---|---|---|---|---|
| 0 | $0 - 1.50 = -1.50$ | 2.25 | .18 | $2.25(.18) = .4050$ |
| 1 | $1 - 1.50 = -.50$ | .25 | .39 | $.25(.39) = .0975$ |
| 2 | $2 - 1.50 = .50$ | .25 | .24 | $.25(.24) = .0600$ |
| 3 | $3 - 1.50 = 1.50$ | 2.25 | .14 | $2.25(.14) = .3150$ |
| 4 | $4 - 1.50 = 2.50$ | 6.25 | .04 | $6.25(.04) = .2500$ |
| 5 | $5 - 1.50 = 3.50$ | 12.25 | .01 | $12.25(.01) = .1225$ |
| | | | | 1.2500 |

$$\sigma^2 = \Sigma(x - \mu)^2 f(x)$$

As equation (5.5) shows, an essential part of the variance formula is the deviation, $x - \mu$, which measures how far a particular value of the random variable is from the expected value, or mean, $\mu$. In computing the variance of a random variable, the deviations are squared and then weighted by the corresponding value of the probability function. The sum of these weighted squared deviations for all values of the random variable is referred to as the *variance*. The notations Var($x$) and $\sigma^2$ are both used to denote the variance of a random variable.

The calculation of the variance for the probability distribution of the number of automobiles sold during a day at DiCarlo Motors is summarized in Table 5.6. We see that the variance is 1.25. The **standard deviation**, $\sigma$, is defined as the positive square root of the variance. Thus, the standard deviation for the number of automobiles sold during a day is

$$\sigma = \sqrt{1.25} = 1.118$$

The standard deviation is measured in the same units as the random variable ($\sigma = 1.118$ automobiles) and therefore is often preferred in describing the variability of a random variable. The variance $\sigma^2$ is measured in squared units and is thus more difficult to interpret.

## Exercises

### Methods

15. The following table provides a probability distribution for the random variable $x$.

| $x$ | $f(x)$ |
|---|---|
| 3 | .25 |
| 6 | .50 |
| 9 | .25 |

    a.   Compute $E(x)$, the expected value of $x$.
    b.   Compute $\sigma^2$, the variance of $x$.
    c.   Compute $\sigma$, the standard deviation of $x$.

16. The following table provides a probability distribution for the random variable $y$.

| $y$ | $f(y)$ |
|-----|--------|
| 2 | .20 |
| 4 | .30 |
| 7 | .40 |
| 8 | .10 |

a. Compute $E(y)$.
b. Compute $\text{Var}(y)$ and $\sigma$.

## Applications

17. A volunteer ambulance service handles 0 to 5 service calls on any given day. The probability distribution for the number of service calls is as follows.

| Number of Service Calls | Probability |
|-------------------------|-------------|
| 0 | .10 |
| 1 | .15 |
| 2 | .30 |
| 3 | .20 |
| 4 | .15 |
| 5 | .10 |

a. What is the expected number of service calls?
b. What is the variance in the number of service calls? What is the standard deviation?

18. The American Housing Survey reported the following data on the number of bedrooms in owner-occupied and renter-occupied houses in central cities (www.census.gov, March 31, 2003).

| | Number of Houses (1000s) | |
|---|---|---|
| Bedrooms | Renter-Occupied | Owner-Occupied |
| 0 | 547 | 23 |
| 1 | 5012 | 541 |
| 2 | 6100 | 3832 |
| 3 | 2644 | 8690 |
| 4 or more | 557 | 3783 |

a. Define a random variable $x$ = number of bedrooms in renter-occupied houses and develop a probability distribution for the random variable. (Let $x = 4$ represent 4 or more bedrooms.)
b. Compute the expected value and variance for the number of bedrooms in renter-occupied houses.
c. Define a random variable $y$ = number of bedrooms in owner-occupied houses and develop a probability distribution for the random variable. (Let $y = 4$ represent 4 or more bedrooms.)
d. Compute the expected value and variance for the number of bedrooms in owner-occupied houses.
e. What observations can you make from a comparison of the number of bedrooms in renter-occupied versus owner-occupied homes?

19. The actual shooting records of four basketball teams showed the probability of making a 2-point basket was .50 and the probability of making a 3-point basket was .39.
    a. What is the expected value of a 2-point shot for these teams?
    b. What is the expected value of a 3-point shot for these teams?
    c. If the probability of making a 2-point basket is greater than the probability of making a 3-point basket, why do coaches allow some players to shoot the 3-point shot if they have the opportunity? Use expected value to explain your answer.

20. The probability distribution for damage claims paid by the Newton Automobile Insurance Company on collision insurance follows.

| Payment ($) | Probability |
|---|---|
| 0 | .90 |
| 400 | .04 |
| 1000 | .03 |
| 2000 | .01 |
| 4000 | .01 |
| 6000 | .01 |

   a. Use the expected collision payment to determine the collision insurance premium that would enable the company to break even.
   b. The insurance company charges an annual rate of $260 for the collision coverage. What is the expected value of the collision policy for a policyholder? (*Hint:* It is the expected payments from the company minus the cost of coverage.) Why does the policyholder purchase a collision policy with this expected value?

21. The following probability distributions of job satisfaction scores for a sample of information systems (IS) senior executives and IS middle managers range from a low of 1 (very dissatisfied) to a high of 5 (very satisfied) (*Computerworld,* May 26, 1997).

| | Probability | |
| Job Satisfaction Score | IS Senior Executives | IS Middle Managers |
|---|---|---|
| 1 | .05 | .04 |
| 2 | .09 | .10 |
| 3 | .03 | .12 |
| 4 | .42 | .46 |
| 5 | .41 | .28 |

   a. What is the expected value of the job satisfaction score for senior executives?
   b. What is the expected value of the job satisfaction score for middle managers?
   c. Compute the variance of job satisfaction scores for executives and middle managers.
   d. Compute the standard deviation of job satisfaction scores for both probability distributions.
   e. Compare the overall job satisfaction of senior executives and middle managers.

22. The demand for a product of Carolina Industries varies greatly from month to month. The probability distribution in the following table, based on the past two years of data, shows the company's monthly demand.

| Unit Demand | Probability |
|---|---|
| 300 | .20 |
| 400 | .30 |
| 500 | .35 |
| 600 | .15 |

a. If the company bases monthly orders on the expected value of the monthly demand, what should Carolina's monthly order quantity be for this product?
b. Assume that each unit demanded generates $70 in revenue and that each unit ordered costs $50. How much will the company gain or lose in a month if it places an order based on your answer to part (a) and the actual demand for the item is 300 units?

23. According to a survey, 95% of subscribers to *The Wall Street Journal Interactive Edition* have a computer at home. For those households, the probability distributions for the number of laptop and desktop computers are given (*The Wall Street Journal Interactive Edition Subscriber Study,* 1999).

| | Probability | |
| Number of Computers | Laptop | Desktop |
| --- | --- | --- |
| 0 | .47 | .06 |
| 1 | .45 | .56 |
| 2 | .06 | .28 |
| 3 | .02 | .10 |

a. What is the expected value of the number of computers per household for each type of computer?
b. What is the variance of the number of computers per household for each type of computer?
c. Make some comparisons between the number of laptops and the number of desktops owned by the *Journal*'s subscribers.

24. The J. R. Ryland Computer Company is considering a plant expansion that will enable the company to begin production of a new computer product. The company's president must determine whether to make the expansion a medium- or large-scale project. An uncertainty is the demand for the new product, which for planning purposes may be low demand, medium demand, or high demand. The probability estimates for demand are .20, .50, and .30, respectively. Letting $x$ and $y$ indicate the annual profit in thousands of dollars, the firm's planners developed the following profit forecasts for the medium- and large-scale expansion projects.

| | | Medium-Scale Expansion Profit | | Large-Scale Expansion Profit | |
| --- | --- | --- | --- | --- | --- |
| | | $x$ | $f(x)$ | $y$ | $f(y)$ |
| Demand | Low | 50 | .20 | 0 | .20 |
| | Medium | 150 | .50 | 100 | .50 |
| | High | 200 | .30 | 300 | .30 |

a. Compute the expected value for the profit associated with the two expansion alternatives. Which decision is preferred for the objective of maximizing the expected profit?
b. Compute the variance for the profit associated with the two expansion alternatives. Which decision is preferred for the objective of minimizing the risk or uncertainty?

## 5.4 Binomial Probability Distribution

The binomial probability distribution is a discrete probability distribution that provides many applications. It is associated with a multiple-step experiment that we call the binomial experiment.

## A Binomial Experiment

A **binomial experiment** exhibits the following four properties.

---

PROPERTIES OF A BINOMIAL EXPERIMENT

1. The experiment consists of a sequence of $n$ identical trials.
2. Two outcomes are possible on each trial. We refer to one outcome as a *success* and the other outcome as a *failure*.
3. The probability of a success, denoted by $p$, does not change from trial to trial. Consequently, the probability of a failure, denoted by $1 - p$, does not change from trial to trial.
4. The trials are independent.

---

*Jakob Bernoulli (1654–1705), the first of the Bernoulli family of Swiss mathematicians, published a treatise on probability that contained the theory of permutations and combinations, as well as the binomial theorem.*

If properties 2, 3, and 4 are present, we say the trials are generated by a Bernoulli process. If, in addition, property 1 is present, we say we have a binomial experiment. Figure 5.2 depicts one possible sequence of successes and failures for a binomial experiment involving eight trials.

In a binomial experiment, our interest is in the *number of successes occurring in the n trials*. If we let $x$ denote the number of successes occurring in the $n$ trials, we see that $x$ can assume the values of $0, 1, 2, 3, \ldots, n$. Because the number of values is finite, $x$ is a *discrete* random variable. The probability distribution associated with this random variable is called the **binomial probability distribution**. For example, consider the experiment of tossing a coin five times and on each toss observing whether the coin lands with a head or a tail on its upward face. Suppose we want to count the number of heads appearing over the five tosses. Does this experiment show the properties of a binomial experiment? What is the random variable of interest? Note that:

1. The experiment consists of five identical trials; each trial involves the tossing of one coin.
2. Two outcomes are possible for each trial: a head or a tail. We can designate head a success and tail a failure.
3. The probability of a head and the probability of a tail are the same for each trial, with $p = .5$ and $1 - p = .5$.
4. The trials or tosses are independent because the outcome on any one trial is not affected by what happens on other trials or tosses.

**FIGURE 5.2**   ONE POSSIBLE SEQUENCE OF SUCCESSES AND FAILURES FOR AN EIGHT-TRIAL BINOMIAL EXPERIMENT

---

*Property 1:*   The experiment consists of
$n = 8$ identical trials.

*Property 2:*   Each trial results in either
success ($S$) or failure ($F$).

| Trials $\longrightarrow$ | 1 | 2 | 3 | 4 | 5 | 6 | 7 | 8 |
|---|---|---|---|---|---|---|---|---|
| Outcomes $\longrightarrow$ | $S$ | $F$ | $F$ | $S$ | $S$ | $F$ | $S$ | $S$ |

---

Thus, the properties of a binomial experiment are satisfied. The random variable of interest is $x =$ the number of heads appearing in the five trials. In this case, $x$ can assume the values of 0, 1, 2, 3, 4, or 5.

As another example, consider an insurance salesperson who visits 10 randomly selected families. The outcome associated with each visit is classified as a success if the family purchases an insurance policy and a failure if the family does not. From past experience, the salesperson knows the probability that a randomly selected family will purchase an insurance policy is .10. Checking the properties of a binomial experiment, we observe that:

1. The experiment consists of 10 identical trials; each trial involves contacting one family.
2. Two outcomes are possible on each trial: the family purchases a policy (success) or the family does not purchase a policy (failure).
3. The probabilities of a purchase and a nonpurchase are assumed to be the same for each sales call, with $p = .10$ and $1 - p = .90$.
4. The trials are independent because the families are randomly selected.

Because the four assumptions are satisfied, this example is a binomial experiment. The random variable of interest is the number of sales obtained in contacting the 10 families. In this case, $x$ can assume the values of 0, 1, 2, 3, 4, 5, 6, 7, 8, 9, and 10.

Property 3 of the binomial experiment is called the *stationarity assumption* and is sometimes confused with property 4, independence of trials. To see how they differ, consider again the case of the salesperson calling on families to sell insurance policies. If, as the day wore on, the salesperson got tired and lost enthusiasm, the probability of success (selling a policy) might drop to .05, for example, by the tenth call. In such a case, property 3 (stationarity) would not be satisfied, and we would not have a binomial experiment. Even if property 4 held—that is, the purchase decisions of each family were made independently—it would not be a binomial experiment if property 3 was not satisfied.

In applications involving binomial experiments, a special mathematical formula, called the *binomial probability function,* can be used to compute the probability of $x$ successes in the $n$ trials. Using probability concepts introduced in Chapter 4, we will show in the context of an illustrative problem how the formula can be developed.

## Martin Clothing Store Problem

Let us consider the purchase decisions of the next three customers who enter the Martin Clothing Store. On the basis of past experience, the store manager estimates the probability that any one customer will make a purchase is .30. What is the probability that two of the next three customers will make a purchase?

Using a tree diagram (Figure 5.3), we can see that the experiment of observing the three customers each making a purchase decision has eight possible outcomes. Using $S$ to denote success (a purchase) and $F$ to denote failure (no purchase), we are interested in experimental outcomes involving two successes in the three trials (purchase decisions). Next, let us verify that the experiment involving the sequence of three purchase decisions can be viewed as a binomial experiment. Checking the four requirements for a binomial experiment, we note that:

1. The experiment can be described as a sequence of three identical trials, one trial for each of the three customers who will enter the store.
2. Two outcomes—the customer makes a purchase (success) or the customer does not make a purchase (failure)—are possible for each trial.
3. The probability that the customer will make a purchase (.30) or will not make a purchase (.70) is assumed to be the same for all customers.
4. The purchase decision of each customer is independent of the decisions of the other customers.

FIGURE 5.3 TREE DIAGRAM FOR THE MARTIN CLOTHING STORE PROBLEM

| First Customer | Second Customer | Third Customer | Experimental Outcome | Value of $x$ |
|---|---|---|---|---|
| | | S | (S, S, S) | 3 |
| | S | F | (S, S, F) | 2 |
| S | F | S | (S, F, S) | 2 |
| | | F | (S, F, F) | 1 |
| | S | S | (F, S, S) | 2 |
| F | | F | (F, S, F) | 1 |
| | F | S | (F, F, S) | 1 |
| | | F | (F, F, F) | 0 |

$S$ = Purchase
$F$ = No purchase
$x$ = Number of customers making a purchase

Hence, the properties of a binomial experiment are present.

The number of experimental outcomes resulting in exactly $x$ successes in $n$ trials can be computed using the following formula.*

NUMBER OF EXPERIMENTAL OUTCOMES PROVIDING EXACTLY $x$ SUCCESSES IN $n$ TRIALS

$$\binom{n}{x} = \frac{n!}{x!(n-x)!} \tag{5.6}$$

where

$$n! = n(n-1)(n-2)\cdots(2)(1)$$

and, by definition,

$$0! = 1$$

Now let us return to the Martin Clothing Store experiment involving three customer purchase decisions. Equation (5.6) can be used to determine the number of experimental

*This formula, introduced in Chapter 4, determines the number of combinations of $n$ objects selected $x$ at a time. For the binomial experiment, this combinatorial formula provides the number of experimental outcomes (sequences of $n$ trials) resulting in $x$ successes.

outcomes involving two purchases; that is, the number of ways of obtaining $x = 2$ successes in the $n = 3$ trials. From equation (5.6) we have

$$\binom{n}{x} = \binom{3}{2} = \frac{3!}{2!(3-2)!} = \frac{(3)(2)(1)}{(2)(1)(1)} = \frac{6}{2} = 3$$

Equation (5.6) shows that three of the experimental outcomes yield two successes. From Figure 5.3 we see these three outcomes are denoted by $(S, S, F)$, $(S, F, S)$, and $(F, S, S)$.

Using equation (5.6) to determine how many experimental outcomes have three successes (purchases) in the three trials, we obtain

$$\binom{n}{x} = \binom{3}{3} = \frac{3!}{3!(3-3)!} = \frac{3!}{3!0!} = \frac{(3)(2)(1)}{3(2)(1)(1)} = \frac{6}{6} = 1$$

From Figure 5.3 we see that the one experimental outcome with three successes is identified by $(S, S, S)$.

We know that equation (5.6) can be used to determine the number of experimental outcomes that result in $x$ successes. If we are to determine the probability of $x$ successes in $n$ trials, however, we must also know the probability associated with each of these experimental outcomes. Because the trials of a binomial experiment are independent, we can simply multiply the probabilities associated with each trial outcome to find the probability of a particular sequence of successes and failures.

The probability of purchases by the first two customers and no purchase by the third customer, denoted $(S, S, F)$, is given by

$$pp(1 - p)$$

With a .30 probability of a purchase on any one trial, the probability of a purchase on the first two trials and no purchase on the third is given by

$$(.30)(.30)(.70) = (.30)^2(.70) = .063$$

Two other experimental outcomes also result in two successes and one failure. The probabilities for all three experimental outcomes involving two successes follow.

| **Trial Outcomes** | | | | **Probability of** |
|---|---|---|---|---|
| **1st Customer** | **2nd Customer** | **3rd Customer** | **Experimental Outcome** | **Experimental Outcome** |
| Purchase | Purchase | No purchase | $(S, S, F)$ | $pp(1 - p) = p^2(1 - p)$ $= (.30)^2(.70) = .063$ |
| Purchase | No purchase | Purchase | $(S, F, S)$ | $p(1 - p)p = p^2(1 - p)$ $= (.30)^2(.70) = .063$ |
| No purchase | Purchase | Purchase | $(F, S, S)$ | $(1 - p)pp = p^2(1 - p)$ $= (.30)^2(.70) = .063$ |

Observe that all three experimental outcomes with two successes have exactly the same probability. This observation holds in general. In any binomial experiment, all sequences of trial outcomes yielding $x$ successes in $n$ trials have the *same probability* of occurrence. The probability of each sequence of trials yielding $x$ successes in $n$ trials follows.

$$\begin{aligned}\text{Probability of a particular}\\ \text{sequence of trial outcomes} = p^x(1-p)^{(n-x)}\\ \text{with } x \text{ successes in } n \text{ trials}\end{aligned} \qquad (5.7)$$

For the Martin Clothing Store, this formula shows that any experimental outcome with two successes has a probability of $p^2(1-p)^{(3-2)} = p^2(1-p)^1 = (.30)^2(.70)^1 = .063$.

Because equation (5.6) shows the number of outcomes in a binomial experiment with $x$ successes and equation (5.7) gives the probability for each sequence involving $x$ successes, we combine equations (5.6) and (5.7) to obtain the following **binomial probability function**.

---

BINOMIAL PROBABILITY FUNCTION

$$f(x) = \binom{n}{x}p^x(1-p)^{(n-x)} \qquad (5.8)$$

where

$$f(x) = \text{the probability of } x \text{ successes in } n \text{ trials}$$
$$n = \text{the number of trials}$$
$$\binom{n}{x} = \frac{n!}{x!(n-x)!}$$
$$p = \text{the probability of a success on any one trial}$$
$$1-p = \text{the probability of a failure on any one trial}$$

---

In the Martin Clothing Store example, let us compute the probability that no customer makes a purchase, exactly one customer makes a purchase, exactly two customers make a purchase, and all three customers make a purchase. The calculations are summarized in Table 5.7, which gives the probability distribution of the number of customers making a purchase. Figure 5.4 is a graph of this probability distribution.

The binomial probability function can be applied to *any* binomial experiment. If we are satisfied that a situation demonstrates the properties of a binomial experiment and if we know the values of $n$ and $p$, we can use equation (5.8) to compute the probability of $x$ successes in the $n$ trials.

TABLE 5.7    PROBABILITY DISTRIBUTION FOR THE NUMBER OF CUSTOMERS
             MAKING A PURCHASE

| $x$ | $f(x)$ |
|---|---|
| 0 | $\dfrac{3!}{0!3!}(.30)^0(.70)^3 = .343$ |
| 1 | $\dfrac{3!}{1!2!}(.30)^1(.70)^2 = .441$ |
| 2 | $\dfrac{3!}{2!1!}(.30)^2(.70)^1 = .189$ |
| 3 | $\dfrac{3!}{3!0!}(.30)^3(.70)^0 = \underline{.027}$ |
|  | $1.000$ |

FIGURE 5.4   GRAPHICAL REPRESENTATION OF THE PROBABILITY DISTRIBUTION
FOR THE NUMBER OF CUSTOMERS MAKING A PURCHASE

If we consider variations of the Martin experiment, such as 10 customers rather than three entering the store, the binomial probability function given by equation (5.8) is still applicable. Suppose we have a binomial experiment with $n = 10$, $x = 4$, and $p = .30$. The probability of making exactly four sales to 10 customers entering the store is

$$f(4) = \frac{10!}{4!6!}(.30)^4(.70)^6 = .2001$$

## Using Tables of Binomial Probabilities

Tables have been developed that give the probability of $x$ successes in $n$ trials for a binomial experiment. The tables are generally easy to use and quicker than equation (5.8). Table 5 of Appendix B provides such a table of binomial probabilities. A portion of this table appears in Table 5.8. To use this table, we must specify the values of $n$, $p$, and $x$ for the binomial experiment of interest. In the example at the top of Table 5.8, we see that the probability of $x = 3$ successes in a binomial experiment with $n = 10$ and $p = .40$ is .2150. You can use equation (5.8) to verify that you would obtain the same answer if you used the binomial probability function directly.

Now let us use Table 5.8 to verify the probability of four successes in 10 trials for the Martin Clothing Store problem. Note that the value of $f(4) = .2001$ can be read directly from the table of binomial probabilities, with $n = 10$, $x = 4$, and $p = .30$.

*With modern calculators, these tables are almost unnecessary. It is easy to evaluate equation (5.8) directly.*

Even though the tables of binomial probabilities are relatively easy to use, it is impossible to have tables that show all possible values of $n$ and $p$ that might be encountered in a binomial experiment. However, with today's calculators, using equation (5.8) to calculate the desired probability is not difficult, especially if the number of trials is not large. In the exercises, you should practice using equation (5.8) to compute the binomial probabilities unless the problem specifically requests that you use the binomial probability table.

**TABLE 5.8    SELECTED VALUES FROM THE BINOMIAL PROBABILITY TABLE**
EXAMPLE: $n = 10, x = 3, p = .40; f(3) = .2150$

| $n$ | $x$ | .05 | .10 | .15 | .20 | $p$ .25 | .30 | .35 | .40 | .45 | .50 |
|---|---|---|---|---|---|---|---|---|---|---|---|
| 9 | 0 | .6302 | .3874 | .2316 | .1342 | .0751 | .0404 | .0207 | .0101 | .0046 | .0020 |
| | 1 | .2985 | .3874 | .3679 | .3020 | .2253 | .1556 | .1004 | .0605 | .0339 | .0176 |
| | 2 | .0629 | .1722 | .2597 | .3020 | .3003 | .2668 | .2162 | .1612 | .1110 | .0703 |
| | 3 | .0077 | .0446 | .1069 | .1762 | .2336 | .2668 | .2716 | .2508 | .2119 | .1641 |
| | 4 | .0006 | .0074 | .0283 | .0661 | .1168 | .1715 | .2194 | .2508 | .2600 | .2461 |
| | 5 | .0000 | .0008 | .0050 | .0165 | .0389 | .0735 | .1181 | .1672 | .2128 | .2461 |
| | 6 | .0000 | .0001 | .0006 | .0028 | .0087 | .0210 | .0424 | .0743 | .1160 | .1641 |
| | 7 | .0000 | .0000 | .0000 | .0003 | .0012 | .0039 | .0098 | .0212 | .0407 | .0703 |
| | 8 | .0000 | .0000 | .0000 | .0000 | .0001 | .0004 | .0013 | .0035 | .0083 | .0176 |
| | 9 | .0000 | .0000 | .0000 | .0000 | .0000 | .0000 | .0001 | .0003 | .0008 | .0020 |
| 10 | 0 | .5987 | .3487 | .1969 | .1074 | .0563 | .0282 | .0135 | .0060 | .0025 | .0010 |
| | 1 | .3151 | .3874 | .3474 | .2684 | .1877 | .1211 | .0725 | .0403 | .0207 | .0098 |
| | 2 | .0746 | .1937 | .2759 | .3020 | .2816 | .2335 | .1757 | .1209 | .0763 | .0439 |
| | 3 | .0105 | .0574 | .1298 | .2013 | .2503 | .2668 | .2522 | **.2150** | .1665 | .1172 |
| | 4 | .0010 | .0112 | .0401 | .0881 | .1460 | .2001 | .2377 | .2508 | .2384 | .2051 |
| | 5 | .0001 | .0015 | .0085 | .0264 | .0584 | .1029 | .1536 | .2007 | .2340 | .2461 |
| | 6 | .0000 | .0001 | .0012 | .0055 | .0162 | .0368 | .0689 | .1115 | .1596 | .2051 |
| | 7 | .0000 | .0000 | .0001 | .0008 | .0031 | .0090 | .0212 | .0425 | .0746 | .1172 |
| | 8 | .0000 | .0000 | .0000 | .0001 | .0004 | .0014 | .0043 | .0106 | .0229 | .0439 |
| | 9 | .0000 | .0000 | .0000 | .0000 | .0000 | .0001 | .0005 | .0016 | .0042 | .0098 |
| | 10 | .0000 | .0000 | .0000 | .0000 | .0000 | .0000 | .0000 | .0001 | .0003 | .0010 |

Statistical software packages such as Minitab and spreadsheet packages such as Excel also provide a capability for computing binomial probabilities. Consider the Martin Clothing Store example with $n = 10$ and $p = .30$. Figure 5.5 shows the binomial probabilities generated by Minitab for all possible values of $x$. Note that these values are the same as those found in the $p = .30$ column of Table 5.8. Appendix 5.1 gives the step-by-step procedure for using Minitab to generate the output in Figure 5.5. Appendix 5.2 describes how Excel can be used to compute binomial probabilities.

## Expected Value and Variance for the Binomial Distribution

In Section 5.3 we provided formulas for computing the expected value and variance of a discrete random variable. In the special case where the random variable has a binomial distribution with a known number of trials $n$ and a known probability of success $p$, the general formulas for the expected value and variance can be simplified. The results follow.

EXPECTED VALUE AND VARIANCE FOR THE BINOMIAL DISTRIBUTION

$$E(x) = \mu = np \tag{5.9}$$

$$\text{Var}(x) = \sigma^2 = np(1 - p) \tag{5.10}$$

**FIGURE 5.5    MINITAB OUTPUT SHOWING BINOMIAL PROBABILITIES FOR THE MARTIN CLOTHING STORE PROBLEM**

| x | P(X = x) |
|------|----------|
| 0.00 | 0.0282 |
| 1.00 | 0.1211 |
| 2.00 | 0.2335 |
| 3.00 | 0.2668 |
| 4.00 | 0.2001 |
| 5.00 | 0.1029 |
| 6.00 | 0.0368 |
| 7.00 | 0.0090 |
| 8.00 | 0.0014 |
| 9.00 | 0.0001 |
| 10.00 | 0.0000 |

For the Martin Clothing Store problem with three customers, we can use equation (5.9) to compute the expected number of customers who will make a purchase.

$$E(x) = np = 3(.30) = .9$$

Suppose that for the next month the Martin Clothing Store forecasts 1000 customers will enter the store. What is the expected number of customers who will make a purchase? The answer is $\mu = np = (1000)(.3) = 300$. Thus, to increase the expected number of purchases, Martin's must induce more customers to enter the store and/or somehow increase the probability that any individual customer will make a purchase after entering.

For the Martin Clothing Store problem with three customers, we see that the variance and standard deviation for the number of customers who will make a purchase are

*The np chart and lot acceptance sampling are quality control procedures that are excellent examples of the use of the binomial distribution. These procedures are discussed in Chapter 20, Statistical Methods for Quality Control.*

$$\sigma^2 = np(1 - p) = 3(.3)(.7) = .63$$
$$\sigma = \sqrt{.63} = .79$$

For the next 1000 customers entering the store, the variance and standard deviation for the number of customers who will make a purchase are

$$\sigma^2 = np(1 - p) = 1000(.3)(.7) = 210$$
$$\sigma = \sqrt{210} = 14.49$$

## NOTES AND COMMENTS

1. The binomial tables in Appendix B show values of $p$ only up to and including $p = .50$. It would appear that such tables cannot be used when the probability of success exceeds $p = .50$. However, they can be used by noting that the probability of $n - x$ failures is also the probability of $x$ successes. When the probability of success is greater than $p = .50$, one can compute the probability of $n - x$ failures instead. The probability of failure, $1 - p$, will be less than .50 when $p > .50$.

2. Some sources present binomial tables in a cumulative form. In using such tables, one must subtract to find the probability of $x$ successes in $n$ trials. For example, $f(2) = P(x \le 2) - P(x \le 1)$. Our tables provide these probabilities directly. To compute cumulative probabilities using our tables, one simply sums the individual probabilities. For example, to compute $P(x \le 2)$ using our tables, we sum $f(0) + f(1) + f(2)$.

## Exercises

### Methods

25. Consider a binomial experiment with two trials and $p = .4$.
    a. Draw a tree diagram for this experiment (see Figure 5.3).
    b. Compute the probability of one success, $f(1)$.
    c. Compute $f(0)$.
    d. Compute $f(2)$.
    e. Compute the probability of at least one success.
    f. Compute the expected value, variance, and standard deviation.

26. Consider a binomial experiment with $n = 10$ and $p = .10$.
    a. Compute $f(0)$.
    b. Compute $f(2)$.
    c. Compute $P(x \leq 2)$.
    d. Compute $P(x \geq 1)$.
    e. Compute $E(x)$.
    f. Compute $\text{Var}(x)$ and $\sigma$.

27. Consider a binomial experiment with $n = 20$ and $p = .70$.
    a. Compute $f(12)$.
    b. Compute $f(16)$.
    c. Compute $P(x \geq 16)$.
    d. Compute $P(x \leq 15)$.
    e. Compute $E(x)$.
    f. Compute $\text{Var}(x)$ and $\sigma$.

### Applications

28. The 1999 Youth and Money Survey, sponsored by the American Savings Education Council, the Employee Benefit Research Institute, and Matthew Greenwald & Associates, talked to 1000 students ages 16–22 about personal finance. The survey found that 33% of the students have their own credit card.
    a. In a sample of six students, what is the probability that two will have their own credit card?
    b. In a sample of six students, what is the probability that at least two will have their own credit card?
    c. In a sample of 10 students, what is the probability that none will have their own credit card?

29. According to a *Business Week*/Harris Poll of 1035 adults, 40% of those surveyed agreed strongly with the proposition that business has too much power over American life (*Business Week*, September 11, 2000). Assume this percentage is representative of the American population. In a sample of 20 individuals taken from a cross-section of the American population, what is the probability that at least five of these individuals will feel that business has too much power over American life?

30. When a new machine is functioning properly, only 3% of the items produced are defective. Assume that we will randomly select two parts produced on the machine and that we are interested in the number of defective parts found.
    a. Describe the conditions under which this situation would be a binomial experiment.
    b. Draw a tree diagram similar to Figure 5.3 showing this problem as a two-trial experiment.
    c. How many experimental outcomes result in exactly one defect being found?
    d. Compute the probabilities associated with finding no defects, exactly one defect, and two defects.

31. Nine percent of undergraduate students carry credit card balances greater than $7000 (*Reader's Digest,* July 2002). Suppose 10 undergraduate students are selected randomly to be interviewed about credit card usage.
    a. Is the selection of 10 students a binomial experiment? Explain.
    b. What is the probability that two of the students will have a credit card balance greater than $7000?
    c. What is the probability that none will have a credit card balance greater than $7000?
    d. What is the probability that at least three will have a credit card balance greater than $7000?

32. Military radar and missile detection systems are designed to warn a country of an enemy attacks. A reliability question is whether a detection system will be able to identify an attack and issue a warning. Assume that a particular detection system has a .90 probability of detecting a missile attack. Use the binomial probability distribution to answer the following questions.
    a. What is the probability that a single detection system will detect an attack?
    b. If two detection systems are installed in the same area and operate independently, what is the probability that at least one of the systems will detect the attack?
    c. If three systems are installed, what is the probability that at least one of the systems will detect the attack?
    d. Would you recommend that multiple detection systems be used? Explain.

33. Fifty percent of Americans think we are in a recession, even though technically we have not had two straight quarters of negative growth (*Business Week,* July 30, 2001). For a sample of 20 Americans, make the following calculations.
    a. Compute the probability that exactly 12 people think we are in a recession.
    b. Compute the probability that no more than five people think we are in a recession.
    c. How many people would you expect to say we are in a recession?
    d. Compute the variance and standard deviation of the number of people who think we are in a recession.

34. Forty percent of business travelers carry either a cell phone or a laptop (*USA Today,* September 12, 2000). For a sample of 15 business travelers, make the following calculations.
    a. Compute the probability that three of the travelers carry a cell phone or laptop.
    b. Compute the probability that 12 of the travelers carry neither a cell phone nor a laptop.
    c. Compute the probability that at least three of the travelers carry a cell phone or a laptop.

35. A university found that 20% of its students withdraw without completing the introductory statistics course. Assume that 20 students registered for the course this quarter.
    a. Compute the probability that two or fewer will withdraw.
    b. Compute the probability that exactly four will withdraw.
    c. Compute the probability that more than three will withdraw.
    d. Compute the expected number of withdrawals.

36. For the special case of a binomial random variable, we stated that the variance could be computed using the formula $\sigma^2 = np(1 - p)$. For the Martin Clothing Store problem with $n = 3$ and $p = .3$ we found $\sigma^2 = np(1 - p) = 3(.3)(.7) = .63$. Use the general definition of variance for a discrete random variable, equation (5.5), and the probabilities in Table 5.7 to verify that the variance is in fact .63.

37. Seventy-two percent of Americans have online access (*CNBC,* December 3, 2001). In a random sample of 30 people, what is the expected number of persons with online access? What are the variance and standard deviation?

 # 5.5　Poisson Probability Distribution

In this section we consider a discrete random variable that is often useful in estimating the number of occurrences over a specified interval of time or space. For example, the random variable of interest might be the number of arrivals at a car wash in one hour, the number

*The Poisson probability distribution is often used to model random arrivals in waiting line situations.*

of repairs needed in 10 miles of highway, or the number of leaks in 100 miles of pipeline. If the following two properties are satisfied, the number of occurrences is a random variable described by the **Poisson probability distribution**.

---

**PROPERTIES OF A POISSON EXPERIMENT**

**1.** The probability of an occurrence is the same for any two intervals of equal length.
**2.** The occurrence or nonoccurrence in any interval is independent of the occurrence or nonoccurrence in any other interval.

---

The **Poisson probability function** is defined by equation (5.11).

---

**POISSON PROBABILITY FUNCTION**

*Siméon Poisson taught mathematics at the Ecole Polytechnique in Paris from 1802 to 1808. In 1837, he published a work entitled, "Researches on the Probability of Criminal and Civil Verdicts," which includes a discussion of what later became known as the Poisson distribution.*

$$f(x) = \frac{\mu^x e^{-\mu}}{x!} \qquad (5.11)$$

where

$$f(x) = \text{the probability of } x \text{ occurrences in an interval}$$
$$\mu = \text{expected value or mean number of occurrences in an interval}$$
$$e = 2.71828$$

---

Before we consider a specific example to see how the Poisson distribution can be applied, note that the number of occurrences, $x$, has no upper limit. It is a discrete random variable that may assume an infinite sequence of values ($x = 0, 1, 2, \ldots$).

## An Example Involving Time Intervals

Suppose that we are interested in the number of arrivals at the drive-up teller window of a bank during a 15-minute period on weekday mornings. If we can assume that the probability of a car arriving is the same for any two time periods of equal length and that the arrival or nonarrival of a car in any time period is independent of the arrival or nonarrival in any other time period, the Poisson probability function is applicable. Suppose these assumptions are satisfied and an analysis of historical data shows that the average number of cars arriving in a 15-minute period of time is 10; in this case, the following probability function applies.

*Bell Labs uses the Poisson distribution to model the arrival of phone calls.*

$$f(x) = \frac{10^x e^{-10}}{x!}$$

The random variable here is $x$ = number of cars arriving in any 15-minute period.

If management wanted to know the probability of exactly five arrivals in 15 minutes, we would set $x = 5$ and thus obtain

$$\begin{array}{l}\text{Probability of exactly} \\ \text{5 arrivals in 15 minutes}\end{array} = f(5) = \frac{10^5 e^{-10}}{5!} = .0378$$

Although this probability was determined by evaluating the probability function with $\mu = 10$ and $x = 5$, it is often easier to refer to a table for the Poisson distribution. The table provides probabilities for specific values of $x$ and $\mu$. We included such a table as Table 7 of Appendix B. For convenience, we reproduced a portion of this table as Table 5.9. Note that to use the table of Poisson probabilities, we need know only the values of $x$ and $\mu$. From Table 5.9

TABLE 5.9   SELECTED VALUES FROM THE POISSON PROBABILITY TABLES
EXAMPLE: $\mu = 10, x = 5; f(5) = .0378$

| | | | | | $\mu$ | | | | | |
|---|---|---|---|---|---|---|---|---|---|---|
| $x$ | **9.1** | **9.2** | **9.3** | **9.4** | **9.5** | **9.6** | **9.7** | **9.8** | **9.9** | **10** |
| 0 | .0001 | .0001 | .0001 | .0001 | .0001 | .0001 | .0001 | .0001 | .0001 | .0000 |
| 1 | .0010 | .0009 | .0009 | .0008 | .0007 | .0007 | .0006 | .0005 | .0005 | .0005 |
| 2 | .0046 | .0043 | .0040 | .0037 | .0034 | .0031 | .0029 | .0027 | .0025 | .0023 |
| 3 | .0140 | .0131 | .0123 | .0115 | .0107 | .0100 | .0093 | .0087 | .0081 | .0076 |
| 4 | .0319 | .0302 | .0285 | .0269 | .0254 | .0240 | .0226 | .0213 | .0201 | .0189 |
| 5 | .0581 | .0555 | .0530 | .0506 | .0483 | .0460 | .0439 | .0418 | .0398 | **.0378** |
| 6 | .0881 | .0851 | .0822 | .0793 | .0764 | .0736 | .0709 | .0682 | .0656 | .0631 |
| 7 | .1145 | .1118 | .1091 | .1064 | .1037 | .1010 | .0982 | .0955 | .0928 | .0901 |
| 8 | .1302 | .1286 | .1269 | .1251 | .1232 | .1212 | .1191 | .1170 | .1148 | .1126 |
| 9 | .1317 | .1315 | .1311 | .1306 | .1300 | .1293 | .1284 | .1274 | .1263 | .1251 |
| 10 | .1198 | .1210 | .1219 | .1228 | .1235 | .1241 | .1245 | .1249 | .1250 | .1251 |
| 11 | .0991 | .1012 | .1031 | .1049 | .1067 | .1083 | .1098 | .1112 | .1125 | .1137 |
| 12 | .0752 | .0776 | .0799 | .0822 | .0844 | .0866 | .0888 | .0908 | .0928 | .0948 |
| 13 | .0526 | .0549 | .0572 | .0594 | .0617 | .0640 | .0662 | .0685 | .0707 | .0729 |
| 14 | .0342 | .0361 | .0380 | .0399 | .0419 | .0439 | .0459 | .0479 | .0500 | .0521 |
| 15 | .0208 | .0221 | .0235 | .0250 | .0265 | .0281 | .0297 | .0313 | .0330 | .0347 |
| 16 | .0118 | .0127 | .0137 | .0147 | .0157 | .0168 | .0180 | .0192 | .0204 | .0217 |
| 17 | .0063 | .0069 | .0075 | .0081 | .0088 | .0095 | .0103 | .0111 | .0119 | .0128 |
| 18 | .0032 | .0035 | .0039 | .0042 | .0046 | .0051 | .0055 | .0060 | .0065 | .0071 |
| 19 | .0015 | .0017 | .0019 | .0021 | .0023 | .0026 | .0028 | .0031 | .0034 | .0037 |
| 20 | .0007 | .0008 | .0009 | .0010 | .0011 | .0012 | .0014 | .0015 | .0017 | .0019 |
| 21 | .0003 | .0003 | .0004 | .0004 | .0005 | .0006 | .0006 | .0007 | .0008 | .0009 |
| 22 | .0001 | .0001 | .0002 | .0002 | .0002 | .0002 | .0003 | .0003 | .0004 | .0004 |
| 23 | .0000 | .0001 | .0001 | .0001 | .0001 | .0001 | .0001 | .0001 | .0002 | .0002 |
| 24 | .0000 | .0000 | .0000 | .0000 | .0000 | .0000 | .0000 | .0001 | .0001 | .0001 |

we see that the probability of five arrivals in a 15-minute period is found by locating the value in the row of the table corresponding to $x = 5$ and the column of the table corresponding to $\mu = 10$. Hence, we obtain $f(5) = .0378$.

*A property of the Poisson distribution is that the mean and variance are equal.*

In the preceding example, the mean of the Poisson distribution is $\mu = 10$ arrivals per 15-minute period. A property of the Poisson distribution is that the mean of the distribution and the variance of the distribution are *equal*. Thus, the variance for the number of arrivals during 15-minute periods is $\sigma^2 = 10$. The standard deviation is $\sigma = \sqrt{10} = 3.16$.

Our illustration involves a 15-minute period, but other time periods can be used. Suppose we want to compute the probability of one arrival in a three-minute period. Because 10 is the expected number of arrivals in a 15-minute period, we see that $10/15 = 2/3$ is the expected number of arrivals in a one-minute period and that $(2/3)(3 \text{ minutes}) = 2$ is the expected number of arrivals in a three-minute period. Thus, the probability of $x$ arrivals in a three-minute time period with $\mu = 2$ is given by the following Poisson probability function.

$$f(x) = \frac{2^x e^{-2}}{x!}$$

The probability of one arrival in a three-minute period is calculated as follows:

$$\text{Probability of exactly 1 arrival in 3 minutes} = f(1) = \frac{2^1 e^{-2}}{1!} = .2707$$

Earlier we computed the probability of five arrivals in a 15-minute period; it was .0378. Note that the probability of one arrival in a 3-minute period (.2707) is not the same. When computing a Poisson probability for a different time interval, we must first convert the mean arrival rate to the time period of interest and then compute the probability.

## An Example Involving Length or Distance Intervals

Let us illustrate an application not involving time intervals in which the Poisson distribution is useful. Suppose we are concerned with the occurrence of major defects in a highway one month after resurfacing. We will assume that the probability of a defect is the same for any two highway intervals of equal length and that the occurrence or nonoccurrence of a defect in any one interval is independent of the occurrence or nonoccurrence of a defect in any other interval. Hence, the Poisson distribution can be applied.

Suppose we learn that major defects one month after resurfacing occur at the average rate of two per mile. Let us find the probability of no major defects in a particular three-mile section of the highway. Because we are interested in an interval with a length of three miles, $\mu = (2 \text{ defects/mile})(3 \text{ miles}) = 6$ represents the expected number of major defects over the three-mile section of highway. Using equation (5.11), the probability of no major defects is $f(0) = 6^0 e^{-6}/0! = .0025$. Thus, it is unlikely that no major defects will occur in the three-mile section. In fact, this example indicates a $1 - .0025 = .9975$ probability of at least one major defect in the three-mile highway section.

### Exercises

## Methods

38. Consider a Poisson distribution with $\mu = 3$.
    a.  Write the appropriate Poisson probability function.
    b.  Compute $f(2)$.
    c.  Compute $f(1)$.
    d.  Compute $P(x \geq 2)$.

39. Consider a Poisson distribution with a mean of two occurrences per time period.
    a.  Write the appropriate Poisson probability function.
    b.  What is the expected number of occurrences in three time periods?
    c.  Write the appropriate Poisson probability function to determine the probability of $x$ occurrences in three time periods.
    d.  Compute the probability of two occurrences in one time period.
    e.  Compute the probability of six occurrences in three time periods.
    f.  Compute the probability of five occurrences in two time periods.

## Applications

40. Phone calls arrive at the rate of 48 per hour at the reservation desk for Regional Airways.
    a.  Compute the probability of receiving three calls in a five-minute interval of time.
    b.  Compute the probability of receiving exactly 10 calls in 15 minutes.
    c.  Suppose no calls are currently on hold. If the agent takes five minutes to complete the current call, how many callers do you expect to be waiting by that time? What is the probability that none will be waiting?
    d.  If no calls are currently being processed, what is the probability that the agent can take three minutes for personal time without being interrupted by a call?

41. During the period of time that a local university takes phone-in registrations, calls come in at the rate of one every two minutes.
    a. What is the expected number of calls in one hour?
    b. What is the probability of three calls in five minutes?
    c. What is the probability of no calls in a five-minute period?

**SELF test**

42. More than 50 million guests stayed at bed and breakfasts (B&Bs) last year. The Web site for the Bed and Breakfast Inns of North America (www.bestInns.net), which averages approximately seven visitors per minute, enables many B&Bs to attract guests without waiting years to be mentioned in guidebooks (*Time,* September 2001).
    a. Compute the probability of no Web site visitors in a 1-minute period.
    b. Compute the probability of two or more Web site visitors in a 1-minute period.
    c. Compute the probability of one or more Web site visitors in a 30-second period.
    d. Compute the probability of five or more Web site visitors in a 1-minute period.

43. Airline passengers arrive randomly and independently at the passenger-screening facility at a major international airport. The mean arrival rate is 10 passengers per minute.
    a. Compute the probability of no arrivals in a 1-minute period.
    b. Compute the probability that three or fewer passengers arrive in a 1-minute period.
    c. Compute the probability of no arrivals in a 15-second period.
    d. Compute the probability of at least one arrival in a 15-second period.

44. Investment activities for subscribers to *The Wall Street Journal Interactive Edition* show that the average number of security transactions per year is approximately 15 (*The Wall Street Journal* Subscriber Study, 1999). Assume that a particular investor makes transactions at this rate. Furthermore, assume that the probability of a transaction for this investor is the same for any two months and transactions in one month are independent of transactions in any other month.
    a. Compute the mean number of transactions per month.
    b. Compute the probability of no transactions during a month.
    c. Compute the probability of exactly one transaction during a month.
    d. Compute the probability of more than one transaction during a month.

45. The National Safety Council reported that air bag-related fatalities dropped to 18 in the year 2000 (www.nsc.org).
    a. Compute the expected number of air bag-related fatalities per month.
    b. Compute the probability of no air bag-related fatalities in a month.
    c. Compute the probability of two or more air bag-related fatalities in a month.

# 5.6 Hypergeometric Probability Distribution

The **hypergeometric probability distribution** is closely related to the binomial distribution. The two probability distributions differ in two key ways. With the hypergeometric distribution, the trials are not independent; and the probability of success changes from trial to trial.

In the usual notation for the hypergeometric distribution, $r$ denotes the number of elements in the population of size $N$ labeled success, and $N - r$ denotes the number of elements in the population labeled failure. The **hypergeometric probability function** is used to compute the probability that in a random selection of $n$ elements, selected without replacement, we obtain $x$ elements labeled success and $n - x$ elements labeled failure. For this outcome to occur, we must obtain $x$ successes from the $r$ successes in the population and $n - x$ failures from the $N - r$ failures. The following hypergeometric probability function provides $f(x)$, the probability of obtaining $x$ successes in a sample of size $n$.

**HYPERGEOMETRIC PROBABILITY FUNCTION**

$$f(x) = \frac{\binom{r}{x}\binom{N-r}{n-x}}{\binom{N}{n}} \qquad \text{for } 0 \le x \le r \qquad (5.12)$$

where

$$f(x) = \text{probability of } x \text{ successes in } n \text{ trials}$$
$$n = \text{number of trials}$$
$$N = \text{number of elements in the population}$$
$$r = \text{number of elements in the population labeled success}$$

Note that $\binom{N}{n}$ represents the number of ways a sample of size $n$ can be selected from a population of size $N$; $\binom{r}{x}$ represents the number of ways that $x$ successes can be selected from a total of $r$ successes in the population; and $\binom{N-r}{n-x}$ represents the number of ways that $n - x$ failures can be selected from a total of $N - r$ failures in the population.

To illustrate the computations involved in using equation (5.12), let us consider the following quality control application. Electric fuses produced by Ontario Electric are packaged in boxes of 12 units each. Suppose an inspector randomly selects 3 of the 12 fuses in a box for testing. If the box contains exactly 5 defective fuses, what is the probability that the inspector will find exactly 1 of the 3 fuses defective? In this application, $n = 3$ and $N = 12$. With $r = 5$ defective fuses in the box the probability of finding $x = 1$ defective fuse is

$$f(1) = \frac{\binom{5}{1}\binom{7}{2}}{\binom{12}{3}} = \frac{\left(\frac{5!}{1!4!}\right)\left(\frac{7!}{2!5!}\right)}{\left(\frac{12!}{3!9!}\right)} = \frac{(5)(21)}{220} = .4773$$

Now suppose that we wanted to know the probability of finding *at least* 1 defective fuse. The easiest way to answer this question is to first compute the probability that the inspector does not find any defective fuses. The probability of $x = 0$ is

$$f(0) = \frac{\binom{5}{0}\binom{7}{3}}{\binom{12}{3}} = \frac{\left(\frac{5!}{0!5!}\right)\left(\frac{7!}{3!4!}\right)}{\left(\frac{12!}{3!9!}\right)} = \frac{(1)(35)}{220} = .1591$$

With a probability of zero defective fuses $f(0) = .1591$, we conclude that the probability of finding at least 1 defective fuse must be $1 - .1591 = .8409$. Thus, there is a reasonably high probability that the inspector will find at least 1 defective fuse.

The mean and variance of a hypergeometric distribution are as follows.

$$E(x) = \mu = n\left(\frac{r}{N}\right) \tag{5.13}$$

$$\text{Var}(x) = \sigma^2 = n\left(\frac{r}{N}\right)\left(1 - \frac{r}{N}\right)\left(\frac{N - n}{N - 1}\right) \tag{5.14}$$

In the preceding example $n = 3$, $r = 5$, and $N = 12$. Thus, the mean and variance for the number of defective fuses is

$$\mu = n\left(\frac{r}{N}\right) = 3\left(\frac{5}{12}\right) = 1.25$$

$$\sigma^2 = n\left(\frac{r}{N}\right)\left(1 - \frac{r}{N}\right)\left(\frac{N - n}{N - 1}\right) = 3\left(\frac{5}{12}\right)\left(1 - \frac{5}{12}\right)\left(\frac{12 - 3}{12 - 1}\right) = .60$$

The standard deviation is $\sigma = \sqrt{.60} = .77$.

## NOTES AND COMMENTS

Consider a hypergeometric distribution with $n$ trials. Let $p = (r/N)$ denote the probability of a success on the first trial. If the population size is large, the term $(N - n)/(N - 1)$ in equation (5.14) approaches 1. As a result, the expected value and variance can be written $E(x) = np$ and $\text{Var}(x) = np(1 - p)$. Note that these expressions are used for expected value and variance of a binomial distribution, as in equations (5.9) and (5.10). When the population size is large, a hypergeometric distribution can be approximated by a binomial distribution with $n$ trials and a probability of success $p = (r/N)$.

## Exercises

### Methods

46. Suppose $N = 10$ and $r = 3$. Compute the hypergeometric probabilities for the following values of $n$ and $x$.
    a.  $n = 4, x = 1$.
    b.  $n = 2, x = 2$.
    c.  $n = 2, x = 0$.
    d.  $n = 4, x = 2$.

47. Suppose $N = 15$ and $r = 4$. What is the probability of $x = 3$ for $n = 10$?

### Applications

48. According to *Beverage Digest*, Coke Classic and Pepsi ranked number one and number two in sales (*The Wall Street Journal Almanac*, 1998). Assume that in a group of 10 individuals, six preferred Coke Classic and four preferred Pepsi. A random sample of three of these individuals is selected.
    a.  What is the probability that exactly two preferred Coke Classic?
    b.  What is the probability that the majority (either two or three) preferred Pepsi?

49. Blackjack, or twenty-one as it is frequently called, is a popular gambling game played in Las Vegas casinos. A player is dealt two cards. Face cards (jacks, queens, and kings) and tens have a point value of 10. Aces have a point value of 1 or 11. A 52-card deck contains 16 cards with a point value of 10 (jacks, queens, kings, and tens) and four aces.
    a. What is the probability that both cards dealt are aces or 10-point cards?
    b. What is the probability that both of the cards are aces?
    c. What is the probability that both of the cards have a point value of 10?
    d. A blackjack is a 10-point card and an ace for a value of 21. Use your answers to parts (a), (b), and (c) to determine the probability that a player is dealt blackjack. (*Hint:* Part (d) is not a hypergeometric problem. Develop your own logical relationship as to how the hypergeometric probabilities from parts (a), (b), and (c) can be combined to answer this question.)

50. Axline Computers manufactures personal computers at two plants, one in Texas and the other in Hawaii. The Texas plant has 40 employees; the Hawaii plant has 20. A random sample of 10 employees is to be asked to fill out a benefits questionnaire.
    a. What is the probability that none of the employees in the sample work at the plant in Hawaii?
    b. What is the probability that one of the employees in the sample works at the plant in Hawaii?
    c. What is the probability that two or more of the employees in the sample work at the plant in Hawaii?
    d. What is the probability that nine of the employees in the sample work at the plant in Texas?

51. Of the 25 students (14 boys and 11 girls) in the sixth-grade class at St. Andrew School, five students were absent Thursday.
    a. What is the probability that two of the absent students were girls?
    b. What is the probability that two of the absent students were boys?
    c. What is the probability that all of the absent students were boys?
    d. What is the probability that none of the absent students were boys?

52. A shipment of 10 items has two defective and eight nondefective items. In the inspection of the shipment, a sample of items will be selected and tested. If a defective item is found, the shipment of 10 items will be rejected.
    a. If a sample of three items is selected, what is the probability that the shipment will be rejected?
    b. If a sample of four items is selected, what is the probability that the shipment will be rejected?
    c. If a sample of five items is selected, what is the probability that the shipment will be rejected?
    d. If management would like a .90 probability of rejecting a shipment with two defective and eight nondefective items, how large a sample would you recommend?

## Summary

A random variable provides a numerical description of the outcome of an experiment. The probability distribution for a random variable describes how the probabilities are distributed over the values the random variable can assume. For any discrete random variable $x$, the probability distribution is defined by a probability function, denoted by $f(x)$, which provides the probability associated with each value of the random variable. Once the probability function is defined, we can compute the expected value, variance, and standard deviation for the random variable.

The binomial distribution can be used to determine the probability of $x$ successes in $n$ trials whenever the experiment has the following properties:

1. The experiment consists of a sequence of $n$ identical trials.
2. Two outcomes are possible on each trial, one called success and the other failure.
3. The probability of a success $p$ does not change from trial to trial. Consequently, the probability of failure, $1 - p$, does not change from trial to trial.
4. The trials are independent.

When the four properties hold, the binomial probability function can be used to determine the probability of obtaining $x$ successes in $n$ trials. Formulas were also presented for the mean and variance of the binomial distribution.

The Poisson distribution is used when it is desirable to determine the probability of obtaining $x$ occurrences over an interval of time or space. The following assumptions are necessary for the Poisson distribution to be applicable.

1. The probability of an occurrence of the event is the same for any two intervals of equal length.
2. The occurrence or nonoccurrence of the event in any interval is independent of the occurrence or nonoccurrence of the event in any other interval.

A third discrete probability distribution, the hypergeometric, was introduced in Section 5.6. Like the binomial, it is used to compute the probability of $x$ successes in $n$ trials. But, in contrast to the binomial, the probability of success changes from trial to trial.

## Glossary

**Random variable** A numerical description of the outcome of an experiment.
**Discrete random variable** A random variable that may assume either a finite number of values or an infinite sequence of values.
**Continuous random variable** A random variable that may assume any numerical value in an interval or collection of intervals.
**Probability distribution** A description of how the probabilities are distributed over the values of the random variable.
**Probability function** A function, denoted by $f(x)$, that provides the probability that $x$ assumes a particular value for a discrete random variable.
**Discrete uniform probability distribution** A probability distribution for which each possible value of the random variable has the same probability.
**Expected value** A measure of the central location of a random variable.
**Variance** A measure of the variability, or dispersion, of a random variable.
**Standard deviation** The positive square root of the variance.
**Binomial experiment** An experiment having the four properties stated at the beginning of Section 5.4.
**Binomial probability distribution** A probability distribution showing the probability of $x$ successes in $n$ trials of a binomial experiment.
**Binomial probability function** The function used to compute binomial probabilities.
**Poisson probability distribution** A probability distribution showing the probability of $x$ occurrences of an event over a specified interval of time or space.
**Poisson probability function** The function used to compute Poisson probabilities.

**Hypergeometric probability distribution** A probability distribution showing the probability of $x$ successes in $n$ trials from a population with $r$ successes and $N$-$r$ failures.
**Hypergeometric probability function** The function used to compute hypergeometric probabilities.

## Key Formulas

**Discrete Uniform Probability Function**

$$f(x) = 1/n \tag{5.3}$$

where

$$n = \text{the number of values the random variable may assume}$$

**Expected Value of a Discrete Random Variable**

$$E(x) = \mu = \Sigma x f(x) \tag{5.4}$$

**Variance of a Discrete Random Variable**

$$\text{Var}(x) = \sigma^2 = \Sigma(x - \mu)^2 f(x) \tag{5.5}$$

**Number of Experimental Outcomes Providing Exactly $x$ Successes in $n$ Trials**

$$\binom{n}{x} = \frac{n!}{x!(n-x)!} \tag{5.6}$$

**Binomial Probability Function**

$$f(x) = \binom{n}{x} p^x (1-p)^{(n-x)} \tag{5.8}$$

**Expected Value for the Binomial Distribution**

$$E(x) = \mu = np \tag{5.9}$$

**Variance for the Binomial Distribution**

$$\text{Var}(x) = \sigma^2 = np(1-p) \tag{5.10}$$

**Poisson Probability Function**

$$f(x) = \frac{\mu^x e^{-\mu}}{x!} \tag{5.11}$$

**Hypergeometric Probability Function**

$$f(x) = \frac{\binom{r}{x}\binom{N-r}{n-x}}{\binom{N}{n}} \qquad \text{for } 0 \le x \le r \tag{5.12}$$

**Expected Value for the Hypergeometric Distribution**

$$E(x) = \mu = n\left(\frac{r}{N}\right) \tag{5.13}$$

**Variance for the Hypergeometric Distribution**

$$\text{Var}(x) = \sigma^2 = n\left(\frac{r}{N}\right)\left(1 - \frac{r}{N}\right)\left(\frac{N-n}{N-1}\right) \tag{5.14}$$

## Supplementary Exercises

53. The *Barron's* Big Money Poll asked 131 investment managers across the United States about their short-term investment outlook (*Barron's,* October 28, 2002). Their responses showed 4% were very bullish, 39% were bullish, 29% were neutral, 21% were bearish, and 7% were very bearish. Let $x$ be the random variable reflecting the level of optimism about the market. Set $x = 5$ for very bullish down through $x = 1$ for very bearish.
    a.  Develop a probability distribution for the level of optimism of investment managers.
    b.  Compute the expected value for the level of optimism.
    c.  Compute the variance and standard deviation for the level of optimism.
    d.  Comment on what your results imply about the level of optimism and its variability.

54. The American Association of Individual Investors publishes an annual guide to the top mutual funds (*The Individual Investor's Guide to the Top Mutual Funds,* 22e, American Association of Individual Investors, 2003). Table 5.10 contains their ratings of the total risk for 29 categories of mutual funds.
    a.  Let $x = 1$ for low risk up through $x = 5$ for high risk, and develop a probability distribution for level of risk.
    b.  What are the expected value and variance for total risk?
    c.  It turns out that 11 of the fund categories were bond funds. For the bond funds, 7 categories were rated low and 4 were rated below average. Compare the total risk of the bond funds with the 17 categories stock funds.

55. The budgeting process for a midwestern college resulted in expense forecasts for the coming year (in $ millions) of $9, $10, $11, $12, and $13. Because the actual expenses are unknown, the following respective probabilities are assigned: .3, .2, .25, .05, and .2.
    a.  Show the probability distribution for the expense forecast.
    b.  What is the expected value of the expense forecast for the coming year?
    c.  What is the variance of the expense forecast for the coming year?
    d.  If income projections for the year are estimated at $12 million, comment on the financial position of the college.

**TABLE 5.10    RISK RATING FOR 29 CATEGORIES OF MUTUAL FUNDS**

| Total Risk | Number of Fund Categories |
|---|---|
| Low | 7 |
| Below Average | 6 |
| Average | 3 |
| Above Average | 6 |
| High | 7 |

56. Kristen DelGuzzi conducted a study of Hamilton County judges and courts over a three-year period (*The Cincinnati Enquirer,* January 11, 1998). One finding was that 4% of the cases decided in Common Pleas Court were appealed.
    a. If 20 cases are heard on a particular day, what is the probability that 3 will be appealed?
    b. If 20 cases are heard on a particular day, what is the probability none will be appealed?
    c. It is not unusual for 1200 cases to be heard in a month. What is the expected number of appeals?
    d. If 1200 cases are heard in a month, what are the variance and standard deviation of the number of appeals?

57. A company is planning to interview Internet users to learn how its proposed Web site will be received by different age groups. According to the Census Bureau, 40% of individuals aged 18 to 54, and 12% of individuals aged 55 and over use the Internet (*Statistical Abstract of the United States,* 2000).
    a. How many people from the 18–54 age group must be contacted to find an expected number of at least 10 Internet users?
    b. How many people from the age group 55 and over must be contacted to find an expected number of at least 10 Internet users?
    c. If you contact the number of 18- to 54-year-old people suggested in part (a), what is the standard deviation of the number who will be Internet users?
    d. If you contact the number of people aged 55 and older suggested in part (b), what is the standard deviation of the number who will be Internet users?

58. Many companies use a quality control technique called acceptance sampling to monitor incoming shipments of parts, raw materials, and so on. In the electronics industry, component parts are commonly shipped from suppliers in large lots. Inspection of a sample of $n$ components can be viewed as the $n$ trials of a binomial experiment. The outcome for each component tested (trial) will be that the component is classified as good or defective. Reynolds Electronics accepts a lot from a particular supplier if the defective components in the lot do not exceed 1%. Suppose a random sample of five items from a recent shipment is tested.
    a. Assume that 1% of the shipment is defective. Compute the probability that no items in the sample are defective.
    b. Assume that 1% of the shipment is defective. Compute the probability that exactly one item in the sample is defective.
    c. What is the probability of observing one or more defective items in the sample if 1% of the shipment is defective?
    d. Would you feel comfortable accepting the shipment if one item were found to be defective? Why or why not?

59. The unemployment rate is 4.1% (*Barron's,* September 4, 2000). Assume that 100 employable people are selected randomly.
    a. What is the expected number of people who are unemployed?
    b. What is the variance and standard deviation of the number of people who are unemployed?

60. In December 1997, the U.S. Department of Justice issued an injunction against Microsoft Corporation for bundling its Internet Explorer® Web browser with its Windows 95® operating system (*Fortune,* February 2, 1998). Public opinion was divided on whether Microsoft was a monopoly. In a *Fortune* poll, 41% of respondents agreed with the statement, "Microsoft is a monopoly." Suppose a sample of 800 people is taken.
    a. How many would you expect to agree that Microsoft is a monopoly?
    b. What is the standard deviation of the number of respondents who believe Microsoft is a monopoly?
    c. What is the standard deviation of the number of respondents who do not believe Microsoft is a monopoly?

61. Cars arrive at a car wash randomly and independently; the probability of an arrival is the same for any two time intervals of equal length. The mean arrival rate is 15 cars per hour. What is the probability that 20 or more cars will arrive during any given hour of operation?

62. A new automated production process averages 1.5 breakdowns per day. Because of the cost associated with a breakdown, management is concerned about the possibility of having three or more breakdowns during a day. Assume that breakdowns occur randomly, that the probability of a breakdown is the same for any two time intervals of equal length, and that breakdowns in one period are independent of breakdowns in other periods. What is the probability of having three or more breakdowns during a day?

63. A regional director responsible for business development in the state of Pennsylvania is concerned about the number of small business failures. If the mean number of small business failures per month is 10, what is the probability that exactly four small businesses will fail during a given month? Assume that the probability of a failure is the same for any two months and that the occurrence or nonoccurrence of a failure in any month is independent of failures in any other month.

64. Customer arrivals at a bank are random and independent; the probability of an arrival in any one-minute period is the same as the probability of an arrival in any other one-minute period. Answer the following questions, assuming a mean arrival rate of three customers per minute.
    a. What is the probability of exactly three arrivals in a one-minute period?
    b. What is the probability of at least three arrivals in a one-minute period?

65. A deck of playing cards contains 52 cards, four of which are aces. What is the probability that the deal of a five-card hand provides:
    a. A pair of aces?
    b. Exactly one ace?
    c. No aces?
    d. At least one ace?

66. Through the week ending September 16, 2001, Tiger Woods was the leading money winner on the PGA Tour, with total earnings of $5,517,777. Of the top 10 money winners, seven players used a Titleist brand golf ball (www.pgatour.com). Suppose that we randomly select two of the top 10 money winners.
    a. What is the probability that exactly one uses a Titleist golf ball?
    b. What is the probability that both use Titleist golf balls?
    c. What is the probability that neither uses a Titleist golf ball?

# Appendix 5.1 Discrete Probability Distributions with Minitab

Statistical packages such as Minitab offer a relatively easy and efficient procedure for computing binomial probabilities. In this appendix, we show the step-by-step procedure for determining the binomial probabilities for the Martin Clothing Store problem in Section 5.4. Recall that the desired binomial probabilities are based on $n = 10$ and $p = .30$. Before beginning the Minitab routine, the user must enter the desired values of the random variable $x$ into a column of the worksheet. We entered the values $0, 1, 2, \ldots, 10$ in column 1 (see Figure 5.5) to generate the entire binomial probability distribution. The Minitab steps to obtain the desired binomial probabilities follow.

**Step 1.** Select the **Calc** menu
**Step 2.** Choose **Probability Distributions**
**Step 3.** Choose **Binomial**
**Step 4.** When the Binomial Distribution dialog box appears:
      Select **Probability**
      Enter 10 in the **Number of trials** box
      Enter .3 in the **Probability of success** box
      Enter C1 in the **Input column** box
      Click **OK**

The Minitab output with the binomial probabilities will appear as shown in Figure 5.5.

Minitab provides Poisson probabilities in a similar manner. The only differences are in step 3, where the Poisson option would be selected, and step 4, where the **Mean** would be entered rather than the number of trials and the probability of success.

# Appendix 5.2   Discrete Probability Distributions with Excel

Excel provides functions for computing probabilities for the binomial, Poisson, and hypergeometric distributions introduced in this chapter. The Excel function for computing binomial probabilities is BINOMDIST. It has four arguments: $x$ (the number of successes), $n$ (the number of trials), $p$ (the probability of success), and cumulative. FALSE is used for the fourth argument (cumulative) if we want the probability of $x$ successes, and TRUE is used for the fourth argument if we want the cumulative probability of $x$ or fewer successes. Here we show how to compute the probabilities of 0 through 10 successes in the Martin Clothing Store problem of Section 5.4 (see Figure 5.5).

As we describe the worksheet development refer to Figure 5.6; the formula worksheet is set in the background, and the value worksheet appears in the foreground. We entered

**FIGURE 5.6    EXCEL WORKSHEET FOR COMPUTING BINOMIAL PROBABILITIES**

| | A | B | C | D |
|---|---|---|---|---|
| 1 | Number of Trials (n) | 10 | | |
| 2 | Probability of Success (p) | 0.3 | | |
| 3 | | | | |
| 4 | | x | f(x) | |
| 5 | | 0 | =BINOMDIST(B5,$B$1,$B$2,FALSE) | |
| 6 | | 1 | =BINOMDIST(B6,$B$1,$B$2,FALSE) | |
| 7 | | 2 | =BINOMDIST(B7,$B$1,$B$2,FALSE) | |
| 8 | | 3 | =BINOMDIST(B8,$B$1,$B$2,FALSE) | |
| 9 | | 4 | =BINOMDIST(B9,$B$1,$B$2,FALSE) | |
| 10 | | 5 | =BINOMDIST(B10,$B$1,$B$2,FALSE) | |
| 11 | | 6 | =BINOMDIST(B11,$B$1,$B$2,FALSE) | |
| 12 | | 7 | =BINOMDIST(B12,$B$1,$B$2,FALSE) | |
| 13 | | 8 | =BINOMDIST(B13,$B$1,$B$2,FALSE) | |
| 14 | | 9 | =BINOMDIST(B14,$B$1,$B$2,FALSE) | |
| 15 | | 10 | =BINOMDIST(B15,$B$1,$B$2,FALSE) | |
| 16 | | | | |

| | A | B | C | D |
|---|---|---|---|---|
| 1 | Number of Trials (n) | 10 | | |
| 2 | Probability of Success (p) | 0.3 | | |
| 3 | | | | |
| 4 | | x | f(x) | |
| 5 | | 0 | 0.0282 | |
| 6 | | 1 | 0.1211 | |
| 7 | | 2 | 0.2335 | |
| 8 | | 3 | 0.2668 | |
| 9 | | 4 | 0.2001 | |
| 10 | | 5 | 0.1029 | |
| 11 | | 6 | 0.0368 | |
| 12 | | 7 | 0.0090 | |
| 13 | | 8 | 0.0014 | |
| 14 | | 9 | 0.0001 | |
| 15 | | 10 | 0.0000 | |
| 16 | | | | |

the number of trials (10) into cell B1, the probability of success into cell B2, and the values for the random variable into cells B5:B15. The following steps will generate the desired probabilities:

**Step 1.** Use the BINOMDIST function to compute the probability of $x = 0$ by entering the following formula into cell C5:

$$=\text{BINOMDIST(B5,\$B\$1,\$B\$2,FALSE)}$$

**Step 2.** Copy the formula in cell C5 into cells C6:C15.

The value worksheet in the foreground of Figure 5.6 shows that the probabilities obtained are the same as in Figure 5.5. Poisson and hypergeometric probabilities can be computed in a similar fashion. The POISSON and HYPERGEOMDIST functions are used. Excel's Insert Function tool can help the user in entering the proper arguments for these functions (see Appendix 2.2).

# CHAPTER 6

# Continuous Probability Distributions

## CONTENTS

## PROCTER & GAMBLE*
### *CINCINNATI, OHIO*

Procter & Gamble (P&G) produces and markets such products as detergents, disposable diapers, over-the-counter pharmaceuticals, dentifrices, bar soaps, mouthwashes, and paper towels. Worldwide, it has the leading brand in more categories than any other consumer products company.

As a leader in the application of statistical methods in decision making, P&G employs people with diverse academic backgrounds: engineering, statistics, operations research, and business. The major quantitative technologies for which these people provide support are probabilistic decision and risk analysis, advanced simulation, quality improvement, and quantitative methods (e.g., linear programming, regression analysis, probability analysis).

The Industrial Chemicals Division of P&G is a major supplier of fatty alcohols derived from natural substances such as coconut oil and from petroleum-based derivatives. The division wanted to know the economic risks and opportunities of expanding its fatty-alcohol production facilities, so it called in P&G's experts in probabilistic decision and risk analysis to help. After structuring and modeling the problem, they determined that the key to profitability was the cost difference between the petroleum- and coconut-based raw materials. Future costs were unknown, but the analysts were able to represent them with the following continuous random variables.

$$x = \text{the coconut oil price per pound of fatty alcohol}$$

and

$$y = \text{the petroleum raw material price per pound of fatty alcohol}$$

Because the key to profitability was the difference between these two random variables, a third random variable, $d = x - y$, was used in the analysis. Experts were interviewed to determine

Some of Procter & Gamble's many well-known products.
© Joe Higgins/South-Western.

the probability distribution for $x$ and $y$. In turn, this information was used to develop a probability distribution for the difference in prices $d$. This continuous probability distribution showed a .90 probability that the price difference would be $.0655 or less and a .50 probability that the price difference would be $.035 or less. In addition, there was only a .10 probability that the price difference would be $.0045 or less.[†]

The Industrial Chemicals Division thought that being able to quantify the impact of raw material price differences was key to reaching a consensus. The probabilities obtained were used in a sensitivity analysis of the raw material price difference. The analysis yielded sufficient insight to form the basis for a recommendation to management.

The use of continuous random variables and their probability distributions was helpful to P&G in analyzing the economic risks associated with its fatty-alcohol production. In this chapter, you will gain an understanding of continuous random variables and their probability distributions including one of the most important probability distributions in statistics, the normal distribution.

*The authors are indebted to Joel Kahn of Procter & Gamble for providing this Statistics in Practice.

[†]The price differences stated here have been modified to protect proprietary data.

In the preceding chapter we discussed discrete random variables and their probability distributions. In this chapter we turn to the study of continuous random variables. Specifically, we discuss three continuous probability distributions: the uniform, the normal, and the exponential.

A fundamental difference separates discrete and continuous random variables in terms of how probabilities are computed. For a discrete random variable, the probability function $f(x)$ provides the probability that the random variable assumes a particular value. With continuous random variables the counterpart of the probability function is the **probability density function**, also denoted by $f(x)$. The difference is that the probability density function does not directly provide probabilities. However, the area under the graph of $f(x)$ corresponding to a given interval does provide the probability that the continuous random variable $x$ assumes a value in that interval. So when we compute probabilities for continuous random variables we are computing the probability that the random variable assumes any value in an interval.

One of the implications of the definition of probability for continuous random variables is that the probability of any particular value of the random variable is zero, because the area under the graph of $f(x)$ at any particular point is zero. In Section 6.1 we demonstrate these concepts for a continuous random variable that has a uniform distribution.

Much of the chapter is devoted to describing and showing applications of the normal distribution. The main importance of normal distribution is its extensive use in statistical inference. The chapter closes with a discussion of the exponential distribution.

## 6.1    Uniform Probability Distribution

*Whenever the probability is proportional to the length of the interval, the random variable is uniformly distributed.*

Consider the random variable $x$ representing the flight time of an airplane traveling from Chicago to New York. Suppose the flight time can be any value in the interval from 120 minutes to 140 minutes. Because the random variable $x$ can assume any value in that interval, $x$ is a continuous rather than a discrete random variable. Let us assume that sufficient actual flight data are available to conclude that the probability of a flight time within any 1-minute interval is the same as the probability of a flight time within any other 1-minute interval contained in the larger interval from 120 to 140 minutes. With every 1-minute interval being equally likely, the random variable $x$ is said to have a **uniform probability distribution**. The probability density function, which defines the uniform distribution for the flight-time random variable, is

$$f(x) = \begin{cases} 1/20 & \text{for } 120 \le x \le 140 \\ 0 & \text{elsewhere} \end{cases}$$

Figure 6.1 is a graph of this probability density function. In general, the uniform probability density function for a random variable $x$ is defined by the following formula.

UNIFORM PROBABILITY DENSITY FUNCTION

$$f(x) = \begin{cases} \dfrac{1}{b - a} & \text{for } a \le x \le b \\ 0 & \text{elsewhere} \end{cases} \tag{6.1}$$

For the flight-time random variable, $a = 120$ and $b = 140$.

FIGURE 6.1    UNIFORM PROBABILITY DENSITY FUNCTION FOR FLIGHT TIME

As noted in the introduction, for a continuous random variable, we consider probability only in terms of the likelihood that a random variable assumes a value within a specified interval. In the flight time example, an acceptable probability question is: What is the probability that the flight time is between 120 and 130 minutes? That is, what is $P(120 \leq x \leq 130)$? Because the flight time must be between 120 and 140 minutes and because the probability is described as being uniform over this interval, we feel comfortable saying $P(120 \leq x \leq 130) = .50$. In the following subsection we show that this probability can be computed as the area under the graph of $f(x)$ from 120 to 130 (see Figure 6.2).

## Area as a Measure of Probability

Let us make an observation about the graph in Figure 6.2. Consider the area under the graph of $f(x)$ in the interval from 120 to 130. The area is rectangular, and the area of a rectangle is simply the width multiplied by the height. With the width of the interval equal to $130 - 120 = 10$ and the height equal to the value of the probability density function $f(x) = 1/20$, we have area = width × height = $10(1/20) = 10/20 = .50$.

FIGURE 6.2    AREA PROVIDES PROBABILITY OF FLIGHT TIME BETWEEN 120
             AND 130 MINUTES

What observation can you make about the area under the graph of $f(x)$ and probability? They are identical! Indeed, this observation is valid for all continuous random variables. Once a probability density function $f(x)$ is identified, the probability that $x$ takes a value between some lower value $x_1$ and some higher value $x_2$ can be found by computing the area under the graph of $f(x)$ over the interval from $x_1$ to $x_2$.

Given the uniform distribution for flight time and using the interpretation of area as probability, we can answer any number of probability questions about flight times. For example, what is the probability of a flight time between 128 and 136 minutes? The width of the interval is $136 - 128 = 8$. With the uniform height of $f(x) = 1/20$, we see that $P(128 \leq x \leq 136) = 8(1/20) = .40$.

Note that $P(120 \leq x \leq 140) = 20(1/20) = 1$; that is, the total area under the graph of $f(x)$ is equal to 1. This property holds for all continuous probability distributions and is the analog of the condition that the sum of the probabilities must equal 1 for a discrete probability function. For a continuous probability density function, we must also require that $f(x) \geq 0$ for all values of $x$. This requirement is the analog of the requirement that $f(x) \geq 0$ for discrete probability functions.

Two major differences stand out between the treatment of continuous random variables and the treatment of their discrete counterparts.

1. We no longer talk about the probability of the random variable assuming a particular value. Instead, we talk about the probability of the random variable assuming a value within some given interval.

*To see that the probability of any single point is 0, refer to Figure 6.2 and compute the probability of a single point, say, $x = 125$. $P(x = 125) = P(125 \leq x \leq 125) = 0(1/20) = 0$.*

2. The probability of the random variable assuming a value within some given interval from $x_1$ to $x_2$ is defined to be the area under the graph of the probability density function between $x_1$ and $x_2$. It implies that the probability of a continuous random variable assuming any particular value exactly is zero, because the area under the graph of $f(x)$ at a single point is zero.

The calculation of the expected value and variance for a continuous random variable is analogous to that for a discrete random variable. However, because the computational procedure involves integral calculus, we leave the derivation of the appropriate formulas to more advanced texts.

For the uniform continuous probability distribution introduced in this section, the formulas for the expected value and variance are

$$E(x) = \frac{a + b}{2}$$

$$\text{Var}(x) = \frac{(b - a)^2}{12}$$

In these formulas, $a$ is the smallest value and $b$ is the largest value that the random variable may assume.

Applying these formulas to the uniform distribution for flight times from Chicago to New York, we obtain

$$E(x) = \frac{(120 + 140)}{2} = 130$$

$$\text{Var}(x) = \frac{(140 - 120)^2}{12} = 33.33$$

The standard deviation of flight times can be found by taking the square root of the variance. Thus, $\sigma = 5.77$ minutes.

## NOTES AND COMMENTS

1. For a continuous random variable the probability of any particular value is zero; thus, $P(a \leq x \leq b) = P(a < x < b)$. This result shows that the probability of a random variable assuming a value in any interval is the same whether or not the endpoints are included.

2. To see more clearly why the height of a probability density function is not a probability, think about a random variable with the following uniform probability distribution.

$$f(x) = \begin{cases} 2 & \text{for } 0 \leq x \leq .5 \\ 0 & \text{elsewhere} \end{cases}$$

The height of the probability density function, $f(x)$, is 2 for values of $x$ between 0 and .5. However, we know probabilities can never be greater than 1. Thus, we see that $f(x)$ cannot be interpreted as the probability of $x$.

## Exercises

### Methods

1. The random variable $x$ is known to be uniformly distributed between 1.0 and 1.5.
   a. Show the graph of the probability density function.
   b. Compute $P(x = 1.25)$.
   c. Compute $P(1.0 \leq x \leq 1.25)$.
   d. Compute $P(1.20 < x < 1.5)$.

2. The random variable $x$ is known to be uniformly distributed between 10 and 20.
   a. Show the graph of the probability density function.
   b. Compute $P(x < 15)$.
   c. Compute $P(12 \leq x \leq 18)$.
   d. Compute $E(x)$.
   e. Compute $\text{Var}(x)$.

### Applications

3. Delta Airlines quotes a flight time of 2 hours, 5 minutes for its flights from Cincinnati to Tampa. Suppose we believe that actual flight times are uniformly distributed between 2 hours and 2 hours, 20 minutes.
   a. Show the graph of the probability density function for flight time.
   b. What is the probability that the flight will be no more than 5 minutes late?
   c. What is the probability that the flight will be more than 10 minutes late?
   d. What is the expected flight time?

4. Most computer languages include a function that can be used to generate random numbers. In Excel, the RAND function can be used to generate random numbers between 0 and 1. If we let $x$ denote a random number generated using RAND, then $x$ is a continuous random variable with the following probability density function.

$$f(x) = \begin{cases} 1 & \text{for } 0 \leq x \leq 1 \\ 0 & \text{elsewhere} \end{cases}$$

   a. Graph the probability density function.
   b. What is the probability of generating a random number between .25 and .75?
   c. What is the probability of generating a random number with a value less than or equal to .30?
   d. What is the probability of generating a random number with a value greater than .60?

5.  The driving distance for the top 100 golfers on the PGA tour is between 284.7 and 310.6 yards (*Golfweek,* March 29, 2003). Assume that the driving distance for these golfers is uniformly distributed over this interval.
    a.  Give a mathematical expression for the probability density function of driving distance.
    b.  What is the probability the driving distance for one of these golfers is less than 290 yards?
    c.  What is the probability the driving distance for one of these golfers is at least 300 yards?
    d.  What is the probability the driving distance for one of these golfers is between 290 and 305 yards?
    e.  How many of these golfers drive the ball at least 290 yards?

6.  The label on a bottle of liquid detergent shows contents to be 12 ounces per bottle. The production operation fills the bottle uniformly according to the following probability density function.

$$f(x) = \begin{cases} 8 & \text{for } 11.975 \le x \le 12.100 \\ 0 & \text{elsewhere} \end{cases}$$

    a.  What is the probability that a bottle will be filled with between 12 and 12.05 ounces?
    b.  What is the probability that a bottle will be filled with 12.02 or more ounces?
    c.  Quality control accepts a bottle that is filled to within .02 ounces of the number of ounces shown on the container label. What is the probability that a bottle of this liquid detergent will fail to meet the quality control standard?

7.  Suppose we are interested in bidding on a piece of land and we know there is one other bidder.* The seller announced that the highest bid in excess of $10,000 will be accepted. Assume that the competitor's bid $x$ is a random variable that is uniformly distributed between $10,000 and $15,000.
    a.  Suppose you bid $12,000. What is the probability that your bid will be accepted?
    b.  Suppose you bid $14,000. What is the probability that your bid will be accepted?
    c.  What amount should you bid to maximize the probability that you get the property?
    d.  Suppose you know someone who is willing to pay you $16,000 for the property. Would you consider bidding less than the amount in part (c)? Why or why not?

 ## 6.2  Normal Probability Distribution

The most important probability distribution for describing a continuous random variable is the **normal probability distribution**. The normal distribution has been used in a wide variety of practical applications in which the random variables are heights and weights of people, test scores, scientific measurements, amounts of rainfall, and so on. It is also widely used in statistical inference, which is the major topic of the remainder of this book. In such applications, the normal distribution provides a description of the likely results obtained through sampling.

*Abraham de Moivre, a French mathematician, published The Doctrine of Chances in 1733. He derived the normal distribution.*

### Normal Curve

The form, or shape, of the normal distribution is illustrated by the bell-shaped normal curve in Figure 6.3. The probability density function that defines the bell-shaped curve of the normal distribution follows.

*This exercise is based on a problem suggested to us by Professor Roger Myerson of Northwestern University.

**FIGURE 6.3   BELL-SHAPED CURVE FOR THE NORMAL DISTRIBUTION**

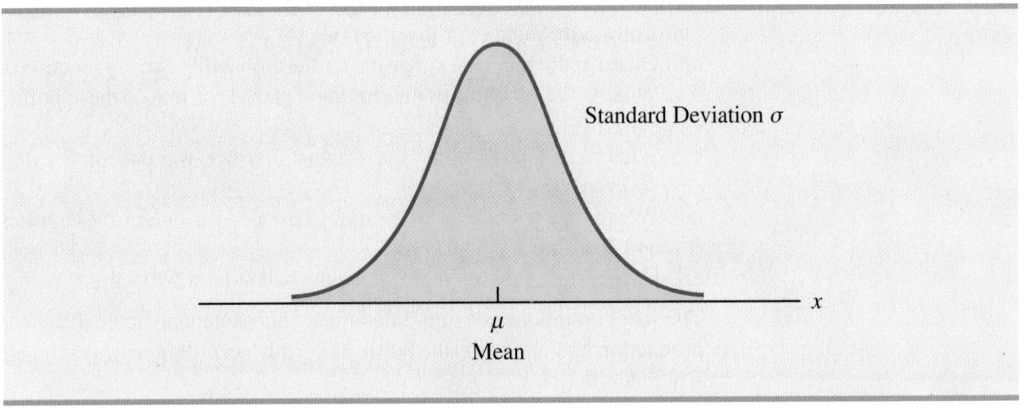

NORMAL PROBABILITY DENSITY FUNCTION

$$f(x) = \frac{1}{\sigma\sqrt{2\pi}} e^{-(x-\mu)^2/2\sigma^2}$$  (6.2)

where

$\mu$ = mean
$\sigma$ = standard deviation
$\pi$ = 3.14159
$e$ = 2.71828

We make several observations about the characteristics of the normal distribution.

*The normal curve has two parameters, $\mu$ and $\sigma$. They determine the location and shape of the normal distribution.*

1. The entire family of normal distributions is differentiated by its mean $\mu$ and its standard deviation $\sigma$.
2. The highest point on the normal curve is at the mean, which is also the median and mode of the distribution.
3. The mean of the distribution can be any numerical value: negative, zero, or positive. Three normal distributions with the same standard deviation but three different means ($-10$, 0, and 20) are shown here.

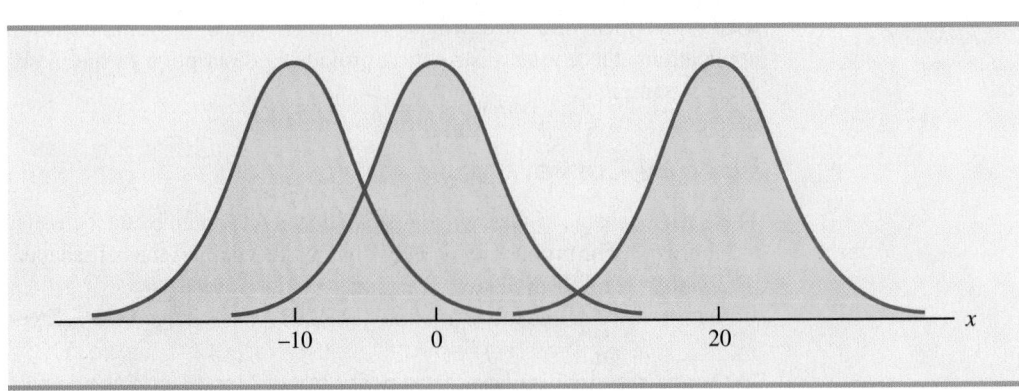

4. The normal distribution is symmetric, with the shape of the curve to the left of the mean a mirror image of the shape of the curve to the right of the mean. The tails of the curve extend to infinity in both directions and theoretically never touch the horizontal axis. Because it is symmetric, the normal distribution is not skewed; its skewness measure is zero.

5. The standard deviation determines how flat and wide the curve is. Larger values of the standard deviation result in wider, flatter curves, showing more variability in the data. Two normal distributions with the same mean but with different standard deviations are shown here.

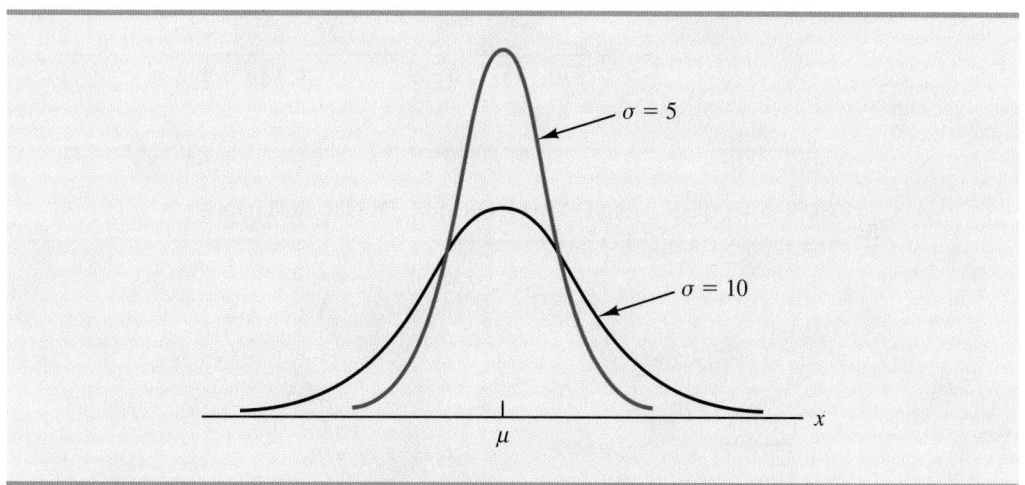

6. Probabilities for the normal random variable are given by areas under the curve. The total area under the curve for the normal distribution is 1. Because the distribution is symmetric, the area under the curve to the left of the mean is .50 and the area under the curve to the right of the mean is .50.

7. The percentage of values in some commonly used intervals are:
   a. 68.3% of the values of a normal random variable are within plus or minus one standard deviation of its mean.
   b. 95.4% of the values of a normal random variable are within plus or minus two standard deviations of its mean.
   c. 99.7% of the values of a normal random variable are within plus or minus three standard deviations of its mean.

*These percentages are the basis for the empirical rule introduced in Section 3.3.*

Figure 6.4 shows properties (a), (b), and (c) graphically.

## Standard Normal Probability Distribution

A random variable that has a normal distribution with a mean of zero and a standard deviation of one is said to have a **standard normal probability distribution**. The letter $z$ is commonly used to designate this particular normal random variable. Figure 6.5 is the graph of the standard normal distribution. It has the same general appearance as other normal distributions, but with the special properties of $\mu = 0$ and $\sigma = 1$.

FIGURE 6.4    AREAS UNDER THE CURVE FOR ANY NORMAL DISTRIBUTION

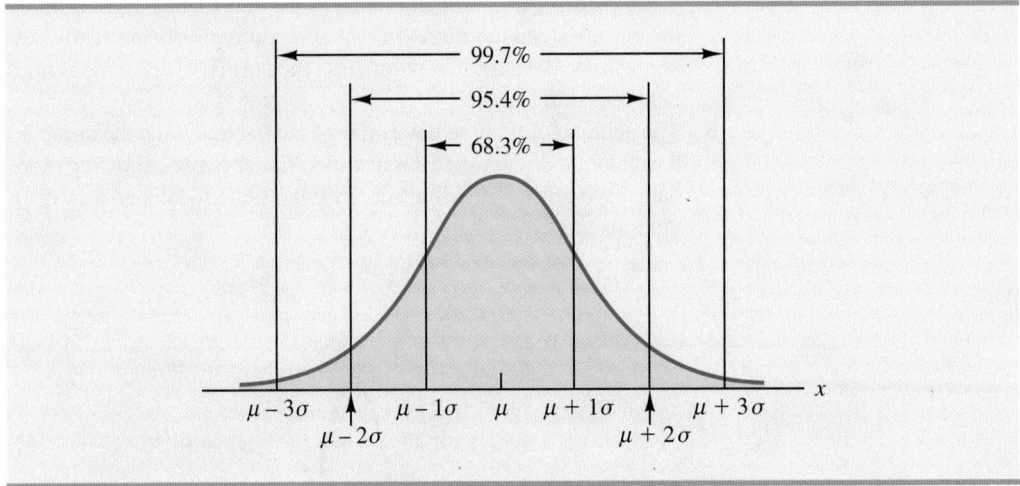

FIGURE 6.5    THE STANDARD NORMAL DISTRIBUTION

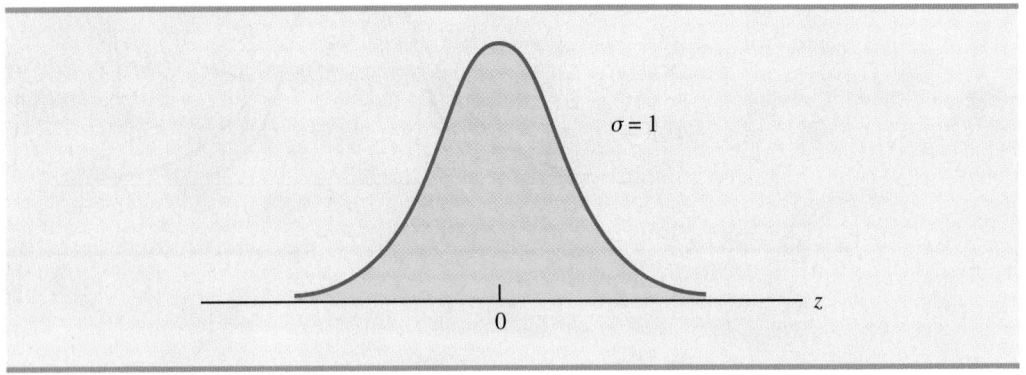

*For the normal probability density function, the height of the curve varies and calculus is required to compute the areas that represent probability.*

Because $\mu = 0$ and $\sigma = 1$, the formula for the standard normal probability density function is a simpler version of equation (6.2).

> **STANDARD NORMAL DENSITY FUNCTION**
>
> $$f(x) = \frac{1}{\sqrt{2\pi}} e^{-z^2/2}$$

As with other continuous random variables, probability calculations with any normal distribution are made by computing areas under the graph of the probability density function. Thus, to find the probability that a normal random variable is within any specific interval, we must compute the area under the normal curve over that interval. For the standard normal distribution, areas under the normal curve have been computed and are available in tables that can be used in computing probabilities. Table 6.1 is such a table; it is also available as Table 1 of Appendix B and inside the front cover of this text.

*Given a z value, we use the standard normal table to find the appropriate probability (an area under the curve).*

To see how the table of areas under the curve for the standard normal distribution (Table 6.1) can be used to find probabilities, let us consider some examples. Later, we will see how this same table can be used to compute probabilities for any normal distribution.

**TABLE 6.1   AREAS, OR PROBABILITIES, FOR THE STANDARD NORMAL DISTRIBUTION**

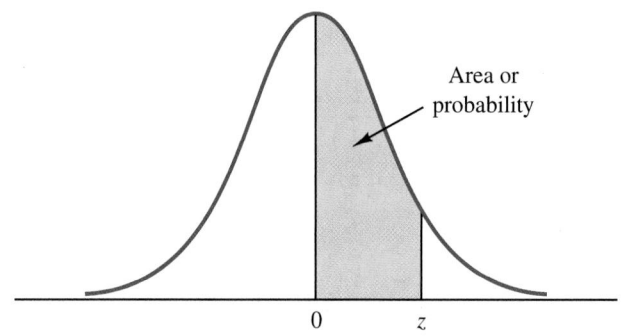

| z | .00 | .01 | .02 | .03 | .04 | .05 | .06 | .07 | .08 | .09 |
|---|---|---|---|---|---|---|---|---|---|---|
| .0 | .0000 | .0040 | .0080 | .0120 | .0160 | .0199 | .0239 | .0279 | .0319 | .0359 |
| .1 | .0398 | .0438 | .0478 | .0517 | .0557 | .0596 | .0636 | .0675 | .0714 | .0753 |
| .2 | .0793 | .0832 | .0871 | .0910 | .0948 | .0987 | .1026 | .1064 | .1103 | .1141 |
| .3 | .1179 | .1217 | .1255 | .1293 | .1331 | .1368 | .1406 | .1443 | .1480 | .1517 |
| .4 | .1554 | .1591 | .1628 | .1664 | .1700 | .1736 | .1772 | .1808 | .1844 | .1879 |
| .5 | .1915 | .1950 | .1985 | .2019 | .2054 | .2088 | .2123 | .2157 | .2190 | .2224 |
| .6 | .2257 | .2291 | .2324 | .2357 | .2389 | .2422 | .2454 | .2486 | .2517 | .2549 |
| .7 | .2580 | .2611 | .2642 | .2673 | .2704 | .2734 | .2764 | .2794 | .2823 | .2852 |
| .8 | .2881 | .2910 | .2939 | .2967 | .2995 | .3023 | .3051 | .3078 | .3106 | .3133 |
| .9 | .3159 | .3186 | .3212 | .3238 | .3264 | .3289 | .3315 | .3340 | .3365 | .3389 |
| 1.0 | .3413 | .3438 | .3461 | .3485 | .3508 | .3531 | .3554 | .3577 | .3599 | .3621 |
| 1.1 | .3643 | .3665 | .3686 | .3708 | .3729 | .3749 | .3770 | .3790 | .3810 | .3830 |
| 1.2 | .3849 | .3869 | .3888 | .3907 | .3925 | .3944 | .3962 | .3980 | .3997 | .4015 |
| 1.3 | .4032 | .4049 | .4066 | .4082 | .4099 | .4115 | .4131 | .4147 | .4162 | .4177 |
| 1.4 | .4192 | .4207 | .4222 | .4236 | .4251 | .4265 | .4279 | .4292 | .4306 | .4319 |
| 1.5 | .4332 | .4345 | .4357 | .4370 | .4382 | .4394 | .4406 | .4418 | .4429 | .4441 |
| 1.6 | .4452 | .4463 | .4474 | .4484 | .4495 | .4505 | .4515 | .4525 | .4535 | .4545 |
| 1.7 | .4554 | .4564 | .4573 | .4582 | .4591 | .4599 | .4608 | .4616 | .4625 | .4633 |
| 1.8 | .4641 | .4649 | .4656 | .4664 | .4671 | .4678 | .4686 | .4693 | .4699 | .4706 |
| 1.9 | .4713 | .4719 | .4726 | .4732 | .4738 | .4744 | .4750 | .4756 | .4761 | .4767 |
| 2.0 | .4772 | .4778 | .4783 | .4788 | .4793 | .4798 | .4803 | .4808 | .4812 | .4817 |
| 2.1 | .4821 | .4826 | .4830 | .4834 | .4838 | .4842 | .4846 | .4850 | .4854 | .4857 |
| 2.2 | .4861 | .4864 | .4868 | .4871 | .4875 | .4878 | .4881 | .4884 | .4887 | .4890 |
| 2.3 | .4893 | .4896 | .4898 | .4901 | .4904 | .4906 | .4909 | .4911 | .4913 | .4916 |
| 2.4 | .4918 | .4920 | .4922 | .4925 | .4927 | .4929 | .4931 | .4932 | .4934 | .4936 |
| 2.5 | .4938 | .4940 | .4941 | .4943 | .4945 | .4946 | .4948 | .4949 | .4951 | .4952 |
| 2.6 | .4953 | .4955 | .4956 | .4957 | .4959 | .4960 | .4961 | .4962 | .4963 | .4964 |
| 2.7 | .4965 | .4966 | .4967 | .4968 | .4969 | .4970 | .4971 | .4972 | .4973 | .4974 |
| 2.8 | .4974 | .4975 | .4976 | .4977 | .4977 | .4978 | .4979 | .4979 | .4980 | .4981 |
| 2.9 | .4981 | .4982 | .4982 | .4983 | .4984 | .4984 | .4985 | .4985 | .4986 | .4986 |
| 3.0 | .4987 | .4987 | .4987 | .4988 | .4988 | .4989 | .4989 | .4989 | .4990 | .4990 |

To begin, let us see how we can compute the probability that the $z$ value for the standard normal random variable will be between .00 and 1.00; that is, $P(.00 \leq z \leq 1.00)$. The darkly shaded region in the following graph shows this probability.

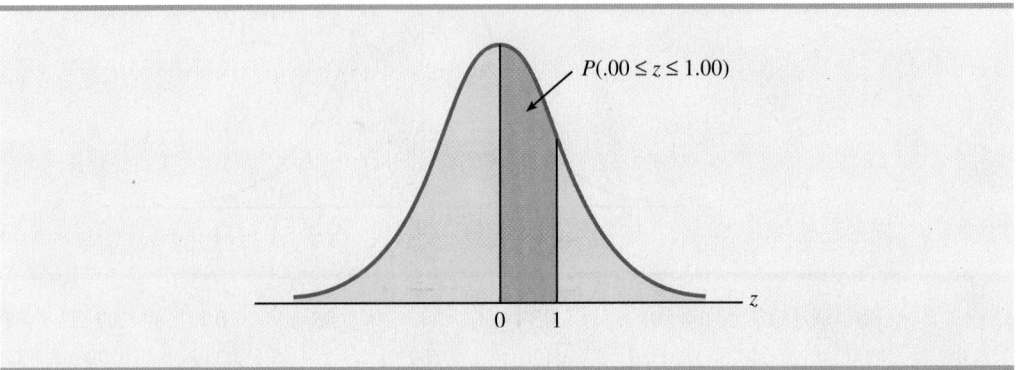

The entries in Table 6.1 give the area under the standard normal curve between the mean, $z = 0$, and a specified value of $z$ (see the graph at the top of the table). In this case, we are interested in the area between $z = 0$ and $z = 1.00$. Thus, we must find the entry in the table corresponding to $z = 1.00$. First we find 1.0 in the left column of the table and then find .00 in the top row of the table. By looking in the body of the table, we find that the 1.0 row and the .00 column intersect at the value of .3413, which gives us the desired probability: $P(.00 \leq z \leq 1.00) = .3413$. A portion of Table 6.1 showing these steps follows.

| $z$ | .00 | .01 | .02 |
|---|---|---|---|
| . | | | |
| . | | | |
| . | | | |
| .9 | .3159 | .3186 | .3212 |
| 1.0 | .3413 | .3438 | .3461 |
| 1.1 | .3643 | .3665 | .3686 |
| 1.2 | .3849 | .3869 | .3888 |
| . | | | |
| . | | | |

$P(.00 \leq z \leq 1.00)$

Using the same approach, we can find $P(.00 \leq z \leq 1.25)$. By first locating the 1.2 row and then moving across to the .05 column, we find $P(.00 \leq z \leq 1.25) = .3944$.

As another example of the use of the table of areas for the standard normal distribution, we compute the probability of obtaining a $z$ value between $z = -1.00$ and $z = 1.00$; that is, $P(-1.00 \leq z \leq 1.00)$.

Note that we already used Table 6.1 to show that the probability of a $z$ value between $z = .00$ and $z = 1.00$ is .3413, and recall that the normal distribution is *symmetric*. Thus, the probability of a $z$ value between $z = .00$ and $z = -1.00$ is the same as the probability of a $z$ value between $z = .00$ and $z = +1.00$. Hence, the probability of a $z$ value between $z = -1.00$ and $z = +1.00$ is

$$P(-1.00 \leq z \leq .00) + P(.00 \leq z \leq 1.00) = .3413 + .3413 = .6826$$

This probability is shown graphically in the following figure.

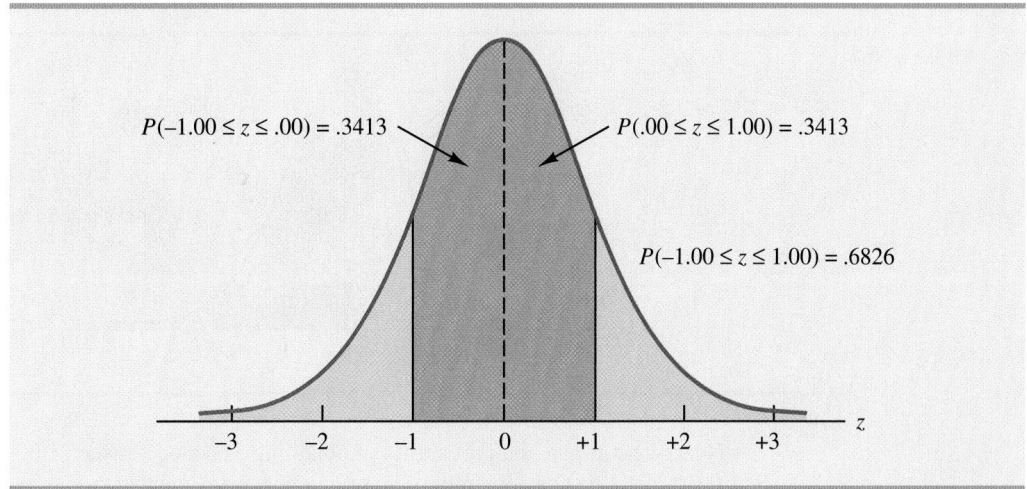

*These probability calculations are the basis for observation 7 on page 231.*

In a similar manner, we can use the values in Table 6.1 to show that the probability of a $z$ value between $-2.00$ and $+2.00$ is $.4772 + .4772 = .9544$ and that the probability of a $z$ value between $-3.00$ and $+3.00$ is $.4987 + .4987 = .9974$. Because we know that the total probability or total area under the curve for any continuous random variable must be $1.0000$, the probability $.9974$ tells us that the value of $z$ will almost always be between $-3.00$ and $+3.00$.

Next, we compute the probability of obtaining a $z$ value of at least $1.58$; that is, $P(z \geq 1.58)$. First, we use the $z = 1.5$ row and the $.08$ column of Table 6.1 to find that $P(.00 \leq z \leq 1.58) = .4429$. Now, because the normal probability distribution is symmetric, we know that 50% of the area under the curve must be to the right of the mean (i.e., $z = 0$) and 50% of the area under the curve must be to the left of the mean. If $.4429$ is the area between the mean and $z = 1.58$, then the area or probability corresponding to $z \geq 1.58$ must be $.5000 - .4429 = .0571$. This probability is shown in the following figure.

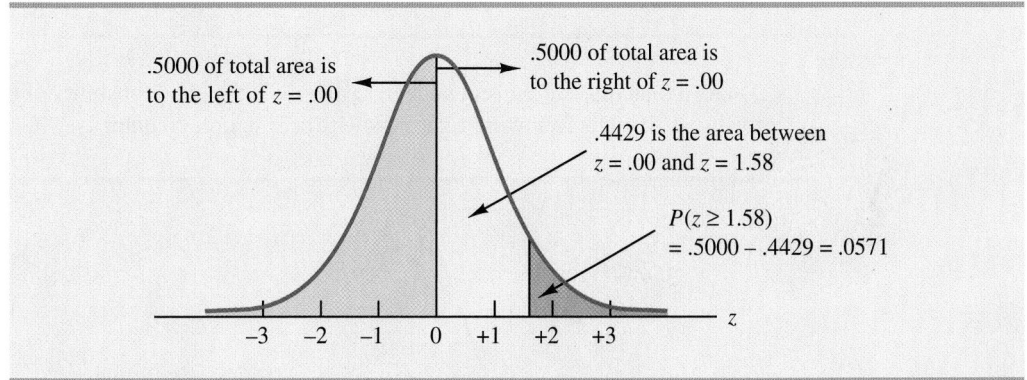

As another illustration, consider the probability that the random variable $z$ assumes a value of $-.50$ or larger; that is, $P(z \geq -.50)$. To make this computation, we note that the probability we are seeking can be written as the sum of two probabilities: $P(z \geq -.50) = P(-.50 \leq z \leq .00) + P(z \geq 0.00)$. We saw previously that $P(z \geq 0.00) = .50$. Also, we know that because the normal distribution is symmetric, $P(-.50 \leq z \leq .00) = P(.00 \leq z \leq .50)$.

Referring to Table 6.1, we find that $P(.00 \leq z \leq .50) = .1915$. Therefore $P(z \geq -.50) = .1915 + .5000 = .6915$. The following graph shows this probability.

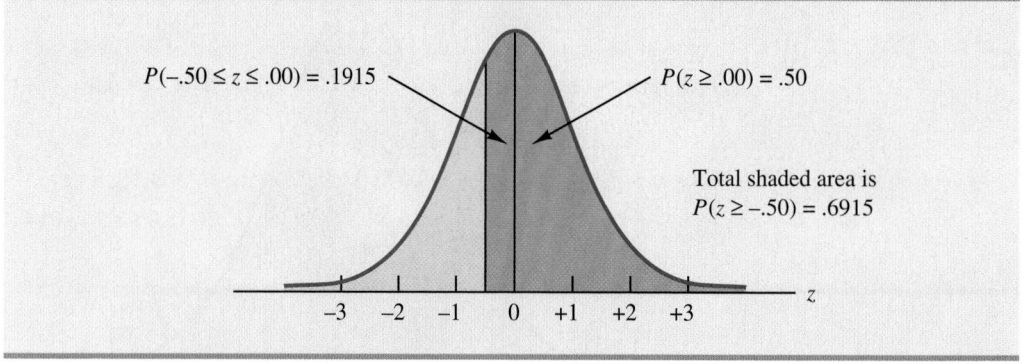

Next, we compute the probability of obtaining a $z$ value between 1.00 and 1.58; that is, $P(1.00 \leq z \leq 1.58)$. From our previous examples, we know that there is a .3413 probability of a $z$ value between $z = 0.00$ and $z = 1.00$ and that there is .4429 probability of a $z$ value between $z = 0.00$ and $z = 1.58$. Hence, there must be a $.4429 - .3413 = .1016$ probability of a $z$ value between $z = 1.00$ and $z = 1.58$. Thus, $P(1.00 \leq z \leq 1.58) = .1016$. This situation is shown graphically in the following figure.

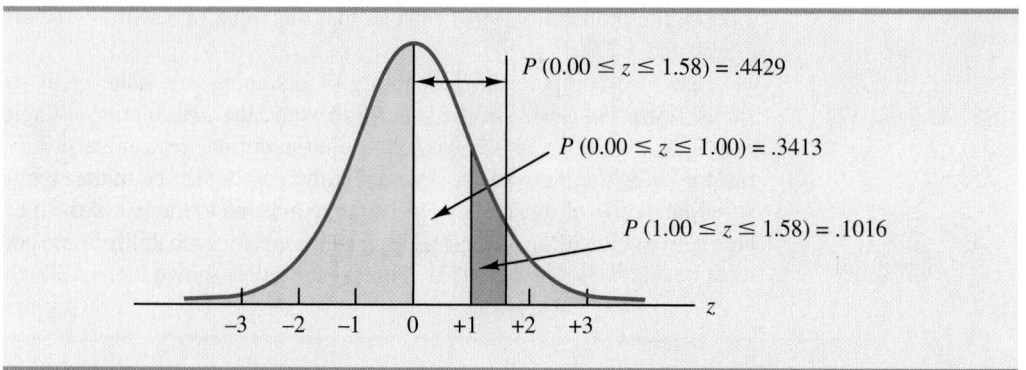

As a final illustration, let us find a $z$ value such that the probability of obtaining a larger $z$ value is .10. The following figure shows this situation graphically.

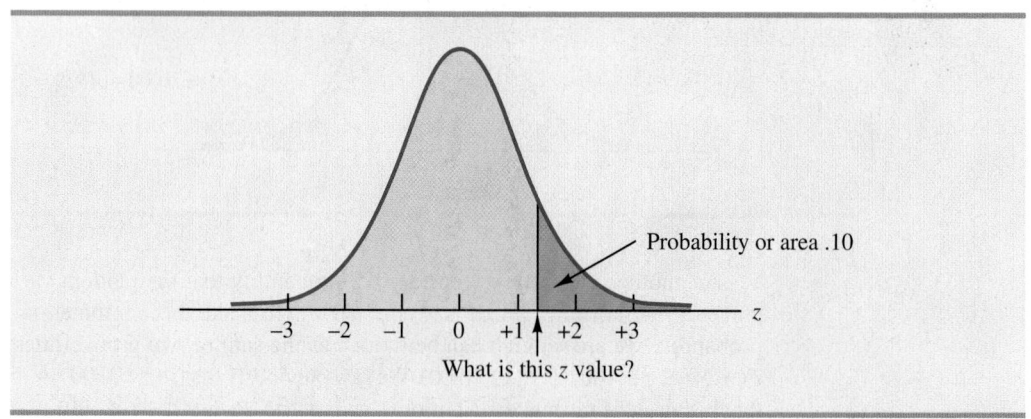

*Given a probability, we can use the standard normal table in an inverse fashion to find the corresponding z value.*

This problem is the inverse of those in the preceding examples. Previously, we specified the $z$ value of interest and then found the corresponding probability, or area. In this example, we are given the probability and asked to find the corresponding $z$ value. To do so, we use the table of probabilities for the standard normal distribution (Table 6.1) somewhat differently.

Recall that the body of Table 6.1 gives the area under the curve between the mean and a particular $z$ value. We are given the information that the area in the upper tail of the curve is .10. Hence, we must determine how much of the area is between the mean and the $z$ value of interest. Because we know that .5000 of the area is to the right of the mean, .5000 − .1000 = .4000 must be the area under the curve between the mean and the desired $z$ value. Scanning the body of the table, we find .3997 as the probability value closest to .4000. The section of the table providing this result follows.

| $z$ | .06 | .07 | .08 | .09 |
|-----|-----|-----|-----|-----|
| . | | | | |
| . | | | | |
| . | | | | |
| **1.0** | .3554 | .3577 | .3599 | .3621 |
| **1.1** | .3770 | .3790 | .3810 | .3830 |
| **1.2** | .3962 | .3980 | .3997 | .4015 |
| **1.3** | .4131 | .4147 | .4162 | .4177 |
| **1.4** | .4279 | .4292 | .4306 | .4319 |
| . | | | | |
| . | | | | |
| . | | | | |

Area value in body
of table closest to .4000

Reading the $z$ value from the left-most column and the top row of the table, we find that the corresponding $z$ value is 1.28. Thus, an area of approximately .4000 (actually .3997) will be between the mean and $z = 1.28$.* In terms of the question originally asked, the probability is approximately .10 that the $z$ value will be larger than 1.28.

The examples illustrate that the table of areas for the standard normal distribution can be used to find probabilities associated with values of the standard normal random variable $z$. Two types of questions can be asked. The first type of question specifies a value, or values, for $z$ and asks us to use the table to determine the corresponding areas, or probabilities. The second type of question provides an area, or probability, and asks us to use the table to determine the corresponding $z$ value. Thus, we need to be flexible in using the standard normal probability table to answer the desired probability question. In most cases, sketching a graph of the standard normal distribution and shading the appropriate area or probability helps to visualize the situation and aids in determining the correct answer.

## Computing Probabilities for Any Normal Distribution

The reason for discussing the standard normal distribution so extensively is that probabilities for all normal distributions are computed by using the standard normal distribution. That is, when we have a normal distribution with any mean $\mu$ and any standard deviation $\sigma$, we answer probability questions about the distribution by first converting to the standard normal distribution. Then we can use Table 6.1 and the appropriate $z$ values to find the

*We could use interpolation in the body of the table to get a better approximation of the $z$ value that corresponds to an area of .4000. Doing so provides one more decimal place of accuracy and yields a $z$ value of 1.282. However, in most practical situations, sufficient accuracy is obtained by simply using the table value closest to the desired probability.

desired probabilities. The formula used to convert any normal random variable $x$ with mean $\mu$ and standard deviation $\sigma$ to the standard normal distribution follows.

*The formula for the standard normal random variable is similar to the formula we introduced in Chapter 3 for computing z-scores for a data set.*

CONVERTING TO THE STANDARD NORMAL DISTRIBUTION

$$z = \frac{x - \mu}{\sigma}$$

(6.3)

A value of $x$ equal to its mean $\mu$ results in $z = (\mu - \mu)/\sigma = 0$. Thus, we see that a value of $x$ equal to its mean $\mu$ corresponds to a value of $z$ at its mean 0. Now suppose that $x$ is one standard deviation greater than its mean; that is, $x = \mu + \sigma$. Applying equation (6.3), we see that the corresponding $z$ value is $z = [(\mu + \sigma) - \mu]/\sigma = \sigma/\sigma = 1$. Thus, a value of $x$ that is one standard deviation above its mean corresponds to $z = 1$. In other words, we can interpret $z$ as the number of standard deviations that the normal random variable $x$ is from its mean $\mu$.

To see how this conversion enables us to compute probabilities for any normal distribution, suppose we have a normal distribution with $\mu = 10$ and $\sigma = 2$. What is the probability that the random variable $x$ is between 10 and 14? Using equation (6.3) we see that at $x = 10$, $z = (x - \mu)/\sigma = (10 - 10)/2 = 0$ and that at $x = 14$, $z = (14 - 10)/2 = 4/2 = 2$. Thus, the answer to our question about the probability of $x$ being between 10 and 14 is given by the equivalent probability that $z$ is between 0 and 2 for the standard normal distribution. In other words, the probability that we are seeking is the probability that the random variable $x$ is between its mean and two standard deviations greater than the mean. Using $z = 2.00$ and Table 6.1, we see that the probability is .4772. Hence the probability that $x$ is between 10 and 14 is .4772.

## Grear Tire Company Problem

We turn now to an application of the normal distribution. Suppose the Grear Tire Company just developed a new steel-belted radial tire that will be sold through a national chain of discount stores. Because the tire is a new product, Grear's managers believe that the mileage guarantee offered with the tire will be an important factor in the acceptance of the product. Before finalizing the tire mileage guarantee policy, Grear's managers want probability information about the number of miles the tires will last.

From actual road tests with the tires, Grear's engineering group estimates the mean tire mileage is $\mu = 36,500$ miles and that the standard deviation is $\sigma = 5000$. In addition, the data collected indicate a normal distribution is a reasonable assumption. What percentage of the tires can be expected to last more than 40,000 miles? In other words, what is the probability that the tire mileage will exceed 40,000? This question can be answered by finding the area of the darkly shaded region in Figure 6.6.

At $x = 40,000$, we have

$$z = \frac{x - \mu}{\sigma} = \frac{40,000 - 36,500}{5000} = \frac{3500}{5000} = .70$$

Refer now to the bottom of Figure 6.6. We see that a value of $x = 40,000$ on the Grear Tire normal distribution corresponds to a value of $z = .70$ on the standard normal distribution. Using Table 6.1, we see that the area between the mean and $z = .70$ is .2580. Referring again to Figure 6.6, we see that the area between $x = 36,500$ and $x = 40,000$ on the Grear Tire normal distribution is the same. Thus, .5000 − .2580 = .2420 is the probability that $x$ will exceed 40,000. We can conclude that about 24.2% of the tires will exceed 40,000 in mileage.

**FIGURE 6.6    GREAR TIRE COMPANY MILEAGE DISTRIBUTION**

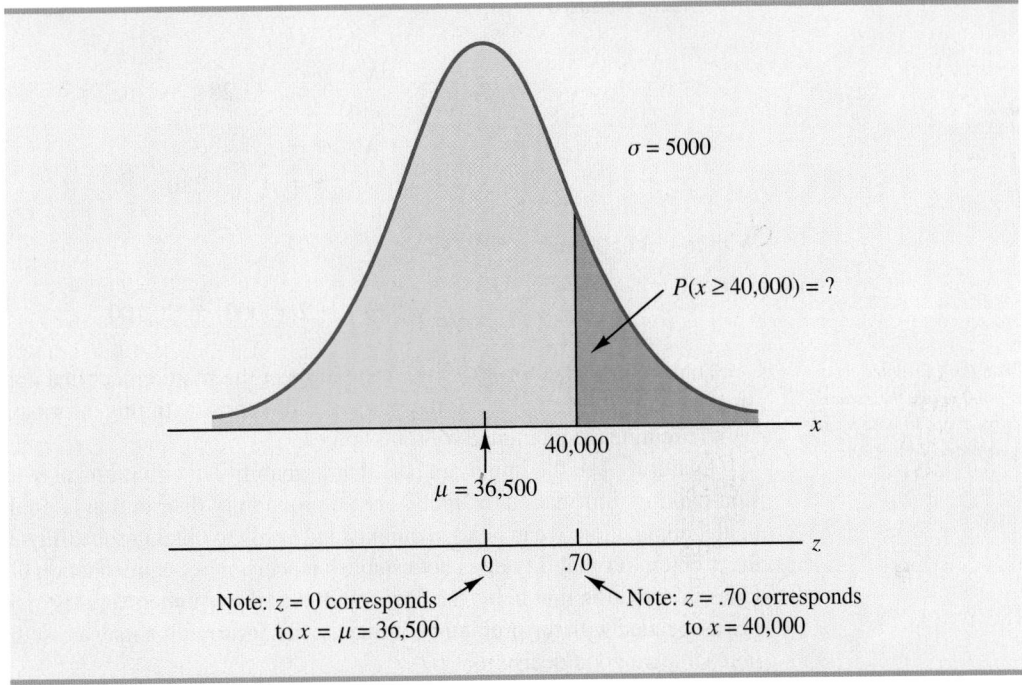

Let us now assume that Grear is considering a guarantee that will provide a discount on replacement tires if the original tires do not exceed the mileage stated in the guarantee. What should the guaranteed mileage be if Grear wants no more than 10% of the tires to be eligible for the discount guarantee? This question is interpreted graphically in Figure 6.7.

According to Figure 6.7, 40% of the area must be between the mean and the unknown guarantee mileage. We look up .4000 in the body of Table 6.1 and see that this area is at approximately 1.28 standard deviations to the left of the mean. That is, $z = -1.28$ is the value of the standard normal random variable corresponding to the desired mileage

**FIGURE 6.7    GREAR'S DISCOUNT GUARANTEE**

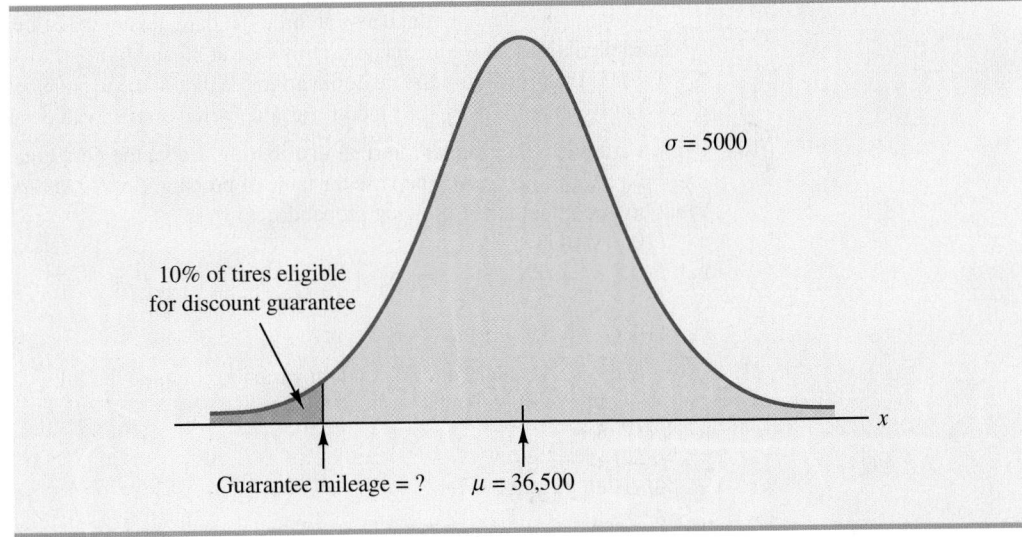

guarantee on the Grear Tire normal distribution. To find the value of $x$ corresponding to $z = -1.28$, we have

$$z = \frac{x - \mu}{\sigma} = -1.28$$
$$x - \mu = -1.28\sigma$$
$$x = \mu - 1.28\sigma$$

With $\mu = 36,500$ and $\sigma = 5000$,

$$x = 36,500 - 1.28(5000) = 30,100$$

*With the guarantee set at 30,000 miles, the actual percentage eligible for the guarantee will be 9.68%.*

Thus, a guarantee of 30,100 miles will meet the requirement that approximately 10% of the tires will be eligible for the guarantee. Perhaps, with this information, the firm will set its tire mileage guarantee at 30,000 miles.

Again, we see the important role that probability distributions play in providing deci-sion-making information. Namely, once a probability distribution is established for a par-ticular application, it can be used quickly and easily to obtain probability information about the problem. Probability does not establish a decision recommendation directly, but it pro-vides information that helps the decision maker better understand the risks and uncertain-ties associated with the problem. Ultimately, this information may assist the decision maker in reaching a good decision.

## Exercises

## Methods

8. Using Figure 6.4 as a guide, sketch a normal curve for a random variable $x$ that has a mean of $\mu = 100$ and a standard deviation of $\sigma = 10$. Label the horizontal axis with values of 70, 80, 90, 100, 110, 120, and 130.

9. A random variable is normally distributed with a mean of $\mu = 50$ and a standard devia-tion of $\sigma = 5$.
   a. Sketch a normal curve for the probability density function. Label the horizontal axis with values of 35, 40, 45, 50, 55, 60, and 65. Figure 6.4 shows that the normal curve almost touches the horizontal axis at three standard deviations below and at three stan-dard deviations above the mean (in this case at 35 and 65).
   b. What is the probability the random variable will assume a value between 45 and 55?
   c. What is the probability the random variable will assume a value between 40 and 60?

10. Draw a graph for the standard normal distribution. Label the horizontal axis at values of $-3, -2, -1, 0, 1, 2$, and 3. Then use the table of probabilities for the standard normal dis-tribution to compute the following probabilities.
    a. $P(0 \leq z \leq 1)$
    b. $P(0 \leq z \leq 1.5)$
    c. $P(0 < z < 2)$
    d. $P(0 < z < 2.5)$

11. Given that $z$ is a standard normal random variable, compute the following probabilities.
    a. $P(-1 \leq z \leq 0)$
    b. $P(-1.5 \leq z \leq 0)$
    c. $P(-2 < z < 0)$
    d. $P(-2.5 \leq z \leq 0)$
    e. $P(-3 \leq z \leq 0)$

12. Given that $z$ is a standard normal random variable, compute the following probabilities.
    a. $P(0 \le z \le .83)$
    b. $P(-1.57 \le z \le 0)$
    c. $P(z > .44)$
    d. $P(z \ge -.23)$
    e. $P(z < 1.20)$
    f. $P(z \le -.71)$

13. Given that $z$ is a standard normal random variable, compute the following probabilities.
    a. $P(-1.98 \le z \le .49)$
    b. $P(.52 \le z \le 1.22)$
    c. $P(-1.75 \le z \le -1.04)$

14. Given that $z$ is a standard normal random variable, find $z$ for each situation.
    a. The area between 0 and $z$ is .4750.
    b. The area between 0 and $z$ is .2291.
    c. The area to the right of $z$ is .1314.
    d. The area to the left of $z$ is .6700.

15. Given that $z$ is a standard normal random variable, find $z$ for each situation.
    a. The area to the left of $z$ is .2119.
    b. The area between $-z$ and $z$ is .9030.
    c. The area between $-z$ and $z$ is .2052.
    d. The area to the left of $z$ is .9948.
    e. The area to the right of $z$ is .6915.

16. Given that $z$ is a standard normal random variable, find $z$ for each situation.
    a. The area to the right of $z$ is .01.
    b. The area to the right of $z$ is .025.
    c. The area to the right of $z$ is .05.
    d. The area to the right of $z$ is .10.

## Applications

17. The average amount parents and children spent per child on back-to-school clothes in Autumn 2001 was $527 (CNBC, September 5, 2001). Assume the standard deviation is $160 and that the amount spent is normally distributed.
    a. What is the probability that the amount spent on a randomly selected child is more than $700?
    b. What is the probability that the amount spent on a randomly selected child is less than $100?
    c. What is the probability that the amount spent on a randomly selected child is between $450 and $700?
    d. What is the probability that the amount spent on a randomly selected child is no more than $300?

18. The average stock price for companies making up the S&P 500 is $30, and the standard deviation is $8.2 (*BusinessWeek*, Special Annual Issue, Spring 2003). Assume the stock prices are normally distributed.
    a. What is the probability a company will have a stock price of at least $40?
    b. What is the probability a company will have a stock price no higher than $20?
    c. How high does a stock price have to be to put a company in the top 10%?

19. The average amount of precipitation in Dallas, Texas, during the month of April is 3.5 inches (*The World Almanac*, 2000). Assume that a normal distribution applies and that the standard deviation is .8 inches.
    a. What percentage of the time does the amount of rainfall in April exceed 5 inches?
    b. What percentage of the time is the amount of rainfall in April less than 3 inches?
    c. A month is classified as extremely wet if the amount of rainfall is in the upper 10% for that month. How much precipitation must fall before a month of April is classified as extremely wet?

20. In January 2003, the American worker spent an average of 77 hours logged on to the Internet while at work (*CNBC*, March 15, 2003). Assume the times are normally distributed and that the standard deviation is 20 hours.
   a. What is the probability a randomly selected worker spent fewer than 50 hours logged on to the Internet?
   b. What percentage of workers spent more than 100 hours logged on to the Internet?
   c. A person is classified as a heavy user if he or she is in the upper 20% of usage. How many hours must a worker have logged on to the Internet to be considered a heavy user?

21. A person must score in the upper 2% of the population on an IQ test to qualify for membership in Mensa, the international high-IQ society (*US Airways Attache*, September, 2000). If IQ scores are normally distributed with a mean of 100 and a standard deviation of 15, what score must a person have to qualify for Mensa?

22. According to the Bureau of Labor Statistics, the average weekly pay for a U.S. production worker was $441.84 (*The World Almanac*, 2000). Assume that available data indicate that production worker wages were normally distributed with a standard deviation of $90.
   a. What is the probability that a worker earned between $400 and $500?
   b. How much did a production worker have to earn to be in the top 20% of wage earners?
   c. For a randomly selected production worker, what is the probability the worker earned less than $250 per week?

23. The time needed to complete a final examination in a particular college course is normally distributed with a mean of 80 minutes and a standard deviation of 10 minutes. Answer the following questions.
   a. What is the probability of completing the exam in one hour or less?
   b. What is the probability that a student will complete the exam in more than 60 minutes but less than 75 minutes?
   c. Assume that the class has 60 students and that the examination period is 90 minutes in length. How many students do you expect will be unable to complete the exam in the allotted time?

24. The daily trading volumes (millions of shares) for stocks traded on the New York Stock Exchange for 12 days in August and September are shown here (*Barron's*, August 7, 2000, September 4, 2000, and September 11, 2000).

| | | |
|---|---|---|
| 917 | 983 | 1,046 |
| 944 | 723 | 783 |
| 813 | 1,057 | 766 |
| 836 | 992 | 973 |

The probability distribution of trading volume is approximately normal.
   a. Compute the mean and standard deviation for the daily trading volume to use as estimates of the population mean and standard deviation.
   b. What is the probability that on a particular day the trading volume will be less than 800 million shares?
   c. What is the probability that trading volume will exceed 1 billion shares?
   d. If the exchange wants to issue a press release on the top 5% of trading days, what volume will trigger a release?

25. The average ticket price for a Washington Redskins football game was $81.89 for the 2001 season (*USA Today*, September 6, 2001). With the additional costs of parking, food, drinks, and souvenirs, the average cost for a family of four to attend a game totaled $442.54. Assume the normal distribution applies and that the standard deviation is $65.
   a. What is the probability that a family of four will spend more than $400?
   b. What is the probability that a family of four will spend $300 or less?
   c. What is the probability that a family of four will spend between $400 and $500?

# 6.3  Normal Approximation of Binomial Probabilities

In Section 5.4 we presented the discrete binomial distribution. Recall that a binomial experiment consists of a sequence of $n$ identical independent trials with each trial having two possible outcomes, a success or a failure. The probability of a success on a trial is the same for all trials and is denoted by $p$. The binomial random variable is the number of successes in the $n$ trials, and probability questions pertain to the probability of $x$ successes in the $n$ trials.

When the number of trials becomes large, evaluating the binomial probability function by hand or with a calculator is difficult. In addition, the binomial tables in Appendix B do not include values of $n$ greater than 20. Hence, when we encounter a binomial distribution problem with a large number of trials, we may want to approximate the binomial distribution. In cases where the number of trials is greater than 20, $np \geq 5$, and $n(1 - p) \geq 5$, the normal distribution provides an easy-to-use approximation of binomial probabilities.

When using the normal approximation to the binomial, we set $\mu = np$ and $\sigma = \sqrt{np(1 - p)}$ in the definition of the normal curve. Let us illustrate the normal approximation to the binomial by supposing that a particular company has a history of making errors in 10% of its invoices. A sample of 100 invoices has been taken, and we want to compute the probability that 12 invoices contain errors. That is, we want to find the binomial probability of 12 successes in 100 trials.

In applying the normal approximation to the binomial, we set $\mu = np = (100)(.1) = 10$ and $\sigma = \sqrt{np(1 - p)} = \sqrt{(100)(.1)(.9)} = 3$. A normal distribution with $\mu = 10$ and $\sigma = 3$ is shown in Figure 6.8.

Recall that, with a continuous probability distribution, probabilities are computed as areas under the probability density function. As a result, the probability of any single value for the random variable is zero. Thus to approximate the binomial probability of 12 successes, we must compute the area under the corresponding normal curve between 11.5 and 12.5. The .5 that we add and subtract from 12 is called a **continuity correction factor**. It is introduced

FIGURE 6.8    NORMAL APPROXIMATION TO A BINOMIAL PROBABILITY DISTRIBUTION WITH $n = 100$ AND $p = .10$ SHOWING THE PROBABILITY OF 12 ERRORS

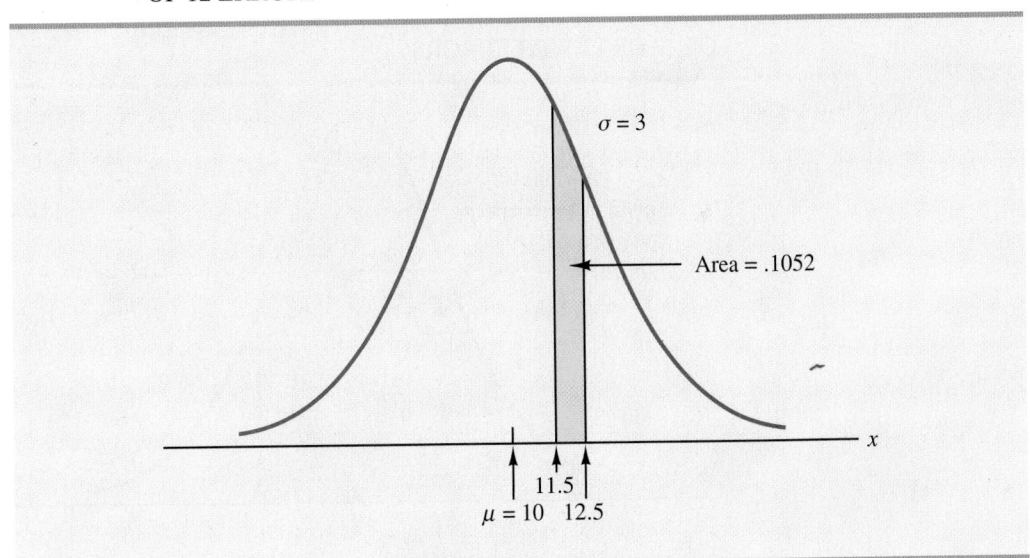

because a continuous distribution is being used to approximate a discrete distribution. Thus, $P(x = 12)$ for the *discrete* binomial distribution is approximated by $P(11.5 \leq x \leq 12.5)$ for the *continuous* normal distribution.

Converting to the standard normal distribution to compute $P(11.5 \leq x \leq 12.5)$, we have

$$z = \frac{x - \mu}{\sigma} = \frac{12.5 - 10.0}{3} = .83 \quad \text{at } x = 12.5$$

and

$$z = \frac{x - \mu}{\sigma} = \frac{11.5 - 10.0}{3} = .50 \quad \text{at } x = 11.5$$

From Table 6.1 we find that the area under the curve (in Figure 6.8) between 10 and 12.5 is .2967. Similarly, the area under the curve between 10 and 11.5 is .1915. Therefore, the area between 11.5 and 12.5 is .2967 − .1915 = .1052. The normal approximation to the probability of 12 successes in 100 trials is .1052.

For another illustration, suppose we want to compute the probability of 13 or fewer errors in the sample of 100 invoices. Figure 6.9 shows the area under the normal curve that approximates this probability. Note that the use of the continuity correction factor results in the value of 13.5 being used to compute the desired probability. The $z$ value corresponding to $x = 13.5$ is

$$z = \frac{13.5 - 10.0}{3.0} = 1.17$$

Table 6.1 shows that the area under the standard normal curve between 0 and 1.17 is .3790. The area under the normal curve approximating the probability of 13 or fewer errors is given by the heavily shaded portion of the graph in Figure 6.9. The probability is .3790 + .5000 = .8790.

**FIGURE 6.9** NORMAL APPROXIMATION TO A BINOMIAL PROBABILITY DISTRIBUTION WITH $n = 100$ AND $p = .10$ SHOWING THE PROBABILITY OF 13 OR FEWER ERRORS

## Exercises

### Methods

26. A binomial probability distribution has $p = .20$ and $n = 100$.
    a. What is the mean and standard deviation?
    b. Is this a situation in which binomial probabilities can be approximated by the normal probability distribution? Explain.
    c. What is the probability of exactly 24 successes?
    d. What is the probability of 18 to 22 successes?
    e. What is the probability of 15 or fewer successes?

27. Assume a binomial probability distribution has $p = .60$ and $n = 200$.
    a. What is the mean and standard deviation?
    b. Is this a situation in which binomial probabilities can be approximated by the normal probability distribution? Explain.
    c. What is the probability of 100 to 110 successes?
    d. What is the probability of 130 or more successes?
    e. What is the advantage of using the normal probability distribution to approximate the binomial probabilities? Use part (d) to explain the advantage.

### Applications

28. President Bush proposed the elimination of taxes on dividends paid to shareholders on the grounds that they result in double taxation. The earnings used to pay dividends are already taxed to the corporation. A survey on this issue revealed that 47% of Americans favor the proposal. By political party, 64% of Republications and 29% of Democrats favor the proposal (*Investor's Business Daily,* January 13, 2003). Suppose a group of 250 Americans gather to hear a speech about the proposal.
    a. What is the probability at least half of the group is in favor of the proposal?
    b. You later find out 150 Republicans and 100 Democrats are present. Now what is your estimate of the expected number in favor of the proposal?
    c. Will a speaker in favor of the proposal be better received by this group than one against the proposal?

29. The unemployment rate is 5.8% (*Bureau of Labor Statistics,* www.bls.gov, April 3, 2003). Suppose that 100 employable people are selected randomly.
    a. What is the expected number who are unemployed?
    b. What is the variance and standard deviation of the number who are unemployed?
    c. What is the probability that exactly 6 are unemployed?
    d. What is the probability that at least 4 are unemployed?

30. In December 1997, the U.S. Department of Justice issued an injunction against Microsoft Corporation for bundling its Internet Explorer Web browser with its Windows 95 operating system (*Fortune,* February 2, 1998). Public opinion was divided on whether Microsoft was a monopoly. In a *Fortune* poll, 41% of respondents agreed with the statement, "Microsoft is a monopoly."
    a. For a sample of 800 people, how many would you expect to agree that Microsoft is a monopoly?
    b. For a sample of 800 people, what is the probability that 300 or fewer agree that Microsoft is a monopoly?
    c. Again for a sample of 800 people, what is the probability that more than 450 do not agree that Microsoft is a monopoly?

31. A Myrtle Beach resort hotel has 120 rooms. In the spring months, hotel room occupancy is approximately 75%.
    a. What is the probability that at least half of the rooms are occupied on a given day?
    b. What is the probability that 100 or more rooms are occupied on a given day?
    c. What is the probability that 80 or fewer rooms are occupied on a given day?

# 6.4 Exponential Probability Distribution

The **exponential probability distribution** may be used for random variables such as the time between arrivals at a car wash, the time required to load a truck, the distance between major defects in a highway, and so on. The exponential probability density function follows.

> **EXPONENTIAL PROBABILITY DENSITY FUNCTION**
>
> $$f(x) = \frac{1}{\mu} e^{-x/\mu} \qquad \text{for } x \geq 0, \mu > 0 \tag{6.4}$$

As an example of the exponential distribution, suppose that $x =$ the time it takes to load a truck at the Schips loading dock follows such a distribution. If the mean, or average, time to load a truck is 15 minutes ($\mu = 15$), the appropriate probability density function is

$$f(x) = \frac{1}{15} e^{-x/15}$$

Figure 6.10 is the graph of this probability density function.

## Computing Probabilities for the Exponential Distribution

*In waiting line applications, the exponential distribution is often used for service time.*

As with any continuous probability distribution, the area under the curve corresponding to an interval provides the probability that the random variable assumes a value in that interval. In the Schips loading dock example, the probability that loading a truck will take 6 minutes or less ($x \leq 6$) is defined to be the area under the curve in Figure 6.10 from $x = 0$ to $x = 6$. Similarly, the probability that loading a truck will take 18 minutes or less ($x \leq 18$)

FIGURE 6.10    EXPONENTIAL DISTRIBUTION FOR THE SCHIPS LOADING DOCK EXAMPLE

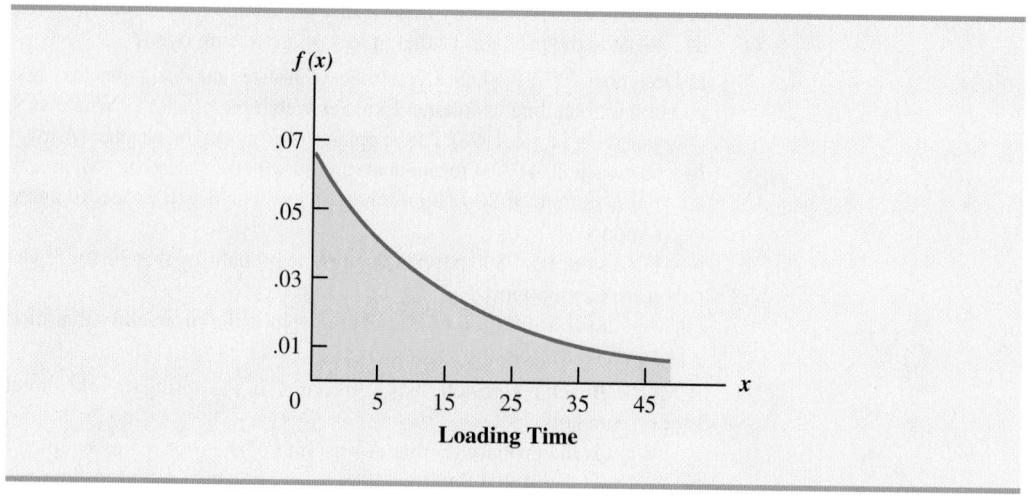

is the area under the curve from $x = 0$ to $x = 18$. Note also that the probability that loading a truck will take between 6 minutes and 18 minutes ($6 \leq x \leq 18$) is given by the area under the curve from $x = 6$ to $x = 18$.

To compute exponential probabilities such as those just described, we use the following formula. It provides the cumulative probability of obtaining a value for the exponential random variable of less than or equal to some specific value denoted by $x_0$.

**EXPONENTIAL DISTRIBUTION: CUMULATIVE PROBABILITIES**

$$P(x \leq x_0) = 1 - e^{-x_0/\mu} \qquad\qquad (6.5)$$

For the Schips loading dock example, $x =$ loading time and $\mu = 15$, which gives us

$$P(x \leq x_0) = 1 - e^{-x_0/15}$$

Hence, the probability that loading a truck will take 6 minutes or less is

$$P(x \leq 6) = 1 - e^{-6/15} = .3297$$

Figure 6.11 shows the area or probability for a loading time of 6 minutes or less.

Using equation (6.5), we calculate the probability of loading a truck in 18 minutes or less.

$$P(x \leq 18) = 1 - e^{-18/15} = .6988$$

Thus, the probability that loading a truck will take between 6 minutes and 18 minutes is equal to $.6988 - .3297 = .3691$. Probabilities for any other interval can be computed similarly.

**FIGURE 6.11    PROBABILITY OF A LOADING TIME OF 6 MINUTES OR LESS**

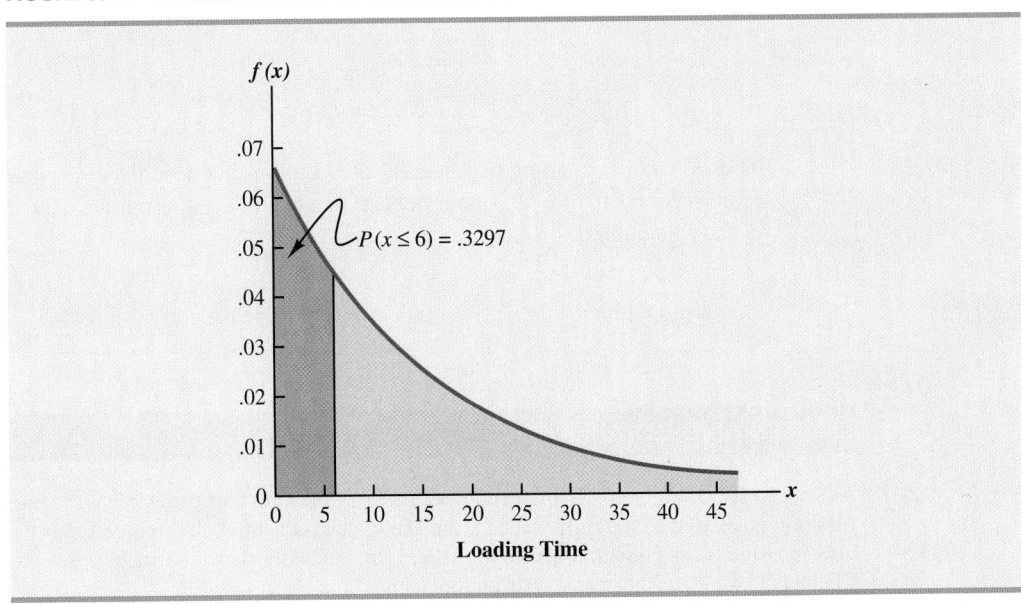

*A property of the exponential distribution is that the mean and standard deviation are equal.*

In the preceding example, the mean time it takes to load a truck is $\mu = 15$ minutes. A property of the exponential distribution is that the mean of the distribution and the standard deviation of the distribution are *equal*. Thus, the standard deviation for the time it takes to load a truck is $\sigma = 15$ minutes. The variance is $\sigma^2 = (15)^2 = 225$.

## Relationship Between the Poisson and Exponential Distributions

In Section 5.5 we introduced the Poisson distribution as a discrete probability distribution that is often useful in examining the number of occurrences of an event over a specified interval of time or space. Recall that the Poisson probability function is

$$f(x) = \frac{\mu^x e^{-\mu}}{x!}$$

where

$$\mu = \text{expected value or mean number of} \\ \text{occurrences over a specified interval}$$

The continuous exponential probability distribution is related to the discrete Poisson distribution. If the Poisson distribution provides an appropriate description of the number of occurrences per interval, the exponential distribution provides a description of the length of the interval between occurrences.

*If arrivals follow a Poisson distribution, the time between arrivals must follow an exponential distribution.*

To illustrate this relationship, suppose the number of cars that arrive at a car wash during 1 hour is described by a Poisson probability distribution with a mean of 10 cars per hour. The Poisson probability function that gives the probability of $x$ arrivals per hour is

$$f(x) = \frac{10^x e^{-10}}{x!}$$

Because the average number of arrivals is 10 cars per hour, the average time between cars arriving is

$$\frac{1 \text{ hour}}{10 \text{ cars}} = .1 \text{ hour/car}$$

Thus, the corresponding exponential distribution that describes the time between the arrivals has a mean of $\mu = .1$ hour per car; as a result, the appropriate exponential probability density function is

$$f(x) = \frac{1}{.1} e^{-x/.1} = 10e^{-10x}$$

### NOTES AND COMMENTS

As we can see in Figure 6.10, the exponential distribution is skewed to the right. Indeed, the skewness measure for exponential distributions is 2. In Chapter 3, we stated that any distribution with a skewness measure above 2 is badly skewed. So the exponential distribution gives us a good idea what a badly skewed distribution looks like.

## Exercises

### Methods

32. Consider the following exponential probability density function.

$$f(x) = \frac{1}{8} e^{-x/8} \qquad \text{for } x \geq 0$$

   a.  Find $P(x \leq 6)$.
   b.  Find $P(x \leq 4)$.
   c.  Find $P(x \geq 6)$.
   d.  Find $P(4 \leq x \leq 6)$.

33. Consider the following exponential probability density function.

$$f(x) = \frac{1}{3} e^{-x/3} \qquad \text{for } x \geq 0$$

   a.  Write the formula for $P(x \leq x_0)$.
   b.  Find $P(x \leq 2)$.
   c.  Find $P(x \geq 3)$.
   d.  Find $P(x \leq 5)$.
   e.  Find $P(2 \leq x \leq 5)$.

### Applications

34. *Internet Magazine* monitors Internet service providers (ISPs) and provides statistics on their performance. The average time to download a web page for free ISPs is approximately 20 seconds for European web pages (*Internet Magazine,* January 2000). Assume the time to download a Web page follows an exponential distribution.
   a.  What is the probability it will take less than 10 seconds to download a Web page?
   b.  What is the probability it will take more than 30 seconds to download a Web page?
   c.  What is the probability it will take between 10 and 30 seconds to download a Web page?

35. The time between arrivals of vehicles at a particular intersection follows an exponential probability distribution with a mean of 12 seconds.
   a.  Sketch this exponential probability distribution.
   b.  What is the probability that the arrival time between vehicles is 12 seconds or less?
   c.  What is the probability that the arrival time between vehicles is 6 seconds or less?
   d.  What is the probability of 30 or more seconds between vehicle arrivals?

36. The lifetime (hours) of an electronic device is a random variable with the following exponential probability density function.

$$f(x) = \frac{1}{50} e^{-x/50} \qquad \text{for } x \geq 0$$

   a.  What is the mean lifetime of the device?
   b.  What is the probability that the device will fail in the first 25 hours of operation?
   c.  What is the probability that the device will operate 100 or more hours before failure?

37. Sparagowski & Associates conducted a study of service times at the drive-up window of fast-food restaurants. The average time between placing an order and receiving the order at McDonald's restaurants was 2.78 minutes (*The Cincinnati Enquirer,* July 9, 2000). Waiting times, such as these, frequently follow an exponential distribution.
   a.  What is the probability that a customer's service time is less than 2 minutes?
   b.  What is the probability that a customer's service time is more than 5 minutes?
   c.  What is the probability that a customer's service time is more than 2.78 minutes?

38. According to Barron's 1998 Primary Reader Survey, the average annual number of investment transactions for a subscriber is 30 (*www.barronsmag.com,* July 28, 2000). Suppose the number of transactions in a year follows the Poisson probability distribution.
    a. Show the probability distribution for the time between investment transactions.
    b. What is the probability of no transactions during the month of January for a particular subscriber?
    c. What is the probability that the next transaction will occur within the next half month for a particular subscriber?

## Summary

This chapter extended the discussion of probability distributions to the case of continuous random variables. The major conceptual difference between discrete and continuous probability distributions involves the method of computing probabilities. With discrete distributions, the probability function $f(x)$ provides the probability that the random variable $x$ assumes various values. With continuous distributions, the probability density function $f(x)$ does not provide probability values directly. Instead, probabilities are given by areas under the curve or graph of the probability density function $f(x)$. Because the area under the curve above a single point is zero, we observe that the probability of any particular value is zero for a continuous random variable.

Three continuous probability distributions—the uniform, normal, and exponential distributions—were treated in detail. The normal distribution is used widely in statistical inference and will be used extensively throughout the remainder of the text.

## Glossary

**Probability density function** A function used to compute probabilities for a continuous random variable. The area under the graph of a probability density function over an interval represents probability.

**Uniform probability distribution** A continuous probability distribution for which the probability that the random variable will assume a value in any interval is the same for each interval of equal length.

**Normal probability distribution** A continuous probability distribution. Its probability density function is bell shaped and determined by its mean $\mu$ and standard deviation $\sigma$.

**Standard normal probability distribution** A normal distribution with a mean of zero and a standard deviation of one.

**Continuity correction factor** A value of .5 that is added to or subtracted from a value of $x$ when the continuous normal distribution is used to approximate the discrete binomial distribution.

**Exponential probability distribution** A continuous probability distribution that is useful in computing probabilities for the time it takes to complete a task.

## Key Formulas

**Uniform Probability Density Function**

$$f(x) = \begin{cases} \dfrac{1}{b - a} & \text{for } a \leq x \leq b \\ 0 & \text{elsewhere} \end{cases} \tag{6.1}$$

**Normal Probability Density Function**

$$f(x) = \frac{1}{\sigma\sqrt{2\pi}} e^{-(x-\mu)^2/2\sigma^2} \tag{6.2}$$

**Converting to the Standard Normal Distribution**

$$z = \frac{x - \mu}{\sigma} \tag{6.3}$$

**Exponential Probability Density Function**

$$f(x) = \frac{1}{\mu} e^{-x/\mu} \qquad \text{for } x \geq 0, \mu > 0 \tag{6.4}$$

**Exponential Distribution: Cumulative Probabilities**

$$P(x \leq x_0) = 1 - e^{-x_0/\mu} \tag{6.5}$$

## Supplementary Exercises

39. A business executive, transferred from Chicago to Atlanta, needs to sell her house in Chicago quickly. The executive's employer has offered to buy the house for $210,000, but the offer expires at the end of the week. The executive does not currently have a better offer, but can afford to leave the house on the market for another month. From conversations with her realtor, the executive believes the price she will get by leaving the house on the market for another month is uniformly distributed between $200,000 and $225,000.
    a. If she leaves the house on the market for another month, what is the mathematical expression for the probability density function of the sales price?
    b. If she leaves it on the market for another month, what is the probability she will get at least $215,000 for the house?
    c. If she leaves it on the market for another month, what is the probability she will get less than $210,000?
    d. Should the executive leave the house on the market for another month? Why or why not?

40. Sixty-eight percent of the debt owed by American families is home mortgage or equity credit (*Federal Reserve Bulletin*, January 1997). The median amount of mortgage debt for families with the head of the household under 35 years old is $63,000. Assume the amount of mortgage debt for this group is normally distributed and the standard deviation is $15,000.
    a. What is the mean amount of mortgage debt for this group?
    b. How much mortgage debt do the 10% with the smallest debt have?
    c. What percent of these families have mortgage debt in excess of $80,000?
    d. The upper 5% of mortgage debt is in excess of what amount?

41. Motorola used the normal distribution to determine the probability of defects and the number of defects expected in a production process (*APICS—The Performance Advantage*, July 1991). Assume a production process produces items with a mean weight of 10 ounces. Calculate the probability of a defect and the expected number of defects for a 1000-unit production run in the following situations.
    a. The process standard deviation is .15, and the process control is set at plus or minus one standard deviation. Units with weights less than 9.85 or greater than 10.15 ounces will be classified as defects.

b.  Through process design improvements, the process standard deviation can be reduced to .05. Assume the process control remains the same, with weights less than 9.85 or greater than 10.15 ounces being classified as defects.

c.  What is the advantage of reducing process variation thereby setting process control limits at a greater number of standard deviations from the mean?

42.  The average annual amount American households spend for daily transportation is $6312 (*Money,* August 2001). Assume that the amount spent is normally distributed.

a.  Suppose you learn that 5% of American households spend less than $1000 for daily transportation. What is the standard deviation of the amount spend?

b.  What is the probability that a household spends between $4000 and $6000?

c.  What is the amount spent by the 3% of households with the highest daily transportation cost?

43.  The sales of High-Brite Toothpaste are believed to be approximately normally distributed, with a mean of 10,000 tubes per week and a standard deviation of 1500 tubes per week.

a.  What is the probability that more than 12,000 tubes will be sold in any given week?

b.  To have a .95 probability that the company will have sufficient stock to cover the weekly demand, how many tubes should be produced?

44.  Ward Doering Auto Sales is considering offering a special service contract that will cover the total cost of any service work required on leased vehicles. From experience, the company manager estimates that yearly service costs are approximately normally distributed, with a mean of $150 and a standard deviation of $25.

a.  If the company offers the service contract to customers for a yearly charge of $200, what is the probability that any one customer's service costs will exceed the contract price of $200?

b.  What is Ward's expected profit per service contract?

45.  The Asian currency crisis of late 1997 and early 1998 was expected to lead to substantial job losses in the United States as inexpensive imports flooded markets. California was expected to be especially hard hit. The Economic Policy Institute estimated that the mean number of job losses in California would be 126,681 (*St. Petersburg Times,* January 24, 1998). Assume the number of jobs lost in California is normally distributed with a standard deviation of 30,000.

a.  What is the probability the number of lost jobs is between 80,000 and 150,000?

b.  What is the probability the number of lost jobs will be less than 50,000?

c.  What cutoff value will provide a .95 probability that the number of lost jobs will not exceed the value?

46.  Assume that the test scores from a college admissions test are normally distributed, with a mean of 450 and a standard deviation of 100.

a.  What percentage of the people taking the test score between 400 and 500?

b.  Suppose someone receives a score of 630. What percentage of the people taking the test score better? What percentage score worse?

c.  If a particular university will not admit anyone scoring below 480, what percentage of the persons taking the test would be acceptable to the university?

47.  According to *Advertising Age,* the average base salary for women working as copywriters in advertising firms is higher than the average base salary for men. The average base salary for women is $67,000 and the average base salary for men is $65,500 (*Working Woman,* July/August 2000). Assume salaries are normally distributed and that the standard deviation is $7,000 for both men and women.

a.  What is the probability of a woman receiving a salary in excess of $75,000?

b.  What is the probability of a man receiving a salary in excess of $75,000?

c.  What is the probability of a woman receiving a salary below $50,000?

d.  How much would a woman have to make to have a higher salary than 99% of her male counterparts?

48. A machine fills containers with a particular product. The standard deviation of filling weights is known from past data to be .6 ounce. If only 2% of the containers hold less than 18 ounces, what is the mean filling weight for the machine? That is, what must $\mu$ equal? Assume the filling weights have a normal distribution.

49. Consider a multiple-choice examination with 50 questions. Each question has four possible answers. Assume that a student who has done the homework and attended lectures has a 75 probability of answering any question correctly.
    a. A student must answer 43 or more questions correctly to obtain a grade of A. What percentage of the students who have done their homework and attended lectures will obtain a grade of A on this multiple-choice examination?
    b. A student who answers 35 to 39 questions correctly will receive a grade of C. What percentage of students who have done their homework and attended lectures will obtain a grade of C on this multiple-choice examination?
    c. A student must answer 30 or more questions correctly to pass the examination. What percentage of the students who have done their homework and attended lectures will pass the examination?
    d. Assume that a student has not attended class and has not done the homework for the course. Furthermore, assume that the student will simply guess at the answer to each question. What is the probability that this student will answer 30 or more questions correctly and pass the examination?

50. A blackjack player at a Las Vegas casino learned that the house will provide a free room if play is for four hours at an average bet of $50. The player's strategy provides a probability of .49 of winning on any one hand, and the player knows that there are 60 hands per hour. Suppose the player plays for four hours at a bet of $50 per hand.
    a. What is the player's expected payoff?
    b. What is the probability the player loses $1000 or more?
    c. What is the probability the player wins?
    d. Suppose the player starts with $1500. What is the probability of going broke?

51. The time in minutes for which a student uses a computer terminal at the computer center of a major university follows an exponential probability distribution with a mean of 36 minutes. Assume a student arrives at the terminal just as another student is beginning to work on the terminal.
    a. What is the probability that the wait for the second student will be 15 minutes or less?
    b. What is the probability that the wait for the second student will be between 15 and 45 minutes?
    c. What is the probability that the second student will have to wait an hour or more?

52. The Web site for the Bed and Breakfast Inns of North America (www.bestinns.net) gets approximately seven visitors per minute (*Time,* September 2001). Suppose the number of Web site visitors per minute follows a Poisson probability distribution.
    a. What is the mean time between visits to the Web site?
    b. Show the exponential probability density function for the time between Web site visits.
    c. What is the probability no one will access the Web site in a 1-minute period?
    d. What is the probability no one will access the Web site in a 12-second period?

53. The average travel time to work for New York City residents is 36.5 minutes (*Time Almanac,* 2001).
    a. Assume the exponential probability distribution is applicable and show the probability density function for the travel time to work for a typical New Yorker.
    b. What is the probability it will take a typical New Yorker between 20 and 40 minutes to travel to work?
    c. What is the probability it will take the typical New Yorker more than 40 minutes to travel to work?

54. The time (in minutes) between telephone calls at an insurance claims office has the following exponential probability distribution.

$$f(x) = .50e^{-.50x} \qquad \text{for } x \geq 0$$

a. What is the mean time between telephone calls?
b. What is the probability of having 30 seconds or less between telephone calls?
c. What is the probability of having 1 minute or less between telephone calls?
d. What is the probability of having 5 or more minutes without a telephone call?

## Case Problem    Specialty Toys

Specialty Toys, Inc., sells a variety of new and innovative children's toys. Management learned that the preholiday season is the best time to introduce a new toy, because many families use this time to look for new ideas for December holiday gifts. When Specialty discovers a new toy with good market potential, it chooses an October market entry date.

In order to get toys in its stores by October, Specialty places one-time orders with its manufacturers in June or July of each year. Demand for children's toys can be highly volatile. If a new toy catches on, a sense of shortage in the market place often increases the demand to high levels and large profits can be realized. However, new toys can also flop, leaving Specialty stuck with high levels of inventory that must be sold at reduced prices. The most important question the company faces is deciding how many units of a new toy should be purchased to meet anticipated sales demand. If too few are purchased, sales will be lost; if too many are purchased, profits will be reduced because of low prices realized in clearance sales.

For the coming season, Specialty plans to introduce a new product called Weather Teddy. This variation of a talking teddy bear is made by a company in Taiwan. When a child presses Teddy's hand, the bear begins to talk. A built-in barometer selects one of five responses that predict the weather conditions. The responses range from "It looks to be a very nice day! Have fun." to "I think it may rain today. Don't forget your umbrella." Tests with the product show that, even though it is not a perfect weather predictor, its predictions are surprisingly good. Several of Specialty's managers claimed Teddy gave predictions of the weather that were as good as many local television weather forecasters.

As usual, Specialty faces the decision of how many Weather Teddy units to order for the coming holiday season. Members of the management team suggested order quantities of 15,000, 18,000, 24,000, or 28,000 units. The wide range of order quantities suggested indicate considerable disagreement concerning the market potential. The product management team asks you for an analysis of the stock-out probabilities for various order quantities, an estimate of the profit potential, and to help make an order quantity recommendation. Specialty expects to sell Weather Teddy for $24 based on a cost of $16 per unit. If inventory remains after the holiday season, Specialty will sell all surplus inventory for $5 per unit. After reviewing the sales history of similar products, Specialty's senior sales forecaster predicted an expected demand of 20,000 units with a 0.90 probability that demand would be between 10,000 units and 30,000 units.

### Managerial Report

Prepare a managerial report that addresses the following issues and recommends an order quantity for the Weather Teddy product.

1. Use the sales forecaster's prediction to describe a normal probability distribution that can be used to approximate the demand distribution. Sketch the distribution and show its mean and standard deviation.

2. Compute the probability of a stock-out for the order quantities suggested by members of the management team.
3. Compute the projected profit for the order quantities suggested by the management team under three scenarios: worst case in which sales = 10,000 units, most likely case in which sales = 20,000 units, and best case in which sales = 30,000 units.
4. One of Specialty's managers felt that the profit potential was so great that the order quantity should have a 70% chance of meeting demand and only a 30% chance of any stock-outs. What quantity would be ordered under this policy, and what is the projected profit under the three sales scenarios?
5. Provide your own recommendation for an order quantity and note the associated profit projections. Provide a rationale for your recommendation.

## Appendix 6.1   Continuous Probability Distributions with Minitab

Let us demonstrate the Minitab procedure for computing continuous probabilities by referring to the Grear Tire Company problem where tire mileage was described by a normal distribution with $\mu = 36,500$ and $\sigma = 5000$. One question asked was: What is the probability that the tire mileage will exceed 40,000 miles?

For continuous probability distributions, Minitab gives a cumulative probability; that is, Minitab gives the probability that the random variable will assume a value less than or equal to a specified constant. For the Grear tire mileage question, Minitab can be used to determine the cumulative probability that the tire mileage will be less than or equal to 40,000 miles. (The specified constant in this case is 40,000.) After obtaining the cumulative probability from Minitab, we must subtract it from 1 to determine the probability that the tire mileage will exceed 40,000 miles.

Prior to using Minitab to compute a probability, one must enter the specified constant into a column of the worksheet. For the Grear tire mileage question we entered the specified constant of 40,000 into column C1 of the Minitab worksheet. The steps in using Minitab to compute the cumulative probability of the normal random variable assuming a value less than or equal to 40,000 follow.

**Step 1.** Select the **Calc** menu
**Step 2.** Choose **Probability Distributions**
**Step 3.** Choose **Normal**
**Step 4.** When the Normal Distribution dialog box appears:
>  Select **Cumulative probability**
>  Enter 36500 in the **Mean** box
>  Enter 5000 in the **Standard deviation** box
>  Enter C1 in the **Input column** box (the column containing 40,000)
>  Click **OK**

After the user clicks **OK,** Minitab prints the cumulative probability that the normal random variable assumes a value less than or equal to 40,000. Minitab shows that this probability is .7580. Because we are interested in the probability that the tire mileage will be greater than 40,000, the desired probability is $1 - .7580 = .2420$.

A second question in the Grear Tire Company problem was: What mileage guarantee should Grear set to ensure that no more than 10% of the tires qualify for the guarantee? Here we are given a probability and want to find the corresponding value for the random variable. Minitab uses an inverse calculation routine to find the value of the random variable associated with a given cumulative probability. First, we must enter the cumulative probability into a column of the Minitab worksheet (say C1). In this case, the desired cumulative probability is .10. Then, the first three steps of the Minitab procedure are as already listed. In step 4, we select **Inverse cumulative probability** instead of **Cumulative probability** and complete the remaining parts of the step. Minitab then displays the mileage guarantee of 30,100 miles.

Minitab is capable of computing probabilities for other continuous probability distributions, including the exponential probability distribution. To compute exponential probabilities, follow the procedure shown previously for the normal probability distribution and choose the **Exponential** option in step 3. Step 4 is as shown, with the exception that entering the standard deviation is not required. Output for cumulative probabilities and inverse cumulative probabilities is identical to that described for the normal probability distribution.

## Appendix 6.2 Continuous Probability Distributions with Excel

Excel provides the capability for computing probabilities for several continuous probability distributions, including the normal and exponential probability distributions. In this appendix, we describe how Excel can be used to compute probabilities for any normal distribution. The procedures for the exponential and other continuous distributions are similar to the one we describe for the normal distribution.

Let us return to the Grear Tire Company problem where the tire mileage was described by a normal distribution with $\mu = 36,500$ and $\sigma = 5000$. Assume we are interested in the probability that tire mileage will exceed 40,000 miles.

Excel's NORMDIST function provides cumulative probabilities for a normal distribution. The general form of the function is NORMDIST $(x, \mu, \sigma,$ cumulative). For the fourth argument, TRUE is specified if a cumulative probability is desired. Thus, to compute the cumulative probability that the tire mileage will be less than or equal to 40,000 miles we would enter the following formula into any cell of an Excel worksheet:

$$=\text{NORMDIST}(40000,36500,5000,\text{TRUE})$$

At this point, .7580 will appear in the cell where the formula was entered, indicating that the probability of tire mileage being less than or equal to 40,000 miles is .7580. Therefore, the probability that tire mileage will exceed 40,000 miles is $1 - .7580 = .2420$.

Excel's NORMINV function uses an inverse computation to find the $x$ value corresponding to a given cumulative probability. For instance, suppose we want to find the guaranteed mileage Grear should offer so that no more than 10% of the tires will be eligible for the guarantee. We would enter the following formula into any cell of an Excel worksheet:

$$=\text{NORMINV}(.1,36500,5000)$$

At this point, 30092 will appear in the cell where the formula was entered indicating that the probability of a tire not lasting 30,092 miles is .10.

The Excel function for computing exponential probabilities is EXPONDIST. Using it is straightforward. But if one needs help specifying the proper values for the arguments, Excel's Insert Function tool can be used (see Appendix 2.2).

# Sampling and Sampling Distributions

## CONTENTS

## MEADWESTVACO CORPORATION*
### STAMFORD, CONNECTICUT

MeadWestvaco Corporation, a leading producer of packaging, coated and specialty papers, consumer and office products, and specialty chemicals, employs more than 30,000 people. It operates worldwide in 33 countries and serves customers located in approximately 100 countries. MeadWestvaco holds a leading position in paper production, with an annual capacity of 1.8 million tons. The company's products include textbook paper, glossy magazine paper, beverage packaging systems, and office products. MeadWestvaco's internal consulting group uses sampling to provide a variety of information that enables the company to obtain significant productivity benefits and remain competitive.

For example, MeadWestvaco maintains large woodland holdings, which supply the trees, or raw material, for many of the company's products. Managers need reliable and accurate information about the timberlands and forests to evaluate the company's ability to meet its future raw material needs. What is the present volume in the forests? What is the past growth of the forests? What is the projected future growth of the forests? With answers to these important questions MeadWestvaco's managers can develop plans for the future, including long-term planting and harvesting schedules for the trees.

How does MeadWestvaco obtain the information it needs about its vast forest holdings? Data collected from sample plots throughout the forests are the basis for learning about the population of trees owned by the company. To identify the sample plots, the timberland holdings are first divided into three sections based on location and types of trees. Using maps and random numbers, MeadWestvaco analysts identify random samples of 1/5- to 1/7-acre plots in each section of the

Random sampling of its forest holdings enables MeadWestvaco Corporation to meet future raw material needs. © Walter Hodges/Corbis.

forest. MeadWestvaco foresters collect data from these sample plots to learn about the forest population.

Foresters throughout the organization participate in the field data collection process. Periodically, two-person teams gather information on each tree in every sample plot. The sample data are entered into the company's continuous forest inventory (CFI) computer system. Reports from the CFI system include a number of frequency distribution summaries containing statistics on types of trees, present forest volume, past forest growth rates, and projected future forest growth and volume. Sampling and the associated statistical summaries of the sample data provide the reports essential for the effective management of MeadWestvaco's forests and timberlands.

In this chapter you will learn about simple random sampling and the sample selection process. In addition, you will learn how statistics such as the sample mean and sample proportion are used to estimate the population mean and population proportion. The important concept of a sampling distribution is also introduced.

*The authors are indebted to Dr. Edward P. Winkofsky for providing this Statistics in Practice.

In Chapter 1, we defined a *population* and a *sample*. The definitions are restated here.

1. A *population* is the set of all the elements of interest in a study.
2. A *sample* is a subset of the population.

Numerical characteristics of a population, such as the mean and standard deviation, are called **parameters**. A primary purpose of statistical inference is to develop estimates and test hypotheses about population parameters using information contained in a sample.

Let us begin by citing two situations in which samples provide estimates of population parameters.

1. A tire manufacturer developed a new tire designed to provide an increase in mileage over the firm's current line of tires. To estimate the mean number of miles provided by the new tires, the manufacturer selected a sample of 120 new tires for testing. The test results provided a sample mean of 36,500 miles. Hence, an estimate of the mean tire mileage for the population of new tires was 36,500 miles.

2. Members of a political party were considering supporting a particular candidate for election to the U.S. Senate, and party leaders wanted an estimate of the proportion of registered voters favoring the candidate. The time and cost associated with contacting every individual in the population of registered voters were prohibitive. Hence, a sample of 400 registered voters was selected and 160 of the 400 voters indicated a preference for the candidate. An estimate of the proportion of the population of registered voters favoring the candidate was $160/400 = .40$.

These two examples illustrate some of the reasons why samples are used. Note that in the tire mileage example, collecting the data on tire life involves wearing out each tire tested. Clearly it is not feasible to test every tire in the population; a sample is the only realistic way to obtain the desired tire mileage data. In the example involving the election, contacting every registered voter in the population is theoretically possible, but the time and cost in doing so are prohibitive; thus, a sample of registered voters is preferred.

*A sample mean provides an estimate of a population mean, and a sample proportion provides an estimate of a population proportion. With estimates such as these, some estimation error can be expected. This chapter provides the basis for determining how large that error might be.*

It is important to realize that sample results provide only *estimates* of the values of the population characteristics. We do not expect the sample mean of 36,500 miles to exactly equal the mean mileage for all tires in the population, nor do we expect exactly .40, or 40%, of the population of registered voters to favor the candidate. The reason is simply that the sample contains only a portion of the population. With proper sampling methods, the sample results will provide "good" estimates of the population parameters. But how good can we expect the sample results to be? Fortunately, statistical procedures are available for answering this question.

In this chapter we show how simple random sampling can be used to select a sample from a population. We then show how data obtained from a simple random sample can be used to compute estimates of a population mean, a population standard deviation, and a population proportion. In addition, we introduce the important concept of a sampling distribution. As we show, knowledge of the appropriate sampling distribution is what enables us to make statements about how close the sample estimates are to the corresponding population parameters. The last section discusses some alternatives to simple random sampling that are often employed in practice.

# 7.1   The Electronics Associates Sampling Problem

The director of personnel for Electronics Associates, Inc. (EAI), has been assigned the task of developing a profile of the company's 2500 managers. The characteristics to be identified include the mean annual salary for the managers and the proportion of managers having completed the company's management training program.

Using the 2500 managers as the population for this study, we can find the annual salary and the training program status for each individual by referring to the firm's personnel records. The data file containing this information for all 2500 managers in the population is on the CD that accompanies the text.

**CD** file

**EAI**

Using the EAI data set and the formulas presented in Chapter 3, we compute the population mean and the population standard deviation for the annual salary data.

$$\text{Population mean:} \quad \mu = \$51,800$$
$$\text{Population standard deviation:} \quad \sigma = \$4000$$

The data for the training program status show that 1500 of the 2500 managers completed the training program. Letting $p$ denote the proportion of the population that completed the training program, we see that $p = 1500/2500 = .60$. The population mean annual salary ($\mu = \$51,800$), the population standard deviation of annual salary ($\sigma = \$4000$), and the population proportion that completed the training program ($p = .60$) are parameters of the population of EAI managers.

*Often the cost of collecting information from a sample is substantially less than from a population, especially when personal interviews must be conducted to collect the information.*

Now, suppose that the necessary information on all the EAI managers was not readily available in the company's database. The question we now consider is how the firm's director of personnel can obtain estimates of the population parameters by using a sample of managers rather than all 2500 managers in the population. Suppose that a sample of 30 managers will be used. Clearly, the time and the cost of developing a profile would be substantially less for 30 managers than for the entire population. If the personnel director could be assured that a sample of 30 managers would provide adequate information about the population of 2500 managers, working with a sample would be preferable to working with the entire population. Let us explore the possibility of using a sample for the EAI study by first considering how we can identify a sample of 30 managers.

 # 7.2  Simple Random Sampling

Several methods can be used to select a sample from a population; one of the most common is **simple random sampling**. The definition of a simple random sample and the process of selecting a simple random sample depend on whether the population is *finite* or *infinite*. Because the EAI sampling problem involves a finite population of 2500 managers, we first consider sampling from a finite population.

## Sampling from a Finite Population

A simple random sample of size $n$ from a finite population of size $N$ is defined as follows.

> **SIMPLE RANDOM SAMPLE (FINITE POPULATION)**
>
> A simple random sample of size $n$ from a finite population of size $N$ is a sample selected such that each possible sample of size $n$ has the same probability of being selected.

One procedure for selecting a simple random sample from a finite population is to choose the elements for the sample one at a time in such a way that, at each step, each of the elements remaining in the population has the same probability of being selected. Sampling $n$ elements in this way will satisfy the definition of a simple random sample from a finite population.

*Computer-generated random numbers can also be used to implement the random sample selection process. Excel provides a function for generating random numbers in its worksheets.*

To select a simple random sample from the finite population of EAI managers, we first assign each manager a number. For example, we can assign the managers the numbers 1 to 2500 in the order that their names appear in the EAI personnel file. Next, we refer to the table of random numbers shown in Table 7.1. Using the first row of the table, each digit, 6, 3, 2, . . . , is a random digit having an equal chance of occurring. Because the largest number in the population list of EAI managers, 2500, has four digits, we will select random numbers from the table in sets or groups of four digits. Even though we may start the selection of random numbers anywhere in the table and move systematically in a direction of our choice, we will

*The random numbers in the table are shown in groups of five for readability.*

use the first row of Table 7.1 and move from left to right. The first 7 four-digit random numbers are

|  |  |  |  |  |  |  |
|---|---|---|---|---|---|---|
| 6327 | 1599 | 8671 | 7445 | 1102 | 1514 | 1807 |

Because the numbers in the table are random, these four-digit numbers are equally likely.

## TABLE 7.1    RANDOM NUMBERS

| | | | | | | | | | |
|---|---|---|---|---|---|---|---|---|---|
| 63271 | 59986 | 71744 | 51102 | 15141 | 80714 | 58683 | 93108 | 13554 | 79945 |
| 88547 | 09896 | 95436 | 79115 | 08303 | 01041 | 20030 | 63754 | 08459 | 28364 |
| 55957 | 57243 | 83865 | 09911 | 19761 | 66535 | 40102 | 26646 | 60147 | 15702 |
| 46276 | 87453 | 44790 | 67122 | 45573 | 84358 | 21625 | 16999 | 13385 | 22782 |
| 55363 | 07449 | 34835 | 15290 | 76616 | 67191 | 12777 | 21861 | 68689 | 03263 |
| 69393 | 92785 | 49902 | 58447 | 42048 | 30378 | 87618 | 26933 | 40640 | 16281 |
| 13186 | 29431 | 88190 | 04588 | 38733 | 81290 | 89541 | 70290 | 40113 | 08243 |
| 17726 | 28652 | 56836 | 78351 | 47327 | 18518 | 92222 | 55201 | 27340 | 10493 |
| 36520 | 64465 | 05550 | 30157 | 82242 | 29520 | 69753 | 72602 | 23756 | 54935 |
| 81628 | 36100 | 39254 | 56835 | 37636 | 02421 | 98063 | 89641 | 64953 | 99337 |
| 84649 | 48968 | 75215 | 75498 | 49539 | 74240 | 03466 | 49292 | 36401 | 45525 |
| 63291 | 11618 | 12613 | 75055 | 43915 | 26488 | 41116 | 64531 | 56827 | 30825 |
| 70502 | 53225 | 03655 | 05915 | 37140 | 57051 | 48393 | 91322 | 25653 | 06543 |
| 06426 | 24771 | 59935 | 49801 | 11082 | 66762 | 94477 | 02494 | 88215 | 27191 |
| 20711 | 55609 | 29430 | 70165 | 45406 | 78484 | 31639 | 52009 | 18873 | 96927 |
| 41990 | 70538 | 77191 | 25860 | 55204 | 73417 | 83920 | 69468 | 74972 | 38712 |
| 72452 | 36618 | 76298 | 26678 | 89334 | 33938 | 95567 | 29380 | 75906 | 91807 |
| 37042 | 40318 | 57099 | 10528 | 09925 | 89773 | 41335 | 96244 | 29002 | 46453 |
| 53766 | 52875 | 15987 | 46962 | 67342 | 77592 | 57651 | 95508 | 80033 | 69828 |
| 90585 | 58955 | 53122 | 16025 | 84299 | 53310 | 67380 | 84249 | 25348 | 04332 |
| 32001 | 96293 | 37203 | 64516 | 51530 | 37069 | 40261 | 61374 | 05815 | 06714 |
| 62606 | 64324 | 46354 | 72157 | 67248 | 20135 | 49804 | 09226 | 64419 | 29457 |
| 10078 | 28073 | 85389 | 50324 | 14500 | 15562 | 64165 | 06125 | 71353 | 77669 |
| 91561 | 46145 | 24177 | 15294 | 10061 | 98124 | 75732 | 00815 | 83452 | 97355 |
| 13091 | 98112 | 53959 | 79607 | 52244 | 63303 | 10413 | 63839 | 74762 | 50289 |

We can now use these four-digit random numbers to give each manager in the population an equal chance of being included in the random sample. The first number, 6327, is greater than 2500. It does not correspond to one of the numbered managers in the population, and hence is discarded. The second number, 1599, is between 1 and 2500. Thus the first manager selected for the random sample is number 1599 on the list of EAI managers. Continuing this process, we ignore the numbers 8671 and 7445 before identifying managers number 1102, 1514, and 1807 to be included in the random sample. This process continues until the simple random sample of 30 EAI managers has been obtained.

In implementing this simple random sample selection process, it is possible that a random number used previously may appear again in the table before the sample of 30 EAI managers has been selected. Because we do not want to select a manager more than one time, any previously used random numbers are ignored because the corresponding manager is already included in the sample. Selecting a sample in this manner is referred to as **sampling without replacement**. If we selected a sample such that previously used random numbers are acceptable and specific managers could be included in the sample two or more times, we would be **sampling with replacement**. Sampling with replacement is a valid way of identifying a simple random sample. However, sampling without replacement is the sampling procedure used most often. When we refer to simple random sampling, we will assume that the sampling is without replacement.

## Sampling from an Infinite Population

*In practice, a population being studied is usually considered infinite if it involves an ongoing process that makes listing or counting every element in the population impossible.*

In some situations, the population is either infinite or so large that for practical purposes it must be treated as infinite. For example, suppose that a fast-food restaurant would like to obtain a profile of its customers by selecting a simple random sample of customers and asking each customer to complete a short questionnaire. In such situations, the on-going process of customer visits to the restaurant can be viewed as coming from an infinite population. The definition of a simple random sample from an infinite population follows.

---

**SIMPLE RANDOM SAMPLE (INFINITE POPULATION)**

A simple random sample from an infinite population is a sample selected such that the following conditions are satisfied.

1. Each element selected comes from the population.
2. Each element is selected independently.

---

*For infinite populations, a sample selection procedure must be specially devised to select the items independently and thus avoid a selection bias that gives higher selection probabilities to certain types of elements.*

For the example of selecting a simple random sample of customers at a fast-food restaurant, the first requirement is satisfied by any customer who comes into the restaurant. The second requirement is satisfied by selecting customers independently. The purpose of the second requirement is to prevent selection bias. Selection bias would occur if, for instance, five consecutive customers selected were all friends who arrived together. We might expect these customers to exhibit similar profiles. Selection bias can be avoided by ensuring that the selection of a particular customer does not influence the selection of any other customer. In other words, the customers must be selected independently.

McDonald's, the fast-food restaurant leader, implemented a simple random sampling procedure for just such a situation. The sampling procedure was based on the fact that some customers presented discount coupons. Whenever a customer presented a discount coupon, the next customer served was asked to complete a customer profile questionnaire. Because arriving customers presented discount coupons randomly, and independently, this sampling plan ensured that customers were selected independently. Thus, the two requirements for a simple random sample from an infinite population were satisfied.

Infinite populations are often associated with an ongoing process that operates continuously over time. For example, parts being manufactured on a production line, transactions occurring at a bank, telephone calls arriving at a technical support center, and customers entering stores may all be viewed as coming from an infinite population. In such cases, a creative sampling procedure ensures that no selection bias occurs and that the sample elements are selected independently.

---

## NOTES AND COMMENTS

1. The number of different simple random samples of size $n$ that can be selected from a finite population of size $N$ is

$$\frac{N!}{n!(N - n)!}$$

In this formula, $N!$ and $n!$ are the factorial computations discussed in Chapter 4. For the EAI problem with $N = 2500$ and $n = 30$, this expression can be used to show that approximately $2.75 \times 10^{69}$ different simple random samples of 30 EAI managers can be obtained.

2. Computer software packages can be used to select a random sample. In the chapter appendixes, we show how Minitab and Excel can be used to select a simple random sample from a finite population.

## Exercises

### Methods

1.  Consider a finite population with five elements labeled A, B, C, D, and E. Ten possible simple random samples of size 2 can be selected.
    a.  List the 10 samples beginning with AB, AC, and so on.
    b.  Using simple random sampling, what is the probability that each sample of size 2 is selected?
    c.  Assume random number 1 corresponds to A, random number 2 corresponds to B, and so on. List the simple random sample of size 2 that will be selected by using the random digits 8 0 5 7 5 3 2.

2.  Assume a finite population has 350 elements. Using the last three digits of each of the following five-digit random numbers (601, 022, 448, . . . ), determine the first four elements that will be selected for the simple random sample.

    98601   73022   83448   02147   34229   27553   84147   93289   14209

### Applications

3.  *Fortune* publishes data on sales, profits, assets, stockholders' equity, market value, and earnings per share for the 500 largest U.S. industrial corporations (*Fortune* 500, 2003). Assume that you want to select a simple random sample of 10 corporations from the *Fortune* 500 list. Use the last three digits in column 9 of Table 7.1, beginning with 554. Read down the column and identify the numbers of the 10 corporations that would be selected.

4.  The 10 most active issues on the New York (NYSE), Nasdaq, and American (AMEX) exchanges with market caps greater than $500 million are as follows (*The Wall Street Journal,* February 21, 2003):

    | | |
    |---|---|
    | Applied Materials | Nasdaq 100 |
    | Cisco Systems | Nextel |
    | Intel | Oracle |
    | Lucent Technologies | SPDR |
    | Microsoft | Sun Microsystems |

    a.  Assume that a random sample of five will be selected for an in-depth study of recent business practices at large, high-volume corporations. Beginning with the first random digit in Table 7.1 and reading down the column, use the single-digit random numbers to select a simple random sample of five companies to be used in this study.
    b.  According to the Notes and Comments information, how many different simple random samples of size 5 can be selected from the list of 10 companies?

5.  A student government organization is interested in estimating the proportion of students who favor a mandatory "pass-fail" grading policy for elective courses. A list of names and addresses of the 645 students enrolled during the current quarter is available from the registrar's office. Using three-digit random numbers in row 10 of Table 7.1 and moving across the row from left to right, identify the first 10 students who would be selected using simple random sampling. The three-digit random numbers begin with 816, 283, and 610.

6.  The *County and City Data Book,* published by the Census Bureau, lists information on 3139 counties throughout the United States. Assume that a national study will collect data from 30 randomly selected counties. Use four-digit random numbers from the last column of Table 7.1 to identify the numbers corresponding to the first five counties selected for the sample. Ignore the first digits and begin with the four-digit random numbers 9945, 8364, 5702, and so on.

7. Assume that we want to identify a simple random sample of 12 of the 372 doctors practicing in a particular city. The doctors' names are available from a local medical organization. Use the eighth column of five-digit random numbers in Table 7.1 to identify the 12 doctors for the sample. Ignore the first two random digits in each five-digit grouping of the random numbers. This process begins with random number 108 and proceeds down the column of random numbers.

8. The following list provides the NCAA top 25 football teams for the 2002 season (*NCAA News*, January 4, 2003). Use the ninth column of the random numbers in Table 7.1, beginning with 13554, to select a simple random sample of six football teams. Begin with team 13 and use the first two digits in each row of the ninth column for your selection process. Which six football teams are selected for the simple random sample?

|  |  |
|---|---|
| 1. Ohio State | 14. Virginia Tech |
| 2. Miami | 15. Penn State |
| 3. Georgia | 16. Auburn |
| 4. Southern California | 17. Notre Dame |
| 5. Oklahoma | 18. Pittsburgh |
| 6. Kansas State | 19. Marshall |
| 7. Texas | 20. West Virginia |
| 8. Iowa | 21. Colorado |
| 9. Michigan | 22. TCU |
| 10. Washington State | 23. Florida State |
| 11. North Carolina State | 24. Florida |
| 12. Boise State | 25. Virginia |
| 13. Maryland | |

9. *The Wall Street Journal* provides the net asset value, the year-to-date percent return, and the three-year percent return for 555 mutual funds (*The Wall Street Journal,* April 25, 2003). Assume that a simple random sample of 12 of the 555 mutual funds will be selected for a follow-up study on the size and performance of mutual funds. Use the fourth column of the random numbers in Table 7.1, beginning with 51102, to select the simple random sample of 12 mutual funds. Begin with mutual fund 102 and use the *last* three digits in each row of the fourth column for your selection process. What are the numbers of the 12 mutual funds in the simple random sample?

10. Indicate whether the following populations should be considered finite or infinite.
    a. All registered voters in the state of California.
    b. All television sets that could be produced by the Allentown, Pennsylvania, plant of the TV-M Company.
    c. All orders that could be processed by a mail-order firm.
    d. All emergency telephone calls that could come into a local police station.
    e. All components that Fibercon, Inc., produced on the second shift on May 17.

## 7.3 Point Estimation

Now that we described how to select a simple random sample, let us return to the EAI problem. A simple random sample of 30 managers and the corresponding data on annual salary and management training program participation are as shown in Table 7.2. The notation $x_1$, $x_2$, and so on is used to denote the annual salary of the first manager in the sample, the annual salary of the second manager in the sample, and so on. Participation in the management training program is indicated by Yes in the management training program column.

To estimate the value of a population parameter, we compute a corresponding characteristic of the sample, referred to as a **sample statistic**. For example, to estimate the population mean $\mu$ and the population standard deviation $\sigma$ for the annual salary of EAI

TABLE 7.2   ANNUAL SALARY AND TRAINING PROGRAM STATUS FOR A SIMPLE
RANDOM SAMPLE OF 30 EAI MANAGERS

| Annual Salary ($) | Management Training Program | Annual Salary ($) | Management Training Program |
|---|---|---|---|
| $x_1 = 49{,}094.30$ | Yes | $x_{16} = 51{,}766.00$ | Yes |
| $x_2 = 53{,}263.90$ | Yes | $x_{17} = 52{,}541.30$ | No |
| $x_3 = 49{,}643.50$ | Yes | $x_{18} = 44{,}980.00$ | Yes |
| $x_4 = 49{,}894.90$ | Yes | $x_{19} = 51{,}932.60$ | Yes |
| $x_5 = 47{,}621.60$ | No | $x_{20} = 52{,}973.00$ | Yes |
| $x_6 = 55{,}924.00$ | Yes | $x_{21} = 45{,}120.90$ | Yes |
| $x_7 = 49{,}092.30$ | Yes | $x_{22} = 51{,}753.00$ | Yes |
| $x_8 = 51{,}404.40$ | Yes | $x_{23} = 54{,}391.80$ | No |
| $x_9 = 50{,}957.70$ | Yes | $x_{24} = 50{,}164.20$ | No |
| $x_{10} = 55{,}109.70$ | Yes | $x_{25} = 52{,}973.60$ | No |
| $x_{11} = 45{,}922.60$ | Yes | $x_{26} = 50{,}241.30$ | No |
| $x_{12} = 57{,}268.40$ | No | $x_{27} = 52{,}793.90$ | No |
| $x_{13} = 55{,}688.80$ | Yes | $x_{28} = 50{,}979.40$ | Yes |
| $x_{14} = 51{,}564.70$ | No | $x_{29} = 55{,}860.90$ | Yes |
| $x_{15} = 56{,}188.20$ | No | $x_{30} = 57{,}309.10$ | No |

managers, we use the data in Table 7.2 to calculate the corresponding sample statistics: the
sample mean $\bar{x}$ and the sample standard deviation $s$. Using the formulas for a sample mean
and a sample standard deviation presented in Chapter 3, the sample mean is

$$\bar{x} = \frac{\Sigma x_i}{n} = \frac{1{,}554{,}420}{30} = \$51{,}814$$

and the sample standard deviation is

$$s = \sqrt{\frac{\Sigma(x_i - \bar{x})^2}{n - 1}} = \sqrt{\frac{325{,}009{,}260}{29}} = \$3348$$

To estimate $p$, the proportion of managers in the population who completed the management training program, we use the corresponding sample proportion $\bar{p}$. Let $x$ denote the
number of managers in the sample who completed the management training program. The
data in Table 7.2 show that $x = 19$. Thus, with a sample size of $n = 30$, the sample proportion is

$$\bar{p} = \frac{x}{n} = \frac{19}{30} = .63$$

By making the preceding computations, we perform the statistical procedure called
*point estimation*. We refer to the sample mean $\bar{x}$ as the **point estimator** of the population
mean $\mu$, the sample standard deviation $s$ as the point estimator of the population standard
deviation $\sigma$, and the sample proportion $\bar{p}$ as the point estimator of the population proportion $p$. The numerical value obtained for $\bar{x}$, $s$, or $\bar{p}$ is called the **point estimate**. Thus, for
the simple random sample of 30 EAI managers shown in Table 7.2, \$51,814 is the point es-
timate of $\mu$, \$3348 is the point estimate of $\sigma$, and .63 is the point estimate of $p$. Table 7.3
summarizes the sample results and compares the point estimates to the actual values of the
population parameters.

**TABLE 7.3**  SUMMARY OF POINT ESTIMATES OBTAINED FROM A SIMPLE RANDOM
SAMPLE OF 30 EAI MANAGERS

| Population Parameter | Parameter Value | Point Estimator | Point Estimate |
|---|---|---|---|
| $\mu$ = Population mean annual salary | $51,800 | $\bar{x}$ = Sample mean annual salary | $51,814 |
| $\sigma$ = Population standard deviation for annual salary | $4000 | $s$ = Sample standard deviation for annual salary | $3348 |
| $p$ = Population proportion having completed the management training program | .60 | $\bar{p}$ = Sample proportion having completed the management training program | .63 |

As evident from Table 7.3, the point estimates differ somewhat from the corresponding
population parameters. This difference is to be expected because a sample, and not a census of the entire population, is being used to develop the point estimates. In the next chapter, we will show how to construct an interval estimate in order to provide information about
how close the point estimate is to the population parameter.

## Exercises

## Methods

**SELF** test

11. The following data are from a simple random sample.

   5   8   10   7   10   14

   a. What is the point estimate of the population mean?
   b. What is the point estimate of the population standard deviation?

12. A survey question for a sample of 150 individuals yielded 75 Yes responses, 55 No responses, and 20 No Opinions.
   a. What is the point estimate of the proportion in the population who respond Yes?
   b. What is the point estimate of the proportion in the population who respond No?

## Applications

**SELF** test

13. A simple random sample of 5 months of sales data provided the following information:

   | *Month:* | 1 | 2 | 3 | 4 | 5 |
   |---|---|---|---|---|---|
   | *Units Sold:* | 94 | 100 | 85 | 94 | 92 |

   a. Develop a point estimate of the population mean number of units sold per month.
   b. Develop a point estimate of the population standard deviation.

14. A sample of 784 children ages 9 to 14 were asked about cash provided by their parents
   (*Consumer Reports,* January 1997). The responses were as follows.

   | Source of Cash | Frequency |
   |---|---|
   | Allowance only | 149 |
   | Handouts & chores plus an allowance | 219 |
   | Handouts & chores but no allowance | 251 |
   | Nothing | 165 |
   | Total | 784 |

a. Develop a point estimate of the proportion of children who receive an allowance as their only source of cash.

b. Develop a point estimate of the proportion of children who receive cash as handouts and for chores, but nothing in the form of an allowance.

c. Considering all sources, develop a point estimate of the proportion of children who receive at least some cash from their parents.

15. *Appliance Magazine* provided estimates of the life expectancy of household appliances (*USA Today,* September 5, 2000). A simple random sample of 10 VCRs shows the following useful life in years.

$$6.5 \quad 8.0 \quad 6.2 \quad 7.4 \quad 7.0 \quad 8.4 \quad 9.5 \quad 4.6 \quad 5.0 \quad 7.4$$

a. Develop a point estimate of the population mean life expectancy for VCRs.

b. Develop a point estimate of the population standard deviation for life expectancy of VCRs.

16. The U.S. Department of Transportation reports statistics on how frequently major airline flights arrive at or before their scheduled arrival times (*Associated Press,* September 8, 2000). Assume that the estimated proportion of flights arriving on time for an airline is based on a sample of 1400 flights. If 1117 of the flights arrive on time, develop a point estimate of the proportion of all flights that arrive on time.

17. A Louis Harris poll used a survey of 1008 adults to learn about how people feel about the economy (*Business Week,* August 7, 2000). Responses were as follow:

| | |
|---|---|
| 595 adults | The economy is growing. |
| 332 adults | The economy is staying about the same. |
| 81 adults | The economy is shrinking. |

Develop a point estimate of the following population parameters.

a. The proportion of all adults who feel the economy is growing.

b. The proportion of all adults who feel the economy is staying about the same.

c. The proportion of all adults who feel the economy is shrinking.

## 7.4   Introduction to Sampling Distributions

In the preceding section we said that the sample mean $\bar{x}$ is the point estimator of the population mean $\mu$, and the sample proportion $\bar{p}$ is the point estimator of the population proportion $p$. For the simple random sample of 30 EAI managers shown in Table 7.2, the point estimate of $\mu$ is $\bar{x} = \$51,814$ and the point estimate of $p$ is $\bar{p} = .63$. Suppose we select another simple random sample of 30 EAI managers and obtain the following point estimates:

Sample mean: $\bar{x} = \$52,670$

Sample proportion: $\bar{p} = .70$

Note that different values of $\bar{x}$ and $\bar{p}$ were obtained. Indeed, a second simple random sample of 30 EAI managers cannot be expected to provide the same point estimates as the first sample.

Now, suppose we repeat the process of selecting a simple random sample of 30 EAI managers over and over again, each time computing the values of $\bar{x}$ and $\bar{p}$. Table 7.4 contains a portion of the results obtained for 500 simple random samples, and Table 7.5 shows the frequency and relative frequency distributions for the 500 $\bar{x}$ values. Figure 7.1 shows the relative frequency histogram for the $\bar{x}$ values.

*The ability to understand the material in subsequent chapters depends heavily on the ability to understand and use the sampling distributions presented in this chapter.*

In Chapter 5 we defined a random variable as a numerical description of the outcome of an experiment. If we consider the process of selecting a simple random sample as an

TABLE 7.4    VALUES OF $\bar{x}$ AND $\bar{p}$ FROM 500 SIMPLE RANDOM SAMPLES
OF 30 EAI MANAGERS

| Sample Number | Sample Mean ($\bar{x}$) | Sample Proportion ($\bar{p}$) |
|---|---|---|
| 1 | 51,814 | .63 |
| 2 | 52,670 | .70 |
| 3 | 51,780 | .67 |
| 4 | 51,588 | .53 |
| . | . | . |
| . | . | . |
| . | . | . |
| 500 | 51,752 | .50 |

experiment, the sample mean $\bar{x}$ is the numerical description of the outcome of the experiment. Thus, the sample mean $\bar{x}$ is a random variable. As a result, just like other random variables, $\bar{x}$ has a mean or expected value, a standard deviation, and a probability distribution. Because the various possible values of $\bar{x}$ are the result of different simple random samples, the probability distribution of $\bar{x}$ is called the **sampling distribution** of $\bar{x}$. Knowledge of this sampling distribution and its properties will enable us to make probability statements about how close the sample mean $\bar{x}$ is to the population mean $\mu$.

Let us return to Figure 7.1. We would need to enumerate every possible sample of 30 managers and compute each sample mean to completely determine the sampling distribution of $\bar{x}$. However, the histogram of 500 $\bar{x}$ values gives an approximation of this sampling distribution. From the approximation we observe the bell-shaped appearance of the distribution. We note that the largest concentration of the $\bar{x}$ values and the mean of the 500 $\bar{x}$ values is near the population mean $\mu = \$51,800$. We will describe the properties of the sampling distribution of $\bar{x}$ more fully in the next section.

The 500 values of the sample proportion $\bar{p}$ are summarized by the relative frequency histogram in Figure 7.2. As in the case of $\bar{x}$, $\bar{p}$ is a random variable. If every possible sample of size 30 were selected from the population and if a value of $\bar{p}$ were computed for each sample, the resulting probability distribution would be the sampling distribution of $\bar{p}$. The relative frequency histogram of the 500 sample values in Figure 7.2 provides a general idea of the appearance of the sampling distribution of $\bar{p}$.

TABLE 7.5    FREQUENCY DISTRIBUTION OF $\bar{x}$ FROM 500 SIMPLE RANDOM SAMPLES
OF 30 EAI MANAGERS

| Mean Annual Salary ($) | Frequency | Relative Frequency |
|---|---|---|
| 49,500.00–49,999.99 | 2 | .004 |
| 50,000.00–50,499.99 | 16 | .032 |
| 50,500.00–50,999.99 | 52 | .104 |
| 51,000.00–51,499.99 | 101 | .202 |
| 51,500.00–51,999.99 | 133 | .266 |
| 52,000.00–52,499.99 | 110 | .220 |
| 52,500.00–52,999.99 | 54 | .108 |
| 53,000.00–53,499.99 | 26 | .052 |
| 53,500.00–53,999.99 | 6 | .012 |
| Totals | 500 | 1.000 |

FIGURE 7.1 RELATIVE FREQUENCY HISTOGRAM OF $\bar{x}$ VALUES FROM 500 SIMPLE
RANDOM SAMPLES OF SIZE 30 EACH

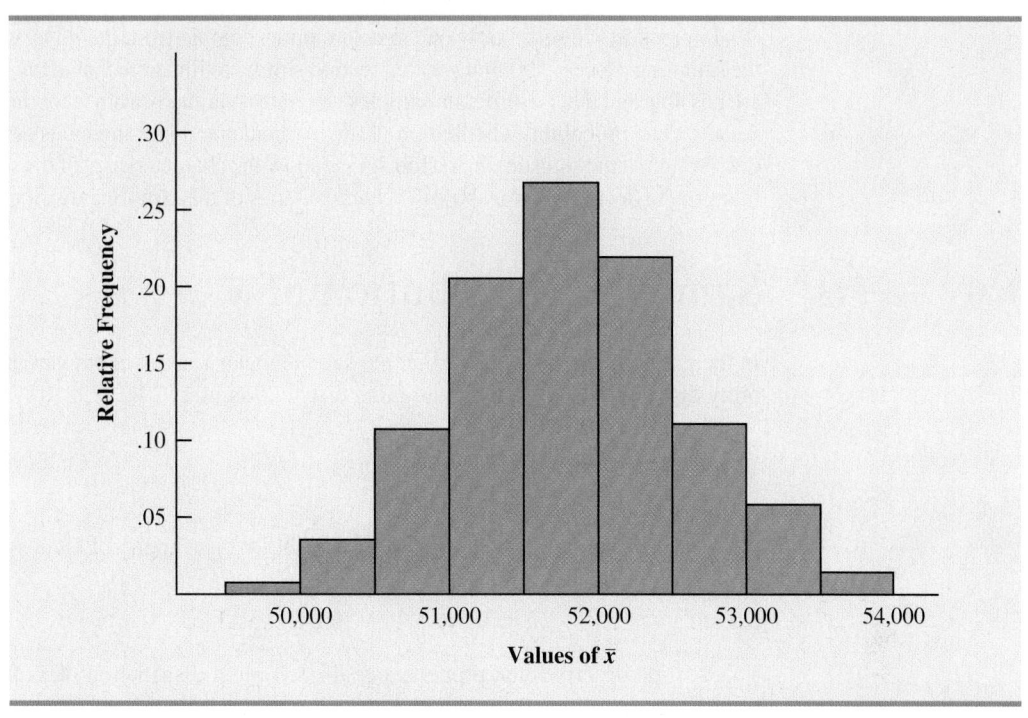

FIGURE 7.2 RELATIVE FREQUENCY HISTOGRAM OF $\bar{p}$ VALUES FROM 500 SIMPLE
RANDOM SAMPLES OF SIZE 30 EACH

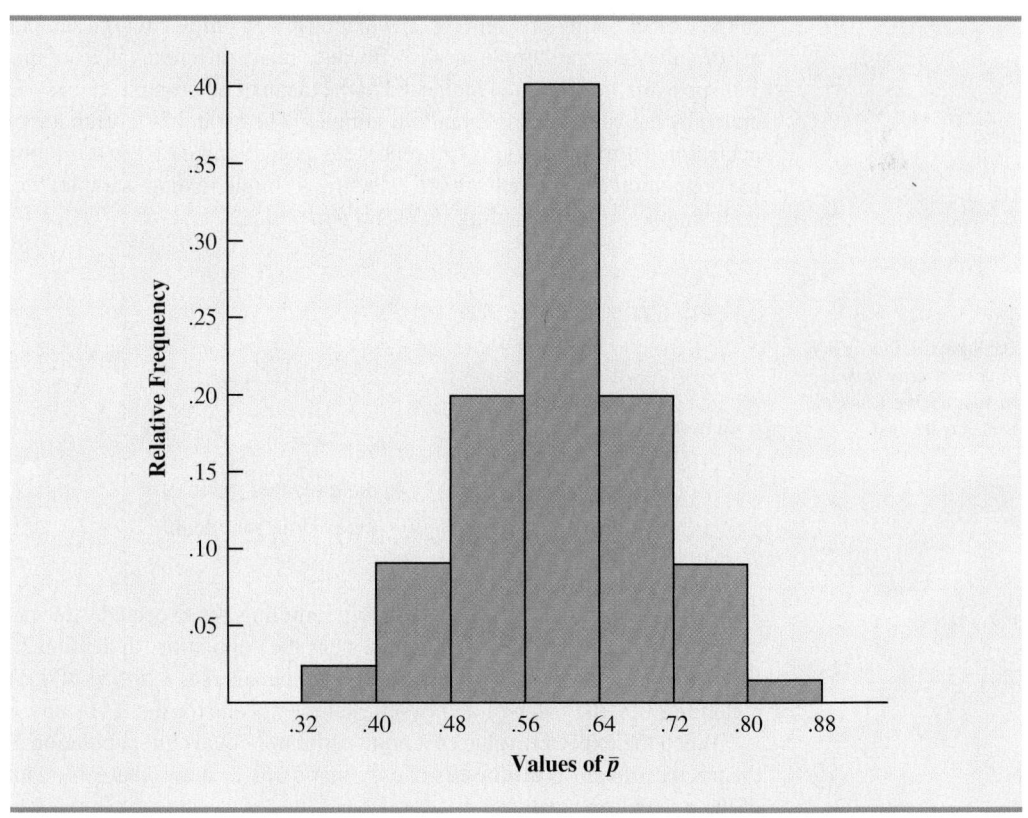

In practice, we select only one simple random sample from the population. We repeated the sampling process 500 times in this section simply to illustrate that many different samples are possible and that the different samples generate a variety of values for the sample statistics $\bar{x}$ and $\bar{p}$. The probability distribution of any particular sample statistic is called the sampling distribution of the statistic. In Section 7.5 we show the characteristics of the sampling distribution of $\bar{x}$. In Section 7.6 we show the characteristics of the sampling distribution of $\bar{p}$.

# 7.5 Sampling Distribution of $\bar{x}$

In the previous section we said that the sample mean $\bar{x}$ is a random variable and its probability distribution is called the sampling distribution of $\bar{x}$.

> **SAMPLING DISTRIBUTION OF $\bar{x}$**
>
> The sampling distribution of $\bar{x}$ is the probability distribution of all possible values of the sample mean $\bar{x}$.

This section describes the properties of the sampling distribution of $\bar{x}$. Just as with other probability distributions we studied, the sampling distribution of $\bar{x}$ has an expected value or mean, a standard deviation, and a characteristic shape or form. Let us begin by considering the mean of all possible $\bar{x}$ values, which is referred to as the expected value of $\bar{x}$.

## Expected Value of $\bar{x}$

In the EAI sampling problem we saw that different simple random samples result in a variety of values for the sample mean $\bar{x}$. Because many different values of the random variable $\bar{x}$ are possible, we are often interested in the mean of all possible values of $\bar{x}$ that can be generated by the various simple random samples. The mean of the $\bar{x}$ random variable is the expected value of $\bar{x}$. Let $E(\bar{x})$ represent the expected value of $\bar{x}$ and $\mu$ represent the mean of the population from which we are selecting a simple random sample. It can be shown that with simple random sampling, $E(\bar{x})$ and $\mu$ are equal.

> **EXPECTED VALUE OF $\bar{x}$**
>
> *The expected value of $\bar{x}$ equals the mean of the population from which the sample is selected.*
>
> $$E(\bar{x}) = \mu \qquad (7.1)$$
>
> where
>
> $$E(\bar{x}) = \text{the expected value of } \bar{x}$$
> $$\mu = \text{the population mean}$$

This result shows that with simple random sampling, the expected value or mean of the sampling distribution of $\bar{x}$ is equal to the mean of the population. In Section 7.1 we saw that the mean annual salary for the population of EAI managers is $\mu = \$51,800$. Thus, according to equation (7.1), the mean of all possible sample means for the EAI study is also $\$51,800$.

When the expected value of a point estimator equals the population parameter, we say the point estimator is **unbiased**. Thus, equation (7.1) shows that $\bar{x}$ is an unbiased estimator of the population mean $\mu$.

## Standard Deviation of $\bar{x}$

Let us define the standard deviation of the sampling distribution of $\bar{x}$. We will use the following notation.

$$\sigma_{\bar{x}} = \text{the standard deviation of } \bar{x}$$
$$\sigma = \text{the standard deviation of the population}$$
$$n = \text{the sample size}$$
$$N = \text{the population size}$$

It can be shown that with simple random sampling, the standard deviation of $\bar{x}$ depends on whether the population is finite or infinite. The two formulas for the standard deviation of $\bar{x}$ follow.

---

STANDARD DEVIATION OF $\bar{x}$

| *Finite Population* | *Infinite Population* | |
|:---:|:---:|:---:|
| $\sigma_{\bar{x}} = \sqrt{\dfrac{N-n}{N-1}}\left(\dfrac{\sigma}{\sqrt{n}}\right)$ | $\sigma_{\bar{x}} = \dfrac{\sigma}{\sqrt{n}}$ | **(7.2)** |

---

In comparing the two formulas in (7.2), we see that the factor $\sqrt{(N-n)/(N-1)}$ is required for the finite population case but not for the infinite population case. This factor is commonly referred to as the **finite population correction factor**. In many practical sampling situations, we find that the population involved, although finite, is "large," whereas the sample size is relatively "small." In such cases the finite population correction factor $\sqrt{(N-n)/(N-1)}$ is close to 1. As a result, the difference between the values of the standard deviation of $\bar{x}$ for the finite and infinite population cases becomes negligible. Then, $\sigma_{\bar{x}} = \sigma/\sqrt{n}$ becomes a good approximation to the standard deviation of $\bar{x}$ even though the population is finite. This observation leads to the following general guideline, or rule of thumb, for computing the standard deviation of $\bar{x}$.

---

USE THE FOLLOWING EXPRESSION TO COMPUTE THE STANDARD DEVIATION OF $\bar{x}$

$$\sigma_{\bar{x}} = \frac{\sigma}{\sqrt{n}} \qquad\qquad (7.3)$$

whenever

1. The population is infinite; or
2. The population is finite *and* the sample size is less than or equal to 5% of the population size; that is, $n/N \le .05$.

---

*Problem 21 shows that when $n/N \le .05$, the finite population correction factor has little effect on the value of $\sigma_{\bar{x}}$.*

In cases where $n/N > .05$, the finite population version of formula (7.2) should be used in the computation of $\sigma_{\bar{x}}$. Unless otherwise noted, throughout the text we will assume that the population size is "large," $n/N \le .05$, and expression (7.3) can be used to compute $\sigma_{\bar{x}}$.

*The term standard error is used throughout statistical inference to refer to the standard deviation of a point estimator.*

To compute $\sigma_{\bar{x}}$, we need to know $\sigma$, the standard deviation of the population. To further emphasize the difference between $\sigma_{\bar{x}}$ and $\sigma$, we refer to the standard deviation of $\bar{x}$, $\sigma_{\bar{x}}$ as the **standard error** of the mean. In general, the term *standard error* refers to the standard deviation of a point estimator. Later we will see that the value of the standard error of the mean is helpful in determining how far the sample mean may be from the population mean. Let us now return to the EAI example and compute the standard error of the mean associated with simple random samples of 30 EAI managers.

In Section 7.1 we saw that the standard deviation of annual salary for the population of 2500 EAI managers is $\sigma = 4000$. In this case, the population is finite, with $N = 2500$. However, with a sample size of 30, we have $n/N = 30/2500 = .012$. Because the sample size is less than 5% of the population size, we can ignore the finite population correction factor and use equation (7.3) to compute the standard error.

$$\sigma_{\bar{x}} = \frac{\sigma}{\sqrt{n}} = \frac{4000}{\sqrt{30}} = 730.3$$

## Form of the Sampling Distribution of $\bar{x}$

The preceding results concerning the expected value and standard deviation for the sampling distribution of $\bar{x}$ are applicable for any population. The final step in identifying the characteristics of the sampling distribution of $\bar{x}$ is to determine the form or shape of the sampling distribution. We will consider two cases: (1) the population has a normal distribution; and (2) the population does not have a normal distribution.

**Population has a normal distribution.** In many situations it is reasonable to assume that the population from which we are selecting a simple random sample has a normal, or nearly normal, distribution. When the population has a normal distribution, the sampling distribution of $\bar{x}$ is normally distributed for any sample size.

**Population does not have a normal distribution.** When the population from which we are selecting a simple random sample does not have a normal distribution, the **central limit theorem** is helpful in identifying the shape of the sampling distribution of $\bar{x}$. A statement of the central limit theorem as it applies to the sampling distribution of $\bar{x}$ follows.

---

CENTRAL LIMIT THEOREM

In selecting simple random samples of size $n$ from a population, the sampling distribution of the sample mean $\bar{x}$ can be approximated by a *normal distribution* as the sample size becomes large.

---

Figure 7.3 shows how the central limit theorem works for three different populations; each column refers to one of the populations. The top panel of the figure shows that none of the populations are normally distributed. However, note what begins to happen to the sampling distribution of $\bar{x}$ as the sample size is increased. When the samples are of size 2, we see that the sampling distribution begins to take on an appearance different from that of the population distribution. For samples of size 5, we see all three sampling distributions beginning to take on a bell-shaped appearance. Finally, the samples of size 30 show all three sampling distributions to be approximately normally distributed. Thus, for sufficiently large samples, the sampling distribution of $\bar{x}$ can be approximated by a normal distribution. However, how large must the sample size be before we can assume that the central limit theorem applies? Statistical researchers investigated this question by studying the sampling

**FIGURE 7.3**    ILLUSTRATION OF THE CENTRAL LIMIT THEOREM
FOR THREE POPULATIONS

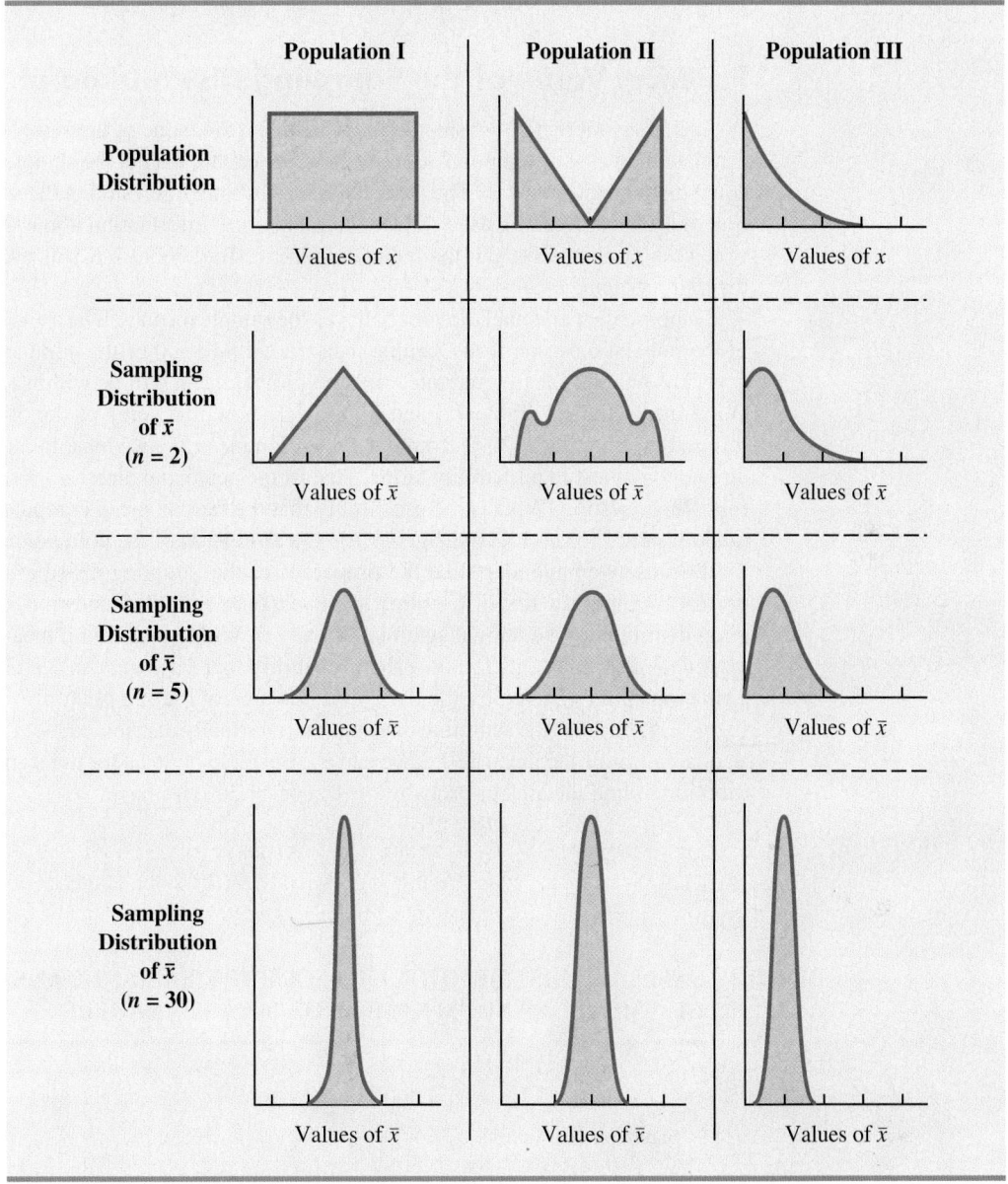

distribution of $\bar{x}$ for a variety of populations and a variety of sample sizes. General statistical practice is to assume that for most applications, the sampling distribution of $\bar{x}$ can be approximated by a normal distribution whenever the sample size is 30 or more.

## Sampling Distribution of $\bar{x}$ for the EAI Problem

Let us return to the EAI problem where we previously showed that $E(\bar{x}) = \$51{,}800$ and $\sigma_{\bar{x}} = 730.3$. At this point, we do not have any information about the population distribution; it may or may not be normally distributed. If the population has a normal distribution, the sampling distribution of $\bar{x}$ is normally distributed. If the population does not have a normal distribution, the simple random sample of 30 managers and the central limit theorem enable us to conclude that the sampling distribution of $\bar{x}$ can be approximated by a normal distribution. In either case, we are comfortable proceeding with the conclusion that the sampling distribution of $\bar{x}$ can be described by the normal distribution shown in Figure 7.4.

## Practical Value of the Sampling Distribution of $\bar{x}$

Whenever a simple random sample is selected and the value of the sample mean is used to estimate the value of the population mean $\mu$, we cannot expect the sample mean to exactly equal the population mean. The practical reason we are interested in the sampling distribution of $\bar{x}$ is that it can be used to provide probability information about the difference between the sample mean and the population mean. To demonstrate this use, let us return to the EAI problem.

Suppose the personnel director believes the sample mean will be an acceptable estimate of the population mean if the sample mean is within $500 of the population mean. However, it is not possible to guarantee that the sample mean will be within $500 of the population mean. Indeed, Table 7.5 and Figure 7.1 show that some of the 500 sample means differed by more than $2000 from the population mean. So we must think of the personnel director's request in probability terms. That is, the personnel director is concerned with the following question: What is the probability that the sample mean computed using a simple random sample of 30 EAI managers will be within $500 of the population mean?

Because we have identified the properties of the sampling distribution of $\bar{x}$ (see Figure 7.4), we will use this distribution to answer the probability question. Refer to the sampling distribution of $\bar{x}$ shown again in Figure 7.5. With a population mean of $51,800, the personnel director wants to know the probability that $\bar{x}$ is between $51,300 and $52,300. This probability is given by the darkly shaded area of the sampling distribution shown in Figure 7.5. Because the sampling distribution is normally distributed, with mean 51,800 and standard error of the mean 730.3, we can use the table of areas for the standard normal distribution to find the area or probability. At $\bar{x} = 51,300$, we have

$$z = \frac{51,300 - 51,800}{730.3} = -.68$$

FIGURE 7.4     SAMPLING DISTRIBUTION OF $\bar{x}$ FOR THE MEAN ANNUAL SALARY OF A SIMPLE RANDOM SAMPLE OF 30 EAI MANAGERS

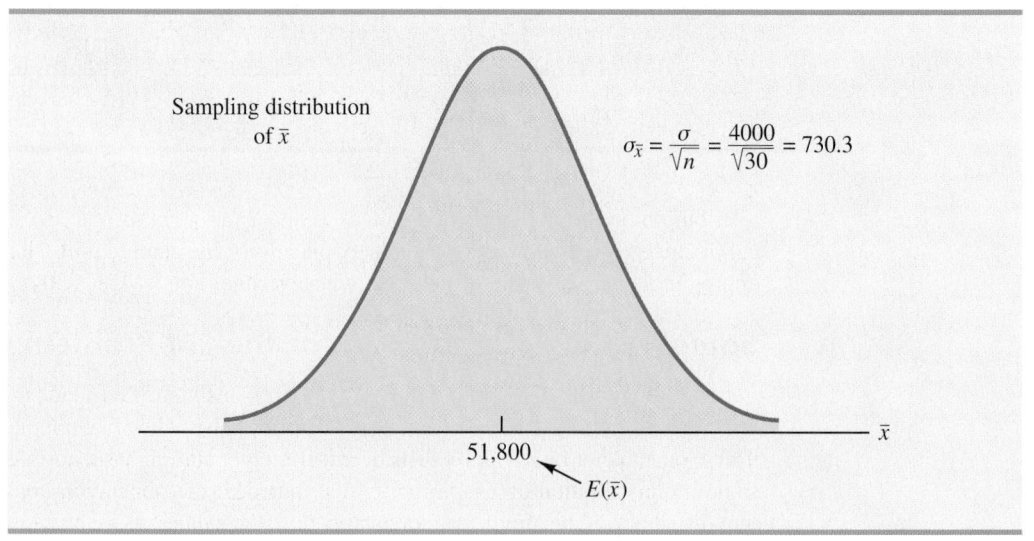

**FIGURE 7.5    THE PROBABILITY OF A SAMPLE MEAN BEING WITHIN $500 OF THE POPULATION MEAN**

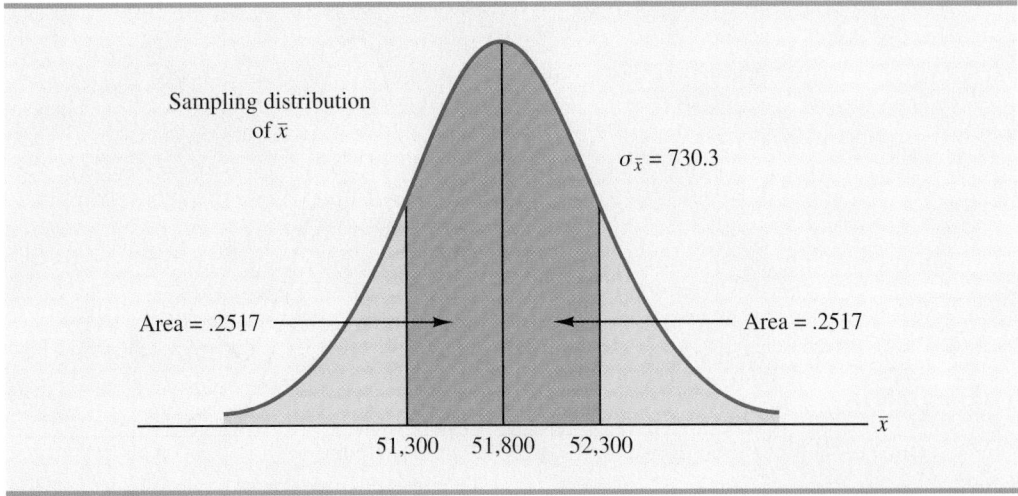

Referring to the standard normal distribution table, we find an area between $z = 0$ and $z = -.68$ of .2517. Similar calculations for $x = 52,300$ show an area between $z = 0$ and $z = +.68$ of .2517. Thus, the probability of the value of the sample mean being between 51,300 and 52,300 is .2517 + .2517 = .5034.

*The sampling distribution of $\bar{x}$ can be used to provide probability information about how close the sample mean $\bar{x}$ is to the population mean $\mu$.*

The preceding computations show that a simple random sample of 30 EAI managers has a .5034 probability of providing a sample mean $\bar{x}$ that is within $500 of the population mean. Thus, there is a $1 - .5034 = .4966$ probability that the difference between $\bar{x}$ and $\mu = \$51,800$ will be more than $500. In other words, a simple random sample of 30 EAI managers has roughly a 50/50 chance of providing a sample mean within the allowable $500. Perhaps a larger sample size should be considered. Let us explore this possibility by considering the relationship between the sample size and the sampling distribution of $\bar{x}$.

## Relationship Between the Sample Size and the Sampling Distribution of $\bar{x}$

Suppose that in the EAI sampling problem we select a simple random sample of 100 EAI managers instead of the 30 originally considered. Intuitively, it would seem that with more data provided by the larger sample size, the sample mean based on $n = 100$ should provide a better estimate of the population mean than the sample mean based on $n = 30$. To see how much better, let us consider the relationship between the sample size and the sampling distribution of $\bar{x}$.

First note that $E(\bar{x}) = \mu$ regardless of the sample size. Thus, the mean of all possible values of $\bar{x}$ is equal to the population mean $\mu$ regardless of the sample size $n$. However, note that the standard error of the mean, $\sigma_{\bar{x}} = \sigma/\sqrt{n}$, is related to the square root of the sample size. Whenever the sample size is increased, the standard error of the mean $\sigma_{\bar{x}}$ decreases. With $n = 30$, the standard error of the mean for the EAI problem is 730.3. However, with the increase in the sample size to $n = 100$, the standard error of the mean is decreased to

$$\sigma_{\bar{x}} = \frac{\sigma}{\sqrt{n}} = \frac{4000}{\sqrt{100}} = 400$$

The sampling distributions of $\bar{x}$ with $n = 30$ and $n = 100$ are shown in Figure 7.6. Because the sampling distribution with $n = 100$ has a smaller standard error, the values of $\bar{x}$ have less variation and tend to be closer to the population mean than the values of $\bar{x}$ with $n = 30$.

FIGURE 7.6    A COMPARISON OF THE SAMPLING DISTRIBUTIONS OF $\bar{x}$ FOR SIMPLE
RANDOM SAMPLES OF $n = 30$ AND $n = 100$ EAI MANAGERS

We can use the sampling distribution of $\bar{x}$ for the case with $n = 100$ to compute the
probability that a simple random sample of 100 EAI managers will provide a sample mean
that is within $500 of the population mean. Because the sampling distribution is normal,
with mean 51,800 and standard error of the mean 400, we can use the standard normal distribution table to find the area or probability. At $\bar{x} = 51,300$ (Figure 7.7), we have

$$z = \frac{51,300 - 51,800}{400} = -1.25$$

FIGURE 7.7    THE PROBABILITY OF A SAMPLE MEAN BEING WITHIN $500
OF THE POPULATION MEAN WHEN A SIMPLE RANDOM SAMPLE
OF 100 EAI MANAGERS IS USED

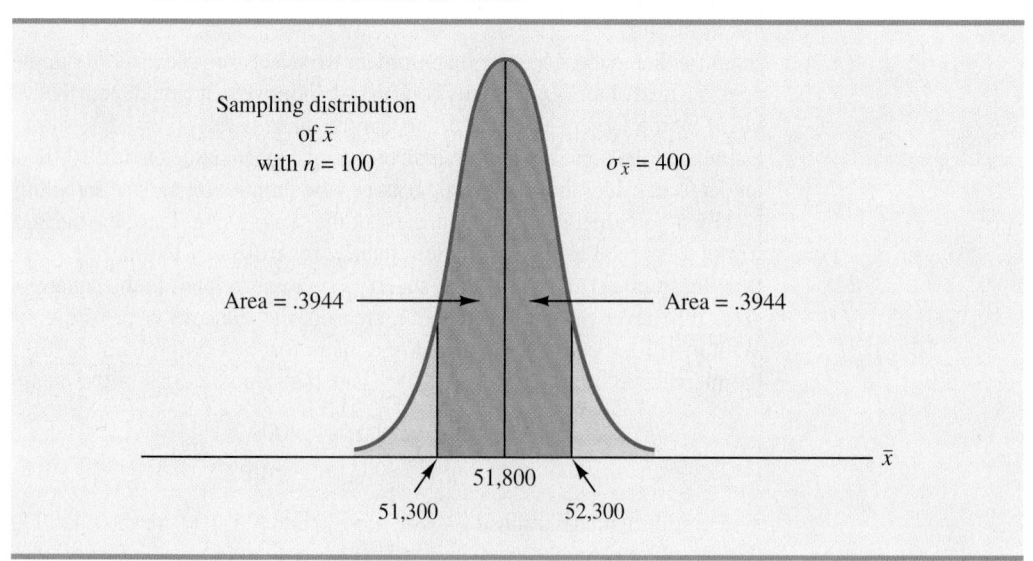

Referring to the standard normal probability distribution table, we find an area between $z = 0$ and $z = -1.25$ of .3944. With a similar calculation for $\bar{x} = 52{,}300$, we see that the probability of the value of the sample mean being between 51,300 and 52,300 is .3944 + .3944 = .7888. Thus, by increasing the sample size from 30 to 100 EAI managers, we have increased the probability of obtaining a sample mean within $500 of the population mean from .5034 to .7888.

The important point in this discussion is that as the sample size is increased, the standard error of the mean decreases. As a result, the larger sample size provides a higher probability that the sample mean is within a specified distance of the population mean.

## NOTES AND COMMENTS

1. In presenting the sampling distribution of $\bar{x}$ for the EAI problem, we took advantage of the fact that the population mean $\mu = 51{,}800$ and the population standard deviation $\sigma = 4000$ were known. However, usually the values of the population mean $\mu$ and the population standard deviation $\sigma$ that are needed to determine the sampling distribution of $\bar{x}$ will be unknown. In Chapter 8 we will show how the sample mean $\bar{x}$ and the sample standard deviation $s$ are used when $\mu$ and $\sigma$ are unknown.

2. The theoretical proof of the central limit theorem requires independent observations in the sample. This condition is met for infinite populations and for finite populations where sampling is done with replacement. Although the central limit theorem does not directly address sampling without replacement from finite populations, general statistical practice applies the findings of the central limit theorem when the population size is large.

## Exercises

### Methods

18.  A population has a mean of 200 and a standard deviation of 50. A simple random sample of size 100 will be taken and the sample mean $\bar{x}$ will be used to estimate the population mean.
     a.  What is the expected value of $\bar{x}$?
     b.  What is the standard deviation of $\bar{x}$?
     c.  Show the sampling distribution of $\bar{x}$.
     d.  What does the sampling distribution of $\bar{x}$ show?

19.  A population has a mean of 200 and a standard deviation of 50. Suppose a simple random sample of size 100 is selected and $\bar{x}$ is used to estimate $\mu$.
     a.  What is the probability that the sample mean will be within $\pm 5$ of the population mean?
     b.  What is the probability that the sample mean will be within $\pm 10$ of the population mean?

20.  Assume the population standard deviation is $\sigma = 25$. Compute the standard error of the mean, $\sigma_{\bar{x}}$, for sample sizes of 50, 100, 150, and 200. What can you say about the size of the standard error of the mean as the sample size is increased?

21.  Suppose a simple random sample of size 50 is selected from a population with $\sigma = 10$. Find the value of the standard error of the mean in each of the following cases (use the finite population correction factor if appropriate).
     a.  The population size is infinite.
     b.  The population size is $N = 50{,}000$.
     c.  The population size is $N = 5000$.
     d.  The population size is $N = 500$.

## Applications

22. Refer to the EAI sampling problem. Suppose a simple random sample of 60 managers is used.
    a. Sketch the sampling distribution of $\bar{x}$ when simple random samples of size 60 are used.
    b. What happens to the sampling distribution of $\bar{x}$ if simple random samples of size 120 are used?
    c. What general statement can you make about what happens to the sampling distribution of $\bar{x}$ as the sample size is increased? Does this generalization seem logical? Explain.

23. In the EAI sampling problem (see Figure 7.5), we showed that for $n = 30$, there was .5034 probability of obtaining a sample mean within $\pm\$500$ of the population mean.
    a. What is the probability that $\bar{x}$ is within $500 of the population mean if a sample of size 60 is used?
    b. Answer part (a) for a sample of size 120.

24. The mean tuition cost at state universities throughout the United States is $4260 per year (*St. Petersburg Times,* December 11, 2002). Use this value as the population mean and assume that the population standard deviation is $\sigma = \$900$. Suppose that a random sample of 50 state universities will be selected.
    a. Show the sampling distribution of $\bar{x}$ where $\bar{x}$ is the sample mean tuition cost for the 50 state universities.
    b. What is the probability that the simple random sample will provide a sample mean within $250 of the population mean?
    c. What is the probability that the simple random sample will provide a sample mean within $100 of the population mean?

25. The College Board American College Testing Program reported a population mean SAT score of $\mu = 1020$ (*The World Almanac 2003*). Assume that the population standard deviation is $\sigma = 100$.
    a. What is the probability that a random sample of 75 students will provide a sample mean SAT score within 10 of the population mean?
    b. What is the probability a random sample of 75 students will provide a sample mean SAT score within 20 of the population mean?

26. The mean annual starting salary for marketing majors is $34,000 (*Time,* May 8, 2000). Assume that for the population of graduates with a marketing major, the mean annual starting salary is $\mu = 34,000$, and the standard deviation is $\sigma = 2000$.
    a. What is the probability that a simple random sample of marketing majors will have a sample mean within $\pm\$250$ of the population mean for each of the following sample sizes: 30, 50, 100, 200, and 400?
    b. What is the advantage of a larger sample size when attempting to estimate the population mean?

27. The mean monthly rental for a two-bedroom apartment in Atlanta is $982 (*Elle,* September 1998). Assume that the population mean is $982 and the population standard deviation is $210.
    a. What is the probability that a simple random sample of 40 two-bedroom apartments will provide a sample mean monthly rental within $\pm\$100$ of the population mean?
    b. What is the probability that a simple random sample of 40 two-bedroom apartments will provide a sample mean monthly rental within $\pm\$25$ of the population mean?
    c. Discuss the results in parts (a) and (b).

28. The average annual cost of automobile insurance is $687 (*National Association of Insurance Commissioners,* January 2003). Use this value as the population mean and assume that the population standard deviation is $\sigma = \$230$. Consider a sample of 45 automobile insurance policies.
    a. Show the sampling distribution of $\bar{x}$ where $\bar{x}$ is the sample mean annual cost of automobile insurance.
    b. What is the probability that the sample mean is within $100 of the population mean?

c.   What is the probability that the sample mean is within $25 of the population mean?

d.   What would you recommend if an insurance agency wanted the sample mean to estimate the population mean within ±$25?

29.   *Money* magazine reported that the average price of a gallon of gasoline in the United States during the first quarter of 2001 was $1.46 (*Money,* August 2001). Assume the price reported by *Money* is the population mean, and the population standard deviation is $\sigma = \$.15$.

a.   What is the probability that the mean price for a sample of 30 gas stations is within $.03 of the population mean?

b.   What is the probability that the mean price for a sample of 50 gas stations is within $.03 of the population mean?

c.   What is the probability that the mean price for a sample 100 gas stations is within $.03 of the population mean?

d.   Would you recommend a sample size of 30, 50, or 100 to have at least a .95 probability that the sample mean is within $.03 of the population mean?

30.   To estimate the mean age for a population of 4000 employees, a simple random sample of 40 employees is selected.

a.   Would you use the finite population correction factor in calculating the standard error of the mean? Explain.

b.   If the population standard deviation is $\sigma = 8.2$ years, compute the standard error both with and without the finite population correction factor. What is the rationale for ignoring the finite population correction factor whenever $n/N \leq .05$?

c.   What is the probability that the sample mean age of the employees will be within ±2 years of the population mean age?

##   Sampling Distribution of $\bar{p}$

The sample proportion $\bar{p}$ is the point estimator of the population proportion $p$. The formula for computing the sample proportion is

$$\bar{p} = \frac{x}{n}$$

where

$x =$ the number of elements in the sample that possess the characteristic of interest

$n =$ sample size

As noted in Section 7.4, the sample proportion $\bar{p}$ is a random variable and its probability distribution is called the sampling distribution of $\bar{p}$.

---

**SAMPLING DISTRIBUTION OF $\bar{p}$**

The sampling distribution of $\bar{p}$ is the probability distribution of all possible values of the sample proportion $\bar{p}$.

---

To determine how close the sample proportion $\bar{p}$ is to the population proportion $p$, we need to understand the properties of the sampling distribution of $\bar{p}$: the expected value of $\bar{p}$, the standard deviation of $\bar{p}$, and the shape or form of the sampling distribution of $\bar{p}$.

## Expected Value of $\bar{p}$

The expected value of $\bar{p}$, the mean of all possible values of $\bar{p}$, is equal to the population proportion $p$.

---

EXPECTED VALUE OF $\bar{p}$

$$E(\bar{p}) = p \qquad\qquad (7.4)$$

where

$$E(\bar{p}) = \text{the expected value of } \bar{p}$$
$$p = \text{the population proportion}$$

---

Because $E(\bar{p}) = p$, $\bar{p}$ is an unbiased estimator of $p$. Recall from Section 7.1 we noted that $p = .60$ for the EAI population, where $p$ is the proportion of the population of managers who participated in the company's management training program. Thus, the expected value of $\bar{p}$ for the EAI sampling problem is .60.

## Standard Deviation of $\bar{p}$

Just as we found for the standard deviation of $\bar{x}$, the standard deviation of $\bar{p}$ depends on whether the population is finite or infinite. The two formulas for computing the standard deviation of $\bar{p}$ follow.

---

STANDARD DEVIATION OF $\bar{p}$

| *Finite Population* | *Infinite Population* |
|:---:|:---:|
| $\sigma_{\bar{p}} = \sqrt{\dfrac{N-n}{N-1}} \sqrt{\dfrac{p(1-p)}{n}}$ | $\sigma_{\bar{p}} = \sqrt{\dfrac{p(1-p)}{n}} \qquad (7.5)$ |

---

Comparing the two formulas in (7.5), we see that the only difference is the use of the finite population correction factor $\sqrt{(N-n)/(N-1)}$.

As was the case with the sample mean $\bar{x}$, the difference between the expressions for the finite population and the infinite population becomes negligible if the size of the finite population is large in comparison to the sample size. We follow the same rule of thumb that we recommended for the sample mean. That is, if the population is finite with $n/N \le .05$, we will use $\sigma_{\bar{p}} = \sqrt{p(1-p)/n}$. However, if the population is finite with $n/N > .05$, the finite population correction factor should be used. Again, unless specifically noted, throughout the text we will assume that the population size is large in relation to the sample size and thus the finite population correction factor is unnecessary.

In Section 7.5 we used standard error of the mean to refer to the standard deviation of $\bar{x}$. We stated that in general the term standard error refers to the standard deviation of a point estimator. Thus, for proportions we use *standard error of the proportion* to refer to the standard deviation of $\bar{p}$. Let us now return to the EAI example and compute the standard error of the proportion associated with simple random samples of 30 EAI managers.

For the EAI study we know that the population proportion of managers who participated in the management training program is $p = .60$. With $n/N = 30/2500 = .012$, we can ignore the finite population correction factor when we compute the standard error of the proportion. For the simple random sample of 30 managers, $\sigma_{\bar{p}}$ is

$$\sigma_{\bar{p}} = \sqrt{\frac{p(1-p)}{n}} = \sqrt{\frac{.60(1-.60)}{30}} = .0894$$

## Form of the Sampling Distribution of $\bar{p}$

Now that we know the mean and standard deviation of the sampling distribution of $\bar{p}$, the final step is to determine the form or shape of the sampling distribution. The sample proportion is $\bar{p} = x/n$. For a simple random sample from a large population, the value of $x$ is a binomial random variable indicating the number of elements in the sample with the characteristic of interest. Because $n$ is a constant, the probability of $x/n$ is the same as the binomial probability of $x$, which means that the sampling distribution of $\bar{p}$ is also a discrete probability distribution and that the probability for each value of $x/n$ is the same as the probability of $x$.

In Chapter 6 we also showed that a binomial distribution can be approximated by a normal distribution whenever the sample size is large enough to satisfy the following two conditions:

$$np \geq 5 \quad \text{and} \quad n(1-p) \geq 5$$

Assuming these two conditions are satisfied, the probability distribution of $x$ in the sample proportion, $\bar{p} = x/n$, can be approximated by a normal distribution. And because $n$ is a constant, the sampling distribution of $\bar{p}$ can also be approximated by a normal distribution. This approximation is stated as follows:

> The sampling distribution of $\bar{p}$ can be approximated by a normal distribution whenever $np \geq 5$ and $n(1-p) \geq 5$.

In practical applications, when an estimate of a population proportion is desired, we find that sample sizes are almost always large enough to permit the use of a normal approximation for the sampling distribution of $\bar{p}$.

Recall that for the EAI sampling problem we know that the population proportion of managers who participated in the training program is $p = .60$. With a simple random sample of size 30, we have $np = 30(.60) = 18$ and $n(1-p) = 30(.40) = 12$. Thus, the sampling distribution of $\bar{p}$ can be approximated by a normal distribution shown in Figure 7.8.

## Practical Value of the Sampling Distribution of $\bar{p}$

The practical value of the sampling distribution of $\bar{p}$ is that it can be used to provide probability information about the difference between the sample proportion and the population proportion. For instance, suppose that in the EAI problem the personnel director wants to know the probability of obtaining a value of $\bar{p}$ that is within .05 of the population proportion of EAI managers who participated in the training program. That is, what is the probability of obtaining a sample with a sample proportion $\bar{p}$ between .55 and .65? The darkly shaded area in Figure 7.9 shows this probability. Using the fact that the sampling distribution of $\bar{p}$ can be approximated by a normal distribution with a mean of .60 and a standard error of the proportion of $\sigma_{\bar{p}} = .0894$, we find that the standard normal random variable corresponding to $\bar{p} = .55$ has a value of $z = (.55 - .60)/.0894 = -.56$. Referring to the

FIGURE 7.8 FIGURE 7.8 SAMPLING DISTRIBUTION OF $\bar{p}$ FOR THE PROPORTION OF EAI MANAGERS WHO PARTICIPATED IN THE MANAGEMENT TRAINING PROGRAM

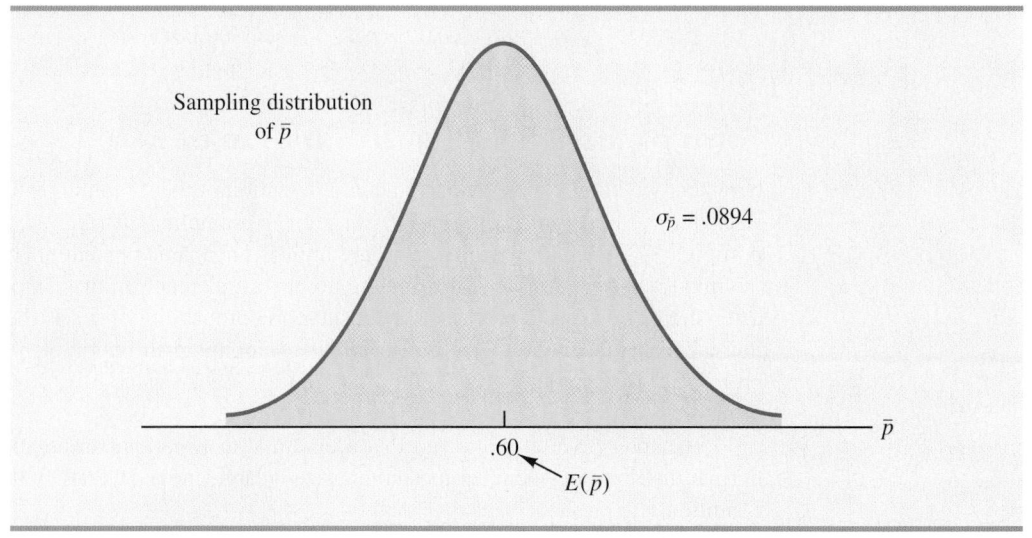

standard normal distribution table, we see that the area between $z = -.56$ and $z = 0$ is .2123. Similarly, at $\bar{p} = .65$ we find an area between $z = 0$ and $z = .56$ of .2123. Thus, the probability of selecting a sample that provides a sample proportion $\bar{p}$ within .05 of the population proportion $p$ is .2123 + .2123 = .4246.

If we consider increasing the sample size to $n = 100$, the standard error of the proportion becomes

$$\sigma_{\bar{p}} = \sqrt{\frac{.60(1 - .60)}{100}} = .049$$

With a sample size of 100 EAI managers, the probability of the sample proportion having a value within .05 of the population proportion can now be computed. Because the sam-

FIGURE 7.9 SAMPLING DISTRIBUTION OF $\bar{p}$ FOR THE EAI SAMPLING PROBLEM

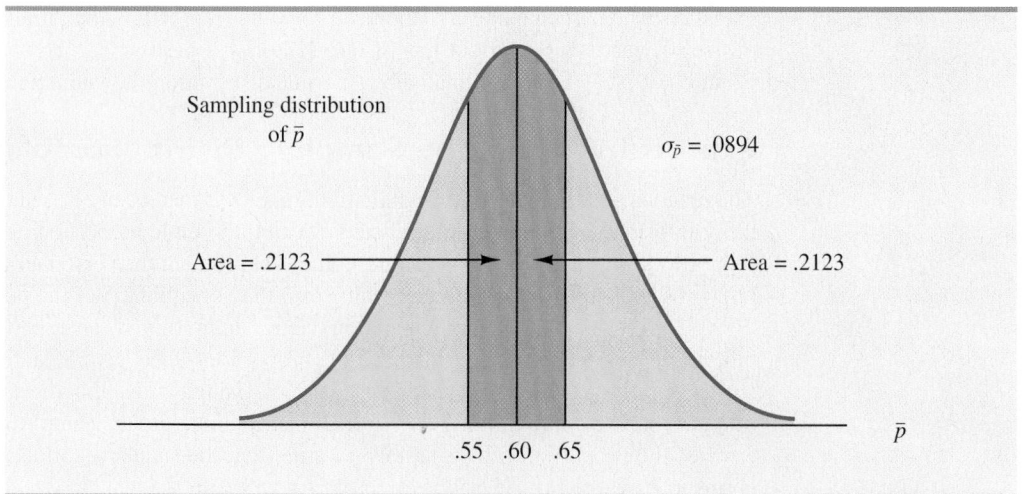

pling distribution is approximately normal, with mean .60 and standard deviation .049, we can use the standard normal distribution table to find the area or probability. At $\bar{p} = .55$, we have $z = (.55 - .60)/.049 = -1.02$. Referring to the standard normal distribution table, we see that the area between $z = -1.02$ and $z = 0$ is .3461. Similarly, at .65 the area between $z = 0$ and $z = 1.02$ is .3461. Thus, if the sample size is increased from 30 to 100, the probability that the sample proportion $\bar{p}$ is within .05 of the population proportion $p$ will increase to $.3461 + .3461 = .6922$.

## Exercises

## Methods

31. A simple random sample of size 100 is selected from a population with $p = .40$.
    a. What is the expected value of $\bar{p}$?
    b. What is the standard error of $\bar{p}$?
    c. Show the sampling distribution of $\bar{p}$.
    d. What does the sampling distribution of $\bar{p}$ show?

32. A population proportion is .40. A simple random sample of size 200 will be taken and the sample proportion $\bar{p}$ will be used to estimate the population proportion.
    a. What is the probability that the sample proportion will be within ±.03 of the population proportion?
    b. What is the probability that the sample proportion will be within ±.05 of the population proportion?

33. Assume that the population proportion is .55. Compute the standard error of the proportion, $\sigma_{\bar{p}}$, for sample sizes of 100, 200, 500, and 1000. What can you say about the size of the standard error of the proportion as the sample size is increased?

34. The population proportion is .30. What is the probability that a sample proportion will be within ±.04 of the population proportion for each of the following sample sizes?
    a. $n = 100$
    b. $n = 200$
    c. $n = 500$
    d. $n = 1000$
    e. What is the advantage of a larger sample size?

## Applications

35. The president of Doerman Distributors, Inc., believes that 30% of the firm's orders come from first-time customers. A simple random sample of 100 orders will be used to estimate the proportion of first-time customers.
    a. Assume that the president is correct and $p = .30$. What is the sampling distribution of $\bar{p}$ for this study?
    b. What is the probability that the sample proportion $\bar{p}$ will be between .20 and .40?
    c. What is the probability that the sample proportion will be between .25 and .35?

36. *Business Week* reported that 56% of the households in the United States have Internet access (May 21, 2001). Use a population proportion $p = .56$ and assume that a sample of 300 households will be selected.
    a. Show the sampling distribution of $\bar{p}$ where $\bar{p}$ is the sample proportion of households that have Internet access.
    b. What is the probability that the sample proportion will be within ±.03 of the population proportion?
    c. Answer part (b) for sample sizes of 600 and 1000.

37. *Time*/CNN voter polls monitored public opinion for the presidential candidates during the 2000 presidential election campaign. One *Time*/CNN poll conducted by Yankelovich Partners, Inc., used a sample of 589 likely voters (*Time,* June 26, 2000). Assume the population proportion for a presidential candidate is $p = .50$. Let $\bar{p}$ be the sample proportion of likely voters favoring the presidential candidate.
   a. Show the sampling distribution of $\bar{p}$.
   b. What is the probability the *Time*/CNN poll will provide a sample proportion within $\pm.04$ of the population proportion?
   c. What is the probability the *Time*/CNN poll will provide a sample proportion within $\pm.03$ of the population proportion?
   d. What is the probability the *Time*/CNN poll will provide a sample proportion within $\pm.02$ of the population proportion?

38. Although most people believe breakfast is the most important meal of the day, 25% of adults skip breakfast (*U.S. News & World Report,* November 10, 1997). Assume the population proportion is $p = .25$, and $\bar{p}$ is the sample proportion of adults who skip breakfast based on a sample of 200 adults.
   a. Show the sampling distribution of $\bar{p}$.
   b. What is the probability that the sample proportion will be within $\pm.03$ of the population proportion?
   c. What is the probability that the sample proportion will be within $\pm.05$ of the population proportion?

39. The *Democrat and Chronicle* reported that 25% of the flights arriving at the San Diego airport during the first five months of 2001 were late (*Democrat and Chronicle,* July 23, 2001). Assume the population proportion is $p = .25$.
   a. Show the sampling distribution of $\bar{p}$, the proportion of late flights in a sample of 1000 flights.
   b. What is the probability that the sample proportion will be within $\pm.03$ of the population proportion if a sample of size 1000 is selected?
   c. Answer part (b) for a sample of 500 flights.

40. The Grocery Manufacturers of America reported that 76% of consumers read the ingredients listed on a product's label. Assume the population proportion is $p = .76$ and a sample of 400 consumers is selected from the population.
   a. Show the sampling distribution of the sample proportion $\bar{p}$ where $\bar{p}$ is the proportion of the sampled consumers who read the ingredients listed on a product's label.
   b. What is the probability that the sample proportion will be within $\pm.03$ of the population proportion?
   c. Answer part (b) for a sample of 750 consumers.

41. The Food Marketing Institute shows that 17% of households spend more than $100 per week on groceries. Assume the population proportion is $p = .17$ and a simple random sample of 800 households will be selected from the population.
   a. Show the sampling distribution of $\bar{p}$, the sample proportion of households spending more than $100 per week on groceries.
   b. What is the probability that the sample proportion will be within $\pm.02$ of the population proportion?
   c. Answer part (b) for a sample of 1600 households.

## 7.7   Properties of Point Estimators

In this chapter we showed how sample statistics such as a sample mean $\bar{x}$, a sample standard deviation $s$, and a sample proportion $\bar{p}$ can be used as point estimators of their corresponding population parameters $\mu$, $\sigma$, and $p$. It is intuitively appealing that each of these sample statistics is the point estimator of its corresponding population parameter. However, before using a sample statistic as a point estimator, statisticians check to see whether the sample statistic demonstrates certain properties associated with good point estimators. In this section we discuss the properties of good point estimators: unbiased, efficiency, and consistency.

Because several different sample statistics can be used as point estimators of different population parameters, we use the following general notation in this section.

$$\theta = \text{the population parameter of interest}$$
$$\hat{\theta} = \text{the sample statistic or point estimator of } \theta$$

The notation $\theta$ is the Greek letter theta, and the notation $\hat{\theta}$ is pronounced "theta-hat." In general, $\theta$ represents any population parameter such as a population mean, population standard deviation, population proportion, and so on; $\hat{\theta}$ represents the corresponding sample statistic such as the sample mean, sample standard deviation, and sample proportion.

## Unbiased

If the expected value of the sample statistic is equal to the population parameter being estimated, the sample statistic is said to be an *unbiased estimator* of the population parameter.

UNBIASED

The sample statistic $\hat{\theta}$ is an unbiased estimator of the population parameter $\theta$ if

$$E(\hat{\theta}) = \theta$$

where

$$E(\hat{\theta}) = \text{the expected value of the sample statistic } \hat{\theta}$$

Hence, the expected value, or mean, of all possible values of an unbiased sample statistic is equal to the population parameter being estimated.

Figure 7.10 shows the cases of unbiased and biased point estimators. In the illustration showing the unbiased estimator, the mean of the sampling distribution is equal to the value of the population parameter. The estimation errors balance out in this case, because sometimes the value of the point estimator $\hat{\theta}$ may be less than $\theta$ and other times it may be greater than $\theta$. In the case of a biased estimator, the mean of the sampling distribution is less than or greater than the value of the population parameter. In the illustration in Panel B of Figure 7.10, $E(\hat{\theta})$ is greater than $\theta$; thus, the sample statistic has a high probability of overestimating the value of the population parameter. The amount of the bias is shown in the figure.

In discussing the sampling distributions of the sample mean and the sample proportion, we stated that $E(\bar{x}) = \mu$ and $E(\bar{p}) = p$. Thus, both $\bar{x}$ and $\bar{p}$ are unbiased estimators of their corresponding population parameters $\mu$ and $p$.

In the case of the sample standard deviation $s$ and the sample variance $s^2$, it can be shown that $E(s^2) = \sigma^2$. Thus, we conclude that the sample variance $s^2$ is an unbiased estimator of the population variance $\sigma^2$. In fact, when we first presented the formulas for the sample variance and the sample standard deviation in Chapter 3, $n - 1$ rather than $n$ was used in the denominator. The reason for using $n - 1$ rather than $n$ is to make the sample variance an unbiased estimator of the population variance.

FIGURE 7.10    EXAMPLES OF UNBIASED AND BIASED POINT ESTIMATORS

## Efficiency

Assume that a simple random sample of $n$ elements can be used to provide two unbiased point estimators of the same population parameter. In this situation, we would prefer to use the point estimator with the smaller standard error, because it tends to provide estimates closer to the population parameter. The point estimator with the smaller standard error is said to have greater **relative efficiency** than the other.

Figure 7.11 shows the sampling distributions of two unbiased point estimators, $\hat{\theta}_1$ and $\hat{\theta}_2$. Note that the standard error of $\hat{\theta}_1$ is less than the standard error of $\hat{\theta}_2$; thus, values of $\hat{\theta}_1$ have a greater chance of being close to the parameter $\theta$ than do values of $\hat{\theta}_2$. Because

FIGURE 7.11    SAMPLING DISTRIBUTIONS OF TWO UNBIASED POINT ESTIMATORS

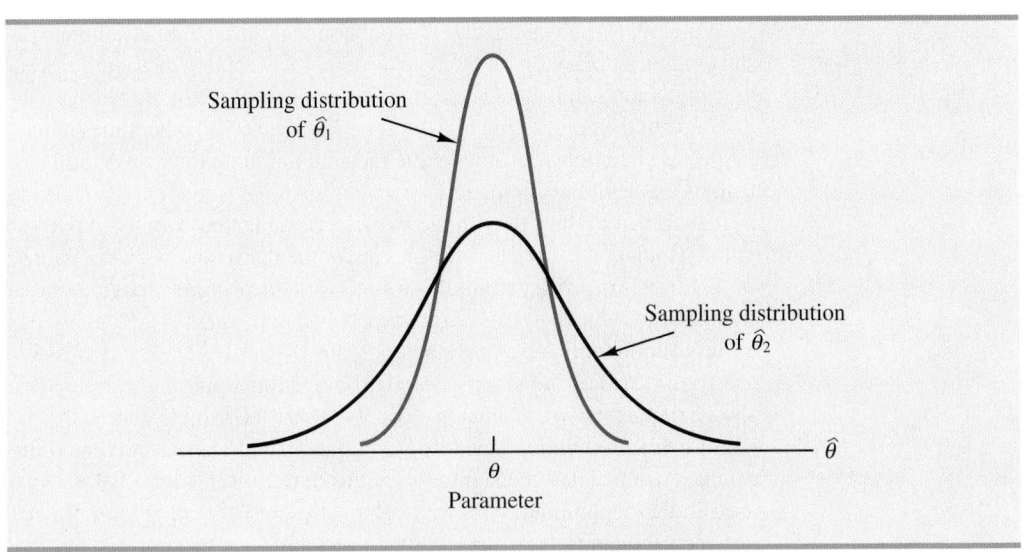

*When sampling from a normal population, the standard error of the sample mean is less than the standard error of the sample median. Thus, the sample mean is more efficient than the sample median.*

the standard error of point estimator $\hat{\theta}_1$ is less than the standard error of point estimator $\hat{\theta}_2$, $\hat{\theta}_1$ is relatively more efficient than $\hat{\theta}_2$ and is the preferred point estimator.

## Consistency

A third property associated with good point estimators is **consistency.** Loosely speaking, a point estimator is consistent if the values of the point estimator tend to become closer to the population parameter as the sample size becomes larger. In other words, a large sample size tends to provide a better point estimate than a small sample size. Note that for the sample mean $\bar{x}$, we showed that the standard error of $\bar{x}$ is given by $\sigma_{\bar{x}} = \sigma/\sqrt{n}$. Because $\sigma_{\bar{x}}$ is related to the sample size such that larger sample sizes provide smaller values for $\sigma_{\bar{x}}$, we conclude that a larger sample size tends to provide point estimates closer to the population mean $\mu$. In this sense, we can say that the sample mean $\bar{x}$ is a consistent estimator of the population mean $\mu$. Using a similar rationale, we can also conclude that the sample proportion $\bar{p}$ is a consistent estimator of the population proportion $p$.

### NOTES AND COMMENTS

In Chapter 3 we stated that the mean and the median are two measures of central location. In this chapter we discussed only the mean. The reason is that in sampling from a normal population, where the population mean and population median are identical, the standard error of the median is approximately 25% larger than the standard error of the mean. Recall that in the EAI problem where $n = 30$, the standard error of the mean is $\sigma_{\bar{x}} = 730.3$. The standard error of the median for this problem would be $1.25 \times (730.3) = 913$. As a result, the sample mean is more efficient and will have a higher probability of being within a specified distance of the population mean.

 ## 7.8   Other Sampling Methods

We described the simple random sampling procedure and discussed the properties of the sampling distributions of $\bar{x}$ and $\bar{p}$ when simple random sampling is used. However, simple random sampling is not the only sampling method available. Such methods as stratified random sampling, cluster sampling, and systematic sampling provide advantages over simple random sampling in some situations. In this section we briefly introduce these alternative sampling methods. A more in-depth treatment is provided in Chapter 22 which is located on the CD that accompanies the text.

*This section provides a brief introduction to sampling methods other than simple random sampling.*

### Stratified Random Sampling

In **stratified random sampling**, the elements in the population are first divided into groups called *strata*, such that each element in the population belongs to one and only one stratum. The basis for forming the strata, such as department, location, age, industry type, and so on, is at the discretion of the designer of the sample. However, the best results are obtained when the elements within each stratum are as much alike as possible. Figure 7.12 is a diagram of a population divided into $H$ strata.

*Stratified random sampling works best when the variance among elements in each stratum is relatively small.*

After the strata are formed, a simple random sample is taken from each stratum. Formulas are available for combining the results for the individual stratum samples into one estimate of the population parameter of interest. The value of stratified random sampling depends on how homogeneous the elements are within the strata. If elements within strata are alike, the strata will have low variances. Thus relatively small sample sizes can be

**FIGURE 7.12**    DIAGRAM FOR STRATIFIED RANDOM SAMPLING

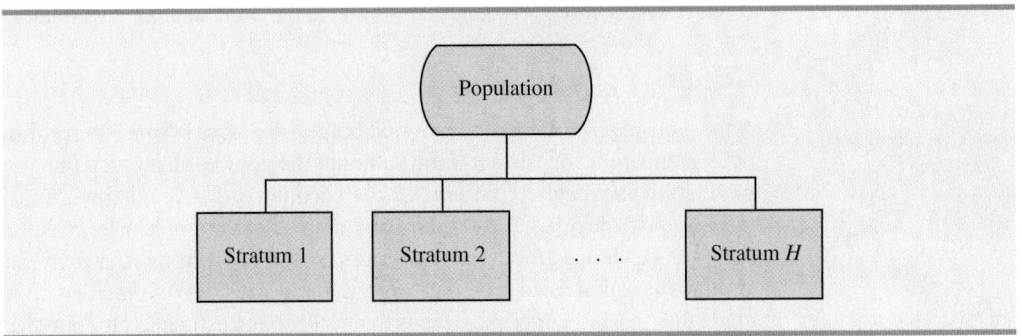

used to obtain good estimates of the strata characteristics. If strata are homogeneous, the stratified random sampling procedure provides results just as precise as those of simple random sampling by using a smaller total sample size.

## Cluster Sampling

*Cluster sampling works best when each cluster provides a small-scale representation of the population.*

In **cluster sampling**, the elements in the population are first divided into separate groups called *clusters*. Each element of the population belongs to one and only one cluster (see Figure 7.13). A simple random sample of the clusters is then taken. All elements within each sampled cluster form the sample. Cluster sampling tends to provide the best results when the elements within the clusters are not alike. In the ideal case, each cluster is a representative small-scale version of the entire population. The value of cluster sampling depends on how representative each cluster is of the entire population. If all clusters are alike in this regard, sampling a small number of clusters will provide good estimates of the population parameters.

One of the primary applications of cluster sampling is area sampling, where clusters are city blocks or other well-defined areas. Cluster sampling generally requires a larger total sample size than either simple random sampling or stratified random sampling. However, it can result in cost savings because of the fact that when an interviewer is sent to a sampled cluster (e.g., a city-block location), many sample observations can be obtained in a relatively short time. Hence, a larger sample size may be obtainable with a significantly lower total cost.

## Systematic Sampling

In some sampling situations, especially those with large populations, it is time-consuming to select a simple random sample by first finding a random number and then counting or searching through the list of the population until the corresponding element is found. An

**FIGURE 7.13**    DIAGRAM FOR CLUSTER SAMPLING

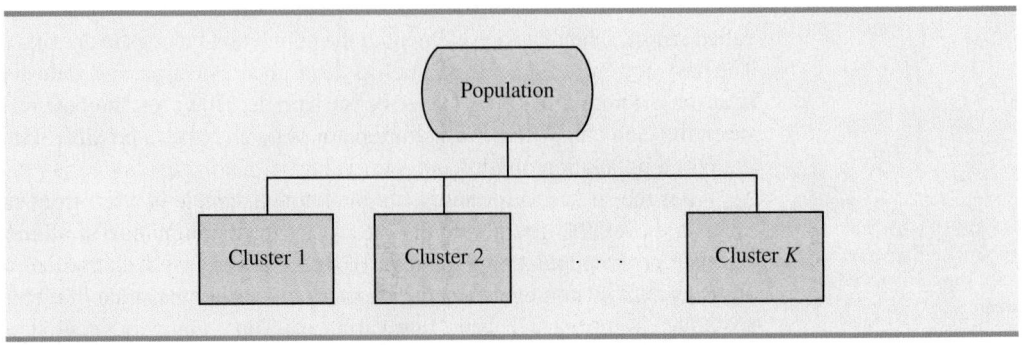

alternative to simple random sampling is **systematic sampling**. For example, if a sample size of 50 is desired from a population containing 5000 elements, we will sample one element for every 5000/50 = 100 elements in the population. A systematic sample for this case involves selecting randomly one of the first 100 elements from the population list. Other sample elements are identified by starting with the first sampled element and then selecting every 100th element that follows in the population list. In effect, the sample of 50 is identified by moving systematically through the population and identifying every 100th element after the first randomly selected element. The sample of 50 usually will be easier to identify in this way than it would be if simple random sampling were used. Because the first element selected is a random choice, a systematic sample is usually assumed to have the properties of a simple random sample. This assumption is especially applicable when the list of elements in the population is a random ordering of the elements.

## Convenience Sampling

The sampling methods discussed thus far are referred to as *probability sampling* techniques. Elements selected from the population have a known probability of being included in the sample. The advantage of probability sampling is that the sampling distribution of the appropriate sample statistic generally can be identified. Formulas such as the ones for simple random sampling presented in this chapter can be used to determine the properties of the sampling distribution. Then the sampling distribution can be used to make probability statements about the error associated with the sample results.

Convenience sampling is a *nonprobability sampling* technique. As the name implies, the sample is identified primarily by convenience. Elements are included in the sample without prespecified or known probabilities of being selected. For example, a professor conducting research at a university may use student volunteers to constitute a sample simply because they are readily available and will participate as subjects for little or no cost. Similarly, an inspector may sample a shipment of oranges by selecting oranges haphazardly from among several crates. Labeling each orange and using a probability method of sampling would be impractical. Samples such as wildlife captures and volunteer panels for consumer research are also convenience samples.

Convenience samples have the advantage of relatively easy sample selection and data collection; however, it is impossible to evaluate the "goodness" of the sample in terms of its representativeness of the population. A convenience sample may provide good results or it may not; no statistically justified procedure allows a probability analysis and inference about the quality of the sample results. Sometimes researchers apply statistical methods designed for probability samples to a convenience sample, arguing that the convenience sample can be treated as though it were a probability sample. However, this argument cannot be supported, and we should be cautious in interpreting the results of convenience samples that are used to make inferences about populations.

## Judgment Sampling

One additional nonprobability sampling technique is **judgment sampling**. In this approach, the person most knowledgeable on the subject of the study selects elements of the population that he or she feels are most representative of the population. Often this method is a relatively easy way of selecting a sample. For example, a reporter may sample two or three senators, judging that those senators reflect the general opinion of all senators. However, the quality of the sample results depends on the judgment of the person selecting the sample. Again, great caution is warranted in drawing conclusions based on judgment samples used to make inferences about populations.

## NOTES AND COMMENTS

We recommend using probability sampling methods: simple random sampling, stratified random sampling, cluster sampling, or systematic sampling. For these methods, formulas are available for evaluating the "goodness" of the sample results in terms of the closeness of the results to the population parameters being estimated. An evaluation of the goodness cannot be made with convenience or judgment sampling. Thus, great care should be used in interpreting the results based on nonprobability sampling methods.

## Summary

In this chapter we presented the concepts of simple random sampling and sampling distributions. We demonstrated how a simple random sample can be selected and how the data collected for the sample can be used to develop point estimates of population parameters. Because different simple random samples provide different values for the point estimators, point estimators such as $\bar{x}$ and $\bar{p}$ are random variables. The probability distribution of such a random variable is called a sampling distribution. In particular, we described the sampling distributions of the sample mean $\bar{x}$ and the sample proportion $\bar{p}$.

In considering the characteristics of the sampling distributions of $\bar{x}$ and $\bar{p}$, we stated that $E(\bar{x}) = \mu$ and $E(\bar{p}) = p$. After developing the standard deviation or standard error formulas for these estimators, we described the conditions necessary for the sampling distributions of $\bar{x}$ and $\bar{p}$ to follow a normal distribution. Other sampling methods including stratified random sampling, cluster sampling, systematic sampling, convenience sampling, and judgment sampling were discussed.

## Glossary

**Parameter** A numerical characteristic of a population, such as a population mean $\mu$, a population standard deviation $\sigma$, a population proportion $p$, and so on.

**Simple random sampling** Finite population: a sample selected such that each possible sample of size $n$ has the same probability of being selected. Infinite population: a sample selected such that each element comes from the same population and the elements are selected independently.

**Sampling without replacement** Once an element has been included in the sample, it is removed from the population and cannot be selected a second time.

**Sampling with replacement** Once an element has been included in the sample, it is returned to the population. A previously selected element can be selected again and therefore may appear in the sample more than once.

**Sample statistic** A sample characteristic, such as a sample mean $\bar{x}$, a sample standard deviation $s$, a sample proportion $\bar{p}$, and so on. The value of the sample statistic is used to estimate the value of the corresponding population parameter.

**Point estimator** The sample statistic, such as $\bar{x}$, $s$, or $\bar{p}$, that provides the point estimate of the population parameter.

**Point estimate** The value of a point estimator used in a particular instance as an estimate of a population parameter.

**Sampling distribution** A probability distribution consisting of all possible values of a sample statistic.

**Unbiased** A property of a point estimator that is present when the expected value of the point estimator is equal to the population parameter it estimates.

**Finite population correction factor** The term $\sqrt{(N - n)/(N - 1)}$ that is used in the formulas for $\sigma_{\bar{x}}$ and $\sigma_{\bar{p}}$ whenever a finite population, rather than an infinite population, is being sampled. The generally accepted rule of thumb is to ignore the finite population correction factor whenever $n/N \leq .05$.

**Standard error** The standard deviation of a point estimator.

**Central limit theorem** A theorem that enables one to use the normal probability distribution to approximate the sampling distribution of $\bar{x}$ whenever the sample size is large.

**Relative efficiency** Given two unbiased point estimators of the same population parameter, the point estimator with the smaller standard deviation is more efficient.

**Consistency** A property of a point estimator that is present whenever larger sample sizes tend to provide point estimates closer to the population parameter.

**Stratified random sampling** A probability sampling method in which the population is first divided into strata and a simple random sample is then taken from each stratum.

**Cluster sampling** A probability sampling method in which the population is first divided into clusters and then a simple random sample of the clusters is taken.

**Systematic sampling** A probability sampling method in which we randomly select one of the first $k$ elements and then select every $k$th element thereafter.

**Convenience sampling** A nonprobability method of sampling whereby elements are selected for the sample on the basis of convenience.

**Judgment sampling** A nonprobability method of sampling whereby elements are selected for the sample based on the judgment of the person doing the study.

## Key Formulas

**Expected Value of $\bar{x}$**

$$E(\bar{x}) = \mu \qquad (7.1)$$

**Standard Deviation of $\bar{x}$ (Standard Error)**

| *Finite Population* | *Infinite Population* |
|---|---|

$$\sigma_{\bar{x}} = \sqrt{\frac{N - n}{N - 1}} \left( \frac{\sigma}{\sqrt{n}} \right) \qquad\qquad \sigma_{\bar{x}} = \frac{\sigma}{\sqrt{n}} \qquad (7.2)$$

**Expected Value of $\bar{p}$**

$$E(\bar{p}) = p \qquad (7.4)$$

**Standard Deviation of $\bar{p}$ (Standard Error)**

| *Finite Population* | *Infinite Population* |
|---|---|

$$\sigma_{\bar{p}} = \sqrt{\frac{N - n}{N - 1}} \sqrt{\frac{p(1 - p)}{n}} \qquad\qquad \sigma_{\bar{p}} = \sqrt{\frac{p(1 - p)}{n}} \qquad (7.5)$$

## Supplementary Exercises

42. *Business Week's* Corporate Scoreboard provides quarterly data on sales, profits, net income, return on equity, price/earnings ratio, and earnings per share for 899 companies (*Business Week,* August 14, 2000). The companies can be numbered 1 to 899 in the order they appear on the Corporate Scoreboard list. Begin at the bottom of the second column of random digits in Table 7.1. Ignoring the first two digits in each group and using three-digit random numbers beginning with 112, read *up* the column to identify the number of (from 1 to 899) the first eight companies to be included in a simple random sample.

43. The mean television viewing time for teens is three hours per day (*Barron's,* November 8, 1999). Assume the population mean is $\mu = 3$ and the population standard deviation is $\sigma = 1.2$ hours. Suppose a sample of 50 teens will be used to monitor television viewing time. Let $\bar{x}$ denote the sample mean viewing time.
    a.  Show the sample distribution of $\bar{x}$.
    b.  What is the probability the sample mean will be within $\pm.25$ hours of the population mean?

44. The mean travel time to work for individuals in Chicago is 31.5 minutes (*1998 Information Please Almanac*). Assume the population mean is $\mu = 31.5$ minutes and the population standard deviation is $\sigma = 12$ minutes. A sample of 50 Chicago residents is selected.
    a.  Show the sampling distribution of $\bar{x}$ where $\bar{x}$ is the sample mean travel time to work for the 50 Chicago residents.
    b.  What is the probability that the sample mean will be within $\pm 1$ minute of the population mean?
    c.  What is the probability that the sample mean will be within $\pm 3$ minutes of the population mean?

45. The U.S. Bureau of Labor Statistics reported the mean hourly wage rate for individuals in executive, administrative, and managerial occupations is $24.07 (*The Wall Street Journal Almanac 1998*). Assume the population mean is $\mu = \$24.07$ and the population standard deviation is $\sigma = \$4.80$. A sample of 120 individuals in executive, administrative, and managerial occupations will be selected.
    a.  What is the probability that the sample mean will be within $\pm\$0.50$ of the population mean?
    b.  What is the probability that the sample mean will be within $\pm\$1.00$ of the population mean?

46. The average annual salary for federal government employees in Indiana is $41,979 (*The World Almanac 2001*). Use this figure as the population mean and assume the population standard deviation is $\sigma = \$5000$. Suppose that a random sample of 50 federal government employees will be selected from the population.
    a.  What is the value of the standard error of the mean?
    b.  What is the probability that the sample mean will be more than $41,979?
    c.  What is the probability the sample mean will be within $1000 of the population mean?
    d.  How would the probability in part (c) change if the sample size were increased to 100?

47. Three firms carry inventories that differ in size. Firm A's inventory contains 2000 items, firm B's inventory contains 5000 items, and firm C's inventory contains 10,000 items. The population standard deviation for the cost of the items in each firm's inventory is $\sigma = 144$. A statistical consultant recommends that each firm take a sample of 50 items from its inventory to provide statistically valid estimates of the average cost per item. Managers of the small firm state that because it has the smallest population, it should be able to make the estimate from a much smaller sample than that required by the larger firms. How-

ever, the consultant states that to obtain the same standard error and thus the same precision in the sample results, all firms should use the same sample size regardless of population size.

    a.   Using the finite population correction factor, compute the standard error for each of the three firms given a sample of size 50.

    b.   What is the probability that for each firm the sample mean $\bar{x}$ will be within $\pm 25$ of the population mean $\mu$?

48.   A researcher reports survey results by stating that the standard error of the mean is 20. The population standard deviation is 500.

    a.   How large was the sample used in this survey?

    b.   What is the probability that the point estimate was within $\pm 25$ of the population mean?

49.   A production process is checked periodically by a quality control inspector. The inspector selects simple random samples of 30 finished products and computes the sample mean product weights $\bar{x}$. If test results over a long period of time show that 5% of the $\bar{x}$ values are over 2.1 pounds and 5% are under 1.9 pounds, what are the mean and the standard deviation for the population of products produced with this process?

50.   As of June 13, 2001, 30.5% of individual investors were bullish on the stock market short term (*AAII Journal,* July 2001). Answer the following questions assuming a sample of 200 individual investors is used.

    a.   Show the sampling distribution of $\bar{p}$, the sample proportion of individual investors who are bullish on the market short term.

    b.   What is the probability that the sample proportion will be within $\pm .04$ of the population proportion?

    c.   What is the probability that the sample proportion will be within $\pm .02$ of the population proportion?

51.   A market research firm conducts telephone surveys with a 40% historical response rate. What is the probability that in a new sample of 400 telephone numbers, at least 150 individuals will cooperate and respond to the questions? In other words, what is the probability that the sample proportion will be at least $150/400 = .375$?

52.   According to ORC International, 71% of Internet users connect their computers to the Internet by normal telephone lines (*USA Today,* January 18, 2000). Assume a population proportion $p = .71$.

    a.   What is the probability that a sample proportion from a simple random sample of 350 Internet users will be within $\pm .05$ of the population proportion?

    b.   What is the probability that a sample proportion from a simple random sample of 350 Internet users will be .75 or greater?

53.   The proportion of individuals insured by the All-Driver Automobile Insurance Company who received at least one traffic ticket during a five-year period is .15.

    a.   Show the sampling distribution of $\bar{p}$ if a random sample of 150 insured individuals is used to estimate the proportion having received at least one ticket.

    b.   What is the probability that the sample proportion will be within $\pm .03$ of the population proportion?

54.   Lori Jeffrey is a successful sales representative for a major publisher of college textbooks. Historically, Lori obtains a book adoption on 25% of her sales calls. Viewing her sales calls for one month as a sample of all possible sales calls, assume that a statistical analysis of the data yields a standard error of the proportion of .0625.

    a.   How large was the sample used in this analysis? That is, how many sales calls did Lori make during the month?

    b.   Let $\bar{p}$ indicate the sample proportion of book adoptions obtained during the month. Show the sampling distribution $\bar{p}$.

    c.   Using the sampling distribution of $\bar{p}$, compute the probability that Lori will obtain book adoptions on 30% or more of her sales calls during a one-month period.

## Appendix 7.1     The Expected Value and Standard Deviation of $\bar{x}$

In this appendix we present the mathematical basis for the expressions for $E(\bar{x})$, the expected value of $\bar{x}$ as given by equation (7.1), and $\sigma_{\bar{x}}$, the standard deviation of $\bar{x}$ as given by equation (7.2).

### Expected Value of $\bar{x}$

Assume a population with mean $\mu$ and variance $\sigma^2$. A simple random sample of size $n$ is selected with individual observations denoted $x_1, x_2, \ldots, x_n$. A sample mean $\bar{x}$ is computed as follows.

$$\bar{x} = \frac{\Sigma x_i}{n}$$

With repeated simple random samples of size $n$, $\bar{x}$ is a random variable that assumes different numerical values depending on the specific $n$ items selected. The expected value of the random variable $\bar{x}$ is the mean of all possible $\bar{x}$ values.

$$\text{Mean of } \bar{x} = E(\bar{x}) = E\left(\frac{\Sigma x_i}{n}\right)$$

$$= \frac{1}{n}[E(x_1 + x_2 + \cdots + x_n)]$$

$$= \frac{1}{n}[E(x_1) + E(x_2) + \cdots + E(x_n)]$$

For any $x_i$ we have $E(x_i) = \mu$, therefore we can write

$$E(\bar{x}) = \frac{1}{n}(\mu + \mu + \cdots + \mu)$$

$$= \frac{1}{n}(n\mu) = \mu$$

This result shows that the mean of all possible $\bar{x}$ values is the same as the population mean $\mu$. That is, $E(\bar{x}) = \mu$.

### Standard Deviation of $\bar{x}$

Again assume a population with mean $\mu$, variance $\sigma^2$, and a sample mean given by

$$\bar{x} = \frac{\Sigma x_i}{n}$$

With repeated simple random samples of size $n$, we know that $\bar{x}$ is a random variable that takes different numerical values depending on the specific $n$ items selected. What follows is the derivation of the expression for the standard deviation of the $\bar{x}$ values, $\sigma_{\bar{x}}$, for the case of an infinite population. The derivation of the expression for $\sigma_{\bar{x}}$ for a finite population when sampling is done without replacement is more difficult and is beyond the scope of this text.

Returning to the infinite population case, recall that a simple random sample from an infinite population consists of observations $x_1, x_2, \ldots, x_n$ that are independent. The following two expressions are general formulas for the variance of random variables.

$$\text{Var}(ax) = a^2 \, \text{Var}(x)$$

where $a$ is a constant and $x$ is a random variable, and

$$\text{Var}(x + y) = \text{Var}(x) + \text{Var}(y)$$

where $x$ and $y$ are *independent* random variables. Using the two preceding equations, we can develop the expression for the variance of the random variable $\bar{x}$ as follows.

$$\text{Var}(\bar{x}) = \text{Var}\!\left(\frac{\Sigma x_i}{n}\right) = \text{Var}\!\left(\frac{1}{n}\Sigma x_i\right)$$

Then, with $1/n$ a constant, we have

$$\text{Var}(\bar{x}) = \left(\frac{1}{n}\right)^2 \text{Var}(\Sigma x_i)$$

$$= \left(\frac{1}{n}\right)^2 \text{Var}(x_1 + x_2 + \cdots + x_n)$$

In the infinite population case, the random variables $x_1, x_2, \ldots, x_n$ are independent, which enables us to write

$$\text{Var}(\bar{x}) = \left(\frac{1}{n}\right)^2 [\text{Var}(x_1) + \text{Var}(x_2) + \cdots + \text{Var}(x_n)]$$

For any $x_i$, we have $\text{Var}(x_i) = \sigma^2$, therefore we have

$$\text{Var}(\bar{x}) = \left(\frac{1}{n}\right)^2 (\sigma^2 + \sigma^2 + \cdots + \sigma^2)$$

With $n$ values of $\sigma^2$ in this expression, we have

$$\text{Var}(\bar{x}) = \left(\frac{1}{n}\right)^2 (n\sigma^2) = \frac{\sigma^2}{n}$$

Taking the square root provides the formula for the standard deviation of $\bar{x}$.

$$\sigma_{\bar{x}} = \sqrt{\text{Var}(\bar{x})} = \frac{\sigma}{\sqrt{n}}$$

# Appendix 7.2   Random Sampling with Minitab

If a list of the elements in a population is available in a Minitab file, Minitab can be used to select a simple random sample. For example, a list of the top 100 metropolitan areas in the United States and Canada are provided in column 1 of the data set MetAreas (*Places Rated Almanac—The Millennium Edition 2000*). Column 2 contains the overall rating of each metropolitan area. The first 10 metropolitan areas in the data set and their corresponding ratings are shown in Table 7.6

Suppose that you would like to select a simple random sample of 30 metropolitan areas in order to do an in-depth study of the cost of living in the United States and Canada. The following steps can be used to select the sample.

**Step 1.** Select the **Calc** pull-down menu
**Step 2.** Choose **Random Data**

**TABLE 7.6    OVERALL RATING FOR THE FIRST 10 METROPOLITAN AREAS IN THE DATA SET METAREAS**

**MetAreas**

| Metropolitan Area | Rating |
|---|---|
| Albany, NY | 64.18 |
| Albuquerque, NM | 66.16 |
| Appleton, WI | 60.56 |
| Atlanta, GA | 69.97 |
| Austin, TX | 71.48 |
| Baltimore, MD | 69.75 |
| Birmingham, AL | 69.59 |
| Boise City, ID | 68.36 |
| Boston, MA | 68.99 |
| Buffalo, NY | 66.10 |

**Step 3.** Choose **Sample From Columns**
**Step 4.** When the Sample From Columns dialog box appears:
        Enter 30 in the **Sample** box
        Enter C1 C2 in the box below
        Enter C3 C4 in the **Store samples in** box
**Step 5.** Click **OK**

The random sample of 30 metropolitan areas appears in columns C3 and C4.

## Appendix 7.3    Random Sampling with Excel

If a list of the elements in a population is available in an Excel file, Excel can be used to select a simple random sample. For example, a list of the top 100 metropolitan areas in the United States and Canada are provided in column A of the data set MetAreas (*Places Rated Almanac—The Millennium Edition 2000*). Column B contains the overall rating of each metropolitan area. The first 10 metropolitan areas in the data set and their corresponding ratings are shown in Table 7.6. Assume that you would like to select a simple random sample of 30 metropolitan areas in order to do an in-depth study of the cost of living in the United States and Canada.

The rows of any Excel data set can be placed in a random order by adding an extra column to the data set and filling the column with random numbers using the =RAND() function. Then using Excel's sort ascending capability on the random number column, the rows of the data set will be reordered randomly. The random sample of size *n* appears in the first *n* rows of the reordered data set.

In the MetAreas data set, labels are in row 1 and the 100 metropolitan areas are in rows 2 to 101. The following steps can be used to select a simple random sample of 30 metropolitan areas.

**Step 1.** Enter =RAND() in cell C2
**Step 2.** Copy cell C2 to cells C3:C101
**Step 3.** Select any cell in Column C
**Step 4.** Click the **Sort Ascending** button on the tool bar

The random sample of 30 metropolitan areas appears in rows 2 to 31 of the reordered data set. The random numbers in column C are no longer necessary and can be deleted if desired.

# CHAPTER 8

# Interval Estimation

## CONTENTS

STATISTICS IN PRACTICE:
FOOD LION

## FOOD LION*
### SALISBURY, NORTH CAROLINA

Founded in 1957 as Food Town, Food Lion is one of the largest supermarket chains in the United States with 1200 stores in 11 Southeastern and Mid-Atlantic states. The company sells more than 24,000 different products and offers nationally and regionally advertised brand-name merchandise, as well as a growing number of high-quality private label products manufactured especially for Food Lion. The company maintains its low price leadership and quality assurance through operating efficiencies such as standard store formats, innovative warehouse design, energy-efficient facilities, and data synchronization with suppliers. Food Lion looks to a future of continued innovation, growth, price leadership, and service to its customers.

Being in an inventory-intense business, Food Lion made the decision to adopt the LIFO (last-in, first-out) method of inventory valuation. This method matches current costs against current revenues, which minimizes the effect of radical price changes on profit and loss results. In addition, the LIFO method reduces net income thereby reducing income taxes during periods of inflation.

Food Lion establishes a LIFO index for each of seven inventory pools: Grocery, Paper/Household, Pet Supplies, Health & Beauty Aids, Dairy, Cigarette/Tobacco, and Beer/Wine. For example, a LIFO index of 1.008 for the Grocery pool would indicate that the company's grocery inventory value at current costs reflects a 0.8% increase due to inflation over the most recent one-year period.

A LIFO index for each inventory pool requires that the year-end inventory count for each product be valued at the current year-end cost and at the preceding year-end cost. To avoid ex-

*The authors are indebted to Keith Cunningham, Tax Director, and Bobby Harkey, Staff Tax Accountant, at Food Lion for providing this Statistics in Practice.

The Food Lion store in the Cambridge Shopping Center, Charlotte, North Carolina. © Courtesy of Food Lion.

cessive time and expense associated with counting the inventory in all 1200 store locations, Food Lion selects a random sample of 50 stores. Year-end physical inventories are taken in each of the sample stores. The current-year and preceding-year costs for each item are then used to construct the required LIFO indexes for each inventory pool.

For a recent year, the sample estimate of the LIFO index for the Health & Beauty Aid inventory pool was 1.015. Using a 95% confidence level, Food Lion computed a margin of error of .006 for the sample estimate. Thus, the interval from 1.009 to 1.021 provided a 95% confidence interval estimate of the population LIFO index. This level of precision was judged to be very good.

In this chapter you will learn how to compute the margin of error associated with sample estimates. You will also learn how to use this information to construct and interpret interval estimates of a population mean and a population proportion.

In Chapter 7, we stated that a point estimator is a sample statistic used to estimate a population parameter. For instance, the sample mean $\bar{x}$ is a point estimator of the population mean $\mu$ and the sample proportion $\bar{p}$ is a point estimator of the population proportion $p$. Because a point estimator cannot be expected to provide the exact value of the population parameter, an **interval estimate** is often computed by adding and subtracting a value, called the **margin of error**, to the point estimate. The general form of an interval estimate is as follows:

$$\text{Point estimate} \pm \text{Margin of error}$$

The purpose of an interval estimate is to provide information about how close the point estimate is to the value of the population parameter.

In this chapter we show how to compute interval estimates of a population mean $\mu$ and a population proportion $p$. The general form of an interval estimate of a population mean is

$$\bar{x} \pm \text{Margin of error}$$

Similarly, the general form of an interval estimate of a population proportion is

$$\bar{p} \pm \text{Margin of error}$$

The sampling distributions of $\bar{x}$ and $\bar{p}$ play key roles in computing these interval estimates.

# 8.1  Population Mean: $\sigma$ Known

In order to develop an interval estimate of a population mean, either the population standard deviation $\sigma$ or the sample standard deviation $s$ must be used to compute the margin of error. Although $\sigma$ is rarely known exactly, historical data or other information available in some applications permit us to obtain a good estimate of the population standard deviation prior to sampling. In such cases, the population standard deviation can, for all practical purposes, be considered known. We refer to such cases as the $\sigma$ **known** case. In this section we show how a simple random sample can be used to construct an interval estimate of a population mean for the $\sigma$ known case.

The development of an interval estimate of a population mean for the $\sigma$ known case can be illustrated by considering the monthly customer service survey conducted by CJW, Inc. CJW provides a Web site for accepting customer orders and providing follow-up service over the Internet. The company prides itself on providing easy online ordering, timely delivery, and prompt response to customer inquiries. Good customer service is critical to the ongoing success of the company.

CJW's quality assurance team uses a customer service survey to measure satisfaction with its Web site and online customer service. Each month, the team sends a questionnaire to a random sample of customers who placed an order or requested service during the previous month. The questionnaire asks customers to rate their satisfaction with such things as ease of placing orders, timely delivery, accurate order filling, and technical advice. The team summarizes each customer's questionnaire by computing an overall satisfaction score $x$ that ranges from 0 (worst possible score) to 100 (best possible score). A sample mean customer satisfaction score $\bar{x}$ is then computed.

The sample mean satisfaction score provides a point estimate of the mean satisfaction score $\mu$ for the population of all CJW customers. With this timely measure of customer service, CJW can promptly take corrective action if a low customer satisfaction score results. The company conducted this satisfaction survey for a number of months, and consistently obtained an estimate near 20 for the standard deviation of satisfaction scores. Based on this historical data, CJW now assumes a known value of $\sigma = 20$ for the population standard deviation. The historical data also show that the population of satisfaction scores follows a normal distribution.

During the most recent month, the quality assurance team surveyed 100 customers ($n = 100$) and obtained a sample mean satisfaction score of $\bar{x} = 82$. This sample mean satisfaction score provides a point estimate of the population mean satisfaction score, $\mu$. In the discussion that follows, we show how to compute the margin of error for this estimate and develop an interval estimate of the population mean.

CJW

## Margin of Error and the Interval Estimate

In Chapter 7 we showed that the sampling distribution of $\bar{x}$ can be used to compute the probability that $\bar{x}$ will be within a given distance of $\mu$. In the CJW example, the historical data show that the population of satisfaction scores is normally distributed with a standard deviation of $\sigma = 20$. So, using what we learned in Chapter 7, we can conclude that the sampling distribution of $\bar{x}$ follows a normal distribution with a standard error of $\sigma_{\bar{x}} = \sigma/\sqrt{n} = 20/\sqrt{100} = 2$. This sampling distribution is shown in Figure 8.1.* Because the sampling distribution shows how values of $\bar{x}$ are distributed around the population mean $\mu$, the sampling distribution of $\bar{x}$ provides information about the possible differences between $\bar{x}$ and $\mu$.

Using the table of areas for the standard normal distribution, we find that 95% of the values of any normally distributed random variable are within $\pm 1.96$ standard deviations of the mean. Thus, when the sampling distribution of $\bar{x}$ is normally distributed, 95% of the $\bar{x}$ values must be within $\pm 1.96\sigma_{\bar{x}}$ of the mean $\mu$. In the CJW example we know that the sampling distribution of $\bar{x}$ is normally distributed with a standard error of $\sigma_{\bar{x}} = 2$. Because $\pm 1.96\sigma_{\bar{x}} = 1.96(2) = 3.92$, we can conclude that 95% of all $\bar{x}$ values obtained using a sample size of $n = 100$ will be within $\pm 3.92$ of the population mean $\mu$. See Figure 8.2.

In the introduction to this chapter we said that the general form of an interval estimate of the population mean $\mu$ is $\bar{x} \pm$ Margin of error. For the CJW example, suppose we set the margin of error equal to 3.92 and compute the interval estimate of $\mu$ using $\bar{x} \pm 3.92$. To provide an interpretation for this interval estimate, let us consider the values of $\bar{x}$ that could be obtained if we took three *different* simple random samples, each consisting of 100 CJW customers. The first sample mean might turn out to have the value shown as $\bar{x}_1$ in Figure 8.3. In this case, Figure 8.3 shows that the interval formed by subtracting 3.92 from $\bar{x}_1$ and adding 3.92 to $\bar{x}_1$ includes the population mean $\mu$. Now consider what happens if the second sample mean turns out to have the value shown as $\bar{x}_2$ in Figure 8.3. Although this sample mean differs from the first sample mean, we see that the interval formed by subtracting 3.92 from $\bar{x}_2$ and adding 3.92 to $\bar{x}_2$ also includes the population mean $\mu$. However, consider what

**FIGURE 8.1**    SAMPLING DISTRIBUTION OF THE SAMPLE MEAN SATISFACTION
SCORE FROM SIMPLE RANDOM SAMPLES OF 100 CUSTOMERS

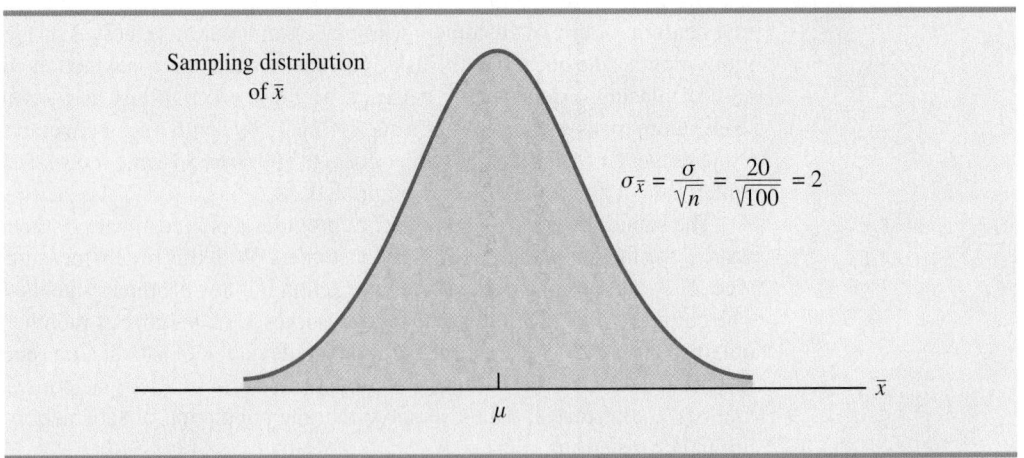

Sampling distribution of $\bar{x}$

$$\sigma_{\bar{x}} = \frac{\sigma}{\sqrt{n}} = \frac{20}{\sqrt{100}} = 2$$

$\mu$

---

*We use the fact that the population of satisfaction scores has a normal distribution to conclude that the sampling distribution of $\bar{x}$ has a normal distribution. If the population did not have a normal distribution, we could rely on the central limit theorem and the sample size of $n = 100$ to conclude that the sampling distribution of $\bar{x}$ is approximately normal. In either case, the sampling distribution of $\bar{x}$ would appear as shown in Figure 8.1.

**FIGURE 8.2**    SAMPLING DISTRIBUTION OF $\bar{x}$ SHOWING THE LOCATION OF SAMPLE MEANS THAT ARE WITHIN 3.92 OF $\mu$

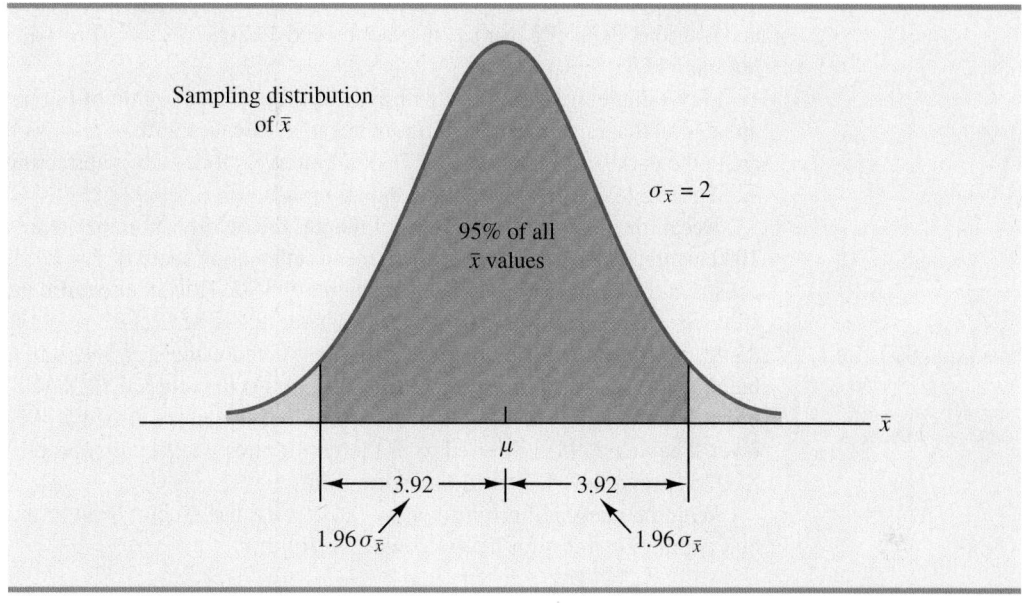

**FIGURE 8.3**    INTERVALS FORMED FROM SELECTED SAMPLE MEANS AT LOCATIONS $\bar{x}_1$, $\bar{x}_2$, AND $\bar{x}_3$

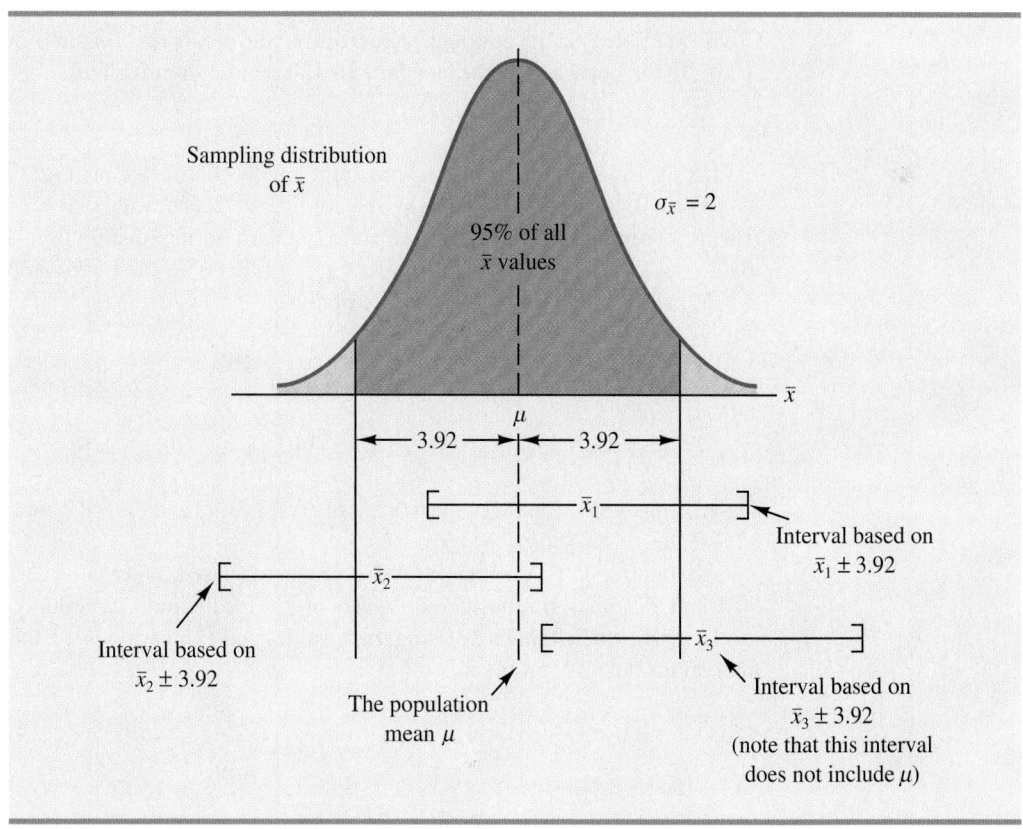

happens if the third sample means turns out to have the value shown as $\bar{x}_3$ in Figure 8.3. In this case, the interval formed by subtracting 3.92 from $\bar{x}_3$ and adding 3.92 to $\bar{x}_3$ does not include the population mean $\mu$. Because $\bar{x}_3$ falls in the upper tail of the sampling distribution and is farther than 3.92 from $\mu$, subtracting and adding 3.92 to $\bar{x}_3$ forms an interval that does not include $\mu$.

Any sample mean $\bar{x}$ that is within the darkly shaded region of Figure 8.3 will provide an interval that contains the population mean $\mu$. Because 95% of all possible sample means are in the darkly shaded region, 95% of all intervals formed by subtracting 3.92 from $\bar{x}$ and adding 3.92 to $\bar{x}$ will include the population mean $\mu$.

*This discussion provides insight as to why the interval is called a 95% confidence interval.*

Recall that during the most recent month, the quality assurance team at CJW surveyed 100 customers and obtained a sample mean satisfaction score of $\bar{x} = 82$. Using $\bar{x} \pm 3.92$ to construct the interval estimate, we obtain $82 \pm 3.92$. Thus, the specific interval estimate of $\mu$ based on the data from the most recent month is $82 - 3.92 = 78.08$ to $82 + 3.92 = 85.92$. Because 95% of all the intervals constructed using $\bar{x} \pm 3.92$ will contain the population mean, we say that we are 95% confident that the interval 78.08 to 85.92 includes the population mean $\mu$. We say that this interval has been established at the 95% **confidence level**. The value .95 is referred to as the **confidence coefficient**, and the interval 78.08 to 85.92 is called the 95% **confidence interval**.

With the margin of error given by $z_{\alpha/2}(\sigma/\sqrt{n})$, the general form of an interval estimate of a population mean for the $\sigma$ known case follows:

---

**INTERVAL ESTIMATE OF A POPULATION MEAN: $\sigma$ KNOWN**

$$\bar{x} \pm z_{\alpha/2} \frac{\sigma}{\sqrt{n}} \tag{8.1}$$

where $(1 - \alpha)$ is the confidence coefficient and $z_{\alpha/2}$ is the $z$ value providing an area $\alpha/2$ in the upper tail of the standard normal probability distribution.

---

Let us use expression (8.1) to construct a 95% confidence interval for the CJW problem. For a 95% confidence interval, the confidence coefficient is $(1 - \alpha) = .95$ and thus, $\alpha = .05$. Using the tables of areas for the standard normal distribution, an area of $\alpha/2 = .05/2 = .025$ in the upper tail provides $z_{.025} = 1.96$. With the CJW sample mean $\bar{x} = 82$, $\sigma = 20$, and a sample size $n = 100$, we obtain

$$82 \pm 1.96 \frac{20}{\sqrt{100}}$$

$$82 \pm 3.92$$

Thus, using expression (8.1), the margin of error is 3.92 and the 95% confidence interval is $82 - 3.92 = 78.08$ to $82 + 3.92 = 85.92$.

Although a 95% confidence level is frequently used, other confidence levels such as 90% and 99% may be considered. Values of $z_{\alpha/2}$ for the most commonly used confidence levels are shown in Table 8.1. Using these values and expression (8.1), the 90% confidence interval for the CJW problem is

$$82 \pm 1.645 \frac{20}{\sqrt{100}}$$

$$82 \pm 3.29$$

**TABLE 8.1    VALUES OF $z_{\alpha/2}$ FOR THE MOST COMMONLY USED CONFIDENCE LEVELS**

| Confidence Level | $\alpha$ | $\alpha/2$ | $z_{\alpha/2}$ |
|---|---|---|---|
| 90% | .10 | .05 | 1.645 |
| 95% | .05 | .025 | 1.960 |
| 99% | .01 | .005 | 2.576 |

Thus, at 90% confidence, the margin of error is 3.29 and the confidence interval is $82 - 3.29 = 78.71$ to $82 + 3.29 = 85.29$. Similarly, the 99% confidence interval is

$$82 \pm 2.576 \frac{20}{\sqrt{100}}$$

$$82 \pm 5.15$$

Thus, at 99% confidence, the margin of error is 5.15 and the confidence interval is $82 - 5.15 = 76.85$ to $82 + 5.15 = 87.15$.

Comparing the results for the 90%, 95%, and 99% confidence levels, we see that in order to have a higher degree of confidence, the margin of error and thus the width of the confidence interval must be larger.

## Practical Advice

If the population follows a normal distribution, the confidence interval provided by expression (8.1) is exact. Therefore, if expression (8.1) were used repeatedly to generate 95% confidence intervals, exactly 95% of the intervals generated would contain the population mean. If the population does not follow a normal distribution, the confidence interval provided by expression (8.1) will be approximate. In this case, the quality of the approximation depends on both the distribution of the population and the sample size.

In most applications, a sample size of $n \geq 30$ is adequate when using expression (8.1) to develop an interval estimate of a population mean. If the population is not normally distributed but is roughly symmetric, sample sizes as small as 15 can be expected to provide good approximate confidence intervals. With smaller sample sizes, expression (8.1) should only be used if the analyst believes, or is willing to assume, that the population distribution is at least approximately normal.

### NOTES AND COMMENTS

1. The interval estimation procedure discussed in this section is based on the assumption that the population standard deviation $\sigma$ is known. By $\sigma$ known we mean that historical data or other information are available that permit us to obtain a good estimate of the population standard deviation prior to taking the sample that will be used to develop an estimate of the population mean. So technically we don't mean that $\sigma$ is actually known with certainty. We just mean that we obtained a good estimate of the standard deviation prior to sampling and thus we won't be using the same sample to estimate both the population mean and the population standard deviation.

2. The sample size $n$ appears in the denominator of the interval estimation expression (8.1). Thus, if a particular sample size provides too wide an interval to be of any practical use, we may want to consider increasing the sample size. With $n$ in the denominator, a larger sample size will provide a smaller margin of error, a narrower interval, and greater precision. The procedure for determining the size of a simple random sample necessary to obtain a desired precision is discussed in Section 8.3.

## Exercises

### Methods

1. A simple random sample of 40 items resulted in a sample mean of 25. The population standard deviation is $\sigma = 5$.
   a. What is the standard error of the mean, $\sigma_{\bar{x}}$?
   b. At 95% confidence, what is the margin of error?

2. A simple random sample of 50 items from a population with $\sigma = 6$ resulted in a sample mean of 32.
   a. Provide a 90% confidence interval for the population mean.
   b. Provide a 95% confidence interval for the population mean.
   c. Provide a 99% confidence interval for the population mean.

3. A simple random sample of 60 items resulted in a sample mean of 80. The population standard deviation is $\sigma = 15$.
   a. Compute the 95% confidence interval for the population mean.
   b. Assume that the same sample mean was obtained from a sample of 120 items. Provide a 95% confidence interval for the population mean.
   c. What is the effect of a larger sample size on the interval estimate?

4. A 95% confidence interval for a population mean was reported to be 152 to 160. If $\sigma = 15$, what sample size was used in this study?

### Applications

5. In an effort to estimate the mean amount spent per customer for dinner at a major Atlanta restaurant, data were collected for a sample of 49 customers. Assume a population standard deviation of $5.
   a. At 95% confidence, what is the margin of error?
   b. If the sample mean is $24.80, what is the 95% confidence interval for the population mean?

6. Nielsen Media Research reported that the household mean television viewing time during the 8 P.M. to 11 P.M. time period is 8.5 hours per week (*The World Almanac,* 2003). Given a sample size of 300 households and a population standard deviation of $\sigma = 3.5$ hours, what is the 95% confidence interval estimate of the mean television viewing time per week during the 8 P.M. to 11 P.M. time period?

7. A survey of small businesses with Web sites found that the average amount spent on a site was $11,500 per year (*Fortune,* March 5, 2001). Given a sample of 60 businesses and a population standard deviation of $\sigma = $4000$, what is the margin of error? Use 95% confidence. What would you recommend if the study required a margin of error of $500?

8. The National Quality Research Center at the University of Michigan provides a quarterly measure of consumer opinions about products and services (*The Wall Street Journal,* February 18, 2003). Based on a customer satisfaction index of 100, a survey of 10 restaurants in the Fast Food/Pizza group showed a sample mean index of 71. Past data indicate that the population standard deviation of the index has been relatively stable with $\sigma = 5$.
   a. What assumption should the researcher be willing to make if a margin of error is desired?
   b. Using 95% confidence, what is the margin of error?
   c. What is the margin of error if 99% confidence is desired?

9. The undergraduate grade point average (GPA) for students admitted to the top graduate business schools was 3.37 (*Best Graduate Schools, U.S. News and World Report,* 2001). Assume this estimate was based on a sample of 120 students admitted to the top schools. Using past years' data, the population standard deviation can be assumed known with $\sigma = .28$. What is the 95% confidence interval estimate of the mean undergraduate GPA for students admitted to the top graduate business schools?

10. The National Association of Independent Colleges and Universities reported that students graduating from public colleges and universities carry an average debt of $12,000 upon graduation (*Kiplinger's Personal Finance Magazine,* November 1998). Assume that this average debt is based on a sample of 245 students and that, based on past studies, the population standard deviation for the debt upon graduation is $2200.

   a.   Develop a 90% confidence interval estimate of the population mean.
   b.   Develop a 95% confidence interval estimate of the population mean.
   c.   Develop a 99% confidence interval estimate of the population mean.
   d.   Discuss what happens to the width of the confidence interval as the confidence level is increased. Does this result seem reasonable? Explain.

 # Population Mean: $\sigma$ Unknown

If an estimate of the population standard deviation $\sigma$ cannot be developed prior to sampling, we must use the sample standard deviation $s$ to estimate $\sigma$. This is the **$\sigma$ unknown** case. When $s$ is used to estimate $\sigma$, the margin of error and the interval estimate for the population mean are based on a probability distribution known as the *t* **distribution**. Although the mathematical development of the *t* distribution is based on the assumption of a normal distribution for the population we are sampling from, research shows that the *t* distribution can be successfully applied in many situations where the population deviates significantly from normal. Later in this section we provide guidelines for using the *t* distribution if the population is not normally distributed.

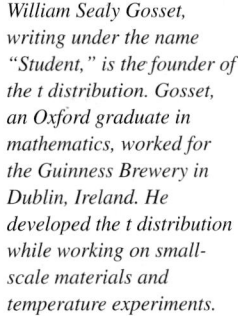

*William Sealy Gosset, writing under the name "Student," is the founder of the t distribution. Gosset, an Oxford graduate in mathematics, worked for the Guinness Brewery in Dublin, Ireland. He developed the t distribution while working on small-scale materials and temperature experiments.*

The *t* distribution is a family of similar probability distributions, with a specific *t* distribution depending on a parameter known as the **degrees of freedom**. The *t* distribution with one degree of freedom is unique, as is the *t* distribution with two degrees of freedom, with three degrees of freedom, and so on. As the number of degrees of freedom increases, the difference between the *t* distribution and the standard normal distribution becomes smaller and smaller. Figure 8.4 shows *t* distributions with 10 and 20 degrees of freedom and

**FIGURE 8.4    COMPARISON OF THE STANDARD NORMAL DISTRIBUTION WITH
*t* DISTRIBUTIONS HAVING 10 AND 20 DEGREES OF FREEDOM**

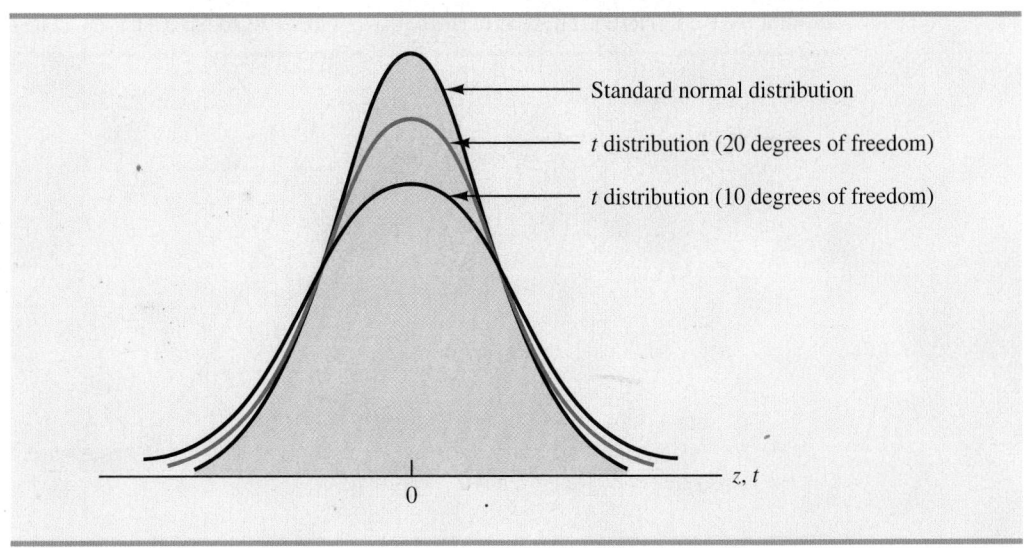

their relationship to the standard normal probability distribution. Note that a *t* distribution with more degrees of freedom exhibits less variability and more closely resembles the standard normal distribution. Note also that the mean of the *t* distribution is zero.

We place a subscript on *t* to indicate the area in the upper tail of the *t* distribution. For example, just as we used $z_{.025}$ to indicate the *z* value providing a .025 area in the upper tail of a standard normal distribution, we will use $t_{.025}$ to indicate a .025 area in the upper tail of a *t* distribution. In general, we will use the notation $t_{\alpha/2}$ to represent a *t* value with an area of $\alpha/2$ in the upper tail of the *t* distribution. See Figure 8.5.

Table 8.2 contains a table for the *t* distribution. This table also appears inside the front cover of the text. Each row in the table corresponds to a separate *t* distribution with the degrees of freedom shown. For example, for a *t* distribution with 10 degrees of freedom, $t_{.025} = 2.228$. Similarly, for a *t* distribution with 20 degrees of freedom, $t_{.025} = 2.086$. As the degrees of freedom continue to increase, $t_{.025}$ approaches $z_{.025} = 1.96$. In fact, the standard normal distribution *z* values can be found in the infinite degrees of freedom row (labeled ∞) of the *t* distribution table. If the degrees of freedom exceed 100, the infinite degrees of freedom row can be used to approximate the actual *t* value; in other words, for more than 100 degrees of freedom, the standard normal *z* value provides a good approximation to the *t* value. Table 2 in Appendix B provides a more extensive *t* distribution table, with all the degrees of freedom from 1 to 100 included.

*As the degrees of freedom increase, the t distribution approaches the standard normal distribution.*

## Margin of Error and the Interval Estimate

In Section 8.1 we showed that an interval estimate of a population mean for the $\sigma$ known case is

$$\bar{x} \pm z_{\alpha/2}\frac{\sigma}{\sqrt{n}}$$

To compute an interval estimate of $\mu$ for the $\sigma$ unknown case, the sample standard deviation *s* is used to estimate $\sigma$ and $z_{\alpha/2}$ is replaced by the *t* distribution value $t_{\alpha/2}$. The margin

**FIGURE 8.5**    *t* DISTRIBUTION WITH $\alpha/2$ AREA OR PROBABILITY IN THE UPPER TAIL

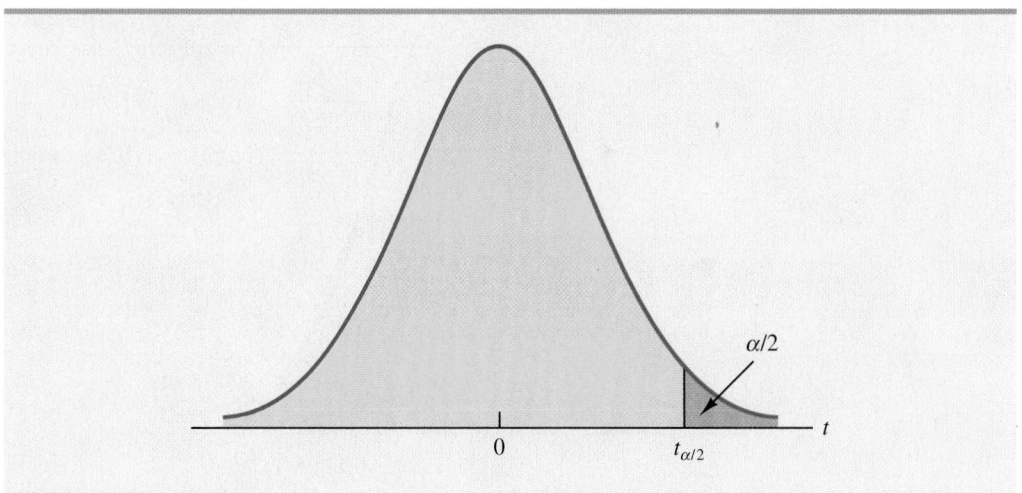

**TABLE 8.2**  *t* DISTRIBUTION TABLE FOR AREAS IN THE UPPER TAIL
EXAMPLE WITH 10 DEGREES OF FREEDOM, $t_{.025} = 2.228$

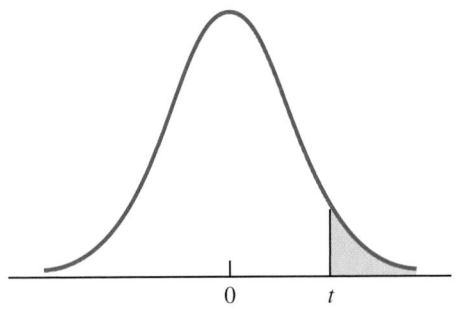

| Degrees of Freedom | Area in Upper Tail | | | | | |
|---|---|---|---|---|---|---|
| | **.20** | **.10** | **.05** | **.025** | **.01** | **.005** |
| 1 | 1.376 | 3.078 | 6.314 | 12.706 | 31.821 | 63.656 |
| 2 | 1.061 | 1.886 | 2.920 | 4.303 | 6.965 | 9.925 |
| 3 | .978 | 1.638 | 2.353 | 3.182 | 4.541 | 5.841 |
| 4 | .941 | 1.533 | 2.132 | 2.776 | 3.747 | 4.604 |
| 5 | .920 | 1.476 | 2.015 | 2.571 | 3.365 | 4.032 |
| 6 | .906 | 1.440 | 1.943 | 2.447 | 3.143 | 3.707 |
| 7 | .896 | 1.415 | 1.895 | 2.365 | 2.998 | 3.499 |
| 8 | .889 | 1.397 | 1.860 | 2.306 | 2.896 | 3.355 |
| 9 | .883 | 1.383 | 1.833 | 2.262 | 2.821 | 3.250 |
| 10 | .879 | 1.372 | 1.812 | 2.228 | 2.764 | 3.169 |
| 11 | .876 | 1.363 | 1.796 | 2.201 | 2.718 | 3.106 |
| 12 | .873 | 1.356 | 1.782 | 2.179 | 2.681 | 3.055 |
| 13 | .870 | 1.350 | 1.771 | 2.160 | 2.650 | 3.012 |
| 14 | .868 | 1.345 | 1.761 | 2.145 | 2.624 | 2.977 |
| 15 | .866 | 1.341 | 1.753 | 2.131 | 2.602 | 2.947 |
| 16 | .865 | 1.337 | 1.746 | 2.120 | 2.583 | 2.921 |
| 17 | .863 | 1.333 | 1.740 | 2.110 | 2.567 | 2.898 |
| 18 | .862 | 1.330 | 1.734 | 2.101 | 2.552 | 2.878 |
| 19 | .861 | 1.328 | 1.729 | 2.093 | 2.539 | 2.861 |
| 20 | .860 | 1.325 | 1.725 | 2.086 | 2.528 | 2.845 |
| 21 | .859 | 1.323 | 1.721 | 2.080 | 2.518 | 2.831 |
| 22 | .858 | 1.321 | 1.717 | 2.074 | 2.508 | 2.819 |
| 23 | .858 | 1.319 | 1.714 | 2.069 | 2.500 | 2.807 |
| 24 | .857 | 1.318 | 1.711 | 2.064 | 2.492 | 2.797 |
| 25 | .856 | 1.316 | 1.708 | 2.060 | 2.485 | 2.787 |
| 26 | .856 | 1.315 | 1.706 | 2.056 | 2.479 | 2.779 |
| 27 | .855 | 1.314 | 1.703 | 2.052 | 2.473 | 2.771 |
| 28 | .855 | 1.313 | 1.701 | 2.048 | 2.467 | 2.763 |
| 29 | .854 | 1.311 | 1.699 | 2.045 | 2.462 | 2.756 |
| 30 | .854 | 1.310 | 1.697 | 2.042 | 2.457 | 2.750 |
| 40 | .851 | 1.303 | 1.684 | 2.021 | 2.423 | 2.704 |
| 50 | .849 | 1.299 | 1.676 | 2.009 | 2.403 | 2.678 |
| 60 | .848 | 1.296 | 1.671 | 2.000 | 2.390 | 2.660 |
| 80 | .846 | 1.292 | 1.664 | 1.990 | 2.374 | 2.639 |
| 100 | .845 | 1.290 | 1.660 | 1.984 | 2.364 | 2.626 |
| ∞ | .842 | 1.282 | 1.645 | 1.960 | 2.326 | 2.576 |

*Note:* A more extensive table is provided as Table 2 of Appendix B.

of error is then given by $t_{\alpha/2}\, s/\sqrt{n}$. With this margin of error, the general expression for an interval estimate of a population mean when $\sigma$ is unknown follows.

---

**INTERVAL ESTIMATE OF A POPULATION MEAN: $\sigma$ UNKNOWN**

$$\bar{x} \pm t_{\alpha/2}\frac{s}{\sqrt{n}} \tag{8.2}$$

where $s$ is the sample standard deviation, $(1 - \alpha)$ is the confidence ~~coefficient~~ level, and $t_{\alpha/2}$ is the $t$ value providing an area of $\alpha/2$ in the upper tail of the $t$ distribution with $n - 1$ degrees of freedom.

---

The reason the number of degrees of freedom associated with the $t$ value in expression (8.2) is $n - 1$ concerns the use of $s$ as an estimate of the population standard deviation $\sigma$. The expression for the sample standard deviation is

$$s = \sqrt{\frac{\Sigma(x_i - \bar{x})^2}{n - 1}}$$

Degrees of freedom refers to the number of independent pieces of information that go into the computation of $\Sigma(x_i - \bar{x})^2$. The $n$ pieces of information involved in computing $\Sigma(x_i - \bar{x})^2$ are as follows: $x_1 - \bar{x}, x_2 - \bar{x}, \ldots, x_n - \bar{x}$. In Section 3.2 we indicated that $\Sigma(x_i - \bar{x}) = 0$ for any data set. Thus, only $n - 1$ of the $x_i - \bar{x}$ values are independent; that is, if we know $n - 1$ of the values, the remaining value can be determined exactly by using the condition that the sum of the $x_i - \bar{x}$ values must be 0. Thus, $n - 1$ is the number of degrees of freedom associated with $\Sigma(x_i - \bar{x})^2$ and hence the number of degrees of freedom for the $t$ distribution in expression (8.2).

To illustrate the interval estimation procedure for the $\sigma$ unknown case, we will consider a study designed to estimate the mean credit card debt for the population of U.S. households. A sample of $n = 85$ households provided the credit card balances shown in Table 8.3. For this situation, no previous estimate of the population standard deviation $\sigma$ is available. Thus,

**TABLE 8.3**    CREDIT CARD BALANCES FOR A SAMPLE OF 85 HOUSEHOLDS

**Balance**

| | | | | | |
|---|---|---|---|---|---|
| 9619 | 5994 | 3344 | 7888 | 7581 | 9980 |
| 5364 | 4652 | 13627 | 3091 | 12545 | 8718 |
| 8348 | 5376 | 968 | 943 | 7959 | 8452 |
| 7348 | 5998 | 4714 | 8762 | 2563 | 4935 |
| 381 | 7530 | 4334 | 1407 | 6787 | 5938 |
| 2998 | 3678 | 4911 | 6644 | 5071 | 5266 |
| 1686 | 3581 | 1920 | 7644 | 9536 | 10658 |
| 1962 | 5625 | 3780 | 11169 | 4459 | 3910 |
| 4920 | 5619 | 3478 | 7979 | 8047 | 7503 |
| 5047 | 9032 | 6185 | 3258 | 8083 | 1582 |
| 6921 | 13236 | 1141 | 8660 | 2153 | |
| 5759 | 4447 | 7577 | 7511 | 8003 | |
| 8047 | 609 | 4667 | 14442 | 6795 | |
| 3924 | 414 | 5219 | 4447 | 5915 | |
| 3470 | 7636 | 6416 | 6550 | 7164 | |

the sample data must be used to estimate both the population mean and the population standard deviation. Using the data in Table 8.3, we compute the sample mean $\bar{x} = \$5900$ and the sample standard deviation $s = \$3058$. With 95% confidence and $n - 1 = 84$ degrees of freedom, Table 2 in Appendix B provides $t_{.025} = 1.989$. We can now use expression (8.2) to compute an interval estimate of the population mean.

$$5900 \pm 1.989 \frac{3058}{\sqrt{85}}$$

$$5900 \pm 660$$

The point estimate of the population mean is $5900, the margin of error is $660, and the 95% confidence interval is $5900 - 660 = \$5240$ to $5900 + 660 = \$6560$. Thus, we are 95% confident than the population mean credit card balance for all households is between $5240 and $6560.

The procedures used by Minitab and Excel to develop confidence intervals for a population mean are described in Appendixes 8.1 and 8.2. For the household credit card balances study, the results of the Minitab interval estimation procedure are shown in Figure 8.6. The sample of 85 households provides a sample mean credit card balance of $5900, a sample standard deviation of $3058, and (after rounding) an estimate of the standard error of the mean of $332, and a 95% confidence interval of $5240 to $6560.

## Practical Advice

If the population follows a normal distribution, the confidence interval provided by expression (8.2) is exact and can be used for any sample size. If the population does not follow a normal distribution, the confidence interval provided by expression (8.2) will be approximate. In this case, the quality of the approximation depends on both the distribution of the population and the sample size.

*Larger sample sizes are needed if the distribution of the population is highly skewed or includes outliers.*

In most applications, a sample size of $n \geq 30$ is adequate when using expression (8.2) to develop an interval estimate of a population mean. However, if the population distribution is highly skewed or contains outliers, most statisticians would recommend increasing the sample size to 50 or more. If the population is not normally distributed but is roughly symmetric, sample sizes as small as 15 can be expected to provide good approximate confidence intervals. With smaller sample sizes, expression (8.2) should only be used if the analyst believes, or is willing to assume, that the population distribution is at least approximately normal.

## Using a Small Sample

In the following example we develop an interval estimate for a population mean when the sample size is small. As we already noted, an understanding of the distribution of the population becomes a factor in deciding whether the interval estimation procedure provides acceptable results.

Scheer Industries is considering a new computer-assisted program to train maintenance employees to do machine repairs. In order to fully evaluate the program, the director of

**FIGURE 8.6** MINITAB CONFIDENCE INTERVAL FOR THE CREDIT CARD BALANCE SURVEY

| Variable | N | Mean | StDev | SE Mean | 95% CI |
|----------|-----|---------|---------|---------|------------------|
| Balance | 85 | 5900.00 | 3058.00 | 331.69 | (5240.40, 6559.60) |

**TABLE 8.4    TRAINING TIME IN DAYS FOR A SAMPLE OF 20 SCHEER INDUSTRIES EMPLOYEES**

**Scheer**

| 52 | 59 | 54 | 42 |
| 44 | 50 | 42 | 48 |
| 55 | 54 | 60 | 55 |
| 44 | 62 | 62 | 57 |
| 45 | 46 | 43 | 56 |

manufacturing requested an estimate of the population mean time required for maintenance employees to complete the computer-assisted training.

A sample of 20 employees is selected, with each employee in the sample completing the training program. Data on the training time in days for the 20 employees are shown in Table 8.4. A histogram of the sample data appears in Figure 8.7. What can we say about the distribution of the population based on this histogram? First, the sample data do not support with certainty the conclusion that the distribution of the population is normal, yet we do not see any evidence of skewness or outliers. Therefore, using the guidelines in the previous subsection, we conclude that an interval estimate based on the *t* distribution appears acceptable for the sample of 20 employees.

We continue by computing the sample mean and sample standard deviation as follows.

$$\bar{x} = \frac{\Sigma x_i}{n} = \frac{1030}{20} = 51.5 \text{ days}$$

$$s = \sqrt{\frac{\Sigma(x_i - \bar{x})^2}{n - 1}} = \sqrt{\frac{889}{20 - 1}} = 6.84 \text{ days}$$

**FIGURE 8.7    HISTOGRAM OF TRAINING TIMES FOR THE SCHEER INDUSTRIES SAMPLE**

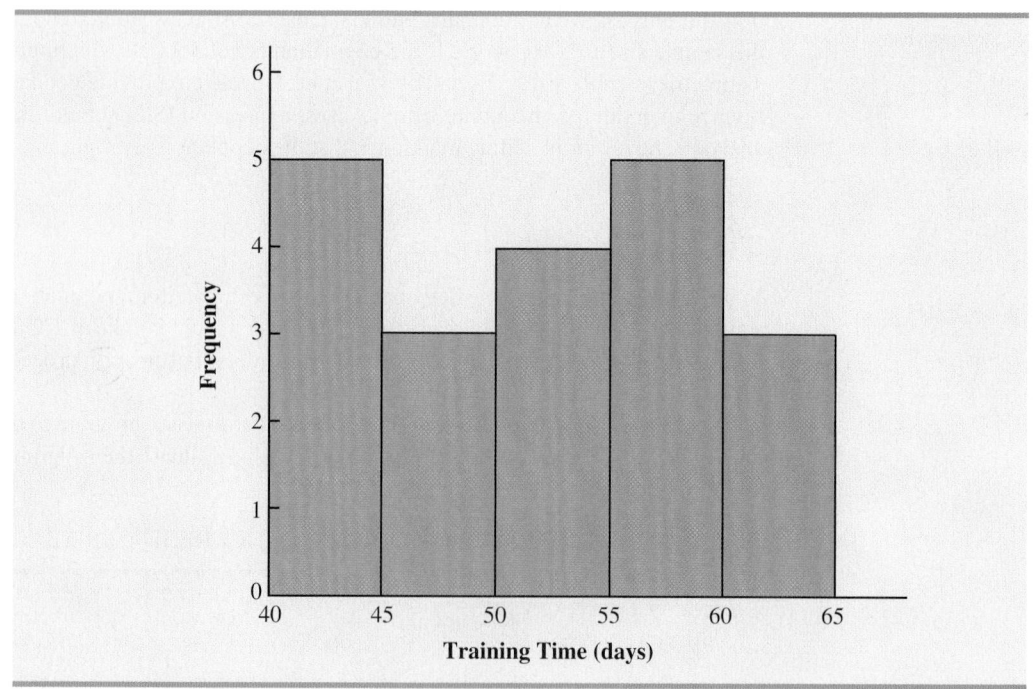

For a 95% confidence interval, we use Table 8.2 and $n - 1 = 19$ degrees of freedom to obtain $t_{.025} = 2.093$. Expression (8.2) provides the interval estimate of the population mean.

$$51.5 \pm 2.093\left(\frac{6.84}{\sqrt{20}}\right)$$

$$51.5 \pm 3.2$$

The point estimate of the population mean is 51.5 days. The margin of error is 3.2 days and the 95% confidence interval is $51.5 - 3.2 = 48.3$ days to $51.5 + 3.2 = 54.7$ days.

Using a histogram of the sample data to learn about the distribution of a population is not always conclusive, but in many cases it provides the only information available. The histogram, along with judgment on the part of the analyst, can often be used to decide if expression (8.2) can be used to develop the interval estimate.

## Summary of Interval Estimation Procedures

We provided two approaches to developing an interval estimate of a population mean. For the $\sigma$ known case, $\sigma$ and the standard normal distribution are used in expression (8.1) to compute the margin of error and to develop the interval estimate. For the $\sigma$ unknown case, the sample standard deviation $s$ and the $t$ distribution are used in expression (8.2) to compute the margin of error and to develop the interval estimate.

A summary of the interval estimation procedures for the two cases is shown in Figure 8.8. In most applications, a sample size of $n \geq 30$ is adequate. If the population has a normal or approximately normal distribution, however, smaller sample sizes may be used. For the $\sigma$ unknown case a sample size of $n \geq 50$ is recommended if the population distribution is believed to be highly skewed or has outliers.

**FIGURE 8.8**    SUMMARY OF INTERVAL ESTIMATION PROCEDURES
FOR A POPULATION MEAN

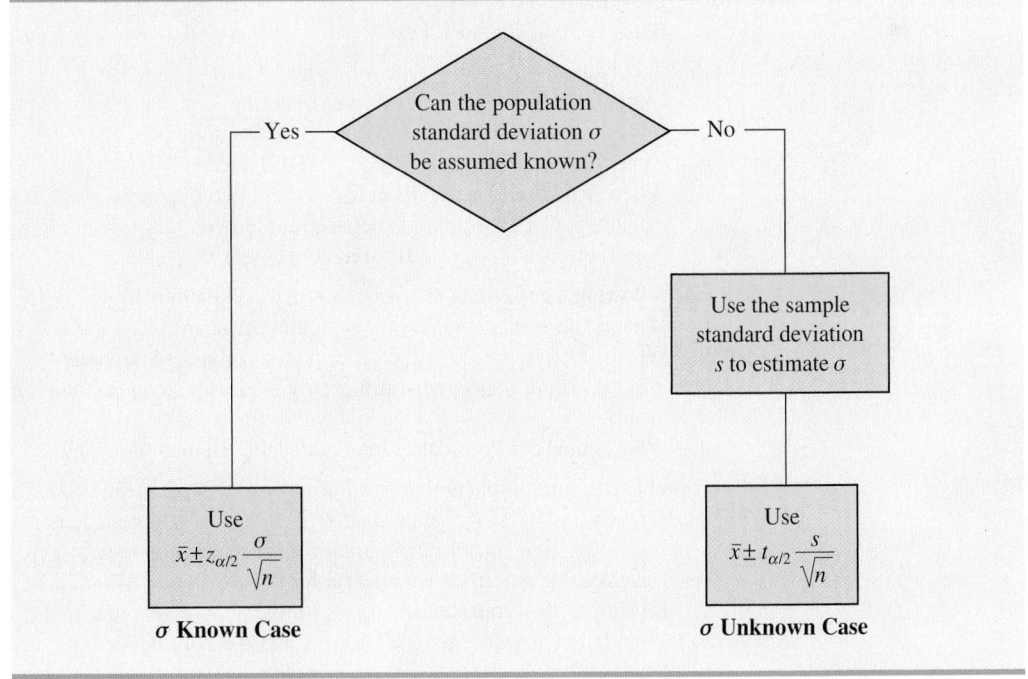

## NOTES AND COMMENTS

1. When $\sigma$ is known, the margin of error, $z_{\alpha/2}(\sigma/\sqrt{n})$, is fixed and is the same for all samples of size $n$. When $\sigma$ is unknown, the margin of error, $t_{\alpha/2}(s/\sqrt{n})$, varies from sample to sample. This variation occurs because the sample standard deviation $s$ varies depending upon the sample selected. A large value for $s$ provides a larger margin of error, while a small value for $s$ provides a smaller margin of error.

2. What happens to confidence interval estimates when the population is skewed? Consider a population that is skewed to the right with large data values stretching the distribution to the right. When such skewness exists, the sample mean $\bar{x}$ and the sample standard deviation $s$ are positively correlated. Larger values of $s$ tend to be associated with larger values of $\bar{x}$. Thus, when $\bar{x}$ is larger than the population mean, $s$ tends to be larger than $\sigma$. This skewness causes the margin of error, $t_{\alpha/2}(s/\sqrt{n})$ to be larger than it would be with $\sigma$ known. The confidence interval with the larger margin of error tends to include the population mean $\mu$ more often than it would if the true value of $\sigma$ were used. But when $\bar{x}$ is smaller than the population mean, the correlation between $\bar{x}$ and $s$ causes the margin of error to be small. In this case, the confidence interval with the smaller margin of error tends to miss the population mean more than it would if we knew $\sigma$ and used it. For this reason, we recommend using larger sample sizes with highly skewed population distributions.

## Exercises

## Methods

11. For a $t$ distribution with 16 degrees of freedom, find the area, or probability, in each region.
    a. To the right of 2.120
    b. To the left of 1.337
    c. To the left of $-1.746$
    d. To the right of 2.583
    e. Between $-2.120$ and 2.120
    f. Between $-1.746$ and 1.746

12. Find the $t$ value(s) for each of the following cases.
    a. Upper tail area of .025 with 12 degrees of freedom
    b. Lower tail area of .05 with 50 degrees of freedom
    c. Upper tail area of .01 with 30 degrees of freedom
    d. Where 90% of the area falls between these two $t$ values with 25 degrees of freedom
    e. Where 95% of the area falls between these two $t$ values with 45 degrees of freedom
    (See Table 2 of Appendix B for a more extensive $t$ table.)

13. The following sample data are from a normal population: 10, 8, 12, 15, 13, 11, 6, 5.
    a. What is the point estimate of the population mean?
    b. What is the point estimate of the population standard deviation?
    c. With 95% confidence, what is the margin of error for the estimation of the population mean?
    d. What is the 95% confidence interval for the population mean?

14. A simple random sample with $n = 54$ provided a sample mean of 22.5 and a sample standard deviation of 4.4. (See Table 2 of Appendix B for a more extensive $t$ table.)
    a. Develop a 90% confidence interval for the population mean.
    b. Develop a 95% confidence interval for the population mean.
    c. Develop a 99% confidence interval for the population mean.
    d. What happens to the margin of error and the confidence interval as the confidence level is increased?

## Applications

15. Sales personnel for Skillings Distributors submit weekly reports listing the customer contacts made during the week. A sample of 65 weekly reports showed a sample mean of 19.5 customer contacts per week. The sample standard deviation was 5.2. Provide 90% and 95% confidence intervals for the population mean number of weekly customer contacts for the sales personnel.

16. The mean number of hours of flying time for pilots at Continental Airlines is 49 hours per month (*The Wall Street Journal,* February 25, 2003). Assume that this mean was based on actual flying times for a sample of 100 Continental pilots and that the sample standard deviation was 8.5 hours.
    a. At 95% confidence, what is the margin of error?
    b. What is the 95% confidence interval estimate of the population mean flying time for the pilots?
    c. The mean number of hours of flying time for pilots at United Airlines is 36 hours per month. Use your results from part (b) to discuss differences between the flying times for the pilots at the two airlines. *The Wall Street Journal* reported United Airlines as having the highest labor cost among all airlines. Does the information in this exercise provide insight as to why United Airlines might expect higher labor costs?

17. The International Air Transport Association surveys business travelers to develop quality ratings for transatlantic gateway airports. The maximum possible rating is 10. Suppose a simple random sample of 50 business travelers is selected and each traveler is asked to provide a rating for the Miami International Airport. The ratings obtained from the sample of 50 business travelers follow.

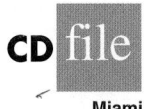

Miami

| 6 | 4 | 6 | 8 | 7 | 7 | 6 | 3 | 3 | 8 | 10 | 4 | 8 |
|---|---|---|---|---|---|---|---|---|---|----|---|---|
| 7 | 8 | 7 | 5 | 9 | 5 | 8 | 4 | 3 | 8 | 5 | 5 | 4 |
| 4 | 4 | 8 | 4 | 5 | 6 | 2 | 5 | 9 | 9 | 8 | 4 | 8 |
| 9 | 9 | 5 | 9 | 7 | 8 | 3 | 10 | 8 | 9 | 6 | | |

Develop a 95% confidence interval estimate of the population mean rating for Miami.

18. Thirty fast-food restaurants including Wendy's, McDonald's, and Burger King were visited during the summer of 2000 (*The Cincinnati Enquirer,* July 9, 2000). During each visit, the customer went to the drive-through and ordered a basic meal such as a "combo" meal or a sandwich, fries, and shake. The time between pulling up to the message board and receiving the filled order was recorded. The times in minutes for the 30 visits are as follows:

FastFood

| 0.9 | 1.0 | 1.2 | 2.2 | 1.9 | 3.6 | 2.8 | 5.2 | 1.8 | 2.1 |
|-----|-----|-----|-----|-----|-----|-----|-----|-----|-----|
| 6.8 | 1.3 | 3.0 | 4.5 | 2.8 | 2.3 | 2.7 | 5.7 | 4.8 | 3.5 |
| 2.6 | 3.3 | 5.0 | 4.0 | 7.2 | 9.1 | 2.8 | 3.6 | 7.3 | 9.0 |

   a. Provide a point estimate of the population mean drive-through time at fast-food restaurants.
   b. At 95% confidence, what is the margin of error?
   c. What is the 95% confidence interval estimate of the population mean?
   d. Discuss skewness that may be present in this population. What suggestion would you make for a repeat of this study?

19. A National Retail Foundation survey found households intended to spend an average of $649 during the December holiday season (*The Wall Street Journal,* December 2, 2002). Assume that the survey included 600 households and that the sample standard deviation was $175.
   a. With 95% confidence, what is the margin of error?
   b. What is the 95% confidence interval estimate of the population mean?
   c. The prior year, the population mean expenditure per household was $632. Discuss the change in holiday season expenditures over the one-year period.

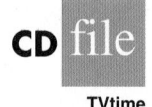

**TVtime**

20. The American Association of Advertising Agencies records data on nonprogram minutes on half-hour, prime-time television shows. Representative data in minutes for a sample of 20 prime-time shows on major networks at 8:30 P.M. follow.

| | | |
|---|---|---|
| 6.0 | 6.6 | 5.8 |
| 7.0 | 6.3 | 6.2 |
| 7.2 | 5.7 | 6.4 |
| 7.0 | 6.5 | 6.2 |
| 6.0 | 6.5 | 7.2 |
| 7.3 | 7.6 | 6.8 |
| 6.0 | 6.2 | |

Assume a normal population and provide a point estimate and a 95% confidence interval for the mean number of nonprogram minutes on half-hour, prime-time television shows at 8:30 P.M.

21. Complaints about rising prescription drug prices caused the U.S. Congress to consider laws that would force pharmaceutical companies to offer prescription discounts to senior citizens without drug benefits. The House Government Reform Committee provided data on the prescription cost for some of the most widely used drugs (*Newsweek*, May 8, 2000). Assume the following data show a sample of the prescription cost in dollars for Zocor, a drug used to lower cholesterol.

| | | | | | | | |
|---|---|---|---|---|---|---|---|
| 110 | 112 | 115 | 99 | 100 | 98 | 104 | 126 |

Given a normal population, what is the 95% confidence interval estimate of the population mean cost for a prescription of Zocor?

22. The number of hours Americans sleep each night varies considerably with 12% of the population sleeping less than six hours to 3% sleeping more than eight hours (*The Macmillan Visual Almanac*, 1996). The following sample of 25 individuals reports hours of sleep per night.

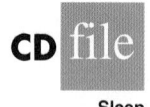

**Sleep**

| | | | | |
|---|---|---|---|---|
| 6.9 | 7.6 | 6.5 | 6.2 | 5.3 |
| 7.8 | 7.0 | 5.5 | 7.6 | 6.7 |
| 7.3 | 6.6 | 7.1 | 6.9 | 6.0 |
| 6.8 | 6.5 | 7.2 | 5.8 | 8.6 |
| 7.6 | 7.1 | 6.0 | 7.2 | 7.7 |

a. What is the point estimate of the population mean number of hours of sleep each night?
b. Given that the population has a normal distribution, develop a 95% confidence interval for the population mean number of hours of sleep each night.

 **8.3** # Determining the Sample Size

In providing practical advice in the two preceding sections, we commented on the role of the sample size in providing good approximate confidence intervals when the population is not normally distributed. In this section, we focus on another aspect of the sample size issue. We describe how to choose a sample size large enough to provide a desired margin of error. To understand how this process is done, we return to the $\sigma$ known case presented in Section 8.1. Using expression (8.1), the interval estimate is

$$\bar{x} \pm z_{\alpha/2}\frac{\sigma}{\sqrt{n}}$$

The quantity $z_{\alpha/2}(\sigma/\sqrt{n})$ is the margin of error. Thus, we see that $z_{\alpha/2}$, the population standard deviation $\sigma$, and the sample size $n$ combine to determine the margin of error. Once we select a confidence coefficient $1 - \alpha$, $z_{\alpha/2}$ can be determined. Then, if we have a value for $\sigma$, we can determine the sample size $n$ needed to provide any desired margin of error. Development of the formula used to compute the required sample size $n$ follows.

Let $E$ = the desired margin of error

$$E = z_{\alpha/2} \frac{\sigma}{\sqrt{n}}$$

*If a desired margin of error is selected prior to sampling, the procedures in this section can be used to determine the sample size necessary to satisfy the margin of error requirement.*

Solving for $\sqrt{n}$, we have

$$\sqrt{n} = \frac{z_{\alpha/2}\sigma}{E}$$

Squaring both sides of this equation, we obtain the following expression for the sample size.

*Equation (8.3) can be used to provide a good sample size recommendation. However, judgment on the part of the analyst should be used to determine whether the final sample size should be adjusted upward.*

**SAMPLE SIZE FOR AN INTERVAL ESTIMATE OF A POPULATION MEAN**

$$n = \frac{(z_{\alpha/2})^2 \sigma^2}{E^2} \qquad (8.3)$$

This sample size provides the desired margin of error at the chosen confidence level.

In equation (8.3) $E$ is the margin of error that the user is willing to accept, and the value of $z_{\alpha/2}$ follows directly from the confidence level to be used in developing the interval estimate. Although user preference must be considered, 95% confidence is the most frequently chosen value ($z_{.025} = 1.96$).

Finally, use of equation (8.3) requires a value for the population standard deviation $\sigma$. However, even if $\sigma$ is unknown, we can use equation (8.3) provided we have a preliminary or *planning value* for $\sigma$. In practice, one of the following procedures can be chosen.

*A planning value for the population standard deviation $\sigma$ must be specified before the sample size can be determined. Three methods of obtaining a planning value for $\sigma$ are discussed here.*

1. Use the estimate of the population standard deviation computed from data of previous studies as the planning value for $\sigma$.
2. Use a pilot study to select a preliminary sample. The sample standard deviation from the preliminary sample can be used as the planning value for $\sigma$.
3. Use judgment or a "best guess" for the value of $\sigma$. For example, we might begin by estimating the largest and smallest data values in the population. The difference between the largest and smallest values provides an estimate of the range for the data. Finally, the range divided by 4 is often suggested as a rough approximation of the standard deviation and thus an acceptable planning value for $\sigma$.

Let us demonstrate the use of equation (8.3) to determine the sample size by considering the following example. A previous study that investigated the cost of renting automobiles in the United States found a mean cost of approximately $55 per day for renting a midsize automobile. Suppose that the organization that conducted this study would like to conduct a new study in order to estimate the population mean daily rental cost for a midsize automobile in the United States. In designing the new study, the project director specifies that the population mean daily rental cost be estimated with a margin of error of $2 and a 95% level of confidence.

The project director specified a desired margin of error of $E = 2$, and the 95% level of confidence indicates $z_{.025} = 1.96$. Thus, we only need a planning value for the population standard deviation $\sigma$ in order to compute the required sample size. At this point, an analyst

*Equation (8.3) provides the minimum sample size needed to satisfy the desired margin of error requirement. If the computed sample size is not an integer, rounding up to the next integer value will provide a margin of error slightly smaller than required.*

reviewed the sample data from the previous study and found that the sample standard deviation for the daily rental cost was $9.65. Using 9.65 as the planning value for $\sigma$, we obtain

$$n = \frac{(z_{\alpha/2})^2 \sigma^2}{E^2} = \frac{(1.96)^2 (9.65)^2}{2^2} = 89.43$$

Thus, the sample size for the new study needs to be at least 89.43 midsize automobile rentals in order to satisfy the project director's $2 margin-of-error requirement. In cases where the computed $n$ is not an integer, we round up to the next integer value; hence, the recommended sample size is 90 midsize automobile rentals.

## Exercises

## Methods

23. How large a sample should be selected to provide a 95% confidence interval with a margin of error of 10? Assume that the population standard deviation is 40.

24. The range for a set of data is estimated to be 36.
    a. What is the planning value for the population standard deviation?
    b. At 95% confidence, how large a sample would provide a margin of error of 3?
    c. At 95% confidence, how large a sample would provide a margin of error of 2?

## Applications

25. Refer to the Scheer Industries example in Section 8.2. Use 6.82 days as a planning value for the population standard deviation.
    a. Assuming 95% confidence, what sample size would be required to obtain a margin of error of 1.5 days?
    b. If the precision statement was made with 90% confidence, what sample size would be required to obtain a margin of error of 2 days?

26. *Bride's* magazine reported that the mean cost of a wedding is $19,000 (*USA Today,* April 17, 2000). Assume that the population standard deviation is $9,400. *Bride's* plans to use an annual survey to monitor the cost of a wedding. Use 95% confidence.
    a. What is the recommended sample size if the desired margin of error is $1000?
    b. What is the recommended sample size if the desired margin of error is $500?
    c. What is the recommended sample size if the desired margin of error is $200?

27. Annual starting salaries for college graduates with degrees in business administration are generally expected to be between $30,000 and $45,000. Assume that a 95% confidence interval estimate of the population mean annual starting salary is desired. What is the planning value for the population standard deviation? How large a sample should be taken if the desired margin of error is
    a. $500?
    b. $200?
    c. $100?
    d. Would you recommend trying to obtain the $100 margin of error? Explain.

28. Smith Travel Research provides information on the one-night cost of hotel rooms throughout the United States (*USA Today,* July 8, 2002). Using $22.50 as the planning value for the population standard deviation, what sample size is recommended for each of the following cases? Use $2 as the desired margin of error.
    a. A 90% confidence interval estimate of the population mean cost of hotel rooms
    b. A 95% confidence interval estimate of the population mean cost of hotel rooms

    c.   A 99% confidence interval estimate of the population mean cost of hotel rooms

    d.   When the desired margin of error is fixed, what happens to the sample size as the confidence level is increased? Would you recommend a 99% confidence level be used by Smith Travel Research? Discuss.

29.  The travel-to-work time for residents of the 15 largest cities in the United States is reported in the *2003 Information Please Almanac.* Suppose that a preliminary simple random sample of residents of San Francisco is used to develop a planning value of 6.25 minutes for the population standard deviation.

    a.   If we want to estimate the population mean travel-to-work time for San Francisco residents with a margin of error of 2 minutes, what sample size should be used? Assume 95% confidence.

    b.   If we want to estimate the population mean travel-to-work time for San Francisco residents with a margin of error of 1 minute, what sample size should be used? Assume 95% confidence.

30.  During the first quarter of 2003, the price/earnings (P/E) ratio for stocks listed on the New York Stock Exchange generally ranged from 5 to 60 (*The Wall Street Journal,* March 7, 2003). Assume that we want to estimate the population mean P/E ratio for all stocks listed on the exchange. How many stocks should be included in the sample if we want a margin of error of 3? Use 95% confidence.

 **8.4**

# Population Proportion

In the introduction to this chapter we said that the general form of an interval estimate of a population proportion $p$ is

$$\bar{p} \pm \text{Margin of error}$$

The sampling distribution of $\bar{p}$ plays a key role in computing the margin of error for this interval estimate.

    In Chapter 7 we said that the sampling distribution of $\bar{p}$ can be approximated by a normal distribution whenever $np \geq 5$ and $n(1 - p) \geq 5$. Figure 8.9 shows the normal approximation

**FIGURE 8.9**   NORMAL APPROXIMATION OF THE SAMPLING DISTRIBUTION OF $\bar{p}$

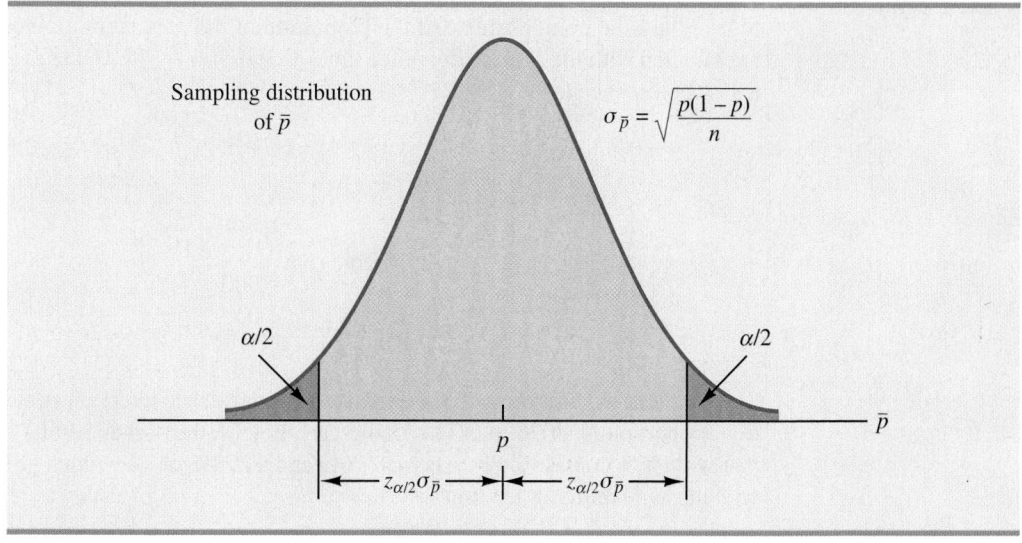

of the sampling distribution of $\bar{p}$. The mean of the sampling distribution of $\bar{p}$ is the population proportion $p$, and the standard error of $\bar{p}$ is

$$\sigma_{\bar{p}} = \sqrt{\frac{p(1 - p)}{n}} \tag{8.4}$$

Because the sampling distribution of $\bar{p}$ is normally distributed, if we choose $z_{\alpha/2}\sigma_{\bar{p}}$ as the margin of error in an interval estimate of a population proportion, we know that $100(1 - \alpha)$ percent of the intervals generated will contain the true population proportion. But $\sigma_{\bar{p}}$ cannot be used directly in the computation of the margin of error because $p$ will not be known; $p$ is what we are trying to estimate. So, $\bar{p}$ is substituted for $p$ and the margin of error for an interval estimate of a population proportion is given by

$$\text{Margin of error} = z_{\alpha/2}\sqrt{\frac{\bar{p}(1 - \bar{p})}{n}} \tag{8.5}$$

The general expression for an interval estimate of a population proportion is as follows.

*When developing confidence intervals for proportions, the quantity $z_{\alpha/2}\sqrt{\bar{p}(1 - \bar{p})/n}$ provides the margin of error.*

### INTERVAL ESTIMATE OF A POPULATION PROPORTION

$$\bar{p} \pm z_{\alpha/2}\sqrt{\frac{\bar{p}(1 - \bar{p})}{n}} \tag{8.6}$$

where $1 - \alpha$ is the confidence coefficient and $z_{\alpha/2}$ is the $z$ value providing an area of $\alpha/2$ in the upper tail of the standard normal distribution.

**CD** file

**TeeTimes**

The following example illustrates the computation of the margin of error and interval estimate for a population proportion. A national survey of 900 women golfers was conducted to learn how women golfers view their treatment at golf courses in the United States. The survey found that 396 of the women golfers were satisfied with the availability of tee times. Thus, the point estimate of the proportion of the population of women golfers who are satisfied with the availability of tee times is 396/900 = .44. Using expression (8.6) and a 95% confidence level,

$$\bar{p} \pm z_{\alpha/2}\sqrt{\frac{\bar{p}(1 - \bar{p})}{n}}$$

$$.44 \pm 1.96\sqrt{\frac{.44(1 - .44)}{900}}$$

$$.44 \pm .0324$$

Thus, the margin of error is .0324 and the 95% confidence interval estimate of the population proportion is .4076 to .4724. Using percentages, the survey results enable us to state that with 95% confidence between 40.76% and 47.24% of all women golfers are satisfied with the availability of tee times.

## Determining the Sample Size

Let us consider the question of how large the sample size should be to obtain an estimate of a population proportion at a specified level of precision. The rationale for the sample size determination in developing interval estimates of $p$ is similar to the rationale used in Section 8.3 to determine the sample size for estimating a population mean.

Previously in this section we said that the margin of error associated with an interval estimate of a population proportion is $z_{\alpha/2}\sqrt{\bar{p}(1-\bar{p})/n}$. The margin of error is based on the values of $z_{\alpha/2}$, the sample proportion $\bar{p}$, and the sample size $n$. Larger sample sizes provide a smaller margin of error and better precision.

Let $E$ denote the desired margin of error.

$$E = z_{\alpha/2}\sqrt{\frac{\bar{p}(1-\bar{p})}{n}}$$

Solving this equation for $n$ provides a formula for the sample size that will provide a margin of error of size $E$.

$$n = \frac{(z_{\alpha/2})^2\bar{p}(1-\bar{p})}{E^2}$$

Note, however, that we cannot use this formula to compute the sample size that will provide the desired margin of error because $\bar{p}$ will not be known until after we select the sample. What we need, then, is a planning value for $\bar{p}$ that can be used to make the computation. Using $p^*$ to denote the planning value for $\bar{p}$, the following formula can be used to compute the sample size that will provide a margin of error of size $E$.

SAMPLE SIZE FOR AN INTERVAL ESTIMATE OF A POPULATION PROPORTION

$$n = \frac{(z_{\alpha/2})^2 p^*(1-p^*)}{E^2} \tag{8.7}$$

In practice, the planning value can be chosen by one of the following procedures.

1. Use the sample proportion from a previous sample of the same or similar units.
2. Use a pilot study to select a preliminary sample. The sample proportion from this sample can be used as the planning value, $p^*$.
3. Use judgment or a "best guess" for the value of $p^*$.
4. If none of the preceding alternatives apply, use a planning value of $p^* = .50$.

Let us return to the survey of women golfers and assume that the company is interested in conducting a new survey to estimate the current proportion of the population of women golfers who are satisfied with the availability of tee times. How large should the sample be if the survey director wants to estimate the population proportion with a margin of error of .025 at 95% confidence? With $E = .025$ and $z_{\alpha/2} = 1.96$, we need a planning value $p^*$ to answer the sample size question. Using the previous survey result of $\bar{p} = .44$ as the planning value $p^*$, equation (8.7) shows that

$$n = \frac{(z_{\alpha/2})^2 p^*(1-p^*)}{E^2} = \frac{(1.96)^2(.44)(1-.44)}{(.025)^2} = 1514.5$$

**TABLE 8.5    SOME POSSIBLE VALUES FOR $p^*(1 - p^*)$**

| $p^*$ | $p^*(1 - p^*)$ | |
|------|---------------|---|
| .10 | $(.10)(.90) = .09$ | |
| .30 | $(.30)(.70) = .21$ | |
| .40 | $(.40)(.60) = .24$ | |
| .50 | $(.50)(.50) = .25$ | ← Largest value for $p^*(1 - p^*)$ |
| .60 | $(.60)(.40) = .24$ | |
| .70 | $(.70)(.30) = .21$ | |
| .90 | $(.90)(.10) = .09$ | |

Thus, the sample size must be at least 1514.5 women golfers to satisfy the margin of error requirement. Rounding up to the next integer value indicates that a sample of 1515 women golfers is recommended to satisfy the margin of error requirement.

The fourth alternative suggested for selecting a planning value $p^*$ is to use $p^* = .50$. This value of $p^*$ is frequently used when no other information is available. To understand why, note that the numerator of equation (8.7) shows that the sample size is proportional to the quantity $p^*(1 - p^*)$. A larger value for the quantity $p^*(1 - p^*)$ will result in a larger sample size. Table 8.5 gives some possible values of $p^*(1 - p^*)$. Note that the largest value of $p^*(1 - p^*)$ occurs when $p^* = .50$. Thus, in case of any uncertainty about an appropriate planning value, we know that $p^* = .50$ will provide the largest sample size recommendation. In effect, we play it safe by recommending the largest possible sample size. If the sample proportion turns out to be different from the .50 planning value, the margin of error will be smaller than anticipated. Thus, in using $p^* = .50$, we guarantee that the sample size will be sufficient to obtain the desired margin of error.

In the survey of women golfers example, a planning value of $p^* = .50$ would have provided the sample size

$$n = \frac{(z_{\alpha/2})^2 p^*(1 - p^*)}{E^2} = \frac{(1.96)^2(.50)(1 - .50)}{(.025)^2} = 1536.6$$

Thus, a slightly larger sample size of 1537 women golfers would be recommended.

## NOTES AND COMMENTS

The margin of error for estimating a population proportion is almost always .10 or less. In national public opinion polls conducted by organizations such as Gallup and Harris, a .03 or .04 margin of error is common. With such margins of error, equation (8.7) will almost always provide a sample size that is large enough to satisfy the requirements of $np \geq 5$ and $n(1 - p) \geq 5$ for using a normal distribution as an approximation for the sampling distribution of $\bar{x}$.

## Exercises

### Methods

31. A simple random sample of 400 individuals provides 100 Yes responses.
    a.  What is the point estimate of the proportion of the population that would provide Yes responses?
    b.  What is your estimate of the standard error of the proportion, $\sigma_{\bar{p}}$?
    c.  Compute the 95% confidence interval for the population proportion.

32. A simple random sample of 800 elements generates a sample proportion $\bar{p} = .70$.
    a. Provide a 90% confidence interval for the population proportion.
    b. Provide a 95% confidence interval for the population proportion.

33. In a survey, the planning value for the population proportion is $p^* = 35$. How large a sample should be taken to provide a 95% confidence interval with a margin of error of .05?

34. At 95% confidence, how large a sample should be taken to obtain a margin of error of .03 for the estimation of a population proportion? Assume that past data are not available for developing a planning value for $\bar{p}$.

## Applications

35. A survey of 611 office workers investigated telephone answering practices, including how often each office worker was able to answer incoming telephone calls and how often incoming telephone calls went directly to voice mail (*USA Today*, April 21, 2002). A total of 281 office workers indicated that they never need voice mail and are able to take every telephone call.
    a. What is the point estimate of the proportion of the population of office workers who are able to take every telephone call?
    b. At 90% confidence, what is the margin of error?
    c. What is the 90% confidence interval for the proportion of the population of office workers who are able to take every telephone call?

36. A survey by the Society for Human Resource Management asked 346 job seekers why employees change jobs so frequently (*The Wall Street Journal*, March 28, 2000). The answer selected most (152 times) was "higher compensation elsewhere."
    a. What is the point estimate of the proportion of job seekers who would select "higher compensation elsewhere" as the reason for changing jobs?
    b. What is the 95% confidence interval estimate of the population proportion?

37. Towers Perrin, a New York human resources consulting firm, conducted a survey of 1100 employees at medium-sized and large companies to determine how dissatisfied were employees with their jobs (*The Wall Street Journal*, January 29, 2003). A total of 473 employees indicated they strongly disliked their current work experience.
    a. What is the point estimate of the proportion of the population of employees who strongly dislike their current work experience?
    b. At 95% confidence, what is the margin of error?
    c. What is the 95% confidence interval for the proportion of the population of employees who strongly dislike their current work experience?
    d. Towers Perrin estimates that it costs employers one-third of an hourly employee's annual salary to find a successor and as much as 1.5 times the annual salary to find a successor for a highly compensated employee. What message did this survey send to employers?

38. Audience profile data collected at the ESPN SportsZone Web site showed that 26% of the users were women (*USA Today*, January 21, 1998). Assume that this percentage was based on a sample of 400 users.
    a. At 95% confidence, what is the margin of error associated with the estimated proportion of users who are women?
    b. What is the 95% confidence interval for the population proportion of ESPN SportsZone Web site users who are women?
    c. How large a sample should be taken if the desired margin of error is .03?

39. An Employee Benefit Research Institute survey explored the reasons small business employers offer a retirement plan to their employees (*USA Today*, April 4, 2000). The reason "competitive advantage in recruitment/retention" was anticipated 33% of the time.
    a. What sample size is recommended if a survey goal is to estimate the proportion of small business employers who offer a retirement plan primarily for "competitive advantage in recruitment/retention" with a margin of error of .03? Use 95% confidence.
    b. Repeat part (a) using 99% confidence.

40. The professional baseball home run record of 61 home runs in a season was held for 37 years by Roger Maris of the New York Yankees. However, between 1998 and 2001, three players—Mark McGwire, Sammy Sosa, and Barry Bonds—broke the standard set by Maris with Bonds holding the current record 73 home runs in a single season. With the long standing home run record being broken and with many other new offensive records being set, suspicion arose that baseball players might be using illegal muscle-building drugs called steroids. A *USA Today*/CNN/Gallup poll found that 86% of baseball fans think professional baseball players should be tested for steroids (*USA Today*, July 8, 2002). If 650 baseball fans were included in the sample, compute the margin of error and the 95% confidence interval for the population proportion of baseball fans who think professional baseball players should be tested for steroids.

41. An American Express retail survey found that 16% of U.S. consumers used the Internet to buy gifts during the 1999 holiday season (*USA Today*, January 18, 2000). If 1285 customers participated in the survey, what is the margin of error and what is the interval estimate of the population proportion of customers using the Internet to buy gifts? Use 95% confidence.

42. A *USA Today*/CNN/Gallup poll for the 2000 presidential campaign sampled 491 potential voters in June (*USA Today*, June 9, 2000). A primary purpose of the poll was to obtain an estimate of the proportion of potential voters who favor each candidate. Assume a planning value of $p^* = .50$ and a 95% confidence level.
    a. For $p^* = .50$, what was the planned margin of error for the June poll?
    b. Closer to the November election, better precision and smaller margins of error are desired. Assume the following margins of error are requested for surveys to be conducted during the presidential campaign. Compute the recommended sample size for each survey.

| Survey | Margin of Error |
|---|---|
| September | .04 |
| October | .03 |
| Early November | .02 |
| Pre-Election Day | .01 |

43. The League of American Theatres and Producers uses an ongoing audience tracking survey that provides up-to-date information about Broadway theater audiences (*Playbill*, Winter 1997). Every week, the League distributes a one-page survey on random theater seats at a rotation roster of Broadway shows. The survey questionnaire takes only five minutes to complete and enables audiences to communicate their views about the theater industry.
    a. How large a sample should be taken if the desired margin of error on any population proportion is .04? Use 95% confidence and a planning value of $p^* = .50$.
    b. Assume that the sample size recommended in part (a) is implemented and that during one week 445 theatergoers indicated that they do not live in New York City. What is the point estimate of the proportion of Broadway audiences that do not live in New York City?
    c. Based on the data in part (b), what is the 95% confidence interval for the population proportion of Broadway audiences that do not live in New York City?

## Summary

In this chapter we presented methods for developing interval estimates of a population mean and a population proportion. A point estimator may or may not provide a good estimate of a population parameter. The use of an interval estimate provides a measure of the precision of an estimate. Both the interval estimate of the population mean and the population proportion are of the form: point estimate $\pm$ margin of error.

We presented interval estimates for a population mean for two cases. In the $\sigma$ known case, historical data or other information is used to develop an estimate of $\sigma$ prior to taking a sample. Analysis of new sample data then proceeds based on the assumption that $\sigma$ is known. In the $\sigma$ unknown case, the sample data are used to estimate both the population mean and the population standard deviation. The final choice of which interval estimation procedure to use depends upon the analyst's understanding of which method provides the best estimate of $\sigma$.

In the $\sigma$ known case, the interval estimation procedure is based on the assumed value of $\sigma$ and the use of the standard normal distribution. In the $\sigma$ unknown case, the interval estimation procedure uses the sample standard deviation $s$ and the $t$ distribution. In both cases the quality of the interval estimates obtained depends on the distribution of the population and the sample size. If the population is normally distributed the interval estimates will be exact in both cases, even for small sample sizes. If the population is not normally distributed, the interval estimates obtained will be approximate. Larger sample sizes will provide better approximations, but the more highly skewed the population is, the larger the sample size needs to be to obtain a good approximation. Practical advice about the sample size necessary to obtain good approximations was included in Sections 8.1 and 8.2.

The general form of the interval estimate for a population proportion is $\bar{p} \pm$ margin of error. In practice the sample sizes used for interval estimates of a population proportion are generally large. Thus, the interval estimation procedure is based on the standard normal distribution.

## Glossary

**Interval estimate** An estimate of a population parameter that provides an interval believed to contain the value of the parameter. For the interval estimates in this chapter, it has the form: point estimate $\pm$ margin of error.

**Margin of error** The $\pm$ value added to and subtracted from a point estimate in order to develop an interval estimate of a population parameter.

**$\sigma$ known** The condition existing when historical data or other information provides a good value for the population standard deviation prior to taking a sample. The interval estimation procedure uses this known value of $\sigma$ in computing the margin of error.

**$\sigma$ unknown** The condition existing when no good basis exists for estimating the population standard deviation prior to taking the sample. The interval estimation procedure uses the sample standard deviation $s$ in computing the margin of error.

**Confidence level** The confidence associated with an interval estimate. For example, if an interval estimation procedure provides intervals such that 95% of the intervals formed using the procedure will include the population parameter, the interval estimate is said to be constructed at the 95% confidence level.

**Confidence coefficient** The confidence level expressed as a decimal value. For example, .95 is the confidence coefficient for a 95% confidence level.

**Confidence interval** Another name for an interval estimate.

**$t$ distribution** A family of probability distributions that can be used to develop an interval estimate of a population mean whenever the population standard deviation $\sigma$ is unknown and is estimated by the sample standard deviation $s$.

**Degrees of freedom** A parameter of the $t$ distribution. When the $t$ distribution is used in the computation of an interval estimate of a population mean, the appropriate $t$ distribution has $n - 1$ degrees of freedom, where $n$ is the size of the simple random sample.

## Key Formulas

**Interval Estimate of a Population Mean: $\sigma$ Known**

$$\bar{x} \pm z_{\alpha/2} \frac{\sigma}{\sqrt{n}} \tag{8.1}$$

**Interval Estimate of a Population Mean: $\sigma$ Unknown**

$$\bar{x} \pm t_{\alpha/2} \frac{s}{\sqrt{n}} \tag{8.2}$$

**Sample Size for an Interval Estimate of a Population Mean**

$$n = \frac{(z_{\alpha/2})^2 \sigma^2}{E^2} \tag{8.3}$$

**Interval Estimate of a Population Proportion**

$$\bar{p} \pm z_{\alpha/2} \sqrt{\frac{\bar{p}(1 - \bar{p})}{n}} \tag{8.6}$$

**Sample Size for an Interval Estimate of a Population Proportion**

$$n = \frac{(z_{\alpha/2})^2 p^*(1 - p^*)}{E^2} \tag{8.7}$$

## Supplementary Exercises

44. A survey of first-time home buyers found that the mean of annual household income was $50,000 (CNBC.com, July 11, 2000). Assume the survey used a sample of 400 first-time home buyers and assume that the population standard deviation is $20,500.
    a. At 95% confidence, what is the margin of error for this study?
    b. What is the 95% confidence interval for the population mean annual household income for first-time home buyers?

45. A survey conducted by the American Automobile Association showed that a family of four spends an average of $215.60 per day while on vacation. Suppose a sample of 64 families of four vacationing at Niagara Falls resulted in a sample mean of $252.45 per day and a sample standard deviation of $74.50.
    a. Develop a 95% confidence interval estimate of the mean amount spent per day by a family of four visiting Niagara Falls.
    b. Based on the confidence interval from part (a), does it appear that the population mean amount spent per day by families visiting Niagara Falls differs from the mean reported by the American Automobile Association? Explain.

46. The motion picture *Harry Potter and the Sorcerer's Stone* shattered the box office debut record previously held by *The Lost World: Jurassic Park* (*The Wall Street Journal,* November 19, 2001). A sample of 100 movie theaters showed that the mean three-day weekend gross was $25,467 per theater. The sample standard deviation was $4980.
    a. What is the margin of error for this study? Use 95% confidence.
    b. What is the 95% confidence interval estimate for the population mean weekend gross per theater?

c. *The Lost World* took in $72.1 million in its first three-day weekend. *Harry Potter and the Sorcerer's Stone* was shown in 3672 theaters. What is an estimate of the total *Harry Potter and the Sorcerer's Stone* took in during its first three-day weekend?

d. An Associated Press article claimed *Harry Potter* "shattered" the box office debut record held by *The Lost World.* Do your results agree with this claim?

47. Arthur D. Little, Inc., estimates that approximately 70% of mail received by a household is advertisements (*Time,* July 14, 1997). A sample of 20 households shows the following data for the number of advertisements received and the total number of pieces of mail received during one week.

**Mail**

| Household | Advertisements | Total Mail | Household | Advertisements | Total Mail |
|---|---|---|---|---|---|
| 1 | 24 | 35 | 11 | 13 | 19 |
| 2 | 9 | 14 | 12 | 16 | 28 |
| 3 | 18 | 30 | 13 | 20 | 27 |
| 4 | 9 | 12 | 14 | 17 | 22 |
| 5 | 15 | 28 | 15 | 21 | 24 |
| 6 | 23 | 33 | 16 | 21 | 33 |
| 7 | 13 | 20 | 17 | 15 | 25 |
| 8 | 17 | 20 | 18 | 15 | 24 |
| 9 | 20 | 23 | 19 | 18 | 24 |
| 10 | 20 | 25 | 20 | 12 | 16 |

a. What is the point estimate of the population mean number of advertisements received per week? What is the 95% confidence interval for the population mean?

b. What is the point estimate of the population mean number of pieces of mail received per week? What is the 95% confidence interval for the population mean?

c. Use the point estimates in parts (a) and (b). Do these estimates agree with the statement that approximately 70% of mailings are advertisements?

**Flights**

48. US Airways conducted a number of studies that indicated a substantial savings could be obtained by encouraging Dividend Miles frequent flyer customers to redeem miles and schedule award flights online (*US Airways Attache,* February 2003). One study collected data on the amount of time required to redeem miles and schedule an award flight over the telephone. A sample showing the time in minutes required for each of 150 award flights scheduled by telephone is contained in the data set Flights. Use Minitab or Excel to help answer the following questions.

a. What is the sample mean number of minutes required to schedule an award flight by telephone?

b. What is the 95% confidence interval for the population mean time to schedule an award flight by telephone?

c. Assume a telephone ticket agent works 7.5 hours per day. How many award flights can one ticket agent be expected to handle a day?

d. Discuss why this information supported US Airways plans to use an online system to reduce costs.

**ActTemps**

49. A survey by Accountemps asked a sample of 200 executives to provide data on the number of minutes per day office workers waste trying to locate mislabeled, misfiled, or misplaced items. Data consistent with this survey are contained in the data set ActTemps.

a. Use ActTemps to develop a point estimate of the number of minutes per day office workers waste trying to locate mislabeled, misfiled, or misplaced items.

b. What is the sample standard deviation?

c. What is the 95% confidence interval for the mean number of minutes wasted per day?

50. Mileage tests are conducted for a particular model of automobile. If a 98% confidence interval with a margin of error of 1 mile per gallon is desired, how many automobiles should be used in the test? Assume that preliminary mileage tests indicate the standard deviation is 2.6 miles per gallon.

51. In developing patient appointment schedules, a medical center wants to estimate the mean time that a staff member spends with each patient. How large a sample should be taken if the desired margin of error is two minutes at a 95% level of confidence? How large a sample should be taken for a 99% level of confidence? Use a planning value for the population standard deviation of eight minutes.

52. Annual salary plus bonus data for chief executive officers are presented in the *Business Week* Annual Pay Survey. A preliminary sample showed that the standard deviation is $675 with data provided in thousands of dollars. How many chief executive officers should be in a sample if we want to estimate the population mean annual salary plus bonus with a margin of error of $100,000? (*Note:* The desired margin of error would be $E = 100$ if the data are in thousands of dollars.) Use 95% confidence.

53. The National Center for Education Statistics reported that 47% of college students work to pay for tuition and living expenses. Assume that a sample of 450 college students was used in the study.
    a. Provide a 95% confidence interval for the population proportion of college students who work to pay for tuition and living expenses.
    b. Provide a 99% confidence interval for the population proportion of college students who work to pay for tuition and living expenses.
    c. What happens to the margin of error as the confidence is increased from 95% to 99%?

54. A *USA Today*/CNN/Gallup survey of 369 working parents found 200 who said they spend too little time with their children because of work commitments.
    a. What is the point estimate of the proportion of the population of working parents who feel they spend too little time with their children because of work commitments?
    b. At 95% confidence, what is the margin of error?
    c. What is the 95% confidence interval estimate of the population proportion of working parents who feel they spend too little time with their children because of work commitments?

55. A *Time*/CNN poll of 1400 American adults asked, "Where would you rather go in your spare time?" The top response by 504 adults was a shopping mall.
    a. What is the point estimate of the proportion of adults who would prefer going to a shopping mall in their spare time?
    b. At 95% confidence, what is the margin of error associated with this estimate?

56. A Roper Starch survey asked employees ages 18 to 29 whether they would prefer better health insurance or a raise in salary (*USA Today,* September 5, 2000). Answer the following questions assuming 340 of 500 employees said they would prefer better health insurance over a raise.
    a. What is the point estimate of the proportion of employees ages 18 to 29 who would prefer better health insurance?
    b. What is the 95% confidence interval estimate of the population proportion?

57. The *2003 Statistical Abstract of the United States* reported the percentage of people 18 years of age and older who smoke. Suppose that a study designed to collect new data on smokers and nonsmokers uses a preliminary estimate of the proportion who smoke of .30.
    a. How large a sample should be taken to estimate the proportion of smokers in the population with a margin of error of .02? Use 95% confidence.
    b. Assume that the study uses your sample size recommendation in part (a) and finds 520 smokers. What is the point estimate of the proportion of smokers in the population?
    c. What is the 95% confidence interval for the proportion of smokers in the population?

58. A well-known bank credit card firm wishes to estimate the proportion of credit card holders who carry a nonzero balance at the end of the month and incur an interest charge. Assume that the desired margin of error is .03 at 98% confidence.

a. How large a sample should be selected if it is anticipated that roughly 70% of the firm's card holders carry a nonzero balance at the end of the month?

b. How large a sample should be selected if no planning value for the proportion could be specified?

59. In a survey, 200 people were asked to identify their major source of news information; 110 stated that their major source was television news.

a. Construct a 95% confidence interval for the proportion of people in the population who consider television their major source of news information.

b. How large a sample would be necessary to estimate the population proportion with a margin of error of .05 at 95% confidence?

60. Although airline schedules and cost are important factors for business travelers when choosing an airline carrier, a *USA Today* survey found that business travelers list an airline's frequent flyer program as the most important factor. From a sample of $n = 1993$ business travelers who responded to the survey, 618 listed a frequent flyer program as the most important factor.

a. What is the point estimate of the proportion of the population of business travelers who believe a frequent flyer program is the most important factor when choosing an airline carrier?

b. Develop a 95% confidence interval estimate of the population proportion.

c. How large a sample would be required to report the margin of error of .01 at 95% confidence? Would you recommend that *USA Today* attempt to provide this degree of precision? Why or why not?

## Case Problem 1    Bock Investment Services

The goal of Bock Investment Services (BIS) is to be the leading money market advisory service in South Carolina. To provide better service for their present clients and to attract new clients, BIS developed a weekly newsletter. BIS is considering adding a new feature to the newsletter that will report the results of a weekly telephone survey of fund managers. To investigate the feasibility of offering this service, and to determine what type of information to include in the newsletter, BIS selected a simple random sample of 45 money market funds. A portion of the data obtained is shown in Table 8.6, which reports fund assets and yields for the past 7 and 30 days. Before calling the money market fund managers to obtain additional data, BIS decided to do some preliminary analysis of the data already collected.

### Managerial Report

1. Use appropriate descriptive statistics to summarize the data on assets and yields for the money market funds.

2. Develop a 95% confidence interval estimate of the mean assets, mean 7-day yield, and mean 30-day yield for the population of money market funds. Provide a managerial interpretation of each interval estimate.

3. Discuss the implication of your findings in terms of how BIS could use this type of information in preparing their weekly newsletter.

4. What other information would you recommend that BIS gather to provide the most useful information to their clients?

## Case Problem 2    Gulf Real Estate Properties

Gulf Real Estate Properties, Inc., is a real estate firm located in Southwest Florida. The company, which advertises itself as "expert in the real estate market," monitors condominium sales by collecting data on location, list price, sale price, and number of days it takes to sell

**TABLE 8.6**  DATA FOR BOCK INVESTMENT SERVICES

**Bock**

| Money Market Fund | Assets ($ millions) | 7-Day Yield (%) | 30-Day Yield (%) |
|---|---|---|---|
| Amcore | 103.9 | 4.10 | 4.08 |
| Alger | 156.7 | 4.79 | 4.73 |
| Arch MM/Trust | 496.5 | 4.17 | 4.13 |
| BT Instit Treas | 197.8 | 4.37 | 4.32 |
| Benchmark Div | 2755.4 | 4.54 | 4.47 |
| Bradford | 707.6 | 3.88 | 3.83 |
| Capital Cash | 1.7 | 4.29 | 4.22 |
| Cash Mgt Trust | 2707.8 | 4.14 | 4.04 |
| Composite | 122.8 | 4.03 | 3.91 |
| Cowen Standby | 694.7 | 4.25 | 4.19 |
| Cortland | 217.3 | 3.57 | 3.51 |
| Declaration | 38.4 | 2.67 | 2.61 |
| Dreyfus | 4832.8 | 4.01 | 3.89 |
| Elfun | 81.7 | 4.51 | 4.41 |
| FFB Cash | 506.2 | 4.17 | 4.11 |
| Federated Master | 738.7 | 4.41 | 4.34 |
| Fidelity Cash | 13272.8 | 4.51 | 4.42 |
| Flex-fund | 172.8 | 4.60 | 4.48 |
| Fortis | 105.6 | 3.87 | 3.85 |
| Franklin Money | 996.8 | 3.97 | 3.92 |
| Freedom Cash | 1079.0 | 4.07 | 4.01 |
| Galaxy Money | 801.4 | 4.11 | 3.96 |
| Government Cash | 409.4 | 3.83 | 3.82 |
| Hanover Cash | 794.3 | 4.32 | 4.23 |
| Heritage Cash | 1008.3 | 4.08 | 4.00 |
| Infinity/Alpha | 53.6 | 3.99 | 3.91 |
| John Hancock | 226.4 | 3.93 | 3.87 |
| Landmark Funds | 481.3 | 4.28 | 4.26 |
| Liquid Cash | 388.9 | 4.61 | 4.64 |
| MarketWatch | 10.6 | 4.13 | 4.05 |
| Merrill Lynch Money | 27005.6 | 4.24 | 4.18 |
| NCC Funds | 113.4 | 4.22 | 4.20 |
| Nationwide | 517.3 | 4.22 | 4.14 |
| Overland | 291.5 | 4.26 | 4.17 |
| Pierpont Money | 1991.7 | 4.50 | 4.40 |
| Portico Money | 161.6 | 4.28 | 4.20 |
| Prudential MoneyMart | 6835.1 | 4.20 | 4.16 |
| Reserve Primary | 1408.8 | 3.91 | 3.86 |
| Schwab Money | 10531.0 | 4.16 | 4.07 |
| Smith Barney Cash | 2947.6 | 4.16 | 4.12 |
| Stagecoach | 1502.2 | 4.18 | 4.13 |
| Strong Money | 470.2 | 4.37 | 4.29 |
| Transamerica Cash | 175.5 | 4.20 | 4.19 |
| United Cash | 323.7 | 3.96 | 3.89 |
| Woodward Money | 1330.0 | 4.24 | 4.21 |

*Source: Barron's,* October 3, 1994.

**TABLE 8.7    SALES DATA FOR GULF REAL ESTATE PROPERTIES**

| Gulf View Condominiums | | | No Gulf View Condominiums | | |
|---|---|---|---|---|---|
| List Price | Sale Price | Days to Sell | List Price | Sale Price | Days to Sell |
| 495.0 | 475.0 | 130 | 217.0 | 217.0 | 182 |
| 379.0 | 350.0 | 71 | 148.0 | 135.5 | 338 |
| 529.0 | 519.0 | 85 | 186.5 | 179.0 | 122 |
| 552.5 | 534.5 | 95 | 239.0 | 230.0 | 150 |
| 334.9 | 334.9 | 119 | 279.0 | 267.5 | 169 |
| 550.0 | 505.0 | 92 | 215.0 | 214.0 | 58 |
| 169.9 | 165.0 | 197 | 279.0 | 259.0 | 110 |
| 210.0 | 210.0 | 56 | 179.9 | 176.5 | 130 |
| 975.0 | 945.0 | 73 | 149.9 | 144.9 | 149 |
| 314.0 | 314.0 | 126 | 235.0 | 230.0 | 114 |
| 315.0 | 305.0 | 88 | 199.8 | 192.0 | 120 |
| 885.0 | 800.0 | 282 | 210.0 | 195.0 | 61 |
| 975.0 | 975.0 | 100 | 226.0 | 212.0 | 146 |
| 469.0 | 445.0 | 56 | 149.9 | 146.5 | 137 |
| 329.0 | 305.0 | 49 | 160.0 | 160.0 | 281 |
| 365.0 | 330.0 | 48 | 322.0 | 292.5 | 63 |
| 332.0 | 312.0 | 88 | 187.5 | 179.0 | 48 |
| 520.0 | 495.0 | 161 | 247.0 | 227.0 | 52 |
| 425.0 | 405.0 | 149 | | | |
| 675.0 | 669.0 | 142 | | | |
| 409.0 | 400.0 | 28 | | | |
| 649.0 | 649.0 | 29 | | | |
| 319.0 | 305.0 | 140 | | | |
| 425.0 | 410.0 | 85 | | | |
| 359.0 | 340.0 | 107 | | | |
| 469.0 | 449.0 | 72 | | | |
| 895.0 | 875.0 | 129 | | | |
| 439.0 | 430.0 | 160 | | | |
| 435.0 | 400.0 | 206 | | | |
| 235.0 | 227.0 | 91 | | | |
| 638.0 | 618.0 | 100 | | | |
| 629.0 | 600.0 | 97 | | | |
| 329.0 | 309.0 | 114 | | | |
| 595.0 | 555.0 | 45 | | | |
| 339.0 | 315.0 | 150 | | | |
| 215.0 | 200.0 | 48 | | | |
| 395.0 | 375.0 | 135 | | | |
| 449.0 | 425.0 | 53 | | | |
| 499.0 | 465.0 | 86 | | | |
| 439.0 | 428.5 | 158 | | | |

**CD** file

**GulfProp**

each unit. Each condominium is classified as *Gulf View* if it is located directly on the Gulf of Mexico or *No Gulf View* if it is located on the bay or a golf course, near but not on the Gulf. Sample data from the multiple listing service in Naples, Florida, provided recent sales data for 40 Gulf View condominiums and 18 No Gulf View condominiums.* Prices are in thousands of dollars. The data are shown in Table 8.7.

---

*Data based on condominium sales reported in the Naples MLS (Coldwell Banker, June 2000).

## Managerial Report

1. Use appropriate descriptive statistics to summarize each of the three variables for the 40 Gulf View condominiums.
2. Use appropriate descriptive statistics to summarize each of the three variables for the 18 No Gulf View condominiums.
3. Compare your summary results. Discuss any specific statistical results that would help a real estate agent understand the condominium market.
4. Develop a 95% confidence interval estimate of the population mean sales price and population mean number of days to sell for Gulf View condominiums. Interpret your results.
5. Develop a 95% confidence interval estimate of the population mean sales price and population mean number of days to sell for No Gulf View condominiums. Interpret your results.
6. Assume the branch manager requested estimates of the mean selling price of Gulf View condominiums with a margin of error of $40,000 and the mean selling price of No Gulf View condominiums with a margin of error of $15,000. Using 95% confidence, how large should the sample sizes be?
7. Gulf Real Estate Properties just signed contracts for two new listings: a Gulf View condominium with a list price of $589,000 and a No Gulf View condominium with a list price of $285,000. What is your estimate of the final selling price and number of days required to sell each of these units?

## Case Problem 3   Metropolitan Research, Inc.

Metropolitan Research, Inc., a consumer research organization, conducts surveys designed to evaluate a wide variety of products and services available to consumers. In one particular study, Metropolitan looked at consumer satisfaction with the performance of automobiles produced by a major Detroit manufacturer. A questionnaire sent to owners of one of the manufacturer's full-sized cars revealed several complaints about early transmission problems. To learn more about the transmission failures, Metropolitan used a sample of actual transmission repairs provided by a transmission repair firm in the Detroit area. The following data show the actual number of miles driven for 50 vehicles at the time of transmission failure.

| 85,092 | 32,609 | 59,465 | 77,437 | 32,534 | 64,090 | 32,464 | 59,902 |
| 39,323 | 89,641 | 94,219 | 116,803 | 92,857 | 63,436 | 65,605 | 85,861 |
| 64,342 | 61,978 | 67,998 | 59,817 | 101,769 | 95,774 | 121,352 | 69,568 |
| 74,276 | 66,998 | 40,001 | 72,069 | 25,066 | 77,098 | 69,922 | 35,662 |
| 74,425 | 67,202 | 118,444 | 53,500 | 79,294 | 64,544 | 86,813 | 116,269 |
| 37,831 | 89,341 | 73,341 | 85,288 | 138,114 | 53,402 | 85,586 | 82,256 |
| 77,539 | 88,798 | | | | | | |

## Managerial Report

1. Use appropriate descriptive statistics to summarize the transmission failure data.
2. Develop a 95% confidence interval for the mean number of miles driven until transmission failure for the population of automobiles with transmission failure. Provide a managerial interpretation of the interval estimate.
3. Discuss the implication of your statistical finding in terms of the belief that some owners of the automobiles experienced early transmission failures.

4. How many repair records should be sampled if the research firm wants the population mean number of miles driven until transmission failure to be estimated with a margin of error of 5000 miles? Use 95% confidence.
5. What other information would you like to gather to evaluate the transmission failure problem more fully?

## Appendix 8.1    Interval Estimation with Minitab

We describe the use of Minitab in constructing confidence intervals for a population mean and a population proportion.

### Population Mean: $\sigma$ Known

CJW

We illustrate using the CJW example in Section 8.1. The satisfaction scores for the sample of 100 customers are in column C1 of a Minitab worksheet. The population standard deviation $\sigma = 20$ is assumed known. The following steps can be used to compute a 95% confidence interval estimate of the population mean.

**Step 1.** Select the **Stat** menu
**Step 2.** Choose **Basic Statistics**
**Step 3.** Choose **1-Sample Z**
**Step 4.** When the 1-Sample Z dialog box appears:
        Enter C1 in the **Samples in columns** box
        Enter 20 in the **Standard deviation** box
**Step 5.** Click **OK**

The Minitab default is a 95% confidence level. In order to specify a different confidence level such as 90%, add the following to step 4.

        Select **Options**
        When the 1-Sample Z-Options dialog box appears:
            Enter 90 in the **Confidence level** box
        Click **OK**

### Population Mean: $\sigma$ Unknown

Balance

We illustrate using the data in Table 8.3 showing the credit card balances for a sample of 85 households. The data are in column C1 of a Minitab worksheet. In this case the population standard deviation $\sigma$ will be estimated by the sample standard deviation $s$. The following steps can be used to compute a 95% confidence interval estimate of the population mean.

**Step 1.** Select the **Stat** menu
**Step 2.** Choose **Basic Statistics**
**Step 3.** Choose **1-Sample t**
**Step 4.** When the 1-Sample t dialog box appears:
        Enter C1 in the **Samples in columns** box
**Step 5.** Click **OK**

The Minitab default is a 95% confidence level. In order to specify a different confidence level such as 90%, add the following to step 4.

        Select **Options**
        When the 1-Sample t-Options dialog box appears:
            Enter 90 in the **Confidence level** box
        Click **OK**

## Population Proportion

**TeeTimes**

We illustrate using the survey data for women golfers presented in Section 8.4. The data are in column C1 of a Minitab worksheet. Individual responses are recorded as Yes if the golfer is satisfied with the availability of tee times and No otherwise. The following steps can be used to compute a 95% confidence interval estimate of the proportion of women golfers who are satisfied with the availability of tee times.

**Step 1.** Select the **Stat** menu
**Step 2.** Choose **Basic Statistics**
**Step 3.** Choose **1 Proportion**
**Step 4.** When the 1 Proportion dialog box appears:
      Enter C1 in the **Samples in columns** box
**Step 5.** Select **Options**
**Step 6.** When the 1 Proportion-Options dialog box appears:
      Select **Use test and interval based on normal distribution**
      Click **OK**
**Step 7.** Click **OK**

The Minitab default is a 95% confidence level. In order to specify a different confidence level such as 90%, enter 90 in the **Confidence Level** box when the 1 Proportion-Options dialog box appears in step 6.

*Note:* Minitab's 1 Proportion routine uses an alphabetical ordering of the responses and selects the *second response* for the population proportion of interest. In the women golfers example, Minitab used the alphabetical ordering No-Yes and then provided the confidence interval for the proportion of Yes responses. Because Yes was the response of interest, the Minitab output was fine. However, if Minitab's alphabetical ordering does not provide the response of interest, select any cell in the column and use the sequence: Editor > Column > Value Order. It will provide you with the option of entering a user-specified order. But you must list the response of interest second in the define-an-order box.

## Appendix 8.2   Interval Estimation Using Excel

We describe the use of Excel in constructing confidence intervals for a population mean and a population proportion.

### Population Mean: $\sigma$ Known

**CJW**

We illustrate using the CJW example in Section 8.1. The population standard deviation $\sigma = 20$ is assumed known. The satisfaction scores for the sample of 100 customers are in column A of an Excel worksheet. The following steps can be used to compute the margin of error for an estimate of the population mean. We begin by using Excel's Descriptive Statistics Tool described in Chapter 3.

**Step 1.** Select the **Tools** menu
**Step 2.** Choose **Data Analysis**
**Step 3.** Choose **Descriptive Statistics** from the list of Analysis Tools
**Step 4.** When the Descriptive Statistics dialog box appears:
      Enter A1:A101 in the **Input Range** box
      Select **Grouped by Columns**
      Select **Labels in First Row**
      Select **Output Range**

Enter C1 in the **Output Range** box
Select **Summary Statistics**
Click **OK**

The summary statistics will appear in columns C and D. Continue by computing the margin of error using Excel's Confidence function as follows:

**Step 5.**  Select cell C16 and enter the label Margin of Error
**Step 6.**  Select cell D16 and enter the Excel formula =CONFIDENCE(.05,20,100)

The three parameters of the Confidence function are:

Alpha = 1 − confidence coefficient = 1 − .95 = .05
The population standard deviation = 20
The sample size = 100 (Note this parameter appears as Count in cell D15)

The point estimate of the population mean is in cell D3 and the margin of error is in cell D16. The point estimate (82) and the margin of error (3.92) allow the confidence interval for the population mean to be easily computed.

## Population Mean: $\sigma$ Unknown

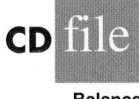

**Balance**

We illustrate using the data in Table 8.2, which show the credit card balances for a sample of 85 households. The data are in column A of an Excel worksheet. The following steps can be used to compute the point estimate and the margin of error for an interval estimate of a population mean. We will use Excel's Descriptive Statistics Tool described in Chapter 3.

**Step 1.**  Select the **Tools** menu
**Step 2.**  Choose **Data Analysis**
**Step 3.**  Choose **Descriptive Statistics** from the list of Analysis Tools
**Step 4.**  When the Descriptive Statistics dialog box appears:
    Enter A1:A86 in the **Input Range** box
    Select **Grouped by Columns**
    Select **Labels in First Row**
    Select **Output Range**
    Enter C1 in the Output Range box
    Select **Summary Statistics**
    Select **Confidence Level for Mean**
        Enter 95 in the Confidence Level for Mean box
    Click **OK**

The summary statistics will appear in columns C and D. The point estimate of the population mean appears in cell D3. The margin of error, labeled "Confidence Level(95.0%)," appears in cell D16. The point estimate ($5900) and the margin of error ($660) allow the confidence interval for the population mean to be easily computed. The output from this Excel procedure is shown in Figure 8.10.

## Population Proportion

We illustrate using the survey data for women golfers presented in Section 8.4. The data are in column A of an Excel worksheet. Individual responses are recorded as Yes if the golfer is satisfied with the availability of tee times and No otherwise. Excel does not offer a built-in routine to handle the estimation of a population proportion; however, it is relatively easy

FIGURE 8.10    INTERVAL ESTIMATION OF THE POPULATION MEAN CREDIT CARD
BALANCE USING EXCEL

| | A | B | C | D | E | F |
|---|---|---|---|---|---|---|
| 1 | **Balance** | | *Balance* | | | |
| 2 | 9619 | | | | | |
| 3 | 5364 | | Mean | 5900 | Point Estimate | |
| 4 | 8348 | | Standard Error | 331.7 | | |
| 5 | 7348 | | Median | 5759 | | |
| 6 | 381 | | Mode | 8047 | | |
| 7 | 2998 | | Standard Deviation | 3058 | | |
| 8 | 1686 | | Sample Variance | 9351364 | | |
| 9 | 1962 | | Kurtosis | 0.2327 | | |
| 10 | 4920 | | Skewness | 0.4076 | | |
| 11 | 5047 | | Range | 14061 | | |
| 12 | 6921 | | Minimum | 381 | | |
| 13 | 5759 | | Maximum | 14442 | | |
| 14 | 8047 | | Sum | 501500 | | |
| 15 | 3924 | | Count | 85 | Margin of Error | |
| 16 | 3470 | | Confidence Level(95.0%) | 660 | | |
| 17 | 5994 | | | | | |
| 81 | 5938 | | | | | |
| 82 | 5266 | | | | | |
| 83 | 10658 | | | | | |
| 84 | 3910 | | | | | |
| 85 | 7503 | | | | | |
| 86 | 1582 | | | | | |
| 87 | | | | | | |

*Note: Rows 18 to 80 are hidden.*

to develop an Excel template that can be used for this purpose. The template shown in Figure 8.11 provides the 95% confidence interval estimate of the proportion of women golfers who are satisfied with the availability of tee times. Note that the background worksheet in Figure 8.11 shows the cell formulas that provide the interval estimation results shown in the foreground worksheet. The following steps are necessary to use the template for this data set.

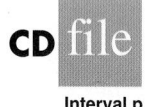

**CD** file

**Interval p**

**Step 1.** Enter the data range A2:A901 into the =COUNTA cell formula in cell D3
**Step 2.** Enter Yes as the response of interest in cell D4
**Step 3.** Enter the data range A2:A901 into the =COUNTIF cell formula in cell D5
**Step 4.** Enter .95 as the confidence coefficient in cell D8

The template automatically provides the confidence interval in cells D15 and D16.

This template can be used to compute the confidence interval for a population proportion for other applications. For instance, to compute the interval estimate for a new data set, enter the new sample data into column A of the worksheet and then make the changes to the four cells as shown. If the new sample data have already been summarized, the sample data do not have to be entered into the worksheet. In this case, enter the sample size into cell D3 and the sample proportion into cell D6; the worksheet template will then provide the confidence interval for the population proportion. The worksheet in Figure 8.11 is available in the file Interval p on the CD that accompanies this book.

FIGURE 8.11   EXCEL TEMPLATE FOR INTERVAL ESTIMATION OF A POPULATION PROPORTION

| | A | B | C | D | E |
|---|---|---|---|---|---|
| 1 | **Response** | | **Interval Estimate of a Population Proportion** | | |
| 2 | Yes | | | | |
| 3 | No | | **Sample Size** | =COUNTA(A2:A901) | |
| 4 | Yes | | **Response of Interest** | Yes | |
| 5 | Yes | | **Count for Response** | =COUNTIF(A2:A901,D4) | |
| 6 | No | | **Sample Proportion** | =D5/D3 | |
| 7 | No | | | | |
| 8 | No | | **Confidence Coefficient** | 0.95 | |
| 9 | Yes | | **z Value** | =NORMSINV(0.5+D8/2) | |
| 10 | Yes | | | | |
| 11 | Yes | | **Standard Error** | =SQRT(D6*(1-D6)/D3) | |
| 12 | No | | **Margin of Error** | =D9*D11 | |
| 13 | No | | | | |
| 14 | Yes | | **Point Estimate** | =D6 | |
| 15 | No | | **Lower Limit** | =D14-D12 | |
| 16 | No | | **Upper Limit** | =D14+D12 | |
| 17 | Yes | | | | |
| 18 | No | | | | |
| 901 | Yes | | | | |
| 902 | | | | | |

*Note: Rows 19 to 900 are hidden.*

| | A | B | C | D | E | F | G |
|---|---|---|---|---|---|---|---|
| 1 | **Response** | | **Interval Estimate of a Population Proportion** | | | | |
| 2 | Yes | | | | | | |
| 3 | No | | **Sample Size** | 900 | | Enter the response of interest. | |
| 4 | Yes | | **Response of Interest** | Yes | | | |
| 5 | Yes | | **Count for Response** | 396 | | | |
| 6 | No | | **Sample Proportion** | 0.4400 | | | |
| 7 | No | | | | | Enter the Confidence Coefficient | |
| 8 | No | | **Confidence Coefficient** | 0.95 | | | |
| 9 | Yes | | **z Value** | 1.960 | | | |
| 10 | Yes | | | | | | |
| 11 | Yes | | **Standard Error** | 0.0165 | | | |
| 12 | No | | **Margin of Error** | 0.0324 | | | |
| 13 | No | | | | | | |
| 14 | Yes | | **Point Estimate** | 0.4400 | | | |
| 15 | No | | **Lower Limit** | 0.4076 | | | |
| 16 | No | | **Upper Limit** | 0.4724 | | | |
| 17 | Yes | | | | | | |
| 18 | No | | | | | | |
| 901 | Yes | | | | | | |
| 902 | | | | | | | |

# Hypothesis Tests

**CONTENTS**

STATISTICS IN PRACTICE:
JOHN MORRELL & COMPANY

## STATISTICS *in* PRACTICE

### JOHN MORRELL & COMPANY*
*CINCINNATI, OHIO*

John Morrell & Company, which began in England in 1827, is considered the oldest continuously operating meat manufacturer in the United States. It is a wholly owned and independently managed subsidiary of Smithfield Foods, Smithfield, Virginia. John Morrell & Company offers an extensive product line of processed meats and fresh pork to consumers under 13 regional brands including John Morrell, E-Z-Cut, Tobin's First Prize, Dinner Bell, Hunter, Kretschmar, Rath, Rodeo, Shenson, Farmers Hickory Brand, Iowa Quality, and Peyton's. Each regional brand enjoys high brand recognition and loyalty among consumers.

Market research at Morrell provides management with up-to-date information on the company's various products and how the products compare with competing brands of similar products. A recent study investigated consumer preference for Morrell's Convenient Cuisine Beef Pot Roast compared to similar beef products from two major competitors. In the three-product comparison test, a sample of consumers was used to indicate how the products rated in terms of taste, appearance, aroma, and overall preference.

One research question concerned whether Morrell's Convenient Cuisine Beef Pot Roast was the preferred choice of more than 50% of the consumer population. Letting $p$ indicate the population proportion preferring Morrell's product, the hypothesis test for the research question is as follows:

$$H_0: p \leq .50$$
$$H_a: p > .50$$

The null hypothesis $H_0$ indicates the preference for Morrell's product is less than or equal to 50%. If the sample data sup-

Convenient Cuisine fully-cooked entrees allow consumers to heat and serve in the same microwaveable tray. © Courtesy of John Morrell's Convenient Cuisine products.

port rejecting $H_0$ in favor of the alternate hypothesis $H_a$, Morrell will draw the research conclusion that in a three-product comparison, their product is preferred by more than 50% of the consumer population.

In an independent taste test study using a sample of 224 consumers in Cincinnati, Milwaukee, and Los Angeles, 150 consumers selected the Morrell Convenient Cuisine Beef Pot Roast as the preferred product. Using statistical hypothesis testing procedures, the null hypothesis $H_0$ was rejected. The study provided statistical evidence supporting $H_a$ and the conclusion that the Morrell product is preferred by more than 50% of the consumer population.

The point estimate of the population proportion was $\bar{p} = 150/224 = .67$. Thus, the sample data provided support for a food magazine advertisement showing that in a three-product taste comparison, Morrell's Convenient Cuisine Beef Pot Roast was "preferred 2 to 1 over the competition."

In this chapter we will discuss how to formulate hypotheses and how to conduct tests like the one used by Morrell. Through the analysis of sample data, we will be able to determine whether a hypothesis should or should not be rejected.

---

*The authors are indebted to Marty Butler, vice president of Marketing, John Morrell, for providing this Statistics in Practice.

---

In Chapters 7 and 8 we showed how a sample could be used to develop point and interval estimates of population parameters. In this chapter we continue the discussion of statistical inference by showing how hypothesis testing can be used to determine whether a statement about the value of a population parameter should or should not be rejected.

In hypothesis testing we begin by making a tentative assumption about a population parameter. This tentative assumption is called the **null hypothesis** and is denoted by $H_0$. We then define another hypothesis, called the **alternative hypothesis**, which is the opposite of what is stated in the null hypothesis. The alternative hypothesis is denoted by $H_a$.

The hypothesis testing procedure uses data from a sample to test the two competing statements indicated by $H_0$ and $H_a$.

This chapter shows how hypothesis tests can be conducted about a population mean and a population proportion. We begin by providing examples that illustrate approaches to developing null and alternative hypotheses.

## 9.1  Developing Null and Alternative Hypotheses

*Learning to formulate hypotheses correctly will take practice. Expect some initial confusion over the proper choice for $H_0$ and $H_a$. The examples in this section show a variety of forms for $H_0$ and $H_a$ depending upon the application.*

In some applications it may not be obvious how the null and alternative hypotheses should be formulated. Care must be taken to structure the hypotheses appropriately so that the hypothesis testing conclusion provides the information the researcher or decision maker wants. Guidelines for establishing the null and alternative hypotheses will be given for three types of situations in which hypothesis testing procedures are commonly employed.

### Testing Research Hypotheses

Consider a particular automobile model that currently attains an average fuel efficiency of 24 miles per gallon. A product research group developed a new fuel injection system specifically designed to increase the miles-per-gallon rating. To evaluate the new system, several will be manufactured, installed in automobiles, and subjected to research-controlled driving tests. Here the product research group is looking for evidence to conclude that the new system *increases* the mean miles-per-gallon rating. In this case, the research hypothesis is that the new fuel injection system will provide a mean miles-per-gallon rating exceeding 24; that is, $\mu > 24$. As a general guideline, a research hypothesis should be stated as the *alternative hypothesis*. Hence, the appropriate null and alternative hypotheses for the study are:

$$H_0: \mu \leq 24$$
$$H_a: \mu > 24$$

*The conclusion that the research hypothesis is true is made if the sample data contradict the null hypothesis.*

If the sample results indicate that $H_0$ cannot be rejected, researchers cannot conclude that the new fuel injection system is better. Perhaps more research and subsequent testing should be conducted. However, if the sample results indicate that $H_0$ can be rejected, researchers can make the inference that $H_a: \mu > 24$ is true. With this conclusion, the researchers gain the statistical support necessary to state that the new system increases the mean number of miles per gallon. Production with the new system should be considered.

In research studies such as these, the null and alternative hypotheses should be formulated so that the rejection of $H_0$ supports the research conclusion. The research hypothesis therefore should be expressed as the alternative hypothesis.

### Testing the Validity of a Claim

As an illustration of testing the validity of a claim, consider the situation of a manufacturer of soft drinks who states that it fills two-liter containers of its products with an average of at least 67.6 fluid ounces. A sample of two-liter containers will be selected, and the contents will be measured to test the manufacturer's claim. In this type of hypothesis testing situation, we generally assume that the manufacturer's claim is true unless the sample evidence is contradictory. Using this approach for the soft-drink example, we would state the null and alternative hypotheses as follows.

$$H_0: \mu \geq 67.6$$
$$H_a: \mu < 67.6$$

*A manufacturer's claim is usually given the benefit of the doubt and stated as the null hypothesis. The conclusion that the claim is false can be made if the null hypothesis is rejected.*

If the sample results indicate $H_0$ cannot be rejected, the manufacturer's claim will not be challenged. However, if the sample results indicate $H_0$ can be rejected, the inference will be made that $H_a$: $\mu < 67.6$ is true. With this conclusion, statistical evidence indicates that the manufacturer's claim is incorrect and that the soft-drink containers are being filled with a mean less than the claimed 67.6 ounces. Appropriate action against the manufacturer may be considered.

In any situation that involves testing the validity of a claim, the null hypothesis is generally based on the assumption that the claim is true. The alternative hypothesis is then formulated so that rejection of $H_0$ will provide statistical evidence that the stated assumption is incorrect. Action to correct the claim should be considered whenever $H_0$ is rejected.

## Testing in Decision-Making Situations

In testing research hypotheses or testing the validity of a claim, action is taken if $H_0$ is rejected. In many instances, however, action must be taken both when $H_0$ cannot be rejected and when $H_0$ can be rejected. In general, this type of situation occurs when a decision maker must choose between two courses of action, one associated with the null hypothesis and another associated with the alternative hypothesis. For example, on the basis of a sample of parts from a shipment just received, a quality control inspector must decide whether to accept the shipment or to return the shipment to the supplier because it does not meet specifications. Assume that specifications for a particular part require a mean length of two inches per part. If the mean length is greater or less than the two-inch standard, the parts will cause quality problems in the assembly operation. In this case, the null and alternative hypotheses would be formulated as follows.

$$H_0: \mu = 2$$
$$H_a: \mu \neq 2$$

If the sample results indicate $H_0$ cannot be rejected, the quality control inspector will have no reason to doubt that the shipment meets specifications, and the shipment will be accepted. However, if the sample results indicate $H_0$ should be rejected, the conclusion will be that the parts do not meet specifications. In this case, the quality control inspector will have sufficient evidence to return the shipment to the supplier. Thus, we see that for these types of situations, action is taken both when $H_0$ cannot be rejected and when $H_0$ can be rejected.

## Summary of Forms for Null and Alternative Hypotheses

The hypothesis tests in this chapter involve two population parameters: the population mean and the population proportion. Depending on the situation, hypothesis tests about a population parameter may take one of three forms: two use inequalities in the null hypothesis; the third uses an equality in the null hypothesis. For hypothesis tests involving a population mean, we let $\mu_0$ denote the hypothesized value and we must choose one of the following three forms for the hypothesis test.

*The three possible forms of hypotheses $H_0$ and $H_a$ are shown here. Note that the equality always appears in the null hypothesis $H_0$.*

$$H_0: \mu \geq \mu_0 \qquad H_0: \mu \leq \mu_0 \qquad H_0: \mu = \mu_0$$
$$H_a: \mu < \mu_0 \qquad H_a: \mu > \mu_0 \qquad H_a: \mu \neq \mu_0$$

For reasons that will be clear later, the first two forms are called one-tailed tests. The third form is called a two-tailed test.

In many situations, the choice of $H_0$ and $H_a$ is not obvious and judgment is necessary to select the proper form. However, as the preceding forms show, the equality part of the expression (either $\geq$, $\leq$, or $=$) *always* appears in the null hypothesis. In selecting the proper form of $H_0$ and $H_a$, keep in mind that the alternative hypothesis is often what the test is attempting to establish. Hence, asking whether the user is looking for evidence to support $\mu < \mu_0$, $\mu > \mu_0$, or $\mu \neq \mu_0$ will help determine $H_a$. The following exercises are designed to provide practice in choosing the proper form for a hypothesis test involving a population mean.

## Exercises

1. The manager of the Danvers-Hilton Resort Hotel stated that the mean guest bill for a weekend is $600 or less. A member of the hotel's accounting staff noticed that the total charges for guest bills have been increasing in recent months. The accountant will use a sample of weekend guest bills to test the manager's claim.
   a. Which form of the hypotheses should be used to test the manager's claim? Explain.

   $$H_0: \mu \geq 600 \qquad H_0: \mu \leq 600 \qquad H_0: \mu = 600$$
   $$H_a: \mu < 600 \qquad H_a: \mu > 600 \qquad H_a: \mu \neq 600$$

   b. What conclusion is appropriate when $H_0$ cannot be rejected?
   c. What conclusion is appropriate when $H_0$ can be rejected?

2. The manager of an automobile dealership is considering a new bonus plan designed to increase sales volume. Currently, the mean sales volume is 14 automobiles per month. The manager wants to conduct a research study to see whether the new bonus plan increases sales volume. To collect data on the plan, a sample of sales personnel will be allowed to sell under the new bonus plan for a one-month period.
   a. Develop the null and alternative hypotheses most appropriate for this research situation.
   b. Comment on the conclusion when $H_0$ cannot be rejected.
   c. Comment on the conclusion when $H_0$ can be rejected.

3. A production line operation is designed to fill cartons with laundry detergent to a mean weight of 32 ounces. A sample of cartons is periodically selected and weighed to determine whether underfilling or overfilling is occurring. If the sample data lead to a conclusion of underfilling or overfilling, the production line will be shut down and adjusted to obtain proper filling.
   a. Formulate the null and alternative hypotheses that will help in deciding whether to shut down and adjust the production line.
   b. Comment on the conclusion and the decision when $H_0$ cannot be rejected.
   c. Comment on the conclusion and the decision when $H_0$ can be rejected.

4. Because of high production-changeover time and costs, a director of manufacturing must convince management that a proposed manufacturing method reduces costs before the new method can be implemented. The current production method operates with a mean cost of $220 per hour. A research study will measure the cost of the new method over a sample production period.
   a. Develop the null and alternative hypotheses most appropriate for this study.
   b. Comment on the conclusion when $H_0$ cannot be rejected.
   c. Comment on the conclusion when $H_0$ can be rejected.

## 9.2 Type I and Type II Errors

The null and alternative hypotheses are competing statements about the population. Either the null hypothesis $H_0$ is true or the alternative hypothesis $H_a$ is true, but not both. Ideally the hypothesis testing procedure should lead to the acceptance of $H_0$ when $H_0$ is true and the

TABLE 9.1    ERRORS AND CORRECT CONCLUSIONS IN HYPOTHESIS TESTING

|  |  | Population Condition | |
|---|---|---|---|
|  |  | $H_0$ True | $H_a$ True |
|  | Accept $H_0$ | Correct Conclusion | Type II Error |
| Conclusion |  |  |  |
|  | Reject $H_0$ | Type I Error | Correct Conclusion |

rejection of $H_0$ when $H_a$ is true. Unfortunately, the correct conclusions are not always possible. Because hypothesis tests are based on sample information, we must allow for the possibility of errors. Table 9.1 illustrates the two kinds of errors that can be made in hypothesis testing.

The first row of Table 9.1 shows what can happen if the conclusion is to accept $H_0$. If $H_0$ is true, this conclusion is correct. However, if $H_a$ is true, we make a **Type II error**; that is, we accept $H_0$ when it is false. The second row of Table 9.1 shows what can happen if the conclusion is to reject $H_0$. If $H_0$ is true, we make a **Type I error**; that is, we reject $H_0$ when it is true. However, if $H_a$ is true, rejecting $H_0$ is correct.

Recall the hypothesis testing illustration discussed in Section 9.1 in which an automobile product research group developed a new fuel injection system designed to increase the miles-per-gallon rating of a particular automobile. With the current model obtaining an average of 24 miles per gallon, the hypothesis test was formulated as follows.

$$H_0: \mu \leq 24$$
$$H_a: \mu > 24$$

The alternative hypothesis, $H_a: \mu > 24$, indicates that the researchers are looking for sample evidence to support the conclusion that the population mean miles per gallon with the new fuel injection system is greater than 24.

In this application, the Type I error of rejecting $H_0$ when it is true corresponds to the researchers claiming that the new system improves the miles-per-gallon rating ($\mu > 24$) when in fact the new system is not any better than the current system. In contrast, the Type II error of accepting $H_0$ when it is false corresponds to the researchers concluding that the new system is not any better than the current system ($\mu \leq 24$) when in fact the new system improves miles-per-gallon performance.

For the miles-per-gallon rating hypothesis test, the null hypothesis is $H_0: \mu \leq 24$. Suppose the null hypothesis is true as an equality; that is, $\mu = 24$. The probability of making a Type I error when the null hypothesis is true as an equality is called the **level of significance**. Thus, for the miles-per-gallon rating hypothesis test, the level of significance is the probability of rejecting $H_0: \mu \leq 24$ when $\mu = 24$. Because of the importance of this concept, we now restate the definition of level of significance.

LEVEL OF SIGNIFICANCE

The level of significance is the probability of making a Type I error when the null hypothesis is true as an equality.

The Greek symbol $\alpha$ (alpha) is used to denote the level of significance, and common choices for $\alpha$ are .05 and .01.

In practice, the person conducting the hypothesis test specifies the level of significance. By selecting $\alpha$, that person is controlling the probability of making a Type I error. If the cost of making a Type I error is high, small values of $\alpha$ are preferred. If the cost of making a Type I error is not too high, larger values of $\alpha$ are typically used. Applications of hypothesis testing that only control for the Type I error are often called *significance tests*. Most applications of hypothesis testing are of this type.

Although most applications of hypothesis testing control for the probability of making a Type I error, they do not always control for the probability of making a Type II error. Hence, if we decide to accept $H_0$, we cannot determine how confident we can be with that decision. Because of the uncertainty associated with making a Type II error, statisticians often recommend that we use the statement "do not reject $H_0$" instead of "accept $H_0$." Using the statement "do not reject $H_0$" carries the recommendation to withhold both judgment and action. In effect, by not directly accepting $H_0$, the statistician avoids the risk of making a Type II error. Whenever the probability of making a Type II error has not been determined and controlled, we will not make the statement "accept $H_0$." In such cases, only two conclusions are possible: *do not reject $H_0$ or reject $H_0$.*

Although controlling for a Type II error in hypothesis testing is not common, it can be done. In Sections 9.7 and 9.8 we will illustrate procedures for determining and controlling the probability of making a Type II error. If proper controls have been established for this error, action based on the "accept $H_0$" conclusion can be appropriate.

*If the sample data are consistent with the null hypothesis $H_0$, we will follow the practice of concluding "do not reject $H_0$." This conclusion is preferred over "accept $H_0$," because the conclusion to accept $H_0$ puts us at risk of making a Type II error.*

## Exercises

5. Americans spend an average of 8.6 minutes per day reading newspapers (*USA Today*, April 10, 1995). A researcher believes that individuals in management positions spend more than the national average time per day reading newspapers. A sample of individuals in management positions will be selected by the researcher. Data on newspaper-reading times will be used to test the following null and alternative hypotheses.

$$H_0: \mu \leq 8.6$$
$$H_a: \mu > 8.6$$

   a. What is the Type I error in this situation? What are the consequences of making this error?
   b. What is the Type II error in this situation? What are the consequences of making this error?

6. The label on a 3-quart container of orange juice claims that the orange juice contains an average of 1 gram of fat or less. Answer the following questions for a hypothesis test that could be used to test the claim on the label.
   a. Develop the appropriate null and alternative hypotheses.
   b. What is the Type I error in this situation? What are the consequences of making this error?
   c. What is the Type II error in this situation? What are the consequences of making this error?

7. Carpetland salespersons average $8000 per week in sales. Steve Contois, the firm's vice president, proposes a compensation plan with new selling incentives. Steve hopes that the results of a trial selling period will enable him to conclude that the compensation plan increases the average sales per salesperson.
   a. Develop the appropriate null and alternative hypotheses.
   b. What is the Type I error in this situation? What are the consequences of making this error?
   c. What is the Type II error in this situation? What are the consequences of making this error?

8.  Suppose a new production method will be implemented if a hypothesis test supports the conclusion that the new method reduces the mean operating cost per hour.
    a.  State the appropriate null and alternative hypotheses if the mean cost for the current production method is $220 per hour.
    b.  What is the Type I error in this situation? What are the consequences of making this error?
    c.  What is the Type II error in this situation? What are the consequences of making this error?

# 9.3   Population Mean: $\sigma$ Known

In Chapter 8 we said that the $\sigma$ known case corresponds to applications in which historical data and/or other information is available that enable us to obtain a good estimate of the population standard deviation prior to sampling. In such cases the population standard deviation can, for all practical purposes, be considered known. In this section we show how to conduct a hypothesis test about a population mean for the $\sigma$ known case.

The methods presented in this section are exact if the sample is selected from a population that is normally distributed. In cases where it is not reasonable to assume the population is normally distributed, these methods are still applicable if the sample size is large enough. We provide some practical advice concerning the population distribution and the sample size at the end of this section.

## One-Tailed Test

**One-tailed tests** about a population mean take one of the following two forms.

| Lower Tail Test | Upper Tail Test |
|---|---|
| $H_0: \mu \geq \mu_0$ | $H_0: \mu \leq \mu_0$ |
| $H_a: \mu < \mu_0$ | $H_a: \mu > \mu_0$ |

Let us consider an example involving a lower tail test.

The Federal Trade Commission (FTC) periodically conducts statistical studies designed to test the claims that manufacturers make about their products. For example, the label on a large can of Hilltop Coffee states that the can contains 3 pounds of coffee. The FTC knows that Hilltop's production process cannot place exactly 3 pounds of coffee in each can, even if the mean filling weight for the population of all cans filled is 3 pounds per can. However, as long as the population mean filling weight is at least 3 pounds per can, the rights of consumers will be protected. Thus, the FTC interprets the label information on a large can of coffee as a claim by Hilltop that the population mean filling weight is at least 3 pounds per can. We will show how the FTC can check Hilltop's claim by conducting a lower tail hypothesis test.

The first step is to develop the null and alternative hypotheses for the test. If the population mean filling weight is at least 3 pounds per can, Hilltop's claim is correct. This establishes the null hypothesis for the test. However, if the population mean weight is less than 3 pounds per can, Hilltop's claim is incorrect. This establishes the alternative hypothesis. With $\mu$ denoting the population mean filling weight, the null and alternative hypotheses are as follows:

$$H_0: \mu \geq 3$$
$$H_a: \mu < 3$$

Note that the hypothesized value of the population mean is $\mu_0 = 3$.

If the sample data indicate that $H_0$ cannot be rejected, the statistical evidence does not support the conclusion that a label violation has occurred. Hence, no action should be taken against Hilltop. However, if the sample data indicate $H_0$ can be rejected, we will conclude that the alternative hypothesis, $H_a$: $\mu < 3$, is true. In this case a conclusion of underfilling and a charge of a label violation against Hilltop would be justified.

Suppose a sample of 36 cans of coffee is selected and the sample mean $\bar{x}$ is computed as an estimate of the population mean $\mu$. If the value of the sample mean $\bar{x}$ is less than 3 pounds, the sample results will cast doubt on the null hypothesis. What we want to know is how much less than 3 pounds must $\bar{x}$ be before we would be willing to declare the difference significant and risk making a Type I error by falsely accusing Hilltop of a label violation. A key factor in addressing this issue is the value the decision maker selects for the level of significance.

As noted in the preceding section, the level of significance, denoted by $\alpha$, is the probability of making a Type I error by rejecting $H_0$ when the null hypothesis is true as an equality. The decision maker must specify the level of significance. If the cost of making a Type I error is high, a small value should be chosen for the level of significance. If the cost is not high, a larger value is more appropriate. In the Hilltop Coffee study, the director of the FTC's testing program made the following statement: "If the company is meeting its weight specifications at $\mu = 3$, I would like a 99% chance of not taking any action against the company. Although I do not want to accuse the company wrongly of underfilling its product, I am willing to risk a 1% chance of making such an error." From the director's statement, we set the level of significance for the hypothesis test at $\alpha = .01$. Thus, we must design the hypothesis test so that the probability of making a Type I error when $\mu = 3$ is .01.

For the Hilltop Coffee study, by developing the null and alternative hypotheses and specifying the level of significance for the test, we carry out the first two steps required in conducting every hypothesis test. We are now ready to perform the third step of hypothesis testing: collect the sample data and compute the value of what is called a test statistic.

**Test statistic**  For the Hilltop Coffee study, previous FTC tests show that the population standard deviation can be assumed known with a value of $\sigma = .18$. In addition, these tests also show that the population of filling weights can be assumed to have a normal distribution. From the study of sampling distributions in Chapter 7 we know that if the population from which we are sampling is normally distributed, the sampling distribution of $\bar{x}$ will also be normally distributed. Thus, for the Hilltop Coffee study, the sampling distribution of $\bar{x}$ is normally distributed. With a known value of $\sigma = .18$ and a sample size of $n = 36$, Figure 9.1 shows the sampling distribution of $\bar{x}$ when the null hypothesis is true

FIGURE 9.1    SAMPLING DISTRIBUTION OF $\bar{x}$ FOR THE HILLTOP COFFEE STUDY WHEN THE NULL HYPOTHESIS IS TRUE AS AN EQUALITY ($\mu_0 = 3$)

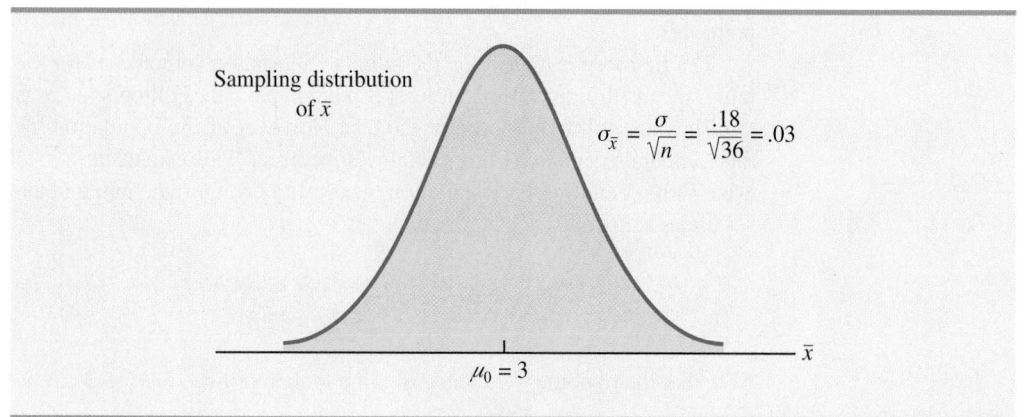

*The standard error of $\bar{x}$ is the standard deviation of the sampling distribution of $\bar{x}$.*

as an equality; that is, when $\mu = \mu_0 = 3$.* Note that the standard error of $\bar{x}$ is given by $\sigma_{\bar{x}} = \sigma/\sqrt{n} = .18/\sqrt{36} = .03$.

Because the sampling distribution of $\bar{x}$ is normally distributed, the sampling distribution of

$$z = \frac{\bar{x} - \mu_0}{\sigma_{\bar{x}}} = \frac{\bar{x} - 3}{.03}$$

is a standard normal distribution. A value of $z = -1$ means that the value of $\bar{x}$ is one standard error below the mean, a value of $z = -2$ means that the value of $\bar{x}$ is two standard errors below the mean, and so on. We can use the standard normal distribution table to find the lower tail probability corresponding to any $z$ value. For instance, the standard normal table shows that the area between the mean and $z = -3.00$ is .4986. Hence, the probability of obtaining a value of $z$ that is three or more standard errors below the mean is $.5000 - .4986 = .0014$. As a result, the probability of obtaining a value of $\bar{x}$ that is 3 or more standard errors below the hypothesized population mean $\mu_0 = 3$ is also .0014. Such a result is unlikely if the null hypothesis is true.

For hypothesis tests about a population mean for the $\sigma$ known case, we use the standard normal random variable $z$ as a **test statistic** to determine whether $\bar{x}$ deviates from the hypothesized value $\mu_0$ enough to justify rejecting the null hypothesis. With $\sigma_{\bar{x}} = \sigma/\sqrt{n}$, the test statistic used in the $\sigma$ known case is as follows.

---

**TEST STATISTIC FOR HYPOTHESIS TESTS ABOUT A POPULATION MEAN: $\sigma$ KNOWN**

$$z = \frac{\bar{x} - \mu_0}{\sigma/\sqrt{n}} \tag{9.1}$$

---

The key question for a lower tail test is: How small must the test statistic $z$ be before we choose to reject the null hypothesis? Two approaches can be used to answer this question.

The first approach uses the value of the test statistic $z$ to compute a probability called a *p*-value. The *p*-value measures the support (or lack of support) provided by the sample for the null hypothesis, and is the basis for determining whether the null hypothesis should be rejected given the level of significance. The second approach requires that we first determine a value for the test statistic called the **critical value**. For a lower tail test, the critical value serves as a benchmark for determining whether the value of the test statistic is small enough to reject the null hypothesis. We begin with the *p*-value approach.

*p*-**value approach**  In practice, the *p*-value approach has become the preferred method of determining whether the null hypothesis can be rejected, especially when using computer software packages such as Minitab and Excel. To begin our discussion of the use of *p*-values in hypothesis testing, we now provide a formal definition for a *p*-value.

---

*p*-VALUE

The *p*-value is a probability, computed using the test statistic, that measures the support (or lack of support) provided by the sample for the null hypothesis.

---

*In constructing sampling distributions for hypothesis tests, it is assumed that $H_0$ is satisfied as an equality.

Because a p-value is a probability, it ranges from 0 to 1. In general, the smaller the p-value, the less support it indicates for the null hypothesis. A small p-value indicates a sample result that is unusual given the assumption that $H_0$ is true. Small p-values lead to rejection of $H_0$, whereas large p-values indicate the null hypothesis should not be rejected.

Two steps are required to use the p-value approach. First, we must use the value of the test statistic to compute the p-value. The method used to compute a p-value depends on whether the test is lower tail, upper tail, or a two-tailed test. For a lower tail test, the p-value is the probability of obtaining a value for the test statistic at least as small as that provided by the sample. Thus, to compute the p-value for the lower tail test in the σ known case, we must find the area under the standard normal curve to the left of the test statistic. After computing the p-value, we must then decide whether it is small enough to reject the null hypothesis; as we will show, this involves comparing it to the level of significance.

Let us now illustrate the p-value approach by computing the p-value for the Hilltop Coffee lower tail test.

**Coffee**

Suppose the sample of 36 Hilltop coffee cans provides a sample mean of $\bar{x} = 2.92$ pounds. Is $\bar{x} = 2.92$ small enough to cause us to reject $H_0$? Because this test is a lower tail test, the p-value is the area under the standard normal curve to the left of the test statistic. Using $\bar{x} = 2.92$, $\sigma = .18$, and $n = 36$, we compute the value of the test statistic z.

$$z = \frac{\bar{x} - \mu_0}{\sigma/\sqrt{n}} = \frac{2.92 - 3}{.18/\sqrt{36}} = -2.67$$

Thus, the p-value is the probability that the test statistic z is less than or equal to −2.67 (the area under the standard normal curve to the left of the test statistic).

Using the standard normal distribution table, we find that the area between the mean and $z = -2.67$ is .4962. Thus, the p-value is $.5000 - .4962 = .0038$. Figure 9.2 shows that $\bar{x} = 2.92$ corresponds to $z = -2.67$ and a p-value $= .0038$. This p-value indicates a small probability of obtaining a sample mean of $\bar{x} = 2.92$ or smaller when sampling from a population with $\mu = 3$. This p-value does not provide much support for the null hypothesis, but is it small enough to cause us to reject $H_0$? The answer depends upon the level of significance for the test.

As noted previously, the director of the FTC's testing program selected a value of .01 for the level of significance. The selection of $\alpha = .01$ means that the director is willing to accept a probability of .01 of rejecting the null hypothesis when it is true as an equality ($\mu_0 = 3$). The sample of 36 coffee cans in the Hilltop Coffee study resulted in a p-value $= .0038$, which means that the probability of obtaining a value of $\bar{x} = 2.92$ or less when the null hypothesis is true as an equality is .0038. Because .0038 is less than or equal to $\alpha = .01$, we reject $H_0$. Therefore, we find sufficient statistical evidence to reject the null hypothesis at the .01 level of significance.

We can now state the general rule for determining whether the null hypothesis can be rejected when using the p-value approach. For a level of significance $\alpha$, the rejection rule using the p-value approach is as follows:

---

REJECTION RULE USING p-VALUE

Reject $H_0$ if p-value $\leq \alpha$

---

In the Hilltop Coffee test, the p-value of .0038 resulted in the rejection of the null hypothesis. Although the basis for making the rejection decision involves a comparison of the p-value to the level of significance specified by the FTC director, the observed p-value of

FIGURE 9.2   *p*-VALUE FOR THE HILLTOP COFFEE STUDY WHEN $\bar{x} = 2.92$ AND $z = -2.67$

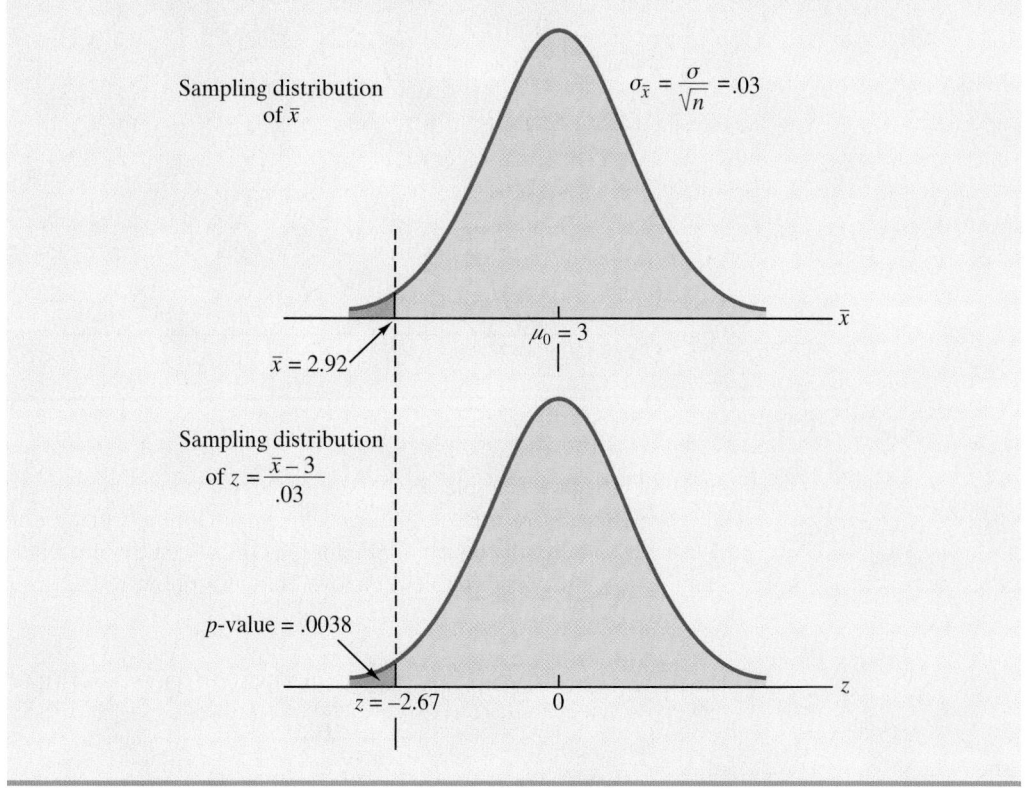

.0038 means that we would reject $H_0$ for any value $\alpha \geq .0038$. For this reason, the *p*-value is also called the *observed level of significance.*

Different decision makers may express different opinions concerning the cost of making a Type I error and may choose a different level of significance. By providing the *p*-value as part of the hypothesis testing results, another decision maker can compare the reported *p*-value to his or her own level of significance and possibly make a different decision with respect to rejecting $H_0$.

**Critical value approach**   For a lower tail test, the critical value is the value of the test statistic that corresponds to an area of $\alpha$ (the level of significance) in the lower tail of the sampling distribution of the test statistic. In other words, the critical value is the largest value of the test statistic that will result in the rejection of the null hypothesis. Let us return to the Hilltop Coffee example and see how this approach works.

In the $\sigma$ known case, the sampling distribution for the test statistic $z$ is a standard normal distribution. Therefore, the critical value is the value of the test statistic that corresponds to an area of $\alpha = .01$ in the lower tail of a standard normal distribution. Using the standard normal distribution table, we find that $z = -2.33$ provides an area of .01 in the lower tail (see Figure 9.3). Thus, if the sample results in a value of the test statistic that is less than or equal to $-2.33$, the corresponding *p*-value will be less than or equal to .01; in this case, we should reject the null hypothesis. Hence, for the Hilltop Coffee study the critical value rejection rule for a level of significance of .01 is

$$\text{Reject } H_0 \text{ if } z \leq -2.33$$

FIGURE 9.3 CRITICAL VALUE FOR THE HILLTOP COFFEE HYPOTHESIS TEST

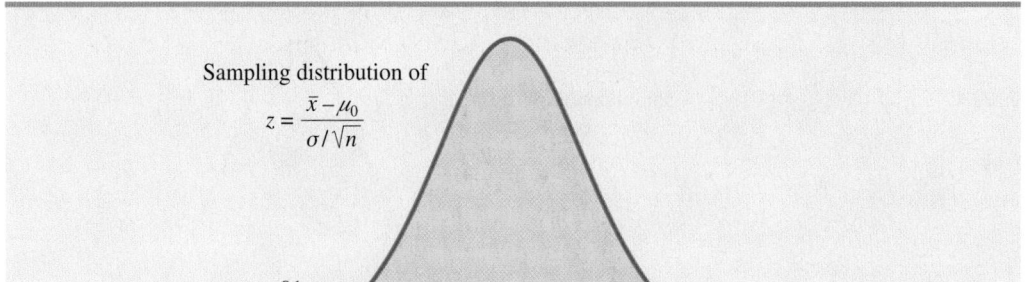

In the Hilltop Coffee example, $\bar{x} = 2.92$ and the test statistic is $z = -2.67$. Because $z = -2.67 < -2.33$, we can reject $H_0$ and conclude that Hilltop Coffee is underfilling cans.

We can generalize the rejection rule for the critical value approach to handle any level of significance. The rejection rule for a lower tail test follows.

---

REJECTION RULE FOR A LOWER TAIL TEST: CRITICAL VALUE APPROACH

Reject $H_0$ if $z \leq -z_\alpha$

where $-z_\alpha$ is the critical value; that is, the $z$ value that provides an area of $\alpha$ in the lower tail of the standard normal distribution.

---

The $p$-value approach to hypothesis testing and the critical value approach will always lead to the same rejection decision; that is, whenever the $p$-value is less than or equal to $\alpha$, the value of the test statistic will be less than or equal to the critical value. The advantage of the $p$-value approach is that the $p$-value tells us *how* significant the results are (the observed level of significance). If we use the critical value approach, we only know that the results are significant at the stated level of significance.

Computer procedures for hypothesis testing provide the $p$-value, so it is rapidly becoming the preferred method of conducting hypothesis tests. If you do not have access to a computer, you may prefer to use the critical value approach. For some probability distributions it is easier to use statistical tables to find a critical value than to use the tables to compute the $p$-value. This topic is discussed further in the next section.

At the beginning of this section, we said that one-tailed tests about a population mean take one of the following two forms:

| Lower Tail Test | Upper Tail Test |
|:---:|:---:|
| $H_0\colon \mu \geq \mu_0$ | $H_0\colon \mu \leq \mu_0$ |
| $H_a\colon \mu < \mu_0$ | $H_a\colon \mu > \mu_0$ |

We used the Hilltop Coffee study to illustrate how to conduct a lower tail test. We can use the same general approach to conduct an upper tail test. The test statistic $z$ is still computed using equation (9.1). But, for an upper tail test, the $p$-value is the probability of obtaining a value for the test statistic at least as large as that provided by the sample. Thus, to compute the $p$-value for the upper tail test in the $\sigma$ known case, we must find the area under the standard normal curve to the right of the test statistic. Using the critical value approach causes us to reject the null hypothesis if the value of the test statistic is greater than or equal to the critical value $z_\alpha$; in other words, we reject $H_0$ if $z \geq z_\alpha$.

## Two-Tailed Test

In hypothesis testing, the general form for a **two-tailed test** about a population mean is as follows:

$$H_0:\ \mu = \mu_0$$
$$H_a:\ \mu \neq \mu_0$$

In this subsection we show how to conduct a two-tailed test about a population mean for the $\sigma$ known case. As an illustration, we consider the hypothesis testing situation facing MaxFlight, Inc.

The U.S. Golf Association (USGA) establishes rules that manufacturers of golf equipment must meet if their products are to be acceptable for use in USGA events. MaxFlight uses a high-technology manufacturing process to produce golf balls with an average distance of 295 yards. Sometimes, however, the process gets out of adjustment and produces golf balls with average distances different from 295 yards. When the average distance falls below 295 yards, the company worries about losing sales because the golf balls do not provide as much distance as advertised. When the average distance passes 295 yards, MaxFlight's golf balls may be rejected by the USGA for exceeding the overall distance standard concerning carry and roll.

MaxFlight's quality control program involves taking periodic samples of 50 golf balls to monitor the manufacturing process. For each sample, a hypothesis test is conducted to determine whether the process has fallen out of adjustment. Let us develop the null and alternative hypotheses. We begin by assuming that the process is functioning correctly; that is, the golf balls being produced have a mean distance of 295 yards. This assumption establishes the null hypothesis. The alternative hypothesis is that the mean distance is not equal to 295 yards. With a hypothesized value of $\mu_0 = 295$, the null and alternative hypotheses for the MaxFlight hypothesis test are as follows:

$$H_0:\ \mu = 295$$
$$H_a:\ \mu \neq 295$$

If the sample mean $\bar{x}$ is significantly less than 295 yards or significantly greater than 295 yards, we will reject $H_0$. In this case, corrective action will be taken to adjust the manufacturing process. On the other hand, if $\bar{x}$ does not deviate from the hypothesized mean $\mu_0 = 295$ by a significant amount, $H_0$ will not be rejected and no action will be taken to adjust the manufacturing process.

The quality control team selected $\alpha = .05$ as the level of significance for the test. Data from previous tests conducted when the process was known to be in adjustment show that the population standard deviation can be assumed known with a value of $\sigma = 12$. Thus, with a sample size of $n = 50$, the standard error of $\bar{x}$ is

$$\sigma_{\bar{x}} = \frac{\sigma}{\sqrt{n}} = \frac{12}{\sqrt{50}} = 1.7$$

Because the sample size is large, the central limit theorem (see Chapter 7) allows us to conclude that the sampling distribution of $\bar{x}$ can be approximated by a normal distribution.

Figure 9.4 shows the sampling distribution of $\bar{x}$ for the MaxFlight hypothesis test with a hypothesized population mean of $\mu_0 = 295$.

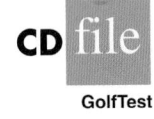

**CD** file

GolfTest

Suppose that a sample of 50 golf balls is selected and that the sample mean is $\bar{x} = 297.6$ yards. This sample mean provides support for the conclusion that the population mean is larger than 295 yards. Is this value of $\bar{x}$ enough larger than 295 to cause us to reject $H_0$ at the .05 level of significance? In the previous section we described two approaches that can be used to answer this question: the $p$-value approach and the critical value approach.

***$p$-value approach*** Recall that the $p$-value is a probability, computed using the test statistic, that measures the support (or lack of support) provided by the sample for the null hypothesis. For a two-tailed test, values of the test statistic in *either* tail show a lack of support for the null hypothesis. For a two-tailed test, the $p$-value is the probability of obtaining a value for the test statistic *at least as unlikely* as that provided by the sample. Let us see how the $p$-value is computed for the MaxFlight hypothesis test.

First we compute the value of the test statistic. For the $\sigma$ known case, the test statistic $z$ is a standard normal random variable. Using Equation (9.1) with $\bar{x} = 297.6$, the value of the test statistic is

$$z = \frac{\bar{x} - \mu_0}{\sigma/\sqrt{n}} = \frac{297.6 - 295}{12/\sqrt{50}} = 1.53$$

Now to compute the $p$-value we must find the probability of obtaining a value for the test statistic *at least as unlikely* as $z = 1.53$. Clearly values of $z \geq 1.53$ are *at least as unlikely*. But, because this is a two-tailed test, values of $z \leq -1.53$ are also *at least as unlikely* as the value of the test statistic provided by the sample. Referring to Figure 9.5, we see that the two-tailed $p$-value in this case is given by $P(z \leq -1.53) + P(z \geq 1.53)$. Because the normal curve is symmetric, we can compute this probability by finding the area under the standard normal curve to the right of $z = 1.53$ and doubling it. The table for the standard normal distribution shows that the area between the mean and $z = 1.53$ is .4370. Thus, the area under the standard normal curve to the right of the test statistic $z = 1.53$ is $.5000 - .4370 = .0630$. Doubling this, we find the $p$-value for the MaxFlight two-tailed hypothesis test is $p$-value $= 2(.0630) = .1260$.

Next we compare the $p$-value to the level of significance to see if the null hypothesis should be rejected. With a level of significance of $\alpha = .05$, we do not reject $H_0$ because the $p$-value $= .1260 > .05$. Because the null hypothesis is not rejected, no action will be taken to adjust the MaxFlight manufacturing process.

**FIGURE 9.4    SAMPLING DISTRIBUTION OF $\bar{x}$ FOR THE MAXFLIGHT HYPOTHESIS TEST**

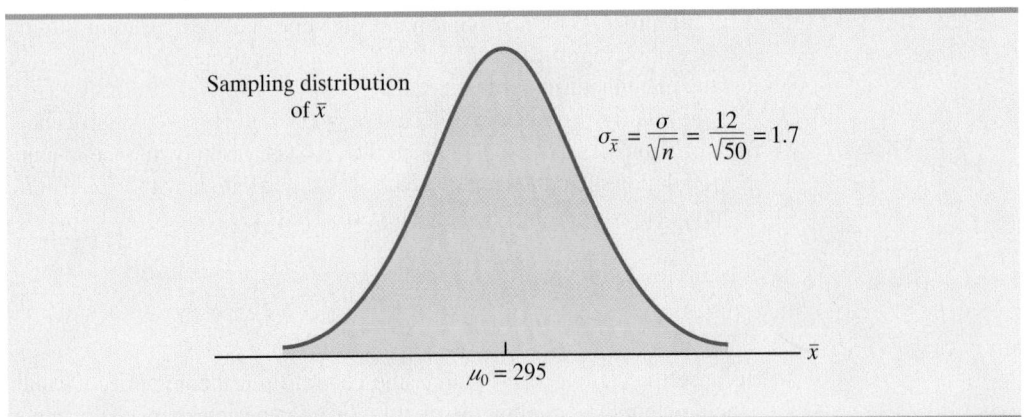

FIGURE 9.5   *p*-VALUE FOR THE MAXFLIGHT HYPOTHESIS TEST

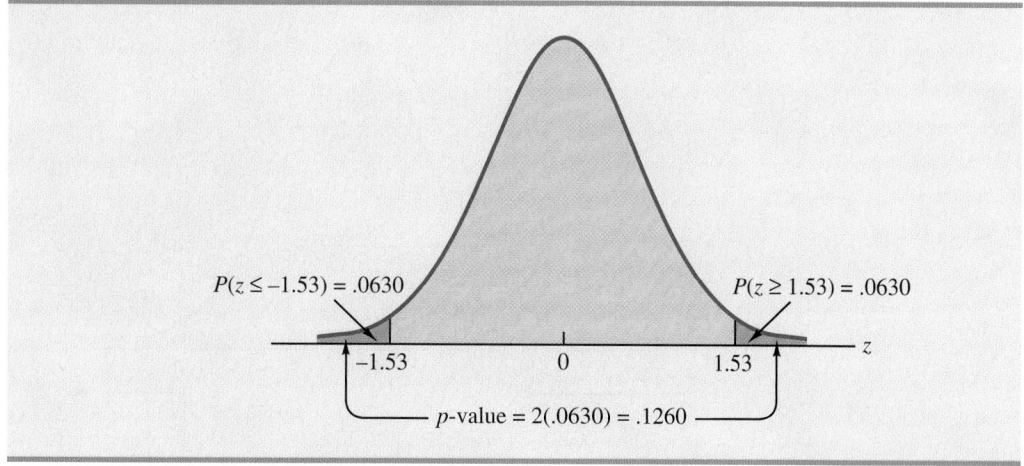

The computation of the *p*-value for a two-tailed test may seem a bit confusing as compared to the computation of the *p*-value for a one-tailed test. But, it can be simplified by following these three steps.

1. Compute the value of the test statistic $z$.
2. If the value of the test statistic is in the upper tail ($z > 0$), find the area under the standard normal curve to the right of $z$. If the value of the test statistic is in the lower tail, find the area under the standard normal curve to the left of $z$.
3. Double the tail area, or probability, obtained in step 2 to obtain the *p*-value.

In practice, the computation of the *p*-value is done automatically when using computer software such as Minitab and Excel. For instance, Figure 9.6 shows the Minitab output for the MaxFlight hypothesis test. The sample mean $\bar{x} = 297.6$, the test statistic $z = 1.53$, and the *p*-value $= .126$ are shown. The step-by-step procedure used to obtain the Minitab output is described in Appendix 9.1.

**Critical value approach**   Before leaving this section, let us see how the test statistic $z$ can be compared to a critical value to make the hypothesis testing decision for a two-tailed test. Figure 9.7 shows that the critical values for the test will occur in both the lower and upper tails of the standard normal distribution. With a level of significance of $\alpha = .05$, the area in each tail beyond the critical values is $\alpha/2 = .05/2 = .025$. Using the table of areas for the standard normal distribution, we find the critical values for the test statistic are

FIGURE 9.6   MINITAB OUTPUT FOR THE MAXFLIGHT HYPOTHESIS TEST

```
Test of mu = 295 vs not = 295
The assumed sigma = 12

Variable      N        Mean       StDev      SE Mean
Yards         50      297.600     11.297      1.697

Variable           95.0% CI              Z          P
Yards         (294.274, 300.926)       1.53       0.126
```

FIGURE 9.7    CRITICAL VALUES FOR THE MAXFLIGHT HYPOTHESIS TEST

$-z_{.025} = -1.96$ and $z_{.025} = 1.96$. Thus, using the critical value approach, the two-tailed rejection rule is

$$\text{Reject } H_0 \text{ if } z \leq 1.96 \text{ or if } z \geq 1.96$$

Because the value of the test statistic for the MaxFlight study is $z = 1.53$, the statistical evidence will not permit us to reject the null hypothesis at the .05 level of significance.

## Summary and Practical Advice

We presented examples of a lower tail test and a two-tailed test about a population mean. Based upon these examples, we can now summarize the hypothesis testing procedures about a population mean for the $\sigma$ known case as shown in Table 9.2. Note that $\mu_0$ is the hypothesized value of the population mean.

The hypothesis testing steps followed in the two examples presented in this section are common to every hypothesis test.

STEPS OF HYPOTHESIS TESTING

**Step 1.** Develop the null and alternative hypotheses.
**Step 2.** Specify the level of significance.
**Step 3.** Collect the sample data and compute the value of the test statistic.

*p-Value Approach*

**Step 4.** Use the value of the test statistic to compute the *p*-value.
**Step 5.** Reject $H_0$ if the *p*-value $\leq \alpha$.

*Critical Value Approach*

**Step 4.** Use the level of significance to determine the critical value and the rejection rule.
**Step 5.** Use the value of the test statistic and the rejection rule to determine whether to reject $H_0$.

TABLE 9.2    SUMMARY OF HYPOTHESIS TESTS ABOUT A POPULATION MEAN: $\sigma$ KNOWN CASE

|  | Lower Tail Test | Upper Tail Test | Two-Tailed Test |
|---|---|---|---|
| **Hypotheses** | $H_0: \mu \geq \mu_0$ $H_a: \mu < \mu_0$ | $H_0: \mu \leq \mu_0$ $H_a: \mu > \mu_0$ | $H_0: \mu = \mu_0$ $H_a: \mu \neq \mu_0$ |
| **Test Statistic** | $z = \dfrac{\bar{x} - \mu_0}{\sigma/\sqrt{n}}$ | $z = \dfrac{\bar{x} - \mu_0}{\sigma/\sqrt{n}}$ | $z = \dfrac{\bar{x} - \mu_0}{\sigma/\sqrt{n}}$ |
| **Rejection Rule: $p$-Value Approach** | Reject $H_0$ if $p$-value $\leq \alpha$ | Reject $H_0$ if $p$-value $\leq \alpha$ | Reject $H_0$ if $p$-value $\leq \alpha$ |
| **Rejection Rule: Critical Value Approach** | Reject $H_0$ if $z \leq -z_\alpha$ | Reject $H_0$ if $z \geq z_\alpha$ | Reject $H_0$ if $z \leq -z_{\alpha/2}$ or if $z \geq z_{\alpha/2}$ |

Practical advice about the sample size for hypothesis tests is similar to the advice we provided about the sample size for interval estimation in Chapter 8. In most applications, a sample size of $n \geq 30$ is adequate when using the hypothesis testing procedure described in this section. In cases where the sample size is less than 30, the distribution of the population from which we are sampling becomes an important consideration. If the population is normally distributed, the hypothesis testing procedure that we described is exact and can be used for any sample size. If the population is not normally distributed but is at least roughly symmetric, sample sizes as small as 15 can be expected to provide acceptable results. With smaller sample sizes, the hypothesis testing procedure presented in this section should only be used if the analyst believes, or is willing to assume, that the population is at least approximately normally distributed.

## Relationship Between Interval Estimation and Hypothesis Testing

We close this section by discussing the relationship between interval estimation and hypothesis testing. In Chapter 8 we showed how to develop a confidence interval estimate of a population mean. For the $\sigma$ known case, the confidence interval estimate of a population mean corresponding to a $1 - \alpha$ confidence coefficient is given by

$$\bar{x} \pm z_{\alpha/2} \frac{\sigma}{\sqrt{n}} \tag{9.2}$$

Conducting a hypothesis test requires us first to develop the hypotheses about the value of a population parameter. In the case of the population mean, the two-tailed test takes the form

$$H_0: \mu = \mu_0$$
$$H_a: \mu \neq \mu_0$$

where $\mu_0$ is the hypothesized value for the population mean. Using the two-tailed critical value approach, we do not reject $H_0$ for values of the sample mean $\bar{x}$ that are within $-z_{\alpha/2}$ and $+z_{\alpha/2}$ standard errors of $\mu_0$. Thus, the do-not-reject region for the sample mean $\bar{x}$ in a two-tailed hypothesis test with a level of significance of $\alpha$ is given by

$$\mu_0 \pm z_{\alpha/2} \frac{\sigma}{\sqrt{n}} \tag{9.3}$$

A close look at expression (9.2) and expression (9.3) provides insight about the relationship between the estimation and hypothesis testing approaches to statistical inference. Note in particular that both procedures require the computation of the values $z_{\alpha/2}$ and $\sigma/\sqrt{n}$. Focusing on $\alpha$, we see that a confidence coefficient of $(1 - \alpha)$ for interval estimation corresponds to a level of significance of $\alpha$ in hypothesis testing. For example, a 95% confidence interval corresponds to a .05 level of significance for hypothesis testing. Furthermore, expressions (9.2) and (9.3) show that, because $z_{\alpha/2}(\sigma/\sqrt{n})$ is the plus or minus value for both expressions, if $\bar{x}$ is in the do-not-reject region defined by (9.3), the hypothesized value $\mu_0$ will be in the confidence interval defined by (9.2). Conversely, if the hypothesized value $\mu_0$ is in the confidence interval defined by (9.2), the sample mean $\bar{x}$ will be in the do-not-reject region for the hypothesis $H_0$: $\mu = \mu_0$ as defined by (9.3). These observations lead to the following procedure for using a confidence interval to conduct a two-tailed hypothesis test.

### A CONFIDENCE INTERVAL APPROACH TO TESTING A HYPOTHESIS OF THE FORM

$$H_0: \mu = \mu_0$$
$$H_a: \mu \neq \mu_0$$

1. Select a simple random sample from the population and use the value of the sample mean $\bar{x}$ to develop the confidence interval for the population mean $\mu$.

$$\bar{x} \pm z_{\alpha/2} \frac{\sigma}{\sqrt{n}}$$

*For a two-tailed hypothesis test, the null hypothesis can be rejected if the confidence interval does not include $\mu_0$.*

2. If the confidence interval contains the hypothesized value $\mu_0$, do not reject $H_0$. Otherwise, reject $H_0$.

Let us return to the MaxFlight hypothesis test, which resulted in the following two-tailed test.

$$H_0: \mu = 295$$
$$H_a: \mu \neq 295$$

To test this hypothesis with a level of significance of $\alpha = .05$, we sampled 50 golf balls and found a sample mean distance of $\bar{x} = 297.6$ yards. Recall that the population standard deviation is $\sigma = 12$. Using these results with $z_{.025} = 1.96$, we find that the 95% confidence interval estimate of the population mean is

$$\bar{x} \pm z_{.025} \frac{\sigma}{\sqrt{n}}$$
$$297.6 \pm 1.96 \frac{12}{\sqrt{50}}$$
$$297.6 \pm 3.3$$

or

$$294.3 \text{ to } 300.9$$

This finding enables the quality control manager to conclude with 95% confidence that the mean distance for the population of golf balls is between 294.3 and 300.9 yards. Because the hypothesized value for the population mean, $\mu_0 = 295$, is in this interval, the hypothesis testing conclusion is that the null hypothesis, $H_0$: $\mu = 295$, cannot be rejected.

Note that this discussion and example pertain to two-tailed hypothesis tests about a population mean. However, the same confidence interval and two-tailed hypothesis testing relationship exists for other population parameters. The relationship can also be extended to one-tailed tests about population parameters. Doing so, however, requires the development of one-sided confidence intervals.

## NOTES AND COMMENTS

**1.** In Appendix 9.2 we show how to compute $p$-values using Excel. The smaller the $p$-value the greater the evidence against $H_0$ and the more the evidence in favor of $H_a$. Here are some guidelines statisticians suggest for interpreting small $p$-values.
- Less than .01—Overwhelming evidence to conclude $H_a$ is true.
- Between .01 and .05—Strong evidence to conclude $H_a$ is true.
- Between .05 and .10—Weak evidence to conclude $H_a$ is true.
- Greater than .10—Insufficient evidence to conclude $H_a$ is true.

## Exercises

*Note to Student:* Some of the exercises that follow ask you to use the $p$-value approach and others ask you to use the critical value approach. Both methods will provide the same hypothesis testing conclusion. We provide exercises with both methods to give you practice using both. In later sections and in following chapters, we will generally emphasize the $p$-value approach as the preferred method, but you may select either based on personal preference.

## Methods

9. Consider the following hypothesis test:

$$H_0: \mu \geq 20$$
$$H_a: \mu < 20$$

A sample of 50 provided a sample mean of 19.4. The population standard deviation is 2.
  a. Compute the value of the test statistic.
  b. What is the $p$-value?
  c. Using $\alpha = .05$, what is your conclusion?
  d. What is the rejection rule using the critical value? What is your conclusion?

10. Consider the following hypothesis test:

$$H_0: \mu \leq 25$$
$$H_a: \mu > 25$$

A sample of 40 provided a sample mean of 26.4. The population standard deviation is 6.
  a. Compute the value of the test statistic.
  b. What is the $p$-value?
  c. At $\alpha = .01$, what is your conclusion?
  d. What is the rejection rule using the critical value? What is your conclusion?

11. Consider the following hypothesis test:

$$H_0: \mu = 15$$
$$H_a: \mu \neq 15$$

A sample of 50 provided a sample mean of 14.15. The population standard deviation is 3.

    a.    Compute the value of the test statistic.
    b.    What is the $p$-value?
    c.    At $\alpha = .05$, what is your conclusion?
    d.    What is the rejection rule using the critical value? What is your conclusion?

12.   Consider the following hypothesis test:

$$H_0: \mu \geq 80$$
$$H_a: \mu < 80$$

A sample of 100 is used and the population standard deviation is 12. Use $\alpha = .01$ to compute the $p$-value and state your conclusion for each of the following sample results.
    a.    $\bar{x} = 78.5$
    b.    $\bar{x} = 77$
    c.    $\bar{x} = 75.5$
    d.    $\bar{x} = 81$

13.   Consider the following hypothesis test:

$$H_0: \mu \leq 50$$
$$H_a: \mu > 50$$

A sample of 60 is used and the population standard deviation is 8. Use the critical value approach to state your conclusion for each of the following sample results. Use $\alpha = .05$.
    a.    $\bar{x} = 52.5$
    b.    $\bar{x} = 51$
    c.    $\bar{x} = 51.8$

14.   Consider the following hypothesis test:

$$H_0: \mu = 22$$
$$H_a: \mu \neq 22$$

A sample of 75 is used and the population standard deviation is 10. Use $\alpha = .01$, compute the $p$-value and state your conclusion for each of the following sample results.
    a.    $\bar{x} = 23$
    b.    $\bar{x} = 25.1$
    c.    $\bar{x} = 20$

## Applications

15.   Individuals filing federal income tax returns prior to March 31 received an average refund of $1056. Consider the population of "last-minute" filers who mail their tax return during the last five days of the income tax period (typically April 10 to April 15).
    a.    A researcher suggests that a reason individuals wait until the last five days is that on average these individuals receive lower refunds than do early filers. Develop appropriate hypotheses such that rejection of $H_0$ will support the researcher's contention.
    b.    For a sample of 400 individuals who filed a tax return between April 10 and 15, the sample mean refund was $910. Based on prior experience a population standard deviation of $\sigma = \$1600$ may be assumed. What is the $p$-value?
    c.    At $\alpha = .05$, what is your conclusion?
    d.    Repeat the preceding hypothesis test using the critical value approach.

16. Reis, Inc., a New York real estate research firm, tracks the cost of apartment rentals in the United States. In mid-2002, the nationwide mean apartment rental rate was $895 per month (*The Wall Street Journal,* July 8, 2002). Assume that, based on the historical quarterly surveys, a population standard deviation of $\sigma = \$225$ is reasonable. In a current study of apartment rental rates, a sample of 180 apartments nationwide provided a sample mean of $915 per month. Do the sample data enable Reis to conclude that the population mean apartment rental rate now exceeds the level reported in 2002?
   a. State the null and alternative hypothesis.
   b. What is the *p*-value?
   c. At $\alpha = .01$, what is your conclusion?
   d. What would you recommend Reis consider doing at this time?

17. The mean length of a work week for the population of workers was reported to be 39.2 hours (*Investor's Business Daily,* September 11, 2000). Suppose that we would like to take a current sample of workers to see whether the mean length of a work week has changed from the previously reported 39.2 hours.
   a. State the hypotheses that will help us determine whether a change occurred in the mean length of a work week.
   b. Suppose a current sample of 112 workers provided a sample mean of 38.5 hours. Use a population standard deviation $\sigma = 4.8$ hours. What is the *p*-value?
   c. At $\alpha = .05$, can the null hypothesis be rejected? What is your conclusion?
   d. Repeat the preceding hypothesis test using the critical value approach.

18. The Florida Department of Labor and Employment Security reported the state mean annual wage was $26,133 (*The Naples Daily News,* February 13, 1999). A hypothesis test of wages by county can be conducted to see whether the mean annual wage for a particular county differs from the state mean.
   a. Formulate the hypotheses that can be used to determine whether the mean annual wage in a county differs from the state mean annual wage of $26,133.
   b. A sample of 550 individuals in Collier County showed a sample mean annual wage of $25,457. Assume a population standard deviation $\sigma = \$7600$. What is the *p*-value?
   c. Using $\alpha = .05$, what is your conclusion?

19. In 2001, the U.S. Department of Labor reported the average hourly earnings for U.S. production workers to be $14.32 per hour (*The World Almanac 2003*). A sample of 75 production workers during 2003 showed a sample mean of $14.68 per hour. Assuming the population standard deviation $\sigma = \$1.45$, can we conclude that an increase occurred in the mean hourly earnings since 2001? Use $\alpha = .05$. What is the *p*-value?

20. The national mean sales price for new one-family homes is $181,900 (*The New York Times Almanac 2000*). A sample of 40 one-family home sales in the South showed a sample mean of $166,400. Use a population standard deviation of $33,500.
   a. Formulate the null and alternative hypotheses that can be used to determine whether the sample data support the conclusion that the population mean sales price for new one-family homes in the South is less than the national mean of $181,900.
   b. What is the value of the test statistic?
   c. What is the *p*-value?
   d. At $\alpha = .01$, what is your conclusion?

21. Fowle Marketing Research, Inc., bases charges to a client on the assumption that telephone surveys can be completed in a mean time of 15 minutes or less. If a longer mean survey time is necessary, a premium rate is charged. Suppose a sample of 35 surveys shows a sample mean of 17 minutes. Use $\sigma = 4$ minutes. Is the premium rate justified?
   a. Formulate the null and alternative hypotheses for this application.
   b. Compute the value of the test statistic.
   c. What is the *p*-value?
   d. At $\alpha = .01$, what is your conclusion?

22.   CCN and ActMedia provided a television channel targeted to individuals waiting in super-market checkout lines. The channel showed news, short features, and advertisements. The length of the program was based on the assumption that the population mean time a shopper stands in a supermarket checkout line is 8 minutes. A sample of actual waiting times will be used to test this assumption and determine whether actual mean waiting time differs from this standard.

    a.   Formulate the hypotheses for this application.

    b.   A sample of 120 shoppers showed a sample mean waiting time of 8.5 minutes. Assume a population standard deviation $\sigma = 3.2$ minutes. What is the $p$-value?

    c.   At $\alpha = .05$, what is your conclusion?

    d.   Compute a 95% confidence interval for the population mean. Does it support your conclusion?

 **9.4** **Population Mean: $\sigma$ Unknown**

In this section we describe how to conduct hypothesis tests about a population mean for the $\sigma$ unknown case. Because the $\sigma$ unknown case corresponds to situations in which an estimate of the population standard deviation cannot be developed prior to sampling, the sample must be used to develop an estimate of both $\mu$ and $\sigma$. Thus, to conduct a hypothesis test about a population mean for the $\sigma$ unknown case, the sample mean $\bar{x}$ is used as an estimate of $\mu$ and the sample standard deviation $s$ is used as an estimate of $\sigma$.

The steps of the hypothesis testing procedure for the $\sigma$ unknown case are the same as those for the $\sigma$ known case described in Section 9.3. But, with $\sigma$ unknown, the computation of the test statistic and $p$-value are a bit different. Recall that for the $\sigma$ known case, the sampling distribution of the test statistic has a standard normal distribution. For the $\sigma$ unknown case, however, the sampling distribution of the test statistic has slightly more variability because the sample is used to develop estimates of both $\mu$ and $\sigma$.

In Section 8.2 we showed that an interval estimate of a population mean for the $\sigma$ unknown case is based on a probability distribution known as the $t$ distribution. Hypothesis tests about a population mean for the $\sigma$ unknown case are also based on the $t$ distribution. In fact, for the $\sigma$ unknown case, the test statistic has a $t$ distribution with $n - 1$ degrees of freedom.

> **TEST STATISTIC FOR HYPOTHESIS TESTS ABOUT A POPULATION MEAN: $\sigma$ UNKNOWN**
>
> $$t = \frac{\bar{x} - \mu_0}{s/\sqrt{n}} \tag{9.4}$$

In Chapter 8 we said that the $t$ distribution is based on an assumption that the population from which we are sampling has a normal distribution. However, research shows that this assumption can be relaxed considerably when the sample size is large enough. We provide some practical advice concerning the population distribution and sample size at the end of the section.

### One-Tailed Test

Let us consider an example of a one-tailed test about a population mean for the $\sigma$ unknown case. A business travel magazine wants to classify transatlantic gateway airports according to the mean rating for the population of business travelers. A rating scale with a low score

**AirRating**

of 0 and a high score of 10 will be used, and airports with a population mean rating greater than 7 will be designated as superior service airports. The  magazine staff surveyed a sample of 60 business travelers at each airport to obtain the ratings data. The sample for London's Heathrow Airport provided a sample mean rating of $\bar{x} = 7.25$ and a sample standard deviation of $s = 1.052$. Do the data indicate that Heathrow should be designated as a superior service airport?

We want to develop a hypothesis test for which the decision to reject $H_0$ will lead to the conclusion that the population mean rating for the Heathrow Airport is *greater* than 7. Thus, an upper tail test with $H_a$: $\mu > 7$ is required. The null and alternative hypotheses for this upper tail test are as follows:

$$H_0: \mu \leq 7$$
$$H_a: \mu > 7$$

We will use $\alpha = .05$ as the level of significance for the test.

Using equation (9.4) with $\bar{x} = 7.25$, $s = 1.052$, and $n = 60$, the value of the test statistic is

$$t = \frac{\bar{x} - \mu_0}{s/\sqrt{n}} = \frac{7.25 - 7}{1.052/\sqrt{60}} = 1.84$$

The sampling distribution of $t$ has $n - 1 = 60 - 1 = 59$ degrees of freedom. Because the test is an upper tail test, the $p$-value is the area under the curve of the $t$ distribution to the right of $t = 1.84$.

The $t$ distribution table provided in most textbooks will not contain sufficient detail to determine the exact $p$-value, such as the $p$-value corresponding to $t = 1.84$. For instance, using Table 2 in Appendix B, the $t$ distribution with 59 degrees of freedom provides the following information.

| Area in Upper Tail | .20 | .10 | .05 | .025 | .01 | .005 |
|---|---|---|---|---|---|---|
| *t* Value (59 df) | 0.848 | 1.296 | 1.671 | 2.001 | 2.391 | 2.662 |

$$t = 1.84$$

We see that $t = 1.84$ is between 1.671 and 2.001. Although the table does not provide the exact $p$-value, the values in the "Area in Upper Tail" row show that the $p$-value must be less than .05 and greater than .025. With a level of significance of $\alpha = .05$, this placement is all we need to know to make the decision to reject the null hypothesis and conclude that Heathrow should be classified as a superior service airport.

*Appendixes 9.1 and 9.2 explain how to obtain the exact p-value using Minitab and Excel.*

Computer packages such as Minitab and Excel can easily determine the exact $p$-value associated with the test statistic $t = 1.84$. For example, the Minitab output in Figure 9.8 shows the sample mean $\bar{x} = 7.25$, the sample standard deviation $s = 1.052$ (rounded), the test statistic $t = 1.84$, and the exact $p$-value = .035 for the Heathrow rating hypothesis test. A $p$-value = .035 < .05 leads to the rejection of the null hypothesis and to the conclusion Heathrow should be classified as a superior service airport. The step-by-step procedure used to obtain the Minitab output shown in Figure 9.8 is described in Appendix 9.1.

The critical value approach can also be used to make the rejection decision. With $\alpha = .05$ and the $t$ distribution with 59 degrees of freedom, $t_{.05} = 1.671$ is the critical value for the test. The rejection rule is thus

$$\text{Reject } H_0 \text{ if } t \geq 1.671$$

FIGURE 9.8    MINITAB OUTPUT FOR THE HEATHROW RATING HYPOTHESIS TEST

```
Test of mu = 7 vs > 7

                                                    95%
                                                   Lower
   Variable    N     Mean      StDev    SE Mean    Bound      T        P
   Rating      60    7.250     1.05163  0.13577    7.02312    1.84     0.035
```

With the test statistic $t = 1.84 \geq 1.671$, $H_0$ is rejected and we can conclude that Heathrow can be classified as a superior service airport.

## Two-Tailed Test

To illustrate how to conduct a two-tailed test about a population mean for the $\sigma$ unknown case, let us consider the hypothesis testing situation facing Holiday Toys. The company manufactures and distributes its products through more than 1000 retail outlets. In planning production levels for the coming winter season, Holiday must decide how many units of each product to produce prior to knowing the actual demand at the retail level. For this year's most important new toy, Holiday's marketing director is expecting demand to average 40 units per retail outlet. Prior to making the final production decision based upon this estimate, Holiday decided to survey a sample of 25 retailers in order to develop more information about the demand for the new product. Each retailer was provided with information about the features of the new toy along with the cost and the suggested selling price. Then each retailer was asked to specify an anticipated order quantity.

With $\mu$ denoting the population mean order quantity per retail outlet, the sample data will·be used to conduct the following two-tailed hypothesis test:

$$H_0: \mu = 40$$
$$H_a: \mu \neq 40$$

If $H_0$ cannot be rejected, Holiday will continue its production planning based on the marketing director's estimate that the population mean order quantity per retail outlet will be $\mu = 40$ units. However, if $H_0$ is rejected. Holiday will immediately reevaluate its production plan for the product. A two-tailed hypothesis test is used because Holiday wants to reevaluate the production plan if the population mean quantity per retail outlet is less than anticipated or greater than anticipated. Because no historical data are available (it's a new product), the population mean $\mu$ and the population standard deviation must both be estimated using $\bar{x}$ and $s$ from the sample data.

**Orders**

The sample of 25 retailers provided a mean of $\bar{x} = 37.4$ and a standard deviation of $s = 11.79$ units. Before going ahead with the use of the $t$ distribution, the analyst constructed a histogram of the sample data in order to check on the form of the population distribution. The histogram of the sample data showed no evidence of skewness or any extreme outliers, so the analyst concluded that the use of the $t$ distribution with $n - 1 = 24$ degrees of freedom was appropriate. Using equation (9.4) with $\bar{x} = 37.4$, $\mu_0 = 40$, $s = 11.79$, and $n = 25$, the value of the test statistic is

$$t = \frac{\bar{x} - \mu_0}{s/\sqrt{n}} = \frac{37.4 - 40}{11.79/\sqrt{25}} = -1.10$$

Because we have a two-tailed test, the *p*-value is two times the area under the curve for the *t* distribution to the left of $t = -1.10$. Using Table 2 in Appendix B, the *t* distribution table for 24 degrees of freedom provides the following information.

| Area in Upper Tail | .20 | .10 | .05 | .025 | .01 | .005 |
|---|---|---|---|---|---|---|
| *t* Value (24 df) | 0.858 | 1.318 | 1.711 | 2.064 | 2.492 | 2.797 |

$t = 1.10$

The *t* distribution table only contains positive *t* values. Because the *t* distribution is symmetric, however, we can find the area under the curve to the right of $t = 1.10$ and double it to find the *p*-value. We see that $t = 1.10$ is between 0.858 and 1.318. From the "Area in Upper Tail" row, we see that the area in the tail to the right of $t = 1.10$ is between .20 and .10. Doubling these amounts, we see that the *p*-value must be between .40 and .20. With a level of significance of $\alpha = .05$, we now know that the *p*-value is greater than $\alpha$. Therefore, $H_0$ cannot be rejected. Sufficient evidence is not available to conclude that Holiday should change its production plan for the coming season. Using Minitab or Excel, we find that the exact *p*-value is .282. Figure 9.9 shows the two areas under the curve of the *t* distribution corresponding to the exact *p*-value.

The test statistic can also be compared to the critical value to make the two-tailed hypothesis testing decision. With $\alpha = .05$ and the *t* distribution with 24 degrees of freedom, $-t_{.025} = -2.064$ and $t_{.025} = 2.064$ are the critical values for the two-tailed test. The rejection rule using the test statistic is

$$\text{Reject } H_0 \text{ if } t \leq -2.064 \text{ or if } t \geq 2.064$$

Based on the test statistic $t = -1.10$, $H_0$ cannot be rejected. This result indicates that Holiday should continue its production planning for the coming season based on the expectation that $\mu = 40$.

## Summary and Practical Advice

Table 9.3 provides a summary of the hypothesis testing procedures about a population mean for the $\sigma$ unknown case. The key difference between these procedures and the ones for the $\sigma$ known case are that $s$ is used, instead of $\sigma$, in the computation of the test statistic. For this reason, the test statistic follows the *t* distribution.

**FIGURE 9.9**    AREA UNDER THE CURVE IN BOTH TAILS PROVIDES THE *p*-VALUE

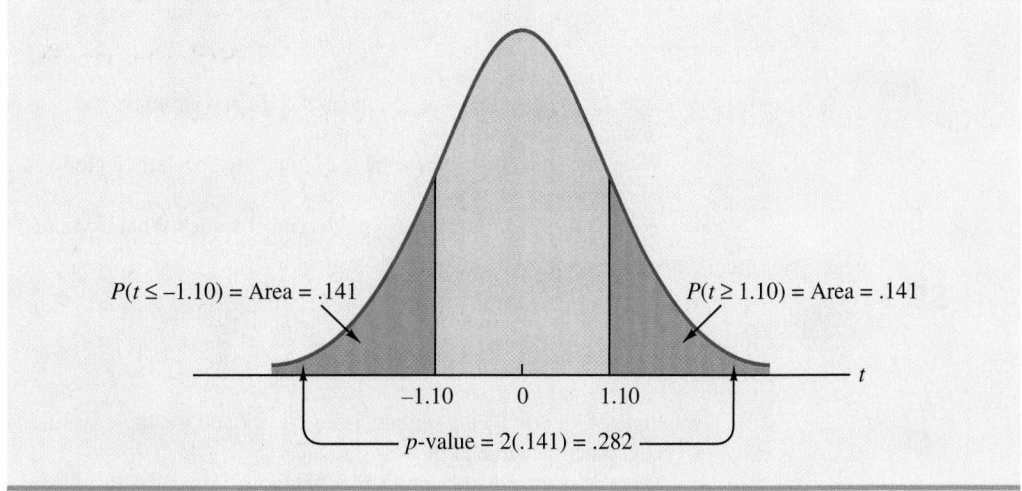

$P(t \leq -1.10) = \text{Area} = .141$    $P(t \geq 1.10) = \text{Area} = .141$

$-1.10$    0    $1.10$    $t$

$p\text{-value} = 2(.141) = .282$

**TABLE 9.3** SUMMARY OF HYPOTHESIS TESTS ABOUT A POPULATION MEAN: $\sigma$ UNKNOWN CASE

|  | Lower Tail Test | Upper Tail Test | Two-Tailed Test |
|---|---|---|---|
| **Hypotheses** | $H_0: \mu \geq \mu_0$ <br> $H_a: \mu < \mu_0$ | $H_0: \mu \leq \mu_0$ <br> $H_a: \mu > \mu_0$ | $H_0: \mu = \mu_0$ <br> $H_a: \mu \neq \mu_0$ |
| **Test Statistic** | $t = \dfrac{\bar{x} - \mu_0}{s/\sqrt{n}}$ | $t = \dfrac{\bar{x} - \mu_0}{s/\sqrt{n}}$ | $t = \dfrac{\bar{x} - \mu_0}{s/\sqrt{n}}$ |
| **Rejection Rule:** <br> **$p$-Value Approach** | Reject $H_0$ if <br> $p$-value $\leq \alpha$ | Reject $H_0$ if <br> $p$-value $\leq \alpha$ | Reject $H_0$ if <br> $p$-value $\leq \alpha$ |
| **Rejection Rule:** <br> **Critical Value** <br> **Approach** | Reject $H_0$ if <br> $t \leq -t_\alpha$ | Reject $H_0$ if <br> $t \geq t_\alpha$ | Reject $H_0$ if <br> $t \leq -t_{\alpha/2}$ <br> or if $t \geq t_{\alpha/2}$ |

The applicability of the hypothesis testing procedures of this section is dependent on the distribution of the population being sampled from and the sample size. When the population is normally distributed, the hypothesis tests described in this section provide exact results for any sample size. When the population is not normally distributed, the procedures are approximations. Nonetheless, we find that sample sizes greater than 50 will provide good results in almost all cases. If the population is approximately normal, small sample sizes (e.g., $n < 15$) can provide acceptable results. In situations where the population cannot be approximated by a normal distribution, sample sizes of $n \geq 15$ will provide acceptable results as long as the population is not significantly skewed and does not contain outliers. If the population is significantly skewed or contains outliers, samples sizes approaching 50 are a good idea.

## Exercises

## Methods

23. Consider the following hypothesis test:

$$H_0: \mu \leq 12$$
$$H_a: \mu > 12$$

A sample of 25 provided a sample mean $\bar{x} = 14$ and a sample standard deviation $s = 4.32$.
 a. Compute the value of the test statistic.
 b. What does the $t$ distribution table (Table 2 in Appendix B) tell you about the $p$-value?
 c. At $\alpha = .05$, what is your conclusion?
 d. What is the rejection rule using the critical value? What is your conclusion?

24. Consider the following hypothesis test:

$$H_0: \mu = 18$$
$$H_a: \mu \neq 18$$

A sample of 48 provided a sample mean $\bar{x} = 17$ and a sample standard deviation $s = 4.5$.
 a. Compute the value of the test statistic.
 b. What does the $t$ distribution table (Table 2 in Appendix B) tell you about the $p$-value?

c.   At $\alpha = .05$, what is your conclusion?

d.   What is the rejection rule using the critical value? What is your conclusion?

25.  Consider the following hypothesis test:

$$H_0: \mu \geq 45$$
$$H_a: \mu < 45$$

A sample of 36 is used. Using $\alpha = .01$, identify the $p$-value and state your conclusion for each of the following sample results.

a.   $\bar{x} = 44$ and $s = 5.2$

b.   $\bar{x} = 43$ and $s = 4.6$

c.   $\bar{x} = 46$ and $s = 5.0$

26.  Consider the following hypothesis test:

$$H_0: \mu = 100$$
$$H_a: \mu \neq 100$$

A sample of 65 is used. Using $\alpha = .05$, identify the $p$-value and state your conclusion for each of the following sample results.

a.   $\bar{x} = 103$ and $s = 11.5$

b.   $\bar{x} = 96.5$ and $s = 11.0$

c.   $\bar{x} = 102$ and $s = 10.5$

## Applications

27.  The Employment and Training Administration reported the U.S. mean unemployment insurance benefit of $238 per week (*The World Almanac,* 2003). A researcher in the state of Virginia anticipated that sample data would show evidence that the mean weekly unemployment insurance benefit in Virginia was below the national level.

a.   Develop appropriate hypotheses such that rejection of $H_0$ will support the researcher's contention.

b.   For a sample of 100 individuals, the sample mean weekly unemployment insurance benefit was $231 with a sample standard deviation of $80. What is the $p$-value?

c.   At $\alpha = .05$, what is your conclusion?

d.   Repeat the preceding hypothesis test using the critical value approach.

28.  The National Association of Professional Baseball Leagues, Inc., reported that attendance for 176 minor league baseball teams reached an all-time high during the 2001 season (*New York Times,* July 28, 2002). On a per-game basis, the mean attendance for minor league baseball was 3530 people per game. Midway through the 2002 season, the president of the association asked for an attendance report that would hopefully show that the mean attendance for 2002 was exceeding the 2001 level.

a.   Formulate hypotheses that could be used determine whether the mean attendance per game in 2002 was greater than the previous year's level.

b.   Assume that a sample of 92 minor league baseball games played during the first half of the 2002 season showed a mean attendance of 3740 people per game with a sample standard deviation of 810. What is the $p$-value?

c.   At $\alpha = .01$, what is your conclusion?

29.  The cost of a one-carat VS2 clarity, H color diamond from Diamond Source USA is $5600 (diasource.com, March 2003). A midwestern jeweler makes calls to contacts in the diamond district of New York City to see whether the mean price of diamonds there differs from $5600.

a.   Formulate hypotheses that can be used to determine whether the mean price in New York City differs from $5600.

b.   Assume that a sample of 25 New York City contacts provided a sample mean price of $5835 and a sample standard deviation of $520. What is the $p$-value?

c.   At $\alpha = .05$, can the null hypothesis be rejected? What is your conclusion?

d.   Repeat the preceding hypothesis test using the critical value approach.

30.  AOL Time Warner Inc.'s CNN has been the longtime ratings leader of cable television news. Nielsen Media Research indicated that the mean CNN viewing audience was 600,000 viewers per day during 2002 (*The Wall Street Journal,* March 10, 2003). Assume that for a sample of 40 days during the first half of 2003, the daily audience was 612,000 viewers with a sample standard deviation of 65,000 viewers.

a.   What are the hypotheses if CNN management would like information on any change in the CNN viewing audience?

b.   What is the *p*-value?

c.   Select your own level of significance. What is your conclusion?

d.   What recommendation would you make to CNN management in this application?

31.  Raftelis Financial Consulting reported that the mean quarterly water bill in the United States is $47.50 (*U.S. News and World Report,* August 12, 2002). Some water systems are operated by public utilities while other water systems are operated by private companies. An economist pointed out that privatization does not equal competition and that monopoly powers provided to public utilities are now being transferred to private companies. The concern is that consumers end up paying higher-than-average rates for water provided by private companies. The water system for Atlanta, Georgia, is provided by a private company. A sample of 64 Atlanta consumers showed a mean quarterly water bill of $51 with a sample standard deviation of $12. At $\alpha = .05$, does the Atlanta sample support the conclusion that above-average rates exist for this private water system? What is your conclusion?

32.  According to the National Automobile Dealers Association, the mean price for used cars is $10,192. A manager of a Kansas City used car dealership reviewed a sample of 50 recent used car sales at the dealership in an attempt to determine whether the population mean price for used cars at this particular dealership differed from the national mean.

a.   Formulate the hypotheses that can be used to determine whether a difference exists in the mean price for used cars at the dealership.

b.   What is the *p*-value based on a sample mean price of $9750 and a sample standard deviation of $1400?

c.   At $\alpha = .05$, what is your conclusion?

33.  Callaway Golf Company's new forged titanium ERC driver has been described as "illegal" because it promises driving distances that exceed the USGA's standard. *Golf Digest* compared actual driving distances with the ERC driver and a USGA-approved driver with a population mean driving distance of 280 yards. Based on nine test drives, the mean driving distance by the ERC driver was 286.9 yards (*Golf Digest,* May 12, 2000). Answer the following questions assuming a sample standard deviation driving distance of 10 yards.   ↳ σ unknown

a.   Formulate the null and alternative hypotheses that can be used to determine whether the new ERC driver has a population mean driving distance greater than 280 yards.

b.   On average, how many yards farther did the golf ball travel with the ERC driver?

c.   At $\alpha = .05$, what is your conclusion?

34.  Joan's Nursery specializes in custom-designed landscaping for residential areas. The estimated labor cost associated with a particular landscaping proposal is based on the number of plantings of trees, shrubs, and so on to be used for the project. For cost-estimating purposes, managers use two hours of labor time for the planting of a medium-sized tree. Actual times from a sample of 10 plantings during the past month follow (times in hours).

| 1.7 | 1.5 | 2.6 | 2.2 | 2.4 | 2.3 | 2.6 | 3.0 | 1.4 | 2.3 |
|-----|-----|-----|-----|-----|-----|-----|-----|-----|-----|

With a .05 level of significance, test to see whether the mean tree-planting time differs from two hours.

a.   State the null and alternative hypotheses.
b.   Compute the sample mean.
c.   Compute the sample standard deviation.
d.   What is the *p*-value?
e.   What is your conclusion?

## 9.5 Population Proportion

In this section we show how to conduct a hypothesis test about a population proportion $p$. Using $p_0$ to denote the hypothesized value for the population proportion, the three forms for a hypothesis test about a population proportion are as follows.

$$
\begin{array}{ccc}
H_0: p \geq p_0 & H_0: p \leq p_0 & H_0: p = p_0 \\
H_a: p < p_0 & H_a: p > p_0 & H_a: p \neq p_0
\end{array}
$$

The first form is called a lower tail test, the second form is called an upper tail test, and the third form is called a two-tailed test.

Hypothesis tests about a population proportion are based on the difference between the sample proportion $\bar{p}$ and the hypothesized population proportion $p_0$. The methods used to conduct the hypothesis test are similar to those used for hypothesis tests about a population mean. The only difference is that we use the sample proportion and its standard error to compute the test statistic. The *p*-value approach or the critical value approach is then used to determine whether the null hypothesis should be rejected.

Let us consider an example involving a situation faced by Pine Creek golf course. Over the past year, 20% of the players at Pine Creek were women. In an effort to increase the proportion of women players, Pine Creek implemented a special promotion designed to attract women golfers. One month after the promotion was implemented, the course manager requested a statistical study to determine whether the proportion of women players at Pine Creek had increased. Because the objective of the study is to determine whether the proportion of women golfers increased, an upper tail test with $H_a: p > .20$ is appropriate. The null and alternative hypotheses for the Pine Creek hypothesis test are as follows:

$$
\begin{array}{c}
H_0: p \leq .20 \\
H_a: p > .20
\end{array}
$$

If $H_0$ can be rejected, the test results will give statistical support for the conclusion that the proportion of women golfers increased and the promotion was beneficial. The course manager specified that a level of significance of $\alpha = .05$ be used in carrying out this hypothesis test.

The next step of the hypothesis testing procedure is to select a sample and compute the value of an appropriate test statistic. To show how this step is done for the Pine Creek upper tail test, we begin with a general discussion of how to compute the value of the test statistic for any form of a hypothesis test about a population proportion. The sampling distribution of $\bar{p}$, the point estimator of the population parameter $p$, is the basis for developing the test statistic.

When the null hypothesis is true as an equality, the expected value of $\bar{p}$ equals the hypothesized value $p_0$; that is, $E(\bar{p}) = p_0$. The standard error of $\bar{p}$ is given by

$$
\sigma_{\bar{p}} = \sqrt{\frac{p_0(1 - p_0)}{n}}
$$

In Chapter 7 we said that if $np \geq 5$ and $n(1 - p) \geq 5$, the sampling distribution of $\bar{p}$ can be approximated by a normal distribution.* Under these conditions, which usually apply in practice, the quantity

$$z = \frac{\bar{p} - p_0}{\sigma_{\bar{p}}} \qquad (9.5)$$

has a standard normal probability distribution. With $\sigma_{\bar{p}} = \sqrt{p_0(1 - p_0)/n}$, the standard normal random variable $z$ is the test statistic used to conduct hypothesis tests about a population proportion.

---

**TEST STATISTIC FOR HYPOTHESIS TESTS ABOUT A POPULATION PROPORTION**

$$z = \frac{\bar{p} - p_0}{\sqrt{\dfrac{p_0(1 - p_0)}{n}}} \qquad (9.6)$$

---

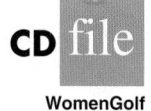

**CD file**

**WomenGolf**

We can now compute the test statistic for the Pine Creek hypothesis test. Suppose a random sample of 400 players was selected, and that 100 of the players were women. The proportion of women golfers in the sample is

$$\bar{p} = \frac{100}{400} = .25$$

Using equation (9.6), the value of the test statistic is

$$z = \frac{\bar{p} - p_0}{\sqrt{\dfrac{p_0(1 - p_0)}{n}}} = \frac{.25 - .20}{\sqrt{\dfrac{.20(1 - .20)}{400}}} = \frac{.05}{.02} = 2.50$$

Because the Pine Creek hypothesis test is an upper tail test, the $p$-value is the probability that $z$ is greater than or equal to $z = 2.50$; that is, it is the area under the standard normal curve to the right of $z = 2.50$. Using the table of areas for the standard normal distribution, we find that the area between the mean and $z = 2.50$ is .4938. Thus, the $p$-value for the Pine Creek test is $.5000 - .4938 = .0062$. Figure 9.10 shows this $p$-value calculation.

Recall that the course manager specified a level of significance of $\alpha = .05$. A $p$-value $= .0062 < .05$ gives sufficient statistical evidence to reject $H_0$ at the .05 level of significance. Thus, the test provides statistical support for the conclusion that the special promotion increased the proportion of women players at the Pine Creek golf course.

The decision whether to reject the null hypothesis can also be made using the critical value approach. The critical value corresponding to an area of .05 in the upper tail of a stan-

---

*In most applications involving hypothesis tests of a population proportion, sample sizes are large enough to use the normal approximation. The exact sampling distribution of $\bar{p}$ is discrete with the probability for each value of $\bar{p}$ given by the binomial distribution. So hypothesis testing is a bit more complicated for small samples when the normal approximation cannot be used.

**FIGURE 9.10    CALCULATION OF THE $p$-VALUE FOR THE PINE CREEK HYPOTHESIS TEST**

Area = .4938

$p$-value = $p(z \geq 2.50)$ = .0062

0    2.5    $z$

dard normal distribution is $z_{.05} = 1.645$. Thus, the rejection rule using the critical value approach is to reject $H_0$ if $z \geq 1.645$. Because $z = 2.50 > 1.645$, $H_0$ is rejected.

Again, we see that the $p$-value approach and the critical value approach lead to the same hypothesis testing conclusion, but the $p$-value approach provides more information. With a $p$-value = .0062, the null hypothesis would be rejected for any level of significance greater than or equal to .0062.

## Summary

The procedure used to conduct a hypothesis test about a population proportion is similar to the procedure used to conduct a hypothesis test about a population mean. Although we only illustrated how to conduct a hypothesis test about a population proportion for an upper tail test, similar procedures can be used for lower tail and two-tailed tests. Table 9.4 provides a summary of the hypothesis tests about a population proportion.

**TABLE 9.4    SUMMARY OF HYPOTHESIS TESTS ABOUT A POPULATION PROPORTION**

|  | **Lower Tail Test** | **Upper Tail Test** | **Two-Tailed Test** |
|---|---|---|---|
| **Hypotheses** | $H_0: p \geq p_0$ <br> $H_a: p < p_0$ | $H_0: p \leq p_0$ <br> $H_a: p > p_0$ | $H_0: p = p_0$ <br> $H_a: p \neq p_0$ |
| **Test Statistic** | $z = \dfrac{\bar{p} - p_0}{\sqrt{\dfrac{p_0(1 - p_0)}{n}}}$ | $z = \dfrac{\bar{p} - p_0}{\sqrt{\dfrac{p_0(1 - p_0)}{n}}}$ | $z = \dfrac{\bar{p} - p_0}{\sqrt{\dfrac{p_0(1 - p_0)}{n}}}$ |
| **Rejection Rule:** <br> **$p$-Value Approach** | Reject $H_0$ if <br> $p$-value $\leq \alpha$ | Reject $H_0$ if <br> $p$-value $\leq \alpha$ | Reject $H_0$ if <br> $p$-value $\leq \alpha$ |
| **Rejection Rule:** <br> **Critical Value** <br> **Approach** | Reject $H_0$ if <br> $z \leq -z_\alpha$ | Reject $H_0$ if <br> $z \geq z_\alpha$ | Reject $H_0$ if <br> $z \leq -z_{\alpha/2}$ <br> or if $z \geq z_{\alpha/2}$ |

## Exercises

## Methods

35. Consider the following hypothesis test:

$$H_0: p = .20$$
$$H_a: p \neq .20$$

A sample of 400 provided a sample proportion $\bar{p} = .175$.

a. Compute the value of the test statistic.
b. What is the $p$-value?
c. At $\alpha = .05$, what is your conclusion?
d. What is the rejection rule using the critical value? What is your conclusion?

36. Consider the following hypothesis test:

$$H_0: p \geq .75$$
$$H_a: p < .75$$

A sample of 300 items was selected. At $\alpha = .05$, compute the $p$-value and state your conclusion for each of the following sample results.

a. $\bar{p} = .68$
b. $\bar{p} = .72$
c. $\bar{p} = .70$
d. $\bar{p} = .77$

## Applications

37. The Heldrich Center for Workforce Development found that 40% of Internet users received more than 10 e-mail messages per day (*USA Today,* May 7, 2000). A similar study on the use of e-mail was repeated in 2002.

a. Formulate the hypotheses that can be used to determine whether the proportion of Internet users receiving more than 10 e-mail messages per day increased.
b. If a sample of 425 Internet users found 189 receiving more than 10 e-mail messages per day, what is the $p$-value?
c. At $\alpha = .05$, what is your conclusion?

38. A study by *Consumer Reports* showed that 64% of supermarket shoppers believe supermarket brands to be as good as national name brands. To investigate whether this result applies to its own product, the manufacturer of a national name-brand ketchup asked a sample of shoppers whether they believed that supermarket ketchup was as good as the national brand ketchup.

a. Formulate the hypotheses that could be used to determine whether the percentage of supermarket shoppers who believe that the supermarket ketchup was as good as the national brand ketchup differed from 64%.
b. If a sample of 100 shoppers showed 52 stating that the supermarket brand was as good as the national brand, what is the $p$-value?
c. At $\alpha = .05$, what is your conclusion?
d. Should the national brand ketchup manufacturer be pleased with this conclusion? Explain.

39. The National Center for Health Statistics released a report that stated 70% of adults do not exercise regularly (*Associated Press,* April 7, 2002). A researcher decided to conduct a study to see whether the National Center for Health Statistics' claim differed on a state-by-state basis.

a. State the null and alternative hypothesis assuming the intent of the researcher is to identify states that differ from the 70% reported by the National Center for Health Statistics.

b. At $\alpha = .05$, what is the research conclusion for the following states:

Wisconsin:  252 of 350 adults did not exercise regularly
California:  189 of 300 adults did not exercise regularly

40. Before the 2003 Super Bowl, ABC predicted that 22% of the Super Bowl audience would express an interest in seeing one of its forthcoming new television shows, including "8 Simple Rules," "Are You Hot?," and "Dragnet." ABC ran commercials for these television shows during the Super Bowl. The day after the Super Bowl, Intermediate Advertising Group of New York sampled 1532 viewers who saw the commercials and found that 414 said that they would watch one of the ABC advertised television shows (*The Wall Street Journal,* January 30, 2003).

a. What is the point estimate of the proportion of the audience that said they would watch the television shows after seeing the television commercials?

b. At $\alpha = .05$, determine whether the intent to watch the ABC television shows significantly increased after seeing the television commercials. Formulate the appropriate hypotheses, compute the $p$-value, and state your conclusion.

c. Why are such studies valuable to companies and advertising firms?

41. Microsoft Outlook is the most widely used e-mail manager. A Microsoft executive claims that Microsoft Outlook is used by at least 75% of Internet users. A sample of Internet users will be used to test this claim.

a. Formulate the hypotheses that can be used to test the claim.

b. A Merrill Lynch study reported that Microsoft Outlook is used by 72% of Internet users (CNBC, June 2000). Assume that the report was based on a sample size of 300 Internet users. What is the $p$-value?

c. At $\alpha = .05$, should the executive's claim of at least 75% be rejected?

42. According to the Census Bureau's American Housing Survey, the primary reason people who move chose their new neighborhood is because the location is convenient to work (*USA Today,* December 24, 2002). Based on 1990 Census Bureau data, we know that 24% of the population of people who moved selected "location convenient to work" as the reason for selecting their new neighborhood. Assume a sample of 300 people who moved during 2003 found 93 did so to be closer to work. Do the sample data support the research conclusion that in 2003 more people are choosing where to live based on how close they will be to their work? What is the point estimate of the proportion of people who moved during 2003 that chose their new neighborhood because the location is convenient to work? What is your research conclusion? Use $\alpha = .05$.

43. An article about driving practices in Strathcona County, Alberta, Canada, claimed that 48% of drivers did not stop at stop sign intersections on county roads (*Edmonton Journal,* July 19, 2000). Two months later, a follow-up study collected data in order to see whether this percentage had changed.

a. Formulate the hypotheses to determine whether the proportion of drivers who did not stop at stop sign intersections had changed.

b. Assume the study found 360 of 800 drivers did not stop at stop sign intersections. What is the sample proportion? What is the $p$-value?

c. At $\alpha = .05$, what is your conclusion?

44. Burger King sponsored what is believed to have been the biggest product giveaway in fast-food history when it initiated "FreeFryDay" on Friday, January 2, 1998. Anyone who stopped at one of Burger King's 7400 restaurants received a free order of the new Burger King fries. A national taste test comparing the new Burger King fries to McDonald's fries was the basis for the Burger King promotion. (*USA Today,* December 10, 1997.) Let $p$ denote the population proportion who prefer the Burger King fries.

a. Formulate the hypotheses that can be used to help determine whether more than 50% of the population prefer the Burger King fries.

b. Of 500 customers who participated in the taste test, 285 expressed a preference for the Burger King fries. What is the sample proportion? What is the $p$-value?

c. At $\alpha = .01$, what is your conclusion?

d. How did the national taste test statistics help Burger King's management decide to implement the "FreeFryDay" campaign? Discuss.

45. Drugstore.com was the first e-commerce company to offer Internet drugstore retailing. Drugstore.com customers were provided the opportunity to buy health, beauty, personal care, wellness, and pharmaceutical replenishment products over the Internet. At the end of 10 months of operation, the company reported that 44% of orders were from repeat customers (*Drugstore.com Annual Report,* January 2, 2000). Assume that Drugstore.com will use a sample of customer orders each quarter to determine whether the proportion of orders from repeat customers changed from the initial $p = .44$.

a. Formulate the null and alternative hypotheses.

b. During the first quarter a sample of 500 orders showed 205 repeat customers. What is the $p$-value? Use $\alpha = .05$. What is your conclusion?

c. During the second quarter a sample of 500 orders showed 245 repeat customers. What is the $p$-value? Use $\alpha = .05$. What is your conclusion?

#   Hypothesis Testing and Decision Making

In Section 9.1 we discussed three types of situations in which hypothesis testing is used:

1. Testing research hypotheses
2. Testing the validity of a claim
3. Testing in decision-making situations

In the first two situations, action is taken only when the null hypothesis $H_0$ is rejected and hence the alternative hypothesis $H_a$ is concluded to be true. In the third situation—decision making—it is necessary to take action when the null hypothesis is not rejected as well as when it is rejected.

The hypothesis testing procedures presented thus far have limited applicability in a decision-making situation because it is not considered appropriate to accept $H_0$ and take action based on the conclusion that $H_0$ is true. The reason for not taking action when the test results indicate *do not reject* $H_0$ is that the decision to accept $H_0$ exposes the decision maker to the risk of making a Type II error; that is, accepting $H_0$ when it is false. With the hypothesis testing procedures described in the preceding sections, the probability of a Type I error is controlled by establishing a level of significance for the test. However, the probability of making the Type II error is not controlled.

Clearly, in certain decision-making situations the decision maker may want—and in some cases may be forced—to take action with both the conclusion *do not reject* $H_0$ and the conclusion *reject* $H_0$. A good illustration of this situation is lot-acceptance sampling, a topic we will discuss in more depth in Chapter 20. For example, a quality control manager must decide to accept a shipment of batteries from a supplier or to return the shipment because of poor quality. Assume that design specifications require batteries from the supplier to have a mean useful life of at least 120 hours. To evaluate the quality of an incoming shipment, a sample of 36 batteries will be selected and tested. On the basis of the sample, a decision must be made to accept the shipment of batteries or to return it to the supplier because of poor quality. Let $\mu$ denote the mean number of hours of useful life for batteries in the shipment. The null and alternative hypotheses about the population mean follow.

$$H_0: \mu \geq 120$$
$$H_a: \mu < 120$$

If $H_0$ is rejected, the alternative hypothesis is concluded to be true. This conclusion indicates that the appropriate action is to return the shipment to the supplier. However, if $H_0$ is not rejected, the decision maker must still determine what action should be taken. Thus, without directly concluding that $H_0$ is true, but merely by not rejecting it, the decision maker will have made the decision to accept the shipment as being of satisfactory quality.

In such decision-making situations, it is recommended that the hypothesis testing procedure be extended to control the probability of making a Type II error. Because a decision will be made and action taken when we do not reject $H_0$, knowledge of the probability of making a Type II error will be helpful. In Sections 9.7 and 9.8 we explain how to compute the probability of making a Type II error and how the sample size can be adjusted to help control the probability of making a Type II error.

 # 9.7  Calculating the Probability of Type II Errors

In this section we show how to calculate the probability of making a Type II error for a hypothesis test about a population mean. We illustrate the procedure by using the lot-acceptance example described in Section 9.6. The null and alternative hypotheses about the mean number of hours of useful life for a shipment of batteries are $H_0: \mu \geq 120$ and $H_a: \mu < 120$. If $H_0$ is rejected, the decision will be to return the shipment to the supplier because the mean hours of useful life are less than the specified 120 hours. If $H_0$ is not rejected, the decision will be to accept the shipment.

Suppose a level of significance of $\alpha = .05$ is used to conduct the hypothesis test. The test statistic in the $\sigma$ known case is

$$z = \frac{\bar{x} - \mu_0}{\sigma/\sqrt{n}} = \frac{\bar{x} - 120}{\sigma/\sqrt{n}}$$

Based on the critical value approach and $z_{.05} = 1.645$, the rejection rule for the lower tail test is

$$\text{Reject } H_0 \text{ if } z \leq -1.645$$

Suppose a sample of 36 batteries will be selected and based upon previous testing the population standard deviation can be assumed known with a value of $\sigma = 12$ hours. The rejection rule indicates that we will reject $H_0$ if

$$z = \frac{\bar{x} - 120}{12/\sqrt{36}} \leq -1.645$$

Solving for $\bar{x}$ in the preceding expression indicates that we will reject $H_0$ if

$$\bar{x} \leq 120 - 1.645\left(\frac{12}{\sqrt{36}}\right) = 116.71$$

Rejecting $H_0$ when $\bar{x} \leq 116.71$ means that we will make the decision to accept the shipment whenever

$$\bar{x} > 116.71$$

With this information, we are ready to compute probabilities associated with making a Type II error. First, recall that we make a Type II error whenever the true shipment mean is less than 120 hours and we make the decision to accept $H_0$: $\mu \geq 120$. Hence, to compute the probability of making a Type II error, we must select a value of $\mu$ less than 120 hours. For example, suppose the shipment is considered to be of poor quality if the batteries have a mean life of $\mu = 112$ hours. If $\mu = 112$ is really true, what is the probability of accepting $H_0$: $\mu \geq 120$ and hence committing a Type II error? Note that this probability is the probability that the sample mean $\bar{x}$ is greater than 116.71 when $\mu = 112$.

Figure 9.11 shows the sampling distribution of $\bar{x}$ when the mean is $\mu = 112$. The shaded area in the upper tail gives the probability of obtaining $\bar{x} > 116.71$. Using the standard normal distribution, we see that at $\bar{x} = 116.71$

$$z = \frac{\bar{x} - \mu}{\sigma/\sqrt{n}} = \frac{116.71 - 112}{12/\sqrt{36}} = 2.36$$

The standard normal distribution table shows that with $z = 2.36$, the area in the upper tail is $.5000 - .4909 = .0091$. Thus, $.0091$ is the probability of making a Type II error when $\mu = 112$. Denoting the probability of making a Type II error as $\beta$, we see that when $\mu = 112$, $\beta = .0091$. Therefore, we can conclude that if the mean of the population is 112 hours, the probability of making a Type II error is only $.0091$.

We can repeat these calculations for other values of $\mu$ less than 120. Doing so will show a different probability of making a Type II error for each value of $\mu$. For example, suppose the shipment of batteries has a mean useful life of $\mu = 115$ hours. Because we will accept $H_0$ whenever $\bar{x} > 116.71$, the z value for $\mu = 115$ is given by

$$z = \frac{\bar{x} - \mu}{\sigma/\sqrt{n}} = \frac{116.71 - 115}{12/\sqrt{36}} = .86$$

**FIGURE 9.11   PROBABILITY OF A TYPE II ERROR WHEN $\mu = 112$**

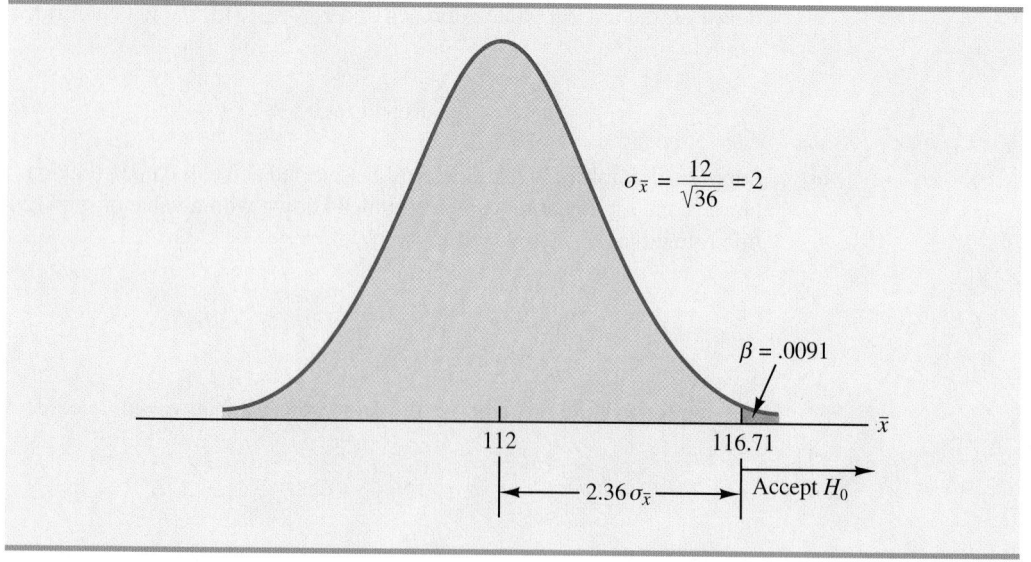

**TABLE 9.5    PROBABILITY OF MAKING A TYPE II ERROR FOR THE LOT-ACCEPTANCE HYPOTHESIS TEST**

| Value of $\mu$ | $z = \dfrac{116.71 - \mu}{12/\sqrt{36}}$ | Probability of a Type II Error ($\beta$) | Power $(1 - \beta)$ |
|---|---|---|---|
| 112 | 2.36 | .0091 | .9909 |
| 114 | 1.36 | .0869 | .9131 |
| 115 | .86 | .1949 | .8051 |
| 116.71 | .00 | .5000 | .5000 |
| 117 | −.15 | .5596 | .4404 |
| 118 | −.65 | .7422 | .2578 |
| 119.999 | −1.645 | .9500 | .0500 |

From the standard normal distribution table, we find that the area in the upper tail of the standard normal distribution for $z = .86$ is $.5000 - .3051 = .1949$. Thus, the probability of making a Type II error is $\beta = .1949$ when the true mean is $\mu = 115$.

*As Table 9.5 shows, the probability of a Type II error depends on the value of the population mean $\mu$. For values of $\mu$ near $\mu_0$, the probability of making the Type II error can be high.*

In Table 9.5 we show the probability of making a Type II error for a variety of values of $\mu$ less than 120. Note that as $\mu$ increases toward 120, the probability of making a Type II error increases toward an upper bound of .95. However, as $\mu$ decreases to values farther below 120, the probability of making a Type II error diminishes. This pattern is what we should expect. When the true population mean $\mu$ is close to the null hypothesis value of $\mu = 120$, the probability is high that we will make a Type II error. However, when the true population mean $\mu$ is far below the null hypothesis value of $\mu = 120$, the probability is low that we will make a Type II error.

The probability of correctly rejecting $H_0$ when it is false is called the **power** of the test. For any particular value of $\mu$, the power is $1 - \beta$; that is, the probability of correctly rejecting the null hypothesis is 1 minus the probability of making a Type II error. Values of power are also listed in Table 9.5. On the basis of these values, the power associated with each value of $\mu$ is shown graphically in Figure 9.12. Such a graph is called a **power curve**.

**FIGURE 9.12    POWER CURVE FOR THE LOT-ACCEPTANCE HYPOTHESIS TEST**

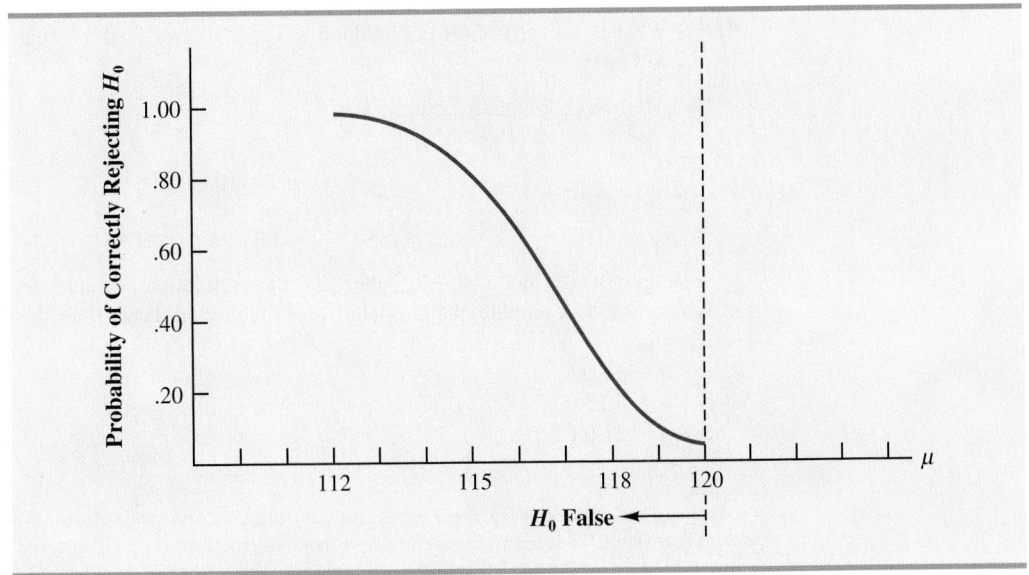

Note that the power curve extends over the values of $\mu$ for which the null hypothesis is false. The height of the power curve at any value of $\mu$ indicates the probability of correctly rejecting $H_0$ when $H_0$ is false.*

In summary, the following step-by-step procedure can be used to compute the probability of making a Type II error in hypothesis tests about a population mean.

1.  Formulate the null and alternative hypotheses.
2.  Use the level of significance $\alpha$ and the critical value approach to determine the critical value and the rejection rule for the test.
3.  Use the rejection rule to solve for the value of the sample mean corresponding to the critical value of the test statistic.
4.  Use the results from step 3 to state the values of the sample mean that lead to the acceptance of $H_0$. These values define the acceptance region for the test.
5.  Use the sampling distribution of $\bar{x}$ for a value of $\mu$ satisfying the alternative hypothesis, and the acceptance region from step 4, to compute the probability that the sample mean will be in the acceptance region. This probability is the probability of making a Type II error at the chosen value of $\mu$.

## Exercises

## Methods

46.  Consider the following hypothesis test.

$$H_0: \mu \geq 10$$
$$H_a: \mu < 10$$

The sample size is 120 and the population standard deviation is assumed known with $\sigma = 5$. Use $\alpha = .05$.

a.  If the population mean is 9, what is the probability that the sample mean leads to the conclusion *do not reject $H_0$*?
b.  What type of error would be made if the actual population mean is 9 and we conclude that $H_0: \mu \geq 10$ is true?
c.  What is the probability of making a Type II error if the actual population mean is 8?

47.  Consider the following hypothesis test.

$$H_0: \mu = 20$$
$$H_a: \mu \neq 20$$

A sample of 200 items will be taken and the population standard deviation is $\sigma = 10$. Use $\alpha = .05$. Compute the probability of making a Type II error if the population mean is:

a.  $\mu = 18.0$
b.  $\mu = 22.5$
c.  $\mu = 21.0$

___

*Another graph, called the *operating characteristic curve*, is sometimes used to provide information about the probability of making a Type II error. The operating characteristic curve shows the probability of accepting $H_0$ and thus provides $\beta$ for the values of $\mu$ where the null hypothesis is false. The probability of making a Type II error can be read directly from this graph.

## Applications

48. Fowle Marketing Research, Inc., bases charges to a client on the assumption that telephone surveys can be completed within 15 minutes or less. If more time is required, a premium rate is charged. With a sample of 35 surveys, a population standard deviation of 4 minutes, and a level of significance of .01, the sample mean will be used to test the null hypothesis $H_0$: $\mu \le 15$.
    a. What is your interpretation of the Type II error for this problem? What is its impact on the firm?
    b. What is the probability of making a Type II error when the actual mean time is $\mu = 17$ minutes?
    c. What is the probability of making a Type II error when the actual mean time is $\mu = 18$ minutes?
    d. Sketch the general shape of the power curve for this test.

49. A consumer research group is interested in testing an automobile manufacturer's claim that a new economy model will travel at least 25 miles per gallon of gasoline ($H_0$: $\mu \ge 25$).
    a. With a .02 level of significance and a sample of 30 cars, what is the rejection rule based on the value of $\bar{x}$ for the test to determine whether the manufacturer's claim should be rejected? Assume that $\sigma$ is 3 miles per gallon.
    b. What is the probability of committing a Type II error if the actual mileage is 23 miles per gallon?
    c. What is the probability of committing a Type II error if the actual mileage is 24 miles per gallon?
    d. What is the probability of committing a Type II error if the actual mileage is 25.5 miles per gallon?

50. *Young Adult* magazine states the following hypotheses about the mean age of its subscribers.

$$H_0: \mu = 28$$
$$H_a: \mu \ne 28$$

    a. What would it mean to make a Type II error in this situation?
    b. The population standard deviation is assumed known at $\sigma = 6$ years and the sample size is 100. With $\alpha = .05$, what is the probability of accepting $H_0$ for $\mu$ equal to 26, 27, 29, and 30?
    c. What is the power at $\mu = 26$? What does this result tell you?

51. A production line operation is tested for filling weight accuracy using the following hypotheses.

| Hypothesis | Conclusion and Action |
|---|---|
| $H_0$: $\mu = 16$ | Filling okay; keep running |
| $H_a$: $\mu \ne 16$ | Filling off standard; stop and adjust machine |

The sample size is 30 and the population standard deviation is $\sigma = .8$. Use $\alpha = .05$.
    a. What would a Type II error mean in this situation?
    b. What is the probability of making a Type II error when the machine is overfilling by .5 ounces?
    c. What is the power of the statistical test when the machine is overfilling by .5 ounces?
    d. Show the power curve for this hypothesis test. What information does it contain for the production manager?

52. Refer to Exercise 48. Assume the firm selects a sample of 50 surveys and repeat parts (b) and (c). What observation can you make about how increasing the sample size affects the probability of making a Type II error?

53. Sparr Investments, Inc., specializes in tax-deferred investment opportunities for its clients. Recently Sparr offered a payroll deduction investment program for the employees of a particular company. Sparr estimates that the employees are currently averaging $100 or less per month in tax-deferred investments. A sample of 40 employees will be used to test Sparr's hypothesis about the current level of investment activity among the population of employees. Assume the employee monthly tax-deferred investment amounts have a standard deviation of $75 and that a .05 level of significance will be used in the hypothesis test.
   a.  What is the Type II error in this situation?
   b.  What is the probability of the Type II error if the actual mean employee monthly investment is $120?
   c.  What is the probability of the Type II error if the actual mean employee monthly investment is $130?
   d.  Assume a sample size of 80 employees is used and repeat parts (b) and (c).

# 9.8  Determining the Sample Size for Hypothesis Tests About a Population Mean

Assume that a hypothesis test is to be conducted about the value of a population mean. The level of significance specified by the user determines the probability of making a Type I error for the test. By controlling the sample size, the user can also control the probability of making a Type II error. Let us show how a sample size can be determined for the following lower tail test about a population mean.

$$H_0: \mu \geq \mu_0$$
$$H_a: \mu < \mu_0$$

The upper panel of Figure 9.13 is the sampling distribution of $\bar{x}$ when $H_0$ is true with $\mu = \mu_0$. For a lower tail test, the critical value of the test statistic is denoted $-z_\alpha$. In the upper panel of the figure the vertical line, labeled $c$, is the corresponding value of $\bar{x}$. Note that, if we reject $H_0$ when $\bar{x} \leq c$, the probability of a Type I error will be $\alpha$. With $z_\alpha$ representing the $z$ value corresponding to an area of $\alpha$ in the upper tail of the standard normal distribution, we compute $c$ using the following formula:

$$c = \mu_0 - z_\alpha \frac{\sigma}{\sqrt{n}} \qquad (9.7)$$

The lower panel of Figure 9.13 is the sampling distribution of $\bar{x}$ when the alternative hypothesis is true with $\mu = \mu_a < \mu_0$. The shaded region shows $\beta$, the probability of a Type II error that the decision maker will be exposed to if the null hypothesis is accepted when $\bar{x} > c$. With $z_\beta$ representing the $z$ value corresponding to an area of $\beta$ in the upper tail of the standard normal distribution, we compute $c$ using the following formula:

$$c = \mu_a + z_\beta \frac{\sigma}{\sqrt{n}} \qquad (9.8)$$

Now what we want to do is to select a value for $c$ so that when we reject $H_0$ and accept $H_a$, the probability of a Type I error is equal to the chosen value of $\alpha$ and the probability of a Type II error is equal to the chosen value of $\beta$. Therefore, both equations (9.7) and (9.8) must provide the same value for $c$. Thus, the following equation must be true.

$$\mu_0 - z_\alpha \frac{\sigma}{\sqrt{n}} = \mu_a + z_\beta \frac{\sigma}{\sqrt{n}}$$

**FIGURE 9.13**    DETERMINING THE SAMPLE SIZE FOR SPECIFIED LEVELS
OF THE TYPE I ($\alpha$) AND TYPE II ($\beta$) ERRORS

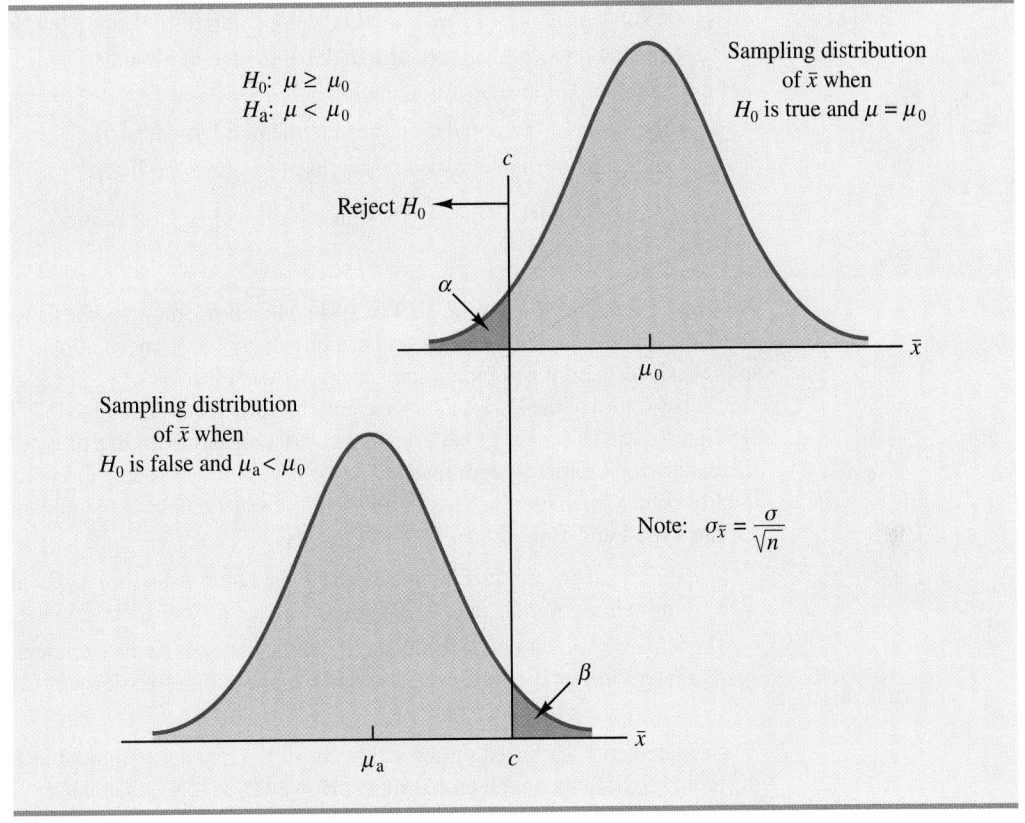

To determine the required sample size, we first solve for the $\sqrt{n}$ as follows.

$$\mu_0 - \mu_a = z_\alpha \frac{\sigma}{\sqrt{n}} + z_\beta \frac{\sigma}{\sqrt{n}}$$

$$\mu_0 - \mu_a = \frac{(z_\alpha + z_\beta)\sigma}{\sqrt{n}}$$

and

$$\sqrt{n} = \frac{(z_\alpha + z_\beta)\sigma}{(\mu_0 - \mu_a)}$$

Squaring both sides of the expression provides the following sample size formula for a one-tailed hypothesis test about a population mean.

SAMPLE SIZE FOR A ONE-TAILED HYPOTHESIS TEST ABOUT A
POPULATION MEAN

$$n = \frac{(z_\alpha + z_\beta)^2 \sigma^2}{(\mu_0 - \mu_a)^2} \tag{9.9}$$

where

$z_\alpha$ = z value providing an area of $\alpha$ in the upper tail of a standard normal distribution

$z_\beta$ = z value providing an area of $\beta$ in the upper tail of a standard normal distribution

$\sigma$ = the population standard deviation

$\mu_0$ = the value of the population mean in the null hypothesis

$\mu_a$ = the value of the population mean used for the Type II error

*Note:* In a two-tailed hypothesis test, use (9.9) with $z_{\alpha/2}$ replacing $z_\alpha$.

Although the logic of equation (9.9) was developed for the hypothesis test shown in Figure 9.13, it holds for any one-tailed test about a population mean. Note that in a two-tailed hypothesis test about a population mean, $z_{\alpha/2}$ is used instead of $z_\alpha$ in equation (9.9).

Let us return to the lot-acceptance example from Sections 9.6 and 9.7. The design specification for the shipment of batteries indicated a mean useful life of at least 120 hours for the batteries. Shipments were rejected if $H_0: \mu \geq 120$ was rejected. Let us assume that the quality control manager makes the following statements about the allowable probabilities for the Type I and Type II errors.

Type I error statement: If the mean life of the batteries in the shipment is $\mu = 120$, I am willing to risk an $\alpha = .05$ probability of rejecting the shipment.

Type II error statement: If the mean life of the batteries in the shipment is five hours under the specification (i.e., $\mu = 115$), I am willing to risk a $\beta = .10$ probability of accepting the shipment.

These statements are based on the judgment of the manager. Someone else might specify different restrictions on the probabilities. However, statements about the allowable probabilities of both errors must be made before the sample size can be determined.

In the example, $\alpha = .05$ and $\beta = .10$. Using the standard normal probability distribution, we have $z_{.05} = 1.645$ and $z_{.10} = 1.28$. From the statements about the error probabilities, we note that $\mu_0 = 120$ and $\mu_a = 115$. Finally, the population standard deviation was assumed known at $\sigma = 12$. By using equation (9.9), we find that the recommended sample size for the lot-acceptance example is

$$n = \frac{(1.645 + 1.28)^2 (12)^2}{(120 - 115)^2} = 49.3$$

Rounding up, we recommend a sample size of 50.

Because both the Type I and Type II error probabilities have been controlled at allowable levels with $n = 50$, the quality control manager is now justified in using the *accept $H_0$* and *reject $H_0$* statements for the hypothesis test. The accompanying inferences are made with allowable probabilities of making Type I and Type II errors.

We can make three observations about the relationship among $\alpha$, $\beta$, and the sample size $n$.

1. Once two of the three values are known, the other can be computed.
2. For a given level of significance $\alpha$, increasing the sample size will reduce $\beta$.
3. For a given sample size, decreasing $\alpha$ will increase $\beta$, whereas increasing $\alpha$ will decrease $\beta$.

The third observation should be kept in mind when the probability of a Type II error is not being controlled. It suggests that one should not choose unnecessarily small values for the level of significance $\alpha$. For a given sample size, choosing a smaller level of significance means more exposure to a Type II error. Inexperienced users of hypothesis testing often think that smaller values of $\alpha$ are always better. They are better if we are concerned only about making a Type I error. However, smaller values of $\alpha$ have the disadvantage of increasing the probability of making a Type II error.

## Exercises

### Methods

54. Consider the following hypothesis test.

$$H_0: \mu \geq 10$$
$$H_a: \mu < 10$$

The sample size is 120 and the population standard deviation is 5. Use $\alpha = .05$. If the actual population mean is 9, the probability of a Type II error is .2912. Suppose the researcher wants to reduce the probability of a Type II error to .10 when the actual population mean is 9. What sample size is recommended?

55. Consider the following hypothesis test.

$$H_0: \mu = 20$$
$$H_a: \mu \neq 20$$

The population standard deviation is 10. Use $\alpha = .05$. How large a sample should be taken if the researcher is willing to accept a .05 probability of making a Type II error when the actual population mean is 22?

### Applications

56. Suppose the project director for the Hilltop Coffee study (see Section 9.3) asked for a .10 probability of claiming that Hilltop was not in violation when it really was underfilling by 1 ounce ($\mu_a = 2.9375$ pounds). What sample size would have been recommended?

57. A special industrial battery must have a life of at least 400 hours. A hypothesis test is to be conducted with a .02 level of significance. If the batteries from a particular production run have an actual mean use life of 385 hours, the production manager wants a sampling procedure that only 10% of the time would show erroneously that the batch is acceptable. What sample size is recommended for the hypothesis test? Use 30 hours as an estimate of the population standard deviation.

58. *Young Adult* magazine states the following hypotheses about the mean age of its subscribers.

$$H_0: \mu = 28$$
$$H_a: \mu \neq 28$$

If the manager conducting the test will permit a .15 probability of making a Type II error when the true mean age is 29, what sample size should be selected? Assume $\sigma = 6$ and a .05 level of significance.

59. An automobile mileage study tested the following hypotheses.

| Hypothesis | Conclusion |
| --- | --- |
| $H_0: \mu \geq 25$ mpg | Manufacturer's claim supported |
| $H_a: \mu < 25$ mpg | Manufacturer's claim rejected; average mileage per gallon less than stated |

For $\sigma = 3$ and a .02 level of significance, what sample size would be recommended if the researcher wants an 80% chance of detecting that $\mu$ is less than 25 miles per gallon when it is actually 24?

## Summary

Hypothesis testing is a statistical procedure that uses sample data to determine whether a statement about the value of a population parameter should or should not be rejected. The hypotheses are two competing statements about a population parameter. One statement is called the null hypothesis, $(H_0)$ and the other statement is called the alternative hypothesis $(H_a)$. In Section 9.1 we provided guidelines for developing hypotheses for three situations frequently encountered in practice.

Whenever historical data or other information provides a basis for assuming that the population standard deviation is known, the hypothesis testing procedure is based on the standard normal distribution. Whenever $\sigma$ is unknown, the sample standard deviation $s$ is used to estimate $\sigma$ and the hypothesis testing procedure is based on the $t$ distribution. In both cases, the quality of results depends on both the form of the population distribution and the sample size. If the population has a normal distribution, both hypothesis testing procedures are applicable, even with small sample sizes. If the population is not normally distributed, larger sample sizes are needed. General guidelines about the sample size were provided in Sections 9.3 and 9.4. In the case of hypothesis tests about a population proportion, the hypothesis testing procedure uses a test statistic based on the standard normal distribution.

In all cases, the value of the test statistic can be used to compute a $p$-value for the test. A $p$-value is a probability, computed using the test statistic, that measures the support (or lack of support) provided by the sample for the null hypothesis. If the $p$-value is less than or equal to the level of significance $\alpha$, the null hypothesis can be rejected.

Hypothesis testing conclusions can also be made by comparing the value of the test statistic to a critical value. For lower tail tests, the null hypothesis is rejected if the value of the test statistic is less than or equal to the critical value. For upper tail tests, the null hypothesis is rejected if the value of the test statistic is greater than or equal to the critical value. Two-tailed tests consist of two critical values: one in the lower tail of the sampling distribution and one in the upper tail. In this case, the null hypothesis is rejected if the value of the test statistic is less than or equal to the critical value in the lower tail or greater than or equal to the critical value in the upper tail.

Extensions of hypothesis testing procedures to include an analysis of the Type II error were also presented. In Section 9.7 we showed how to compute the probability of making a Type II error. In Section 9.8 we showed how to determine a sample size that will control for both the probability of making a Type I error and a Type II error.

## Glossary

**Null hypothesis** The hypothesis tentatively assumed true in the hypothesis testing procedure.
**Alternative hypothesis** The hypothesis concluded to be true if the null hypothesis is rejected.
**Type I error** The error of rejecting $H_0$ when it is true.
**Type II error** The error of accepting $H_0$ when it is false.
**Level of significance** The probability of making a Type I error when the null hypothesis is true as an equality.
**One-tailed test** A hypothesis test in which rejection of the null hypothesis occurs for values of the test statistic in one tail of its sampling distribution.
**Test statistic** A statistic whose value helps determine whether a null hypothesis can be rejected.
**$p$-value** A probability, computed using the test statistic, that measures the support (or lack of support) provided by the sample for the null hypothesis. For a lower tail test, the $p$-value is the probability of obtaining a value for the test statistic at least as small as that provided by the sample. For an upper tail test, the $p$-value is the probability of obtaining a value for

the test statistic at least as large as that provided by the sample. For a two-tailed test, the $p$-value is the probability of obtaining a value for the test statistic at least as unlikely as that provided by the sample.

**Critical value** A value that is compared with the test statistic to determine whether $H_0$ should be rejected.

**Two-tailed test** A hypothesis test in which rejection of the null hypothesis occurs for values of the test statistic in either tail of its sampling distribution.

**Power** The probability of correctly rejecting $H_0$ when it is false.

**Power curve** A graph of the probability of rejecting $H_0$ for all possible values of the population parameter not satisfying the null hypothesis. The power curve provides the probability of correctly rejecting the null hypothesis.

## Key Formulas

**Test Statistic for Hypothesis Tests About a Population Mean: $\sigma$ Known**

$$z = \frac{\bar{x} - \mu_0}{\sigma/\sqrt{n}}$$ (9.1)

**Test Statistic for Hypothesis Tests About a Population Mean: $\sigma$ Unknown**

$$t = \frac{\bar{x} - \mu_0}{s/\sqrt{n}}$$ (9.4)

**Test Statistic for Hypothesis Tests About a Population Proportion**

$$z = \frac{\bar{p} - p_0}{\sqrt{\dfrac{p_0(1 - p_0)}{n}}}$$ (9.6)

**Sample Size for a One-Tailed Hypothesis Test About a Population Mean**

$$n = \frac{(z_\alpha + z_\beta)^2 \sigma^2}{(\mu_0 - \mu_a)^2}$$ (9.9)

In a two-tailed test, replace $z_\alpha$ with $z_{\alpha/2}$.

## Supplementary Exercises

60.  A production line operates with a mean filling weight of 16 ounces per container. Over-filling or underfilling presents a serious problem and when detected requires the operator to shut down the production line to readjust the filling mechanism. From past data, a population standard deviation $\sigma = .8$ ounces is assumed. A quality control inspector selects a sample of 30 items every hour and at that time makes the decision of whether to shut down the line for readjustment. The level of significance is $\alpha = .05$.
   a.  State the hypothesis test for this quality control application.
   b.  If a sample mean of $\bar{x} = 16.32$ ounces were found, what is the $p$-value? What action would you recommend?
   c.  If a sample mean of $\bar{x} = 15.82$ ounces were found, what is the $p$-value? What action would you recommend?
   d.  Use the critical value approach. What is the rejection rule for the preceding hypothesis testing procedure? Repeat parts (b) and (c). Do you reach the same conclusion?

61. At Western University the historical mean of scholarship examination scores for freshman applications is 900. A historical population standard deviation $\sigma = 180$ is assumed known. Each year, the assistant dean uses a sample of applications to determine whether the mean examination score for the new freshman applications has changed.
    a. State the hypotheses.
    b. What is the 95% confidence interval estimate of the population mean examination score if a sample of 200 applications provided a sample mean $\bar{x} = 935$?
    c. Use the confidence interval to conduct a hypothesis test. Using $\alpha = .05$, what is your conclusion?
    d. What is the $p$-value?

62. The population mean annual salary for public school teachers in the state of New York is $45,250. A sample mean annual salary of public school teachers in New York City is $47,000 (*Time,* April 3, 2000). Assume the New York City results are based on a sample of 95 teachers. Assume the population standard deviation is $\sigma = \$6300$.
    a. Formulate the null and alternative hypotheses that can be used to determine whether the sample data support the conclusion that public school teachers in New York City have a higher mean salary than the public school teachers in the state of New York.
    b. What is the $p$-value?
    c. Use $\alpha = .01$. What is your conclusion?

63. According to the National Association of Colleges and Employers, the 2000 mean annual salary of business degree graduates in accounting was $37,000 (*Time,* May 8, 2000). In a follow-up study in June 2001, a sample of 48 graduating accounting majors provided a sample mean of $38,100 and a sample standard deviation of $5200.
    a. Formulate the null and alternative hypotheses that can be used to determine whether the sample data support the conclusion that June 2001 graduates in accounting have a mean salary greater than the 2000 mean annual salary of $37,000.
    b. What is the $p$-value?
    c. Use $\alpha = .05$. What is your conclusion?

64. The College Board reported that the average number of freshman class applications to public colleges and universities is 6000 (*USA Today,* December 26, 2002). During a recent application/enrollment period, a sample of 32 colleges and universities showed that the sample mean number of freshman class applications was 5812 with a sample standard deviation of 1140. Do the data indicate a change in the mean number of applications? Use $\alpha = .05$.

65. The *Motor Trend New Car Buyer's Guide* listed the Ford Taurus as having a highway fuel efficiency of 30 miles per gallon. A consumer interest group conducts automobile mileage tests seeking statistical evidence to identify instances where automobile manufacturers overstate the miles-per-gallon rating for a particular model.
    a. State the hypotheses that would enable the consumer interest group to conclude that the Ford Taurus fuel efficiency is less than the published 30 miles per gallon.
    b. A sample of 50 mileage tests with the Ford Taurus showed a sample mean of 29.6 miles per gallon and a sample standard deviation of 1.8 miles per gallon. What is the $p$-value?
    c. What conclusion should be drawn from the sample results? Use $\alpha = .01$.
    d. Repeat the preceding hypothesis test using the critical value approach.

66. The chamber of commerce of a Florida Gulf Coast community advertises that area residential property is available at a mean cost of $125,000 or less per lot. Suppose a sample of 32 properties provided a sample mean of $130,000 per lot and a sample standard deviation of $12,500. Using a .05 level of significance, test the validity of the advertising claim.

67. The population mean earnings per share for financial services corporations including American Express, E*TRADE Group, Goldman Sachs, and Merrill Lynch was $3 (*Business Week,* August 14, 2000). In 2001, a sample of 10 financial services corporations provided the following earnings per share data:

| 1.92 | 2.16 | 3.63 | 3.16 | 4.02 | 3.14 | 2.20 | 2.34 | 3.05 | 2.38 |
|------|------|------|------|------|------|------|------|------|------|

a. Formulate the null and alternative hypotheses that can be used to determine whether the population mean earnings per share in 2001 differ from the $3 reported in 2000.
b. Compute the sample mean.
c. Compute the sample standard deviation.
d. What is the $p$-value?
e. Use $\alpha = .05$. What is your conclusion?

68. A study by the Center for Disease Control (CDC) found that 23.3% of adults are smokers and that roughly 70% of those who do smoke indicate that they want to quit (*Associated Press,* July 26, 2002). CDC reported that, of people who smoked at some point in their lives, 50% have been able to kick the habit. Part of the study suggested that the success rate for quitting rose by education level. Assume that a sample of 100 college graduates who smoked at some point in their lives showed that 64 had been able to successfully stop smoking.
    a. State the hypotheses that can be used to determine whether the population of college graduates has a success rate higher than the overall population when it comes to breaking the smoking habit.
    b. Given the sample data, what is the proportion of college graduates who, having smoked at some point in their lives, were able to stop smoking?
    c. What is the $p$-value? At $\alpha = .01$, what is your hypothesis testing conclusion?

69. An airline promotion to business travelers is based on the assumption that two-thirds of business travelers use a laptop computer on overnight business trips.
    a. State the hypotheses that can be used to test the assumption.
    b. What is the sample proportion from an American Express sponsored survey that found 355 of 546 business travelers use a laptop computer on overnight business trips?
    c. What is the $p$-value?
    d. Use $\alpha = .05$. What is your conclusion?

70. Shell Oil office workers were asked which work schedule appealed most: working five 8-hour days a week or working four 10-hour days a week (*USA Today,* September 11, 2000). Let $p =$ the proportion of the office worker population preferring the four-10-hour-days work week.
    a. State the hypotheses if Shell management is interested in statistical support that shows more than 50% of office workers prefer the four-10-hour-days work week.
    b. What is the sample proportion if a sample of 105 office workers showed 67 preferred the four-10-hour-days schedule?
    c. What is the $p$-value? Use $\alpha = .01$. What is your conclusion?

71. The Department of Transportation reported Amtrak trains had a 78% on-time arrival record over the previous 12 months (*USA Today,* November 23, 1998). Assume that in 2001, a study found 330 of 400 Amtrak trains arrived on time. Does the sample indicate the Amtrak arrival rate has changed? Test at $\alpha = .05$.
    a. What is the sample proportion of Amtrak trains arriving on time?
    b. What is the $p$-value?
    c. What is your conclusion?

72. A radio station in Myrtle Beach announced that at least 90% of the hotels and motels would be full for the Memorial Day weekend. The station advised listeners to make reservations in advance if they planned to be in the resort over the weekend. On Saturday night a sample of 58 hotels and motels showed 49 with a no-vacancy sign and 9 with vacancies. What is your reaction to the radio station's claim after seeing the sample evidence? Use $\alpha = .05$ in making the statistical test. What is the $p$-value?

73. Environmental health indicators include air quality, water quality, and food quality. Twenty-five years ago, 47% of U.S. food samples contained pesticide residues (*U.S. News & World Report,* April 17, 2000). In a recent study, 44 of 125 food samples contained pesticide residues.
    a. State the hypotheses that can be used to show that the population proportion declined.
    b. What is the sample proportion?

c. What is the *p*-value?

d. Use $\alpha = .01$. What is your conclusion?

74. Shorney Construction Company bids on projects assuming that the mean idle time per worker is 72 or fewer minutes per day. A sample of 30 construction workers will be used to test this assumption. Assume that the population standard deviation is 20 minutes.

a. State the hypotheses to be tested.

b. What is the probability of making a Type II error when the population mean idle time is 80 minutes?

c. What is the probability of making a Type II error when the population mean idle time is 75 minutes?

d. What is the probability of making a Type II error when the population mean idle time is 70 minutes?

e. Sketch the power curve for this problem.

75. A federal funding program is available to low-income neighborhoods. To qualify for the funding, a neighborhood must have a mean household income of less than $15,000 per year. Neighborhoods with mean annual household income of $15,000 or more do not qualify. Funding decisions are based on a sample of residents in the neighborhood. A hypothesis test with a .02 level of significance is conducted. If the funding guidelines call for a maximum probability of .05 of not funding a neighborhood with a mean annual household income of $14,000, what sample size should be used in the funding decision study? Use $\sigma = \$4000$ as a planning value.

76. $H_0: \mu = 120$ and $H_a: \mu \neq 120$ are used to test whether a bath soap production process is meeting the standard output of 120 bars per batch. Use a .05 level of significance for the test and a planning value of 5 for the standard deviation.

a. If the mean output drops to 117 bars per batch, the firm wants to have a 98% chance of concluding that the standard production output is not being met. How large a sample should be selected?

b. With your sample size from part (a), what is the probability of concluding that the process is operating satisfactorily for each of the following actual mean outputs: 117, 118, 119, 121, 122, and 123 bars per batch? That is, what is the probability of a Type II error in each case?

## Case Problem 1   Quality Associates, Inc.

Quality Associates, Inc., a consulting firm, advises its clients about sampling and statistical procedures that can be used to control their manufacturing processes. In one particular application, a client gave Quality Associates a sample of 800 observations taken during a time in which that client's process was operating satisfactorily. The sample standard deviation for these data was .21; hence, with so much data, the population standard deviation was assumed to be .21. Quality Associates then suggested that random samples of size 30 be taken periodically to monitor the process on an ongoing basis. By analyzing the new samples, the client could quickly learn whether the process was operating satisfactorily. When the process was not operating satisfactorily, corrective action could be taken to eliminate the problem. The design specification indicated the mean for the process should be 12. The hypothesis test suggested by Quality Associates follows.

$$H_0: \mu = 12$$
$$H_a: \mu \neq 12$$

Corrective action will be taken any time $H_0$ is rejected.

The following samples were collected at hourly intervals during the first day of operation of the new statistical process control procedure. These data are available in the data set Quality.

| Sample 1 | Sample 2 | Sample 3 | Sample 4 |
|----------|----------|----------|----------|
| 11.55 | 11.62 | 11.91 | 12.02 |
| 11.62 | 11.69 | 11.36 | 12.02 |
| 11.52 | 11.59 | 11.75 | 12.05 |
| 11.75 | 11.82 | 11.95 | 12.18 |
| 11.90 | 11.97 | 12.14 | 12.11 |
| 11.64 | 11.71 | 11.72 | 12.07 |
| 11.80 | 11.87 | 11.61 | 12.05 |
| 12.03 | 12.10 | 11.85 | 11.64 |
| 11.94 | 12.01 | 12.16 | 12.39 |
| 11.92 | 11.99 | 11.91 | 11.65 |
| 12.13 | 12.20 | 12.12 | 12.11 |
| 12.09 | 12.16 | 11.61 | 11.90 |
| 11.93 | 12.00 | 12.21 | 12.22 |
| 12.21 | 12.28 | 11.56 | 11.88 |
| 12.32 | 12.39 | 11.95 | 12.03 |
| 11.93 | 12.00 | 12.01 | 12.35 |
| 11.85 | 11.92 | 12.06 | 12.09 |
| 11.76 | 11.83 | 11.76 | 11.77 |
| 12.16 | 12.23 | 11.82 | 12.20 |
| 11.77 | 11.84 | 12.12 | 11.79 |
| 12.00 | 12.07 | 11.60 | 12.30 |
| 12.04 | 12.11 | 11.95 | 12.27 |
| 11.98 | 12.05 | 11.96 | 12.29 |
| 12.30 | 12.37 | 12.22 | 12.47 |
| 12.18 | 12.25 | 11.75 | 12.03 |
| 11.97 | 12.04 | 11.96 | 12.17 |
| 12.17 | 12.24 | 11.95 | 11.94 |
| 11.85 | 11.92 | 11.89 | 11.97 |
| 12.30 | 12.37 | 11.88 | 12.23 |
| 12.15 | 12.22 | 11.93 | 12.25 |

**Quality**

## Managerial Report

1. Conduct a hypothesis test for each sample at the .01 level of significance and determine what action, if any, should be taken. Provide the test statistic and $p$-value for each test.
2. Compute the standard deviation for each of the four samples. Does the assumption of .21 for the population standard deviation appear reasonable?
3. Compute limits for the sample mean $\bar{x}$ around $\mu = 12$ such that, as long as a new sample mean is within those limits, the process will be considered to be operating satisfactorily. If $\bar{x}$ exceeds the upper limit or if $\bar{x}$ is below the lower limit, corrective action will be taken. These limits are referred to as upper and lower control limits for quality control purposes.
4. Discuss the implications of changing the level of significance to a larger value. What mistake or error could increase if the level of significance is increased?

## Case Problem 2    Unemployment Study

Each month the U.S. Bureau of Labor Statistics publishes a variety of unemployment statistics, including the number of individuals who are unemployed and the mean length of time the individuals have been unemployed. For November 1998, the Bureau of Labor Statistics reported that the national mean length of time of unemployment was 14.6 weeks.

The mayor of Philadelphia requested a study on the status of unemployment in the Philadelphia area. A sample of 50 unemployed residents of Philadelphia included data on their age and the number of weeks without a job. A portion of the data collected in November 1998 follows. The complete data set is available in the data file BLS.

**BLS**

| Age | Weeks | Age | Weeks | Age | Weeks |
|-----|-------|-----|-------|-----|-------|
| 56 | 22 | 22 | 11 | 25 | 12 |
| 35 | 19 | 48 | 6 | 25 | 1 |
| 22 | 7 | 48 | 22 | 59 | 33 |
| 57 | 37 | 25 | 5 | 49 | 26 |
| 40 | 18 | 40 | 20 | 33 | 13 |

## Managerial Report

1. Use descriptive statistics to summarize the data.
2. Develop a 95% confidence interval estimate of the mean age of unemployed individuals in Philadelphia.
3. Conduct a hypothesis test to determine whether the mean duration of unemployment in Philadelphia is greater than the national mean duration of 14.6 weeks. Use a .01 level of significance. What is your conclusion?
4. Is there a relationship between the age of an unemployed individual and the number of weeks of unemployment? Explain.

## Appendix 9.1 Hypothesis Testing with Minitab

We describe the use of Minitab to conduct hypothesis tests about a population mean and a population proportion.

### Population Mean: $\sigma$ Known

We illustrate using the MaxFlight golf ball distance example in Section 9.3. The data are in column C1 of a Minitab worksheet. The population standard deviation $\sigma = 12$ is assumed known and the level of significance is $\alpha = .05$. The following steps can be used to test the hypothesis $H_0: \mu = 280$ versus $H_a: \mu \neq 280$.

**GolfTest**

**Step 1.** Select the **Stat** menu
**Step 2.** Choose **Basic Statistics**
**Step 3.** Choose **1-Sample Z**
**Step 4.** When the 1-Sample Z dialog box appears:
    Enter C1 in the **Samples in columns** box
    Enter 12 in the **Standard deviation** box
    Enter 295 in the **Test mean** box
    Select **Options**
**Step 5.** When the 1-Sample Z-Options dialog box appears:
    Enter 95 in the **Confidence level** box*
    Select **not equal** in the **Alternative** box
    Click **OK**
**Step 6.** Click **OK**

---

*Minitab provides both hypothesis testing and interval estimation results simultaneously. The user may select any confidence level for the interval estimate of the population mean: 95% confidence is suggested here.

In addition to the hypothesis testing results, Minitab provides a 95% confidence interval for the population mean.

The procedure can be easily modified for a one-tailed hypothesis test by selecting the less than or greater than option in the **Alternative** box in step 5.

## Population Mean: $\sigma$ Unknown

**AirRating**

The ratings that 60 business travelers gave for Heathrow Airport are entered in column C1 of a Minitab worksheet. The level of significance for the test is $\alpha = .05$, and the population standard deviation $\sigma$ will be estimated by the sample standard deviation $s$. The following steps can be used to test the hypothesis $H_0: \mu \leq 7$ against $H_a: \mu > 7$.

**Step 1.** Select the **Stat** menu
**Step 2.** Choose **Basic Statistics**
**Step 3.** Choose **1-Sample t**
**Step 4.** When the 1-Sample t dialog box appears:
        Enter C1 in the **Samples in columns** box
        Enter 7 in the **Test mean** box
        Select **Options**
**Step 5.** When the 1-Sample t-options dialog box appears:
        Enter 95 in the **Confidence level** box*
        Select **greater than** in the **Alternative** box
        Click **OK**
**Step 6.** Click **OK**

The Heathrow Airport rating study involved a greater than alternative hypothesis. The preceding steps can be easily modified for other hypothesis tests by selecting the less than or not equal options in the **Alternative** box in step 5.

## Population Proportion

**WomenGolf**

We illustrate using the Pine Creek golf course example in Section 9.5. The data with responses Female and Male are in column C1 of a Minitab worksheet. Minitab uses an alphabetical ordering of the responses and selects the *second response* for the population proportion of interest. In this example, Minitab uses the alphabetical ordering Female-Male to provide results for the population proportion of Male responses. Because Female is the response of interest, we change Minitab's ordering as follows: Select any cell in the column and use the sequence: Editor > Column > Value Order. Then choose the option of entering a user-specified order. Make sure that the responses are ordered Male-Female in the **Define-an-order** box. Minitab's 1 Proportion routine will then provide the hypothesis test results for the population proportion of female golfers. We proceed as follows:

**Step 1.** Select the **Stat** menu
**Step 2.** Choose **Basic Statistics**
**Step 3.** Choose **1 Proportion**
**Step 4.** When the 1 Proportion dialog box appears:
        Enter C1 in the **Samples in Columns** box
        Select **Options**
**Step 5.** When the 1 Proportion-Options dialog box appears:
        Enter 95 in the **Confidence level** box
        Enter .20 in the **Test proportion** box
        Select greater than in the **Alternative** box
        Select **Use test and interval based on normal distribution**
        Click **OK**
**Step 6.** Click **OK**

## Appendix 9.2   Hypothesis Testing with Excel

Excel does not provide built-in routines for the hypothesis tests presented in this chapter. To handle these situations, we present Excel worksheets that we designed to test hypotheses about a population mean and a population proportion. The worksheets are easy to use and can be modified to handle any sample data. The worksheets are available on the CD that accompanies this book.

### Population Mean: $\sigma$ Known

We illustrate using the MaxFlight golf ball distance example in Section 9.3. The data are in column A of an Excel worksheet. The population standard deviation $\sigma = 12$ is assumed known and the level of significance is $\alpha = .05$. The following steps can be used to test the hypothesis $H_0: \mu = 280$ versus $H_a: \mu \neq 280$.

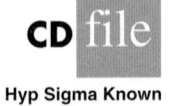

**Hyp Sigma Known**

Refer to Figure 9.14 as we describe the procedure. The worksheet in the background shows the cell formulas used to compute the results shown in the foreground worksheet. The data are entered into cells A2:A51. The following steps are necessary to use the template for this data set.

> **Step 1.** Enter the data range A2:A51 into the =COUNT cell formula in cell D4
> **Step 2.** Enter the data range A2:A51 into the =AVERAGE cell formula in cell D5
> **Step 3.** Enter the population standard deviation $\sigma = 12$ in cell D6
> **Step 4.** Enter the hypothesized value for the population mean 280 in cell D8

The remaining cell formulas automatically provide the standard error, the value of the test statistic $z$, and three $p$-values. Because the alternative hypothesis ($\mu_0 \neq 280$) indicates a two-tailed test, the $p$-value (Two Tail) in cell D15 is used to make the rejection decision. With $p$-value $= .1255 > \alpha = .05$, the null hypothesis cannot be rejected. The $p$-values in cells D13 or D14 would be used if the hypothesis involved a one-tailed test.

This template can be used to make hypothesis testing computations for other applications. For instance, to conduct a hypothesis test for a new data set, enter the new sample data into column A of the worksheet. Modify the formulas in cells D4 and D5 to correspond to the new data range. Enter the population standard deviation into cell D6 and the hypothesized value for the population mean into cell D8 to obtain the results. If the new sample data have already been summarized, the new sample data do not have to be entered into the worksheet. In this case, enter the sample size into cell D4, the sample mean into cell D5, the population standard deviation into cell D6, and the hypothesized value for the population mean into cell D8 to obtain the results. The worksheet in Figure 9.14 is available in the file Hyp Sigma Known on the CD that accompanies this book.

### Population Mean: $\sigma$ Unknown

We illustrate using the Heathrow Airport rating example in Section 9.4. The data are in column A of an Excel worksheet. The population standard deviation $\sigma$ is unknown and will be estimated by the sample standard deviation $s$. The level of significance is $\alpha = .05$. The following steps can be used to test the hypothesis $H_0: \mu \leq 7$ versus $H_a: \mu > 7$.

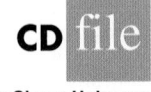

**Hyp Sigma Unknown**

Refer to Figure 9.15 as we describe the procedure. The background worksheet shows the cell formulas used to compute the results shown in the foreground version of the worksheet. The data are entered into cells A2:A61. The following steps are necessary to use the template for this data set.

**Step 1.** Enter the data range A2:A61 into the =COUNT cell formula in cell D4
**Step 2.** Enter the data range A2:A61 into the =AVERAGE cell formula in cell D5
**Step 3.** Enter the data range A2:A61 into the =STDEV cell formula in cell D6
**Step 4.** Enter the hypothesized value for the population mean 7 into cell D8

The remaining cell formulas automatically provide the standard error, the value of the test statistic $t$, the number of degrees of freedom, and three $p$-values. Because the alternative hypothesis ($\mu > 7$) indicates an upper tail test, the $p$-value (Upper Tail) in cell D15 is used

**FIGURE 9.14**   EXCEL WORKSHEET FOR HYPOTHESIS TESTS ABOUT A POPULATION MEAN
WITH $\sigma$ KNOWN

| | A | B | C | D | E |
|---|---|---|---|---|---|
| 1 | Yards | | **Hypothesis Test About a Population Mean** | | |
| 2 | 288 | | **With σ Known** | | |
| 3 | 267 | | | | |
| 4 | 274 | | **Sample Size** | =COUNT(A2:A51) | |
| 5 | 283 | | **Sample Mean** | =AVERAGE(A2:A51) | |
| 6 | 268 | | **Population Std. Deviation** | 12 | |
| 7 | 302 | | | | |
| 8 | 282 | | **Hypothesized Value** | 280 | |
| 9 | 293 | | | | |
| 10 | 302 | | **Standard Error** | =D6/SQRT(D4) | |
| 11 | 279 | | **Test Statistic z** | =(D5-D8)/D10 | |
| 12 | 270 | | | | |
| 13 | 276 | | **p-value (Lower Tail)** | =NORMSDIST(D11) | |
| 14 | 290 | | **p-value (Upper Tail)** | =1-D13 | |
| 15 | 276 | | **p-value (Two Tail)** | =2*MIN(D13,D14) | |
| 16 | 297 | | | | |
| 17 | 291 | | | | |
| 49 | 288 | | | | |
| 50 | 286 | | | | |
| 51 | 277 | | | | |
| 52 | | | | | |

*Note: Rows 18 to 48 are hidden.*

| | A | B | C | D | E |
|---|---|---|---|---|---|
| 1 | Yards | | **Hypothesis Test About a Population Mean** | | |
| 2 | 288 | | **With σ Known** | | |
| 3 | 267 | | | | |
| 4 | 274 | | **Sample Size** | 50 | |
| 5 | 283 | | **Sample Mean** | 282.6 | |
| 6 | 268 | | **Population Std. Deviation** | 12 | |
| 7 | 302 | | | | |
| 8 | 282 | | **Hypothesized Value** | 280 | |
| 9 | 293 | | | | |
| 10 | 302 | | **Standard Error** | 1.70 | |
| 11 | 279 | | **Test Statistic z** | 1.53 | |
| 12 | 270 | | | | |
| 13 | 276 | | **p-value (Lower Tail)** | 0.9372 | |
| 14 | 290 | | **p-value (Upper Tail)** | 0.0628 | |
| 15 | 276 | | **p-value (Two Tail)** | 0.1255 | |
| 16 | 297 | | | | |
| 17 | 291 | | | | |
| 49 | 288 | | | | |
| 50 | 286 | | | | |
| 51 | 277 | | | | |
| 52 | | | | | |

FIGURE 9.15   EXCEL WORKSHEET FOR HYPOTHESIS TESTS ABOUT A POPULATION MEAN
WITH $\sigma$ UNKNOWN

|  | A | B | C | D | E |
|---|---|---|---|---|---|
| 1 | Rating |  | Hypothesis Test About a Population Mean |  |  |
| 2 | 5 |  | With $\sigma$ Unknown |  |  |
| 3 | 7 |  |  |  |  |
| 4 | 8 |  | Sample Size | =COUNT(A2:A61) |  |
| 5 | 7 |  | Sample Mean | =AVERAGE(A2:A61) |  |
| 6 | 8 |  | Sample Std. Deviation | =STDEV(A2:A61) |  |
| 7 | 8 |  |  |  |  |
| 8 | 8 |  | Hypothesized Value | 7 |  |
| 9 | 7 |  |  |  |  |
| 10 | 8 |  | Standard Error | =D6/SQRT(D4) |  |
| 11 | 10 |  | Test Statistic t | =(D5-D8)/D10 |  |
| 12 | 6 |  | Degrees of Freedom | =D4-1 |  |
| 13 | 7 |  |  |  |  |
| 14 | 8 |  | p-value (Lower Tail) | =IF(D11<0,TDIST(-D11,D12,1),1-TDIST(D11,D12,1)) |  |
| 15 | 8 |  | p-value (Upper Tail) | =1-D14 |  |
| 16 | 9 |  | p-value (Two Tail) | =2*MIN(D14,D15) |  |
| 17 | 7 |  |  |  |  |
| 59 | 7 |  |  |  |  |
| 60 | 7 |  |  |  |  |
| 61 | 8 |  |  |  |  |
| 62 |  |  |  |  |  |

Note: Rows 18 to 58 are
hidden.

|  | A | B | C | D | E |
|---|---|---|---|---|---|
| 1 | Rating |  | Hypothesis Test About a Population Mean |  |  |
| 2 | 5 |  | With $\sigma$ Unknown |  |  |
| 3 | 7 |  |  |  |  |
| 4 | 8 |  | Sample Size | 60 |  |
| 5 | 7 |  | Sample Mean | 7.25 |  |
| 6 | 8 |  | Sample Std. Deviation | 1.05 |  |
| 7 | 8 |  |  |  |  |
| 8 | 8 |  | Hypothesized Value | 7 |  |
| 9 | 7 |  |  |  |  |
| 10 | 8 |  | Standard Error | 0.136 |  |
| 11 | 10 |  | Test Statistic t | 1.841 |  |
| 12 | 6 |  | Degrees of Freedom | 59 |  |
| 13 | 7 |  |  |  |  |
| 14 | 8 |  | p-value (Lower Tail) | 0.9647 |  |
| 15 | 8 |  | p-value (Upper Tail) | 0.0353 |  |
| 16 | 9 |  | p-value (Two Tail) | 0.0706 |  |
| 17 | 7 |  |  |  |  |
| 59 | 7 |  |  |  |  |
| 60 | 7 |  |  |  |  |
| 61 | 8 |  |  |  |  |
| 62 |  |  |  |  |  |

to make the decision. With $p$-value $= .0353 < \alpha = .05$, the null hypothesis is rejected. The $p$-values in cells D14 or D16 would be used if the hypotheses involved a lower tail test or a two-tailed test.

This template can be used to make hypothesis testing computations for other applications. For instance, to conduct a hypothesis test for a new data set, enter the new sample data into column A of the worksheet and modify the formulas in cells D4, D5, and D6 to correspond to the new data range. Enter the hypothesized value for the population mean into cell D8 to obtain the results. If the new sample data have already been summarized, the new sample data do not have to be entered into the worksheet. In this case, enter the sample size into cell D4, the sample mean into cell D5, the sample standard deviation into cell D6, and the hypothesized value for the population mean into cell D8 to obtain the results. The worksheet in Figure 9.15 is available in the file Hyp Sigma Unknown on the CD that accompanies this book.

## Population Proportion

**Hypothesis p**

We illustrate using the Pine Creek golf course survey data presented in Section 9.5. The data of Male or Female golfer are in column A of an Excel worksheet. Refer to Figure 9.16 as we describe the procedure. The background worksheet shows the cell formulas used to compute the results shown in the foreground worksheet. The data are entered into

**FIGURE 9.16**   EXCEL WORKSHEET FOR HYPOTHESIS TESTS ABOUT A POPULATION PROPORTION

|  | A | B | C | D | E |
|---|---|---|---|---|---|
| 1 | Golfer | | Interval Estimate of a Population Proportion | | |
| 2 | Female | | | | |
| 3 | Male | | Sample Size | =COUNTA(A2:A401) | |
| 4 | Female | | Response of Interest | Female | |
| 5 | Male | | Count for Response | =COUNTIF(A2:A401,D4) | |
| 6 | Male | | Sample Proportion | =D5/D3 | |
| 7 | Female | | | | |
| 8 | Male | | Hypothesized Value | 0.20 | |
| 9 | Male | | | | |
| 10 | Female | | Standard Error | =SQRT(D8*(1-D8)/D3) | |
| 11 | Male | | Test Statistic z | =(D6-D8)/D10 | |
| 12 | Male | | | | |
| 13 | Male | | p-value (Lower Tail) | =NORMSDIST(D11) | |
| 14 | Male | | p-value (Upper Tail) | =1-D13 | |
| 15 | Male | | p-value (TwoTail) | =2*MIN(D13,D14) | |
| 16 | Female | | | | |
| 400 | Male | | | | |
| 401 | Male | | | | |
| 402 | | | | | |

|  | A | B | C | D | E |
|---|---|---|---|---|---|
| 1 | Golfer | | Interval Estimate of a Population Proportion | | |
| 2 | Female | | | | |
| 3 | Male | | Sample Size | 400 | |
| 4 | Female | | Response of Interest | Female | |
| 5 | Male | | Count for Response | 100 | |
| 6 | Male | | Sample Proportion | 0.2500 | |
| 7 | Female | | | | |
| 8 | Male | | Hypothesized Value | 0.20 | |
| 9 | Male | | | | |
| 10 | Female | | Standard Error | 0.0200 | |
| 11 | Male | | Test Statistic z | 2.50 | |
| 12 | Male | | | | |
| 13 | Male | | p-value (Lower Tail) | 0.9938 | |
| 14 | Male | | p-value (Upper Tail) | 0.0062 | |
| 15 | Male | | p-value (TwoTail) | 0.0124 | |
| 16 | Female | | | | |
| 400 | Male | | | | |
| 401 | Male | | | | |
| 402 | | | | | |

*Note: Rows 17 to 399 are hidden.*

cell A2:A401. The following steps can be used to test the hypothesis $H_0: p \leq .20$ versus $H_a: p > .20$.

**Step 1.** Enter the data range A2:A401 into the =COUNTA cell formula in cell D3
**Step 2.** Enter Female as the response of interest in cell D4
**Step 3.** Enter the data range A2:A401 into the =COUNTIF cell formula in cell D5
**Step 4.** Enter the hypothesized value for the population proportion .20 into cell D8

The remaining cell formulas automatically provide the standard error, the value of the test statistic $z$, and three $p$-values. Because the alternative hypothesis ($p_0 > .20$) indicates an upper tail test, the $p$-value (Upper Tail) in cell D14 is used to make the decision. With $p$-value $= .0062 < \alpha = .05$, the null hypothesis is rejected. The $p$-values in cells D13 or D15 would be used if the hypothesis involved a lower tail test or a two-tailed test.

This template can be used to make hypothesis testing computations for other applications. For instance, to conduct a hypothesis test for a new data set, enter the new sample data into column A of the worksheet. Modify the formulas in cells D3 and D5 to correspond to the new data range. Enter the response of interest into cell D4 and the hypothesized value for the population proportion into cell D8 to obtain the results. If the new sample data have already been summarized, the new sample data do not have to be entered into the worksheet. In this case, enter the sample size into cell D3, the sample proportion into cell D6, and the hypothesized value for the population proportion into cell D8 to obtain the results. The worksheet in Figure 9.16 is available in the file Hypothesis p on the CD that accompanies this book.

# CHAPTER 10

# Statistical Inference About Means and Proportions with Two Populations

## CONTENTS

STATISTICS IN PRACTICE: FISONS
CORPORATION

## FISONS CORPORATION
*ROCHESTER, NEW YORK*

Fisons Corporation, Rochester, New York, is a unit of Fisons Plc., UK. Fisons opened its United States operations in 1966.

Fisons' Pharmaceutical Division uses extensive statistical procedures to test and develop new drugs. The testing process in the pharmaceutical industry usually consists of three stages: (1) preclinical testing, (2) testing for long-term usage and safety, and (3) clinical efficacy testing. At each successive stage, the chance that a drug will pass the rigorous tests decreases; however, the cost of further testing increases dramatically. Industry surveys indicate that on average the research and development for one new drug costs $250 million and takes 12 years. Hence, it is important to eliminate unsuccessful new drugs in the early stages of the testing process, as well as identify promising ones for further testing.

Statistics plays a major role in pharmaceutical research, where government regulations are stringent and rigorously enforced. In preclinical testing, a two- or three-population statistical study typically is used to determine whether a new drug should continue to be studied in the long-term usage and safety program. The populations may consist of the new drug, a control, and a standard drug. The preclinical testing process begins when a new drug is sent to the pharmacology group for evaluation of efficacy—the capacity of the drug to produce the desired effects. As part of the process, a statistician is asked to design an experiment that can be used to test the new drug. The design must specify the sample size and the statistical methods of analysis. In a two-population study, one sample is used to obtain data on the efficacy of the new drug (population 1) and a second sample is used to obtain data on the efficacy of a standard drug (population 2). Depending on the intended use, the new and standard drugs are tested in such disciplines as neurology, cardiology, and immunology. In most studies, the statistical method involves hypothesis testing for the difference between the means of the new drug population and the standard drug population. If a new drug

Statistical methods are used to test and develop new drugs. © Mark Richards/PhotoEdit.

lacks efficacy or produces undesirable effects in comparison with the standard drug, the new drug is rejected and withdrawn from further testing. Only new drugs that show promising comparisons with the standard drugs are forwarded to the long-term usage and safety testing program.

Further data collection and multipopulation studies are conducted in the long-term usage and safety testing program and in the clinical testing programs. The Food and Drug Administration (FDA) requires that statistical methods be defined prior to such testing to avoid data-related biases. In addition, to avoid human biases, some of the clinical trials are double or triple blind. That is, neither the subject nor the investigator knows what drug is administered to whom. If the new drug meets all requirements in relation to the standard drug, a new drug application (NDA) is filed with the FDA. The application is rigorously scrutinized by statisticians and scientists at the agency.

In this chapter you will learn how to construct interval estimates and make hypothesis tests about means and proportions with two populations. Techniques will be presented for analyzing independent random samples as well as matched samples.

In Chapters 8 and 9 we showed how to develop interval estimates and conduct hypothesis tests for situations involving a single population mean and a single population proportion. In this chapter we continue our discussion of statistical inference by showing how interval estimates and hypothesis tests can be developed for situations involving two populations, when the difference between the two population means or the two population proportions is of prime importance. For example, we may want to develop an interval estimate of the difference between the mean starting salary for a population of men and the mean starting salary for a population of women or conduct a hypothesis test to determine whether any difference is present between the proportion of defective parts in a population of parts produced by supplier A and the proportion of defective parts in a population of parts produced by supplier B. We begin our discussion of statistical inference about two populations by showing how to develop interval estimates and conduct hypothesis tests about the difference between the means of two populations when the standard deviations of the two populations are assumed known.

# 10.1   Inferences About the Difference Between Two Population Means: $\sigma_1$ and $\sigma_2$ Known

Letting $\mu_1$ denote the mean of population 1 and $\mu_2$ denote the mean of population 2, we will focus on inferences about the difference between the means: $\mu_1 - \mu_2$. To make an inference about this difference, we select a simple random sample of $n_1$ units from population 1 and a second simple random sample of $n_2$ units from population 2. The two samples, taken separately and independently, are referred to as **independent simple random samples**. In this section, we assume that information is available such that the two population standard deviations, $\sigma_1$ and $\sigma_2$, can be assumed known prior to collecting the samples. We refer to this situation as the $\sigma_1$ and $\sigma_2$ known case. In the following example we show how to compute a margin of error and develop an interval estimate of the difference between the two population means when $\sigma_1$ and $\sigma_2$ are known.

## Interval Estimation of $\mu_1 - \mu_2$

Greystone Department Stores, Inc., operates two stores in Buffalo, New York: one is in the inner city and the other is in a suburban shopping center. The regional manager noticed that products that sell well in one store do not always sell well in the other. The manager believes this situation may be attributable to differences in customer demographics at the two locations. Customers may differ in age, education, income, and so on. Suppose the manager asks us to investigate the difference between the mean ages of the customers who shop at the two stores.

Let us define population 1 as all customers who shop at the inner-city store and population 2 as all customers who shop at the suburban store.

$\mu_1$ = mean of population 1 (i.e., the mean age of all customers who shop at the inner-city store)

$\mu_2$ = mean of population 2 (i.e., the mean age of all customers who shop at the suburban store)

The difference between the two population means is $\mu_1 - \mu_2$.

To estimate $\mu_1 - \mu_2$, we will select a simple random sample of $n_1$ customers from population 1 and a simple random sample of $n_2$ customers from population 2. We then compute the two sample means.

$\bar{x}_1$ = sample mean age for the simple random sample of $n_1$ inner-city customers

$\bar{x}_2$ = sample mean age for the simple random sample of $n_2$ suburban customers

The point estimator of the difference between the two population means is the difference between the two sample means.

---

**POINT ESTIMATOR OF THE DIFFERENCE BETWEEN TWO POPULATION MEANS**

$$\bar{x}_1 - \bar{x}_2 \qquad \text{(10.1)}$$

---

Figure 10.1 provides an overview of the process used to estimate the difference between two population means based on two independent simple random samples.

*The standard error of $\bar{x}_1 - \bar{x}_2$ is the standard deviation of the sampling distribution of $\bar{x}_1 - \bar{x}_2$.*

As with other point estimators, the point estimator $\bar{x}_1 - \bar{x}_2$ has a standard error that describes the variation in the sampling distribution of the estimator. With two independent simple random samples, the standard error of $\bar{x}_1 - \bar{x}_2$ is as follows:

$$\sigma_{\bar{x}_1 - \bar{x}_2} = \sqrt{\frac{\sigma_1^2}{n_1} + \frac{\sigma_2^2}{n_2}} \qquad \text{(10.2)}$$

If both populations have a normal distribution, or if the sample sizes are large enough that the central limit theorem enables us to conclude that the sampling distributions of $\bar{x}_1$ and $\bar{x}_2$ can be approximated by a normal distribution, the sampling distribution of $\bar{x}_1 - \bar{x}_2$ will have a normal distribution with mean given by $\mu_1 - \mu_2$.

As we showed in Chapter 8, an interval estimate is given by a point estimate $\pm$ a margin of error. In the case of estimation of the difference between two population means, an interval estimate will take the following form:

$$\bar{x}_1 - \bar{x}_2 \pm \text{Margin of error}$$

**FIGURE 10.1    ESTIMATING THE DIFFERENCE BETWEEN TWO POPULATION MEANS**

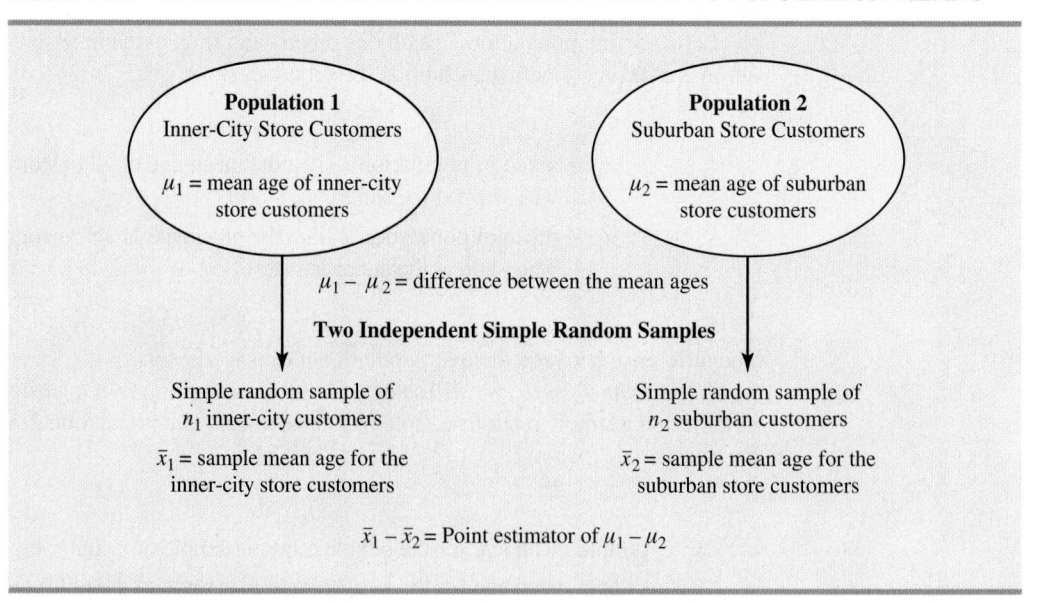

With the sampling distribution of $\bar{x}_1 - \bar{x}_2$ having a normal distribution, we can write the margin of error as follows:

*The margin of error is given by multiplying the standard error by $z_{\alpha/2}$.*

$$\text{Margin of error} = z_{\alpha/2}\sigma_{\bar{x}_1 - \bar{x}_2} = z_{\alpha/2}\sqrt{\frac{\sigma_1^2}{n_1} + \frac{\sigma_2^2}{n_2}} \tag{10.3}$$

Thus the interval estimate of the difference between two population means is as follows:

> **INTERVAL ESTIMATE OF THE DIFFERENCE BETWEEN TWO POPULATION MEANS: $\sigma_1$ AND $\sigma_2$ KNOWN**
>
> $$\bar{x}_1 - \bar{x}_2 \pm z_{\alpha/2}\sqrt{\frac{\sigma_1^2}{n_1} + \frac{\sigma_2^2}{n_2}} \tag{10.4}$$
>
> where $1 - \alpha$ is the confidence coefficient.

Let us return to the Greystone example. Based on data from previous customer demographic studies, the two population standard deviations are known with $\sigma_1 = 9$ years and $\sigma_2 = 10$ years. The data collected from the two independent simple random samples of Greystone customers provided the following results.

|  | **Inner City Store** | **Suburban Store** |
|---|---|---|
| Sample Size | $n_1 = 36$ | $n_2 = 49$ |
| Sample Mean | $\bar{x}_1 = 40$ years | $\bar{x}_2 = 35$ years |

Using expression (10.1), we find that the point estimate of the difference between the mean ages of the two populations is $\bar{x}_1 - \bar{x}_2 = 40 - 35 = 5$ years. Thus, we estimate that the customers at the inner-city store have a mean age five years greater than the mean age of the suburban store customers. We can now use expression (10.4) to compute the margin of error and provide the interval estimate of $\mu_1 - \mu_2$. Using 95% confidence and $z_{\alpha/2} = z_{.025} = 1.96$, we have

$$\bar{x}_1 - \bar{x}_2 \pm z_{\alpha/2}\sqrt{\frac{\sigma_1^2}{n_1} + \frac{\sigma_2^2}{n_2}}$$

$$40 - 35 \pm 1.96\sqrt{\frac{9^2}{36} + \frac{10^2}{49}}$$

$$5 \pm 4.06$$

Thus, the margin of error is 4.06 years and the 95% confidence interval estimate of the difference between the two population means is $5 - 4.06 = .94$ years to $5 + 4.06 = 9.06$ years.

## Hypothesis Tests About $\mu_1 - \mu_2$

Let us consider hypothesis tests about the difference between two population means. Using $D_0$ to denote the hypothesized difference between $\mu_1$ and $\mu_2$, the three forms for a hypothesis test are as follows:

$$\begin{array}{ccc} H_0: \mu_1 - \mu_2 \geq D_0 & H_0: \mu_1 - \mu_2 \leq D_0 & H_0: \mu_1 - \mu_2 = D_0 \\ H_a: \mu_1 - \mu_2 < D_0 & H_a: \mu_1 - \mu_2 > D_0 & H_a: \mu_1 - \mu_2 \neq D_0 \end{array}$$

In many applications, $D_0 = 0$. Using the two-tailed test as an example, when $D_0 = 0$ the null hypothesis is $H_0: \mu_1 - \mu_2 = 0$. In this case, the null hypothesis is that $\mu_1$ and $\mu_2$ are equal. Rejection of $H_0$ leads to the conclusion that $H_a: \mu_1 - \mu_2 \neq 0$ is true; that is, $\mu_1$ and $\mu_2$ are not equal.

The steps for conducting hypothesis tests presented in Chapter 9 are applicable here. We must choose a level of significance, compute the value of the test statistic and find the $p$-value to determine whether the null hypothesis should be rejected. With two independent simple random samples, we showed that the point estimator $\bar{x}_1 - \bar{x}_2$ has a standard error $\sigma_{\bar{x}_1 - \bar{x}_2}$ given by expression (10.2) and the distribution of $\bar{x}_1 - \bar{x}_2$ can be described by a normal distribution. In this case, the test statistic for the difference between two population means when $\sigma_1$ and $\sigma_2$ are known is as follows.

TEST STATISTIC FOR HYPOTHESIS TESTS ABOUT $\mu_1 - \mu_2$: $\sigma_1$ AND $\sigma_2$ KNOWN

$$z = \frac{(\bar{x}_1 - \bar{x}_2) - D_0}{\sqrt{\dfrac{\sigma_1^2}{n_1} + \dfrac{\sigma_2^2}{n_2}}} \qquad (10.5)$$

Let us demonstrate the use of this test statistic in the following hypothesis testing example.

As part of a study to evaluate differences in education quality between two training centers, a standardized examination is given to individuals who are trained at the centers. The difference between the mean examination scores is used to assess quality differences between the centers. The population means for the two centers are as follows.

$$\mu_1 = \text{the mean examination score for the population}$$
$$\text{of individuals trained at center A}$$

$$\mu_2 = \text{the mean examination score for the population}$$
$$\text{of individuals trained at center B}$$

We begin with the tentative assumption that no difference exists between the training quality provided at the two centers. Hence, in terms of the mean examination scores, the null hypothesis is that $\mu_1 - \mu_2 = 0$. If sample evidence leads to the rejection of this hypothesis, we will conclude that the mean examination scores differ for the two populations. This conclusion indicates a quality differential between the two centers and suggests that a follow-up study investigating the reason for the differential may be warranted. The null and alternative hypotheses for this two-tailed test are written as follows.

$$H_0: \mu_1 - \mu_2 = 0$$
$$H_a: \mu_1 - \mu_2 \neq 0$$

The standardized examination given previously in a variety of settings always resulted in an examination score standard deviation near 10 points. Thus, we will use this information to assume that the population standard deviations are known with $\sigma_1 = 10$ and $\sigma_2 = 10$. An $\alpha = .05$ level of significance is specified for the study.

Independent simple random samples of $n_1 = 30$ individuals from training center A and $n_2 = 40$ individuals from training center B are taken. The respective sample means are $\bar{x}_1 = 82$ and $\bar{x}_2 = 78$. Do these data suggest a significant difference between the population means at the two training centers? To help answer this question, we compute the test statistic using equation (10.5).

$$z = \frac{(\bar{x}_1 - \bar{x}_2) - D_0}{\sqrt{\dfrac{\sigma_1^2}{n_1} + \dfrac{\sigma_2^2}{n_2}}} = \frac{(82 - 78) - 0}{\sqrt{\dfrac{10^2}{30} + \dfrac{10^2}{40}}} = 1.66$$

Next let us compute the $p$-value for this two-tailed test. Because the test statistic $z$ is in the upper tail, we first compute the area under the curve to the right of $z = 1.66$. Using the standard normal distribution table, the area between the mean and $z = 1.66$ is .4515. Thus, the area in the upper tail of the distribution is $.5000 - .4515 = .0485$. Because this test is a two-tailed test, we must double the tail area: $p$-value $= 2(.0485) = .0970$. Following the usual rule to reject $H_0$ if $p$-value $\leq \alpha$, we see that the $p$-value of .0970 does not allow us to reject $H_0$ at the .05 level of significance. The sample results do not provide sufficient evidence to conclude the training centers differ in quality.

In this chapter we will use the $p$-value approach to hypothesis testing as described in Chapter 9. However, if you prefer, the test statistic and the critical value rejection rule may be used. With $\alpha = .05$ and $z_{\alpha/2} = z_{.025} = 1.96$, the rejection rule employing the critical value approach would be reject $H_0$ if $z \leq -1.96$ or if $z \geq 1.96$. With $z = 1.66$, we reach the same do not reject $H_0$ conclusion.

In the preceding example, we demonstrated a two-tailed hypothesis test about the difference between two population means. Lower tail and upper tail tests can also be considered. These tests use the same test statistic as given in equation (10.5). The procedure for computing the $p$-value and the rejection rules for these one-tailed tests are the same as those presented in Chapter 9.

## Practical Advice

In most applications of the interval estimation and hypothesis testing procedures presented in this section, random samples with $n_1 \geq 30$ and $n_2 \geq 30$ are adequate. In cases where either or both sample sizes are less than 30, the distributions of the populations become important considerations. In general, with smaller sample sizes, it is more important for the analyst to be satisfied that it is reasonable to assume that the distributions of the two populations are at least approximately normal.

## Exercises

## Methods

1. Consider the following results for two independent random samples taken from two populations.

| Sample 1 | Sample 2 |
|---|---|
| $n_1 = 50$ | $n_2 = 35$ |
| $\bar{x}_1 = 13.6$ | $\bar{x}_2 = 11.6$ |
| $\sigma_1 = 2.2$ | $\sigma_2 = 3.0$ |

a.   What is the point estimate of the difference between the two population means?
b.   Provide a 90% confidence interval for the difference between the two population means.
c.   Provide a 95% confidence interval for the difference between the two population means.

2. Consider the following hypothesis test.

$$H_0: \mu_1 - \mu_2 \leq 0$$
$$H_a: \mu_1 - \mu_2 > 0$$

The following results are for two independent samples taken from the two populations.

| Sample 1 | Sample 2 |
|---|---|
| $n_1 = 40$ | $n_2 = 50$ |
| $\bar{x}_1 = 25.2$ | $\bar{x}_2 = 22.8$ |
| $\sigma_1 = 5.2$ | $\sigma_2 = 6.0$ |

    a. What is the value of the test statistic?
    b. What is the *p*-value?
    c. With $\alpha = .05$, what is your hypothesis testing conclusion?

3. Consider the following hypothesis test.

$$H_0: \mu_1 - \mu_2 = 0$$
$$H_a: \mu_1 - \mu_2 \neq 0$$

The following results are for two independent samples taken from the two populations.

| Sample 1 | Sample 2 |
|---|---|
| $n_1 = 80$ | $n_2 = 70$ |
| $\bar{x}_1 = 104$ | $\bar{x}_2 = 106$ |
| $\sigma_1 = 8.4$ | $\sigma_2 = 7.6$ |

    a. What is the value of the test statistic?
    b. What is the *p*-value?
    c. With $\alpha = .05$, what is your hypothesis testing conclusion?

## Applications

4. Gasoline prices reached record high levels in 16 states during 2003 (*The Wall Street Journal*, March 7, 2003). Two of the affected states were California and Florida. The American Automobile Association reported a sample mean price of $2.04 per gallon in California and a sample mean price of $1.72 per gallon in Florida. Use a sample size of 40 for the California data and a sample size of 35 for the Florida data. Assume that prior studies indicate a population standard deviation of .10 in California and .08 in Florida are reasonable.
    a. What is a point estimate of the difference between the population mean prices per gallon in California and Florida?
    b. At 95% confidence, what is the margin of error?
    c. What is the 95% confidence interval estimate of the difference between the population mean prices per gallon in the two states?

5. A Cornell University study of wage differentials between men and women reported that one of the reasons wages for men are higher than wages for women is that men tend to have more years of work experience than women (*Business Week*, August 28, 2000). Assume the following sample summaries show the years of experience for each group.

| Men | Women |
|---|---|
| $n_1 = 100$ | $n_2 = 85$ |
| $\bar{x}_1 = 14.9$ years | $\bar{x}_2 = 10.3$ years |
| $\sigma_1 = 5.2$ years | $\sigma_2 = 3.8$ years |

   a. What is the point estimate of the difference between the two population means?

   b. At 95% confidence, what is the margin of error?

   c. What is the 95% confidence interval estimate of the difference between the two population means?

6. The nation's 40,000 mortgage brokerages are some of the most profitable small businesses in the United States. These low-profile companies find loans for customers in exchange for commissions. Mortgage Bankers Association of America provides data on the average size of loans handled by mortgage brokerages (*The Wall Street Journal*, February 24, 2003). Using sample data consistent with the Mortgage Bankers Association data, a sample of 270 loans made in 2002 provided a mean loan of $175,000. Data for 2001 showed a sample of 250 loans made with a mean loan of $165,000. Based on historical loan data, the population standard deviations for the loan amounts can be assumed known at $55,000 in 2002 and $50,000 in 2001. Do the sample data indicate an increase in the mean loan amount between 2001 and 2002? Use $\alpha = .05$.

*[handwritten: $H_0: \mu_1 > \mu_2$   $H_a: \mu_1 > \mu_2$]*

*[handwritten: $H_0: \mu_1 - \mu_2 \le 0$   $H_a: \mu_1 - \mu_2 > 0$]*

7. The Greystone Department Store age study provided the following data on the ages of customers from independent random samples taken at the two store locations.

| Inner-City Store | Suburban Store |
|---|---|
| $n_1 = 36$ | $n_2 = 49$ |
| $\bar{x}_1 = 40$ years | $\bar{x}_2 = 35$ years |
| $\sigma_1 = 9$ years | $\sigma_2 = 10$ years |

   a. State the hypotheses that could be used to detect a difference between the population mean ages at the two stores.

   b. What is the value of the test statistic?

   c. What is the *p*-value?

   d. At $\alpha = .05$, what is your conclusion?

*[handwritten: e) Theo critical value method:  $z_{\alpha/2} = 1.96$  since $z$ is $> z_{\alpha/2}$ then reject $H_0$ ......]*

8. Arnold Palmer and Tiger Woods are two of the best golfers to ever play the game. To show how these two golfers would compare if both were playing at the top of their game, the following sample data provide the results of 18-hole scores during a PGA tournament competition. Palmer's scores are from his 1960 season, while Woods' scores are from his 1999 season (*Golf Magazine*, February 2000).

| Palmer, 1960 | Woods, 1999 |
|---|---|
| $n_1 = 112$ | $n_2 = 84$ |
| $\bar{x}_1 = 69.95$ | $\bar{x}_2 = 69.56$ |

Use the sample results to test the hypothesis of no difference between the population mean 18-hole scores for the two golfers.

   a. Assume a population standard deviation of 2.5 for both golfers. What is the value of the test statistic?

   b. What is the *p*-value?

   c. At $\alpha = .01$, what is your conclusion?

*[handwritten: d) Critical value $z = 1.08$ is NOT $< z_{\alpha/2} = 2.5 > 5$ don't reject $H_0$]*

# Inferences About the Difference Between Two Population Means: $\sigma_1$ and $\sigma_2$ Unknown

In this section we extend the discussion of inferences about the difference between two population means to the case when the two population standard deviations, $\sigma_1$ and $\sigma_2$, are unknown. In this case, we will use the sample standard deviations, $s_1$ and $s_2$, to estimate the unknown population standard deviations. When we use the sample standard deviations, the interval estimation and hypothesis testing procedures will be based on the $t$ distribution rather than the standard normal distribution.

## Interval Estimation of $\mu_1 - \mu_2$

In the following example we show how to compute a margin of error and develop an interval estimate of the difference between two population means when $\sigma_1$ and $\sigma_2$ are unknown. Clearwater National Bank is conducting a study designed to identify differences between checking account practices by customers at two of its branch banks. A simple random sample of 28 checking accounts is selected from the Cherry Grove Branch and an independent simple random sample of 22 checking accounts is selected from the Beechmont Branch. The current checking account balance is recorded for each of the checking accounts. A summary of the account balances follows:

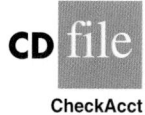

**CheckAcct**

|  | **Cherry Grove** | **Beechmont** |
|---|---|---|
| Sample Size | $n_1 = 28$ | $n_2 = 22$ |
| Sample Mean | $\bar{x}_1 = \$1025$ | $\bar{x}_2 = \$910$ |
| Sample Standard Deviation | $s_1 = \$150$ | $s_2 = \$125$ |

Clearwater National Bank would like to estimate the difference between the mean checking account balance maintained by the population of Cherry Grove customers and the population of Beechmont customers. Let us develop the margin of error and an interval estimate of the difference between these two population means.

In Section 10.1, we provided the following interval estimate for the case when the population standard deviations, $\sigma_1$ and $\sigma_2$, are known.

$$\bar{x}_1 - \bar{x}_2 \pm z_{\alpha/2} \sqrt{\frac{\sigma_1^2}{n_1} + \frac{\sigma_2^2}{n_2}}$$

*When $\sigma_1$ and $\sigma_2$ are estimated by $s_1$ and $s_2$, the t distribution is used to make inferences about the difference between two population means.*

With $\sigma_1$ and $\sigma_2$ unknown, we will use the sample standard deviations $s_1$ and $s_2$ to estimate $\sigma_1$ and $\sigma_2$ and replace $z_{\alpha/2}$ with $t_{\alpha/2}$. As a result, the interval estimate of the difference between two population means is given by the following expression:

> **INTERVAL ESTIMATE OF THE DIFFERENCE BETWEEN TWO POPULATION MEANS: $\sigma_1$ AND $\sigma_2$ UNKNOWN**
>
> $$\bar{x}_1 - \bar{x}_2 \pm t_{\alpha/2} \sqrt{\frac{s_1^2}{n_1} + \frac{s_2^2}{n_2}} \qquad (10.6)$$
>
> where $1 - \alpha$ is the confidence coefficient.

In this expression, the use of the $t$ distribution is an approximation, but it provides excellent results and is relatively easy to use. The only difficulty that we encounter in using expression (10.6) is determining the appropriate degrees of freedom for $t_{\alpha/2}$. Statistical software packages compute the appropriate degrees of freedom automatically. The formula used is as follows:

$$df = \frac{\left(\dfrac{s_1^2}{n_1} + \dfrac{s_2^2}{n_2}\right)^2}{\dfrac{1}{n_1 - 1}\left(\dfrac{s_1^2}{n_1}\right)^2 + \dfrac{1}{n_2 - 1}\left(\dfrac{s_2^2}{n_2}\right)^2} \qquad (10.7)$$

Let us return to the Clearwater National Bank example and show how to use expression (10.6) to provide a 95% confidence interval estimate of the difference between the population mean checking account balances at the two branch banks. The sample data show $n_1 = 28$, $\bar{x}_1 = \$1025$, and $s_1 = \$150$ for the Cherry Grove branch, and $n_2 = 22$, $\bar{x}_2 = \$910$, and $s_2 = \$125$ for the Beechmont branch. The calculation for degrees of freedom for $t_{\alpha/2}$ is as follows:

$$df = \frac{\left(\dfrac{s_1^2}{n_1} + \dfrac{s_2^2}{n_2}\right)^2}{\dfrac{1}{n_1 - 1}\left(\dfrac{s_1^2}{n_1}\right)^2 + \dfrac{1}{n_2 - 1}\left(\dfrac{s_2^2}{n_2}\right)^2} = \frac{\left(\dfrac{150^2}{28} + \dfrac{125^2}{22}\right)^2}{\dfrac{1}{28 - 1}\left(\dfrac{150^2}{28}\right)^2 + \dfrac{1}{22 - 1}\left(\dfrac{125^2}{22}\right)^2} = 47.8$$

We round the noninteger degrees of freedom *down* to 47 to provide a larger $t$-value and a more conservative interval estimate. Using the $t$ distribution table with 47 degrees of freedom, we find $t_{.025} = 2.012$. Using expression (10.6), we develop the 95% confidence interval estimate of the difference between the two population means as follows.

$$\bar{x}_1 - \bar{x}_2 \pm t_{.025}\sqrt{\frac{s_1^2}{n_1} + \frac{s_2^2}{n_2}}$$

$$1025 - 910 \pm 2.012\sqrt{\frac{150^2}{28} + \frac{125^2}{22}}$$

$$115 \pm 78$$

The point estimate of the difference between the population mean checking account balances at the two branches is $115. The margin of error is $78, and the 95% confidence interval estimate of the difference between the two population means is $115 - 78 = \$37$ to $115 + 78 = \$193$.

*This suggestion should help if you are using equation (10.7) to calculate the degrees of freedom by hand.*

The computation of the degrees of freedom (equation (10.7)) is cumbersome if you are doing the calculation by hand, but it is easily implemented with a computer software package. However, note that the expressions $s_1^2/n_1$ and $s_2^2/n_2$ appear in both expression (10.6) and equation (10.7). These values only need to be computed once in order to evaluate both (10.6) and (10.7).

## Hypothesis Tests About $\mu_1 - \mu_2$

Let us now consider hypothesis tests about the difference between the means of two populations when the population standard deviations $\sigma_1$ and $\sigma_2$ are unknown. Letting $D_0$ denote the hypothesized difference between $\mu_1$ and $\mu_2$, Section 10.1 showed that the test statistic used for the case where $\sigma_1$ and $\sigma_2$ are known is as follows.

$$z = \frac{(\bar{x}_1 - \bar{x}_2) - D_0}{\sqrt{\dfrac{\sigma_1^2}{n_1} + \dfrac{\sigma_2^2}{n_2}}}$$

The test statistic, $z$, follows the standard normal distribution.

When $\sigma_1$ and $\sigma_2$ are unknown, we use $s_1$ as an estimator of $\sigma_1$ and $s_2$ as an estimator of $\sigma_2$. Substituting these sample standard deviations for $\sigma_1$ and $\sigma_2$ provides the following test statistic when $\sigma_1$ and $\sigma_2$ are unknown.

---

TEST STATISTIC FOR HYPOTHESIS TESTS ABOUT $\mu_1 - \mu_2$: $\sigma_1$ AND $\sigma_2$ UNKNOWN

$$t = \frac{(\bar{x}_1 - \bar{x}_2) - D_0}{\sqrt{\dfrac{s_1^2}{n_1} + \dfrac{s_2^2}{n_2}}} \tag{10.8}$$

The degrees of freedom for $t$ are given by equation (10.7).

---

Let us demonstrate the use of this test statistic in the following hypothesis testing example.

Consider a new computer software package developed to help systems analysts reduce the time required to design, develop, and implement an information system. To evaluate the benefits of the new software package, a random sample of 24 systems analysts is selected. Each analyst is given specifications for a hypothetical information system. Then 12 of the analysts are instructed to produce the information system by using current technology. The other 12 analysts are trained in the use of the new software package and then instructed to use it to produce the information system.

This study involves two populations: a population of systems analysts using the current technology and a population of systems analysts using the new software package. In terms of the time required to complete the information system design project, the population means are as follow.

$\mu_1$ = the mean project completion time for systems analysts using the current technology

$\mu_2$ = the mean project completion time for systems analysts using the new software package

The researcher in charge of the new software evaluation project hopes to show that the new software package will provide a shorter mean project completion time. Thus, the researcher is looking for evidence to conclude that $\mu_2$ is less than $\mu_1$; in this case, the difference between the two population means, $\mu_1 - \mu_2$, will be greater than zero. The research hypothesis $\mu_1 - \mu_2 > 0$ is stated as the alternative hypothesis. Thus, the hypothesis test becomes

$$H_0: \mu_1 - \mu_2 \leq 0$$
$$H_a: \mu_1 - \mu_2 > 0$$

We will use $\alpha = .05$ as the level of significance.

Suppose that the 24 analysts complete the study with the results shown in Table 10.1. Using the test statistic in equation (10.8), we have

$$t = \frac{(\bar{x}_1 - \bar{x}_2) - D_0}{\sqrt{\dfrac{s_1^2}{n_1} + \dfrac{s_2^2}{n_2}}} = \frac{(325 - 286) - 0}{\sqrt{\dfrac{40^2}{12} + \dfrac{44^2}{12}}} = 2.27$$

**TABLE 10.1   COMPLETION TIME DATA AND SUMMARY STATISTICS
FOR THE SOFTWARE TESTING STUDY**

**SoftwareTest**

|  | Current Technology | New Software |
|---|---|---|
|  | 300 | 274 |
|  | 280 | 220 |
|  | 344 | 308 |
|  | 385 | 336 |
|  | 372 | 198 |
|  | 360 | 300 |
|  | 288 | 315 |
|  | 321 | 258 |
|  | 376 | 318 |
|  | 290 | 310 |
|  | 301 | 332 |
|  | 283 | 263 |

**Summary Statistics**

| | | |
|---|---|---|
| Sample size | $n_1 = 12$ | $n_2 = 12$ |
| Sample mean | $\bar{x}_1 = 325$ hours | $\bar{x}_2 = 286$ hours |
| Sample standard deviation | $s_1 = 40$ | $s_2 = 44$ |

Computing the degrees of freedom using equation (10.7), we have

$$df = \frac{\left(\dfrac{s_1^2}{n_1} + \dfrac{s_2^2}{n_2}\right)^2}{\dfrac{1}{n_1 - 1}\left(\dfrac{s_1^2}{n_1}\right)^2 + \dfrac{1}{n_2 - 1}\left(\dfrac{s_2^2}{n_2}\right)^2} = \frac{\left(\dfrac{40^2}{12} + \dfrac{44^2}{12}\right)^2}{\dfrac{1}{12 - 1}\left(\dfrac{40^2}{12}\right)^2 + \dfrac{1}{12 - 1}\left(\dfrac{44^2}{12}\right)^2} = 21.8$$

Rounding down, we will use a $t$ distribution with 21 degrees of freedom. This row of the $t$ distribution table is as follows:

| Area in Upper Tail | .20 | .10 | .05 | .025 | .01 | .005 |
|---|---|---|---|---|---|---|
| $t$ Value (21 df) | 0.859 | 1.323 | 1.721 | 2.080 | 2.518 | 2.831 |

$t = 2.27$

*Using the t distribution table, we can only determine a range for the p-value. Use of the computer is required to determine the exact p-value.*

With an upper tail test, the $p$-value is the area in the upper tail to the right of $t = 2.27$. From the above results, we see that the $p$-value is between .025 and .01. Thus, the $p$-value is less than $\alpha = .05$ and $H_0$ is rejected. The sample results enable the researcher to conclude that $\mu_1 - \mu_2 > 0$, or $\mu_1 > \mu_2$. Thus, the research study supports the conclusion that the new software package provides a smaller population mean completion time.

Minitab can be used to analyze data for testing hypotheses about the difference between two population means. The output comparing the current and new software technology is shown in Figure 10.2. The last line of the output shows $t = 2.27$ and $p$-value $= .017$. Note that Minitab used equation (10.7) to compute 21 degrees of freedom for this analysis.

## Practical Advice

*Whenever possible, equal sample sizes, $n_1 = n_2$, are recommended.*

The interval estimation and hypothesis testing procedures presented in this section are robust and can be used with relatively small sample sizes. In most applications, equal or nearly equal sample sizes such that the total sample size $n_1 + n_2$ is at least 20 can be

**FIGURE 10.2** MINITAB OUTPUT FOR THE HYPOTHESIS TEST OF THE CURRENT AND NEW SOFTWARE TECHNOLOGY

```
Two-sample T for Current vs New
             N      Mean     StDev    SE Mean
Current     12     325.0      40.0        12
New         12     286.0      44.0        13

Difference = mu Current - mu New
Estimate for difference:  39.0000
95% lower bound for difference = 9.4643
T-Test of difference = 0 (vs >):  T-Value = 2.27  P-Value = 0.017  DF = 21
```

expected to provide very good results even if the populations are not normal. Larger sample sizes are recommended if the distributions of the populations are highly skewed or contain outliers. Smaller sample sizes should only be used if the analyst is satisfied that the distributions of the populations are at least approximately normal.

## NOTES AND COMMENTS

Another approach used to make inferences about the difference between two population means when $\sigma_1$ and $\sigma_2$ are unknown is based on the assumption that the two population standard deviations are *equal* ($\sigma_1 = \sigma_2 = \sigma$). Under this assumption, the two sample standard deviations are combined to provide the following *pooled sample variance:*

$$s_p^2 = \frac{(n_1 - 1)s_1^2 + (n_2 - 1)s_2^2}{n_1 + n_2 - 2}$$

The $t$ test statistic becomes

$$t = \frac{(\bar{x}_1 - \bar{x}_2) - D_0}{s_p\sqrt{\dfrac{1}{n_1} + \dfrac{1}{n_2}}}$$

and has $n_1 + n_2 - 2$ degrees of freedom. At this point, the computation of the $p$-value and the interpretation of the sample results are identical to the procedures discussed earlier in this section.

A difficulty with this procedure is that the assumption that the two population standard deviations are equal is usually difficult to verify. Unequal population standard deviations are frequently encountered. Using the pooled procedure may not provide satisfactory results especially if the sample sizes $n_1$ and $n_2$ are quite different.

The $t$ procedure that we presented in this section does not require the assumption of equal population standard deviations and can be applied whether the population standard deviations are equal or not. It is a more general procedure and is recommended for most applications.

## Exercises

### Methods

**SELF** test

9. Consider the following results for independent random samples taken from two populations.

| Sample 1 | Sample 2 |
|---|---|
| $n_1 = 20$ | $n_2 = 30$ |
| $\bar{x}_1 = 22.5$ | $\bar{x}_2 = 20.1$ |
| $s_1 = 2.5$ | $s_2 = 4.8$ |

a. What is the point estimate of the difference between the two population means?
b. What is the degrees of freedom for the $t$ distribution?
c. At 95% confidence, what is the margin of error?
d. What is the 95% confidence interval for the difference between the two population means?

10. Consider the following hypothesis test.

$$H_0: \mu_1 - \mu_2 = 0$$
$$H_a: \mu_1 - \mu_2 \neq 0$$

The following results are from independent samples taken from two populations.

| Sample 1 | Sample 2 |
|----------|----------|
| $n_1 = 35$ | $n_2 = 40$ |
| $\bar{x}_1 = 13.6$ | $\bar{x}_2 = 10.1$ |
| $s_1 = 5.2$ | $s_2 = 8.5$ |

a. What is the value of the test statistic?
b. What is the degrees of freedom for the $t$ distribution?
c. What is the $p$-value?
d. At $\alpha = .05$, what is your conclusion?

11. Consider the following data for two independent random samples taken from two normal populations.

| Sample 1 | 10 | 7 | 13 | 7 | 9 | 8 |
|----------|----|----|----|----|----|----|
| Sample 2 | 8 | 7 | 8 | 4 | 6 | 9 |

a. Compute the two sample means.
b. Compute the two sample standard deviations.
c. What is the point estimate of the difference between the two population means?
d. What is the 90% confidence interval estimate of the difference between the two population means?

## Applications

12. The U.S. Department of Transportation provides the number of miles that residents of the 75 largest metropolitan areas travel per day in a car. Suppose that for a simple random sample of 50 Buffalo residents the mean is 22.5 miles a day and the standard deviation is 8.4 miles a day, and for an independent simple random sample of 40 Boston residents the mean is 18.6 miles a day and the standard deviation is 7.4 miles a day.
a. What is the point estimate of the difference between the mean number of miles that Buffalo residents travel per day and the mean number of miles that Boston residents travel per day?
b. What is the 95% confidence interval for the difference between the two population means?

13. The International Air Transport Association surveyed business travelers to determine ratings of various international airports. The maximum possible score was 10. Suppose 50 business travelers were asked to rate the Miami airport and 50 other business travelers were asked to rate the Los Angeles airport. The rating scores follow.

**Airport**

**Miami**

| 6 | 4 | 6 | 8 | 7 | 7 | 6 | 3 | 3 | 8 | 10 | 4 | 8 |
|---|---|---|---|---|---|---|---|---|---|----|---|---|
| 7 | 8 | 7 | 5 | 9 | 5 | 8 | 4 | 3 | 8 | 5 | 5 | 4 |
| 4 | 4 | 8 | 4 | 5 | 6 | 2 | 5 | 9 | 9 | 8 | 4 | 8 |
| 9 | 9 | 5 | 9 | 7 | 8 | 3 | 10 | 8 | 9 | 6 | | |

**Los Angeles**

| 10 | 9 | 6 | 7 | 8 | 7 | 9 | 8 | 10 | 7 | 6 | 5 | 7 |
|----|---|---|---|---|----|----|---|----|----|----|---|---|
| 3 | 5 | 6 | 8 | 7 | 10 | 8 | 4 | 7 | 8 | 6 | 9 | 9 |
| 5 | 3 | 1 | 8 | 9 | 6 | 8 | 5 | 4 | 6 | 10 | 9 | 8 |
| 3 | 2 | 7 | 9 | 5 | 3 | 10 | 3 | 5 | 10 | 8 | | |

Develop a 95% confidence interval estimate of the difference between the mean ratings of the Miami and Los Angeles airports.

14. The National Association of Home Builders provided data on the cost of the most popular home remodeling projects (*USA Today*, June 17, 1997). Sample data on cost in thousands of dollars for two types of remodeling projects are as follows.

| Kitchen | Master Bedroom |
|---------|----------------|
| 25.2 | 18.0 |
| 17.4 | 22.9 |
| 22.8 | 26.4 |
| 21.9 | 24.8 |
| 19.7 | 26.9 |
| 23.0 | 17.8 |
| 19.7 | 24.6 |
| 16.9 | 21.0 |
| 21.8 | |
| 23.6 | |

a. Develop a point estimate of the difference between the population mean remodeling costs for the two types of projects.

b. Develop a 90% confidence interval for the difference between the two population means.

15. Suppose selected independent random samples of 15 unionized women and 20 nonunionized women in manufacturing and provide the following hourly wage rates.

**Union**

**Union Workers**

| 22.40 | 18.90 | 16.70 | 14.05 | 16.20 | 20.00 | 16.10 | 16.30 | 19.10 |
|-------|-------|-------|-------|-------|-------|-------|-------|-------|
| 16.50 | 18.50 | 19.80 | 17.00 | 14.30 | 17.20 | | | |

**Nonunion Workers**

| 17.60 | 14.40 | 16.60 | 15.00 | 17.65 | 15.00 | 17.55 | 13.30 | 11.20 |
|-------|-------|-------|-------|-------|-------|-------|-------|-------|
| 15.90 | 19.20 | 11.85 | 16.65 | 15.20 | 15.30 | 17.00 | 15.10 | 14.30 |
| 13.90 | 14.50 | | | | | | | |

a.  What is the point estimate of the difference between hourly wages for the two populations?

b.  Develop a 95% confidence interval estimate of the difference between the two population means.

c.  Does there appear to be any difference in the mean wage rate for these two groups? Explain.

16.  Coastal areas of the United States including Cape Cod, the Outer Banks, the Carolinas, and the Gulf Coast had relatively high population growth rates during the 1990s. Data were collected on residents living in the coastal communities as well as on residents living in noncoastal areas throughout the United States (*USA Today,* July 21, 2000). Assume that the following sample results were obtained on the ages of individuals in the two populations:

| Coastal Areas | Noncoastal Areas |
|---|---|
| $n_1 = 150$ | $n_2 = 175$ |
| $\bar{x}_1 = 39.3$ years | $\bar{x}_2 = 35.4$ years |
| $s_1 = 16.8$ years | $s_2 = 15.2$ years |

Test the hypothesis of no difference between the two population means. Use $\alpha = .05$.

a.  Formulate the null and alternative hypotheses.

b.  What is the value of the test statistic?

c.  What is the $p$-value?

d.  What is your conclusion?

17.  Injuries to major league baseball players have been increasing in recent years. For the period 1992 to 2001, league expansion caused major league baseball rosters to increase 15%. However, the number of players being put on the disabled list due to injury increased 32% over the same period (*USA Today,* July 8, 2002). A research question addressed whether major league baseball players being put on the disabled list are on the list longer in 2001 than players put on the disabled list a decade earlier.

a.  Using the population mean number of days a player is on the disabled list, formulate null and alternative hypotheses that can be used to test the research question.

b.  Assume that the following data apply:

| | 2001 Season | 1992 Season |
|---|---|---|
| Sample Players | $n_1 = 45$ | $n_2 = 38$ |
| Sample Mean Days | $\bar{x}_1 = 60$ days | $\bar{x}_2 = 51$ days |
| Sample Std Deviation | $s_1 = 18$ days | $s_2 = 15$ days |

What is the point estimate of the difference between population mean days on the disabled list for 2001 compared to 1992? What is the percent increase in the number of days on the disabled list?

c.  Use $\alpha = .01$. What is your conclusion about number of days on the disabled list? What is the $p$-value?

d.  Do these data suggest that major league baseball should be concerned about the situation?

18. The mean time to locate flight information on Internet Web sites of the major airline companies is generally 2 to 3 minutes (*USA Today,* September 11, 2000). Sample results representative of the times for Delta Airlines and Northwest Airlines are as follows:

| Delta | Northwest |
|---|---|
| $n_1 = 32$ | $n_2 = 25$ |
| $\bar{x}_1 = 2.5$ minutes | $\bar{x}_2 = 2.1$ minutes |
| $s_1 = .8$ minutes | $s_2 = 1.1$ minutes |

   a. Formulate the hypotheses if the purpose is to test for a significant difference between the population mean times for the two airlines.
   b. Compute the value of the test statistic.
   c. What is the *p*-value?
   d. At $\alpha = .05$, what is your conclusion?

19. Periodically, Merrill Lynch customers are asked to evaluate Merrill Lynch financial consultants and services (2000 Merrill Lynch Client Satisfaction Survey). Higher ratings on the client satisfaction survey indicate better service with 7 the maximum service rating. Independent samples of service ratings for two financial consultants are summarized here. Consultant A has 10 years of experience while consultant B has 1 year of experience. Use $\alpha = .05$ and test to see whether the consultant with more experience has the higher population mean service rating.

| Consultant A | Consultant B |
|---|---|
| $n_1 = 16$ | $n_2 = 10$ |
| $\bar{x}_1 = 6.82$ | $\bar{x}_2 = 6.25$ |
| $s_1 = .64$ | $s_2 = .75$ |

   a. State the null and alternative hypotheses.
   b. Compute the value of the test statistic.
   c. What is the *p*-value?
   d. What is your conclusion?

20. Educational testing companies provide tutoring, classroom learning, and practice tests in an effort to help students perform better on tests such as the Scholastic Aptitude Test (SAT). The test preparation companies claim that their courses will improve SAT score performances by an average of 120 points (*The Wall Street Journal,* January 23, 2003). A researcher is uncertain of this claim and believes that 120 points may be an overstatement in an effort to encourage students to take the test preparation course. In an evaluation study of one test preparation service, the researcher collects SAT score data for 35 students who took the test preparation course and 48 students who did not take the course.

   a. Formulate the hypotheses that can be used to test the researcher's belief that the improvement in SAT scores may be less than the stated average of 120 points.
   b. Use $\alpha = .05$ and the following data. What is your conclusion?

|  | Course | No Course |
|---|---|---|
| Sample Mean | 1058 | 983 |
| Sample Standard Deviation | 90 | 105 |

c.  What is the point estimate of the improvement in the average SAT scores provided by the test preparation course? Provide a 95% confidence interval estimate of the improvement.

d.  What advice would you have for the researcher after seeing the confidence interval?

# 10.3  Inferences About the Difference Between Two Population Means: Matched Samples

Suppose employees at a manufacturing company can use two different methods to perform a production task. To maximize production output, the company wants to identify the method with the smaller population mean completion time. Let $\mu_1$ denote the population mean completion time for production method 1 and $\mu_2$ denote the population mean completion time for production method 2. With no preliminary indication of the preferred production method, we begin by tentatively assuming that the two production methods have the same population mean completion time. Thus, the null hypothesis is $H_0: \mu_1 - \mu_2 = 0$. If this hypothesis is rejected, we can conclude that the population mean completion times differ. In this case, the method providing the smaller mean completion time would be recommended. The null and alternative hypotheses are written as follows.

$$H_0: \mu_1 - \mu_2 = 0$$
$$H_a: \mu_1 - \mu_2 \neq 0$$

In choosing the sampling procedure that will be used to collect production time data and test the hypotheses, we consider two alternative designs. One is based on **independent samples** and the other is based on **matched samples.**

1.  *Independent sample design:* A simple random sample of workers is selected and each worker in the sample uses method 1. A second independent simple random sample of workers is selected and each worker in this sample uses method 2. The test of the difference between population means is based on the procedures in Section 10.2.
2.  *Matched sample design:* One simple random sample of workers is selected. Each worker first uses one method and then uses the other method. The order of the two methods is assigned randomly to the workers, with some workers performing method 1 first and others performing method 2 first. Each worker provides a pair of data values, one value for method 1 and another value for method 2.

In the matched sample design the two production methods are tested under similar conditions (i.e., with the same workers); hence this design often leads to a smaller sampling error than the independent sample design. The primary reason is that in a matched sample design, variation between workers is eliminated because the same workers are used for both production methods.

Let us demonstrate the analysis of a matched sample design by assuming it is the method used to test the difference between population means for the two production methods. A random sample of six workers is used. The data on completion times for the six workers are given in Table 10.2. Note that each worker provides a pair of data values, one for each production method. Also note that the last column contains the difference in completion times $d_i$ for each worker in the sample.

The key to the analysis of the matched sample design is to realize that we consider only the column of differences. Therefore, we have six data values (.6, −.2, .5, .3, .0, and .6) that will be used to analyze the difference between population means of the two production methods.

**TABLE 10.2    TASK COMPLETION TIMES FOR A MATCHED SAMPLE DESIGN**

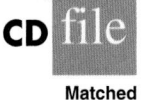

**CD file**

**Matched**

| Worker | Completion Time for Method 1 (minutes) | Completion Time for Method 2 (minutes) | Difference in Completion Times ($d_i$) |
|---|---|---|---|
| 1 | 6.0 | 5.4 | .6 |
| 2 | 5.0 | 5.2 | −.2 |
| 3 | 7.0 | 6.5 | .5 |
| 4 | 6.2 | 5.9 | .3 |
| 5 | 6.0 | 6.0 | .0 |
| 6 | 6.4 | 5.8 | .6 |

Let $\mu_d$ = the mean of the *difference* values for the population of workers. With this notation, the null and alternative hypotheses are rewritten as follows.

$$H_0: \mu_d = 0$$
$$H_a: \mu_d \neq 0$$

If $H_0$ is rejected, we can conclude that the population mean completion times differ.

*Other than the use of the d notation, the formulas for the sample mean and sample standard deviation are the same ones used previously in the text.*

The $d$ notation is a reminder that the matched sample provides *difference* data. The sample mean and sample standard deviation for the six difference values in Table 10.2 follow.

$$\bar{d} = \frac{\Sigma d_i}{n} = \frac{1.8}{6} = .30$$

$$s_d = \sqrt{\frac{\Sigma(d_i - \bar{d})^2}{n - 1}} = \sqrt{\frac{.56}{5}} = .335$$

*It is not necessary to make the assumption that the population has a normal distribution if the sample size is large. Sample size guidelines for using the t distribution were presented in Chapters 8 and 9.*

With the small sample of $n = 6$ workers, we need to make the assumption that the population of differences has a normal distribution. This assumption is necessary so that we may use the $t$ distribution for hypothesis testing and interval estimation procedures. Based on this assumption, the following test statistic has a $t$ distribution with $n - 1$ degrees of freedom.

$$t = \frac{\bar{d} - \mu_d}{s_d/\sqrt{n}} \tag{10.9}$$

*Once the difference data are computed, the t distribution procedure for matched samples is the same as the one-population estimation and hypothesis testing procedures described in Chapters 8 and 9.*

Let us use equation (10.9) to test the hypotheses $H_0: \mu_d = 0$ and $H_a: \mu_d \neq 0$, using $\alpha = .05$. Substituting the sample results $\bar{d} = .30$, $s_d = .335$, and $n = 6$ into equation (10.9), we compute the value of the test statistic.

$$t = \frac{\bar{d} - \mu_d}{s_d/\sqrt{n}} = \frac{.30 - 0}{.335/\sqrt{6}} = 2.20$$

Now let us compute the $p$-value for this two-tailed test. Because $t = 2.20 > 0$, the test statistic is in the upper tail of the $t$ distribution. With $t = 2.20$, the area in the upper tail to the right of the test statistic can be found by using the $t$ distribution table with degrees of freedom $= n - 1 = 6 - 1 = 5$. Information from the 5 degrees of freedom row of the $t$ distribution table is as follows:

| Area in Upper Tail | .20 | .10 | .05 | .025 | .01 | .005 |
|---|---|---|---|---|---|---|
| **$t$ Value (5 df)** | 0.920 | 1.476 | 2.015 | 2.571 | 3.365 | 4.032 |

$$t = 2.20$$

Thus, we see that the area in the upper tail is between .05 and .025. Because this test is a two-tailed test, we double these values to conclude that the $p$-value is between .10 and .05. This $p$-value is greater than $\alpha = .05$. Thus, the null hypothesis $H_0$: $\mu_d = 0$ is not rejected. Using Minitab and the data in Table 10.2, we find the $p$-value $= .080$.

In addition we can obtain an interval estimate of the difference between the two population means by using the single population methodology of Chapter 8. At 95% confidence, the calculation follows.

$$\bar{d} \pm t_{.025} \frac{s_d}{\sqrt{n}}$$

$$.3 \pm 2.571 \left( \frac{.335}{\sqrt{6}} \right)$$

$$.3 \pm .35$$

Thus, the margin of error is .35 and the 95% confidence interval for the difference between the population means of the two production methods is $-.05$ minutes to .65 minutes.

## NOTES AND COMMENTS

1. In the example presented in this section, workers performed the production task with first one method and then the other method. This example illustrates a matched sample design in which each sampled element (worker) provides a pair of data values. It is also possible to use different but "similar" elements to provide the pair of data values. For example, a worker at one location could be matched with a similar worker at another location (similarity based on age, education, gender, experience, etc.). The pairs of workers would provide the difference data that could be used in the matched sample analysis.

2. A matched sample procedure for inferences about two population means generally provides better precision than the independent sample approach, therefore it is the recommended design. However, in some applications the matching cannot be achieved, or perhaps the time and cost associated with matching are excessive. In such cases, the independent sample design should be used.

## Exercises

## Methods

21.  Consider the following hypothesis test.

$$H_0: \mu_d \le 0$$
$$H_a: \mu_d > 0$$

The following data are from matched samples taken from two populations.

| | | Population | |
|---|---|---|---|
| Element | | 1 | 2 |
| 1 | | 21 | 20 |
| 2 | | 28 | 26 |
| 3 | | 18 | 18 |
| 4 | | 20 | 20 |
| 5 | | 26 | 24 |

a. Compute the difference value for each element.
b. Compute $\bar{d}$.
c. Compute the standard deviation $s_d$.
d. Conduct a hypothesis test using $\alpha = .05$. What is your conclusion?

22. The following data are from matched samples taken from two populations.

| | | Population | |
|---|---|---|---|
| Element | | 1 | 2 |
| 1 | | 11 | 8 |
| 2 | | 7 | 8 |
| 3 | | 9 | 6 |
| 4 | | 12 | 7 |
| 5 | | 13 | 10 |
| 6 | | 15 | 15 |
| 7 | | 15 | 14 |

a. Compute the difference value for each element.
b. Compute $\bar{d}$.
c. Compute the standard deviation $s_d$.
d. What is the point estimate of the difference between the two population means?
e. Provide a 95% confidence interval for the difference between the two population means.

## Applications

23. A market research firm used a sample of individuals to rate the purchase potential of a particular product before and after the individuals saw a new television commercial about the product. The purchase potential ratings were based on a 0 to 10 scale, with higher values indicating a higher purchase potential. The null hypothesis stated that the mean rating "after" would be less than or equal to the mean rating "before." Rejection of this hypothesis would show that the commercial improved the mean purchase potential rating. Use $\alpha = .05$ and the following data to test the hypothesis and comment on the value of the commercial.

| | Purchase Rating | | | | Purchase Rating | |
|---|---|---|---|---|---|---|
| Individual | After | Before | | Individual | After | Before |
| 1 | 6 | 5 | | 5 | 3 | 5 |
| 2 | 6 | 4 | | 6 | 9 | 8 |
| 3 | 7 | 7 | | 7 | 7 | 5 |
| 4 | 4 | 3 | | 8 | 6 | 6 |

24. A sample of 10 international telephone calls provided Sprint and WorldCom calling rates per minute for calls from the United States (*World Traveler,* July 2000).

| Country | Sprint | WorldCom |
|---------|--------|----------|
| Australia | .46 | .26 |
| Belgium | .69 | .40 |
| Brazil | .92 | .53 |
| Colombia | .55 | .53 |
| Denmark | .50 | .26 |
| France | .46 | .26 |
| Germany | .46 | .26 |
| Hong Kong | .92 | .40 |
| Japan | .69 | .40 |
| United Kingdom | .46 | .26 |

Provide a 95% confidence interval estimate of the difference between the two population means.

25. The cost of transportation from the airport to the downtown area depends on the method of transportation. One-way costs for taxi and shuttle bus transportation for a sample of 10 major cities follow. Provide a 95% confidence interval for the mean cost increase associated with taxi transportation.

| City | Taxi ($) | Shuttle Bus ($) | City | Taxi ($) | Shuttle Bus ($) |
|------|----------|-----------------|------|----------|-----------------|
| Atlanta | 15.00 | 7.00 | Minneapolis | 16.50 | 7.50 |
| Chicago | 22.00 | 12.50 | New Orleans | 18.00 | 7.00 |
| Denver | 11.00 | 5.00 | New York (LaGuardia) | 16.00 | 8.50 |
| Houston | 15.00 | 4.50 | Philadelphia | 20.00 | 8.00 |
| Los Angeles | 26.00 | 11.00 | Washington, D.C. | 10.00 | 5.00 |

26. Rental car gasoline prices per gallon were sampled at eight major airports. Data for Hertz and National car rental companies follow (*USA Today,* April 4, 2000).

| Airport | Hertz | National |
|---------|-------|----------|
| Boston Logan | 1.55 | 1.56 |
| Chicago O'Hare | 1.62 | 1.59 |
| Los Angeles | 1.72 | 1.78 |
| Miami | 1.65 | 1.49 |
| New York (JFK) | 1.72 | 1.51 |
| New York (LaGuardia) | 1.67 | 1.50 |
| Orange County, CA | 1.68 | 1.77 |
| Washington (Dulles) | 1.52 | 1.41 |

Use $\alpha = .05$ to test the hypothesis of no difference between the population mean prices per gallon for the two companies.

27. A survey was made of Book-of-the-Month-Club members to ascertain whether members spend more time watching television than they do reading. Assume a sample of 15 respondents provided the following data on weekly hours of television watching and weekly hours of reading. Using a .05 level of significance, can you conclude that Book-of-the-Month-Club members spend more hours per week watching television than reading?

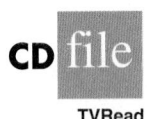

**TVRead**

| Respondent | Television | Reading | Respondent | Television | Reading |
|---|---|---|---|---|---|
| 1 | 10 | 6 | 9 | 4 | 7 |
| 2 | 14 | 16 | 10 | 8 | 8 |
| 3 | 16 | 8 | 11 | 16 | 5 |
| 4 | 18 | 10 | 12 | 5 | 10 |
| 5 | 15 | 10 | 13 | 8 | 3 |
| 6 | 14 | 8 | 14 | 19 | 10 |
| 7 | 10 | 14 | 15 | 11 | 6 |
| 8 | 12 | 14 | | | |

28. StreetInsider.com reported 2002 earnings per share data for a sample of major companies (February 12, 2003). Prior to 2002, financial analysts predicted the 2002 earnings per share for these same companies (*Barron's,* September 10, 2001). Use the following data to comment on differences between actual and estimated earnings per share.

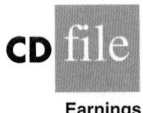

**Earnings**

| Company | Actual | Predicted |
|---|---|---|
| AT&T | 1.29 | 0.38 |
| American Express | 2.01 | 2.31 |
| Citigroup | 2.59 | 3.43 |
| Coca-Cola | 1.60 | 1.78 |
| DuPont | 1.84 | 2.18 |
| Exxon-Mobil | 2.72 | 2.19 |
| General Electric | 1.51 | 1.71 |
| Johnson & Johnson | 2.28 | 2.18 |
| McDonald's | 0.77 | 1.55 |
| Wal-Mart | 1.81 | 1.74 |

a. Use $\alpha = .05$ and test for any difference between the population mean actual and population mean estimated earnings per share. What is the $p$-value? What is your conclusion?
b. What is the point estimate of the difference between the two means? Did the analysts tend to underestimate or overestimate the earnings?
c. At 95% confidence, what is the margin of error for the estimate in part (b)? What would you recommend based on this information?

29. A manufacturer produces both a deluxe and a standard model of an automatic sander designed for home use. Selling prices obtained from a sample of retail outlets follow.

| | Model Price ($) | | | Model Price ($) | |
|---|---|---|---|---|---|
| Retail Outlet | Deluxe | Standard | Retail Outlet | Deluxe | Standard |
| 1 | 39 | 27 | 5 | 40 | 30 |
| 2 | 39 | 28 | 6 | 39 | 34 |
| 3 | 45 | 35 | 7 | 35 | 29 |
| 4 | 38 | 30 | | | |

a.   The manufacturer's suggested retail prices for the two models show a $10 price differential. Use a .05 level of significance and test that the mean difference between the prices of the two models is $10.
b.   What is the 95% confidence interval for the difference between the mean prices of the two models?

 # Inferences About the Difference Between Two Population Proportions

Letting $p_1$ denote the proportion for population 1 and $p_2$ denote the proportion for population 2, we next consider inferences about the difference between the two population proportions: $p_1 - p_2$. To make an inference about this difference, we will select two independent random samples consisting of $n_1$ units from population 1 and $n_2$ units from population 2.

## Interval Estimation of $p_1 - p_2$

In the following example, we show how to compute a margin of error and develop an interval estimate of the difference between two population proportions.

A tax preparation firm is interested in comparing the quality of work at two of its regional offices. By randomly selecting samples of tax returns prepared at each office and verifying the sample returns' accuracy, the firm will be able to estimate the proportion of erroneous returns prepared at each office. Of particular interest is the difference between these proportions.

$p_1$ = proportion of erroneous returns for population 1 (office 1)
$p_2$ = proportion of erroneous returns for population 2 (office 2)
$\bar{p}_1$ = sample proportion for a simple random sample from population 1
$\bar{p}_2$ = sample proportion for a simple random sample from population 2

The difference between the two population proportions is given by $p_1 - p_2$. The point estimator of $p_1 - p_2$ is as follows.

POINT ESTIMATOR OF THE DIFFERENCE BETWEEN TWO POPULATION
PROPORTIONS

$$\bar{p}_1 - \bar{p}_2 \tag{10.10}$$

Thus, the point estimator of the difference between two population proportions is the difference between the sample proportions of two independent simple random samples.

As with other point estimators, the point estimator $\bar{p}_1 - \bar{p}_2$ has a sampling distribution that reflects the possible values of $\bar{p}_1 - \bar{p}_2$ if we repeatedly took two independent random samples. The mean of this sampling distribution is $p_1 - p_2$ and the standard error of $\bar{p}_1 - \bar{p}_2$ is as follows:

$$\sigma_{\bar{p}_1 - \bar{p}_2} = \sqrt{\frac{p_1(1 - p_1)}{n_1} + \frac{p_2(1 - p_2)}{n_2}} \tag{10.11}$$

If the sample sizes are large enough that $n_1 p_1$, $n_1(1 - p_1)$, $n_2 p_2$, and $n_2(1 - p_2)$ are all greater than or equal to 5, the sampling distribution of $\bar{p}_1 - \bar{p}_2$ can be approximated by a normal distribution.

As we showed previously, an interval estimate is given by a point estimate ± a margin of error. In the estimation of the difference between two population proportions, an interval estimate will take the following form:

$$\bar{p}_1 - \bar{p}_2 \pm \text{Margin of error}$$

With the sampling distribution of $\bar{p}_1 - \bar{p}_2$ approximated by a normal distribution, we would like to use $z_{\alpha/2}\sigma_{\bar{p}_1 - \bar{p}_2}$ as the margin of error. However, $\sigma_{\bar{p}_1 - \bar{p}_2}$ given by equation (10.11) cannot be used directly because the two population proportions, $p_1$ and $p_2$, are unknown. Using the sample proportion $\bar{p}_1$ to estimate $p_1$ and the sample proportion $\bar{p}_2$ to estimate $p_2$, the margin of error is as follows.

$$\text{Margin of error} = z_{\alpha/2}\sqrt{\frac{\bar{p}_1(1 - \bar{p}_1)}{n_1} + \frac{\bar{p}_2(1 - \bar{p}_2)}{n_2}} \qquad (10.12)$$

The general form of an interval estimate of the difference between two population proportions is as follows.

**INTERVAL ESTIMATE OF THE DIFFERENCE BETWEEN TWO POPULATION PROPORTIONS**

$$\bar{p}_1 - \bar{p}_2 \pm z_{\alpha/2}\sqrt{\frac{\bar{p}_1(1 - \bar{p}_1)}{n_1} + \frac{\bar{p}_2(1 - \bar{p}_2)}{n_2}} \qquad (10.13)$$

where $1 - \alpha$ is the confidence coefficient.

Returning to the tax preparation example, we find that independent simple random samples from the two offices provide the following information.

| **Office 1** | **Office 2** |
| --- | --- |
| $n_1 = 250$ | $n_2 = 300$ |
| Number of returns with errors = 35 | Number of returns with errors = 27 |

**TaxPrep**

The sample proportions for the two offices follow.

$$\bar{p}_1 = \frac{35}{250} = .14$$

$$\bar{p}_2 = \frac{27}{300} = .09$$

The point estimate of the difference between the proportions of erroneous tax returns for the two populations is $\bar{p}_1 - \bar{p}_2 = .14 - .09 = .05$. Thus, we estimate that office 1 has a .05, or 5%, greater error rate than office 2.

Expression (10.13) can now be used to provide a margin of error and interval estimate of the difference between the two population proportions. Using a 90% confidence interval with $z_{\alpha/2} = z_{.05} = 1.645$, we have

$$\bar{p}_1 - \bar{p}_2 \pm z_{\alpha/2} \sqrt{\frac{\bar{p}_1(1 - \bar{p}_1)}{n_1} + \frac{\bar{p}_2(1 - \bar{p}_2)}{n_2}}$$

$$.14 - .09 \pm 1.645 \sqrt{\frac{.14(1 - .14)}{250} + \frac{.09(1 - .09)}{300}}$$

$$.05 \pm .045$$

Thus, the margin of error is .045, and the 90% confidence interval is .005 to .095.

## Hypothesis Tests About $p_1 - p_2$

Let us now consider hypothesis tests about the difference between the proportions of two populations. We focus on tests involving no difference between the two population proportions. In this case, the three forms for a hypothesis test are as follows:

*All hypotheses considered use 0 as the difference of interest.*

$$
\begin{array}{lll}
H_0: p_1 - p_2 \geq 0 & H_0: p_1 - p_2 \leq 0 & H_0: p_1 - p_2 = 0 \\
H_a: p_1 - p_2 < 0 & H_a: p_1 - p_2 > 0 & H_a: p_1 - p_2 \neq 0
\end{array}
$$

When we assume $H_0$ is true as an equality, we have $p_1 - p_2 = 0$, which is the same as saying that the population proportions are equal, $p_1 = p_2$.

We will base the test statistic on the sampling distribution of the point estimator $\bar{p}_1 - \bar{p}_2$. In equation (10.11), we showed that the standard error of $\bar{p}_1 - \bar{p}_2$ is given by

$$\sigma_{\bar{p}_1 - \bar{p}_2} = \sqrt{\frac{p_1(1 - p_1)}{n_1} + \frac{p_2(1 - p_2)}{n_2}}$$

Under the assumption $H_0$ is true as an equality, the population proportions are equal and $p_1 = p_2 = p$. In this case, $\sigma_{\bar{p}_1 - \bar{p}_2}$ becomes

$$\sigma_{\bar{p}_1 - \bar{p}_2} = \sqrt{\frac{p(1 - p)}{n_1} + \frac{p(1 - p)}{n_2}} = \sqrt{p(1 - p)\left(\frac{1}{n_1} + \frac{1}{n_2}\right)} \qquad (10.14)$$

With $p$ unknown, we pool, or combine, the point estimators from the two samples ($\bar{p}_1$ and $\bar{p}_2$) to obtain a single point estimator of $p$ as follows:

$$\bar{p} = \frac{n_1\bar{p}_1 + n_2\bar{p}_2}{n_1 + n_2} \qquad (10.15)$$

This **pooled estimator** of $p$ is a weighted average of $\bar{p}_1$ and $\bar{p}_2$.

Substituting $\bar{p}$ for $p$ in equation (10.14), we obtain an estimate of the standard error of $\bar{p}_1 - \bar{p}_2$. This estimate of the standard error is used in the test statistic. The general form of the test statistic for hypothesis tests about the difference between two population proportions is the point estimator divided by the estimate of $\sigma_{\bar{p}_1 - \bar{p}_2}$.

TEST STATISTIC FOR HYPOTHESIS TESTS ABOUT $p_1 - p_2$

$$z = \frac{(\bar{p}_1 - \bar{p}_2)}{\sqrt{\bar{p}(1 - \bar{p})\left(\frac{1}{n_1} + \frac{1}{n_2}\right)}} \qquad (10.16)$$

This test statistic applies to large sample situations where $n_1p_1$, $n_1(1 - p_1)$, $n_2p_2$, and $n_2(1 - p_2)$ are all greater than or equal to 5.

Let us return to the tax preparation firm example and assume that the firm wants to use a hypothesis test to determine whether the error proportions differ between the two offices. A two-tailed test is required. The null and alternative hypotheses are as follows:

$$H_0: p_1 - p_2 = 0$$
$$H_a: p_1 - p_2 \neq 0$$

If $H_0$ is rejected, the firm can conclude that the error rates at the two offices differ. We will use $\alpha = .10$ as the level of significance.

The sample data previously collected showed $\bar{p}_1 = .14$ for the $n_1 = 250$ returns sampled at office 1 and $\bar{p}_2 = .09$ for the $n_2 = 300$ returns sampled at office 2. We continue by computing the pooled estimate of $p$.

$$\bar{p} = \frac{n_1\bar{p}_1 + n_2\bar{p}_2}{n_1 + n_2} = \frac{250(.14) + 300(.09)}{250 + 300} = .1127$$

Using this pooled estimate and the difference between the sample proportions, the value of the test statistic is as follows.

$$z = \frac{(\bar{p}_1 - \bar{p}_2)}{\sqrt{\bar{p}(1 - \bar{p})\left(\dfrac{1}{n_1} + \dfrac{1}{n_2}\right)}} = \frac{(.14 - .09)}{\sqrt{.1127(1 - .1127)\left(\dfrac{1}{250} + \dfrac{1}{300}\right)}} = 1.85$$

In computing the $p$-value for this two-tailed test, we first note that $z = 1.85$ is in the upper tail of the standard normal distribution. Using $z = 1.85$ and the standard normal distribution table, we find the area in the upper tail is $.5000 - .4678 = .0322$. Doubling this area for a two-tailed test, we find the $p$-value $= 2(.0322) = .0644$. With the $p$-value less than $\alpha = .10$, $H_0$ is rejected at the .10 level of significance. The firm can conclude that the error rates differ between the two offices. This hypothesis testing conclusion is consistent with the earlier interval estimation results that showed the interval estimate of the difference between the population error rates at the two offices to be .005 to .095, with Office 1 having the higher error rate.

## Exercises

## Methods

30. Consider the following results for independent samples taken from two populations.

| Sample 1 | Sample 2 |
|---|---|
| $n_1 = 400$ | $n_2 = 300$ |
| $\bar{p}_1 = .48$ | $\bar{p}_2 = .36$ |

a. What is the point estimate of the difference between the two population proportions?
b. Develop a 90% confidence interval for the difference between the two population proportions.
c. Develop a 95% confidence interval for the difference between the two population proportions.

31. Consider the hypothesis test

$$H_0: p_1 - p_2 \leq 0$$
$$H_a: p_1 - p_2 > 0$$

The following results are for independent samples taken from the two populations.

| Sample 1 | Sample 2 |
|----------|----------|
| $n_1 = 200$ | $n_2 = 300$ |
| $\bar{p}_1 = .22$ | $\bar{p}_2 = .16$ |

a. What is the $p$-value?

b. With $\alpha = .05$, what is your hypothesis testing conclusion?

## Applications

32. A *Business Week*/Harris survey asked senior executives at large corporations their opinions about the economic outlook for the future. One question was "Do you think that there will be an increase in the number of full-time employees at your company over the next 12 months?" In the current survey, 220 of 400 executives answered yes, while in a previous year survey, 192 of 400 executives had answered yes. Provide a 95% confidence interval estimate for the difference between the proportions at the two points in time. What is your interpretation of the interval estimate?

33. A Gallup poll found that 16% of 505 men and 25% of 496 women surveyed favored a law forbidding the sale of all beer, wine, and liquor throughout the nation. Develop a 95% confidence interval for the difference between the proportion of women who favor such a ban and the proportion of men who favor such a ban.

34. A CNN/*USA Today* poll evaluated the popularity of major league baseball after the Mark McGwire and Sammy Sosa record-setting home-run chase during the 1998 season. A sample of 1082 found 682 people responding yes to the question "Are you a fan of major league baseball?" (*USA Today*, September 17, 1998). During the baseball strike of April 1995, a sample of 1008 found only 413 people responding yes to the same question.
    a. Use the sample proportions to estimate the fan support for major league baseball in 1998 and in 1995. What is the point estimate of the increase in major league baseball fan support from the strike in 1995 to the McGwire/Sosa home-run chase of 1998?
    b. Develop a 95% confidence interval estimate of the increase in fan support.

35. Slot machines are the favorite game at casinos throughout the United States (*Harrah's Survey 2002: Profile of the American Gamble*). The following sample data show the number of women and number of men who selected slot machines as their favorite game.

| | Women | Men |
|--|-------|-----|
| Sample Size | 320 | 250 |
| Favorite Game—Slots | 256 | 165 |

a. What is the point estimate of the proportion of women who say slots is their favorite game?

b. What is the point estimate of the proportion of men who say slots is their favorite game?

c. Provide a 95% confidence interval estimate of the difference between the proportion of women and proportion of men who say slots is their favorite game.

36. The Bureau of Transportation tracks the flight arrival performances of the 10 biggest airlines in the United States (*The Wall Street Journal,* March 4, 2003). Flights that arrive within 15 minutes of schedule are considered on time. Using sample data consistent with Bureau of Transportation statistics reported in January 2001 and January 2002, consider the following:

> January 2001    A sample of 924 flights showed 742 on time.
> January 2002    A sample of 841 flights showed 714 on time.

    a. What is the point estimate of on-time flights in January 2001?
    b. What is the point estimate of on-time flights in January 2002?
    c. Let $p_1$ denote the population proportion of on-time flights in January 2001 and $p_2$ denote the population proportion of on-time flights in January 2002. State the hypotheses that could be tested to determine whether the major airlines improved on-time flight performance during the one-year period.
    d. At $\alpha = .05$, what is your conclusion? What is the $p$-value?

37. In a test of the quality of two television commercials, each commercial was shown in a separate test area six times over a one-week period. The following week a telephone survey was conducted to identify individuals who had seen the commercials. Those individuals were asked to state the primary message in the commercials. The following results were recorded.

| | Commercial A | Commercial B |
|---|---|---|
| **Number Who Saw Commercial** | 150 | 200 |
| **Number Who Recalled Message** | 63 | 60 |

    a. Use $\alpha = .05$ and test the hypothesis that there is no difference in the recall proportions for the two commercials.
    b. Compute a 95% confidence interval for the difference between the recall proportions for the two populations.

38. The stock market declined in early 2000 with many stocks dropping below their 1997 highs. In fact, 81.5% of New York Stock Exchange (NYSE) stocks and 72.4% of NASDAQ stocks were trading below their 1997 highs (*Barron's,* May 22, 2000). If the data were based on 232 NYSE stocks and 210 NASDAQ stocks, test the hypothesis $H_0$: $p_1 - p_2 = 0$ with $\alpha = .05$. What is the $p$-value? What is your conclusion?

39. A 2003 *New York Times*/CBS News poll sampled 523 adults who were planning a vacation during the next six months and found that 141 were expecting to travel by airplane (*New York Times New Service,* March 2, 2003). A similar survey question in a May 1993 *New York Times*/CBS News poll found that of 477 adults who were planning a vacation in the next six months, 81 were expecting to travel by airplane.
    a. State the hypotheses that can be used to determine whether a significant change occurred in the population proportion planning to travel by airplane over the 10-year period.
    b. What is the sample proportion expecting to travel by airplane in 2003? In 1993?
    c. Use $\alpha = .01$ and test for a significant difference. What is your conclusion?
    d. Discuss reasons that might provide an explanation for this conclusion.

## Summary

In this chapter we discussed procedures for developing interval estimates and conducting hypothesis tests involving two populations. First, we showed how to make inferences about the difference between two population means when independent simple random samples are selected. We first considered the case where the population standard deviations, $\sigma_1$ and $\sigma_2$, could be assumed known. The standard normal distribution $z$ was used to develop the interval estimate and served as the test statistic for hypothesis tests. We then considered the case where the population standard deviations were unknown and estimated by the sample standard deviations $s_1$ and $s_2$. In this case, the $t$ distribution was used to develop the interval estimate and served as the test statistic for hypothesis tests.

Inferences about the difference between two population means were then discussed for the matched sample design. In the matched sample design each element provides a pair of data values, one from each population. The difference between the paired data values is then used in the statistical analysis. The matched sample design is generally preferred to the independent sample design because the matched-sample procedure often improves the precision of the estimate.

Finally, interval estimation and hypothesis testing about the difference between two population proportions were discussed. Statistical procedures for analyzing the difference between two population proportions are similar to the procedures for analyzing the difference between two population means.

## Glossary

**Independent samples** Samples selected from two populations in such a way that the elements making up one sample are chosen independently of the elements making up the other sample.

**Matched samples** Samples in which each data value of one sample is matched with a corresponding data value of the other sample.

**Pooled estimator of $p$** An estimator of a population proportion obtained by computing a weighted average of the point estimators obtained from two independent samples.

## Key Formulas

**Point Estimator of the Difference Between Two Population Means**

$$\bar{x}_1 - \bar{x}_2 \tag{10.1}$$

**Standard Error of $\bar{x}_1 - \bar{x}_2$**

$$\sigma_{\bar{x}_1 - \bar{x}_2} = \sqrt{\frac{\sigma_1^2}{n_1} + \frac{\sigma_2^2}{n_2}} \tag{10.2}$$

**Interval Estimate of the Difference Between Two Population Means: $\sigma_1$ and $\sigma_2$ Known**

$$\bar{x}_1 - \bar{x}_2 \pm z_{\alpha/2} \sqrt{\frac{\sigma_1^2}{n_1} + \frac{\sigma_2^2}{n_2}} \tag{10.4}$$

**Test Statistic for Hypothesis Tests About $\mu_1 - \mu_2$: $\sigma_1$ and $\sigma_2$ Known**

$$z = \frac{(\bar{x}_1 - \bar{x}_2) - D_0}{\sqrt{\dfrac{\sigma_1^2}{n_1} + \dfrac{\sigma_2^2}{n_2}}} \tag{10.5}$$

**Interval Estimate of the Difference Between Two Population Means: $\sigma_1$ and $\sigma_2$ Unknown**

$$\bar{x}_1 - \bar{x}_2 \pm t_{\alpha/2}\sqrt{\frac{s_1^2}{n_1} + \frac{s_2^2}{n_2}} \tag{10.6}$$

**Degrees of Freedom for the $t$ Distribution Using Two Independent Random Samples**

$$df = \frac{\left(\dfrac{s_1^2}{n_1} + \dfrac{s_2^2}{n_2}\right)^2}{\dfrac{1}{n_1 - 1}\left(\dfrac{s_1^2}{n_1}\right)^2 + \dfrac{1}{n_2 - 1}\left(\dfrac{s_2^2}{n_2}\right)^2} \tag{10.7}$$

**Test Statistic for Hypothesis Tests About $\mu_1 - \mu_2$: $\sigma_1$ and $\sigma_2$ Unknown**

$$t = \frac{(\bar{x}_1 - \bar{x}_2) - D_0}{\sqrt{\dfrac{s_1^2}{n_1} + \dfrac{s_2^2}{n_2}}} \tag{10.8}$$

**Test Statistic for Hypothesis Tests Involving Matched Samples**

$$t = \frac{\bar{d} - \mu_d}{s_d/\sqrt{n}} \tag{10.9}$$

**Point Estimate of the Difference Between Two Population Proportions**

$$\bar{p}_1 - \bar{p}_2 \tag{10.10}$$

**Standard Error of $\bar{p}_1 - \bar{p}_2$**

$$\sigma_{\bar{p}_1 - \bar{p}_2} = \sqrt{\frac{p_1(1 - p_1)}{n_1} + \frac{p_2(1 - p_2)}{n_2}} \tag{10.11}$$

**Interval Estimate of the Difference Between Two Population Proportions**

$$\bar{p}_1 - \bar{p}_2 \pm z_{\alpha/2}\sqrt{\frac{\bar{p}_1(1 - \bar{p}_1)}{n_1} + \frac{\bar{p}_2(1 - \bar{p}_2)}{n_2}} \tag{10.13}$$

**Standard Error of $\bar{p}_1 - \bar{p}_2$ When $p_1 = p_2 = p$**

$$\sigma_{\bar{p}_1 - \bar{p}_2} = \sqrt{p(1 - p)\left(\frac{p(1 - p)}{n_1}\right)} \tag{10.14}$$

**Pooled Estimator of $p$ When $p_1 = p_2 = p$**

$$\bar{p} = \frac{n_1\bar{p}_1 + n_2\bar{p}_2}{n_1 + n_2} \tag{10.15}$$

**Test Statistic for Hypothesis Tests About $p_1 - p_2$**

$$z = \frac{(\bar{p}_1 - \bar{p}_2)}{\sqrt{\bar{p}(1 - \bar{p})\left(\dfrac{1}{n_1} + \dfrac{1}{n_2}\right)}} \tag{10.16}$$

## Supplementary Exercises

40. Starting annual salaries for individuals with master's and bachelor's degrees in business were collected in two independent random samples. Use the following data to develop a 90% confidence interval estimate of the increase in starting salary that can be expected upon completion of a master's program.

|  Master's Degree  |  Bachelor's Degree  |
|---|---|
| $n_1 = 60$ | $n_2 = 80$ |
| $\bar{x}_1 = \$45{,}000$ | $\bar{x}_2 = \$35{,}000$ |
| $\sigma_1 = \$4000$ | $\sigma_2 = \$3500$ |

41. Safegate Foods, Inc., is redesigning the checkout lanes in its supermarkets throughout the country and is considering two designs. Tests on customer checkout times conducted at two stores where the two new systems have been installed result in the following summary of the data.

|  System A  |  System B  |
|---|---|
| $n_1 = 120$ | $n_2 = 100$ |
| $\bar{x}_1 = 4.1$ minutes | $\bar{x}_2 = 3.4$ minutes |
| $\sigma_1 = 2.2$ minutes | $\sigma_2 = 1.5$ minutes |

Test at the .05 level of significance to determine whether the population mean checkout times of the two systems differ. Which system is preferred?

42. Mutual funds are classified as *load* or *no-load* funds. Load funds require an investor to pay an initial fee based on a percentage of the amount invested in the fund. The no-load funds do not require this initial fee. Some financial advisors argue that the load mutual funds may be worth the extra fee because these funds provide a higher mean rate of return than the no-load mutual funds. A sample of 30 load mutual funds and a sample of 30 no-load mutual funds were selected from *Barron's Lipper Mutual Funds Quarterly,* January 12, 1998. Data were collected on the annual return for the funds over a five-year period. The data are contained in the data set Mutual. The data for the first five load and first five no-load mutual funds are as follows.

| Mutual Funds—Load | Return | Mutual Funds—No Load | Return |
|---|---|---|---|
| American National Growth | 15.51 | Amana Income Fund | 13.24 |
| Arch Small Cap Equity | 14.57 | Berger One Hundred | 12.13 |
| Bartlett Cap Basic | 17.73 | Columbia International Stock | 12.17 |
| Calvert World International | 10.31 | Dodge & Cox Balanced | 16.06 |
| Colonial Fund A | 16.23 | Evergreen Fund | 17.61 |

a. Formulate $H_0$ and $H_a$ such that rejection of $H_0$ leads to the conclusion that the load mutual funds have a higher mean annual return over the five-year period.

b. Use the 60 mutual funds in the data set Mutual to conduct the hypothesis test. What is the *p*-value? At $\alpha = .05$, what is your conclusion?

43. Samples of final examination scores for two statistics classes with different instructors provided the following results.

| Instructor A | Instructor B |
|---|---|
| $n_1 = 12$ | $n_2 = 15$ |
| $\bar{x}_1 = 72$ | $\bar{x}_2 = 78$ |
| $s_1 = 8$ | $s_2 = 10$ |

With $\alpha = .05$, test whether these data are sufficient to conclude that the population mean grades for the two classes differ.

44. The Educational Testing Service conducted a study to investigate differences between the scores of male and female students on the Scholastic Aptitude Test. The study identified a random sample of 562 female and 852 male students who achieved the same high score on the mathematics portion of the test. That is, the female and male students were viewed as having similarly high abilities in mathematics. The SAT verbal scores for the two samples are as follows.

| Female Students | Male Students |
|---|---|
| $\bar{x}_1 = 547$ | $\bar{x}_2 = 525$ |
| $s_1 = 83$ | $s_2 = 78$ |

a. Do the data support the conclusion that given a population of female students and a population of male students with similarly high mathematical abilities, the female students will score significantly higher on the verbal portion? Test at a .01 level of significance. What is your conclusion?

b. Provide a 95% confidence interval for the difference between the population mean scores.

45. The Asian economy faltered during the last few months of 1997. Investors anticipated that the downturn in the Asian economy would have a negative effect on the earnings of companies in the United States during the fourth quarter of 1997. The following sample data show the earnings per share for the fourth quarter of 1996 and the fourth quarter of 1997 (*The Wall Street Journal,* January 28, 1998).

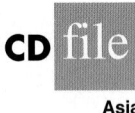

**Asia**

| Company | Earnings 1996 | Earnings 1997 |
|---|---|---|
| Atlantic Richfield | 1.16 | 1.17 |
| Balchem Corp. | 0.16 | 0.13 |
| Black & Decker Corp. | 0.97 | 1.02 |
| Dial Corp. | 0.18 | 0.23 |
| DSC Communications | 0.15 | −0.32 |
| Eastman Chemical | 0.77 | 0.36 |
| Excel Communications | 0.28 | −0.14 |
| Federal Signal | 0.40 | 0.29 |
| Ford Motor Company | 0.97 | 1.45 |
| GTE Corp | 0.81 | 0.73 |
| ITT Industries | 0.59 | 0.60 |

| Company | Earnings 1996 | Earnings 1997 |
|---|---|---|
| Kimberly-Clark | 0.61 | $-0.27$ |
| Minnesota Mining & Mfr. | 0.91 | 0.89 |
| Procter & Gamble | 0.63 | 0.71 |

   a.  Formulate $H_0$ and $H_a$ such that rejection of $H_0$ leads to the conclusion that the mean earnings per share for the fourth quarter of 1997 are less than for the fourth quarter of 1996.

   b.  Use the data in the file Asia to conduct the hypothesis test. At $\alpha = .05$, what is your conclusion?

46. In a *Business Week*/Harris poll asking 1035 adults how well U.S. companies competed in the global economy, 704 respondents answered good/excellent (*Business Week,* September 11, 2000). In a similar poll of 1004 adults in 1996, 582 respondents answered good/excellent. Can the sample results be used to conclude that the proportion of adults responding good/excellent has increased over the four years from 1996 to 2000?

   a.  State the null and alternative hypotheses.

   b.  Compute the *p*-value.

   c.  At $\alpha = .01$, what is your conclusion?

47. A large automobile insurance company selected samples of single and married male policyholders and recorded the number who made an insurance claim over the preceding three-year period.

| Single Policyholders | Married Policyholders |
|---|---|
| $n_1 = 400$ | $n_2 = 900$ |
| Number making claims $= 76$ | Number making claims $= 90$ |

   a.  Use $\alpha = .05$ and test to determine whether the claim rates differ between single and married male policyholders.

   b.  Provide a 95% confidence interval for the difference between the proportions for the two populations.

48. Medical tests were conducted to learn about drug-resistant tuberculosis. Of 142 cases tested in New Jersey, nine were found to be drug-resistant. Of 268 cases tested in Texas, five were found to be drug-resistant. Do these data suggest a statistically significant difference between the proportions of drug-resistant cases in the two states? Use a .02 level of significance. What is the *p*-value and what is your conclusion?

## Case Problem   Par, Inc.

Par, Inc., is a major manufacturer of golf equipment. Management believes that Par's market share could be increased with the introduction of a cut-resistant, longer-lasting golf ball. Therefore, the research group at Par has been investigating a new golf ball coating designed to resist cuts and provide a more durable ball. The tests with the coating have been promising.

One of the researchers voiced concern about the effect of the new coating on driving distances. Par would like the new cut-resistant ball to offer driving distances comparable to those of the current-model golf ball. To compare the driving distances for the two balls, 40 balls of both the new and current models were subjected to distance tests. The testing was performed with a mechanical hitting machine so that any difference between the mean distances for the two models could be attributed to a difference in the two models. The results of the tests, with distances measured to the nearest yard, follow. These data are available on the CD that accompanies the text.

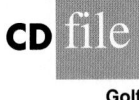
Golf

| Model | | Model | | Model | | Model | |
|---|---|---|---|---|---|---|---|
| Current | New | Current | New | Current | New | Current | New |
| 264 | 277 | 270 | 272 | 263 | 274 | 281 | 283 |
| 261 | 269 | 287 | 259 | 264 | 266 | 274 | 250 |
| 267 | 263 | 289 | 264 | 284 | 262 | 273 | 253 |
| 272 | 266 | 280 | 280 | 263 | 271 | 263 | 260 |
| 258 | 262 | 272 | 274 | 260 | 260 | 275 | 270 |
| 283 | 251 | 275 | 281 | 283 | 281 | 267 | 263 |
| 258 | 262 | 265 | 276 | 255 | 250 | 279 | 261 |
| 266 | 289 | 260 | 269 | 272 | 263 | 274 | 255 |
| 259 | 286 | 278 | 268 | 266 | 278 | 276 | 263 |
| 270 | 264 | 275 | 262 | 268 | 264 | 262 | 279 |

## Managerial Report

1. Formulate and present the rationale for a hypothesis test that Par could use to compare the driving distances of the current and new golf balls.
2. Analyze the data to provide the hypothesis testing conclusion. What is the *p*-value for your test? What is your recommendation for Par, Inc.?
3. Provide descriptive statistical summaries of the data for each model.
4. What is the 95% confidence interval for the population mean of each model, and what is the 95% confidence interval for the difference between the means of the two populations?
5. Do you see a need for larger sample sizes and more testing with the golf balls? Discuss.

## Appendix 10.1  Inferences About Two Populations Using Minitab

We describe the use of Minitab to develop interval estimates and conduct hypothesis tests about the difference between two population means and the difference between two population proportions. Minitab provides both interval estimation and hypothesis testing results within the same module. Thus, the Minitab procedure is the same for both types of inferences. In the examples that follow, we will demonstrate interval estimation and hypothesis testing for the same two samples. We note that Minitab does not provide a routine for inferences about the difference between two population means when the population standard deviations $\sigma_1$ and $\sigma_2$ are known.

### Difference Between Two Population Means: $\sigma_1$ and $\sigma_2$ Unknown

CheckAcct

We will use the data for the checking account balances example presented in Section 10.2. The checking account balances at the Cherry Grove branch are in column C1, and the checking account balances at the Beechmont branch are in column C2. In this example, we will use the Minitab 2-Sample *t* procedure to provide a 95% confidence interval estimate of the difference between population means for the checking account balances at the two branch banks. The output of the procedure also provides the *p*-value for the hypothesis test: $H_0: \mu_1 - \mu_2 = 0$ versus $H_a: \mu_1 - \mu_2 \neq 0$. The following steps are necessary to execute the procedure:

**Step 1.** Select the **Stat** menu
**Step 2.** Choose **Basic Statistics**
**Step 3.** Choose **2-Sample t**
**Step 4.** When the 2-Sample t (Test and Confidence Interval) dialog box appears:
    Select **Samples in different columns**
    Enter C1 in the **First** box
    Enter C2 in the **Second** box
    Select **Options**
**Step 5.** When the Options dialog box appears:
    Enter 95 in the **Confidence level** box
    Enter 0 in the **Test difference** box
    Enter not equal in the **Alternative** box
    Click **OK**
**Step 6.** Click **OK**

The 95% confidence interval estimate is $37 to $193 as described in Section 10.2. The *p*-value = .005 shows the null hypothesis of equal population means can be rejected at the $\alpha = .01$ level of significance. In other applications, step 5 may be modified to provide different confidence levels, different hypothesized values, and different forms of the hypotheses.

## Difference Between Two Population Means with Matched Samples

**Matched**

We use the data on production times in Table 10.2 to illustrate the matched-sample procedure. The completion times for method 1 are entered into column C1 and the completion times for method 2 are entered into column C2. The Minitab steps for a matched sample are as follows:

**Step 1.** Select the **Stat** menu
**Step 2.** Choose **Basic Statistics**
**Step 3.** Choose **Paired t**
**Step 4.** When the Paired t (Test and Confidence Interval) dialog box appears:
    Select **Samples in columns**
    Enter C1 in the **First sample** box
    Enter C2 in the **Second sample** box
    Select **Options**
**Step 5.** When the Options dialog box appears:
    Enter 95 in the **Confidence level**
    Enter 0 in the **Test difference** box
    Enter not equal in the **Alternative** box
    Click **OK**
**Step 6.** Click **OK**

Step 5 may be modified to provide different confidence levels, different hypothesized values, and different forms of the hypothesis.

## Difference Between Two Population Proportions

**TaxPrep**

We will use the data on tax preparation errors presented in Section 10.4. The sample results for 250 tax returns prepared at Office 1 are in column C1 and the sample results for 300 tax returns prepared at Office 2 are in column C2. Yes denotes an error was found in the tax return and No indicates no error was found. The procedure we describe provides both a 95%

confidence interval estimate of the difference between the two population proportions and hypothesis testing results for $H_0: p_1 - p_2 = 0$ and $H_a: p_1 - p_2 \neq 0$.

**Step 1.** Select the **Stat** menu
**Step 2.** Choose **Basic Statistics**
**Step 3.** Choose **2 Proportions**
**Step 4.** When the 2 Proportions (Test and Confidence Interval) dialog box appears:
Select **Samples in different columns**
Enter C1 in the **First** box
Enter C2 in the **Second** box
Select **Options**
**Step 5.** When the 2 Proportions-Options dialog box appears:
Enter 95 in the **Confidence level** box
Enter 0 in the **Test difference** box
Enter not equal in the **Alternative** box
Select **Use pooled estimate of p for test**
Click **OK**
**Step 6.** Click **OK**

Step 5 may be modified to provide different confidence levels, different hypothesized values and different forms of the hypotheses.

In the tax preparation example, the data are qualitative. Yes and No are used to indicate whether an error is present. In modules involving proportions, Minitab calculates proportions for the response coming second in alphabetic order. Thus, in the tax preparation example, Minitab computes the proportion of Yes responses, which is the proportion we wanted.

If Minitab's alphabetical ordering does not compute the proportion for the response of interest, we can fix it. Select any cell in the data column, go to the Minitab menu bar, and select Editor > Column > Value Order. This sequence will provide the option of entering a user-specified order. Simply make sure that the response of interest is listed second in the define-an-order box. Minitab's 2 Proportion routine will then provide the confidence interval and hypothesis testing results for the population proportion of interest.

Finally, we note that Minitab's 2 Proportion routine uses a computational procedure different from the procedure described in the text. Thus, the Minitab output can be expected to provide slightly different interval estimates and slightly different p-values. However, results from the two methods should be close and are expected to provide the same interpretation and conclusion.

## Appendix 10.2    Inferences About Two Populations Using Excel

We describe the use of Excel to conduct hypothesis tests about the difference between two population means.* We begin with inferences about the difference between the means of two populations when the population standard deviations $\sigma_1$ and $\sigma_2$ are known.

### Difference Between Two Population Means: $\sigma_1$ and $\sigma_2$ Known

**CD** file

**ExamScores**

We will use the examination scores for the two training centers discussed in Section 10.1. The label Center A is in cell A1 and the label Center B is in cell B1. The examination scores for Center A are in cells A2:A31 and examination scores for Center B are in cells B2:B41. The

---

*Excel's data analysis tools provide hypothesis testing procedures for the difference between two population means. No routines are available for interval estimation of the difference between two population means nor for inferences about the difference between two population proportions.

population standard deviations are assumed known with $\sigma_1 = 10$ and $\sigma_2 = 10$. The Excel routine will request the input of variances which are $\sigma_1^2 = 100$ and $\sigma_2^2 = 100$. The following steps can be used to conduct a hypothesis test about the difference between the two population means.

**Step 1.** Select the **Tools** menu
**Step 2.** Choose **Data Analysis**
**Step 3.** When the Data Analysis dialog box appears:
         Choose **z-Test: Two Sample for Means**
         Click **OK**
**Step 4.** When the z-Test: Two Sample for Means dialog box appears:
         Enter A1:A31 in the **Variable 1 Range** box
         Enter B1:B41 in the **Variable 2 Range** box
         Enter 0 in the **Hypothesized Mean Difference** box
         Enter 100 in the **Variable 1 Variance** box
         Enter 100 in the **Variable 2 Variance** box
         Select **Labels**
         Enter .05 in the **Alpha** box
         Select **Output Range** and enter C1 in the box
         Click **OK**

## Difference Between Two Population Means: $\sigma_1$ and $\sigma_2$ Unknown

**SoftwareTest**

We use the data for the software testing study in Table 10.1. The data are already entered into an Excel worksheet with the label Current in cell A1 and the label New in cell B1. The completion times for the current technology are in cells A2:A13, and the completion times for the new software are in cells B2:B13. The following steps can be used to conduct a hypothesis test about the difference between two population means with $\sigma_1$ and $\sigma_2$ unknown.

**Step 1.** Select **Tools** menu
**Step 2.** Choose **Data Analysis**
**Step 3.** When the Data Analysis dialog box appears:
         Choose **t-Test: Two Sample Assuming Unequal Variances**
         Click **OK**
**Step 4.** When the t-Test: Two Sample Assuming Unequal Variances dialog box appears:
         Enter A1:A13 in the **Variable 1 Range** box
         Enter B1:B13 in the **Variable 2 Range** box
         Enter 0 in the **Hypothesized Mean Difference** box
         Select **Labels**
         Enter .05 in the **Alpha** box
         Select **Output Range** and enter C1 in the box
         Click **OK**

## Difference Between Two Population Means with Matched Samples

**Matched**

We use the matched-sample completion times in Table 10.2 to illustrate. The data are entered into a worksheet with the label Method 1 in cell A1 and the label Method 2 in cell B1. The completion times for method 1 are in cells A2:A7 and the completion times for method 2 are in cells B2:B7. The Excel procedure uses the steps previously described for the *t*-Test except the user chooses the **t-Test: Paired Two Sample for Means** data analysis tool in step 3. The variable 1 range is A1:A7 and the variable 2 range is B1:B7.

# Inferences About Population Variances

CONTENTS

## U.S. GENERAL ACCOUNTING OFFICE*
_WASHINGTON, D.C._

The U.S. General Accounting Office (GAO) is an independent, nonpolitical audit organization in the legislative branch of the federal government. GAO evaluators determine the effectiveness of current and proposed federal programs. To carry out their duties, evaluators must be proficient in records review, legislative research, and statistical analysis techniques.

In one case, GAO evaluators studied a Department of Interior program established to help clean up the nation's rivers and lakes. As part of this program, federal grants were made to small cities throughout the United States. Congress asked the GAO to determine how effectively the program was operating. To do so, the GAO examined records and visited the sites of several waste treatment plants.

One objective of the GAO audit was to ensure that the effluent (treated sewage) at the plants met certain standards. Among other things the audits reviewed sample data on the oxygen content, the pH level, and the amount of suspended solids in the effluent. A requirement of the program was that a variety of tests be taken daily at each plant and that the collected data be sent periodically to the state engineering department. The GAO's investigation of the data showed whether various characteristics of the effluent were within acceptable limits.

For example, the mean or average pH level of the effluent was examined carefully. In addition, the variance in the reported pH levels was reviewed. The following hypothesis test was conducted about the variance in pH level for the population of effluent.

$$H_0: \sigma^2 = \sigma_0^2$$
$$H_a: \sigma^2 \neq \sigma_0^2$$

In this test, $\sigma_0^2$ is the population variance in pH level expected at a properly functioning plant. In one particular plant, the

Effluent at this facility must fall within a statistically determined pH range. © John Boyner/Corbis.

null hypothesis was rejected. Further analysis showed that this plant had a variance in pH level that was significantly less than normal.

The auditors visited the plant to examine the measuring equipment and to discuss their statistical findings with the plant manager. The auditors found that the measuring equipment was not being used because the operator did not know how to work it. Instead, the operator had been told by an engineer what level of pH was acceptable and had simply recorded similar values without actually conducting the test. The unusually low variance in this plant's data resulted in rejection of $H_0$. The GAO suspected that other plants might have similar problems and recommended an operator training program to improve the data collection aspect of the pollution control program.

In this chapter you will learn how to conduct statistical inferences about the variances of one and two populations. Two new distributions, the chi-square distribution and the $F$ distribution, will be introduced and used to make interval estimates and hypothesis tests about population variances.

*The authors thank Mr. Art Foreman and Mr. Dale Ledman of the U.S. General Accounting Office for providing this Statistics in Practice.

In the preceding four chapters we examined methods of statistical inference involving population means and population proportions. In this chapter we expand the discussion to situations involving inferences about population variances. As an example of a case in which a variance can provide important decision-making information, consider the production process of filling containers with a liquid detergent product. The filling mechanism for the process is adjusted so that the mean filling weight is 16 ounces per container. Although a mean of 16 ounces is desired, the variance of the filling weights is also critical.

That is, even with the filling mechanism properly adjusted for the mean of 16 ounces, we cannot expect every container to have exactly 16 ounces. By selecting a sample of containers, we can compute a sample variance for the number of ounces placed in a container. This value will serve as an estimate of the variance for the population of containers being filled by the production process. If the sample variance is modest, the production process will be continued. However, if the sample variance is excessive, overfilling and underfilling may be occurring even though the mean is correct at 16 ounces. In this case, the filling mechanism will be readjusted in an attempt to reduce the filling variance for the containers.

*In many manufacturing applications, controlling the process variance is extremely important in maintaining quality.*

In the first section we consider inferences about the variance of a single population. Subsequently, we will discuss procedures that can be used to make inferences about the variances of two populations.

 ## 11.1  Inferences About a Population Variance

The sample variance

$$s^2 = \frac{\Sigma(x_i - \bar{x})^2}{n - 1}$$ (11.1)

is the point estimator of the population variance $\sigma^2$. In using the sample variance as a basis for making inferences about a population variance, the sampling distribution of the quantity $(n - 1)s^2/\sigma^2$ is helpful. This sampling distribution is described as follows.

**SAMPLING DISTRIBUTION OF $(n - 1)s^2/\sigma^2$**

Whenever a simple random sample of size $n$ is selected from a normal population, the sampling distribution of

*The chi-square distribution is based on sampling from a normal population.*

$$\frac{(n - 1)s^2}{\sigma^2}$$ (11.2)

has a chi-square distribution with $n - 1$ degrees of freedom.

Figure 11.1 shows some possible forms of the sampling distribution of $(n - 1)s^2/\sigma^2$.

Tables of areas or probabilities are readily available for the chi-square distribution. Since the sampling distribution of $(n - 1)s^2/\sigma^2$ is known to have a chi-square distribution whenever a simple random sample of size $n$ is selected from a normal population, we can use the chi-square distribution to develop interval estimates and conduct hypothesis tests about a population variance.

### Interval Estimation

To show how the chi-square distribution can be used to develop a confidence interval estimate of a population variance $\sigma^2$, suppose that we are interested in estimating the population variance for the production filling process mentioned at the beginning of this chapter. A sample of 20 containers is taken, and the sample variance for the filling quantities is found to be $s^2 = .0025$. However, we know we cannot expect the variance of a sample of 20 containers to provide the exact value of the variance for the population of containers filled by the production process. Hence, our interest will be in developing an interval estimate for the population variance.

FIGURE 11.1    EXAMPLES OF THE SAMPLING DISTRIBUTION OF $(n-1)s^2/\sigma^2$
(A CHI-SQUARE DISTRIBUTION)

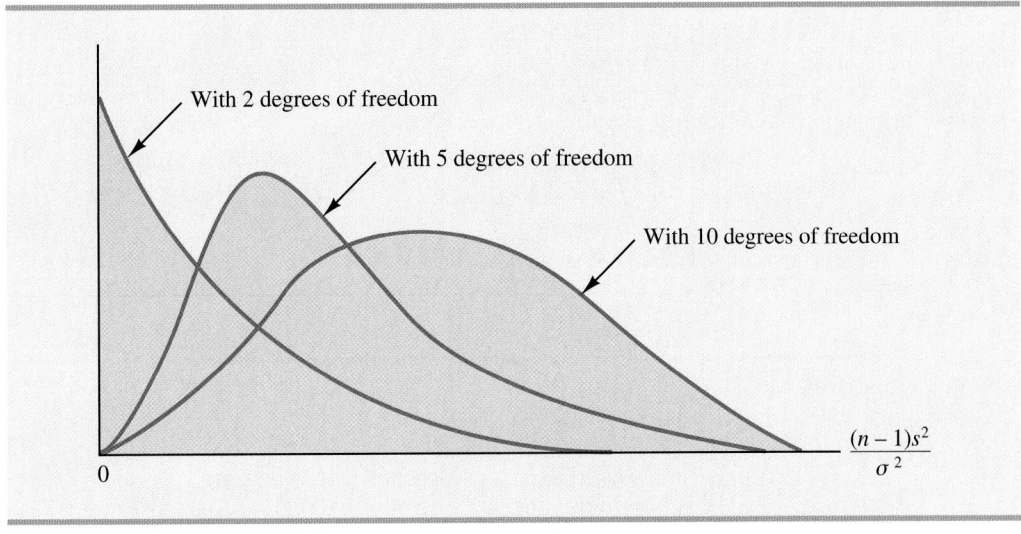

With 2 degrees of freedom

With 5 degrees of freedom

With 10 degrees of freedom

$\dfrac{(n-1)s^2}{\sigma^2}$

We will use the notation $\chi_\alpha^2$ to denote the value for the chi-square distribution that provides an area or probability of $\alpha$ to the *right* of the $\chi_\alpha^2$ value. For example, in Figure 11.2 the chi-square distribution with 19 degrees of freedom is shown with $\chi_{.025}^2 = 32.852$ indicating that 2.5% of the chi-square values are to the right of 32.852, and $\chi_{.975}^2 = 8.907$ indicating that 97.5% of the chi-square values are to the right of 8.907. Refer to Table 11.1 and verify that these chi-square values with 19 degrees of freedom (19th row of the table) are correct. Table 3 of Appendix B provides a more extensive table of chi-square values.

From the graph in Figure 11.2 we see that .95, or 95%, of the chi-square values are between $\chi_{.975}^2$ and $\chi_{.025}^2$. That is, there is a .95 probability of obtaining a $\chi^2$ value such that

$$\chi_{.975}^2 \leq \chi^2 \leq \chi_{.025}^2$$

FIGURE 11.2    A CHI-SQUARE DISTRIBUTION WITH 19 DEGREES OF FREEDOM

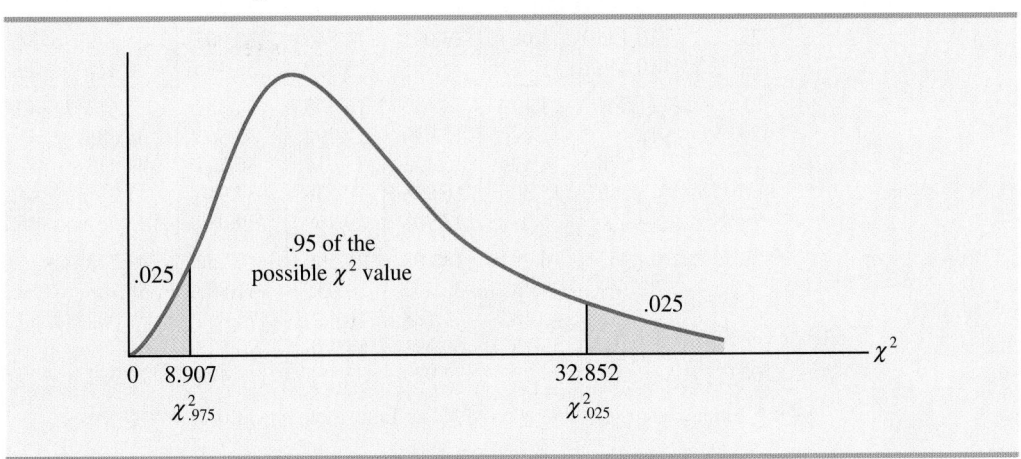

.025

.95 of the
possible $\chi^2$ value

.025

$\chi^2$

0    8.907

$\chi_{.975}^2$

32.852

$\chi_{.025}^2$

**TABLE 11.1**    SELECTED VALUES FROM THE CHI-SQUARE DISTRIBUTION TABLE*

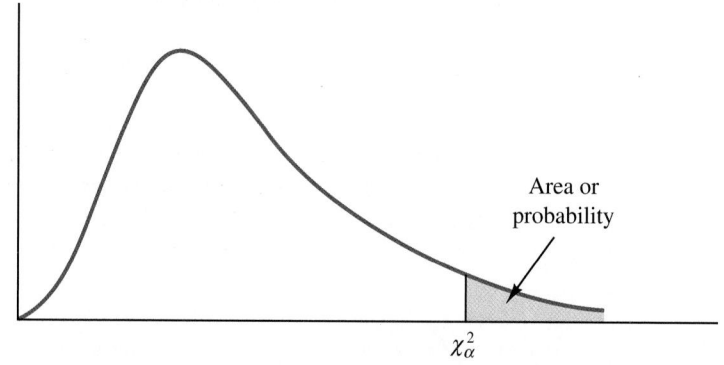

| Degrees of Freedom | Area in Upper Tail | | | | | | | |
|---|---|---|---|---|---|---|---|---|
| | **.99** | **.975** | **.95** | **.90** | **.10** | **.05** | **.025** | **.01** |
| 1 | .000 | .001 | .004 | .016 | 2.706 | 3.841 | 5.024 | 6.635 |
| 2 | .020 | .051 | .103 | .211 | 4.605 | 5.991 | 7.378 | 9.210 |
| 3 | .115 | .216 | .352 | .584 | 6.251 | 7.815 | 9.348 | 11.345 |
| 4 | .297 | .484 | .711 | 1.064 | 7.779 | 9.488 | 11.143 | 13.277 |
| 5 | .554 | .831 | 1.145 | 1.610 | 9.236 | 11.070 | 12.832 | 15.086 |
| 6 | .872 | 1.237 | 1.635 | 2.204 | 10.645 | 12.592 | 14.449 | 16.812 |
| 7 | 1.239 | 1.690 | 2.167 | 2.833 | 12.017 | 14.067 | 16.013 | 18.475 |
| 8 | 1.647 | 2.180 | 2.733 | 3.490 | 13.362 | 15.507 | 17.535 | 20.090 |
| 9 | 2.088 | 2.700 | 3.325 | 4.168 | 14.684 | 16.919 | 19.023 | 21.666 |
| 10 | 2.558 | 3.247 | 3.940 | 4.865 | 15.987 | 18.307 | 20.483 | 23.209 |
| 11 | 3.053 | 3.816 | 4.575 | 5.578 | 17.275 | 19.675 | 21.920 | 24.725 |
| 12 | 3.571 | 4.404 | 5.226 | 6.304 | 18.549 | 21.026 | 23.337 | 26.217 |
| 13 | 4.107 | 5.009 | 5.892 | 7.041 | 19.812 | 22.362 | 24.736 | 27.688 |
| 14 | 4.660 | 5.629 | 6.571 | 7.790 | 21.064 | 23.685 | 26.119 | 29.141 |
| 15 | 5.229 | 6.262 | 7.261 | 8.547 | 22.307 | 24.996 | 27.488 | 30.578 |
| 16 | 5.812 | 6.908 | 7.962 | 9.312 | 23.542 | 26.296 | 28.845 | 32.000 |
| 17 | 6.408 | 7.564 | 8.672 | 10.085 | 24.769 | 27.587 | 30.191 | 33.409 |
| 18 | 7.015 | 8.231 | 9.390 | 10.865 | 25.989 | 28.869 | 31.526 | 34.805 |
| 19 | 7.633 | 8.907 | 10.117 | 11.651 | 27.204 | 30.144 | 32.852 | 36.191 |
| 20 | 8.260 | 9.591 | 10.851 | 12.443 | 28.412 | 31.410 | 34.170 | 37.566 |
| 21 | 8.897 | 10.283 | 11.591 | 13.240 | 29.615 | 32.671 | 35.479 | 38.932 |
| 22 | 9.542 | 10.982 | 12.338 | 14.041 | 30.813 | 33.924 | 36.781 | 40.289 |
| 23 | 10.196 | 11.689 | 13.091 | 14.848 | 32.007 | 35.172 | 38.076 | 41.638 |
| 24 | 10.856 | 12.401 | 13.848 | 15.659 | 33.196 | 36.415 | 39.364 | 42.980 |
| 25 | 11.524 | 13.120 | 14.611 | 16.473 | 34.382 | 37.652 | 40.646 | 44.314 |
| 26 | 12.198 | 13.844 | 15.379 | 17.292 | 35.563 | 38.885 | 41.923 | 45.642 |
| 27 | 12.878 | 14.573 | 16.151 | 18.114 | 36.741 | 40.113 | 43.195 | 46.963 |
| 28 | 13.565 | 15.308 | 16.928 | 18.939 | 37.916 | 41.337 | 44.461 | 48.278 |
| 29 | 14.256 | 16.047 | 17.708 | 19.768 | 39.087 | 42.557 | 45.722 | 49.588 |
| 30 | 14.953 | 16.791 | 18.493 | 20.599 | 40.256 | 43.773 | 46.979 | 50.892 |
| 40 | 22.164 | 24.433 | 26.509 | 29.051 | 51.805 | 55.758 | 59.342 | 63.691 |
| 60 | 37.485 | 40.482 | 43.188 | 46.459 | 74.397 | 79.082 | 83.298 | 88.379 |
| 80 | 53.540 | 57.153 | 60.391 | 64.278 | 96.578 | 101.879 | 106.629 | 112.329 |
| 100 | 70.065 | 74.222 | 77.929 | 82.358 | 118.498 | 124.342 | 129.561 | 135.807 |

*Note: A more extensive table is provided as Table 3 of Appendix B.

We stated in expression (11.2) that $(n - 1)s^2/\sigma^2$ follows a chi-square distribution, therefore we can substitute $(n - 1)s^2/\sigma^2$ for $\chi^2$ and write

$$\chi^2_{.975} \leq \frac{(n - 1)s^2}{\sigma^2} \leq \chi^2_{.025} \tag{11.3}$$

In effect, expression (11.3) provides an interval estimate in that .95, or 95%, of all possible values for $(n - 1)s^2/\sigma^2$ will be in the interval $\chi^2_{.975}$ to $\chi^2_{.025}$. We now need to do some algebraic manipulations with expression (11.3) to develop an interval estimate for the population variance $\sigma^2$. Working with the leftmost inequality in expression (11.3), we have

$$\chi^2_{.975} \leq \frac{(n - 1)s^2}{\sigma^2}$$

Thus

$$\sigma^2 \chi^2_{.975} \leq (n - 1)s^2$$

or

$$\sigma^2 \leq \frac{(n - 1)s^2}{\chi^2_{.975}} \tag{11.4}$$

Performing similar algebraic manipulations with the rightmost inequality in expression (11.3) gives

$$\frac{(n - 1)s^2}{\chi^2_{.025}} \leq \sigma^2 \tag{11.5}$$

The results of expressions (11.4) and (11.5) can be combined to provide

$$\frac{(n - 1)s^2}{\chi^2_{.025}} \leq \sigma^2 \leq \frac{(n - 1)s^2}{\chi^2_{.975}} \tag{11.6}$$

Because expression (11.3) is true for 95% of the $(n - 1)s^2/\sigma^2$ values, expression (11.6) provides a 95% confidence interval estimate for the population variance $\sigma^2$.

Let us return to the problem of providing an interval estimate for the population variance of filling quantities. Recall that the sample of 20 containers provided a sample variance of $s^2 = .0025$. With a sample size of 20, we have 19 degrees of freedom. As shown in Figure 11.2, we have already determined that $\chi^2_{.975} = 8.907$ and $\chi^2_{.025} = 32.852$. Using these values in expression (11.6) provides the following interval estimate for the population variance.

$$\frac{(19)(.0025)}{32.852} \leq \sigma^2 \leq \frac{(19)(.0025)}{8.907}$$

or

*A confidence interval for a population standard deviation can be found by computing the square roots of the lower limit and upper limit of the confidence interval for the population variance.*

$$.0014 \leq \sigma^2 \leq .0053$$

Taking the square root of these values provides the following 95% confidence interval for the population standard deviation.

$$.0380 \leq \sigma \leq .0730$$

Thus, we illustrated the process of using the chi-square distribution to establish interval estimates of a population variance and a population standard deviation. Note specifically that because $\chi^2_{.975}$ and $\chi^2_{.025}$ were used, the interval estimate has a .95 confidence coefficient. Extending expression (11.6) to the general case of any confidence coefficient, we have the following interval estimate of a population variance.

---

**INTERVAL ESTIMATE OF A POPULATION VARIANCE**

$$\frac{(n-1)s^2}{\chi^2_{\alpha/2}} \leq \sigma^2 \leq \frac{(n-1)s^2}{\chi^2_{(1-\alpha/2)}} \qquad (11.7)$$

where the $\chi^2$ values are based on a chi-square distribution with $n-1$ degrees of freedom and where $1-\alpha$ is the confidence coefficient.

---

## Hypothesis Testing

Using $\sigma^2_0$ to denote the hypothesized value for the population variance, the three forms for a hypothesis test about a population variance are as follows:

$$H_0: \sigma^2 \geq \sigma^2_0 \qquad H_0: \sigma^2 \leq \sigma^2_0 \qquad H_0: \sigma^2 = \sigma^2_0$$
$$H_a: \sigma^2 < \sigma^2_0 \qquad H_a: \sigma^2 > \sigma^2_0 \qquad H_a: \sigma^2 \neq \sigma^2_0$$

These three forms are similar to the three forms that we used to conduct one-tailed and two-tailed hypothesis tests about population means and proportions in Chapters 9 and 10.

The procedure for conducting a hypothesis test about a population variance uses the hypothesized value for the population variance $\sigma^2_0$ and the sample variance $s^2$ to compute the value of a $\chi^2$ test statistic. Assuming that the population has a normal distribution, the test statistic is as follows:

---

**TEST STATISTIC FOR HYPOTHESIS TESTS ABOUT A POPULATION VARIANCE**

$$\chi^2 = \frac{(n-1)s^2}{\sigma^2_0} \qquad (11.8)$$

where $\chi^2$ has a chi-square distribution with $n-1$ degrees of freedom.

---

After computing the value of the $\chi^2$ test statistic, either the $p$-value approach or the critical value approach may be used to determine whether the null hypothesis can be rejected.

Let us consider the following example. The St. Louis Metro Bus Company wants to promote an image of reliability by encouraging its drivers to maintain consistent schedules. As a standard policy the company would like arrival times at bus stops to have low variability. In terms of the variance of arrival times, the company standard specifies an arrival time variance of 4 or less when arrival times are measured in minutes. The following hypothesis test is formulated to help the company determine whether the arrival time population variance is excessive.

$$H_0: \sigma^2 \leq 4$$
$$H_a: \sigma^2 > 4$$

In tentatively assuming $H_0$ is true, we are assuming that the population variance of arrival times is within the company guideline. We reject $H_0$ if the sample evidence indicates that the population variance exceeds the guideline. In this case, follow-up steps should be taken to reduce the population variance. We conduct the hypothesis test using a level of significance of $\alpha = .05$.

Suppose that a random sample of 24 bus arrivals taken at a downtown intersection provide a sample variance of $s^2 = 4.9$. Assuming that the population distribution of arrival times is approximately normal, the value of the test statistic is as follows.

$$\chi^2 = \frac{(n-1)s^2}{\sigma_0^2} = \frac{(24-1)(4.9)}{4} = 28.18$$

The chi-square distribution with $n - 1 = 24 - 1 = 23$ degrees of freedom is shown in Figure 11.3. Because this is an upper tail test, the area under the curve to the right of the test statistic $\chi^2 = 28.18$ is the $p$-value for the test.

Like the $t$ distribution table, the chi-square distribution table does not contain sufficient detail to enable us to determine the $p$-value exactly. However, we can use the chi-square distribution table to obtain a range for the $p$-value. For example, using Table 11.1, we find the following information for a chi-square distribution with 23 degrees of freedom.

| Area in Upper Tail | .10 | .05 | .025 | .01 |
|---|---|---|---|---|
| $\chi^2$ Value (23 df) | 32.007 | 35.172 | 38.076 | 41.638 |

$$\chi^2 = 28.18$$

*Reject $H_0$ if $p$-value $\leq \alpha$ applies to this hypothesis test. Appendixes 11.1 and 11.2 show how Minitab and Excel can be used to compute the $p$-value.*

Because $\chi^2 = 28.18$ is less than 32.007, the area in upper tail (the $p$-value) is greater than .10. With the $p$-value $> \alpha = .05$, we cannot reject the null hypothesis. The sample does not support the conclusion that the population variance of the arrival times is excessive.

Because of the difficulty of determining the exact $p$-value directly from the chi-square distribution table, a computer software package such as Minitab or Excel is helpful. Appendixes 11.1 and 11.2 describe the procedures used to show that with 23 degrees of freedom, $\chi^2 = 28.18$ provides a $p$-value $= .2091$.

As with other hypothesis testing procedures, the critical value approach can also be used to draw the hypothesis testing conclusion. With $\alpha = .05$, $\chi^2_{.05}$ provides the critical value for

**FIGURE 11.3    CHI-SQUARE DISTRIBUTION FOR THE ST. LOUIS METRO BUS EXAMPLE**

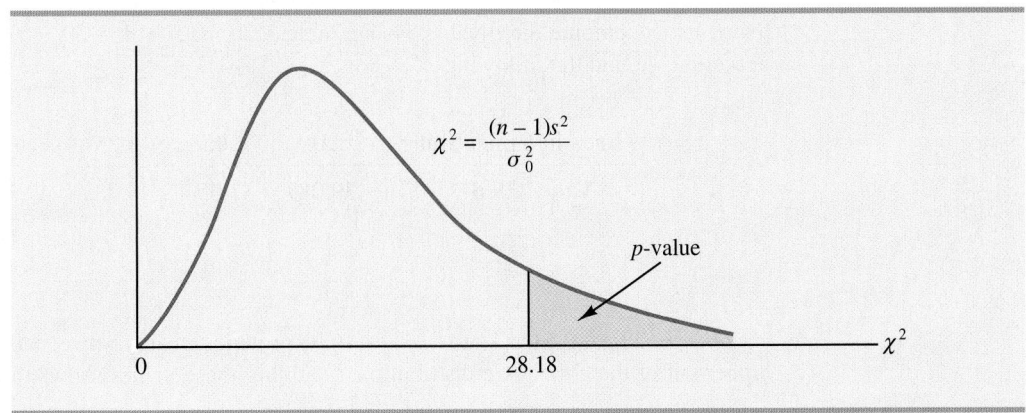

the upper tail hypothesis test. Using Table 11.1 and 23 degrees of freedom, $\chi^2_{.05} = 35.172$. Thus, the rejection rule for the bus arrival time example is as follows:

$$\text{Reject } H_0 \text{ if } \chi^2 \geq 35.172$$

Because the value of the test statistic is $\chi^2 = 28.18$, we cannot reject the null hypothesis.

In practice, upper tail tests as presented here are the most frequently encountered tests about a population variance. In situations involving arrival times, production times, filling weights, part dimensions, and so on, low variances are desirable, whereas large variances are unacceptable. With a statement about the maximum allowable population variance, we can test the null hypothesis that the population variance is less than or equal to the maximum allowable value against the alternative hypothesis that the population variance is greater than the maximum allowable value. With this test structure, corrective action will be taken whenever rejection of the null hypothesis indicates the presence of an excessive population variance.

As we saw with population means and proportions, other forms of hypotheses tests can be developed. Let us demonstrate a two-tailed test about a population variance by considering a situation faced by a bureau of motor vehicles. Historically, the variance in test scores for individuals applying for driver's licenses has been $\sigma^2 = 100$. A new examination with new test questions has been developed. Administrators of the bureau of motor vehicles would like the variance in the test scores for the new examination to remain at the historical level. To evaluate the variance in the new examination test scores, the following two-tailed hypothesis test has been proposed.

$$H_0: \sigma^2 = 100$$
$$H_a: \sigma^2 \neq 100$$

Rejection of $H_0$ will indicate that a change in the variance has occurred and suggest that some questions in the new examination may need revision to make the variance of the new test scores similar to the variance of the old test scores. A sample of 30 applicants for driver's licenses will be given the new version of the examination. We will use a level of significance $\alpha = .05$ to conduct the hypothesis test.

The sample of 30 examination scores provided a sample variance $s^2 = 162$. The value of the chi-square test statistic is as follows:

$$\chi^2 = \frac{(n-1)s^2}{\sigma_0^2} = \frac{(30-1)(162)}{100} = 46.98$$

Now, let us compute the $p$-value. Using Table 11.1 and $n - 1 = 30 - 1 = 29$ degrees of freedom, we find the following.

| Area in Upper Tail | .10 | .05 | .025 | .01 |
|---|---|---|---|---|
| $\chi^2$ Value (29 df) | 39.087 | 42.557 | 45.722 | 49.588 |

$$\chi^2 = 46.98$$

Thus, the value of the test statistic $\chi^2 = 46.98$ provides an area between .025 and .01 in the upper tail of the chi-square distribution. Doubling these values shows that the two-tailed

$p$-value is between .05 and .02. Minitab or Excel can be used to show the exact $p$-value = .0374. With $p$-value $\leq \alpha = .05$, we reject $H_0$ and conclude that the new examination test scores have a population variance different from the historical variance of $\sigma^2 = 100$. A summary of the hypothesis testing procedures for a population variance is shown in Table 11.2.

**TABLE 11.2    SUMMARY OF HYPOTHESIS TESTS ABOUT A POPULATION VARIANCE**

|  | **Lower Tail Test** | **Upper Tail Test** | **Two-Tailed Test** |
|---|---|---|---|
| **Hypotheses** | $H_0: \sigma^2 \geq \sigma_0^2$ $H_a: \sigma^2 < \sigma_0^2$ | $H_0: \sigma^2 \leq \sigma_0^2$ $H_a: \sigma^2 > \sigma_0^2$ | $H_0: \sigma^2 = \sigma_0^2$ $H_a: \sigma^2 \neq \sigma_0^2$ |
| **Test Statistic** | $\chi^2 = \dfrac{(n-1)s^2}{\sigma_0^2}$ | $\chi^2 = \dfrac{(n-1)s^2}{\sigma_0^2}$ | $\chi^2 = \dfrac{(n-1)s^2}{\sigma_0^2}$ |
| **Rejection Rule:** $p$-**value Approach** | Reject $H_0$ if $p$-value $\leq \alpha$ | Reject $H_0$ if $p$-value $\leq \alpha$ | Reject $H_0$ if $p$-value $\leq \alpha$ |
| **Rejection Rule:** **Critical Value** **Approach** | Reject $H_0$ if $\chi^2 \leq \chi^2_{(1-\alpha)}$ | Reject $H_0$ if $\chi^2 \geq \chi^2_{\alpha}$ | Reject $H_0$ if $\chi^2 \leq \chi^2_{(1-\alpha/2)}$ or if $\chi^2 \geq \chi^2_{\alpha/2}$ |

## Exercises

### Methods

1. Find the following chi-square distribution values from Table 11.1 or Table 3 of Appendix B.
   a. $\chi^2_{.05}$ with df = 5
   b. $\chi^2_{.025}$ with df = 15
   c. $\chi^2_{.975}$ with df = 20
   d. $\chi^2_{.01}$ with df = 10
   e. $\chi^2_{.95}$ with df = 18

2. A sample of 20 items provides a sample standard deviation of 5.
   a. Compute the 90% confidence interval estimate of the population variance.
   b. Compute the 95% confidence interval estimate of the population variance.
   c. Compute the 95% confidence interval estimate of the population standard deviation.

3. A sample of 16 items provides a sample standard deviation of 9.5. Test the following hypotheses using $\alpha = .05$. What is your conclusion? Use both the $p$-value approach and the critical value approach.

$$H_0: \sigma^2 \leq 50$$
$$H_a: \sigma^2 > 50$$

### Applications

4. The variance in drug weights is critical in the pharmaceutical industry. For a specific drug, with weights measured in grams, a sample of 18 units provided a sample variance of $s^2 = .36$.
   a. Construct a 90% confidence interval estimate of the population variance for the weight of this drug.
   b. Construct a 90% confidence interval estimate of the population standard deviation.

5. The daily car rental rates for a sample of eight cities follow.

| City | Daily Car Rental Rate ($) |
|---|---|
| Atlanta | 47 |
| Chicago | 50 |
| Dallas | 53 |
| New Orleans | 45 |
| Phoenix | 40 |
| Pittsburgh | 43 |
| San Francisco | 39 |
| Seattle | 37 |

a. Compute the variance and the standard deviation for these data.
b. What is the 95% confidence interval estimate of the variance of car rental rates for the population?
c. What is the 95% confidence interval estimate of the standard deviation for the population?

6. The Oppenheimer Capital Appreciation mutual fund provided a 17.6% average annual return over a five-year period (*Fortune,* August 18, 1997). Assume that the following data show the annual returns for each of the five years: 10.8, 34.2, 4.2, 9.4, and 29.4. The standard deviation of the annual returns can be used as a measure of risk, with a larger standard deviation indicating more variation and therefore more uncertainty in the annual returns.
a. Use the data as a sample of five annual returns to determine the sample standard deviation measure of risk for the Oppenheimer Capital Appreciation mutual fund.
b. What is the 95% confidence interval for the population standard deviation of annual returns for the Oppenheimer Capital Appreciation mutual fund?

7. A sample of eight earnings per share estimates for 1998 is shown here (*Barron's,* December 8, 1997).

| Company | Estimated Earnings per Share |
|---|---|
| AT&T | 2.92 |
| Caterpillar | 4.65 |
| Eastman Kodak | 4.27 |
| Exxon | 3.09 |
| Hewlett-Packard | 3.57 |
| IBM | 7.04 |
| McDonald's | 2.64 |
| Wal-Mart | 1.74 |

a. Compute the sample variance and sample standard deviation for these data.
b. What is the 95% confidence interval for the population variance?
c. What is the 95% confidence interval for the population standard deviation?

8. A group of 12 security analysts provided estimates of the year 2001 earnings per share for Qualcomm, Inc. (*Zacks.com,* June 13, 2000). The data are as follows:

1.40    1.40    1.45    1.49    1.37    1.27    1.40    1.55    1.40    1.42    1.48    1.63

a. Compute the sample variance for the earnings per share estimate.
b. Compute the sample standard deviation for the earnings per share estimate.
c. Provide 95% confidence interval estimates of the population variance and the population standard deviation.

9. An automotive part must be machined to close tolerances to be acceptable to customers. Production specifications call for a maximum variance in the lengths of the parts of .0004. Suppose the sample variance for 30 parts turns out to be $s^2 = .0005$. Using $\alpha = .05$, test to see whether the population variance specification is being violated.

10. The average useful life of a VCR is 6 years with a standard deviation of .75 year (*Consumer Reports 1995 Buying Guide*). A sample of the useful life of 30 television sets provided a sample standard deviation of .95 year. Construct a hypothesis test that can be used to determine whether the standard deviation of the useful life of television sets is significantly greater than the standard deviation of the useful life of VCRs. With a .05 level of significance, what is your conclusion?

11. Home mortgage interest rates for 30-year fixed-rate loans vary throughout the country. During the summer of 2000, data available from various parts of the country suggested that the standard deviation of the interest rates was .096 (*The Wall Street Journal*, September 8, 2000). The corresponding variance in interest rates would be $(.096)^2 = .009216$. Consider a follow-up study in the summer of 2001. The interest rates for 30-year fixed rate loans at a sample of 20 lending institutions had a sample standard deviation of .114. Conduct a hypothesis test using $H_0: \sigma^2 = .009216$ to see whether the sample data indicate that the variability in interest rates changed. Use $\alpha = .05$. What is your conclusion?

12. A *Fortune* study found that the variance in the number of vehicles owned or leased by subscribers to *Fortune* magazine is .94. Assume a sample of 12 subscribers to another magazine provided the following data on the number of vehicles owned or leased: 2, 1, 2, 0, 3, 2, 2, 1, 2, 1, 0, and 1.
   a. Compute the sample variance in the number of vehicles owned or leased by the 12 subscribers.
   b. Test the hypothesis $H_0: \sigma^2 = .94$ to determine whether the variance in the number of vehicles owned or leased by subscribers of the other magazine differs from $\sigma^2 = .94$ for *Fortune*. At a .05 level of significance, what is your conclusion?

## (11.2)  Inferences About Two Population Variances

In some statistical applications we may want to compare the variances in product quality resulting from two different production processes, the variances in assembly times for two assembly methods, or the variances in temperatures for two heating devices. In making comparisons about the two population variances, we will be using data collected from two independent random samples, one from population 1 and another from population 2. The two sample variances $s_1^2$ and $s_2^2$ will be the basis for making inferences about the two population variances $\sigma_1^2$ and $\sigma_2^2$. Whenever the variances of two normal populations are equal ($\sigma_1^2 = \sigma_2^2$), the sampling distribution of the ratio of the two sample variances $s_1^2/s_2^2$ is as follows.

---

**SAMPLING DISTRIBUTION OF $s_1^2/s_2^2$ WHEN $\sigma_1^2 = \sigma_2^2$**

Whenever independent simple random samples of sizes $n_1$ and $n_2$ are selected from two normal populations with equal variances, the sampling distribution of

$$\frac{s_1^2}{s_2^2}$$

(11.9)

has an $F$ distribution with $n_1 - 1$ degrees of freedom for the numerator and $n_2 - 1$ degrees of freedom for the denominator; $s_1^2$ is the sample variance for the random sample of $n_1$ items from population 1, and $s_2^2$ is the sample variance for the random sample of $n_2$ items from population 2.

Figure 11.4 is a graph of the $F$ distribution with 20 degrees of freedom for both the numerator and denominator. As can be seen from this graph, the $F$ distribution is not symmetric, and the $F$ values can never be negative. The shape of any particular $F$ distribution depends on its numerator and denominator degrees of freedom.

We will use $F_\alpha$ to denote the value of $F$ that provides an area or probability of $\alpha$ in the upper tail of the distribution. For example, as noted in Figure 11.4, $F_{.05}$ denotes the upper tail area of .05 for an $F$ distribution with 20 degrees of freedom for the numerator and 20 degrees of freedom for the denominator. The specific value of $F_{.05}$ can be found by referring to the $F$ distribution table, a portion of which is shown in Table 11.3. Using 20 degrees of freedom for the numerator, 20 degrees of freedom for the denominator, and the row corresponding to an area of .05 in the upper tail, we find $F_{.05} = 2.12$. Note that the table can be used to find $F$ values for upper tail areas of .10, .05, .025 and .01. See Table 4 of Appendix B for a more extensive table for the $F$ distribution.

Let us show how the $F$ distribution can be used to conduct a hypothesis test about the variances of two populations. We begin with a test of the equality of two population variances. The hypotheses are stated as follows.

$$H_0: \sigma_1^2 = \sigma_2^2$$
$$H_a: \sigma_1^2 \neq \sigma_2^2$$

We make the tentative assumption that the population variances are equal. If $H_0$ is rejected, we will draw the conclusion that the population variances are not equal.

The procedure used to conduct the hypothesis test requires two independent random samples, one from each population. The two sample variances are then computed. We refer to the population providing the *larger* sample variance as population 1. Thus, a sample size of $n_1$ and a sample variance of $s_1^2$ correspond to population 1, and a sample size of $n_2$ and a sample

**FIGURE 11.4**    *F* DISTRIBUTION WITH 20 DEGREES OF FREEDOM FOR THE NUMERATOR AND 20 DEGREES OF FREEDOM FOR THE DENOMINATOR

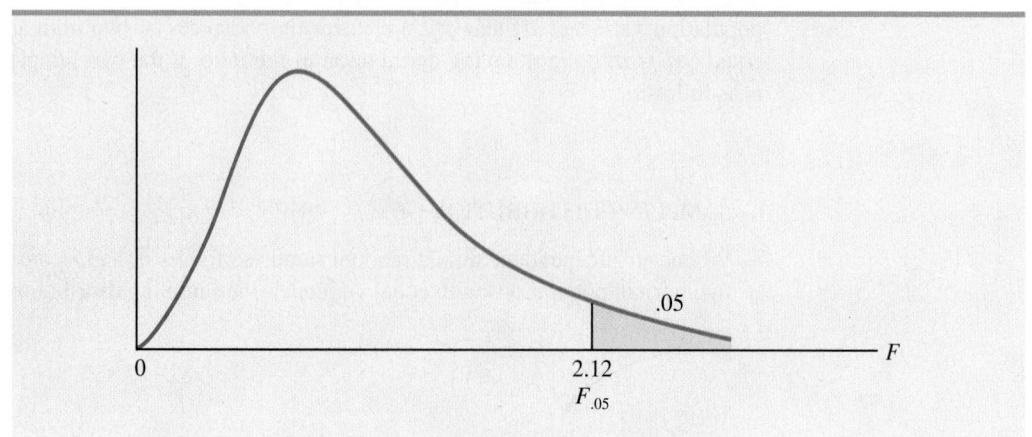

**TABLE 11.3** SELECTED VALUES FROM THE *F* DISTRIBUTION TABLE*

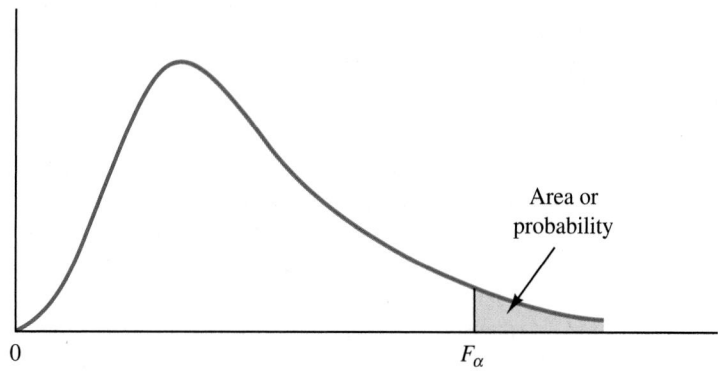

| Denominator Degrees of Freedom | Area in Upper Tail | Numerator Degrees of Freedom | | | | |
|---|---|---|---|---|---|---|
| | | **10** | **15** | **20** | **25** | **30** |
| **10** | .10 | 2.32 | 2.24 | 2.20 | 2.17 | 2.16 |
| | .05 | 2.98 | 2.85 | 2.77 | 2.73 | 2.70 |
| | .025 | 3.72 | 3.52 | 3.42 | 3.35 | 3.31 |
| | .01 | 4.85 | 4.56 | 4.41 | 4.31 | 4.25 |
| **15** | .10 | 2.06 | 1.97 | 1.92 | 1.89 | 1.87 |
| | .05 | 2.54 | 2.40 | 2.33 | 2.28 | 2.25 |
| | .025 | 3.06 | 2.86 | 2.76 | 2.69 | 2.64 |
| | .01 | 3.80 | 3.52 | 3.37 | 3.28 | 3.21 |
| **20** | .10 | 1.94 | 1.84 | 1.79 | 1.76 | 1.74 |
| | .05 | 2.35 | 2.20 | 2.12 | 2.07 | 2.04 |
| | .025 | 2.77 | 2.57 | 2.46 | 2.40 | 2.35 |
| | .01 | 3.37 | 3.09 | 2.94 | 2.84 | 2.78 |
| **25** | .10 | 1.87 | 1.77 | 1.72 | 1.68 | 1.66 |
| | .05 | 2.24 | 2.09 | 2.01 | 1.96 | 1.92 |
| | .025 | 2.61 | 2.41 | 2.30 | 2.23 | 2.18 |
| | .01 | 3.13 | 2.85 | 2.70 | 2.60 | 2.54 |
| **30** | .10 | 1.82 | 1.72 | 1.67 | 1.63 | 1.61 |
| | .05 | 2.16 | 2.01 | 1.93 | 1.88 | 1.84 |
| | .025 | 2.51 | 2.31 | 2.20 | 2.12 | 2.07 |
| | .01 | 2.98 | 2.70 | 2.55 | 2.45 | 2.39 |

*Note:* A more extensive table is provided as Table 4 of Appendix B.

variance of $s_2^2$ correspond to population 2. Based on the assumption that both populations have a normal distribution, the ratio of sample variances provides the following *F* test statistic.

**TEST STATISTIC FOR HYPOTHESIS TESTS ABOUT POPULATION VARIANCES WITH $\sigma_1^2 = \sigma_2^2$**

$$F = \frac{s_1^2}{s_2^2}$$

(11.10)

> Denoting the population with the larger sample variance as population 1, the test statistic has an $F$ distribution with $n_1 - 1$ degrees of freedom for the numerator and $n_2 - 1$ degrees of freedom for the denominator.

Because the $F$ test statistic is constructed with the larger sample variance $s_1^2$ in the numerator, the value of the test statistic will be in the upper tail of the $F$ distribution. Therefore, the $F$ distribution table as shown in Table 11.3 and in Table 4 of Appendix B need only provide upper tail areas or probabilities. If we did not construct the test statistic in this manner, lower tail areas or probabilities would be needed. In this case, additional calculations or more extensive $F$ distribution tables would be required. Let us now consider an example of a hypothesis test about the equality of two population variances.

Dullus County Schools is renewing its school bus service contract for the coming year and must select one of two bus companies, the Milbank Company or the Gulf Park Company. We will use the variance of the arrival or pickup/delivery times as a primary measure of the quality of the bus service. Low variance values indicate the more consistent and higher-quality service. If the variances of arrival times associated with the two services are equal, Dullus School administrators will select the company offering the better financial terms. However, if the sample data on bus arrival times for the two companies indicate a significant difference between the variances, the administrators may want to give special consideration to the company with the better or lower variance service. The appropriate hypotheses follow.

$$H_0: \sigma_1^2 = \sigma_2^2$$
$$H_a: \sigma_1^2 \neq \sigma_2^2$$

If $H_0$ can be rejected, the conclusion of unequal service quality is appropriate. We will use a level of significance of $\alpha = .10$ to conduct the hypothesis test.

**SchoolBus**

A sample of 26 arrival times for the Milbank service provides a sample variance of 48 and a sample of 16 arrival times for the Gulf Park service provides a sample variance of 20. Because the Milbank sample provided the larger sample variance, we will denote Milbank as population 1. Using equation (11.10), the value of the test statistic is

$$F = \frac{s_1^2}{s_2^2} = \frac{48}{20} = 2.40$$

The corresponding $F$ distribution has $n_1 - 1 = 26 - 1 = 25$ numerator degrees of freedom and $n_2 - 1 = 16 - 1 = 15$ denominator degrees of freedom.

As with other hypothesis testing procedures, we can use the $p$-value approach or the critical value approach to obtain the hypothesis testing conclusion. Table 11.3 shows the following areas in the upper tail and corresponding $F$ values for an $F$ distribution with 25 numerator degrees of freedom and 15 denominator degrees of freedom.

| Area in Upper Tail | .10 | .05 | .025 | .01 |
|---|---|---|---|---|
| $F$ Value ($df_1 = 25$, $df_2 = 15$) | 1.89 | 2.28 | 2.69 | 3.28 |

$$F = 2.40$$

Because $F = 2.40$ is between 2.28 and 2.69, the area in the upper tail of the distribution is between .05 and .025. Since this is a two-tailed test, we double the upper tail area, which results in a $p$-value between .10 and .05. For this test, we selected $\alpha = .10$ as the level of significance, which gives us a $p$-value $< \alpha = .10$. Thus, the null hypothesis is rejected. This finding leads to the conclusion that the two bus services differ in terms of pickup/delivery time variances. The recommendation is that the Dullus County School administrators give special consideration to the better or lower variance service offered by the Gulf Park Company.

We can use Minitab or Excel to show that the test statistic $F = 2.40$ provides a two-tailed $p$-value $= .0811$. With $.0811 < \alpha = .10$, the null hypothesis of equal population variances is rejected.

To use the critical value approach to conduct the two-tailed hypothesis test at the $\alpha = .10$ level of significance, we would select critical values with an area of $\alpha/2 = .10/2 = .05$ in each tail of the distribution. Because the value of the test statistic computed using equation (11.10) will always be in the upper tail, we only need to determine the upper tail critical value. From Table 11.3, we see that $F_{.05} = 2.28$. Thus, even though we use a two-tailed test, the rejection rule is stated as follows.

$$\text{Reject } H_0 \text{ if } F \geq 2.28$$

Because the test statistic $F = 2.40$ is greater than 2.28, we reject $H_0$ and conclude that the two bus services differ in terms of pickup/delivery time variances.

One-tailed tests involving two population variances are also possible. In this case, we use the $F$ distribution to determine whether one population variance is significantly greater than the other. A one-tailed hypothesis test about two population variances will always be formulated as an *upper tail* test:

$$H_0: \sigma_1^2 \leq \sigma_2^2$$
$$H_a: \sigma_1^2 > \sigma_2^2$$

*A one-tailed hypothesis test about two population variances can always be formulated as an upper tail test. This approach eliminates the need for lower tail F values.*

This form of the hypothesis test always places the $p$-value and the critical value in the upper tail of the $F$ distribution. As a result, only upper tail $F$ values will be needed, simplifying both the computations and the table for the $F$ distribution.

Let us demonstrate the use of the $F$ distribution to conduct a one-tailed test about the variances of two populations by considering a public opinion survey. Samples of 31 men and 41 women will be used to study attitudes about current political issues. The researcher conducting the study wants to test to see whether the sample data indicate that women show a greater variation in attitude on political issues than men. In the form of the one-tailed hypothesis test given previously, women will be denoted as population 1 and men will be denoted as population 2. The hypothesis test will be stated as follows.

$$H_0: \sigma_{\text{women}}^2 \leq \sigma_{\text{men}}^2$$
$$H_a: \sigma_{\text{women}}^2 > \sigma_{\text{men}}^2$$

A rejection of $H_0$ gives the researcher the statistical support necessary to conclude that women show a greater variation in attitude on political issues.

With the sample variance for women in the numerator and the sample variance for men in the denominator, the $F$ distribution will have $n_1 - 1 = 41 - 1 = 40$ numerator degrees of freedom and $n_2 - 1 = 31 - 1 = 30$ denominator degrees of freedom. We will use a level of significance $\alpha = .05$ to conduct the hypothesis test. The survey results provide a sample variance of $s_1^2 = 120$ for women and a sample variance of $s_2^2 = 80$ for men. The test statistic is as follows.

$$F = \frac{s_1^2}{s_2^2} = \frac{120}{80} = 1.50$$

TABLE 11.4   SUMMARY OF HYPOTHESIS TESTS ABOUT TWO POPULATION VARIANCES

|  | **Upper Tail Test** | **Two-Tailed Test** |
|---|---|---|
| **Hypotheses** | $H_0: \sigma_1^2 \leq \sigma_2^2$ <br> $H_a: \sigma_1^2 > \sigma_2^2$ | $H_0: \sigma_1^2 = \sigma_2^2$ <br> $H_a: \sigma_1^2 \neq \sigma_2^2$ <br><br> Note: Population 1 has the larger sample variance |
| **Test Statistic** | $F = \dfrac{s_1^2}{s_2^2}$ | $F = \dfrac{s_1^2}{s_2^2}$ |
| **Rejection Rule:** *p*-value | Reject $H_0$ if <br> *p*-value $\leq \alpha$ | Reject $H_0$ if <br> *p*-value $\leq \alpha$ |
| **Rejection Rule:** Critical Value Approach | Reject $H_0$ if <br> $F \geq F_\alpha$ | Reject $H_0$ if <br> $F \geq F_{\alpha/2}$ |

Referring to Table 4 in Appendix B, we find that an $F$ distribution with 40 numerator degrees of freedom and 30 denominator degrees of freedom has $F_{.10} = 1.57$. Because the test statistic $F = 1.50$ is less than 1.57, the area in the upper tail must be greater than .10. Thus, we can conclude that the *p*-value is greater than .10. Using Minitab or Excel provides a *p*-value $= .1256$. Because the *p*-value $> \alpha = .05$, $H_0$ cannot be rejected. Hence, the sample results do not support the conclusion that women show greater variation in attitude on political issues than men. Table 11.4 provides a summary of hypothesis tests about two population variances.

## NOTES AND COMMENTS

Research confirms the fact that the $F$ distribution is sensitive to the assumption of normal populations. The $F$ distribution should not be used unless it is reasonable to assume that both populations are at least approximately normally distributed.

## Exercises

## Methods

13. Find the following $F$ distribution values from Table 4 of Appendix B.
    a.  $F_{.05}$ with degrees of freedom 5 and 10
    b.  $F_{.025}$ with degrees of freedom 20 and 15
    c.  $F_{.01}$ with degrees of freedom 8 and 12
    d.  $F_{.10}$ with degrees of freedom 10 and 20

14. A sample of 16 items from population 1 has a sample variance $s_1^2 = 5.8$ and a sample of 21 items from population 2 has a sample variance $s_2^2 = 2.4$. Test the following hypotheses at the .05 level of significance.

$$H_0: \sigma_1^2 \leq \sigma_2^2$$
$$H_a: \sigma_1^2 > \sigma_2^2$$

    a.  What is your conclusion using the *p*-value approach?
    b.  Repeat the test using the critical value approach.

15. Consider the following hypothesis test.

$$H_0: \sigma_1^2 = \sigma_2^2$$
$$H_a: \sigma_1^2 \neq \sigma_2^2$$

a. What is your conclusion if $n_1 = 21$, $s_1^2 = 8.2$, $n_2 = 26$, and $s_2^2 = 4.0$? Use $\alpha = .05$ and the $p$-value approach.
b. Repeat the test using the critical value approach.

## Applications

16. Media Metrix and Jupiter Communications gathered data on the time adults and the time teens spend online during a month (*USA Today*, September 14, 2000). The study concluded that on average, adults spend more time online than teens. Assume that a follow-up study sampled 26 adults and 30 teens. The standard deviations of the time online during a month were 94 minutes and 58 minutes, respectively. Do the sample results support the conclusion that adults have a greater variance in online time than teens? Use $\alpha = .01$. What is the $p$-value?

17. Most individuals are aware of the fact that the average annual repair cost for an automobile depends on the age of the automobile. A researcher is interested in finding out whether the variance of the annual repair costs also increases with the age of the automobile. A sample of 26 automobiles 4 years old showed a sample standard deviation for annual repair costs of $170 and a sample of 25 automobiles 2 years old showed a sample standard deviation for annual repair costs of $100.
a. State the null and alternative versions of the research hypothesis that the variance in annual repair costs is larger for the older automobiles.
b. At a .01 level of significance, what is your conclusion? What is the $p$-value? Discuss the reasonableness of your findings.

18. The standard deviation in the 12-month earnings per share for 10 companies in the airline industry was 4.27 and the standard deviation in the 12-month earnings per share for 7 companies in the automotive industry was 2.27 (*Business Week*, August 14, 2000). Conduct a test for equal variances at $\alpha = .05$. What is your conclusion about the variability in earnings per share for the airline industry and the automotive industry?

19. The variance in a production process is an important measure of the quality of the process. A large variance often signals an opportunity for improvement in the process by finding ways to reduce the process variance. Conduct a statistical test to determine whether there is a significant difference between the variances in the bag weights for the two machines. Use a .05 level of significance. What is your conclusion? Which machine, if either, provides the greater opportunity for quality improvements?

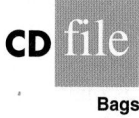

**Bags**

| Machine 1 | 2.95 | 3.45 | 3.50 | 3.75 | 3.48 | 3.26 | 3.33 | 3.20 |
|-----------|------|------|------|------|------|------|------|------|
|           | 3.16 | 3.20 | 3.22 | 3.38 | 3.90 | 3.36 | 3.25 | 3.28 |
|           | 3.20 | 3.22 | 2.98 | 3.45 | 3.70 | 3.34 | 3.18 | 3.35 |
|           | 3.12 |      |      |      |      |      |      |      |
| Machine 2 | 3.22 | 3.30 | 3.34 | 3.28 | 3.29 | 3.25 | 3.30 | 3.27 |
|           | 3.38 | 3.34 | 3.35 | 3.19 | 3.35 | 3.05 | 3.36 | 3.28 |
|           | 3.30 | 3.28 | 3.30 | 3.20 | 3.16 | 3.33 |      |      |

*Calculate Using Excel*

20. On the basis of data provided by a Romac salary survey, the variance in annual salaries for seniors in public accounting firms is approximately 2.1 and the variance in annual salaries for managers in public accounting firms is approximately 11.1. The salary data were provided in thousands of dollars. Assuming that the salary data were based on samples of 25 seniors and 26 managers, test the hypothesis that the population variances in the salaries are equal. At a .05 level of significance, what is your conclusion?

21. The Dow Jones Industrial Average varies as investors buy and sell shares of the 30 stocks that make up the average. Samples of the Dow Jones Industrial Average taken at different times during the first five days of November 1997 and the first five days of December 1997 are as follow (*Barron's*, December 8, 1997).

| November | December |
|----------|----------|
| 7493 | 8066 |
| 7525 | 8209 |
| 7760 | 7842 |
| 7499 | 7943 |
| 7555 | 7846 |
| 7690 | 8071 |
| 7668 | 8055 |
| 7600 | 8159 |
| 7516 | 7828 |
| 7711 | 8109 |

a. Compute the variances of the Dow Jones Industrial Average for the two time periods.
b. Use a .05 level of significance and test to determine whether the population variances for the two time periods are equal. What is the *p*-value? What is your conclusion?

22. A research hypothesis is that the variance of stopping distances of automobiles on wet pavement is substantially greater than the variance of stopping distances of automobiles on dry pavement. In the research study, 16 automobiles traveling at the same speeds are tested for stopping distances on wet pavement and then tested for stopping distances on dry pavement. On wet pavement, the standard deviation of stopping distances is 32 feet. On dry pavement, the standard deviation is 16 feet.

a. At a .05 level of significance, do the sample data justify the conclusion that the variance in stopping distances on wet pavement is greater than the variance in stopping distances on dry pavement? What is the *p*-value?
b. What are the implications of your statistical conclusions in terms of driving safety recommendations?

## Summary

In this chapter we presented statistical procedures that can be used to make inferences about population variances. In the process we introduced two new probability distributions: the chi-square distribution and the $F$ distribution. The chi-square distribution can be used as the basis for interval estimation and hypothesis tests about the variance of a normal population.

We illustrated the use of the $F$ distribution in hypothesis tests about the variances of two normal populations. In particular, we showed that with independent simple random samples of sizes $n_1$ and $n_2$ selected from two normal populations with equal variances $\sigma_1^2 = \sigma_2^2$, the sampling distribution of the ratio of the two sample variances $s_1^2/s_2^2$ has an $F$ distribution with $n_1 - 1$ degrees of freedom for the numerator and $n_2 - 1$ degrees of freedom for the denominator.

## Key Formulas

**Interval Estimate of a Population Variance**

$$\frac{(n-1)s^2}{\chi^2_{\alpha/2}} \leq \sigma^2 \leq \frac{(n-1)s^2}{\chi^2_{(1-\alpha/2)}}$$

(11.7)

**Test Statistic for Hypothesis Tests About a Population Variance**

$$\chi^2 = \frac{(n-1)s^2}{\sigma_0^2} \tag{11.8}$$

**Test Statistic for Hypothesis Tests About Population Variances with $\sigma_1^2 = \sigma_2^2$**

$$F = \frac{s_1^2}{s_2^2} \tag{11.10}$$

## Supplementary Exercises

23. Because of staffing decisions, managers of the Gibson-Marimont Hotel are interested in the variability in the number of rooms occupied per day during a particular season of the year. A sample of 20 days of operation shows a sample mean of 290 rooms occupied per day and a sample standard deviation of 30 rooms.
    a. What is the point estimate of the population variance?
    b. Provide a 90% confidence interval estimate of the population variance.
    c. Provide a 90% confidence interval estimate of the population standard deviation.

24. Initial public offerings (IPOs) of stocks are on average underpriced. The standard deviation measures the dispersion, or variation, in the underpricing-overpricing indicator. A sample of 13 Canadian IPOs that were subsequently traded on the Toronto Stock Exchange had a standard deviation of 14.95. Develop a 95% confidence interval estimate of the population standard deviation for the underpricing-overpricing indicator.

25. The estimated daily living costs for an executive traveling to various major cities follow. The estimates include a single room at a four-star hotel, beverages, breakfast, taxi fares, and incidental costs.

**Travel**

| City | Daily Living Cost | City | Daily Living Cost |
|------|------|------|------|
| Bangkok | $242.87 | Madrid | $283.56 |
| Bogota | 260.93 | Mexico City | 212.00 |
| Bombay | 139.16 | Milan | 284.08 |
| Cairo | 194.19 | Paris | 436.72 |
| Dublin | 260.76 | Rio de Janeiro | 240.87 |
| Frankfurt | 355.36 | Seoul | 310.41 |
| Hong Kong | 346.32 | Tel Aviv | 223.73 |
| Johannesburg | 165.37 | Toronto | 181.25 |
| Lima | 250.08 | Warsaw | 238.20 |
| London | 326.76 | Washington, D.C. | 250.61 |

    a. Compute the sample mean.
    b. Compute the sample standard deviation.
    c. Compute a 95% confidence interval for the population standard deviation.

26. Part variability is critical in the manufacturing of ball bearings. Large variances in the size of the ball bearings cause bearing failure and rapid wearout. Production standards call for a maximum variance of .0001 when the bearing sizes are measured in inches. A sample of 15 bearings shows a sample standard deviation of .014 inches.
    a. Use $\alpha = .10$ to determine whether the sample indicates that the maximum acceptable variance is being exceeded.
    b. Compute the 90% confidence interval estimate of the variance of the ball bearings in the population.

27. The filling variance for boxes of cereal is designed to be .02 or less. A sample of 41 boxes of cereal shows a sample standard deviation of .16 ounces. Use $\alpha = .05$ to determine whether the variance in the cereal box fillings is exceeding the design specification.

28. City Trucking, Inc., claims consistent delivery times for its routine customer deliveries. A sample of 22 truck deliveries shows a sample variance of 1.5. Test to determine whether $H_0: \sigma^2 \leq 1$ can be rejected. Use $\alpha = .10$.

29. Using a sample of 9 days over the past 6 months, a dentist treated the following numbers of patients: 22, 25, 20, 18, 15, 22, 24, 19, and 26. If the number of patients seen per day is normally distributed, would an analysis of these sample data reject the hypothesis that the variance in the number of patients seen per day is equal to 10? Use a .10 level of significance. What is your conclusion?

30. A sample standard deviation for the number of passengers taking a particular airline flight is 8. A 95% confidence interval estimate of the population standard deviation is 5.86 passengers to 12.62 passengers.
    a. Was a sample size of 10 or 15 used in the statistical analysis?
    b. Suppose the sample standard deviation of $s = 8$ was based on a sample of 25 flights. What change would you expect in the confidence interval for the population standard deviation? Compute a 95% confidence interval estimate of $\sigma$ with a sample size of 25.

31. Each day the major stock markets have a group of leading gainers in price (stocks that go up the most). On one day the standard deviation in the percent change for a sample of 10 NASDAQ leading gainers was 15.8. On the same day, the standard deviation in the percent change for a sample of 10 NYSE leading gainers was 7.9 (*USA Today*, September 14, 2000). Conduct a test for equal population variances to see whether it can be concluded that there is a difference in the volatility of the leading gainers on the two exchanges. Use $\alpha = .10$. What is your conclusion?

32. The grade point averages of 352 students who completed a college course in financial accounting have a standard deviation of .940. The grade point averages of 73 students who dropped out of the same course have a standard deviation of .797. Do the data indicate a difference between the variances of grade point averages for students who completed a financial accounting course and students who dropped out? Use a .05 level of significance. *Note:* $F_{.025}$ with 351 and 72 degrees of freedom is 1.466.

33. The accounting department analyzes the variance of the weekly unit costs reported by two production departments. A sample of 16 cost reports for each of the two departments shows cost variances of 2.3 and 5.4, respectively. Is this sample sufficient to conclude that the two production departments differ in terms of unit cost variance? Use $\alpha = .10$.

34. Two new assembly methods are tested and the variances in assembly times are reported. Use $\alpha = .10$ and test for equality of the two population variances.

|  | Method A | Method B |
|---|---|---|
| Sample Size | $n_1 = 31$ | $n_2 = 25$ |
| Sample Variation | $s_1^2 = 25$ | $s_2^2 = 12$ |

## Case Problem  Air Force Training Program

An Air Force introductory course in electronics uses a personalized system of instruction whereby each student views a videotaped lecture and then is given a programmed instruction text. The students work independently with the text until they have completed the training and passed a test. Of concern is the varying pace at which the students complete this portion of their training program. Some students are able to cover the programmed instruction text relatively quickly, whereas other students work much longer with the text and require additional time to complete the course. The fast students wait until the slow students complete the introductory course before the entire group proceeds together with other aspects of their training.

A proposed alternative system involves use of computer-assisted instruction. In this method, all students view the same videotaped lecture and then each is assigned to a computer terminal for further instruction. The computer guides the student, working independently, through the self-training portion of the course.

To compare the proposed and current methods of instruction, an entering class of 122 students was assigned randomly to one of the two methods. One group of 61 students used the current programmed-text method and the other group of 61 students used the proposed computer-assisted method. The time in hours was recorded for each student in the study. The following data are provided on the CD that accompanies the text in the data set Training.

**Course Completion Times (hours) for Current Training Method**

| 76 | 76 | 77 | 74 | 76 | 74 | 74 | 77 | 72 | 78 | 73 |
|----|----|----|----|----|----|----|----|----|----|----|
| 78 | 75 | 80 | 79 | 72 | 69 | 79 | 72 | 70 | 70 | 81 |
| 76 | 78 | 72 | 82 | 72 | 73 | 71 | 70 | 77 | 78 | 73 |
| 79 | 82 | 65 | 77 | 79 | 73 | 76 | 81 | 69 | 75 | 75 |
| 77 | 79 | 76 | 78 | 76 | 76 | 73 | 77 | 84 | 74 | 74 |
| 69 | 79 | 66 | 70 | 74 | 72 |    |    |    |    |    |

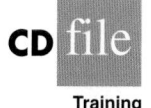

**CD file**

Training

**Course Completion Times (hours) for Proposed Computer-Assisted Method**

| 74 | 75 | 77 | 78 | 74 | 80 | 73 | 73 | 78 | 76 | 76 |
|----|----|----|----|----|----|----|----|----|----|----|
| 74 | 77 | 69 | 76 | 75 | 72 | 75 | 72 | 76 | 72 | 77 |
| 73 | 77 | 69 | 77 | 75 | 76 | 74 | 77 | 75 | 78 | 72 |
| 77 | 78 | 78 | 76 | 75 | 76 | 76 | 75 | 76 | 80 | 77 |
| 76 | 75 | 73 | 77 | 77 | 77 | 79 | 75 | 75 | 72 | 82 |
| 76 | 76 | 74 | 72 | 78 | 71 |    |    |    |    |    |

## Managerial Report

1. Use appropriate descriptive statistics to summarize the training time data for each method. What similarities or differences do you observe from the sample data?
2. Use the methods of Chapter 10 to comment on any difference between the population means for the two methods. Discuss your findings.
3. Compute the standard deviation and variance for each training method. Conduct a hypothesis test about the equality of population variances for the two training methods. Discuss your findings.
4. What conclusion can you reach about any differences between the two methods? What is your recommendation? Explain.
5. Can you suggest other data or testing that might be desirable before making a final decision on the training program to be used in the future?

## Appendix 11.1 Population Variances with Minitab

We describe how to use Minitab to compute the $p$-values for the chi-square test statistic and $F$ test statistic. These $p$-values can be used in hypothesis tests about the variance of one population or the variances of two populations.

### One Population

**BusTimes**

We will use the data for the St. Louis Metro Bus example in Section 11.1. The arrival times appear in column C1. In order to compute the $p$-value for a hypothesis test about a population variance, the user must first compute the sample variance and the corresponding chi-square test statistic* $\chi^2 = 28.18$. With the hypotheses $H_0$: $\sigma^2 \leq 4$ and $H_a$: $\sigma^2 > 4$, Minitab can be used to compute the following upper tail $p$-value.

> **Step 1.** Select the **Calc** menu
> **Step 2.** Choose **Probability Distributions**
> **Step 3.** Choose **Chi-Square**
> **Step 4.** When the Chi-Square Distribution dialog box appears:
>> Select **Cumulative probability**
>> Enter 23 in the **Degrees of freedom** box
>> Select **Input constant** and enter 28.18 in the box
>> Click **OK**

This procedure provides the cumulative probability of .7909, which is the area under the curve to the left of $\chi^2 = 28.18$. Because the $p$-value is the upper tail area or probability, $p$-value $= 1 - .7909 = .2091$. If the test is a lower tail test, the cumulative probability is the $p$-value. For a two-tailed test, the $p$-value is double the smaller of the lower tail area and the upper tail area.

### Two Populations

**SchoolBus**

We will use the data for the Dullus County School bus study in Section 11.2. The arrival times for Milbank appear in column C1, and the arrival times for Gulf Park appear in column C2. The following Minitab procedure can be used to conduct hypothesis test $H_0$: $\sigma_1^2 = \sigma_2^2$ and $H_a$: $\sigma_1^2 \neq \sigma_2^2$.

> **Step 1.** Select the **Stat** menu
> **Step 2.** Choose **Basic Statistics**
> **Step 3.** Choose **2-Variances**
> **Step 4.** When the 2-Variances dialog box appears:
>> Select **Samples in different columns**
>> Enter C1 in the **First** box
>> Enter C2 in the **Second** box
>> Click **OK**

Information about the test will be displayed in the section entitled F-Test (normal distribution) showing the test statistic $F = 2.40$ and the $p$-value $= .081$. This Minitab procedure specifically performs the two-tailed test for the equality of population variances. Thus, if this Minitab routine is used for a one-tailed test, remembering that the area in one tail is one-half of the area for the two-tailed $p$-value should make it relatively easy to compute the $p$-value for the one-tailed test.

---

*Using Minitab to compute a sample variance $s^2$ was discussed in Chapter 3. The corresponding chi-square test statistic given by equation (11.8) can be obtained with a relatively easy hand calculation.

# Appendix 11.2    Population Variances with Excel

We describe how to use Excel to compute the $p$-values for the chi-square test statistic and $F$ test statistic. These $p$-values can be used in hypothesis tests about the variance of one population or the variances of two populations.

## One Population

**Hyp Variance**

We will use the data for the St. Louis Metro Bus example in Section 11.1. The data are already entered into column A of an Excel worksheet. The following steps can be used to test the hypothesis $H_0: \sigma^2 \le 4$ versus $H_a: \sigma^2 > 4$. Refer to Figure 11.5 as we describe the procedure. The worksheet in the background shows the cell formulas used to compute the results shown in the foreground. The data are entered into cells A2:A25. The following steps are necessary to use the template for the data set.

**Step 1.** Enter the data range A2:A25 into the =COUNT formula in cell D3.
**Step 2.** Enter the data range A2:A25 into the =VAR formula in cell D4.
**Step 3.** Enter the hypothesized value for the population variance in cell D6.

**FIGURE 11.5**    EXCEL WORKSHEET FOR THE ST. LOUIS METRO BUS HYPOTHESIS TEST

| | A | B | C | D | E |
|---|---|---|---|---|---|
| 1 | Times | | **Hypothesis Test About a Population Variance** | | |
| 2 | 15.7 | | | | |
| 3 | 16.9 | | Sample Size | =COUNT(A2:A25) | |
| 4 | 12.8 | | Sample Variance | =VAR(A2:A25) | |
| 5 | 15.6 | | | | |
| 6 | 14.0 | | Hypothesized Value | 4 | |
| 7 | 16.2 | | | | |
| 8 | 14.8 | | Test Statistic | =(D3-1)*D4/D6 | |
| 9 | 19.8 | | | | |
| 10 | 13.2 | | $p$-value (Lower Tail) | =1-D11 | |
| 11 | 15.3 | | $p$-value (Upper Tail) | =CHIDIST(D8,D3-1) | |
| 12 | 14.7 | | $p$-value (Two Tail) | =2*MIN(D10,D11) | |
| 13 | 10.2 | | | | |
| 24 | 14.2 | | | | |
| 25 | 12.7 | | | | |
| 26 | | | | | |

| | A | B | C | D | E |
|---|---|---|---|---|---|
| 1 | Times | | **Hypothesis Test About a Population Variance** | | |
| 2 | 15.7 | | | | |
| 3 | 16.9 | | Sample Size | 24 | |
| 4 | 12.8 | | Sample Variance | 4.9 | |
| 5 | 15.6 | | | | |
| 6 | 14.0 | | Hypothesized Value | 4 | |
| 7 | 16.2 | | | | |
| 8 | 14.8 | | Test Statistic | 28.18 | |
| 9 | 19.8 | | | | |
| 10 | 13.2 | | $p$-value (Lower Tail) | 0.7909 | |
| 11 | 15.3 | | $p$-value (Upper Tail) | 0.2091 | |
| 12 | 14.7 | | $p$-value (Two Tail) | 0.4181 | |
| 13 | 10.2 | | | | |
| 24 | 14.2 | | | | |
| 25 | 12.7 | | | | |
| 26 | | | | | |

*Note: Rows 14 to 23 are hidden.*

The remaining cell formulas automatically provide the value of the test statistic and three $p$-values. Because the alternative hypothesis $(\sigma^2 > 4)$ indicates an upper tail test, the $p$-value (Upper Tail) shows the $p$-value is .2091. The $p$-values in cells D10 and D12 would be used for a lower tail or a two-tailed hypothesis test.

This template can be used to make hypothesis testing computations for other applications. For instance, to use another data set, copy the new sample data into column A of the worksheet. Modify the formulas in cells D3 and D4 to correspond to the new data range. Enter the hypothesized value for the population variance into cell D6 to obtain the results. If the sample data have already been summarized, the new sample data do not have to be entered into the worksheet. In this case, enter the sample size into cell D3, the sample variance into cell D4, and the hypothesized value for the population variance into cell D6 to obtain the results. The worksheet in Figure 11.5 is available in the file Hyp Variance on the CD that accompanies this text.

## Two Populations

**SchoolBus**

We will use the data for the Dullus County School bus study in Section 11.2. The Excel worksheet has the label Milbank in cell A1 and the label Gulf Park in cell B1. The times for the Milbank sample are in cells A2:A26 and the times for the Gulf Park sample are in cells B2:B17. The steps to conduct the hypothesis test $H_0$: $\sigma_1^2 = \sigma_2^2$ and $H_a$: $\sigma_1^2 \neq \sigma_2^2$ are as follow:

**Step 1.** Select the **Tools** menu
**Step 2.** Choose **Data Analysis**
**Step 3.** When the Data Analysis dialog box appears:
Choose **F-Test Two-Sample for Variances**
Click **OK**
**Step 4.** When the F-Test Two Sample for Variances dialog box appears:
Enter A1:A27 in the **Variable 1 Range** box
Enter B1:B17 in the **Variable 2 Range** box
Select **Labels**
Enter .05 in the **Alpha** box
(*Note:* This Excel procedure uses alpha as the area in the upper tail.)
Select **Output Range** and enter C1 in the box
Click **OK**

The output $P(F \leq f) = .0405$ is the one-tailed area associated with the test statistic $F = 2.40$. Thus, the two-tailed $p$-value is $2(.0405) = .081$. If the hypothesis test had been a one-tailed test, the one-tailed area in the cell labeled $P(F \leq f)$ provides the information necessary to determine the $p$-value for the test.

# Tests of Goodness of Fit and Independence

**CONTENTS**

## UNITED WAY*
### ROCHESTER, NEW YORK

United Way of Greater Rochester is a nonprofit organization dedicated to improving the quality of life for all people in the seven counties it serves by meeting the community's most important human care needs.

The annual United Way/Red Cross fund-raising campaign, conducted each spring, funds hundreds of programs offered by more than 200 service providers. These providers meet a wide variety of human needs—physical, mental, and social—and serve people of all ages, backgrounds, and economic means.

Because of enormous volunteer involvement, United Way of Greater Rochester is able to hold its operating costs at just eight cents of every dollar raised.

The United Way of Greater Rochester decided to conduct a survey to learn more about community perceptions of charities. Focus-group interviews were held with professional, service, and general worker groups to get preliminary information on perceptions. The information obtained was then used to help develop the questionnaire for the survey. The questionnaire was pretested, modified, and distributed to 440 individuals; 323 completed questionnaires were obtained.

A variety of descriptive statistics, including frequency distributions and crosstabulations, were provided from the data collected. An important part of the analysis involved the use of contingency tables and chi-square tests of independence. One use of such statistical tests was to determine whether perceptions of administrative expenses were independent of occupation.

The hypotheses for the test of independence were:

$H_0$: Perception of United Way administrative expenses is independent of the occupation of the respondent.

$H_a$: Perception of United Way administrative expenses is not independent of the occupation of the respondent.

Statistical surveys help United Way adjust its program to better meet the needs of the people it serves. © Tony Freeman/PhotoEdit.

Two questions in the survey provided the data for the statistical test. One question obtained data on perceptions of the percentage of funds going to administrative expenses (up to 10%, 11–20%, and 21% or more). The other question asked for the occupation of the respondent.

The chi-square test at a .05 level of significance led to rejection of the null hypothesis of independence and to the conclusion that perceptions of United Way's administrative expenses did vary by occupation. Actual administrative expenses were less than 9%, but 35% of the respondents perceived that administrative expenses were 21% or more. Hence, many had inaccurate perceptions of administrative costs. In this group, production-line, clerical, sales, and professional-technical employees had more inaccurate perceptions than other groups.

The community perceptions study helped United Way of Rochester to develop adjustments to its program and fund-raising activities. In this chapter, you will learn how a statistical test of independence, such as that described here, is conducted.

---

*The authors are indebted to Dr. Philip R. Tyler, Marketing Consultant to the United Way, for providing this Statistics in Practice.

In Chapter 11 we showed how the chi-square distribution could be used in estimation and in hypothesis tests about a population variance. In Chapter 12, we introduce two additional hypothesis testing procedures, both based on the use of the chi-square distribution. Like other hypothesis testing procedures, these tests compare sample results with those that are expected when the null hypothesis is true. The conclusion of the hypothesis test is based on how "close" the sample results are to the expected results.

In the following section we introduce a goodness of fit test for a multinomial population. Later we discuss the test for independence using contingency tables and then show goodness of fit tests for the Poisson and normal distributions.

## 12.1 Goodness of Fit Test: A Multinomial Population

In this section we consider the case in which each element of a population is assigned to one and only one of several classes or categories. Such a population is a **multinomial population**. The multinomial distribution can be thought of as an extension of the binomial distribution to the case of three or more categories of outcomes. On each trial of a multinomial experiment, one and only one of the outcomes occurs. Each trial of the experiment is assumed to be independent, and the probabilities of the outcomes remain the same for each trial.

*The assumptions for the multinomial experiment parallel those for the binomial experiment with the exception that the multinomial has three or more outcomes per trial.*

As an example, consider the market share study being conducted by Scott Marketing Research. Over the past year market shares stabilized at 30% for company A, 50% for company B, and 20% for company C. Recently company C developed a "new and improved" product to replace its current entry in the market. Company C retained Scott Marketing Research to determine whether the new product will alter market shares.

In this case, the population of interest is a multinomial population; each customer is classified as buying from company A, company B, or company C. Thus, we have a multinomial population with three outcomes. Let us use the following notation for the proportions.

$$p_A = \text{market share for company A}$$
$$p_B = \text{market share for company B}$$
$$p_C = \text{market share for company C}$$

Scott Marketing Research will conduct a sample survey and compute the proportion preferring each company's product. A hypothesis test will then be conducted to see whether the new product caused a change in market shares. Assuming that company C's new product will not alter the market shares, the null and alternative hypotheses are stated as follows.

$$H_0: p_A = .30, p_B = .50, \text{ and } p_C = .20$$
$$H_a: \text{The population proportions are not}$$
$$p_A = .30, p_B = .50, \text{ and } p_C = .20$$

If the sample results lead to the rejection of $H_0$, Scott Marketing Research will have evidence that the introduction of the new product affects market shares.

Let us assume that the market research firm has used a consumer panel of 200 customers for the study. Each individual was asked to specify a purchase preference among the three alternatives: company A's product, company B's product, and company C's new product. The 200 responses are summarized here.

*The consumer panel of 200 customers in which each individual is asked to select one of three alternatives is equivalent to a multinomial experiment consisting of 200 trials.*

| Observed Frequency | | |
|---|---|---|
| **Company A's Product** | **Company B's Product** | **Company C's New Product** |
| 48 | 98 | 54 |

We now can perform a **goodness of fit test** that will determine whether the sample of 200 customer purchase preferences is consistent with the null hypothesis. The goodness of fit test is based on a comparison of the sample of *observed* results with the *expected* results under the assumption that the null hypothesis is true. Hence, the next step is to compute expected purchase preferences for the 200 customers under the assumption that $p_A = .30$, $p_B = .50$, and $p_C = .20$. Doing so provides the expected results.

**Expected Frequency**

| Company A's Product | Company B's Product | Company C's New Product |
|:---:|:---:|:---:|
| 200(.30) = 60 | 200(.50) = 100 | 200(.20) = 40 |

Thus, we see that the expected frequency for each category is found by multiplying the sample size of 200 by the hypothesized proportion for the category.

The goodness of fit test now focuses on the differences between the observed frequencies and the expected frequencies. Large differences between observed and expected frequencies cast doubt on the assumption that the hypothesized proportions or market shares are correct. Whether the differences between the observed and expected frequencies are "large" or "small" is a question answered with the aid of the following test statistic.

---

**TEST STATISTIC FOR GOODNESS OF FIT**

$$\chi^2 = \sum_{i=1}^{k} \frac{(f_i - e_i)^2}{e_i} \qquad (12.1)$$

where

$f_i$ = observed frequency for category $i$

$e_i$ = expected frequency for category $i$

$k$ = the number of categories

*Note:* The test statistic has a chi-square distribution with $k - 1$ degrees of freedom provided that the expected frequencies are 5 *or more* for all categories.

---

Let us continue with the Scott Market Research example and use the sample data to test the hypothesis that the multinomial population retains the proportions $p_A = .30$, $p_B = .50$, and $p_C = .20$. We will use an $\alpha = .05$ level of significance. We proceed by using the observed and expected frequencies to compute the value of the test statistic. With the expected frequencies all 5 or more, the computation of the chi-square test statistic is shown in Table 12.1. Thus, we have $\chi^2 = 7.34$.

*The test for goodness of fit is always a one-tailed test with the rejection occurring in the upper tail of the chi-square distribution.*

We will reject the null hypothesis if the differences between the observed and expected frequencies are *large*. Large differences between the observed and expected frequencies will result in a large value for the test statistic. Thus the test of goodness of fit will always be an upper tail test. We can use the upper tail area for the test statistic and the *p*-value approach to determine whether the null hypothesis can be rejected. With $k - 1 = 3 - 1 = 2$ degrees of freedom, the chi-square table (Table 3 of Appendix B) provides the following:

*An introduction to the chi-square distribution and the use of the chi-square table were presented in Section 11.1.*

| Area in Upper Tail | .10 | .05 | .025 | .01 |
|:---|:---:|:---:|:---:|:---:|
| $\chi^2$ **Value (2 df)** | 4.605 | 5.991 | 7.378 | 9.210 |

$$\chi^2 = 7.34$$

**TABLE 12.1**  COMPUTATION OF THE CHI-SQUARE TEST STATISTIC FOR THE SCOTT MARKETING RESEARCH MARKET SHARE STUDY

| Category | Hypothesized Proportion | Observed Frequency $(f_i)$ | Expected Frequency $(e_i)$ | Difference $(f_i - e_i)$ | Squared Difference $(f_i - e_i)^2$ | Squared Difference Divided by Expected Frequency $(f_i - e_i)^2/e_i$ |
|---|---|---|---|---|---|---|
| Company A | .30 | 48 | 60 | $-12$ | 144 | 2.40 |
| Company B | .50 | 98 | 100 | $-2$ | 4 | 0.04 |
| Company C | .20 | 54 | 40 | 14 | 196 | 4.90 |
| Total | | 200 | | | | $\chi^2 = 7.34$ |

The test statistic $\chi^2 = 7.34$ is between 5.991 and 7.378. Thus, the corresponding upper tail area or $p$-value must be between .05 and .025. With $p$-value $\leq \alpha = .05$, we reject $H_0$ and conclude that the introduction of the new product by company C will alter the current market share structure. Minitab or Excel can be used to show $\chi^2 = 7.34$ provides a $p$-value $= .0255$

Instead of using the $p$-value, we could use the critical value approach to draw the same conclusion. With $\alpha = .05$ and 2 degrees of freedom, the critical value for the test statistic is $\chi^2_{.05} = 5.991$. The upper tail rejection rule becomes

$$\text{Reject } H_0 \text{ if } \chi^2 \geq 5.991$$

With $7.34 > 5.991$, we reject $H_0$. The $p$-value approach and critical value approach provide the same hypothesis testing conclusion.

Although no further conclusions can be made as a result of the test, we can compare the observed and expected frequencies informally to obtain an idea of how the market share structure may change. Considering company C, we find that the observed frequency of 54 is larger than the expected frequency of 40. Because the expected frequency was based on current market shares, the larger observed frequency suggests that the new product will have a positive effect on company C's market share. Comparisons of the observed and expected frequencies for the other two companies indicate that company C's gain in market share will hurt company A more than company B.

Let us summarize the general steps that can be used to conduct a goodness of fit test for a hypothesized multinomial population distribution.

**MULTINOMIAL DISTRIBUTION GOODNESS OF FIT TEST: A SUMMARY**

1. State the null and alternative hypotheses.

   $H_0$: The population follows a multinomial distribution with specified probabilities for each of the $k$ categories

   $H_a$: The population does not follow a multinomial distribution with the specified probabilities for each of the $k$ categories

2. Select a random sample and record the observed frequencies $f_i$ for each category.

3. Assume the null hypothesis is true and determine the expected frequency $e_i$ in each category by multiplying the category probability by the sample size.

**4.** Compute the value of the test statistic.

$$\chi^2 = \sum_{i=1}^{k} \frac{(f_i - e_i)^2}{e_i}$$

**5.** Rejection rule:

| | |
|---|---|
| *p*-value approach: | Reject $H_0$ if *p*-value $\leq \alpha$ |
| Critical value approach: | Reject $H_0$ if $\chi^2 \geq \chi^2_\alpha$ |

where $\alpha$ is the level of significance for the test and there are $k - 1$ degrees of freedom.

## Exercises

### Methods

1. Test the following hypotheses by using the $\chi^2$ goodness of fit test.

$$H_0: p_A = .40, p_B = .40, \text{ and } p_C = .20$$
$$H_a: \text{The population proportions are not}$$
$$p_A = .40, p_B = .40, \text{ and } p_C = .20$$

A sample of size 200 yielded 60 in category A, 120 in category B, and 20 in category C. Use $\alpha = .01$ and test to see whether the proportions are as stated in $H_0$.
   a. Use the *p*-value approach.
   b. Repeat the test using the critical value approach.

2. Suppose we have a multinomial population with four categories: A, B, C, and D. The null hypothesis is that the proportion of items is the same in every category. The null hypothesis is

$$H_0: p_A = p_B = p_C = p_D = .25$$

A sample of size 300 yielded the following results.

A: 85　B: 95　C: 50　D: 70

Use $\alpha = .05$ to determine whether $H_0$ should be rejected. What is the *p*-value?

### Applications

3. During the first 13 weeks of the television season, the Saturday evening 8:00 P.M. to 9:00 P.M. audience proportions were recorded as ABC 29%, CBS 28%, NBC 25%, and independents 18%. A sample of 300 homes two weeks after a Saturday night schedule revision yielded the following viewing audience data: ABC 95 homes, CBS 70 homes, NBC 89 homes, and independents 46 homes. Test with $\alpha = .05$ to determine whether the viewing audience proportions changed.

4. M&M/MARS, makers of M&M® Chocolate Candies, conducted a national poll in which more than 10 million people indicated their preference for a new color. The tally of this poll resulted in the replacement of tan-colored M&Ms with a new blue color. In the brochure "Colors," made available by M&M/MARS Consumer Affairs, the distribution of colors for the plain candies is as follows:

| Brown | Yellow | Red | Orange | Green | Blue |
|-------|--------|-----|--------|-------|------|
| 30% | 20% | 20% | 10% | 10% | 10% |

In a study reported in *Chance* (no. 4, 1996), samples of 1-pound bags were used to determine whether the reported percentages were indeed valid. The following results were obtained for one sample of 506 plain candies.

| Brown | Yellow | Red | Orange | Green | Blue |
|-------|--------|-----|--------|-------|------|
| 177 | 135 | 79 | 41 | 36 | 38 |

Use $\alpha = .05$ to determine whether these data support the percentages reported by the company.

5. One of the questions on the *Business Week* Subscriber Study was, "When making investment purchases, do you use full service or discount brokerage firms?" Survey results showed that 264 respondents use full service brokerage firms only, 255 use discount brokerage firms only, and 229 use both full service and discount firms. Use $\alpha = .10$ to determine whether there are any differences in preference among the three service choices.

6. Negative appeal is recognized as an effective method of persuasion in advertising. A study in *The Journal of Advertising* reported the results of a content analysis of guilt advertisements in 24 magazines. The number of ads with guilt appeals that appeared in selected magazine types follow.

| Magazine Type | Number of Ads with Guilt Appeals |
|---------------|:---:|
| News and opinion | 20 |
| General editorial | 15 |
| Family-oriented | 30 |
| Business/financial | 22 |
| Female-oriented | 16 |
| African-American | 12 |

Using $\alpha = .10$ test to see whether the proportion of ads with guilt appeals differs among the six types of magazines.

7. *The Wall Street Journal's* Shareholder Scoreboard tracks the performance of 1000 major U.S. companies (*The Wall Street Journal,* March 10, 2003). The performance of each company is rated based on the annual total return, including stock price changes and the reinvestment of dividends. Ratings are assigned by dividing all 1000 companies into five groups from A (top 20%), B (next 20%), to E (bottom 20%). Shown here are the one-year ratings for a sample of 60 of the largest companies. Do the largest companies differ in performance from the performance of the 1000 companies in the Shareholder Scoreboard? Use $\alpha = .05$.

| A | B | C | D | E |
|---|---|---|---|---|
| 5 | 8 | 15 | 20 | 12 |

8. How well do airline companies serve their customers? A study showed the following customer ratings: 3% excellent, 28% good, 45% fair, and 24% poor (*Business Week,* September 11, 2000). In a follow-up study of service by telephone companies, assume that a sample of 400 adults found the following customer ratings: 24 excellent, 124 good, 172 fair, and 80 poor. Is the distribution of the customer ratings for telephone companies different from the distribution of customer ratings for airline companies? Test with $\alpha = .01$. What is your conclusion?

## 12.2  Test of Independence

Another important application of the chi-square distribution involves using sample data to test for the independence of two variables. Let us illustrate the test of independence by considering the study conducted by the Alber's Brewery of Tucson, Arizona. Alber's manufactures and distributes three types of beer: light, regular, and dark. In an analysis of the market segments for the three beers, the firm's market research group raised the question of whether preferences for the three beers differ among male and female beer drinkers. If beer preference is independent of the gender of the beer drinker, one advertising campaign will be initiated for all of Alber's beers. However, if beer preference depends on the gender of the beer drinker, the firm will tailor its promotions to different target markets.

A test of independence addresses the question of whether the beer preference (light, regular, or dark) is independent of the gender of the beer drinker (male, female). The hypotheses for this test of independence are:

$H_0$: Beer preference is independent of the gender of the beer drinker
$H_a$: Beer preference is not independent of the gender of the beer drinker

Table 12.2 can be used to describe the situation being studied. After identification of the population as all male and female beer drinkers, a sample can be selected and each individual asked to state his or her preference for the three Alber's beers. Every individual in the sample will be classified in one of the six cells in the table. For example, an individual may be a male preferring regular beer (cell (1,2)), a female preferring light beer (cell (2,1)), a female preferring dark beer (cell (2,3)), and so on. Because we have listed all possible combinations of beer preference and gender or, in other words, listed all possible contingencies, Table 12.2 is called a **contingency table.** The test of independence uses the contingency table format and for that reason is sometimes referred to as a *contingency table test.*

Suppose a simple random sample of 150 beer drinkers is selected. After tasting each beer, the individuals in the sample are asked to state their preference or first choice. The crosstabulation in Table 12.3 summarizes the responses for the study. As we see, the data for the test of independence are collected in terms of counts or frequencies for each cell or

*To test whether two variables are independent, one sample is selected and crosstabulation is used to summarize the data for the two variables simultaneously.*

TABLE 12.2   CONTINGENCY TABLE FOR BEER PREFERENCE AND GENDER OF BEER DRINKER

| | | Beer Preference | | |
|---|---|---|---|---|
| | | Light | Regular | Dark |
| Gender | **Male** | cell(1,1) | cell(1,2) | cell(1,3) |
| | **Female** | cell(2,1) | cell(2,2) | cell(2,3) |

**TABLE 12.3    SAMPLE RESULTS FOR BEER PREFERENCES OF MALE AND FEMALE BEER DRINKERS (OBSERVED FREQUENCIES)**

|  |  | Beer Preference | | | |
|---|---|---|---|---|---|
|  |  | **Light** | **Regular** | **Dark** | **Total** |
| Gender | **Male** | 20 | 40 | 20 | 80 |
|  | **Female** | 30 | 30 | 10 | 70 |
|  | Total | 50 | 70 | 30 | 150 |

category. Of the 150 individuals in the sample, 20 were men who favored light beer, 40 were men who favored regular beer, 20 were men who favored dark beer, and so on.

The data in Table 12.3 are the observed frequencies for the six classes or categories. If we can determine the expected frequencies under the assumption of independence between beer preference and gender of the beer drinker, we can use the chi-square distribution to determine whether there is a significant difference between observed and expected frequencies.

Expected frequencies for the cells of the contingency table are based on the following rationale. First we assume that the null hypothesis of independence between beer preference and gender of the beer drinker is true. Then we note that in the entire sample of 150 beer drinkers, a total of 50 prefer light beer, 70 prefer regular beer, and 30 prefer dark beer. In terms of fractions we conclude that $50/150 = 1/3$ of the beer drinkers prefer light beer, $70/150 = 7/15$ prefer regular beer, and $30/150 = 1/5$ prefer dark beer. If the *independence* assumption is valid, we argue that these fractions must be applicable to both male and female beer drinkers. Thus, under the assumption of independence, we would expect the sample of 80 male beer drinkers to show that $(1/3)80 = 26.67$ prefer light beer, $(7/15)80 = 37.33$ prefer regular beer, and $(1/5)80 = 16$ prefer dark beer. Application of the same fractions to the 70 female beer drinkers provides the expected frequencies shown in Table 12.4.

Let $e_{ij}$ denote the expected frequency for the contingency table category in row $i$ and column $j$. With this notation, let us reconsider the expected frequency calculation for males (row $i = 1$) who prefer regular beer (column $j = 2$); that is, expected frequency $e_{12}$. Following the preceding argument for the computation of expected frequencies, we can show that

$$e_{12} = (7/15)80 = 37.33$$

This expression can be written slightly differently as

$$e_{12} = (7/15)80 = (70/150)80 = \frac{(80)(70)}{150} = 37.33$$

**TABLE 12.4    EXPECTED FREQUENCIES IF BEER PREFERENCE IS INDEPENDENT OF THE GENDER OF THE BEER DRINKER**

|  |  | Beer Preference | | | |
|---|---|---|---|---|---|
|  |  | **Light** | **Regular** | **Dark** | **Total** |
| Gender | **Male** | 26.67 | 37.33 | 16.00 | 80 |
|  | **Female** | 23.33 | 32.67 | 14.00 | 70 |
|  | Total | 50.00 | 70.00 | 30.00 | 150 |

Note that 80 in the expression is the total number of males (row 1 total), 70 is the total number of individuals preferring regular beer (column 2 total), and 150 is the total sample size. Hence, we see that

$$e_{12} = \frac{(\text{Row 1 Total})(\text{Column 2 Total})}{\text{Sample Size}}$$

Generalization of the expression shows that the following formula provides the expected frequencies for a contingency table in the test of independence.

**EXPECTED FREQUENCIES FOR CONTINGENCY TABLES UNDER THE ASSUMPTION OF INDEPENDENCE**

$$e_{ij} = \frac{(\text{Row } i \text{ Total})(\text{Column } j \text{ Total})}{\text{Sample Size}} \tag{12.2}$$

Using the formula for male beer drinkers who prefer dark beer, we find an expected frequency of $e_{13} = (80)(30)/150 = 16.00$, as shown in Table 12.4. Use equation (12.2) to verify the other expected frequencies shown in Table 12.4.

The test procedure for comparing the observed frequencies of Table 12.3 with the expected frequencies of Table 12.4 is similar to the goodness of fit calculations made in Section 12.1. Specifically, the $\chi^2$ value based on the observed and expected frequencies is computed as follows.

**TEST STATISTIC FOR INDEPENDENCE**

$$\chi^2 = \sum_i \sum_j \frac{(f_{ij} - e_{ij})^2}{e_{ij}} \tag{12.3}$$

where

$f_{ij}$ = observed frequency for contingency table category in row $i$ and column $j$

$e_{ij}$ = expected frequency for contingency table category in row $i$ and column $j$ based on the assumption of independence

*Note:* With $n$ rows and $m$ columns in the contingency table, the test statistic has a chi-square distribution with $(n - 1)(m - 1)$ degrees of freedom provided that the expected frequencies are five or more for all categories.

The double summation in equation (12.3) is used to indicate that the calculation must be made for all the cells in the contingency table.

By reviewing the expected frequencies in Table 12.4, we see that the expected frequencies are five or more for each category. We therefore proceed with the computation of the chi-square test statistic. The calculations necessary to compute the chi-square test statistic for determining whether beer preference is independent of the gender of the beer drinker are shown in Table 12.5. We see that the value of the test statistic is $\chi^2 = 6.12$.

**TABLE 12.5**   COMPUTATION OF THE CHI-SQUARE TEST STATISTIC FOR DETERMINING WHETHER BEER PREFERENCE IS INDEPENDENT OF THE GENDER OF THE BEER DRINKER

| Gender | Beer Preference | Observed Frequency $(f_{ij})$ | Expected Frequency $(e_{ij})$ | Difference $(f_{ij} - e_{ij})$ | Squared Difference $(f_{ij} - e_{ij})^2$ | Squared Difference Divided by Expected Frequency $(f_{ij} - e_{ij})^2/e_{ij}$ |
|---|---|---|---|---|---|---|
| Male | Light | 20 | 26.67 | −6.67 | 44.44 | 1.67 |
| Male | Regular | 40 | 37.33 | 2.67 | 7.11 | 0.19 |
| Male | Dark | 20 | 16.00 | 4.00 | 16.00 | 1.00 |
| Female | Light | 30 | 23.33 | 6.67 | 44.44 | 1.90 |
| Female | Regular | 30 | 32.67 | −2.67 | 7.11 | 0.22 |
| Female | Dark | 10 | 14.00 | −4.00 | 16.00 | 1.14 |
| | Total | 150 | | | | $\chi^2 = 6.12$ |

*The test for independence is always a one-tailed test with the rejection region in the upper tail of the chi-square distribution.*

The number of degrees of freedom for the appropriate chi-square distribution is computed by multiplying the number of rows minus 1 by the number of columns minus 1. With two rows and three columns, we have $(2 - 1)(3 - 1) = 3$ degrees of freedom. Just like the test for goodness of fit, the test for independence rejects $H_0$ if the differences between observed and expected frequencies provide a large value for the test statistic. Thus the test for independence is also an upper tail test. Using the chi-square table (Table 3 of Appendix B), we conclude that the upper tail area or $p$-value at $\chi^2 = 6.12$ is between .025 and .05. Excel shows $p$-value = .0468. At the .05 level of significance, $p$-value $\leq \alpha = .05$. We reject the null hypothesis of independence and conclude that beer preference is not independent of the gender of the beer drinker.

Computer software packages such as Minitab and Excel can simplify the computations for a test of independence and provide the $p$-value for the test. The steps used to obtain computer results for a test of independence are presented in Appendixes 12.1 and 12.2. The Minitab output for the Alber's Brewery test of independence is shown in Figure 12.1.

Although no further conclusions can be made as a result of the test, we can compare the observed and expected frequencies informally to obtain an idea about the dependence between beer preference and gender. Refer to Tables 12.3 and 12.4. We see that male beer

**FIGURE 12.1**   MINITAB OUTPUT FOR THE ALBER'S BREWERY TEST OF INDEPENDENCE

```
        Expected counts are printed below observed counts

                   Light    Regular    Dark    Total
             1       20        40        20       80
                   26.67     37.33     16.00

             2       30        30        10       70
                   23.33     32.67     14.00

        Total        50        70        30      150

        DF = 2,  P-Value = 0.047
```

drinkers have higher observed than expected frequencies for both regular and dark beers, whereas female beer drinkers have a higher observed than expected frequency only for light beer. These observations give us insight about the beer preference differences between male and female beer drinkers.

Let us summarize the steps in a contingency table test of independence.

---

**TEST OF INDEPENDENCE: A SUMMARY**

1. State the null and alternative hypotheses.

   $H_0$: The column variable is independent of the row variable
   $H_a$: The column variable is not independent of the row variable

2. Select a random sample and record the observed frequencies for each cell of the contingency table.
3. Use equation (12.2) to compute the expected frequency for each cell.
4. Use equation (12.3) to compute the value of the test statistic.
5. Rejection rule:

   | | |
   |---|---|
   | $p$-value approach: | Reject $H_0$ if $p$-value $\leq \alpha$ |
   | Critical value approach: | Reject $H_0$ if $\chi^2 \geq \chi_\alpha^2$ |

   where $\alpha$ is the level of significance, with $n$ rows and $m$ columns providing $(n - 1)(m - 1)$ degrees of freedom.

---

## NOTES AND COMMENTS

The test statistic for the chi-square tests in this chapter requires an expected frequency of five for each category. When a category has fewer than five, it is often appropriate to combine two adjacent categories to obtain an expected frequency of five or more in each category.

---

## Exercises

## Methods

9. The following $2 \times 3$ contingency table contains observed frequencies for a sample of 200. Test for independence of the row and column variables using the $\chi^2$ test with $\alpha = .05$.

| Row Variable | Column Variable | | |
|---|---|---|---|
| | A | B | C |
| P | 20 | 44 | 50 |
| Q | 30 | 26 | 30 |

10. The following 3 × 3 contingency table contains observed frequencies for a sample of 240. Test for independence of the row and column variables using the $\chi^2$ test with $\alpha = .05$.

|  | Column Variable | | |
|---|---|---|---|
| Row Variable | A | B | C |
| P | 20 | 30 | 20 |
| Q | 30 | 60 | 25 |
| R | 10 | 15 | 30 |

# Applications

11. One of the questions on the *Business Week* Subscriber Study was, "In the past 12 months, when traveling for business, what type of airline ticket did you purchase most often?" The data obtained are shown in the following contingency table.

| | Type of Flight | |
|---|---|---|
| Type of Ticket | Domestic Flights | International Flights |
| First class | 29 | 22 |
| Business/executive class | 95 | 121 |
| Full fare economy/coach class | 518 | 135 |

Use $\alpha = .05$ and test for the independence of type of flight and type of ticket. What is your conclusion?

12. In a study of brand loyalty in the automotive industry, new-car customers were asked whether the make of their new car was the same as the make of their previous car (*Business Week,* May 8, 2000). The breakdown of 600 responses shows the brand loyalty for domestic, European, and Asian cars.

| | Manufacturer | | |
|---|---|---|---|
| Purchased | Domestic | European | Asian |
| Same Make | 125 | 55 | 68 |
| Different Make | 140 | 105 | 107 |

a. Test a hypothesis to determine whether brand loyalty is independent of the manufacturer. Use $\alpha = .05$. What is your conclusion?
b. If a significant difference is found, which manufacturer appears to have the greatest brand loyalty?

13. Starting positions for business and engineering graduates are classified by industry as shown in the following table.

| | Industry | | | |
|---|---|---|---|---|
| Degree Major | Oil | Chemical | Electrical | Computer |
| Business | 30 | 15 | 15 | 40 |
| Engineering | 30 | 30 | 20 | 20 |

Use $\alpha = .01$ and test for independence of degree major and industry type.

14. A study conducted by Marist Institute for Public Opinion asked men and women to indicate which person is the most difficult to buy holiday gifts for (*USA Today,* December 15, 1997). Suppose that the following data were obtained in a follow-up study consisting of 100 men and 100 women.

| Most Difficult to Buy For | Gender | |
|---|---|---|
| | Men | Women |
| Spouse | 37 | 25 |
| Parents | 28 | 31 |
| Children | 7 | 19 |
| Siblings | 8 | 3 |
| In-laws | 4 | 10 |
| Other relatives | 16 | 12 |

Use $\alpha = .05$ and test for independence of gender and the most difficult person to buy for. What is your conclusion?

15. Negative appeal is recognized as an effective method of persuasion in advertising. A study in *The Journal of Advertising* reported the results of a content analysis of guilt and fear advertisements in 24 magazines. The number of ads with guilt and fear appeals that appeared in selected magazine types follows.

| Magazine Type | Type of Appeal | |
|---|---|---|
| | Number of Ads With Guilt Appeals | Number of Ads With Fear Appeals |
| News and opinion | 20 | 10 |
| General editorial | 15 | 11 |
| Family-oriented | 30 | 19 |
| Business/financial | 22 | 17 |
| Female-oriented | 16 | 14 |
| African-American | 12 | 15 |

Use the chi-square test of independence with a .01 level of significance to analyze the data. What is your conclusion?

16. Businesses are increasingly placing orders online. The Performance Measurement Group collected data on the rates of correctly filled electronic orders by industry (*Investor's Business Daily,* May 8, 2000). Assume a sample of 700 electronic orders provided the following results.

| Order | Industry | | | |
|---|---|---|---|---|
| | Pharmaceutical | Consumer | Computers | Telecommunications |
| Correct | 207 | 136 | 151 | 178 |
| Incorrect | 3 | 4 | 9 | 12 |

a. Test a hypothesis to determine whether order fulfillment is independent of industry. Use $\alpha = .05$. What is your conclusion?

b. Which industry has the highest percentage of correctly filled orders?

17.  Three suppliers provide the following data on defective parts.

| | | Part Quality | |
| --- | --- | --- | --- |
| **Supplier** | **Good** | **Minor Defect** | **Major Defect** |
| A | 90 | 3 | 7 |
| B | 170 | 18 | 7 |
| C | 135 | 6 | 9 |

Use $\alpha = .05$ and test for independence between supplier and part quality. What does the result of your analysis tell the purchasing department?

18.  A study of educational levels of voters and their political party affiliations yielded the following results.

| | | Party Affiliation | |
| --- | --- | --- | --- |
| **Educational Level** | **Democratic** | **Republican** | **Independent** |
| **Did not complete high school** | 40 | 20 | 10 |
| **High school degree** | 30 | 35 | 15 |
| **College degree** | 30 | 45 | 25 |

Use $\alpha = .01$ and determine whether party affiliation is independent of the educational level of the voters.

19.  On the syndicated Siskel and Ebert television show the hosts often created the impression that they strongly disagreed about which movies were best. An article in *Chance* (no. 2, 1997) reported the results of ratings of 160 movies by Siskel and Ebert. Each review is categorized as Pro ("thumbs up"), Con ("thumbs down"), or Mixed.

| | | Ebert Rating | |
| --- | --- | --- | --- |
| **Siskel Rating** | **Con** | **Mixed** | **Pro** |
| **Con** | 24 | 8 | 13 |
| **Mixed** | 8 | 13 | 11 |
| **Pro** | 10 | 9 | 64 |

Use the chi-square test of independence with a .01 level of significance to analyze the data. What is your conclusion?

# 12.3 Goodness of Fit Test: Poisson and Normal Distributions

In Section 12.1 we introduced the goodness of fit test for a multinomial population. In general, the goodness of fit test can be used with any hypothesized probability distribution. In this section we illustrate the goodness of fit test procedure for cases in which the population is hypothesized to have a Poisson or a normal distribution. As we shall see, the goodness of fit test and the use of the chi-square distribution for the test follow the same general procedure used for the goodness of fit test in Section 12.1.

## Poisson Distribution

Let us illustrate the goodness of fit test for the case in which the hypothesized population distribution is a Poisson distribution. As an example, consider the arrival of customers at Dubek's Food Market in Tallahassee, Florida. Because of some recent staffing problems, Dubek's managers asked a local consulting firm to assist with the scheduling of clerks for the checkout lanes. After reviewing the checkout lane operation, the consulting firm will make a recommendation for a clerk-scheduling procedure. The procedure, based on a mathematical analysis of waiting lines, is applicable only if the number of customers arriving during a specified time period follows the Poisson distribution. Therefore, before the scheduling process is implemented, data on customer arrivals must be collected and a statistical test conducted to see whether an assumption of a Poisson distribution for arrivals is reasonable.

We define the arrivals at the store in terms of the *number of customers* entering the store during 5-minute intervals. Hence, the following null and alternative hypotheses are appropriate for the Dubek's Food Market study.

$H_0$: The number of customers entering the store during 5-minute intervals
    has a Poisson probability distribution

$H_a$: The number of customers entering the store during 5-minute intervals
    does not have a Poisson distribution

If a sample of customer arrivals indicates $H_0$ cannot be rejected, Dubek's will proceed with the implementation of the consulting firm's scheduling procedure. However, if the sample leads to the rejection of $H_0$, the assumption of the Poisson distribution for the arrivals cannot be made, and other scheduling procedures will be considered.

To test the assumption of a Poisson distribution for the number of arrivals during weekday morning hours, a store employee randomly selects a sample of 128 5-minute intervals during weekday mornings over a three-week period. For each 5-minute interval in the sample, the store employee records the number of customer arrivals. In summarizing the data, the employee determines the number of 5-minute intervals having no arrivals, the number of 5-minute intervals having one arrival, the number of 5-minute intervals having two arrivals, and so on. These data are summarized in Table 12.6.

Table 12.6 gives the observed frequencies for the 10 categories. We now want to use a goodness of fit test to determine whether the sample of 128 time periods supports the hypothesized Poisson distribution. To conduct the goodness of fit test, we need to consider the expected frequency for each of the 10 categories under the assumption that the Poisson distribution of arrivals is true. That is, we need to compute the expected number of time periods in which no customers, one customer, two customers, and so on would arrive if, in fact, the customer arrivals follow a Poisson distribution.

The Poisson probability function, which was first introduced in Chapter 5, is

$$f(x) = \frac{\mu^x e^{-\mu}}{x!} \qquad (12.4)$$

In this function, $\mu$ represents the mean or expected number of customers arriving per 5-minute period, $x$ is the random variable indicating the number of customers arriving during a 5-minute period, and $f(x)$ is the probability that $x$ customers will arrive in a 5-minute interval.

Before we use equation (12.4) to compute Poisson probabilities, we must obtain an estimate of $\mu$, the mean number of customer arrivals during a 5-minute time period. The sample mean for the data in Table 12.6 provides this estimate. With no customers arriving in two 5-minute time periods, one customer arriving in eight 5-minute time periods, and so on, the total number of customers who arrived during the sample of 128 5-minute time pe-

**TABLE 12.6**

OBSERVED FREQUENCY OF DUBEK'S CUSTOMER ARRIVALS FOR A SAMPLE OF 128 5-MINUTE TIME PERIODS

| Number of Customers Arriving | Observed Frequency |
|---|---|
| 0 | 2 |
| 1 | 8 |
| 2 | 10 |
| 3 | 12 |
| 4 | 18 |
| 5 | 22 |
| 6 | 22 |
| 7 | 16 |
| 8 | 12 |
| 9 | 6 |
| Total | 128 |

riods is given by $0(2) + 1(8) + 2(10) + \cdots + 9(6) = 640$. The 640 customer arrivals over the sample of 128 periods provide a mean arrival rate of $\mu = 640/128 = 5$ customers per 5-minute period. With this value for the mean of the Poisson distribution, an estimate of the Poisson probability function for Dubek's Food Market is

$$f(x) = \frac{5^x e^{-5}}{x!} \qquad\qquad (12.5)$$

This probability function can be evaluated for different values of $x$ to determine the probability associated with each category of arrivals. These probabilities, which can also be found in Table 7 of Appendix B, are given in Table 12.7. For example, the probability of zero customers arriving during a 5-minute interval is $f(0) = .0067$, the probability of one customer arriving during a 5-minute interval is $f(1) = .0337$, and so on. As we saw in Section 12.1, the expected frequencies for the categories are found by multiplying the probabilities by the sample size. For example, the expected number of periods with zero arrivals is given by $(.0067)(128) = .86$, the expected number of periods with one arrival is given by $(.0337)(128) = 4.31$, and so on.

*When the expected number in some category is less than five, the assumptions for the $\chi^2$ test are not satisfied. When this happens, adjacent categories can be combined to increase the expected number to five.*

Before we make the usual chi-square calculations to compare the observed and expected frequencies, note that in Table 12.7, four of the categories have an expected frequency less than five. This condition violates the requirements for use of the chi-square distribution. However, expected category frequencies less than five cause no difficulty, because adjacent categories can be combined to satisfy the "at least five" expected frequency requirement. In particular, we will combine 0 and 1 into a single category and then combine 9 with "10 or more" into another single category. Thus, the rule of a minimum expected frequency of five in each category is satisfied. Table 12.8 shows the observed and expected frequencies after combining categories.

As in Section 12.1, the goodness of fit test focuses on the differences between observed and expected frequencies, $f_i - e_i$. Thus, we will use the observed and expected frequencies shown in Table 12.8, to compute the chi-square test statistic.

$$\chi^2 = \sum_{i=1}^{k} \frac{(f_i - e_i)^2}{e_i}$$

**TABLE 12.7    EXPECTED FREQUENCY OF DUBEK'S CUSTOMER ARRIVALS,**
**ASSUMING A POISSON DISTRIBUTION WITH $\mu = 5$**

| Number of Customers Arriving ($x$) | Poisson Probability $f(x)$ | Expected Number of 5-Minute Time Periods With $x$ Arrivals, $128\,f(x)$ |
|:---:|:---:|:---:|
| 0 | .0067 | 0.86 |
| 1 | .0337 | 4.31 |
| 2 | .0842 | 10.78 |
| 3 | .1404 | 17.97 |
| 4 | .1755 | 22.46 |
| 5 | .1755 | 22.46 |
| 6 | .1462 | 18.71 |
| 7 | .1044 | 13.36 |
| 8 | .0653 | 8.36 |
| 9 | .0363 | 4.65 |
| 10 or more | .0318 | 4.07 |
| | Total | 128.00 |

**TABLE 12.8**   OBSERVED AND EXPECTED FREQUENCIES FOR DUBEK'S CUSTOMER ARRIVALS AFTER COMBINING CATEGORIES

| Number of Customers Arriving | Observed Frequency $(f_i)$ | Expected Frequency $(e_i)$ |
|:---:|:---:|:---:|
| 0 or 1 | 10 | 5.17 |
| 2 | 10 | 10.78 |
| 3 | 12 | 17.97 |
| 4 | 18 | 22.46 |
| 5 | 22 | 22.46 |
| 6 | 22 | 18.72 |
| 7 | 16 | 13.37 |
| 8 | 12 | 8.36 |
| 9 or more | 6 | 8.72 |
| Total | 128 | 128.00 |

The calculations necessary to compute the chi-square test statistic are shown in Table 12.9. The value of the test statistic is $\chi^2 = 10.96$.

In general, the chi-square distribution for a goodness of fit test has $k - p - 1$ degrees of freedom, where $k$ is the number of categories and $p$ is the number of population parameters estimated from the sample data. For the Poisson distribution goodness of fit test, Table 12.9 shows $k = 9$ categories. Because the sample data were used to estimate the mean of the Poisson distribution, $p = 1$. Thus, there are $k - p - 1 = k - 2$ degrees of freedom. With $k = 9$, we have $9 - 2 = 7$ degrees of freedom.

Suppose we test the null hypothesis that the probability distribution for the customer arrivals is a Poisson distribution with a .05 level of significance. To test this hypothesis, we need to determine the $p$-value for the test statistic $\chi^2 = 10.96$ by finding the area in the upper tail of a chi-square distribution with 7 degrees of freedom. Using Table 3 of Appendix B, we find that

**TABLE 12.9**   COMPUTATION OF THE CHI-SQUARE TEST STATISTIC FOR THE DUBEK'S FOOD MARKET STUDY

| Number of Customers Arriving $(x)$ | Observed Frequency $(f_i)$ | Expected Frequency $(e_i)$ | Difference $(f_i - e_i)$ | Squared Difference $(f_i - e_i)^2$ | Squared Difference Divided by Expected Frequency $(f_i - e_i)^2/e_i$ |
|:---:|:---:|:---:|:---:|:---:|:---:|
| 0 or 1 | 10 | 5.17 | 4.83 | 23.28 | 4.50 |
| 2 | 10 | 10.78 | −0.78 | 0.61 | 0.06 |
| 3 | 12 | 17.97 | −5.97 | 35.62 | 1.98 |
| 4 | 18 | 22.46 | −4.46 | 19.89 | 0.89 |
| 5 | 22 | 22.46 | −0.46 | 0.21 | 0.01 |
| 6 | 22 | 18.72 | 3.28 | 10.78 | 0.58 |
| 7 | 16 | 13.37 | 2.63 | 6.92 | 0.52 |
| 8 | 12 | 8.36 | 3.64 | 13.28 | 1.59 |
| 9 or more | 6 | 8.72 | −2.72 | 7.38 | 0.85 |
| Total | 128 | 128.00 | | | $\chi^2 = 10.96$ |

$\chi^2 = 10.96$ provides an area in the upper tail greater than .10. Thus, we know that the $p$-value is greater than .10. Minitab or Excel show $p$-value = .1403. With $p$-value $> \alpha = .05$, we cannot reject $H_0$. Hence, the assumption of a Poisson probability distribution for weekday morning customer arrivals cannot be rejected. As a result, Dubek's management may proceed with the consulting firm's scheduling procedure for weekday mornings.

---

POISSON DISTRIBUTION GOODNESS OF FIT TEST: A SUMMARY

1. State the null and alternative hypotheses.

$H_0$: The population has a Poisson distribution

$H_a$: The population does not have a Poisson distribution

2. Select a random sample and
   a. Record the observed frequency $f_i$ for each value of the Poisson random variable.
   b. Compute the mean number of occurrences $\mu$.
3. Compute the expected frequency of occurrences $e_i$ for each value of the Poisson random variable. Multiply the sample size by the Poisson probability of occurrence for each value of the Poisson random variable. If there are fewer than five expected occurrences for some values, combine adjacent values and reduce the number of categories as necessary.
4. Compute the value of the test statistic.

$$\chi^2 = \sum_{i=1}^{k} \frac{(f_i - e_i)^2}{e_i}$$

5. Rejection rule:

$p$-value approach:     Reject $H_0$ if $p$-value $\leq \alpha$

Critical value approach:   Reject $H_0$ if $\chi^2 \geq \chi_\alpha^2$

where $\alpha$ is the level of significance and there are $k - 2$ degrees of freedom.

---

## Normal Distribution

The goodness of fit test for a normal distribution is also based on the use of the chi-square distribution. It is similar to the procedure we discussed for the Poisson distribution. In particular, observed frequencies for several categories of sample data are compared to expected frequencies under the assumption that the population has a normal distribution. Because the normal distribution is continuous, we must modify the way the categories are defined and how the expected frequencies are computed. Let us demonstrate the goodness of fit test for a normal distribution by considering the job applicant test data for Chemline, Inc., listed in Table 12.10.

Chemline hires approximately 400 new employees annually for its four plants located throughout the United States. The personnel director asks whether a normal distribution applies for the population of test scores. If such a distribution can be used, the distribution would be helpful in evaluating specific test scores; that is, scores in the upper 20%, lower 40%, and so on, could be identified quickly. Hence, we want to test the null hypothesis that the population of test scores has a normal distribution.

**TABLE 12.10**

CHEMLINE
EMPLOYEE
APTITUDE TEST
SCORES FOR
50 RANDOMLY
CHOSEN JOB
APPLICANTS

| 71 | 66 | 61 | 65 | 54 | 93 |
|----|----|----|----|----|----|
| 60 | 86 | 70 | 70 | 73 | 73 |
| 55 | 63 | 56 | 62 | 76 | 54 |
| 82 | 79 | 76 | 68 | 53 | 58 |
| 85 | 80 | 56 | 61 | 61 | 64 |
| 65 | 62 | 90 | 69 | 76 | 79 |
| 77 | 54 | 64 | 74 | 65 | 65 |
| 61 | 56 | 63 | 80 | 56 | 71 |
| 79 | 84 |    |    |    |    |

**Chemline**

*With a continuous probability distribution, establish intervals such that each interval has an expected frequency of five or more.*

Let us first use the data in Table 12.10 to develop estimates of the mean and standard deviation of the normal distribution that will be considered in the null hypothesis. We use the sample mean $\bar{x}$ and the sample standard deviation $s$ as point estimators of the mean and standard deviation of the normal distribution. The calculations follow.

$$\bar{x} = \frac{\Sigma x_i}{n} = \frac{3421}{50} = 68.42$$

$$s = \sqrt{\frac{\Sigma(x_i - \bar{x})^2}{n-1}} = \sqrt{\frac{5310.0369}{49}} = 10.41$$

Using these values, we state the following hypotheses about the distribution of the job applicant test scores.

$H_0$: The population of test scores has a normal distribution with mean 68.42 and standard deviation 10.41

$H_a$: The population of test scores does not have a normal distribution with mean 68.42 and standard deviation 10.41

The hypothesized normal distribution is shown in Figure 12.2.

Now let us consider a way of defining the categories for a goodness of fit test involving a normal distribution. For the discrete probability distribution in the Poisson distribution test, the categories were readily defined in terms of the number of customers arriving, such as 0, 1, 2, and so on. However, with the continuous normal probability distribution, we must use a different procedure for defining the categories. We need to define the categories in terms of *intervals* of test scores.

Recall the rule of thumb for an expected frequency of at least five in each interval or category. We define the categories of test scores such that the expected frequencies will be at least five for each category. With a sample size of 50, one way of establishing categories is to divide the normal distribution into 10 equal-probability intervals (see Figure 12.3). With a sample size of 50, we would expect five outcomes in each interval or category, and the rule of thumb for expected frequencies would be satisfied.

Let us look more closely at the procedure for calculating the category boundaries. When the normal probability distribution is assumed, the standard normal distribution tables can

**FIGURE 12.2**    HYPOTHESIZED NORMAL DISTRIBUTION OF TEST SCORES FOR THE CHEMLINE JOB APPLICANTS

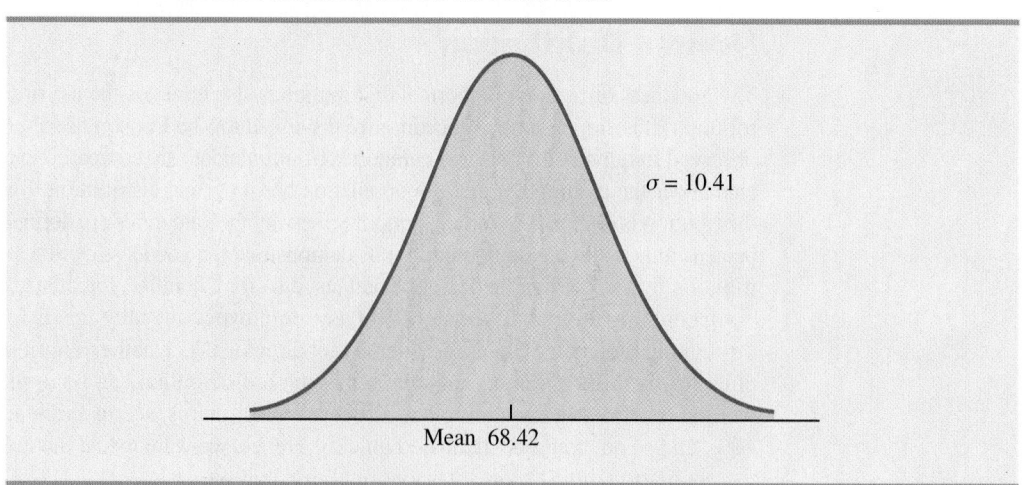

$\sigma = 10.41$

Mean 68.42

FIGURE 12.3   NORMAL DISTRIBUTION FOR THE CHEMLINE EXAMPLE
WITH 10 EQUAL-PROBABILITY INTERVALS

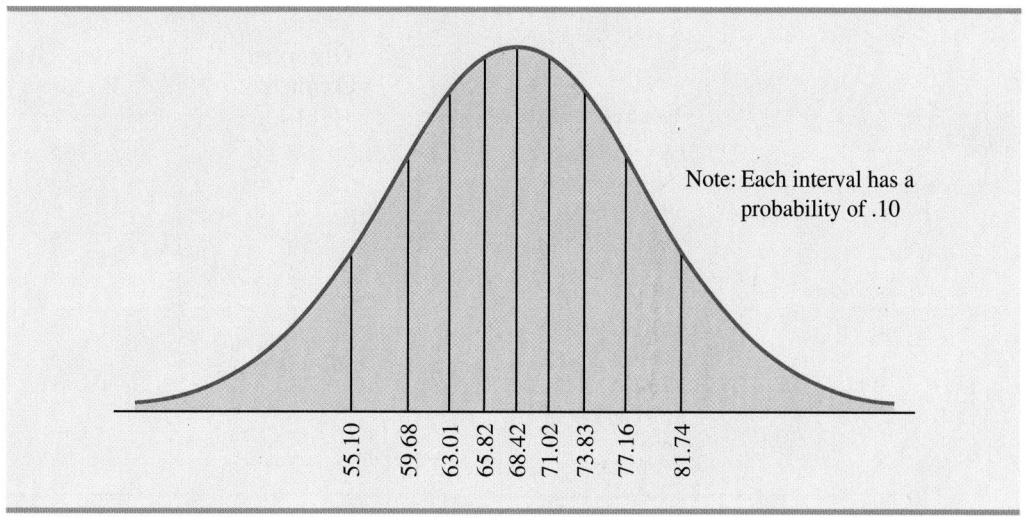

Note: Each interval has a
probability of .10

55.10  59.68  63.01  65.82  68.42  71.02  73.83  77.16  81.74

be used to determine these boundaries. First consider the test score cutting off the lowest
10% of the test scores. From Table 1 of Appendix B we find that the $z$ value for this test
score is $-1.28$. Therefore, the test score of $x = 68.42 - 1.28(10.41) = 55.10$ provides this
cutoff value for the lowest 10% of the scores. For the lowest 20%, we find $z = -.84$, and
thus $x = 68.42 - .84(10.41) = 59.68$. Working through the normal distribution in that way
provides the following test score values.

| | |
|---|---|
| Lower 10%: | $68.42 - 1.28(10.41) = 55.10$ |
| Lower 20%: | $68.42 - .84(10.41) = 59.68$ |
| Lower 30%: | $68.42 - .52(10.41) = 63.01$ |
| Lower 40%: | $68.42 - .25(10.41) = 65.82$ |
| Mid-score: | $68.42 + 0(10.41) = 68.42$ |
| Upper 40%: | $68.42 + .25(10.41) = 71.02$ |
| Upper 30%: | $68.42 + .52(10.41) = 73.83$ |
| Upper 20%: | $68.42 + .84(10.41) = 77.16$ |
| Upper 10%: | $68.42 + 1.28(10.41) = 81.74$ |

These cutoff or interval boundary points are identified on the graph in Figure 12.3.

With the categories or intervals of test scores now defined and with the known expected frequency of five per category, we can return to the sample data of Table 12.10 and
determine the observed frequencies for the categories. Doing so provides the results in
Table 12.11.

With the results in Table 12.11, the goodness of fit calculations proceed exactly as before. Namely, we compare the observed and expected results by computing a $\chi^2$ value. The
computations necessary to compute the chi-square test statistic are shown in Table 12.12.
We see that the value of the test statistic is $\chi^2 = 7.2$.

To determine whether the computed $\chi^2$ value of 7.2 is large enough to reject $H_0$, we
need to refer to the appropriate chi-square distribution tables. Using the rule for computing
the number of degrees of freedom for the goodness of fit test, we have $k - p - 1 =
10 - 2 - 1 = 7$ degrees of freedom based on $k = 10$ categories and $p = 2$ parameters
(mean and standard deviation) estimated from the sample data.

**TABLE 12.11**  OBSERVED AND EXPECTED FREQUENCIES FOR CHEMLINE JOB APPLICANT TEST SCORES

| Test Score Interval | Observed Frequency $(f_i)$ | Expected Frequency $(e_i)$ |
|---|---|---|
| Less than 55.10 | 5 | 5 |
| 55.10 to 59.68 | 5 | 5 |
| 59.68 to 63.01 | 9 | 5 |
| 63.01 to 65.82 | 6 | 5 |
| 65.82 to 68.42 | 2 | 5 |
| 68.42 to 71.02 | 5 | 5 |
| 71.02 to 73.83 | 2 | 5 |
| 73.83 to 77.16 | 5 | 5 |
| 77.16 to 81.74 | 5 | 5 |
| 81.74 and Over | 6 | 5 |
| Total | 50 | 50 |

**TABLE 12.12**  COMPUTATION OF THE CHI-SQUARE TEST STATISTIC FOR THE CHEMLINE JOB APPLICANT EXAMPLE

| Test Score Interval | Observed Frequency $(f_i)$ | Expected Frequency $(e_i)$ | Difference $(f_i - e_i)$ | Squared Difference $(f_i - e_i)^2$ | Squared Difference Divided by Expected Frequency $(f_i - e_i)^2/e_i$ |
|---|---|---|---|---|---|
| Less than 55.10 | 5 | 5 | 0 | 0 | 0.0 |
| 55.10 to 59.68 | 5 | 5 | 0 | 0 | 0.0 |
| 59.68 to 63.01 | 9 | 5 | 4 | 16 | 3.2 |
| 63.01 to 65.82 | 6 | 5 | 1 | 1 | 0.2 |
| 65.82 to 68.42 | 2 | 5 | $-3$ | 9 | 1.8 |
| 68.42 to 71.02 | 5 | 5 | 0 | 0 | 0.0 |
| 71.02 to 73.83 | 2 | 5 | $-3$ | 9 | 1.8 |
| 73.83 to 77.16 | 5 | 5 | 0 | 0 | 0.0 |
| 77.16 to 81.74 | 5 | 5 | 0 | 0 | 0.0 |
| 81.74 and Over | 6 | 5 | 1 | 1 | 0.2 |
| Total | 50 | 50 | | | $\chi^2 = 7.2$ |

*Estimating the two parameters of the normal distribution will cause a loss of two degrees of freedom in the $\chi^2$ test.*

Suppose that we test the null hypothesis that the distribution for the test scores is a normal distribution with a .10 level of significance. To test this hypothesis, we need to determine the $p$-value for the test statistic $\chi^2 = 7.2$ by finding the area in the upper tail of a chi-square distribution with 7 degrees of freedom. Using Table 3 of Appendix B, we find that $\chi^2 = 7.2$ provides an area in the upper tail greater than .10. Thus, we know that the $p$-value is greater than .10. Excel shows $p$-value = .4084. With $p$-value $> \alpha = .10$, the hypothesis that the probability distribution for the Chemline job applicant test scores is a normal distribution cannot be rejected. The normal distribution may be applied to assist in the interpretation of test scores. A summary of the goodness fit test for a normal distribution follows.

NORMAL DISTRIBUTION GOODNESS OF FIT TEST: A SUMMARY

1. State the null and alternative hypotheses.

   $H_0$: The population has a normal distribution
   $H_a$: The population does not have a normal distribution

2. Select a random sample and
   **a.** Compute the sample mean and sample standard deviation.
   **b.** Define intervals of values so that the expected frequency is at least five for each interval. Using equal probability intervals is a good approach.
   **c.** Record the observed frequency of data values $f_i$ in each interval defined.
3. Compute the expected number of occurrences $e_i$ for each interval of values defined in step 2(b). Multiply the sample size by the probability of a normal random variable being in the interval.
4. Compute the value of the test statistic.

$$\chi^2 = \sum_{i=1}^{k} \frac{(f_i - e_i)^2}{e_i}$$

5. Rejection rule:

   $p$-value approach:        Reject $H_0$ if $p$-value $\leq \alpha$
   Critical value approach:   Reject $H_0$ if $\chi^2 \geq \chi_\alpha^2$

   where $\alpha$ is the level of significance and there are $k - 3$ degrees of freedom.

## Exercises

## Methods

20. Data on the number of occurrences per time period and observed frequencies follow. Use $\alpha = .05$ and the goodness of fit test to see whether the data fit a Poisson distribution.

| Number of Occurrences | Observed Frequency |
|:---:|:---:|
| 0 | 39 |
| 1 | 30 |
| 2 | 30 |
| 3 | 18 |
| 4 | 3 |

21. The following data are believed to have come from a normal distribution. Use the goodness of fit test and $\alpha = .05$ to test this claim.

| | | | | | | | | | | | | | | |
|---|---|---|---|---|---|---|---|---|---|---|---|---|---|---|
| 17 | 23 | 22 | 24 | 19 | 23 | 18 | 22 | 20 | 13 | 11 | 21 | 18 | 20 | 21 |
| 21 | 18 | 15 | 24 | 23 | 23 | 43 | 29 | 27 | 26 | 30 | 28 | 33 | 23 | 29 |

## Applications

22. The number of automobile accidents per day in a particular city is believed to have a Poisson distribution. A sample of 80 days during the past year gives the following data. Do these data support the belief that the number of accidents per day has a Poisson distribution? Use $\alpha = .05$.

| Number of Accidents | Observed Frequency (days) |
|---|---|
| 0 | 34 |
| 1 | 25 |
| 2 | 11 |
| 3 | 7 |
| 4 | 3 |

23. The number of incoming phone calls at a company switchboard during 1-minute intervals is believed to have a Poisson distribution. Use $\alpha = .10$ and the following data to test the assumption that the incoming phone calls follow a Poisson distribution.

| Number of Incoming Phone Calls During a 1-Minute Interval | Observed Frequency |
|---|---|
| 0 | 15 |
| 1 | 31 |
| 2 | 20 |
| 3 | 15 |
| 4 | 13 |
| 5 | 4 |
| 6 | 2 |
| Total | 100 |

24. The weekly demand for a product is believed to be normally distributed. Use a goodness of fit test and the following data to test this assumption. Use $\alpha = .10$. The sample mean is 24.5 and the sample standard deviation is 3.

| | | | | |
|---|---|---|---|---|
| 18 | 20 | 22 | 27 | 22 |
| 25 | 22 | 27 | 25 | 24 |
| 26 | 23 | 20 | 24 | 26 |
| 27 | 25 | 19 | 21 | 25 |
| 26 | 25 | 31 | 29 | 25 |
| 25 | 28 | 26 | 28 | 24 |

25. Use $\alpha = .01$ and conduct a goodness of fit test to see whether the following sample appears to have been selected from a normal distribution.

| | | | | | | | | | | | | | | |
|---|---|---|---|---|---|---|---|---|---|---|---|---|---|---|
| 55 | 86 | 94 | 58 | 55 | 95 | 55 | 52 | 69 | 95 | 90 | 65 | 87 | 50 | 56 |
| 55 | 57 | 98 | 58 | 79 | 92 | 62 | 59 | 88 | 65 | | | | | |

After you complete the goodness of fit calculations, construct a histogram of the data. Does the histogram representation support the conclusion reached with the goodness of fit test? (*Note:* $\bar{x} = 71$ and $s = 17$.)

## Summary

In this chapter we introduced the goodness of fit test and the test of independence, both of which are based on the use of the chi-square distribution. The purpose of the goodness of fit test is to determine whether a hypothesized probability distribution can be used as a model for a particular population of interest. The computations for conducting the goodness of fit test involve comparing observed frequencies from a sample with expected frequencies when the hypothesized probability distribution is assumed true. A chi-square distribution is used to determine whether the differences between observed and expected frequencies are large enough to reject the hypothesized probability distribution. We illustrated the goodness of fit test for multinomial, Poisson, and normal distributions.

A test of independence for two variables is an extension of the methodology employed in the goodness of fit test for a multinomial population. A contingency table is used to determine the observed and expected frequencies. Then a chi-square value is computed. Large chi-square values, caused by large differences between observed and expected frequencies, lead to the rejection of the null hypothesis of independence.

## Glossary

**Multinomial population** A population in which each element is assigned to one and only one of several categories. The multinomial distribution extends the binomial distribution from two to three or more outcomes.

**Goodness of fit test** A statistical test conducted to determine whether to reject a hypothesized probability distribution for a population.

**Contingency table** A table used to summarize observed and expected frequencies for a test of independence.

## Key Formulas

**Test Statistic for Goodness of Fit**

$$\chi^2 = \sum_{i=1}^{k} \frac{(f_i - e_i)^2}{e_i} \tag{12.1}$$

**Expected Frequencies for Contingency Tables Under the Assumption of Independence**

$$e_{ij} = \frac{(\text{Row } i \text{ Total})(\text{Column } j \text{ Total})}{\text{Sample Size}} \tag{12.2}$$

**Test Statistic for Independence**

$$\chi^2 = \sum_{i}\sum_{j} \frac{(f_{ij} - e_{ij})^2}{e_{ij}} \tag{12.3}$$

## Supplementary Exercises

26. In setting sales quotas, the marketing manager makes the assumption that order potentials are the same for each of four sales territories. A sample of 200 sales follows. Should the manager's assumption be rejected? Use $\alpha = .05$.

| Sales Territories | | | |
|---|---|---|---|
| **I** | **II** | **III** | **IV** |
| 60 | 45 | 59 | 36 |

27. Seven percent of mutual fund investors rate corporate stocks "very safe," 58% rate them "somewhat safe," 24% rate them "not very safe," 4% rate them "not at all safe," and 7% are "not sure." A *Business Week*/Harris poll asked 529 mutual fund investors how they would rate corporate bonds on safety. The responses are as follows.

| Safety Rating | Frequency |
|---|---|
| Very safe | 48 |
| Somewhat safe | 323 |
| Not very safe | 79 |
| Not at all safe | 16 |
| Not sure | 63 |
| Total | 529 |

Do mutual fund investors' attitudes toward corporate bonds differ from their attitudes toward corporate stocks? Support your conclusion with a statistical test. Use $\alpha = .01$.

28. A community park will open soon. A sample of 140 individuals are asked to state their preference for when they would most like to visit the park. The sample results follow.

| Weekday | Saturday | Sunday | Holiday |
|---|---|---|---|
| 20 | 20 | 40 | 60 |

In developing a staffing plan, should the park manager plan on the same number of individuals visiting the park each day? Support your conclusion with a statistical test. Use $\alpha = .05$.

29. A regional transit authority is concerned about the number of riders on one of its bus routes. In setting up the route, the assumption is that the number of riders is the same on every day from Monday through Friday. Using the following data, test with $\alpha = .05$ to determine whether the transit authority's assumption is correct.

| Day | Number of Riders |
|---|---|
| Monday | 13 |
| Tuesday | 16 |
| Wednesday | 28 |
| Thursday | 17 |
| Friday | 16 |

30. The results of *Computerworld's* Annual Job Satisfaction Survey showed that 28% of Information Systems (IS) managers are very satisfied with their job, 46% are somewhat satisfied, 12% are neither satisfied or dissatisfied, 10% are somewhat dissatisfied, and 4% are very dissatisfied. Suppose that a sample of 500 computer programmers yielded the following results.

| Category | Number of Respondents |
|---|---|
| Very satisfied | 105 |
| Somewhat satisfied | 235 |
| Neither | 55 |
| Somewhat dissatisfied | 90 |
| Very dissatisfied | 15 |

Use $\alpha = .05$ and test to determine whether the job satisfaction for computer programmers is different from the job satisfaction for IS managers.

31. A sample of parts provided the following contingency table data on part quality by production shift.

| Shift | Number Good | Number Defective |
|---|---|---|
| First | 368 | 32 |
| Second | 285 | 15 |
| Third | 176 | 24 |

Use $\alpha = .05$ and test the hypothesis that part quality is independent of the production shift. What is your conclusion?

32. *The Wall Street Journal* Subscriber Study showed data on the employment status of subscribers. Sample results corresponding to subscribers of the eastern and western editions are shown here.

| | Region | |
|---|---|---|
| Employment Status | Eastern Edition | Western Edition |
| Full-time | 1105 | 574 |
| Part-time | 31 | 15 |
| Self-employed/consultant | 229 | 186 |
| Not employed | 485 | 344 |

Use $\alpha = .05$ and test the hypothesis that employment status is independent of the region. What is your conclusion?

33. A lending institution supplied the following data on loan approvals by four loan officers. Use $\alpha = .05$ and test to determine whether the loan approval decision is independent of the loan officer reviewing the loan application.

| | Loan Approval Decision | |
|---|---|---|
| Loan Officer | Approved | Rejected |
| Miller | 24 | 16 |
| McMahon | 17 | 13 |
| Games | 35 | 15 |
| Runk | 11 | 9 |

34. Data on the marital status of men and women ages 20 to 29 were obtained as part of a national survey. The results from a sample of 350 men and 400 women follow. These data are representative of results published in the *U.S. Current Population Report* (*The Statistical Abstract of the United States,* 1999).

| | Marital Status | | |
|---|---|---|---|
| Gender | Never Married | Married | Divorced |
| Men | 234 | 106 | 10 |
| Women | 216 | 168 | 16 |

a. Use $\alpha = .01$ and test for independence between marital status and gender. What is your conclusion?
b. Summarize the percent in each marital status category for men and for women.

35. The following crosstabulation shows industry type and P/E ratio for 100 companies in the consumer products and banking industries.

| | | P/E Ratio | | | | | |
|---|---|---|---|---|---|---|---|
| | | 5–9 | 10–14 | 15–19 | 20–24 | 25–29 | Total |
| Industry | Consumer | 4 | 10 | 18 | 10 | 8 | 50 |
| | Banking | 14 | 14 | 12 | 6 | 4 | 50 |
| | Total | 18 | 24 | 30 | 16 | 12 | 100 |

Does there appear to be a relationship between industry type and P/E ratio? Support your conclusion with a statistical test using $\alpha = .05$.

36. The following data were collected on the number of emergency ambulance calls for an urban county and a rural county in Virginia.

| | | Day of Week | | | | | | | |
|---|---|---|---|---|---|---|---|---|---|
| | | Sun | Mon | Tue | Wed | Thur | Fri | Sat | Total |
| County | Urban | 61 | 48 | 50 | 55 | 63 | 73 | 43 | 393 |
| | Rural | 7 | 9 | 16 | 13 | 9 | 14 | 10 | 78 |
| | Total | 68 | 57 | 66 | 68 | 72 | 87 | 53 | 471 |

Conduct a test for independence using $\alpha = .05$. What is your conclusion?

37. A random sample of final examination grades for a college course follows.

| 55 | 85 | 72 | 99 | 48 | 71 | 88 | 70 | 59 | 98 | 80 | 74 | 93 | 85 | 74 |
| 82 | 90 | 71 | 83 | 60 | 95 | 77 | 84 | 73 | 63 | 72 | 95 | 79 | 51 | 85 |
| 76 | 81 | 78 | 65 | 75 | 87 | 86 | 70 | 80 | 64 | | | | | |

Use $\alpha = .05$ and test to determine whether a normal distribution should be rejected as being representative of the population's distribution of grades.

38. The office occupancy rates were reported for four California metropolitan areas. Do the following data suggest that the office vacancies were independent of metropolitan area? Use a .05 level of significance. What is your conclusion?

| Occupancy Status | Los Angeles | San Diego | San Francisco | San Jose |
| --- | --- | --- | --- | --- |
| Occupied | 160 | 116 | 192 | 174 |
| Vacant | 40 | 34 | 33 | 26 |

39. A salesperson makes four calls per day. A sample of 100 days gives the following frequencies of sales volumes.

| Number of Sales | Observed Frequency (days) |
| --- | --- |
| 0 | 30 |
| 1 | 32 |
| 2 | 25 |
| 3 | 10 |
| 4 | 3 |
| Total | 100 |

Records show sales are made to 30% of all sales calls. Assuming independent sales calls, the number of sales per day should follow a binomial distribution. The binomial probability function presented in Chapter 5 is

$$f(x) = \frac{n!}{x!(n-x)!} p^x (1-p)^{n-x}$$

For this exercise, assume that the population has a binomial distribution with $n = 4$, $p = .30$, and $x = 0, 1, 2, 3,$ and 4.

a. Compute the expected frequencies for $x = 0, 1, 2, 3,$ and 4 by using the binomial probability function. Combine categories if necessary to satisfy the requirement that the expected frequency is five or more for all categories.

b. Use the goodness of fit test to determine whether the assumption of a binomial distribution should be rejected. Use $\alpha = .05$. Because no parameters of the binomial distribution were estimated from the sample data, the degrees of freedom are $k - 1$ when $k$ is the number of categories.

## Case Problem   A Bipartisan Agenda for Change

In a study conducted by Zogby International for the *Democrat and Chronicle,* more than 700 New Yorkers were polled to determine whether the New York state government works. Respondents surveyed were asked questions involving pay cuts for state legislators, restrictions on lobbyists, terms limits for legislators, and whether state citizens should be able to put matters directly on the state ballot for a vote (*Democrat and Chronicle,* December 7, 1997). The results regarding several proposed reforms had broad support, crossing all demographic and political lines.

Suppose that a follow-up survey of 100 individuals who live in the western region of New York was conducted. The party affiliation (Democrat, Independent, Republican) of each individual surveyed was recorded, as well as their responses to the following three questions.

1. Should legislative pay be cut for every day the state budget is late?
   Yes _____   No _____
2. Should there be more restrictions on lobbyists?
   Yes _____   No _____
3. Should there be term limits requiring that legislators serve a fixed number of years?
   Yes _____   No _____

NYReform

The responses were coded using 1 for a *yes* response and 2 for a *no* response. The complete data set is available on the data disk in the data set named NYReform.

## Managerial Report

1. Use descriptive statistics to summarize the data from this study. What are your preliminary conclusions about the independence of the response (Yes or No) and party affiliation for each of the three questions in the survey?
2. With regard to question 1, test for the independence of the response (Yes and No) and party affiliation. Use $\alpha = .05$.
3. With regard to question 2, test for the independence of the response (Yes and No) and party affiliation. Use $\alpha = .05$.
4. With regard to question 3, test for the independence of the response (Yes and No) and party affiliation. Use $\alpha = .05$.
5. Does it appear that there is broad support for change across all political lines? Explain.

## Appendix 12.1 Tests of Goodness of Fit and Independence Using Minitab

### Goodness of Fit Test

This Minitab procedure can be used for goodness of fit tests for the multinomial distribution in Section 12.1 and the Poisson and normal distributions in Section 12.3. The user must obtain the observed frequencies, calculate the expected frequencies, and enter both the observed and expected frequencies in a Minitab worksheet. Column C1 is labeled Observed and contains the observed frequencies. Column C2 is labeled Expected and contains the expected frequencies. Use the Scott Marketing Research example presented in Section 12.1, open a Minitab worksheet, and enter the observed frequencies 48, 98, and 54 in column C1 and enter the expected frequencies 60, 100, and 40 in column C2. The Minitab steps for the goodness of fit test follow.

**Step 1.** Select the **Calc** menu
**Step 2.** Choose **Calculator**

**Step 3.** When the Calculator dialog box appears:

Enter ChiSquare in the **Store result in variable** box

Enter Sum((C1-C2)**2/C2)) in the **Expression** box

Click **OK**

**Step 4.** Select the **Calc** menu

**Step 5.** Choose **Probability Distributions**

**Step 6.** Choose **Chi-Square**

**Step 7.** When the Chi-Square Distribution dialog box appears:

Select **Cumulative probability**

Enter 2 in the **Degrees of freedom** box

Select **Input column** and enter ChiSquare in the box

Click **OK**

The Minitab output provides the cumulative probability .9745, which is the area under the curve to the left of $\chi^2 = 7.34$. The area remaining in the upper tail is the $p$-value. Thus, we have $p$-value $= 1 - .9745 = .0255$.

## Test of Independence

We begin with a new Minitab worksheet and enter the observed frequency data for the Alber's Brewery example from Section 12.2 into columns 1, 2, and 3, respectively. Thus, we entered the observed frequencies corresponding to a light beer preference (20 and 30) in C1, the observed frequencies corresponding to a regular beer preference (40 and 30) in C2, and the observed frequencies corresponding to a dark beer preference (20 and 10) in C3. The Minitab steps for the test of independence are as follows.

**Step 1.** Select the **Stat** menu

**Step 2.** Select **Tables**

**Step 3.** Choose **Chi-Square Test (Table in Worksheet)**

**Step 4.** When the Chi-Square Test dialog box appears:

Enter C1-C3 in the **Columns containing the table** box

Click **OK**

# Appendix 12.2   Tests of Goodness of Fit and Independence Using Excel

## Goodness of Fit Test

**FitTest**

This Excel procedure can be used for goodness of fit tests for the multinomial distribution in Section 12.1 and the Poisson and normal distributions in Section 12.3. The user must obtain the observed frequencies, calculate the expected frequencies, and enter both the observed and expected frequencies in an Excel worksheet.

The observed frequencies and expected frequencies for the Scott Market Research example presented in Section 12.1 are entered in columns A and B as shown in Figure 12.4. The test statistic $\chi^2 = 7.34$ is calculated in column D. With $k = 3$ categories, the user enters the degrees of freedom $k - 1 = 3 - 1 = 2$ in cell D11. The CHIDIST function provides the $p$-value in cell D13. The background worksheet shows the cell formulas.

## Test of Independence

**Independence**

The Excel procedure for the test of independence requires the user to obtain the observed frequencies and enter them in the worksheet. The Alber's Brewery example from Section 12.2 provides the observed frequencies, which are entered in cells B7 to D8 as shown in the worksheet in Figure 12.5. The cell formulas in the background worksheet show the procedure used to compute the expected frequencies. With two rows and three columns, the user enters the degrees of freedom $(2 - 1)(3 - 1) = 2$ in cell E22. The CHITEST function provides the $p$-value in cell E24.

**FIGURE 12.4**   EXCEL WORKSHEET FOR THE SCOTT MARKETING RESEARCH GOODNESS OF FIT TEST

|   | A | B | C | D | E |
|---|---|---|---|---|---|
| 1 | **Goodness of Fit Test** | | | | |
| 2 | | | | | |
| 3 | Observed | Expected | | | |
| 4 | Frequency | Frequency | | Calculations | |
| 5 | 48 | 60 | | =(A5-B5)^2/B5 | |
| 6 | 98 | 100 | | =(A6-B6)^2/B6 | |
| 7 | 54 | 40 | | =(A7-B7)^2/B7 | |
| 8 | | | | | |
| 9 | | | Test Statistic | =SUM(D5:D7) | |
| 10 | | | | | |
| 11 | | | Degrees of Freedom | 2 | |
| 12 | | | | | |
| 13 | | | p-Value | =CHIDIST(D9,D11) | |
| 14 | | | | | |

|   | A | B | C | D | E |
|---|---|---|---|---|---|
| 1 | **Goodness of Fit Test** | | | | |
| 2 | | | | | |
| 3 | Observed | Expected | | | |
| 4 | Frequency | Frequency | | Calculations | |
| 5 | 48 | 60 | | 2.40 | |
| 6 | 98 | 100 | | 0.04 | |
| 7 | 54 | 40 | | 4.90 | |
| 8 | | | | | |
| 9 | | | Test Statistic | 7.34 | |
| 10 | | | | | |
| 11 | | | Degrees of Freedom | 2 | |
| 12 | | | | | |
| 13 | | | p-Value | 0.0255 | |
| 14 | | | | | |

**FIGURE 12.5    EXCEL WORKSHEET FOR THE ALBER'S BREWERY TEST OF INDEPENDENCE**

|    | A | B | C | D | E | F |
|----|---|---|---|---|---|---|
| 1 | **Test of Independence** | | | | | |
| 2 | | | | | | |
| 3 | Observed Frequencies | | | | | |
| 4 | | | | | | |
| 5 | | | Beer Preference | | | |
| 6 | Gender | Light | Regular | Dark | Total | |
| 7 | Male | 20 | 40 | 20 | =SUM(B7:D7) | |
| 8 | Female | 30 | 30 | 10 | =SUM(B8:D8) | |
| 9 | Total | =SUM(B7:B8) | =SUM(C7:C8) | =SUM(D7:D8) | =SUM(E7:E8) | |
| 10 | | | | | | |
| 11 | | | | | | |
| 12 | Expected Frequencies | | | | | |
| 13 | | | | | | |
| 14 | | | Beer Preference | | | |
| 15 | Gender | Light | Regular | Dark | Total | |
| 16 | Male | =E7*B$9/$E$9 | =E7*C$9/$E$9 | =E7*D$9/$E$9 | =SUM(B16:D16) | |
| 17 | Female | =E8*B$9/$E$9 | =E8*C$9/$E$9 | =E8*D$9/$E$9 | =SUM(B17:D17) | |
| 18 | Total | =SUM(B16:B17) | =SUM(C16:C17) | =SUM(D16:D17) | =SUM(E16:E17) | |
| 19 | | | | | | |
| 20 | | | | Test Statistic | =CHIINV(E24,E22) | |
| 21 | | | | | | |
| 22 | | | | Degrees of Freedom | 2 | |
| 23 | | | | | | |
| 24 | | | | p-value | =CHITEST(C7:E8,C16:E17) | |
| 25 | | | | | | |

|    | A | B | C | D | E | F |
|----|---|---|---|---|---|---|
| 1 | **Test of Independence** | | | | | |
| 2 | | | | | | |
| 3 | Observed Frequencies | | | | | |
| 4 | | | | | | |
| 5 | | | Beer Preference | | | |
| 6 | Gender | Light | Regular | Dark | Total | |
| 7 | Male | 20 | 40 | 20 | 80 | |
| 8 | Female | 30 | 30 | 10 | 70 | |
| 9 | Total | 50 | 70 | 30 | 150 | |
| 10 | | | | | | |
| 11 | | | | | | |
| 12 | Expected Frequencies | | | | | |
| 13 | | | | | | |
| 14 | | | Beer Preference | | | |
| 15 | Gender | Light | Regular | Dark | Total | |
| 16 | Male | 26.67 | 37.33 | 16 | 80 | |
| 17 | Female | 23.33 | 32.67 | 14 | 70 | |
| 18 | Total | 50 | 70 | 30 | 150 | |
| 19 | | | | | | |
| 20 | | | | Test Statistic | 6.12 | |
| 21 | | | | | | |
| 22 | | | | Degrees of Freedom | 2 | |
| 23 | | | | | | |
| 24 | | | | p-value | 0.0468 | |
| 25 | | | | | | |

# CHAPTER 13

# Analysis of Variance and Experimental Design

**CONTENTS**

## BURKE MARKETING SERVICES, INC.*
*CINCINNATI, OHIO*

Burke Marketing Services, Inc., is one of the most experienced market research firms in the industry. Burke writes more proposals, on more projects, every day than any other market research company in the world. Supported by state-of-the-art technology, Burke offers a wide variety of research capabilities, providing answers to nearly any marketing question.

In one study, a firm retained Burke to evaluate potential new versions of a children's dry cereal. To maintain confidentiality, we refer to the cereal manufacturer as the Anon Company. The four key factors that Anon's product developers thought would enhance the taste of the cereal were the following:

1. Ratio of wheat to corn in the cereal flake
2. Type of sweetener: sugar, honey, or artificial
3. Presence or absence of flavor bits with a fruit taste
4. Short or long cooking time

Burke designed an experiment to determine what effects these four factors had on cereal taste. For example, one test cereal was made with a specified ratio of wheat to corn, sugar as the sweetener, flavor bits, and a short cooking time; another test cereal was made with a different ratio of wheat to corn and the other three factors the same, and so on. Groups of children then taste-tested the cereals and stated what they thought about the taste of each.

Analysis of variance was the statistical method used to study the data obtained from the taste tests. The results of the analysis showed the following:

_____

*The authors are indebted to Dr. Ronald Tatham of Burke Marketing Services for providing this Statistics in Practice.

Burke's research provides valuable statistical information on what customers want from a product. © Mary Kate Denny/PhotoEdit.

- The flake composition and sweetener type were highly influential in taste evaluation.
- The flavor bits actually detracted from the taste of the cereal.
- The cooking time had no effect on the taste.

This information helped Anon identify the factors that would lead to the best-tasting cereal.

The experimental design employed by Burke and the subsequent analysis of variance were helpful in making a product design recommendation. In this chapter, we will see how such procedures are carried out.

---

*Sir Ronald Alymer Fisher (1890–1962) invented the branch of statistics known as experimental design. In addition to being accomplished in statistics, he was a noted scientist in the field of genetics.*

In this chapter we introduce a statistical procedure called *analysis of variance* (ANOVA). First, we show how ANOVA can be used to test for the equality of three or more population means using data obtained from an observational study. Then, we discuss the use of ANOVA for analyzing data obtained from three types of experimental studies: a completely randomized design, a randomized block design, and a factorial experiment. In the following chapters we will see that ANOVA plays a key role in analyzing the results of regression analysis involving both experimental and observational data.

##  An Introduction to Analysis of Variance

National Computer Products, Inc. (NCP), manufactures printers and fax machines at plants located in Atlanta, Dallas, and Seattle. To measure how much employees at these plants know about total quality management, a random sample of six employees was selected from each plant and given a quality awareness examination. The examination scores obtained for these 18 employees are listed in Table 13.1. The sample means, sample variances, and sample standard deviations for each group are also provided. Managers want to use these data to test the hypothesis that the mean examination score is the same for all three plants.

We will define population 1 as all employees at the Atlanta plant, population 2 as all employees at the Dallas plant, and population 3 as all employees at the Seattle plant. Let

$$\mu_1 = \text{mean examination score for population 1}$$
$$\mu_2 = \text{mean examination score for population 2}$$
$$\mu_3 = \text{mean examination score for population 3}$$

Although we will never know the actual values of $\mu_1$, $\mu_2$, and $\mu_3$, we want to use the sample results to test the following hypotheses.

$$H_0: \mu_1 = \mu_2 = \mu_3$$
$$H_a: \text{Not all population means are equal}$$

*If $H_0$ is rejected, we cannot conclude that all population means are different. Rejecting $H_0$ means that at least two population means have different values.*

As we will demonstrate shortly, analysis of variance is a statistical procedure that can be used to determine whether the observed differences in the three sample means are large enough to reject $H_0$.

In the introduction to this chapter we stated that analysis of variance can be used to analyze data obtained from both an observational study and an experimental study. In order to provide a common set of terminology for discussing the use of analysis of variance in both types of studies, we need to introduce the concepts of a response variable, a factor, and a treatment.

The two variables in the NCP example are plant location and score on the quality awareness examination. Because the objective is to determine whether the mean examination score is the same for plants located in Atlanta, Dallas, and Seattle, examination score is referred to as the dependent or *response variable* and plant location as the independent variable or *factor*. In general, the values of a factor selected for investigation are referred to as levels of the factor or *treatments*. Thus, in the NCP example the three treatments are Atlanta, Dallas, and Seattle. These three treatments define the populations of interest in the NCP example. For each treatment or population, the response variable is the examination score.

**TABLE 13.1   EXAMINATION SCORES FOR 18 EMPLOYEES**

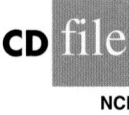

CD file

NCP

| Observation | Plant 1 Atlanta | Plant 2 Dallas | Plant 3 Seattle |
|---|---|---|---|
| 1 | 85 | 71 | 59 |
| 2 | 75 | 75 | 64 |
| 3 | 82 | 73 | 62 |
| 4 | 76 | 74 | 69 |
| 5 | 71 | 69 | 75 |
| 6 | 85 | 82 | 67 |
| Sample mean | 79 | 74 | 66 |
| Sample variance | 34 | 20 | 32 |
| Sample standard deviation | 5.83 | 4.47 | 5.66 |

## Assumptions for Analysis of Variance

Three assumptions are required to use analysis of variance.

*If the sample sizes are equal, analysis of variance is not sensitive to departures from the assumption of normally distributed populations.*

1. **For each population, the response variable is normally distributed.** Implication: In the NCP example, the examination scores (response variable) must be normally distributed at each plant.
2. **The variance of the response variable, denoted $\sigma^2$, is the same for all of the populations.** Implication: In the NCP example, the variance of examination scores must be the same for all three plants.
3. **The observations must be independent.** Implication: In the NCP example, the examination score for each employee must be independent of the examination score for any other employee.

## A Conceptual Overview

If the means for the three populations are equal, we would expect the three sample means to be close together. In fact, the closer the three sample means are to one another, the more evidence we have for the conclusion that the population means are equal. Alternatively, the more the sample means differ, the more evidence we have for the conclusion that the population means are not equal. In other words, if the variability among the sample means is "small," it supports $H_0$; if the variability among the sample means is "large," it supports $H_a$.

If the null hypothesis, $H_0: \mu_1 = \mu_2 = \mu_3$, is true, we can use the variability among the sample means to develop an estimate of $\sigma^2$. First, note that if the assumptions for analysis of variance are satisfied, each sample will have come from the same normal distribution with mean $\mu$ and variance $\sigma^2$. Recall from Chapter 7 that the sampling distribution of the sample mean $\bar{x}$ for a simple random sample of size $n$ from a normal population will be normally distributed with mean $\mu$ and variance $\sigma^2/n$. Figure 13.1 illustrates such a sampling distribution.

Thus, if the null hypothesis is true, we can think of each of the three sample means, $\bar{x}_1 = 79$, $\bar{x}_2 = 74$, and $\bar{x}_3 = 66$, from Table 13.1 as values drawn at random from the sampling distribution shown in Figure 13.1. In this case, the mean and variance of the three $\bar{x}$ values can be used to estimate the mean and variance of the sampling distribution. When the sample sizes are equal, as in the NCP example, the best estimate of the mean of the

**FIGURE 13.1    SAMPLING DISTRIBUTION OF $\bar{x}$ GIVEN $H_0$ IS TRUE**

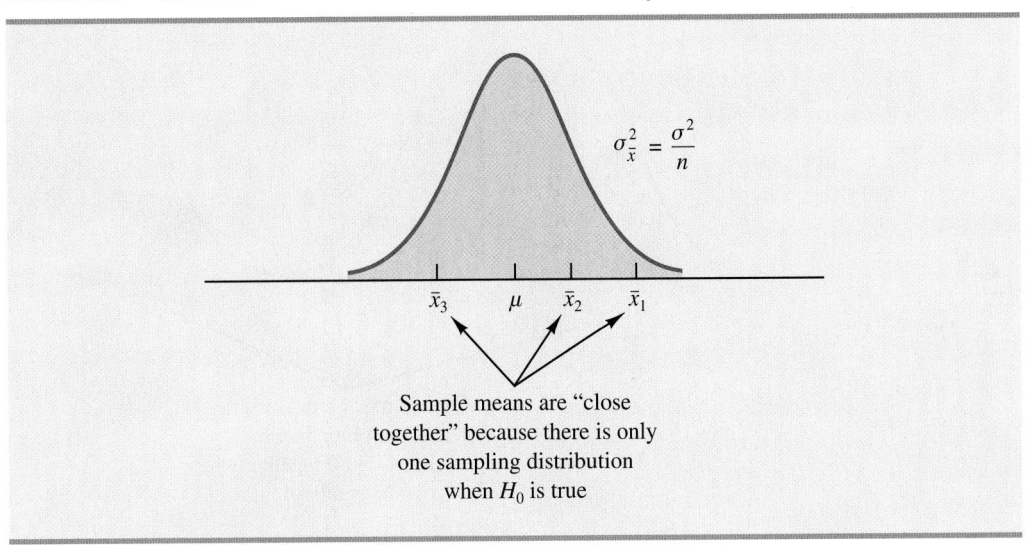

$$\sigma_{\bar{x}}^2 = \frac{\sigma^2}{n}$$

$\bar{x}_3 \quad \mu \quad \bar{x}_2 \quad \bar{x}_1$

Sample means are "close together" because there is only one sampling distribution when $H_0$ is true sampling distribution of $\bar{x}$ is the mean or average of the sample means. Thus, in the NCP example, an estimate of the mean of the sampling distribution of $\bar{x}$ is $(79 + 74 + 66)/3 = 73$. We refer to this estimate as the *overall sample mean*. An estimate of the variance of the sampling distribution of $\bar{x}$, $\sigma_{\bar{x}}^2$, is provided by the variance of the three sample means.

$$s_{\bar{x}}^2 = \frac{(79 - 73)^2 + (74 - 73)^2 + (66 - 73)^2}{3 - 1} = \frac{86}{2} = 43$$

Because $\sigma_{\bar{x}}^2 = \sigma^2/n$, solving for $\sigma^2$ gives

$$\sigma^2 = n\sigma_{\bar{x}}^2$$

Hence,

$$\text{Estimate of } \sigma^2 = n \text{ (Estimate of } \sigma_{\bar{x}}^2) = ns_{\bar{x}}^2 = 6(43) = 258$$

The result, $ns_{\bar{x}}^2 = 258$, is referred to as the *between-treatments* estimate of $\sigma^2$.

The between-treatments estimate of $\sigma^2$ is based on the assumption that the null hypothesis is true. In this case, each sample comes from the same population, and there is only one sampling distribution of $\bar{x}$. To illustrate what happens when $H_0$ is false, suppose the population means all differ. Note that because the three samples are from normal populations with different means, they will result in three different sampling distributions. Figure 13.2 shows that in this case, the sample means are not as close together as they were when $H_0$ was true. Thus, $s_{\bar{x}}^2$ will be larger, causing the between-treatments estimate of $\sigma^2$ to be larger. In general, when the population means are not equal, the between-treatments estimate will overestimate the population variance $\sigma^2$.

The variation within each of the samples also has an effect on the conclusion we reach in analysis of variance. When a simple random sample is selected from each population, each of the sample variances provides an unbiased estimate of $\sigma^2$. Hence, we can combine or pool the individual estimates of $\sigma^2$ into one overall estimate. The estimate of $\sigma^2$ obtained in this way is called the *pooled* or *within-treatments* estimate of $\sigma^2$. Because each sample variance provides an estimate of $\sigma^2$ based only on the variation within each sample, the within-treatments estimate of $\sigma^2$ is not affected by whether the population means are equal.

**FIGURE 13.2**    SAMPLING DISTRIBUTIONS OF $\bar{x}$ GIVEN $H_0$ IS FALSE

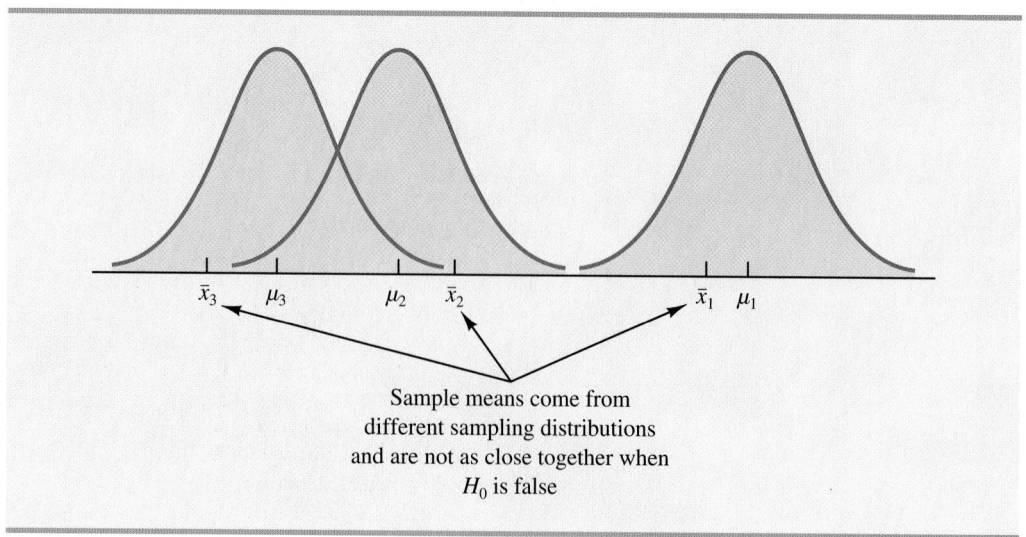

Sample means come from
different sampling distributions
and are not as close together when
$H_0$ is false

When the sample sizes are equal, the within-treatments estimate of $\sigma^2$ can be obtained by computing the average of the individual sample variances. For the NCP example we obtain

$$\text{Within-treatments estimate of } \sigma^2 = \frac{34 + 20 + 32}{3} = \frac{86}{3} = 28.67$$

In the NCP example, the between-treatments estimate of $\sigma^2$ (258) is much larger than the within-treatments estimate of $\sigma^2$ (28.67). In fact, the ratio of these two estimates is $258/28.67 = 9.00$. Recall, however, that the between-treatments approach provides a good estimate of $\sigma^2$ only if the null hypothesis is true; if the null hypothesis is false, the between-treatments approach overestimates $\sigma^2$. The within-treatments approach provides a good estimate of $\sigma^2$ in either case. Thus, if the null hypothesis is true, the two estimates will be similar and their ratio will be close to 1. If the null hypothesis is false, the between-treatments estimate will be larger than the within-treatments estimate, and their ratio will be large. In the next section we will show how large this ratio must be to reject $H_0$.

In summary, the logic behind ANOVA is based on the development of two independent estimates of the common population variance $\sigma^2$. One estimate of $\sigma^2$ is based on the variability among the sample means themselves, and the other estimate of $\sigma^2$ is based on the variability of the data within each sample. By comparing these two estimates of $\sigma^2$, we will be able to determine whether the population means are equal.

## NOTES AND COMMENTS

In Sections 10.1 and 10.2 we presented statistical methods for testing the hypothesis that the means of two populations are equal. ANOVA can also be used to test the hypothesis that the means of two populations are equal. In practice, however, analysis of variance is usually not used except when dealing with three or more population means.

## 13.2  Analysis of Variance: Testing for the Equality of $k$ Population Means

Analysis of variance can be used to test for the equality of $k$ population means. The general form of the hypotheses tested is

$$H_0: \mu_1 = \mu_2 = \cdots = \mu_k$$
$$H_a: \text{Not all population means are equal}$$

where

$$\mu_j = \text{mean of the } j\text{th population}$$

We assume that a simple random sample of size $n_j$ has been selected from each of the $k$ populations or treatments. For the resulting sample data, let

$$x_{ij} = \text{value of observation } i \text{ for treatment } j$$
$$n_j = \text{number of observations for treatment } j$$
$$\bar{x}_j = \text{sample mean for treatment } j$$
$$s_j^2 = \text{sample variance for treatment } j$$
$$s_j = \text{sample standard deviation for treatment } j$$

The formulas for the sample mean and sample variance for treatment $j$ are as follow.

$$\bar{x}_j = \frac{\sum_{i=1}^{n_j} x_{ij}}{n_j} \tag{13.1}$$

$$s_j^2 = \frac{\sum_{i=1}^{n_j} (x_{ij} - \bar{x}_j)^2}{n_j - 1} \tag{13.2}$$

The overall sample mean, denoted $\bar{\bar{x}}$, is the sum of all the observations divided by the total number of observations. That is,

$$\bar{\bar{x}} = \frac{\sum_{j=1}^{k} \sum_{i=1}^{n_j} x_{ij}}{n_T} \tag{13.3}$$

where

$$n_T = n_1 + n_2 + \cdots + n_k \tag{13.4}$$

If the size of each sample is $n$, $n_T = kn$; in this case equation (13.3) reduces to

$$\bar{\bar{x}} = \frac{\sum_{j=1}^{k} \sum_{i=1}^{n_j} x_{ij}}{kn} = \frac{\sum_{j=1}^{k} \sum_{i=1}^{n_j} x_{ij}/n}{k} = \frac{\sum_{j=1}^{k} \bar{x}_j}{k} \tag{13.5}$$

In other words, whenever the sample sizes are the same, the overall sample mean is just the average of the $k$ sample means.

Because each sample in the NCP example consists of $n = 6$ observations, the overall sample mean can be computed by using equation (13.5). For the data in Table 13.1 we obtained the following result.

$$\bar{\bar{x}} = \frac{79 + 74 + 66}{3} = 73$$

If the null hypothesis is true ($\mu_1 = \mu_2 = \mu_3 = \mu$), the overall sample mean of 73 is the best estimate of the population mean $\mu$.

## Between-Treatments Estimate of Population Variance

In the preceding section, we introduced the concept of a between-treatments estimate of $\sigma^2$ and showed how to compute it when the sample sizes were equal. This estimate of $\sigma^2$ is called the *mean square due to treatments* and is denoted MSTR. The general formula for computing MSTR is

$$\text{MSTR} = \frac{\sum_{j=1}^{k} n_j (\bar{x}_j - \bar{\bar{x}})^2}{k - 1} \tag{13.6}$$

The numerator in equation (13.6) is called the *sum of squares due to treatments* and is denoted SSTR. The denominator, $k - 1$, represents the degrees of freedom associated with SSTR. Hence, the mean square due to treatments can be computed by the following formula.

---

**MEAN SQUARE DUE TO TREATMENTS**

$$\text{MSTR} = \frac{\text{SSTR}}{k - 1} \tag{13.7}$$

where

$$\text{SSTR} = \sum_{j=1}^{k} n_j (\bar{x}_j - \bar{\bar{x}})^2 \tag{13.8}$$

---

If $H_0$ is true, MSTR provides an unbiased estimate of $\sigma^2$. However, if the means of the $k$ populations are not equal, MSTR is not an unbiased estimate of $\sigma^2$; in fact, in that case, MSTR should overestimate $\sigma^2$.

For the NCP data in Table 13.1, we obtain the following results.

$$\text{SSTR} = \sum_{j=1}^{k} n_j (\bar{x}_j - \bar{\bar{x}})^2 = 6(79 - 73)^2 + 6(74 - 73)^2 + 6(66 - 73)^2 = 516$$

$$\text{MSTR} = \frac{\text{SSTR}}{k - 1} = \frac{516}{2} = 258$$

## Within-Treatments Estimate of Population Variance

Earlier, we introduced the concept of a within-treatments estimate of $\sigma^2$ and showed how to compute it when the sample sizes were equal. This estimate of $\sigma^2$ is called the *mean square due to error* and is denoted MSE. The general formula for computing MSE is

$$\text{MSE} = \frac{\sum_{j=1}^{k} (n_j - 1) s_j^2}{n_T - k} \tag{13.9}$$

The numerator in equation (13.9) is called the *sum of squares due to error* and is denoted SSE. The denominator of MSE is referred to as the degrees of freedom associated with SSE. Hence, the formula for MSE can also be stated as follows.

---

**MEAN SQUARE DUE TO ERROR**

$$\text{MSE} = \frac{\text{SSE}}{n_T - k} \tag{13.10}$$

where

$$\text{SSE} = \sum_{j=1}^{k} (n_j - 1) s_j^2 \tag{13.11}$$

---

Note that MSE is based on the variation within each of the treatments; it is not influenced by whether the null hypothesis is true. Thus, MSE always provides an unbiased estimate of $\sigma^2$.

For the NCP data in Table 13.1 we obtain the following results.

$$\text{SSE} = \sum_{j=1}^{k}(n_j - 1)s_j^2 = (6 - 1)34 + (6 - 1)20 + (6 - 1)32 = 430$$

$$\text{MSE} = \frac{\text{SSE}}{n_T - k} = \frac{430}{18 - 3} = \frac{430}{15} = 28.67$$

## Comparing the Variance Estimates: The $F$ Test

*An introduction to the F distribution and the use of the F distribution table were presented in Section 11.2.*

If the null hypothesis is true, MSTR and MSW provide two independent, unbiased estimates of $\sigma^2$. Based on the material covered in Chapter 11 we know that for normal populations, the sampling distribution of the ratio of two independent estimates of $\sigma^2$ follows an $F$ distribution. Hence, if the null hypothesis is true and the ANOVA assumptions are valid, the sampling distribution of MSTR/MSE is an $F$ distribution with numerator degrees of freedom equal to $k - 1$ and denominator degrees of freedom equal to $n_T - k$. In other words, if the null hypothesis is true, the value of MSTR/MSE should appear to have been selected from this $F$ distribution.

However, if the null hypothesis is false the value of MSTR/MSE will be inflated because MSTR overestimates $\sigma^2$. Hence, we will reject $H_0$ if the resulting value of MSTR/MSE appears to be too large to have been selected from an $F$ distribution with $k - 1$ numerator degrees of freedom and $n_T - k$ denominator degrees of freedom. Because the decision to reject $H_0$ is based on the value of MSTR/MSE, the test statistic used to test for the equality of $k$ population means is as follows.

TEST STATISTIC FOR THE EQUALITY OF $k$ POPULATION MEANS

$$F = \frac{\text{MSTR}}{\text{MSE}} \qquad \qquad (13.12)$$

The test statistic follows an $F$ distribution with $k - 1$ degrees of freedom in the numerator and $n_T - k$ degrees of freedom in the denominator.

Let us return to the National Computer Products example and use a level of significance $\alpha = .05$ to conduct the hypothesis test. The value of the test statistic is

$$F = \frac{\text{MSTR}}{\text{MSE}} = \frac{258}{28.67} = 9$$

The numerator degrees of freedom is $k - 1 = 3 - 1 = 2$ and the denominator degrees of freedom is $n_T - k = 18 - 3 = 15$. Because we will only reject the null hypothesis for large values of the test statistic, the $p$-value is the upper tail area of the $F$ distribution to the right of the test statistic $F = 9$. Figure 13.3 shows the sampling distribution of $F = \text{MSTR/MSE}$, the value of the test statistic, and the upper tail area that is the $p$-value for the hypothesis test.

From Table 4 of Appendix B we find the following areas in the upper tail of an $F$ distribution with 2 numerator degrees of freedom and 15 denominator degrees of freedom.

| Area in Upper Tail | .10 | .05 | .025 | .01 |
|---|---|---|---|---|
| $F$ Value (df$_1$ = 2, df$_2$ = 15) | 2.70 | 3.68 | 4.77 | 6.36 |

$F = 9$

**FIGURE 13.3**   COMPUTATION OF $p$-VALUE USING THE SAMPLING DISTRIBUTION
OF MSTR/MSE

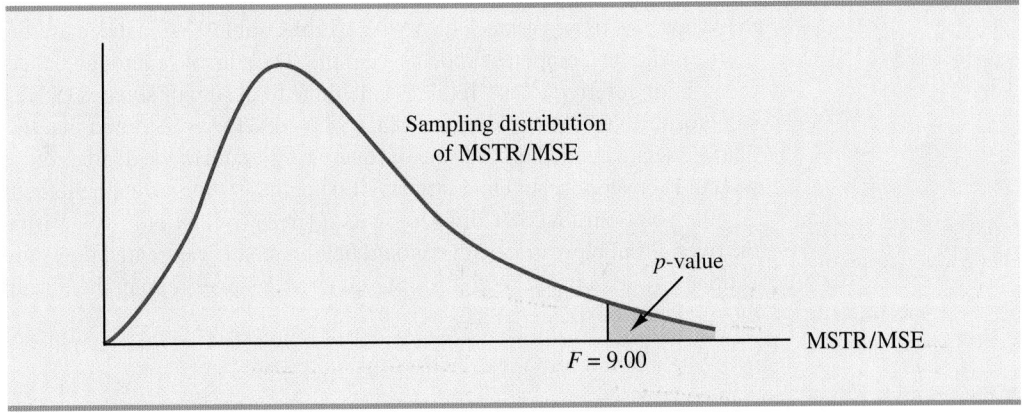

Because $F = 9$ is greater than 6.36, the area in the upper tail at $F = 9$ is less than .01. Thus, the $p$-value is less than .01. With $p$-value $\le \alpha = .05$, $H_0$ is rejected. The test provides sufficient evidence to conclude that the means of the three populations are not equal. In other words, analysis of variance supports the conclusion that the population mean examination scores at the three NCP plants are not equal.

Because the $F$ table only provides values for upper tail areas of .10, .05, .025, and .01, we cannot determine the exact $p$-value directly from the table. Minitab or Excel provide the $p$-value as part of the standard ANOVA output. Appendixes 13.1 and 13.2 show the procedures that can be used. For the NCP example, the exact $p$-value corresponding to the test statistic $F = 9$ is .003.

As with other hypothesis testing procedures, the critical value approach may also be used. With $\alpha = .05$, the critical $F$ value occurs with an area of .05 in the upper tail of an $F$ distribution with 2 and 15 degrees of freedom. From the $F$ distribution table, we find $F_{.05} = 3.68$. Hence, the appropriate upper tail rejection rule for the NCP example is

$$\text{Reject } H_0 \text{ if } F \ge 3.68$$

With $F = 9$, we reject $H_0$ and conclude that the means of the three populations are not equal. A summary of the overall procedure for testing for the equality of $k$ population means follows.

TEST FOR THE EQUALITY OF $k$ POPULATION MEANS

$$H_0: \mu_1 = \mu_2 = \cdots = \mu_k$$
$$H_a: \text{Not all population means are equal}$$

TEST STATISTIC

$$F = \frac{\text{MSTR}}{\text{MSE}}$$

REJECTION RULE

$p$-value approach:       Reject $H_0$ if $p$-value $\le \alpha$

Critical value approach:    Reject $H_0$ if $F \ge F_\alpha$

where the value of $F_\alpha$ is based on an $F$ distribution with $k - 1$ numerator degrees of freedom and $n_T - k$ denominator degrees of freedom.

## ANOVA Table

The results of the preceding calculations can be displayed conveniently in a table referred to as the analysis of variance or **ANOVA table**. Table 13.2 is the analysis of variance table for the National Computer Products example. The sum of squares associated with the source of variation referred to as "Total" is called the total sum of squares (SST). Note that the results for the NCP example suggest that SST = SSTR + SSE, and that the degrees of freedom associated with this total sum of squares is the sum of the degrees of freedom associated with the between-treatments estimate of $\sigma^2$ and the within-treatments estimate of $\sigma^2$.

We point out that SST divided by its degrees of freedom $n_T - 1$ is nothing more than the overall sample variance that would be obtained if we treated the entire set of 18 observations as one data set. With the entire data set as one sample, the formula for computing the total sum of squares, SST, is

$$\text{SST} = \sum_{j=1}^{k} \sum_{i=1}^{n_j} (x_{ij} - \bar{\bar{x}})^2 \tag{13.13}$$

It can be shown that the results we observed for the analysis of variance table for the NCP example also apply to other problems. That is,

$$\text{SST} = \text{SSTR} + \text{SSE} \tag{13.14}$$

*Analysis of variance can be thought of as a statistical procedure for partitioning the total sum of squares into separate components.*

In other words, SST can be partitioned into two sums of squares: the sum of squares due to treatments and the sum of squares due to error. Note also that the degrees of freedom corresponding to SST, $n_T - 1$, can be partitioned into the degrees of freedom corresponding to SSTR, $k - 1$, and the degrees of freedom corresponding to SSE, $n_T - k$. The analysis of variance can be viewed as the process of **partitioning** the total sum of squares and the degrees of freedom into their corresponding sources: treatments and error. Dividing the sum of squares by the appropriate degrees of freedom provides the variance estimates and the $F$ value used to test the hypothesis of equal population means.

## Computer Results for Analysis of Variance

Because of the widespread availability of statistical computer packages, analysis of variance computations with large sample sizes or a large number of populations can be performed easily. In Figure 13.4 we show output for the NCP example obtained from the Minitab computer package. The first part of the computer output contains the familiar ANOVA table format. Comparing Figure 13.4 with Table 13.2, we see that the same information is available, although some of the headings are slightly different. The heading

**TABLE 13.2**   ANALYSIS OF VARIANCE TABLE FOR THE NCP EXAMPLE

| Source of Variation | Sum of Squares | Degrees of Freedom | Mean Square | $F$ |
|---|---|---|---|---|
| Treatments | 516 | 2 | 258.00 | 9.00 |
| Error | 430 | 15 | 28.67 | |
| Total | 946 | 17 | | |

**FIGURE 13.4    MINITAB OUTPUT FOR THE NCP ANALYSIS OF VARIANCE**

```
Analysis of Variance
Source     DF       SS       MS        F        p
Factor      2     516.0    258.0     9.00     0.003
Error      15     430.0     28.7
Total      17     946.0
                                  Individual 95% Cis For Mean
                                  Based on Pooled StDev
 Level      N      Mean     StDev   ---+---------+---------+---------+---
 Atlanta    6     79.000    5.831                          (-----*-----)
 Dallas     6     74.000    4.472                 (-----*-----)
 Seattle    6     66.000    5.657    (-----*-----)
                                  ---+---------+---------+---------+---
 Pooled StDev =    5.354         63.0      70.0      77.0      84.0
```

Source is used for the source of variation column, and Factor identifies the treatments row. The sum of squares and degrees of freedom columns are interchanged, and a $p$-value is provided for the $F$ test. Thus, at the $\alpha = .05$ level of significance, we reject $H_0$ because the $p$ value $= 0.003 < \alpha = .05$.

Note that following the ANOVA table the computer output contains the respective sample sizes, the sample means, and the standard deviations. In addition, Minitab provides a figure that shows individual 95% confidence interval estimates of each population mean. In developing these confidence interval estimates, Minitab uses MSE as the estimate of $\sigma^2$. Thus, the square root of MSE provides the best estimate of the population standard deviation $\sigma$. This estimate of $\sigma$ on the computer output is Pooled StDev; it is equal to 5.354. To provide an illustration of how these interval estimates are developed, we will compute a 95% confidence interval estimate of the population mean for the Atlanta plant.

From our study of interval estimation in Chapter 8, we know that the general form of an interval estimate of a population mean is

$$\bar{x} \pm t_{\alpha/2}\frac{s}{\sqrt{n}} \tag{13.15}$$

where $s$ is the estimate of the population standard deviation $\sigma$. In the analysis of variance the best estimate of $\sigma$ is provided by the square root of MSE or the Pooled StDev, therefore we use a value of 5.354 for $s$ in expression (13.15). The degrees of freedom for the $t$ value is 15, the degrees of freedom associated with the within-treatments estimate of $\sigma^2$. Hence, with $t_{.025} = 2.131$ we obtain

$$79 \pm 2.131\frac{5.354}{\sqrt{6}} = 79 \pm 4.66$$

Thus, the individual 95% confidence interval for the Atlanta plant goes from $79 - 4.66 = 74.34$ to $79 + 4.66 = 83.66$. Because the sample sizes are equal for the NCP example, the individual confidence intervals for the Dallas and Seattle plants are also constructed by adding and subtracting 4.66 from each sample mean. Thus, in the figure provided by Minitab we see that the widths of the confidence intervals are the same.

## NOTES AND COMMENTS

**1.** The overall sample mean can also be computed as a weighted average of the $k$ sample means.

$$\bar{\bar{x}} = \frac{n_1 \bar{x}_1 + n_2 \bar{x}_2 + \cdots + n_k \bar{x}_k}{n_T}$$

In problems where the sample means are provided, this formula is simpler than equation (13.3) for computing the overall mean.

**2.** If each sample consists of $n$ observations, equation (13.6) can be written as

$$\text{MSTR} = \frac{n \sum\limits_{j=1}^{k} (\bar{x}_j - \bar{\bar{x}})^2}{k-1} = n \left[ \frac{\sum\limits_{j=1}^{k} (\bar{x}_j - \bar{\bar{x}})^2}{k-1} \right]$$
$$= n s_{\bar{x}}^2$$

Note that this result is the same as presented in Section 13.1 when we introduced the concept of the between-treatments estimate of $\sigma^2$. Equation (13.6) is simply a generalization of this result to the unequal sample-size case.

**3.** If each sample has $n$ observations, $n_T = kn$; thus, $n_T - k = k(n - 1)$, and equation (13.9) can be rewritten as

$$\text{MSE} = \frac{\sum\limits_{j=1}^{k} (n-1) s_j^2}{k(n-1)} = \frac{(n-1) \sum\limits_{j=1}^{k} s_j^2}{k(n-1)} = \frac{\sum\limits_{j=1}^{k} s_j^2}{k}$$

In other words, if the sample sizes are the same, MSE is just the average of the $k$ sample variances. Note that it is the same result we used in Section 13.1 when we introduced the concept of the within-treatments estimate of $\sigma^2$.

**4.** Confidence interval estimates for each of the $k$ population means can be developed using

$$\bar{x} \pm t_{\alpha/2} \frac{\sqrt{\text{MSE}}}{\sqrt{n}}$$

The degrees of freedom for the $t$ value are the degrees of freedom associated with the within-treatments estimate of $\sigma^2$.

## Exercises

## Methods

1. Five observations were selected from each of three populations. The data obtained follow.

| Observation | Sample 1 | Sample 2 | Sample 3 |
|---|---|---|---|
| 1 | 32 | 44 | 33 |
| 2 | 30 | 43 | 36 |
| 3 | 30 | 44 | 35 |
| 4 | 26 | 46 | 36 |
| 5 | 32 | 48 | 40 |
| Sample mean | 30 | 45 | 36 |
| Sample variance | 6.00 | 4.00 | 6.50 |

a. Compute the between-treatments estimate of $\sigma^2$.
b. Compute the within-treatments estimate of $\sigma^2$.
c. At the $\alpha = .05$ level of significance, can we reject the null hypothesis that the means of the three populations are equal?
d. Set up the ANOVA table for this problem.

2. Four observations were selected from each of three populations. The data obtained follow.

| Observation | Sample 1 | Sample 2 | Sample 3 |
|---|---|---|---|
| 1 | 165 | 174 | 169 |
| 2 | 149 | 164 | 154 |

| Observation | Sample 1 | Sample 2 | Sample 3 |
|---|---|---|---|
| 3 | 156 | 180 | 161 |
| 4 | 142 | 158 | 148 |
| Sample mean | 153 | 169 | 158 |
| Sample variance | 96.67 | 97.33 | 82.00 |

   a.   Compute the between-treatments estimate of $\sigma^2$.
   b.   Compute the within-treatments estimate of $\sigma^2$.
   c.   At the $\alpha = .05$ level of significance, can we reject the null hypothesis that the three population means are equal? Explain.
   d.   Set up the ANOVA table for this problem.

3.   Samples were selected from three populations. The data obtained follow.

| | Sample 1 | Sample 2 | Sample 3 |
|---|---|---|---|
| | 93 | 77 | 88 |
| | 98 | 87 | 75 |
| | 107 | 84 | 73 |
| | 102 | 95 | 84 |
| | | 85 | 75 |
| | | 82 | |
| $\bar{x}_j$ | 100 | 85 | 79 |
| $s_j^2$ | 35.33 | 35.60 | 43.50 |

   a.   Compute the between-treatments estimate of $\sigma^2$.
   b.   Compute the within-treatments estimate of $\sigma^2$.
   c.   At the $\alpha = .05$ level of significance, can we reject the null hypothesis that the three population means are equal? Explain.
   d.   Set up the ANOVA table for this problem.

4.   A random sample of 16 observations was selected from each of four populations. A portion of the ANOVA table follows.

| Source of Variation | Sum of Squares | Degrees of Freedom | Mean Square | F |
|---|---|---|---|---|
| Treatments | | | 400 | |
| Error | | | | |
| Total | 1500 | | | |

   a.   Provide the missing entries for the ANOVA table.
   b.   At the $\alpha = .05$ level of significance, can we reject the null hypothesis that the means of the four populations are equal?

5.   Random samples of 25 observations were selected from each of three populations. For these data, SSTR = 120 and SSE = 216.
   a.   Set up the ANOVA table for this problem.
   b.   At the $\alpha = .05$ level of significance, can we reject the null hypothesis that the three population means are equal?

## Applications

6. To test whether the mean time needed to mix a batch of material is the same for machines produced by three manufacturers, the Jacobs Chemical Company obtained the following data on the time (in minutes) needed to mix the material. Use these data to test whether the population mean times for mixing a batch of material differ for the three manufacturers. Use $\alpha = .05$.

| Manufacturer | | |
|---|---|---|
| **1** | **2** | **3** |
| 20 | 28 | 20 |
| 26 | 26 | 19 |
| 24 | 31 | 23 |
| 22 | 27 | 22 |

7. Managers at all levels of an organization need adequate information to perform their respective tasks. One study investigated the effect the source has on the dissemination of information. In this particular study the sources of information were a superior, a peer, and a subordinate. In each case, a measure of dissemination was obtained, with higher values indicating greater dissemination of information. Use $\alpha = .05$ and the following data to test whether the source of information significantly affects dissemination. What is your conclusion, and what does it suggest about the use and dissemination of information?

| **Superior** | **Peer** | **Subordinate** |
|---|---|---|
| 8 | 6 | 6 |
| 5 | 6 | 5 |
| 4 | 7 | 7 |
| 6 | 5 | 4 |
| 6 | 3 | 3 |
| 7 | 4 | 5 |
| 5 | 7 | 7 |
| 5 | 6 | 5 |

8. A study investigated the perception of corporate ethical values among individuals specializing in marketing. Use $\alpha = .05$ and the following data (higher scores indicate higher ethical values) to test for significant differences in perception among the three groups.

| **Marketing Managers** | **Marketing Research** | **Advertising** |
|---|---|---|
| 6 | 5 | 6 |
| 5 | 5 | 7 |
| 4 | 4 | 6 |
| 5 | 4 | 5 |
| 6 | 5 | 6 |
| 4 | 4 | 6 |

9. A study reported in the *Journal of Small Business Management* concluded that self-employed individuals experience higher job stress than individuals who are not self-employed. In this study job stress was assessed with a 15-item scale designed to measure various aspects of ambiguity and role conflict. Ratings for each of the 15 items were made using a scale with 1–5 response options ranging from strong agreement to strong disagreement. The sum of the ratings for the 15 items for each individual surveyed is between

15 and 75, with higher values indicating a higher degree of job stress. Suppose that a similar approach, using a 20-item scale with 1–5 response options, was used to measure the job stress of individuals for 15 randomly selected real estate agents, 15 architects, and 15 stockbrokers. The results obtained follow.

**CD file**

**Stress**

| Real Estate Agent | Architect | Stockbroker |
|:---:|:---:|:---:|
| 81 | 43 | 65 |
| 48 | 63 | 48 |
| 68 | 60 | 57 |
| 69 | 52 | 91 |
| 54 | 54 | 70 |
| 62 | 77 | 67 |
| 76 | 68 | 83 |
| 56 | 57 | 75 |
| 61 | 61 | 53 |
| 65 | 80 | 71 |
| 64 | 50 | 54 |
| 69 | 37 | 72 |
| 83 | 73 | 65 |
| 85 | 84 | 58 |
| 75 | 58 | 58 |

Use $\alpha = .05$ to test for any significant difference in job stress among the three professions.

10. *Condé Nast Traveler* conducts an annual survey in which readers rate their favorite cruise ships. Ratings are provided for small ships (carrying up to 500 passengers), medium ships (carrying 500 to 1,500 passengers), and large ships (carrying a minimum of 1,500 passengers). The following data show the service ratings for eight randomly selected small ships, eight randomly selected medium ships, and eight randomly selected large ships. All ships are rated on a 100-point scale, with higher values indicating better service (*Condé Nast Traveler,* February 2003).

**CD file**

**Ships**

| Small Ships | | Medium Ships | | Large Ships | |
|---|---|---|---|---|---|
| **Name** | **Rating** | **Name** | **Rating** | **Name** | **Rating** |
| Hanseactic | 90.5 | Amsterdam | 91.1 | Century | 89.2 |
| Mississippi Queen | 78.2 | Crystal Symphony | 98.9 | Disney Wonder | 90.2 |
| Philae | 92.3 | Maasdam | 94.2 | Enchantment of the Seas | 85.9 |
| Royal Clipper | 95.7 | Noordam | 84.3 | Grand Princess | 84.2 |
| Seabourn Pride | 94.1 | Royal Princess | 84.8 | Infinity | 90.2 |
| Seabourn Spirit | 100 | Ryndam | 89.2 | Legend of the Seas | 80.6 |
| Silver Cloud | 91.8 | Statendam | 86.4 | Paradise | 75.8 |
| Silver Wind | 95 | Veendam | 88.3 | Sun Princess | 82.3 |

Use $\alpha = .05$ to test for any significant difference in the mean service ratings among the three sizes of cruise ships.

## 13.3  Multiple Comparison Procedures

When we use analysis of variance to test whether the means of *k* populations are equal, rejection of the null hypothesis allows us to conclude only that the population means are *not all equal.* In some cases we will want to go a step further and determine where the differences among means occur. The purpose of this section is to introduce two **multiple comparison procedures** that can be used to conduct statistical comparisons between pairs of population means.

## Fisher's LSD

Suppose that analysis of variance provides statistical evidence to reject the null hypothesis of equal population means. In this case, Fisher's least significant difference (LSD) procedure can be used to determine where the differences occur. To illustrate the use of Fisher's LSD procedure in making pairwise comparisons of population means, recall the NCP example introduced in Section 13.1. Using analysis of variance, we concluded that the population mean examination scores are not the same at the three plants. In this case, the follow-up question is: We believe the plants differ, but where do the differences occur? That is, do the means of populations 1 and 2 differ? Or those of populations 1 and 3? Or those of populations 2 and 3?

In Chapter 10 we presented a statistical procedure for testing the hypothesis that the means of two populations are equal. With a slight modification in how we estimate the population variance, Fisher's LSD procedure is based on the $t$ test statistic presented for the two-population case. The following table summarizes Fisher's LSD procedure.

FISHER'S LSD PROCEDURE

$$H_0: \mu_i = \mu_j$$
$$H_a: \mu_i \neq \mu_j$$

TEST STATISTIC

$$t = \frac{\bar{x}_i - \bar{x}_j}{\sqrt{MSE\left(\frac{1}{n_i} + \frac{1}{n_j}\right)}} \qquad (13.16)$$

REJECTION RULE

$p$-value approach:         Reject $H_0$ if $p$-value $\leq \alpha$
Critical value approach:   Reject $H_0$ if $t \leq -t_{\alpha/2}$ or $t \geq t_{\alpha/2}$

where the value of $t_{\alpha/2}$ is based on a $t$ distribution with $n_T - k$ degrees of freedom.

Let us now apply this procedure to determine whether there is a significant difference between the means of population 1 (Atlanta) and population 2 (Dallas) at the $\alpha = .05$ level of significance. Table 13.1 shows that the sample mean is 79 for the Atlanta plant and 74 for the Dallas plant. Table 13.2 shows that the value of MSE is 28.67; it is the estimate of $\sigma^2$ and is based on 15 degrees of freedom. For the NCP data the value of the test statistic is

$$t = \frac{79 - 74}{\sqrt{28.67\left(\frac{1}{6} + \frac{1}{6}\right)}} = 1.62$$

The $t$ distribution table (Table 2 in Appendix B) shows that with 15 degrees of freedom $t = 1.341$ for an area of .10 in the upper tail and $t = 1.753$ for an area of .05 in the upper tail. Because the test statistic $t = 1.62$ is between 1.341 and 1.753, we know that the area in the upper tail must be between .05 and .10. Because this test is a two-tailed test, we double these values to conclude that the $p$-value is between .10 and .20. Minitab or Excel can be used to show that the $p$-value corresponding to $t = 1.62$ is .1261. Because the $p$-value is greater than $\alpha = .05$, we cannot reject the null hypothesis. Hence, we cannot conclude that the population mean score at the Atlanta plant is different from the population mean score at the Dallas plant.

Many practitioners find it easier to determine how large the difference between the sample means must be to reject $H_0$. In this case the test statistic is $\bar{x}_i - \bar{x}_j$, and the test is conducted by the following procedure.

---

**FISHER'S LSD PROCEDURE BASED ON THE TEST STATISTIC $\bar{x}_i - \bar{x}_j$**

$$H_0: \mu_i = \mu_j$$
$$H_a: \mu_i \neq \mu_j$$

TEST STATISTIC

$$\bar{x}_i - \bar{x}_j$$

REJECTION RULE AT A LEVEL OF SIGNIFICANCE $\alpha$

$$\text{Reject } H_0 \text{ if } |\bar{x}_i - \bar{x}_j| > \text{LSD}$$

where

$$\text{LSD} = t_{\alpha/2}\sqrt{\text{MSE}\left(\frac{1}{n_i} + \frac{1}{n_j}\right)} \qquad (13.17)$$

---

For the NCP example the value of LSD is

$$\text{LSD} = 2.131\sqrt{28.67\left(\frac{1}{6} + \frac{1}{6}\right)} = 6.59$$

Note that when the sample sizes are equal, only one value for LSD is computed. In such cases we can simply compare the magnitude of the difference between any two sample means with the value of LSD. For example, the difference between the sample means for population 1 (Atlanta) and population 3 (Seattle) is $79 - 66 = 13$. This difference is greater than 6.59, which means we can reject the null hypothesis that the population mean examination score for the Atlanta plant is equal to the population mean score for the Seattle plant. Similarly, with the difference between the sample means for populations 2 and 3 of $74 - 66 = 8 > 6.59$, we can also reject the hypothesis that the population mean examination score for the Dallas plant is equal to the population mean examination score for the Seattle plant. In effect, our conclusion is that the Atlanta and Dallas plants both differ from the Seattle plant.

Fisher's LSD can also be used to develop a confidence interval estimate of the difference between the means of two populations. The general procedure follows.

---

**CONFIDENCE INTERVAL ESTIMATE OF THE DIFFERENCE BETWEEN TWO POPULATION MEANS USING FISHER'S LSD PROCEDURE**

$$\bar{x}_i - \bar{x}_j \pm \text{LSD} \tag{13.18}$$

where

$$\text{LSD} = t_{\alpha/2}\sqrt{\text{MSE}\left(\frac{1}{n_i} + \frac{1}{n_j}\right)} \tag{13.19}$$

and $t_{\alpha/2}$ is based on a $t$ distribution with $n_T - k$ degrees of freedom.

---

If the confidence interval in expression (13.18) includes the value zero, we cannot reject the hypothesis that the two population means are equal. However, if the confidence interval does not include the value zero, we conclude that there is a difference between the population means. For the NCP example, recall that LSD = 6.59 (corresponding to $t_{.025} = 2.131$). Thus, a 95% confidence interval estimate of the difference between the means of populations 1 and 2 is $79 - 74 \pm 6.59 = 5 \pm 6.59 = -1.59$ to 11.59; because this interval includes zero, we cannot reject the hypothesis that the two population means are equal.

## Type I Error Rates

We began the discussion of Fisher's LSD procedure with the premise that analysis of variance gave us statistical evidence to reject the null hypothesis of equal population means. We showed how Fisher's LSD procedure can be used in such cases to determine where the differences occur. Technically, it is referred to as a *protected* or *restricted* LSD test because it is employed only if we first find a significant $F$ value by using analysis of variance. To see why this distinction is important in multiple comparison tests, we need to explain the difference between a *comparisonwise* Type I error rate and an *experimentwise* Type I error rate.

In the NCP example we used Fisher's LSD procedure to make three pairwise comparisons.

| **Test 1** | **Test 2** | **Test 3** |
|---|---|---|
| $H_0: \mu_1 = \mu_2$ | $H_0: \mu_1 = \mu_3$ | $H_0: \mu_2 = \mu_3$ |
| $H_a: \mu_1 \neq \mu_2$ | $H_a: \mu_1 \neq \mu_3$ | $H_a: \mu_2 \neq \mu_3$ |

In each case, we used a level of significance of $\alpha = .05$. Therefore, for each test, if the null hypothesis is true, the probability that we will make a Type I error is $\alpha = .05$; hence, the probability that we will not make a Type I error on each test is $1 - .05 = .95$. In discussing multiple comparison procedures we refer to this probability of a Type I error ($\alpha = .05$) as the **comparisonwise Type I error rate**; comparisonwise Type I error rates indicate the level of significance associated with a single pairwise comparison.

Let us now consider a slightly different question. What is the probability that in making three pairwise comparisons, we will commit a Type I error on at least one of the three tests? To answer this question, note that the probability that we will not make a Type I error on any of the three tests is $(.95)(.95)(.95) = .8574$.* Therefore, the probability of making at least one Type I error is $1 - .8574 = .1426$. Thus, when we use Fisher's LSD procedure to make all three pairwise comparisons, the Type I error rate associated with this approach is not .05, but actually .1426; we refer to this error rate as the *overall* or **experimentwise Type I error rate**. To avoid confusion, we denote the experimentwise Type I error rate as $\alpha_{EW}$.

The experimentwise Type I error rate gets larger for problems with more populations. For example, a problem with five populations has 10 possible pairwise comparisons. If we tested all possible pairwise comparisons by using Fisher's LSD with a comparisonwise error rate of $\alpha = .05$, the experimentwise Type I error rate would be $1 - (1 - .05)^{10} = .40$. In such cases, practitioners look to alternatives that provide better control over the experimentwise error rate.

One alternative for controlling the overall experimentwise error rate, referred to as the Bonferroni adjustment, involves using a smaller comparisonwise error rate for each test. For example, if we want to test $C$ pairwise comparisons and want the maximum probability of making a Type I error for the overall experiment to be $\alpha_{EW}$, we simply use a comparisonwise error rate equal to $\alpha_{EW}/C$. In the NCP example, if we want to use Fisher's LSD procedure to test all three pairwise comparisons with a maximum experimentwise error rate of $\alpha_{EW} = .05$, we set the comparisonwise error rate to be $\alpha = .05/3 = .017$. For a problem with five populations and 10 possible pairwise comparisons, the Bonferroni adjustment would suggest a comparisonwise error rate of $.05/10 = .005$. Recall from our discussion of hypothesis testing in Chapter 9 that for a fixed sample size, any decrease in the probability of making a Type I error will result in an increase in the probability of making a Type II error, which corresponds to accepting the hypothesis that the two population means are equal when in fact they are not equal. As a result, many practitioners are reluctant to perform individual tests with a low comparisonwise Type I error rate because of the increased risk of making a Type II error.

Several other procedures, such as Tukey's procedure and Duncan's multiple range test, have been developed to help in such situations. However, there is considerable controversy in the statistical community as to which procedure is "best." The truth is that no one procedure is best for all types of problems.

## Exercises

## Methods

11.   In exercise 1, five observations were selected from each of three populations. For these data, $\bar{x}_1 = 30$, $\bar{x}_2 = 45$, $\bar{x}_3 = 36$, and MSE = 5.5. At the $\alpha = .05$ level of significance, the null hypothesis of equal population means was rejected. In the following calculations, use $\alpha = .05$.

   a.   Use Fisher's LSD procedure to test whether there is a significant difference between the means of populations 1 and 2, populations 1 and 3, and populations 2 and 3.

   b.   Use Fisher's LSD procedure to develop a 95% confidence interval estimate of the difference between the means of populations 1 and 2.

---

*The assumption is that the three tests are independent, and hence the joint probability of the three events can be obtained by simply multiplying the individual probabilities. In fact, the three tests are not independent because MSE is used in each test; therefore, the error involved is even greater than that shown.

12. Four observations were selected from each of three populations. The data obtained are shown. In the following calculations, use $\alpha = .05$.

|  | Sample 1 | Sample 2 | Sample 3 |
|---|---|---|---|
|  | 63 | 82 | 69 |
|  | 47 | 72 | 54 |
|  | 54 | 88 | 61 |
|  | 40 | 66 | 48 |
| $\bar{x}_j$ | 51 | 77 | 58 |
| $s_j^2$ | 96.67 | 97.34 | 81.99 |

a. Use analysis of variance to test for a significant difference among the means of the three populations.
b. Use Fisher's LSD procedure to see which means are different.

## Applications

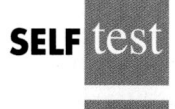

13. Refer to exercise 6. At the $\alpha = .05$ level of significance, use Fisher's LSD procedure to test for the equality of the means for manufacturers 1 and 3. What conclusion can you draw after carrying out this test?

14. Refer to exercise 13. Use Fisher's LSD procedure to develop a 95% confidence interval estimate of the difference between the means of population 1 and population 2.

15. Refer to exercise 8. At the $\alpha = .05$ level of significance, we can conclude that there are differences in the perceptions for marketing managers, marketing research specialists, and advertising specialists. Use the procedures in this section to determine where the differences occur. Use $\alpha = .05$.

16. To test for any significant difference in the number of hours between breakdowns for four machines, the following data were obtained.

| Machine 1 | Machine 2 | Machine 3 | Machine 4 |
|---|---|---|---|
| 6.4 | 8.7 | 11.1 | 9.9 |
| 7.8 | 7.4 | 10.3 | 12.8 |
| 5.3 | 9.4 | 9.7 | 12.1 |
| 7.4 | 10.1 | 10.3 | 10.8 |
| 8.4 | 9.2 | 9.2 | 11.3 |
| 7.3 | 9.8 | 8.8 | 11.5 |

a. At the $\alpha = .05$ level of significance, what is the difference, if any, in the population mean times among the four machines?
b. Use Fisher's LSD procedure to test for the equality of the means for machines 2 and 4. Use a .05 level of significance.

17. Refer to exercise 16. Use the Bonferroni adjustment to test for a significant difference between all pairs of means. Assume that a maximum overall experimentwise error rate of .05 is desired.

18. Refer to exercise 10. At the .05 level of significance, we can conclude that there are differences between the mean service ratings of small ships, medium ships, and large ships. Use the procedures in this section to determine where the differences occur. Use $\alpha = .05$.

# An Introduction to Experimental Design

*Cause-and-effect relationships can be difficult to establish in observational studies; such relationships are easier to establish in experimental studies.*

Statistical studies can be classified as being either experimental or observational. In an experimental study, variables of interest are identified. Then, one or more factors in the study are controlled so that data can be obtained about how the factors influence the variables. In *observational* or *nonexperimental* studies, no attempt is made to control the factors. A survey (see Chapter 21) is perhaps the most common type of observational study.

The NCP example that we used to introduce analysis of variance is an illustration of an observational statistical study. To measure how much NCP employees knew about total quality management, a random sample of six employees was selected from each of NCP's three plants and given a quality-awareness examination. The examination scores for these employees were then analyzed by analysis of variance to test the hypothesis that the population mean examination scores were equal for the three plants.

As an example of an experimental statistical study, let us consider the problem facing Chemitech, Inc. Chemitech developed a new filtration system for municipal water supplies. The components for the new filtration system will be purchased from several suppliers, and Chemitech will assemble the components at its plant in Columbia, South Carolina. The industrial engineering group is responsible for determining the best assembly method for the new filtration system. After considering a variety of possible approaches, the group narrows the alternatives to three: method A, method B, and method C. These methods differ in the sequence of steps used to assemble the product. Managers at Chemitech want to determine which assembly method can produce the greatest number of filtration systems per week.

In the Chemitech experiment, assembly method is the independent variable or **factor**. Because three assembly methods correspond to this factor, we say that three treatments are associated with this experiment; each **treatment** corresponds to each of the three assembly methods. The Chemitech problem is an example of a **single-factor experiment** involving a qualitative factor (method of assembly). Other experiments may consist of multiple factors; some factors may be qualitative and some may be quantitative.

The three assembly methods or treatments define the three populations of interest for the Chemitech experiment. One population is all Chemitech employees who use assembly method A, another is those who use method B, and the third is those who use method C. Note that for each population the dependent or response variable is the number of filtration systems assembled per week, and the primary statistical objective of the experiment is to determine whether the mean number of units produced per week is the same for all three populations.

*Randomization is the process of assigning the treatments to the experimental units at random. Prior to the work of Sir R. A. Fisher, treatments were assigned on a systematic or subjective basis.*

Suppose a random sample of three employees is selected from all assembly workers at the Chemitech production facility. In experimental design terminology, the three randomly selected workers are the **experimental units**. The experimental design that we will use for the Chemitech problem is called a **completely randomized design**. This type of design requires that each of the three assembly methods or treatments be assigned randomly to one of the experimental units or workers. For example, method A might be randomly assigned to the second worker, method B to the first worker, and method C to the third worker. The concept of *randomization,* as illustrated in this example, is an important principle of all experimental designs.

Note that this experiment would result in only one measurement or number of units assembled for each treatment. To obtain additional data for each assembly method, we must repeat or replicate the basic experimental process. Suppose, for example, that instead of selecting just three workers at random we selected 15 workers and then randomly assigned each of the three treatments to five of the workers. Because each method of assembly is assigned to five workers, we say that five replicates have been obtained. The process of *replication* is another important principle of experimental design. Figure 13.5 shows the completely randomized design for the Chemitech experiment.

**FIGURE 13.5**     COMPLETELY RANDOMIZED DESIGN FOR EVALUATING
THE CHEMITECH ASSEMBLY METHOD EXPERIMENT

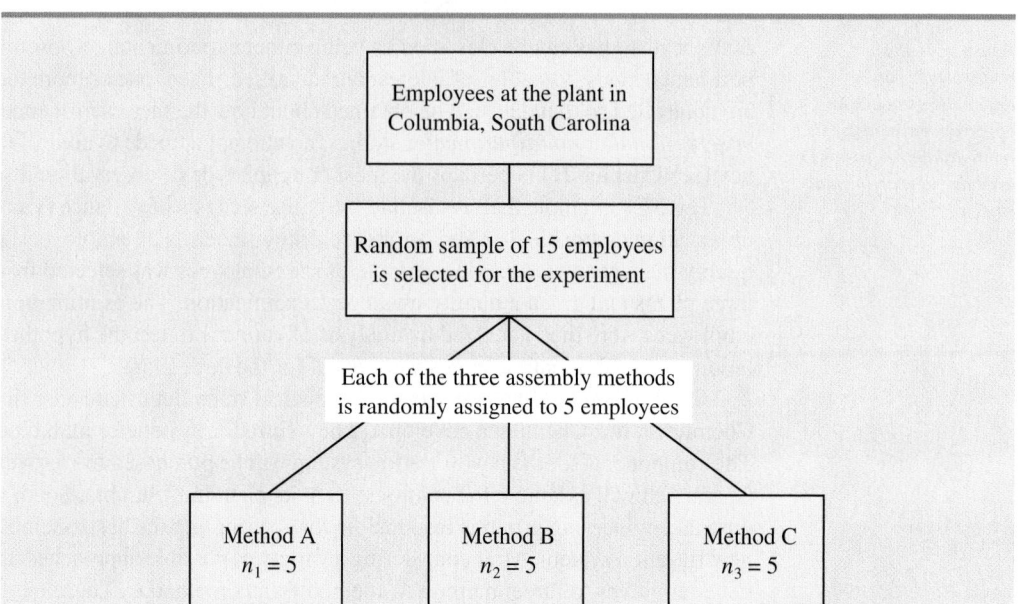

## Data Collection

Once we are satisfied with the experimental design, we proceed by collecting and analyzing the data. In the Chemitech case, the employees would be instructed in how to perform the assembly method assigned to them and then would begin assembling the new filtration systems using that method. After this assignment and training, the number of units assembled by each employee during one week is as shown in Table 13.3. The sample mean number of units produced with each of the three assembly methods is reported in the following table.

| Assembly Method | Mean Number Produced |
|-----------------|----------------------|
| A | 62 |
| B | 66 |
| C | 52 |

From these data, method B appears to result in higher production rates than either of the other methods.

The real issue is whether the three sample means observed are different enough for us to conclude that the means of the populations corresponding to the three methods of assembly are different. To write this question in statistical terms, we introduce the following notation.

$\mu_1$ = mean number of units produced per week for method A
$\mu_2$ = mean number of units produced per week for method B
$\mu_3$ = mean number of units produced per week for method C

TABLE 13.3  NUMBER OF UNITS PRODUCED BY 15 WORKERS

ChemTech

| Observation | Method | | |
|---|---|---|---|
| | A | B | C |
| 1 | 58 | 58 | 48 |
| 2 | 64 | 69 | 57 |
| 3 | 55 | 71 | 59 |
| 4 | 66 | 64 | 47 |
| 5 | 67 | 68 | 49 |
| Sample mean | 62 | 66 | 52 |
| Sample variance | 27.5 | 26.5 | 31.0 |
| Sample standard deviation | 5.24 | 5.15 | 5.57 |

Although we will never know the actual values of $\mu_1$, $\mu_2$, and $\mu_3$, we want to use the sample means to test the following hypotheses.

$$H_0: \mu_1 = \mu_2 = \mu_3$$
$$H_a: \text{Not all population means are equal}$$

The problem we face in analyzing data from a completely randomized experimental design is the same problem we faced when we first introduced analysis of variance as a method for testing whether the means of more than two populations are equal. In the next section we will show how analysis of variance is applied in problem situations such as the Chemitech assembly method experiment.

## NOTES AND COMMENTS

1. Randomization in experimental design is the analog of probability sampling in an observational study.
2. In many medical experiments, potential bias is eliminated by using a double-blind study. In such studies neither the physician applying the treatment nor the subject knows which treatment is being applied. Many other types of experiments could benefit from this type of study.

## 13.5 Completely Randomized Designs

The hypotheses we want to test when analyzing the data from a completely randomized design are exactly the same as the general form of the hypotheses we presented in Section 13.2.

$$H_0: \mu_1 = \mu_2 = \cdots = \mu_k$$
$$H_a: \text{Not all population means are equal}$$

Hence, to test for the equality of means in situations where the data are collected in a completely randomized experimental design, we can use analysis of variance as introduced in Sections 13.1 and 13.2. Recall that analysis of variance requires the calculation of two independent estimates of the population variance $\sigma^2$.

## Between-Treatments Estimate of Population Variance

The between-treatments estimate of $\sigma^2$ is referred to as the *mean square due to treatments* and is denoted MSTR. The formula for computing MSTR follows:

$$\text{MSTR} = \frac{\sum_{j=1}^{k} n_j(\bar{x}_j - \bar{\bar{x}})^2}{k-1} \tag{13.20}$$

The numerator in equation (13.20) is called the *sum of squares between* or *sum of squares due to treatments* and is denoted SSTR. The denominator $k-1$ represents the degrees of freedom associated with SSTR.

For the Chemitech data in Table 13.3, we obtain the following results (note: $\bar{\bar{x}} = 60$).

$$\text{SSTR} = \sum_{j=1}^{k} n_j(\bar{x}_j - \bar{\bar{x}})^2 = 5(62-60)^2 + 5(66-60)^2 + 5(52-60)^2 = 520$$

$$\text{MSTR} = \frac{\text{SSTR}}{k-1} = \frac{520}{3-1} = 260$$

## Within-Treatments Estimate of Population Variance

The within-treatments estimate of $\sigma^2$ is referred to as the *mean square due to error* and is denoted MSE. The formula for computing MSE follows.

$$\text{MSE} = \frac{\sum_{j=1}^{k}(n_j - 1)s_j^2}{n_T - k} \tag{13.21}$$

The numerator in equation (13.21) is called the *sum of squares within* or *sum of squares due to error* and is denoted SSE. The denominator of MSE is referred to as the degrees of freedom associated with SSE.

For the Chemitech data in Table 13.3, we obtain the following results.

$$\text{SSE} = \sum_{j=1}^{k}(n_j - 1)s_j^2 = 4(27.5) + 4(26.5) + 4(31) = 340$$

$$\text{MSE} = \frac{\text{SSE}}{n_T - k} = \frac{340}{15-3} = 28.33$$

## Comparing the Variance Estimates: The $F$ Test

If the null hypothesis is true and the ANOVA assumptions are valid, the sampling distribution of MSTR/MSE is an $F$ distribution with numerator degrees of freedom equal to $k-1$ and denominator degrees of freedom equal to $n_T - k$. Recall also that if the means of the $k$ populations are not equal, the value of MSTR/MSE will be inflated because MSTR overestimates $\sigma^2$. Hence we will reject $H_0$ if the resulting value of MSTR/MSE appears to be too large to have been selected at random from an $F$ distribution with degrees of freedom $k-1$ in the numerator and $n_T - k$ in the denominator.

Let us return to the Chemitech problem and use a level of significance $\alpha = .05$ to conduct the hypothesis test. The value of the test statistic is

$$F = \frac{\text{MSTR}}{\text{MSE}} = \frac{260}{28.33} = 9.18$$

The numerator degrees of freedom is $k - 1 = 3 - 1 = 2$ and the denominator degrees of freedom is $n_T - k = 15 - 3 = 12$. Because we will only reject the null hypothesis for large values of the test statistic, the $p$-value is the area under the $F$ distribution to the right of $F = 9.18$. From Table 4 of Appendix B we find that the $F$ value with an area of .01 in the upper tail is 6.93. Because the area in the upper tail for an $F$ value of 9.18 must be less than .01, the $p$-value for the Chemitech hypothesis test is less than .01. Alternatively, we can use Minitab or Excel to show that the exact $p$-value corresponding to $F = 9.18$ is .0038. With $p$-value $\leq \alpha = .05$, $H_0$ is rejected. The test gives us sufficient evidence to conclude that not all the population means are equal.

## ANOVA Table

We can now write the result that shows how the total sum of squares, SST, is partitioned.

$$\text{SST} = \text{SSTR} + \text{SSE} \qquad\qquad \textbf{(13.22)}$$

This result also holds true for the degrees of freedom associated with each of these sums of squares; that is, the total degrees of freedom is the sum of the degrees of freedom associated with SSTR and SSE. The general form of the ANOVA table for a completely randomized design is shown in Table 13.4; Table 13.5 is the corresponding ANOVA table for the Chemitech problem.

## Pairwise Comparisons

We can use Fisher's LSD procedure to test all possible pairwise comparisons for the Chemitech problem. At the 5% level of significance, the $t$ distribution table shows that with $n_T - k = 15 - 3 = 12$ degrees of freedom, $t_{.025} = 2.179$. Using MSE = 28.33 in equation (13.17), we obtain Fisher's least significant difference.

$$\text{LSD} = t_{\alpha/2}\sqrt{\text{MSE}\left(\frac{1}{n_i} + \frac{1}{n_j}\right)} = 2.179\sqrt{28.33\left(\frac{1}{5} + \frac{1}{5}\right)} = 7.34$$

**TABLE 13.4**   ANOVA TABLE FOR A COMPLETELY RANDOMIZED DESIGN

| Source of Variation | Sum of Squares | Degrees of Freedom | Mean Square | $F$ |
|---|---|---|---|---|
| Treatments | SSTR | $k - 1$ | $\text{MSTR} = \dfrac{\text{SSTR}}{k - 1}$ | $\dfrac{\text{MSTR}}{\text{MSE}}$ |
| Error | SSE | $n_T - k$ | $\text{MSE} = \dfrac{\text{SSE}}{n_T - k}$ | |
| Total | SST | $n_T - 1$ | | |

**TABLE 13.5**   ANOVA TABLE FOR THE CHEMITECH PROBLEM

| Source of Variation | Sum of Squares | Degrees of Freedom | Mean Square | F |
|---|---|---|---|---|
| Treatments | 520 | 2 | 260.00 | 9.18 |
| Error | 340 | 12 | 28.33 | |
| Total | 860 | 14 | | |

If the magnitude of the difference between any two sample means exceeds 7.34, we can reject the hypothesis that the corresponding population means are equal. For the Chemitech data in Table 13.3, we obtain the following results.

| Sample Differences | Significant? |
|---|---|
| Method A − Method B = 62 − 66 = −4 | No |
| Method A − Method C = 62 − 52 = 10 | Yes |
| Method B − Method C = 66 − 52 = 14 | Yes |

Thus, the difference in the population means is attributable to the difference between the means for method A and method C and the difference between the means for method B and method C. Methods A and B therefore are preferred to method C. However, more testing should be done to compare method A with method B. The current study does not provide sufficient evidence to conclude that these two methods differ.

## Exercises

## Methods

19. The following data are from a completely randomized design.

| Observation | Treatment | | |
|---|---|---|---|
| | A | B | C |
| 1 | 162 | 142 | 126 |
| 2 | 142 | 156 | 122 |
| 3 | 165 | 124 | 138 |
| 4 | 145 | 142 | 140 |
| 5 | 148 | 136 | 150 |
| 6 | 174 | 152 | 128 |
| $\bar{x}_j$ | 156 | 142 | 134 |
| $s_j^2$ | 164.4 | 131.2 | 110.4 |

   a. Compute the sum of squares between treatments.
   b. Compute the mean square between treatments.
   c. Compute the sum of squares due to error.
   d. Compute the mean square due to error.
   e. At the $\alpha = .05$ level of significance, test whether the means for the three treatments are equal.

20. Refer to exercise 19.
    a. Set up the ANOVA table.
    b. At the $\alpha = .05$ level of significance, use Fisher's least significant difference procedure to test all possible pairwise comparisons. What conclusion can you draw after carrying out this procedure?

21. In a completely randomized experimental design, seven experimental units were used for each of the five levels of the factor. Complete the following ANOVA table.

| Source of Variation | Sum of Squares | Degrees of Freedom | Mean Square | F |
|---|---|---|---|---|
| Treatments | 300 | | | |
| Error | | | | |
| Total | 460 | | | |

22. Refer to exercise 21.
    a. What hypotheses are implied in this problem?
    b. At the $\alpha = .05$ level of significance, can we reject the null hypothesis in part (a)? Explain.

23. In an experiment designed to test the output levels of three different treatments, the following results were obtained: SST = 400, SSTR = 150, $n_T = 19$. Set up the ANOVA table and test for any significant difference between the mean output levels of the three treatments. Use $\alpha = .05$.

24. In a completely randomized experimental design, 12 experimental units were used for the first treatment, 15 for the second treatment, and 20 for the third treatment. Complete the following analysis of variance. At a .05 level of significance, is there a significant difference between the treatments?

| Source of Variation | Sum of Squares | Degrees of Freedom | Mean Square | F |
|---|---|---|---|---|
| Treatments | 1200 | | | |
| Error | | | | |
| Total | 1800 | | | |

25. Develop the analysis of variance computations for the following experimental design. At $\alpha = .05$, is there a significant difference between the treatment means?

**Exer25**

| | Treatment | | |
|---|---|---|---|
| | **A** | **B** | **C** |
| | 136 | 107 | 92 |
| | 120 | 114 | 82 |
| | 113 | 125 | 85 |
| | 107 | 104 | 101 |
| | 131 | 107 | 89 |
| | 114 | 109 | 117 |
| | 129 | 97 | 110 |
| | 102 | 114 | 120 |
| | | 104 | 98 |
| | | 89 | 106 |
| $\bar{x}_j$ | 119 | 107 | 100 |
| $s_j^2$ | 146.86 | 96.44 | 173.78 |

## Applications

26. Three different methods for assembling a product were proposed by an industrial engineer. To investigate the number of units assembled correctly with each method, 30 employees were randomly selected and randomly assigned to the three proposed methods in such a way that each method was used by 10 workers. The number of units assembled correctly was recorded, and the analysis of variance procedure was applied to the resulting data set. The following results were obtained: SST = 10,800; SSTR = 4560.
   a. Set up the ANOVA table for this problem.
   b. Use $\alpha = .05$ to test for any significant difference in the means for the three assembly methods.

27. In an experiment designed to test the breaking strength of four types of cables, the following results were obtained: SST = 85.05, SSTR = 61.64, $n_T = 24$. Set up the ANOVA table and test for any significant difference in the mean breaking strength of the four cables. Use $\alpha = .05$.

28. To study the effect of temperature on yield in a chemical process, five batches were produced at each of three temperature levels. The results follow. Construct an analysis of variance table. Use a .05 level of significance to test whether the temperature level has an effect on the mean yield of the process.

| | Temperature | |
|---|---|---|
| **50°C** | **60°C** | **70°C** |
| 34 | 30 | 23 |
| 24 | 31 | 28 |
| 36 | 34 | 28 |
| 39 | 23 | 30 |
| 32 | 27 | 31 |

29. Auditors must make judgments about various aspects of an audit on the basis of their own direct experience, indirect experience, or a combination of the two. In a study, auditors were asked to make judgments about the frequency of errors to be found in an audit. The judgments by the auditors were then compared to the actual results. Suppose the following data were obtained from a similar study; lower scores indicate better judgments.

**AudJudg**

| Direct | Indirect | Combination |
|---|---|---|
| 17.0 | 16.6 | 25.2 |
| 18.5 | 22.2 | 24.0 |
| 15.8 | 20.5 | 21.5 |
| 18.2 | 18.3 | 26.8 |
| 20.2 | 24.2 | 27.5 |
| 16.0 | 19.8 | 25.8 |
| 13.3 | 21.2 | 24.2 |

Use $\alpha = .05$ to test to see whether the basis for the judgment affects the quality of the judgment. What is your conclusion?

30. Four different paints are advertised as having the same drying time. To check the manufacturer's claims, five samples were tested for each of the paints. The time in minutes until the paint was dry enough for a second coat to be applied was recorded. The following data were obtained.

**Paint**

| Paint 1 | Paint 2 | Paint 3 | Paint 4 |
|---------|---------|---------|---------|
| 128 | 144 | 133 | 150 |
| 137 | 133 | 143 | 142 |
| 135 | 142 | 137 | 135 |
| 124 | 146 | 136 | 140 |
| 141 | 130 | 131 | 153 |

At the $\alpha = .05$ level of significance, test to see whether the mean drying time is the same for each type of paint.

31. A well-known automotive magazine took three top-of-the-line midsize automobiles manufactured in the United States, test-drove them, and compared them on a variety of criteria. In the area of gasoline mileage performance, five automobiles of each brand were each test-driven 500 miles; the miles per gallon data obtained follow. Use the analysis of variance procedure with $\alpha = .05$ to determine whether there is a significant difference in the mean number of miles per gallon for the three types of automobiles.

| Automobile | | |
|---|---|---|
| A | B | C |
| 19 | 19 | 24 |
| 21 | 20 | 26 |
| 20 | 22 | 23 |
| 19 | 21 | 25 |
| 21 | 23 | 27 |

32. Refer to exercise 29. Use Fisher's least significant difference procedure to test all possible pairwise comparisons. What conclusion can you draw after carrying out this procedure? Use $\alpha = .05$.

33. Refer to exercise 31. Use Fisher's least significant difference procedure to test all possible pairwise comparisons. What conclusion can you draw after carrying out this procedure? Use $\alpha = .05$.

## (13.6) Randomized Block Design

Thus far we considered the completely randomized experimental design. Recall that to test for a difference among treatment means, we computed an $F$ value by using the ratio

$$F = \frac{\text{MSTR}}{\text{MSE}} \tag{13.23}$$

*A completely randomized design is useful when the experimental units are homogeneous. If the experimental units are heterogeneous, **blocking** is often used to form homogeneous groups.*

A problem can arise whenever differences due to extraneous factors (ones not considered in the experiment) cause the MSE term in this ratio to become large. In such cases, the $F$ value in equation (13.23) can become small, signaling no difference among treatment means when in fact such a difference exists.

In this section we present an experimental design known as a **randomized block design**. Its purpose is to control some of the extraneous sources of variation by removing such variation from the MSE term. This design tends to provide a better estimate of the true error variance and leads to a more powerful hypothesis test in terms of the ability to detect differences among treatment means. To illustrate, let us consider a stress study for air traffic controllers.

## Air Traffic Controller Stress Test

A study measuring the fatigue and stress of air traffic controllers resulted in proposals for modification and redesign of the controller's work station. After consideration of several designs for the work station, three specific alternatives are selected as having the best potential for reducing controller stress. The key question is: To what extent do the three alternatives differ in terms of their effect on controller stress? To answer this question, we need to design an experiment that will provide measurements of air traffic controller stress under each alternative.

In a completely randomized design, a random sample of controllers would be assigned to each work station alternative. However, controllers are believed to differ substantially in their ability to handle stressful situations. What is high stress to one controller might be only moderate or even low stress to another. Hence, when considering the within-group source of variation (MSE), we must realize that this variation includes both random error and error due to individual controller differences. In fact, managers expected controller variability to be a major contributor to the MSE term.

*Experimental studies in business often involve experimental units that are highly heterogeneous; as a result, randomized block designs are often employed.*

One way to separate the effect of the individual differences is to use a randomized block design. Such a design will identify the variability stemming from individual controller differences and remove it from the MSE term. The randomized block design calls for a single sample of controllers. Each controller in the sample is tested with each of the three work station alternatives. In experimental design terminology, the work station is the *factor of interest* and the controllers are the *blocks*. The three treatments or populations associated with the work station factor correspond to the three work station alternatives. For simplicity, we refer to the work station alternatives as system A, system B, and system C.

*Blocking in experimental design is similar to stratification in sampling.*

The *randomized* aspect of the randomized block design is the random order in which the treatments (systems) are assigned to the controllers. If every controller were to test the three systems in the same order, any observed difference in systems might be due to the order of the test rather than to true differences in the systems.

To provide the necessary data, the three work station alternatives were installed at the Cleveland Control Center in Oberlin, Ohio. Six controllers were selected at random and assigned to operate each of the systems. A follow-up interview and a medical examination of each controller participating in the study provided a measure of the stress for each controller on each system. The data are reported in Table 13.6.

Table 13.7 is a summary of the stress data collected. In this table we include column totals (treatments) and row totals (blocks) as well as some sample means that will be help-

**TABLE 13.6**   A RANDOMIZED BLOCK DESIGN FOR THE AIR TRAFFIC CONTROLLER STRESS TEST

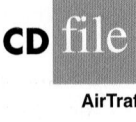

| | | Treatments | | |
| --- | --- | --- | --- | --- |
| | | System A | System B | System C |
| **Blocks** | **Controller 1** | 15 | 15 | 18 |
| | **Controller 2** | 14 | 14 | 14 |
| | **Controller 3** | 10 | 11 | 15 |
| | **Controller 4** | 13 | 12 | 17 |
| | **Controller 5** | 16 | 13 | 16 |
| | **Controller 6** | 13 | 13 | 13 |

**TABLE 13.7   SUMMARY OF STRESS DATA FOR THE AIR TRAFFIC CONTROLLER STRESS TEST**

|  |  | Treatments | | | Row or Block Totals | Block Means |
|--|--|------------|--|--|---------------------|-------------|
|  |  | System A | System B | System C |  |  |
| Blocks | Controller 1 | 15 | 15 | 18 | 48 | $\bar{x}_{1.} = 48/3 = 16.0$ |
|  | Controller 2 | 14 | 14 | 14 | 42 | $\bar{x}_{2.} = 42/3 = 14.0$ |
|  | Controller 3 | 10 | 11 | 15 | 36 | $\bar{x}_{3.} = 36/3 = 12.0$ |
|  | Controller 4 | 13 | 12 | 17 | 42 | $\bar{x}_{4.} = 42/3 = 14.0$ |
|  | Controller 5 | 16 | 13 | 16 | 45 | $\bar{x}_{5.} = 45/3 = 15.0$ |
|  | Controller 6 | 13 | 13 | 13 | 39 | $\bar{x}_{6.} = 39/3 = 13.0$ |
| Column or Treatment Totals |  | 81 | 78 | 93 | 252 | $\bar{\bar{x}} = \dfrac{252}{18} = 14.0$ |
| Treatment Means |  | $\bar{x}_{.1} = \dfrac{81}{6}$ $= 13.5$ | $\bar{x}_{.2} = \dfrac{78}{6}$ $= 13.0$ | $\bar{x}_{.3} = \dfrac{93}{6}$ $= 15.5$ |  |  |

ful in making the sum of squares computations for the ANOVA procedure. Because lower stress values are viewed as better, the sample data seem to favor system B with its mean stress rating of 13. However, the usual question remains: Do the sample results justify the conclusion that the population mean stress levels for the three systems differ? That is, are the differences statistically significant? An analysis of variance computation similar to the one performed for the completely randomized design can be used to answer this statistical question.

## ANOVA Procedure

The ANOVA procedure for the randomized block design requires us to partition the sum of squares total (SST) into three groups: sum of squares due to treatments, sum of squares due to blocks, and sum of squares due to error. The formula for this partitioning follows.

$$\text{SST} = \text{SSTR} + \text{SSBL} + \text{SSE} \tag{13.24}$$

This sum of squares partition is summarized in the ANOVA table for the randomized block design as shown in Table 13.8. The notation used in the table is

$$k = \text{the number of treatments}$$
$$b = \text{the number of blocks}$$
$$n_T = \text{the total sample size } (n_T = kb)$$

Note that the ANOVA table also shows how the $n_T - 1$ total degrees of freedom are partitioned such that $k - 1$ degrees of freedom go to treatments, $b - 1$ go to blocks, and $(k - 1)(b - 1)$ go to the error term. The mean square column shows the sum of squares divided by the degrees of freedom, and $F = \text{MSTR/MSE}$ is the $F$ ratio used to test for a significant difference among the treatment means. The primary contribution of the randomized block design is that, by including blocks, we remove the individual controller differences from the MSE term and obtain a more powerful test for the stress differences in the three work station alternatives.

**TABLE 13.8** ANOVA TABLE FOR THE RANDOMIZED BLOCK DESIGN WITH $k$ TREATMENTS AND $b$ BLOCKS

| Source of Variation | Sum of Squares | Degrees of Freedom | Mean Square | $F$ |
|---|---|---|---|---|
| Treatments | SSTR | $k - 1$ | $MSTR = \dfrac{SSTR}{k - 1}$ | $\dfrac{MSTR}{MSE}$ |
| Blocks | SSBL | $b - 1$ | $MSBL = \dfrac{SSBL}{b - 1}$ | |
| Error | SSE | $(k - 1)(b - 1)$ | $MSE = \dfrac{SSE}{(k - 1)(b - 1)}$ | |
| Total | SST | $n_T - 1$ | | |

## Computations and Conclusions

To compute the $F$ statistic needed to test for a difference among treatment means with a randomized block design, we need to compute MSTR and MSE. To calculate these two mean squares, we must first compute SSTR and SSE; in doing so, we will also compute SSBL and SST. To simplify the presentation, we perform the calculations in four steps. In addition to $k$, $b$, and $n_T$ as previously defined, the following notation is used.

$x_{ij}$ = value of the observation corresponding to treatment $j$ in block $i$
$\bar{x}_{.j}$ = sample mean of the $j$th treatment
$\bar{x}_{i.}$ = sample mean for the $i$th block
$\bar{\bar{x}}$ = overall sample mean

**Step 1.** Compute the total sum of squares (SST).

$$SST = \sum_{i=1}^{b} \sum_{j=1}^{k} (x_{ij} - \bar{\bar{x}})^2 \tag{13.25}$$

**Step 2.** Compute the sum of squares due to treatments (SSTR).

$$SSTR = b \sum_{j=1}^{k} (\bar{x}_{.j} - \bar{\bar{x}})^2 \tag{13.26}$$

**Step 3.** Compute the sum of squares due to blocks (SSBL).

$$SSBL = k \sum_{i=1}^{b} (\bar{x}_{i.} - \bar{\bar{x}})^2 \tag{13.27}$$

**Step 4.** Compute the sum of squares due to error (SSE).

$$SSE = SST - SSTR - SSBL \tag{13.28}$$

For the air traffic controller data in Table 13.7, these steps lead to the following sums of squares.

**Step 1.** $SST = (15 - 14)^2 + (15 - 14)^2 + (18 - 14)^2 + \cdots + (13 - 14)^2 = 70$
**Step 2.** $SSTR = 6[(13.5 - 14)^2 + (13.0 - 14)^2 + (15.5 - 14)^2] = 21$
**Step 3.** $SSBL = 3[(16 - 14)^2 + (14 - 14)^2 + (12 - 14)^2 + (14 - 14)^2 + (15 - 14)^2 + (13 - 14)^2] = 30$
**Step 4.** $SSE = 70 - 21 - 30 = 19$

These sums of squares divided by their degrees of freedom provide the corresponding mean square values shown in Table 13.9.

Let us use a level of significance $\alpha = .05$ to conduct the hypothesis test. The value of the test statistic is

$$F = \frac{\text{MSTR}}{\text{MSE}} = \frac{10.5}{1.9} = 5.53$$

The numerator degrees of freedom is $k - 1 = 3 - 1 = 2$ and the denominator degrees of freedom is $(k - 1)(b - 1) = (3 - 1)(6 - 1) = 10$. Because we will only reject the null hypothesis for large values of the test statistic, the $p$-value is the area under the $F$ distribution to the right of $F = 5.53$. From Table 4 of Appendix B we find that with the degrees of freedom 2 and 10, $F = 5.53$ is between $F_{.025} = 5.46$ and $F_{.01} = 7.56$. As a result, the area in the upper tail, or the $p$-value, is between .01 and .025. Alternatively, we can use Minitab or Excel to show that the exact $p$-value for $F = 5.53$ is .0241. With $p$-value $\leq \alpha = .05$, we reject the null hypothesis $H_0: \mu_1 = \mu_2 = \mu_3$ and conclude that the population mean stress levels differ for the three work station alternatives.

Some general comments can be made about the randomized block design. The experimental design described in this section is a *complete* block design; the word "complete" indicates that each block is subjected to all $k$ treatments. That is, all controllers (blocks) were tested with all three systems (treatments). Experimental designs in which some but not all treatments are applied to each block are referred to as *incomplete* block designs. A discussion of incomplete block designs is beyond the scope of this text.

Because each controller in the air traffic controller stress test was required to use all three systems, this approach guarantees a complete block design. In some cases, however, blocking is carried out with "similar" experimental units in each block. For example, assume that in a pretest of air traffic controllers, the population of controllers was divided into groups ranging from extremely high-stress individuals to extremely low-stress individuals. The blocking could still be accomplished by having three controllers from each of the stress classifications participate in the study. Each block would then consist of three controllers in the same stress group. The randomized aspect of the block design would be the random assignment of the three controllers in each block to the three systems.

Finally, note that the ANOVA table shown in Table 13.8 provides an $F$ value to test for treatment effects but *not* for blocks. The reason is that the experiment was designed to test a single factor—work station design. The blocking based on individual stress differences was conducted to remove such variation from the MSE term. However, the study was not designed to test specifically for individual differences in stress.

Some analysts compute $F = \text{MSB}/\text{MSE}$ and use that statistic to test for significance of the blocks. Then they use the result as a guide to whether the same type of blocking would be desired in future experiments. However, if individual stress difference is to be a factor in the study, a different experimental design should be used. A test of significance on blocks should not be performed as a basis for a conclusion about a second factor.

**TABLE 13.9    ANOVA TABLE FOR THE AIR TRAFFIC CONTROLLER STRESS TEST**

| Source of Variation | Sum of Squares | Degrees of Freedom | Mean Square | F |
|---|---|---|---|---|
| Treatments | 21 | 2 | 10.5 | 10.5/1.9 = 5.53 |
| Blocks | 30 | 5 | 6.0 | |
| Error | 19 | 10 | 1.9 | |
| Total | 70 | 17 | | |

## NOTES AND COMMENTS

The error degrees of freedom are less for a randomized block design than for a completely randomized design because $b - 1$ degrees of freedom are lost for the $b$ blocks. If $n$ is small, the potential effects due to blocks can be masked because of the loss of error degrees of freedom; for large $n$, the effects are minimized.

## Exercises

### Methods

34. Consider the experimental results for the following randomized block design. Make the calculations necessary to set up the analysis of variance table.

|        |   | **Treatments** | | |
|--------|---|---|---|---|
|        |   | **A** | **B** | **C** |
|        | **1** | 10 | 9 | 8 |
|        | **2** | 12 | 6 | 5 |
| Blocks | **3** | 18 | 15 | 14 |
|        | **4** | 20 | 18 | 18 |
|        | **5** | 8 | 7 | 8 |

Use $\alpha = .05$ to test for any significant differences.

35. The following data were obtained for a randomized block design involving five treatments and three blocks: SST = 430, SSTR = 310, SSBL = 85. Set up the ANOVA table and test for any significant differences. Use $\alpha = .05$.

36. An experiment has been conducted for four treatments with eight blocks. Complete the following analysis of variance table.

| Source of Variation | Sum of Squares | Degrees of Freedom | Mean Square | F |
|---|---|---|---|---|
| Treatments | 900 | | | |
| Blocks | 400 | | | |
| Error | | | | |
| Total | 1800 | | | |

Use $\alpha = .05$ to test for any significant differences.

### Applications

37. An automobile dealer conducted a test to determine if the time in minutes needed to complete a minor engine tune-up depends on whether a computerized engine analyzer or an electronic analyzer is used. Because tune-up time varies among compact, intermediate, and full-sized cars, the three types of cars were used as blocks in the experiment. The data obtained follow.

|  |  | Analyzer | |
|---|---|---|---|
|  |  | **Computerized** | **Electronic** |
|  | **Compact** | 50 | 42 |
| **Car** | **Intermediate** | 55 | 44 |
|  | **Full-sized** | 63 | 46 |

Use $\alpha = .05$ to test for any significant differences.

38. Five different auditing procedures were compared in terms of total audit time. To control for possible variation due to the person conducting the audit, four accountants were selected randomly and treated as blocks in the experiment. The following values were obtained by the ANOVA procedure: SST = 100, SSTR = 45, SSBL = 36. Use $\alpha = .05$ to test for any significant difference in the mean total audit time for the five auditing procedures.

39. An important factor in selecting software for word-processing and database management systems is the time required to learn how to use the system. To evaluate three file management systems, a firm designed a test involving five word-processing operators. Because operator variability was believed to be a significant factor, each of the five operators was trained on each of the three file management systems. The data obtained follow.

|  |  | System | |
|---|---|---|---|
|  | **A** | **B** | **C** |
| **1** | 16 | 16 | 24 |
| **2** | 19 | 17 | 22 |
| **Operator**   **3** | 14 | 13 | 19 |
| **4** | 13 | 12 | 18 |
| **5** | 18 | 17 | 22 |

Use $\alpha = .05$ to test for any difference in the mean training time (in hours) for the three systems.

40. A study reported in the *Journal of the American Medical Association* investigated the cardiac demands of heavy snow shoveling. Ten healthy men underwent exercise testing with a treadmill and a cycle ergometer modified for arm cranking. The men then cleared two tracts of heavy, wet snow by using a lightweight plastic snow shovel and an electric snow thrower. Each subject's heart rate, blood pressure, oxygen uptake, and perceived exertion during snow removal were compared with the values obtained during treadmill and arm-crank ergometer testing. Suppose the following table gives the heart rates in beats per minute for each of the 10 subjects.

**Snow**

| Subject | Treadmill | Arm-Crank Ergometer | Snow Shovel | Snow Thrower |
|---|---|---|---|---|
| 1 | 177 | 205 | 180 | 98 |
| 2 | 151 | 177 | 164 | 120 |
| 3 | 184 | 166 | 167 | 111 |
| 4 | 161 | 152 | 173 | 122 |
| 5 | 192 | 142 | 179 | 151 |
| 6 | 193 | 172 | 205 | 158 |
| 7 | 164 | 191 | 156 | 117 |
| 8 | 207 | 170 | 160 | 123 |
| 9 | 177 | 181 | 175 | 127 |
| 10 | 174 | 154 | 191 | 109 |

At the .05 level of significance, test for any significant differences.

# 13.7 Factorial Experiments

The experimental designs we considered thus far enable us to draw statistical conclusions about one factor. However, in some experiments we want to draw conclusions about more than one variable or factor. **Factorial experiments** and their corresponding ANOVA computations are valuable designs when simultaneous conclusions about two or more factors are required. The term *factorial* is used because the experimental conditions include all possible combinations of the factors. For example, for *a* levels of factor A and *b* levels of factor B, the experiment will involve collecting data on *ab* treatment combinations. In this section we will show the analysis for a two-factor factorial experiment. The basic approach can be extended to experiments involving more than two factors.

As an illustration of a two-factor factorial experiment, we will consider a study involving the Graduate Management Admissions Test (GMAT), a standardized test used by graduate schools of business to evaluate an applicant's ability to pursue a graduate program in that field. Scores on the GMAT range from 200 to 800, with higher scores implying higher aptitude.

In an attempt to improve students' performance on the GMAT exam, a major Texas university is considering offering the following three GMAT preparation programs.

1.  A three-hour review session covering the types of questions generally asked on the GMAT.
2.  A one-day program covering relevant exam material, along with the taking and grading of a sample exam.
3.  An intensive 10-week course involving the identification of each student's weaknesses and the setting up of individualized programs for improvement.

Hence, one factor in this study is the GMAT preparation program, which has three treatments: three-hour review, one-day program, and 10-week course. Before selecting the preparation program to adopt, further study will be conducted to determine how the proposed programs affect GMAT scores.

The GMAT is usually taken by students from three colleges: the College of Business, the College of Engineering, and the College of Arts and Sciences. Therefore, a second factor of interest in the experiment is whether a student's undergraduate college affects the GMAT score. This second factor, undergraduate college, also has three treatments: business, engineering, and arts and sciences. The factorial design for this experiment with three treatments corresponding to factor A, the preparation program, and three treatments corresponding to factor B, the undergraduate college, will have a total of $3 \times 3 = 9$ treatment combinations. These treatment combinations or experimental conditions are summarized in Table 13.10.

**TABLE 13.10**   NINE TREATMENT COMBINATIONS FOR THE TWO-FACTOR GMAT EXPERIMENT

|  |  | Factor B: College | | |
|---|---|---|---|---|
|  |  | **Business** | **Engineering** | **Arts and Sciences** |
| Factor A: | **Three-hour review** | 1 | 2 | 3 |
| Preparation | **One-day program** | 4 | 5 | 6 |
| Program | **10-week course** | 7 | 8 | 9 |

Assume that a sample of two students will be selected corresponding to each of the nine treatment combinations shown in Table 13.10: two business students will take the three-hour review, two will take the one-day program, and two will take the 10-week course. In addition, two engineering students and two arts and sciences students will take each of the three preparation programs. In experimental design terminology, the sample size of two for each treatment combination indicates that we have two **replications**. Additional replications and a larger sample size could easily be used, but we elect to minimize the computational aspects for this illustration.

This experimental design requires that six students who plan to attend graduate school be randomly selected from *each* of the three undergraduate colleges. Then two students from each college should be assigned randomly to each preparation program, resulting in a total of 18 students being used in the study.

Let us assume that the randomly selected students participated in the preparation programs and then took the GMAT. The scores obtained are reported in Table 13.11.

The analysis of variance computations with the data in Table 13.11 will provide answers to the following questions.

- **Main effect (factor A):** Do the preparation programs differ in terms of effect on GMAT scores?
- **Main effect (factor B):** Do the undergraduate colleges differ in terms of effect on GMAT scores?
- **Interaction effect (factors A and B):** Do students in some colleges do better on one type of preparation program whereas others do better on a different type of preparation program?

The term **interaction** refers to a new effect that we can now study because we used a factorial experiment. If the interaction effect has a significant impact on the GMAT scores, we can conclude that the effect of the type of preparation program depends on the undergraduate college.

## ANOVA Procedure

The ANOVA procedure for the two-factor factorial experiment is similar to the completely randomized experiment and the randomized block experiment in that we again partition the sum of squares and the degrees of freedom into their respective sources. The formula for partitioning the sum of squares for the two-factor factorial experiments follows.

$$SST = SSA + SSB + SSAB + SSE \qquad \text{(13.29)}$$

**TABLE 13.11    GMAT SCORES FOR THE TWO-FACTOR EXPERIMENT**

GMAT

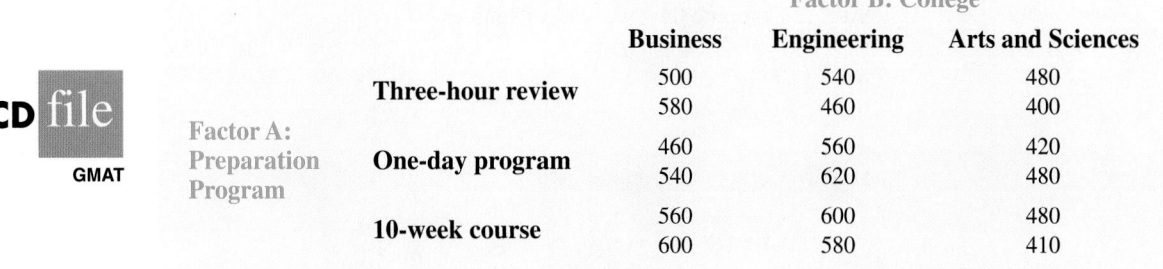

|  |  | Factor B: College | | |
|---|---|---|---|---|
|  |  | **Business** | **Engineering** | **Arts and Sciences** |
| | **Three-hour review** | 500 | 540 | 480 |
| | | 580 | 460 | 400 |
| Factor A: Preparation Program | **One-day program** | 460 | 560 | 420 |
| | | 540 | 620 | 480 |
| | **10-week course** | 560 | 600 | 480 |
| | | 600 | 580 | 410 |

**TABLE 13.12**   ANOVA TABLE FOR THE TWO-FACTOR FACTORIAL EXPERIMENT WITH $r$ REPLICATIONS

| Source of Variation | Sum of Squares | Degrees of Freedom | Mean Square | $F$ |
|---|---|---|---|---|
| Factor A | SSA | $a - 1$ | $\text{MSA} = \dfrac{\text{SSA}}{a - 1}$ | $\dfrac{\text{MSA}}{\text{MSE}}$ |
| Factor B | SSB | $b - 1$ | $\text{MSB} = \dfrac{\text{SSB}}{b - 1}$ | $\dfrac{\text{MSB}}{\text{MSE}}$ |
| Interaction | SSAB | $(a - 1)(b - 1)$ | $\text{MSAB} = \dfrac{\text{SSAB}}{(a - 1)(b - 1)}$ | $\dfrac{\text{MSAB}}{\text{MSE}}$ |
| Error | SSE | $ab(r - 1)$ | $\text{MSE} = \dfrac{\text{SSE}}{ab(r - 1)}$ | |
| Total | SST | $n_T - 1$ | | |

The partitioning of the sum of squares and degrees of freedom is summarized in Table 13.12. The following notation is used.

$a$ = number of levels of factor A

$b$ = number of levels of factor B

$r$ = number of replications

$n_T$ = total number of observations taken in the experiment; $n_T = abr$

## Computations and Conclusions

To compute the $F$ statistics needed to test for the significance of factor A, factor B, and interaction, we need to compute MSA, MSB, MSAB, and MSE. To calculate these four mean squares, we must first compute SSA, SSB, SSAB, and SSE; in doing so we will also compute SST. To simplify the presentation, we perform the calculations in five steps. In addition to $a$, $b$, $r$, and $n_T$ as previously defined, the following notation is used.

$x_{ijk}$ = observation corresponding to the $k$th replicate taken from treatment $i$ of factor A and treatment $j$ of factor B

$\bar{x}_{i\cdot}$ = sample mean for the observations in treatment $i$ (factor A)

$\bar{x}_{\cdot j}$ = sample mean for the observations in treatment $j$ (factor B)

$\bar{x}_{ij}$ = sample mean for the observations corresponding to the combination of treatment $i$ (factor A) and treatment $j$ (factor B)

$\bar{\bar{x}}$ = overall sample mean of all $n_T$ observations

**Step 1.**  Compute the total sum of squares.

$$\text{SST} = \sum_{i=1}^{a}\sum_{j=1}^{b}\sum_{k=1}^{r}(x_{ijk} - \bar{\bar{x}})^2 \qquad \textbf{(13.30)}$$

**Step 2.**  Compute the sum of squares for factor A.

$$\text{SSA} = br\sum_{i=1}^{a}(\bar{x}_{i\cdot} - \bar{\bar{x}})^2 \qquad \textbf{(13.31)}$$

**Step 3.** Compute the sum of squares for factor B.

$$\text{SSB} = ar \sum_{j=1}^{b} (\bar{x}_{\cdot j} - \bar{\bar{x}})^2 \qquad (13.32)$$

**Step 4.** Compute the sum of squares for interaction.

$$\text{SSAB} = r \sum_{i=1}^{a} \sum_{j=1}^{b} (\bar{x}_{ij} - \bar{x}_{i\cdot} - \bar{x}_{\cdot j} + \bar{\bar{x}})^2 \qquad (13.33)$$

**Step 5.** Compute the sum of squares due to error.

$$\text{SSE} = \text{SST} - \text{SSA} - \text{SSB} - \text{SSAB} \qquad (13.34)$$

Table 13.13 reports the data collected in the experiment and the various sums that will help us with the sum of squares computations. Using equations (13.30) through (13.34), we calculate the following sums of squares for the GMAT two-factor factorial experiment.

**Step 1.**   $\text{SST} = (500 - 515)^2 + (580 - 515)^2 + (540 - 515)^2 + \cdots +$
$(410 - 515)^2 = 82{,}450$

**Step 2.**   $\text{SSA} = (3)(2)[(493.33 - 515)^2 + (513.33 - 515)^2 +$
$(538.33 - 515)^2] = 6100$

**Step 3.**   $\text{SSB} = (3)(2)[(540 - 515)^2 + (560 - 515)^2 + (445 - 515)^2] = 45{,}300$

**Step 4.** $\text{SSAB} = 2[(540 - 493.33 - 540 + 515)^2 + (500 - 493.33 -$
$560 + 515)^2 + \cdots + (445 - 538.33 - 445 + 515)^2] = 11{,}200$

**Step 5.**   $\text{SSE} = 82{,}450 - 6100 - 45{,}300 - 11{,}200 = 19{,}850$

These sums of squares divided by their corresponding degrees of freedom, as shown in Table 13.14, provide the appropriate mean square values for testing the two main effects (preparation program and undergraduate college) and the interaction effect.

Let us use a level of significance $\alpha = .05$ to conduct the hypothesis tests for the two-factor GMAT study. Because of the computational effort involved in any modest- to large-size factorial experiment, the computer usually plays an important role in performing the analysis of variance computations and in the calculation of the $p$-values used to make the hypothesis testing decisions. Figure 13.6 shows the Minitab output for the analysis of variance for the GMAT two-factor factorial experiment. The $p$-value used to test for significant differences among the three preparation programs (factor A) is .299. Because the $p$-value $=$ .299 is greater than $\alpha = .05$, there is no significant difference in the mean GMAT test scores for the three preparation programs. However, for the undergraduate college effect, the $p$-value $= .005$ is less than $\alpha = .05$; thus, there is a significant difference in the mean GMAT test scores among the three undergraduate colleges. Finally, because the $p$-value of .350 for the interaction effect is greater than $\alpha = .05$, there is no significant interaction effect. Therefore, the study provides no reason to believe that the three preparation programs differ in their ability to prepare students from the different colleges for the GMAT.

Undergraduate college was found to be a significant factor. Checking the calculations in Table 13.13, we see that the sample means are: business students $\bar{x}_{\cdot 1} = 540$, engineering students $\bar{x}_{\cdot 2} = 560$, and arts and sciences students $\bar{x}_{\cdot 3} = 445$. Tests on individual treatment means can be conducted; yet after reviewing the three sample means, we would anticipate no difference in preparation for business and engineering graduates. However, the arts and sciences students appear to be significantly less prepared for the GMAT than students in the other colleges. Perhaps this observation will lead the university to consider other options for assisting these students in preparing for graduate management admission tests.

**TABLE 13.13** GMAT SUMMARY DATA FOR THE TWO-FACTOR EXPERIMENT

| Factor A: Preparation Program | Factor B: College | | | Row Totals | Factor A Means |
|---|---|---|---|---|---|
| | **Business** | **Engineering** | **Arts and Sciences** | | |
| **Three-hour review** (Treatment combination totals) | 500 <br> 580 <br> 1080 <br> $\bar{x}_{11} = \dfrac{1080}{2} = 540$ | 540 <br> 460 <br> 1000 <br> $\bar{x}_{12} = \dfrac{1000}{2} = 500$ | 480 <br> 400 <br> 880 <br> $\bar{x}_{13} = \dfrac{880}{2} = 440$ | 2960 | $\bar{x}_{1\cdot} = \dfrac{2960}{6} = 493.33$ |
| **One-day program** | 460 <br> 540 <br> 1000 <br> $\bar{x}_{21} = \dfrac{1000}{2} = 500$ | 560 <br> 620 <br> 1180 <br> $\bar{x}_{22} = \dfrac{1180}{2} = 590$ | 420 <br> 480 <br> 900 <br> $\bar{x}_{23} = \dfrac{900}{2} = 450$ | 3080 | $\bar{x}_{2\cdot} = \dfrac{3080}{6} = 513.33$ |
| **10-week course** | 560 <br> 600 <br> 1160 <br> $\bar{x}_{31} = \dfrac{1160}{2} = 580$ | 600 <br> 580 <br> 1180 <br> $\bar{x}_{32} = \dfrac{1180}{2} = 590$ | 480 <br> 410 <br> 890 <br> $\bar{x}_{33} = \dfrac{890}{2} = 445$ | 3230 | $\bar{x}_{3\cdot} = \dfrac{3230}{6} = 538.33$ |
| **Column Totals** | 3240 | 3360 | 2670 | 9270 | ⟵ Overall total |
| **Factor B Means** | $\bar{x}_{\cdot 1} = \dfrac{3240}{6} = 540$ | $\bar{x}_{\cdot 2} = \dfrac{3360}{6} = 560$ | $\bar{x}_{\cdot 3} = \dfrac{2670}{6} = 445$ | $\bar{\bar{x}} = \dfrac{9270}{18} = 515$ | |

530

TABLE 13.14    ANOVA TABLE FOR THE TWO-FACTOR GMAT STUDY

| Source of Variation | Sum of Squares | Degrees of Freedom | Mean Square | F |
|---|---|---|---|---|
| Factor A | 6,100 | 2 | 3,050 | $3{,}050/2206 = 1.38$ |
| Factor B | 45,300 | 2 | 22,650 | $22{,}650/2206 = 10.27$ |
| Interaction | 11,200 | 4 | 2,800 | $2{,}800/2206 = 1.27$ |
| Error | 19,850 | 9 | 2,206 | |
| Total | 82,450 | 17 | | |

FIGURE 13.6    MINITAB OUTPUT FOR THE GMAT TWO-FACTOR DESIGN

| SOURCE | DF | SS | MS | F | P |
|---|---|---|---|---|---|
| Factor A | 2 | 6100 | 3050 | 1.38 | 0.299 |
| Factor B | 2 | 45300 | 22650 | 10.27 | 0.005 |
| Interaction | 4 | 11200 | 2800 | 1.27 | 0.350 |
| Error | 9 | 19850 | 2206 | | |
| Total | 17 | 82450 | | | |

## Exercises

### Methods

41.  A factorial experiment involving two levels of factor A and three levels of factor B resulted in the following data.

|  |  | Factor B | | |
|---|---|---|---|---|
|  |  | **Level 1** | **Level 2** | **Level 3** |
| Factor A | **Level 1** | 135<br>165 | 90<br>66 | 75<br>93 |
|  | **Level 2** | 125<br>95 | 127<br>105 | 120<br>136 |

Test for any significant main effects and any interaction. Use $\alpha = .05$.

42.  The calculations for a factorial experiment involving four levels of factor A, three levels of factor B, and three replications resulted in the following data: SST = 280, SSA = 26, SSB = 23, SSAB = 175. Set up the ANOVA table and test for any significant main effects and any interaction effect. Use $\alpha = .05$.

### Applications

43.  A mail-order catalog firm designed a factorial experiment to test the effect of the size of a magazine advertisement and the advertisement design on the number of catalog requests received (data in 1000s). Three advertising designs and two different-size advertisements were considered. The data obtained follow. Use the ANOVA procedure for

factorial designs to test for any significant effects due to type of design, size of advertisement, or interaction. Use $\alpha = .05$.

|  |  | Size of Advertisement | |
|---|---|---|---|
|  |  | **Small** | **Large** |
|  | **A** | 8 | 12 |
|  |  | 12 | 8 |
| **Design** | **B** | 22 | 26 |
|  |  | 14 | 30 |
|  | **C** | 10 | 18 |
|  |  | 18 | 14 |

44. An amusement park studied methods for decreasing the waiting time (minutes) for rides by loading and unloading riders more efficiently. Two alternative loading/unloading methods have been proposed. To account for potential differences due to the type of ride and the possible interaction between the method of loading and unloading and the type of ride, a factorial experiment was designed. Use the following data to test for any significant effect due to the loading and unloading method, the type of ride, and interaction. Use $\alpha = .05$.

|  | Type of Ride | | |
|---|---|---|---|
|  | **Roller Coaster** | **Screaming Demon** | **Log Flume** |
| **Method 1** | 41 | 52 | 50 |
|  | 43 | 44 | 46 |
| **Method 2** | 49 | 50 | 48 |
|  | 51 | 46 | 44 |

45. The U.S. Bureau of Labor Statistics collects information on the earnings of men and women for different occupations. Suppose that a reporter for *The Tampa Tribune* wanted to investigate whether there were any differences between the weekly salaries of men and women employed as financial managers, computer programmers, and pharmacists. A sample of five men and women was selected from each of the three occupations, and the weekly salary for each individual in the sample was recorded. The data obtained follow.

**Salaries**

| Weekly Salary ($) | Occupation | Gender |
|---|---|---|
| 872 | Financial Manager | Male |
| 859 | Financial Manager | Male |
| 1028 | Financial Manager | Male |
| 1117 | Financial Manager | Male |
| 1019 | Financial Manager | Male |
| 519 | Financial Manager | Female |
| 702 | Financial Manager | Female |
| 805 | Financial Manager | Female |
| 558 | Financial Manager | Female |
| 591 | Financial Manager | Female |
| 747 | Computer Programmer | Male |
| 766 | Computer Programmer | Male |
| 901 | Computer Programmer | Male |
| 690 | Computer Programmer | Male |

| Weekly Salary ($) | Occupation | Gender |
|---|---|---|
| 881 | Computer Programmer | Male |
| 884 | Computer Programmer | Female |
| 765 | Computer Programmer | Female |
| 685 | Computer Programmer | Female |
| 700 | Computer Programmer | Female |
| 671 | Computer Programmer | Female |
| 1105 | Pharmacist | Male |
| 1144 | Pharmacist | Male |
| 1085 | Pharmacist | Male |
| 903 | Pharmacist | Male |
| 998 | Pharmacist | Male |
| 813 | Pharmacist | Female |
| 985 | Pharmacist | Female |
| 1006 | Pharmacist | Female |
| 1034 | Pharmacist | Female |
| 817 | Pharmacist | Female |

At the $\alpha = .05$ level of significance, test for any significant effect due to occupation, gender, and interaction.

46. A study reported in *The Accounting Review* examined the separate and joint effects of two levels of time pressure (low and moderate) and three levels of knowledge (naive, declarative, and procedural) on key word selection behavior in tax research. Subjects were given a tax case containing a set of facts, a tax issue, and a key word index consisting of 1336 key words. They were asked to select the key words they believed would refer them to a tax authority relevant to resolving the tax case. Prior to the experiment, a group of tax experts determined that the text contained 19 relevant key words. Subjects in the naive group had little or no declarative or procedural knowledge, subjects in the declarative group had significant declarative knowledge but little or no procedural knowledge, and subjects in the procedural group had significant declarative knowledge and procedural knowledge. Declarative knowledge consists of knowledge of both the applicable tax rules and the technical terms used to describe such rules. Procedural knowledge is knowledge of the rules that guide the tax researcher's search for relevant key words. Subjects in the low time pressure situation were told they had 25 minutes to complete the problem, an amount of time which should be "more than adequate" to complete the case; subjects in the moderate time pressure situation were told they would have "only" 11 minutes to complete the case. Suppose 25 subjects were selected for each of the six treatment combinations and the sample means for each treatment combination are as follows (standard deviations are in parentheses).

|  |  | Knowledge | | |
|---|---|---|---|---|
|  |  | Naive | Declarative | Procedural |
|  | Low | 1.13 (1.12) | 1.56 (1.33) | 2.00 (1.54) |
| Time Pressure |  |  |  |  |
|  | Moderate | 0.48 (0.80) | 1.68 (1.36) | 2.86 (1.80) |

Use the ANOVA procedure to test for any significant differences due to time pressure, knowledge, and interaction. Use a .05 level of significance. Assume that the total sum of squares for this experiment is 327.50.

## Summary

In this chapter we showed how analysis of variance can be used to test for differences among means of several populations or treatments. We introduced the completely randomized design, the randomized block design, and the two-factor factorial experiment. The completely randomized design and the randomized block design are used to draw conclusions about differences in the means of a single factor. The primary purpose of blocking in the randomized block design is to remove extraneous sources of variation from the error term. Such blocking provides a better estimate of the true error variance and a better test to determine whether the population or treatment means of the factor differ significantly.

We showed that the basis for the statistical tests used in analysis of variance and experimental design is the development of two independent estimates of the population variance $\sigma^2$. In the single-factor case, one estimator is based on the variation between the treatments; this estimator provides an unbiased estimate of $\sigma^2$ only if the means $\mu_1, \mu_2, \ldots,$ $\mu_k$ are all equal. A second estimator of $\sigma^2$ is based on the variation of the observations within each sample; this estimator will always provide an unbiased estimate of $\sigma^2$. By computing the ratio of these two estimators (the $F$ statistic) we developed a rejection rule for determining whether to reject the null hypothesis that the population or treatment means are equal. In all the experimental designs considered, the partitioning of the sum of squares and degrees of freedom into their various sources enabled us to compute the appropriate values for the analysis of variance calculations and tests. We also showed how Fisher's LSD procedure and the Bonferroni adjustment can be used to perform pairwise comparisons to determine which means are different.

## Glossary

**ANOVA table** A table used to summarize the analysis of variance computations and results. It contains columns showing the source of variation, the sum of squares, the degrees of freedom, the mean square, and the $F$ value(s).

**Partitioning** The process of allocating the total sum of squares and degrees of freedom to the various components.

**Multiple comparison procedures** Statistical procedures that can be used to conduct statistical comparisons between pairs of population means.

**Comparisonwise Type I error rate** The probability of a Type I error associated with a single pairwise comparison.

**Experimentwise Type I error rate** The probability of making a Type I error on at least one of several pairwise comparisons.

**Factor** Another word for the independent variable of interest.

**Treatments** Different levels of a factor.

**Single-factor experiment** An experiment involving only one factor with $k$ populations or treatments.

**Experimental units** The objects of interest in the experiment.

**Completely randomized design** An experimental design in which the treatments are randomly assigned to the experimental units.

**Blocking** The process of using the same or similar experimental units for all treatments. The purpose of blocking is to remove a source of variation from the error term and hence provide a more powerful test for a difference in population or treatment means.

**Randomized block design** An experimental design employing blocking.

**Factorial experiment** An experimental design that allows statistical conclusions about two or more factors.

**Replications** The number of times each experimental condition is repeated in an experiment.
**Interaction** The effect produced when the levels of one factor interact with the levels of another factor in influencing the response variable.

## Key Formulas

## Testing for the Equality of $k$ Population Means

### Sample Mean for Treatment $j$

$$\bar{x}_j = \frac{\sum_{i=1}^{n_j} x_{ij}}{n_j} \tag{13.1}$$

### Sample Variance for Treatment $j$

$$s_j^2 = \frac{\sum_{i=1}^{n_j} (x_{ij} - \bar{x}_j)^2}{n_j - 1} \tag{13.2}$$

### Overall Sample Mean

$$\bar{\bar{x}} = \frac{\sum_{j=1}^{k} \sum_{i=1}^{n_j} x_{ij}}{n_T} \tag{13.3}$$

$$n_T = n_1 + n_2 + \cdots + n_k \tag{13.4}$$

### Mean Square Due to Treatments

$$\text{MSTR} = \frac{\text{SSTR}}{k - 1} \tag{13.7}$$

### Sum of Squares Due to Treatments

$$\text{SSTR} = \sum_{j=1}^{k} n_j (\bar{x}_j - \bar{\bar{x}})^2 \tag{13.8}$$

### Mean Square Due to Error

$$\text{MSE} = \frac{\text{SSE}}{n_T - k} \tag{13.10}$$

### Sum of Squares Due to Error

$$\text{SSE} = \sum_{j=1}^{k} (n_j - 1) s_j^2 \tag{13.11}$$

### Test Statistic for the Equality of $k$ Population Means

$$F = \frac{\text{MSTR}}{\text{MSE}} \tag{13.12}$$

**Total Sum of Squares**

$$SST = \sum_{j=1}^{k} \sum_{i=1}^{n_j} (x_{ij} - \bar{\bar{x}})^2 \tag{13.13}$$

**Partitioning of Sum of Squares**

$$SST = SSTR + SSE \tag{13.14}$$

## Multiple Comparison Procedures

**Test Statistic for Fisher's LSD Procedure**

$$t = \frac{\bar{x}_i - \bar{x}_j}{\sqrt{MSE\left(\dfrac{1}{n_i} + \dfrac{1}{n_j}\right)}} \tag{13.16}$$

**Fisher's LSD**

$$LSD = t_{\alpha/2}\sqrt{MSE\left(\frac{1}{n_i} + \frac{1}{n_j}\right)} \tag{13.17}$$

## Completely Randomized Designs

**Mean Square Due to Treatments**

$$MSTR = \frac{\displaystyle\sum_{j=1}^{k} n_j (\bar{x}_j - \bar{\bar{x}})^2}{k - 1} \tag{13.20}$$

**Mean Square Due to Error**

$$MSE = \frac{\displaystyle\sum_{j=1}^{k} (n_j - 1)s_j^2}{n_T - k} \tag{13.21}$$

*F* **Test Statistic**

$$F = \frac{MSTR}{MSE} \tag{13.23}$$

## Randomized Block Designs

**Total Sum of Squares**

$$SST = \sum_{i=1}^{b} \sum_{j=1}^{k} (x_{ij} - \bar{\bar{x}})^2 \tag{13.25}$$

**Sum of Squares Due to Treatments**

$$SSTR = b \sum_{j=1}^{k} (\bar{x}_{\cdot j} - \bar{\bar{x}})^2 \tag{13.26}$$

**Sum of Squares Due to Blocks**

$$SSBL = k \sum_{i=1}^{b} (\bar{x}_{i\cdot} - \bar{\bar{x}})^2 \qquad (13.27)$$

**Sum of Squares Due to Error**

$$SSE = SST - SSTR - SSBL \qquad (13.28)$$

# Factorial Experiments

**Total Sum of Squares**

$$SST = \sum_{i=1}^{a} \sum_{j=1}^{b} \sum_{k=1}^{r} (x_{ijk} - \bar{\bar{x}})^2 \qquad (13.30)$$

**Sum of Squares for Factor A**

$$SSA = br \sum_{i=1}^{a} (\bar{x}_{i\cdot} - \bar{\bar{x}})^2 \qquad (13.31)$$

**Sum of Squares for Factor B**

$$SSB = ar \sum_{j=1}^{b} (\bar{x}_{\cdot j} - \bar{\bar{x}})^2 \qquad (13.32)$$

**Sum of Squares for Interaction**

$$SSAB = r \sum_{i=1}^{a} \sum_{j=1}^{b} (\bar{x}_{ij} - \bar{x}_{i\cdot} - \bar{x}_{\cdot j} + \bar{\bar{x}})^2 \qquad (13.33)$$

**Sum of Squares for Error**

$$SSE = SST - SSA - SSB - SSAB \qquad (13.34)$$

## Supplementary Exercises

47. A simple random sample of the asking prices (in thousands of dollars) of four houses currently for sale in each of two residential areas resulted in the following data.

| Area 1 | Area 2 |
|--------|--------|
| 92 | 90 |
| 89 | 102 |
| 98 | 96 |
| 105 | 88 |

   a. Use the ANOVA procedure to test whether the mean asking price is the same. Use $\alpha = .05$.
   b. Suppose that data were collected for another residential area. The asking prices for the simple random sample from the third area were $81,000, $86,000, $75,000, and $90,000. Is the mean asking price the same for all three areas? Use $\alpha = .05$.

48. Buyers of sport utility vehicles (SUVs) and pickup trucks find a wide choice in today's marketplace. One of the factors that is important to many buyers is the resale value of the vehicle. The following table shows the resale value (%) after two years for 10 SUVs, 10 small pickup trucks, and 10 large pickup trucks (*Kiplinger's New Cars & Trucks 2000 Buyer's Guide*).

**Trucks**

| Sport Utility | Resale Value | Small Pickup | Resale Value |
|---|---|---|---|
| Chevrolet Blazer LS | 55 | Chevrolet S-10 Extended Cab | 46 |
| Ford Explorer Sport | 57 | Dodge Dakota Club Cab Sport | 53 |
| GMC Yukon XL 1500 | 67 | Ford Ranger XLT Regular Cab | 48 |
| Honda CR-V | 65 | Ford Ranger XLT Supercab | 55 |
| Isuzu VehiCross | 62 | GMC Sonoma Regular Cab | 44 |
| Jeep Cherokee Limited | 57 | Isuzu Hombre Spacecab | 41 |
| Mercury Mountaineer | 59 | Mazda B4000 SE Cab Plus | 51 |
| Nissan Pathfinder XE | 54 | Nissan Frontier XE Regular Cab | 51 |
| Toyota 4Runner | 55 | Toyota Tacoma Xtracab | 49 |
| Toyota RAV4 | 55 | Toyota Tacoma Xtracab V6 | 50 |

| Full-Size Pickup | Resale Value |
|---|---|
| Chevrolet K2500 | 60 |
| Chevrolet Silverado 2500 Ext | 64 |
| Dodge Ram 1500 | 54 |
| Dodge Ram Quad Cab 2500 | 63 |
| Dodge Ram Regular Cab 2500 | 59 |
| Ford F150 XL | 58 |
| Ford F-350 Super Duty Crew Cab XL | 64 |
| GMC New Sierra 1500 Ext Cab | 68 |
| Toyota Tundra Access Cab Limited | 53 |
| Toyota Tundra Regular Cab | 58 |

At the $\alpha = .05$ level of significance, test for any significant difference in the mean resale value for the three types of vehicles.

49. *Money* magazine reports percentage returns and expense ratios for stock and bond funds. The following data are the expense ratios for 10 midcap stock funds, 10 small-cap stock funds, 10 hybrid stock funds, and 10 specialty stock funds (*Money,* March 2003).

**Funds**

| Midcap | Small-Cap | Hybrid | Specialty |
|---|---|---|---|
| 1.2 | 2.0 | 2.0 | 1.6 |
| 1.1 | 1.2 | 2.7 | 2.7 |
| 1.0 | 1.7 | 1.8 | 2.6 |
| 1.2 | 1.8 | 1.5 | 2.5 |
| 1.3 | 1.5 | 2.5 | 1.9 |
| 1.8 | 2.3 | 1.0 | 1.5 |
| 1.4 | 1.9 | 0.9 | 1.6 |
| 1.4 | 1.3 | 1.9 | 2.7 |
| 1.0 | 1.2 | 1.4 | 2.2 |
| 1.4 | 1.3 | 0.3 | 0.7 |

Use $\alpha = .05$ to test for any significant difference in the mean expense ratio among the four types of stock funds.

50.   A study reported in the *Journal of Small Business Management* concluded that self-employed individuals do not experience higher job satisfaction than individuals who are not self-employed. In this study, job satisfaction is measured using 18 items, each of which is rated using a Likert-type scale with 1–5 response options ranging from strong agreement to strong disagreement. A higher score on this scale indicates a higher degree of job satisfaction. The sum of the ratings for the 18 items, ranging from 18–90, is used as the measure of job satisfaction. Suppose that this approach was used to measure the job satisfaction for lawyers, physical therapists, cabinetmakers, and systems analysts. The results obtained for a sample of 10 individuals from each profession follow.

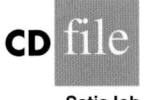

**SatisJob**

| Lawyer | Physical Therapist | Cabinetmaker | Systems Analyst |
|--------|--------------------|--------------|-----------------|
| 44 | 55 | 54 | 44 |
| 42 | 78 | 65 | 73 |
| 74 | 80 | 79 | 71 |
| 42 | 86 | 69 | 60 |
| 53 | 60 | 79 | 64 |
| 50 | 59 | 64 | 66 |
| 45 | 62 | 59 | 41 |
| 48 | 52 | 78 | 55 |
| 64 | 55 | 84 | 76 |
| 38 | 50 | 60 | 62 |

At the $\alpha = .05$ level of significance, test for any difference in the job satisfaction among the four professions.

51.   Crown Plaza Hotels and Resorts offered special weekend rates at hotels at resorts nationwide. A sample of 30 properties from three regions of the country provided the following room rates (*USA Today*, April 14, 2000).

**Resorts**

| West | Rate ($) | South | Rate ($) | Northeast | Rate ($) |
|------|----------|-------|----------|-----------|----------|
| Albuquerque | 89 | Atlanta | 105 | Albany | 89 |
| Irvine | 79 | Dallas | 80 | Boston | 139 |
| Las Vegas | 119 | Greenville | 79 | Hartford | 85 |
| Los Angeles | 99 | Houston | 79 | New York | 159 |
| Palo Alto | 109 | Jackson | 69 | Philadelphia | 99 |
| Phoenix | 149 | Macon | 69 | Pittsfield | 99 |
| Portland | 79 | Miami | 89 | Providence | 149 |
| San Francisco | 139 | Orlando | 119 | Washington | 159 |
| San Jose | 99 | Richmond | 109 | White Plains | 109 |
| Seattle | 119 | Tampa | 119 | Worcester | 124 |

At the $\alpha = .05$ level of significance, test whether the mean rates are the same for the three regions.

52.   To investigate whether there is any difference in the annual compensation for art directors at advertising agencies, suppose that a sample of 10 art directors was selected from each of four regions: West, South, North Central, and Northeast. The base salary (in thousands of dollars) for each of the individuals sampled follows.

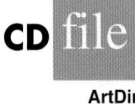

**ArtDir**

| West | South | North Central | Northeast |
|------|-------|---------------|-----------|
| 60.9 | 50.8 | 49.5 | 65.9 |
| 45.9 | 39.6 | 42.3 | 58.6 |
| 62.1 | 44.2 | 35.5 | 49.3 |

*(continued)*

| West | South | North Central | Northeast |
|------|-------|---------------|-----------|
| 66.6 | 40.0 | 49.1 | 52.9 |
| 68.0 | 53.9 | 56.7 | 48.5 |
| 65.0 | 45.4 | 41.4 | 52.9 |
| 49.4 | 61.1 | 51.3 | 52.4 |
| 62.3 | 42.3 | 49.4 | 48.1 |
| 62.6 | 38.4 | 42.1 | 46.5 |
| 57.2 | 38.3 | 55.7 | 45.9 |

At the $\alpha = .05$ level of significance, test whether the mean base salary for art directors is the same for each of the four regions.

53. The National Football League rates prospects by position on a scale that ranges from 5 to 9. The ratings are interpreted as follows: 8–9 should start the first year; 7.0–7.9 should start; 6.0–6.9 will make the team as backup; and 5.0–5.9, can make the club and contribute. The following table shows the ratings for three positions for 40 NFL prospects (*USA Today*, April 14, 2000). Does there appear to be any significant effect on the rating due to the player's position?

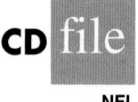

NFL

| Wide Receiver | | Guard | | Offensive Tackle | |
|---------------|--------|-------|--------|------------------|--------|
| **Name** | **Rating** | **Name** | **Rating** | **Name** | **Rating** |
| Peter Warrick | 9.0 | Cosey Coleman | 7.4 | Chris Samuels | 8.5 |
| Plaxico Burress | 8.8 | Travis Claridge | 7.0 | Stockar McDougle | 8.0 |
| Sylvester Morris | 8.3 | Kaulana Noa | 6.8 | Chris McIngosh | 7.8 |
| Travis Taylor | 8.1 | Leander Jordan | 6.7 | Adrian Klemm | 7.6 |
| Laveranues Coles | 8.0 | Chad Clifton | 6.3 | Todd Wade | 7.3 |
| Dez White | 7.9 | Manula Savea | 6.1 | Marvel Smith | 7.1 |
| Jerry Porter | 7.4 | Ryan Johanningmeir | 6.0 | Michael Thompson | 6.8 |
| Ron Dugans | 7.1 | Mark Tauscher | 6.0 | Bobby Williams | 6.8 |
| Todd Pinkston | 7.0 | Blaine Saipaia | 6.0 | Darnell Alford | 6.4 |
| Dennis Northcutt | 7.0 | Richard Mercier | 5.8 | Terrance Beadles | 6.3 |
| Anthony Lucas | 6.9 | Damion McIntosh | 5.3 | Tutan Reyes | 6.1 |
| Darrell Jackson | 6.6 | Jeno James | 5.5 | Greg Robinson-Ran | 6.0 |
| Danny Farmer | 6.5 | Al Jackson | 5.5 | | |
| Sherrod Gideon | 6.4 | | | | |
| Trevor Gaylor | 6.2 | | | | |

54. In a completely randomized experimental design, three brands of paper towels were tested for their ability to absorb water. Equal-size towels were used, with four sections of towels tested per brand. The absorbency rating data follow. At a .05 level of significance, does there appear to be a difference in the ability of the brands to absorb water?

| Brand | | |
|-------|-------|-------|
| *x* | *y* | *z* |
| 91 | 99 | 83 |
| 100 | 96 | 88 |
| 88 | 94 | 89 |
| 89 | 99 | 76 |

55. *Business 2.0*'s first annual employment survey provided data showing the typical annual salary for 97 different jobs. The following data show the annual salary for 30 different jobs in three fields: computer software and hardware, construction, and engineering (*Business 2.0,* March 2003).

| Computers | | Construction | | Engineering | |
|---|---|---|---|---|---|
| **Job** | **Salary** | **Job** | **Salary** | **Job** | **Salary** |
| Data Mgr. | 94 | Administrator | 55 | Aeronautical | 75 |
| Mfg. Mgr. | 90 | Architect | 53 | Agricultural | 70 |
| Programmer | 63 | Architect Mgr. | 77 | Chemical | 88 |
| Project Mgr. | 84 | Const. Mgr. | 60 | Civil | 77 |
| Software Dev. | 73 | Foreperson | 41 | Electrical | 89 |
| Sr. Design | 75 | Interior Design | 54 | Mechanical | 85 |
| Staff Systems | 94 | Landscape Architect | 51 | Mining | 96 |
| Systems Analyst | 77 | Sr. Estimator | 64 | Nuclear | 105 |

**CD file**

**JobSalary**

Use $\alpha = .05$ to test for any significant difference in the mean annual salary among the three job fields.

56. Three different assembly methods have been proposed for a new product. A completely randomized experimental design was chosen to determine which assembly method results in the greatest number of parts produced per hour, and 30 workers were randomly selected and assigned to use one of the proposed methods. The number of units produced by each worker follows.

| Method | | |
|---|---|---|
| **A** | **B** | **C** |
| 97 | 93 | 99 |
| 73 | 100 | 94 |
| 93 | 93 | 87 |
| 100 | 55 | 66 |
| 73 | 77 | 59 |
| 91 | 91 | 75 |
| 100 | 85 | 84 |
| 86 | 73 | 72 |
| 92 | 90 | 88 |
| 95 | 83 | 86 |

**CD file**

**Assembly**

Use these data and test to see whether the mean number of parts produced is the same with each method. Use $\alpha = .05$.

57. Hargreaves Automotive Parts, Inc., wanted to compare the mileage for four different types of brake linings. Thirty linings of each type were produced and placed on a fleet of rental cars. The number of miles that each brake lining lasted until it no longer met the required federal safety standard was recorded, and an average value was computed for each type of lining. The following data were obtained.

| Type | Sample Size | Sample Mean | Standard Deviation |
|---|---|---|---|
| A | 30 | 32,000 | 1450 |
| B | 30 | 27,500 | 1525 |
| C | 30 | 34,200 | 1650 |
| D | 30 | 30,300 | 1400 |

Test to see whether the corresponding population means are equal. Use $\alpha = .05$.

58. A manufacturer of batteries for electronic toys and calculators is considering three new battery designs. Data were collected to determine whether the mean lifetime in hours is the same for each of the three designs.

| Design A | Design B | Design C |
|----------|----------|----------|
| 78 | 112 | 115 |
| 98 | 99 | 101 |
| 88 | 101 | 100 |
| 96 | 116 | 120 |

Test to see whether the population means are equal. Use $\alpha = .05$.

59. In a study conducted to investigate browsing activity by shoppers, each shopper was initially classified as a nonbrowser, light browser, or heavy browser. For each shopper, the study obtained a measure to determine how comfortable the shopper was in a store. Higher scores indicated greater comfort. Suppose the following data were collected.

**CD file**

**Browsing**

| Nonbrowser | Light Browser | Heavy Browser |
|------------|---------------|---------------|
| 4 | 5 | 5 |
| 5 | 6 | 7 |
| 6 | 5 | 5 |
| 3 | 4 | 7 |
| 3 | 7 | 4 |
| 4 | 4 | 6 |
| 5 | 6 | 5 |
| 4 | 5 | 7 |

a. Use $\alpha = .05$ to test for differences among comfort levels for the three types of browsers.
b. Use Fisher's LSD procedure to compare the comfort levels of nonbrowsers and light browsers. Use $\alpha = .05$. What is your conclusion?

60. A research firm tests the miles-per-gallon characteristics of three brands of gasoline. Because of different gasoline performance characteristics in different brands of automobiles, five brands of automobiles are selected and treated as blocks in the experiment; that is, each brand of automobile is tested with each type of gasoline. The results of the experiment (in miles per gallon) follow.

| | | Gasoline Brands | | |
|--|--|--|--|--|
| | | I | II | III |
| | A | 18 | 21 | 20 |
| | B | 24 | 26 | 27 |
| Automobiles | C | 30 | 29 | 34 |
| | D | 22 | 25 | 24 |
| | E | 20 | 23 | 24 |

a. At $\alpha = .05$, is there a significant difference in the mean miles-per-gallon characteristics of the three brands of gasoline?

b. Analyze the experimental data using the ANOVA procedure for completely randomized designs. Compare your findings with those obtained in part (a). What is the advantage of attempting to remove the block effect?

61. Wegman's Food Markets and Tops Friendly Markets are the major grocery chains in the Rochester, New York, area. When Wal-Mart opened a Supercenter in one of the Rochester suburbs, experts predicted that Wal-Mart would undersell both local stores. The *Democrat and Chronicle* obtained the price data in the following table for a 15-item market basket (*Democrat and Chronicle,* March 17, 2002).

**Grocery**

| Item | Tops | Wal-Mart | Wegmans |
|---|---|---|---|
| Bananas (1 lb.) | 0.49 | 0.48 | 0.49 |
| Campbell's soup (10.75 oz.) | 0.60 | 0.54 | 0.77 |
| Chicken breasts (3 lbs.) | 10.47 | 8.61 | 8.07 |
| Colgate toothpaste (6.2 oz.) | 1.99 | 2.40 | 1.97 |
| Large eggs (1 dozen) | 1.59 | 0.88 | 0.79 |
| Heinz ketchup (36 oz.) | 2.59 | 1.78 | 2.59 |
| Jell-O (cherry, 3 oz.) | 0.67 | 0.42 | 0.65 |
| Jif peanut butter (18 oz.) | 2.29 | 1.78 | 2.09 |
| Milk (fat free, 1/2 gal.) | 1.34 | 1.24 | 1.34 |
| Oscar Meyer hotdogs (1 lb.) | 3.29 | 1.50 | 3.39 |
| Ragu pasta sauce (1 lb., 10 oz.) | 2.09 | 1.50 | 1.25 |
| Ritz crackers (1 lb.) | 3.29 | 2.00 | 3.39 |
| Tide detergent (liquid, 100 oz.) | 6.79 | 5.24 | 5.99 |
| Tropicana orange juice (1/2 gal.) | 2.50 | 2.50 | 2.50 |
| Twizzlers (strawberry, 1 lb.) | 1.19 | 1.27 | 1.69 |

At the .05 level of significance, test for any significant difference in the mean price for the 15-item shopping basket for the three stores.

62. Each month *Internet Magazine* accesses more than 100 Internet service providers (ISPs) in order to check the availability of the ISP and test the speed of the connection by measuring the time (seconds) it takes to download a number of popular Web pages. The following data show the download time for 22 free ISPs for Web sites located in the United Kingdom, United States, and Europe (*Internet Magazine,* January 2000).

**ISP**

| ISP Name | U.K. | U.S. | Europe |
|---|---|---|---|
| Abel Gratis | 10.62 | 14.64 | 17.08 |
| Breathe | 11.67 | 14.14 | 19.86 |
| btclick.com | 12.12 | 16.43 | 21.30 |
| Bun | 11.13 | 14.09 | 15.83 |
| Cable & Wireless Life | 9.99 | 13.07 | 18.43 |
| conX | 12.63 | 15.97 | 22.12 |
| Freebeeb | 11.71 | 15.52 | 19.57 |
| Free-Online | 13.77 | 13.98 | 23.35 |
| Freeserve | 10.65 | 13.62 | 25.56 |

(*continued*)

| ISP Name | U.K. | U.S. | Europe |
|---|---|---|---|
| FreeUK | 12.20 | 14.96 | 18.95 |
| Icom-Web | 9.62 | 11.66 | 15.91 |
| IPNet | 13.82 | 16.70 | 22.86 |
| I-way Soho | 14.86 | 12.86 | 19.32 |
| LineOne | 12.01 | 17.82 | 21.88 |
| Madasafish | 13.38 | 15.59 | 19.61 |
| NetDirect Online | 11.71 | 15.52 | 19.57 |
| Netscape Online | 10.84 | 12.66 | 16.52 |
| Screaming.net (BT Line) | 13.23 | 15.91 | 23.08 |
| Telinco Internet Services | 12.83 | 15.34 | 18.76 |
| UK Online | 10.39 | 13.28 | 21.04 |
| UKPeople | 13.79 | 19.82 | 19.76 |
| Virgin Net | 12.17 | 15.47 | 21.94 |

At $\alpha = .05$, is there a significant difference in the mean download time for Web sites located in the United Kingdom, United States, and Europe?

63. A factorial experiment was designed to test for any significant differences in the time needed to perform English to foreign language translations with two computerized language translators. Because the type of language translated was also considered a significant factor, translations were made with both systems for three different languages: Spanish, French, and German. Use the following data for translation time in hours.

| | Language | | |
|---|---|---|---|
| | **Spanish** | **French** | **German** |
| System 1 | 8 <br> 12 | 10 <br> 14 | 12 <br> 16 |
| System 2 | 6 <br> 10 | 14 <br> 16 | 16 <br> 22 |

Test for any significant differences due to language translator, type of language, and interaction. Use $\alpha = .05$.

64. A manufacturing company designed a factorial experiment to determine whether the number of defective parts produced by two machines differed and if the number of defective parts produced also depended on whether the raw material needed by each machine was loaded manually or by an automatic feed system. The following data give the numbers of defective parts produced. Use $\alpha = .05$ to test for any significant effect due to machine, loading system, and interaction.

| | Loading System | |
|---|---|---|
| | **Manual** | **Automatic** |
| Machine 1 | 30 <br> 34 | 30 <br> 26 |
| Machine 2 | 20 <br> 22 | 24 <br> 28 |

# Case Problem 1   Wentworth Medical Center

As part of a long-term study of individuals 65 years of age or older, sociologists and physicians at the Wentworth Medical Center in upstate New York investigated the relationship between geographic location and depression. A sample of 60 individuals, all in reasonably good health, was selected; 20 individuals were residents of Florida, 20 were residents of New York, and 20 were residents of North Carolina. Each of the individuals sampled was given a standardized test to measure depression. The data collected follow; higher test scores indicate higher levels of depression. These data are available on the data disk in the file Medical1.

A second part of the study considered the relationship between geographic location and depression for individuals 65 years of age or older who had a chronic health condition such as arthritis, hypertension, and/or heart ailment. A sample of 60 individuals with such conditions was identified. Again, 20 were residents of Florida, 20 were residents of New York, and 20 were residents of North Carolina. The levels of depression recorded for this study follow. These data are available on the CD accompanying the text in the file named Medical2.

**CD** file
Medical1

**CD** file
Medical2

| Data from Medical1 | | | Data from Medical2 | | |
|---|---|---|---|---|---|
| Florida | New York | North Carolina | Florida | New York | North Carolina |
| 3 | 8 | 10 | 13 | 14 | 10 |
| 7 | 11 | 7 | 12 | 9 | 12 |
| 7 | 9 | 3 | 17 | 15 | 15 |
| 3 | 7 | 5 | 17 | 12 | 18 |
| 8 | 8 | 11 | 20 | 16 | 12 |
| 8 | 7 | 8 | 21 | 24 | 14 |
| 8 | 8 | 4 | 16 | 18 | 17 |
| 5 | 4 | 3 | 14 | 14 | 8 |
| 5 | 13 | 7 | 13 | 15 | 14 |
| 2 | 10 | 8 | 17 | 17 | 16 |
| 6 | 6 | 8 | 12 | 20 | 18 |
| 2 | 8 | 7 | 9 | 11 | 17 |
| 6 | 12 | 3 | 12 | 23 | 19 |
| 6 | 8 | 9 | 15 | 19 | 15 |
| 9 | 6 | 8 | 16 | 17 | 13 |
| 7 | 8 | 12 | 15 | 14 | 14 |
| 5 | 5 | 6 | 13 | 9 | 11 |
| 4 | 7 | 3 | 10 | 14 | 12 |
| 7 | 7 | 8 | 11 | 13 | 13 |
| 3 | 8 | 11 | 17 | 11 | 11 |

## Managerial Report

1. Use descriptive statistics to summarize the data from the two studies. What are your preliminary observations about the depression scores?
2. Use analysis of variance on both data sets. State the hypotheses being tested in each case. What are your conclusions?
3. Use inferences about individual treatment means where appropriate. What are your conclusions?
4. Discuss extensions of this study or other analyses that you feel might be helpful.

**Case Problem 2**   # Compensation for ID Professionals

For the preceding 10 years *Industrial Distribution* tracked compensation of industrial distribution (ID) professionals. Results for the 358 respondents in the 1997 Annual Salary Survey showed that 27% of the respondents work for companies with sales over $40 million, with the typical ID professional working for a $12 million firm. Those who work for small to mid-sized companies (between $6 million and $20 million) report higher earnings than those in larger firms. The lowest paid employees work for firms with sales of less than $1 million. The typical outside salesperson made $50,000 in 1996, and the typical inside salesperson earned just $30,000 (*Industrial Distribution*, November 1997). Suppose that a local chapter of ID professionals in the greater San Francisco area conducted a survey of its membership to study the relationship, if any, between the years of experience and salary for individuals employed in outside and inside sales positions. On the survey, respondents were asked to specify one of three levels of years of experience: low (1–10 years), medium (11–20 years), and high (21 or more years). A portion of the data obtained follow. The complete data set, consisting of 120 observations, is available on the CD accompanying the text in the file named IDSalary.

IDSalary

| Observation | Salary $ | Position | Experience |
|---|---|---|---|
| 1 | 28938 | Inside | Medium |
| 2 | 27694 | Inside | Medium |
| 3 | 45515 | Outside | Low |
| 4 | 27031 | Inside | Medium |
| 5 | 37283 | Outside | Low |
| 6 | 32718 | Inside | Low |
| 7 | 54081 | Outside | High |
| 8 | 23621 | Inside | Low |
| 9 | 47835 | Outside | High |
| 10 | 29768 | Inside | Medium |
| . | . | . | . |
| . | . | . | . |
| . | . | . | . |
| 115 | 33080 | Inside | High |
| 116 | 53702 | Outside | Medium |
| 117 | 58131 | Outside | Medium |
| 118 | 32788 | Inside | High |
| 119 | 28070 | Inside | Medium |
| 120 | 35259 | Outside | Low |

## Managerial Report

1. Use descriptive statistics to summarize the data.
2. Develop a 95% confidence interval estimate of the mean annual salary for all salespersons, regardless of years of experience and type of position.
3. Develop a 95% confidence interval estimate of the mean salary for outside salespersons. Compare your results with the national value reported by *Industrial Distribution*.
4. Develop a 95% confidence interval estimate of the mean salary for inside salespersons. Compare your results with the national value reported by *Industrial Distribution*.

**5.** Ignoring the years of experience, develop a 95% confidence interval estimate of the mean difference between the annual salary for outside salespersons and the mean annual salary for inside salespersons. What is your conclusion?

**6.** Use analysis of variance to test for any significant differences due to position. Use a .05 level of significance, and for now, ignore the effect of years of experience.

**7.** Use analysis of variance to test for any significant differences due to years of experience. Use a .05 level of significance, and for now, ignore the effect of position.

**8.** At the .05 level of significance test for any significant differences due to position, years of experience, and interaction. Use inferences about individual treatment means where appropriate.

## Appendix 13.1   Analysis of Variance and Experimental Design with Minitab

### Single-Factor Observational Studies and Completely Randomized Designs

In Section 13.2 we showed how analysis of variance could be used to test for the equality of $k$ population means using data from an observational study. In Section 13.5 we showed how the same approach could be used to test for the equality of $k$ population means in situations where the data have been collected in a completely randomized design. To illustrate how Minitab can be used to test for the equality of $k$ population means for both of these cases, we show how to test whether the mean examination score is the same at each plant in the National Computer Products example introduced in Section 13.1. The examination score data are entered into the first three columns of a Minitab worksheet; column 1 is labeled Atlanta, column 2 is labeled Dallas, and column 3 is labeled Seattle. The following steps produce the Minitab output in Figure 13.4

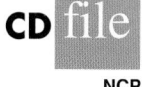

**NCP**

**Step 1.** Select the **Stat** menu
**Step 2.** Choose **ANOVA**
**Step 3.** Choose **One-way (Unstacked)**
**Step 4.** When the One-way Analysis of Variance dialog box appears:
  Enter C1-C3 in the **Responses (in separate columns)** box
  Click **OK**

### Randomized Block Designs

In Section 13.6 we showed how analysis of variance could be used to test for the equality of $k$ population means using data from a randomized block design. To illustrate how Minitab can be used for this type of experimental design, we show how to test whether the mean stress levels for air traffic controllers is the same for three work stations. The stress level scores shown in Table 13.6 are entered into column 1 of a Minitab worksheet. Coding the treatments as 1 for System A, 2 for System B, and 3 for System C, the coded values for the treatments are entered into column 2 of the worksheet. Finally, the corresponding number of each controller (1, 2, 3, 4, 5, 6) is entered into column 3. Thus, the values in the first row of the worksheet are 15, 1, 1; the values in row 2 are 15, 2, 1; the values in row 3 are 18, 3, 1; the values in row 4 are 14, 1, 2; and so on. The following steps produce the Minitab output corresponding to the ANOVA table shown in Table 13.9.

**Step 1.** Select the **Stat** menu
**Step 2.** Choose **ANOVA**

**Step 3.** Choose **Two-way**
**Step 4.** When the Two-way Analysis of Variance dialog box appears:
      Enter C1 in the **Response** box
      Enter C2 in the **Row factor** box
      Enter C3 in the **Column factor** box
      Select **Fit additive model**
      Click **OK**

## Factorial Experiments

In Section 13.7 we showed how analysis of variance could be used to test for the equality of $k$ population means using data from a factorial experiment. To illustrate how Minitab can be used for this type of experimental design, we show how to analyze the data for the two-factor GMAT experiment introduced in that section. The GMAT scores shown in Table 13.11 are entered into column 1 of a Minitab worksheet; column 1 is labeled Score, column 2 is labeled Factor A, and column 3 is labeled Factor B. Coding the factor A preparation programs as 1 for the three-hour review, 2 for the one-day program, and 3 for the 10-week course, the coded values for factor A are entered into column 2 of the worksheet. Coding the factor B colleges as 1 for Business, 2 for Engineering, and 3 for Arts and Sciences, the coded values for factor B are entered into column 3. Thus, the values in the first row of the worksheet are 500, 1, 1; the values in row 2 are 580, 1, 1; the values in row 3 are 540, 1, 2; the values in row 4 are 460, 1, 2; and so on. The following steps produce the Minitab output corresponding to the ANOVA table shown in Figure 13.6.

**Step 1.** Select the **Stat** menu
**Step 2.** Choose **ANOVA**
**Step 3.** Choose **Two-way**
**Step 4.** When the Two-way Analysis of Variance dialog box appears:
      Enter C1 in the **Response** box
      Enter C2 in the **Row factor** box
      Enter C3 in the **Column factor** box
      Click **OK**

## Appendix 13.2   Analysis of Variance and Experimental Design with Excel

### Single-Factor Observational Studies and Completely Randomized Designs

In Section 13.2 we showed how analysis of variance could be used to test for the equality of $k$ population means using data from an observational study. In Section 13.5 we showed how the same approach could be used to test for equality of $k$ population means in situations where the data are collected in a completely randomized design. To illustrate how Excel can be used to test for the equality of $k$ population means for both of these cases, we show how to test whether the mean examination score is the same at each plant in the National Computer Products example introduced in Section 13.1. The examination score data are entered into worksheet rows 2 to 7 of columns B, C, and D as shown in Figure 13.7. Note that cells A2:A7 are used to identify the observations at each of the plants. The following steps are used to obtain the output shown in

**CD** file

**NCP**

**FIGURE 13.7   EXCEL SOLUTION FOR THE NCP ANALYSIS OF VARIANCE EXAMPLE**

|    | A | B | C | D | E | F | G | H |
|----|---|---|---|---|---|---|---|---|
| 1 | **Observation** | **Atlanta** | **Dallas** | **Seattle** | | | | |
| 2 | 1 | 85 | 71 | 59 | | | | |
| 3 | 2 | 75 | 75 | 64 | | | | |
| 4 | 3 | 82 | 73 | 62 | | | | |
| 5 | 4 | 76 | 74 | 69 | | | | |
| 6 | 5 | 71 | 69 | 75 | | | | |
| 7 | 6 | 85 | 82 | 67 | | | | |
| 8 | | | | | | | | |
| 9 | Anova: Single Factor | | | | | | | |
| 10 | | | | | | | | |
| 11 | SUMMARY | | | | | | | |
| 12 | *Groups* | *Count* | *Sum* | *Average* | *Variance* | | | |
| 13 | Atlanta | 6 | 474 | 79 | 34 | | | |
| 14 | Dallas | 6 | 444 | 74 | 20 | | | |
| 15 | Seattle | 6 | 396 | 66 | 32 | | | |
| 16 | | | | | | | | |
| 17 | | | | | | | | |
| 18 | ANOVA | | | | | | | |
| 19 | *Source of Variation* | *SS* | *df* | *MS* | *F* | *P-value* | *F crit* | |
| 20 | Between Groups | 516 | 2 | 258 | 9 | 0.0027 | 3.68 | |
| 21 | Within Groups | 430 | 15 | 28.6667 | | | | |
| 22 | | | | | | | | |
| 23 | Total | 946 | 17 | | | | | |
| 24 | | | | | | | | |

cells A9:G23; the ANOVA portion of this output corresponds to the ANOVA table shown in Table 13.2.

> **Step 1.** Select the **Tools** menu
> **Step 2.** Choose **Data Analysis**
> **Step 3.** Choose **Anova: Single-Factor** from the list of Analysis Tools
> Click **OK**
> **Step 4.** When the Anova: Single-Factor dialog box appears:
> Enter B1:D7 in **Input Range** box
> Select **Columns**
> Select **Labels in First Row**
> Select **Output Range** and enter A9 in the box
> Click **OK**

## Randomized Block Designs

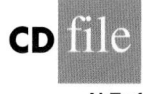

**AirTraf**

In Section 13.6 we showed how analysis of variance could be used to test for the equality of *k* population means using data from a randomized block design. To illustrate how Excel can be used for this type of experimental design, we show how to test whether the mean stress levels for air traffic controllers are the same for three work stations. The stress level scores shown in Table 13.6 are entered into worksheet rows 2 to 7 of columns B, C, and D as shown in Figure 13.8. The cells in rows 2 to 7 of column A contain the number of each

**FIGURE 13.8    EXCEL SOLUTION FOR THE AIR TRAFFIC CONTROLLER STRESS TEST**

| | A | B | C | D | E | F | G | H |
|---|---|---|---|---|---|---|---|---|
| 1 | **Controller** | **System A** | **System B** | **System C** | | | | |
| 2 | 1 | 15 | 15 | 18 | | | | |
| 3 | 2 | 14 | 14 | 14 | | | | |
| 4 | 3 | 10 | 11 | 15 | | | | |
| 5 | 4 | 13 | 12 | 17 | | | | |
| 6 | 5 | 16 | 13 | 16 | | | | |
| 7 | 6 | 13 | 13 | 13 | | | | |
| 8 | | | | | | | | |
| 9 | Anova: Two-Factor Without Replication | | | | | | | |
| 10 | | | | | | | | |
| 11 | *SUMMARY* | *Count* | *Sum* | *Average* | *Variance* | | | |
| 12 | 1 | 3 | 48 | 16 | 3 | | | |
| 13 | 2 | 3 | 42 | 14 | 0 | | | |
| 14 | 3 | 3 | 36 | 12 | 7 | | | |
| 15 | 4 | 3 | 42 | 14 | 7 | | | |
| 16 | 5 | 3 | 45 | 15 | 3 | | | |
| 17 | 6 | 3 | 39 | 13 | 0 | | | |
| 18 | | | | | | | | |
| 19 | System A | 6 | 81 | 13.5 | 4.3 | | | |
| 20 | System B | 6 | 78 | 13 | 2 | | | |
| 21 | System C | 6 | 93 | 15.5 | 3.5 | | | |
| 22 | | | | | | | | |
| 23 | | | | | | | | |
| 24 | ANOVA | | | | | | | |
| 25 | *Source of Variation* | *SS* | *df* | *MS* | *F* | *P-value* | *F crit* | |
| 26 | Rows | 30 | 5 | 6 | 3.16 | 0.0574 | 3.33 | |
| 27 | Columns | 21 | 2 | 10.5 | 5.53 | 0.0242 | 4.10 | |
| 28 | Error | 19 | 10 | 1.9 | | | | |
| 29 | | | | | | | | |
| 30 | Total | 70 | 17 | | | | | |
| 31 | | | | | | | | |

controller (1, 2, 3, 4, 5, 6). The following steps produce the Excel output corresponding to the ANOVA table shown in Table 13.9.

**Step 1.** Select the **Tools** menu
**Step 2.** Choose **Data Analysis**
**Step 3.** Choose **Anova: Two-Factor Without Replication** from the list of Analysis Tools
　　　　　Click **OK**
**Step 4.** When the Anova: Two-Factor Without Replication dialog box appears:
　　　　　Enter A1:D7 in **Input Range** box
　　　　　Select **Labels**
　　　　　Select **Output Range** and enter A9 in the box
　　　　　Click **OK**

## Factorial Experiments

In Section 13.7 we showed how analysis of variance could be used to test for the equality of $k$ population means using data from a factorial experiment. To illustrate how Excel can be used for this type of experimental design, we show how to analyze the data for the two-factor GMAT experiment introduced in that section. The GMAT scores shown in Table 13.11 are entered into worksheet rows 2 to 7 of columns B, C, and D as shown in Figure 13.9. The following steps are used to obtain the output shown in

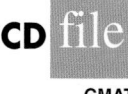

**CD file**

**GMAT**

**FIGURE 13.9**   EXCEL SOLUTION FOR THE TWO-FACTOR GMAT EXPERIMENT

| | A | B | C | D | E | F | G | H |
|---|---|---|---|---|---|---|---|---|
| 1 | | **Business** | **Engineering** | **Arts and Sciences** | | | | |
| 2 | 3-hour review | 500 | 540 | 480 | | | | |
| 3 | | 580 | 460 | 400 | | | | |
| 4 | 1-day program | 460 | 560 | 420 | | | | |
| 5 | | 540 | 620 | 480 | | | | |
| 6 | 10-week course | 560 | 600 | 480 | | | | |
| 7 | | 600 | 580 | 410 | | | | |
| 8 | | | | | | | | |
| 9 | Anova: Two-Factor With Replication | | | | | | | |
| 10 | | | | | | | | |
| 11 | SUMMARY | Business | Engineering | Arts and Sciences | Total | | | |
| 12 | *3-hour review* | | | | | | | |
| 13 | Count | 2 | 2 | 2 | 6 | | | |
| 14 | Sum | 1080 | 1000 | 880 | 2960 | | | |
| 15 | Average | 540 | 500 | 440 | 493.3333 | | | |
| 16 | Variance | 3200 | 3200 | 3200 | 3946.667 | | | |
| 17 | | | | | | | | |
| 18 | *1-day program* | | | | | | | |
| 19 | Count | 2 | 2 | 2 | 6 | | | |
| 20 | Sum | 1000 | 1180 | 900 | 3080 | | | |
| 21 | Average | 500 | 590 | 450 | 513.3333 | | | |
| 22 | Variance | 3200 | 1800 | 1800 | 5386.667 | | | |
| 23 | | | | | | | | |
| 24 | *10-week course* | | | | | | | |
| 25 | Count | 2 | 2 | 2 | 6 | | | |
| 26 | Sum | 1160 | 1180 | 890 | 3230 | | | |
| 27 | Average | 580 | 590 | 445 | 538.3333 | | | |
| 28 | Variance | 800 | 200 | 2450 | 5936.667 | | | |
| 29 | | | | | | | | |
| 30 | *Total* | | | | | | | |
| 31 | Count | 6 | 6 | 6 | | | | |
| 32 | Sum | 3240 | 3360 | 2670 | | | | |
| 33 | Average | 540 | 560 | 445 | | | | |
| 34 | Variance | 2720 | 3200 | 1510 | | | | |
| 35 | | | | | | | | |
| 36 | | | | | | | | |
| 37 | ANOVA | | | | | | | |
| 38 | *Source of Variation* | SS | df | MS | F | P-value | F crit | |
| 39 | Sample | 6100 | 2 | 3050 | 1.38 | 0.2994 | 4.26 | |
| 40 | Columns | 45300 | 2 | 22650 | 10.27 | 0.0048 | 4.26 | |
| 41 | Interaction | 11200 | 4 | 2800 | 1.27 | 0.3503 | 3.63 | |
| 42 | Within | 19850 | 9 | 2205.5556 | | | | |
| 43 | | | | | | | | |
| 44 | Total | 82450 | 17 | | | | | |
| 45 | | | | | | | | |

cells A9:G44; the ANOVA portion of this output corresponds to the ANOVA table shown in Table 13.14.

**Step 1.** Select the **Tools** menu

**Step 2.** Choose **Data Analysis**

**Step 3.** Choose **Anova: Two-Factor With Replication** from the list of Analysis Tools
Click **OK**

**Step 4.** When the Anova: Two-Factor With Replication dialog box appears:
Enter A1:D7 in **Input Range** box
Enter 2 in **Rows per sample** box
Select **Output Range** and enter A10 in the box
Click **OK**

# CHAPTER 14

# Simple Linear Regression

## CONTENTS

## ALLIANCE DATA SYSTEMS*
*DALLAS, TEXAS*

Alliance Data Systems (ADS) provides transaction processing, credit services, and marketing services for clients in the rapidly growing customer relationship management (CRM) industry. ADS clients are concentrated in four industries: retail, petroleum/convenience stores, utilities, and transportation. In 1983, Alliance began offering end-to-end credit processing services to the retail, petroleum, and casual dining industries; today they employ more than 6500 employees who provide services to clients around the world. Operating more than 140,000 point-of-sale terminals in the United States alone, ADS processes in excess of 2.5 billion transactions annually. The company ranks second in the United States in private label credit services by representing 49 private label programs with nearly 72 million cardholders. In 2001, ADS made an initial public offering and is now listed on the New York Stock Exchange.

As one of its marketing services, ADS designs direct mail campaigns and promotions. With its database containing information on the spending habits of more than 100 million consumers, ADS can target those consumers most likely to benefit from a direct mail promotion. The Analytical Development Group uses regression analysis to build models that measure and predict the responsiveness of consumers to direct market campaigns. Some regression models predict the probability of purchase for individuals receiving a promotion, and others predict the amount spent by those consumers making a purchase.

For one particular campaign, a retail store chain wanted to attract new customers. To predict the effect of the campaign, ADS analysts selected a sample from the consumer database, sent the sampled individuals promotional materials, and then collected transaction data on the consumers' response. Sample data were collected on the amount of purchase made by the consumers responding to the campaign, as well as a variety of consumer-specific variables thought to be useful in predicting sales. The consumer-specific variable that contributed most to predicting the amount purchased was the total amount of credit purchases at related stores over the past 39 months. ADS analysts

*The authors are indebted to Philip Clemance, Director of Analytical Development at Alliance Data Systems, for providing this Statistics in Practice.

Alliance Data analysts discuss use of a regression model to predict sales for a direct marketing campaign. © Courtesy of Alliance Data Systems.

developed an estimated regression equation relating the amount of purchase to the amount spent at related stores:

$$\hat{y} = 26.7 + 0.00205x$$

where

$$\hat{y} = \text{amount of purchase}$$
$$x = \text{amount spent at related stores}$$

Using this equation, we could predict that someone spending \$10,000 over the past 39 months at related stores would spend \$47.20 when responding to the direct mail promotion. In this chapter, you will learn how to develop this type of estimated regression equation.

The final model developed by ADS analysts also included several other variables that increased the predictive power of the preceding equation. Some of these variables included the absence/presence of a bank credit card, estimated income, and the average amount spent per trip at a selected store. In the following chapter, we will learn how such additional variables can be incorporated into a multiple regression model.

Managerial decisions often are based on the relationship between two or more variables. For example, after considering the relationship between advertising expenditures and sales, a marketing manager might attempt to predict sales for a given level of advertising expenditures. In another case, a public utility might use the relationship between the daily high temperature and the demand for electricity to predict electricity usage on the basis of next month's anticipated daily high temperatures. Sometimes a manager will rely on intuition to judge how two variables are related. However, if data can be obtained, a statistical procedure called *regression analysis* can be used to develop an equation showing how the variables are related.

*The statistical methods used in studying the relationship between two variables were first employed by Sir Francis Galton (1822–1911). Galton was interested in studying the relationship between a father's height and the son's height. Galton's disciple, Karl Pearson (1857–1936), analyzed the relationship between the father's height and the son's height for 1078 pairs of subjects.*

In regression terminology, the variable being predicted is called the **dependent variable**. The variable or variables being used to predict the value of the dependent variable are called the **independent variables**. For example, in analyzing the effect of advertising expenditures on sales, a marketing manager's desire to predict sales would suggest making sales the dependent variable. Advertising expenditure would be the independent variable used to help predict sales. In statistical notation, $y$ denotes the dependent variable and $x$ denotes the independent variable.

In this chapter we consider the simplest type of regression analysis involving one independent variable and one dependent variable in which the relationship between the variables is approximated by a straight line. It is called **simple linear regression**. Regression analysis involving two or more independent variables is called multiple regression analysis; multiple regression and cases involving curvilinear relationships are covered in Chapters 15 and 16.

# 14.1   Simple Linear Regression Model

Armand's Pizza Parlors is a chain of Italian-food restaurants located in a five-state area. Armand's most successful locations are near college campuses. The managers believe that quarterly sales for these restaurants (denoted by $y$) are related positively to the size of the student population (denoted by $x$); that is, restaurants near campuses with a large student population tend to generate more sales than those located near campuses with a small student population. Using regression analysis, we can develop an equation showing how the dependent variable $y$ is related to the independent variable $x$.

## Regression Model and Regression Equation

In the Armand's Pizza Parlors example, the population consists of all the Armand's restaurants. For every restaurant in the population, there is a value of $x$ (student population) and a corresponding value of $y$ (quarterly sales). The equation that describes how $y$ is related to $x$ and an error term is called the **regression model**. The regression model used in simple linear regression follows.

SIMPLE LINEAR REGRESSION MODEL

$$y = \beta_0 + \beta_1 x + \epsilon \qquad (14.1)$$

$\beta_0$ and $\beta_1$ are referred to as the parameters of the model, and $\epsilon$ (the Greek letter epsilon) is a random variable referred to as the error term. The error term accounts for the variability in $y$ that cannot be explained by the linear relationship between $x$ and $y$.

The population of all Armand's restaurants can also be viewed as a collection of sub-populations, one for each distinct value of $x$. For example, one subpopulation consists of all Armand's restaurants located near college campuses with 8000 students; another subpopulation consists of all Armand's restaurants located near college campuses with 9000 students; and so on. Each subpopulation has a corresponding distribution of $y$ values. Thus, a distribution of $y$ values is associated with restaurants located near campuses with 8000 students; a distribution of $y$ values is associated with restaurants located near campuses with 9000 students; and so on. Each distribution of $y$ values has its own mean or expected value. The equation that describes how the expected value of $y$, denoted $E(y)$, is related to $x$ is called the **regression equation**. The regression equation for simple linear regression follows.

---

SIMPLE LINEAR REGRESSION EQUATION

$$E(y) = \beta_0 + \beta_1 x \tag{14.2}$$

---

The graph of the simple linear regression equation is a straight line; $\beta_0$ is the $y$-intercept of the regression line, $\beta_1$ is the slope, and $E(y)$ is the mean or expected value of $y$ for a given value of $x$.

Examples of possible regression lines are shown in Figure 14.1. The regression line in Panel A shows that the mean value of $y$ is related positively to $x$, with larger values of $E(y)$ associated with larger values of $x$. The regression line in Panel B shows the mean value of $y$ is related negatively to $x$, with smaller values of $E(y)$ associated with larger values of $x$. The regression line in Panel C shows the case in which the mean value of $y$ is not related to $x$; that is, the mean value of $y$ is the same for every value of $x$.

## Estimated Regression Equation

If the values of the population parameters $\beta_0$ and $\beta_1$ were known, we could use equation (14.2) to compute the mean value of $y$ for a given value of $x$. In practice, the parameter values are not known, and must be estimated using sample data. Sample statistics (denoted $b_0$ and $b_1$) are computed as estimates of the population parameters $\beta_0$ and $\beta_1$. Substituting the values of the sample statistics $b_0$ and $b_1$ for $\beta_0$ and $\beta_1$ in the regression equation, we obtain

**FIGURE 14.1** POSSIBLE REGRESSION LINES IN SIMPLE LINEAR REGRESSION

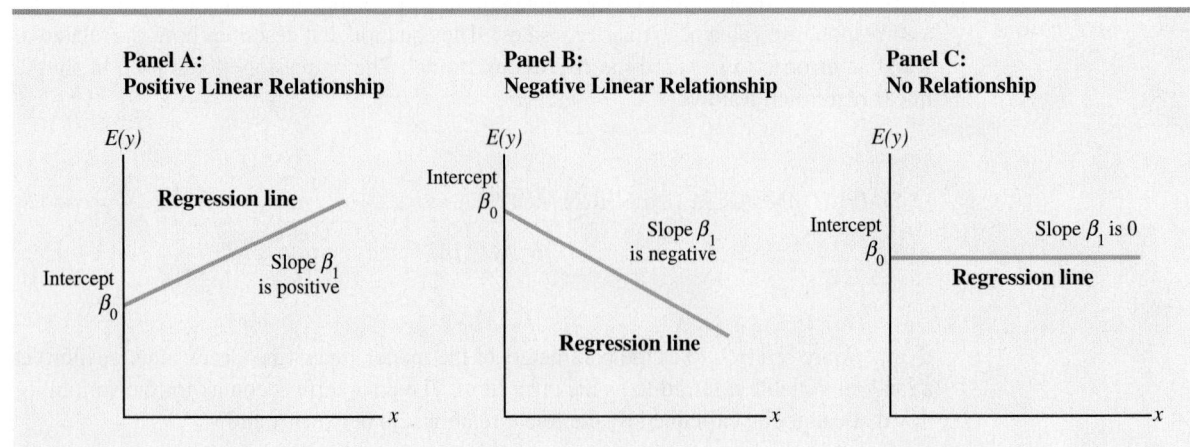

the **estimated regression equation**. The estimated regression equation for simple linear regression follows.

---

ESTIMATED SIMPLE LINEAR REGRESSION EQUATION

$$\hat{y} = b_0 + b_1 x \qquad (14.3)$$

---

The graph of the estimated simple linear regression equation is called the *estimated regression line*; $b_0$ is the $y$ intercept and $b_1$ is the slope. In the next section, we show how the least squares method can be used to compute the values of $b_0$ and $b_1$ in the estimated regression equation.

In general, $\hat{y}$ is the point estimator of $E(y)$, the mean value of $y$ for a given value of $x$. Thus, to estimate the mean or expected value of quarterly sales for all restaurants located near campuses with 10,000 students, Armand's would substitute the value of 10,000 for $x$ in equation (14.3). In some cases, however, Armand's may be more interested in predicting sales for one particular restaurant. For example, suppose Armand's would like to predict quarterly sales for the restaurant located near Talbot College, a school with 10,000 students. As it turns out, the best estimate of $y$ for a given value of $x$ is also provided by $\hat{y}$. Thus, to predict quarterly sales for the restaurant located near Talbot College, Armand's would also substitute the value of 10,000 for $x$ in equation (14.3).

Because the value of $\hat{y}$ provides both a point estimate of $E(y)$ for a given value of $x$ and a point estimate of an individual value of $y$ for a given value of $x$, we will refer to $\hat{y}$ simply as the *estimated value of y*. Figure 14.2 provides a summary of the estimation process for simple linear regression.

**FIGURE 14.2   THE ESTIMATION PROCESS IN SIMPLE LINEAR REGRESSION**

*The estimation of $\beta_0$ and $\beta_1$ is a statistical process much like the estimation of $\mu$ discussed in Chapter 7. $\beta_0$ and $\beta_1$ are the unknown parameters of interest, and $b_0$ and $b_1$ are the sample statistics used to estimate the parameters.*

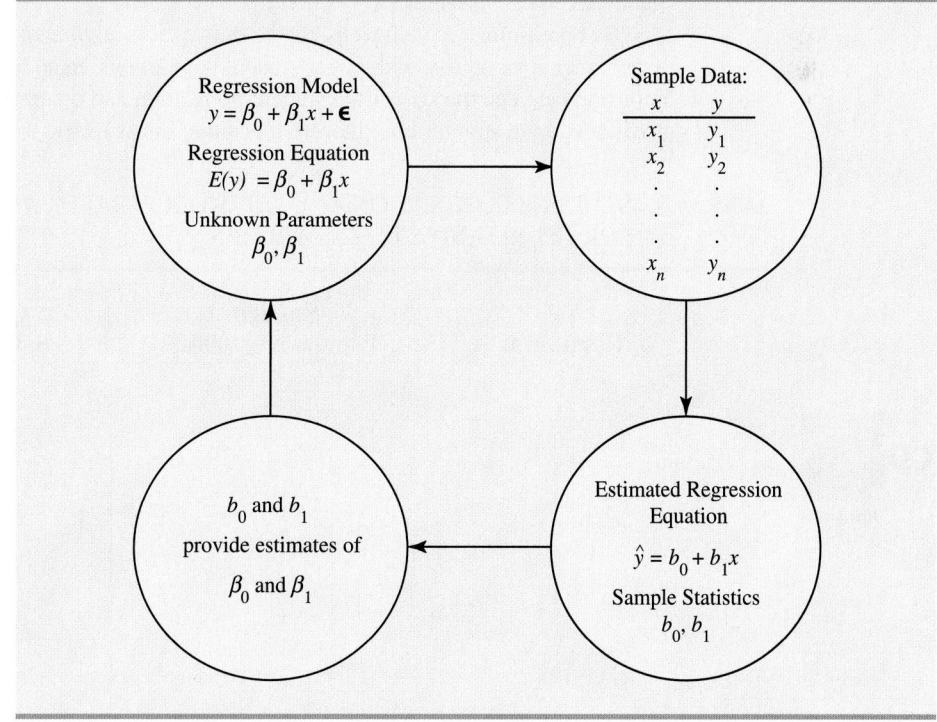

1. Regression analysis cannot be interpreted as a procedure for establishing a cause-and-effect relationship between variables. It can only indicate how or to what extent variables are associated with each other. Any conclusions about cause and effect must be based upon the judgment of those individuals most knowledgeable about the application.

2. The regression equation in simple linear regression is $E(y) = \beta_0 + \beta_1 x$. More advanced texts in regression analysis often write the regression equation as $E(y|x) = \beta_0 + \beta_1 x$ to emphasize that the regression equation provides the mean value of $y$ for a given value of $x$.

# 14.2   Least Squares Method

*In simple linear regression, each observation consists of two values: one for the independent variable and one for the dependent variable.*

The **least squares method** is a procedure for using sample data to find the estimated regression equation. To illustrate the least squares method, suppose data were collected from a sample of 10 Armand's Pizza Parlor restaurants located near college campuses. For the $i$th observation or restaurant in the sample, $x_i$ is the size of the student population (in thousands) and $y_i$ is the quarterly sales (in thousands of dollars). The values of $x_i$ and $y_i$ for the 10 restaurants in the sample are summarized in Table 14.1. We see that restaurant 1, with $x_1 = 2$ and $y_1 = 58$, is near a campus with 2000 students and has quarterly sales of $58,000. Restaurant 2, with $x_2 = 6$ and $y_2 = 105$, is near a campus with 6000 students and has quarterly sales of $105,000. The largest sales value is for restaurant 10, which is near a campus with 26,000 students and has quarterly sales of $202,000.

Figure 14.3 is a scatter diagram of the data in Table 14.1. Student population is shown on the horizontal axis and quarterly sales is shown on the vertical axis. **Scatter diagrams** for regression analysis are constructed with the independent variable $x$ on the horizontal axis and the dependent variable $y$ on the vertical axis. The scatter diagram enables us to observe the data graphically and to draw preliminary conclusions about the possible relationship between the variables.

What preliminary conclusions can be drawn from Figure 14.3? Quarterly sales appear to be higher at campuses with larger student populations. In addition, for these data the relationship between the size of the student population and quarterly sales appears to be approximated by a straight line; indeed, a positive linear relationship is indicated between $x$

**CD file**

**Armand's**

**TABLE 14.1**   STUDENT POPULATION AND QUARTERLY SALES DATA
FOR 10 ARMAND'S PIZZA PARLORS

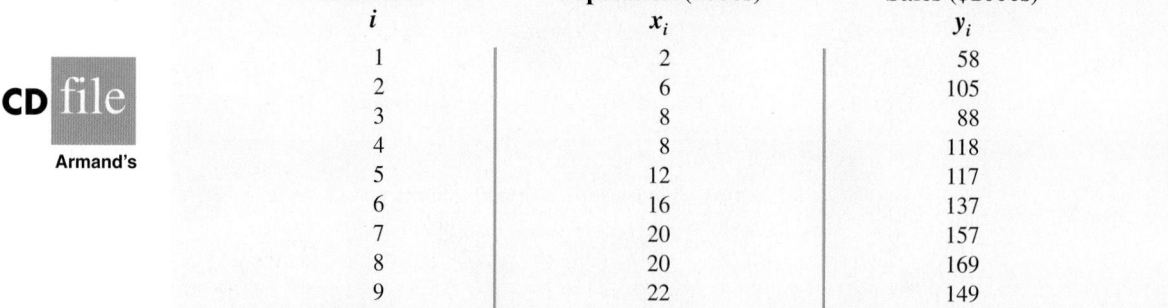

| Restaurant $i$ | Student Population (1000s) $x_i$ | Quarterly Sales ($1000s) $y_i$ |
|---|---|---|
| 1 | 2 | 58 |
| 2 | 6 | 105 |
| 3 | 8 | 88 |
| 4 | 8 | 118 |
| 5 | 12 | 117 |
| 6 | 16 | 137 |
| 7 | 20 | 157 |
| 8 | 20 | 169 |
| 9 | 22 | 149 |
| 10 | 26 | 202 |

FIGURE 14.3  SCATTER DIAGRAM OF STUDENT POPULATION AND QUARTERLY
SALES FOR ARMAND'S PIZZA PARLORS

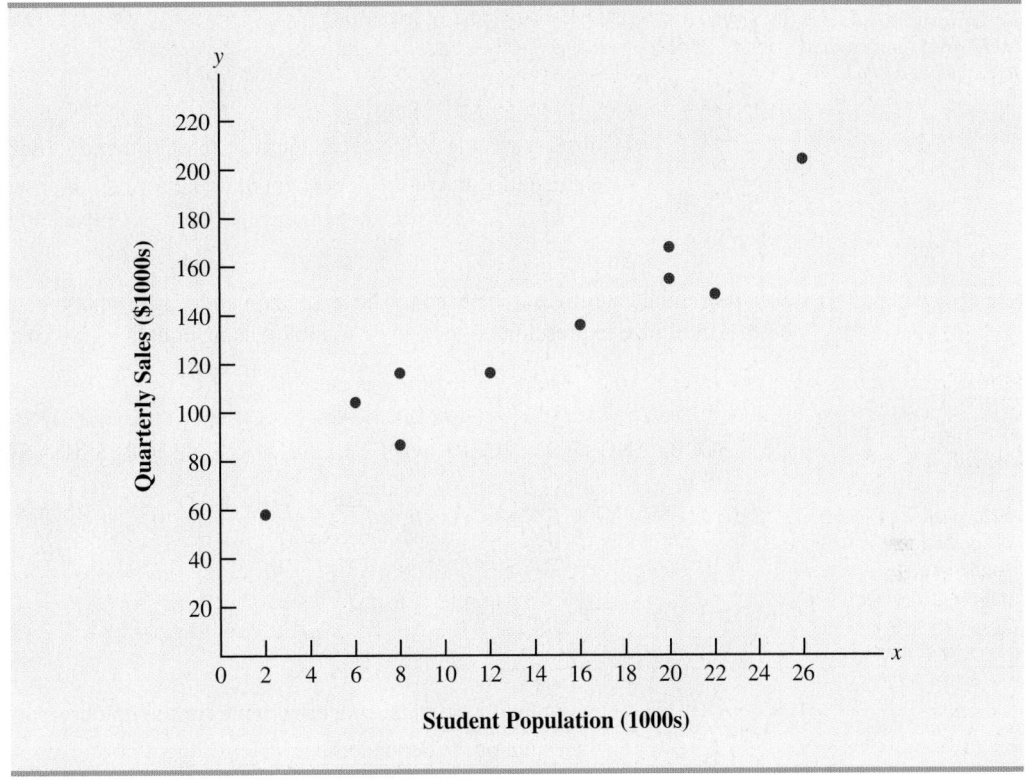

and $y$. We therefore choose the simple linear regression model to represent the relationship
between quarterly sales and student population. Given that choice, our next task is to use
the sample data in Table 14.1 to determine the values of $b_0$ and $b_1$ in the estimated simple
linear regression equation. For the $i$th restaurant, the estimated regression equation provides

$$\hat{y}_i = b_0 + b_1 x_i \tag{14.4}$$

where

$\hat{y}_i$ = estimated value of quarterly sales ($1000s) for the $i$th restaurant

$b_0$ = the $y$ intercept of the estimated regression line

$b_1$ = the slope of the estimated regression line

$x_i$ = size of the student population (1000s) for the $i$th restaurant

With $y_i$ denoting the observed (actual) sales for restaurant $i$ and $\hat{y}_i$ in equation (14.4) representing the estimated value of sales for restaurant $i$, every restaurant in the sample will have
an observed value of sales $y_i$ and an estimated value of sales $\hat{y}_i$. For the estimated regression line to provide a good fit to the data, we want the differences between the observed
sales values and the estimated sales values to be small.

The least squares method uses the sample data to provide the values of $b_0$ and $b_1$ that
minimize the *sum of the squares of the deviations* between the observed values of the dependent variable $y_i$ and the estimated values of the dependent variable. The criterion for the
least squares method is given by expression (14.5).

LEAST SQUARES CRITERION

*Carl Friedrich Gauss (1777–1855) proposed the least squares method.*

$$\min \Sigma(y_i - \hat{y}_i)^2 \qquad (14.5)$$

where

$y_i$ = observed value of the dependent variable for the $i$th observation
$\hat{y}_i$ = estimated value of the dependent variable for the $i$th observation

Differential calculus can be used to show (see Appendix 14.1) that the values of $b_0$ and $b_1$ that minimize expression (14.5) can be found by using equations (14.6) and (14.7).

SLOPE AND $y$-INTERCEPT FOR THE ESTIMATED REGRESSION EQUATION*

*In computing $b_1$ with a calculator, carry as many significant digits as possible in the intermediate calculations. We recommend carrying at least four significant digits.*

$$b_1 = \frac{\Sigma(x_i - \bar{x})(y_i - \bar{y})}{\Sigma(x_i - \bar{x})^2} \qquad (14.6)$$

$$b_0 = \bar{y} - b_1\bar{x} \qquad (14.7)$$

where

$x_i$ = value of the independent variable for the $i$th observation
$y_i$ = value of the dependent variable for the $i$th observation
$\bar{x}$ = mean value for the independent variable
$\bar{y}$ = mean value for the dependent variable
$n$ = total number of observations

Some of the calculations necessary to develop the least squares estimated regression equation for Armand's Pizza Parlors are shown in Table 14.2. With the sample of 10 restaurants, we have $n = 10$ observations. Because equations (14.6) and (14.7) require $\bar{x}$ and $\bar{y}$ we begin the calculations by computing $\bar{x}$ and $\bar{y}$.

$$\bar{x} = \frac{\Sigma x_i}{n} = \frac{140}{10} = 14$$

$$\bar{y} = \frac{\Sigma y_i}{n} = \frac{1300}{10} = 130$$

Using equations (14.6) and (14.7) and the information in Table 14.2, we can compute the slope and intercept of the estimated regression equation for Armand's Pizza Parlors. The calculation of the slope ($b_1$) proceeds as follows.

---

*An alternate formula for $b_1$ is

$$b_1 = \frac{\Sigma x_i y_i - (\Sigma x_i \Sigma y_i)/n}{\Sigma x_i^2 - (\Sigma x_i)^2/n}$$

This form of equation (14.6) is often recommended when using a calculator to compute $b_1$.

TABLE 14.2   CALCULATIONS FOR THE LEAST SQUARES ESTIMATED REGRESSION
EQUATION FOR ARMAND PIZZA PARLORS

| Restaurant $i$ | $x_i$ | $y_i$ | $x_i - \bar{x}$ | $y_i - \bar{y}$ | $(x_i - \bar{x})(y_i - \bar{y})$ | $(x_i - \bar{x})^2$ |
|---|---|---|---|---|---|---|
| 1 | 2 | 58 | $-12$ | $-72$ | 864 | 144 |
| 2 | 6 | 105 | $-8$ | $-25$ | 200 | 64 |
| 3 | 8 | 88 | $-6$ | $-42$ | 252 | 36 |
| 4 | 8 | 118 | $-6$ | $-12$ | 72 | 36 |
| 5 | 12 | 117 | $-2$ | $-13$ | 26 | 4 |
| 6 | 16 | 137 | 2 | 7 | 14 | 4 |
| 7 | 20 | 157 | 6 | 27 | 162 | 36 |
| 8 | 20 | 169 | 6 | 39 | 234 | 36 |
| 9 | 22 | 149 | 8 | 19 | 152 | 64 |
| 10 | 26 | 202 | 12 | 72 | 864 | 144 |
| Totals | 140 | 1300 | | | 2840 | 568 |
| | $\Sigma x_i$ | $\Sigma y_i$ | | | $\Sigma(x_i - \bar{x})(y_i - \bar{y})$ | $\Sigma(x_i - \bar{x})^2$ |

$$b_1 = \frac{\Sigma(x_i - \bar{x})(y_i - \bar{y})}{\Sigma(x_i - \bar{x})^2}$$

$$= \frac{2840}{568}$$

$$= 5$$

The calculation of the $y$ intercept ($b_0$) follows.

$$b_0 = \bar{y} - b_1\bar{x}$$
$$= 130 - 5(14)$$
$$= 60$$

Thus, the estimated regression equation is

$$\hat{y} = 60 + 5x$$

Figure 14.4 shows the graph of this equation on the scatter diagram.

The slope of the estimated regression equation ($b_1 = 5$) is positive, implying that as student population increases, sales increase. In fact, we can conclude (based on sales measured in $1000s and student population in 1000s) that an increase in the student population of 1000 is associated with an increase of $5000 in expected sales; that is, quarterly sales are expected to increase by $5 per student.

*Using the estimated regression equation to make predictions outside the range of the values of the independent variable should be done with caution because outside that range we cannot be sure that the same relationship is valid.*

If we believe the least squares estimated regression equation adequately describes the relationship between $x$ and $y$, it would seem reasonable to use the estimated regression equation to predict the value of $y$ for a given value of $x$. For example, if we wanted to predict quarterly sales for a restaurant to be located near a campus with 16,000 students, we would compute

$$\hat{y} = 60 + 5(16) = 140$$

Hence, we would predict quarterly sales of $140,000 for this restaurant. In the following sections we will discuss methods for assessing the appropriateness of using the estimated regression equation for estimation and prediction.

**FIGURE 14.4**   GRAPH OF THE ESTIMATED REGRESSION EQUATION FOR ARMAND'S PIZZA PARLORS: $\hat{y} = 60 + 5x$

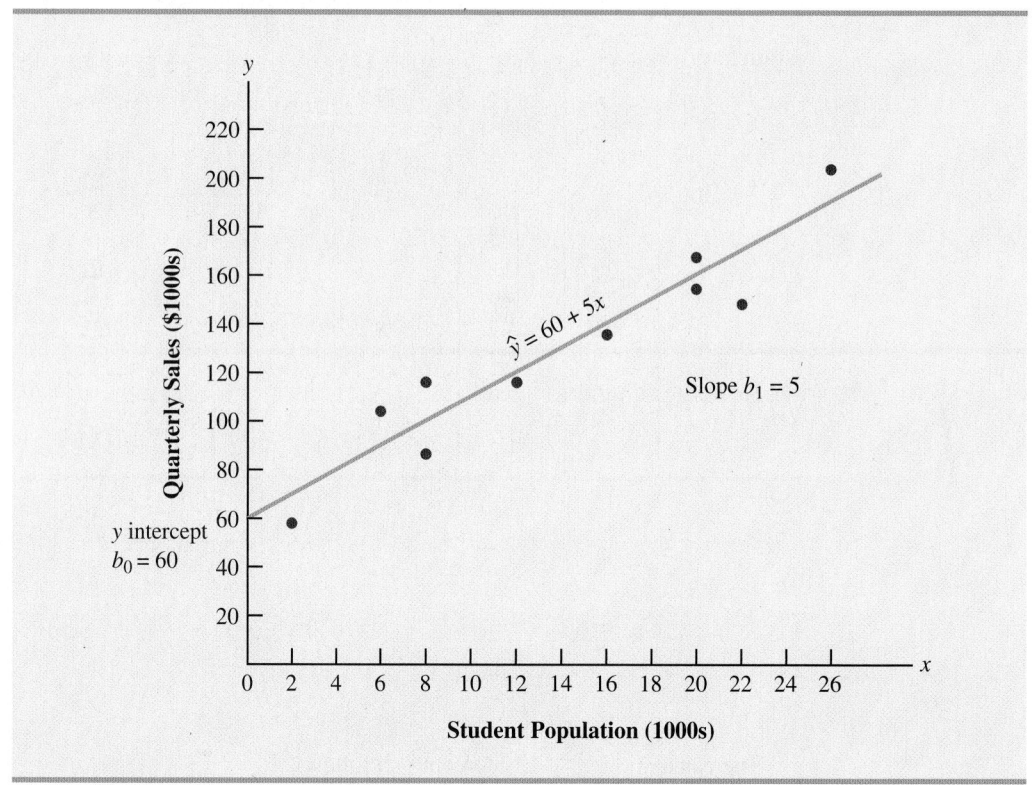

## NOTES AND COMMENTS

The least squares method provides an estimated regression equation that minimizes the sum of squared deviations between the observed values of the dependent variable $y_i$ and the estimated values of the dependent variable $\hat{y}_i$. This least squares criterion is used to choose the equation that provides the best fit. If some other criterion were used, such as minimizing the sum of the absolute deviations between $y_i$ and $\hat{y}_i$, a different equation would be obtained. In practice, the least squares method is the most widely used.

## Exercises

## Methods

1.   Given are five observations for two variables, $x$ and $y$.

| $x_i$ | 1 | 2 | 3 | 4 | 5 |
|-------|---|---|---|---|----|
| $y_i$ | 3 | 7 | 5 | 11 | 14 |

a.   Develop a scatter diagram for these data.
b.   What does the scatter diagram developed in part (a) indicate about the relationship between the two variables?

    c.  Try to approximate the relationship between $x$ and $y$ by drawing a straight line through the data.

    d.  Develop the estimated regression equation by computing the values of $b_0$ and $b_1$ using equations (14.6) and (14.7).

    e.  Use the estimated regression equation to predict the value of $y$ when $x = 4$.

2.  Given are five observations for two variables, $x$ and $y$.

| $x_i$ | 2 | 3 | 5 | 1 | 8 |
|-------|----|----|----|----|----|
| $y_i$ | 25 | 25 | 20 | 30 | 16 |

    a.  Develop a scatter diagram for these data.

    b.  What does the scatter diagram developed in part (a) indicate about the relationship between the two variables?

    c.  Try to approximate the relationship between $x$ and $y$ by drawing a straight line through the data.

    d.  Develop the estimated regression equation by computing the values of $b_0$ and $b_1$ using equations (14.6) and (14.7).

    e.  Use the estimated regression equation to predict the value of $y$ when $x = 6$.

3.  Given are five observations collected in a regression study on two variables.

| $x_i$ | 2 | 4 | 5 | 7 | 8 |
|-------|---|---|---|---|---|
| $y_i$ | 2 | 3 | 2 | 6 | 4 |

    a.  Develop a scatter diagram for these data.

    b.  Develop the estimated regression equation for these data.

    c.  Use the estimated regression equation to predict the value of $y$ when $x = 4$.

## Applications

4.  The following data were collected on the height (inches) and weight (pounds) of women swimmers.

| Height | 68 | 64 | 62 | 65 | 66 |
|--------|-----|-----|-----|-----|-----|
| Weight | 132 | 108 | 102 | 115 | 128 |

    a.  Develop a scatter diagram for these data with height as the independent variable.

    b.  What does the scatter diagram developed in part (a) indicate about the relationship between the two variables?

    c.  Try to approximate the relationship between height and weight by drawing a straight line through the data.

    d.  Develop the estimated regression equation by computing the values of $b_0$ and $b_1$.

    e.  If a swimmer's height is 63 inches, what would you estimate her weight to be?

5.  Technological advances helped make inflatable paddlecraft suitable for backcountry use. These blow-up rubber boats, which can be rolled into a bundle not much bigger than a golf bag, are large enough to accommodate one or two paddlers and their camping gear. *Canoe & Kayak* magazine tested boats from nine manufacturers to determine how they would perform on a three-day wilderness paddling trip. One of the criteria in their evaluation was the baggage capacity of the boat, evaluated using a 4-point rating scale from 1 (lowest rating) to 4 (highest rating). The following data show the baggage capacity rating and the price of the boat (*Canoe & Kayak,* March 2003).

| Boat | Baggage Capacity | Price ($) |
|---|---|---|
| S14 | 4 | 1595 |
| Orinoco | 4 | 1399 |
| Outside Pro | 4 | 1890 |
| Explorer 380X | 3 | 795 |
| River XK2 | 2.5 | 600 |
| Sea Tiger | 4 | 1995 |
| Maverik II | 3 | 1205 |
| Starlite 100 | 2 | 583 |
| Fat Pack Cat | 3 | 1048 |

a. Develop a scatter diagram for these data with baggage capacity rating as the independent variable.
b. What does the scatter diagram developed in part (a) indicate about the relationship between baggage capacity and price?
c. Draw a straight line through the data to approximate a linear relationship between baggage capacity and price.
d. Use the least squares method to develop the estimated regression equation.
e. Provide an interpretation for the slope of the estimated regression equation.
f. Predict the price for a boat with a baggage capacity rating of 3.

6. Wageweb conducts surveys of salary data and presents summaries on its Web site. Based on salary data as of October 1, 2002, Wageweb reported that the average annual salary for sales vice presidents was $142,111, with an average annual bonus of $15,432 (Wageweb.com, March 13, 2003). Assume the following data are a sample of the annual salary and bonus for 10 sales vice presidents. Data are in thousands of dollars.

| Vice President | Salary | Bonus |
|---|---|---|
| 1 | 135 | 12 |
| 2 | 115 | 14 |
| 3 | 146 | 16 |
| 4 | 167 | 19 |
| 5 | 165 | 22 |
| 6 | 176 | 24 |
| 7 | 98 | 7 |
| 8 | 136 | 17 |
| 9 | 163 | 18 |
| 10 | 119 | 11 |

a. Develop a scatter diagram for these data with salary as the independent variable.
b. What does the scatter diagram developed in part (a) indicate about the relationship between salary and bonus?
c. Use the least squares method to develop the estimated regression equation.
d. Provide an interpretation for the slope of the estimated regression equation.
e. Predict the bonus for a vice president with an annual salary of $120,000.

7. The Dow Jones Industrial Average (DJIA) and the Standard & Poor's 500 (S&P) indexes are both used as measures of overall movement in the stock market. The DJIA is based on the price movements of 30 large companies; the S&P 500 is an index composed of

500 stocks. Some say the S&P 500 is a better measure of stock market performance because it is broader based. The closing prices for the DJIA and the S&P 500 for 10 weeks,
beginning with February 11, 2000, follow (*Barron's,* April 17, 2000).

**DowS&P**

| Date | DJIA | S&P |
|------|------|-----|
| February 11 | 10425 | 1387 |
| February 18 | 10220 | 1346 |
| February 25 | 9862 | 1333 |
| March 3 | 10367 | 1409 |
| March 10 | 9929 | 1395 |
| March 17 | 10595 | 1464 |
| March 24 | 11113 | 1527 |
| March 31 | 10922 | 1499 |
| April 7 | 11111 | 1516 |
| April 14 | 10306 | 1357 |

a. Develop a scatter diagram for these data with DJIA as the independent variable.
b. Develop the least squares estimated regression equation.
c. Suppose the closing price for the DJIA is 11,000. Estimate the closing price for the
S&P 500.

8. Mountain bikes that cost less than $1000 now contain many of the high-quality compo-
nents that until recently were only available on high-priced models. Today, even sub-$1000
models often offer supple suspensions, clipless pedals, and highly engineered frames. An
interesting question is whether higher price still buys a higher level of handling, as measured by the bike's sidetrack capability. To measure sidetrack capability, *Outside Magazine* used a rating scale from 1 to 5, with 1 representing an average rating and 5 representing
an excellent rating. The sidetrack capability and the price for 10 mountain bikes tested by
*Outside Magazine* follow (*Outside Magazine Buyer's Guide,* 2001).

**MtnBikes**

| Manufacturer and Model | Sidetrack Capability | Price ($) |
|------------------------|:-------------------:|:---------:|
| Raleigh M80 | 1 | 600 |
| Marin Bear Valley Feminina | 1 | 649 |
| GT Avalanche 2.0 | 2 | 799 |
| Kona Jake the Snake | 1 | 899 |
| Schwinn Moab 2 | 3 | 950 |
| Giant XTC NRS 3 | 4 | 1100 |
| Fisher Paragon Genesisters | 4 | 1149 |
| Jamis Dakota XC | 3 | 1300 |
| Trek Fuel 90 | 5 | 1550 |
| Specialized Stumpjumper M4 | 4 | 1625 |

a. Develop a scatter diagram for these data with sidetrack capability as the independent
variable.
b. Does it appear that higher priced models have a higher level of handling? Explain.
c. Develop the least squares estimated regression equation.
d. What is the estimated price for a mountain bike if it has a sidetrack capability rating
of 4?

9. A sales manager collected the following data on annual sales and years of experience.

| Salesperson | Years of Experience | Annual Sales ($1000s) |
|---|---|---|
| 1 | 1 | 80 |
| 2 | 3 | 97 |
| 3 | 4 | 92 |
| 4 | 4 | 102 |
| 5 | 6 | 103 |
| 6 | 8 | 111 |
| 7 | 10 | 119 |
| 8 | 10 | 123 |
| 9 | 11 | 117 |
| 10 | 13 | 136 |

a. Develop a scatter diagram for these data with years of experience as the independent variable.
b. Develop an estimated regression equation that can be used to predict annual sales given the years of experience.
c. Use the estimated regression equation to predict annual sales for a salesperson with 9 years of experience.

10. *PC World* provided ratings for the top 15 notebook PCs (*PC World,* February 2000). The performance score is a measure of how fast a PC can run a mix of common business applications as compared to how fast a baseline machine can run them. For example, a PC with a performance score of 200 is twice as fast as the baseline machine. A 100-point scale was used to provide an overall rating for each notebook tested in the study. A score in the 90s is exceptional, while one in the 70s is above average. The performance scores and the overall ratings for the 15 notebooks follow.

PCs

| | Performance Score | Overall Rating |
|---|---|---|
| AMS Tech Roadster 15CTA380 | 115 | 67 |
| Compaq Armada M700 | 191 | 78 |
| Compaq Prosignia Notebook 150 | 153 | 79 |
| Dell Inspiron 3700 C466GT | 194 | 80 |
| Dell Inspiron 7500 R500VT | 236 | 84 |
| Dell Latitude Cpi A366XT | 184 | 76 |
| Enpower ENP-313 Pro | 184 | 77 |
| Gateway Solo 9300LS | 216 | 92 |
| HP Pavilion Notebook PC | 185 | 83 |
| IBM ThinkPad I Series 1480 | 183 | 78 |
| Micro Express NP7400 | 189 | 77 |
| Micron TransPort NX PII-400 | 202 | 78 |
| NEC Versa SX | 192 | 78 |
| Sceptre Soundx 5200 | 141 | 73 |
| Sony VAIO PCG-F340 | 187 | 77 |

a. Develop a scatter diagram for these data with performance score as the independent variable.
b. Develop the least squares estimated regression equation.
c. Estimate the overall rating for a new PC that has a performance score of 225.

11. Although delays at major airports are now less frequent, it helps to know which airports are likely to throw off your schedule. In addition, if your plane is late arriving at a particular airport where you must make a connection, how likely is it that the departure will be

late and thus increase your chances of making the connection? The following data show the percentage of late arrivals and departures during August for 13 airports (*Business 2.0*, February 2002).

**Airport**

| Airport | Late Arrivals (%) | Late Departures (%) |
|---|---|---|
| Atlanta | 24 | 22 |
| Charlotte | 20 | 20 |
| Chicago | 30 | 29 |
| Cincinnati | 20 | 19 |
| Dallas | 20 | 22 |
| Denver | 23 | 23 |
| Detroit | 18 | 19 |
| Houston | 20 | 16 |
| Minneapolis | 18 | 18 |
| Phoenix | 21 | 22 |
| Pittsburgh | 25 | 22 |
| Salt Lake City | 18 | 17 |
| St. Louis | 16 | 16 |

a. Develop a scatter diagram for these data with the percentage of late arrivals as the independent variable.
b. What does the scatter diagram developed in part (a) indicate about the relationship between late arrivals and late departures?
c. Use the least squares method to develop the estimated regression equation.
d. Provide an interpretation for the slope of the estimated regression equation.
e. Suppose the percentage of late arrivals at the Philadelphia airport for August was 22%. What is an estimate of the percentage of late departures?

12. The following table gives the number of employees and the revenue (in millions of dollars) for 20 companies (*Fortune*, April 17, 2000).

**EmpRev**

| | Employees | Revenue ($millions) |
|---|---|---|
| Sprint | 77,600 | 19,930 |
| Chase Manhattan | 74,801 | 33,710 |
| Computer Sciences | 50,000 | 7,660 |
| Wells Fargo | 89,355 | 21,795 |
| Sunbeam | 12,200 | 2,398 |
| CBS | 29,000 | 7,510 |
| Time Warner | 69,722 | 27,333 |
| Steelcase | 16,200 | 2,743 |
| Georgia-Pacific | 57,000 | 17,796 |
| Toro | 1,275 | 4,673 |
| American Financial | 9,400 | 3,334 |
| Fluor | 53,561 | 12,417 |
| Phillips Petroleum | 15,900 | 13,852 |
| Cardinal Health | 36,000 | 25,034 |
| Borders Group | 23,500 | 2,999 |
| MCI Worldcom | 77,000 | 37,120 |
| Consolidated Edison | 14,269 | 7,491 |
| IBP | 45,000 | 14,075 |
| Super Value | 50,000 | 17,421 |
| H&R Block | 4,200 | 1,669 |

a. Develop a scatter diagram for these data with number of employees as the independent variable.

b. What does the scatter diagram developed in part (a) indicate about the relationship between number of employees and revenue?

c. Develop the estimated regression equation for these data.

d. Use the estimated regression equation to predict the revenue for a firm with 75,000 employees.

13. To the Internal Revenue Service, the reasonableness of total itemized deductions depends on the taxpayer's adjusted gross income. Large deductions, which include charity and medical deductions, are more reasonable for taxpayers with large adjusted gross incomes. If a taxpayer claims larger than average itemized deductions for a given level of income, the chances of an IRS audit are increased. Data (in thousands of dollars) on adjusted gross income and the average or reasonable amount of itemized deductions follow.

| Adjusted Gross Income ($1000s) | Reasonable Amount of Itemized Deductions ($1000s) |
|---|---|
| 22 | 9.6 |
| 27 | 9.6 |
| 32 | 10.1 |
| 48 | 11.1 |
| 65 | 13.5 |
| 85 | 17.7 |
| 120 | 25.5 |

a. Develop a scatter diagram for these data with adjusted gross income as the independent variable.

b. Use the least squares method to develop the estimated regression equation.

c. Estimate a reasonable level of total itemized deductions for a taxpayer with an adjusted gross income of $52,500. If this taxpayer claimed itemized deductions of $20,400, would the IRS agent's request for an audit appear justified? Explain.

14. Starting salaries for accountants and auditors in Rochester, New York, trail those of many U.S. cities. The following data show the starting salary (in thousands of dollars) and the cost of living index for Rochester and nine other metropolitan areas (*Democrat and Chronicle,* September 1, 2002). The cost of living index, based on a city's food, housing, taxes, and other costs, ranges from 0 (most expensive) to 100 (least expensive).

**CD file**

**Salaries**

| Metropolitan Area | Index | Salary ($1000s) |
|---|---|---|
| Oklahoma City | 82.44 | 23.9 |
| Tampa/St. Petersburg/Clearwater | 79.89 | 24.5 |
| Indianapolis | 55.53 | 27.4 |
| Buffalo/Niagara Falls | 41.36 | 27.7 |
| Atlanta | 39.38 | 27.1 |
| Rochester | 28.05 | 25.6 |
| Sacramento | 25.50 | 28.7 |
| Raleigh/Durham/Chapel Hill | 13.32 | 26.7 |
| San Diego | 3.12 | 27.8 |
| Honolulu | 0.57 | 28.3 |

a. Develop a scatter diagram for these data with the cost of living index as the independent variable.

b. Develop the estimated regression equation relating the cost of living index to the starting salary.

c. Estimate the starting salary for a metropolitan area with a cost of living index of 50.

# Coefficient of Determination

For the Armand's Pizza Parlors example, we developed the estimated regression equation $\hat{y} = 60 + 5x$ to approximate the linear relationship between the size of the student population $x$ and quarterly sales $y$. A question now is: How well does the estimated regression equation fit the data? In this section, we show that the **coefficient of determination** provides a measure of the goodness of fit for the estimated regression equation.

For the $i$th observation, the difference between the observed value of the dependent variable, $y_i$, and the estimated value of the dependent variable, $\hat{y}_i$, is called the *$i$th residual*. The $i$th residual represents the error in using $\hat{y}_i$ to estimate $y_i$. Thus, for the $i$th observation, the residual is $y_i - \hat{y}_i$. The sum of squares of these residuals or errors is the quantity that is minimized by the least squares method. This quantity, also known as the *sum of squares due to error*, is denoted by SSE.

> SUM OF SQUARES DUE TO ERROR
> $$\text{SSE} = \Sigma(y_i - \hat{y}_i)^2 \tag{14.8}$$

The value of SSE is a measure of the error in using the estimated regression equation to estimate the values of the dependent variable in the sample.

In Table 14.3 we show the calculations required to compute the sum of squares due to error for the Armand's Pizza Parlors example. For instance, for restaurant 1 the values of the independent and dependent variables are $x_1 = 2$ and $y_1 = 58$. Using the estimated regression equation, we find that the estimated value of quarterly sales for restaurant 1 is $\hat{y}_1 = 60 + 5(2) = 70$. Thus, the error in using $\hat{y}_1$ to estimate $y_1$ for restaurant 1 is $y_1 - \hat{y}_1 = 58 - 70 = -12$. The squared error, $(-12)^2 = 144$, is shown in the last column of Table 14.3. After computing and squaring the residuals for each restaurant in the sample, we sum them to obtain SSE = 1530. Thus, SSE = 1530 measures the error in using the estimated regression equation $\hat{y} = 60 + 5x$ to predict sales.

Now suppose we are asked to develop an estimate of quarterly sales without knowledge of the size of the student population. Without knowledge of any related variables, we would

**TABLE 14.3    CALCULATION OF SSE FOR ARMAND'S PIZZA PARLORS**

| Restaurant $i$ | $x_i$ = Student Population (1000s) | $y_i$ = Quarterly Sales ($1000s) | Predicted Sales $\hat{y}_i = 60 + 5x_i$ | Error $y_i - \hat{y}_i$ | Squared Error $(y_i - \hat{y}_i)^2$ |
|---|---|---|---|---|---|
| 1 | 2 | 58 | 70 | −12 | 144 |
| 2 | 6 | 105 | 90 | 15 | 225 |
| 3 | 8 | 88 | 100 | −12 | 144 |
| 4 | 8 | 118 | 100 | 18 | 324 |
| 5 | 12 | 117 | 120 | −3 | 9 |
| 6 | 16 | 137 | 140 | −3 | 9 |
| 7 | 20 | 157 | 160 | −3 | 9 |
| 8 | 20 | 169 | 160 | 9 | 81 |
| 9 | 22 | 149 | 170 | −21 | 441 |
| 10 | 26 | 202 | 190 | 12 | 144 |
| | | | | | SSE = 1530 |

**TABLE 14.4**   COMPUTATION OF THE TOTAL SUM OF SQUARES FOR ARMAND'S PIZZA PARLORS

| Restaurant $i$ | $x_i$ = Student Population (1000s) | $y_i$ = Quarterly Sales ($1000s) | Deviation $y_i - \bar{y}$ | Squared Deviation $(y_i - \bar{y})^2$ |
|---|---|---|---|---|
| 1 | 2 | 58 | −72 | 5,184 |
| 2 | 6 | 105 | −25 | 625 |
| 3 | 8 | 88 | −42 | 1,764 |
| 4 | 8 | 118 | −12 | 144 |
| 5 | 12 | 117 | −13 | 169 |
| 6 | 16 | 137 | 7 | 49 |
| 7 | 20 | 157 | 27 | 729 |
| 8 | 20 | 169 | 39 | 1,521 |
| 9 | 22 | 149 | 19 | 361 |
| 10 | 26 | 202 | 72 | 5,184 |
| | | | | SST = 15,730 |

use the sample mean as an estimate of quarterly sales at any given restaurant. Table 14.2 shows that for the sales data, $\Sigma y_i = 1300$. Hence, the mean value of quarterly sales for the sample of 10 Armand's restaurants is $\bar{y} = \Sigma y_i/n = 1300/10 = 130$. In Table 14.4 we show the sum of squared deviations obtained by using the sample mean $\bar{y} = 130$ to estimate the value of quarterly sales for each restaurant in the sample. For the $i$th restaurant in the sample, the difference $y_i - \bar{y}$ provides a measure of the error involved in using $\bar{y}$ to estimate sales. The corresponding sum of squares, called the *total sum of squares,* is denoted SST.

TOTAL SUM OF SQUARES

$$SST = \Sigma(y_i - \bar{y})^2 \tag{14.9}$$

The sum at the bottom of the last column in Table 14.4 is the total sum of squares for Armand's Pizza Parlors; it is SST = 15,730.

In Figure 14.5 we show the estimated regression line $\hat{y} = 60 + 5x$ and the line corresponding to $\bar{y} = 130$. Note that the points cluster more closely around the estimated regression line than they do about the line $\bar{y} = 130$. For example, for the 10th restaurant in the sample we see that the error is much larger when $\bar{y} = 130$ is used as an estimate of $y_{10}$ than when $\hat{y}_{10} = 60 + 5(26) = 190$ is used. We can think of SST as a measure of how well the observations cluster about the $\bar{y}$ line and SSE as a measure of how well the observations cluster about the $\hat{y}$ line.

To measure how much the $\hat{y}$ values on the estimated regression line deviate from $\bar{y}$, another sum of squares is computed. This sum of squares, called the *sum of squares due to regression,* is denoted SSR.

SUM OF SQUARES DUE TO REGRESSION

$$SSR = \Sigma(\hat{y}_i - \bar{y})^2 \tag{14.10}$$

**FIGURE 14.5**   DEVIATIONS ABOUT THE ESTIMATED REGRESSION LINE AND THE LINE
$y = \bar{y}$ FOR ARMAND'S PIZZA PARLORS

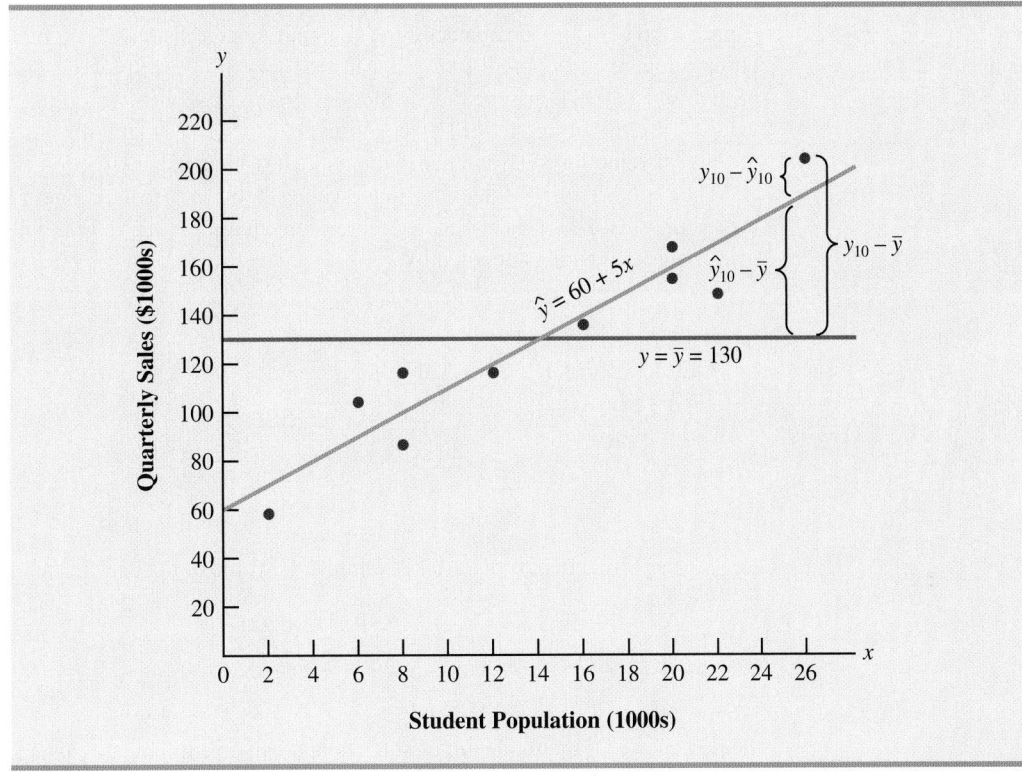

From the preceding discussion, we should expect that SST, SSR, and SSE are related.
Indeed, the relationship among these three sums of squares provides one of the most important results in statistics.

*SSR can be thought of as
the explained portion of
SST, and SSE can be
thought of as the
unexplained portion of SST.*

RELATIONSHIP AMONG SST, SSR, AND SSE

$$SST = SSR + SSE \qquad (14.11)$$

where

$SST$ = total sum of squares
$SSR$ = sum of squares due to regression
$SSE$ = sum of squares due to error

Equation (14.11) shows that the total sum of squares can be partitioned into two components, the regression sum of squares and the sum of squares due to error. Hence, if the values of any two of these sum of squares are known, the third sum of squares can be computed easily. For instance, in the Armand's Pizza Parlors example, we already know that
$SSE = 1530$ and $SST = 15{,}730$; therefore, solving for SSR in equation (14.11), we find that
the sum of squares due to regression is

$$SSR = SST - SSE = 15{,}730 - 1530 = 14{,}200$$

Now let us see how the three sums of squares, SST, SSR, and SSE, can be used to provide a measure of the goodness of fit for the estimated regression equation. The estimated regression equation would provide a perfect fit if every value of the dependent variable $y_i$ happened to lie on the estimated regression line. In this case, $y_i - \hat{y}_i$ would be zero for each observation, resulting in SSE = 0. Because SST = SSR + SSE, we see that for a perfect fit SSR must equal SST, and the ratio (SSR/SST) must equal one. Poorer fits will result in larger values for SSE. Solving for SSE in equation (14.11), we see that SSE = SST − SSR. Hence, the largest value for SSE (and hence the poorest fit) occurs when SSR = 0 and SSE = SST.

The ratio SSR/SST, which will take values between zero and one, is used to evaluate the goodness of fit for the estimated regression equation. This ratio is called the *coefficient of determination* and is denoted by $r^2$.

COEFFICIENT OF DETERMINATION

$$r^2 = \frac{SSR}{SST}$$

(14.12)

For the Armand's Pizza Parlors example, the value of the coefficient of determination is

$$r^2 = \frac{SSR}{SST} = \frac{14{,}200}{15{,}730} = .9027$$

When we express the coefficient of determination as a percentage, $r^2$ can be interpreted as the percentage of the total sum of squares that can be explained by using the estimated regression equation. For Armand's Pizza Parlors, we can conclude that 90.27% of the total sum of squares can be explained by using the estimated regression equation $\hat{y} = 60 + 5x$ to predict quarterly sales. In other words, 90.27% of the variability in sales can be explained by the linear relationship between the size of the student population and sales. We should be pleased to find such a good fit for the estimated regression equation.

## Correlation Coefficient

In Chapter 3 we introduced the **correlation coefficient** as a descriptive measure of the strength of linear association between two variables, $x$ and $y$. Values of the correlation coefficient are always between −1 and +1. A value of +1 indicates that the two variables $x$ and $y$ are perfectly related in a positive linear sense. That is, all data points are on a straight line that has a positive slope. A value of −1 indicates that $x$ and $y$ are perfectly related in a negative linear sense, with all data points on a straight line that has a negative slope. Values of the correlation coefficient close to zero indicate that $x$ and $y$ are not linearly related.

In Section 3.5 we presented the equation for computing the sample correlation coefficient. If a regression analysis has already been performed and the coefficient of determination $r^2$ computed, the sample correlation coefficient can be computed as follows.

SAMPLE CORRELATION COEFFICIENT

$$r_{xy} = (\text{sign of } b_1)\sqrt{\text{Coefficient of determination}}$$
$$= (\text{sign of } b_1)\sqrt{r^2}$$

(14.13)

where

$$b_1 = \text{the slope of the estimated regression equation } \hat{y} = b_0 + b_1x$$

The sign for the sample correlation coefficient is positive if the estimated regression equation has a positive slope ($b_1 > 0$) and negative if the estimated regression equation has a negative slope ($b_1 < 0$).

For the Armand's Pizza Parlor example, the value of the coefficient of determination corresponding to the estimated regression equation $\hat{y} = 60 + 5x$ is .9027. Because the slope of the estimated regression equation is positive, equation (14.13) shows that the sample correlation coefficient is $+\sqrt{.9027} = +.9501$. With a sample correlation coefficient of $r_{xy} = +.9501$, we would conclude that a strong positive linear association exists between $x$ and $y$.

In the case of a linear relationship between two variables, both the coefficient of determination and the sample correlation coefficient provide measures of the strength of the relationship. The coefficient of determination provides a measure between zero and one whereas the sample correlation coefficient provides a measure between $-1$ and $+1$. Although the sample correlation coefficient is restricted to a linear relationship between two variables, the coefficient of determination can be used for nonlinear relationships and for relationships that have two or more independent variables. Thus, the coefficient of determination provides a wider range of applicability.

## NOTES AND COMMENTS

1. In developing the least squares estimated regression equation and computing the coefficient of determination, we made no probabilistic assumptions about the error term $\epsilon$, and no statistical tests for significance of the relationship between $x$ and $y$ were conducted. Larger values of $r^2$ imply that the least squares line provides a better fit to the data; that is, the observations are more closely grouped about the least squares line. But, using only $r^2$, we can draw no conclusion about whether the relationship between $x$ and $y$ is statistically significant. Such a conclusion must be based on considerations that involve the sample size and the properties of the appropriate sampling distributions of the least squares estimators.

2. As a practical matter, for typical data found in the social sciences, values of $r^2$ as low as .25 are often considered useful. For data in the physical and life sciences, $r^2$ values of .60 or greater are often found; in fact, in some cases, $r^2$ values greater than .90 can be found. In business applications, $r^2$ values vary greatly, depending on the unique characteristics of each application.

## Exercises

### Methods

15.   The data from exercise 1 follow.

| $x_i$ | 1 | 2 | 3 | 4 | 5 |
|-------|---|---|---|---|---|
| $y_i$ | 3 | 7 | 5 | 11 | 14 |

The estimated regression equation for these data is $\hat{y} = .20 + 2.60x$.
   a.   Compute SSE, SST, and SSR using equations (14.8), (14.9), and (14.10).
   b.   Compute the coefficient of determination $r^2$. Comment on the goodness of fit.
   c.   Compute the sample correlation coefficient.

16. The data from exercise 2 follow.

| $x_i$ | 2 | 3 | 5 | 1 | 8 |
|-------|----|----|----|----|----|
| $y_i$ | 25 | 25 | 20 | 30 | 16 |

The estimated regression equation for these data is $\hat{y} = 30.33 - 1.88x$.
a. Compute SSE, SST, and SSR.
b. Compute the coefficient of determination $r^2$. Comment on the goodness of fit.
c. Compute the sample correlation coefficient.

17. The data from exercise 3 follow.

| $x_i$ | 2 | 4 | 5 | 7 | 8 |
|-------|---|---|---|---|---|
| $y_i$ | 2 | 3 | 2 | 6 | 4 |

The estimated regression equation for these data is $\hat{y} = .75 + .51x$. What percentage of the total sum of squares can be accounted for by the estimated regression equation? What is the value of the sample correlation coefficient?

## Applications

18. The following data are the monthly salaries $y$ and the grade point averages $x$ for students who obtained a bachelor's degree in business administration with a major in information systems. The estimated regression equation for these data is $\hat{y} = 1790.5 + 581.1x$.

| GPA | Monthly Salary ($) |
|-----|--------------------|
| 2.6 | 3300 |
| 3.4 | 3600 |
| 3.6 | 4000 |
| 3.2 | 3500 |
| 3.5 | 3900 |
| 2.9 | 3600 |

a. Compute SST, SSR, and SSE.
b. Compute the coefficient of determination $r^2$. Comment on the goodness of fit.
c. What is the value of the sample correlation coefficient?

19. The data from exercise 7 follow.

|  | x = DJIA | y = S&P |
|--|----------|---------|
| February 11 | 10425 | 1387 |
| February 18 | 10220 | 1346 |
| February 25 | 9862 | 1333 |
| March 3 | 10367 | 1409 |
| March 10 | 9929 | 1395 |
| March 17 | 10595 | 1464 |
| March 24 | 11113 | 1527 |
| March 31 | 10922 | 1499 |
| April 7 | 11111 | 1516 |
| April 14 | 10306 | 1357 |

The estimated regression equation for these data is $\hat{y} = -137.63 + .1489x$. What percentage of the total sum of squares can be accounted for by the estimated regression equation? Comment on the goodness of fit. What is the sample correlation coefficient?

20. The typical household income and typical home price for a sample of 18 cities follow (*Places Rated Almanac,* 2000). Data are in thousands of dollars.

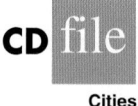

**Cities**

|  | Income | Home Price |
|---|---|---|
| Akron, OH | 74.1 | 114.9 |
| Atlanta, GA | 82.4 | 126.9 |
| Birmingham, AL | 71.2 | 130.9 |
| Bismarck, ND | 62.8 | 92.8 |
| Cleveland, OH | 79.2 | 135.8 |
| Columbia, SC | 66.8 | 116.7 |
| Denver, CO | 82.6 | 161.9 |
| Detroit, MI | 85.3 | 145.0 |
| Fort Lauderdale, FL | 75.8 | 145.3 |
| Hartford, CT | 89.1 | 162.1 |
| Lancaster, PA | 75.2 | 125.9 |
| Madison, WI | 78.8 | 145.2 |
| Naples, FL | 100.0 | 173.6 |
| Nashville, TN | 77.3 | 125.9 |
| Philadelphia, PA | 87.0 | 151.5 |
| Savannah, GA | 67.8 | 108.1 |
| Toledo, OH | 71.2 | 101.1 |
| Washington, DC | 97.4 | 191.9 |

a. Use these data to develop an estimated regression equation that could be used to estimate the typical home price for a city given the typical household income.
b. Compute $r^2$. Would you feel comfortable using this estimated regression equation to estimate the typical home price for a city?
c. Estimate the typical home price for a city with a typical household income of $95,000.

21. An important application of regression analysis in accounting is in the estimation of cost. By collecting data on volume and cost and using the least squares method to develop an estimated regression equation relating volume and cost, an accountant can estimate the cost associated with a particular manufacturing volume. Consider the following sample of production volumes and total cost data for a manufacturing operation.

| Production Volume (units) | Total Cost ($) |
|---|---|
| 400 | 4000 |
| 450 | 5000 |
| 550 | 5400 |
| 600 | 5900 |
| 700 | 6400 |
| 750 | 7000 |

a. Use these data to develop an estimated regression equation that could be used to predict the total cost for a given production volume.
b. What is the variable cost per unit produced?
c. Compute the coefficient of determination. What percentage of the variation in total cost can be explained by production volume?
d. The company's production schedule shows 500 units must be produced next month. What is the estimated total cost for this operation?

22. *PC World* provided ratings for the top five small-office laser printers and five corporate laser printers (*PC World,* February 2003). The highest rated small-office laser printer was the Minolta-QMS PagePro 1250W, with an overall rating of 91. The highest rated corporate

laser printer, the Xerox Phaser 4400/N, had an overall rating of 83. The following data show the speed for plain text printing in pages per minute (ppm) and the price for each printer.

**Printers**

| Name | Type | Speed (ppm) | Price ($) |
|------|------|-------------|-----------|
| Minolta-QMS PagePro 1250W | Small Office | 12 | 199 |
| Brother HL-1850 | Small Office | 10 | 499 |
| Lexmark E320 | Small Office | 12.2 | 299 |
| Minolta-QMS PagePro 1250E | Small Office | 10.3 | 299 |
| HP Laserjet 1200 | Small Office | 11.7 | 399 |
| Xerox Phaser 4400/N | Corporate | 17.8 | 1850 |
| Brother HL-2460N | Corporate | 16.1 | 1000 |
| IBM Infoprint 1120n | Corporate | 11.8 | 1387 |
| Lexmark W812 | Corporate | 19.8 | 2089 |
| Oki Data B8300n | Corporate | 28.2 | 2200 |

a. Develop the estimated regression equation with speed as the independent variable.
b. Compute $r^2$. What percentage of the variation in cost can be explained by the printing speed?
c. What is the sample correlation coefficient between speed and price? Does it reflect a strong or weak relationship between printing speed and cost?

## 14.4 Model Assumptions

In conducting a regression analysis, we begin by making an assumption about the appropriate model for the relationship between the dependent and independent variable(s). For the case of simple linear regression, the assumed regression model is

$$y = \beta_0 + \beta_1 x + \epsilon$$

Then, the least squares method is used to develop values for $b_0$ and $b_1$, the estimates of the model parameters $\beta_0$ and $\beta_1$, respectively. The resulting estimated regression equation is

$$\hat{y} = b_0 + b_1 x$$

We saw that the value of the coefficient of determination ($r^2$) is a measure of the goodness of fit of the estimated regression equation. However, even with a large value of $r^2$, the estimated regression equation should not be used until further analysis of the appropriateness of the assumed model has been conducted. An important step in determining whether the assumed model is appropriate involves testing for the significance of the relationship. The tests of significance in regression analysis are based on the following assumptions about the error term $\epsilon$.

---

**ASSUMPTIONS ABOUT THE ERROR TERM $\epsilon$ IN THE REGRESSION MODEL**

$$y = \beta_0 + \beta_1 x + \epsilon$$

1. The error term $\epsilon$ is a random variable with a mean or expected value of zero; that is, $E(\epsilon) = 0$.

   *Implication:* $\beta_0$ and $\beta_1$ are constants, therefore $E(\beta_0) = \beta_0$ and $E(\beta_1) = \beta_1$; thus, for a given value of $x$, the expected value of $y$ is

$$E(y) = \beta_0 + \beta_1 x \qquad \text{(14.14)}$$

As we indicated previously, equation (14.14) is referred to as the regression equation.

2. The variance of $\epsilon$, denoted by $\sigma^2$, is the same for all values of $x$.
   *Implication:* The variance of $y$ about the regression line equals $\sigma^2$ and is the same for all values of $x$.

3. The values of $\epsilon$ are independent.
   *Implication:* The value of $\epsilon$ for a particular value of $x$ is not related to the value of $\epsilon$ for any other value of $x$; thus, the value of $y$ for a particular value of $x$ is not related to the value of $y$ for any other value of $x$.

4. The error term $\epsilon$ is a normally distributed random variable.
   *Implication:* Because $y$ is a linear function of $\epsilon$, $y$ is also a normally distributed random variable.

Figure 14.6 illustrates the model assumptions and their implications; note that in this graphical interpretation, the value of $E(y)$ changes according to the specific value of $x$ considered. However, regardless of the $x$ value, the probability distribution of $\epsilon$ and hence the probability distributions of $y$ are normally distributed, each with the same variance. The specific value of the error $\epsilon$ at any particular point depends on whether the actual value of $y$ is greater than or less than $E(y)$.

At this point, we must keep in mind that we are also making an assumption or hypothesis about the form of the relationship between $x$ and $y$. That is, we assume that a straight

**FIGURE 14.6   ASSUMPTIONS FOR THE REGRESSION MODEL**

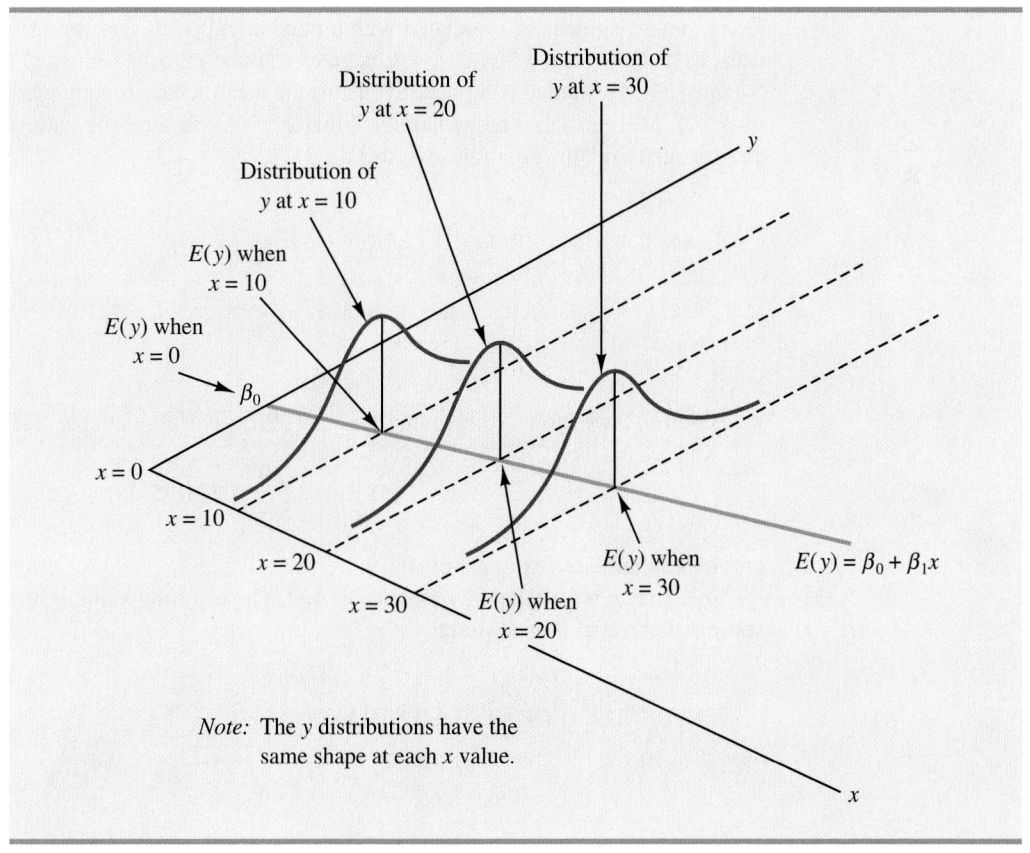

*Note:* The $y$ distributions have the same shape at each $x$ value.

line represented by $\beta_0 + \beta_1 x$ is the basis for the relationship between the variables. We must not lose sight of the fact that some other model, for instance $y = \beta_0 + \beta_1 x^2 + \epsilon$, may turn out to be a better model for the underlying relationship.

# 14.5 Testing for Significance

In a simple linear regression equation, the mean or expected value of $y$ is a linear function of $x$: $E(y) = \beta_0 + \beta_1 x$. If the value of $\beta_1$ is zero, $E(y) = \beta_0 + (0)x = \beta_0$. In this case, the mean value of $y$ does not depend on the value of $x$ and hence we would conclude that $x$ and $y$ are not linearly related. Alternatively, if the value of $\beta_1$ is not equal to zero, we would conclude that the two variables are related. Thus, to test for a significant regression relationship, we must conduct a hypothesis test to determine whether the value of $\beta_1$ is zero. Two tests are commonly used. Both require an estimate of $\sigma^2$, the variance of $\epsilon$ in the regression model.

## Estimate of $\sigma^2$

From the regression model and its assumptions we can conclude that $\sigma^2$, the variance of $\epsilon$, also represents the variance of the $y$ values about the regression line. Recall that the deviations of the $y$ values about the estimated regression line are called residuals. Thus, SSE, the sum of squared residuals, is a measure of the variability of the actual observations about the estimated regression line. The **mean square error** (MSE) provides the estimate of $\sigma^2$; it is SSE divided by its degrees of freedom.

With $\hat{y}_i = b_0 + b_1 x_i$, SSE can be written as

$$\text{SSE} = \Sigma(y_i - \hat{y}_i)^2 = \Sigma(y_i - b_0 - b_1 x_i)^2$$

Every sum of squares is associated with a number called its degrees of freedom. Statisticians have shown that SSE has $n - 2$ degrees of freedom because two parameters ($\beta_0$ and $\beta_1$) must be estimated to compute SSE. Thus, the mean square is computed by dividing SSE by $n - 2$. MSE provides an unbiased estimator of $\sigma^2$. Because the value of MSE provides an estimate of $\sigma^2$, the notation $s^2$ is also used.

---

**MEAN SQUARE ERROR (ESTIMATE OF $\sigma^2$)**

$$s^2 = \text{MSE} = \frac{\text{SSE}}{n - 2} \tag{14.15}$$

---

In Section 14.3 we showed that for the Armand's Pizza Parlors example, SSE = 1530; hence,

$$s^2 = \text{MSE} = \frac{1530}{8} = 191.25$$

provides an unbiased estimate of $\sigma^2$.

To estimate $\sigma$ we take the square root of $s^2$. The resulting value, $s$, is referred to as the **standard error of the estimate**.

---

**STANDARD ERROR OF THE ESTIMATE**

$$s = \sqrt{\text{MSE}} = \sqrt{\frac{\text{SSE}}{n - 2}} \tag{14.16}$$

---

For the Armand's Pizza Parlors example, $s = \sqrt{\text{MSE}} = \sqrt{191.25} = 13.829$. In the following discussion, we use the standard error of the estimate in the tests for a significant relationship between $x$ and $y$.

## $t$ **Test**

The simple linear regression model is $y = \beta_0 + \beta_1 x + \epsilon$. If $x$ and $y$ are linearly related, we must have $\beta_1 \neq 0$. The purpose of the $t$ test is to see whether we can conclude that $\beta_1 \neq 0$. We will use the sample data to test the following hypotheses about the parameter $\beta_1$.

$$H_0 : \beta_1 = 0$$
$$H_a : \beta_1 \neq 0$$

If $H_0$ is rejected, we will conclude that $\beta_1 \neq 0$ and that a statistically significant relationship exists between the two variables. However, if $H_0$ cannot be rejected, we will have insufficient evidence to conclude that a significant relationship exists. The properties of the sampling distribution of $b_1$, the least squares estimator of $\beta_1$, provide the basis for the hypothesis test.

First, let us consider what would happen if we used a different random sample for the same regression study. For example, suppose that Armand's Pizza Parlors used the sales records of a different sample of 10 restaurants. A regression analysis of this new sample might result in an estimated regression equation similar to our previous estimated regression equation $\hat{y} = 60 + 5x$. However, it is doubtful that we would obtain exactly the same equation (with an intercept of exactly 60 and a slope of exactly 5). Indeed, $b_0$ and $b_1$, the least squares estimators, are sample statistics with their own sampling distributions. The properties of the sampling distribution of $b_1$ follow.

---

**SAMPLING DISTRIBUTION OF $b_1$**

*Expected Value*

$$E(b_1) = \beta_1$$

*Standard Deviation*

$$\sigma_{b_1} = \frac{\sigma}{\sqrt{\Sigma(x_i - \bar{x})^2}} \tag{14.17}$$

*Distribution Form*

Normal

---

Note that the expected value of $b_1$ is equal to $\beta_1$, so $b_1$ is an unbiased estimator of $\beta_1$.

Because we do not know the value of $\sigma$, we develop an estimate of $\sigma_{b_1}$, denoted $s_{b_1}$, by estimating $\sigma$ with $s$ in equation (14.17). Thus, we obtain the following estimate of $\sigma_{b_1}$.

*The standard deviation of $b_1$ is also referred to as the standard error of $b_1$. Thus, $s_{b_1}$ provides an estimate of the standard error of $b_1$.*

---

**ESTIMATED STANDARD DEVIATION OF $b_1$**

$$s_{b_1} = \frac{s}{\sqrt{\Sigma(x_i - \bar{x})^2}} \tag{14.18}$$

---

For Armand's Pizza Parlors, $s = 13.829$. Hence, using $\Sigma(x_i - \bar{x})^2 = 568$ as shown in Table 14.2, we have

$$s_{b_1} = \frac{13.829}{\sqrt{568}} = .5803$$

as the estimated standard deviation of $b_1$.

The $t$ test for a significant relationship is based on the fact that the test statistic

$$\frac{b_1 - \beta_1}{s_{b_1}}$$

follows a $t$ distribution with $n - 2$ degrees of freedom. If the null hypothesis is true, then $\beta_1 = 0$ and $t = b_1/s_{b_1}$.

Let us conduct this test of significance for Armand's Pizza Parlors at the $\alpha = .01$ level of significance. The test statistic is

$$t = \frac{b_1}{s_{b_1}} = \frac{5}{.5803} = 8.62$$

*Appendixes 14.3 and 14.4 show how Minitab and Excel can be used to compute the p-value.*

The $t$ distribution table shows that with $n - 2 = 10 - 2 = 8$ degrees of freedom, $t = 3.355$ provides an area of .005 in the upper tail. Thus, the area in the upper tail of the $t$ distribution corresponding to the test statistic $t = 8.62$ must be less than .005. Because this test is a two-tailed test, we double this value to conclude that the $p$-value associated with $t = 8.62$ must be less than $2(.005) = .01$. Minitab or Excel show the $p$-value $= .000$. Because the $p$-value is less than $\alpha = .01$, we reject $H_0$ and conclude that $\beta_1$ is not equal to zero. This evidence is sufficient to conclude that a significant relationship exists between student population and quarterly sales. A summary of the $t$ test for significance in simple linear regression follows.

---

$t$ TEST FOR SIGNIFICANCE IN SIMPLE LINEAR REGRESSION

$$H_0: \beta_1 = 0$$
$$H_a: \beta_1 \neq 0$$

TEST STATISTIC

$$t = \frac{b_1}{s_{b_1}} \tag{14.19}$$

REJECTION RULE

        $p$-value approach:       Reject $H_0$ if $p$-value $\leq \alpha$

        Critical value approach:   Reject $H_0$ if $t \leq -t_{\alpha/2}$ or if $t \geq t_{\alpha/2}$

where $t_{\alpha/2}$ is based on a $t$ distribution with $n - 2$ degrees of freedom.

---

## Confidence Interval for $\beta_1$

The form of a confidence interval for $\beta_1$ is as follows:

$$b_1 \pm t_{\alpha/2} s_{b_1}$$

The point estimator is $b_1$ and the margin of error is $t_{\alpha/2}s_{b_1}$. The confidence coefficient associated with this interval is $1 - \alpha$, and $t_{\alpha/2}$ is the $t$ value providing an area of $\alpha/2$ in the upper tail of a $t$ distribution with $n - 2$ degrees of freedom. For example, suppose that we wanted to develop a 99% confidence interval estimate of $\beta_1$ for Armand's Pizza Parlors. From Table 2 of Appendix B we find that the $t$ value corresponding to $\alpha = .01$ and $n - 2 = 10 - 2 = 8$ degrees of freedom is $t_{.005} = 3.355$. Thus, the 99% confidence interval estimate of $\beta_1$ is

$$b_1 \pm t_{\alpha/2}s_{b_1} = 5 \pm 3.355(.5803) = 5 \pm 1.95$$

or 3.05 to 6.95.

In using the $t$ test for significance, the hypotheses tested were

$$H_0: \beta_1 = 0$$
$$H_a: \beta_1 \neq 0$$

At the $\alpha = .01$ level of significance, we can use the 99% confidence interval as an alternative for drawing the hypothesis testing conclusion for the Armand's data. Because 0, the hypothesized value of $\beta_1$, is not included in the confidence interval (3.05 to 6.95), we can reject $H_0$ and conclude that a significant statistical relationship exists between the size of the student population and quarterly sales. In general, a confidence interval can be used to test any two-sided hypothesis about $\beta_1$. If the hypothesized value of $\beta_1$ is contained in the confidence interval, do not reject $H_0$. Otherwise, reject $H_0$.

## $F$ **Test**

An $F$ test, based on the $F$ probability distribution, can also be used to test for significance in regression. With only one independent variable, the $F$ test will provide the same conclusion as the $t$ test; that is, if the $t$ test indicates $\beta_1 \neq 0$ and hence a significant relationship, the $F$ test will also indicate a significant relationship. But with more than one independent variable, only the $F$ test can be used to test for an overall significant relationship.

The logic behind the use of the $F$ test for determining whether the regression relationship is statistically significant is based on the development of two independent estimates of $\sigma^2$. We explained how MSE provides an estimate of $\sigma^2$. If the null hypothesis $H_0: \beta_1 = 0$ is true, the sum of squares due to regression, SSR, divided by its degrees of freedom provides another independent estimate of $\sigma^2$. This estimate is called the *mean square due to regression,* or simply the *mean square regression,* and is denoted MSR. In general,

$$\text{MSR} = \frac{\text{SSR}}{\text{Regression degrees of freedom}}$$

For the models we consider in this text, the regression degrees of freedom is always equal to the number of independent variables in the model:

$$\text{MSR} = \frac{\text{SSR}}{\text{Number of independent variables}} \tag{14.20}$$

Because we consider only regression models with one independent variable in this chapter, we have MSR = SSR/1 = SSR. Hence, for Armand's Pizza Parlors, MSR = SSR = 14,200.

If the null hypothesis $(H_0: \beta_1 = 0)$ is true, MSR and MSE are two independent estimates of $\sigma^2$ and the sampling distribution of MSR/MSE follows an $F$ distribution with numerator degrees of freedom equal to one and denominator degrees of freedom equal to $n - 2$. Therefore, when $\beta_1 = 0$, the value of MSR/MSE should be close to one. However, if the null hypothesis is false ($\beta_1 \neq 0$), MSR will overestimate $\sigma^2$ and the value of MSR/MSE will be inflated; thus, large values of MSR/MSE lead to the rejection of $H_0$ and the conclusion that the relationship between $x$ and $y$ is statistically significant.

Let us conduct the $F$ test for the Armand's Pizza Parlors example. The test statistic is

$$F = \frac{\text{MSR}}{\text{MSE}} = \frac{14{,}200}{191.25} = 74.25$$

*The F test and the t test provide identical results for simple linear regression.*

The $F$ distribution table (Table 4 of Appendix B) shows that with one degree of freedom in the denominator and $n - 2 = 10 - 2 = 8$ degrees of freedom in the denominator, $F = 11.26$ provides an area of .01 in the upper tail. Thus, the area in the upper tail of the $F$ distribution corresponding to the test statistic $F = 74.25$ must be less than .01. Thus, we conclude that the $p$-value must be less than .01. Minitab or Excel show the $p$-value = .000. Because the $p$-value is less than $\alpha = .01$, we reject $H_0$ and conclude that a significant relationship exists between the size of the student population and quarterly sales. A summary of the $F$ test for significance in simple linear regression follows.

---

**$F$ TEST FOR SIGNIFICANCE IN SIMPLE LINEAR REGRESSION**

$$H_0: \beta_1 = 0$$
$$H_a: \beta_1 \neq 0$$

*If $H_0$ is false, MSE still provides an unbiased estimate of $\sigma^2$ and MSR overestimates $\sigma^2$. If $H_0$ is true, both MSE and MSR provide unbiased estimates of $\sigma^2$; in this case the value of MSR/MSE should be close to 1.*

**TEST STATISTIC**

$$F = \frac{\text{MSR}}{\text{MSE}} \tag{14.21}$$

**REJECTION RULE**

| | |
|---|---|
| $p$-value approach: | Reject $H_0$ if $p$-value $\leq \alpha$ |
| Critical value approach: | Reject $H_0$ if $F \geq F_\alpha$ |

where $F_\alpha$ is based on an $F$ distribution with 1 degree of freedom in the numerator and $n - 2$ degrees of freedom in the denominator.

---

In Chapter 13 we covered analysis of variance (ANOVA) and showed how an **ANOVA table** could be used to provide a convenient summary of the computational aspects of analysis of variance. A similar ANOVA table can be used to summarize the results of the $F$ test for significance in regression. Table 14.5 is the general form of the ANOVA table for simple linear regression. Table 14.6 is the ANOVA table with the $F$ test computations performed for Armand's Pizza Parlors. Regression, Error, and Total are the labels for the three sources of variation, with SSR, SSE, and SST appearing as the corresponding sum of squares in column 2. The degrees of freedom, 1 for SSR, $n - 2$ for SSE, and $n - 1$ for SST, are shown in column 3. Column 4 contains the values of MSR and MSE and column 5 contains the value of $F = $ MSR/MSE. Almost all computer printouts of regression analysis include an ANOVA table summary of the $F$ test for significance.

**TABLE 14.5    GENERAL FORM OF THE ANOVA TABLE FOR SIMPLE LINEAR REGRESSION**

*In every analysis of variance table the total sum of squares is the sum of the regression sum of squares and the error sum of squares; in addition, the total degrees of freedom is the sum of the regression degrees of freedom and the error degrees of freedom.*

| Source of Variation | Sum of Squares | Degrees of Freedom | Mean Square | F |
|---|---|---|---|---|
| Regression | SSR | 1 | $MSR = \dfrac{SSR}{1}$ | $F = \dfrac{MSR}{MSE}$ |
| Error | SSE | $n - 2$ | $MSE = \dfrac{SSE}{n - 2}$ | |
| Total | SST | $n - 1$ | | |

## Some Cautions About the Interpretation of Significance Tests

Rejecting the null hypothesis $H_0: \beta_1 = 0$ and concluding that the relationship between $x$ and $y$ is significant does not enable us to conclude that a cause-and-effect relationship is present between $x$ and $y$. Concluding a cause-and-effect relationship is warranted only if the analyst can provide some type of theoretical justification that the relationship is in fact causal. In the Armand's Pizza Parlors example, we can conclude that there is a significant relationship between the size of the student population $x$ and quarterly sales $y$; moreover, the estimated regression equation $\hat{y} = 60 + 5x$ provides the least squares estimate of the relationship. We cannot, however, conclude that changes in student population $x$ *cause* changes in quarterly sales $y$ just because we identified a statistically significant relationship. The appropriateness of such a cause-and-effect conclusion is left to supporting theoretical justification and to good judgment on the part of the analyst. Armand's managers felt that increases in the student population were a likely cause of increased quarterly sales. Thus, the result of the significance test enabled them to conclude that a cause-and-effect relationship was present.

*Regression analysis, which can be used to identify how variables are associated with one another, cannot be used as evidence of a cause-and-effect relationship.*

In addition, just because we are able to reject $H_0: \beta_1 = 0$ and demonstrate statistical significance does not enable us to conclude that the relationship between $x$ and $y$ is linear. We can state only that $x$ and $y$ are related and that a linear relationship explains a significant portion of the variability in $y$ over the range of values for $x$ observed in the sample. Figure 14.7 illustrates this situation. The test for significance calls for the rejection of the null hypothesis $H_0: \beta_1 = 0$ and leads to the conclusion that $x$ and $y$ are significantly related, but the figure shows that the actual relationship between $x$ and $y$ is not linear. Although the

**TABLE 14.6    ANOVA TABLE FOR THE ARMAND'S PIZZA PARLORS PROBLEM**

| Source of Variation | Sum of Squares | Degrees of Freedom | Mean Square | F |
|---|---|---|---|---|
| Regression | 14,200 | 1 | $\dfrac{14{,}200}{1} = 14{,}200$ | $\dfrac{14{,}200}{191.25} = 74.25$ |
| Error | 1,530 | 8 | $\dfrac{1530}{8} = 191.25$ | |
| Total | 15,730 | 9 | | |

FIGURE 14.7   EXAMPLE OF A LINEAR APPROXIMATION OF A NONLINEAR
RELATIONSHIP

linear approximation provided by $\hat{y} = b_0 + b_1 x$ is good over the range of $x$ values observed in the sample, it becomes poor for $x$ values outside that range.

Given a significant relationship, we should feel confident in using the estimated regression equation for predictions corresponding to $x$ values within the range of the $x$ values observed in the sample. For Armand's Pizza Parlors, this range corresponds to values of $x$ between 2 and 26. Unless other reasons indicate that the model is valid beyond this range, predictions outside the range of the independent variable should be made with caution. For Armand's Pizza Parlors, because the regression relationship has been found significant at the .01 level, we should feel confident using it to predict sales for restaurants where the associated student population is between 2000 and 26,000.

## NOTES AND COMMENTS

1. The assumptions made about the error term (Section 14.4) are what allow the tests of statistical significance in this section. The properties of the sampling distribution of $b_1$ and the subsequent $t$ and $F$ tests follow directly from these assumptions.

2. Do not confuse statistical significance with practical significance. With very large sample sizes, statistically significant results can be obtained for small values of $b_1$; in such cases, one must exercise care in concluding that the relationship has practical significance.

3. A test of significance for a linear relationship between $x$ and $y$ can also be performed by using the sample correlation coefficient $r_{xy}$. With $\rho_{xy}$ denoting the population correlation coefficient, the hypotheses are as follows.

$$H_0: \rho_{xy} = 0$$
$$H_a: \rho_{xy} \neq 0$$

A significant relationship can be concluded if $H_0$ is rejected. The details of this test are provided in Appendix 14.2. However, the $t$ and $F$ tests presented previously in this section give the same result as the test for significance using the correlation coefficient. Conducting a test for significance using the correlation coefficient therefore is not necessary if a $t$ or $F$ test has already been conducted.

## Exercises

### Methods

23.  The data from exercise 1 follow.

| $x_i$ | 1 | 2 | 3 | 4 | 5 |
|-------|---|---|---|---|---|
| $y_i$ | 3 | 7 | 5 | 11 | 14 |

a.  Compute the mean square error using equation (14.15).
b.  Compute the standard error of the estimate using equation (14.16).
c.  Compute the estimated standard deviation of $b_1$ using equation (14.18).
d.  Use the $t$ test to test the following hypotheses ($\alpha = .05$):

$$H_0: \beta_1 = 0$$
$$H_a: \beta_1 \neq 0$$

e.  Use the $F$ test to test the hypotheses in part (d) at a .05 level of significance. Present the results in the analysis of variance table format.

24.  The data from exercise 2 follow.

| $x_i$ | 2 | 3 | 5 | 1 | 8 |
|-------|----|----|----|----|----|
| $y_i$ | 25 | 25 | 20 | 30 | 16 |

a.  Compute the mean square error using equation (14.15).
b.  Compute the standard error of the estimate using equation (14.16).
c.  Compute the estimated standard deviation of $b_1$ using equation (14.18).
d.  Use the $t$ test to test the following hypotheses ($\alpha = .05$):

$$H_0: \beta_1 = 0$$
$$H_a: \beta_1 \neq 0$$

e.  Use the $F$ test to test the hypotheses in part (d) at a .05 level of significance. Present the results in the analysis of variance table format.

25.  The data from exercise 3 follow.

| $x_i$ | 2 | 4 | 5 | 7 | 8 |
|-------|---|---|---|---|---|
| $y_i$ | 2 | 3 | 2 | 6 | 4 |

a.  What is the value of the standard error of the estimate?
b.  Test for a significant relationship by using the $t$ test. Use $\alpha = .05$.
c.  Use the $F$ test to test for a significant relationship. Use $\alpha = .05$. What is your conclusion?

### Applications

26.  In exercise 18 the data on grade point average and monthly salary were as follows.

| GPA | Monthly Salary ($) | GPA | Monthly Salary ($) |
|-----|--------------------|-----|--------------------|
| 2.6 | 3300 | 3.2 | 3500 |
| 3.4 | 3600 | 3.5 | 3900 |
| 3.6 | 4000 | 2.9 | 3600 |

a.  Does the *t* test indicate a significant relationship between grade point average and monthly salary? What is your conclusion? Use $\alpha = .05$.

b.  Test for a significant relationship using the *F* test. What is your conclusion? Use $\alpha = .05$.

c.  Show the ANOVA table.

27. *Outside Magazine* tested 10 different models of day hikers and backpacking boots. The following data show the upper support and price for each model tested. Upper support was measured using a rating from 1 to 5, with a rating of 1 denoting average upper support and a rating of 5 denoting excellent upper support (*Outside Magazine Buyer's Guide,* 2001).

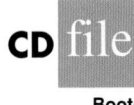

**Boots**

| Manufacturer and Model | Upper Support | Price ($) |
| --- | --- | --- |
| Salomon Super Raid | 2 | 120 |
| Merrell Chameleon Prime | 3 | 125 |
| Teva Challenger | 3 | 130 |
| Vasque Fusion GTX | 3 | 135 |
| Boreal Maigmo | 3 | 150 |
| L.L. Bean GTX Super Guide | 5 | 189 |
| Lowa Kibo | 5 | 190 |
| Asolo AFX 520 GTX | 4 | 195 |
| Raichle Mt. Trail GTX | 4 | 200 |
| Scarpa Delta SL M3 | 5 | 220 |

a.  Use these data to develop an estimated regression equation to estimate the price of a day hiker and backpacking boot given the upper support rating.

b.  At the .05 level of significance, determine whether upper support and price are related.

c.  Would you feel comfortable using the estimated regression equation developed in part (a) to estimate the price for a day hiker or backpacking boot given the upper support rating?

d.  Estimate the price for a day hiker with an upper support rating of 4.

28. Refer to exercise 10, where an estimated regression equation relating the performance score and the overall rating for notebook PCs was developed. At the .05 level of significance, test whether performance score and overall rating are related. Show the ANOVA table. What is your conclusion?

29. Refer to exercise 21, where data on production volume and cost were used to develop an estimated regression equation relating production volume and cost for a particular manufacturing operation. Use $\alpha = .05$ to test whether the production volume is significantly related to the total cost. Show the ANOVA table. What is your conclusion?

30. Refer to exercise 22 where the following data were used to determine whether the price of a printer is related to the speed for plain text printing (*PC World,* February 2003).

**Printers**

| Name | Type | Speed (ppm) | Price ($) |
| --- | --- | --- | --- |
| Minolta-QMS PagePro 1250W | Small Office | 12 | 199 |
| Brother HL-1850 | Small Office | 10 | 499 |
| Lexmark E320 | Small Office | 12.2 | 299 |
| Minolta-QMS PagePro 1250E | Small Office | 10.3 | 299 |
| HP Laserjet 1200 | Small Office | 11.7 | 399 |
| Xerox Phaser 4400/N | Corporate | 17.8 | 1850 |
| Brother HL-2460N | Corporate | 16.1 | 1000 |

| Name | Type | Speed (ppm) | Price ($) |
|------|------|-------------|-----------|
| IBM Infoprint 1120n | Corporate | 11.8 | 1387 |
| Lexmark W812 | Corporate | 19.8 | 2089 |
| Oki Data B8300n | Corporate | 28.2 | 2200 |

Does the evidence indicate a significant relationship between printing speed and price? Conduct the appropriate statistical test and state your conclusion. Use $\alpha = .05$.

31. Refer to Exercise 20, where an estimated regression equation was developed relating typical household income and typical home price. Test whether the typical household income for a city and the typical home price are related at the .01 level of significance.

# 14.6　Using the Estimated Regression Equation for Estimation and Prediction

When using the simple linear regression model we are making an assumption about the relationship between $x$ and $y$. We then use the least squares method to obtain the estimated simple linear regression equation. If a significant relationship exists between $x$ and $y$, and the coefficient of determination shows that the fit is good, the estimated regression equation should be useful for estimation and prediction.

## Point Estimation

In the Armand's Pizza Parlors example, the estimated regression equation $\hat{y} = 60 + 5x$ provides an estimate of the relationship between the size of the student population $x$ and quarterly sales $y$. We can use the estimated regression equation to develop a point estimate of the mean value of $y$ for a particular value of $x$ or to predict an individual value of $y$ corresponding to a given value of $x$. For instance, suppose Armand's managers want a point estimate of the mean quarterly sales for all restaurants located near college campuses with 10,000 students. Using the estimated regression equation $\hat{y} = 60 + 5x$, we see that for $x = 10$ (or 10,000 students), $\hat{y} = 60 + 5(10) = 110$. Thus, a point estimate of the mean quarterly sales for all restaurants located near campuses with 10,000 students is $110,000.

Now suppose Armand's managers want to predict sales for an individual restaurant located near Talbot College, a school with 10,000 students. In this case we are not interested in the mean value for all restaurants located near campuses with 10,000 students; we are just interested in predicting quarterly sales for one individual restaurant. As it turns out, the point estimate for an individual value of $y$ is the same as the point estimate for the mean value of $y$. Hence, we would predict quarterly sales of $\hat{y} = 60 + 5(10) = 110$ or $110,000 for this one restaurant.

## Interval Estimation

*Confidence intervals and prediction intervals show the precision of the regression results. Narrower intervals provide a higher degree of precision.*

Point estimates do not provide any information about the precision associated with an estimate. For that we must develop interval estimates much like those in Chapters 8, 10, and 11. The first type of interval estimate, a **confidence interval**, is an interval estimate of the *mean value of y* for a given value of $x$. The second type of interval estimate, a **prediction interval**, is used whenever we want an interval estimate of an *individual value of y* for a given value of $x$. The point estimate of the mean value of $y$ is the same as the point estimate of an individual value of $y$. But, the interval estimates we obtain for the two cases are different. The margin of error is larger for a prediction interval.

## Confidence Interval for the Mean Value of $y$

The estimated regression equation provides a point estimate of the mean value of $y$ for a given value of $x$. In developing the confidence interval, we will use the following notation.

$x_p$ = the particular or given value of the independent variable $x$

$y_p$ = the value of the dependent variable $y$ corresponding to the given $x_p$

$E(y_p)$ = the mean or expected value of the dependent variable $y$ corresponding to the given $x_p$

$\hat{y}_p = b_0 + b_1 x_p$ = the point estimate of $E(y_p)$ when $x = x_p$

Using this notation to estimate the mean sales for all Armand's restaurants located near a campus with 10,000 students, we have $x_p = 10$, and $E(y_p)$ denotes the unknown mean value of sales for all restaurants where $x_p = 10$. The point estimate of $E(y_p)$ is provided by $\hat{y}_p = 60 + 5(10) = 110$.

In general, we cannot expect $\hat{y}_p$ to equal $E(y_p)$ exactly. If we want to make an inference about how close $\hat{y}_p$ is to the true mean value $E(y_p)$, we will have to estimate the variance of $\hat{y}_p$. The formula for estimating the variance of $\hat{y}_p$ given $x_p$, denoted by $s_{\hat{y}_p}^2$, is

$$s_{\hat{y}_p}^2 = s^2 \left[ \frac{1}{n} + \frac{(x_p - \bar{x})^2}{\Sigma(x_i - \bar{x})^2} \right] \qquad (14.22)$$

The estimate of the standard deviation of $\hat{y}_p$ is given by the square root of equation (14.22).

$$s_{\hat{y}_p} = s \sqrt{\frac{1}{n} + \frac{(x_p - \bar{x})^2}{\Sigma(x_i - \bar{x})^2}} \qquad (14.23)$$

The computational results for Armand's Pizza Parlors in Section 14.5 provided $s = 13.829$. With $x_p = 10$, $\bar{x} = 14$, and $\Sigma(x_i - \bar{x})^2 = 568$, we can use equation (14.23) to obtain

$$s_{\hat{y}_p} = 13.829 \sqrt{\frac{1}{10} + \frac{(10 - 14)^2}{568}}$$

$$= 13.829 \sqrt{.1282} = 4.95$$

The general expression for a confidence interval follows.

---

CONFIDENCE INTERVAL FOR $E(y_p)$

*The margin of error associated with this internal estimate is $t_{\alpha/2} s_{\hat{y}_p}$.*

$$\hat{y}_p \pm t_{\alpha/2} s_{\hat{y}_p} \qquad (14.24)$$

where the confidence coefficient is $1 - \alpha$ and $t_{\alpha/2}$ is based on a $t$ distribution with $n - 2$ degrees of freedom.

---

Using expression (14.24) to develop a 95% confidence interval of the mean quarterly sales for all Armand's restaurants located near campuses with 10,000 students, we need the value of $t$ for $\alpha/2 = .025$ and $n - 2 = 10 - 2 = 8$ degrees of freedom. Using Table 2 of Appendix B, we have $t_{.025} = 2.306$. Thus, with $\hat{y}_p = 110$ and a margin of error of $t_{\alpha/2} s_{\hat{y}_p} = 2.306(4.95) = 11.415$, the 95% confidence interval estimate is

$$110 \pm 11.415$$

In dollars, the 95% confidence interval for the mean quarterly sales of all restaurants near campuses with 10,000 students is $110,000 \pm \$11,415$. Therefore, the 95% confidence interval for the mean quarterly sales when the student population is 10,000 is $98,585 to $121,415.

Note that the estimated standard deviation of $\hat{y}_p$ given by equation (14.23) is smallest when $x_p = \bar{x}$ and the quantity $x_p - \bar{x} = 0$. In this case, the estimated standard deviation of $\hat{y}_p$ becomes

$$s_{\hat{y}_p} = s\sqrt{\frac{1}{n} + \frac{(\bar{x} - \bar{x})^2}{\Sigma(x_i - \bar{x})^2}} = s\sqrt{\frac{1}{n}}$$

This result implies that we can make the best or most precise estimate of the mean value of $y$ whenever $x_p = \bar{x}$. In fact, the further $x_p$ is from $\bar{x}$ the larger $x_p - \bar{x}$ becomes. As a result, confidence intervals for the mean value of $y$ will become wider as $x_p$ deviates more from $\bar{x}$. This pattern is shown graphically in Figure 14.8.

## Prediction Interval for an Individual Value of $y$

Suppose that instead of estimating the mean value of sales for all Armand's restaurants located near campuses with 10,000 students, we want to estimate the sales for an individual restaurant located near Talbot College, a school with 10,000 students. As noted previously,

**FIGURE 14.8**   CONFIDENCE INTERVALS FOR THE MEAN SALES $y$ AT GIVEN VALUES OF STUDENT POPULATION $x$

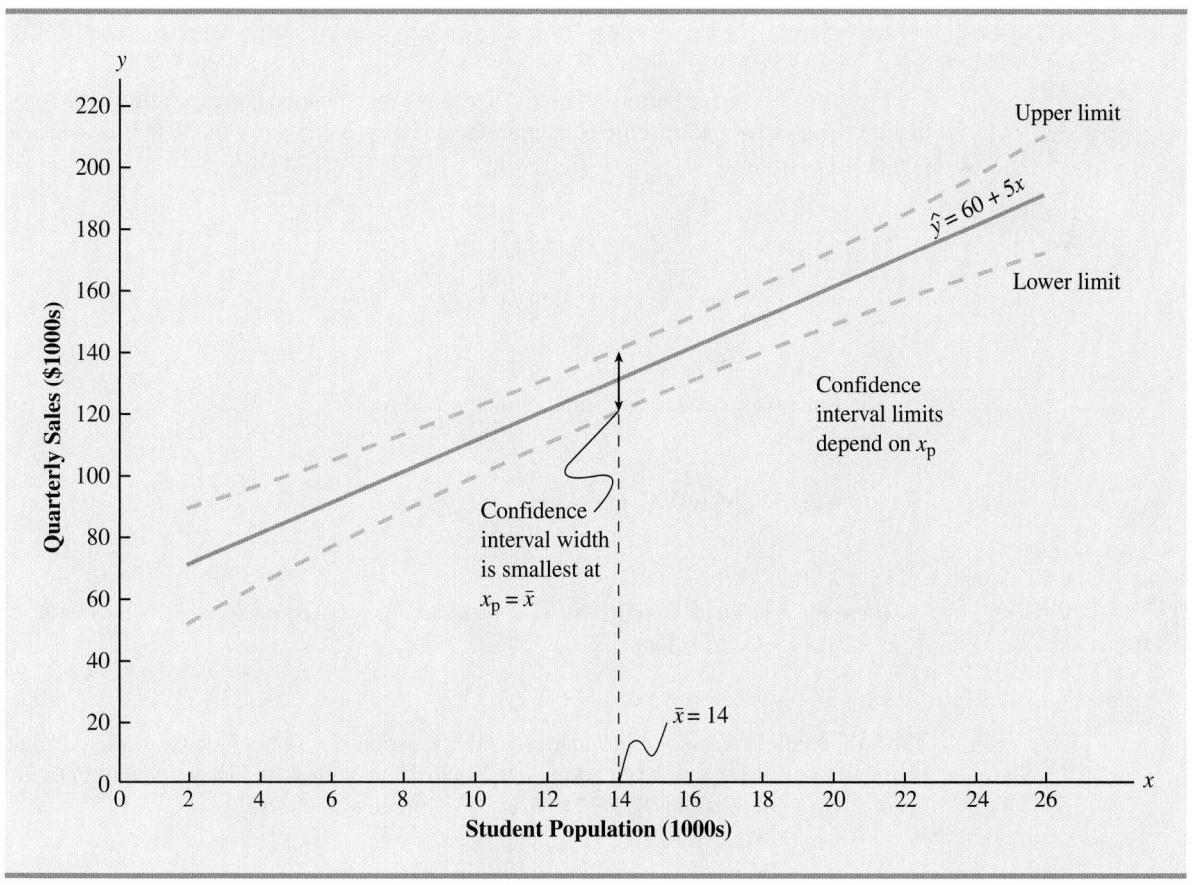

the point estimate of $y_p$, the value of $y$ corresponding to the given $x_p$, is provided by the estimated regression equation $\hat{y}_p = b_0 + b_1 x_p$. For the restaurant at Talbot College, we have $x_p = 10$ and a corresponding predicted quarterly sales of $\hat{y}_p = 60 + 5(10) = 110$, or \$110,000. Note that this value is the same as the point estimate of the mean sales for all restaurants located near campuses with 10,000 students.

To develop a prediction interval, we must first determine the variance associated with using $\hat{y}_p$ as an estimate of an individual value of $y$ when $x = x_p$. This variance is made up of the sum of the following two components.

1. The variance of individual $y$ values about the mean $E(y_p)$, an estimate of which is given by $s^2$
2. The variance associated with using $\hat{y}_p$ to estimate $E(y_p)$, an estimate of which is given by $s_{\hat{y}_p}^2$

The formula for estimating the variance of an individual value of $y_p$, denoted by $s_{ind}^2$, is

$$s_{ind}^2 = s^2 + s_{\hat{y}_p}^2$$
$$= s^2 + s^2 \left[ \frac{1}{n} + \frac{(x_p - \bar{x})^2}{\Sigma(x_i - \bar{x})^2} \right]$$
$$= s^2 \left[ 1 + \frac{1}{n} + \frac{(x_p - \bar{x})^2}{\Sigma(x_i - \bar{x})^2} \right] \tag{14.25}$$

Hence, an estimate of the standard deviation of an individual value of $y_p$ is given by

$$s_{ind} = s \sqrt{1 + \frac{1}{n} + \frac{(x_p - \bar{x})^2}{\Sigma(x_i - \bar{x})^2}} \tag{14.26}$$

For Armand's Pizza Parlors, the estimated standard deviation corresponding to the prediction of sales for one specific restaurant located near a campus with 10,000 students is computed as follows.

$$s_{ind} = 13.829 \sqrt{1 + \frac{1}{10} + \frac{(10 - 14)^2}{568}}$$
$$= 13.829 \sqrt{1.1282}$$
$$= 14.69$$

The general expression for a prediction interval follows.

PREDICTION INTERVAL FOR $y_p$

*The margin of error associated with this interval estimate is $t_{\alpha/2} s_{ind}$.*

$$\hat{y}_p \pm t_{\alpha/2} s_{ind} \tag{14.27}$$

where the confidence coefficient is $1 - \alpha$ and $t_{\alpha/2}$ is based on a $t$ distribution with $n - 2$ degrees of freedom.

The 95% prediction interval for quarterly sales at Armand's Talbot College restaurant can be found by using $t_{.025} = 2.306$ and $s_{ind} = 14.69$. Thus, with $\hat{y}_p = 110$ and a margin of error of $t_{\alpha/2} s_{ind} = 2.306(14.69) = 33.875$, the 95% prediction interval is

$$110 \pm 33.875$$

**FIGURE 14.9    CONFIDENCE AND PREDICTION INTERVALS FOR SALES $y$ AT GIVEN VALUES OF STUDENT POPULATION $x$**

In dollars, this prediction interval is $110,000 ± $33,875 or $76,125 to $143,875. Note that the prediction interval for an individual restaurant located near a campus with 10,000 students is wider than the confidence interval for the mean sales of all restaurants located near campuses with 10,000 students. The difference reflects the fact that we are able to estimate the mean value of $y$ more precisely than we can an individual value of $y$.

Both confidence interval estimates and prediction interval estimates are most precise when the value of the independent variable is $x_p = \bar{x}$. The general shapes of confidence intervals and the wider prediction intervals are shown together in Figure 14.9.

## Exercises

### Methods

32.  The data from exercise 1 follow.

| $x_i$ | 1 | 2 | 3 | 4 | 5 |
|-------|---|---|---|---|----|
| $y_i$ | 3 | 7 | 5 | 11 | 14 |

a.  Use equation (14.23) to estimate the standard deviation of $\hat{y}_p$ when $x = 4$.
b.  Use expression (14.24) to develop a 95% confidence interval for the expected value of $y$ when $x = 4$.

c.   Use equation (14.26) to estimate the standard deviation of an individual value of $y$ when $x = 4$.

d.   Use expression (14.27) to develop a 95% prediction interval for $y$ when $x = 4$.

33.   The data from exercise 2 follow.

| $x_i$ | 2 | 3 | 5 | 1 | 8 |
|-------|----|----|----|----|----|
| $y_i$ | 25 | 25 | 20 | 30 | 16 |

a.   Estimate the standard deviation of $\hat{y}_p$ when $x = 3$.

b.   Develop a 95% confidence interval for the expected value of $y$ when $x = 3$.

c.   Estimate the standard deviation of an individual value of $y$ when $x = 3$.

d.   Develop a 95% prediction interval for $y$ when $x = 3$.

34.   The data from exercise 3 follow.

| $x_i$ | 2 | 4 | 5 | 7 | 8 |
|-------|----|----|----|----|----|
| $y_i$ | 2 | 3 | 2 | 6 | 4 |

Develop the 95% confidence and prediction intervals when $x = 3$. Explain why these two intervals are different.

## Applications

35.   In exercise 18, the data on grade point average $x$ and monthly salary $y$ provided the estimated regression equation $\hat{y} = 1790.5 + 581.1x$.

a.   Develop a 95% confidence interval for the mean starting salary for all students with a 3.0 GPA.

b.   Develop a 95% prediction interval for the starting salary for Joe Heller, a student with a GPA of 3.0.

PCs

36.   In exercise 10, data on the performance score ($x$) and the overall rating ($y$) for notebook PCs provided the estimated regression equation $\hat{y} = 51.819 + .1452x$ (*PC World*, February 2000).

a.   Develop a point estimate of the overall rating for a PC with a performance score of 200.

b.   Develop a 95% confidence interval for the mean overall score for all PCs with a performance score of 200.

c.   Suppose that a new PC developed by Dell has a performance score of 200. Develop a 95% prediction interval for the overall score for this new PC.

d.   Discuss the differences in your answers to parts (b) and (c).

37.   In exercise 13, data were given on the adjusted gross income $x$ and the amount of itemized deductions taken by taxpayers. Data were reported in thousands of dollars. With the estimated regression equation $\hat{y} = 4.68 + .16x$, the point estimate of a reasonable level of total itemized deductions for a taxpayer with an adjusted gross income of $52,500 is $13,080.

a.   Develop a 95% confidence interval for the mean amount of total itemized deductions for all taxpayers with an adjusted gross income of $52,500.

b.   Develop a 95% prediction interval estimate for the amount of total itemized deductions for a particular taxpayer with an adjusted gross income of $52,500.

c.   If the particular taxpayer referred to in part (b) claimed total itemized deductions of $20,400, would the IRS agent's request for an audit appear to be justified?

d.   Use your answer to part (b) to give the IRS agent a guideline as to the amount of total itemized deductions a taxpayer with an adjusted gross income of $52,500 should claim before an audit is recommended.

38.   Refer to Exercise 21, where data on the production volume $x$ and total cost $y$ for a particular manufacturing operation were used to develop the estimated regression equation $\hat{y} = 1246.67 + 7.6x$.

a.   The company's production schedule shows that 500 units must be produced next month. What is the point estimate of the total cost for next month?

b. Develop a 99% prediction interval for the total cost for next month.

c. If an accounting cost report at the end of next month shows that the actual production cost during the month was $6000, should managers be concerned about incurring such a high total cost for the month? Discuss.

39. Almost all U.S. light-rail systems use electric cars that run on tracks built at street level. The Federal Transit Administration claims light-rail is one of the safest modes of travel, with an accident rate of .99 accidents per million passenger miles as compared to 2.29 for buses. The following data show the miles of track and the weekday ridership in thousands of passengers for six light-rail systems (*USA Today*, January 7, 2003).

| City | Miles of Track | Ridership (1000s) |
|------|----------------|-------------------|
| Cleveland | 15 | 15 |
| Denver | 17 | 35 |
| Portland | 38 | 81 |
| Sacramento | 21 | 31 |
| San Diego | 47 | 75 |
| San Jose | 31 | 30 |
| St. Louis | 34 | 42 |

a. Use these data to develop an estimated regression equation that could be used to predict the ridership given the miles of track.

b. Did the estimated regression equation provide a good fit? Explain.

c. Develop a 95% confidence interval for the mean weekday ridership for all light-rail systems with 30 miles of track.

d. Suppose that Charlotte is considering construction of a light-rail system with 30 miles of track. Develop a 95% prediction interval for the weekday ridership for the Charlotte system. Do you think that the prediction interval you developed would be of value to Charlotte planners in anticipating the number of weekday riders for their new light-rail system? Explain.

#  Computer Solution

Performing the regression analysis computations without the help of a computer can be quite time consuming. In this section we discuss how the computational burden can be minimized by using a computer software package such as Minitab.

We entered Armand's student population and sales data into a Minitab worksheet. The independent variable was named Pop and the dependent variable was named Sales to assist with interpretation of the computer output. Using Minitab, we obtained the printout for Armand's Pizza Parlors shown in Figure 14.10.* The interpretation of this printout follows.

1. Minitab prints the estimated regression equation as Sales = 60.0 + 5.00 Pop.

2. A table is printed that shows the values of the coefficients $b_0$ and $b_1$, the standard deviation of each coefficient, the $t$ value obtained by dividing each coefficient value by its standard deviation, and the $p$-value associated with the $t$ test. Because the $p$-value is zero (to three decimal places), the sample results indicate that the null hypothesis ($H_0$: $\beta_1 = 0$) should be rejected. Alternatively, we could compare 8.62 (located in the $t$-ratio column) to the appropriate critical value. This procedure for the $t$ test was described in Section 14.5.

---

*The Minitab steps necessary to generate the output are given in Appendix 14.3.

**FIGURE 14.10    MINITAB OUTPUT FOR THE ARMAND'S PIZZA PARLORS PROBLEM**

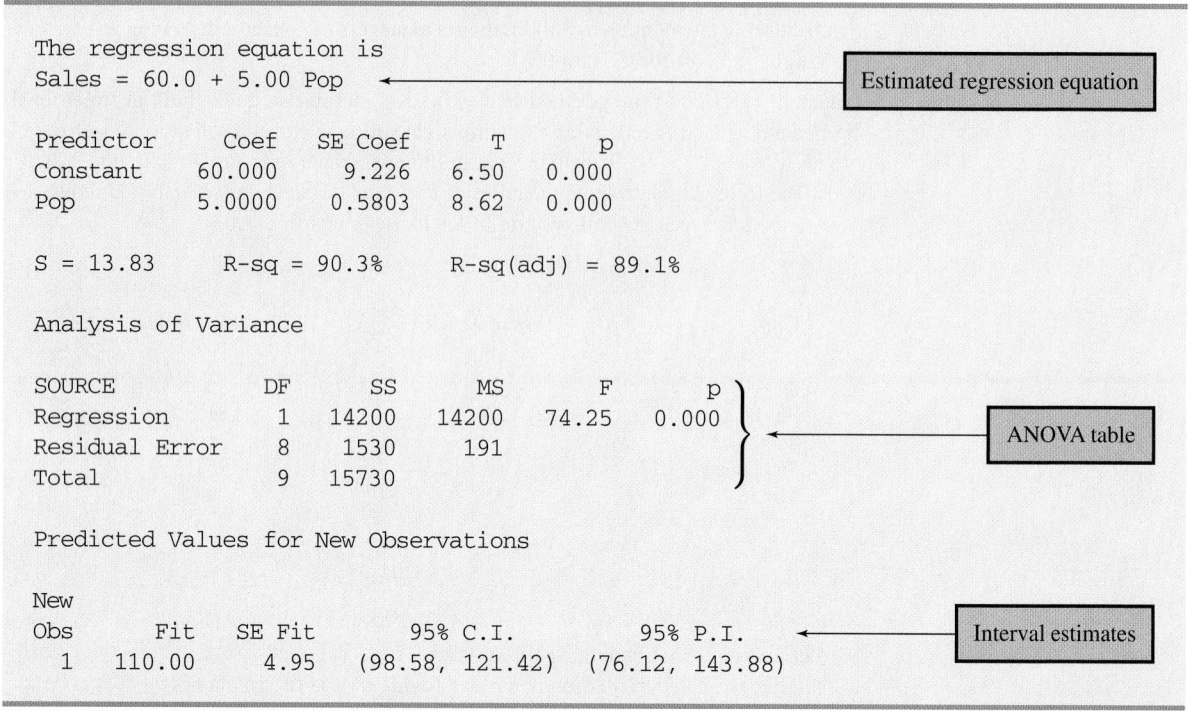

```
The regression equation is
Sales = 60.0 + 5.00 Pop          ◄──────────── Estimated regression equation

Predictor     Coef    SE Coef      T        p
Constant    60.000      9.226    6.50    0.000
Pop         5.0000     0.5803    8.62    0.000

S = 13.83    R-sq = 90.3%     R-sq(adj) = 89.1%

Analysis of Variance

SOURCE           DF      SS      MS       F       p  ⎫
Regression        1   14200   14200   74.25   0.000  ⎬── ANOVA table
Residual Error    8    1530     191                  ⎪
Total             9   15730                          ⎭

Predicted Values for New Observations

New
Obs     Fit   SE Fit       95% C.I.          95% P.I.     ◄── Interval estimates
  1  110.00     4.95   (98.58, 121.42)   (76.12, 143.88)
```

3. Minitab prints the standard error of the estimate, $s = 13.83$, as well as information about the goodness of fit. Note that "R-sq = 90.3%" is the coefficient of determination expressed as a percentage. The value "R-Sq (adj) = 89.1%" is discussed in Chapter 15.

4. The ANOVA table is printed below the heading Analysis of Variance. Minitab uses the label Residual Error for the error source of variation. Note that DF is an abbreviation for degrees of freedom and that MSR is given as 14,200 and MSE as 191. The ratio of these two values provides the $F$ value of 74.25 and the corresponding $p$-value of 0.000. Because the $p$-value is zero (to three decimal places), the relationship between Sales and Pop is judged statistically significant.

5. The 95% confidence interval estimate of the expected sales and the 95% prediction interval estimate of sales for an individual restaurant located near a campus with 10,000 students are printed below the ANOVA table. The confidence interval is (98.58, 121.42) and the prediction interval is (76.12, 143.88) as we showed in Section 14.6.

## Exercises

## Applications

**SELF** test

40. The commercial division of a real estate firm is conducting a regression analysis of the relationship between $x$, annual gross rents (in thousands of dollars), and $y$, selling price (in thousands of dollars) for apartment buildings. Data were collected on several properties recently sold and the following computer output was obtained.

```
The regression equation is
Y = 20.0 + 7.21 X

Predictor       Coef      SE Coef        T
Constant      20.000       3.2213     6.21
X              7.210       1.3626     5.29

Analysis of Variance

SOURCE                DF            SS
Regression             1       41587.3
Residual Error         7
Total                  8       51984.1
```

a. How many apartment buildings were in the sample?
b. Write the estimated regression equation.
c. What is the value of $s_{b_1}$?
d. Use the $F$ statistic to test the significance of the relationship at a .05 level of significance.
e. Estimate the selling price of an apartment building with gross annual rents of $50,000.

41. Following is a portion of the computer output for a regression analysis relating $y$ = maintenance expense (dollars per month) to $x$ = usage (hours per week) of a particular brand of computer terminal.

```
The regression equation is
Y = 6.1092 + .8951 X

Predictor       Coef      SE Coef
Constant      6.1092       0.9361
X             0.8951       0.1490

Analysis of Variance

SOURCE                DF            SS          MS
Regression             1       1575.76     1575.76
Residual Error         8        349.14       43.64
Total                  9       1924.90
```

a. Write the estimated regression equation.
b. Use a $t$ test to determine whether monthly maintenance expense is related to usage at the .05 level of significance.
c. Use the estimated regression equation to predict monthly maintenance expense for any terminal that is used 25 hours per week.

42. A regression model relating $x$, number of salespersons at a branch office, to $y$, annual sales at the office (in thousands of dollars) provided the following computer output from a regression analysis of the data.

```
The regression equation is
Y = 80.0 + 50.00 X

Predictor        Coef     SE Coef        T
Constant         80.0      11.333      7.06
X                50.0       5.482      9.12

Analysis of Variance

SOURCE              DF          SS          MS
Regression           1      6828.6      6828.6
Residual Error      28      2298.8        82.1
Total               29      9127.4
```

a. Write the estimated regression equation.
b. How many branch offices were involved in the study?
c. Compute the *F* statistic and test the significance of the relationship at a .05 level of significance.
d. Predict the annual sales at the Memphis branch office. This branch employs 12 salespersons.

43. Health experts recommend that runners drink 4 ounces of water every 15 minutes they run. Although handheld bottles work well for many types of runs, all-day cross-country runs require hip-mounted or over-the-shoulder hydration systems. In addition to carrying more water, hip-mounted or over-the-shoulder hydration systems offer more storage space for food and extra clothing. As the capacity increases, however, the weight and cost of these larger-capacity systems also increase. The following data show the weight (ounces) and the price for 26 hip-mounted or over-the-shoulder hydration systems (*Trail Runner Gear Guide,* 2003).

**CD** file

**Hydration1**

| Model | Weight (oz.) | Price ($) |
|---|---|---|
| Fastdraw | 3 | 10 |
| Fastdraw Plus | 4 | 12 |
| Fitness | 5 | 12 |
| Access | 7 | 20 |
| Access Plus | 8 | 25 |
| Solo | 9 | 25 |
| Serenade | 9 | 35 |
| Solitaire | 11 | 35 |
| Gemini | 21 | 45 |
| Shadow | 15 | 40 |
| SipStream | 18 | 60 |
| Express | 9 | 30 |
| Lightning | 12 | 40 |
| Elite | 14 | 60 |
| Extender | 16 | 65 |
| Stinger | 16 | 65 |
| GelFlask Belt | 3 | 20 |
| GelDraw | 1 | 7 |
| GelFlask Clip-on Holster | 2 | 10 |
| GelFlask Holster SS | 1 | 10 |
| Strider (W) | 8 | 30 |

| Model | Weight (oz.) | Price ($) |
|---|---|---|
| Walkabout (W) | 14 | 40 |
| Solitude I.C.E. | 9 | 35 |
| Getaway I.C.E. | 19 | 55 |
| Profile I.C.E. | 14 | 50 |
| Traverse I.C.E. | 13 | 60 |

a. Use these data to develop an estimated regression equation that could be used to predict the price of a hydration system given its weight.
b. Test the significance of the relationship at the .05 level of significance.
c. Did the estimated regression equation provide a good fit? Explain.
d. Assume that the estimated regression equation developed in part (a) will also apply to hydration systems produced by other companies. Develop a 95% confidence interval estimate of the price for all hydration systems that weigh 10 ounces.
e. Assume that the estimated regression equation developed in part (a) will also apply to hydration systems produced by other companies. Develop a 95% prediction interval estimate of the price for the Back Draft system produced by Eastern Mountain Sports. The Back Draft system weighs 10 ounces.

44. Cushman & Wakefield, Inc., collects data showing the office building vacancy rates and rental rates for markets in the United States. The following data show the overall vacancy rates (%) and the average rental rates (per square foot) for the central business district for 18 selected markets.

**CD file**

**OffRates**

| Market | Vacancy Rate (%) | Average Rate ($) |
|---|---|---|
| Atlanta | 21.9 | 18.54 |
| Boston | 6.0 | 33.70 |
| Hartford | 22.8 | 19.67 |
| Baltimore | 18.1 | 21.01 |
| Washington | 12.7 | 35.09 |
| Philadelphia | 14.5 | 19.41 |
| Miami | 20.0 | 25.28 |
| Tampa | 19.2 | 17.02 |
| Chicago | 16.0 | 24.04 |
| San Francisco | 6.6 | 31.42 |
| Phoenix | 15.9 | 18.74 |
| San Jose | 9.2 | 26.76 |
| West Palm Beach | 19.7 | 27.72 |
| Detroit | 20.0 | 18.20 |
| Brooklyn | 8.3 | 25.00 |
| Downtown, NY | 17.1 | 29.78 |
| Midtown, NY | 10.8 | 37.03 |
| Midtown South, NY | 11.1 | 28.64 |

a. Develop a scatter diagram for these data; plot the vacancy rate on the horizontal axis.
b. Does there appear to be any relationship between vacancy rates and rental rates?
c. Develop the estimated regression equation that could be used to predict the average rental rate given the overall vacancy rate.
d. Test the significance of the relationship at the .05 level of significance.

e.  Did the estimated regression equation provide a good fit? Explain.
f.  Predict the expected rental rate for markets with a 25% vacancy rate in the central business district.
g.  The overall vacancy rate in the central business district in Ft. Lauderdale is 11.3%. Predict the expected rental rate for Ft. Lauderdale.

# 14.8   Residual Analysis: Validating Model Assumptions

**Residual analysis** *is the primary tool for determining whether the assumed regression model is appropriate.*

As we noted previously, the *residual* for observation $i$ is the difference between the observed value of the dependent variable ($y_i$) and the estimated value of the dependent variable ($\hat{y}_i$).

---

RESIDUAL FOR OBSERVATION $i$

$$y_i - \hat{y}_i \qquad\qquad (14.28)$$

where

$y_i$ is the observed value of the dependent variable
$\hat{y}_i$ is the estimated value of the dependent variable

---

In other words, the $i$th residual is the error resulting from using the estimated regression equation to predict the value of the dependent variable. The residuals for the Armand's Pizza Parlors example are computed in Table 14.7. The observed values of the dependent variable are in the second column and the estimated values of the dependent variable, obtained using the estimated regression equation $\hat{y} = 60 + 5x$, are in the third column. An analysis of the corresponding residuals in the fourth column will help determine whether the assumptions made about the regression model are appropriate.

Let us now review the regression assumptions for the Armand's Pizza Parlors example. A simple linear regression model was assumed.

$$y = \beta_0 + \beta_1 x + \epsilon \qquad\qquad (14.29)$$

This model indicates that we assumed quarterly sales ($y$) to be a linear function of the size of the student population ($x$) plus an error term $\epsilon$. In Section 14.4 we made the following assumptions about the error term $\epsilon$.

1.  $E(\epsilon) = 0$.
2.  The variance of $\epsilon$, denoted by $\sigma^2$, is the same for all values of $x$.
3.  The values of $\epsilon$ are independent.
4.  The error term $\epsilon$ has a normal distribution.

These assumptions provide the theoretical basis for the $t$ test and the $F$ test used to determine whether the relationship between $x$ and $y$ is significant, and for the confidence and prediction interval estimates presented in Section 14.6. If the assumptions about the error term $\epsilon$ appear questionable, the hypothesis tests about the significance of the regression relationship and the interval estimation results may not be valid.

The residuals provide the best information about $\epsilon$; hence an analysis of the residuals is an important step in determining whether the assumptions for $\epsilon$ are appropriate. Much of

**TABLE 14.7    RESIDUALS FOR ARMAND'S PIZZA PARLORS**

| Student Population $x_i$ | Sales $y_i$ | Estimated Sales $\hat{y}_i = 60 + 5x_i$ | Residuals $y_i - \hat{y}_i$ |
|---|---|---|---|
| 2 | 58 | 70 | −12 |
| 6 | 105 | 90 | 15 |
| 8 | 88 | 100 | −12 |
| 8 | 118 | 100 | 18 |
| 12 | 117 | 120 | −3 |
| 16 | 137 | 140 | −3 |
| 20 | 157 | 160 | −3 |
| 20 | 169 | 160 | 9 |
| 22 | 149 | 170 | −21 |
| 26 | 202 | 190 | 12 |

residual analysis is based on an examination of graphical plots. In this section, we discuss the following residual plots.

1. A plot of the residuals against values of the independent variable $x$
2. A plot of residuals against the predicted values of the dependent variable $\hat{y}$
3. A standardized residual plot
4. A normal probability plot

## Residual Plot Against $x$

A **residual plot** against the independent variable $x$ is a graph in which the values of the independent variable are represented by the horizontal axis and the corresponding residual values are represented by the vertical axis. A point is plotted for each residual. The first coordinate for each point is given by the value of $x_i$ and the second coordinate is given by the corresponding value of the residual $y_i - \hat{y}_i$. For a residual plot against $x$ with the Armand's Pizza Parlors data from Table 14.7, the coordinates of the first point are $(2, -12)$, corresponding to $x_1 = 2$ and $y_1 - \hat{y}_1 = -12$; the coordinates of the second point are $(6, 15)$, corresponding to $x_2 = 6$ and $y_2 - \hat{y}_2 = 15$, and so on. Figure 14.11 shows the resulting residual plot.

Before interpreting the results for this residual plot, let us consider some general patterns that might be observed in any residual plot. Three examples appear in Figure 14.12. If the assumption that the variance of $\epsilon$ is the same for all values of $x$ and the assumed regression model is an adequate representation of the relationship between the variables, the residual plot should give an overall impression of a horizontal band of points such as the one in Panel A of Figure 14.12. However, if the variance of $\epsilon$ is not the same for all values of $x$—for example, if variability about the regression line is greater for larger values of $x$—a pattern such as the one in Panel B of Figure 14.12 could be observed. In this case, the assumption of a constant variance of $\epsilon$ is violated. Another possible residual plot is shown in Panel C. In this case, we would conclude that the assumed regression model is not an adequate representation of the relationship between the variables. A curvilinear regression model or multiple regression model should be considered.

Now let us return to the residual plot for Armand's Pizza Parlors shown in Figure 14.11. The residuals appear to approximate the horizontal pattern in Panel A of Figure 14.12. Hence, we conclude that the residual plot does not provide evidence that the assumptions made for Armand's regression model should be challenged. At this point, we are confident in the conclusion that Armand's simple linear regression model is valid.

**FIGURE 14.11    PLOT OF THE RESIDUALS AGAINST THE INDEPENDENT VARIABLE $x$ FOR ARMAND'S PIZZA PARLORS**

Experience and good judgment are always factors in the effective interpretation of residual plots. Seldom does a residual plot conform precisely to one of the patterns in Figure 14.12. Yet analysts who frequently conduct regression studies and frequently review residual plots become adept at understanding the differences between patterns that are reasonable and patterns that indicate the assumptions of the model should be questioned. A residual plot provides one technique to assess the validity of the assumptions for a regression model.

## Residual Plot Against $\hat{y}$

Another residual plot represents the predicted value of the dependent variable $\hat{y}$ on the horizontal axis and the residual values on the vertical axis. A point is plotted for each residual. The first coordinate for each point is given by $\hat{y}_i$ and the second coordinate is given by the corresponding value of the $i$th residual $y_i - \hat{y}_i$. With the Armand's data from Table 14.7, the coordinates of the first point are $(70, -12)$, corresponding to $\hat{y}_1 = 70$ and $y_1 - \hat{y}_1 = -12$; the coordinates of the second point are $(90, 15)$, and so on. Figure 14.13 provides the residual plot. Note that the pattern of this residual plot is the same as the pattern of the residual plot against the independent variable $x$. It is not a pattern that would lead us to question the model assumptions. For simple linear regression, both the residual plot against $x$ and the residual plot against $\hat{y}$ provide the same pattern. For multiple regression analysis, the residual plot against $\hat{y}$ is more widely used because of the presence of more than one independent variable.

## Standardized Residuals

Many of the residual plots provided by computer software packages use a standardized version of the residuals. As demonstrated in preceding chapters, a random variable is standardized by subtracting its mean and dividing the result by its standard deviation. With the

**FIGURE 14.12    RESIDUAL PLOTS FROM THREE REGRESSION STUDIES**

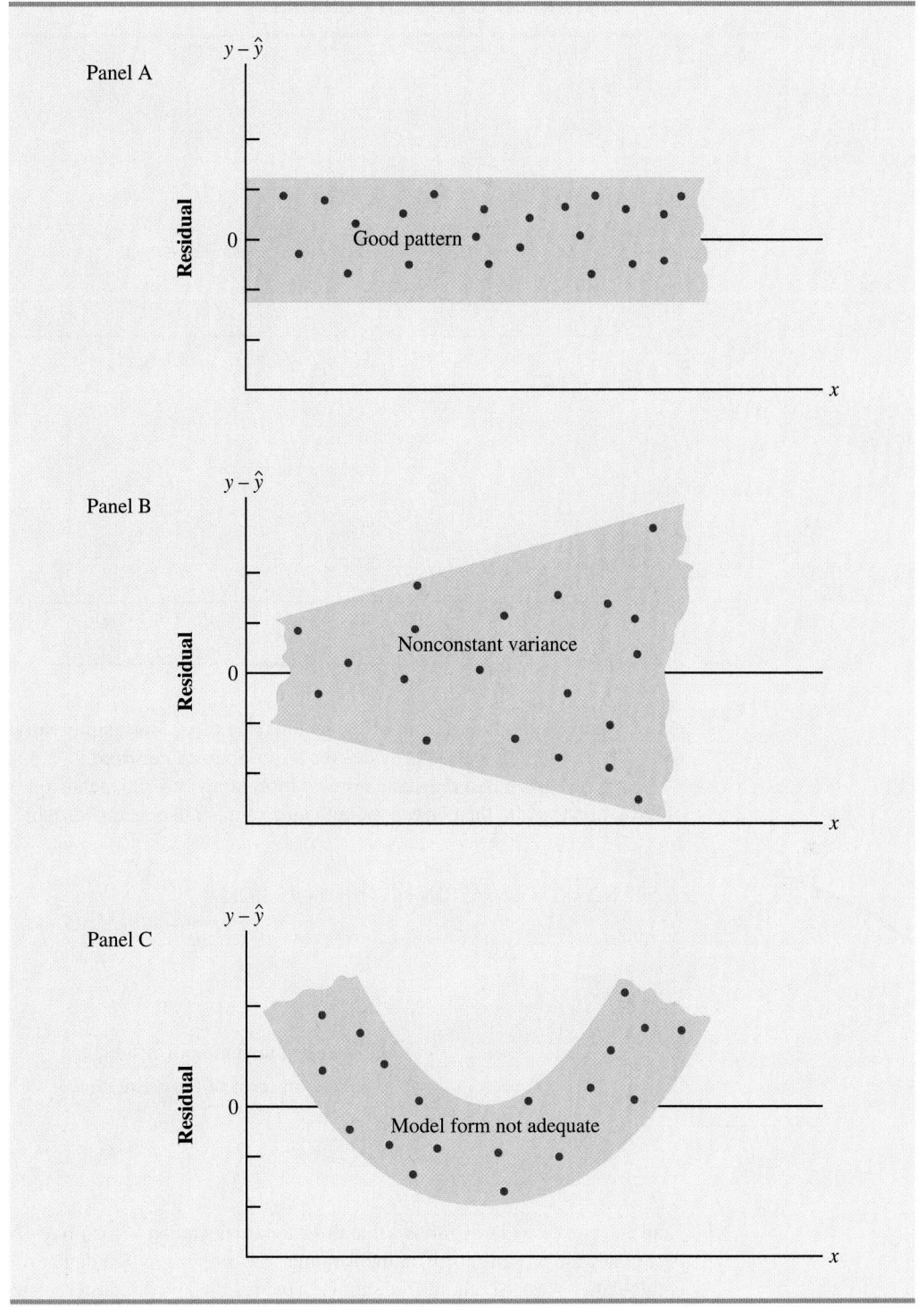

**FIGURE 14.13    PLOT OF THE RESIDUALS AGAINST THE PREDICTED VALUES $\hat{y}$
FOR ARMAND'S PIZZA PARLORS**

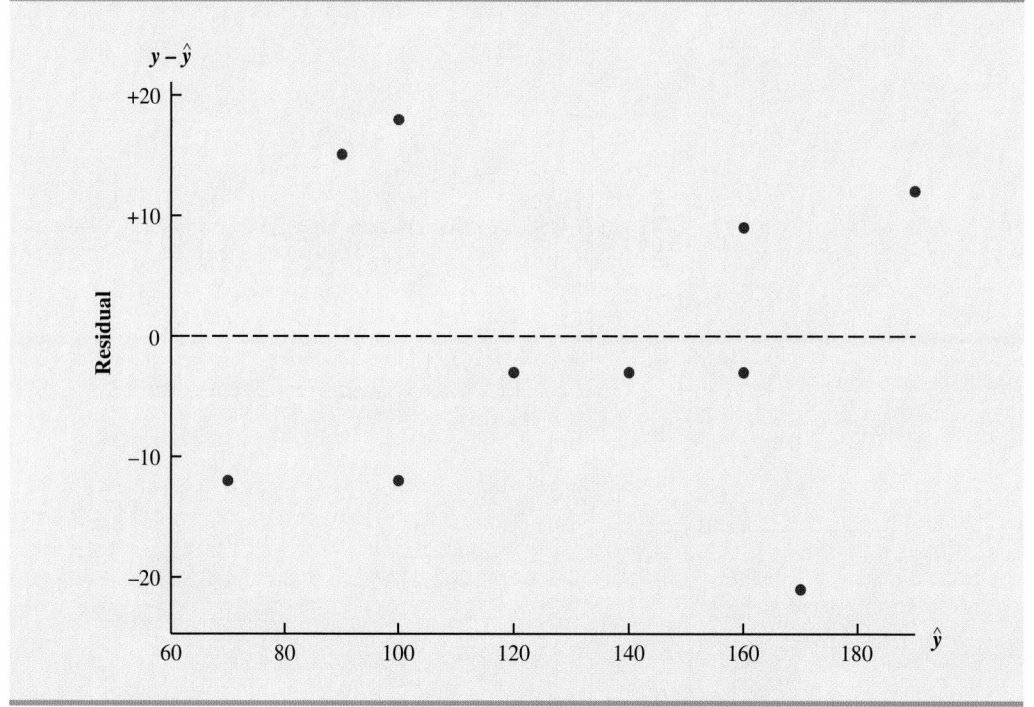

least squares method, the mean of the residuals is zero. Thus, simply dividing each residual by its standard deviation provides the **standardized residual**.

It can be shown that the standard deviation of residual $i$ depends on the standard error of the estimate $s$ and the corresponding value of the independent variable $x_i$.

STANDARD DEVIATION OF THE $i$th RESIDUAL*

$$s_{y_i - \hat{y}_i} = s\sqrt{1 - h_i} \qquad (14.30)$$

where

$$s_{y_i - \hat{y}_i} = \text{the standard deviation of residual } i$$
$$s = \text{the standard error of the estimate}$$
$$h_i = \frac{1}{n} + \frac{(x_i - \bar{x})^2}{\Sigma(x_i - \bar{x})^2} \qquad (14.31)$$

Note that equation (14.30) shows that the standard deviation of the $i$th residual depends on $x_i$ because of the presence of $h_i$ in the formula.[†] Once the standard deviation of each residual is calculated, we can compute the standardized residual by dividing each residual by its corresponding standard deviation.

---

*This equation actually provides an estimate of the standard deviation of the $i$th residual, because $s$ is used instead of $\sigma$.
[†]$h_i$ is referred to as the *leverage* of observation $i$. Leverage will be discussed further when we consider influential observations in Section 14.9.

STANDARDIZED RESIDUAL FOR OBSERVATION $i$

$$\frac{y_i - \hat{y}_i}{s_{y_i - \hat{y}_i}} \qquad\qquad (14.32)$$

Table 14.8 shows the calculation of the standardized residuals for Armand's Pizza Parlors. Recall that previous calculations showed $s = 13.829$. Figure 14.14 is the plot of the standardized residuals against the independent variable $x$.

*Small departures from normality do not have a great effect on the statistical tests used in regression analysis.*

The standardized residual plot can provide insight about the assumption that the error term $\epsilon$ has a normal distribution. If this assumption is satisfied, the distribution of the standardized residuals should appear to come from a standard normal probability distribution.* Thus, when looking at a standardized residual plot, we should expect to see approximately 95% of the standardized residuals between $-2$ and $+2$. We see in Figure 14.14 that for the Armand's example all standardized residuals are between $-2$ and $+2$. Therefore, on the basis of the standardized residuals, this plot gives us no reason to question the assumption that $\epsilon$ has a normal distribution.

Because of the effort required to compute the estimated values of $\hat{y}$, the residuals, and the standardized residuals, most statistical packages provide these values as optional regression output. Hence, residual plots can be easily obtained. For large problems computer packages are the only practical means for developing the residual plots discussed in this section.

## Normal Probability Plot

Another approach for determining the validity of the assumption that the error term has a normal distribution is the **normal probability plot**. To show how a normal probability plot is developed, we introduce the concept of *normal scores*.

Suppose 10 values are selected randomly from a normal probability distribution with a mean of zero and a standard deviation of one, and that the sampling process is repeated over and over with the values in each sample of 10 ordered from smallest to largest. For now, let

**TABLE 14.8**   COMPUTATION OF STANDARDIZED RESIDUALS FOR ARMAND'S PIZZA PARLORS

| Restaurant $i$ | $x_i$ | $x_i - \bar{x}$ | $(x_i - \bar{x})^2$ | $\dfrac{(x_i - \bar{x})^2}{\Sigma(x_i - \bar{x})^2}$ | $h_i$ | $s_{y_i - \hat{y}_i}$ | $y_i - \hat{y}_i$ | Standardized Residual |
|---|---|---|---|---|---|---|---|---|
| 1 | 2 | $-12$ | 144 | .2535 | .3535 | 11.1193 | $-12$ | $-1.0792$ |
| 2 | 6 | $-8$ | 64 | .1127 | .2127 | 12.2709 | 15 | 1.2224 |
| 3 | 8 | $-6$ | 36 | .0634 | .1634 | 12.6493 | $-12$ | $-.9487$ |
| 4 | 8 | $-6$ | 36 | .0634 | .1634 | 12.6493 | 18 | 1.4230 |
| 5 | 12 | $-2$ | 4 | .0070 | .1070 | 13.0682 | $-3$ | $-.2296$ |
| 6 | 16 | 2 | 4 | .0070 | .1070 | 13.0682 | $-3$ | $-.2296$ |
| 7 | 20 | 6 | 36 | .0634 | .1634 | 12.6493 | $-3$ | $-.2372$ |
| 8 | 20 | 6 | 36 | .0634 | .1634 | 12.6493 | 9 | .7115 |
| 9 | 22 | 8 | 64 | .1127 | .2127 | 12.2709 | $-21$ | $-1.7114$ |
| 10 | 26 | 12 | 144 | .2535 | .3535 | 11.1193 | 12 | 1.0792 |
|  |  | Total | 568 |  |  |  |  |  |

*Note:* The values of the residuals were computed in Table 14.7.

---

*Because $s$ is used instead of $\sigma$ in equation (14.30), the probability distribution of the standardized residuals is not technically normal. However, in most regression studies, the sample size is large enough that a normal approximation is very good.

**FIGURE 14.14**    PLOT OF THE STANDARDIZED RESIDUALS AGAINST THE
INDEPENDENT VARIABLE $x$ FOR ARMAND'S PIZZA PARLORS

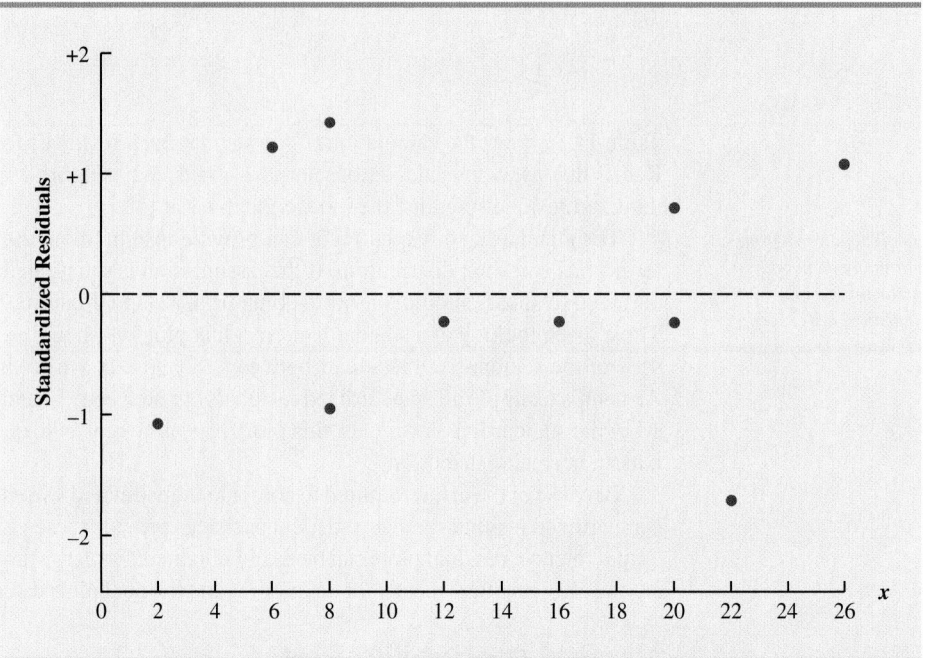

**TABLE 14.9**

NORMAL SCORES
FOR $n = 10$

| Order Statistic | Normal Score |
|---|---|
| 1 | −1.55 |
| 2 | −1.00 |
| 3 | −.65 |
| 4 | −.37 |
| 5 | −.12 |
| 6 | .12 |
| 7 | .37 |
| 8 | .65 |
| 9 | 1.00 |
| 10 | 1.55 |

**TABLE 14.10**

NORMAL SCORES
AND ORDERED
STANDARDIZED
RESIDUALS FOR
ARMAND'S PIZZA
PARLORS

| Normal Scores | Ordered Standardized Residuals |
|---|---|
| −1.55 | −1.7114 |
| −1.00 | −1.0792 |
| −.65 | −.9487 |
| −.37 | −.2372 |
| −.12 | −.2296 |
| .12 | −.2296 |
| .37 | .7115 |
| .65 | 1.0792 |
| 1.00 | 1.2224 |
| 1.55 | 1.4230 |

us consider only the smallest value in each sample. The random variable representing the smallest value obtained in repeated sampling is called the first-order statistic.

Statisticians show that for samples of size 10 from a standard normal probability distribution, the expected value of the first-order statistic is −1.55. This expected value is called a normal score. For the case with a sample of size $n = 10$, there are 10 order statistics and 10 normal scores (see Table 14.9). In general, a data set consisting of $n$ observations will have $n$ order statistics and hence $n$ normal scores.

Let us now show how the 10 normal scores can be used to determine whether the standardized residuals for Armand's Pizza Parlors appear to come from a standard normal probability distribution. We begin by ordering the 10 standardized residuals from Table 14.8. The 10 normal scores and the ordered standardized residuals are shown together in Table 14.10. If the normality assumption is satisfied, the smallest standardized residual should be close to the smallest normal score, the next smallest standardized residual should be close to the next smallest normal score, and so on. If we were to develop a plot with the normal scores on the horizontal axis and the corresponding standardized residuals on the vertical axis, the plotted points should cluster closely around a 45-degree line passing through the origin if the standardized residuals are approximately normally distributed. Such a plot is referred to as a *normal probability plot*.

Figure 14.15 is the normal probability plot for the Armand's Pizza Parlors example. Judgment is used to determine whether the pattern observed deviates from the line enough to conclude that the standardized residuals are not from a standard normal probability distribution. In Figure 14.15, we see that the points are grouped closely about the line. We therefore conclude that the assumption of the error term having a normal probability distribution is reasonable. In general, the more closely the points are clustered about the 45-degree line, the stronger the evidence supporting the normality assumption. Any substantial curvature in the normal probability plot is evidence that the residuals have not come from a normal distribution. Normal scores and the associated normal probability plot can be obtained easily from statistical packages such as Minitab.

**FIGURE 14.15   NORMAL PROBABILITY PLOT FOR ARMAND'S PIZZA PARLORS**

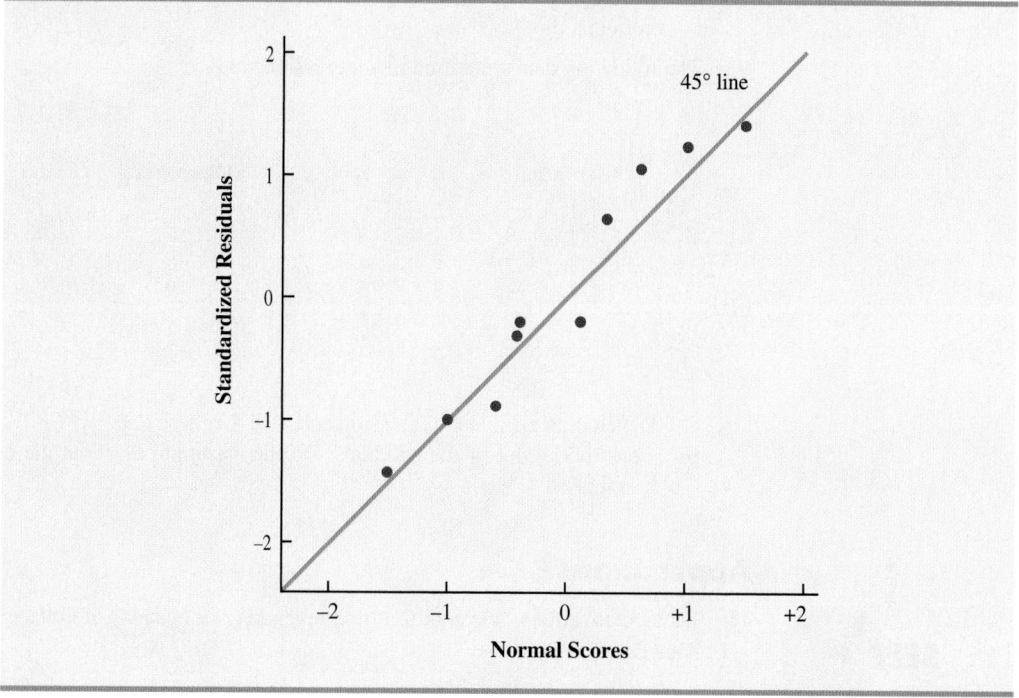

## NOTES AND COMMENTS

1. We use residual and normal probability plots to validate the assumptions of a regression model. If our review indicates that one or more assumptions are questionable, a different regression model or a transformation of the data should be considered. The appropriate corrective action when the assumptions are violated must be based on good judgment; recommendations from an experienced statistician can be valuable.

2. Analysis of residuals is the primary method statisticians use to verify that the assumptions associated with a regression model are valid. Even if no violations are found, it does not necessarily follow that the model will yield good predictions. However, if additional statistical tests support the conclusion of significance and the coefficient of determination is large, we should be able to develop good estimates and predictions using the estimated regression equation.

## Exercises

### Methods

**SELF** test

45. Given are data for two variables, $x$ and $y$.

| $x_i$ | 6 | 11 | 15 | 18 | 20 |
|---|---|---|---|---|---|
| $y_i$ | 6 | 8 | 12 | 20 | 30 |

a. Develop an estimated regression equation for these data.
b. Compute the residuals.
c. Develop a plot of the residuals against the independent variable $x$. Do the assumptions about the error terms seem to be satisfied?

d.  Compute the standardized residuals.
e.  Develop a plot of the standardized residuals against $\hat{y}$. What conclusions can you draw from this plot?

46.  The following data were used in a regression study.

| Observation | $x_i$ | $y_i$ | Observation | $x_i$ | $y_i$ |
|---|---|---|---|---|---|
| 1 | 2 | 4 | 6 | 7 | 6 |
| 2 | 3 | 5 | 7 | 7 | 9 |
| 3 | 4 | 4 | 8 | 8 | 5 |
| 4 | 5 | 6 | 9 | 9 | 11 |
| 5 | 7 | 4 | | | |

a.  Develop an estimated regression equation for these data.
b.  Construct a plot of the residuals. Do the assumptions about the error term seem to be satisfied?

## Applications

47.  Data on advertising expenditures and revenue (in thousands of dollars) for the Four Seasons Restaurant follow.

| Advertising Expenditures | Revenue |
|---|---|
| 1 | 19 |
| 2 | 32 |
| 4 | 44 |
| 6 | 40 |
| 10 | 52 |
| 14 | 53 |
| 20 | 54 |

a.  Let $x$ equal advertising expenditures and $y$ equal revenue. Use the method of least squares to develop a straight line approximation of the relationship between the two variables.
b.  Test whether revenue and advertising expenditures are related at a .05 level of significance.
c.  Prepare a residual plot of $y - \hat{y}$ versus $\hat{y}$. Use the result from part (a) to obtain the values of $\hat{y}$.
d.  What conclusions can you draw from residual analysis? Should this model be used, or should we look for a better one?

48.  Refer to Exercise 9, where an estimated regression equation relating years of experience and annual sales was developed.
a.  Compute the residuals and construct a residual plot for this problem.
b.  Do the assumptions about the error terms seem reasonable in light of the residual plot?

49.  American Depository Receipts (ADRs) are certificates traded on the NYSE representing shares of a foreign company held on deposit in a bank in its home country. The following table shows the price/earnings (P/E) ratio and the percentage return on investment (ROE) for 10 Indian companies that are likely new ADRs (*Bloomberg Personal Finance*, April 2000).

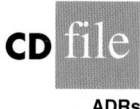

|                              | ROE   | P/E    |
|------------------------------|-------|--------|
| Bharti Televentures          | 6.43  | 36.88  |
| Gujarat Ambuja Cements       | 13.49 | 27.03  |
| Hindalco Industries          | 14.04 | 10.83  |
| ICICI                        | 20.67 | 5.15   |
| Mahanagar Telephone Nigam    | 22.74 | 13.35  |
| NIIT                         | 46.23 | 95.59  |
| Pentamedia Graphics          | 28.90 | 54.85  |
| Satyam Computer Services     | 54.01 | 189.21 |
| Silverline Technologies      | 28.02 | 75.86  |
| Videsh Sanchar Nigam         | 27.04 | 13.17  |

a. Use a computer package to develop an estimated regression equation relating $y$ = P/E and $x$ = ROE.

b. Construct a residual plot of the standardized residuals against the independent variable.

c. Do the assumptions about the error terms and model form seem reasonable in light of the residual plot?

## 14.9  Residual Analysis: Outliers and Influential Observations

In Section 14.8 we showed how residual analysis could be used to determine when violations of assumptions about the regression model occur. In this section, we discuss how residual analysis can be used to identify observations that can be classified as outliers or as being especially influential in determining the estimated regression equation. Some steps that should be taken when such observations occur are discussed.

### Detecting Outliers

Figure 14.16 is a scatter diagram for a data set that contains an **outlier,** a data point (observation) that does not fit the trend shown by the remaining data. Outliers represent observations that are suspect and warrant careful examination. They may represent erroneous

**FIGURE 14.16    A DATA SET WITH AN OUTLIER**

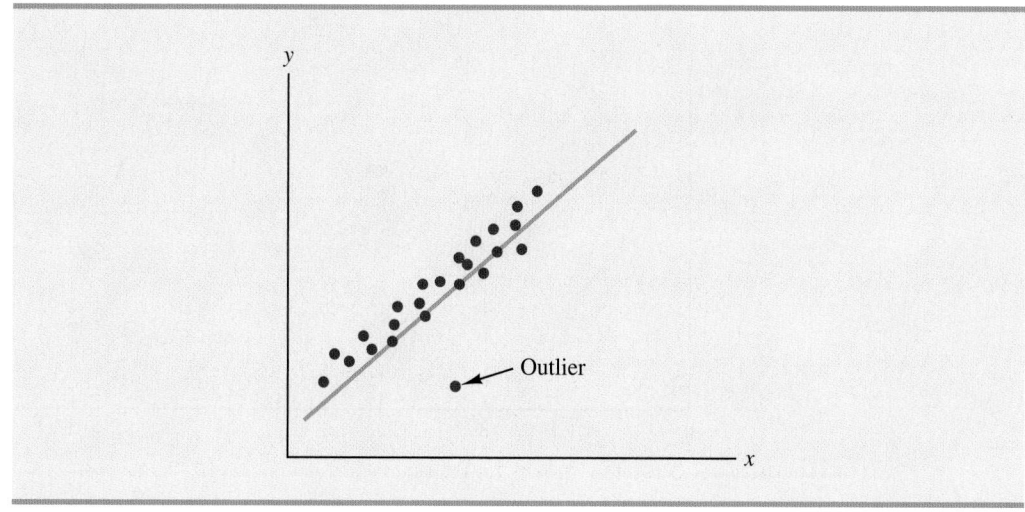

TABLE 14.11

DATA SET
ILLUSTRATING
THE EFFECT
OF AN OUTLIER

| $x_i$ | $y_i$ |
|-------|-------|
| 1 | 45 |
| 1 | 55 |
| 2 | 50 |
| 3 | 75 |
| 3 | 40 |
| 3 | 45 |
| 4 | 30 |
| 4 | 35 |
| 5 | 25 |
| 6 | 15 |

data; if so, the data should be corrected. They may signal a violation of model assumptions; if so, another model should be considered. Finally, they may simply be unusual values that occurred by chance. In this case, they should be retained.

To illustrate the process of detecting outliers, consider the data set in Table 14.11; Figure 14.17 is a scatter diagram. Except for observation 4 ($x_4 = 3$, $y_4 = 75$), a pattern suggesting a negative linear relationship is apparent. Indeed, given the pattern of the rest of the data, we would expect $y_4$ to be much smaller and hence would identify the corresponding observation as an outlier. For the case of simple linear regression, one can often detect outliers by simply examining the scatter diagram.

The standardized residuals can also be used to identify outliers. If an observation deviates greatly from the pattern of the rest of the data (e.g., the outlier in Figure 14.16), the corresponding standardized residual will be large in absolute value. Many computer packages automatically identify observations with standardized residuals that are large in absolute value. In Figure 14.18 we show the Minitab output from a regression analysis of the data in Table 14.11. The next to last line of the output shows that the standardized residual for observation 4 is 2.67. Minitab identifies any observation with a standardized residual of less than $-2$ or greater than $+2$ as an unusual observation; in such cases, the observation is printed on a separate line with an R next to the standardized residual, as shown in Figure 14.18. With normally distributed errors, standardized residuals should be outside these limits approximately 5% of the time.

In deciding how to handle an outlier, we should first check to see whether it is a valid observation. Perhaps an error was made in initially recording the data or in entering the data into the computer file. For example, suppose that in checking the data for the outlier in Table 14.17, we find an error; the correct value for observation 4 is $x_4 = 3$, $y_4 = 30$. Figure 14.19 is the Minitab output obtained after correction of the value of $y_4$. We see that using the incorrect data value substantially affected the goodness of fit. With the correct data, the value of R-sq increased from 49.7% to 83.8% and the value of $b_0$ decreased from 64.958 to 59.237. The slope of the line changed from $-7.331$ to $-6.949$. The identification of the outlier enabled us to correct the data error and improve the regression results.

FIGURE 14.17    SCATTER DIAGRAM FOR OUTLIER DATA SET

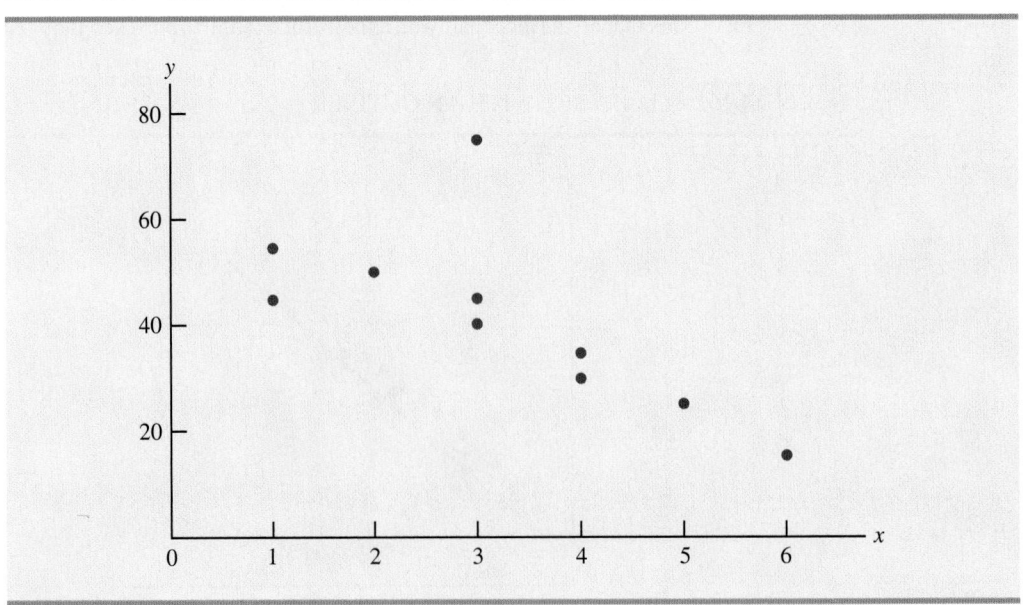

**FIGURE 14.18**    MINITAB OUTPUT FOR REGRESSION ANALYSIS OF THE OUTLIER
DATA SET

```
The regression equation is
y = 65.0 - 7.33 x

Predictor    Coef   SE Coef      T      p
Constant   64.958     9.258   7.02  0.000
X          -7.331     2.608  -2.81  0.023

S = 12.67   R-sq = 49.7%   R-sq(adj) = 43.4%

Analysis of Variance

SOURCE          DF       SS      MS      F      p
Regression       1   1268.2  1268.2   7.90  0.023
Residual Error   8   1284.3   160.5
Total            9   2552.5

Unusual Observations
Obs    x       y    Fit  SE Fit  Residual  St Resid
  4  3.00   75.00  42.97    4.04     32.03      2.67R

R denotes an observation with a large standardized residual.
```

## Detecting Influential Observations

Sometimes one or more observations exert a strong influence on the results obtained. Figure 14.20 shows an example of an **influential observation** in simple linear regression. The estimated regression line has a negative slope. However, if the influential observation were dropped from the data set, the slope of the estimated regression line would change from negative to positive and the y-intercept would be smaller. Clearly, this one observation is

**FIGURE 14.19**    MINITAB OUTPUT FOR THE REVISED OUTLIER DATA SET

```
The regression equation is
Y = 59.2 - 6.95 X

Predictor    Coef   SE Coef      T      p
Constant   59.237     3.835  15.45  0.000
X          -6.949     1.080  -6.43  0.000

S = 5.248   R-sq = 83.8%   R-sq(adj) = 81.8%

Analysis of Variance

SOURCE          DF       SS      MS      F      p
Regression       1   1139.7  1139.7  41.38  0.000
Residual Error   8    220.3    27.5
Total            9   1360.0
```

**FIGURE 14.20**    A DATA SET WITH AN INFLUENTIAL OBSERVATION

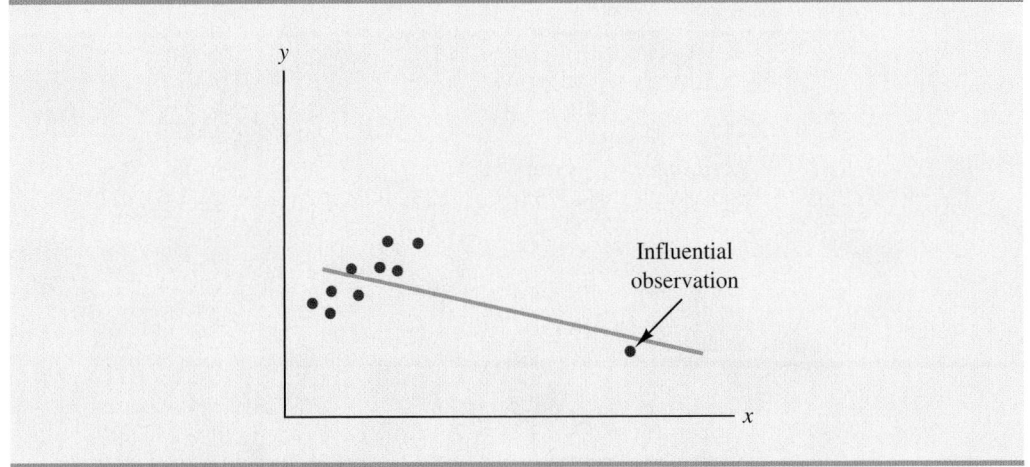

much more influential in determining the estimated regression line than any of the others; dropping one of the other observations from the data set would have little effect on the estimated regression equation.

Influential observations can be identified from a scatter diagram when only one independent variable is present. An influential observation may be an outlier (an observation with a *y* value that deviates substantially from the trend), it may correspond to an *x* value far away from its mean (e.g., see Figure 14.20), or it may be caused by a combination of the two (a somewhat off-trend *y* value and a somewhat extreme *x* value).

Because influential observations may have such a dramatic effect on the estimated regression equation, they must be examined carefully. We should first check to make sure that no error was made in collecting or recording the data. If an error occurred, it can be corrected and a new estimated regression equation can be developed. If the observation is valid, we might consider ourselves fortunate to have it. Such a point, if valid, can contribute to a better understanding of the appropriate model and can lead to a better estimated regression equation. The presence of the influential observation in Figure 14.20, if valid, would suggest trying to obtain data on intermediate values of *x* to understand better the relationship between *x* and *y*.

Observations with extreme values for the independent variables are called **high leverage points**. The influential observation in Figure 14.20 is a point with high leverage. The leverage of an observation is determined by how far the values of the independent variables are from their mean values. For the single-independent-variable case, the leverage of the *i*th observation, denoted $h_i$, can be computed by using equation (14.33).

LEVERAGE OF OBSERVATION *i*

$$h_i = \frac{1}{n} + \frac{(x_i - \bar{x})^2}{\Sigma(x_i - \bar{x})^2} \qquad (14.33)$$

From the formula, it is clear that the farther $x_i$ is from its mean $\bar{x}$, the higher the leverage of observation *i*.

Many statistical packages automatically identify observations with high leverage as part of the standard regression output. As an illustration of how the Minitab statistical package identifies points with high leverage, let us consider the data set in Table 14.12.

**FIGURE 14.21**   SCATTER DIAGRAM FOR THE DATA SET WITH A HIGH LEVERAGE
OBSERVATION

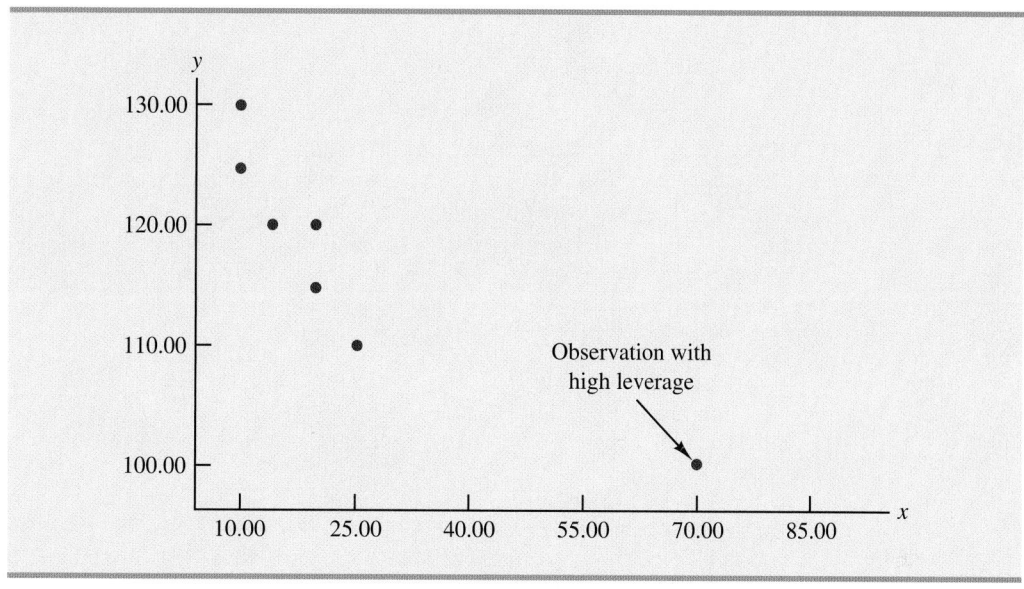

**TABLE 14.12**

**DATA SET WITH A
HIGH LEVERAGE
OBSERVATION**

| $x_i$ | $y_i$ |
|-----|-----|
| 10 | 125 |
| 10 | 130 |
| 15 | 120 |
| 20 | 115 |
| 20 | 120 |
| 25 | 110 |
| 70 | 100 |

*Computer software
packages are essential for
performing the
computations to identify
influential observations.
Minitab's selection rule is
discussed here.*

From Figure 14.21, a scatter diagram for the data set in Table 14.12, it is clear that observation 7 ($x = 70$, $y = 100$) is an observation with an extreme value of $x$. Hence, we would expect it to be identified as a point with high leverage. For this observation, the leverage is computed by using equation (14.33) as follows.

$$h_7 = \frac{1}{n} + \frac{(x_7 - \bar{x})^2}{\Sigma(x_i - \bar{x})^2} = \frac{1}{7} + \frac{(70 - 24.286)^2}{2621.43} = .94$$

For the case of simple linear regression, Minitab identifies observations as having high leverage if $h_i > 6/n$; for the data set in Table 14.12, $6/n = 6/7 = .86$. Because $h_7 = .94 > .86$, Minitab will identify observation 7 as an observation whose $x$ value gives it large influence. Figure 14.22 shows the Minitab output for a regression analysis of this data set. Observation 7 ($x = 70$, $y = 100$) is identified as having large influence; it is printed on a separate line at the bottom, with an X in the right margin.

Influential observations that are caused by an interaction of large residuals and high leverage can be difficult to detect. Diagnostic procedures are available that take both into account in determining when an observation is influential. One such measure, called Cook's $D$ statistic, will be discussed in Chapter 15.

## NOTES AND COMMENTS

Once an observation is identified as potentially influential because of a large residual or high leverage, its impact on the estimated regression equation should be evaluated. More advanced texts discuss diagnostics for doing so. However, if one is not familiar with the more advanced material, a simple procedure is to run the regression analysis with and without the observation. This approach will reveal the influence of the observation on the results.

FIGURE 14.22   MINITAB OUTPUT FOR THE DATA SET WITH A HIGH LEVERAGE
OBSERVATION

```
The regression equation is
y = 127 - 0.425 x

Predictor       Coef   SE Coef        T        p
Constant     127.466     2.961    43.04    0.000
X            -0.42507   0.09537    -4.46    0.007

S = 4.883    R-sq = 79.9%   R-sq(adj) = 75.9%

Analysis of Variance

SOURCE              DF       SS       MS       F        p
Regression           1   473.65   473.65   19.87    0.007
Residual Error       5   119.21    23.84
Total                6   592.86

Unusual Observations
Obs     x      y     Fit   SE Fit   Residual   St Resid
  7   70.0  100.00  97.71    4.73      2.29        1.91 X

X denotes an observation whose X value gives it large influence.
```

## Exercises

## Methods

50.  Consider the following data for two variables, $x$ and $y$.

| $x_i$ | 135 | 110 | 130 | 145 | 175 | 160 | 120 |
|-------|-----|-----|-----|-----|-----|-----|-----|
| $y_i$ | 145 | 100 | 120 | 120 | 130 | 130 | 110 |

a.   Compute the standardized residuals for these data. Do there appear to be any outliers
in the data? Explain.
b.   Plot the standardized residuals against $\hat{y}$. Does this plot reveal any outliers?
c.   Develop a scatter diagram for these data. Does the scatter diagram indicate any outliers in the data? In general, what implications does this finding have for simple linear regression?

51.  Consider the following data for two variables, $x$ and $y$.

| $x_i$ | 4 | 5 | 7 | 8 | 10 | 12 | 12 | 22 |
|-------|---|---|---|---|----|----|----|----|
| $y_i$ | 12 | 14 | 16 | 15 | 18 | 20 | 24 | 19 |

a.   Compute the standardized residuals for these data. Do there appear to be any outliers
in the data? Explain.
b.   Compute the leverage values for these data. Do there appear to be any influential observations in these data? Explain.
c.   Develop a scatter diagram for these data. Does the scatter diagram indicate any influential observations? Explain.

## Applications

52. The following data show the media expenditures ($ millions) and the shipments in bbls. (millions) for 10 major brands of beer.

**Beer**

| Brand | Media Expenditures ($ millions) | Shipments |
|---|---|---|
| Budweiser | 120.0 | 36.3 |
| Bud Light | 68.7 | 20.7 |
| Miller Lite | 100.1 | 15.9 |
| Coors Light | 76.6 | 13.2 |
| Busch | 8.7 | 8.1 |
| Natural Light | 0.1 | 7.1 |
| Miller Genuine Draft | 21.5 | 5.6 |
| Miller High Life | 1.4 | 4.4 |
| Busch Light | 5.3 | 4.3 |
| Milwaukee's Best | 1.7 | 4.3 |

a. Develop the estimated regression equation for these data.
b. Use residual analysis to determine whether any outliers and/or influential observations are present. Briefly summarize your findings and conclusions.

53. Health experts recommend that runners drink 4 ounces of water every 15 minutes they run. Runners who run three to eight hours need a larger-capacity hip-mounted or over-the-shoulder hydration system. The following data show the liquid volume (fl oz) and the price for 26 Ultimate Direction hip-mounted or over-the-shoulder hydration systems (*Trail Runner Gear Guide*, 2003).

**Hydration2**

| Model | Volume (fl oz) | Price ($) |
|---|---|---|
| Fastdraw | 20 | 10 |
| Fastdraw Plus | 20 | 12 |
| Fitness | 20 | 12 |
| Access | 20 | 20 |
| Access Plus | 24 | 25 |
| Solo | 20 | 25 |
| Serenade | 20 | 35 |
| Solitaire | 20 | 35 |
| Gemini | 40 | 45 |
| Shadow | 64 | 40 |
| SipStream | 96 | 60 |
| Express | 20 | 30 |
| Lightning | 28 | 40 |
| Elite | 40 | 60 |
| Extender | 40 | 65 |
| Stinger | 32 | 65 |
| GelFlask Belt | 4 | 20 |
| GelDraw | 4 | 7 |
| GelFlask Clip-on Holster | 4 | 10 |
| GelFlask Holster SS | 4 | 10 |
| Strider (W) | 20 | 30 |
| Walkabout (W) | 230 | 40 |
| Solitude I.C.E. | 20 | 35 |
| Getaway I.C.E. | 40 | 55 |
| Profile I.C.E. | 64 | 50 |
| Traverse I.C.E. | 64 | 60 |

a. Develop the estimated regression equation that can be used to predict the price of a hydration system given its liquid volume.

b. Use residual analysis to determine whether any outliers or influential observations are present. Briefly summarize your findings and conclusions.

54. The market capitalization and the salary of the chief executive officer (CEO) for 20 companies are shown in the following table (*The Wall Street Journal,* February 24, 2000, and April 6, 2000).

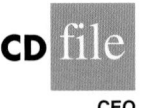
CEO

| | Market Cap. ($ millions) | CEO Salary ($1000s) |
|---|---|---|
| Anheuser-Busch | 32,977.4 | 1,130 |
| AT&T | 162,365.1 | 1,400 |
| Charles Schwab | 31,363.8 | 800 |
| Chevron | 56,849.0 | 1,350 |
| DuPont | 68,848.0 | 1,000 |
| General Electric | 507,216.8 | 3,325 |
| Gillette | 44,180.1 | 978 |
| IBM | 194,455.9 | 2,000 |
| Johnson & Johnson | 143,131.0 | 1,365 |
| Kimberly-Clark | 35,377.5 | 950 |
| Merrill Lynch | 31,062.1 | 700 |
| Motorola | 92,923.7 | 1,275 |
| Philip Morris | 54,421.2 | 1,625 |
| Procter & Gamble | 144,152.9 | 1,318.3 |
| Qualcomm | 116,840.8 | 773 |
| Schering-Plough | 62,259.4 | 1,200 |
| Sun Microsystems | 120,966.5 | 116 |
| Texaco | 30,040.7 | 950 |
| USWest | 36,450.8 | 897 |
| Walt Disney | 61,288.1 | 750 |

a. Develop the estimated regression equation that can be used to predict the CEO salary given the market capitalization.

b. Use residual analysis to determine whether any outliers and/or influential observations are present. Briefly summarize your findings and conclusions.

## Summary

In this chapter we showed how regression analysis can be used to determine how a dependent variable $y$ is related to an independent variable $x$. In simple linear regression, the regression model is $y = \beta_0 + \beta_1 x + \epsilon$. The simple linear regression equation $E(y) = \beta_0 + \beta_1 x$ describes how the mean or expected value of $y$ is related to $x$. We used sample data and the least squares method to develop the estimated regression equation $\hat{y} = b_0 + b_1 x$. In effect, $b_0$ and $b_1$ are the sample statistics used to estimate the unknown model parameters $\beta_0$ and $\beta_1$.

The coefficient of determination was presented as a measure of the goodness of fit for the estimated regression equation; it can be interpreted as the proportion of the variation in the dependent variable $y$ that can be explained by the estimated regression equation. We reviewed correlation as a descriptive measure of the strength of a linear relationship between two variables.

The assumptions about the regression model and its associated error term $\epsilon$ were discussed, and $t$ and $F$ tests, based on those assumptions, were presented as a means for determining whether the relationship between two variables is statistically significant. We showed how to use the estimated regression equation to develop confidence interval estimates of the mean value of $y$ and prediction interval estimates of individual values of $y$.

The chapter concluded with a section on the computer solution of regression problems and two sections on the use of residual analysis to validate the model assumptions and to identify outliers and influential observations.

## Glossary

**Dependent variable** The variable that is being predicted or explained. It is denoted by $y$.

**Independent variable** The variable that is doing the predicting or explaining. It is denoted by $x$.

**Simple linear regression** Regression analysis involving one independent variable and one dependent variable in which the relationship between the variables is approximated by a straight line.

**Regression model** The equation describing how $y$ is related to $x$ and an error term; in simple linear regression, the regression model is $y = \beta_0 + \beta_1 x + \epsilon$.

**Regression equation** The equation that describes how the mean or expected value of the dependent variable is related to the independent variable; in simple linear regression, $E(y) = \beta_0 + \beta_1 x$.

**Estimated regression equation** The estimate of the regression equation developed from sample data by using the least squares method. For simple linear regression, the estimated regression equation is $\hat{y} = b_0 + b_1 x$.

**Least squares method** A procedure used to develop the estimated regression equation. The objective is to minimize $\Sigma(y_i - \hat{y}_i)^2$.

**Scatter diagram** A graph of bivariate data in which the independent variable is on the horizontal axis and the dependent variable is on the vertical axis.

**Coefficient of determination** A measure of the goodness of fit of the estimated regression equation. It can be interpreted as the proportion of the variability in the dependent variable $y$ that is explained by the estimated regression equation.

***i*th residual** The difference between the observed value of the dependent variable and the value predicted using the estimated regression equation; for the $i$th observation the $i$th residual is $y_i - \hat{y}_i$.

**Correlation coefficient** A measure of the strength of the linear relationship between two variables (previously discussed in Chapter 3).

**Mean square error** The unbiased estimate of the variance of the error term $\sigma^2$. It is denoted by MSE or $s^2$.

**Standard error of the estimate** The square root of the mean square error, denoted by $s$. It is the estimate of $\sigma$, the standard deviation of the error term $\epsilon$.

**ANOVA table** The analysis of variance table used to summarize the computations associated with the $F$ test for significance.

**Confidence interval** The interval estimate of the mean value of $y$ for a given value of $x$.

**Prediction interval** The interval estimate of an individual value of $y$ for a given value of $x$.

**Residual analysis** The analysis of the residuals used to determine whether the assumptions made about the regression model appear to be valid. Residual analysis is also used to identify outliers and influential observations.

**Residual plot** Graphical representation of the residuals that can be used to determine whether the assumptions made about the regression model appear to be valid.

**Standardized residual** The value obtained by dividing a residual by its standard deviation.

**Normal probability plot** A graph of the standardized residuals plotted against values of the normal scores. This plot helps determine whether the assumption that the error term has a normal probability distribution appears to be valid.

**Outlier** A data point or observation that does not fit the trend shown by the remaining data.

**Influential observation** An observation that has a strong influence or effect on the regression results.

**High leverage points** Observations with extreme values for the independent variables.

## Key Formulas

**Simple Linear Regression Model**

$$y = \beta_0 + \beta_1 x + \epsilon \tag{14.1}$$

**Simple Linear Regression Equation**

$$E(y) = \beta_0 + \beta_1 x \tag{14.2}$$

**Estimated Simple Linear Regression Equation**

$$\hat{y} = b_0 + b_1 x \tag{14.3}$$

**Least Squares Criterion**

$$\min \Sigma(y_i - \hat{y}_i)^2 \tag{14.5}$$

**Slope and y-Intercept for the Estimated Regression Equation**

$$b_1 = \frac{\Sigma(x_i - \bar{x})(y_i - \bar{y})}{\Sigma(x_i - \bar{x})^2} \tag{14.6}$$

$$b_0 = \bar{y} - b_1\bar{x} \tag{14.7}$$

**Sum of Squares Due to Error**

$$SSE = \Sigma(y_i - \hat{y}_i)^2 \tag{14.8}$$

**Total Sum of Squares**

$$SST = \Sigma(y_i - \bar{y})^2 \tag{14.9}$$

**Sum of Squares Due to Regression**

$$SSR = \Sigma(\hat{y}_i - \bar{y})^2 \tag{14.10}$$

**Relationship Among SST, SSR, and SSE**

$$SST = SSR + SSE \tag{14.11}$$

**Coefficient of Determination**

$$r^2 = \frac{SSR}{SST} \tag{14.12}$$

**Sample Correlation Coefficient**

$$r_{xy} = (\text{sign of } b_1)\sqrt{\text{Coefficient of determination}}$$
$$= (\text{sign of } b_1)\sqrt{r^2} \tag{14.13}$$

**Mean Square Error (Estimate of $\sigma^2$)**

$$s^2 = \text{MSE} = \frac{\text{SSE}}{n-2} \tag{14.15}$$

**Standard Error of the Estimate**

$$s = \sqrt{\text{MSE}} = \sqrt{\frac{\text{SSE}}{n-2}} \tag{14.16}$$

**Standard Deviation of $b_1$**

$$\sigma_{b_1} = \frac{\sigma}{\sqrt{\Sigma(x_i - \bar{x})^2}} \tag{14.17}$$

**Estimated Standard Deviation of $b_1$**

$$s_{b_1} = \frac{s}{\sqrt{\Sigma(x_i - \bar{x})^2}} \tag{14.18}$$

**$t$ Test Statistic**

$$t = \frac{b_1}{s_{b_1}} \tag{14.19}$$

**Mean Square Regression**

$$\text{MSR} = \frac{\text{SSR}}{\text{Number of independent variables}} \tag{14.20}$$

**$F$ Test Statistic**

$$F = \frac{\text{MSR}}{\text{MSE}} \tag{14.21}$$

**Estimated Standard Deviation of $\hat{y}_p$**

$$s_{\hat{y}_p} = s\sqrt{\frac{1}{n} + \frac{(x_p - \bar{x})^2}{\Sigma(x_i - \bar{x})^2}} \tag{14.23}$$

**Confidence Interval for $E(y_p)$**

$$\hat{y}_p \pm t_{\alpha/2}s_{\hat{y}_p} \tag{14.24}$$

**Estimated Standard Deviation of an Individual Value**

$$s_{\text{ind}} = s\sqrt{1 + \frac{1}{n} + \frac{(x_p - \bar{x})^2}{\Sigma(x_i - \bar{x})^2}} \tag{14.26}$$

**Prediction Interval for $y_p$**

$$\hat{y}_p \pm t_{\alpha/2}s_{\text{ind}} \tag{14.27}$$

**Residual for Observation $i$**

$$y_i - \hat{y}_i \tag{14.28}$$

**Standard Deviation of the $i$th Residual**

$$s_{y_i - \hat{y}_i} = s\sqrt{1 - h_i} \qquad (14.30)$$

**Standardized Residual for Observation $i$**

$$\frac{y_i - \hat{y}_i}{s_{y_i - \hat{y}_i}} \qquad (14.32)$$

**Leverage of Observation $i$**

$$h_i = \frac{1}{n} + \frac{(x_i - \bar{x})^2}{\Sigma(x_i - \bar{x})^2} \qquad (14.33)$$

## Supplementary Exercises

55. Does a high value of $r^2$ imply that two variables are causally related? Explain.

56. In your own words, explain the difference between an interval estimate of the mean value of $y$ for a given $x$ and an interval estimate for an individual value of $y$ for a given $x$.

57. What is the purpose of testing whether $\beta_1 = 0$? If we reject $\beta_1 = 0$, does it imply a good fit?

58. The data in the following table show the number of shares selling (millions) and the expected price (average of projected low price and projected high price) for 10 selected initial public stock offerings.

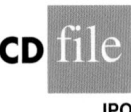

**CD file**

**IPO**

| Company | Shares Selling | Expected Price ($) |
|---|---|---|
| American Physician | 5.0 | 15 |
| Apex Silver Mines | 9.0 | 14 |
| Dan River | 6.7 | 15 |
| Franchise Mortgage | 8.75 | 17 |
| Gene Logic | 3.0 | 11 |
| International Home Foods | 13.6 | 19 |
| PRT Group | 4.6 | 13 |
| Rayovac | 6.7 | 14 |
| RealNetworks | 3.0 | 10 |
| Software AG Systems | 7.7 | 13 |

a. Develop an estimated regression equation with the number of shares selling as the independent variable and the expected price as the dependent variable.
b. At the .05 level of significance, is there a significant relationship between the two variables?
c. Did the estimated regression equation provide a good fit? Explain.
d. Use the estimated regression equation to estimate the expected price for a firm considering an initial public offering of 6 million shares.

59. Corporate share repurchase programs are often touted as a benefit for shareholders. But Robert Gabele, director of insider research for First Call/Thomson Financial, noted that many of these programs are undertaken solely to acquire stock for a company's incentive options for top managers. Across all companies, existing stock options in 1998 represented 6.2 percent of all common shares outstanding. The following data show the number of shares covered by option grants and the number of shares outstanding for 13 companies (*Bloomberg Personal Finance,* January/February 2000).

**Options**

| | Shares of Option Grants Outstanding (millions) | Common Shares Outstanding (millions) |
|---|---|---|
| Adobe Systems | 20.3 | 61.8 |
| Apple Computer | 52.7 | 160.9 |
| Applied Materials | 109.1 | 375.4 |
| Autodesk | 15.7 | 58.9 |
| Best Buy | 44.2 | 203.8 |
| Fruit of the Loom | 14.2 | 66.9 |
| ITT Industries | 18.0 | 87.9 |
| Merrill Lynch | 89.9 | 365.5 |
| Novell | 120.2 | 335.0 |
| Parametric Technology | 78.3 | 269.3 |
| Reebok International | 12.8 | 56.1 |
| Silicon Graphics | 52.6 | 188.8 |
| Toys R Us | 54.8 | 247.6 |

a.  Develop the estimated regression equation that could be used to estimate the number of shares of option grants outstanding given the number of common shares outstanding.

b.  Use the estimated regression equation to estimate the number of shares of option grants outstanding for a company that has 150 million shares of common stock outstanding.

c.  Do you believe the estimated regression equation would provide a good prediction of the number of shares of option grants outstanding? Use $r^2$ to support your answer.

60. *Bloomberg Personal Finance* (July/August 2001) reported the market beta for Texas Instruments was 1.46. Market betas for individual stocks are determined by simple linear regression. For each stock, the dependent variable is its quarterly percentage return (capital appreciation plus dividends) minus the percentage return that could be obtained from a risk-free investment (the Treasury Bill rate is used as the risk-free rate). The independent variable is the quarterly percentage return (capital appreciation plus dividends) for the stock market (S&P 500) minus the percentage return from a risk-free investment. An estimated regression equation is developed with quarterly data; the market beta for the stock is the slope of the estimated regression equation $(b_1)$. The value of the market beta is often interpreted as a measure of the risk associated with the stock. Market betas greater than 1 indicate that the stock is more volatile than the market average; market betas less than 1 indicate that the stock is less volatile than the market average. Suppose that the following figures are the differences between the percentage return and the risk-free return for 10 quarters for the S&P 500 and Horizon Technology.

| S&P 500 | Horizon |
|---|---|
| 1.2 | −0.7 |
| −2.5 | −2.0 |
| −3.0 | −5.5 |
| 2.0 | 4.7 |
| 5.0 | 1.8 |
| 1.2 | 4.1 |
| 3.0 | 2.6 |
| −1.0 | 2.0 |
| .5 | −1.3 |
| 2.5 | 5.5 |

a. Develop an estimated regression equation that can be used to determine the market beta for Horizon Technology. What is Horizon Technology's market beta?
b. Test for a significant relationship at the .05 level of significance.
c. Did the estimated regression equation provide a good fit? Explain.
d. Use the market betas of Texas Instruments and Horizon Technology to compare the risk associated with the two stocks.

61. The daily high and low temperatures for 20 cities follow (*USA Today,* May 9, 2000).

**HighLow**

| | Low | High |
|---|---|---|
| Athens | 54 | 75 |
| Bangkok | 74 | 92 |
| Cairo | 57 | 84 |
| Copenhagen | 39 | 64 |
| Dublin | 46 | 64 |
| Havana | 68 | 86 |
| Hong Kong | 72 | 81 |
| Johannesburg | 50 | 61 |
| London | 48 | 73 |
| Manila | 75 | 93 |
| Melbourne | 50 | 66 |
| Montreal | 52 | 64 |
| Paris | 55 | 77 |
| Rio de Janeiro | 61 | 80 |
| Rome | 54 | 81 |
| Seoul | 50 | 64 |
| Singapore | 75 | 90 |
| Sydney | 55 | 68 |
| Tokyo | 59 | 79 |
| Vancouver | 43 | 57 |

a. Develop a scatter diagram with low temperature on the horizontal axis and high temperature on the vertical axis.
b. What does the scatter diagram developed in part (a) indicate about the relationship between the two variables?
c. Develop the estimated regression equation that could be used to predict the high temperature given the low temperature.
d. Test for a significant relationship at the .05 level of significance.
e. Did the estimated regression equation provide a good fit? Explain.
f. What is the value of the sample correlation coefficient?

62. Jensen Tire & Auto is in the process of deciding whether to purchase a maintenance contract for its new computer wheel alignment and balancing machine. Managers feel that maintenance expense should be related to usage, and they collected the following information on weekly usage (hours) and annual maintenance expense (in hundreds of dollars).

| Weekly Usage (hours) | Annual Maintenance Expense |
|---|---|
| 13 | 17.0 |
| 10 | 22.0 |
| 20 | 30.0 |
| 28 | 37.0 |
| 32 | 47.0 |
| 17 | 30.5 |
| 24 | 32.5 |

| Weekly Usage (hours) | Annual Maintenance Expense |
|---|---|
| 31 | 39.0 |
| 40 | 51.5 |
| 38 | 40.0 |

a. Develop the estimated regression equation that relates annual maintenance expense to weekly usage.
b. Test the significance of the relationship in part (a) at a .05 level of significance.
c. Jensen expects to use the new machine 30 hours per week. Develop a 95% prediction interval for the company's annual maintenance expense.
d. If the maintenance contract costs $3000 per year, would you recommend purchasing it? Why or why not?

63. In a manufacturing process the assembly line speed (feet per minute) was thought to affect the number of defective parts found during the inspection process. To test this theory, managers devised a situation in which the same batch of parts was inspected visually at a variety of line speeds. They collected the following data.

| Line Speed | Number of Defective Parts Found |
|---|---|
| 20 | 21 |
| 20 | 19 |
| 40 | 15 |
| 30 | 16 |
| 60 | 14 |
| 40 | 17 |

a. Develop the estimated regression equation that relates line speed to the number of defective parts found.
b. At a .05 level of significance, determine whether line speed and number of defective parts found are related.
c. Did the estimated regression equation provide a good fit to the data?
d. Develop a 95% confidence interval to predict the mean number of defective parts for a line speed of 50 feet per minute.

64. A sociologist was hired by a large city hospital to investigate the relationship between the number of unauthorized days that employees are absent per year and the distance (miles) between home and work for the employees. A sample of 10 employees was chosen, and the following data were collected.

| Distance to Work | Number of Days Absent |
|---|---|
| 1 | 8 |
| 3 | 5 |
| 4 | 8 |
| 6 | 7 |
| 8 | 6 |
| 10 | 3 |
| 12 | 5 |
| 14 | 2 |
| 14 | 4 |
| 18 | 2 |

a.  Develop a scatter diagram for these data. Does a linear relationship appear reasonable? Explain.
b.  Develop the least squares estimated regression equation.
c.  Is there a significant relationship between the two variables? Use $\alpha = .05$.
d.  Did the estimated regression equation provide a good fit? Explain.
e.  Use the estimated regression equation developed in part (b) to develop a 95% confidence interval for the expected number of days absent for employees living 5 miles from the company.

65.  The regional transit authority for a major metropolitan area wants to determine whether there is any relationship between the age of a bus and the annual maintenance cost. A sample of 10 buses resulted in the following data.

| Age of Bus (years) | Maintenance Cost ($) |
|---|---|
| 1 | 350 |
| 2 | 370 |
| 2 | 480 |
| 2 | 520 |
| 2 | 590 |
| 3 | 550 |
| 4 | 750 |
| 4 | 800 |
| 5 | 790 |
| 5 | 950 |

a.  Develop the least squares estimated regression equation.
b.  Test to see whether the two variables are significantly related with $\alpha = .05$.
c.  Did the least squares line provide a good fit to the observed data? Explain.
d.  Develop a 95% prediction interval for the maintenance cost for a specific bus that is 4 years old.

66.  A marketing professor at Givens College is interested in the relationship between hours spent studying and total points earned in a course. Data collected on 10 students who took the course last quarter follow.

| Hours Spent Studying | Total Points Earned |
|---|---|
| 45 | 40 |
| 30 | 35 |
| 90 | 75 |
| 60 | 65 |
| 105 | 90 |
| 65 | 50 |
| 90 | 90 |
| 80 | 80 |
| 55 | 45 |
| 75 | 65 |

a.  Develop an estimated regression equation showing how total points earned is related to hours spent studying.
b.  Test the significance of the model with $\alpha = .05$.
c.  Predict the total points earned by Mark Sweeney. He spent 95 hours studying.
d.  Develop a 95% prediction interval for the total points earned by Mark Sweeney.

67. The Transactional Records Access Clearinghouse at Syracuse University reported data showing the odds of an Internal Revenue Service audit. The following table shows the average adjusted gross income reported and the percent of the returns that were audited for 20 selected IRS districts.

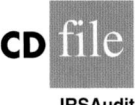

**IRSAudit**

| District | Adjusted Gross Income ($) | Percent Audited |
|---|---|---|
| Los Angeles | 36,664 | 1.3 |
| Sacramento | 38,845 | 1.1 |
| Atlanta | 34,886 | 1.1 |
| Boise | 32,512 | 1.1 |
| Dallas | 34,531 | 1.0 |
| Providence | 35,995 | 1.0 |
| San Jose | 37,799 | 0.9 |
| Cheyenne | 33,876 | 0.9 |
| Fargo | 30,513 | 0.9 |
| New Orleans | 30,174 | 0.9 |
| Oklahoma City | 30,060 | 0.8 |
| Houston | 37,153 | 0.8 |
| Portland | 34,918 | 0.7 |
| Phoenix | 33,291 | 0.7 |
| Augusta | 31,504 | 0.7 |
| Albuquerque | 29,199 | 0.6 |
| Greensboro | 33,072 | 0.6 |
| Columbia | 30,859 | 0.5 |
| Nashville | 32,566 | 0.5 |
| Buffalo | 34,296 | 0.5 |

a. Develop the estimated regression equation that could be used to predict the percent audited given the average adjusted gross income reported.
b. At the .05 level of significance, determine whether the adjusted gross income and the percent audited are related.
c. Did the estimated regression equation provide a good fit? Explain.
d. Use the estimated regression equation developed in part (a) to calculate a 95% confidence interval for the expected percent audited for districts with an average adjusted gross income of $35,000.

## Case Problem 1  Spending and Student Achievement

Is the educational achievement level of students related to how much the state in which they reside spends on education? In many communities taxpayers are asking this important question as school districts request tax revenue increases for education. In this case, you will be asked to analyze data on spending and achievement scores in order to determine whether there is any relationship between spending and student achievement in the public schools.

The federal government's National Assessment of Educational Progress (NAEP) program is frequently used to measure the educational achievement of students. Table 14.13 shows the total current spending per pupil per year, and the composite NAEP test score for 35 states that participated in the NAEP program. These data are available on the CD accompanying the text in the file named NAEP. The composite test score is the sum of the math, science, and reading scores on the 1996 (1994 for reading) NAEP test. Pupils tested are in grade 8, except for reading, which is given to fourth-graders only. The maximum possible score is 1300. Table 14.14 shows the spending per pupil for 13 states that did not

**TABLE 14.13**   SPENDING PER PUPIL AND COMPOSITE TEST SCORES FOR STATES THAT PARTICIPATED IN THE NAEP PROGRAM

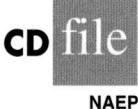

**NAEP**

| State | Spending per Pupil ($) | Composite Test Score |
|---|---|---|
| Louisiana | 4049 | 581 |
| Mississippi | 3423 | 582 |
| California | 4917 | 580 |
| Hawaii | 5532 | 580 |
| South Carolina | 4304 | 603 |
| Alabama | 3777 | 604 |
| Georgia | 4663 | 611 |
| Florida | 4934 | 611 |
| New Mexico | 4097 | 614 |
| Arkansas | 4060 | 615 |
| Delaware | 6208 | 615 |
| Tennessee | 3800 | 618 |
| Arizona | 4041 | 618 |
| West Virginia | 5247 | 625 |
| Maryland | 6100 | 625 |
| Kentucky | 5020 | 626 |
| Texas | 4520 | 627 |
| New York | 8162 | 628 |
| North Carolina | 4521 | 629 |
| Rhode Island | 6554 | 638 |
| Washington | 5338 | 639 |
| Missouri | 4483 | 641 |
| Colorado | 4772 | 644 |
| Indiana | 5128 | 649 |
| Utah | 3280 | 650 |
| Wyoming | 5515 | 657 |
| Connecticut | 7629 | 657 |
| Massachusetts | 6413 | 658 |
| Nebraska | 5410 | 660 |
| Minnesota | 5477 | 661 |
| Iowa | 5060 | 665 |
| Montana | 4985 | 667 |
| Wisconsin | 6055 | 667 |
| North Dakota | 4374 | 671 |
| Maine | 5561 | 675 |

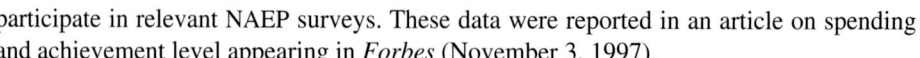

participate in relevant NAEP surveys. These data were reported in an article on spending and achievement level appearing in *Forbes* (November 3, 1997).

## Managerial Report

1. Develop numerical and graphical summaries of the data.
2. Use regression analysis to investigate the relationship between the amount spent per pupil and the composite score on the NAEP test. Discuss your findings.
3. Do you think that the estimated regression equation developed for these data could be used to estimate the composite test scores for the states that did not participate in the NAEP program?

TABLE 14.14    SPENDING PER PUPIL FOR STATES THAT DID NOT PARTICIPATE
IN THE NAEP PROGRAM

| State | Spending per Pupil ($) |
|---|---|
| Idaho | 3602 |
| South Dakota | 4067 |
| Oklahoma | 4265 |
| Nevada | 4658 |
| Kansas | 5164 |
| Illinois | 5297 |
| New Hampshire | 5387 |
| Ohio | 5438 |
| Oregon | 5588 |
| Vermont | 6269 |
| Michigan | 6391 |
| Pennsylvania | 6579 |
| Alaska | 7890 |

4. Suppose that you only considered states that spend at least $4000 per pupil but not more than $6000 per pupil. For these states, does the relationship between the two variables appear to be any different than for the complete data set? Discuss the results of your findings and whether you think deleting states with spending less than $4000 per year and more than $6000 per pupil is appropriate.
5. Develop estimates of the composite test scores for the states that did not participate in the NAEP program.
6. Based upon your analyses, do you think that the educational achievement level of students is related to how much the state spends on education?

## Case Problem 2    U.S. Department of Transportation

As part of a study on transportation safety, the U.S. Department of Transportation collected data on the number of fatal accidents per 1000 licenses and the percentage of licensed drivers under the age of 21 in a sample of 42 cities. Data collected over a one-year period follow. These data are available on the CD accompanying the text in the file named Safety.

**Safety**

| Percent Under 21 | Fatal Accidents per 1000 Licenses | Percent Under 21 | Fatal Accidents per 1000 Licenses |
|---|---|---|---|
| 13 | 2.962 | 17 | 4.100 |
| 12 | 0.708 | 8 | 2.190 |
| 8 | 0.885 | 16 | 3.623 |
| 12 | 1.652 | 15 | 2.623 |
| 11 | 2.091 | 9 | 0.835 |
| 17 | 2.627 | 8 | 0.820 |
| 18 | 3.830 | 14 | 2.890 |
| 8 | 0.368 | 8 | 1.267 |
| 13 | 1.142 | 15 | 3.224 |
| 8 | 0.645 | 10 | 1.014 |

*(continued)*

| Percent Under 21 | Fatal Accidents per 1000 Licenses | Percent Under 21 | Fatal Accidents per 1000 Licenses |
|---|---|---|---|
| 9 | 1.028 | 10 | 0.493 |
| 16 | 2.801 | 14 | 1.443 |
| 12 | 1.405 | 18 | 3.614 |
| 9 | 1.433 | 10 | 1.926 |
| 10 | 0.039 | 14 | 1.643 |
| 9 | 0.338 | 16 | 2.943 |
| 11 | 1.849 | 12 | 1.913 |
| 12 | 2.246 | 15 | 2.814 |
| 14 | 2.855 | 13 | 2.634 |
| 14 | 2.352 | 9 | 0.926 |
| 11 | 1.294 | 17 | 3.256 |

## Managerial Report

1. Develop numerical and graphical summaries of the data.
2. Use regression analysis to investigate the relationship between the number of fatal accidents and the percentage of drivers under the age of 21. Discuss your findings.
3. What conclusion and recommendations can you derive from your analysis?

## Case Problem 3    Alumni Giving

Alumni donations are an important source of revenue for colleges and universities. If administrators could determine the factors that influence increases in the percentage of alumni who make a donation, they might be able to implement policies that could lead to increased revenues. Research shows that students who are more satisfied with their contact with teachers are more likely to graduate. As a result, one might suspect that smaller class sizes and lower student-faculty ratios might lead to a higher percentage of satisfied graduates, which in turn might lead to increases in the percentage of alumni who make a donation. Table 14.15 shows data for 48 national universities (*America's Best Colleges,* Year 2000 Edition). The column labeled % of Classes Under 20 shows the percentage of classes offered with fewer than 20 students. The column labeled Student/Faculty Ratio is the number of students enrolled divided by the total number of faculty. Finally, the column labeled Alumni Giving Rate is the percentage of alumni that made a donation to the university.

## Managerial Report

1. Develop numerical and graphical summaries of the data.
2. Use regression analysis to develop an estimated regression equation that could be used to predict the alumni giving rate given the percentage of classes with fewer than 20 students.
3. Use regression analysis to develop an estimated regression equation that could be used to predict the alumni giving rate given the student-faculty ratio.
4. Which of the two estimated regression equations provides the best fit? For this estimated regression equation, perform an analysis of the residuals and discuss your findings and conclusions.
5. What conclusions and recommendations can you derive from your analysis?

**TABLE 14.15    DATA FOR 48 NATIONAL UNIVERSITIES**

Alumni

| | % of Classes Under 20 | Student/Faculty Ratio | Alumni Giving Rate |
|---|---|---|---|
| Boston College | 39 | 13 | 25 |
| Brandeis University | 68 | 8 | 33 |
| Brown University | 60 | 8 | 40 |
| California Institute of Technology | 65 | 3 | 46 |
| Carnegie Mellon University | 67 | 10 | 28 |
| Case Western Reserve Univ. | 52 | 8 | 31 |
| College of William and Mary | 45 | 12 | 27 |
| Columbia University | 69 | 7 | 31 |
| Cornell University | 72 | 13 | 35 |
| Dartmouth College | 61 | 10 | 53 |
| Duke University | 68 | 8 | 45 |
| Emory University | 65 | 7 | 37 |
| Georgetown University | 54 | 10 | 29 |
| Harvard University | 73 | 8 | 46 |
| Johns Hopkins University | 64 | 9 | 27 |
| Lehigh University | 55 | 11 | 40 |
| Massachusetts Inst. of Technology | 65 | 6 | 44 |
| New York University | 63 | 13 | 13 |
| Northwestern University | 66 | 8 | 30 |
| Pennsylvania State Univ. | 32 | 19 | 21 |
| Princeton University | 68 | 5 | 67 |
| Rice University | 62 | 8 | 40 |
| Stanford University | 69 | 7 | 34 |
| Tufts University | 67 | 9 | 29 |
| Tulane University | 56 | 12 | 17 |
| U. of California–Berkeley | 58 | 17 | 18 |
| U. of California–Davis | 32 | 19 | 7 |
| U. of California–Irvine | 42 | 20 | 9 |
| U. of California–Los Angeles | 41 | 18 | 13 |
| U. of California–San Diego | 48 | 19 | 8 |
| U. of California–Santa Barbara | 45 | 20 | 12 |
| U. of Chicago | 65 | 4 | 36 |
| U. of Florida | 31 | 23 | 19 |
| U. of Illinois–Urbana Champaign | 29 | 15 | 23 |
| U. of Michigan–Ann Arbor | 51 | 15 | 13 |
| U. of North Carolina–Chapel Hill | 40 | 16 | 26 |
| U. of Notre Dame | 53 | 13 | 49 |
| U. of Pennsylvania | 65 | 7 | 41 |
| U. of Rochester | 63 | 10 | 23 |
| U. of Southern California | 53 | 13 | 22 |
| U. of Texas–Austin | 39 | 21 | 13 |
| U. of Virginia | 44 | 13 | 28 |
| U. of Washington | 37 | 12 | 12 |
| U. of Wisconsin–Madison | 37 | 13 | 13 |
| Vanderbilt University | 68 | 9 | 31 |
| Wake Forest University | 59 | 11 | 38 |
| Washington University–St. Louis | 73 | 7 | 33 |
| Yale University | 77 | 7 | 50 |

## Case Problem 4  Major League Baseball Team Values

A group led by John Henry paid $700 million to purchase the Boston Red Sox, even though the Red Sox have not won the World Series since 1918 and posted an operating loss of $11.4 million for 2001. Moreover, *Forbes* magazine estimates that the current value of the team is actually $426 million. *Forbes* attributes the difference between the current value for a team and the price investors are willing to pay to the fact that the purchase of a team often includes the acquisition of a grossly undervalued cable network. For instance, in purchasing the Boston Red Sox, the new owners also got an 80% interest in the New England Sports Network. Table 14.16 shows data for the 30 major league teams (*Forbes*, April 15, 2002). The column labeled Value contains the values of the teams based on current stadium deals, without deduction for debt. The column labeled Income indicates the earnings before interest, taxes, and depreciation.

### Managerial Report

1. Develop numerical and graphical summaries of the data.
2. Use regression analysis to investigate the relationship between value and income. Discuss your findings.

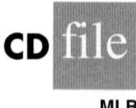

MLB

TABLE 14.16   DATA FOR MAJOR LEAGUE BASEBALL TEAMS

| Team | Value | Revenue | Income |
|---|---|---|---|
| New York Yankees | 730 | 215 | 18.7 |
| New York Mets | 482 | 169 | 14.3 |
| Los Angeles Dodgers | 435 | 143 | −29.6 |
| Boston Red Sox | 426 | 152 | −11.4 |
| Atlanta Braves | 424 | 160 | 9.5 |
| Seattle Mariners | 373 | 166 | 14.1 |
| Cleveland Indians | 360 | 150 | −3.6 |
| Texas Rangers | 356 | 134 | −6.5 |
| San Francisco Giants | 355 | 142 | 16.8 |
| Colorado Rockies | 347 | 129 | 6.7 |
| Houston Astros | 337 | 125 | 4.1 |
| Baltimore Orioles | 319 | 133 | 3.2 |
| Chicago Cubs | 287 | 131 | 7.9 |
| Arizona Diamondbacks | 280 | 127 | −3.9 |
| St. Louis Cardinals | 271 | 123 | −5.1 |
| Detroit Tigers | 262 | 114 | 12.3 |
| Pittsburgh Pirates | 242 | 108 | 9.5 |
| Milwaukee Brewers | 238 | 108 | 18.8 |
| Philadelphia Phillies | 231 | 94 | 2.6 |
| Chicago White Sox | 223 | 101 | −3.8 |
| San Diego Padres | 207 | 92 | 5.7 |
| Cincinnati Reds | 204 | 87 | 4.3 |
| Anaheim Angels | 195 | 103 | 5.7 |
| Toronto Blue Jays | 182 | 91 | −20.6 |
| Oakland Athletics | 157 | 90 | 6.8 |
| Kansas City Royals | 152 | 85 | 2.2 |
| Tampa Bay Devil Rays | 142 | 92 | −6.1 |
| Florida Marlins | 137 | 81 | 1.4 |
| Minnesota Twins | 127 | 75 | 3.6 |
| Montreal Expos | 108 | 63 | −3.4 |

**3.** Use regression analysis to investigate the relationship between value and revenue. Discuss your findings.

**4.** What conclusions and recommendations can you derive from your analysis?

## Appendix 14.1    Calculus-Based Derivation of Least Squares Formulas

As mentioned in the chapter, the least squares method is a procedure for determining the values of $b_0$ and $b_1$ that minimize the sum of squared residuals. The sum of squared residuals is given by

$$\Sigma(y_i - \hat{y}_i)^2$$

Substituting $\hat{y}_i = b_0 + b_1 x_i$, we get

$$\Sigma(y_i - b_0 - b_1 x_i)^2 \tag{14.34}$$

as the expression that must be minimized.

To minimize expression (14.34), we must take the partial derivatives with respect to $b_0$ and $b_1$, set them equal to zero, and solve. Doing so, we get

$$\frac{\partial \Sigma(y_i - b_0 - b_1 x_i)^2}{\partial b_0} = -2\Sigma(y_i - b_0 - b_1 x_i) = 0 \tag{14.35}$$

$$\frac{\partial \Sigma(y_i - b_0 - b_1 x_i)^2}{\partial b_1} = -2\Sigma x_i(y_i - b_0 - b_1 x_i) = 0 \tag{14.36}$$

Dividing equation (14.35) by two and summing each term individually yields

$$-\Sigma y_i + \Sigma b_0 + \Sigma b_1 x_i = 0$$

Bringing $\Sigma y_i$ to the other side of the equal sign and noting that $\Sigma b_0 = n b_0$, we obtain

$$n b_0 + (\Sigma x_i) b_1 = \Sigma y_i \tag{14.37}$$

Similar algebraic simplification applied to equation (14.36) yields

$$(\Sigma x_i) b_0 + (\Sigma x_i^2) b_1 = \Sigma x_i y_i \tag{14.38}$$

Equations (14.37) and (14.38) are known as the *normal equations*. Solving equation (14.37) for $b_0$ yields

$$b_0 = \frac{\Sigma y_i}{n} - b_1 \frac{\Sigma x_i}{n} \tag{14.39}$$

Using equation (14.39) to substitute for $b_0$ in equation (14.38) provides

$$\frac{\Sigma x_i \Sigma y_i}{n} - \frac{(\Sigma x_i)^2}{n} b_1 + (\Sigma x_i^2) b_1 = \Sigma x_i y_i \tag{14.40}$$

By rearranging the terms in equation (14.40), we obtain

$$b_1 = \frac{\Sigma x_i y_i - (\Sigma x_i \Sigma y_i)/n}{\Sigma x_i^2 - (\Sigma x_i)^2/n} = \frac{\Sigma(x_i - \bar{x})(y_i - \bar{y})}{\Sigma(x_i - \bar{x})^2} \qquad (14.41)$$

Because $\bar{x} = \Sigma y_i/n$ and $\bar{x} = \Sigma x_i/n$, we can rewrite equation (14.39) as

$$b_0 = \bar{y} - b_1 \bar{x} \qquad (14.42)$$

Equations (14.41) and (14.42) are the formulas (14.6) and (14.7) we used in the chapter to compute the coefficients in the estimated regression equation.

# Appendix 14.2    A Test for Significance Using Correlation

Using the sample correlation coefficient $r_{xy}$, we can determine whether the linear relationship between $x$ and $y$ is significant by testing the following hypotheses about the population correlation coefficient $\rho_{xy}$.

$$H_0\!: \rho_{xy} = 0$$
$$H_a\!: \rho_{xy} \neq 0$$

If $H_0$ is rejected, we can conclude that the population correlation coefficient is not equal to zero and that the linear relationship between the two variables is significant. This test for significance follows.

A TEST FOR SIGNIFICANCE USING CORRELATION

$$H_0\!: \rho_{xy} = 0$$
$$H_a\!: \rho_{xy} \neq 0$$

TEST STATISTIC

$$t = r_{xy} \sqrt{\frac{n - 2}{1 - r_{xy}^2}} \qquad (14.43)$$

REJECTION RULE

$p$-value approach:      Reject $H_0$ if $p$-value $\leq \alpha$
Critical value approach: Reject $H_0$ if $t \leq -t_{\alpha/2}$ or if $t \geq t_{\alpha/2}$

where $t_{\alpha/2}$ is based on a $t$ distribution with $n - 2$ degrees of freedom.

In Section 14.4, we found that the sample with $n = 10$ provided the sample correlation coefficient for student population and quarterly sales of $r_{xy} = .9501$. The test statistic is

$$t = r_{xy} \sqrt{\frac{n - 2}{1 - r_{xy}^2}} = .9501 \sqrt{\frac{10 - 2}{1 - (.9501)^2}} = 8.61$$

The $t$ distribution table shows that with $n - 2 = 10 - 2 = 8$ degrees of freedom, $t = 3.355$ provides an area of .005 in the upper tail. Thus, the area in the upper tail of the $t$ distribution corresponding to the test statistic $t = 8.61$ must be less than .005. Because this test is a two-tailed test, we double this value to conclude that the $p$-value associated with $t = 8.62$ must be less than $2(.005) = .01$. Minitab or Excel show the $p$-value $= .000$. Because the $p$-value is less than $\alpha = .01$, we reject $H_0$ and conclude that $\rho_{xy}$ is not equal to zero. This evidence is sufficient to conclude that a significant linear relationship exists between student population and quarterly sales.

Note that the test statistic $t$ and the conclusion of a significant relationship are identical to the results obtained in Section 14.5 for the $t$ test conducted using Armand's estimated regression equation $\hat{y} = 60 + 5x$. Performing regression analysis provides the conclusion of a significant relationship between $x$ and $y$ and in addition provides the equation showing how the variables are related. Most analysts therefore use modern computer packages to perform regression analysis and find that using correlation as a test of significance is unnecessary.

## Appendix 14.3   Regression Analysis with Minitab

**Armand's**

In Section 14.7 we discussed the computer solution of regression problems by showing Minitab's output for the Armand's Pizza Parlors problem. In this appendix, we describe the steps required to generate the Minitab computer solution. First, the data must be entered in a Minitab worksheet. Student population data are entered in column C1 and quarterly sales data are entered in column C2. The variable names Pop and Sales are entered as the column headings on the worksheet. In subsequent steps, we refer to the data by using the variable names Pop and Sales or the column indicators C1 and C2. The following steps describe how to use Minitab to produce the regression results shown in Figure 14.10.

**Step 1.** Select the **Stat** menu
**Step 2.** Select the **Regression** menu
**Step 3.** Choose **Regression**
**Step 4.** When the Regression dialog box appears:
        Enter Sales in the **Response** box
        Enter Pop in the **Predictors** box
        Click the **Options** button
    When the Regression-Options dialog box appears:
        Enter 10 in the **Prediction intervals for new observations** box
        Click **OK**
    When the Regression dialog box reappears:
        Click **OK**

The Minitab regression dialog box provides additional capabilities that can be obtained by selecting the desired options. For instance, to obtain a residual plot that shows the predicted value of the dependent variable $\hat{y}$ on the horizontal axis and the standardized residual values on the vertical axis, step 4 would be as follows:

**Step 4.** When the Regression dialog box appears:
        Enter Sales in the **Response** box
        Enter Pop in the **Predictors** box
        Click the **Graphs** button

When the Regression-Graphs dialog box appears:
Select **Standardized** under Residuals for Plots
Select **Residuals versus fits** under Residual Plots
Click **OK**
When the Regression dialog box reappears:
Click **OK**

# Appendix 14.4  Regression Analysis with Excel

**CD** file

**Armand's**

In this appendix we will illustrate how Excel's Regression tool can be used to perform the regression analysis computations for the Armand's Pizza Parlors problem. Refer to Figure 14.23 as we describe the steps involved. The labels Restaurant, Population, and Sales are entered into cells A1:C1 of the worksheet. To identify each of the 10 observations, we entered the numbers 1 through 10 into cells A2:A11. The sample data are entered into cells B2:C11. The following steps describe how to use Excel to produce the regression results.

**Step 1.** Select the **Tools** menu
**Step 2.** Choose **Data Analysis**
**Step 3.** Choose **Regression** from the list of Analysis Tools
**Step 4.** Click **OK**

FIGURE 14.23    EXCEL SOLUTION TO THE ARMAND'S PIZZA PARLORS PROBLEM

|  | A | B | C | D | E | F | G | H | I | J |
|---|---|---|---|---|---|---|---|---|---|---|
| 1 | **Restaurant** | **Population** | **Sales** |  |  |  |  |  |  |  |
| 2 | 1 | 2 | 58 |  |  |  |  |  |  |  |
| 3 | 2 | 6 | 105 |  |  |  |  |  |  |  |
| 4 | 3 | 8 | 88 |  |  |  |  |  |  |  |
| 5 | 4 | 8 | 118 |  |  |  |  |  |  |  |
| 6 | 5 | 12 | 117 |  |  |  |  |  |  |  |
| 7 | 6 | 16 | 137 |  |  |  |  |  |  |  |
| 8 | 7 | 20 | 157 |  |  |  |  |  |  |  |
| 9 | 8 | 20 | 169 |  |  |  |  |  |  |  |
| 10 | 9 | 22 | 149 |  |  |  |  |  |  |  |
| 11 | 10 | 26 | 202 |  |  |  |  |  |  |  |
| 12 |  |  |  |  |  |  |  |  |  |  |
| 13 | SUMMARY OUTPUT |  |  |  |  |  |  |  |  |  |
| 14 |  |  |  |  |  |  |  |  |  |  |
| 15 | *Regression Statistics* |  |  |  |  |  |  |  |  |  |
| 16 | Multiple R | 0.9501 |  |  |  |  |  |  |  |  |
| 17 | R Square | 0.9027 |  |  |  |  |  |  |  |  |
| 18 | Adjusted R Square | 0.8906 |  |  |  |  |  |  |  |  |
| 19 | Standard Error | 13.8293 |  |  |  |  |  |  |  |  |
| 20 | Observations | 10 |  |  |  |  |  |  |  |  |
| 21 |  |  |  |  |  |  |  |  |  |  |
| 22 | ANOVA |  |  |  |  |  |  |  |  |  |
| 23 |  | *df* | *SS* | *MS* | *F* | *Significance F* |  |  |  |  |
| 24 | Regression | 1 | 14200 | 14200 | 74.2484 | 2.55E-05 |  |  |  |  |
| 25 | Residual | 8 | 1530 | 191.25 |  |  |  |  |  |  |
| 26 | Total | 9 | 15730 |  |  |  |  |  |  |  |
| 27 |  |  |  |  |  |  |  |  |  |  |
| 28 |  | *Coefficients* | *Standard Error* | *t Stat* | *P-value* | *Lower 95%* | *Upper 95%* | *Lower 99.0%* | *Upper 99.0%* |  |
| 29 | Intercept | 60 | 9.2260 | 6.5033 | 0.0002 | 38.7247 | 81.2753 | 29.0431 | 90.9569 |  |
| 30 | Population | 5 | 0.5803 | 8.6167 | 2.55E-05 | 3.6619 | 6.3381 | 3.0530 | 6.9470 |  |
| 31 |  |  |  |  |  |  |  |  |  |  |

**Step 5.** When the Regression dialog box appears:

> Enter C1:C11 in the **Input Y Range** box
> Enter B1:B11 in the **Input X Range** box
> Select **Labels**
> Select **Confidence Level**
> Enter 99 in the **Confidence Level** box
> Select **Output Range**
> Enter A13 in the **Output Range** box
>> (Any upper-left-hand corner cell indicating where the output is to begin may be entered here.)
> Click **OK**

The first section of the output, titled *Regression Statistics,* contains summary statistics such as the coefficient of determination (R Square). The second section of the output, titled ANOVA, contains the analysis of variance table. The last section of the output, which is not titled, contains the estimated regression coefficients and related information. We will begin our discussion of the interpretation of the regression output with the information contained in cells A28:I30.

## Interpretation of Estimated Regression Equation Output

The $y$ intercept of the estimated regression line, $b_0 = 60$, is shown in cell B29, and the slope of the estimated regression line, $b_1 = 5$, is shown in cell B30. The label Intercept in cell A29 and the label Population in cell A30 are used to identify these two values.

In Section 14.5 we showed that the estimated standard deviation of $b_1$ is $s_{b_1} = .5803$. Note that the value in cell C30 is .5803. The label Standard Error in cell C28 is Excel's way of indicating that the value in cell C30 is the standard error, or standard deviation, of $b_1$. Recall that the $t$ test for a significant relationship required the computation of the $t$ statistic, $t = b_1/s_{b_1}$. For the Armand's data, the value of $t$ that we computed was $t = 5/.5803 = 8.62$. The label in cell D28, $t$ *Stat,* reminds us that cell D30 contains the value of the $t$ test statistic.

The value in cell E30 is the $p$-value associated with the $t$ test for significance. Excel has displayed the $p$-value in cell E30 using scientific notation. To obtain the decimal value, we move the decimal point 5 places to the left, obtaining a value of .0000255. Because the $p$-value $= .0000255 < \alpha = .01$, we can reject $H_0$ and conclude that we have a significant relationship between student population and quarterly sales.

The information in cells F28:I30 can be used to develop confidence interval estimates of the $y$ intercept and slope of the estimated regression equation. Excel always provides the lower and upper limits for a 95% confidence interval. Recall that in step 4 we selected Confidence Level and entered 99 in the Confidence Level box. As a result, Excel's Regression tool also provides the lower and upper limits for a 99% confidence interval. The value in cell H30 is the lower limit for the 99% confidence interval estimate of $\beta_1$ and the value in cell I30 is the upper limit. Thus, after rounding, the 99% confidence interval estimate of $\beta_1$ is 3.05 to 6.95. The values in cells F30 and G30 provide the lower and upper limits for the 95% confidence interval. Thus, the 95% confidence interval is 3.66 to 6.34.

## Interpretation of ANOVA Output

The information in cells A22:F26 is a summary of the analysis of variance computations. The three sources of variation are labeled Regression, Residual, and Total. The label *df* in cell B23 stands for degrees of freedom, the label *SS* in cell C23 stands for sum of squares, and the label *MS* in cell D23 stands for mean square.

In Section 14.5 we stated that the mean square error, obtained by dividing the error or residual sum of squares by its degrees of freedom, provides an estimate of $\sigma^2$. The value in cell D25, 191.25, is the mean square error for the Armand's regression output. In Section 14.5 we showed that an $F$ test could also be used to test for significance in regression. The value in cell F24, .0000255, is the $p$-value associated with the $F$ test for significance. Because the $p$-value $= .0000255 < \alpha = .01$, we can reject $H_0$ and conclude that we have a significant relationship between student population and quarterly sales. The label Excel uses to identify the $p$-value for the $F$ test for significance, shown in cell F23, is *Significance F*.

*The label Significance F may be more meaningful if you think of the value in cell F24 as the observed level of significance for the F test.*

## Interpretation of Regression Statistics Output

The coefficient of determination, .9027, appears in cell B17; the corresponding label, R Square, is shown in cell A17. The square root of the coefficient of determination provides the sample correlation coefficient of .9501 shown in cell B16. Note that Excel uses the label Multiple R (cell A16) to identify this value. In cell A19, the label Standard Error is used to identify the value of the standard error of the estimate shown in cell B19. Thus, the standard error of the estimate is 13.8293. We caution the reader to keep in mind that in the Excel output, the label Standard Error appears in two different places. In the Regression Statistics section of the output, the label Standard Error refers to the estimate of $\sigma$. In the Estimated Regression Equation section of the output, the label *Standard Error* refers to $s_{b_1}$ the standard deviation of the sampling distribution of $b_1$.

# CHAPTER 15

# Multiple Regression

**CONTENTS**

## INTERNATIONAL PAPER*
*PURCHASE, NEW YORK*

International Paper is the world's largest paper and forest products company. The company employs more than 117,000 people in its operations in nearly 50 countries, and exports its products to more than 130 nations. International Paper produces building materials such as lumber and plywood; consumer packaging materials such as disposable cups and containers; industrial packaging materials such as corrugated boxes and shipping containers; and a variety of papers for use in photocopiers, printers, books, and advertising materials.

To make paper products, pulp mills process wood chips and chemicals to produce wood pulp. The wood pulp is then used at a paper mill to produce paper products. In the production of white paper products, the pulp must be bleached to remove any discoloration. A key bleaching agent used in the process is chlorine dioxide, which, because of its combustible nature, is usually produced at a pulp mill facility and then piped in solution form into the bleaching tower of the pulp mill. To improve one of the processes used to produce chlorine dioxide, researchers studied the process's control and efficiency. One aspect of the study looked at the chemical-feed rate for chlorine dioxide production.

To produce the chlorine dioxide, four chemicals flow at metered rates into the chlorine dioxide generator. The chlorine dioxide produced in the generator flows to an absorber where chilled water absorbs the chlorine dioxide gas to form a chlorine dioxide solution. The solution is then piped into the paper mill. A key part of controlling the process involves the chemical-feed rates. Historically, experienced operators set the chemical-feed rates, but this approach led to overcontrol by the operators. Consequently, chemical engineers at the mill requested that a set of control equations, one for each chemical feed, be developed to aid the operators in setting the rates.

Multiple regression analysis assisted in the development of a better bleaching process for making white paper products. © Lester Lefkowitz/Corbis.

Using multiple regression analysis, statistical analysts developed an estimated multiple regression equation for each of the four chemicals used in the process. Each equation related the production of chlorine dioxide to the amount of chemical used and the concentration level of the chlorine dioxide solution. The resulting set of four equations was programmed into a microcomputer at each mill. In the new system, operators enter the concentration of the chlorine dioxide solution and the desired production rate; the computer software then calculates the chemical feed needed to achieve the desired production rate. After the operators began using the control equations, the chlorine dioxide generator efficiency increased, and the number of times the concentrations fell within acceptable ranges increased significantly.

This example shows how multiple regression analysis can be used to develop a better bleaching process for producing white paper products. In this chapter we will discuss how computer software packages are used for such purposes. Most of the concepts introduced in Chapter 14 for simple linear regression can be directly extended to the multiple regression case.

*The authors are indebted to Marian Williams and Bill Griggs for providing this Statistics in Practice. This application was originally developed at Champion International Corporation, which became part of International Paper in 2000.

In Chapter 14 we presented simple linear regression and demonstrated its use in developing an estimated regression equation that describes the relationship between two variables. Recall that the variable being predicted or explained is called the dependent variable and the variable being used to predict or explain the dependent variable is called the independent variable. In this chapter we continue our study of regression analysis by considering situations involving two or more independent variables. This subject area, called **multiple regression analysis**, enables us to consider more factors and thus obtain better estimates than are possible with simple linear regression.

 # 15.1 Multiple Regression Model

Multiple regression analysis is the study of how a dependent variable $y$ is related to two or more independent variables. In the general case, we will use $p$ to denote the number of independent variables.

## Regression Model and Regression Equation

The concepts of a regression model and a regression equation introduced in the preceding chapter are applicable in the multiple regression case. The equation that describes how the dependent variable $y$ is related to the independent variables $x_1, x_2, \ldots x_p$ and an error term is called the **multiple regression model**. We begin with the assumption that the multiple regression model takes the following form.

---

MULTIPLE REGRESSION MODEL

$$y = \beta_0 + \beta_1 x_1 + \beta_2 x_2 + \cdots + \beta_p x_p + \epsilon \qquad \text{(15.1)}$$

---

In the multiple regression model, $\beta_0, \beta_1, \beta_2, \ldots, \beta_p$ are the parameters and $\epsilon$ (the Greek letter epsilon) is a random variable. A close examination of this model reveals that $y$ is a linear function of $x_1, x_2, \ldots, x_p$ (the $\beta_0 + \beta_1 x_1 + \beta_2 x_2 + \cdots + \beta_p x_p$ part) plus an error term $\epsilon$. The error term accounts for the variability in $y$ that cannot be explained by the linear effect of the $p$ independent variables.

In Section 15.4 we will discuss the assumptions for the multiple regression model and $\epsilon$. One of the assumptions is that the mean or expected value of $\epsilon$ is zero. A consequence of this assumption is that the mean or expected value of $y$, denoted $E(y)$, is equal to $\beta_0 + \beta_1 x_1 + \beta_2 x_2 + \cdots + \beta_p x_p$. The equation that describes how the mean value of $y$ is related to $x_1, x_2, \ldots, x_p$ is called the **multiple regression equation**.

---

MULTIPLE REGRESSION EQUATION

$$E(y) = \beta_0 + \beta_1 x_1 + \beta_2 x_2 + \cdots + \beta_p x_p \qquad \text{(15.2)}$$

---

## Estimated Multiple Regression Equation

If the values of $\beta_0, \beta_1, \beta_2, \ldots, \beta_p$ were known, equation (15.2) could be used to compute the mean value of $y$ at given values of $x_1, x_2, \ldots, x_p$. Unfortunately, these parameter values will not, in general, be known and must be estimated from sample data. A simple random sample is used to compute sample statistics $b_0, b_1, b_2, \ldots, b_p$ that are used as the point estimators of the parameters $\beta_0, \beta_1, \beta_2, \ldots, \beta_p$. These sample statistics provide the following **estimated multiple regression equation**.

---

ESTIMATED MULTIPLE REGRESSION EQUATION

$$\hat{y} = b_0 + b_1x_1 + b_2x_2 + \cdots + b_px_p \qquad \text{(15.3)}$$

where

$$b_0, b_1, b_2, \ldots, b_p \text{ are the estimates of } \beta_0, \beta_1, \beta_2, \ldots, \beta_p$$
$$\hat{y} = \text{estimated value of the dependent variable}$$

---

The estimation process for multiple regression is shown in Figure 15.1.

## (15.2) Least Squares Method

In Chapter 14, we used the **least squares method** to develop the estimated regression equation that best approximated the straight-line relationship between the dependent and independent variables. This same approach is used to develop the estimated multiple regression equation. The least squares criterion is restated as follows.

---

LEAST SQUARES CRITERION

$$\min \Sigma(y_i - \hat{y}_i)^2 \qquad \text{(15.4)}$$

---

**FIGURE 15.1** THE ESTIMATION PROCESS FOR MULTIPLE REGRESSION

*In simple linear regression, $b_0$ and $b_1$ were the sample statistics used to estimate the parameters $\beta_0$ and $\beta_1$. Multiple regression parallels this statistical inference process, with $b_0$, $b_1$, $b_2$, ... $b_p$ denoting the sample statistics used to estimate the parameters $\beta_0$, $\beta_1$, $\beta_2$, ..., $\beta_p$.*

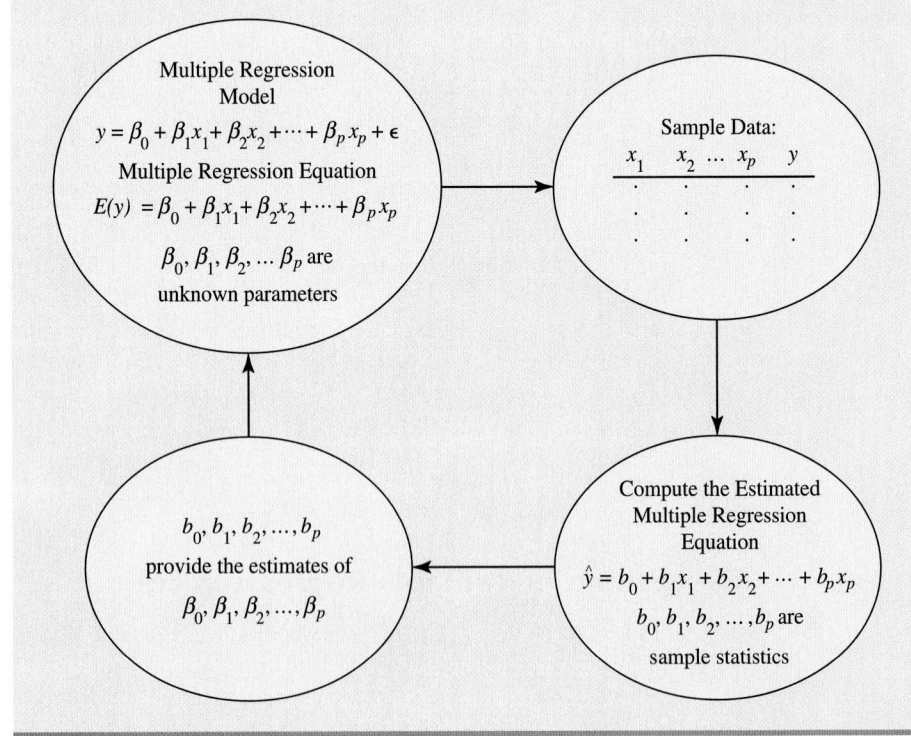

where

$y_i$ = observed value of the dependent variable for the $i$th observation
$\hat{y}_i$ = estimated value of the dependent variable for the $i$th observation

The estimated values of the dependent variable are computed by using the estimated multiple regression equation,

$$\hat{y} = b_0 + b_1 x_1 + b_2 x_2 + \cdots + b_p x_p$$

As expression (15.4) shows, the least squares method uses sample data to provide the values of $b_0, b_1, b_2, \ldots, b_p$ that make the sum of squared residuals [the deviations between the observed values of the dependent variable ($y_i$) and the estimated values of the dependent variable ($\hat{y}_i$)] a minimum.

In Chapter 14 we presented formulas for computing the least squares estimators $b_0$ and $b_1$ for the estimated simple linear regression equation $\hat{y} = b_0 + b_1 x$. With relatively small data sets, we were able to use those formulas to compute $b_0$ and $b_1$ by manual calculations. In multiple regression, however, the presentation of the formulas for the regression coefficients $b_0, b_1, b_2, \ldots, b_p$ involves the use of matrix algebra and is beyond the scope of this text. Therefore, in presenting multiple regression, we focus on how computer software packages can be used to obtain the estimated regression equation and other information. The emphasis will be on how to interpret the computer output rather than on how to make the multiple regression computations.

## An Example: Butler Trucking Company

As an illustration of multiple regression analysis, we will consider a problem faced by the Butler Trucking Company, an independent trucking company in southern California. A major portion of Butler's business involves deliveries throughout its local area. To develop better work schedules, the managers want to estimate the total daily travel time for their drivers.

Initially the managers believed that the total daily travel time would be closely related to the number of miles traveled in making the daily deliveries. A simple random sample of 10 driving assignments provided the data shown in Table 15.1 and the scatter diagram shown in Figure 15.2. After reviewing this scatter diagram, the managers hypothesized that the simple linear regression model $y = \beta_0 + \beta_1 x_1 + \epsilon$ could be used to describe the relationship between the total travel time ($y$) and the number of miles traveled ($x_1$). To estimate

TABLE 15.1   PRELIMINARY DATA FOR BUTLER TRUCKING

| Driving Assignment | $x_1$ = Miles Traveled | $y$ = Travel Time (hours) |
|---|---|---|
| 1 | 100 | 9.3 |
| 2 | 50 | 4.8 |
| 3 | 100 | 8.9 |
| 4 | 100 | 6.5 |
| 5 | 50 | 4.2 |
| 6 | 80 | 6.2 |
| 7 | 75 | 7.4 |
| 8 | 65 | 6.0 |
| 9 | 90 | 7.6 |
| 10 | 90 | 6.1 |

FIGURE 15.2   SCATTER DIAGRAM OF PRELIMINARY DATA FOR BUTLER TRUCKING

the parameters $\beta_0$ and $\beta_1$, the least squares method was used to develop the estimated regression equation.

$$\hat{y} = b_0 + b_1 x_1 \tag{15.5}$$

In Figure 15.3, we show the Minitab computer output from applying simple linear regression to the data in Table 15.1. The estimated regression equation is

$$\hat{y} = 1.27 + .0678 x_1$$

At the .05 level of significance, the $F$ value of 15.81 and its corresponding $p$-value of .004 indicate that the relationship is significant; that is, we can reject $H_0$: $\beta_1 = 0$ because the $p$-value is less than $\alpha = .05$. Note that the same conclusion is obtained from the $t$ value of 3.98 and its associated $p$-value of .004. Thus, we can conclude that the relationship between the total travel time and the number of miles traveled is significant; longer travel times are associated with more miles traveled. With a coefficient of determination (expressed as a percentage) of $R$-sq $= 66.4\%$, we see that 66.4% of the variability in travel time can be explained by the linear effect of the number of miles traveled. This finding is fairly good, but the managers might want to consider adding a second independent variable to explain some of the remaining variability in the dependent variable.

In attempting to identify another independent variable, the managers felt that the number of deliveries could also contribute to the total travel time. The Butler Trucking data, with the number of deliveries added, are shown in Table 15.2. The Minitab computer solution with both miles traveled ($x_1$) and number of deliveries ($x_2$) as independent variables is shown in Figure 15.4. The estimated regression equation is

$$\hat{y} = -.869 + .0611 x_1 + .923 x_2 \tag{15.6}$$

FIGURE 15.3    MINITAB OUTPUT FOR BUTLER TRUCKING WITH ONE
INDEPENDENT VARIABLE

*In the Minitab output the variable names* Miles *and* Time *were entered as the column headings on the worksheet; thus,* $x_1$ = Miles *and* $y$ = Time.

```
The regression equation is
Time = 1.27 + 0.0678 Miles

Predictor      Coef   SE Coef      T      p
Constant      1.274     1.401   0.91  0.390
Miles       0.06783   0.01706   3.98  0.004

S = 1.002   R-sq = 66.4%   R-sq(adj) = 62.2%

Analysis of Variance

SOURCE            DF       SS       MS      F      p
Regression         1   15.871   15.871  15.81  0.004
Residual Error     8    8.029    1.004
Total              9   23.900
```

In the next section we will discuss the use of the coefficient of multiple determination in measuring how good a fit is provided by this estimated regression equation. Before doing so, let us examine more carefully the values of $b_1$ = .0611 and $b_2$ = .923 in equation (15.6).

## Note on Interpretation of Coefficients

One observation can be made at this point about the relationship between the estimated regression equation with only the miles traveled as an independent variable and the equation that includes the number of deliveries as a second independent variable. The value of $b_1$ is not the same in both cases. In simple linear regression, we interpret $b_1$ as an estimate of the change in $y$ for a one-unit change in the independent variable. In multiple regression analysis, this interpretation must be modified somewhat. That is, in multiple regression analysis, we interpret each regression coefficient as follows: $b_i$ represents an estimate of the change in $y$ corresponding to a one-unit change in $x_i$ when all other independent variables are held constant. In the Butler Trucking example involving two independent variables, $b_1$ = .0611. Thus,

TABLE 15.2    DATA FOR BUTLER TRUCKING WITH MILES TRAVELED ($x_1$) AND
NUMBER OF DELIVERIES ($x_2$) AS THE INDEPENDENT VARIABLES

**CD file**

**Butler**

| Driving Assignment | $x_1$ = Miles Traveled | $x_2$ = Number of Deliveries | $y$ = Travel Time (hours) |
|---|---|---|---|
| 1 | 100 | 4 | 9.3 |
| 2 | 50 | 3 | 4.8 |
| 3 | 100 | 4 | 8.9 |
| 4 | 100 | 2 | 6.5 |
| 5 | 50 | 2 | 4.2 |
| 6 | 80 | 2 | 6.2 |
| 7 | 75 | 3 | 7.4 |
| 8 | 65 | 4 | 6.0 |
| 9 | 90 | 3 | 7.6 |
| 10 | 90 | 2 | 6.1 |

**FIGURE 15.4    MINITAB OUTPUT FOR BUTLER TRUCKING WITH TWO
INDEPENDENT VARIABLES**

*In the Minitab output the
variable names Miles,
Deliv, and Time were
entered as the column
headings on the worksheet;
thus, $x_1$ = Miles, $x_2$ =
Deliv, and y = Time.*

```
The regression equation is
Time = - 0.869 + 0.0611 Miles + 0.923 Deliveries

Predictor         Coef    SE Coef        T      p
Constant       -0.8687     0.9515    -0.91  0.392
Miles         0.061135   0.009888     6.18  0.000
Deliveries      0.9234     0.2211     4.18  0.004


S = 0.5731    R-sq = 90.4%    R-sq(adj) = 87.6%

Analysis of Variance

SOURCE             DF       SS       MS      F      p
Regression          2   21.601   10.800  32.88  0.000
Residual Error      7    2.299    0.328
Total               9   23.900
```

.0611 hours is an estimate of the expected increase in travel time corresponding to an increase
of one mile in the distance traveled when the number of deliveries is held constant. Similarly,
because $b_2$ = .923, an estimate of the expected increase in travel time corresponding to an increase of one delivery when the number of miles traveled is held constant is .923 hours.

## Exercises

*Note to student:* The exercises involving data in this and subsequent sections were designed
to be solved using a computer software package.

## Methods

1. The estimated regression equation for a model involving two independent variables and
   10 observations follows.

   $$\hat{y} = 29.1270 + .5906x_1 + .4980x_2$$

   a. Interpret $b_1$ and $b_2$ in this estimated regression equation.
   b. Estimate y when $x_1$ = 180 and $x_2$ = 310.

2. Consider the following data for a dependent variable y and two independent variables, $x_1$
   and $x_2$.

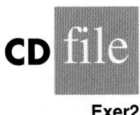

Exer2

| $x_1$ | $x_2$ | y |
|---|---|---|
| 30 | 12 | 94 |
| 47 | 10 | 108 |
| 25 | 17 | 112 |
| 51 | 16 | 178 |
| 40 | 5 | 94 |
| 51 | 19 | 175 |
| 74 | 7 | 170 |

| $x_1$ | $x_2$ | $y$ |
|-------|-------|-----|
| 36 | 12 | 117 |
| 59 | 13 | 142 |
| 76 | 16 | 211 |

a. Develop an estimated regression equation relating $y$ to $x_1$. Estimate $y$ if $x_1 = 45$.
b. Develop an estimated regression equation relating $y$ to $x_2$. Estimate $y$ if $x_2 = 15$.
c. Develop an estimated regression equation relating $y$ to $x_1$ and $x_2$. Estimate $y$ if $x_1 = 45$ and $x_2 = 15$.

3. In a regression analysis involving 30 observations, the following estimated regression equation was obtained.

$$\hat{y} = 17.6 + 3.8x_1 - 2.3x_2 + 7.6x_3 + 2.7x_4$$

a. Interpret $b_1$, $b_2$, $b_3$, and $b_4$ in this estimated regression equation.
b. Estimate $y$ when $x_1 = 10$, $x_2 = 5$, $x_3 = 1$, and $x_4 = 2$.

## Applications

4. A shoe store developed the following estimated regression equation relating sales to inventory investment and advertising expenditures.

$$\hat{y} = 25 + 10x_1 + 8x_2$$

where

$$x_1 = \text{inventory investment (\$1000s)}$$
$$x_2 = \text{advertising expenditures (\$1000s)}$$
$$y = \text{sales (\$1000s)}$$

a. Estimate sales resulting from a $15,000 investment in inventory and an advertising budget of $10,000.
b. Interpret $b_1$ and $b_2$ in this estimated regression equation.

5. The owner of Showtime Movie Theaters, Inc., would like to estimate weekly gross revenue as a function of advertising expenditures. Historical data for a sample of eight weeks follow.

Showtime

| Weekly Gross Revenue ($1000s) | Television Advertising ($1000s) | Newspaper Advertising ($1000s) |
|---|---|---|
| 96 | 5.0 | 1.5 |
| 90 | 2.0 | 2.0 |
| 95 | 4.0 | 1.5 |
| 92 | 2.5 | 2.5 |
| 95 | 3.0 | 3.3 |
| 94 | 3.5 | 2.3 |
| 94 | 2.5 | 4.2 |
| 94 | 3.0 | 2.5 |

a. Develop an estimated regression equation with the amount of television advertising as the independent variable.
b. Develop an estimated regression equation with both television advertising and newspaper advertising as the independent variables.

c.  Is the estimated regression equation coefficient for television advertising expenditures the same in part (a) and in part (b)? Interpret the coefficient in each case.

d.  What is the estimate of the weekly gross revenue for a week when $3500 is spent on television advertising and $1800 is spent on newspaper advertising?

6.  The following table reports the horsepower, curb weight, and the speed at ¼ mile for 16 sports and GT cars (*1998 Road & Track Sports & GT Cars*).

**CD file**

**Auto1**

| Sports & GT Car | Curb Weight (lb.) | Horsepower | Speed at ¼ mile (mph) |
|---|---|---|---|
| Acura Integra Type R | 2577 | 195 | 90.7 |
| Acura NSX-T | 3066 | 290 | 108.0 |
| BMW Z3 2.8 | 2844 | 189 | 93.2 |
| Chevrolet Camaro Z28 | 3439 | 305 | 103.2 |
| Chevrolet Corvette Convertible | 3246 | 345 | 102.1 |
| Dodge Viper RT/10 | 3319 | 450 | 116.2 |
| Ford Mustang GT | 3227 | 225 | 91.7 |
| Honda Prelude Type SH | 3042 | 195 | 89.7 |
| Mercedes-Benz CLK320 | 3240 | 215 | 93.0 |
| Mercedes-Benz SLK230 | 3025 | 185 | 92.3 |
| Mitsubishi 3000GT VR-4 | 3737 | 320 | 99.0 |
| Nissan 240SX SE | 2862 | 155 | 84.6 |
| Pontiac Firebird Trans Am | 3455 | 305 | 103.2 |
| Porsche Boxster | 2822 | 201 | 93.2 |
| Toyota Supra Turbo | 3505 | 320 | 105.0 |
| Volvo C70 | 3285 | 236 | 97.0 |

a.  Use curb weight as the independent variable and the speed at ¼ mile as the dependent variable. What is the estimated regression equation?

b.  Use curb weight and horsepower as two independent variables and the speed at ¼ mile as the dependent variable. What is the estimated regression equation?

c.  The 1999 Porsche 911 Carrera has been advertised as having a curb weight of 2910 pounds and an engine with 296 horsepower. Use the results in part (b) to predict the speed at ¼ mile for the Porsche 911.

7.  Designers of backpacks use exotic material such as supernylon Delrin, high-density polyethylene, aircraft aluminum, and thermomolded foam to make packs that fit comfortably and distribute weight to eliminate pressure points. The following data show the capacity (cubic inches), comfort rating, and price for 10 backpacks tested by *Outside Magazine*. Comfort was measured using a rating from 1 to 5, with a rating of 1 denoting average comfort and a rating of 5 denoting excellent comfort (*Outside Buyer's Guide,* 2001).

**CD file**

**Backpack**

| Manufacturer and Model | Capacity | Comfort | Price |
|---|---|---|---|
| Camp Trails Paragon II | 4330 | 2 | $190 |
| EMS 5500 | 5500 | 3 | 219 |
| Lowe Alpomayo 90+20 | 5500 | 4 | 249 |
| Marmot Muir | 4700 | 3 | 249 |
| Kelly Bigfoot 5200 | 5200 | 4 | 250 |
| Gregory Whitney | 5500 | 4 | 340 |
| Osprey 75 | 4700 | 4 | 389 |
| Arc'Teryx Bora 95 | 5500 | 5 | 395 |
| Dana Design Terraplane LTW | 5800 | 5 | 439 |
| The Works @ Mystery Ranch Jazz | 5000 | 5 | 525 |

    a.   Determine the estimated regression equation that can be used to predict the price of a backpack given the capacity and the comfort rating.

    b.   Interpret $b_1$ and $b_2$.

    c.   Predict the price for a backpack with a capacity of 4500 cubic inches and a comfort rating of 4.

8.   The following table gives the annual return, the safety rating (0 = riskiest, 10 = safest), and the annual expense ratio for 20 foreign funds (*Mutual Funds,* March 2000).

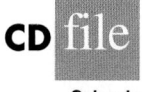

**ForFunds**

| | Safety Rating | Annual Expense Ratio (%) | Annual Return (%) |
|---|---|---|---|
| Accessor Int'l Equity "Adv" | 7.1 | 1.59 | 49 |
| Aetna "I" International | 7.2 | 1.35 | 52 |
| Amer Century Int'l Discovery "Inv" | 6.8 | 1.68 | 89 |
| Columbia International Stock | 7.1 | 1.56 | 58 |
| Concert Inv "A" Int'l Equity | 6.2 | 2.16 | 131 |
| Dreyfus Founders Int'l Equity "F" | 7.4 | 1.80 | 59 |
| Driehaus International Growth | 6.5 | 1.88 | 99 |
| Excelsior "Inst" Int'l Equity | 7.0 | 0.90 | 53 |
| Julius Baer International Equity | 6.9 | 1.79 | 77 |
| Marshall International Stock "Y" | 7.2 | 1.49 | 54 |
| MassMutual Int'l Equity "S" | 7.1 | 1.05 | 57 |
| Morgan Grenfell Int'l Sm Cap "Inst" | 7.7 | 1.25 | 61 |
| New England "A" Int'l Equity | 7.0 | 1.83 | 88 |
| Pilgrim Int'l Small Cap "A" | 7.0 | 1.94 | 122 |
| Republic International Equity | 7.2 | 1.09 | 71 |
| Sit International Growth | 6.9 | 1.50 | 51 |
| Smith Barney "A" Int'l Equity | 7.0 | 1.28 | 60 |
| State St Research "S" Int'l Equity | 7.1 | 1.65 | 50 |
| Strong International Stock | 6.5 | 1.61 | 93 |
| Vontobel International Equity | 7.0 | 1.50 | 47 |

    a.   Develop an estimated regression equation relating the annual return to the safety rating and the annual expense ratio.

    b.   Estimate the annual return for a firm that has a safety rating of 7.5 and annual expense ratio of 2.

9.   Two experts provided subjective lists of school districts that they think are among the best in the country. For each school district the average class size, the combined SAT score, and the percentage of students who attended a four-year college were provided.

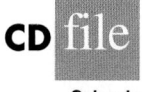

**Schools**

| District | Average Class Size | Combined SAT Score | % Attend Four-Year College |
|---|---|---|---|
| Blue Springs, MO | 25 | 1083 | 74 |
| Garden City, NY | 18 | 997 | 77 |
| Indianapolis, IN | 30 | 716 | 40 |
| Newport Beach, CA | 26 | 977 | 51 |
| Novi, MI | 20 | 980 | 53 |
| Piedmont, CA | 28 | 1042 | 75 |
| Pittsburg, PA | 21 | 983 | 66 |
| Scarsdale, NY | 20 | 1110 | 87 |
| Wayne, PA | 22 | 1040 | 85 |
| Weston, MA | 21 | 1031 | 89 |
| Farmingdale, NY | 22 | 947 | 81 |

*(continued)*

| District | Average Class Size | Combined SAT Score | % Attend Four-Year College |
|---|---|---|---|
| Mamaroneck, NY | 20 | 1000 | 69 |
| Mayfield, OH | 24 | 1003 | 48 |
| Morristown, NJ | 22 | 972 | 64 |
| New Rochelle, NY | 23 | 1039 | 55 |
| Newtown Square, PA | 17 | 963 | 79 |
| Omaha, NE | 23 | 1059 | 81 |
| Shaker Heights, OH | 23 | 940 | 82 |

   a.  Using these data, develop an estimated regression equation relating the percentage of students who attend a four-year college to the average class size and the combined SAT score.
   b.  Estimate the percentage of students who attend a four-year college if the average class size is 20 and the combined SAT score is 1000.

10. *Auto Rental News* provided the following data, which show the number of cars in service (1000s), the number of locations, and the rental revenue ($ millions) for 15 car rental companies (*The Wall Street Journal Almanac 1998*).

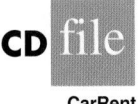

**CarRent**

| Company | Cars | Locations | Revenue |
|---|---|---|---|
| Alamo | 130 | 171 | 1180 |
| Avis | 190 | 1130 | 1500 |
| Budget | 126 | 1052 | 1500 |
| Dollar | 63.5 | 450 | 560 |
| Enterprise | 315.1 | 2636 | 2060 |
| FRCS (Ford) | 55.25 | 1784 | 312.5 |
| Hertz | 250 | 1200 | 2400 |
| National | 135 | 935 | 1200 |
| Payless | 15 | 100 | 47 |
| PROP (Chrysler) | 27 | 1500 | 160 |
| Rent-A-Wreck | 10.9 | 460 | 78 |
| Snappy | 15.5 | 259 | 85 |
| Thrifty | 34 | 480 | 340 |
| U-Save | 13.5 | 500 | 95 |
| Value | 18 | 45 | 150.1 |

   a.  Determine the estimated regression equation that can be used to predict the rental revenue given the number of cars in service.
   b.  Provide an interpretation for the slope of the estimated regression equation developed in part (a).
   c.  Determine the estimated regression equation that can be used to predict the rental revenue given the number of cars in service and the number of locations.

## 15.3 Multiple Coefficient of Determination

In simple linear regression we showed that the total sum of squares can be partitioned into two components: the sum of squares due to regression and the sum of squares due to error. The same procedure applies to the sum of squares in multiple regression.

RELATIONSHIP AMONG SST, SSR, AND SSE

$$SST = SSR + SSE \qquad (15.7)$$

where

$$SST = \text{total sum of squares} = \Sigma(y_i - \bar{y})^2$$
$$SSR = \text{sum of squares due to regression} = \Sigma(\hat{y}_i - \bar{y})^2$$
$$SSE = \text{sum of squares due to error} = \Sigma(y_i - \hat{y}_i)^2$$

Because of the computational difficulty in computing the three sums of squares, we rely on computer packages to determine those values. The analysis of variance part of the Minitab output in Figure 15.4 shows the three values for the Butler Trucking problem with two independent variables: SST = 23.900, SSR = 21.601, and SSE = 2.299. With only one independent variable (number of miles traveled), the Minitab output in Figure 15.3 shows that SST = 23.900, SSR = 15.871, and SSE = 8.029. The value of SST is the same in both cases because it does not depend on $\hat{y}$, but SSR increases and SSE decreases when a second independent variable (number of deliveries) is added. The implication is that the estimated multiple regression equation provides a better fit for the observed data.

In Chapter 14, we used the coefficient of determination, $r^2 = SSR/SST$, to measure the goodness of fit for the estimated regression equation. The same concept applies to multiple regression. The term **multiple coefficient of determination** indicates that we are measuring the goodness of fit for the estimated multiple regression equation. The multiple coefficient of determination, denoted $R^2$, is computed as follows.

MULTIPLE COEFFICIENT OF DETERMINATION

$$R^2 = \frac{SSR}{SST} \tag{15.8}$$

The multiple coefficient of determination can be interpreted as the proportion of the variability in the dependent variable that can be explained by the estimated multiple regression equation. Hence, when multiplied by 100, it can be interpreted as the percentage of the variability in $y$ that can be explained by the estimated regression equation.

In the two-independent-variable Butler Trucking example, with SSR = 21.601 and SST = 23.900, we have

$$R^2 = \frac{21.601}{23.900} = .904$$

Therefore, 90.4% of the variability in travel time $y$ is explained by the estimated multiple regression equation with miles traveled and number of deliveries as the independent variables. In Figure 15.4, we see that the multiple coefficient of determination is also provided by the Minitab output; it is denoted by R-sq = 90.4%.

*Adding independent variables causes the prediction errors to become smaller, thus reducing the sum of squares due to error, SSE. Because SSR = SST − SSE, when SSE becomes smaller, SSR becomes larger, causing $R^2$ = SSR/SST to increase.*

Figure 15.3 shows that the R-sq value for the estimated regression equation with only one independent variable, number of miles traveled ($x_1$), is 66.4%. Thus, the percentage of the variability in travel times that is explained by the estimated regression equation increases from 66.4% to 90.4% when number of deliveries is added as a second independent variable. In general, $R^2$ always increases as independent variables are added to the model.

Many analysts prefer adjusting $R^2$ for the number of independent variables to avoid overestimating the impact of adding an independent variable on the amount of variability explained by the estimated regression equation. With $n$ denoting the number of observations and $p$ denoting the number of independent variables, the **adjusted multiple coefficient of determination** is computed as follows.

*If a variable is added to the model, $R^2$ becomes larger even if the variable added is not statistically significant. The adjusted multiple coefficient of determination compensates for the number of independent variables in the model.*

ADJUSTED MULTIPLE COEFFICIENT OF DETERMINATION

$$R_a^2 = 1 - (1 - R^2)\frac{n - 1}{n - p - 1} \qquad (15.9)$$

For the Butler Trucking example with $n = 10$ and $p = 2$, we have

$$R_a^2 = 1 - (1 - .904)\frac{10 - 1}{10 - 2 - 1} = .88$$

Thus, after adjusting for the two independent variables, we have an adjusted multiple coefficient of determination of .88. This value is provided by the Minitab output in Figure 15.4 as R-sq(adj) = 87.6%; the value we calculated differs because we used a rounded value of $R^2$ in the calculation.

## NOTES AND COMMENTS

If the value of $R^2$ is small and the model contains a large number of independent variables, the adjusted coefficient of determination can take a nega-tive value; in such cases, Minitab sets the adjusted coefficient of determination to zero.

## Exercises

## Methods

11. In exercise 1, the following estimated regression equation based on 10 observations was presented.

    $$\hat{y} = 29.1270 + .5906x_1 + .4980x_2$$

    The values of SST and SSR are 6724.125 and 6216.375, respectively.
    a.  Find SSE.
    b.  Compute $R^2$.
    c.  Compute $R_a^2$.
    d.  Comment on the goodness of fit.

12. In exercise 2, 10 observations were provided for a dependent variable $y$ and two independent variables $x_1$ and $x_2$; for these data SST = 15,182.9, and SSR = 14,052.2.
    a.  Compute $R^2$.
    b.  Compute $R_a^2$.
    c.  Does the estimated regression equation explain a large amount of the variability in the data? Explain.

13. In exercise 3, the following estimated regression equation based on 30 observations was presented.

    $$\hat{y} = 17.6 + 3.8x_1 - 2.3x_2 + 7.6x_3 + 2.7x_4$$

    The values of SST and SSR are 1805 and 1760, respectively.
    a.  Compute $R^2$.
    b.  Compute $R_a^2$.
    c.  Comment on the goodness of fit.

## Applications

14.  In exercise 4, the following estimated regression equation relating sales to inventory investment and advertising expenditures was given.

$$\hat{y} = 25 + 10x_1 + 8x_2$$

The data used to develop the model came from a survey of 10 stores; for those data, SST = 16,000 and SSR = 12,000.
   a.  For the estimated regression equation given, compute $R^2$.
   b.  Compute $R_a^2$.
   c.  Does the model appear to explain a large amount of variability in the data? Explain.

15.  In exercise 5, the owner of Showtime Movie Theaters, Inc., used multiple regression analysis to predict gross revenue ($y$) as a function of television advertising ($x_1$) and newspaper advertising ($x_2$). The estimated regression equation was

$$\hat{y} = 83.2 + 2.29x_1 + 1.30x_2$$

The computer solution provided SST = 25.5 and SSR = 23.435.
   a.  Compute and interpret $R^2$ and $R_a^2$.
   b.  When television advertising was the only independent variable, $R^2 = .653$ and $R_a^2 = .595$. Do you prefer the multiple regression results? Explain.

16.  In exercise 6, data were given on curb weight, horsepower, and speed of a sports and GT car at $\frac{1}{4}$ mile for 16 cars (*1998 Road & Track Sports & GT Cars*).
   a.  Did the estimated regression equation that uses only curb weight to predict the speed at $\frac{1}{4}$ mile provide a good fit? Explain.
   b.  Discuss the benefits of using both the curb weight and the horsepower to predict the speed at $\frac{1}{4}$ mile.

17.  In exercise 9, an estimated regression equation was developed relating the percentage of students who attend a four-year college to the average class size and the combined SAT score.
   a.  Compute and interpret $R^2$ and $R_a^2$.
   b.  Does the estimated regression equation provide a good fit to the data? Explain.

18.  Refer to exercise 10, where data were reported on the number of cars in service (1000s), the number of locations, and the rental revenue ($ millions) for 15 car rental companies (*The Wall Street Journal Almanac 1998*).
   a.  In part (c) of exercise 10, an estimated regression equation was developed relating the rental revenue to the number of cars in service and the number of locations. What are the values of $R^2$ and $R_a^2$?
   b.  Does the estimated regression equation provide a good fit to the data? Explain.

# 15.4  Model Assumptions

In Section 15.1 we introduced the following multiple regression model.

> **MULTIPLE REGRESSION MODEL**
>
> $$y = \beta_0 + \beta_1 x_1 + \beta_2 x_2 + \cdots + \beta_p x_p + \epsilon \qquad (15.10)$$

The assumptions about the error term $\epsilon$ in the multiple regression model parallel those for the simple linear regression model.

**ASSUMPTIONS ABOUT THE ERROR TERM $\epsilon$ IN THE MULTIPLE REGRESSION MODEL** $y = \beta_0 + \beta_1 x_1 + \cdots + \beta_p x_p + \epsilon$

1.  The error $\epsilon$ is a random variable with mean or expected value of zero; that is, $E(\epsilon) = 0$.
    *Implication:* For given values of $x_1, x_2, \ldots, x_p$, the expected, or average, value of $y$ is given by

    $$E(y) = \beta_0 + \beta_1 x_1 + \beta_2 x_2 + \cdots + \beta_p x_p. \qquad \textbf{(15.11)}$$

    Equation (15.11) is the multiple regression equation we introduced in Section 15.1. In this equation, $E(y)$ represents the average of all possible values of $y$ that might occur for the given values of $x_1, x_2, \ldots, x_p$.
2.  The variance of $\epsilon$ is denoted by $\sigma^2$ and is the same for all values of the independent variables $x_1, x_2, \ldots, x_p$.
    *Implication:* The variance of $y$ about the regression line equals $\sigma^2$ and is the same for all values of $x_1, x_2, \ldots, x_p$.
3.  The values of $\epsilon$ are independent.
    *Implication:* The size of the error for a particular set of values for the independent variables is not related to the size of the error for any other set of values.
4.  The error $\epsilon$ is a normally distributed random variable reflecting the deviation between the $y$ value and the expected value of $y$ given by $\beta_0 + \beta_1 x_1 + \beta_2 x_2 + \cdots + \beta_p x_p$.
    *Implication:* Because $\beta_0, \beta_1, \ldots, \beta_p$ are constants for the given values of $x_1, x_2, \ldots, x_p$, the dependent variable $y$ is also a normally distributed random variable.

To obtain more insight about the form of the relationship given by equation (15.11), consider the following two-independent-variable multiple regression equation.

$$E(y) = \beta_0 + \beta_1 x_1 + \beta_2 x_2$$

The graph of this equation is a plane in three-dimensional space. Figure 15.5 provides an example of such a graph. Note that the value of $\epsilon$ shown is the difference between the actual $y$ value and the expected value of $y$, $E(y)$, when $x_1 = x_1^*$ and $x_2 = x_2^*$.

In regression analysis, the term *response variable* is often used in place of the term *dependent variable*. Furthermore, since the multiple regression equation generates a plane or surface, its graph is called a *response surface*.

## (15.5) Testing for Significance

In this section we show how to conduct significance tests for a multiple regression relationship. The significance tests we used in simple linear regression were a $t$ test and an $F$ test. In simple linear regression, both tests provide the same conclusion; that is, if the null hypothesis is rejected, we conclude that $\beta_1 \neq 0$. In multiple regression, the $t$ test and the $F$ test have different purposes.

1.  The $F$ test is used to determine whether a significant relationship exists between the dependent variable and the set of all the independent variables; we will refer to the $F$ test as the test for *overall significance*.

**FIGURE 15.5**   GRAPH OF THE REGRESSION EQUATION FOR MULTIPLE REGRESSION
ANALYSIS WITH TWO INDEPENDENT VARIABLES

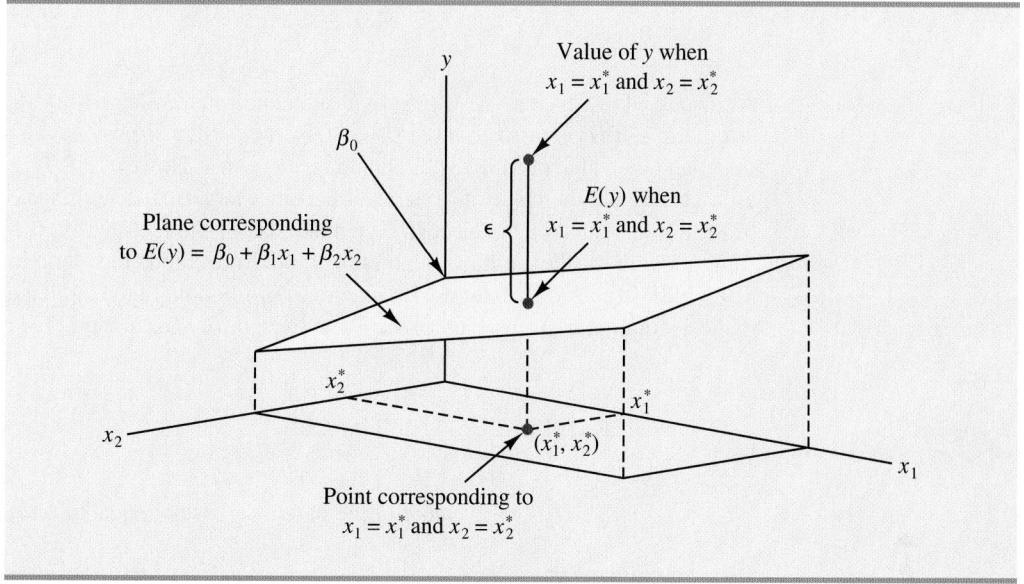

2. If the $F$ test shows an overall significance, the $t$ test is used to determine whether each of the individual independent variables is significant. A separate $t$ test is conducted for each of the independent variables in the model; we refer to each of these $t$ tests as a test for *individual significance.*

In the material that follows, we will explain the $F$ test and the $t$ test and apply each to the Butler Trucking Company example.

## $F$ **Test**

The multiple regression model as defined in Section 15.4 is

$$y = \beta_0 + \beta_1 x_1 + \beta_2 x_2 + \cdots + \beta_p x_p + \epsilon$$

The hypotheses for the $F$ test involve the parameters of the multiple regression model.

$H_0: \beta_1 = \beta_2 = \cdots = \beta_p = 0$
$H_a:$ One or more of the parameters is not equal to zero

If $H_0$ is rejected, the test gives us sufficient statistical evidence to conclude that one or more of the parameters is not equal to zero and that the overall relationship between $y$ and the set of independent variables $x_1, x_2, \ldots, x_p$ is significant. However, if $H_0$ cannot be rejected, we do not have sufficient evidence to conclude that a significant relationship is present.

Before describing the steps of the $F$ test, we need to review the concept of *mean square.* A mean square is a sum of squares divided by its corresponding degrees of freedom. In the multiple regression case, the total sum of squares has $n - 1$ degrees of freedom, the sum of squares due to regression (SSR) has $p$ degrees of freedom, and the sum of squares due to error has $n - p - 1$ degrees of freedom. Hence, the mean square due to regression (MSR) is SSR/$p$ and the mean square due to error (MSE) is SSE/$(n - p - 1)$.

$$\text{MSR} = \frac{\text{SSR}}{p} \qquad\qquad \textbf{(15.12)}$$

and

$$\text{MSE} = \frac{\text{SSE}}{n - p - 1} \tag{15.13}$$

As discussed in Chapter 14, MSE provides an unbiased estimate of $\sigma^2$, the variance of the error term $\epsilon$. If $H_0: \beta_1 = \beta_2 = \cdots = \beta_p = 0$ is true, MSR also provides an unbiased estimate of $\sigma^2$, and the value of MSR/MSE should be close to 1. However, if $H_0$ is false, MSR overestimates $\sigma^2$ and the value of MSR/MSE becomes larger. To determine how large the value of MSR/MSE must be to reject $H_0$, we make use of the fact that if $H_0$ is true and the assumptions about the multiple regression model are valid, the sampling distribution of MSR/MSE is an $F$ distribution with $p$ degrees of freedom in the numerator and $n - p - 1$ in the denominator. A summary of the $F$ test for significance in multiple regression follows.

---

**$F$ TEST FOR OVERALL SIGNIFICANCE**

$H_0: \beta_1 = \beta_2 = \cdots = \beta_p = 0$
$H_a$: One or more of the parameters is not equal to zero

**TEST STATISTIC**

$$F = \frac{\text{MSR}}{\text{MSE}} \tag{15.14}$$

**REJECTION RULE**

| | |
|---|---|
| $p$-value approach: | Reject $H_0$ if $p$-value $\leq \alpha$ |
| Critical value approach: | Reject $H_0$ if $F \geq F_\alpha$ |

where $F_\alpha$ is based on an $F$ distribution with $p$ degrees of freedom in the numerator and $n - p - 1$ degrees of freedom in the denominator.

---

Let us apply the $F$ test to the Butler Trucking Company multiple regression problem. With two independent variables, the hypotheses are written as follows.

$$H_0: \beta_1 = \beta_2 = 0$$
$$H_a: \beta_1 \text{ and/or } \beta_2 \text{ is not equal to zero}$$

Figure 15.6 is the Minitab output for the multiple regression model with miles traveled ($x_1$) and number of deliveries ($x_2$) as the two independent variables. In the analysis of variance part of the output, we see that MSR = 10.8 and MSE = .328. Using equation (15.14), we obtain the test statistic.

$$F = \frac{10.8}{.328} = 32.9$$

Note that the $F$ value on the Minitab output is $F = 32.88$; the value we calculated differs because we used rounded values for MSR and MSE in the calculation. Using $\alpha = .01$, the $p$-value = 0.000 in the last column of the analysis of variance table (Figure 15.6) indicates that we can reject $H_0: \beta_1 = \beta_2 = 0$ because the $p$-value is less than $\alpha = .01$. Alternatively,

**FIGURE 15.6**    MINITAB OUTPUT FOR BUTLER TRUCKING WITH TWO INDEPENDENT
VARIABLES, MILES TRAVELED ($x_1$) AND NUMBER OF DELIVERIES ($x_2$)

```
The regression equation is
Time = - 0.869 + 0.0611 Miles + 0.923 Deliveries

Predictor        Coef    SE Coef        T       p
Constant      -0.8687     0.9515    -0.91   0.392
Miles        0.061135   0.009888     6.18   0.000
Deliveries     0.9234     0.2211     4.18   0.004

S = 0.5731    R-sq = 90.4%   R-sq(adj) = 87.6%

Analysis of Variance

SOURCE            DF       SS       MS       F       p
Regression         2   21.601   10.800   32.88   0.000
Residual Error     7    2.299    0.328
Total              9   23.900
```

Table 4 of Appendix B shows that with two degrees of freedom in the numerator and seven degrees of freedom in the denominator, $F_{.01} = 9.55$. With $32.9 > 9.55$, we reject $H_0\colon \beta_1 = \beta_2 = 0$ and conclude that a significant relationship is present between travel time $y$ and the two independent variables, miles traveled and number of deliveries.

As noted previously, the mean square error provides an unbiased estimate of $\sigma^2$, the variance of the error term $\epsilon$. Referring to Figure 15.6, we see that the estimate of $\sigma^2$ is MSE = .328. The square root of MSE is the estimate of the standard deviation of the error term. As defined in Section 14.5, this standard deviation is called the standard error of the estimate and is denoted $s$. Hence, we have $s = \sqrt{\text{MSE}} = \sqrt{.328} = .573$. Note that the value of the standard error of the estimate appears in the Minitab output in Figure 15.6.

Table 15.3 is the general analysis of variance (ANOVA) table that provides the $F$ test results for a multiple regression model. The value of the $F$ test statistic appears in the last column and can be compared to $F_\alpha$ with $p$ degrees of freedom in the numerator and $n - p - 1$ degrees of freedom in the denominator to make the hypothesis test conclusion. By reviewing the Minitab output for Butler Trucking Company in Figure 15.6, we see that Minitab's analysis of variance table contains this information. Moreover, Minitab also provides the $p$-value corresponding to the $F$ test statistic.

**TABLE 15.3**    ANOVA TABLE FOR A MULTIPLE REGRESSION MODEL WITH $p$
INDEPENDENT VARIABLES

| Source | Sum of Squares | Degrees of Freedom | Mean Square | $F$ |
|---|---|---|---|---|
| Regression | SSR | $p$ | $\text{MSR} = \dfrac{\text{SSR}}{p}$ | $F = \dfrac{\text{MSR}}{\text{MSE}}$ |
| Error | SSE | $n - p - 1$ | $\text{MSE} = \dfrac{\text{SSE}}{n - p - 1}$ | |
| Total | SST | $n - 1$ | | |

## t Test

If the $F$ test shows that the multiple regression relationship is significant, a $t$ test can be conducted to determine the significance of each of the individual parameters. The $t$ test for individual significance follows.

---

$t$ TEST FOR INDIVIDUAL SIGNIFICANCE

For any parameter $\beta_i$

$$H_0: \beta_i = 0$$
$$H_a: \beta_i \neq 0$$

TEST STATISTIC

$$t = \frac{b_i}{s_{b_i}} \tag{15.15}$$

REJECTION RULE

$p$-value approach:        Reject $H_0$ if $p$-value $\leq \alpha$

Critical value approach:   Reject $H_0$ if $t \leq t_{\alpha/2}$ or if $t \geq t_{\alpha/2}$

where $t_{\alpha/2}$ is based on a $t$ distribution with $n - p - 1$ degrees of freedom.

---

In the test statistic, $s_{b_i}$ is the estimate of the standard deviation of $b_i$. The value of $s_{b_i}$ will be provided by the computer software package.

Let us conduct the $t$ test for the Butler Trucking regression problem. Refer to the section of Figure 15.6 that shows the Minitab output for the $t$-ratio calculations. Values of $b_1$, $b_2$, $s_{b_1}$, and $s_{b_2}$ are as follows.

$$b_1 = .061135 \quad s_{b_1} = .009888$$
$$b_2 = .9234 \quad s_{b_2} = .2211$$

Using equation (15.15), we obtain the test statistic for the hypotheses involving parameters $\beta_1$ and $\beta_2$.

$$t = .061135/.009888 = 6.18$$
$$t = .9234/.2211 = 4.18$$

Note that both of these $t$-ratio values and the corresponding $p$-values are provided by the Minitab output in Figure 15.6. Using $\alpha = .01$, the $p$-values of .000 and .004 on the Minitab output indicate that we can reject $H_0: \beta_1 = 0$ and $H_0: \beta_2 = 0$. Hence, both parameters are statistically significant. Alternatively, Table 2 of Appendix B shows that with $n - p - 1 = 10 - 2 - 1 = 7$ degrees of freedom, $t_{.005} = 3.499$. With $6.18 > 3.499$, we reject $H_0: \beta_1 = 0$. Similarly, with $4.18 > 3.499$, we reject $H_0: \beta_2 = 0$.

## Multicollinearity

We used the term *independent variable* in regression analysis to refer to any variable being used to predict or explain the value of the dependent variable. The term does not mean, however, that the independent variables themselves are independent in any statistical sense. On the contrary, most independent variables in a multiple regression problem are correlated to some degree with one another. For example, in the Butler Trucking example involving the two independent variables $x_1$ (miles traveled) and $x_2$ (number of deliveries), we could treat the miles traveled as the dependent variable and the number of deliveries as the independent variable to determine whether those two variables are themselves related. We could then compute the sample correlation coefficient $r_{x_1 x_2}$ to determine the extent to which the variables are related. Doing so yields $r_{x_1 x_2} = .16$. Thus, we find some degree of linear association between the two independent variables. In multiple regression analysis, **multicollinearity** refers to the correlation among the independent variables.

To provide a better perspective of the potential problems of multicollinearity, let us consider a modification of the Butler Trucking example. Instead of $x_2$ being the number of deliveries, let $x_2$ denote the number of gallons of gasoline consumed. Clearly, $x_1$ (the miles traveled) and $x_2$ are related; that is, we know that the number of gallons of gasoline used depends on the number of miles traveled. Hence, we would conclude logically that $x_1$ and $x_2$ are highly correlated independent variables.

Assume that we obtain the equation $\hat{y} = b_0 + b_1 x_1 + b_2 x_2$ and find that the $F$ test shows the relationship to be significant. Then suppose we conduct a $t$ test on $\beta_1$ to determine whether $\beta_1 \neq 0$, and we cannot reject $H_0: \beta_1 = 0$. Does this result mean that travel time is not related to miles traveled? Not necessarily. What it probably means is that with $x_2$ already in the model, $x_1$ does not make a significant contribution to determining the value of $y$. This interpretation makes sense in our example; if we know the amount of gasoline consumed, we do not gain much additional information useful in predicting $y$ by knowing the miles traveled. Similarly, a $t$ test might lead us to conclude $\beta_2 = 0$ on the grounds that, with $x_1$ in the model, knowledge of the amount of gasoline consumed does not add much.

To summarize, in $t$ tests for the significance of individual parameters, the difficulty caused by multicollinearity is that it is possible to conclude that none of the individual parameters are significantly different from zero when an $F$ test on the overall multiple regression equation indicates a significant relationship. This problem is avoided when there is little correlation among the independent variables.

*A sample correlation coefficient greater than +0.70 or less than −0.70 for two independent variables is a rule of thumb warning of potential problems with multicollinearity.*

Statisticians have developed several tests for determining whether multicollinearity is high enough to cause problems. According to the rule of thumb test, multicollinearity is a potential problem if the absolute value of the sample correlation coefficient exceeds .7 for any two of the independent variables. The other types of tests are more advanced and beyond the scope of this text.

*When the independent variables are highly correlated, it is not possible to determine the separate effect of any particular independent variable on the dependent variable.*

If possible, every attempt should be made to avoid including independent variables that are highly correlated. In practice, however, strict adherence to this policy is rarely possible. When decision makers have reason to believe substantial multicollinearity is present, they must realize that separating the effects of the individual independent variables on the dependent variable is difficult.

## NOTES AND COMMENTS

Ordinarily, multicollinearity does not affect the way in which we perform our regression analysis or interpret the output from a study. However, when multicollinearity is severe—that is, when two or more of the independent variables are highly correlated with one another—we can have difficulty interpreting the results of $t$ tests on the individual parameters. In addition to the type of problem illustrated in this section, severe cases of multicollinearity have been shown to result in least squares estimates that have the wrong sign. That is,

in simulated studies where researchers created the underlying regression model and then applied the least squares technique to develop estimates of $\beta_0$, $\beta_1, \beta_2$, and so on, it has been shown that under conditions of high multicollinearity the least squares estimates can have a sign opposite that of the parameter being estimated. For example, $\beta_2$ might actually be $+10$ and $\beta_2$, its estimate, might turn out to be $-2$. Thus, little faith can be placed in the individual coefficients if multicollinearity is present to a high degree.

## Exercises

### Methods

19. In exercise 1, the following estimated regression equation based on 10 observations was presented.

$$\hat{y} = 29.1270 + .5906x_1 + .4980x_2$$

Here SST = 6724.125, SSR = 6216.375, $s_{b_1}$ = .0813, and $s_{b_2}$ = .0567.
   a. Compute MSR and MSE.
   b. Compute $F$ and perform the appropriate $F$ test. Use $\alpha = .05$.
   c. Perform a $t$ test for the significance of $\beta_1$. Use $\alpha = .05$.
   d. Perform a $t$ test for the significance of $\beta_2$. Use $\alpha = .05$.

20. Refer to the data presented in exercise 2. The estimated regression equation for these data is

$$\hat{y} = -18.4 + 2.01x_1 + 4.74x_2$$

Here SST = 15,182.9, SSR = 14,052.2, $s_{b_1}$ = .2471, and $s_{b_2}$ = .9484.
   a. Test for a significant relationship among $x_1$, $x_2$, and $y$. Use $\alpha = .05$.
   b. Is $\beta_1$ significant? Use $\alpha = .05$.
   c. Is $\beta_2$ significant? Use $\alpha = .05$.

21. The following estimated regression equation was developed for a model involving two independent variables.

$$\hat{y} = 40.7 + 8.63x_1 + 2.71x_2$$

After $x_2$ was dropped from the model, the least squares method was used to obtain an estimated regression equation involving only $x_1$ as an independent variable.

$$\hat{y} = 42.0 + 9.01x_1$$

   a. Give an interpretation of the coefficient of $x_1$ in both models.
   b. Could multicollinearity explain why the coefficient of $x_1$ differs in the two models? If so, how?

### Applications

22. In exercise 4 the following estimated regression equation relating sales to inventory investment and advertising expenditures was given.

$$\hat{y} = 25 + 10x_1 + 8x_2$$

The data used to develop the model came from a survey of 10 stores; for these data SST = 16,000 and SSR = 12,000.
   a. Compute SSE, MSE, and MSR.
   b. Use an $F$ test and a .05 level of significance to determine whether there is a relationship among the variables.

23. Refer to Exercise 5.
   a. Use $\alpha = .01$ to test the hypotheses

$$H_0: \beta_1 = \beta_2 = 0$$
$$H_a: \beta_1 \text{ and/or } \beta_2 \text{ is not equal to zero}$$

for the model $y = \beta_0 + \beta_1 x_1 + \beta_2 x_2 + \epsilon$, where

$$x_1 = \text{television advertising (\$1000s)}$$
$$x_2 = \text{newspaper advertising (1000s)}$$

b.  Use $\alpha = .05$ to test the significance of $\beta_1$. Should $x_1$ be dropped from the model?

c.  Use $\alpha = .05$ to test the significance of $\beta_2$. Should $x_2$ be dropped from the model?

24.  Refer to the data in exercise 6. Use curb weight and horsepower to predict the speed of a sports and GT car at $\frac{1}{4}$ mile.

a.  Use the $F$ test to determine the overall significance of the relationship. What is your conclusion at the .05 level of significance?

b.  Use the $t$ test to determine the significance of each independent variable. What is your conclusion at the .05 level of significance?

25.  *Barron's* conducts an annual review of online brokers, including both brokers that can be accessed via a Web browser, as well as direct-access brokers that connect customers directly with the broker's network server. Each broker's offerings and performance are evaluated in six areas, using a point value of 0–5 in each category. The results are weighted to obtain an overall score, and a final star rating, ranging from zero to five stars, is assigned to each broker. Trade execution, ease of use, and range of offerings are three of the areas evaluated. A point value of 5 in the trade execution area means the order entry and execution process flowed easily from one step to the next. A value of 5 in the ease of use area means that the site was easy to use and can be tailored to show what the user wants to see. A value of 5 in the range offerings area means that all of the investment transactions can be executed online. The following data show the point values for trade execution, ease of use, range of offerings, and the star rating for a sample of 10 of the online brokers that *Barron's* evaluated (*Barron's,* March 10, 2003).

**CD file**

**Brokers**

| Broker | Trade Execution | Use | Range | Rating |
|--------|-----------------|-----|-------|--------|
| Wall St. Access | 3.7 | 4.5 | 4.8 | 4.0 |
| E*TRADE (Power) | 3.4 | 3.0 | 4.2 | 3.5 |
| E*TRADE (Standard) | 2.5 | 4.0 | 4.0 | 3.5 |
| Preferred Trade | 4.8 | 3.7 | 3.4 | 3.5 |
| my Track | 4.0 | 3.5 | 3.2 | 3.5 |
| TD Waterhouse | 3.0 | 3.0 | 4.6 | 3.5 |
| Brown & Co. | 2.7 | 2.5 | 3.3 | 3.0 |
| Brokerage America | 1.7 | 3.5 | 3.1 | 3.0 |
| Merrill Lynch Direct | 2.2 | 2.7 | 3.0 | 2.5 |
| Strong Funds | 1.4 | 3.6 | 2.5 | 2.0 |

a.  Determine the estimated regression equation that can be used to predict the star rating given the point values for execution, ease of use, and range of offerings.

b.  Use the $F$ test to determine the overall significance of the relationship. What is the conclusion at the .05 level of significance?

c.  Use the $t$ test to determine the significance of each independent variable. What is your conclusion at the .05 level of significance?

d.  Remove any independent variable that is not significant from the estimated regression equation. What is your recommended estimated regression equation? Compare the $R^2$ with the value of $R^2$ from part (a). Discuss the differences.

26.  In exercise 10 an estimated regression equation was developed relating the rental revenue to the number of cars in service and the number of locations.

a.  Test for a significant relationship between the dependent variable and the two independent variables. Use $\alpha = .05$.

b.  Is the number of cars in service significant? Use $\alpha = .05$.

c.  Is the number of locations significant? Use $\alpha = .05$.

# 15.6 Using the Estimated Regression Equation for Estimation and Prediction

The procedures for estimating the mean value of $y$ and predicting an individual value of $y$ in multiple regression are similar to those in regression analysis involving one independent variable. First, recall that in Chapter 14 we showed that the point estimate of the expected value of $y$ for a given value of $x$ was the same as the point estimate of an individual value of $y$. In both cases, we used $\hat{y} = b_0 + b_1 x$ as the point estimate.

In multiple regression we use the same procedure. That is, we substitute the given values of $x_1, x_2, \ldots, x_p$ into the estimated regression equation and use the corresponding value of $\hat{y}$ as the point estimate. Suppose that for the Butler Trucking example we want to use the estimated regression equation involving $x_1$ (miles traveled) and $x_2$ (number of deliveries) to develop two interval estimates:

1. A *confidence interval* of the mean travel time for all trucks that travel 100 miles and make two deliveries
2. A *prediction interval* of the travel time for *one specific* truck that travels 100 miles and makes two deliveries

Using the estimated regression equation $\hat{y} = -.869 + .0611x_1 + .923x_2$ with $x_1 = 100$ and $x_2 = 2$, we obtain the following value of $\hat{y}$.

$$\hat{y} = -.869 + .0611(100) + .923(2) = 7.09$$

Hence, the point estimate of travel time in both cases is approximately seven hours.

To develop interval estimates for the mean value of $y$ and for an individual value of $y$, we use a procedure similar to that for regression analysis involving one independent variable. The formulas required are beyond the scope of the text, but computer packages for multiple regression analysis will often provide confidence intervals once the values of $x_1$, $x_2, \ldots, x_p$ are specified by the user. In Table 15.4 we show the 95% confidence and prediction intervals for the Butler Trucking example for selected values of $x_1$ and $x_2$; these values were obtained using Minitab. Note that the interval estimate for an individual value of $y$ is wider than the interval estimate for the expected value of $y$. This difference simply reflects the fact that for given values of $x_1$ and $x_2$ we can estimate the mean travel time for all trucks with more precision than we can predict the travel time for one specific truck.

**TABLE 15.4**  THE 95% CONFIDENCE AND PREDICTION INTERVALS FOR BUTLER TRUCKING

| Value of $x_1$ | Value of $x_2$ | Confidence Interval | | Prediction Interval | |
|---|---|---|---|---|---|
| | | **Lower Limit** | **Upper Limit** | **Lower Limit** | **Upper Limit** |
| 50 | 2 | 3.146 | 4.924 | 2.414 | 5.656 |
| 50 | 3 | 4.127 | 5.789 | 3.368 | 6.548 |
| 50 | 4 | 4.815 | 6.948 | 4.157 | 7.607 |
| 100 | 2 | 6.258 | 7.926 | 5.500 | 8.683 |
| 100 | 3 | 7.385 | 8.645 | 6.520 | 9.510 |
| 100 | 4 | 8.135 | 9.742 | 7.362 | 10.515 |

## Exercises

## Methods

27. In exercise 1, the following estimated regression equation based on 10 observations was presented.

$$\hat{y} = 29.1270 + .5906x_1 + .4980x_2$$

    a. Develop a point estimate of the mean value of $y$ when $x_1 = 180$ and $x_2 = 310$.
    b. Develop a point estimate for an individual value of $y$ when $x_1 = 180$ and $x_2 = 310$.

28. Refer to the data in exercise 2. The estimated regression equation for those data is

$$\hat{y} = -18.4 + 2.01x_1 + 4.74x_2$$

    a. Develop a 95% confidence interval for the mean value of $y$ when $x_1 = 45$ and $x_2 = 15$.
    b. Develop a 95% prediction interval for $y$ when $x_1 = 45$ and $x_2 = 15$.

## Applications

29. In exercise 5, the owner of Showtime Movie Theaters, Inc., used multiple regression analysis to predict gross revenue ($y$) as a function of television advertising ($x_1$) and newspaper advertising ($x_2$). The estimated regression equation was

$$\hat{y} = 83.2 + 2.29x_1 + 1.30x_2$$

    a. What is the gross revenue expected for a week when $3500 is spent on television advertising ($x_1 = 3.5$) and $1800 is spent on newspaper advertising ($x_2 = 1.8$)?
    b. Provide a 95% confidence interval for the mean revenue of all weeks with the expenditures listed in part (a).
    c. Provide a 95% prediction interval for next week's revenue, assuming that the advertising expenditures will be allocated as in part (a).

30. In exercise 6, data were given on curb weight, horsepower, and speed at ¼ mile for 16 sports and GT cars (*1998 Road and Track Sports & GT Cars*).
    a. Estimate the ¼-mile speed of a 1999 Porsche 911 Carrera that has a curb weight of 2910 pounds and a horsepower of 296.
    b. Provide a 95% confidence interval for the ¼-mile speed of all sports and GT cars with the characteristics listed in part (a).
    c. Provide a 95% prediction interval for the 1999 Porsche 911 Carrera described in part (a).

31. In exercise 9, an estimated regression equation was developed relating the percentage of students who attend a four-year college to the average class size and the combined SAT score.
    a. Develop a 95% confidence interval for the mean percentage of students who attend a four-year college for a school district that has an average class size of 25 and whose students have a combined SAT score of 1000.
    b. Suppose that a school district in Conway, South Carolina, has an average class size of 25 and a combined SAT score of 950. Develop a 95% prediction interval for the percentage of students who attend a four-year college.

# 15.7 Qualitative Independent Variables

*The independent variables may be qualitative or quantitative.*

Thus far, the examples we considered involved quantitative independent variables such as student population, distance traveled, and number of deliveries. In many situations, however, we must work with **qualitative independent variables** such as gender (male, female), method of payment (cash, credit card, check), and so on. The purpose of this section is to show how qualitative variables are handled in regression analysis. To illustrate the use and interpretation of a qualitative independent variable, we will consider a problem facing the managers of Johnson Filtration, Inc.

## An Example: Johnson Filtration, Inc.

Johnson Filtration, Inc., provides maintenance service for water-filtration systems throughout southern Florida. Customers contact Johnson with requests for maintenance service on their water-filtration systems. To estimate the service time and the service cost, Johnson's managers want to predict the repair time necessary for each maintenance request. Hence, repair time in hours is the dependent variable. Repair time is believed to be related to two factors, the number of months since the last maintenance service and the type of repair problem (mechanical or electrical). Data for a sample of 10 service calls are reported in Table 15.5.

Let $y$ denote the repair time in hours and $x_1$ denote the number of months since the last maintenance service. The regression model that uses only $x_1$ to predict $y$ is

$$y = \beta_0 + \beta_1 x_1 + \epsilon$$

Using Minitab to develop the estimated regression equation, we obtained the output shown in Figure 15.7. The estimated regression equation is

$$\hat{y} = 2.15 + .304x_1 \tag{15.16}$$

At the .05 level of significance, the $p$-value of .016 for the $t$ (or $F$) test indicates that the number of months since the last service is significantly related to repair time. R-sq = 53.4% indicates that $x_1$ alone explains 53.4% of the variability in repair time.

To incorporate the type of failure into the regression model, we define the following variable.

$$x_2 = \begin{cases} 0 \text{ if the type of repair is mechanical} \\ 1 \text{ if the type of repair is electrical} \end{cases}$$

**TABLE 15.5**  DATA FOR THE JOHNSON FILTRATION EXAMPLE

| Service Call | Months Since Last Service | Type of Repair | Repair Time in Hours |
|---|---|---|---|
| 1 | 2 | electrical | 2.9 |
| 2 | 6 | mechanical | 3.0 |
| 3 | 8 | electrical | 4.8 |
| 4 | 3 | mechanical | 1.8 |
| 5 | 2 | electrical | 2.9 |
| 6 | 7 | electrical | 4.9 |
| 7 | 9 | mechanical | 4.2 |
| 8 | 8 | mechanical | 4.8 |
| 9 | 4 | electrical | 4.4 |
| 10 | 6 | electrical | 4.5 |

FIGURE 15.7   MINITAB OUTPUT FOR JOHNSON FILTRATION WITH MONTHS
SINCE LAST SERVICE ($x_1$) AS THE INDEPENDENT VARIABLE

*In the Minitab output the variable names* Months *and* Time *were entered as the column headings on the worksheet; thus,* $x_1$ = Months *and* $y$ = Time.

```
The regression equation is
Time = 2.15 + 0.304 Months


Predictor      Coef   SE Coef      T       p
Constant     2.1473    0.6050    3.55   0.008
Months       0.3041    0.1004    3.03   0.016


S = 0.7810    R-sq = 53.4%    R-sq(adj) = 47.6%


Analysis of Variance

SOURCE            DF         SS         MS       F       p
Regression         1     5.5960     5.5960    9.17   0.016
Residual Error     8     4.8800     0.6100
Total              9    10.4760
```

In regression analysis $x_2$ is called a **dummy** or *indicator* **variable**. Using this dummy variable, we can write the multiple regression model as

$$y = \beta_0 + \beta_1 x_1 + \beta_2 x_2 + \epsilon$$

Table 15.6 is the revised data set that includes the values of the dummy variable. Using Minitab and the data in Table 15.6, we can develop estimates of the model parameters. The Minitab output in Figure 15.8 shows that the estimated multiple regression equation is

$$\hat{y} = .93 + .388 x_1 + 1.26 x_2 \tag{15.17}$$

At the .05 level of significance, the $p$-value of .001 associated with the $F$ test ($F = 21.36$) indicates that the regression relationship is significant. The $t$ test part of the printout in

TABLE 15.6   DATA FOR THE JOHNSON FILTRATION EXAMPLE WITH TYPE OF REPAIR
INDICATED BY A DUMMY VARIABLE ($x_2$ = 0 FOR MECHANICAL; $x_2$ = 1
FOR ELECTRICAL)

**CD file**

**Johnson**

| Customer | Months Since Last Service ($x_1$) | Type of Repair ($x_2$) | Repair Time in Hours ($y$) |
|---|---|---|---|
| 1 | 2 | 1 | 2.9 |
| 2 | 6 | 0 | 3.0 |
| 3 | 8 | 1 | 4.8 |
| 4 | 3 | 0 | 1.8 |
| 5 | 2 | 1 | 2.9 |
| 6 | 7 | 1 | 4.9 |
| 7 | 9 | 0 | 4.2 |
| 8 | 8 | 0 | 4.8 |
| 9 | 4 | 1 | 4.4 |
| 10 | 6 | 1 | 4.5 |

**FIGURE 15.8    MINITAB OUTPUT FOR JOHNSON FILTRATION WITH MONTHS SINCE LAST SERVICE $(x_1)$ AND TYPE OF REPAIR $(x_2)$ AS THE INDEPENDENT VARIABLES**

*In the Minitab output the variable names* Months, Type, *and* Time *were entered as the column headings on the worksheet; thus, $x_1$ =* Months, $x_2$ = Type, *and y =* Time.

```
The regression equation is
Time = 0.930 + 0.388 Months + 1.26 Type

Predictor      Coef   SE Coef      T      p
Constant     0.9305    0.4670   1.99  0.087
Months      0.38762   0.06257   6.20  0.000
Type         1.2627    0.3141   4.02  0.005


S = 0.4590    R-sq = 85.9%    R-sq(adj) = 81.9%

Analysis of Variance

SOURCE          DF        SS       MS       F      p
Regression       2    9.0009   4.5005   21.36  0.001
Residual Error   7    1.4751   0.2107
Total            9   10.4760
```

Figure 15.8 shows that both months since last service ( *p*-value = .000) and type of repair ( *p*-value = .005) are statistically significant. In addition, R-sq = 85.9% and R-sq(adj) = 81.9% indicate that the estimated regression equation does a good job of explaining the variability in repair times. Thus, equation (15.17) should prove helpful in estimating the repair time necessary for the various service calls.

## Interpreting the Parameters

The multiple regression equation for the Johnson Filtration example is

$$E(y) = \beta_0 + \beta_1 x_1 + \beta_2 x_2 \tag{15.18}$$

To understand how to interpret the parameters $\beta_0$, $\beta_1$, and $\beta_2$ when a qualitative variable is present, consider the case when $x_2 = 0$ (mechanical repair). Using $E(y \mid \text{mechanical})$ to denote the mean or expected value of repair time *given* a mechanical repair, we have

$$E(y \mid \text{mechanical}) = \beta_0 + \beta_1 x_1 + \beta_2(0) = \beta_0 + \beta_1 x_1 \tag{15.19}$$

Similarly, for an electrical repair $(x_2 = 1)$, we have

$$E(y \mid \text{electrical}) = \beta_0 + \beta_1 x_1 + \beta_2(1) = \beta_0 + \beta_1 x_1 + \beta_2 \tag{15.20}$$
$$= (\beta_0 + \beta_2) + \beta_1 x_1$$

Comparing equations (15.19) and (15.20), we see that the mean repair time is a linear function of $x_1$ for both mechanical and electrical repairs. The slope of both equations is $\beta_1$, but the *y*-intercept differs. The *y*-intercept is $\beta_0$ in equation (15.19) for mechanical repairs and $(\beta_0 + \beta_2)$ in equation (15.20) for electrical repairs. The interpretation of $\beta_2$ is that it indicates the difference between the mean repair time for an electrical repair and the mean repair time for a mechanical repair.

If $\beta_2$ is positive, the mean repair time for an electrical repair will be greater than that for a mechanical repair; if $\beta_2$ is negative, the mean repair time for an electrical repair will be less than that for a mechanical repair. Finally, if $\beta_2 = 0$, there is no difference in the mean repair time between electrical and mechanical repairs and the type of repair is not related to the repair time.

Using the estimated multiple regression equation $\hat{y} = .93 + .388x_1 + 1.26x_2$, we see that .93 is the estimate of $\beta_0$ and 1.26 is the estimate of $\beta_2$. Thus, when $x_2 = 0$ (mechanical repair)

$$\hat{y} = .93 + .388x_1 \qquad\qquad (15.21)$$

and when $x_2 = 1$ (electrical repair)

$$\begin{aligned} \hat{y} &= .93 + .388x_1 + 1.26(1) \qquad\qquad (15.22) \\ &= 2.19 + .388x_1 \end{aligned}$$

In effect, the use of a dummy variable for type of repair provides two equations that can be used to predict the repair time, one corresponding to mechanical repairs and one corresponding to electrical repairs. In addition, with $b_2 = 1.26$, we learn that, on average, electrical repairs require 1.26 hours longer than mechanical repairs.

Figure 15.9 is the plot of the Johnson data from Table 15.6. Repair time in hours ( $y$ ) is represented by the vertical axis and months since last service ($x_1$) is represented by the horizontal axis. A data point for a mechanical repair is indicated by an M and a data point for

**FIGURE 15.9    SCATTER DIAGRAM FOR THE JOHNSON FILTRATION REPAIR DATA
FROM TABLE 15.6**

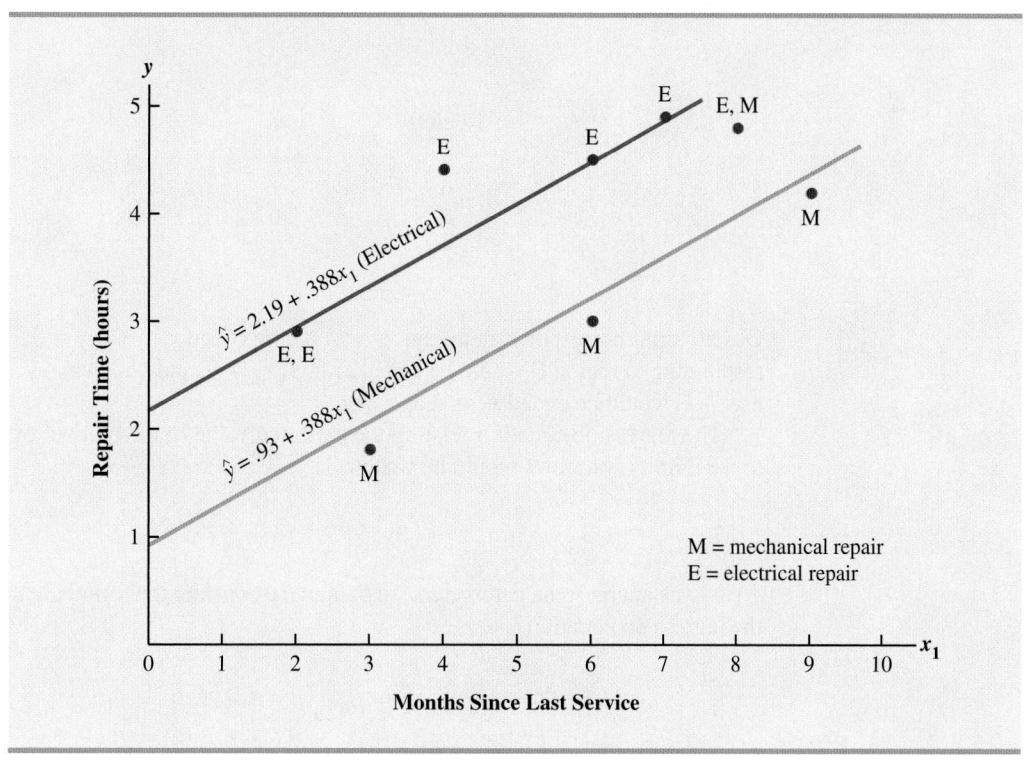

an electrical repair is indicated by an E. Equations (15.21) and (15.22) are plotted on the graph to show graphically the two equations that can be used to predict the repair time, one corresponding to mechanical repairs and one corresponding to electrical repairs.

## More Complex Qualitative Variables

*A qualitative variable with k levels must be modeled using k − 1 dummy variables. Care must be taken in defining and interpreting the dummy variables.*

Because the qualitative variable for the Johnson Filtration example had two levels (mechanical and electrical), defining a dummy variable with zero indicating a mechanical repair and one indicating an electrical repair was easy. However, when a qualitative variable has more than two levels, care must be taken in both defining and interpreting the dummy variables. As we will show, if a qualitative variable has $k$ levels, $k − 1$ dummy variables are required, with each dummy variable being coded as 0 or 1.

For example, suppose a manufacturer of copy machines organized the sales territories for a particular state into three regions: A, B, and C. The managers want to use regression analysis to help predict the number of copiers sold per week. With the number of units sold as the dependent variable, they are considering several independent variables (the number of sales personnel, advertising expenditures, and so on). Suppose the managers believe sales region is also an important factor in predicting the number of copiers sold. Because sales region is a qualitative variable with three levels, A, B and C, we will need $3 − 1 = 2$ dummy variables to represent the sales region. Each variable can be coded 0 or 1 as follows.

$$x_1 = \begin{cases} 1 \text{ if sales region B} \\ 0 \text{ otherwise} \end{cases}$$

$$x_2 = \begin{cases} 1 \text{ if sales region C} \\ 0 \text{ otherwise} \end{cases}$$

With this definition, we have the following values of $x_1$ and $x_2$.

| Region | $x_1$ | $x_2$ |
|--------|-------|-------|
| A | 0 | 0 |
| B | 1 | 0 |
| C | 0 | 1 |

Observations corresponding to region A would be coded $x_1 = 0$, $x_2 = 0$; observations corresponding to region B would be coded $x_1 = 1$, $x_2 = 0$; and observations corresponding to region C would be coded $x_1 = 0$, $x_2 = 1$.

The regression equation relating the expected value of the number of units sold, $E(y)$, to the dummy variables would be written as

$$E(y) = \beta_0 + \beta_1 x_1 + \beta_2 x_2$$

To help us interpret the parameters $\beta_0$, $\beta_1$, and $\beta_2$, consider the following three variations of the regression equation.

$$E(y \mid \text{region A}) = \beta_0 + \beta_1(0) + \beta_2(0) = \beta_0$$
$$E(y \mid \text{region B}) = \beta_0 + \beta_1(1) + \beta_2(0) = \beta_0 + \beta_1$$
$$E(y \mid \text{region C}) = \beta_0 + \beta_1(0) + \beta_2(1) = \beta_0 + \beta_2$$

Thus, $\beta_0$ is the mean or expected value of sales for region A; $\beta_1$ is the difference between the mean number of units sold in region B and the mean number of units sold in region A; and $\beta_2$ is the difference between the mean number of units sold in region C and the mean number of units sold in region A.

Two dummy variables were required because sales region is a qualitative variable with three levels. But the assignment of $x_1 = 0, x_2 = 0$ to indicate region A, $x_1 = 1, x_2 = 0$ to indicate region B, and $x_1 = 0, x_2 = 1$ to indicate region C was arbitrary. For example, we could have chosen $x_1 = 1$, $x_2 = 0$ to indicate region A, $x_1 = 0$, $x_2 = 0$ to indicate region B, and $x_1 = 0, x_2 = 1$ to indicate region C. In that case, $\beta_1$ would have been interpreted as the mean difference between regions A and B and $\beta_2$ as the mean difference between regions C and B.

The important point to remember is that when a qualitative variable has $k$ levels, $k - 1$ dummy variables are required in the multiple regression analysis. Thus, if the sales region example had a fourth region, labeled D, three dummy variables would be necessary. For example, the three dummy variables can be coded as follows.

$$x_1 = \begin{cases} 1 \text{ if sales region B} \\ 0 \text{ otherwise} \end{cases} \qquad x_2 = \begin{cases} 1 \text{ if sales region C} \\ 0 \text{ otherwise} \end{cases} \qquad x_3 = \begin{cases} 1 \text{ if sales region D} \\ 0 \text{ otherwise} \end{cases}$$

## Exercises

### Methods

32. Consider a regression study involving a dependent variable $y$, a quantitative independent variable $x_1$, and a qualitative variable with two levels (level 1 and level 2).
    a. Write a multiple regression equation relating $x_1$ and the qualitative variable to $y$.
    b. What is the expected value of $y$ corresponding to level 1 of the qualitative variable?
    c. What is the expected value of $y$ corresponding to level 2 of the qualitative variable?
    d. Interpret the parameters in your regression equation.

33. Consider a regression study involving a dependent variable $y$, a quantitative independent variable $x_1$, and a qualitative independent variable with three possible levels (level 1, level 2, and level 3).
    a. How many dummy variables are required to represent the qualitative variable?
    b. Write a multiple regression equation relating $x_1$ and the qualitative variable to $y$.
    c. Interpret the parameters in your regression equation.

### Applications

34. Management proposed the following regression model to predict sales at a fast-food outlet.

$$y = \beta_0 + \beta_1 x_1 + \beta_2 x_2 + \beta_3 x_3 + \epsilon$$

where

$$x_1 = \text{number of competitors within one mile}$$
$$x_2 = \text{population within one mile (1000s)}$$
$$x_3 = \begin{cases} 1 \text{ if drive-up window present} \\ 0 \text{ otherwise} \end{cases}$$
$$y = \text{sales (\$1000s)}$$

The following estimated regression equation was developed after 20 outlets were surveyed.

$$\hat{y} = 10.1 - 4.2x_1 + 6.8x_2 + 15.3x_3$$

a. What is the expected amount of sales attributable to the drive-up window?
b. Predict sales for a store with two competitors, a population of 8000 within one mile, and no drive-up window.
c. Predict sales for a store with one competitor, a population of 3000 within one mile, and a drive-up window.

35. Refer to the Johnson Filtration problem introduced in this section. Suppose that in addition to information on the number of months since the machine was serviced and whether a mechanical or an electrical failure had occurred, the managers obtained a list showing which repairperson performed the service. The revised data follow.

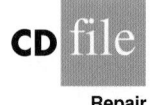

**CD file**

Repair

| Repair Time in Hours | Months Since Last Service | Type of Repair | Repairperson |
|---|---|---|---|
| 2.9 | 2 | Electrical | Dave Newton |
| 3.0 | 6 | Mechanical | Dave Newton |
| 4.8 | 8 | Electrical | Bob Jones |
| 1.8 | 3 | Mechanical | Dave Newton |
| 2.9 | 2 | Electrical | Dave Newton |
| 4.9 | 7 | Electrical | Bob Jones |
| 4.2 | 9 | Mechanical | Bob Jones |
| 4.8 | 8 | Mechanical | Bob Jones |
| 4.4 | 4 | Electrical | Bob Jones |
| 4.5 | 6 | Electrical | Dave Newton |

a. Ignore for now the months since the last maintenance service $(x_1)$ and the repairperson who performed the service. Develop the estimated simple linear regression equation to predict the repair time ($y$) given the type of repair $(x_2)$. Recall that $x_2 = 0$ if the type of repair is mechanical and 1 if the type of repair is electrical.
b. Does the equation that you developed in part (a) provide a good fit for the observed data? Explain.
c. Ignore for now the months since the last maintenance service and the type of repair associated with the machine. Develop the estimated simple linear regression equation to predict the repair time given the repairperson who performed the service. Let $x_3 = 0$ if Bob Jones performed the service and $x_3 = 1$ if Dave Newton performed the service.
d. Does the equation that you developed in part (c) provide a good fit for the observed data? Explain.

36. This problem is an extension of the situation described in exercise 35.
a. Develop the estimated regression equation to predict the repair time given the number of months since the last maintenance service, the type of repair, and the repairperson who performed the service.
b. At the .05 level of significance, test whether the estimated regression equation developed in part (a) represents a significant relationship between the independent variables and the dependent variable.
c. Is the addition of the independent variable $x_3$, the repairperson who performed the service, statistically significant? Use $\alpha = .05$. What explanation can you give for the results observed?

37. The National Football League rates prospects by position on a scale that ranges from 5 to 9. The ratings are interpreted as follows: 8–9 should start the first year; 7.0–7.9 should start; 6.0–6.9 will make the team as backup; and 5.0–5.9 can make the club and contribute. The following table shows the position, weight, speed (for 40 yards), and ratings for 25 NFL prospects (*USA Today*, April 14, 2000).

**Football**

| | Position | Weight (pounds) | Speed (seconds) | Rating |
|---|---|---|---|---|
| Cosey Coleman | Guard | 322 | 5.38 | 7.4 |
| Travis Claridge | Guard | 303 | 5.18 | 7.0 |
| Kaulana Noa | Guard | 317 | 5.34 | 6.8 |
| Leander Jordan | Guard | 330 | 5.46 | 6.7 |
| Chad Clifton | Guard | 334 | 5.18 | 6.3 |
| Manula Savea | Guard | 308 | 5.32 | 6.1 |
| Ryan Johanningmeir | Guard | 310 | 5.28 | 6.0 |
| Mark Tauscher | Guard | 318 | 5.37 | 6.0 |
| Blaine Saipaia | Guard | 321 | 5.25 | 6.0 |
| Richard Mercier | Guard | 295 | 5.34 | 5.8 |
| Damion McIntosh | Guard | 328 | 5.31 | 5.3 |
| Jeno James | Guard | 320 | 5.64 | 5.0 |
| Al Jackson | Guard | 304 | 5.20 | 5.0 |
| Chris Samuels | Offensive tackle | 325 | 4.95 | 8.5 |
| Stockar McDougle | Offensive tackle | 361 | 5.50 | 8.0 |
| Chris McIngosh | Offensive tackle | 315 | 5.39 | 7.8 |
| Adrian Klemm | Offensive tackle | 307 | 4.98 | 7.6 |
| Todd Wade | Offensive tackle | 326 | 5.20 | 7.3 |
| Marvel Smith | Offensive tackle | 320 | 5.36 | 7.1 |
| Michael Thompson | Offensive tackle | 287 | 5.05 | 6.8 |
| Bobby Williams | Offensive tackle | 332 | 5.26 | 6.8 |
| Darnell Alford | Offensive tackle | 334 | 5.55 | 6.4 |
| Terrance Beadles | Offensive tackle | 312 | 5.15 | 6.3 |
| Tutan Reyes | Offensive tackle | 299 | 5.35 | 6.1 |
| Greg Robinson-Ran | Offensive tackle | 333 | 5.59 | 6.0 |

a. Develop a dummy variable that will account for the player's position.
b. Develop an estimated regression equation to show how rating is related to position, weight, and speed.
c. At the .05 level of significance, test whether the estimated regression equation developed in part (b) indicates a significant relationship between the independent variables and the dependent variable.
d. Does the estimated regression equation provide a good fit for the observed data? Explain.
e. Is position a significant factor in the player's rating? Use $\alpha = .05$. Explain.
f. Suppose a new offensive tackle prospect who weighs 300 pounds ran the 40 yards in 5.1 seconds. Use the estimated regression equation developed in part (b) to estimate the rating for this player.

38. A 10-year study conducted by the American Heart Association provided data on how age, blood pressure, and smoking relate to the risk of strokes. Assume that the following data are from a portion of this study. Risk is interpreted as the probability (times 100) that the patient will have a stroke over the next 10-year period. For the smoking variable, define a dummy variable with 1 indicating a smoker and 0 indicating a nonsmoker.

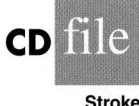

**Stroke**

| Risk | Age | Pressure | Smoker |
|---|---|---|---|
| 12 | 57 | 152 | No |
| 24 | 67 | 163 | No |
| 13 | 58 | 155 | No |
| 56 | 86 | 177 | Yes |
| 28 | 59 | 196 | No |
| 51 | 76 | 189 | Yes |

*(continued)*

| Risk | Age | Pressure | Smoker |
|------|-----|----------|--------|
| 18 | 56 | 155 | Yes |
| 31 | 78 | 120 | No |
| 37 | 80 | 135 | Yes |
| 15 | 78 | 98 | No |
| 22 | 71 | 152 | No |
| 36 | 70 | 173 | Yes |
| 15 | 67 | 135 | Yes |
| 48 | 77 | 209 | Yes |
| 15 | 60 | 199 | No |
| 36 | 82 | 119 | Yes |
| 8 | 66 | 166 | No |
| 34 | 80 | 125 | Yes |
| 3 | 62 | 117 | No |
| 37 | 59 | 207 | Yes |

a. Develop an estimated regression equation that relates risk of a stroke to the person's age, blood pressure, and whether the person is a smoker.

b. Is smoking a significant factor in the risk of a stroke? Explain. Use $\alpha = .05$.

c. What is the probability of a stroke over the next 10 years for Art Speen, a 68-year-old smoker who has blood pressure of 175? What action might the physician recommend for this patient?

 **Residual Analysis**

In Chapter 14 we pointed out that standardized residuals were frequently used in residuals plots and in the identification of outliers. The general formula for the standardized residual for observation $i$ follows.

---

STANDARDIZED RESIDUAL FOR OBSERVATION $i$

$$\frac{y_i - \hat{y}_i}{s_{y_i - \hat{y}_i}} \qquad (15.23)$$

where

$s_{y_i - \hat{y}_i} = $ the standard deviation of residual $i$

---

The general formula for the standard deviation of residual $i$ is defined as follows.

---

STANDARD DEVIATION OF RESIDUAL $i$

$$s_{y_i - \hat{y}_i} = s\sqrt{1 - h_i} \qquad (15.24)$$

where

$s = $ standard error of the estimate

$h_i = $ leverage of observation $i$

---

As we stated in Chapter 14, the **leverage** of an observation is determined by how far the values of the independent variables are from their means. The computation of $h_i$, $s_{y_i - \hat{y}_i}$, and hence the standardized residual for observation $i$ in multiple regression analysis is too complex to be done by hand. However, the standardized residuals can be easily obtained as part of the output from statistical software packages. Table 15.7 lists the predicted values, the residuals, and the standardized residuals for the Butler Trucking example presented previously in this chapter; we obtained these values by using the Minitab statistical software package. The predicted values in the table are based on the estimated regression equation $\hat{y} = -.869 + .0611x_1 + .923x_2$.

The standardized residuals and the predicted values of $y$ from Table 15.7 are used in Figure 15.10, the standardized residual plot for the Butler Trucking multiple regression example. This standardized residual plot does not indicate any unusual abnormalities. Also, all of the standardized residuals are between $-2$ and $+2$; hence, we have no reason to question the assumption that the error term $\epsilon$ is normally distributed. We conclude that the model assumptions are reasonable.

A normal probability plot also can be used to determine whether the distribution of $\epsilon$ appears to be normal. The procedure and interpretation for a normal probability plot were discussed in Section 14.8. The same procedure is appropriate for multiple regression. Again, we would use a statistical software package to perform the computations and provide the normal probability plot.

## Detecting Outliers

An **outlier** is an observation that is unusual in comparison with the other data; in other words, an outlier does not fit the pattern of the other data. In Chapter 14 we showed an example of an outlier and discussed how standardized residuals can be used to detect outliers. Minitab classifies an observation as an outlier if the value of its standardized residual is less than $-2$ or greater than $+2$. Applying this rule to the standardized residuals for the Butler Trucking example (see Table 15.7), we do not detect any outliers in the data set.

In general, the presence of one or more outliers in a data set tends to increase $s$, the standard error of the estimate, and hence increase $s_{y - \hat{y}_i}$, the standard deviation of residual $i$. Because $s_{y_i - \hat{y}_i}$ appears in the denominator of the formula for the standardized residual (15.23), the size of the standardized residual will decrease as $s$ increases. As a result, even though a residual may be unusually large, the large denominator in expression (15.23) may cause the standardized residual rule to fail to identify the observation as being an outlier. We can

**TABLE 15.7**    RESIDUALS AND STANDARDIZED RESIDUALS FOR THE BUTLER TRUCKING REGRESSION ANALYSIS

| Miles Traveled $(x_1)$ | Deliveries $(x_2)$ | Travel Time $(y)$ | Predicted Value $(\hat{y})$ | Residual $(y - \hat{y})$ | Standardized Residual |
|---|---|---|---|---|---|
| 100 | 4 | 9.3 | 8.93846 | 0.361541 | 0.78344 |
| 50 | 3 | 4.8 | 4.95830 | −0.158304 | −0.34962 |
| 100 | 4 | 8.9 | 8.93846 | −0.038460 | −0.08334 |
| 100 | 2 | 6.5 | 7.09161 | −0.591609 | −1.30929 |
| 50 | 2 | 4.2 | 4.03488 | 0.165121 | 0.38167 |
| 80 | 2 | 6.2 | 5.86892 | 0.331083 | 0.65431 |
| 75 | 3 | 7.4 | 6.48667 | 0.913331 | 1.68917 |
| 65 | 4 | 6.0 | 6.79875 | −0.798749 | −1.77372 |
| 90 | 3 | 7.6 | 7.40369 | 0.196311 | 0.36703 |
| 90 | 2 | 6.1 | 6.48026 | −0.380263 | −0.77639 |

FIGURE 15.10   STANDARDIZED RESIDUAL PLOT FOR BUTLER TRUCKING

circumvent this difficulty by using a form of the standardized residuals called **studentized deleted residuals**.

## Studentized Deleted Residuals and Outliers

Suppose the $i$th observation is deleted from the data set and a new estimated regression equation is developed with the remaining $n - 1$ observations. Let $s_{(i)}$ denote the standard error of the estimate based on the data set with the $i$th observation deleted. If we compute the standard deviation of residual $i$ (15.24) using $s_{(i)}$ instead of $s$, and then compute the standardized residual for observation $i$ (15.23) using the revised $s_{y_i - \hat{y}_i}$ value, the resulting standardized residual is called a studentized deleted residual. If the $i$th observation is an outlier, $s_{(i)}$ will be less than $s$. The absolute value of the $i$th studentized deleted residual therefore will be larger than the absolute value of the standardized residual. In this sense, studentized deleted residuals may detect outliers that standardized residuals do not detect.

Many statistical software packages provide an option for obtaining studentized deleted residuals. Using Minitab, we obtained the studentized deleted residuals for the Butler Trucking example; the results are reported in Table 15.8. The $t$ distribution can be used to determine whether the studentized deleted residuals indicate the presence of outliers. Recall that $p$ denotes the number of independent variables and $n$ denotes the number of observations. Hence, if we delete the $i$th observation, the number of observations in the reduced data set is $n - 1$; in this case the error sum of squares has $(n - 1) - p - 1$ degrees of freedom. For the Butler Trucking example with $n = 10$ and $p = 2$, the degrees of freedom for the error sum of squares with the $i$th observation deleted is $9 - 2 - 1 = 6$. At a .05 level of significance, the $t$ distribution (Table 2 of Appendix B) shows that with six degrees of freedom, $t_{.025} = 2.447$. If the value of the $i$th studentized deleted residual is less than $-2.447$ or greater than $+2.447$, we can conclude that the $i$th observation is an outlier. The studentized deleted residuals in Table 15.8 do not exceed those limits; therefore, we conclude that outliers are not present in the data set.

TABLE 15.8    STUDENTIZED DELETED RESIDUALS FOR BUTLER TRUCKING

| Miles Traveled $(x_1)$ | Deliveries $(x_2)$ | Travel Time $(y)$ | Standardized Residual | Studentized Deleted Residual |
|---|---|---|---|---|
| 100 | 4 | 9.3 | 0.78344 | 0.75939 |
| 50 | 3 | 4.8 | −0.34962 | −0.32654 |
| 100 | 4 | 8.9 | −0.08334 | −0.07720 |
| 100 | 2 | 6.5 | −1.30929 | −1.39494 |
| 50 | 2 | 4.2 | 0.38167 | 0.35709 |
| 80 | 2 | 6.2 | 0.65431 | 0.62519 |
| 75 | 3 | 7.4 | 1.68917 | 2.03187 |
| 65 | 4 | 6.0 | −1.77372 | −2.21314 |
| 90 | 3 | 7.6 | 0.36703 | 0.34312 |
| 90 | 2 | 6.1 | −0.77639 | −0.75190 |

## Influential Observations

In Section 14.9 we discussed how the leverage of an observation can be used to identify observations for which the value of the independent variable may have a strong influence on the regression results. As we indicated in the discussion of standardized residuals, the leverage of an observation, denoted $h_i$, measures how far the values of the independent variables are from their mean values. The leverage values are easily obtained as part of the output from statistical software packages. Minitab computes the leverage values and uses the rule of thumb $h_i > 3(p + 1)/n$ to identify **influential observations**. For the Butler Trucking example with $p = 2$ independent variables and $n = 10$ observations, the critical value for leverage is $3(2 + 1)/10 = .9$. The leverage values for the Butler Trucking example obtained by using Minitab are reported in Table 15.9. Because $h_i$ does not exceed .9, we do not detect influential observations in the data set.

## Using Cook's Distance Measure to Identify Influential Observations

A problem that can arise in using leverage to identify influential observations is that an observation can be identified as having high leverage and not necessarily be influential in terms of the resulting estimated regression equation. For example, Table 15.10 is a data set

TABLE 15.9    LEVERAGE AND COOK'S DISTANCE MEASURES FOR BUTLER TRUCKING

| Miles Traveled $(x_1)$ | Deliveries $(x_2)$ | Travel Time $(y)$ | Leverage $(h_i)$ | Cook's D $(D_i)$ |
|---|---|---|---|---|
| 100 | 4 | 9.3 | .351704 | .110994 |
| 50 | 3 | 4.8 | .375863 | .024536 |
| 100 | 4 | 8.9 | .351704 | .001256 |
| 100 | 2 | 6.5 | .378451 | .347923 |
| 50 | 2 | 4.2 | .430220 | .036663 |
| 80 | 2 | 6.2 | .220557 | .040381 |
| 75 | 3 | 7.4 | .110009 | .117562 |
| 65 | 4 | 6.0 | .382657 | .650029 |
| 90 | 3 | 7.6 | .129098 | .006656 |
| 90 | 2 | 6.1 | .269737 | .074217 |

**TABLE 15.10**

DATA SET
ILLUSTRATING
POTENTIAL
PROBLEM USING
THE LEVERAGE
CRITERION

| $x_i$ | $y_i$ | Leverage $h_i$ |
|---|---|---|
| 1 | 18 | .204170 |
| 1 | 21 | .204170 |
| 2 | 22 | .164205 |
| 3 | 21 | .138141 |
| 4 | 23 | .125977 |
| 4 | 24 | .125977 |
| 5 | 26 | .127715 |
| 15 | 39 | .909644 |

consisting of eight observations and their corresponding leverage values (obtained by using Minitab). Because the leverage for the eighth observation is .91 > .75 (the critical leverage value), this observation is identified as influential. Before reaching any final conclusions, however, let us consider the situation from a different perspective.

Figure 15.11 shows the scatter diagram and the estimated regression equation corresponding to the data set in Table 15.10. We used Minitab to develop the following estimated regression equation for these data.

$$\hat{y} = 18.2 + 1.39x$$

The straight line in Figure 15.11 is the graph of this equation. Now, let us delete the observation $x = 15$, $y = 39$ from the data set and fit a new estimated regression equation to the remaining seven observations; the new estimated regression equation is

$$\hat{y} = 18.1 + 1.42x$$

We note that the $y$-intercept and slope of the new estimated regression equation are not significantly different from the values obtained by using all the data. Although the leverage criterion identified the eighth observation as influential, this observation clearly had little

**FIGURE 15.11**   SCATTER DIAGRAM FOR THE DATA SET IN TABLE 15.10

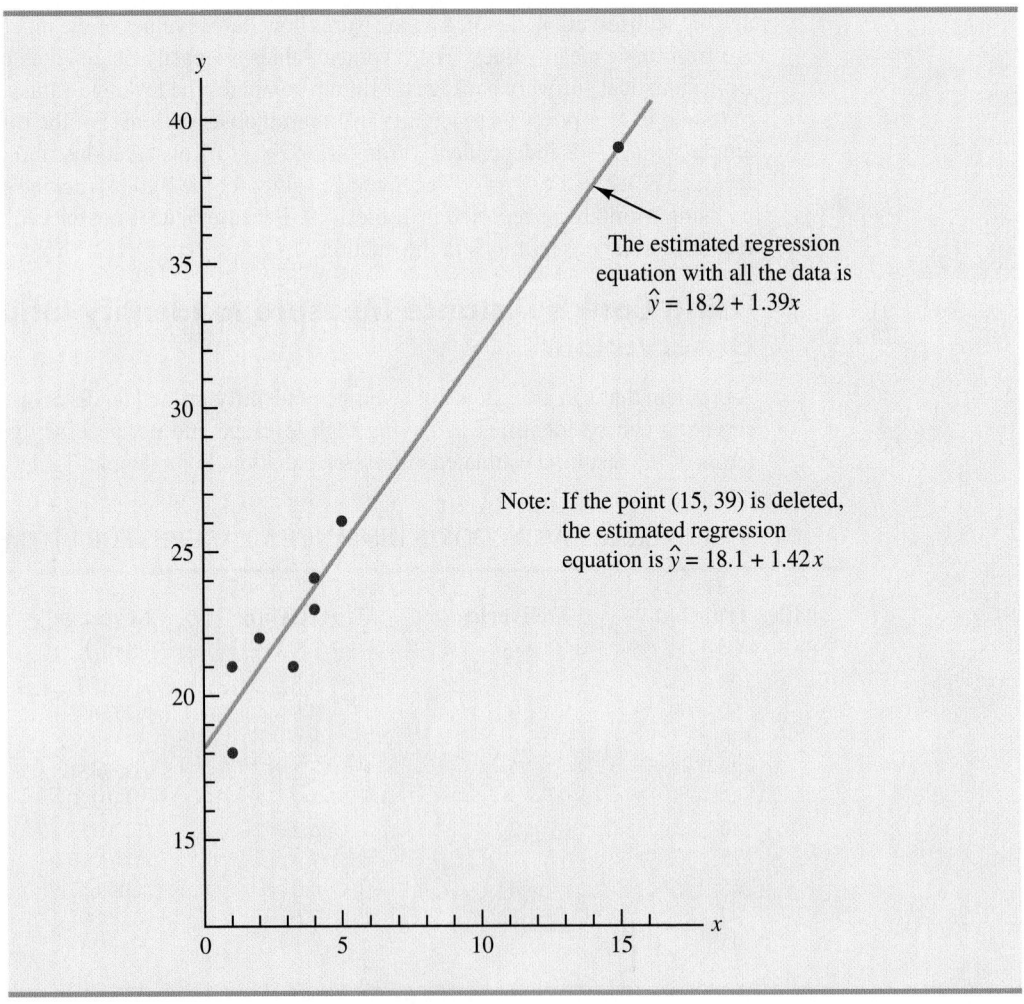

influence on the results obtained. Thus, in some situations using only leverage to identify influential observations can lead to wrong conclusions.

**Cook's distance measure** uses both the leverage of observation $i$, $h_i$, and the residual for observation $i$, $(y_i - \hat{y}_i)$, to determine whether the observation is influential.

---

COOK'S DISTANCE MEASURE

$$D_i = \frac{(y_i - \hat{y}_i)^2}{(p - 1)s^2}\left[\frac{h_i}{(1 - h_i)^2}\right] \qquad (15.25)$$

where

$$D_i = \text{Cook's distance measure for observation } i$$
$$y_i - \hat{y}_i = \text{the residual for observation } i$$
$$h_i = \text{the leverage for observation } i$$
$$p = \text{the number of independent variables}$$
$$s = \text{the standard error of the estimate}$$

---

The value of Cook's distance measure will be large and indicate an influential observation if the residual or the leverage is large. As a rule of thumb, values of $D_i > 1$ indicate that the $i$th observation is influential and should be studied further. The last column of Table 15.9 provides Cook's distance measure for the Butler Trucking problem as given by Minitab. Observation 8 with $D_i = .650029$ has the most influence. However, applying the rule $D_i > 1$, we should not be concerned about the presence of influential observations in the Butler Trucking data set.

## NOTES AND COMMENTS

1. The procedures for identifying outliers and influential observations provide warnings about the potential effects some observations may have on the regression results. Each outlier and influential observation warrants careful examination. If data errors are found, the errors can be corrected and the regression analysis repeated. In general, outliers and influential observations should not be removed from the data set unless clear evidence shows that they are not based on elements of the population being studied and should not have been included in the original data set.

2. To determine whether the value of Cook's distance measure $D_i$ is large enough to conclude that the $i$th observation is influential, we can also compare the value of $D_i$ to the 50th percentile of an $F$ distribution (denoted $F_{.50}$) with $p + 1$ numerator degrees of freedom and $n - p - 1$ denominator degrees of freedom. $F$ tables corresponding to a .50 level of significance must be available to carry out the test. The rule of thumb we provided ($D_i > 1$) is based on the fact that the table value is close to one for a wide variety of cases.

## Exercises

### Methods

**SELF** test

39. Data for two variables, $x$ and $y$, follow.

| $x_i$ | 1 | 2 | 3 | 4 | 5 |
|-------|---|---|---|----|----|
| $y_i$ | 3 | 7 | 5 | 11 | 14 |

a. Develop the estimated regression equation for these data.
b. Plot the standardized residuals versus $\hat{y}$. Do there appear to be any outliers in these data? Explain.
c. Compute the studentized deleted residuals for these data. At the .05 level of significance, can any of these observations be classified as an outlier? Explain.

40. Data for two variables, $x$ and $y$, follow.

| $x_i$ | 22 | 24 | 26 | 28 | 40 |
|-------|----|----|----|----|----|
| $y_i$ | 12 | 21 | 31 | 35 | 70 |

a. Develop the estimated regression equation for these data.
b. Compute the studentized deleted residuals for these data. At the .05 level of significance, can any of these observations be classified as an outlier? Explain.
c. Compute the leverage values for these data. Do there appear to be any influential observations in these data? Explain.
d. Compute Cook's distance measure for these data. Are any observations influential? Explain.

## Applications

41. Exercise 5 gave the following data on weekly gross revenue, television advertising, and newspaper advertising for Showtime Movie Theaters.

Showtime

| Weekly Gross Revenue ($1000s) | Television Advertising ($1000s) | Newspaper Advertising ($1000s) |
|---|---|---|
| 96 | 5.0 | 1.5 |
| 90 | 2.0 | 2.0 |
| 95 | 4.0 | 1.5 |
| 92 | 2.5 | 2.5 |
| 95 | 3.0 | 3.3 |
| 94 | 3.5 | 2.3 |
| 94 | 2.5 | 4.2 |
| 94 | 3.0 | 2.5 |

a. Find an estimated regression equation relating weekly gross revenue to television and newspaper advertising.
b. Plot the standardized residuals against $\hat{y}$. Does the residual plot support the assumptions about $\epsilon$? Explain.
c. Check for any outliers in these data. What are your conclusions?
d. Are there any influential observations? Explain.

42. Exercise 6 provided data on the curb weight, horsepower, and ¼-mile speed for 16 popular sports and GT cars. Suppose that the price of each sports and GT car is also available. The complete data set is as follows:

Auto2

| Sports & GT Car | Price ($1000s) | Curb Weight (lb.) | Horsepower | Speed at ¼ mile (mph) |
|---|---|---|---|---|
| Accura Integra Type R | 25.035 | 2577 | 195 | 90.7 |
| Accura NSX-T | 93.758 | 3066 | 290 | 108.0 |
| BMW Z3 2.8 | 40.900 | 2844 | 189 | 93.2 |
| Chevrolet Camaro Z28 | 24.865 | 3439 | 305 | 103.2 |
| Chevrolet Corvette Convertible | 50.144 | 3246 | 345 | 102.1 |
| Dodge Viper RT/10 | 69.742 | 3319 | 450 | 116.2 |

| Sports & GT Car | Price ($1000s) | Curb Weight (lb.) | Horsepower | Speed at ¼ mile (mph) |
|---|---|---|---|---|
| Ford Mustang GT | 23.200 | 3227 | 225 | 91.7 |
| Honda Prelude Type SH | 26.382 | 3042 | 195 | 89.7 |
| Mercedes-Benz CLK320 | 44.988 | 3240 | 215 | 93.0 |
| Mercedes-Benz SLK230 | 42.762 | 3025 | 185 | 92.3 |
| Mitsubishi 3000GT VR-4 | 47.518 | 3737 | 320 | 99.0 |
| Nissan 240SX SE | 25.066 | 2862 | 155 | 84.6 |
| Pontiac Firebird Trans Am | 27.770 | 3455 | 305 | 103.2 |
| Porsche Boxster | 45.560 | 2822 | 201 | 93.2 |
| Toyota Supra Turbo | 40.989 | 3505 | 320 | 105.0 |
| Volvo C70 | 41.120 | 3285 | 236 | 97.0 |

a. Find the estimated regression equation, which uses price and horsepower to predict ¼-mile speed.

b. Plot the standardized residuals against $\hat{y}$. Does the residual plot support the assumption about $\epsilon$? Explain.

c. Check for any outliers. What are your conclusions?

d. Are there any influential observations? Explain.

43. In exercise 9, data were provided showing the percentage of students who attend a four-year college, the average class size, and the combined SAT score.

a. Develop an estimated regression equation that can be used to predict the percentage of students who attend a four-year college given the combined SAT score.

b. Based on the estimated regression equation developed in part (a), do these data contain any outliers or influential observations? Explain.

c. Develop an estimated regression equation that can be used to predict the percentage of students who attend a four-year college given the average class size and the combined SAT score.

d. Based upon the estimated regression equation developed in part (c), do these data contain any outliers and/or influential observations? Explain.

##  Logistic Regression

In many regression applications the dependent variable may only assume two discrete values. For instance, a bank might like to develop an estimated regression equation for predicting whether a person will be approved for a credit card. The dependent variable can be coded as $y = 1$ if the bank approves the request for a credit card and $y = 0$ if the bank rejects the request for a credit card. Using logistic regression we can estimate the probability that the bank will approve the request for a credit card given a particular set of values for the chosen independent variables.

Let us consider an application of logistic regression involving a direct mail promotion being used by Simmons Stores. Simmons owns and operates a national chain of women's apparel stores. Five thousand copies of an expensive four-color sales catalog have been printed, and each catalog includes a coupon that provides a $50 discount on purchases of $200 or more. The catalogs are expensive and Simmons would like to send them to only those customers who have the highest probability of making a $200 purchase using the discount coupons.

Management thinks that annual spending at Simmons Stores and whether a customer has a Simmons credit card are two variables that might be helpful in predicting whether a customer who receives the catalog will use the coupon to make a $200 purchase. Simmons conducted a pilot study using a random sample of 50 Simmons credit card customers and

TABLE 15.11   SAMPLE DATA FOR SIMMONS STORES

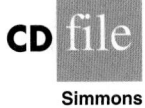
**CD** file

**Simmons**

| Customer | Annual Spending ($1000) | Simmons Card | Purchase |
|---|---|---|---|
| 1 | 2.291 | 1 | 0 |
| 2 | 3.215 | 1 | 0 |
| 3 | 2.135 | 1 | 0 |
| 4 | 3.924 | 0 | 0 |
| 5 | 2.528 | 1 | 0 |
| 6 | 2.473 | 0 | 1 |
| 7 | 2.384 | 0 | 0 |
| 8 | 7.076 | 0 | 0 |
| 9 | 1.182 | 1 | 1 |
| 10 | 3.345 | 0 | 0 |

50 other customers who do not have a Simmons credit card. Simmons sent the catalog to each of the 100 customers selected. At the end of a test period, Simmons noted whether the customer made a purchase (coded 1 if the customer made a purchase and 0 if not). The sample data for the first 10 catalog recipients are shown in Table 15.11. The amount each customer spent last year at Simmons is shown in thousands of dollars and the credit card information has been coded as 1 if the customer has a Simmons credit card and 0 if not. In the Purchase column, a 1 is recorded if the sampled customer used the $50 discount coupon to make a purchase of $200 or more.

We might think of building a multiple regression model using the data in Table 15.11 to help Simmons predict whether a catalog recipient will make a purchase. We would use Annual Spending and Simmons Card as independent variables and Purchase as the dependent variable. Because the dependent variable may only assume the values of 0 or 1, however, the ordinary multiple regression model is not applicable. This example shows the type of situation for which logistic regression was developed. Let us see how logistic regression can be used to help Simmons predict which type of customer is most likely to take advantage of their promotion.

## Logistic Regression Equation

In many ways logistic regression is like ordinary regression. It requires a dependent variable, $y$, and one or more independent variables. In multiple regression analysis, the mean or expected value of $y$, is referred to as the multiple regression equation.

$$E(y) = \beta_0 + \beta_1 x_1 + \beta_2 x_2 + \ldots + \beta_p x_p \tag{15.26}$$

In logistic regression, statistical theory as well as practice has shown that the relationship between $E(y)$ and $x_1, x_2, \ldots, x_p$ is better described by the following nonlinear equation.

LOGISTIC REGRESSION EQUATION

$$E(y) = \frac{e^{\beta_0 + \beta_1 x_1 + \beta_2 x_2 + \cdots + \beta_p x_p}}{1 + e^{\beta_0 + \beta_1 x_1 + \beta_2 x_2 + \cdots + \beta_p x_p}} \tag{15.27}$$

If the two values of the dependent variable $y$ are coded as 0 or 1, the value of $E(y)$ in equation (15.27) provides the *probability* that $y = 1$ given a particular set of values for the independent variables $x_1, x_2, \ldots, x_p$. Because of the interpretation of $E(y)$ as a probability, the **logistic regression equation** is often written as follows.

---

INTERPRETATION OF $E(y)$ AS A PROBABILITY IN LOGISTIC REGRESSION

$$E(y) = P(y = 1 \mid x_1, x_2, \ldots, x_p) \tag{15.28}$$

---

To provide a better understanding of the characteristics of the logistic regression equation, suppose the model involves only one independent variable $x$ and the values of the model parameters are $\beta_0 = -7$ and $\beta_1 = 3$. The logistic regression equation corresponding to these parameter values is

$$E(y) = P(y = 1 \mid x) = \frac{e^{\beta_0 + \beta_1 x}}{1 + e^{\beta_0 + \beta_1 x}} = \frac{e^{-7 + 3x}}{1 + e^{-7 + 3x}} \tag{15.29}$$

Figure 15.12 shows a graph of equation (15.29). Note that the graph is S-shaped. The value of $E(y)$ ranges from 0 to 1, with the value of $E(y)$ gradually approaching 1 as the value of $x$ becomes larger and the value of $E(y)$ approaching 0 as the value of $x$ becomes smaller. Note also that the values of $E(y)$, representing probability, increase fairly rapidly as $x$ increases from 2 to 3. The fact that the values of $E(y)$ range from 0 to 1 and that the curve is S-shaped makes equation (15.29) ideally suited to model the probability the dependent variable is equal to 1.

## Estimating the Logistic Regression Equation

In simple linear and multiple regression the least squares method is used to compute $b_0$, $b_1, \ldots, b_p$ as estimates of the model parameters $(\beta_0, \beta_1, \ldots, \beta_p)$. The nonlinear form of the logistic regression equation makes the method of computing estimates more complex and

**FIGURE 15.12**    LOGISTIC REGRESSION EQUATION FOR $\beta_0 = -7$ AND $\beta_1 = 3$

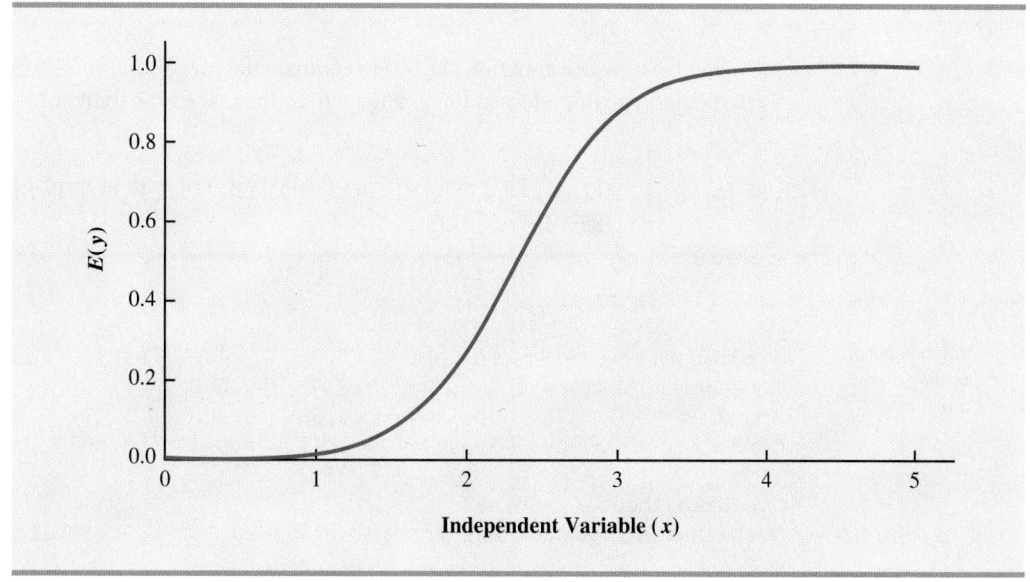

beyond the scope of this text. We will use computer software to provide the estimates. The **estimated logistic regression equation** is

---

### ESTIMATED LOGISTIC REGRESSION EQUATION

$$\hat{y} = \text{estimate of } P(y = 1 \mid x_1, x_2, \ldots, x_p) = \frac{e^{b_0 + b_1 x_1 + b_2 x_2 + \cdots + b_p x_p}}{1 + e^{b_0 + b_1 x_1 + b_2 x_2 + \cdots + b_p x_p}} \qquad (15.30)$$

---

Here, $\hat{y}$ provides an estimate of the probability that $y = 1$, given a particular set of values for the independent variables.

Let us now return to the Simmons Stores example. The variables in the study are defined as follows:

$$y = \begin{cases} 0 \text{ if the customer made no purchase during the test period} \\ 1 \text{ if the customer made a purchase during the test period} \end{cases}$$

$$x_1 = \text{annual spending at Simmons Stores (\$1000s)}$$

$$x_2 = \begin{cases} 0 \text{ if the customer does not have a Simmons credit card} \\ 1 \text{ if the customer has a Simmons credit card} \end{cases}$$

Thus, we choose a logistic regression equation with two independent variables.

$$E(y) = \frac{e^{\beta_0 + \beta_1 x_1 + \beta_2 x_2}}{1 + e^{\beta_0 + \beta_1 x_1 + \beta_2 x_2}} \qquad (15.31)$$

*In Appendix 15.3 we show how Minitab is used to generate the output in Figure 15.13.*

Using the sample data (see Table 15.11), Minitab's binary logistic regression procedure was used to compute estimates of the model parameters $\beta_0$, $\beta_1$, and $\beta_2$. A portion of the output obtained is shown in Figure 15.13. We see that $b_0 = -2.1464$, $b_1 = 0.3416$, and $b_2 = 1.0987$. Thus, the estimated logistic regression equation is

$$\hat{y} = \frac{e^{b_0 + b_1 x_1 + b_2 x_2}}{1 + e^{b_0 + b_1 x_1 + b_2 x_2}} = \frac{e^{-2.1464 + 0.3416 x_1 + 1.0987 x_2}}{1 + e^{-2.1464 + 0.3416 x_1 + 1.0987 x_2}} \qquad (15.32)$$

We can now use equation (15.32) to estimate the probability of making a purchase for a particular type of customer. For example, to estimate the probability of making a purchase

**FIGURE 15.13    PARTIAL LOGISTIC REGRESSION OUTPUT FOR THE SIMMONS STORES EXAMPLE**

*In the Minitab output, $x_1$ = Spending and $x_2$ = Card.*

```
Logistic Regression Table
                                                Odds       95% CI
Predictor      Coef    SE Coef      Z       p   Ratio   Lower  Upper
Constant    -2.1464     0.5772   -3.72   0.000
Spending     0.3416     0.1287    2.66   0.008    1.41   1.09   1.81
Card         1.0987     0.4447    2.47   0.013    3.00   1.25   7.17

Log-Likelihood = -60.487
Test that all slopes are zero: G = 13.628, DF = 2, P-Value = 0.001
```

for customers that spend \$2000 annually and do not have a Simmons credit card, we substitute $x_1 = 2$ and $x_2 = 0$ into equation (15.32).

$$\hat{y} = \frac{e^{-2.1464+0.3416(2)+1.0987(0)}}{1 + e^{-2.1464+0.3416(2)+1.0987(0)}} = \frac{e^{-1.4632}}{1 + e^{-1.4632}} = \frac{.2315}{1.2315} = 0.1880$$

Thus, an estimate of the probability of making a purchase for this particular group of customers is approximately 0.19. Similarly, to estimate the probability of making a purchase for customers that spent \$2000 last year and have a Simmons credit card, we substitute $x_1 = 2$ and $x_2 = 1$ into equation (15.32).

$$\hat{y} = \frac{e^{-2.1464+0.3416(2)+1.0987(1)}}{1 + e^{-2.1464+0.3416(2)+1.0987(1)}} = \frac{e^{-0.3645}}{1 + e^{-0.3645}} = \frac{.6945}{1.6945} = 0.4099$$

Thus, for this group of customers, the probability of making a purchase is approximately 0.41. It appears that the probability of making a purchase is much higher for customers with a Simmons credit card. Before reaching any conclusions, however, we need to assess the statistical significance of our model.

## Testing for Significance

Testing for significance in logistic regression is similar to testing for significance in multiple regression. First we conduct a test for overall significance. For the Simmons Stores example, the hypotheses for the test of overall significance follow:

$$H_0: \beta_1 = \beta_2 = 0$$
$$H_a: \text{One or both of the parameters is not equal to zero}$$

The test for overall significance is based upon the value of a $G$ test statistic. If the null hypothesis is true, the sampling distribution of $G$ follows a chi-square distribution with degrees of freedom equal to the number of independent variables in the model. Although the computation of $G$ is beyond the scope of the book, the value of $G$ and its corresponding $p$-value are provided as part of Minitab's binary logistic regression output. Referring to the last line in Figure 15.13, we see that the value of $G$ is 13.628, its degrees of freedom are 2, and its $p$-value is 0.001. Thus, at any level of significance $\alpha \geq .001$, we would reject the null hypothesis and conclude that the overall model is significant.

If the $G$ test shows an overall significance, a $z$ test can be used to determine whether each of the individual independent variables is making a significant contribution to the overall model. For the independent variables $x_i$, the hypotheses are

$$H_0: \beta_i = 0$$
$$H_a: \beta_i \neq 0$$

If the null hypothesis is true, the value of the estimated coefficient divided by its standard error follows a standard normal probability distribution. The column labeled Z in the Minitab output contains the values of $z_i = b_i/s_{b_i}$ for each of the estimated coefficients and the column labeled p contains the corresponding $p$-values. Suppose we use $\alpha = .05$ to test for the significance of the independent variables in the Simmons model. For the independent variable $x_1$ the $z$ value is 2.66 and the corresponding $p$-value is .008. Thus, at the .05 level of significance we can reject $H_0: \beta_1 = 0$. In a similar fashion we can also reject $H_0: \beta_2 = 0$ because the $p$-value corresponding to $z = 2.47$ is .013. Hence, at the .05 level of significance, both independent variables are statistically significant.

## Managerial Use

We described how to develop the estimated logistic regression equation and how to test it for significance. Let us now use it to make a decision recommendation concerning the Simmons Stores catalog promotion. For Simmons Stores, we already computed $P(y = 1|x_1 = 2, x_2 = 1) = .4099$ and $P(y = 1|x_1 = 2, x_2 = 0) = .1880$. These probabilities indicate that for customers with annual spending of $2000 the presence of a Simmons credit card increases the probability of making a purchase using the discount coupon. In Table 15.12 we show estimated probabilities for values of annual spending ranging from $1000 to $7000 for both customers who have a Simmons credit card and customers who do not have a Simmons credit card. How can Simmons use this information to better target customers for the new promotion? Suppose Simmons wants to send the promotional catalog only to customers who have a 0.40 or higher probability of making a purchase. Using the estimated probabilities in Table 15.12, Simmons promotion strategy would be:

**Customers who have a Simmons credit card:** Send the catalog to every customer that spent $2000 or more last year.

**Customers who do not have a Simmons credit card:** Send the catalog to every customer that spent $6000 or more last year.

Looking at the estimated probabilities further, we see that the probability of making a purchase for customers who do not have a Simmons credit card, but spend $5000 annually is 0.3921. Thus, Simmons may want to consider revising this strategy by including those customers who do not have a credit card as long as they spent $5000 or more last year.

## Interpreting the Logistic Regression Equation

Interpreting a regression equation involves relating the independent variables to the business question that the equation was developed to answer. With logistic regression, it is difficult to interpret the relation between the independent variables and the probability that $y = 1$ directly because the logistic regression equation is nonlinear. However, statisticians have shown that the relationship can be interpreted indirectly using a concept called the odds ratio.

The **odds in favor of an event occurring** is defined as the probability the event will occur divided by the probability the event will not occur. In logistic regression the event of interest is always $y = 1$. Given a particular set of values for the independent variables, the odds in favor of $y = 1$ can be calculated as follows:

$$\text{odds} = \frac{P(y = 1|x_1, x_2, \ldots, x_p)}{P(y = 0|x_1, x_2, \ldots, x_p)} = \frac{P(y = 1|x_1, x_2, \ldots, x_p)}{1 - P(y = 1|x_1, x_2, \ldots, x_p)} \quad (15.33)$$

The **odds ratio** measures the impact on the odds of a one-unit increase in only one of the independent variables. The odds ratio is the odds that $y = 1$ given that one of the inde-

**TABLE 15.12   ESTIMATED PROBABILITIES FOR SIMMONS STORES**

|  |  | Annual Spending | | | | | | |
|---|---|---|---|---|---|---|---|---|
|  |  | **$1000** | **$2000** | **$3000** | **$4000** | **$5000** | **$6000** | **$7000** |
| Credit | **Yes** | 0.3305 | 0.4099 | 0.4943 | 0.5790 | 0.6593 | 0.7314 | 0.7931 |
| Card | **No** | 0.1413 | 0.1880 | 0.2457 | 0.3143 | 0.3921 | 0.4758 | 0.5609 |

pendent variables has been increased by one unit ($odds_1$) divided by the odds that $y = 1$ given no change in the values for the independent variables ($odds_0$).

### ODDS RATIO

$$\text{Odds Ratio} = \frac{odds_1}{odds_0}$$ (15.34)

For example, suppose we want to compare the odds of making a purchase for customers who spend \$2000 annually and have a Simmons credit card ($x_1 = 2$ and $x_2 = 1$) to the odds of making a purchase for customers who spend \$2000 annually and do not have a Simmons credit card ($x_1 = 2$ and $x_2 = 0$). We are interested in interpreting the effect of a one-unit increase in the independent variable $x_2$. In this case

$$odds_1 = \frac{P(y = 1 | x_1 = 2, x_2 = 1)}{1 - P(y = 1 | x_1 = 2, x_2 = 1)}$$

and

$$odds_0 = \frac{P(y = 1 | x_1 = 2, x_2 = 0)}{1 - P(y = 1 | x_1 = 2, x_2 = 0)}$$

Previously we showed that an estimate of the probability that $y = 1$ given $x_1 = 2$ and $x_2 = 1$ is .4099, and an estimate of the probability that $y = 1$ given $x_1 = 2$ and $x_2 = 0$ is .1880. Thus,

$$\text{estimate of } odds_1 = \frac{.4099}{1 - .4099} = .6946$$

and

$$\text{estimate of } odds_0 = \frac{.1880}{1 - .1880} = .2315$$

The estimated odds ratio is

$$\text{Estimated odds ratio} = \frac{.6946}{.2315} = 3.00$$

Thus, we can conclude that the estimated odds in favor of making a purchase for customers who spent \$2000 last year and have a Simmons credit card are 3 times greater than the estimated odds in favor of making a purchase for customers who spent \$2000 last year and do not have a Simmons credit card.

The odds ratio for each independent variable is computed while holding all the other independent variables constant. But it does not matter what constant values are used for the other independent variables. For instance, if we computed the odds ratio for the Simmons credit card variable ($x_2$) using \$3000, instead of \$2000, as the value for the annual spending variable ($x_1$), we would still obtain the same value for the estimated odds ratio (3.00). Thus, we can conclude that the estimated odds of making a purchase for customers who have a Simmons credit card are 3 times greater than the estimated odds of making a purchase for customers who do not have a Simmons credit card.

The odds ratio is standard output for logistic regression software packages. Refer to the Minitab output in Figure 15.13. The column with the heading Odds Ratio contains the estimated odds ratios for each of the independent variables. The estimated odds ratio for $x_1$ is 1.41 and the estimated odds ratio for $x_2$ is 3.00. We already showed how to interpret the estimated odds ratio for the binary independent variable $x_2$. Let us now consider the interpretation of the estimated odds ratio for the continuous independent variable $x_1$.

The value of 1.41 in the Odds Ratio column of the Minitab output tells us that the estimated odds in favor of making a purchase for customers who spent $3000 last year is 1.41 times greater than the estimated odds in favor of making a purchase for customers who spent $2000 last year. Moreover, this interpretation is true for any one-unit change in $x_1$. For instance, the estimated odds in favor of making a purchase for someone who spent $5000 last year is 1.41 times greater than the odds in favor of making a purchase for a customer who spent $4000 last year. But suppose we are interested in the change in the odds for an increase of more than one unit for an independent variable. Note that $x_1$ can range from 1 to 7. The odds ratio as printed by the Minitab output does not answer this question. To answer this question we must explore the relationship between the odds ratio and the regression coefficients.

A unique relationship exists between the odds ratio for a variable and its corresponding regression coefficient. For each independent variable in a logistic regression equation it can be shown that

$$\text{Odds ratio} = e^{\beta_i}$$

To illustrate this relationship, consider the independent variable $x_1$ in the Simmons example. The estimated odds ratio for $x_1$ is

$$\text{Estimated odds ratio} = e^{b_1} = e^{.3416} = 1.41$$

Similarly, the estimated odds ratio for $x_2$ is

$$\text{Estimated odds ratio} = e^{b_2} = e^{1.0987} = 3.00$$

This relationship between the odds ratio and the coefficients of the independent variables makes it easy to compute estimates of the odds ratios once we develop estimates of the model parameters. Moreover, it also provides us with the ability to investigate changes in the odds ratio of more than or less than one unit for a continuous independent variable.

The odds ratio for an independent variable represents the change in the odds for a one-unit change in the independent variable holding all the other independent variables constant. Suppose that we want to consider the effect of a change of more than one unit, say $c$ units. For instance, suppose in the Simmons example that we want to compare the odds of making a purchase for customers who spend $5000 annually ($x_1 = 5$) to the odds of making a purchase for customers who spend $2000 annually ($x_1 = 2$). In this case $c = 5 - 2 = 3$ and the corresponding estimated odds ratio is

$$e^{cb_1} = e^{3(.3416)} = e^{1.0248} = 2.79$$

This result indicates that the estimated odds of making a purchase for customers who spend $5000 annually is 2.79 times greater than the estimated odds of making a purchase for customers who spend $2000 annually. In other words, the estimated odds ratio for an increase of $3000 in annual spending is 2.79.

In general, the odds ratio enables us to compare the odds for two different events. If the value of the odds ratio is 1, the odds for both events are the same. Thus, if the independent variable we are considering (such as Simmons credit card status) has a positive impact on the probability of the event occurring, the corresponding odds ratio will be greater than 1. Most logistic regression software packages provide a confidence interval for the odds ratio. The Minitab output in Figure 15.13 provides a 95% confidence interval for each of the odds ratios. For example, the point estimate of the odds ratio for $x_1$ is 1.41 and the 95% confidence interval is 1.09 to 1.81. Because the confidence interval does not contain the value of 1, we can conclude that $x_1$, has a significant effect on the estimated odds ratio. Similarly, the 95% confidence interval for the odds ratio for $x_2$ is 1.25 to 7.17. Because this interval does not contain the value of 1, we can also conclude that $x_2$ has a significant effect on the odds ratio.

## Logit Transformation

An interesting relationship can be observed between the odds in favor of $y = 1$ and the exponent for $e$ in the logistic regression equation. It can be shown that

$$\ln(\text{odds}) = \beta_0 + \beta_1 x_1 + \beta_2 x_2 + \cdots + \beta_p x_p$$

This equation shows that the natural logarithm of the odds in favor of $y = 1$ is a linear function of the independent variables. This linear function is called the **logit**. We will use the notation $g(x_1, x_2, \ldots, x_p)$ to denote the logit.

> **LOGIT**
>
> $$g(x_1, x_2, \ldots, x_p) = \beta_0 + \beta_1 x_1 + \beta_2 x_2 + \cdots + \beta_p x_p \qquad \textbf{(15.35)}$$

Substituting $g(x_1, x_2, \ldots, x_p)$ for $\beta_1 + \beta_1 x_1 + \beta_2 x_2 + \cdots + \beta_p x_p$ in equation (15.27), we can write the logistic regression equation as

$$E(y) = \frac{e^{g(x_1, x_2, \ldots, x_p)}}{1 + e^{g(x_1, x_2, \ldots, x_p)}} \qquad \textbf{(15.36)}$$

Once we estimate the parameters in the logistic regression equation, we can compute an estimate of the logit. Using $\hat{g}(x_1, x_2, \ldots, x_p)$ to denote the **estimated logit**, we obtain

> **ESTIMATED LOGIT**
>
> $$\hat{g}(x_1, x_2, \ldots, x_p) = b_0 + b_1 x_1 + b_2 x_2 + \cdots + b_p x_p \qquad \textbf{(15.37)}$$

Thus, in terms of the estimated logit, the estimated regression equation is

$$\hat{y} = \frac{e^{b_0 + b_1 x_1 + b_2 x_2 + \cdots + b_p x_p}}{1 + e^{b_0 + b_1 x_1 + b_2 x_2 + \cdots + b_p x_p}} = \frac{e^{\hat{g}(x_1, x_2, \ldots, x_p)}}{1 + e^{\hat{g}(x_1, x_2, \ldots, x_p)}} \qquad \textbf{(15.38)}$$

For the Simmons Stores example, the estimated logit is

$$\hat{g}(x_1, x_2) = -2.1464 + 0.3416x_1 + 1.0987x_2$$

and the estimated regression equation is

$$\hat{y} = \frac{e^{\hat{g}(x_1, x_2)}}{1 + e^{\hat{g}(x_1, x_2)}} = \frac{e^{-2.1464 + 0.3416x_1 + 1.0987x_2}}{1 + e^{-2.1464 + 0.3416x_1 + 1.0987x_2}}$$

Thus, because of the unique relationship between the estimated logit and the estimated logistic regression equation, we can compute the estimated probabilities for Simmons Stores by dividing $e^{\hat{g}(x_1, x_2)}$ by $1 + e^{\hat{g}(x_1, x_2)}$.

## NOTES AND COMMENTS

1. Because of the unique relationship between the estimated coefficients in the model and the corresponding odds ratios, the overall test for significance based upon the $G$ statistic is also a test of overall significance for the odds ratios. In addition, the $z$ test for the individual significance of a model parameter also provides a statistical test of significance for the corresponding odds ratio.

2. In simple and multiple regression, the coefficient of determination is used to measure the goodness of fit. In logistic regression, no single measure provides a similar interpretation. A discussion of goodness of fit is beyond the scope of our introductory treatment of logistic regression.

## Exercises

### Applications

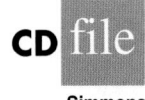

**CD file**

**Simmons**

44. Refer to the Simmons Stores example introduced in this section. The dependent variable is coded as $y = 1$ if the customer makes a purchase and 0 if not. Suppose that the only information available to help predict whether the customer will make a purchase is the customer's credit card status, coded as $x = 1$ if the customer has a Simmons credit card and $x = 0$ if not.
   a. Write the logistic regression equation relating $x$ to $y$.
   b. What is the interpretation of $E(y)$ when $x = 0$?
   c. For the Simmons data in Table 15.11, use Minitab to compute the estimated logit.
   d. Use the estimated logit computed in part (c) to compute an estimate of the probability of making a purchase for customers who do not have a Simmons credit card and an estimate of the probability of making a purchase for customers who have a Simmons credit card.
   e. What is the estimate of the odds ratio? What is its interpretation?

45. In Table 15.12 we provided estimates of the probability of a purchase in the Simmons Stores catalog promotion. A different value is obtained for each combination of values for the independent variables.
   a. Compute the odds in favor of a purchase for a customer with annual spending of $4000 who does not have a Simmons credit card ($x_1 = 4$, $x_2 = 0$).
   b. Use the information in Table 15.12 and part (a) to compute the odds ratio for the Simmons credit card variable $x_2 = 0$, holding annual spending constant at $x_1 = 4$.
   c. In the text, the odds ratio for the credit card variable was computed using the information in the $2000 column of Table 15.12. Did you get the same value for the odds ratio in part (b)?

46. Community Bank would like to increase the number of customers who use payroll direct deposit. Management is considering a new sales campaign that will require each branch manager to call each customer who does not currently use payroll direct deposit. As an incentive to sign up for payroll direct deposit, each customer contacted will be offered free checking for two years. Because of the time and cost associated with the new campaign, management would like to focus their efforts on customers who have the highest probability of signing up for payroll direct deposit. Management believes that the average monthly balance in a customer's checking account may be a useful predictor of whether the customer will sign up for direct payroll deposit. To investigate the relationship between these two variables, Commu-

nity Bank tried the new campaign using a sample of 50 checking account customers that do not currently use payroll direct deposit. The sample data show the average monthly checking account balance (in hundreds of dollars) and whether the customer contacted signed up for payroll direct deposit (coded 1 if the customer signed up for payroll direct deposit and 0 if not). The data are contained in the data set named Bank; a portion of the data follows.

**Bank**

| Customer | x = Monthly Balance | y = Direct Deposit |
|---|---|---|
| 1 | 1.22 | 0 |
| 2 | 1.56 | 0 |
| 3 | 2.10 | 0 |
| 4 | 2.25 | 0 |
| 5 | 2.89 | 0 |
| 6 | 3.55 | 0 |
| 7 | 3.56 | 0 |
| 8 | 3.65 | 1 |
| . | . | . |
| . | . | . |
| . | . | . |
| 48 | 18.45 | 1 |
| 49 | 24.98 | 0 |
| 50 | 26.05 | 1 |

a. Write the logistic regression equation relating $x$ to $y$.
b. For the Community Bank data, use Minitab to compute the estimated logistic regression equation.
c. Conduct a test of significance using the $G$ test statistic. Use $\alpha = .05$.
d. Estimate the probability that customers with an average monthly balance of $1000 will sign up for direct payroll deposit.
e. Suppose Community Bank only wants to contact customers who have a .50 or higher probability of signing up for direct payroll deposit. What is the average monthly balance required to achieve this level of probability?
f. What is the estimate of the odds ratio? What is its interpretation?

47. Over the past few years the percentage of students who leave Lakeland College at the end of the first year has increased. Last year Lakeland started a voluntary one-week orientation program to help first-year students adjust to campus life. If Lakeland is able to show that the orientation program has a positive effect on retention, they will consider making the program a requirement for all first-year students. Lakeland's administration also suspects that students with lower GPAs have a higher probability of leaving Lakeland at the end of the first year. In order to investigate the relation of these variables to retention, Lakeland selected a random sample of 100 students from last year's entering class. The data are contained in the data set named Lakeland; a portion of the data follows.

**Lakeland**

| Student | GPA | Program | Return |
|---|---|---|---|
| 1 | 3.78 | 1 | 1 |
| 2 | 2.38 | 0 | 1 |
| 3 | 1.30 | 0 | 0 |
| 4 | 2.19 | 1 | 0 |
| 5 | 3.22 | 1 | 1 |
| 6 | 2.68 | 1 | 1 |
| . | . | . | . |
| . | . | . | . |
| . | . | . | . |
| 98 | 2.57 | 1 | 1 |
| 99 | 1.70 | 1 | 1 |
| 100 | 3.85 | 1 | 1 |

The dependent variable was coded as $y = 1$ if the student returned to Lakeland for the sophomore year and $y = 0$ if not. The two independent variables are:

$$x_1 = \text{GPA at the end of the first semester}$$

$$x_2 = \begin{cases} 0 \text{ if the student did not attend the orientation program} \\ 1 \text{ if the student attended the orientation program} \end{cases}$$

a. Write the logistic regression equation relating $x_1$ and $x_2$ to $y$.
b. What is the interpretation of $E(y)$ when $x_2 = 0$?
c. Use both independent variables and Minitab to compute the estimated logit.
d. Conduct a test for overall significance using $\alpha = .05$.
e. Use $\alpha = .05$ to determine whether each of the independent variables is significant.
f. Use the estimated logit computed in part (c) to compute an estimate of the probability that students with a 2.5 grade point average who did not attend the orientation program will return to Lakeland for their sophomore year. What is the estimated probability for students with a 2.5 grade point average who attended the orientation program?
g. What is the estimate of the odds ratio for the orientation program? Interpret it.
h. Would you recommend making the orientation program a required activity? Why or why not?

48. *Consumer Reports* conducted a taste test on 19 brands of boxed chocolates. The following data show the price per serving, based on the FDA serving size of 1.4 ounces, and the quality rating for the 19 chocolates tested (*Consumer Reports*, February 2002).

**Chocolate**

| Manufacturer | Price | Rating |
|---|---|---|
| Bernard Callebaut | 3.17 | Very Good |
| Candinas | 3.58 | Excellent |
| Fannie May | 1.49 | Good |
| Godiva | 2.91 | Very Good |
| Hershey's | 0.76 | Good |
| L.A. Burdick | 3.70 | Very Good |
| La Maison du Chocolate | 5.08 | Excellent |
| Leonidas | 2.11 | Very Good |
| Lindt | 2.20 | Good |
| Martine's | 4.76 | Excellent |
| Michael Recchiuti | 7.05 | Very Good |
| Neuchatel | 3.36 | Good |
| Neuchatel Sugar Free | 3.22 | Good |
| Richard Donnelly | 6.55 | Very Good |
| Russell Stover | 0.70 | Good |
| See's | 1.06 | Very Good |
| Teuscher Lake of Zurich | 4.66 | Very Good |
| Whitman's | 0.70 | Fair |
| Whitman's Sugar Free | 1.21 | Fair |

Suppose that you would like to determine whether products that cost more rate higher in quality. For the purpose of this exercise, use the following binary dependent variable:

$$y = 1 \text{ if the quality rating is very good or excellent and } 0 \text{ if good or fair}$$

a. Write the logistic regression equation relating $x = $ price per serving to $y$.
b. Use Minitab to compute the estimated logit.
c. Use the estimated logit computed in part (b) to compute an estimate of the probability a chocolate that has a price per serving of $4.00 will have a quality rating of very good or excellent.
d. What is the estimate of the odds ratio? What is its interpretation?

## Summary

In this chapter, we introduced multiple regression analysis as an extension of simple linear regression analysis presented in Chapter 14. Multiple regression analysis enables us to understand how a dependent variable is related to two or more independent variables. The regression equation $E(y) = \beta_0 + \beta_1 x_1 + \beta_2 x_2 + \cdots + \beta_p x_p$ shows that the expected value or mean value of the dependent variable $y$ is related to the values of the independent variables $x_1, x_2, \ldots, x_p$. Sample data and the least squares method are used to develop the estimated regression equation $\hat{y} = b_0 + b_1 x_1 + b_2 x_2 + \ldots + b_p x_p$. In effect $b_0, b_1, b_2, \ldots, b_p$ are sample statistics used to estimate the unknown model parameters $\beta_0, \beta_1, \beta_2, \ldots, \beta_p$. Computer printouts were used throughout the chapter to emphasize the fact that statistical software packages are the only realistic means of performing the numerous computations required in multiple regression analysis.

The multiple coefficient of determination was presented as a measure of the goodness of fit of the estimated regression equation. It determines the proportion of the variation of $y$ that can be explained by the estimated regression equation. The adjusted multiple coefficient of determination is a similar measure of goodness of fit that adjusts for the number of independent variables and thus avoids overestimating the impact of adding more independent variables.

An $F$ test and a $t$ test were presented as ways to determine statistically whether the relationship among the variables is significant. The $F$ test is used to determine whether there is a significant overall relationship between the dependent variable and the set of all independent variables. The $t$ test is used to determine whether there is a significant relationship between the dependent variable and an individual independent variable given the other independent variables in the regression model. Correlation among the independent variables, known as multicollinearity, was discussed.

The section on qualitative independent variables showed how dummy variables can be used to incorporate qualitative data into multiple regression analysis. The section on residual analysis showed how residual analysis can be used to validate the model assumptions, detect outliers, and identify influential observations. Standardized residuals, leverage, studentized deleted residuals, and Cook's distance measure were discussed. The chapter concluded with a section on how logistic regression can be used to model situations in which the dependent variable may only assume two values.

## Glossary

**Multiple regression analysis** Regression analysis involving two or more independent variables.

**Multiple regression model** The mathematical equation that describes how the dependent variable $y$ is related to the independent variables $x_1, x_2, \ldots, x_p$ and an error term $\epsilon$.

**Multiple regression equation** The mathematical equation relating the expected value or mean value of the dependent variable to the values of the independent variables; that is $E(y) = \beta_0 + \beta_1 x_1 + \beta_2 x_2 + \ldots + \beta_p x_p$.

**Estimated multiple regression equation** The estimate of the multiple regression equation based on sample data and the least squares method; it is $\hat{y} = b_0 + b_1 x_1 + b_2 x_2 + \ldots + b_p x_p$.

**Least squares method** The method used to develop the estimated regression equation. It minimizes the sum of squared residuals (the deviations between the observed values of the dependent variable, $y_i$, and the estimated values of the dependent variable, $\hat{y}_i$).

**Multiple coefficient of determination** A measure of the goodness of fit of the estimated multiple regression equation. It can be interpreted as the proportion of the variability in the dependent variable that is explained by the estimated regression equation.

**Adjusted multiple coefficient of determination** A measure of the goodness of fit of the estimated multiple regression equation that adjusts for the number of independent variables in the model and thus avoids overestimating the impact of adding more independent variables.

**Multicollinearity** The term used to describe the correlation among the independent variables.

**Qualitative independent variable** An independent variable with qualitative data.

**Dummy variable** A variable used to model the effect of qualitative independent variables. A dummy variable may take only the value zero or one.

**Leverage** A measure of how far the values of the independent variables are from their mean values.

**Outlier** An observation that does not fit the pattern of the other data.

**Studentized deleted residuals** Standardized residuals that are based on a revised standard error of the estimate obtained by deleting observation $i$ from the data set and then performing the regression analysis and computations.

**Influential observation** An observation that has a strong influence on the regression results.

**Cook's distance measure** A measure of the influence of an observation based on both the leverage of observation $i$ and the residual for observation $i$.

**Logistic regression equation** The mathematical equation relating $E(y)$, the probability that $y = 1$, to the values of the independent variables; that is, $E(y) = P(y = 1|x_1, x_2, \ldots, x_p) = \dfrac{e^{\beta_0 + \beta_1 x_1 + \beta_2 x_2 + \cdots + \beta_p x_p}}{1 + e^{\beta_0 + \beta_1 x_1 + \beta_2 x_2 + \cdots + \beta_p x_p}}$.

**Estimated logistic regression equation** The estimate of the logistic regression equation based on sample data; that is, $\hat{y} = $ estimate of $P(y = 1|x_1, x_2, \ldots, x_p) = \dfrac{e^{b_0 + b_1 x_1 + b_2 x_2 + \cdots + b_p x_p}}{1 + e^{b_0 + b_1 x_1 + b_2 x_2 + \cdots + b_p x_p}}$.

**Odds in favor of an event occurring** The probability the event will occur divided by the probability the event will not occur.

**Odds ratio** The odds that $y = 1$ given that one of the independent variables increased by one unit (odds$_1$) divided by the odds that $y = 1$ given no change in the values for the independent variables (odds$_0$); that is, Odds ratio $=$ odds$_1$/odds$_0$.

**Logit** The natural logarithm of the odds in favor of $y = 1$; that is, $g(x_1, x_2, \ldots, x_p) = \beta_0 + \beta_1 x_1 + \beta_2 x_2 + \cdots + \beta_p x_p$.

**Estimated logit** An estimate of the logit based on sample data; that is, $\hat{g}(x_1, x_2, \ldots, x_p) = b_0 + b_1 x_1 + b_2 x_2 + \cdots + b_p x_p$.

## Key Formulas

**Multiple Regression Model**

$$y = \beta_0 + \beta_1 x_1 + \beta_2 x_2 + \cdots + \beta_p x_p + \epsilon \tag{15.1}$$

**Multiple Regression Equation**

$$E(y) = \beta_0 + \beta_1 x_1 + \beta_2 x_2 + \cdots + \beta_p x_p \tag{15.2}$$

**Estimated Multiple Regression Equation**

$$\hat{y} = b_0 + b_1 x_1 + b_2 x_2 + \cdots + b_p x_p \tag{15.3}$$

**Least Squares Criterion**

$$\min \Sigma (y_i - \hat{y}_i)^2 \tag{15.4}$$

**Relationship Among SST, SSR, and SSE**

$$SST = SSR + SSE \qquad \text{(15.7)}$$

**Multiple Coefficient of Determination**

$$R^2 = \frac{SSR}{SST} \qquad \text{(15.8)}$$

**Adjusted Multiple Coefficient of Determination**

$$R_a^2 = 1 - (1 - R^2)\frac{n-1}{n-p-1} \qquad \text{(15.9)}$$

**Mean Square Regression**

$$MSR = \frac{SSR}{p} \qquad \text{(15.12)}$$

**Mean Square Error**

$$MSE = \frac{SSE}{n-p-1} \qquad \text{(15.13)}$$

**$F$ Test Statistic**

$$F = \frac{MSR}{MSE} \qquad \text{(15.14)}$$

**$t$ Test Statistic**

$$t = \frac{b_i}{s_{b_i}} \qquad \text{(15.15)}$$

**Standardized Residual for Observation $i$**

$$\frac{y_i - \hat{y}_i}{s_{y_i - \hat{y}_i}} \qquad \text{(15.23)}$$

**Standard Deviation of Residual $i$**

$$s_{y_i - \hat{y}_i} = s\sqrt{1 - h_i} \qquad \text{(15.24)}$$

**Cook's Distance Measure**

$$D_i = \frac{(y_i - \hat{y}_i)^2}{(p-1)s^2}\left[\frac{h_i}{(1-h_i)^2}\right] \qquad \text{(15.25)}$$

**Logistic Regression Equation**

$$E(y) = \frac{e^{\beta_0 + \beta_1 x_1 + \beta_2 x_2 + \cdots + \beta_p x_p}}{1 + e^{\beta_0 + \beta_1 x_1 + \beta_2 x_2 + \cdots + \beta_p x_p}} \qquad \text{(15.27)}$$

**Estimated Logistic Regression Equation**

$$\hat{y} = \text{estimate of } P(y = 1 | x_1, x_2, \ldots, x_p) = \frac{e^{b_0 + b_1 x_1 + b_2 x_2 + \cdots + b_p x_p}}{1 + e^{b_0 + b_1 x_1 + b_2 x_2 + \cdots + b_p x_p}} \quad \textbf{(15.30)}$$

**Odds Ratio**

$$\text{Odds ratio} = \frac{\text{odds}_1}{\text{odds}_0} \quad \textbf{(15.34)}$$

**Logit**

$$g(x_1, x_2, \ldots, x_p) = \beta_0 + \beta_1 x_1 + \beta_2 x_2 + \cdots + \beta_p x_p \quad \textbf{(15.35)}$$

**Estimated Logit**

$$\hat{g}(x_1, x_2, \ldots, x_p) = b_0 + b_1 x_1 + b_2 x_2 + \cdots + b_p x_p \quad \textbf{(15.37)}$$

## Supplementary Exercises

49. The admissions officer for Clearwater College developed the following estimated regression equation relating the final college GPA to the student's SAT mathematics score and high-school GPA.

$$\hat{y} = -1.41 + .0235 x_1 + .00486 x_2$$

where

$$x_1 = \text{high-school grade point average}$$
$$x_2 = \text{SAT mathematics score}$$
$$y = \text{final college grade point average}$$

a. Interpret the coefficients in this estimated regression equation.
b. Estimate the final college GPA for a student who has a high-school average of 84 and a score of 540 on the SAT mathematics test.

50. The personnel director for Electronics Associates developed the following estimated regression equation relating an employee's score on a job satisfaction test to his or her length of service and wage rate.

$$\hat{y} = 14.4 - 8.69 x_1 + 13.5 x_2$$

where

$$x_1 = \text{length of service (years)}$$
$$x_2 = \text{wage rate (dollars)}$$
$$y = \text{job satisfaction test score (higher scores}$$
$$\text{indicate greater job satisfaction)}$$

a. Interpret the coefficients in this estimated regression equation.
b. Develop an estimate of the job satisfaction test score for an employee who has four years of service and makes $6.50 per hour.

51. A partial computer output from a regression analysis follows.

```
The regression equation is
Y = 8.103 + 7.602 X1 + 3.111 X2

Predictor              Coef           SE Coef              T
Constant             _____          2.667            _____
X1                   _____          2.105            _____
X2                   _____          0.613            _____

S = 3.335      R-sq = 92.3%       R-sq(adj) = _____%

Analysis of Variance

SOURCE                 DF             SS             MS          F
Regression           _____         1612          _____      _____
Residual Error         12           _____        _____
Total                _____         _____
```

a. Compute the appropriate $t$-ratios.
b. Test for the significance of $\beta_1$ and $\beta_2$ at $\alpha = .05$.
c. Compute the entries in the DF, SS, and MS columns.
d. Compute $R_a^2$.

52. Recall that in exercise 49, the admissions officer for Clearwater College developed the following estimated regression equation relating final college GPA to the student's SAT mathematics score and high-school GPA.

$$\hat{y} = -1.41 + .0235x_1 + .00486x_2$$

where

$$x_1 = \text{high-school grade point average}$$
$$x_2 = \text{SAT mathematics score}$$
$$y = \text{final college grade point average}$$

A portion of the Minitab computer output follows.

```
The regression equation is
Y = -1.41 + .0235 X1 + .00486 X2

Predictor              Coef           SE Coef              T
Constant             -1.4053         0.4848            _____
X1                   0.023467        0.008666          _____
X2                   _____         0.001077          _____

S = 0.1298     R-sq = _____     R-sq(adj) = _____

Analysis of Variance

SOURCE                 DF             SS             MS          F
Regression           _____        1.76209        _____      _____
Residual Error       _____        _____         _____
Total                  9           1.88000
```

a. Complete the missing entries in this output.
b. Compute $F$ and test at a .05 level of significance to see whether a significant relationship is present.
c. Did the estimated regression equation provide a good fit to the data? Explain.
d. Use the $t$ test and $\alpha = .05$ to test $H_0: \beta_1 = 0$ and $H_0: \beta_2 = 0$.

53. Recall that in exercise 50 the personnel director for Electronics Associates developed the following estimated regression equation relating an employee's score on a job satisfaction test to length of service and wage rate.

$$\hat{y} = 14.4 - 8.69x_1 + 13.5x_2$$

where

$$x_1 = \text{length of service (years)}$$
$$x_2 = \text{wage rate (dollars)}$$
$$y = \text{job satisfaction test score (higher scores indicate greater job satisfaction)}$$

A portion of the Minitab computer output follows.

```
The regression equation is
Y = 14.4 - 8.69 X1 + 13.52 X2

Predictor          Coef          SE Coef            T
Constant         14.448            8.191         1.76
X1                                 1.555         _____
X2               13.517            2.085         _____

S = 3.773      R-sq = _____%   R-sq(adj) = _____%

Analysis of Variance

SOURCE            DF             SS            MS           F
Regression         2          _____        _____      _____
Residual Error  _____         71.17        _____
Total              7          720.0
```

a. Complete the missing entries in this output.
b. Compute $F$ and test using $\alpha = .05$ to see whether a significant relationship is present.
c. Did the estimated regression equation provide a good fit to the data? Explain.
d. Use the $t$ test and $\alpha = .05$ to test $H_0: \beta_1 = 0$ and $H_0: \beta_2 = 0$.

54. *SmartMoney* magazine evaluated 65 metropolitan areas to determine where home values are headed. An ideal city would get a score of 100 if all factors measured were as favorable as possible. Areas with a score of 60 or greater are considered to be primed for price appreciation, and areas with a score of below 50 may see housing values erode. Two of the factors evaluated were the recession resistance of the area and its affordability. Both of these factors were rated using a scale ranging from 0 (low score) to 10 (high score). The data obtained for a sample of 20 cities evaluated by *SmartMoney* follow (*SmartMoney*, February 2002).

| Metro Area | Recession Resistance | Affordability | Score |
|---|---|---|---|
| Tucson | 10 | 7 | 70.7 |
| Fort Worth | 10 | 7 | 68.5 |
| San Antonio | 6 | 8 | 65.5 |
| Richmond | 8 | 6 | 63.6 |
| Indianapolis | 4 | 8 | 62.5 |
| Philadelphia | 0 | 10 | 61.9 |
| Atlanta | 2 | 6 | 60.7 |
| Phoenix | 4 | 5 | 60.3 |
| Cincinnati | 2 | 7 | 57.0 |
| Miami | 6 | 5 | 56.5 |
| Hartford | 0 | 7 | 56.2 |
| Birmingham | 0 | 8 | 55.7 |
| San Diego | 8 | 2 | 54.6 |
| Raleigh | 2 | 7 | 50.9 |
| Oklahoma City | 1 | 6 | 49.6 |
| Orange County | 4 | 2 | 49.1 |
| Denver | 4 | 4 | 48.6 |
| Los Angeles | 0 | 7 | 45.7 |
| Detroit | 0 | 5 | 44.3 |
| New Orleans | 0 | 5 | 41.2 |

**HomeValue**

a.  Develop an estimated regression equation that can be used to predict the score given the recession resistance rating. At the .05 level of significance, test for a significant relationship.
b.  Did the estimated regression equation developed in part (a) provide a good fit to the data? Explain.
c.  Develop an estimated regression equation that can be used to predict the score given the recession resistance rating and the affordability rating. At the .05 level of significance, test for overall significance.

55.  Following are data on price, curb weight, horsepower, time to go from 0 to 60 miles per hour, and the speed at $\frac{1}{4}$ mile for 16 sports and GT cars (*1998 Road & Track Sports & GT Cars*).

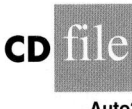

**Auto3**

| | Price ($1000s) | Curb Weight (lb.) | Horse-power | 0 to 60 (seconds) | Speed at $\frac{1}{4}$ mile (mph) |
|---|---|---|---|---|---|
| Acura Integra Type R | 25.035 | 2577 | 195 | 7.0 | 90.7 |
| Acura NSX-T | 93.758 | 3066 | 290 | 5.0 | 108.0 |
| BMW Z3 2.8 | 40.900 | 2844 | 189 | 6.6 | 93.2 |
| Chevrolet Camaro Z28 | 24.865 | 3439 | 305 | 5.4 | 103.2 |
| Chevrolet Corvette Convertible | 50.144 | 3246 | 345 | 5.2 | 102.1 |
| Dodge Viper RT/10 | 69.742 | 3319 | 450 | 4.4 | 116.2 |
| Ford Mustang GT | 23.200 | 3227 | 225 | 6.8 | 91.7 |
| Honda Prelude Type SH | 26.382 | 3042 | 195 | 7.7 | 89.7 |
| Mercedes-Benz CLK320 | 44.988 | 3240 | 215 | 7.2 | 93.0 |
| Mercedes-Benz SLK230 | 42.762 | 3025 | 185 | 6.6 | 92.3 |
| Mitsubishi 3000GT VR-4 | 47.518 | 3737 | 320 | 5.7 | 99.0 |
| Nissan 240SX SE | 25.066 | 2862 | 155 | 9.1 | 84.6 |
| Pontiac Firebird Trans Am | 27.770 | 3455 | 305 | 5.4 | 103.2 |
| Porsche Boxster | 45.560 | 2822 | 201 | 6.1 | 93.2 |
| Toyota Supra Turbo | 40.989 | 3505 | 320 | 5.3 | 105.0 |
| Volvo C70 | 41.120 | 3285 | 236 | 6.3 | 97.0 |

a. Develop an estimated regression equation with price, curb weight, horsepower, and time to go from 0 to 60 mph as four independent variables to predict the speed at $\frac{1}{4}$ mile.

b. Use the $F$ test to determine the significance of the regression results. At a .05 level of significance, what is your conclusion?

c. Use the $t$ test to determine the significance of each independent variable. At a .05 level of significance, what is your conclusion?

d. Delete any independent variable that is not significant and provide your recommended estimated regression equation.

e. Develop a standardized residual plot. Does the pattern of the residual plot appear to be reasonable?

f. Do the data contain any outliers?

g. Do the data contain any influential observations?

56. The U.S. Department of Energy's *Fuel Economy Guide* provides fuel efficiency data for cars and trucks. A portion of the data for 35 standard pickup trucks produced by Chevrolet and General Motors follows (http://www.fueleconomy.gov, March 21, 2003). The column labeled Drive identifies whether the vehicle has two-wheel drive (2WD) or four-wheel drive (4WD). The column labeled Displacement shows the engine's displacement in liters, the column labeled Cylinders specifies the number of cylinders the engine has, and the column labeled Transmission shows whether the truck has an automatic transmission or a manual transmission. The column labeled City MPG shows the fuel efficiency rating for the truck for city driving in terms of miles per gallon (mpg).

| Truck | Name | Drive | Displacement | Cylinders | Transmission | City MPG |
|---|---|---|---|---|---|---|
| 1 | C1500 Silverado | 2WD | 4.3 | 6 | Auto | 15 |
| 2 | C1500 Silverado | 2WD | 4.3 | 6 | Manual | 15 |
| 3 | C1500 Silverado | 2WD | 4.8 | 8 | Auto | 15 |
| 4 | C1500 Silverado | 2WD | 4.8 | 8 | Manual | 16 |
| 5 | C1500 Silverado | 2WD | 5.3 | 8 | Auto | 11 |
| . | . | . | . | . | . | . |
| . | . | . | . | . | . | . |
| . | . | . | . | . | . | . |
| 32 | K1500 Sierra | 4WD | 5.3 | 8 | Auto | 15 |
| 33 | K1500 Sierra | 4WD | 5.3 | 8 | Auto | 15 |
| 34 | Sonoma | 4WD | 4.3 | 6 | Auto | 17 |
| 35 | Sonoma | 4WD | 4.3 | 6 | Manual | 15 |

*CD file*

FuelEcon

a. Develop an estimated regression equation that can be used to predict the fuel efficiency for city driving given the engine's displacement. Test for significance using $\alpha = .05$.

b. Consider the addition of the dummy variable Drive4, where the value of Drive4 is 0 if the truck has two-wheel drive and 1 if the truck has four-wheel drive. Develop the estimated regression equation that can be used to predict the fuel efficiency for city driving given the engine's displacement and the dummy variable Drive4.

c. Use $\alpha = .05$ to determine whether the dummy variable added in part (b) is significant.

d. Consider the addition of the dummy variable EightCyl, where the value of EightCyl is 0 if the truck's engine has six cylinders and 1 if the truck's engine has eight cylinders. Develop the estimated regression equation that can be used to predict the fuel efficiency for city driving given the engine's displacement and the dummy variables Drive4 and EightCyl.

e. For the estimated regression equation developed in part (d), test for overall significance and individual significance using $\alpha = .05$.

57. Today's marketplace offers a wide choice to buyers of sport utility vehicles (SUVs) and pickup trucks. An important factor to many buyers is the resale value of the vehicle. The following table shows the resale value (%) after two years and the suggested retail price for 10 SUVs, 10 small pickup trucks, and 10 large pickup trucks (*Kiplinger's New Cars & Trucks 2000 Buyer's Guide*).

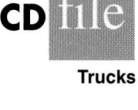

**Trucks**

| | Type of Vehicle | Suggested Retail Price ($) | Resale Value (%) |
|---|---|---|---|
| Chevrolet Blazer LS | sport utility | 19,495 | 55 |
| Ford Explorer Sport | sport utility | 20,495 | 57 |
| GMC Yukon XL 1500 | sport utility | 26,789 | 67 |
| Honda CR-V | sport utility | 18,965 | 65 |
| Isuzu VehiCross | sport utility | 30,186 | 62 |
| Jeep Cherokee Limited | sport utility | 25,745 | 57 |
| Mercury Mountaineer Monterrey | sport utility | 29,895 | 59 |
| Nissan Pathfinder XE | sport utility | 26,919 | 54 |
| Toyota 4Runner | sport utility | 22,418 | 55 |
| Toyota RAV4 | sport utility | 17,148 | 55 |
| Chevrolet S-10 Extended Cab | small pickup | 18,847 | 46 |
| Dodge Dakota Club Cab Sport | small pickup | 16,870 | 53 |
| Ford Ranger XLT Regular Cab | small pickup | 18,510 | 48 |
| Ford Ranger XLT Supercab | small pickup | 20,225 | 55 |
| GMC Sonoma Regular Cab | small pickup | 16,938 | 44 |
| Isuzu Hombre Spacecab | small pickup | 18,820 | 41 |
| Mazda B4000 SE Cab Plus | small pickup | 23,050 | 51 |
| Nissan Frontier XE Regular Cab | small pickup | 12,110 | 51 |
| Toyota Tacoma Xtracab | small pickup | 18,228 | 49 |
| Toyota Tacoma Xtracab V6 | small pickup | 19,318 | 50 |
| Chevrolet K2500 | full-size pickup | 24,417 | 60 |
| Chevrolet Silverado 2500 Ext | full-size pickup | 24,140 | 64 |
| Dodge Ram 1500 | full-size pickup | 17,460 | 54 |
| Dodge Ram Quad Cab 2500 | full-size pickup | 32,770 | 63 |
| Dodge Ram Regular Cab 2500 | full-size pickup | 23,140 | 59 |
| Ford F150 XL | full-size pickup | 22,875 | 58 |
| Ford F-350 Super Duty Crew Cab XL | full-size pickup | 34,295 | 64 |
| GMC New Sierra 1500 Ext Cab | full-size pickup | 27,089 | 68 |
| Toyota Tundra Access Cab Limited | full-size pickup | 25,605 | 53 |
| Toyota Tundra Regular Cab | full-size pickup | 15,835 | 58 |

a. Develop an estimated regression equation that can be used to predict the resale value given the suggested retail price. At the .05 level of significance, test for a significant relationship.
b. Did the estimated regression equation developed in part (a) provide a good fit to the data? Explain.
c. Develop an estimated regression equation that can be used to predict the resale value given the suggested retail price and the type of vehicle.
d. Use the $F$ test to determine the significance of the regression results. At a .05 level of significance, what is your conclusion?

## Case Problem 1   Consumer Research, Inc.

Consumer Research, Inc., is an independent agency that conducts research on consumer attitudes and behaviors for a variety of firms. In one study, a client asked for an investigation of consumer characteristics that can be used to predict the amount charged by credit card users. Data were collected on annual income, household size, and annual credit card charges for a sample of 50 consumers. The following data are on the CD accompanying the text in the data set named Consumer.

**Consumer**

| Income ($1000s) | Household Size | Amount Charged ($) | Income ($1000s) | Household Size | Amount Charged ($) |
|---|---|---|---|---|---|
| 54 | 3 | 4016 | 54 | 6 | 5573 |
| 30 | 2 | 3159 | 30 | 1 | 2583 |
| 32 | 4 | 5100 | 48 | 2 | 3866 |
| 50 | 5 | 4742 | 34 | 5 | 3586 |
| 31 | 2 | 1864 | 67 | 4 | 5037 |
| 55 | 2 | 4070 | 50 | 2 | 3605 |
| 37 | 1 | 2731 | 67 | 5 | 5345 |
| 40 | 2 | 3348 | 55 | 6 | 5370 |
| 66 | 4 | 4764 | 52 | 2 | 3890 |
| 51 | 3 | 4110 | 62 | 3 | 4705 |
| 25 | 3 | 4208 | 64 | 2 | 4157 |
| 48 | 4 | 4219 | 22 | 3 | 3579 |
| 27 | 1 | 2477 | 29 | 4 | 3890 |
| 33 | 2 | 2514 | 39 | 2 | 2972 |
| 65 | 3 | 4214 | 35 | 1 | 3121 |
| 63 | 4 | 4965 | 39 | 4 | 4183 |
| 42 | 6 | 4412 | 54 | 3 | 3730 |
| 21 | 2 | 2448 | 23 | 6 | 4127 |
| 44 | 1 | 2995 | 27 | 2 | 2921 |
| 37 | 5 | 4171 | 26 | 7 | 4603 |
| 62 | 6 | 5678 | 61 | 2 | 4273 |
| 21 | 3 | 3623 | 30 | 2 | 3067 |
| 55 | 7 | 5301 | 22 | 4 | 3074 |
| 42 | 2 | 3020 | 46 | 5 | 4820 |
| 41 | 7 | 4828 | 66 | 4 | 5149 |

## Managerial Report

1. Use methods of descriptive statistics to summarize the data. Comment on the findings.
2. Develop estimated regression equations, first using annual income as the independent variable and then using household size as the independent variable. Which variable is the better predictor of annual credit card charges? Discuss your findings.
3. Develop an estimated regression equation with annual income and household size as the independent variables. Discuss your findings.
4. What is the predicted annual credit card charge for a three-person household with an annual income of $40,000?
5. Discuss the need for other independent variables that could be added to the model. What additional variables might be helpful?

## Case Problem 2 NFL Quarterback Rating

The National Football League (NFL) records weekly performance statistics for individuals and teams. These data can be obtained by accessing the home page for the NFL at http://www.nfl.com. For many fans, one of the most interesting statistics is the rating used to evaluate the passing performance of quarterbacks. Four categories are used as a basis for compiling a passing rating:

1.  Percentage of touchdown passes per attempt
2.  Percentage of completions per attempt
3.  Percentage of interceptions per attempt
4.  Average yards gained per attempt

To illustrate how to compute the rating, consider the performance for Steve Young, the highest rated quarterback in the NFL in 1997. For the 1997 season, Steve Young attempted 356 passes, completed 241 passes for a total of 3029 yards, and had 19 touchdown passes and 6 interceptions. Five steps are needed to compute the passing rating for Steve Young.

**Step 1.** Compute the ratio of the number of touchdowns (19) to the number of passes attempted (356); the value obtained is $19/356 = 0.0534$. Divide this result by 0.05 to obtain the value for the touchdown component of the rating; the value obtained is $0.0534/0.05 = 1.0680$.

**Step 2.** Compute the ratio of the number of passes completed (241) to the number of passes attempted (356); the value obtained is $241/356 = 0.6770$. Subtract 0.3 from this result and divide by 0.2 to obtain the value for the second component of the rating; the value obtained is $(0.6770 - 0.3)/0.2 = 1.8850$.

**Step 3.** Compute the ratio of the number of interceptions (6) to the number of passes attempted (356); the value obtained is $6/356 = 0.0169$. Subtract this value from 0.095 and divide the result by 0.04 to obtain the value for the interceptions component of the rating; the value obtained is $(0.095 - 0.0169)/0.04 = 1.9525$.

**Step 4.** Compute the ratio of the number of passing yards (3029) to the number of passes attempted (356); the value obtained is $3029/356 = 8.5084$. Subtract 3 from this result and divide by 4 to obtain the value for the yards component of the rating; the value obtained is $(8.5084 - 3)/4 = 1.3771$.

**Step 5.** Add the sum of steps 1 through 4, multiply by 100 and divide by 6. The sum of steps 1 through 4 is $1.0680 + 1.8850 + 1.9525 + 1.3771 = 6.2826$. After multiplying by 100 and dividing by 6 we obtain 104.7100 or 104.7; this figure is the passing rating reported by the NFL for Steve Young.

The passing data reported by the NFL for the 1997 season are available on the CD accompanying the text in the data set named NFL. The labels for the columns are defined as follows:

| | |
|---|---|
| Att | Number of passes attempted. |
| Comp | Number of passes completed. |
| Comp% | Number of passes completed divided by the number of passes attempted times 100. |
| Yds | Number of yards obtained passing. |
| Yds/Att | Number of yards obtained passing divided by the number of passes attempted. |
| TD | Number of touchdowns obtained passing. |
| TD% | Number of touchdowns divided by the number of passes attempted times 100. |
| Long | Longest pass completed. |
| Int | Number of interceptions thrown. |
| Int% | Number of interceptions divided by the number of passes attempted. |
| Rating | The quarterback passing rating. |

## Managerial Report

1.  Use methods of descriptive statistics to summarize the data. Comment on the findings.
2.  Develop an estimated regression equation that can be used to predict Int% given the value of Comp%. Discuss your findings.

3.  Develop an estimated regression equation that can be used to predict Rating. Discuss your findings and comment on how your estimated regression equation relates to the previous discussion of computing passing ratings.
4.  If the NFL hired you to compute the passing ratings for next year, what approach would you use? Explain.

## Case Problem 3   Predicting Student Proficiency Test Scores

In order to predict how a school district would have scored when accounting for poverty and other income measures, *The Cincinnati Enquirer* gathered data from the Ohio Department of Education's Education Management Services and the Ohio Department of Taxation (*The Cincinnati Enquirer,* November 30, 1997). First, the newspaper obtained passage-rate data on the math, reading, science, writing, and citizenship proficiency exams given to fourth-, sixth-, ninth-, and 12th-graders in early 1996. By combining these data, they computed an overall percentage of students that passed the tests for each district.

The percentage of a school district's students on Aid for Dependent Children (ADC), the percentage who qualify for free or reduced-price lunches, and the district's median family income were also recorded. A portion of the data collected for the 608 school districts follows. The complete data set is available on the CD accompanying the text in the data set named Enquirer.

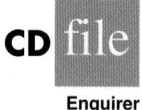

**CD** file

Enquirer

| Rank | School District | County | % Passed | % on ADC | % Free Lunch | Median Income ($) |
|---|---|---|---|---|---|---|
| 1 | Ottawa Hills Local | Lucas | 93.85 | 0.11 | 0.00 | 48231 |
| 2 | Wyoming City | Hamilton | 93.08 | 2.95 | 4.59 | 42672 |
| 3 | Oakwood City | Montgomery | 92.92 | 0.20 | 0.38 | 42403 |
| 4 | Madeira City | Hamilton | 92.37 | 1.50 | 4.83 | 32889 |
| 5 | Indian Hill Ex Vill | Hamilton | 91.77 | 1.23 | 2.70 | 44135 |
| 6 | Solon City | Cuyahoga | 90.77 | 0.68 | 2.24 | 34993 |
| 7 | Chagrin Falls Ex Vill | Cuyahoga | 89.89 | 0.47 | 0.44 | 38921 |
| 8 | Mariemont City | Hamilton | 89.80 | 3.00 | 2.97 | 31823 |
| 9 | Upper Arlington City | Franklin | 89.77 | 0.24 | 0.92 | 38358 |
| 10 | Granville Ex Vill | Licking | 89.22 | 1.14 | 0.00 | 36235 |

The data have been ranked based on the values in the column labeled % Passed; these data are the overall percentage of students passing the tests. Data in the column labeled % on ADC are the percentage of each school district's students on ADC, and the data in the column labeled % Free Lunch are the percentage of students who qualify for free or reduced-price lunches. The column labeled Median Income shows each district's median family income. Also shown for each school district is the county in which the school district is located. Note that in some cases the value in the % Free Lunch column is 0, indicating that the district did not participate in the free lunch program.

## Managerial Report

Use the methods presented in this and previous chapters to analyze this data set. Present a summary of your analysis, including key statistical results, conclusions, and recommendations, in a managerial report. Include any technical material you feel is appropriate in an appendix.

**Case Problem 4**   # Alumni Giving

Alumni donations are an important source of revenue for colleges and universities. If administrators could determine the factors that could lead to increases in the percentage of alumni who make a donation, they might be able to implement policies that could lead to increased revenues. Research shows that students who are more satisfied with their contact with teachers are more likely to graduate. As a result, one might suspect that smaller class sizes and lower student-faculty ratios might lead to a higher percentage of satisfied graduates, which in turn might lead to increases in the percentage of alumni who make a donation. Table 15.13 shows data for 48 national universities (*America's Best Colleges,* Year 2000 Edition). The column labeled Graduation Rate is the percentage of students who initially enrolled at the university and graduated. The column labeled % of Classes Under 20 shows the percentage of classes offered with fewer than 20 students. The column labeled Student-Faculty Ratio is the number of students enrolled divided by the total number of faculty. Finally, the column labeled Alumni Giving Rate is the percentage of alumni who made a donation to the university.

## Managerial Report

1. Use methods of descriptive statistics to summarize the data.
2. Develop an estimated regression equation that can be used to predict the alumni giving rate given the number of students who graduate. Discuss your findings.
3. Develop an estimated regression equation that could be used to predict the alumni giving rate using the data provided.
4. What conclusions and recommendations can you derive from your analysis?

**Appendix 15.1**   # Multiple Regression with Minitab

In Section 15.2 we discussed the computer solution of multiple regression problems by showing Minitab's output for the Butler Trucking Company problem. In this appendix we describe the steps required to generate the Minitab computer solution. First, the data must be entered in a Minitab worksheet. The miles traveled are entered in column C1, the number of deliveries are entered in column C2, and the travel times (hours) are entered in column C3. The variable names Miles, Deliv, and Time were entered as the column headings on the worksheet. In subsequent steps, we refer to the data by using the variable names Miles, Deliv, and Time or the column indicators C1, C2, and C3. The following steps describe how to use Minitab to produce the regression results shown in Figure 15.4.

**Butler**

> **Step 1.** Select the **Stat** menu
> **Step 2.** Select the **Regression** menu
> **Step 3.** Choose **Regression**
> **Step 4.** When the **Regression** dialog box appears
> > Enter Time in the **Response** box
> > Enter Miles and Deliv in the **Predictors** box
> > Click **OK**

**Appendix 15.2**   # Multiple Regression with Excel

In Section 15.2 we discussed the computer solution of multiple regression problems by showing Minitab's output for the Butler Trucking Company problem. In this appendix we describe how to use Excel's Regression tool to develop the estimated multiple regression

TABLE 15.13    DATA FOR 48 NATIONAL UNIVERSITIES

**Alumni**

| | State | Graduation Rate | % of Classes Under 20 | Student-Faculty Ratio | Alumni Giving Rate |
|---|---|---|---|---|---|
| Boston College | MA | 85 | 39 | 13 | 25 |
| Brandeis University | MA | 79 | 68 | 8 | 33 |
| Brown University | RI | 93 | 60 | 8 | 40 |
| California Institute of Technology | CA | 85 | 65 | 3 | 46 |
| Carnegie Mellon University | PA | 75 | 67 | 10 | 28 |
| Case Western Reserve Univ. | OH | 72 | 52 | 8 | 31 |
| College of William and Mary | VA | 89 | 45 | 12 | 27 |
| Columbia University | NY | 90 | 69 | 7 | 31 |
| Cornell University | NY | 91 | 72 | 13 | 35 |
| Dartmouth College | NH | 94 | 61 | 10 | 53 |
| Duke University | NC | 92 | 68 | 8 | 45 |
| Emory University | GA | 84 | 65 | 7 | 37 |
| Georgetown University | PA | 91 | 54 | 10 | 29 |
| Harvard University | MA | 97 | 73 | 8 | 46 |
| Johns Hopkins University | MD | 89 | 64 | 9 | 27 |
| Lehigh University | PA | 81 | 55 | 11 | 40 |
| Massachusetts Inst. of Technology | MA | 92 | 65 | 6 | 44 |
| New York University | NY | 72 | 63 | 13 | 13 |
| Northwestern University | IL | 90 | 66 | 8 | 30 |
| Pennsylvania State Univ. | PA | 80 | 32 | 19 | 21 |
| Princeton University | NJ | 95 | 68 | 5 | 67 |
| Rice University | TX | 92 | 62 | 8 | 40 |
| Stanford University | CA | 92 | 69 | 7 | 34 |
| Tufts University | MA | 87 | 67 | 9 | 29 |
| Tulane University | LA | 72 | 56 | 12 | 17 |
| U. of California–Berkeley | CA | 83 | 58 | 17 | 18 |
| U. of California–Davis | CA | 74 | 32 | 19 | 7 |
| U. of California–Irvine | CA | 74 | 42 | 20 | 9 |
| U. of California–Los Angeles | CA | 78 | 41 | 18 | 13 |
| U. of California–San Diego | CA | 80 | 48 | 19 | 8 |
| U. of California–Santa Barbara | CA | 70 | 45 | 20 | 12 |
| U. of Chicago | IL | 84 | 65 | 4 | 36 |
| U. of Florida | FL | 67 | 31 | 23 | 19 |
| U. of Illinois–Urbana Champaign | IL | 77 | 29 | 15 | 23 |
| U. of Michigan–Ann Arbor | MI | 83 | 51 | 15 | 13 |
| U. of North Carolina–Chapel Hill | NC | 82 | 40 | 16 | 26 |
| U. of Notre Dame | IN | 94 | 53 | 13 | 49 |
| U. of Pennsylvania | PA | 90 | 65 | 7 | 41 |
| U. of Rochester | NY | 76 | 63 | 10 | 23 |
| U. of Southern California | CA | 70 | 53 | 13 | 22 |
| U. of Texas–Austin | TX | 66 | 39 | 21 | 13 |
| U. of Virginia | VA | 92 | 44 | 13 | 28 |
| U. of Washington | WA | 70 | 37 | 12 | 12 |
| U. of Wisconsin–Madison | WI | 73 | 37 | 13 | 13 |
| Vanderbilt University | TN | 82 | 68 | 9 | 31 |
| Wake Forest University | NC | 82 | 59 | 11 | 38 |
| Washington University–St. Louis | MO | 86 | 73 | 7 | 33 |
| Yale University | CT | 94 | 77 | 7 | 50 |

**Butler**

equation for the Butler Trucking problem. Refer to Figure 15.14 as we describe the tasks involved. First, the labels Assignment, Miles, Deliveries, and Time are entered into cells A1:D1 of the worksheet, and the sample data into cells B2:D11. The numbers 1–10 in cells A2:A11 identify each observation.

The following steps describe how to use the Regression tool for the multiple regression analysis.

**Step 1.** Select the **Tools** menu
**Step 2.** Choose **Data Analysis**
**Step 3.** Choose **Regression** from the list of Analysis Tools
**Step 4.** When the Regression dialog box appears
     Enter D1:D11 in the **Input Y Range** box
     Enter B1:C11 in the **Input X Range** box
     Select **Labels**
     Select **Confidence Level**
     Enter 99 in the **Confidence Level** box
     Select **Output Range**
     Enter A13 in the **Output Range** box (to identify the upper left corner of the section of the worksheet where the output will appear)
     Click **OK**

**FIGURE 15.14   EXCEL OUTPUT FOR BUTLER TRUCKING WITH TWO INDEPENDENT VARIABLES**

|  | A | B | C | D | E | F | G | H | I | J |
|---|---|---|---|---|---|---|---|---|---|---|
| 1 | Assignment | Miles | Deliveries | Time | | | | | | |
| 2 | 1 | 100 | 4 | 9.3 | | | | | | |
| 3 | 2 | 50 | 3 | 4.8 | | | | | | |
| 4 | 3 | 100 | 4 | 8.9 | | | | | | |
| 5 | 4 | 100 | 2 | 6.5 | | | | | | |
| 6 | 5 | 50 | 2 | 4.2 | | | | | | |
| 7 | 6 | 80 | 2 | 6.2 | | | | | | |
| 8 | 7 | 75 | 3 | 7.4 | | | | | | |
| 9 | 8 | 65 | 4 | 6 | | | | | | |
| 10 | 9 | 90 | 3 | 7.6 | | | | | | |
| 11 | 10 | 90 | 2 | 6.1 | | | | | | |
| 12 | | | | | | | | | | |
| 13 | SUMMARY OUTPUT | | | | | | | | | |
| 14 | | | | | | | | | | |
| 15 | *Regression Statistics* | | | | | | | | | |
| 16 | Multiple R | 0.9507 | | | | | | | | |
| 17 | R Square | 0.9038 | | | | | | | | |
| 18 | Adjusted R Square | 0.8763 | | | | | | | | |
| 19 | Standard Error | 0.5731 | | | | | | | | |
| 20 | Observations | 10 | | | | | | | | |
| 21 | | | | | | | | | | |
| 22 | ANOVA | | | | | | | | | |
| 23 | | *df* | *SS* | *MS* | *F* | *Significance F* | | | | |
| 24 | Regression | 2 | 21.6006 | 10.8003 | 32.8784 | 0.0003 | | | | |
| 25 | Residual | 7 | 2.2994 | 0.3285 | | | | | | |
| 26 | Total | 9 | 23.9 | | | | | | | |
| 27 | | | | | | | | | | |
| 28 | | *Coefficients* | *Standard Error* | *t Stat* | *P-value* | *Lower 95%* | *Upper 95%* | *Lower 99.0%* | *Upper 99.0%* | |
| 29 | Intercept | -0.8687 | 0.9515 | -0.9129 | 0.3916 | -3.1188 | 1.3813 | -4.1986 | 2.4612 | |
| 30 | Miles | 0.0611 | 0.0099 | 6.1824 | 0.0005 | 0.0378 | 0.0845 | 0.0265 | 0.0957 | |
| 31 | Deliveries | 0.9234 | 0.2211 | 4.1763 | 0.0042 | 0.4006 | 1.4463 | 0.1496 | 1.6972 | |
| 32 | | | | | | | | | | |

In the Excel output shown in Figure 15.14 the label for the independent variable $x_1$ is Miles (see cell A30), and the label for the independent variable $x_2$ is Deliveries (see cell A31). The estimated regression equation is

$$\hat{y} = -.8687 + .0611x_1 + .9234x_2$$

Note that using Excel's Regression tool for multiple regression is almost the same as using it for simple linear regression. The major difference is that in the multiple regression case a larger range of cells is required in order to identify the independent variables.

## Appendix 15.3  Logistic Regression with Minitab

**CD** file

Simmons

Minitab calls logistic regression with a dependent variable that can only assume the values 0 and 1 Binary Logistic Regression. In this appendix we describe the steps required to use Minitab's Binary Logistic Regression procedure to generate the computer output for the Simmons Stores problem shown in Figure 15.13. First, the data must be entered in a Minitab worksheet. The amounts customers spent last year at Simmons (in thousands of dollars) are entered into column C2, the credit card data (1 if a Simmons card; 0 otherwise) are entered into column C3, and the purchase data (1 if the customer made a purchase; 0 otherwise) are entered in column C4. The variable names Spending, Card, and Purchase are entered as the column headings on the worksheet. In subsequent steps, we refer to the data by using the variable names Spending, Card, and Purchase or the column indicators C2, C3, and C4. The following steps will generate the logistic regression output.

**Step 1.** Select the **Stat** menu
**Step 2.** Select the **Regression** menu
**Step 3.** Choose **Binary Logistic Regression**
**Step 4.** When the **Binary Logistic Regression** dialog box appears
        Enter Purchase in the **Response** box
        Enter Spending and Card in the **Model** box
        Click **OK**

The information in Figure 15.13 will now appear as a portion of the output.

# CHAPTER 16

# Regression Analysis: Model Building

## MONSANTO COMPANY*
### *ST. LOUIS, MISSOURI*

Monsanto Company traces its roots to one entrepreneur's investment of $500 and a dusty warehouse on the Mississippi riverfront, where in 1901 John F. Queeney began manufacturing saccharin. Today, Monsanto is one of the nation's largest chemical companies, producing more than a thousand products ranging from industrial chemicals to synthetic playing surfaces used in modern sports stadiums. Monsanto is a worldwide corporation with manufacturing facilities, laboratories, technical centers, and marketing operations in 65 countries.

Monsanto's Nutrition Chemical Division manufactures and markets a methionine supplement used in poultry, swine, and cattle feed products. Because poultry growers work with high volumes and low profit margins, cost-effective poultry feed products with the best possible nutrition value are needed. Optimal feed composition will result in rapid growth and high final body weight for a given level of feed intake. The chemical industry works closely with poultry growers to optimize poultry feed products. Ultimately, success depends on keeping the cost of poultry low in comparison with the cost of beef and other meat products.

Monsanto used regression analysis to model the relationship between body weight $y$ and the amount of methionine $x$ added to the poultry feed. Initially, the following simple linear estimated regression equation was developed.

$$\hat{y} = .21 + .42x$$

This estimated regression equation proved statistically significant; however, the analysis of the residuals indicated that a curvilinear relationship would be a better model of the relationship between body weight and methionine.

Monsanto researchers used regression analysis to develop an optimal feed composition for poultry growers. © PhotoDisc/Getty Images.

Further research conducted by Monsanto showed that although small amounts of methionine tended to increase body weight, at some point body weight leveled off and additional amounts of the methionine were of little or no benefit. In fact, when the amount of methionine increased beyond nutritional requirements, body weight tended to decline. The following estimated multiple regression equation was used to model the curvilinear relationship between body weight and methionine.

$$\hat{y} = -1.89 + 1.32x - .506x^2$$

Use of the regression results enabled Monsanto to determine the optimal level of methionine to be used in poultry feed products.

In this chapter we will extend the discussion of regression analysis by showing how curvilinear models such as the one used by Monsanto can be developed. In addition, we will describe a variety of tools that help determine which independent variables lead to the best estimated regression equation.

*The authors are indebted to James R. Ryland and Robert M. Schisla, Senior Research Specialists, Monsanto Nutrition Chemical Division, for providing this Statistics in Practice.

Model building is the process of developing an estimated regression equation that describes the relationship between a dependent variable and one or more independent variables. The major issues in model building are finding the proper functional form of the relationship and selecting the independent variables to be included in the model. In Section 16.1 we establish the framework for model building by introducing the concept of a general linear model. Section 16.2, which provides the foundation for the more sophisticated computer-based procedures, introduces a general approach for determining when to add or delete independent variables. In Section 16.3 we consider a larger regression problem involving eight independent variables and 25 observations; this problem is used to illustrate the variable selection procedures presented in Section 16.4, including stepwise regression, the forward selection procedure, the backward elimination procedure, and best-subsets regression. In Section 16.5 we show how the Durbin-Watson test can be used to detect serial or autocorrelation, and in Section 16.6 we show how regression analysis can be used for analysis of variance and experimental design problems.

 # 16.1  General Linear Model

Suppose we collected data for one dependent variable $y$ and $k$ independent variables $x_1$, $x_2, \ldots, x_k$. Our objective is to use these data to develop an estimated regression equation that provides the best relationship between the dependent and independent variables. As a general framework for developing more complex relationships among the independent variables, we introduce the concept of a **general linear model** involving $p$ independent variables.

*If you can write a regression model in the form of equation (16.1), the standard multiple regression procedures described in Chapter 15 are applicable.*

> **GENERAL LINEAR MODEL**
> $$y = \beta_0 + \beta_1 z_1 + \beta_2 z_2 + \cdots + \beta_p z_p + \epsilon \qquad (16.1)$$

**TABLE 16.1**

**DATA FOR THE REYNOLDS EXAMPLE**

| Months Employed | Scales Sold |
|---|---|
| 41 | 375 |
| 106 | 296 |
| 76 | 317 |
| 10 | 376 |
| 22 | 162 |
| 12 | 150 |
| 85 | 367 |
| 111 | 308 |
| 40 | 189 |
| 51 | 235 |
| 9 | 83 |
| 12 | 112 |
| 6 | 67 |
| 56 | 325 |
| 19 | 189 |

**Reynolds**

In equation (16.1), each of the independent variables $z_j$ (where $j = 1, 2, \ldots, p$) is a function of $x_1, x_2, \ldots, x_k$ (the variables for which data are collected). In some cases, each $z_j$ may be a function of only one $x$ variable. The simplest case is when we collect data for just one variable $x_1$ and want to estimate $y$ by using a straight-line relationship. In this case $z_1 = x_1$ and equation (16.1) becomes

$$y = \beta_0 + \beta_1 x_1 + \epsilon \qquad (16.2)$$

Equation (16.2) is the simple linear regression model introduced in Chapter 14 with the exception that the independent variable is labeled $x_1$ instead of $x$. In the statistical modeling literature, this model is called a *simple first-order model with one predictor variable*.

## Modeling Curvilinear Relationships

More complex types of relationships can be modeled with equation (16.1). To illustrate, let us consider the problem facing Reynolds, Inc., a manufacturer of industrial scales and laboratory equipment. Managers at Reynolds want to investigate the relationship between length of employment of their salespeople and the number of electronic laboratory scales sold. Table 16.1 gives the number of scales sold by 15 randomly selected salespeople for the most recent sales period and the number of months each salesperson has been employed by the firm. Figure 16.1 is the scatter diagram for these data. The scatter diagram indicates a possible curvilinear relationship between the length of time employed and the number of units sold. Before considering how to develop a curvilinear relationship for Reynolds, let us consider the Minitab output in Figure 16.2 corresponding to a simple first-order model; the estimated regression is

$$\text{Sales} = 111 + 2.38 \text{ Months}$$

where

$$\text{Sales} = \text{number of electronic laboratory scales sold}$$
$$\text{Months} = \text{the number of months the salesperson has been employed}$$

**FIGURE 16.1** SCATTER DIAGRAM FOR THE REYNOLDS EXAMPLE

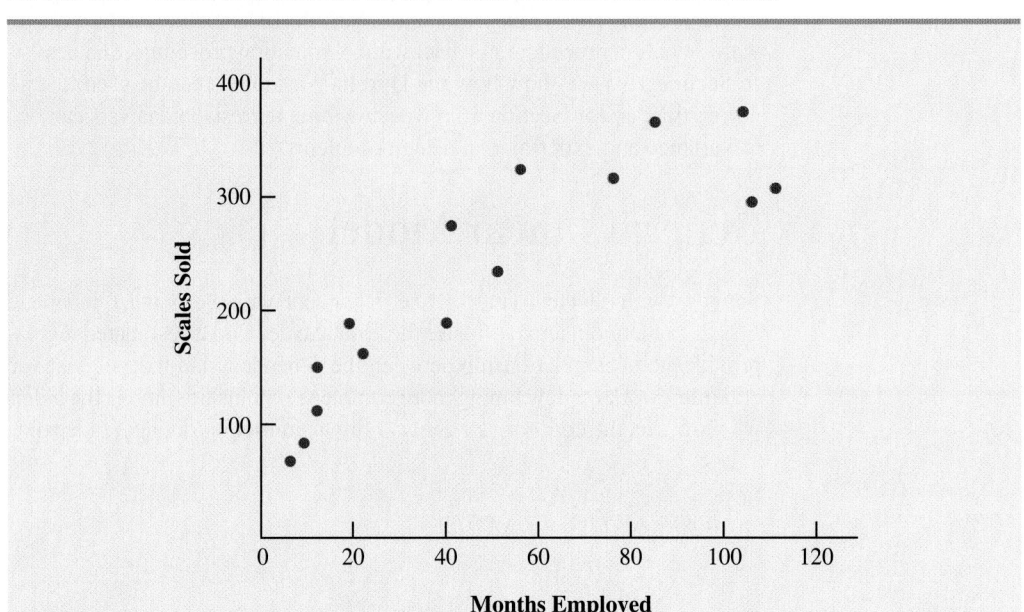

Figure 16.3 is the corresponding standardized residual plot. Although the computer output shows that the relationship is significant ($p$-value $= .000$) and that a linear relationship explains a high percentage of the variability in sales (R-sq $= 78.1\%$), the standardized residual plot suggests that a curvilinear relationship is needed.

To account for the curvilinear relationship, we set $z_1 = x_1$ and $z_2 = x_1^2$ in equation (16.1) to obtain the model

$$y = \beta_0 + \beta_1 x_1 + \beta_2 x_1^2 + \epsilon \qquad (16.3)$$

This model is called a *second-order model with one predictor variable*. To develop an estimated regression equation corresponding to this second-order model, the statistical soft-

**FIGURE 16.2** MINITAB OUTPUT FOR THE REYNOLDS EXAMPLE: FIRST-ORDER MODEL

```
The regression equation is
Sales = 111 + 2.38 Months

Predictor    Coef   SE Coef     T      p
Constant    111.23   21.63    5.14  0.000
Months      2.3768   0.3489   6.81  0.000

S = 49.52   R-sq = 78.1%   R-sq(adj) = 76.4%

Analysis of Variance

SOURCE          DF      SS       MS      F      p
Regression       1   113783   113783  46.41  0.000
Residual Error  13    31874     2452
Total           14   145657
```

**FIGURE 16.3    STANDARDIZED RESIDUAL PLOT FOR THE REYNOLDS EXAMPLE: FIRST-ORDER MODEL**

ware package we are using needs the original data in Table 16.1, as well as that data corresponding to adding a second independent variable that is the square of the number of months the employee has been with the firm. In Figure 16.4 we show the Minitab output corresponding to the second-order model; the estimated regression equation is

*The data for the* MonthsSq *independent variable is obtained by squaring the values of* Months.

$$\text{Sales} = 45.3 + 6.34 \text{ Months} - .0345 \text{ MonthsSq}$$

where

$$\text{MonthsSq} = \text{the square of the number of months the}$$
$$\text{salesperson has been employed}$$

Figure 16.5 is the corresponding standardized residual plot. It shows that the previous curvilinear pattern has been removed. At the .05 level of significance, the computer output shows that the overall model is significant ($p$-value for the $F$ test is 0.000); note also that the $p$-value corresponding to the $t$-ratio for MonthsSq ($p$-value = .002) is less than .05, and hence we can conclude that adding MonthsSq to the model involving Months is significant. With an R-sq(adj) value of 88.6%, we should be pleased with the fit provided by this estimated regression equation. More important, however, is seeing how easy it is to handle curvilinear relationships in regression analysis.

Clearly, many types of relationships can be modeled by using equation (16.1). The regression techniques with which we have been working are definitely not limited to linear, or straight-line, relationships. In multiple regression analysis the word *linear* in the term "general linear model" refers only to the fact that $\beta_0, \beta_1, \ldots, \beta_p$ all have exponents of 1; it does not imply that the relationship between $y$ and the $x_i$'s is linear. Indeed, in this section we have seen one example of how equation (16.1) can be used to model a curvilinear relationship.

**FIGURE 16.4    MINITAB OUTPUT FOR THE REYNOLDS EXAMPLE: SECOND-ORDER MODEL**

```
The regression equation is
Sales = 45.3 + 6.34 Months - 0.0345 MonthsSq

Predictor        Coef    SE Coef       T       p
Constant        45.35      22.77    1.99   0.070
Months          6.345      1.058    6.00   0.000
MonthsSq   -0.034486   0.008948   -3.85   0.002

S = 34.45   R-sq = 90.2%   R-sq(adj) = 88.6%

Analysis of Variance

SOURCE            DF       SS      MS       F       p
Regression         2   131413   65707   55.36   0.000
Residual Error    12    14244    1187
Total             14   145657
```

**FIGURE 16.5    STANDARDIZED RESIDUAL PLOT FOR THE REYNOLDS EXAMPLE: SECOND-ORDER MODEL**

## Interaction

If the original data set consists of observations for $y$ and two independent variables $x_1$ and $x_2$, we can develop a second-order model with two predictor variables by setting $z_1 = x_1$, $z_2 = x_2$, $z_3 = x_1^2$, $z_4 = x_2^2$, and $z_5 = x_1 x_2$ in the general linear model of equation (16.1). The model obtained is

$$y = \beta_0 + \beta_1 x_1 + \beta_2 x_2 + \beta_3 x_1^2 + \beta_4 x_2^2 + \beta_5 x_1 x_2 + \epsilon \qquad (16.4)$$

In this second-order model, the variable $z_5 = x_1 x_2$ is added to account for the potential effects of the two variables acting together. This type of effect is called **interaction**.

To provide an illustration of interaction and what it means, let us review the regression study conducted by Tyler Personal Care for one of its new shampoo products. Two factors believed to have the most influence on sales are unit selling price and advertising expenditure. To investigate the effects of these two variables on sales, prices of $2.00, $2.50, and $3.00 were paired with advertising expenditures of $50,000 and $100,000 in 24 test markets. The unit sales (in thousands) that were observed are reported in Table 16.2.

Table 16.3 is a summary of these data. Note that the mean sales corresponding to a price of $2.00 and an advertising expenditure of $50,000 is 461,000, and the mean sales corresponding to a price of $2.00 and an advertising expenditure of $100,000 is 808,000. Hence, with price held constant at $2.00, the difference in mean sales between advertising expenditures of $50,000 and $100,000 is $808,000 - 461,000 = 347,000$ units. When the price of the product is $2.50, the difference in mean sales is $646,000 - 364,000 = 282,000$ units. Finally, when the price is $3.00, the difference in mean sales is $375,000 - 332,000 = 43,000$ units. Clearly, the difference in mean sales between advertising expenditures of $50,000 and $100,000 depends on the price of the product. In other words, at higher selling prices, the effect of increased advertising expenditure diminishes. These observations provide evidence of interaction between the price and advertising expenditure variables.

To provide another perspective of interaction, Figure 16.6 shows the mean sales for the six price-advertising expenditure combinations. This graph also shows that the effect of advertising expenditure on mean sales depends on the price of the product; we again see the

TABLE 16.2   DATA FOR THE TYLER PERSONAL CARE EXAMPLE

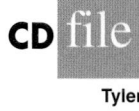

Tyler

| Price | Advertising Expenditure ($1000s) | Sales (1000s) | Price | Advertising Expenditure ($1000s) | Sales (1000s) |
|---|---|---|---|---|---|
| $2.00 | 50 | 478 | $2.00 | 100 | 810 |
| $2.50 | 50 | 373 | $2.50 | 100 | 653 |
| $3.00 | 50 | 335 | $3.00 | 100 | 345 |
| $2.00 | 50 | 473 | $2.00 | 100 | 832 |
| $2.50 | 50 | 358 | $2.50 | 100 | 641 |
| $3.00 | 50 | 329 | $3.00 | 100 | 372 |
| $2.00 | 50 | 456 | $2.00 | 100 | 800 |
| $2.50 | 50 | 360 | $2.50 | 100 | 620 |
| $3.00 | 50 | 322 | $3.00 | 100 | 390 |
| $2.00 | 50 | 437 | $2.00 | 100 | 790 |
| $2.50 | 50 | 365 | $2.50 | 100 | 670 |
| $3.00 | 50 | 342 | $3.00 | 100 | 393 |

**TABLE 16.3** MEAN UNIT SALES (1000s) FOR THE TYLER PERSONAL CARE EXAMPLE

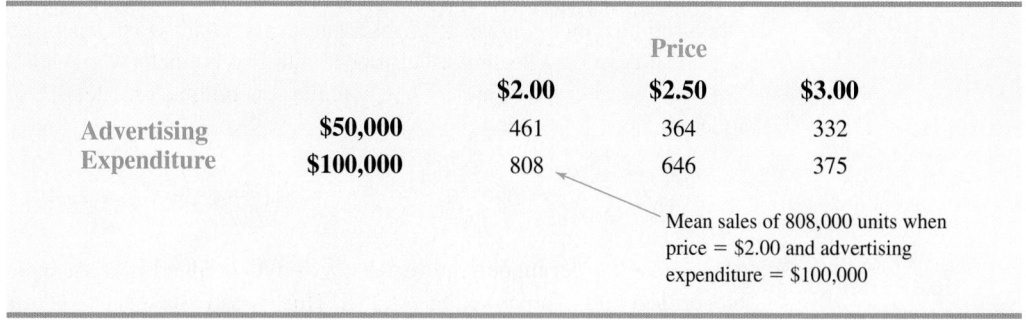

| | | Price | | |
|---|---|---|---|---|
| | | **$2.00** | **$2.50** | **$3.00** |
| **Advertising** | **$50,000** | 461 | 364 | 332 |
| **Expenditure** | **$100,000** | 808 | 646 | 375 |

Mean sales of 808,000 units when
price = $2.00 and advertising
expenditure = $100,000

**FIGURE 16.6** MEAN SALES AS A FUNCTION OF SELLING PRICE
AND ADVERTISING EXPENDITURE

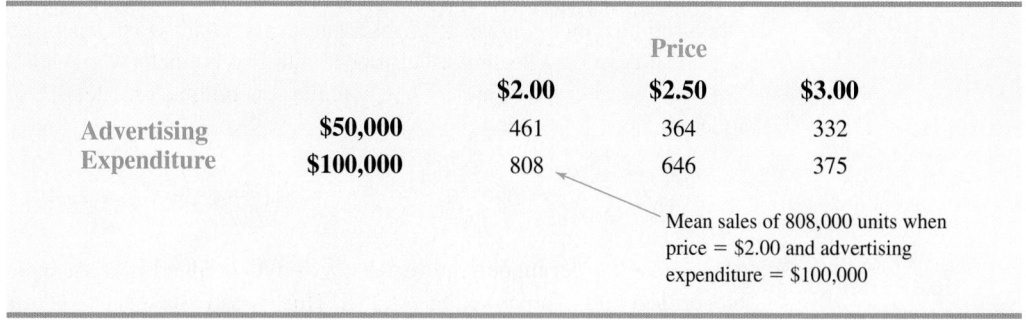

effect of interaction. When interaction between two variables is present, we cannot study the effect of one variable on the response $y$ independently of the other variable. In other words, meaningful conclusions can be developed only if we consider the joint effect that both variables have on the response.

To account for the effect of interaction, we will use the following regression model.

$$y = \beta_0 + \beta_1 x_1 + \beta_2 x_2 + \beta_3 x_1 x_2 + \epsilon \qquad (16.5)$$

where

$$y = \text{unit sales (1000s)}$$
$$x_1 = \text{price (\$)}$$
$$x_2 = \text{advertising expenditure (\$1000s)}$$

Note that equation (16.5) reflects Tyler's belief that the number of units sold depends linearly on selling price and advertising expenditure (accounted for by the $\beta_1 x_1$ and $\beta_2 x_2$ terms), and that there is interaction between the two variables (accounted for by the $\beta_3 x_1 x_2$ term).

To develop an estimated regression equation, a general linear model involving three independent variables ($z_1$, $z_2$, and $z_3$) was used.

$$y = \beta_0 + \beta_1 z_1 + \beta_2 z_2 + \beta_3 z_3 + \epsilon \qquad (16.6)$$

where

$$z_1 = x_1$$
$$z_2 = x_2$$
$$z_3 = x_1 x_2$$

Figure 16.7 is the Minitab output corresponding to the interaction model for the Tyler Personal Care example. The resulting estimated regression equation is

$$\text{Sales} = -276 + 175 \text{ Price} + 19.7 \text{ AdvExp} - 6.08 \text{ PriceAdv}$$

where

$$\text{Sales} = \text{unit sales (1000s)}$$
$$\text{Price} = \text{price of the product (\$)}$$
$$\text{AdvExp} = \text{advertising expenditure (\$1000s)}$$
$$\text{PriceAdv} = \text{interaction term (Price times AdvExp)}$$

*The data for the* PriceAdv *independent variable is obtained by multiplying each value of* Price *times the corresponding value of* AdvExp.

Because the model is significant ($p$-value for the $F$ test is 0.000) and the $p$-value corresponding to the $t$ test for PriceAdv is 0.000, we conclude that interaction is significant given the linear effect of the price of the product and the advertising expenditure. Thus, the regression results show that the effect of advertising expenditure on sales depends on the price.

## Transformations Involving the Dependent Variable

In showing how the general linear model can be used to model a variety of possible relationships between the independent variables and the dependent variable, we have focused attention on transformations involving one or more of the independent variables. Often it

**FIGURE 16.7   MINITAB OUTPUT FOR THE TYLER PERSONAL CARE EXAMPLE**

```
The regression equation is
Sales = - 276 + 175 Price + 19.7 AdvExpen - 6.08 PriceAdv

Predictor      Coef  SE Coef        T      p
Constant     -275.8    112.8    -2.44  0.024
Price        175.00    44.55     3.93  0.001
Adver        19.680     1.427   13.79  0.000
PriceAdv    -6.0800    0.5635  -10.79  0.000

S = 28.17   R-sq = 97.8%   R-sq(adj) = 97.5%

Analysis of Variance

SOURCE            DF       SS      MS       F      p
Regression         3   709316  236439  297.87  0.000
Residual Error    20    15875     794
Total             23   725191
```

**TABLE 16.4**

**MILES-PER-GALLON RATINGS AND WEIGHTS FOR 12 AUTOMOBILES**

| Weight | Miles per Gallon |
|--------|------------------|
| 2289 | 28.7 |
| 2113 | 29.2 |
| 2180 | 34.2 |
| 2448 | 27.9 |
| 2026 | 33.3 |
| 2702 | 26.4 |
| 2657 | 23.9 |
| 2106 | 30.5 |
| 3226 | 18.1 |
| 3213 | 19.5 |
| 3607 | 14.3 |
| 2888 | 20.9 |

**MPG**

is worthwhile to consider transformations involving the dependent variable $y$. As an illustration of when we might want to transform the dependent variable, consider the data in Table 16.4, which shows the miles-per-gallon ratings and weights for 12 automobiles. The scatter diagram in Figure 16.8 indicates a negative linear relationship between these two variables. Therefore, we use a simple first-order model to relate the two variables. The Minitab output is shown in Figure 16.9; the resulting estimated regression equation is

$$MPG = 56.1 - 0.0116 \text{ Weight}$$

where

$$MPG = \text{miles-per-gallon rating}$$
$$Weight = \text{weight of the car in pounds}$$

The model is significant ($p$-value for the $F$ test is 0.000) and the fit is very good (R-sq = 93.5%). However, we note in Figure 16.9 that observation 3 is identified as having a large standardized residual.

Figure 16.10 is the standardized residual plot corresponding to the first-order model. The pattern we observe does not look like the horizontal band we should expect to find if the assumptions about the error term are valid. Instead, the variability in the residuals appears to increase as the value of $\hat{y}$ increases. In other words, we see the wedge-shaped pattern referred to in Chapters 14 and 15 as being indicative of a nonconstant variance. We are not justified in reaching any conclusions about the statistical significance of the resulting estimated regression equation when the underlying assumptions for the tests of significance do not appear to be satisfied.

Often the problem of nonconstant variance can be corrected by transforming the dependent variable to a different scale. For instance, if we work with the logarithm of the dependent variable instead of the original dependent variable, the effect will be to compress the values of the dependent variable and thus diminish the effects of nonconstant variance. Most statistical packages provide the ability to apply logarithmic transformations using either the base 10 (common logarithm) or the base $e = 2.71828 \ldots$ (natural logarithm). We

FIGURE 16.8    SCATTER DIAGRAM FOR THE MILES-PER-GALLON PROBLEM

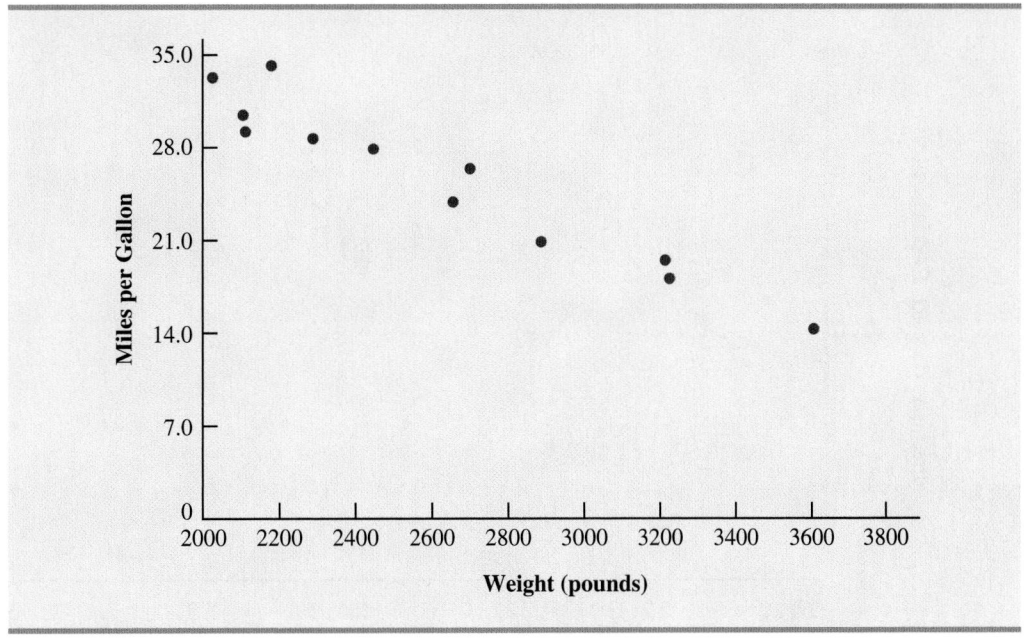

FIGURE 16.9    MINITAB OUTPUT FOR THE MILES-PER-GALLON PROBLEM

```
The regression equation is
MPG = 56.1 - 0.0116 Weight

Predictor         Coef    SE Coef        T       p
Constant        56.096      2.582    21.72   0.000
Weight      -0.0116436   0.0009677   -12.03   0.000

S = 1.671    R-sq = 93.5%    R-sq(adj) = 92.9%

Analysis of Variance

SOURCE            DF        SS        MS        F       p
Regression         1    403.98    403.98   144.76   0.000
Residual Error    10     27.91      2.79
Total             11    431.88

Unusual Observations
Obs  Weight     MPG      Fit   SE Fit   Residual   St Resid
  3    2180   34.200   30.713    0.644      3.487      2.26R

R denotes an observation with a large standardized residual.
```

FIGURE 16.10 STANDARDIZED RESIDUAL PLOT FOR THE MILES-PER-GALLON PROBLEM

applied a natural logarithmic transformation to the miles-per-gallon data and developed the estimated regression equation relating weight to the natural logarithm of miles-per-gallon. The regression results obtained by using the natural logarithm of miles-per-gallon as the dependent variable, labeled LogeMPG in the output, are shown in Figure 16.11; Figure 16.12 is the corresponding standardized residual plot.

Looking at the residual plot in Figure 16.12, we see that the wedge-shaped pattern has now disappeared. Moreover, none of the observations are identified as having a large stan-

FIGURE 16.11 MINITAB OUTPUT FOR THE MILES-PER-GALLON PROBLEM:
LOGARITHMIC TRANSFORMATION

```
The regression equation is
LogeMPG = 4.52 -0.000501 Weight

Predictor          Coef      SE Coef         T      p
Constant        4.52423      0.09932     45.55  0.000
Weight       -0.00050110  0.00003722    -13.46  0.000

S = 0.06425    R-sq = 94.8%   R-sq(adj) = 94.2%

Analysis of Variance

SOURCE          DF        SS         MS       F      p
Regression       1   0.74822    0.74822  181.22  0.000
Residual Error  10   0.04129    0.00413
Total           11   0.78950
```

**FIGURE 16.12**   STANDARDIZED RESIDUAL PLOT FOR THE MILES-PER-GALLON PROBLEM: LOGARITHMIC TRANSFORMATION

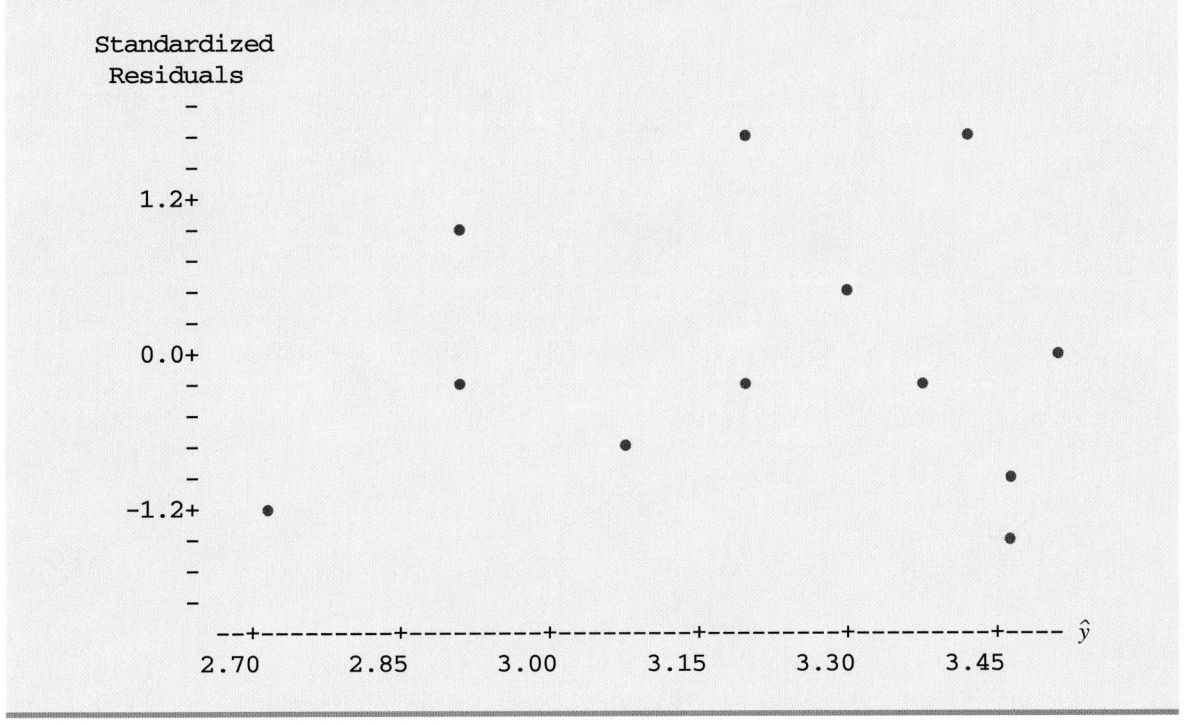

dardized residual. The model with the logarithm of miles per gallon as the dependent variable is statistically significant and provides an excellent fit to the observed data. Hence, we would recommend using the estimated regression equation

$$\text{Log}_e\text{MPG} = 4.52 - 0.000501 \text{ Weight}$$

To estimate the miles-per-gallon rating for an automobile that weighs 2500 pounds, we first develop an estimate of the logarithm of the miles-per-gallon rating.

$$\text{Log}_e\text{MPG} = 4.52 - 0.000501(2500) = 3.2675$$

The miles-per-gallon estimate is obtained by finding the number whose natural logarithm is 3.2675. Using a calculator with an exponential function, or raising $e$ to the power 3.2675, we obtain 26.2 miles per gallon.

Another approach to problems of nonconstant variance is to use $1/y$ as the dependent variable instead of $y$. This type of transformation is called a *reciprocal transformation*. For instance, if the dependent variable is measured in miles per gallon, the reciprocal transformation would result in a new dependent variable whose units would be 1/(miles per gallon) or gallons per mile. In general, there is no way to determine whether a logarithmic transformation or a reciprocal transformation will perform best without actually trying each of them.

## Nonlinear Models That Are Intrinsically Linear

Models in which the parameters $(\beta_0, \beta_1, \ldots, \beta_p)$ have exponents other than 1 are called nonlinear models. However, for the case of the exponential model, we can perform a transformation of variables that will enable us to perform regression analysis with equation (16.1), the general linear model. The exponential model involves the following regression equation.

$$E(y) = \beta_0 \beta_1^x \qquad (16.7)$$

This model is appropriate when the dependent variable $y$ increases or decreases by a constant percentage, instead of by a fixed amount, as $x$ increases.

As an example, suppose sales for a product $y$ are related to advertising expenditure $x$ (in thousands of dollars) according to the following exponential model.

$$E(y) = 500(1.2)^x$$

Thus, for $x = 1$, $E(y) = 500(1.2)^1 = 600$; for $x = 2$, $E(y) = 500(1.2)^2 = 720$; and for $x = 3$, $E(y) = 500(1.2)^3 = 864$. Note that $E(y)$ is not increasing by a constant amount in this case, but by a constant percentage; the percentage increase is 20%.

We can transform this nonlinear model to a linear model by taking the logarithm of both sides of equation (16.7).

$$\log E(y) = \log \beta_0 + x \log \beta_1 \qquad (16.8)$$

Now if we let $y' = \log E(y)$, $\beta_0' = \log \beta_0$, and $\beta_1' = \log \beta_1$, we can rewrite equation (16.8) as

$$y' = \beta_0' + \beta_1' x$$

It is clear that the formulas for simple linear regression can now be used to develop estimates of $\beta_0'$ and $\beta_1'$. Denoting the estimates as $b_0'$ and $b_1'$ leads to the following estimated regression equation.

$$\hat{y}' = b_0' + b_1' x \qquad (16.9)$$

To obtain predictions of the original dependent variable $y$ given a value of $x$, we would first substitute the value of $x$ into equation (16.9) and compute $\hat{y}'$. The antilog of $\hat{y}'$ would be the prediction of $y$, or the expected value of $y$.

Many nonlinear models cannot be transformed into an equivalent linear model. However, such models have had limited use in business and economic applications. Furthermore, the mathematical background needed for study of such models is beyond the scope of this text.

## Exercises

## Methods

1. Consider the following data for two variables, $x$ and $y$.

| $x$ | 22 | 24 | 26 | 30 | 35 | 40 |
|---|---|---|---|---|---|---|
| $y$ | 12 | 21 | 33 | 35 | 40 | 36 |

   a. Develop an estimated regression equation for the data of the form $\hat{y} = b_0 + b_1 x$.
   b. Use the results from part (a) to test for a significant relationship between $x$ and $y$. Use $\alpha = .05$.
   c. Develop a scatter diagram for the data. Does the scatter diagram suggest an estimated regression equation of the form $\hat{y} = b_0 + b_1 x + b_2 x^2$? Explain.

d. Develop an estimated regression equation for the data of the form $\hat{y} = b_0 + b_1 x + b_2 x^2$.

e. Refer to part (d). Is the relationship between $x$, $x^2$, and $y$ significant? Use $\alpha = .05$.

f. Predict the value of $y$ when $x = 25$.

2. Consider the following data for two variables, $x$ and $y$.

| $x$ | 9 | 32 | 18 | 15 | 26 |
|---|---|---|---|---|---|
| $y$ | 10 | 20 | 21 | 16 | 22 |

a. Develop an estimated regression equation for the data of the form $\hat{y} = b_0 + b_1 x$. Comment on the adequacy of this equation for predicting $y$.

b. Develop an estimated regression equation for the data of the form $\hat{y} = b_0 + b_1 x + b_2 x^2$. Comment on the adequacy of this equation for predicting $y$.

c. Predict the value of $y$ when $x = 20$.

3. Consider the following data for two variables, $x$ and $y$.

| $x$ | 2 | 3 | 4 | 5 | 7 | 7 | 7 | 8 | 9 |
|---|---|---|---|---|---|---|---|---|---|
| $y$ | 4 | 5 | 4 | 6 | 4 | 6 | 9 | 5 | 11 |

a. Does there appear to be a linear relationship between $x$ and $y$? Explain.

b. Develop the estimated regression equation relating $x$ and $y$.

c. Plot the standardized residuals versus $\hat{y}$ for the estimated regression equation developed in part (b). Do the model assumptions appear to be satisfied? Explain.

d. Perform a logarithmic transformation on the dependent variable $y$. Develop an estimated regression equation using the transformed dependent variable. Do the model assumptions appear to be satisfied by using the transformed dependent variable? Does a reciprocal transformation work better in this case? Explain.

## Applications

4. A highway department is studying the relationship between traffic flow and speed. The following model has been hypothesized.

$$y = \beta_0 + \beta_1 x + \epsilon$$

where

$$y = \text{traffic flow in vehicles per hour}$$
$$x = \text{vehicle speed in miles per hour}$$

The following data were collected during rush hour for six highways leading out of the city.

| Traffic Flow ($y$) | Vehicle Speed ($x$) |
|---|---|
| 1256 | 35 |
| 1329 | 40 |
| 1226 | 30 |
| 1335 | 45 |
| 1349 | 50 |
| 1124 | 25 |

a. Develop an estimated regression equation for the data.

b. Use $\alpha = .01$ to test for a significant relationship.

5. In working further with the problem of exercise 4, statisticians suggested the use of the following curvilinear estimated regression equation.

$$\hat{y} = b_0 + b_1 x + b_2 x^2$$

a. Use the data of exercise 4 to estimate the parameters of this estimated regression equation.
b. Use $\alpha = .01$ to test for a significant relationship.
c. Estimate the traffic flow in vehicles per hour at a speed of 38 miles per hour.

6. A study of emergency service facilities investigated the relationship between the number of facilities and the average distance traveled to provide the emergency service. The following table gives the data collected.

| Number of Facilities | Average Distance (miles) |
|---|---|
| 9 | 1.66 |
| 11 | 1.12 |
| 16 | .83 |
| 21 | .62 |
| 27 | .51 |
| 30 | .47 |

a. Develop a scatter diagram for these data, treating average distance traveled as the dependent variable.
b. Does a simple linear model appear to be appropriate? Explain.
c. Develop an estimated regression equation for the data that you believe will best explain the relationship between these two variables.

7. An important factor in purchasing a suitable computer monitor is the field of view. If a monitor has a wide field of view slight head turns can still provide an acceptable image and someone standing next to the monitor can still clearly see the image on the screen. In a review of 19-inch LCD monitors, *PCWORLD* found that although all the monitors they tested claimed a 170-degree arc—both horizontally and vertically—the actual angles for the monitors ranged from 108 to 167 degrees. The following data show the horizontal viewing angle for eight 19-inch monitors and *PCWORLD*'s overall rating based upon image quality, price, features, and support policies (*PCWORLD*, February 2003).

**Monitors**

| Monitor | Angle | Rating |
|---|---|---|
| Samsung SyncMaster 191T | 167 | 86 |
| ViewSonic VX900 | 159 | 82 |
| Sceptre Technologies X9S-Naga | 126 | 81 |
| Planar PL191M | 108 | 81 |
| Dell UltraSharp 1900FP | 153 | 81 |
| AOC LM914 | 123 | 81 |
| KDS USA Radius Rad-9 | 118 | 80 |
| NEC MultiSync LCD 1920NX | 123 | 80 |
| Iiyama Pro Lite 4821DT-BK | 119 | 80 |

a. Develop a scatter diagram for these data with horizontal viewing angles as the independent variable.
b. Does a simple linear regression model appear to be appropriate?
c. Develop an estimated regression equation for the data you believe will best explain the relationship between these two variables.

8. In Europe the number of Internet users varies widely from country to country. In 1999, 44.3% of all Swedes used the Internet, while in France the audience was less than 10%. The disparities are expected to persist even though Internet usage is expected to grow dramatically over the next several years. The following table shows the number of Internet users in 1999 and the projected number of users in 2005 for European countries.

**Internet**

| | 1999 Internet Users (%) | 2005 Projected Users (%) |
|---|---|---|
| Austria | 12.6 | 53.4 |
| Belgium | 24.2 | 60.2 |
| Denmark | 40.4 | 71.2 |
| Finland | 40.9 | 71.4 |
| France | 9.7 | 53.1 |
| Germany | 15.0 | 59.6 |
| Greece | 3.4 | 15.8 |
| Ireland | 12.1 | 46.7 |
| Italy | 8.4 | 34.4 |
| Netherlands | 18.6 | 61.4 |
| Norway | 38.0 | 71.7 |
| Portugal | 4.63 | 36.6 |
| Spain | 7.4 | 39.9 |
| Sweden | 44.3 | 71.9 |
| Switzerland | 28.1 | 66.7 |
| United Kingdom | 23.6 | 66.8 |

a. Develop a scatter diagram of the data using the 1999 Internet user percentage as the independent variable. Does a simple linear regression model appear to be appropriate? Discuss.
b. Develop an estimated multiple regression equation with $x$ = the number of 1999 Internet users and $x^2$ as the two independent variables.
c. Consider the nonlinear relationship shown by equation (16.7). Use logarithms to develop an estimated regression equation for this model.
d. Do you prefer the estimated regression equation developed in part (b) or part (c)? Explain.

9. Almost all U.S. light-rail systems use electric cars that run on tracks built at street level. According to the Federal Transit Administration, light-rail is one of the safest modes of travel, with an accident rate of .99 accidents per million passenger miles as compared to 2.29 for buses. The following data show the miles of track and the weekday ridership in thousands of passengers for selected light-rail systems (*USA Today,* January 7, 2003).

**LightRail**

| City | Miles | Riders |
|---|---|---|
| Los Angeles | 22 | 70 |
| San Diego | 47 | 75 |
| Portland | 38 | 81 |
| Sacramento | 21 | 31 |
| San Jose | 31 | 30 |
| San Francisco | 73 | 164 |
| Philadelphia | 69 | 84 |
| Boston | 51 | 231 |
| Denver | 17 | 35 |
| Salt Lake City | 18 | 28 |

*(continued)*

| City | Miles | Riders |
|------|-------|--------|
| Dallas | 44 | 39 |
| New Orleans | 16 | 14 |
| St. Louis | 34 | 42 |
| Pittsburgh | 18 | 25 |
| Buffalo | 6 | 23 |
| Cleveland | 15 | 15 |
| Newark | 9 | 8 |

a.  Develop a scatter diagram for these data, treating the number of miles of track as the independent variable. Does a simple linear regression model appear to be appropriate?

b.  Use a simple linear regression model to develop an estimated regression equation to predict the weekday ridership given the miles of track. Construct a standardized residual plot. Based upon the standardized residual plot, does a simple linear regression model appear to be appropriate?

c.  Perform a logarithmic transformation on the dependent variable. Develop an estimated regression equation using the transformed dependent variable. Do the model assumptions appear to be satisfied by using the transformed dependent variable?

d.  Perform a reciprocal transformation on the dependent variable. Develop an estimated regression equation using the transformed dependent variable.

e.  What estimated regression equation would you recommend? Explain.

##  16.2  Determining When to Add or Delete Variables

In this section we will show how an $F$ test can be used to determine whether it is advantageous to add one or more independent variables to a multiple regression model. This test is based on a determination of the amount of reduction in the error sum of squares resulting from adding one or more independent variables to the model. We will first illustrate how the test can be used in the context of the Butler Trucking example.

In Chapter 15, the Butler Trucking example was introduced to illustrate the use of multiple regression analysis. Recall that the managers wanted to develop an estimated regression equation to predict total daily travel time for trucks using two independent variables: miles traveled and number of deliveries. With miles traveled $x_1$ as the only independent variable, the least squares procedure provided the following estimated regression equation.

$$\hat{y} = 1.27 + .0678x_1$$

In Chapter 15 we showed that the error sum of squares for this model was SSE = 8.029. When $x_2$, the number of deliveries, was added as a second independent variable, we obtained the following estimated regression equation.

$$\hat{y} = -.869 + .0611x_1 + .923x_2$$

The error sum of squares for this model was SSE = 2.299. Clearly, adding $x_2$ resulted in a reduction of SSE. The question we want to answer is: Does adding the variable $x_2$ lead to a *significant* reduction in SSE?

We use the notation SSE($x_1$) to denote the error sum of squares when $x_1$ is the only independent variable in the model, SSE($x_1, x_2$) to denote the error sum of squares when $x_1$ and

$x_2$ are both in the model, and so on. Hence, the reduction in SSE resulting from adding $x_2$ to the model involving just $x_1$ is

$$\text{SSE}(x_1) - \text{SSE}(x_1, x_2) = 8.029 - 2.299 = 5.730$$

An $F$ test is conducted to determine whether this reduction is significant.

The numerator of the $F$ statistic is the reduction in SSE divided by the number of independent variables added to the original model. Here only one variable, $x_2$, has been added; thus, the numerator of the $F$ statistic is

$$\frac{\text{SSE}(x_1) - \text{SSE}(x_1, x_2)}{1} = 5.730$$

The result is a measure of the reduction in SSE per independent variable added to the model. The denominator of the $F$ statistic is the mean square error for the model that includes all of the independent variables. For Butler Trucking this corresponds to the model containing both $x_1$ and $x_2$; thus, $p = 2$ and

$$\text{MSE} = \frac{\text{SSE}(x_1, x_2)}{n - p - 1} = \frac{2.299}{7} = .3284$$

The following $F$ statistic provides the basis for testing whether the addition of $x_2$ is statistically significant.

$$F = \frac{\dfrac{\text{SSE}(x_1) - \text{SSE}(x_1, x_2)}{1}}{\dfrac{\text{SSE}(x_1, x_2)}{n - p - 1}} \tag{16.10}$$

The numerator degrees of freedom for this $F$ test is equal to the number of variables added to the model, and the denominator degrees of freedom is equal to $n - p - 1$.

For the Butler Trucking problem, we obtain

$$F = \frac{\dfrac{5.730}{1}}{\dfrac{2.299}{7}} = \frac{5.730}{.3284} = 17.45$$

Refer to Table 4 of Appendix B. We find that for a level of significance of $\alpha = .05$, $F_{.05} = 5.59$. Because $F = 17.45 > F_{.05} = 5.59$, we can reject the null hypothesis that $x_2$ is not statistically significant; in other words, adding $x_2$ to the model involving only $x_1$ results in a significant reduction in the error sum of squares.

When we want to test for the significance of adding only one more independent variable to a model, the result found with the $F$ test just described could also be obtained by using the $t$ test for the significance of an individual parameter (described in Section 15.4). Indeed, the $F$ statistic we just computed is the square of the $t$ statistic used to test the significance of an individual parameter.

Because the $t$ test is equivalent to the $F$ test when only one independent variable is being added to the model, we can now further clarify the proper use of the $t$ test for testing the significance of an individual parameter. If an individual parameter is not significant, the corresponding variable can be dropped from the model. However, if the $t$ test shows that two or more parameters are not significant, no more than one independent variable can ever be dropped from a model on the basis of a *t* test; if one variable is dropped, a second variable that was not significant initially might become significant.

We now turn to a consideration of whether the addition of more than one independent variable—as a set—results in a significant reduction in the error sum of squares.

## General Case

Consider the following multiple regression model involving $q$ independent variables, where $q < p$.

$$y = \beta_0 + \beta_1 x_1 + \beta_2 x_2 + \cdots + \beta_q x_q + \epsilon \tag{16.11}$$

If we add variables $x_{q+1}, x_{q+2}, \ldots, x_p$ to this model, we obtain a model involving $p$ independent variables.

$$\begin{aligned} y = \beta_0 + \beta_1 x_1 + \beta_2 x_2 + \cdots + \beta_q x_q \\ + \beta_{q+1} x_{q+1} + \beta_{q+2} x_{q+2} + \cdots + \beta_p x_p + \epsilon \end{aligned} \tag{16.12}$$

To test whether the addition of $x_{q+1}, x_{q+2}, \ldots, x_p$ is statistically significant, the null and alternative hypotheses can be stated as follows.

$$H_0: \beta_{q+1} = \beta_{q+2} = \cdots = \beta_p = 0$$
$$H_a: \text{One or more of the parameters is not equal to zero}$$

The following $F$ statistic provides the basis for testing whether the additional independent variables are statistically significant.

$$F = \frac{\dfrac{\text{SSE}(x_1, x_2, \ldots, x_q) - \text{SSE}(x_1, x_2, \ldots, x_q, x_{q+1}, \ldots, x_p)}{p - q}}{\dfrac{\text{SSE}(x_1, x_2, \ldots, x_q, x_{q+1}, \ldots, x_p)}{n - p - 1}} \tag{16.13}$$

This computed $F$ value is then compared with $F_\alpha$, the table value with $p - q$ numerator degrees of freedom and $n - p - 1$ denominator degrees of freedom. If $F > F_\alpha$, we reject $H_0$ and conclude that the set of additional independent variables is statistically significant. Note that for the special case where $q = 1$ and $p = 2$, equation (16.13) reduces to equation (16.10).

*Many computer packages, such as Minitab, provide extra sums of squares corresponding to the order in which each independent variable enters the model; in such cases, the computation of the F test for determining whether to add or delete a set of variables is simplified.*

Many students find equation (16.13) somewhat complex. To provide a simpler description of this $F$ ratio, we can refer to the model with the smaller number of independent variables as the reduced model and the model with the larger number of independent variables as the full model. If we let SSE(reduced) denote the error sum of squares for the reduced model and SSE(full) denote the error sum of squares for the full model, we can write the numerator of (16.13) as

$$\frac{\text{SSE(reduced)} - \text{SSE(full)}}{\text{number of extra terms}} \tag{16.14}$$

Note that "number of extra terms" denotes the difference between the number of independent variables in the full model and the number of independent variables in the reduced model. The denominator of equation (16.13) is the error sum of squares for the full model divided by the corresponding degrees of freedom; in other words, the denominator is the mean square error for the full model. Denoting the mean square error for the full model as MSE(full) enables us to write it as

$$F = \frac{\dfrac{\text{SSE(reduced)} - \text{SSE(full)}}{\text{number of extra terms}}}{\text{MSE(full)}} \qquad (16.15)$$

To illustrate the use of this $F$ statistic, suppose we have a regression problem involving 30 observations. One model with the independent variables $x_1$, $x_2$, and $x_3$ has an error sum of squares of 150 and a second model with the independent variables $x_1$, $x_2$, $x_3$, $x_4$, and $x_5$ has an error sum of squares of 100. Did the addition of the two independent variables $x_4$ and $x_5$ result in a significant reduction in the error sum of squares?

First, note that the degrees of freedom for SST is $30 - 1 = 29$ and that the degrees of freedom for the regression sum of squares for the full model is five (the number of independent variables in the full model). Thus, the degrees of freedom for the error sum of squares for the full model is $29 - 5 = 24$, and hence MSE(full) $= 100/24 = 4.17$. Therefore the $F$ statistic is

$$F = \frac{\dfrac{150 - 100}{2}}{4.17} = 6.00$$

This computed $F$ value is compared with the table $F$ value with two numerator and 24 denominator degrees of freedom. At the .05 level of significance, Table 4 of Appendix B shows $F_{.05} = 3.40$. Because $F = 6.00$ is greater than 3.40, we conclude that the addition of variables $x_4$ and $x_5$ is statistically significant.

## Use of $p$-Values

The $p$-value criterion can also be used to determine whether it is advantageous to add one or more independent variables to a multiple regression model. In the preceding example, we showed how to perform an $F$ test to determine if the addition of two independent variables, $x_4$ and $x_5$, to a model with three independent variables, $x_1$, $x_2$, and $x_3$, was statistically significant. For this example, the computed $F$ statistic was 6.00 and we concluded (by comparing $F = 6.00$ to the critical value $F_{.05} = 3.40$) that the addition of variables $x_4$ and $x_5$ was significant. The $p$-value associated with $F = 6.00$ (2 numerator and 24 denominator degrees of freedom) is .008. With a $p$-value $= .008 < \alpha = .05$, we also conclude that the addition of the two independent variables is statistically significant. It is difficult to determine the $p$-value directly from tables of the $F$ distribution, but computer software packages, such as Minitab or Excel, make computing the $p$-value easy.

### NOTES AND COMMENTS

Computation of the $F$ statistic can also be based on the difference in the regression sums of squares. To show this form of the $F$ statistic, we first note that

$$\text{SSE(reduced)} = \text{SST} - \text{SSR(reduced)}$$
$$\text{SSE(full)} = \text{SST} - \text{SSR(full)}$$

Hence

$$\text{SSE(reduced)} - \text{SSE(full)} = [\text{SST} - \text{SSR(reduced)}] - [\text{SST} - \text{SSR(full)}]$$
$$= \text{SSR (full)} - \text{SSR(reduced)}$$

Thus,

$$F = \frac{\dfrac{SSR(\text{full}) - SSR(\text{reduced})}{\text{number of extra terms}}}{MSE(\text{full})}$$

## Exercises

## Methods

10. In a regression analysis involving 27 observations, the following estimated regression equation was developed.

$$\hat{y} = 25.2 + 5.5x_1$$

For this estimated regression equation SST = 1550 and SSE = 520.

a. At $\alpha = .05$, test whether $x_1$ is significant.

Suppose that variables $x_2$ and $x_3$ are added to the model and the following regression equation is obtained.

$$\hat{y} = 16.3 + 2.3x_1 + 12.1x_2 - 5.8x_3$$

For this estimated regression equation SST = 1550 and SSE = 100.

b. Use an $F$ test and a .05 level of significance to determine whether $x_2$ and $x_3$ contribute significantly to the model.

11. In a regression analysis involving 30 observations, the following estimated regression equation was obtained.

$$\hat{y} = 17.6 + 3.8x_1 - 2.3x_2 + 7.6x_3 + 2.7x_4$$

For this estimated regression equation SST = 1805 and SSR = 1760.

a. At $\alpha = .05$, test the significance of the relationship among the variables.

Suppose variables $x_1$ and $x_4$ are dropped from the model and the following estimated regression equation is obtained.

$$\hat{y} = 11.1 - 3.6x_2 + 8.1x_3$$

For this model SST = 1805 and SSR = 1705.

b. Compute SSE$(x_1, x_2, x_3, x_4)$.
c. Compute SSE$(x_2, x_3)$.
d. Use an $F$ test and a .05 level of significance to determine whether $x_1$ and $x_4$ contribute significantly to the model.

## Applications

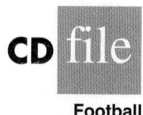

12. The following table gives some of the data available for 14 teams in the National Football League after 15 games.

| | | | | | Interceptions | |
| Team | Won–Lost | Total Points | Rushing Yards | Passing Yards | Made by Team | Made by Opponent |
| --- | --- | --- | --- | --- | --- | --- |
| Atlanta | 5–10 | 305 | 1907 | 2473 | 19 | 23 |
| Chicago | 12–3 | 187 | 2134 | 2718 | 14 | 24 |
| Dallas | 3–12 | 358 | 1858 | 3386 | 24 | 10 |

| Team | Won–Lost | Total Points | Rushing Yards | Passing Yards | Interceptions Made by Team | Interceptions Made by Opponent |
|------|----------|--------------|---------------|---------------|----------------------------|--------------------------------|
| Detroit | 4–11 | 292 | 1184 | 1971 | 15 | 12 |
| Green Bay | 3–12 | 298 | 1274 | 3046 | 22 | 20 |
| St. Louis Rams | 9–6 | 277 | 1882 | 3604 | 17 | 22 |
| Minnesota | 10–5 | 206 | 1744 | 3633 | 16 | 35 |
| New Orleans | 9–6 | 274 | 1843 | 2963 | 15 | 17 |
| N.Y. Giants | 10–5 | 277 | 1492 | 3096 | 14 | 15 |
| Philadelphia | 9–6 | 312 | 1812 | 3247 | 17 | 29 |
| Phoenix | 7–8 | 372 | 1909 | 3633 | 19 | 14 |
| San Francisco | 10–5 | 256 | 2453 | 3131 | 14 | 21 |
| Tampa Bay | 4–11 | 340 | 1650 | 3169 | 33 | 18 |
| Washington | 7–8 | 367 | 1377 | 3930 | 24 | 14 |

 a. Develop an estimated regression equation that can be used to predict the total points scored given the number of interceptions made by the team.

 b. Develop an estimated regression equation that can be used to predict the total points scored given the number of interceptions made by the team, the number of rushing yards, and the number of interceptions made by the opponents.

 c. At a .05 level of significance, test to see whether the addition of the number of rushing yards and the number of interceptions made by the opponents contributes significantly to the estimated regression equation developed in part (a). Explain.

13. Refer to exercise 12.

 a. Develop an estimated regression equation that relates the total points scored to the number of passing yards, the number of interceptions made by the team, and the number of interceptions made by the opponents.

 b. Develop an estimated regression equation using the independent variables in part (a) and the number of rushing yards.

 c. At a .05 level of significance, did the number of rushing yards contribute significantly to the estimated regression equation developed in part (a)? Explain.

14. A 10-year study conducted by the American Heart Association provided data on how age, blood pressure, and smoking relate to the risk of strokes. Data from a portion of this study follow. Risk is interpreted as the probability (times 100) that a person will have a stroke over the next 10-year period. For the smoker variable, 1 indicates a smoker and 0 indicates a nonsmoker.

| Risk | Age | Blood Pressure | Smoker |
|------|-----|----------------|--------|
| 12 | 57 | 152 | 0 |
| 24 | 67 | 163 | 0 |
| 13 | 58 | 155 | 0 |
| 56 | 86 | 177 | 1 |
| 28 | 59 | 196 | 0 |
| 51 | 76 | 189 | 1 |
| 18 | 56 | 155 | 1 |
| 31 | 78 | 120 | 0 |
| 37 | 80 | 135 | 1 |
| 15 | 78 | 98 | 0 |
| 22 | 71 | 152 | 0 |
| 36 | 70 | 173 | 1 |

CD file

**Stroke**

(*continued*)

| Risk | Age | Blood Pressure | Smoker |
|------|-----|----------------|--------|
| 15 | 67 | 135 | 1 |
| 48 | 77 | 209 | 1 |
| 15 | 60 | 199 | 0 |
| 36 | 82 | 119 | 1 |
| 8 | 66 | 166 | 0 |
| 34 | 80 | 125 | 1 |
| 3 | 62 | 117 | 0 |
| 37 | 59 | 207 | 1 |

a. Develop an estimated regression equation that can be used to predict the risk of stroke given the age and blood-pressure level.

b. Consider adding two independent variables to the model developed in part (a), one for the interaction between age and blood-pressure level and the other for whether the person is a smoker. Develop an estimated regression equation using these four independent variables.

c. At a .05 level of significance, test to see whether the addition of the interaction term and the smoker variable contribute significantly to the estimated regression equation developed in part (a).

15. The National Football League rates prospects by position on a scale that ranges from 5 to 9. The ratings are interpreted as follows: 8–9 should start the first year; 7.0–7.9 should start; 6.0–6.9 will make the team as backup; and 5.0–5.9 can make the club and contribute. The following table shows the position, weight, speed (for 40 yards), and ratings for 40 NFL prospects (*USA Today,* April 14, 2000).

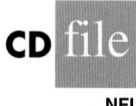

**CD** file

**NFL**

| Observation | Name | Position | Weight | Speed | Rating |
|-------------|------|----------|--------|-------|--------|
| 1 | Peter Warrick | Wide receiver | 194 | 4.53 | 9.0 |
| 2 | Plaxico Burress | Wide receiver | 231 | 4.52 | 8.8 |
| 3 | Sylvester Morris | Wide receiver | 216 | 4.59 | 8.3 |
| 4 | Travis Taylor | Wide receiver | 199 | 4.36 | 8.1 |
| 5 | Laveranues Coles | Wide receiver | 192 | 4.29 | 8.0 |
| 6 | Dez White | Wide receiver | 218 | 4.49 | 7.9 |
| 7 | Jerry Porter | Wide receiver | 221 | 4.55 | 7.4 |
| 8 | Ron Dugans | Wide receiver | 206 | 4.47 | 7.1 |
| 9 | Todd Pinkston | Wide receiver | 169 | 4.37 | 7.0 |
| 10 | Dennis Northcutt | Wide receiver | 175 | 4.43 | 7.0 |
| 11 | Anthony Lucas | Wide receiver | 194 | 4.51 | 6.9 |
| 12 | Darrell Jackson | Wide receiver | 197 | 4.56 | 6.6 |
| 13 | Danny Farmer | Wide receiver | 217 | 4.60 | 6.5 |
| 14 | Sherrod Gideon | Wide receiver | 173 | 4.57 | 6.4 |
| 15 | Trevor Gaylor | Wide receiver | 199 | 4.57 | 6.2 |
| 16 | Cosey Coleman | Guard | 322 | 5.38 | 7.4 |
| 17 | Travis Claridge | Guard | 303 | 5.18 | 7.0 |
| 18 | Kaulana Noa | Guard | 317 | 5.34 | 6.8 |
| 19 | Leander Jordan | Guard | 330 | 5.46 | 6.7 |
| 20 | Chad Clifton | Guard | 334 | 5.18 | 6.3 |
| 21 | Manula Savea | Guard | 308 | 5.32 | 6.1 |
| 22 | Ryan Johanningmeir | Guard | 310 | 5.28 | 6.0 |
| 23 | Mark Tauscher | Guard | 318 | 5.37 | 6.0 |
| 24 | Blaine Saipaia | Guard | 321 | 5.25 | 6.0 |
| 25 | Richard Mercier | Guard | 295 | 5.34 | 5.8 |
| 26 | Damion McIntosh | Guard | 328 | 5.31 | 5.3 |
| 27 | Jeno James | Guard | 320 | 5.64 | 5.0 |

| Observation | Name | Position | Weight | Speed | Rating |
|---|---|---|---|---|---|
| 28 | Al Jackson | Guard | 304 | 5.20 | 5.0 |
| 29 | Chris Samuels | Offensive tackle | 325 | 4.95 | 8.5 |
| 30 | Stockar McDougle | Offensive tackle | 361 | 5.50 | 8.0 |
| 31 | Chris McIngosh | Offensive tackle | 315 | 5.39 | 7.8 |
| 32 | Adrian Klemm | Offensive tackle | 307 | 4.98 | 7.6 |
| 33 | Todd Wade | Offensive tackle | 326 | 5.20 | 7.3 |
| 34 | Marvel Smith | Offensive tackle | 320 | 5.36 | 7.1 |
| 35 | Michael Thompson | Offensive tackle | 287 | 5.05 | 6.8 |
| 36 | Bobby Williams | Offensive tackle | 332 | 5.26 | 6.8 |
| 37 | Darnell Alford | Offensive tackle | 334 | 5.55 | 6.4 |
| 38 | Terrance Beadles | Offensive tackle | 312 | 5.15 | 6.3 |
| 39 | Tutan Reyes | Offensive tackle | 299 | 5.35 | 6.1 |
| 40 | Greg Robinson-Ran | Offensive tackle | 333 | 5.59 | 6.0 |

a.   Develop dummy variables that will account for the player's position.
b.   Develop an estimated regression equation to show how rating is related to position, weight, and speed.
c.   At the .05 level of significance, test whether the estimated regression equation developed in part (b) represents a significant relationship between the independent variables and the dependent variable.
d.   Is position a significant factor in the player's rating? Use $\alpha = .05$. Explain.

#  Analysis of a Larger Problem

In introducing multiple regression analysis, we used the Butler Trucking example extensively. The small size of this problem was an advantage in exploring introductory concepts, but would make it difficult to illustrate some of the variable selection issues involved in model building. To provide an illustration of the variable selection procedures discussed in the next section, we introduce a data set consisting of 25 observations on eight independent variables. Permission to use these data was provided by Dr. David W. Cravens of the Department of Marketing at Texas Christian University. Consequently, we refer to the data set as the Cravens data.*

The Cravens data are for a company that sells products in several sales territories, each of which is assigned to a single sales representative. A regression analysis was conducted to determine whether a variety of predictor (independent) variables could explain sales in each territory. A random sample of 25 sales territories resulted in the data in Table 16.5; the variable definitions are given in Table 16.6.

As a preliminary step, let us consider the sample correlation coefficients between each pair of variables. Figure 16.13 is the correlation matrix obtained using Minitab. Note that the sample correlation coefficient between Sales and Time is .623, between Sales and Poten is .598, and so on.

Looking at the sample correlation coefficients between the independent variables, we see that the correlation between Time and Accounts is .758; hence, if Accounts were used as an independent variable, Time would not add much more explanatory power to the model. Recall the rule-of-thumb test from the discussion of multicollinearity in Section 15.4: multicollinearity can cause problems if the absolute value of the sample correlation coefficient

*For details see David W. Cravens, Robert B. Woodruff, and Joe C. Stamper, "An Analytical Approach for Evaluating Sales Territory Performance," *Journal of Marketing*, 36 (January 1972): 31–37. Copyright © 1972 American Marketing Association.

TABLE 16.5    CRAVENS DATA

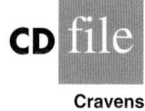

Cravens

| Sales | Time | Poten | AdvExp | Share | Change | Accounts | Work | Rating |
|---|---|---|---|---|---|---|---|---|
| 3,669.88 | 43.10 | 74,065.1 | 4,582.9 | 2.51 | 0.34 | 74.86 | 15.05 | 4.9 |
| 3,473.95 | 108.13 | 58,117.3 | 5,539.8 | 5.51 | 0.15 | 107.32 | 19.97 | 5.1 |
| 2,295.10 | 13.82 | 21,118.5 | 2,950.4 | 10.91 | −0.72 | 96.75 | 17.34 | 2.9 |
| 4,675.56 | 186.18 | 68,521.3 | 2,243.1 | 8.27 | 0.17 | 195.12 | 13.40 | 3.4 |
| 6,125.96 | 161.79 | 57,805.1 | 7,747.1 | 9.15 | 0.50 | 180.44 | 17.64 | 4.6 |
| 2,134.94 | 8.94 | 37,806.9 | 402.4 | 5.51 | 0.15 | 104.88 | 16.22 | 4.5 |
| 5,031.66 | 365.04 | 50,935.3 | 3,140.6 | 8.54 | 0.55 | 256.10 | 18.80 | 4.6 |
| 3,367.45 | 220.32 | 35,602.1 | 2,086.2 | 7.07 | −0.49 | 126.83 | 19.86 | 2.3 |
| 6,519.45 | 127.64 | 46,176.8 | 8,846.2 | 12.54 | 1.24 | 203.25 | 17.42 | 4.9 |
| 4,876.37 | 105.69 | 42,053.2 | 5,673.1 | 8.85 | 0.31 | 119.51 | 21.41 | 2.8 |
| 2,468.27 | 57.72 | 36,829.7 | 2,761.8 | 5.38 | 0.37 | 116.26 | 16.32 | 3.1 |
| 2,533.31 | 23.58 | 33,612.7 | 1,991.8 | 5.43 | −0.65 | 142.28 | 14.51 | 4.2 |
| 2,408.11 | 13.82 | 21,412.8 | 1,971.5 | 8.48 | 0.64 | 89.43 | 19.35 | 4.3 |
| 2,337.38 | 13.82 | 20,416.9 | 1,737.4 | 7.80 | 1.01 | 84.55 | 20.02 | 4.2 |
| 4,586.95 | 86.99 | 36,272.0 | 10,694.2 | 10.34 | 0.11 | 119.51 | 15.26 | 5.5 |
| 2,729.24 | 165.85 | 23,093.3 | 8,618.6 | 5.15 | 0.04 | 80.49 | 15.87 | 3.6 |
| 3,289.40 | 116.26 | 26,878.6 | 7,747.9 | 6.64 | 0.68 | 136.58 | 7.81 | 3.4 |
| 2,800.78 | 42.28 | 39,572.0 | 4,565.8 | 5.45 | 0.66 | 78.86 | 16.00 | 4.2 |
| 3,264.20 | 52.84 | 51,866.1 | 6,022.7 | 6.31 | −0.10 | 136.58 | 17.44 | 3.6 |
| 3,453.62 | 165.04 | 58,749.8 | 3,721.1 | 6.35 | −0.03 | 138.21 | 17.98 | 3.1 |
| 1,741.45 | 10.57 | 23,990.8 | 861.0 | 7.37 | −1.63 | 75.61 | 20.99 | 1.6 |
| 2,035.75 | 13.82 | 25,694.9 | 3,571.5 | 8.39 | −0.43 | 102.44 | 21.66 | 3.4 |
| 1,578.00 | 8.13 | 23,736.3 | 2,845.5 | 5.15 | 0.04 | 76.42 | 21.46 | 2.7 |
| 4,167.44 | 58.44 | 34,314.3 | 5,060.1 | 12.88 | 0.22 | 136.58 | 24.78 | 2.8 |
| 2,799.97 | 21.14 | 22,809.5 | 3,552.0 | 9.14 | −0.74 | 88.62 | 24.96 | 3.9 |

exceeds .7 for any two of the independent variables. If possible, then, we should avoid including both Time and Accounts in the same regression model. The sample correlation coefficient of .549 between Change and Rating is also high and may warrant further consideration.

Looking at the sample correlation coefficients between Sales and each of the independent variables can give us a quick indication of which independent variables are, by themselves, good predictors. We see that the single best predictor of Sales is Accounts, because

TABLE 16.6    VARIABLE DEFINITIONS FOR THE CRAVENS DATA

| Variable | Definition |
|---|---|
| Sales | Total sales credited to the sales representative |
| Time | Length of time employed in months |
| Poten | Market potential; total industry sales in units for the sales territory* |
| AdvExp | Advertising expenditure in the sales territory |
| Share | Market share; weighted average for the past four years |
| Change | Change in the market share over the previous four years |
| Accounts | Number of accounts assigned to the sales representative* |
| Work | Workload; a weighted index based on annual purchases and concentrations of accounts |
| Rating | Sales representative overall rating on eight performance dimensions; an aggregate rating on a 1–7 scale |

*These data were coded to preserve confidentiality.

FIGURE 16.13    SAMPLE CORRELATION COEFFICIENTS FOR THE CRAVENS DATA

|          | Sales  | Time   | Poten  | AdvExp | Share  | Change | Accounts | Work   |
|----------|--------|--------|--------|--------|--------|--------|----------|--------|
| Time     | 0.623  |        |        |        |        |        |          |        |
| Poten    | 0.598  | 0.454  |        |        |        |        |          |        |
| AdvExp   | 0.596  | 0.249  | 0.174  |        |        |        |          |        |
| Share    | 0.484  | 0.106  | -0.211 | 0.264  |        |        |          |        |
| Change   | 0.489  | 0.251  | 0.268  | 0.377  | 0.085  |        |          |        |
| Accounts | 0.754  | 0.758  | 0.479  | 0.200  | 0.403  | 0.327  |          |        |
| Work     | -0.117 | -0.179 | -0.259 | -0.272 | 0.349  | -0.288 | -0.199   |        |
| Rating   | 0.402  | 0.101  | 0.359  | 0.411  | -0.024 | 0.549  | 0.229    | -0.277 |

it has the highest sample correlation coefficient (.754). Recall that for the case of one independent variable, the square of the sample correlation coefficient is the coefficient of determination. Thus, Accounts can explain $(.754)^2(100)$, or 56.85%, of the variability in Sales. The next most important independent variables are Time, Poten, and AdvExp, each with a sample correlation coefficient of approximately .6.

Although there are potential multicollinearity problems, let us consider developing an estimated regression equation using all eight independent variables. The Minitab computer package provided the results in Figure 16.14. The eight-variable multiple regression model has an adjusted coefficient of determination of 88.3%. Note, however, that the $p$-values for the $t$ tests of individual parameters show that only Poten, AdvExp, and Share are significant at the $\alpha = .05$ level, given the effect of all the other variables. Hence, we might be

FIGURE 16.14    MINITAB OUTPUT FOR THE MODEL INVOLVING ALL EIGHT
INDEPENDENT VARIABLES

```
The regression equation is
Sales = - 1508 + 2.01 Time + 0.0372 Poten + 0.151 AdvExp + 199 Share
          + 291 Change + 5.55 Accounts + 19.8 Work + 8 Rating

Predictor       Coef    SE Coef       T       p
Constant      1507.8      778.6   -1.94   0.071
Time           2.010      1.931    1.04   0.313
Poten       0.037205   0.008202    4.54   0.000
AdvExp       0.15099    0.04711    3.21   0.006
Share         199.02      67.03    2.97   0.009
Change        290.9       186.8    1.56   0.139
Accounts      5.551       4.776    1.16   0.262
Work          19.79       33.68    0.59   0.565
Rating          8.2       128.5    0.06   0.950


S = 449.0   R-sq = 92.2%    R-sq(adj) = 88.3%


Analysis of Variance

SOURCE           DF          SS        MS       F       p
Regression        8    38153568   4769196   23.65   0.000
Residual Error   16     3225984    201624
Total            24    41379552
```

**FIGURE 16.15**   MINITAB OUTPUT FOR THE MODEL INVOLVING Poten, AdvExp, AND Share

```
The regression equation is
Sales = - 1604 + 0.0543 Poten + 0.167 AdvExp + 283 Share

Predictor       Coef    SE Coef       T      p
Constant      -1603.6     505.6    -3.17  0.005
Poten        0.054286  0.007474     7.26  0.000
AdvExp        0.16748   0.04427     3.78  0.001
Share          282.75     48.76     5.80  0.000

S = 545.5   R-sq = 84.9%   R-sq(adj) = 82.7%

Analysis of Variance

SOURCE          DF         SS        MS       F      p
Regression       3   35130240  11710080   39.35  0.000
Residual Error  21    6249310    297586
Total           24   41379552
```

inclined to investigate the results that would be obtained if we used just those three variables. Figure 16.15 shows the Minitab results obtained for the estimated regression equation with those three variables. We see that the estimated regression equation has an adjusted coefficient of determination of 82.7%, which, although not quite as good as that for the eight-independent-variable estimated regression equation, is high.

How can we find an estimated regression equation that will do the best job given the data available? One approach is to compute all possible regressions. That is, we could develop eight one-variable estimated regression equations (each of which corresponds to one of the independent variables), 28 two-variable estimated regression equations (the number of combinations of eight variables taken two at a time), and so on. In all, for the Cravens data, 255 different estimated regression equations involving one or more independent variables would have to be fitted to the data.

With the excellent computer packages available today, it is possible to compute all possible regressions. But doing so involves a great amount of computation and requires the model builder to review a large volume of computer output, much of which is associated with obviously poor models. Statisticians prefer a more systematic approach to selecting the subset of independent variables that provide the best estimated regression equation. In the next section, we introduce some of the more popular approaches.

# 16.4   Variable Selection Procedures

*Variable selection procedures are particularly useful in the early stages of building a model, but they cannot substitute for experience and judgment on the part of the analyst.*

In this section we discuss four **variable selection procedures**: stepwise regression, forward selection, backward elimination, and best-subsets regression. Given a data set with several possible independent variables, we can use these procedures to identify which independent variables provide the best model. The first three procedures are iterative; at each step of the procedure a single independent variable is added or deleted and the new model is evaluated. The process continues until a stopping criterion indicates that the procedure cannot find a better model. The last procedure (best subsets) is not a one-variable-at-a-time procedure; it evaluates regression models involving different subsets of the independent variables.

In the stepwise regression, forward selection, and backward elimination procedures, the criterion for selecting an independent variable to add or delete from the model at each step is based on the $F$ statistic introduced in Section 16.2. Suppose, for instance, that we are considering adding $x_2$ to a model involving $x_1$ or deleting $x_2$ from a model involving $x_1$ and $x_2$. To test whether the addition or deletion of $x_2$ is statistically significant, the null and alternative hypotheses can be stated as follows:

$$H_0: \beta_2 = 0$$
$$H_a: \beta_2 \neq 0$$

In Section 16.2 (see equation (16.10)) we showed that

$$F = \frac{\dfrac{\text{SSE}(x_1) - \text{SSE}(x_1, x_2)}{1}}{\dfrac{\text{SSE}(x_1, x_2)}{n - p - 1}}$$

can be used as a criterion for determining whether the presence of $x_2$ in the model causes a significant reduction in the error sum of squares. The $p$-value corresponding to this $F$ statistic is the criterion used to determine whether an independent variable should be added or deleted from the regression model. The usual rejection rule applies: Reject $H_0$ if $p$-value $\leq \alpha$.

## Stepwise Regression

The stepwise regression procedure begins each step by determining whether any of the variables *already in the model* should be removed. It does so by first computing an $F$ statistic and a corresponding $p$-value for each independent variable in the model. The level of significance $\alpha$ for determining whether an independent variable should be removed from the model is referred to in Minitab as *Alpha to remove.* If the $p$-value for any independent variable is greater than *Alpha to remove,* the independent variable with the largest $p$-value is removed from the model and the stepwise regression procedure begins a new step.

If no independent variable can be removed from the model, the procedure attempts to enter another independent variable into the model. It does so by first computing an $F$ statistic and corresponding $p$-value for each independent variable that is not in the model. The level of significance $\alpha$ for determining whether an independent variable should be entered into the model is referred to in Minitab as *Alpha to enter.* The independent variable with the smallest $p$-value is entered into the model provided its $p$-value is less than *Alpha to enter.* The procedure continues in this manner until no independent variables can be deleted from or added to the model.

Figure 16.16 shows the results obtained by using the Minitab stepwise regression procedure for the Cravens data using values of .05 for *Alpha to remove* and .05 for *Alpha to enter.* The stepwise procedure terminated after four steps. The estimated regression equation identified by the Minitab stepwise regression procedure is

$$\hat{y} = -1441.93 + 9.2 \text{ Accounts} + .175 \text{ AdvExp} + .0382 \text{ Poten} + 190 \text{ Share}$$

*Because the one-at-a-time procedures do not consider every possible subset for a given number of independent variables, they will not necessarily select the model with the highest R-sq value.*

Note also in Figure 16.16 that $s = \sqrt{\text{MSE}}$ has been reduced from 881 with the best one-variable model (using Accounts) to 454 after four steps. The value of R-sq has been increased from 56.85% to 90.04%, and the recommended estimated regression equation has an R-Sq(adj) value of 88.05%.

In summary, at each step of the stepwise regression procedure the first consideration is to see whether any independent variable can be removed from the current model. If none

FIGURE 16.16    MINITAB STEPWISE REGRESSION OUTPUT FOR THE CRAVENS DATA

```
Alpha-to-Enter: 0.05      Alpha-to-Remove: 0.05

Response is Sales on 8 predictors, with N = 25

      Step        1        2        3        4
  Constant   709.32    50.29  -327.24 -1441.93

  Accounts     21.7     19.0     15.6      9.2
  T-Value      5.50     6.41     5.19     3.22
  P-Value     0.000    0.000    0.000    0.004

  AdvExp                0.227    0.216    0.175
  T-Value               4.50     4.77     4.74
  P-Value               0.000    0.000    0.000

  Poten                         0.0219   0.0382
  T-Value                         2.53     4.79
  P-Value                        0.019    0.000

  Share                                    190
  T-Value                                 3.82
  P-Value                                0.001

  S             881      650      583      454
  R-Sq        56.85    77.51    82.77    90.04
  R-Sq(adj)   54.97    75.47    80.31    88.05
  C-p          67.6     27.2     18.4      5.4
```

of the independent variables can be removed from the model, the procedure checks to see whether any of the independent variables that are not currently in the model can be entered. Because of the nature of the stepwise regression procedure, an independent variable can enter the model at one step, be removed at a subsequent step, and then enter the model at a later step. The procedure stops when no independent variables can be removed from or entered into the model.

## Forward Selection

The forward selection procedure starts with no independent variables. It adds variables one at a time using the same procedure as stepwise regression for determining whether an independent variable should be entered into the model. However, the forward selection procedure does not permit a variable to be removed from the model once it has been entered. The procedure stops if the $p$-value for each of the independent variables not in the model is greater than *Alpha to enter.*

The estimated regression equation obtained using Minitab's forward selection procedure is

$$\hat{y} = -1441.93 + 9.2 \text{ Accounts} + .175 \text{ AdvExp} + .0382 \text{ Poten} + 190 \text{ Share}$$

Thus, for the Cravens data, the forward selection procedure (using .05 for *Alpha to enter*) leads to the same estimated regression equation as the stepwise procedure.

## Backward Elimination

The backward elimination procedure begins with a model that includes all the independent variables. It then deletes one independent variable at a time using the same procedure as stepwise regression. However, the backward elimination procedure does not permit an independent variable to be reentered once it has been removed. The procedure stops when none of the independent variables in the model have a *p*-value greater than *Alpha to remove.*

The estimated regression equation obtained using Minitab's backward elimination procedure for the Cravens data (using .05 for *Alpha to remove*) is

$$\hat{y} = -1312 + 3.8 \text{ Time} + .0444 \text{ Poten} + .152 \text{ AdvExp} + 259 \text{ Share}$$

Comparing the estimated regression equation identified using the backward elimination procedure to the estimated regression equation identified using the forward selection procedure, we see that three independent variables—AdvExp, Poten, and Share—are common to both. However, the backward elimination procedure has included Time instead of Accounts.

*Forward selection and backward elimination may lead to different models.*

Forward selection and backward elimination are the two extremes of model building; the forward selection procedure starts with no independent variables in the model and adds independent variables one at a time, whereas the backward elimination procedure starts with all independent variables in the model and deletes variables one at a time. The two procedures may lead to the same estimated regression equation. It is possible, however, for them to lead to two different estimated regression equations, as we saw with the Cravens data. Deciding which estimated regression equation to use remains a topic for discussion. Ultimately, the analyst's judgment must be applied. The best-subsets model building procedure we discuss next provides additional model-building information to be considered before a final decision is made.

## Best-Subsets Regression

Stepwise regression, forward selection, and backward elimination are approaches to choosing the regression model by adding or deleting independent variables one at a time. None of them guarantees that the best model for a given number of variables will be found. Hence, these one-variable-at-a-time methods are properly viewed as heuristics for selecting a good regression model.

Some software packages use a procedure called best-subsets regression that enables the user to find, given a specified number of independent variables, the best regression model. Minitab has such a procedure. Figure 16.17 is a portion of the computer output obtained by using the best-subsets procedure for the Cravens data set.

This output identifies the two best one-variable estimated regression equations, the two best two-variable equations, the two best three-variable equations, and so on. The criterion used in determining which estimated regression equations are best for any number of predictors is the value of the coefficient of determination (R-sq). For instance, Accounts, with an R-sq = 56.8%, provides the best estimated regression equation using only one independent variable; AdvExp and Accounts, with an R-sq = 77.5%, provides the best estimated regression equation using two independent variables; and Poten, AdvExp, and Share, with an R-sq = 84.9%, provides the best estimated regression equation with three independent variables. For the Cravens data, the adjusted coefficient of determination (Adj. R-sq = 89.4%) is largest for the model with six independent variables: Time, Poten, AdvExp, Share, Change, and Accounts. However, the best model with four independent variables (Poten, AdvExp, Share, Accounts) has an adjusted coefficient of determination almost as high (88.1%). All other things being equal, a simpler model with fewer variables is usually preferred.

FIGURE 16.17   PORTION OF MINITAB BEST-SUBSETS REGRESSION OUTPUT

```
                                                         A
                                                         c
                                                  A   C  c   R
                                               P  d S  h o   a
                                               T  o v  h a u W t
                                               i  t E  a n n o I
                         Adj.                  m  e x  r g t r n
     Vars   R-sq         R-sq         s        e  n p  e e s K g

       1    56.8         55.0       881.09                 X
       1    38.8         36.1      1049.3      X
       2    77.5         75.5       650.39           X     X
       2    74.6         72.3       691.11        X     X
       3    84.9         82.7       545.52        X X X
       3    82.8         80.3       582.64        X X     X
       4    90.0         88.1       453.84        X X X   X
       4    89.6         87.5       463.93      X X X X
       5    91.5         89.3       430.21      X X X X X
       5    91.2         88.9       436.75        X X X X X
       6    92.0         89.4       427.99      X X X X X X
       6    91.6         88.9       438.20        X X X X X X
       7    92.2         89.0       435.66      X X X X X X X
       7    92.0         88.8       440.29      X X X X X X   X
       8    92.2         88.3       449.02      X X X X X X X X
```

## Making the Final Choice

The analysis performed on the Cravens data to this point is good preparation for choosing a final model, but more analysis should be conducted before the final choice. As we noted in Chapters 14 and 15, a careful analysis of the residuals should be done. We want the residual plot for the chosen model to resemble approximately a horizontal band. Let us assume the residuals are not a problem and that we want to use the results of the best-subsets procedure to help choose the model.

The best-subsets procedure shows us that the best four-variable model contains the independent variables Poten, AdvExp, Share, and Accounts. This result also happens to be the four-variable model identified with the stepwise regression procedure. Table 16.7 is helpful in making the final choice. It shows several possible models consisting of some or all of these four independent variables.

TABLE 16.7   SELECTED MODELS INVOLVING ACCOUNTS, AdvExp, Poten, AND Share

| Model | Independent Variables | Adj. R-sq |
|-------|----------------------|-----------|
| 1 | Accounts | 55.0 |
| 2 | AdvExp, Accounts | 75.5 |
| 3 | Poten, Share | 72.3 |
| 4 | Poten, AdvExp, Accounts | 80.3 |
| 5 | Poten, AdvExp, Share | 82.7 |
| 6 | Poten, AdvExp, Share, Accounts | 88.1 |

From Table 16.7, we see that the model with just AdvExp and Accounts is good. The adjusted coefficient of determination is 75.5%, and the model with all four variables provides only a 12.6-percentage-point improvement. The simpler two-variable model might be preferred, for instance, if it is difficult to measure market potential (Poten). However, if the data are readily available and highly accurate predictions of sales are needed, the model builder would clearly prefer the model with all four variables.

## NOTES AND COMMENTS

1. The stepwise procedure requires that Alpha to remove be greater than or equal to Alpha to enter. This requirement prevents the same variable from being removed and then reentered at the same step.
2. Functions of the independent variables can be used to create new independent variables for use with any of the procedures in this section. For instance, if we wanted $x_1 x_2$ in the model to account for interaction, we would use the data for $x_1$ and $x_2$ to create the data for $z = x_1 x_2$.
3. None of the procedures that add or delete variables one at a time can be guaranteed to identify the best regression model. But they are excellent approaches to finding good models—especially when little multicollinearity is present.

## Exercises

### Applications

16. Two experts provided subjective lists of school districts that they think are among the best in the country. For each school district, the following data were obtained: average class size, instructional spending per student, average teacher salary, combined SAT score, percentage of students taking the SAT, and percentage of graduates attending a four-year college.

Schools

| City | Average Class Size | Instructional Spending per Student ($) | Average Teacher Salary ($) | Combined SAT Score/ (% Taking Test) | Attend Four-Year College (%) |
|---|---|---|---|---|---|
| Blue Springs, MO | 25 | 3,060 | 29,359 | 1083/(8) | 74 |
| Garden City, NY | 18 | 9,700 | 51,000 | 997/(99) | 77 |
| Indianapolis, IN | 30 | 3,222 | 30,482 | 716/(42) | 40 |
| Newport Beach, CA (Newport–Mesa) | 26 | 4,028 | 37,043 | 977/(46) | 51 |
| Novi, MI | 20 | 3,067 | 39,797 | 980/(15) | 53 |
| Piedmont, CA (Piedmont City) | 28 | 4,208 | 37,274 | 1,042/(91) | 75 |
| Pittsburgh, PA (Fox Chapel area) | 21 | 4,884 | 37,156 | 983/(80) | 66 |
| Scarsdale, NY (Edgemont) | 20 | 9,853 | 31,555 | 1,110/(98) | 87 |
| Wayne, PA (Radnor Township) | 22 | 5,022 | 40,406 | 1,040/(95) | 85 |
| Weston, MA | 21 | 4,680 | 39,800 | 1,031/(99) | 89 |
| Farmingdale, NY | 22 | 6,729 | 45,846 | 947/(75) | 81 |
| Mamaroneck, NY | 20 | 10,405 | 49,625 | 1,000/(90) | 69 |
| Mayfield, OH | 24 | 5,881 | 36,228 | 1,003/(25) | 48 |
| Morristown, NJ | 22 | 6,300 | 37,000 | 972/(80) | 64 |
| New Rochelle, NY | 23 | 8,875 | 41,650 | 1,039/(80) | 55 |
| Newtown Square, PA (Marple–Newtown) | 17 | 5,313 | 38,000 | 963/(75) | 79 |
| Omaha, NB (Westside) | 23 | 4,815 | 32,500 | 1,059/(31) | 81 |
| Shaker Heights, OH | 23 | 4,370 | 38,639 | 940/(56) | 82 |

Let the dependent variable be the percentage of graduates attending a four-year college.

a. Develop the best one-variable estimated regression equation.

b. Use the stepwise procedure to develop the best estimated regression equation.

c. Use the backward elimination procedure to develop the best estimated regression equation.

d. Use the best-subsets regression procedure to develop the best estimated regression equation.

17. Refer to the data in exercise 12. Let the dependent variable be the number of wins.

a. Develop the best one-variable estimated regression equation.

b. Use the stepwise procedure to develop the best estimated regression equation.

c. Use the backward elimination procedure to develop the best estimated regression equation.

d. Use the best-subsets regression procedure to develop the best estimated regression equation.

18. The Ladies Professional Golfers Association (LPGA) maintains statistics on performance and earnings for members of the LPGA Tour. Year-end LPGA Tour statistics for 1997 follow (*Golfweek,* December 6, 1997). Scoring Avg. is the average score per 18 holes of golf; Driving Distance is the average number of yards per drive; Fairways is the percentage of drives landing in the fairway; Greens is the percentage of times a player was able to hit the green in regulation; Putts is the average number of putts per round; and Sand Saves is the percentage of times a player was able to get "up and down" once in a greenside sand bunker. A green is considered hit in regulation if any part of the ball is touching the putting surface and the number of strokes taken to hit the green is not more than the value of par minus two.

**CD file**

**LPGATour**

| Player | Scoring Avg. | Driving Distance | Fairways | Greens | Putts | Sand Saves |
|---|---|---|---|---|---|---|
| Annika Sorenstam | 70.04 | 249.00 | 75.4 | 73.2 | 29.67 | 47.3 |
| Karrie Webb | 70.00 | 254.60 | 72.1 | 75.1 | 30.20 | 38.0 |
| Kelly Robbins | 70.35 | 256.00 | 69.3 | 78.6 | 29.96 | 44.9 |
| Chris Johnson | 70.84 | 249.40 | 66.9 | 70.4 | 30.17 | 39.6 |
| Tammie Green | 71.24 | 239.40 | 70.4 | 68.6 | 29.64 | 47.2 |
| Juli Inkster | 70.64 | 251.60 | 69.0 | 69.8 | 29.35 | 46.0 |
| Liselotte Neumann | 71.28 | 243.50 | 66.6 | 65.9 | 29.36 | 48.4 |
| Laura Davies | 70.86 | 258.40 | 56.4 | 68.8 | 29.90 | 40.0 |
| Nancy Lopez | 70.70 | 245.50 | 73.4 | 73.0 | 30.23 | 43.1 |
| Betsy King | 71.52 | 245.70 | 65.9 | 66.9 | 29.63 | 37.6 |
| Lorie Kane | 71.47 | 243.30 | 74.9 | 69.4 | 30.22 | 47.8 |
| Michelle McGann | 71.52 | 256.20 | 57.8 | 69.6 | 30.05 | 51.0 |
| Donna Andrews | 71.01 | 230.60 | 79.1 | 71.7 | 29.94 | 42.3 |
| Colleen Walkeer | 72.31 | 230.00 | 73.6 | 63.3 | 29.58 | 40.9 |
| Rosie Jones | 71.77 | 227.20 | 77.0 | 66.0 | 29.86 | 41.0 |
| Lisa Hackney | 71.34 | 246.00 | 69.8 | 65.1 | 29.91 | 36.4 |
| Jane Geddes | 71.34 | 261.20 | 64.5 | 70.0 | 30.15 | 44.2 |
| Alison Nicholas | 72.31 | 241.70 | 71.8 | 66.4 | 30.43 | 39.4 |
| Pat Hurst | 72.14 | 251.50 | 62.4 | 69.1 | 30.58 | 29.9 |
| Cindy Figg-Currier | 71.90 | 237.20 | 70.1 | 68.0 | 30.40 | 39.3 |

a. If the average score per 18 holes of golf is the dependent variable, what is the best one-variable estimated regression equation? What does the estimated regression equation suggest for players on the LPGA Tour?

b. Use the methods in this section to develop the best estimated multiple regression equation for estimating a player's average score.

c.  Does the estimated regression equation developed in part (b) appear reasonable in terms of interpretation?

d.  Michele Redman has the following data: Driving Distance 231.6 yards, Fairways 75.7%, Greens 65.2%, Putts 30.69, and Sand Saves 50.5%. Estimate the average score for this professional golfer.

19.  A sample of 16 companies taken from the *Stock Investor Pro* database was used to obtain the following data on the price/earnings (P/E) ratio, the gross profit margin, and the sales growth for each company (*Stock Investor Pro*, American Association of Individual Investors, August 21, 1997). The data in the Industry column are codes used to define the industry for each company: 1 = energy-international oil; 2 = health-drugs; and 3 = other.

**StkData**

|  | P/E Ratio | Gross Profit Margin (%) | Sales Growth (%) | Industry |
|---|---|---|---|---|
| Abbott Laboratories | 22.3 | 23.7 | 10.0 | 2 |
| American Home Products | 22.6 | 21.1 | 5.3 | 2 |
| Amoco | 16.7 | 11.0 | 16.5 | 1 |
| Bristol Meyers Squibb Co. | 25.9 | 26.6 | 9.4 | 2 |
| Chevron | 18.3 | 11.6 | 18.4 | 1 |
| Exxon | 18.7 | 9.8 | 8.3 | 1 |
| General Electric Company | 13.1 | 13.4 | 13.1 | 3 |
| Hewlett-Packard | 23.3 | 9.7 | 21.9 | 3 |
| IBM | 17.3 | 11.5 | 5.6 | 3 |
| Merck & Co. Inc. | 26.2 | 25.6 | 18.9 | 2 |
| Mobil | 18.7 | 8.2 | 8.1 | 1 |
| Pfizer | 34.6 | 25.1 | 12.8 | 2 |
| Pharmacia & Upjohn, Inc. | 22.3 | 15.0 | 2.7 | 2 |
| Procter & Gamble Co. | 5.4 | 14.9 | 5.4 | 3 |
| Texaco | 12.3 | 7.3 | 23.7 | 1 |
| Travelers Group Inc. | 28.7 | 17.8 | 28.7 | 3 |

Develop an estimated regression equation that can be used to predict price/earnings ratio. Briefly discuss the process you used to develop a recommended estimated regression equation for these data.

20.  Refer to exercise 14. Using age, blood pressure, whether a person is a smoker, and any interaction involving those variables, develop an estimated regression equation that can be used to predict risk. Briefly describe the process you used to develop an estimated regression equation for these data.

# (16.5) Residual Analysis

In Chapters 14 and 15 we showed how residual plots can be used to detect violations of assumptions about the regression model. We looked for violations of assumptions about the error term $\epsilon$ and the assumed functional form of the model. Some of the actions that can be taken when such violations are detected were already discussed in this chapter. When a different functional form is needed, curvilinear and interaction terms can be included through the use of the general linear model. When several independent variables are considered, the variable selection procedures of the preceding section may be appropriate.

In Chapters 14 and 15 we also discussed how residual analysis can be used to identify observations that can be classified as outliers or as being influential in determining the estimated regression equation. Some steps that should be taken when such observations are found were noted. In many regression studies involving data collected over time, a special type of correlation among the error terms can cause problems; it is called **serial correlation** or **autocorrelation**. In this section we show how the **Durbin-Watson test** can be used to detect significant autocorrelation.

## Autocorrelation and the Durbin-Watson Test

Often, the data used for regression studies in business and economics are collected over time. It is not uncommon for the value of $y$ at time $t$, denoted by $y_t$, to be related to the value of $y$ at previous time periods. In such cases, we say autocorrelation (also called serial correlation) is present in the data. If the value of $y$ in time period $t$ is related to its value in time period $t - 1$, first-order autocorrelation is present. If the value of $y$ in time period $t$ is related to the value of $y$ in time period $t - 2$, second-order autocorrelation is present, and so on.

When autocorrelation is present, one of the assumptions of the regression model is violated: the error terms are not independent. In the case of first-order autocorrelation, the error at time $t$, denoted $\epsilon_t$, will be related to the error at time period $t - 1$, denoted $\epsilon_{t-1}$. Two cases of first-order autocorrelation are illustrated in Figure 16.18. Panel A is the case of positive autocorrelation; panel B is the case of negative autocorrelation. With positive autocorrelation we expect a positive residual in one period to be followed by a positive residual in the next period, a negative residual in one period to be followed by a negative residual in the next period, and so on. With negative autocorrelation, we expect a positive residual in one period to be followed by a negative residual in the next period, then a positive residual, and so on.

When autocorrelation is present, serious errors can be made in performing tests of statistical significance based upon the assumed regression model. It is therefore important to be able to detect autocorrelation and take corrective action. We will show how the Durbin-Watson statistic can be used to detect first-order autocorrelation.

Suppose the values of $\epsilon$ are not independent but are related in the following manner:

$$\epsilon_t = \rho \epsilon_{t-1} + z_t \tag{16.16}$$

where $\rho$ is a parameter with an absolute value less than one and $z_t$ is a normally and independently distributed random variable with a mean of zero and a variance of $\sigma^2$. From equa-

**FIGURE 16.18**    TWO DATA SETS WITH FIRST-ORDER AUTOCORRELATION

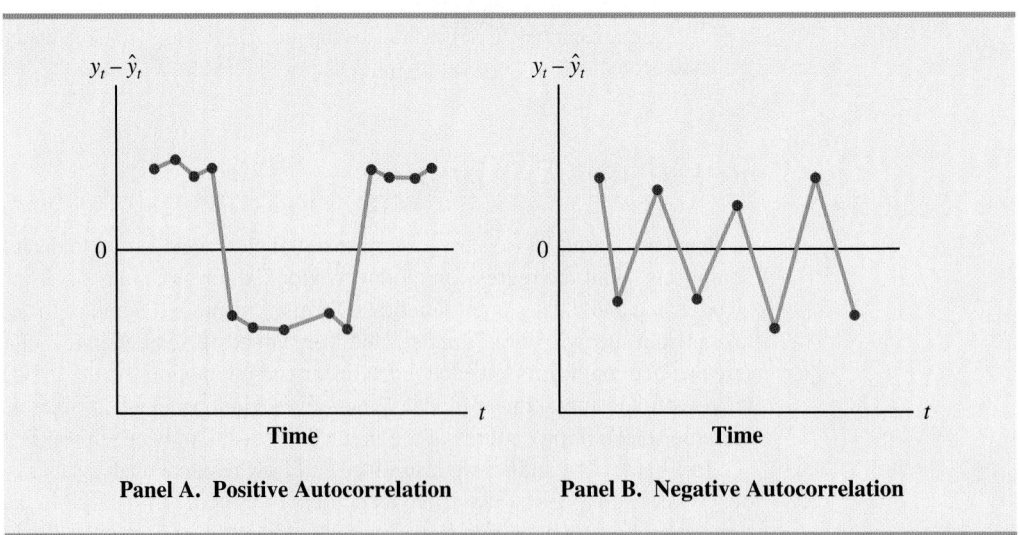

**Panel A.  Positive Autocorrelation**                    **Panel B.  Negative Autocorrelation**

tion (16.16) we see that if $\rho = 0$, the error terms are not related, and each has a mean of zero and a variance of $\sigma^2$. In this case, there is no autocorrelation and the regression assumptions are satisfied. If $\rho > 0$, we have positive autocorrelation; if $\rho < 0$, we have negative autocorrelation. In either of these cases, the regression assumptions about the error term are violated.

The Durbin-Watson test for autocorrelation uses the residuals to determine whether $\rho = 0$. To simplify the notation for the Durbin-Watson statistic, we denote the $i$th residual by $e_i = y_i - \hat{y}_i$. The Durbin-Watson test statistic is computed as follows.

**DURBIN-WATSON TEST STATISTIC**

$$d = \frac{\sum_{t=2}^{n}(e_t - e_{t-1})^2}{\sum_{t=1}^{n}e_t^2} \tag{16.17}$$

If successive values of the residuals are close together (positive autocorrelation), the value of the Durbin-Watson test statistic will be small. If successive values of the residuals are far apart (negative autocorrelation), the value of the Durbin-Watson statistic will be large.

The Durbin-Watson test statistic ranges in value from zero to four, with a value of two indicating no autocorrelation is present. Durbin and Watson developed tables that can be used to determine when their test statistic indicates the presence of autocorrelation. Table 16.8 shows lower and upper bounds ($d_L$ and $d_U$) for hypothesis tests using $\alpha = .05$, $\alpha = .025$, and $\alpha = .01$; $n$ denotes the number of observations. The null hypothesis to be tested is always that there is no autocorrelation.

$$H_0\text{: } \rho = 0$$

The alternative hypothesis to test for positive autocorrelation is

$$H_a\text{: } \rho > 0$$

The alternative hypothesis to test for negative autocorrelation is

$$H_a\text{: } \rho < 0$$

A two-sided test is also possible. In this case the alternative hypothesis is

$$H_a\text{: } \rho \neq 0$$

Figure 16.19 shows how the values of $d_L$ and $d_U$ in Table 16.8 are used to test for autocorrelation. Panel A illustrates the test for positive autocorrelation. If $d < d_L$, we conclude that positive autocorrelation is present. If $d_L \leq d \leq d_U$, we say the test is inconclusive. If $d > d_U$, we conclude that there is no evidence of positive autocorrelation.

Panel B illustrates the test for negative autocorrelation. If $d > 4 - d_L$, we conclude that negative autocorrelation is present. If $4 - d_U \leq d \leq 4 - d_L$, we say the test is inconclusive. If $d < 4 - d_U$, we conclude that there is no evidence of negative autocorrelation.

**TABLE 16.8    CRITICAL VALUES FOR THE DURBIN-WATSON TEST FOR AUTOCORRELATION**

*NOTE:* Entries in the table are the critical values for a one-tailed Durbin-Watson test for autocorrelation. For a two-tailed test, the level of significance is doubled.

**Significance Points of $d_L$ and $d_U$: $\alpha = .05$**

**Number of Independent Variables**

| n | 1 $d_L$ | 1 $d_U$ | 2 $d_L$ | 2 $d_U$ | 3 $d_L$ | 3 $d_U$ | 4 $d_L$ | 4 $d_U$ | 5 $d_L$ | 5 $d_U$ |
|---|---|---|---|---|---|---|---|---|---|---|
| 15 | 1.08 | 1.36 | 0.95 | 1.54 | 0.82 | 1.75 | 0.69 | 1.97 | 0.56 | 2.21 |
| 16 | 1.10 | 1.37 | 0.98 | 1.54 | 0.86 | 1.73 | 0.74 | 1.93 | 0.62 | 2.15 |
| 17 | 1.13 | 1.38 | 1.02 | 1.54 | 0.90 | 1.71 | 0.78 | 1.90 | 0.67 | 2.10 |
| 18 | 1.16 | 1.39 | 1.05 | 1.53 | 0.93 | 1.69 | 0.82 | 1.87 | 0.71 | 2.06 |
| 19 | 1.18 | 1.40 | 1.08 | 1.53 | 0.97 | 1.68 | 0.86 | 1.85 | 0.75 | 2.02 |
| 20 | 1.20 | 1.41 | 1.10 | 1.54 | 1.00 | 1.68 | 0.90 | 1.83 | 0.79 | 1.99 |
| 21 | 1.22 | 1.42 | 1.13 | 1.54 | 1.03 | 1.67 | 0.93 | 1.81 | 0.83 | 1.96 |
| 22 | 1.24 | 1.43 | 1.15 | 1.54 | 1.05 | 1.66 | 0.96 | 1.80 | 0.86 | 1.94 |
| 23 | 1.26 | 1.44 | 1.17 | 1.54 | 1.08 | 1.66 | 0.99 | 1.79 | 0.90 | 1.92 |
| 24 | 1.27 | 1.45 | 1.19 | 1.55 | 1.10 | 1.66 | 1.01 | 1.78 | 0.93 | 1.90 |
| 25 | 1.29 | 1.45 | 1.21 | 1.55 | 1.12 | 1.66 | 1.04 | 1.77 | 0.95 | 1.89 |
| 26 | 1.30 | 1.46 | 1.22 | 1.55 | 1.14 | 1.65 | 1.06 | 1.76 | 0.98 | 1.88 |
| 27 | 1.32 | 1.47 | 1.24 | 1.56 | 1.16 | 1.65 | 1.08 | 1.76 | 1.01 | 1.86 |
| 28 | 1.33 | 1.48 | 1.26 | 1.56 | 1.18 | 1.65 | 1.10 | 1.75 | 1.03 | 1.85 |
| 29 | 1.34 | 1.48 | 1.27 | 1.56 | 1.20 | 1.65 | 1.12 | 1.74 | 1.05 | 1.84 |
| 30 | 1.35 | 1.49 | 1.28 | 1.57 | 1.21 | 1.65 | 1.14 | 1.74 | 1.07 | 1.83 |
| 31 | 1.36 | 1.50 | 1.30 | 1.57 | 1.23 | 1.65 | 1.16 | 1.74 | 1.09 | 1.83 |
| 32 | 1.37 | 1.50 | 1.31 | 1.57 | 1.24 | 1.65 | 1.18 | 1.73 | 1.11 | 1.82 |
| 33 | 1.38 | 1.51 | 1.32 | 1.58 | 1.26 | 1.65 | 1.19 | 1.73 | 1.13 | 1.81 |
| 34 | 1.39 | 1.51 | 1.33 | 1.58 | 1.27 | 1.65 | 1.21 | 1.73 | 1.15 | 1.81 |
| 35 | 1.40 | 1.52 | 1.34 | 1.58 | 1.28 | 1.65 | 1.22 | 1.73 | 1.16 | 1.80 |
| 36 | 1.41 | 1.52 | 1.35 | 1.59 | 1.29 | 1.65 | 1.24 | 1.73 | 1.18 | 1.80 |
| 37 | 1.42 | 1.53 | 1.36 | 1.59 | 1.31 | 1.66 | 1.25 | 1.72 | 1.19 | 1.80 |
| 38 | 1.43 | 1.54 | 1.37 | 1.59 | 1.32 | 1.66 | 1.26 | 1.72 | 1.21 | 1.79 |
| 39 | 1.43 | 1.54 | 1.38 | 1.60 | 1.33 | 1.66 | 1.27 | 1.72 | 1.22 | 1.79 |
| 40 | 1.44 | 1.54 | 1.39 | 1.60 | 1.34 | 1.66 | 1.29 | 1.72 | 1.23 | 1.79 |
| 45 | 1.48 | 1.57 | 1.43 | 1.62 | 1.38 | 1.67 | 1.34 | 1.72 | 1.29 | 1.78 |
| 50 | 1.50 | 1.59 | 1.46 | 1.63 | 1.42 | 1.67 | 1.38 | 1.72 | 1.34 | 1.77 |
| 55 | 1.53 | 1.60 | 1.49 | 1.64 | 1.45 | 1.68 | 1.41 | 1.72 | 1.38 | 1.77 |
| 60 | 1.55 | 1.62 | 1.51 | 1.65 | 1.48 | 1.69 | 1.44 | 1.73 | 1.41 | 1.77 |
| 65 | 1.57 | 1.63 | 1.54 | 1.66 | 1.50 | 1.70 | 1.47 | 1.73 | 1.44 | 1.77 |
| 70 | 1.58 | 1.64 | 1.55 | 1.67 | 1.52 | 1.70 | 1.49 | 1.74 | 1.46 | 1.77 |
| 75 | 1.60 | 1.65 | 1.57 | 1.68 | 1.54 | 1.71 | 1.51 | 1.74 | 1.49 | 1.77 |
| 80 | 1.61 | 1.66 | 1.59 | 1.69 | 1.56 | 1.72 | 1.53 | 1.74 | 1.51 | 1.77 |
| 85 | 1.62 | 1.67 | 1.60 | 1.70 | 1.57 | 1.72 | 1.55 | 1.75 | 1.52 | 1.77 |
| 90 | 1.63 | 1.68 | 1.61 | 1.70 | 1.59 | 1.73 | 1.57 | 1.75 | 1.54 | 1.78 |
| 95 | 1.64 | 1.69 | 1.62 | 1.71 | 1.60 | 1.73 | 1.58 | 1.75 | 1.56 | 1.78 |
| 100 | 1.65 | 1.69 | 1.63 | 1.72 | 1.61 | 1.74 | 1.59 | 1.76 | 1.57 | 1.78 |

*(continued)*

TABLE 16.8    (*Continued*)

### Significance Points of $d_L$ and $d_U$: $\alpha = .025$
### Number of Independent Variables

| | 1 | | 2 | | 3 | | 4 | | 5 | |
|---|---|---|---|---|---|---|---|---|---|---|
| $n$ | $d_L$ | $d_U$ | $d_L$ | $d_U$ | $d_L$ | $d_U$ | $d_L$ | $d_U$ | $d_L$ | $d_U$ |
| 15 | 0.95 | 1.23 | 0.83 | 1.40 | 0.71 | 1.61 | 0.59 | 1.84 | 0.48 | 2.09 |
| 16 | 0.98 | 1.24 | 0.86 | 1.40 | 0.75 | 1.59 | 0.64 | 1.80 | 0.53 | 2.03 |
| 17 | 1.01 | 1.25 | 0.90 | 1.40 | 0.79 | 1.58 | 0.68 | 1.77 | 0.57 | 1.98 |
| 18 | 1.03 | 1.26 | 0.93 | 1.40 | 0.82 | 1.56 | 0.72 | 1.74 | 0.62 | 1.93 |
| 19 | 1.06 | 1.28 | 0.96 | 1.41 | 0.86 | 1.55 | 0.76 | 1.72 | 0.66 | 1.90 |
| 20 | 1.08 | 1.28 | 0.99 | 1.41 | 0.89 | 1.55 | 0.79 | 1.70 | 0.70 | 1.87 |
| 21 | 1.10 | 1.30 | 1.01 | 1.41 | 0.92 | 1.54 | 0.83 | 1.69 | 0.73 | 1.84 |
| 22 | 1.12 | 1.31 | 1.04 | 1.42 | 0.95 | 1.54 | 0.86 | 1.68 | 0.77 | 1.82 |
| 23 | 1.14 | 1.32 | 1.06 | 1.42 | 0.97 | 1.54 | 0.89 | 1.67 | 0.80 | 1.80 |
| 24 | 1.16 | 1.33 | 1.08 | 1.43 | 1.00 | 1.54 | 0.91 | 1.66 | 0.83 | 1.79 |
| 25 | 1.18 | 1.34 | 1.10 | 1.43 | 1.02 | 1.54 | 0.94 | 1.65 | 0.86 | 1.77 |
| 26 | 1.19 | 1.35 | 1.12 | 1.44 | 1.04 | 1.54 | 0.96 | 1.65 | 0.88 | 1.76 |
| 27 | 1.21 | 1.36 | 1.13 | 1.44 | 1.06 | 1.54 | 0.99 | 1.64 | 0.91 | 1.75 |
| 28 | 1.22 | 1.37 | 1.15 | 1.45 | 1.08 | 1.54 | 1.01 | 1.64 | 0.93 | 1.74 |
| 29 | 1.24 | 1.38 | 1.17 | 1.45 | 1.10 | 1.54 | 1.03 | 1.63 | 0.96 | 1.73 |
| 30 | 1.25 | 1.38 | 1.18 | 1.46 | 1.12 | 1.54 | 1.05 | 1.63 | 0.98 | 1.73 |
| 31 | 1.26 | 1.39 | 1.20 | 1.47 | 1.13 | 1.55 | 1.07 | 1.63 | 1.00 | 1.72 |
| 32 | 1.27 | 1.40 | 1.21 | 1.47 | 1.15 | 1.55 | 1.08 | 1.63 | 1.02 | 1.71 |
| 33 | 1.28 | 1.41 | 1.22 | 1.48 | 1.16 | 1.55 | 1.10 | 1.63 | 1.04 | 1.71 |
| 34 | 1.29 | 1.41 | 1.24 | 1.48 | 1.17 | 1.55 | 1.12 | 1.63 | 1.06 | 1.70 |
| 35 | 1.30 | 1.42 | 1.25 | 1.48 | 1.19 | 1.55 | 1.13 | 1.63 | 1.07 | 1.70 |
| 36 | 1.31 | 1.43 | 1.26 | 1.49 | 1.20 | 1.56 | 1.15 | 1.63 | 1.09 | 1.70 |
| 37 | 1.32 | 1.43 | 1.27 | 1.49 | 1.21 | 1.56 | 1.16 | 1.62 | 1.10 | 1.70 |
| 38 | 1.33 | 1.44 | 1.28 | 1.50 | 1.23 | 1.56 | 1.17 | 1.62 | 1.12 | 1.70 |
| 39 | 1.34 | 1.44 | 1.29 | 1.50 | 1.24 | 1.56 | 1.19 | 1.63 | 1.13 | 1.69 |
| 40 | 1.35 | 1.45 | 1.30 | 1.51 | 1.25 | 1.57 | 1.20 | 1.63 | 1.15 | 1.69 |
| 45 | 1.39 | 1.48 | 1.34 | 1.53 | 1.30 | 1.58 | 1.25 | 1.63 | 1.21 | 1.69 |
| 50 | 1.42 | 1.50 | 1.38 | 1.54 | 1.34 | 1.59 | 1.30 | 1.64 | 1.26 | 1.69 |
| 55 | 1.45 | 1.52 | 1.41 | 1.56 | 1.37 | 1.60 | 1.33 | 1.64 | 1.30 | 1.69 |
| 60 | 1.47 | 1.54 | 1.44 | 1.57 | 1.40 | 1.61 | 1.37 | 1.65 | 1.33 | 1.69 |
| 65 | 1.49 | 1.55 | 1.46 | 1.59 | 1.43 | 1.62 | 1.40 | 1.66 | 1.36 | 1.69 |
| 70 | 1.51 | 1.57 | 1.48 | 1.60 | 1.45 | 1.63 | 1.42 | 1.66 | 1.39 | 1.70 |
| 75 | 1.53 | 1.58 | 1.50 | 1.61 | 1.47 | 1.64 | 1.45 | 1.67 | 1.42 | 1.70 |
| 80 | 1.54 | 1.59 | 1.52 | 1.62 | 1.49 | 1.65 | 1.47 | 1.67 | 1.44 | 1.70 |
| 85 | 1.56 | 1.60 | 1.53 | 1.63 | 1.51 | 1.65 | 1.49 | 1.68 | 1.46 | 1.71 |
| 90 | 1.57 | 1.61 | 1.55 | 1.64 | 1.53 | 1.66 | 1.50 | 1.69 | 1.48 | 1.71 |
| 95 | 1.58 | 1.62 | 1.56 | 1.65 | 1.54 | 1.67 | 1.52 | 1.69 | 1.50 | 1.71 |
| 100 | 1.59 | 1.63 | 1.57 | 1.65 | 1.55 | 1.67 | 1.53 | 1.70 | 1.51 | 1.72 |

(*continued*)

TABLE 16.8   (*Continued*)

**Significance Points of $d_L$ and $d_U$: $\alpha = .01$**

**Number of Independent Variables**

| | 1 | | 2 | | 3 | | 4 | | 5 | |
|---|---|---|---|---|---|---|---|---|---|---|
| $n$ | $d_L$ | $d_U$ | $d_L$ | $d_U$ | $d_L$ | $d_U$ | $d_L$ | $d_U$ | $d_L$ | $d_U$ |
| 15 | 0.81 | 1.07 | 0.70 | 1.25 | 0.59 | 1.46 | 0.49 | 1.70 | 0.39 | 1.96 |
| 16 | 0.84 | 1.09 | 0.74 | 1.25 | 0.63 | 1.44 | 0.53 | 1.66 | 0.44 | 1.90 |
| 17 | 0.87 | 1.10 | 0.77 | 1.25 | 0.67 | 1.43 | 0.57 | 1.63 | 0.48 | 1.85 |
| 18 | 0.90 | 1.12 | 0.80 | 1.26 | 0.71 | 1.42 | 0.61 | 1.60 | 0.52 | 1.80 |
| 19 | 0.93 | 1.13 | 0.83 | 1.26 | 0.74 | 1.41 | 0.65 | 1.58 | 0.56 | 1.77 |
| 20 | 0.95 | 1.15 | 0.86 | 1.27 | 0.77 | 1.41 | 0.68 | 1.57 | 0.60 | 1.74 |
| 21 | 0.97 | 1.16 | 0.89 | 1.27 | 0.80 | 1.41 | 0.72 | 1.55 | 0.63 | 1.71 |
| 22 | 1.00 | 1.17 | 0.91 | 1.28 | 0.83 | 1.40 | 0.75 | 1.54 | 0.66 | 1.69 |
| 23 | 1.02 | 1.19 | 0.94 | 1.29 | 0.86 | 1.40 | 0.77 | 1.53 | 0.70 | 1.67 |
| 24 | 1.04 | 1.20 | 0.96 | 1.30 | 0.88 | 1.41 | 0.80 | 1.53 | 0.72 | 1.66 |
| 25 | 1.05 | 1.21 | 0.98 | 1.30 | 0.90 | 1.41 | 0.83 | 1.52 | 0.75 | 1.65 |
| 26 | 1.07 | 1.22 | 1.00 | 1.31 | 0.93 | 1.41 | 0.85 | 1.52 | 0.78 | 1.64 |
| 27 | 1.09 | 1.23 | 1.02 | 1.32 | 0.95 | 1.41 | 0.88 | 1.51 | 0.81 | 1.63 |
| 28 | 1.10 | 1.24 | 1.04 | 1.32 | 0.97 | 1.41 | 0.90 | 1.51 | 0.83 | 1.62 |
| 29 | 1.12 | 1.25 | 1.05 | 1.33 | 0.99 | 1.42 | 0.92 | 1.51 | 0.85 | 1.61 |
| 30 | 1.13 | 1.26 | 1.07 | 1.34 | 1.01 | 1.42 | 0.94 | 1.51 | 0.88 | 1.61 |
| 31 | 1.15 | 1.27 | 1.08 | 1.34 | 1.02 | 1.42 | 0.96 | 1.51 | 0.90 | 1.60 |
| 32 | 1.16 | 1.28 | 1.10 | 1.35 | 1.04 | 1.43 | 0.98 | 1.51 | 0.92 | 1.60 |
| 33 | 1.17 | 1.29 | 1.11 | 1.36 | 1.05 | 1.43 | 1.00 | 1.51 | 0.94 | 1.59 |
| 34 | 1.18 | 1.30 | 1.13 | 1.36 | 1.07 | 1.43 | 1.01 | 1.51 | 0.95 | 1.59 |
| 35 | 1.19 | 1.31 | 1.14 | 1.37 | 1.08 | 1.44 | 1.03 | 1.51 | 0.97 | 1.59 |
| 36 | 1.21 | 1.32 | 1.15 | 1.38 | 1.10 | 1.44 | 1.04 | 1.51 | 0.99 | 1.59 |
| 37 | 1.22 | 1.32 | 1.16 | 1.38 | 1.11 | 1.45 | 1.06 | 1.51 | 1.00 | 1.59 |
| 38 | 1.23 | 1.33 | 1.18 | 1.39 | 1.12 | 1.45 | 1.07 | 1.52 | 1.02 | 1.58 |
| 39 | 1.24 | 1.34 | 1.19 | 1.39 | 1.14 | 1.45 | 1.09 | 1.52 | 1.03 | 1.58 |
| 40 | 1.25 | 1.34 | 1.20 | 1.40 | 1.15 | 1.46 | 1.10 | 1.52 | 1.05 | 1.58 |
| 45 | 1.29 | 1.38 | 1.24 | 1.42 | 1.20 | 1.48 | 1.16 | 1.53 | 1.11 | 1.58 |
| 50 | 1.32 | 1.40 | 1.28 | 1.45 | 1.24 | 1.49 | 1.20 | 1.54 | 1.16 | 1.59 |
| 55 | 1.36 | 1.43 | 1.32 | 1.47 | 1.28 | 1.51 | 1.25 | 1.55 | 1.21 | 1.59 |
| 60 | 1.38 | 1.45 | 1.35 | 1.48 | 1.32 | 1.52 | 1.28 | 1.56 | 1.25 | 1.60 |
| 65 | 1.41 | 1.47 | 1.38 | 1.50 | 1.35 | 1.53 | 1.31 | 1.57 | 1.28 | 1.61 |
| 70 | 1.43 | 1.49 | 1.40 | 1.52 | 1.37 | 1.55 | 1.34 | 1.58 | 1.31 | 1.61 |
| 75 | 1.45 | 1.50 | 1.42 | 1.53 | 1.39 | 1.56 | 1.37 | 1.59 | 1.34 | 1.62 |
| 80 | 1.47 | 1.52 | 1.44 | 1.54 | 1.42 | 1.57 | 1.39 | 1.60 | 1.36 | 1.62 |
| 85 | 1.48 | 1.53 | 1.46 | 1.55 | 1.43 | 1.58 | 1.41 | 1.60 | 1.39 | 1.63 |
| 90 | 1.50 | 1.54 | 1.47 | 1.56 | 1.45 | 1.59 | 1.43 | 1.61 | 1.41 | 1.64 |
| 95 | 1.51 | 1.55 | 1.49 | 1.57 | 1.47 | 1.60 | 1.45 | 1.62 | 1.42 | 1.64 |
| 100 | 1.52 | 1.56 | 1.50 | 1.58 | 1.48 | 1.60 | 1.46 | 1.63 | 1.44 | 1.65 |

*Source:* J. Durbin and G. S. Watson, "Testing for Serial Correlation in Least Squares Regression II," *Biometrika,* 38 (1951), 159–178.

FIGURE 16.19   HYPOTHESIS TEST FOR AUTOCORRELATION USING
THE DURBIN-WATSON TEST

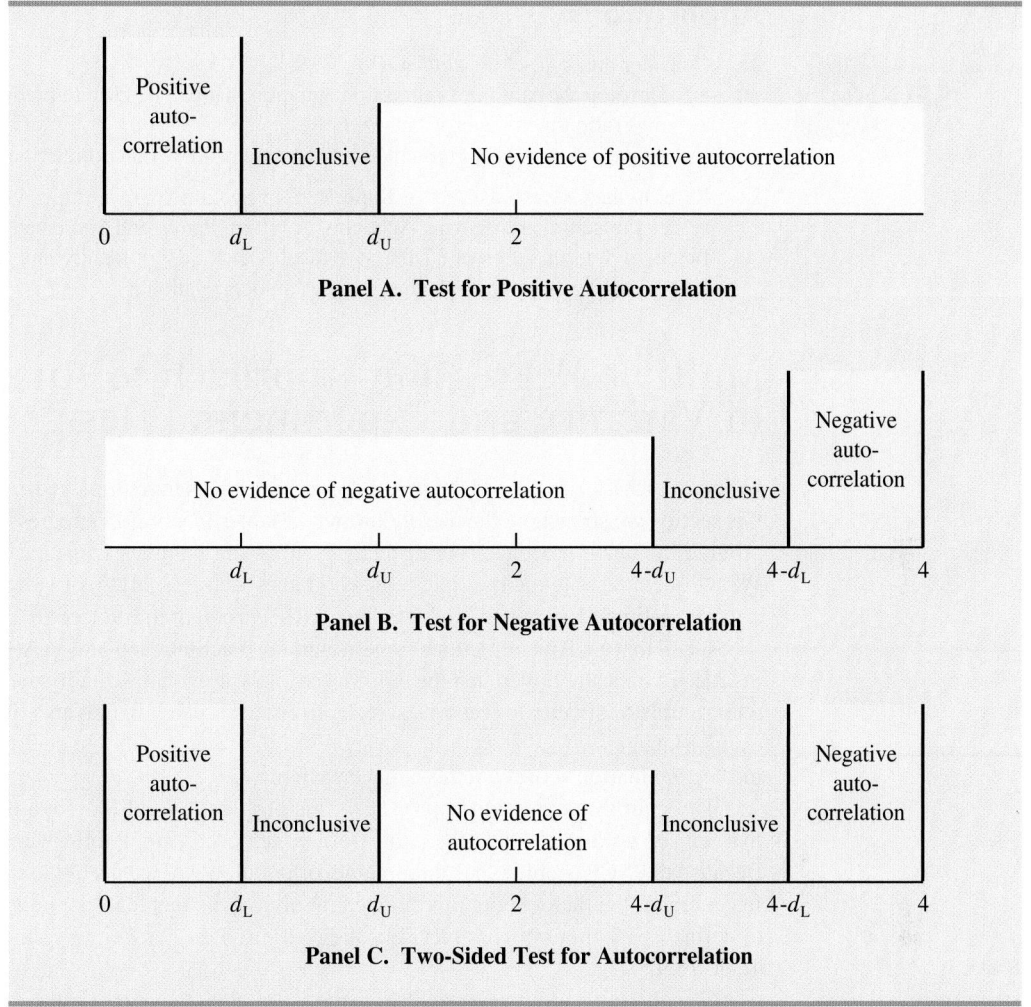

**Panel A.   Test for Positive Autocorrelation**

**Panel B.   Test for Negative Autocorrelation**

**Panel C.   Two-Sided Test for Autocorrelation**

Panel C illustrates the two-sided test. If $d < d_L$ or $d > 4 - d_L$, we reject $H_0$ and conclude that autocorrelation is present. If $d_L \leq d \leq d_U$ or $4 - d_U \leq d \leq 4 - d_L$, we say the test is inconclusive. If $d_U < d < 4 - d_U$, we conclude that there is no evidence of autocorrelation.

If significant autocorrelation is identified, we should investigate whether we omitted one or more key independent variables that have time-ordered effects on the dependent variable. If no such variables can be identified, including an independent variable that measures the time of the observation (for instance, the value of this variable could be one for the first observation, two for the second observation, and so on) will sometimes eliminate or reduce the autocorrelation. When these attempts to reduce or remove autocorrelation do not work, transformations on the dependent or independent variables can prove helpful; a discussion of such transformations can be found in more advanced texts on regression analysis.

Note that the Durbin-Watson tables list the smallest sample size as 15. The reason is that the test is generally inconclusive for smaller sample sizes; in fact, many statisticians believe the sample size should be at least 50 for the test to produce worthwhile results.

## Exercises

### Applications

21. Consider the data set in exercise 19.
    a. Develop the estimated regression equation that can be used to predict the price/earnings ratio given the profit margin.
    b. At the .05 level of significance, test for any positive autocorrelation in the data.

22. Refer to the Cravens data set in Table 16.6. In Section 16.3 we showed that the estimated regression equation involving Accounts, AdvExp, Poten, and Share had an adjusted coefficient of determination of 88.1%. Use the .05 level of significance and apply the Durbin-Watson test to determine whether positive autocorrelation is present.

 **16.6** # Multiple Regression Approach to Analysis of Variance and Experimental Design

In Section 15.7 we discussed the use of dummy variables in multiple regression analysis. In this section we show how the use of dummy variables in a multiple regression equation can provide another approach to solving analysis of variance and experimental design problems. We will demonstrate the multiple regression approach to analysis of variance by applying it to the National Computer Products, Inc. (NCP) problem introduced in Chapter 13.

Recall that NCP manufactures printers and fax machines at plants in Atlanta, Dallas, and Seattle. To measure how much the employees know about total quality management, a random sample of six employees was selected from each plant and given a quality-awareness exam. Managers want to use the exam scores of the 18 employees to determine whether the mean examination scores are the same at each plant.

We begin the regression approach to this problem by defining two dummy variables that will be used to indicate the plant from which each sample observation was selected. Because the NCP problem has three plants or populations, we need two dummy variables. In general, if the factor being investigated involves $k$ distinct levels or populations, we need to define $k - 1$ dummy variables. For the NCP problem we define $x_1$ and $x_2$ as shown in Table 16.9.

We can use the dummy variables $x_1$ and $x_2$ to relate the score on the quality-awareness examination $y$ to the plant at which the employee works.

$E(y)$ = Expected value of the score on the quality-awareness examination
$$= \beta_0 + \beta_1 x_1 + \beta_2 x_2$$

Thus, if we are interested in the expected value of the examination score for an employee who works at the Atlanta plant, our procedure for assigning numerical values to the dummy variables $x_1$ and $x_2$ would result in setting $x_1 = x_2 = 0$. The multiple regression equation then reduces to

$$E(y) = \beta_0 + \beta_1(0) + \beta_2(0) = \beta_0$$

We can interpret $\beta_0$ as the expected value of the examination score for employees who work at the Atlanta plant. In other words, $\beta_0$ is the mean examination score for employees at the Atlanta plant.

Next let us consider the forms of the multiple regression equation for each of the other plants. For the Dallas plant, $x_1 = 1$ and $x_2 = 0$, and

$$E(y) = \beta_0 + \beta_1(1) + \beta_2(0) = \beta_0 + \beta_1$$

**TABLE 16.9**

**NCP PROBLEM WITH DUMMY VARIABLES**

| $x_1$ | $x_2$ | |
|---|---|---|
| 0 | 0 | Observation is associated with the Atlanta plant |
| 1 | 0 | Observation is associated with the Dallas plant |
| 0 | 1 | Observation is associated with the Seattle plant |

**TABLE 16.10   INPUT DATA FOR THE NCP PROBLEM**

| Atlanta | | | Dallas | | | Seattle | | |
|---|---|---|---|---|---|---|---|---|
| $x_1$ | $x_2$ | $y$ | $x_1$ | $x_2$ | $y$ | $x_1$ | $x_2$ | $y$ |
| 0 | 0 | 85 | 1 | 0 | 71 | 0 | 1 | 59 |
| 0 | 0 | 75 | 1 | 0 | 75 | 0 | 1 | 64 |
| 0 | 0 | 82 | 1 | 0 | 73 | 0 | 1 | 62 |
| 0 | 0 | 76 | 1 | 0 | 74 | 0 | 1 | 69 |
| 0 | 0 | 71 | 1 | 0 | 69 | 0 | 1 | 75 |
| 0 | 0 | 85 | 1 | 0 | 82 | 0 | 1 | 67 |

For the Seattle plant, $x_1 = 0$ and $x_2 = 1$, and

$$E(y) = \beta_0 + \beta_1(0) + \beta_2(1) = \beta_0 + \beta_2$$

We see that $\beta_0 + \beta_1$ represents the mean examination score for employees at the Dallas plant, and $\beta_0 + \beta_2$ represents the mean examination score for employees at the Seattle plant.

We now want to estimate the coefficients $\beta_0$, $\beta_1$, and $\beta_2$ and hence develop an estimate of the mean examination score for each plant. The sample data consisting of 18 observations of $x_1$, $x_2$, and $y$ were entered into Minitab. The actual input data and the output from Minitab are in Table 16.10 and Figure 16.20, respectively.

In Figure 16.20, we see that the estimates of $\beta_0$, $\beta_1$, and $\beta_2$ are $b_0 = 79$, $b_1 = -5$, and $b_2 = -13$. Thus, the best estimate of the mean examination score for each plant is as follows.

| Plant | Estimate of $E(y)$ |
|---|---|
| Atlanta | $b_0 = 79$ |
| Dallas | $b_0 + b_1 = 79 - 5 = 74$ |
| Seattle | $b_0 + b_2 = 79 - 13 = 66$ |

**FIGURE 16.20   MULTIPLE REGRESSION OUTPUT FOR THE NCP PROBLEM**

```
The regression equation is
Y = 79.0 - 5.00 X1 - 13.0 X2

Predictor      Coef   SE Coef      T       p
Constant     79.000     2.186   36.14   0.000
X1           -5.000     3.091   -1.62   0.127
X2          -13.000     3.091   -4.21   0.001

S = 5.354    R-sq = 54.5%    R-sq(adj) = 48.5%

Analysis of Variance

SOURCE            DF      SS       MS      F      p
Regression         2   516.00   258.00   9.00   0.003
Residual Error    15   430.00    28.67
Total             17   946.00
```

Note that the best estimate of the mean examination score for each plant obtained from the regression analysis is the same as the sample mean found previously by applying the ANOVA procedure.

Now let us see how we can use the output from the multiple regression package to perform the ANOVA test on the difference in the means for the three plants. First, we observe that if there is no difference in the means,

$$E(y) \text{ for the Dallas plant} - E(y) \text{ for the Atlanta plant} = 0$$
$$E(y) \text{ for the Seattle plant} - E(y) \text{ for the Atlanta plant} = 0$$

Because $\beta_0$ equals $E(y)$ for the Atlanta plant and $\beta_0 + \beta_1$ equals $E(y)$ for the Dallas plant, the first difference is equal to $(\beta_0 + \beta_1) - \beta_0 = \beta_1$. Moreover, because $\beta_0 + \beta_2$ equals $E(y)$ for the Seattle plant, the second difference is equal to $(\beta_0 + \beta_2) - \beta_0 = \beta_2$. We would conclude that there is no difference in the three means if $\beta_1 = 0$ and $\beta_2 = 0$. Hence, the null hypothesis for a test for difference of means can be stated as

$$H_0: \beta_1 = \beta_2 = 0$$

Recall that to test this type of null hypothesis about the significance of the regression relationship, we must compare the value of MSR/MSE to the critical value from an $F$ distribution with numerator and denominator degrees of freedom equal to the degrees of freedom for the regression sum of squares and the error sum of squares, respectively. In the current problem, the regression sum of squares has two degrees of freedom and the error sum of squares has 15 degrees of freedom. Thus, we obtain the following values for MSR and MSE.

$$\text{MSR} = \frac{\text{SSR}}{2} = \frac{516}{2} = 258$$

$$\text{MSE} = \frac{\text{SSE}}{15} = \frac{430}{15} = 28.67$$

Hence, the computed $F$ value is

$$F = \frac{\text{MSR}}{\text{MSE}} = \frac{258}{28.67} = 9.00$$

The Minitab output in Figure 16.20 shows that the $p$-value corresponding to $F = 9.00$ is .003. At a .05 level of significance, we reject $H_0: \beta_1 = \beta_2 = 0$ because $p$-value $= .003 < \alpha = .05$ and conclude that the means for the three plants are different. Alternatively, the critical value of $F$ with two numerator degrees of freedom and 15 denominator degrees of freedom is 3.68. Because the observed value of $F$ is greater than the critical value of 3.68, we also reject the null hypothesis $H_0: \beta_1 = \beta_2 = 0$.

## Exercises

### Methods

23. Consider a completely randomized design involving four treatments: A, B, C, and D. Write a multiple regression equation that can be used to analyze these data. Define all variables.

24. Write a multiple regression equation that can be used to analyze the data for a randomized block design involving three treatments and two blocks. Define all variables.

25. Write a multiple regression equation that can be used to analyze the data for a two-factorial design with two levels for factor A and three levels for factor B. Define all variables.

## Applications

26. The Jacobs Chemical Company wants to estimate the mean time (minutes) required to mix a batch of material on machines produced by three different manufacturers. To limit the cost of testing, four batches of material were mixed on machines produced by each of the three manufacturers. The times needed to mix the material follow.

| Manufacturer 1 | Manufacturer 2 | Manufacturer 3 |
|:--------------:|:--------------:|:--------------:|
| 20 | 28 | 20 |
| 26 | 26 | 19 |
| 24 | 31 | 23 |
| 22 | 27 | 22 |

   a. Write a multiple regression equation that can be used to analyze the data.
   b. What are the best estimates of the coefficients in your regression equation?
   c. In terms of the regression equation coefficients, what hypotheses must we test to see whether the mean time to mix a batch of material is the same for all three manufacturers?
   d. For a $\alpha = .05$ level of significance, what conclusion should be drawn?

27. Four different paints are advertised as having the same drying time. To check the manufacturers' claims, five samples were tested for each of the paints. The time in minutes until the paint was dry enough for a second coat to be applied was recorded for each sample. The data obtained follow.

| Paint 1 | Paint 2 | Paint 3 | Paint 4 |
|:-------:|:-------:|:-------:|:-------:|
| 128 | 144 | 133 | 150 |
| 137 | 133 | 143 | 142 |
| 135 | 142 | 137 | 135 |
| 124 | 146 | 136 | 140 |
| 141 | 130 | 131 | 153 |

   a. Use $\alpha = .05$ to test for any significant differences in mean drying time among the paints.
   b. What is your estimate of mean drying time for paint 2? How is it obtained from the computer output?

28. An automobile dealer conducted a test to determine whether the time needed to complete a minor engine tune-up depends on whether a computerized engine analyzer or an electronic analyzer is used. Because tune-up time varies among compact, intermediate, and full-sized cars, the three types of cars were used as blocks in the experiment. The data (time in minutes) obtained follow.

|  |  | Car | | |
|---|---|:---:|:---:|:---:|
|  |  | Compact | Intermediate | Full Size |
| Analyzer | Computerized | 50 | 55 | 63 |
|  | Electronic | 42 | 44 | 46 |

Use $\alpha = .05$ to test for any significant differences.

29. A mail-order catalog firm designed a factorial experiment to test the effect of the size of a magazine advertisement and the advertisement design on the number (in thousands) of catalog requests received. Three advertising designs and two sizes of advertisements were considered. The following data were obtained. Test for any significant effects due to type of design, size of advertisement, or interaction. Use $\alpha = .05$.

|  |  | Size of Advertisement | |
|---|---|---|---|
|  |  | **Small** | **Large** |
|  | **A** | 8 | 12 |
|  |  | 12 | 8 |
| Design | **B** | 22 | 26 |
|  |  | 14 | 30 |
|  | **C** | 10 | 18 |
|  |  | 18 | 14 |

## Summary

In this chapter we discussed several concepts used by model builders in identifying the best estimated regression equation. First, we introduced the concept of a general linear model to show how the methods discussed in Chapters 14 and 15 could be extended to handle curvilinear relationships and interaction effects. Then we discussed how transformations involving the dependent variable could be used to account for problems such as nonconstant variance in the error term.

In many applications of regression analysis, a large number of independent variables are considered. We presented a general approach based on an $F$ statistic for adding or deleting variables from a regression model. We then introduced a larger problem involving 25 observations and eight independent variables. We saw that one issue encountered in solving larger problems is finding the best subset of the independent variables. To help in that task, we discussed several variable selection procedures: stepwise regression, forward selection, backward elimination, and best-subsets regression.

In Section 16.5, we extended the applications of residual analysis to show the Durbin-Watson test for autocorrelation. The chapter concluded with a discussion of how multiple regression models could be developed to provide another approach for solving analysis of variance and experimental design problems.

## Glossary

**General linear model** A model of the form $y = \beta_0 + \beta_1 z_1 + \beta_2 z_2 + \cdots + \beta_p z_p + \epsilon$, where each of the independent variables $z_j (j = 1, 2, \ldots, p)$ is a function of $x_1, x_2, \ldots, x_k$, the variables for which data have been collected.

**Interaction** The effect of two independent variables acting together.

**Variable selection procedures** Methods for selecting a subset of the independent variables for a regression model.

**Autocorrelation** Correlation in the errors that arises when the error terms at successive points in time are related.

**Serial correlation** Same as autocorrelation.

**Durbin-Watson test** A test to determine whether first-order autocorrelation is present.

## Key Formulas

**General Linear Model**

$$y = \beta_0 + \beta_1 z_1 + \beta_2 z_2 + \cdots + \beta_p z_p + \epsilon \tag{16.1}$$

**F Test Statistic for Adding or Deleting $p - q$ Variables**

$$F = \frac{\dfrac{\text{SSE}(x_1, x_2, \ldots, x_q) - \text{SSE}(x_1, x_2, \ldots, x_q, x_{q+1}, \ldots, x_p)}{p - q}}{\dfrac{\text{SSE}(x_1, x_2, \ldots, x_q, x_{q+1}, \ldots, x_p)}{n - p - 1}} \tag{16.13}$$

**First-Order Autocorrelation**

$$\epsilon_t = \rho \epsilon_{t-1} + z_t \tag{16.16}$$

**Durbin-Watson Test Statistic**

$$d = \frac{\sum\limits_{t=2}^{n} (e_t - e_{t-1})^2}{\sum\limits_{t=1}^{n} e_t^2} \tag{16.17}$$

## Supplementary Exercises

30.   Many international funds offer more reasonable equity valuations than those found in the United States. Because international markets often move in different directions than the U.S. market, investments in foreign markets can also reduce an investor's overall risk. The following table shows the fund type (load or no-load), expense ratio (%), safety rating (0 = riskiest, 10 = safest), and the one-year performance through December 10, 1999, for 20 international funds (*Mutual Funds,* February 2000).

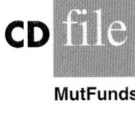

**CD file**

**MutFunds**

| | Fund Type | Expense Ratio (%) | Safety Rating | Performance (%) |
|---|---|---|---|---|
| ABN AMRO Int'l Equity "Com" | No-load | 1.38 | 6.9 | 36 |
| Accessor Int'l Equity "Adv" | No-load | 1.59 | 7.1 | 42 |
| Artisan International | No-load | 1.45 | 6.8 | 72 |
| Columbia Int'l Stock | No-load | 1.56 | 7.1 | 54 |
| Concert Inv. "A" Int'l Equity | Load | 2.16 | 6.3 | 116 |
| Diversified Invstr Int'l Eqty | No-load | 1.40 | 7.3 | 54 |
| Driehaus Int'l Growth | No-load | 1.88 | 6.5 | 92 |
| Founders Passport | No-load | 1.52 | 7.0 | 86 |
| Guardian Baillie Fifford Int'l "A" | Load | 1.62 | 7.1 | 37 |
| Jamestown Int'l Equity | No-load | 1.56 | 7.1 | 35 |
| Julius Baer Int'l Equity | No-load | 1.79 | 6.9 | 71 |
| Aetna "I" Int'l | No-load | 1.35 | 7.3 | 46 |
| Pilgrim Int'l Value "A" | Load | 1.80 | 7.1 | 42 |
| Fidelity Diversified Int'l | No-load | 1.48 | 7.5 | 42 |
| Putnam "A" Int'l Growth | Load | 1.59 | 6.9 | 55 |
| Sit Int'l Growth | No-load | 1.50 | 6.9 | 49 |
| Touchstone Int'l Equity "A" | Load | 1.60 | 7.5 | 35 |
| United Int'l Growth "A" | Load | 1.28 | 7.1 | 47 |
| Vontobel Int'l Equity | No-load | 1.50 | 7.0 | 43 |
| Waddell & Reed Int'l Growth "B" | Load | 2.46 | 7.0 | 75 |

a. Use the methods in this chapter to develop an estimated regression equation that can be used to estimate the performance of a fund on the basis of the data provided.

b. Did the estimated regression equation developed in part (a) provide a good fit? Explain.

c. Acorn International is a no-load fund that has an annual expense ratio of 1.12% and a safety rating of 7.6. Use the estimated regression equation developed in part (a) to estimate the one-year performance for Acorn International.

31. A study investigated the relationship between audit delay (Delay), the length of time from a company's fiscal year-end to the date of the auditor's report, and variables that describe the client and the auditor. Some of the independent variables that were included in this study follow.

Industry    A dummy variable coded 1 if the firm was an industrial company or 0 if the firm was a bank, savings and loan, or insurance company.

Public    A dummy variable coded 1 if the company was traded on an organized exchange or over the counter; otherwise coded 0.

Quality    A measure of overall quality of internal controls, as judged by the auditor, on a five-point scale ranging from "virtually none" (1) to "excellent" (5).

Finished    A measure ranging from 1 to 4, as judged by the auditor, where 1 indicates "all work performed subsequent to year-end" and 4 indicates "most work performed prior to year-end."

A sample of 40 companies provided the following data.

**Audit**

| Delay | Industry | Public | Quality | Finished |
|-------|----------|--------|---------|----------|
| 62 | 0 | 0 | 3 | 1 |
| 45 | 0 | 1 | 3 | 3 |
| 54 | 0 | 0 | 2 | 2 |
| 71 | 0 | 1 | 1 | 2 |
| 91 | 0 | 0 | 1 | 1 |
| 62 | 0 | 0 | 4 | 4 |
| 61 | 0 | 0 | 3 | 2 |
| 69 | 0 | 1 | 5 | 2 |
| 80 | 0 | 0 | 1 | 1 |
| 52 | 0 | 0 | 5 | 3 |
| 47 | 0 | 0 | 3 | 2 |
| 65 | 0 | 1 | 2 | 3 |
| 60 | 0 | 0 | 1 | 3 |
| 81 | 1 | 0 | 1 | 2 |
| 73 | 1 | 0 | 2 | 2 |
| 89 | 1 | 0 | 2 | 1 |
| 71 | 1 | 0 | 5 | 4 |
| 76 | 1 | 0 | 2 | 2 |
| 68 | 1 | 0 | 1 | 2 |
| 68 | 1 | 0 | 5 | 2 |
| 86 | 1 | 0 | 2 | 2 |
| 76 | 1 | 1 | 3 | 1 |
| 67 | 1 | 0 | 2 | 3 |
| 57 | 1 | 0 | 4 | 2 |
| 55 | 1 | 1 | 3 | 2 |
| 54 | 1 | 0 | 5 | 2 |
| 69 | 1 | 0 | 3 | 3 |

| Delay | Industry | Public | Quality | Finished |
|-------|----------|--------|---------|----------|
| 82 | 1 | 0 | 5 | 1 |
| 94 | 1 | 0 | 1 | 1 |
| 74 | 1 | 1 | 5 | 2 |
| 75 | 1 | 1 | 4 | 3 |
| 69 | 1 | 0 | 2 | 2 |
| 71 | 1 | 0 | 4 | 4 |
| 79 | 1 | 0 | 5 | 2 |
| 80 | 1 | 0 | 1 | 4 |
| 91 | 1 | 0 | 4 | 1 |
| 92 | 1 | 0 | 1 | 4 |
| 46 | 1 | 1 | 4 | 3 |
| 72 | 1 | 0 | 5 | 2 |
| 85 | 1 | 0 | 5 | 1 |

    a.    Develop the estimated regression equation using all of the independent variables.

    b.    Did the estimated regression equation developed in part (a) provide a good fit? Explain.

    c.    Develop a scatter diagram showing Delay as a function of Finished. What does this scatter diagram indicate about the relationship between Delay and Finished?

    d.    On the basis of your observations about the relationship between Delay and Finished, develop an alternative estimated regression equation to the one developed in (a) to explain as much of the variability in Delay as possible.

32.  Refer to the data in exercise 31. Consider a model in which only Industry is used to predict Delay. At a .01 level of significance, test for any positive autocorrelation in the data.

33.  Refer to the data in exercise 31.

    a.    Develop an estimated regression equation that can be used to predict Delay by using Industry and Quality.

    b.    Plot the residuals obtained from the estimated regression equation developed in part (a) as a function of the order in which the data are presented. Does any autocorrelation appear to be present in the data? Explain.

    c.    At the .05 level of significance, test for any positive autocorrelation in the data.

34.  A study was conducted to investigate browsing activity by shoppers. Shoppers were classified as nonbrowsers, light browsers, and heavy browsers. For each shopper in the study, a measure was obtained to determine how comfortable the shopper was in the store. Higher scores indicated greater comfort. Assume that the following data are from this study. Use a .05 level of significance to test for differences in comfort levels among the three types of browsers.

**CD** file

**Browsing**

| Nonbrowser | Light Browser | Heavy Browser |
|------------|---------------|---------------|
| 4 | 5 | 5 |
| 5 | 6 | 7 |
| 6 | 5 | 5 |
| 3 | 4 | 7 |
| 3 | 7 | 4 |
| 4 | 4 | 6 |
| 5 | 6 | 5 |
| 4 | 5 | 7 |

35. The following data show the percentage changes in the Dow Jones Industrial Average (DJIA) in each of the four years of eight presidential terms (*1998 Stock Trader's Almanac*). Use regression analysis to determine what effect party and year of term in office have on the change in the Dow Jones Industrial Average.

**CD file**

**Election**

| President | Party | Year Elected | Year of Term | Year's Change in DJIA |
|---|---|---|---|---|
| Johnson | Democrat | 1964 | First | 10.9 |
| Johnson | Democrat | | Second | −18.9 |
| Johnson | Democrat | | Third | 15.2 |
| Johnson | Democrat | | Fourth | 4.3 |
| Nixon | Republican | 1968 | First | −15.2 |
| Nixon | Republican | | Second | 4.8 |
| Nixon | Republican | | Third | 6.1 |
| Nixon | Republican | | Fourth | 14.6 |
| Nixon | Republican | 1972 | First | −16.6 |
| Nixon | Republican | | Second | −27.6 |
| Nixon* | Republican | | Third | 38.3 |
| Nixon* | Republican | | Fourth | 17.9 |
| Carter | Democrat | 1976 | First | −17.3 |
| Carter | Democrat | | Second | −3.1 |
| Carter | Democrat | | Third | 4.2 |
| Carter | Democrat | | Fourth | 14.9 |
| Reagan | Republican | 1980 | First | −9.2 |
| Reagan | Republican | | Second | 19.6 |
| Reagan | Republican | | Third | 20.3 |
| Reagan | Republican | | Fourth | −3.7 |
| Reagan | Republican | 1984 | First | −27.7 |
| Reagan | Republican | | Second | 22.6 |
| Reagan | Republican | | Third | 2.3 |
| Reagan | Republican | | Fourth | 11.8 |
| Bush | Republican | 1988 | First | 27.0 |
| Bush | Republican | | Second | −4.3 |
| Bush | Republican | | Third | 20.3 |
| Bush | Republican | | Fourth | 4.2 |
| Clinton | Democrat | 1992 | First | 13.7 |
| Clinton | Democrat | | Second | 2.1 |
| Clinton | Democrat | | Third | 33.5 |
| Clinton | Democrat | | Fourth | 26.0 |

*Because President Nixon resigned from office in August 1974, Gerald Ford became president and completed the remainder of Nixon's term in office.

36. *Money* magazine reported price and related data for 418 of the most popular vehicles of the 2003 model year. One of the variables reported was the vehicle's resale value, expressed as a percentage of the manufacturer's suggested resale price. The data were classified according to size and type of vehicle. The following table shows the resale value for 10 randomly selected small cars, 10 randomly selected mid-size cars, 10 randomly selected luxury cars, and 10 randomly selected sports cars (*Money,* March 2003).

**CD file**

**Resale**

| Small | Mid-size | Luxury | Sports |
|---|---|---|---|
| 26 | 26 | 36 | 41 |
| 31 | 29 | 38 | 39 |
| 41 | 41 | 38 | 30 |

| Small | Mid-size | Luxury | Sports |
|-------|----------|--------|--------|
| 32 | 27 | 39 | 34 |
| 27 | 26 | 35 | 40 |
| 34 | 33 | 26 | 43 |
| 31 | 27 | 40 | 42 |
| 38 | 29 | 47 | 39 |
| 27 | 35 | 41 | 44 |
| 42 | 39 | 32 | 50 |

Use $\alpha = .05$ and test for any significant difference in the mean resale value among the four types of vehicles.

## Case Problem 1    Unemployment Study

A study provided data on variables that may be related to the number of weeks a manufacturing worker has been jobless. The dependent variable in the study (Weeks) was defined as the number of weeks a worker has been jobless due to a layoff. The following independent variables were used in the study.

| | |
|---|---|
| Age | The age of the worker |
| Educ | The number of years of education |
| Married | A dummy variable: 1 if married, 0 otherwise |
| Head | A dummy variable: 1 if the head of household, 0 otherwise |
| Tenure | The number of years on the previous job |
| Manager | A dummy variable: 1 if management occupation, 0 otherwise |
| Sales | A dummy variable: 1 if sales occupation, 0 otherwise |

Assume the following data were collected for 50 displaced workers. These data are available on the CD accompanying the text in the file named Layoffs.

### Managerial Report

Use the methods presented in this and previous chapters to analyze this data set. Present a summary of your analysis, including key statistical results, conclusions, and recommendations, in a managerial report. Include any appropriate technical material (computer output, residual plots, etc.) in an appendix.

| Weeks | Age | Educ | Married | Head | Tenure | Manager | Sales |
|-------|-----|------|---------|------|--------|---------|-------|
| 37 | 30 | 14 | 1 | 1 | 1 | 0 | 0 |
| 62 | 27 | 14 | 1 | 0 | 6 | 0 | 0 |
| 49 | 32 | 10 | 0 | 1 | 11 | 0 | 0 |
| 73 | 44 | 11 | 1 | 0 | 2 | 0 | 0 |
| 8 | 21 | 14 | 1 | 1 | 2 | 0 | 0 |

**CD file**

**Layoffs**

*(continued)*

| Weeks | Age | Educ | Married | Head | Tenure | Manager | Sales |
|-------|-----|------|---------|------|--------|---------|-------|
| 15 | 26 | 13 | 1 | 0 | 7 | 1 | 0 |
| 52 | 26 | 15 | 1 | 0 | 6 | 0 | 0 |
| 72 | 33 | 13 | 0 | 1 | 6 | 0 | 0 |
| 11 | 27 | 12 | 1 | 1 | 8 | 0 | 0 |
| 13 | 33 | 12 | 0 | 1 | 2 | 0 | 0 |
| 39 | 20 | 11 | 1 | 0 | 1 | 0 | 0 |
| 59 | 35 | 7 | 1 | 1 | 6 | 0 | 0 |
| 39 | 36 | 17 | 0 | 1 | 9 | 1 | 0 |
| 44 | 26 | 12 | 1 | 1 | 8 | 0 | 0 |
| 56 | 36 | 15 | 0 | 1 | 8 | 0 | 0 |
| 31 | 38 | 16 | 1 | 1 | 11 | 0 | 1 |
| 62 | 34 | 13 | 0 | 1 | 13 | 0 | 0 |
| 25 | 27 | 19 | 1 | 0 | 8 | 0 | 0 |
| 72 | 44 | 13 | 1 | 0 | 22 | 0 | 0 |
| 65 | 45 | 15 | 1 | 1 | 6 | 0 | 0 |
| 44 | 28 | 17 | 0 | 1 | 3 | 0 | 1 |
| 49 | 25 | 10 | 1 | 1 | 1 | 0 | 0 |
| 80 | 31 | 15 | 1 | 0 | 12 | 0 | 0 |
| 7 | 23 | 15 | 1 | 0 | 2 | 0 | 0 |
| 14 | 24 | 13 | 1 | 1 | 7 | 0 | 0 |
| 94 | 62 | 13 | 0 | 1 | 8 | 0 | 0 |
| 48 | 31 | 16 | 1 | 0 | 11 | 0 | 0 |
| 82 | 48 | 18 | 0 | 1 | 30 | 0 | 0 |
| 50 | 35 | 18 | 1 | 1 | 5 | 0 | 0 |
| 37 | 33 | 14 | 0 | 1 | 6 | 0 | 1 |
| 62 | 46 | 15 | 0 | 1 | 6 | 0 | 0 |
| 37 | 35 | 8 | 0 | 1 | 6 | 0 | 0 |
| 40 | 32 | 9 | 1 | 1 | 13 | 0 | 0 |
| 16 | 40 | 17 | 1 | 0 | 8 | 1 | 0 |
| 34 | 23 | 12 | 1 | 1 | 1 | 0 | 0 |
| 4 | 36 | 16 | 0 | 1 | 8 | 0 | 1 |
| 55 | 33 | 12 | 1 | 0 | 10 | 0 | 1 |
| 39 | 32 | 16 | 0 | 1 | 11 | 0 | 0 |
| 80 | 62 | 15 | 1 | 0 | 16 | 0 | 1 |
| 19 | 29 | 14 | 1 | 1 | 12 | 0 | 0 |
| 98 | 45 | 12 | 1 | 0 | 17 | 0 | 0 |
| 30 | 38 | 15 | 0 | 1 | 6 | 0 | 1 |
| 22 | 40 | 8 | 1 | 1 | 16 | 0 | 1 |
| 57 | 42 | 13 | 1 | 0 | 2 | 1 | 0 |
| 64 | 45 | 16 | 1 | 1 | 22 | 0 | 0 |
| 22 | 39 | 11 | 1 | 1 | 4 | 0 | 0 |
| 27 | 27 | 15 | 1 | 0 | 10 | 0 | 1 |
| 20 | 42 | 14 | 1 | 1 | 6 | 1 | 0 |
| 30 | 31 | 10 | 1 | 1 | 8 | 0 | 0 |
| 23 | 33 | 13 | 1 | 1 | 8 | 0 | 0 |

## Case Problem 2    Fuel Economy for Cars

**Cars**

Posted on every new car sold in the United States is a fuel economy rating that shows the miles per gallon the car is expected to achieve in actual city and highway use. Data showing these ratings for all cars and trucks are available in the U.S. Department of Energy's *Fuel Economy Guide.* A portion of the data for 230 cars is available on the CD accompanying the text in the file named Cars (http://www.fueleconomy.gov, March 21, 2003). Descriptions for the data, which appear on the disk, follow.

| | |
|---|---|
| Class | The class of the car (Compact, Midsize, Large) |
| Manufacturer | The manufacturer of the car |
| carline name | The name of the car |
| displ | The displacement of the engine in liters |
| cyl | The number of cylinders in the engine (4, 6, 8) |
| trans | The type of transmission (Automatic, Manual) |
| cty | The fuel economy rating for city driving in miles per gallon |
| hwy | The fuel economy rating for highway driving in miles per gallon |

### Managerial Report

Use the methods presented in this and previous chapters to analyze this data set. The objective of your study is to develop an estimated regression equation that can be used to estimate the fuel economy rating for city driving and an estimated regression equation that can be used to estimate the fuel economy rating for highway driving. Present a summary of your analysis, including key statistical results, conclusions, and recommendations, in a managerial report. Include any appropriate technical material (computer output, residual plots, etc.) in an appendix.

## Case Problem 3    Predicting Graduation Rates for Colleges and Universities

The percentage of students who enroll at a college or university and actually graduate is an important statistic for university administrators. Some of the factors related to the graduation rate include the percentage of classes with fewer than 20 students, the percentage of classes with more than 50 students, the student-faculty ratio, the percentage of students who apply to the university and are admitted, the percentage of first-year students in the top 10% of their high school class, and the academic reputation of the university. To study the effect of these factors on the graduation rate, data for 48 national universities was collected (*America's Best Colleges,* Year 2000 Edition). These data are available on the CD accompanying the text in the file named GradRate. Descriptions for data, which appear on the disk, follow.

**GradRate**

| | |
|---|---|
| Region | The region of the country in which the university is located (North, South, Midwest, West) |
| Graduation Rate | The percentage of students who enroll at the university and graduate |
| % of Classes Under 20 | The percentage of classes with fewer than 20 students |

| % of Classes of 50 or More | The percentage of classes with more than 50 students |
| Student-Faculty Ratio | The ratio of the number of students enrolled divided by the total number of faculty |
| Acceptance Rate | The percentage of students who apply and are accepted |
| 1st-Year Students in Top 10% of HS Class | The percentage of students admitted who were in the top 10% of their high school class |
| Academic Reputation Score | A measure of the school's reputation determined by surveying administrators at other universities: measured on a scale from 1 (marginal) to 5 (distinguished) |

## Managerial Report

Use the methods presented in this and previous chapters to analyze this data set. Present a summary of your analysis, including key statistical results, conclusions, and recommendations, in a managerial report. Include any appropriate technical material (computer output, residual plots, etc.) in an appendix.

# CHAPTER 17

# Index Numbers

**CONTENTS**

## U.S. DEPARTMENT OF LABOR, BUREAU OF LABOR STATISTICS
*WASHINGTON, D.C.*

The U.S. Department of Labor, through its Bureau of Labor Statistics, compiles and distributes indexes and statistics that are indicators of business and economic activity in the United States. For instance, the Bureau compiles and publishes the Consumer Price Index, the Producer Price Index, and statistics on average hours and earnings of various groups of workers. Perhaps the most widely quoted index produced by the Bureau of Labor Statistics is the Consumer Price Index. It is often used as a measure of inflation.

In February 2003, the Bureau of Labor Statistics reported that the Consumer Price Index (CPI) increased by .6% from January. This increase followed a .3% increase in January and seemed to indicate a pickup in the rate of inflation. The Bureau also reported that the core rate of inflation was up only .1% in February. The core rate excludes the volatile food and energy components of the CPI and is sometimes regarded as a better indicator of inflationary pressures. The index of gasoline prices rose 9.9% in February and was a major reason for the increase in the CPI index.

The Bureau of Labor Statistics reported that the Producer Price Index (PPI) increased by 1% in February 2003. The PPI measures price changes in wholesale markets and is often seen as a leading indicator of changes in the Consumer Price Index.

The Bureau of Labor Statistics computes the Consumer Price Index from data collected on the sale of goods and services. © AP/Wide World Photos.

Much of the increase, however, was due to increased prices for energy goods. With energy goods removed, the PPI actually decreased in February. Taking this factor into account, the PPI change was not generally regarded as inflationary.

In this chapter we will see how various indexes, such as the Consumer and Producer Price Indexes, are computed and how they should be interpreted.

Each month the U.S. government publishes a variety of indexes designed to help individuals understand current business and economic conditions. Perhaps the most widely known and cited of these indexes is the Consumer Price Index (CPI). As its name implies, the CPI is an indicator of what is happening to prices consumers pay for items purchased. Specifically, the CPI measures changes in price over a period of time. With a given starting point or *base period* and its associated index of 100, the CPI can be used to compare current period consumer prices with those in the base period. For example, a CPI of 125 reflects the condition that consumer prices as a whole are running approximately 25% above the base period prices for the same items. Although relatively few individuals know exactly what this number means, they do know enough about the CPI to understand that an increase means higher prices.

Even though the CPI is perhaps the best-known index, many other governmental and private-sector indexes are available to help us measure and understand how economic conditions in one period compare with economic conditions in other periods. The purpose of this chapter is to describe the most widely used types of indexes. We will begin by constructing some simple index numbers to gain a better understanding of how indexes are computed.

**Price Relatives**

## 17.1

**TABLE 17.1**

**UNLEADED GASOLINE COST**

| Year | Price per Gallon ($) |
|------|----------------------|
| 1984 | 1.21 |
| 1985 | 1.20 |
| 1986 | .93 |
| 1987 | .95 |
| 1988 | .95 |
| 1989 | 1.02 |
| 1990 | 1.16 |
| 1991 | 1.14 |
| 1992 | 1.13 |
| 1993 | 1.11 |
| 1994 | 1.11 |
| 1995 | 1.15 |
| 1996 | 1.23 |
| 1997 | 1.23 |
| 1998 | 1.06 |
| 1999 | 1.17 |
| 2000 | 1.51 |
| 2003 | 1.46 |
| 2002 | 1.36 |

*Source:* U.S. Energy Information Administration.

The simplest form of a price index shows how the current price per unit for a given item compares to a base period price per unit for the same item. For example, Table 17.1 reports the cost of one gallon of unleaded gasoline for the years 1984 through 2002. To facilitate comparisons with other years, the actual cost-per-gallon figure can be converted to a **price relative**, which expresses the unit price in each period as a percentage of the unit price in a base period.

$$\text{Price relative in period } t = \frac{\text{Price in period } t}{\text{Base period price}} (100) \qquad (17.1)$$

For the gasoline prices in Table 17.1 and with 1984 as the base year, the price relatives for one gallon of unleaded gasoline in the years 1984 through 2002 can be calculated. These price relatives are listed in Table 17.2. Note how easily the price in any one year can be compared with the price in the base year by knowing the price relative. For example, the price relative of 76.9 in 1986 shows that the gasoline cost in 1986 was 23.1% below the 1984 base-year cost. Similarly, the 2002 price relative of 112.4 shows a 12.4% increase in gasoline cost in 2002 from the 1984 base-year cost. Price relatives, such as the ones for unleaded gasoline, are extremely helpful in terms of understanding and interpreting changing economic and business conditions over time.

## 17.2 Aggregate Price Indexes

Although price relatives can be used to identify price changes over time for individual items, we are often more interested in the general price change for a group of items taken as a whole. For example, if we want an index that measures the change in the overall cost of living over time, we will want the index to be based on the price changes for a variety of items, including food, housing, clothing, transportation, medical care, and so on. An **aggregate price index** is developed for the specific purpose of measuring the combined change of a group of items.

**TABLE 17.2**

**PRICE RELATIVES FOR ONE GALLON OF UNLEADED GASOLINE (1984–2002)**

| Year | Price Relative (Base 1984) |
|------|----------------------------|
| 1984 | (1.21/1.21)100 = 100.0 |
| 1985 | (1.20/1.21)100 =  99.2 |
| 1986 | (.93/1.21)100 =  76.9 |
| 1987 | (.95/1.21)100 =  78.5 |
| 1988 | (.95/1.21)100 =  78.5 |
| 1989 | (1.02/1.21)100 =  84.3 |
| 1990 | (1.16/1.21)100 =  95.9 |
| 1991 | (1.14/1.21)100 =  94.2 |
| 1992 | (1.13/1.21)100 =  93.4 |
| 1993 | (1.11/1.21)100 =  91.7 |
| 1994 | (1.11/1.21)100 =  91.7 |
| 1995 | (1.15/1.21)100 =  95.0 |
| 1996 | (1.23/1.21)100 = 101.7 |
| 1997 | (1.23/1.21)100 = 101.7 |
| 1998 | (1.06/1.21)100 =  87.6 |
| 1999 | (1.17/1.21)100 =  96.7 |
| 2000 | (1.51/1.21)100 = 124.8 |
| 2001 | (1.46/1.21)100 = 120.7 |
| 2002 | (1.36/1.21)100 = 112.4 |

Consider the development of an aggregate price index for a group of items categorized as normal automotive operating expenses. For illustration, we limit the items included in the group to gasoline, oil, tire, and insurance expenses.

Table 17.3 gives the data for the four components of our automotive operating expense index for the years 1984 and 2002. With 1984 as the base period, an aggregate price index for the four components will give us a measure of the change in normal automotive operating expenses over the 1984–2002 period.

An unweighted aggregate index can be developed by simply summing the unit prices in the year of interest (e.g., 2002) and dividing that sum by the sum of the unit prices in the base year (1984). Let

$$P_{it} = \text{unit price for item } i \text{ in period } t$$
$$P_{i0} = \text{unit price for item } i \text{ in the base period}$$

An unweighted aggregate price index in period $t$, denoted by $I_t$, is given by

$$I_t = \frac{\Sigma P_{it}}{\Sigma P_{i0}} (100) \qquad (17.2)$$

where the sums are for all items in the group.

**TABLE 17.3   DATA FOR AUTOMOTIVE OPERATING EXPENSE INDEX**

| | Unit Price ($) | |
|---|---|---|
| Item | 1984 | 2002 |
| Gallon of gasoline | 1.21 | 1.36 |
| Quart of oil | 1.50 | 2.20 |
| Tires | 80.00 | 145.00 |
| Insurance policy | 300.00 | 700.00 |

An unweighted aggregate index for normal automotive operating expenses in 2002 ($t = 2002$) is given by

$$I_{2002} = \frac{1.36 + 2.20 + 145.00 + 700.00}{1.21 + 1.50 + 80.00 + 300.00}(100)$$

$$= \frac{848.56}{382.71}(100) = 222$$

From the unweighted aggregate price index, we might conclude that the price of normal automotive operating expenses increased 122% over the period from 1984 to 2002. But note that the unweighted aggregate approach to establishing a composite price index for automotive expenses is heavily influenced by the items with large per-unit prices. Consequently, items with relatively low unit prices such as gasoline and oil are dominated by the high unit-price items such as tires and insurance. The unweighted aggregate index for automotive operating expenses is too heavily influenced by price changes in tires and insurance.

Because of the sensitivity of an unweighted index to one or more high-priced items, this form of aggregate index is not widely used. A weighted aggregate price index provides a better comparison when usage quantities differ.

*If quantity of usage is the same for each item, an unweighted index gives the same value as a weighted index. In practice, however, quantities of usage are rarely the same.*

The philosophy behind the **weighted aggregate price index** is that each item in the group should be weighted according to its importance. In most cases, the quantity of usage is the best measure of importance. Hence, one must obtain a measure of the quantity of usage for the various items in the group. Table 17.4 gives annual usage information for each item of automotive operating expense based on the typical operation of a mid-size automobile for approximately 15,000 miles per year. The quantity weights listed show the expected annual usage for this type of driving situation.

Let $Q_i$ = quantity of usage for item $i$. The weighted aggregate price index in period $t$ is given by

$$I_t = \frac{\Sigma P_{it}Q_i}{\Sigma P_{i0}Q_i}(100) \tag{17.3}$$

**TABLE 17.4**

**ANNUAL USAGE INFORMATION FOR AUTOMOTIVE OPERATING EXPENSE INDEX**

| Item | Quantity Weights* |
|---|---|
| Gallons of gasoline | 1000 |
| Quarts of oil | 15 |
| Tires | 2 |
| Insurance policy | 1 |

*Based on 15,000 miles per year. Tire usage is based on a 30,000-mile tire life.

where the sums are for all items in the group. Applied to our automotive operating expenses, the weighted aggregate price index is based on dividing total operating costs in 2002 by total operating costs in 1984.

Let $t = 2002$, and use the quantity weights in Table 17.4. We obtain the following weighted aggregate price index for automotive operating expenses in 2002.

$$I_{2002} = \frac{1.36(1000) + 2.20(15) + 145.00(2) + 700.00(1)}{1.21(1000) + 1.50(15) + 80.00(2) + 300.00(1)}(100)$$

$$= \frac{2383}{1692.5}(100) = 141$$

From this weighted aggregate price index, we would conclude that the price of automotive operating expenses has increased 41% over the period from 1984 through 2002.

Clearly, compared with the unweighted aggregate index, the weighted index provides a more accurate indication of the price change for automotive operating expenses over the 1984–2002 period. Taking the quantity of usage of gasoline into account helps to offset the large increase in insurance costs. The weighted index shows a more moderate increase in automotive operating expenses than the unweighted index. In general, the weighted aggregate index with quantities of usage as weights is the preferred method for establishing a price index for a group of items.

In the weighted aggregate price index formula (17.3), note that the quantity term $Q_i$ does not have a second subscript to indicate the time period. The reason is that the quantities $Q_i$ are considered fixed and do not vary with time as the prices do. The fixed weights or quantities are specified by the designer of the index at levels believed to be representative of typical usage. Once established, they are held constant or fixed for all periods of time the index is in use. Indexes for years other than 2002 require the gathering of new price data $P_{it}$, but the weighting quantities $Q_i$ remain the same.

In a special case of the fixed-weight aggregate index, the quantities are determined from base-year usages. In this case we write $Q_i = Q_{i0}$, with the zero subscript indicating base-year quantity weights; formula (17.3) becomes

$$I_t = \frac{\Sigma P_{it} Q_{i0}}{\Sigma P_{i0} Q_{i0}} (100) \tag{17.4}$$

Whenever the fixed quantity weights are determined from base-year usage, the weighted aggregate index is given the name **Laspeyres index**.

Another option for determining quantity weights is to revise the quantities each period. A quantity $Q_{it}$ is determined for each year that the index is computed. The weighted aggregate index in period $t$ with these quantity weights is given by

$$I_t = \frac{\Sigma P_{it} Q_{it}}{\Sigma P_{i0} Q_{it}} (100) \tag{17.5}$$

Note that the same quantity weights are used for the base period (period 0) and for period $t$. However, the weights are based on usage in period $t$, not the base period. This weighted aggregate index is known as the **Paasche index**. It has the advantage of being based on current usage patterns. However, this method of computing a weighted aggregate index presents two disadvantages: the normal usage quantities $Q_{it}$ must be redetermined each year, thus adding to the time and cost of data collection, and each year the index numbers for previous years must be recomputed to reflect the effect of the new quantity weights. Because of these disadvantages, the Laspeyres index is more widely used. The automotive operating expense index was computed with base-period quantities; hence, it is a Laspeyres index. Had usage figures for 2002 been used, it would be a Paasche index. Indeed, because of more fuel efficient cars, gasoline usage decreased and a Paasche index differs from a Laspeyres index.

## Exercises

## Methods

1. The following table reports prices and usage quantities for two items in 2001 and 2003.

| | Quantity | | Unit Price ($) | |
| Item | 2001 | 2003 | 2001 | 2003 |
| --- | --- | --- | --- | --- |
| A | 1500 | 1800 | 7.50 | 7.75 |
| B | 2 | 1 | 630.00 | 1500.00 |

a.  Compute price relatives for each item in 2003 using 2001 as the base period.
b.  Compute an unweighted aggregate price index for the two items in 2003 using 2001 as the base period.
c.  Compute a weighted aggregate price index for the two items using the Laspeyres method.
d.  Compute a weighted aggregate price index for the two items using the Paasche method.

2.  An item with a price relative of 132 cost $10.75 in 2003. Its base year was 1992.
a.  What was the percentage increase or decrease in cost of the item over the 11-year period?
b.  What did the item cost in 1992?

## Applications

3.  A large manufacturer purchases an identical component from three independent suppliers that differ in unit price and quantity supplied. The relevant data for 2001 and 2003 are given here.

|        |                 | Unit Price ($) | |
| Supplier | Quantity (2001) | 2001 | 2003 |
| --- | --- | --- | --- |
| A | 150 | 5.45 | 6.00 |
| B | 200 | 5.60 | 5.95 |
| C | 120 | 5.50 | 6.20 |

a.  Compute the price relatives for each of the component suppliers separately. Compare the price increases by the suppliers over the two-year period.
b.  Compute an unweighted aggregate price index for the component part in 2003.
c.  Compute a 2003 weighted aggregate price index for the component part. What is the interpretation of this index for the manufacturing firm?

4.  R&B Beverages, Inc., provides a complete line of beer, wine, and soft drink products for distribution through retail outlets in central Iowa. Unit price data for 1999 and 2003 and quantities sold in cases for 1999 follow.

|      | 1999 Quantity | Unit Price ($) | |
| Item | (cases) | 1999 | 2003 |
| --- | --- | --- | --- |
| Beer | 35,000 | 15.00 | 16.25 |
| Wine | 5,000 | 60.00 | 64.00 |
| Soft drink | 60,000 | 9.80 | 10.00 |

Compute a weighted aggregate index for the R&B Beverage sales in 2003, with 1999 as the base period.

5.  Under the LIFO inventory valuation method, a price index for inventory must be established for tax purposes. The quantity weights are based on year-ending inventory levels. Use the beginning-of-the-year price per unit as the base-period price and develop a weighted aggregate index for the total inventory value at the end of the year. What type of weighted aggregate price index must be developed for the LIFO inventory valuation?

|         | Ending    | Unit Price ($) | |
| Product | Inventory | Beginning | Ending |
| --- | --- | --- | --- |
| A | 500 | .15 | .19 |
| B | 50 | 1.60 | 1.80 |
| C | 100 | 4.50 | 4.20 |
| D | 40 | 12.00 | 13.20 |

# 17.3 Computing an Aggregate Price Index from Price Relatives

In Section 17.1 we defined the concept of a price relative and showed how a price relative can be computed with knowledge of the current-period unit price and the base-period unit price. We now want to show how aggregate price indexes like the ones developed in Section 17.2 can be computed directly from information about the price relative of each item in the group. Because of the limited use of unweighted indexes, we restrict our attention to weighted aggregate price indexes. Let us return to the automotive operating expense index of the preceding section. The necessary information for the four items is given in Table 17.5.

*One must be sure prices and quantities are in the same units. For example, if prices are per case, quantity must be the number of cases and not, for instance, the number of individual units.*

Let $w_i$ be the weight applied to the price relative for item $i$. The general expression for a weighted average of price relatives is given by

$$I_t = \frac{\sum \dfrac{P_{it}}{P_{i0}}(100)w_i}{\sum w_i} \tag{17.6}$$

The proper choice of weights in equation (17.6) will enable us to compute a weighted aggregate price index from the price relatives. The proper choice of weights is given by multiplying the base-period price by the quantity of usage.

$$w_i = P_{i0}Q_i \tag{17.7}$$

Substituting $w_i = P_{i0}Q_i$ into equation (17.6) provides the following expression for a weighted price relatives index.

$$I_t = \frac{\sum \dfrac{P_{it}}{P_{i0}}(100)(P_{i0}Q_i)}{\sum P_{i0}Q_i} \tag{17.8}$$

With the canceling of the $P_{i0}$ terms in the numerator, an equivalent expression for the weighted price relatives index is

$$I_t = \frac{\sum P_{it}Q_i}{\sum P_{i0}Q_i}(100)$$

Thus, we see that the weighted price relatives index with $w_i = P_{i0}Q_i$ provides a price index identical to the weighted aggregate index presented in Section 17.2 by equation (17.3). Use

**TABLE 17.5**    PRICE RELATIVES FOR AUTOMOTIVE OPERATING EXPENSE INDEX

| | Unit Price ($) | | | |
| Item | 1984 $(P_0)$ | 2002 $(P_t)$ | Price Relative $(P_t/P_0)100$ | Annual Usage |
|---|---|---|---|---|
| Gallon of gasoline | 1.21 | 1.36 | 112.4 | 1000 |
| Quart of oil | 1.50 | 2.20 | 146.7 | 15 |
| Tires | 80.00 | 145.00 | 181.3 | 2 |
| Insurance policy | 300.00 | 700.00 | 233.3 | 1 |

**TABLE 17.6**   AUTOMOTIVE OPERATING EXPENSE INDEX (1984–2002) BASED ON WEIGHTED PRICE RELATIVES

| Item | Price Relatives $(P_{it}/P_{i0})(100)$ | Base Price ($) $P_{i0}$ | Quantity $Q_i$ | Weight $w_i = P_{i0}Q_i$ | Weighted Price Relatives $(P_{it}/P_{i0})(100)w_i$ |
|---|---|---|---|---|---|
| Gasoline | 112.4 | 1.21 | 1000 | 1,210.0 | 136,004.00 |
| Oil | 146.7 | 1.50 | 15 | 22.5 | 3,300.75 |
| Tires | 181.3 | 80.00 | 2 | 160.0 | 29,008.00 |
| Insurance | 233.3 | 300.00 | 1 | 300.0 | 69,990.00 |
| | | | Totals | 1,692.5 | 238,302.75 |

$$I_{2002} = \frac{238,302.75}{1,692.5} = 141$$

of base-period quantities (i.e., $Q_i = Q_{i0}$) in equation (17.7) leads to a Laspeyres index. Use of current-period quantities (i.e., $Q_i = Q_{it}$) in equation (17.7) leads to a Paasche index.

Let us return to the automotive operating expense data. We can use the price relatives in Table 17.5 and equation (17.6) to compute a weighted average of price relatives. The results obtained by using the weights specified by equation (17.7) are reported in Table 17.6. The index number 141 represents a 41% increase in automotive operating expenses, which is the same as the increase identified by the weighted aggregate index computation in Section 17.2.

## Exercises

### Methods

6. Price relatives for three items, along with base-period prices and usage are shown in the following table. Compute a weighted aggregate price index for the current period.

| | | Base Period | |
|---|---|---|---|
| Item | Price Relative | Price | Usage |
| A | 150 | 22.00 | 20 |
| B | 90 | 5.00 | 50 |
| C | 120 | 14.00 | 40 |

### Applications

7. The Mitchell Chemical Company produces a special industrial chemical that is a blend of three chemical ingredients. The beginning-year cost per pound, the ending-year cost per pound, and the blend proportions follow.

| | Cost per Pound ($) | | Quantity (pounds) |
|---|---|---|---|
| Ingredient | Beginning | Ending | per 100 Pounds of Product |
| A | 2.50 | 3.95 | 25 |
| B | 8.75 | 9.90 | 15 |
| C | .99 | .95 | 60 |

a.  Compute the price relatives for the three ingredients.

b.  Compute a weighted average of the price relatives to develop a one-year cost index for raw materials used in the product. What is your interpretation of this index value?

8.  An investment portfolio consists of four stocks. The purchase price, current price, and number of shares are reported in the following table.

| Stock | Purchase Price/Share ($) | Current Price/Share ($) | Number of Shares |
|---|---|---|---|
| Holiday Trans | 15.50 | 17.00 | 500 |
| NY Electric | 18.50 | 20.25 | 200 |
| KY Gas | 26.75 | 26.00 | 500 |
| PQ Soaps | 42.25 | 45.50 | 300 |

Construct a weighted average of price relatives as an index of the performance of the portfolio to date. Interpret this price index.

9.  Compute the price relatives for the R&B Beverages products in exercise 4. Use a weighted average of price relatives to show that this method provides the same index as the weighted aggregate method.

# Some Important Price Indexes

We identified the procedures used to compute price indexes for single items or groups of items. Now let us consider some price indexes that are important measures of business and economic conditions. Specifically, we consider the Consumer Price Index, the Producer Price Index, and the Dow Jones averages.

## Consumer Price Index

*The CPI includes charges for services (e.g., doctor and dentist bills) and all taxes directly associated with the purchase and use of an item.*

The **Consumer Price Index (CPI)**, published monthly by the U.S. Bureau of Labor Statistics, is the primary measure of the cost of living in the United States. The group of items used to develop the index consists of a *market basket* of 400 items including food, housing, clothing, transportation, and medical items. The CPI is a weighted aggregate price index with fixed weights.* The weight applied to each item in the market basket derives from a usage survey of urban families throughout the United States.

The February 2003 CPI, computed with a 1982–1984 base index of 100, was 183.1. This figure means that the cost of purchasing the market basket of goods and services increased 83.1% since the base period 1982–1984. The 50-year time series of the CPI from 1950 to 2000 is shown in Figure 17.1. Note how the CPI measure reflects the sharp inflationary behavior of the economy in the late 1970s and early 1980s.

## Producer Price Index

*The PPI is designed as a measure of price changes for domestic goods; imports are not included.*

The **Producer Price Index (PPI)**, also published monthly by the U.S. Bureau of Labor Statistics, measures the monthly changes in prices in primary markets in the United States. The PPI is based on prices for the first transaction of each product in nonretail markets. All

---

*The Bureau of Labor Statistics actually publishes two Consumer Price Indexes: one for all urban consumers (CPI-U) and a revised Consumer Price Index for urban wage earners and clerical workers (CPI-W). The CPI-U is the one most widely quoted, and it is published regularly in *The Wall Street Journal*.

**FIGURE 17.1**   CONSUMER PRICE INDEX, 1950–2000 WITH BASE 1982–1984 = 100

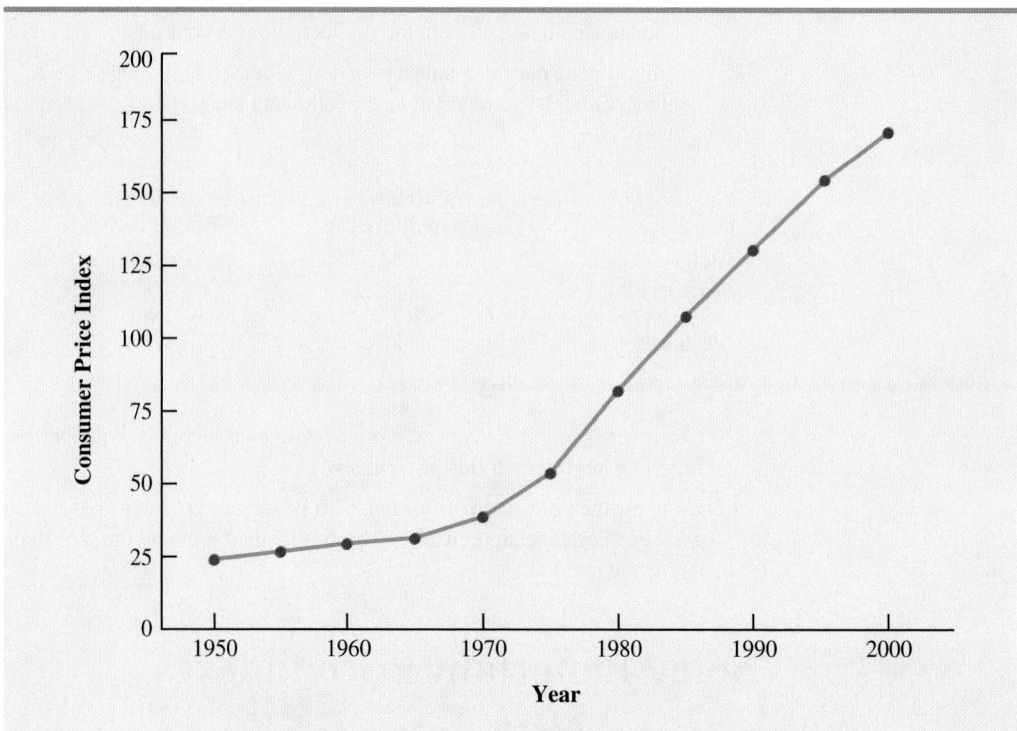

commodities sold in commercial transactions in these markets are represented. The survey covers raw, manufactured, and processed goods at each level of processing and includes the output of industries classified as manufacturing, agriculture, forestry, fishing, mining, gas and electricity, and public utilities. One of the common uses of this index is as a leading indicator of the future trend of consumer prices and the cost of living. An increase in the PPI reflects producer price increases that will eventually be passed on to the consumer through higher retail prices.

Weights for the various items in the PPI are based on the value of shipments. The weighted average of price relatives is calculated by the Laspeyres method. The February 2003 PPI, computed with a 1982 base index of 100, was 142.5.

## Dow Jones Averages

The **Dow Jones averages** are indexes designed to show price trends and movements on the New York Stock Exchange. The best known of the Dow Jones indexes is the Dow Jones Industrial Average (DJIA), which is based on common stock prices of 30 large companies. It is the sum of these stock prices divided by a number, which is revised from time to time to adjust for stock splits and switching of companies in the index. Unlike the other price indexes that we studied, it is not expressed as a percentage of base-year prices. The specific firms used in February 2003 to compute the DJIA are listed in Table 17.7.

Other Dow Jones averages are computed for 20 transportation stocks and for 15 utility stocks. The Dow Jones averages are computed and published daily in *The Wall Street Journal* and other financial publications.

*Charles Henry Dow published his first stock average on July 3, 1884, in the* Customer's Afternoon Letter. *Eleven stocks, nine of which were railroad issues, were included in the first index. An average comparable to the DJIA was first published on October 1, 1928.*

TABLE 17.7   THE 30 COMPANIES USED IN THE DOW JONES INDUSTRIAL AVERAGE
(MARCH 2003)

| | | |
|---|---|---|
| Alcoa | Eastman Kodak | Johnson & Johnson |
| Altria Group | Exxon Mobil | J. P. Morgan Chase |
| American Express | General Electric | McDonald's |
| AT&T | General Motors | Merck |
| Boeing | Hewlett-Packard | Microsoft |
| Caterpillar | Home Depot | Minnesota Mining |
| Citigroup | Honeywell Int'l | Procter & Gamble |
| Coca-Cola | IBM | SBC Communications |
| Disney | Intel | United Technologies |
| DuPont | International Paper | Wal-Mart Stores |

*Source: Barron's,* March 10, 2003.

 **17.5** Deflating a Series By Price Indexes

*Time series are deflated to remove the effects of inflation.*

Many business and economic series reported over time, such as company sales, industry sales, and inventories, are measured in dollar amounts. These time series often show an increasing growth pattern over time, which is generally interpreted as indicating an increase in the physical volume associated with the activities. For example, a total dollar amount of inventory up by 10% might be interpreted to mean that the physical inventory is 10% larger. Such interpretations can be misleading if a time series is measured in terms of dollars, and the total dollar amount is a combination of both price and quantity changes. Hence, in periods when price changes are significant, the changes in the dollar amounts may not be indicative of quantity changes unless we are able to adjust the time series to eliminate the price change effect.

For example, from 1976 to 1980, the total amount of spending in the construction industry increased approximately 75%. That figure suggests excellent growth in construction activity. However, construction prices were increasing just as fast as—or sometimes even faster than—the 75% rate. In fact, while total construction spending was increasing, construction activity was staying relatively constant or, as in the case of new housing starts, decreasing. To interpret construction activity correctly for the 1976–1980 period, we must adjust the total spending series by a price index to remove the price increase effect. Whenever we remove the price increase effect from a time series, we say we are *deflating the series.*

In relation to personal income and wages, we often hear discussions about issues such as "real wages" or the "purchasing power" of wages. These concepts are based on the notion of deflating an hourly wage index. For example, Figure 17.2 shows the pattern of hourly wages of production workers for the period 1998–2002. We see a trend of wage increases from $12.78 per hour to $14.77 per hour. Should production workers be pleased with this growth in hourly wages? The answer depends on what happened to the purchasing power of their wages. If we can compare the purchasing power of the $12.78 hourly wage in 1998 with the purchasing power of the $14.77 hourly wage in 2002, we will be better able to judge the relative improvement in wages.

Table 17.8 reports both the hourly wage rate and the CPI for the period 1998–2002. With these data, we will show how the CPI can be used to deflate the index of hourly wages. The deflated series is found by dividing the hourly wage rate in each year by the corresponding value of the CPI and multiplying by 100. The deflated hourly wage index

FIGURE 17.2    ACTUAL HOURLY WAGES OF PRODUCTION WORKERS

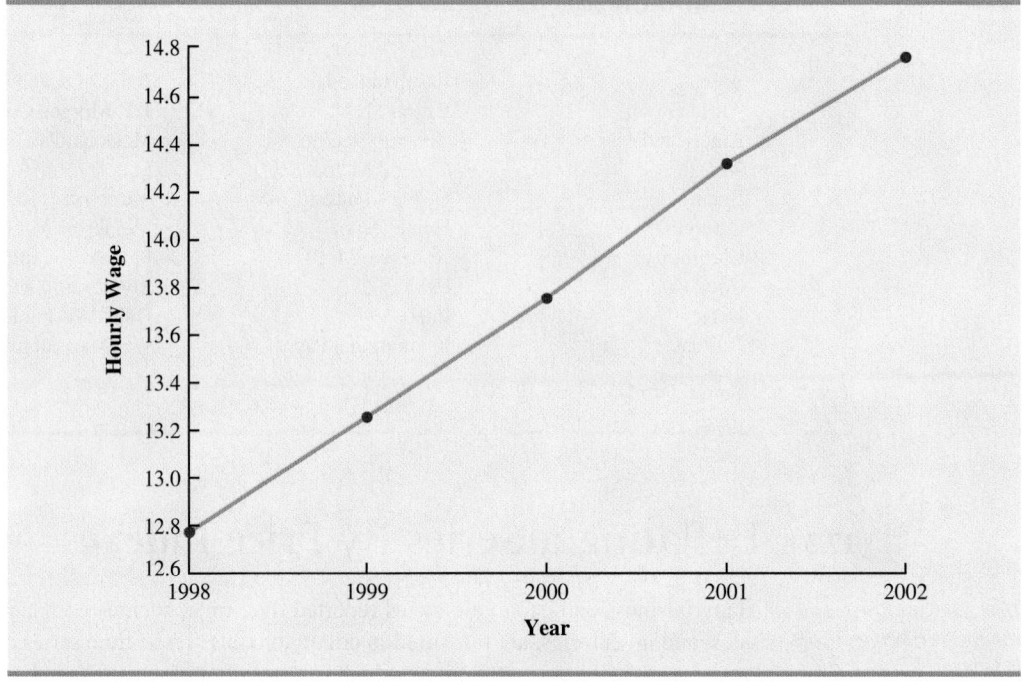

for production workers is given in Table 17.9; Figure 17.3 is a graph showing the deflated, or real, wages.

What does the deflated series of wages tell us about the real wages or purchasing power of workers during the 1998–2002 period? In terms of base period dollars (1982–1984 = 100), the hourly wage rate remained relatively flat over the period. After removing the inflationary effect we see that the purchasing power of the workers has not changed much. This effect is seen in Figure 17.3. Thus, the advantage of using price indexes to deflate a series is that they give us a clearer picture of the real dollar changes that are occurring.

*Real wages are a better measure of purchasing power than actual wages. Indeed, many union contracts call for wages to be adjusted in accordance with changes in the cost of living.*

This process of deflating a series measured over time has an important application in the computation of the gross domestic product (GDP). The GDP is the total value of all

TABLE 17.8    HOURLY WAGES OF PRODUCTION WORKERS AND CONSUMER PRICE
INDEX: 1998–2002

| Year | Hourly Wage ($) | CPI (1982–1984 Base) |
|------|-----------------|----------------------|
| 1998 | 12.78 | 163.0 |
| 1999 | 13.24 | 166.6 |
| 2000 | 13.76 | 172.2 |
| 2001 | 14.31 | 177.1 |
| 2002 | 14.77 | 179.9 |

*Source:* Bureau of Labor Statistics.

TABLE 17.9   DEFLATED SERIES OF HOURLY WAGES FOR PRODUCTION WORKERS

| Year | Deflated Hourly Wage |
|------|----------------------|
| 1998 | ($12.77/163.0)(100) = $7.84 |
| 1999 | ($13.24/166.6)(100) = $7.95 |
| 2000 | ($13.76/172.2)(100) = $7.99 |
| 2001 | ($14.31/177.1)(100) = $8.08 |
| 2002 | ($14.77/179.9)(100) = $8.21 |

FIGURE 17.3   REAL HOURLY WAGES OF PRODUCTION WORKERS (1982–1984 = 100)

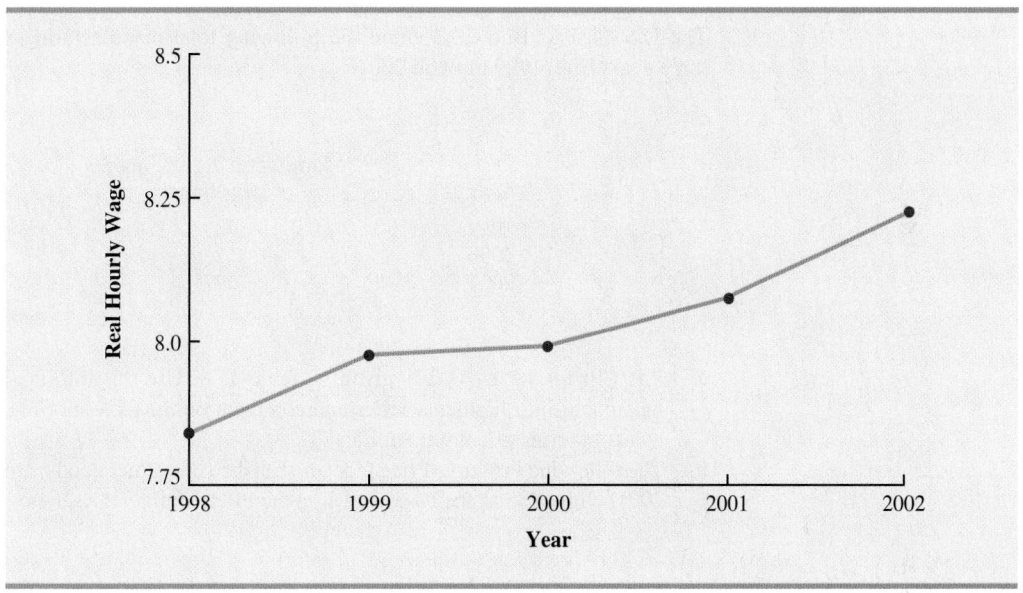

goods and services produced in a given country. Obviously, over time the GDP will show gains that are in part due to price increases if the GDP is not deflated by a price index. Therefore, to adjust the total value of goods and services to reflect actual changes in the volume of goods and services produced and sold, the GDP must be computed with a price index deflator. The process is similar to that discussed in the real wages computation.

## Exercises

### Applications

10. Average hourly wages for manufacturing workers in 1980 were $7.27; in 2000, they were $14.36. The CPI in 1980 was 82.4; in 2000 it was 172.2.
    a.  Deflate the hourly wage rates in 1980 and 2000 to find the real wage rates.
    b.  What is the percentage change in actual hourly wages from 1980 to 2000?
    c.  What is the percentage change in real wages from 1980 to 2000?

11. Average hourly wages for workers in service industries for the four years from 1998 through 2001 are reported here. Use the Consumer Price Index information in Table 17.8 to deflate the wages series. Calculate the percentage increase in real wages and salaries from 1999 to 2001.

| Year | Hourly Wages |
|------|--------------|
| 1998 | 8.13 |
| 1999 | 8.45 |
| 2000 | 8.65 |
| 2001 | 9.15 |

*Source:* Bureau of Labor Statistics.

12. The U.S. Census Bureau reported the following total manufacturing shipments for the three years from 1999 through 2001.

| Year | Manufacturing Shipments ($ billions) |
|------|--------------------------------------|
| 1999 | 4032 |
| 2000 | 4218 |
| 2001 | 3971 |

a. The CPI for 1998–2002 is given in Table 17.8. Use this information to deflate the manufacturing shipments series and comment on the pattern of manufacturers' shipments in terms of constant dollars.

b. The following Producer Price Indexes (finished consumer goods) are for 1999 through 2001, with 1982 as the base year. Use the PPI to deflate the series.

| Year | PPI (1982 = 100) |
|------|------------------|
| 1999 | 133.0 |
| 2000 | 138.0 |
| 2001 | 140.7 |

c. Do you feel that the CPI or the PPI is more appropriate to use as a deflator for manufacturing shipments?

13. Dooley Retail Outlets' total retail sales volumes for selected years since 1982 is shown in the following table. Also shown is the CPI with the index base of 1982–1984. Deflate the sales volume figures on the basis of 1982–1984 constant dollars, and comment on the firm's sales volumes in terms of deflated dollars.

| Year | Retail Sales ($) | CPI (1982–1984 base) |
|------|------------------|----------------------|
| 1982 | 380,000 | 96.5 |
| 1987 | 520,000 | 113.6 |
| 1992 | 700,000 | 140.3 |
| 1997 | 870,000 | 160.5 |
| 2002 | 940,000 | 179.9 |

# 17.6   Price Indexes: Other Considerations

In the preceding sections we described several methods used to compute price indexes, discussed the use of some important indexes, and presented a procedure for using price indexes to deflate a time series. Several other issues must be considered to enhance our understanding of how price indexes are constructed and how they are used. Some are discussed in this section.

## Selection of Items

The primary purpose of a price index is to measure the price change over time for a specified class of items, products, and so on. Whenever the class of items is very large, the index cannot be based on all items in the class. Rather, a sample of representative items must be used. By collecting price and quantity information for the sampled items, we hope to obtain a good idea of the price behavior of all items that the index is representing. For example, in the Consumer Price Index the total number of items that might be considered in the population of normal purchase items for a consumer could be 2000 or more. However, the index is based on the price-quantity characteristics of just 400 items. The selection of the specific items in the index is not a trivial task. Surveys of user purchase patterns as well as good judgment go into the selection process. A simple random sample is not used to select the 400 items.

After the initial selection process, the group of items in the index must be periodically reviewed and revised whenever purchase patterns change. Thus, the issue of which items to include in an index must be resolved before an index can be developed and again before it is revised.

## Selection of a Base Period

Most indexes are established with a base-period value of 100 at some specific time. All future values of the index are then related to the base-period value. What base period is appropriate for an index is not an easy question to answer. It must be based on the judgment of the developer of the index.

Many of the indexes established by the U.S. government as of 2000 use a 1982 base period. As a general guideline, the base period should not be too far from the current period. For example, a Consumer Price Index with a 1945 base period would be difficult for most individuals to understand because of unfamiliarity with conditions in 1945. The base period for most indexes therefore is adjusted periodically to a more recent period of time. The CPI base period was changed from 1967 to the 1982–1984 average in 1988. The PPI currently uses 1982 as its base period (i.e., 1982 = 100).

## Quality Changes

The purpose of a price index is to measure changes in prices over time. Ideally, price data are collected for the same set of items at several times, and then the index is computed. A basic assumption is that the prices are identified for the same items each period. A problem is encountered when a product changes in quality from one period to the next. For example, a manufacturer may alter the quality of a product by using less expensive materials, fewer features, and so on, from year to year. The price may go up in following years, but the price is for a lower-quality product. Consequently, the price may actually go up more than is represented by the list price for the item. It is difficult, if not impossible, to adjust an index for decreases in the quality of an item.

A substantial quality improvement also may cause an increase in the price of a product. A portion of the price related to the quality improvement should be excluded from the index computation. However, adjusting an index for a price increase that is related to higher quality of an item is extremely difficult, if not impossible.

Although common practice is to ignore minor quality changes in developing a price index, major quality changes must be addressed because they can alter the product description from period to period. If a product description is changed, the index must be modified to account for it; in some cases, the product might be deleted from the index.

In some situations, however, a substantial improvement in quality is followed by a decrease in the price. This less typical situation has been the case with personal computers during the 1990s and early 2000s.

## 17.7 Quantity Indexes

In addition to the price indexes described in the preceding sections, other types of indexes are useful. In particular, one other application of index numbers is to measure changes in quantity levels over time. This type of index is called a **quantity index**.

Recall that in the development of the weighted aggregate price index in Section 17.2, to compute an index number for period $t$ we needed data on unit prices at a base period ($P_0$) and period $t$ ($P_t$). Equation (17.3) provided the weighted aggregate price index as

$$I_t = \frac{\Sigma P_{it} Q_i}{\Sigma P_{i0} Q_i} (100)$$

The numerator, $\Sigma P_{it} Q_i$, represents the total value of fixed quantities of the index items in period $t$. The denominator, $\Sigma P_{i0} Q_i$, represents the total value of the same fixed quantities of the index items in year 0.

Computation of a weighted aggregate quantity index is similar to that of a weighted aggregate price index. Quantities for each item are measured in the base period and period $t$, with $Q_{i0}$ and $Q_{it}$, respectively, representing those quantities for item $i$. The quantities are then weighted by a fixed price, the value added, or some other factor. The "value added" to a product is the sales value minus the cost of purchased inputs. The formula for computing a weighted aggregate quantity index for period $t$ is

$$I_t = \frac{\Sigma Q_{it} w_i}{\Sigma Q_{i0} w_i} (100) \tag{17.9}$$

In some quantity indexes the weight for item $i$ is taken to be the base-period price ($P_{i0}$), in which case the weighted aggregate quantity index is

$$I_t = \frac{\Sigma Q_{it} P_{i0}}{\Sigma Q_{i0} P_{i0}} (100) \tag{17.10}$$

Quantity indexes can also be computed on the basis of weighted quantity relatives. One formula for this version of a quantity index follows.

$$I_t = \frac{\Sigma \dfrac{Q_{it}}{Q_{i0}} (Q_{i0} P_i)}{\Sigma Q_{i0} P_i} (100) \tag{17.11}$$

This formula is the quantity version of the weighted price relatives formula developed in Section 17.3 as in equation (17.8).

The **Index of Industrial Production and Capacity Utilization**, developed by the Federal Reserve Board, is probably the best-known quantity index. It is reported monthly and the base period is 1997. The index is designed to measure changes in volume of production levels for a variety of manufacturing classifications in addition to mining and utilities. In January 2003 the index was 111.0.

## Exercises

### Methods

14. Data on quantities of three items sold in 1995 and 2003 are given here along with the sales prices of the items in 1995. Compute a weighted aggregate quantity index for 2003.

| | Quantity Sold | | |
|---|---|---|---|
| Item | 1995 | 2003 | Price/Unit 1995 ($) |
| A | 350 | 300 | 18.00 |
| B | 220 | 400 | 4.90 |
| C | 730 | 850 | 15.00 |

### Applications

15. A trucking firm handles four commodities for a particular distributor. Total shipments for the commodities in 1994 and 2003, as well as the 1994 prices, are reported in the following table.

| | Shipments | | Price/Shipment |
|---|---|---|---|
| Commodity | 1994 | 2003 | 1994 |
| A | 120 | 95 | $1200 |
| B | 86 | 75 | $1800 |
| C | 35 | 50 | $2000 |
| D | 60 | 70 | $1500 |

Develop a weighted aggregate quantity index with a 1994 base. Comment on the growth or decline in quantities over the 1994–2003 period.

16. An automobile dealer reports the 1992 and 2003 sales for three models in the following table. Compute quantity relatives and use them to develop a weighted aggregate quantity index for 2003 using the two years of data.

| | Sales | | Mean Price per Sale |
|---|---|---|---|
| Model | 1992 | 2003 | (1992) |
| Sedan | 200 | 170 | $15,200 |
| Sport | 100 | 80 | $17,000 |
| Wagon | 75 | 60 | $16,800 |

## Summary

Price and quantity indexes are important measures of changes in price and quantity levels within the business and economic environment. Price relatives are simply the ratio of the current unit price of an item to a base-period unit price multiplied by 100, with a value of 100 indicating no difference in the current and base-period prices. Aggregate price indexes are created as a composite measure of the overall change in prices for a given group of items or products. Usually the items in an aggregate price index are weighted by their quantity of usage. A weighted aggregate price index can also be computed by weighting the price relatives by the usage quantities for the items in the index.

The Consumer Price Index and the Producer Price Index are both widely quoted indexes with 1982–1984 and 1982, respectively, as base years. The Dow Jones Industrial Average is another widely quoted price index. It is a weighted sum of the prices of 30 common stocks listed on the New York Stock Exchange. Unlike many other indexes, it is not stated as a percentage of some base-period value.

Often price indexes are used to deflate some other economic series reported over time. We saw how the CPI could be used to deflate hourly wages to obtain an index of real wages. Selection of the items to be included in the index, selection of a base period for the index, and adjustment for changes in quality are important additional considerations in the development of an index number. Quantity indexes were briefly discussed, and the Index of Industrial Production and Capacity Utilization was mentioned as an important quantity index.

## Glossary

**Price relative** A price index for a given item that is computed by dividing a current unit price by a base-period unit price and multiplying the result by 100.

**Aggregate price index** A composite price index based on the prices of a group of items.

**Weighted aggregate price index** A composite price index in which the prices of the items in the composite are weighted by their relative importance.

**Laspeyres index** A weighted aggregate price index in which the weight for each item is its base-period quantity.

**Paasche index** A weighted aggregate price index in which the weight for each item is its current-period quantity.

**Consumer Price Index** A monthly price index that uses the price changes in a market basket of consumer goods and services to measure the changes in consumer prices over time.

**Producer Price Index** A monthly price index designed to measure changes in prices of goods sold in primary markets (i.e., first purchase of a commodity in nonretail markets).

**Dow Jones averages** Aggregate price indexes designed to show price trends and movements on the New York Stock Exchange.

**Quantity index** An index designed to measure changes in quantities over time.

**Index of Industrial Production and Capacity Utilization** A quantity index designed to measure changes in the physical volume or production levels of industrial goods over time.

## Key Formulas

**Price Relative in Period $t$**

$$\frac{\text{Price in period } t}{\text{Base period price}} (100) \tag{17.1}$$

Unweighted Aggregate Price Index in Period $t$

$$I_t = \frac{\Sigma P_{it}}{\Sigma P_{i0}}(100)$$　　　　　　　　　(17.2)

Weighted Aggregate Price Index in Period $t$

$$I_t = \frac{\Sigma P_{it}Q_i}{\Sigma P_{i0}Q_i}(100)$$　　　　　　　　　(17.3)

Weighted Average of Price Relatives

$$I_t = \frac{\Sigma \dfrac{P_{it}}{P_{i0}}(100)w_i}{\Sigma w_i}$$　　　　　　　　　(17.6)

Weighting Factor for Equation (17.6)

$$w_i = P_{i0}Q_i$$　　　　　　　　　(17.7)

Weighted Aggregate Quantity Index

$$I_t = \frac{\Sigma Q_{it}w_i}{\Sigma Q_{i0}w_i}(100)$$　　　　　　　　　(17.9)

## Supplementary Exercises

17.  The median sales prices for new single-family houses for the years 1998–2001 are as follows (*Statistical Abstract of the United States*, 2002).

| Year | Price ($1000s) |
|------|----------------|
| 1998 | 152.5 |
| 1999 | 161.0 |
| 2000 | 169.0 |
| 2001 | 175.2 |

a.  Use 1998 as the base year and develop a price index for new single-family homes over this four-year period.
b.  Use 1999 as the base year and develop a price index for new single-family homes over this four-year period.

18.  Nickerson Manufacturing Company has the following data on quantities shipped and unit costs for each of its four products:

| Products | Base-Period Quantities (2000) | Mean Shipping Cost per Unit ($) 2000 | Mean Shipping Cost per Unit ($) 2003 |
|----------|-------------------------------|------|------|
| A | 2000 | 10.50 | 15.90 |
| B | 5000 | 16.25 | 32.00 |
| C | 6500 | 12.20 | 17.40 |
| D | 2500 | 20.00 | 35.50 |

a. Compute the price relative for each product.
b. Compute a weighted aggregate price index that reflects the shipping cost change over the four-year period.

19. Use the price data in exercise 18 to compute a Paasche index for the shipping cost if 2003 quantities are 4000, 3000, 7500, and 3000 for each of the four products.

20. Boran Stockbrokers, Inc., selects four stocks for the purpose of developing its own index of stock market behavior. Prices per share for a 2001 base period, January 2003, and March 2003 follow. Base-year quantities are set on the basis of historical volumes for the four stocks.

| Stock | Industry | 2001 Quantity | 2001 Base | January 2003 | March 2003 |
|-------|----------|--------------|-----------|--------------|------------|
| | | | | Price per Share ($) | |
| A | Oil | 100 | 31.50 | 22.75 | 22.50 |
| B | Computer | 150 | 65.00 | 49.00 | 47.50 |
| C | Steel | 75 | 40.00 | 32.00 | 29.50 |
| D | Real Estate | 50 | 18.00 | 6.50 | 3.75 |

Use the 2001 base period to compute the Boran index for January 2003 and March 2003. Comment on what the index tells you about what is happening in the stock market.

21. Compute the price relatives for the four stocks making up the Boran index in exercise 20. Use the weighted aggregates of price relatives to compute the January 2003 and March 2003 Boran indexes.

22. Consider the following price relatives and quantity information for grain production in Iowa (*Statistical Abstract of the United States,* 2002).

| Product | 1991 Quantities (millions of bushels) | Base Price per Bushel ($) | 1991–2001 Price Relatives |
|---------|--------------------------------------|---------------------------|---------------------------|
| Corn | 1427 | 2.30 | 91 |
| Soybeans | 350 | 5.51 | 78 |

What is the 2001 weighted aggregate price index for the Iowa grains?

23. Fresh fruit price and quantity data for the years 1988 and 2001 follow (*Statistical Abstract of the United States,* 2002). Quantity data reflect per capita consumption in pounds and prices are per pound.

| Fruit | 1988 per Capita Consumption (pounds) | 1988 Price ($/pound) | 2001 Price ($/pound) |
|-------|--------------------------------------|----------------------|----------------------|
| Bananas | 24.3 | .41 | .51 |
| Apples | 19.9 | .71 | .87 |
| Oranges | 13.9 | .56 | .71 |
| Pears | 3.2 | .64 | .98 |

a. Compute a price relative for each product.
b. Compute a weighted aggregate price index for fruit products. Comment on the change in fruit prices over the 13-year period.

24. Starting faculty salaries (nine-month basis) for assistant professors of business administration at a major Midwestern university follow. Use the CPI to deflate the salary data to constant dollars. Comment on the trend in salaries in higher education as indicated by these data.

| Year | Starting Salary ($) | CPI (1982–1984 Base) |
|------|---------------------|----------------------|
| 1970 | 14,000 | 38.8 |
| 1975 | 17,500 | 53.8 |
| 1980 | 23,000 | 82.4 |
| 1985 | 37,000 | 107.6 |
| 1990 | 53,000 | 130.7 |
| 1995 | 65,000 | 152.4 |
| 2000 | 80,000 | 172.2 |

25. The five-year historical prices per share for a particular stock and the Consumer Price Index with a 1982–1984 base period follow.

| Year | Price per Share ($) | CPI (1982–1984 Base) |
|------|---------------------|----------------------|
| 1998 | 51.00 | 163.0 |
| 1999 | 54.00 | 166.6 |
| 2000 | 58.00 | 172.2 |
| 2001 | 59.50 | 177.1 |
| 2002 | 59.00 | 179.9 |

Deflate the stock price series and comment on the investment aspects of this stock.

26. A major manufacturing company reports the quantity and product value information for 2000 and 2004 in the table that follows. Compute a weighted aggregate quantity index for the data. Comment on what this quantity index means.

| | Quantities | | |
|---------|------|------|-------------|
| Product | 2000 | 2004 | Values ($) |
| A | 800 | 1200 | 30.00 |
| B | 600 | 500 | 20.00 |
| C | 200 | 500 | 25.00 |

# Forecasting

## CONTENTS

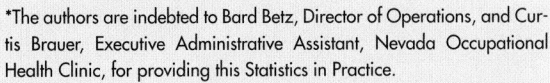

## NEVADA OCCUPATIONAL HEALTH CLINIC*
*SPARKS, NEVADA*

Nevada Occupational Health Clinic is a privately owned medical clinic in Sparks, Nevada. The clinic specializes in industrial medicine, operating at the same site for more than 20 years. In the beginning of 1991, the clinic entered a rapid growth phase in which monthly billings increased from $57,000 to more than $300,000 in 26 months. The clinic was still undergoing dramatic growth when the main clinic building burned to the ground on April 6, 1993.

The clinic's insurance policy covered physical property and equipment as well as loss of income due to the interruption of regular business operations. Settling the property insurance claim was a relatively straightforward matter of determining the value of the physical property and equipment lost during the fire. However, determining the value of the income lost during the seven months that it took to rebuild the clinic was a complicated matter involving negotiations between the business owners and the insurance company. No preestablished rules could help calculate "what would have happened" to the clinic's billings if the

A 1993 fire closed the Nevada Occupational Health Clinic for seven months. © PhotoDisc/Getty Images.

fire had not occurred. To estimate the lost income, the clinic used a forecasting method to project the growth in business that would have been realized during the seven-month lost-business period. The actual history of billings prior to the fire provided the basis for a forecasting model with linear trend and seasonal components as discussed in this chapter. This forecasting model enabled the clinic to establish an accurate estimate of the loss, which eventually was accepted by the insurance company.

*The authors are indebted to Bard Betz, Director of Operations, and Curtis Brauer, Executive Administrative Assistant, Nevada Occupational Health Clinic, for providing this Statistics in Practice.

An essential aspect of managing any organization is planning for the future. Indeed, the long-run success of an organization is closely related to how well management is able to anticipate the future and develop appropriate strategies. Good judgment, intuition, and an awareness of the state of the economy may give a manager a rough idea or "feeling" of what is likely to happen in the future. However, converting that feeling into a number that can be used as next quarter's sales volume or next year's raw material cost is difficult. The purpose of this chapter is to introduce several forecasting methods.

Suppose we are asked to provide quarterly forecasts of the sales volume for a particular product during the coming one-year period. Production schedules, raw material purchasing, inventory policies, and sales quotas will all be affected by the quarterly forecasts we provide. Consequently, poor forecasts may result in poor planning and hence increased costs for the firm. How should we go about providing the quarterly sales volume forecasts?

We will certainly want to review the actual sales data for the product in past periods. Using these historical data, we can identify the general level of sales and any trend such as an increase or decrease in sales volume over time. A further review of the data might reveal a seasonal pattern such as peak sales occurring in the third quarter of each year and sales volume bottoming out during the first quarter. By reviewing historical data, we can often develop a better understanding of the pattern of past sales, leading to better predictions of future sales for the product.

Historical sales form a time series. A **time series** is a set of observations on a variable measured at successive points in time or over successive periods of time. In this chapter,

*Most companies can forecast total demand for all products with errors of less than 5%. However, forecasting demand for individual products can result in significantly higher errors.*

*A forecast is simply a prediction of what will happen in the future. Managers must learn to accept the fact that regardless of the technique used, they will not be able to develop perfect forecasts.*

we will introduce several procedures for analyzing time series. The objective of such analyses is to provide good **forecasts** or predictions of future values of the time series.

Forecasting methods can be classified as quantitative or qualitative. Quantitative forecasting methods can be used when (1) past information about the variable being forecast is available, (2) the information can be quantified, and (3) a reasonable assumption is that the pattern of the past will continue into the future. In such cases, a forecast can be developed using a time series method or a causal method.

If the historical data are restricted to past values of the variable, the forecasting procedure is called a *time series method.* The objective of time series methods is to discover a pattern in the historical data and then extrapolate the pattern into the future; the forecast is based solely on past values of the variable and/or on past forecast errors. In this chapter we discuss three time series methods: smoothing (moving averages, weighted moving averages, and exponential smoothing), trend projection, and trend projection adjusted for seasonal influence.

Causal forecasting methods are based on the assumption that the variable we are forecasting has a cause-effect relationship with one or more other variables. In this chapter we discuss the use of regression analysis as a causal forecasting method. For instance, the sales volume for many products is influenced by advertising expenditures, so regression analysis may be used to develop an equation showing how these two variables are related. Then, once the advertising budget is set for the next period, we could substitute this value into the equation to develop a prediction or forecast of the sales volume for that period. Note that if a time series method was used to develop the forecast, advertising expenditures would not be considered; that is, a time series method would base the forecast solely on past sales.

Qualitative methods generally involve the use of expert judgment to develop forecasts. For instance, a panel of experts might develop a consensus forecast of the prime rate for a year from now. An advantage of qualitative procedures is that they can be applied when the information on the variable being forecast cannot be quantified and when historical data are either not applicable or unavailable. Figure 18.1 provides an overview of the types of forecasting methods.

# Components of a Time Series

The pattern or behavior of the data in a time series involves several components. The usual assumption is that four separate components—trend, cyclical, seasonal, and irregular—combine to provide specific values for the time series. Let us look more closely at each of these components.

## Trend Component

In time series analysis, the measurements may be taken every hour, day, week, month, or year, or at any other regular interval.* Although time series data generally exhibit random fluctuations, the time series may still show gradual shifts or movements to relatively higher or lower values over a longer period of time. The gradual shifting of the time series is referred to as the **trend** in the time series; this shifting or trend is usually the result of long-term factors such as changes in the population, demographic characteristics of the population, technology, and/or consumer preferences.

For example, a manufacturer of photographic equipment may see substantial month-to-month variability in the number of cameras sold. However, in reviewing the sales over the past 10 to 15 years, the manufacturer may find a gradual increase in the annual sales volume.

---

*We limit our discussion to time series in which the values of the series are recorded at equal intervals. Cases in which the observations are not made at equal intervals are beyond the scope of this text.

FIGURE 18.1   OVERVIEW OF FORECASTING METHODS

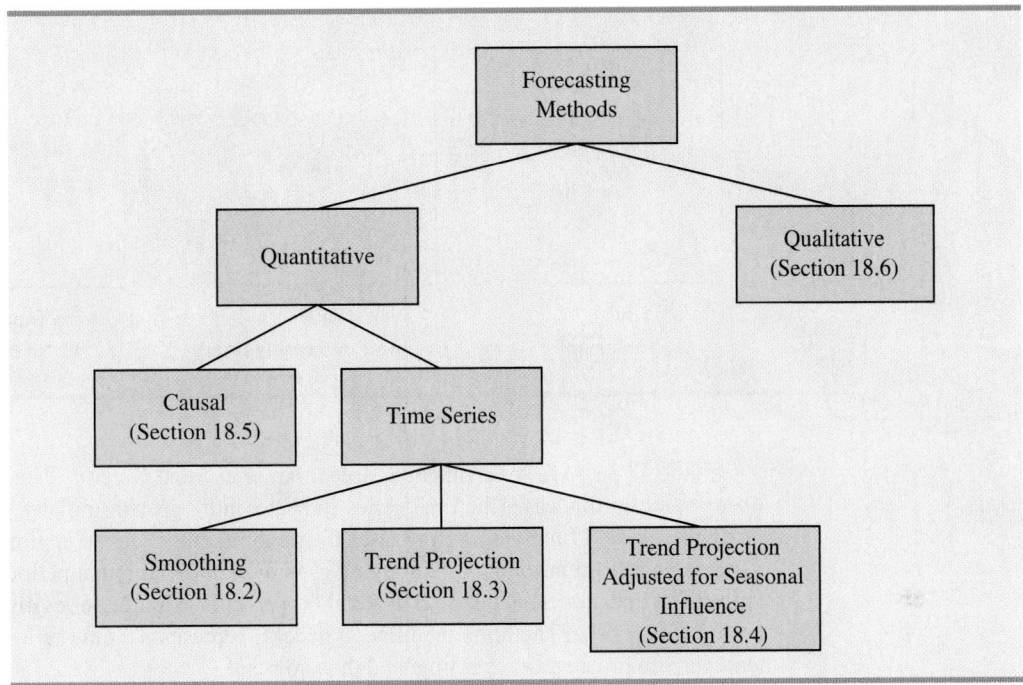

Suppose the sales volume was approximately 17,000 cameras in 1991, 23,000 cameras in 1996, and 25,000 cameras in 2001. This gradual growth in sales over time shows an upward trend for the time series. Figure 18.2 shows a straight line that may be a good approximation of the trend in camera sales. Although the trend for camera sales appears to be linear and increasing over time, sometimes the trend in a time series can be described better by some other patterns.

FIGURE 18.2   LINEAR TREND OF CAMERA SALES

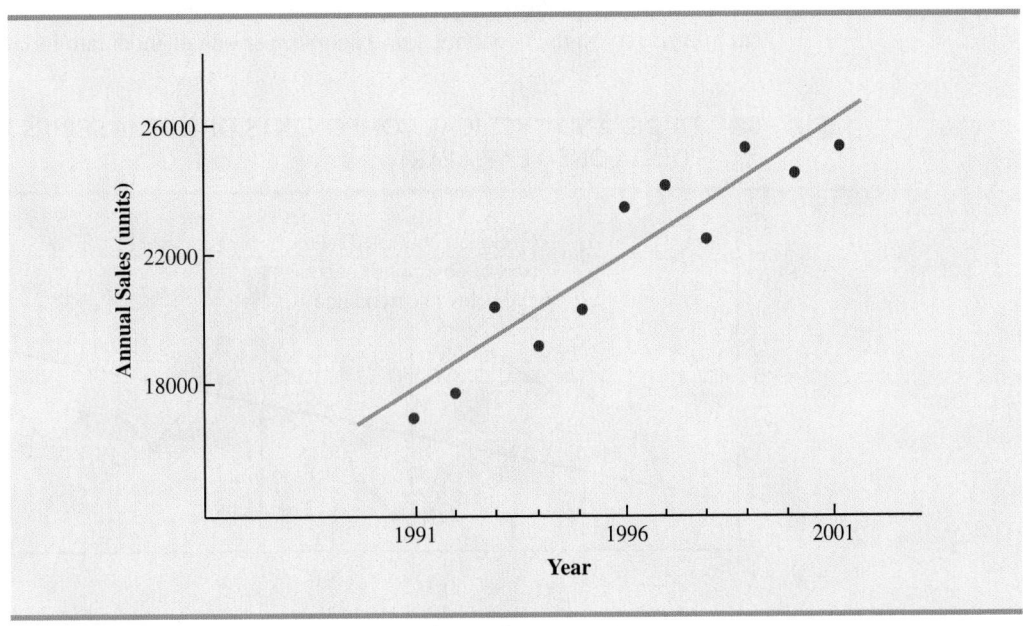

FIGURE 18.3    EXAMPLES OF SOME POSSIBLE TIME SERIES TREND PATTERNS

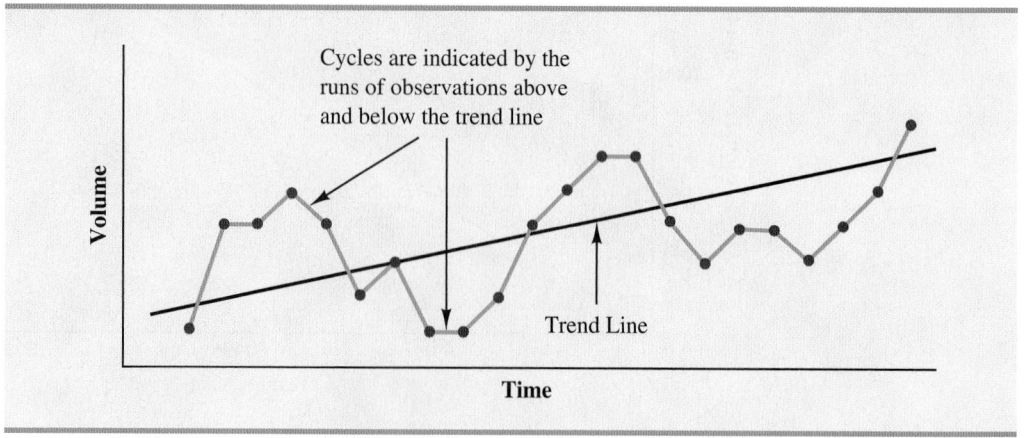

A. Nonlinear    B. Linear decreasing trend    C. No trend

Figure 18.3 shows some other possible time series trend patterns. Panel A shows a nonlinear trend; in this case, the time series indicates little growth initially, then a period of rapid growth, and finally a leveling off. This trend might be a good approximation of sales for a product from introduction through a growth period and into a period of market saturation. The linear decreasing trend in panel B is useful for a time series displaying a steady decrease over time. The horizontal line in panel C represents a time series with no consistent increase or decrease over time and thus no trend.

## Cyclical Component

Although a time series may exhibit a trend over long periods of time, all future values of the time series will not fall exactly on the trend line. In fact, time series often show alternating sequences of points below and above the trend line. Any recurring sequence of points above and below the trend line lasting more than one year can be attributed to the **cyclical component** of the time series. Figure 18.4 shows the graph of a time series with an obvious cyclical component. The observations are taken at intervals one year apart.

Many time series exhibit cyclical behavior with regular runs of observations below and above the trend line. Generally, this component of the time series is due to multiyear cyclical movements in the economy. For example, periods of moderate inflation followed by

FIGURE 18.4    TREND AND CYCLICAL COMPONENTS OF A TIME SERIES WITH DATA
POINTS ONE YEAR APART

periods of rapid inflation can lead to time series that alternate below and above a generally increasing trend line (e.g., a time series for housing costs).

## Seasonal Component

Whereas the trend and cyclical components of a time series are identified by analyzing multi-year movements in historical data, many time series show a regular pattern over one-year periods. For example, a manufacturer of swimming pools expects low sales activity in the fall and winter months, with peak sales in the spring and summer months. Manufacturers of snow removal equipment and heavy clothing, however, expect just the opposite yearly pattern. Not surprisingly, the component of the time series that represents the variability in the data due to seasonal influences is called the **seasonal component**. Although we generally think of seasonal movement in a time series as occurring within one year, the seasonal component can also be used to represent any regularly repeating pattern that is less than one year in duration. For example, daily traffic volume data show within-the-day "seasonal" behavior, with peak levels occurring during rush hours, moderate flow during the rest of the day and early evening, and light flow from midnight to early morning.

## Irregular Component

The **irregular component** of the time series is the residual, or "catch-all," factor that accounts for the deviations of the actual time series values from those expected given the effects of the trend, cyclical, and seasonal components. The irregular component is caused by the short-term, unanticipated, and nonrecurring factors that affect the time series. Because this component accounts for the random variability in the time series, it is unpredictable. We cannot attempt to predict its impact on the time series.

# 18.2    Smoothing Methods

*Many manufacturing environments require forecasts for thousands of items weekly or monthly. Thus, in choosing a forecasting technique, simplicity and ease of use are important criteria. The data requirements for the techniques presented in this section are minimal, and the techniques are easy to use and understand.*

In this section we discuss three forecasting methods: moving averages, weighted moving averages, and exponential smoothing. The objective of each of these methods is to "smooth out" the random fluctuations caused by the irregular component of the time series, therefore they are referred to as smoothing methods. Smoothing methods are appropriate for a stable time series—that is, one that exhibits no significant trend, cyclical, or seasonal effects—because they adapt well to changes in the level of the time series. However, without modification, they do not work as well when significant trend, cyclical, or seasonal variations are present.

Smoothing methods are easy to use and generally provide a high level of accuracy for short-range forecasts, such as a forecast for the next time period. One of the methods, exponential smoothing, has minimal data requirements and thus is a good method to use when forecasts are required for large numbers of items.

## Moving Averages

The **moving averages** method uses the average of the most recent $n$ data values in the time series as the forecast for the next period. Mathematically, the moving average calculation is made as follows.

MOVING AVERAGE

$$\text{Moving average} = \frac{\Sigma(\text{most recent } n \text{ data values})}{n} \qquad (18.1)$$

| Week | Sales (1000s of gallons) |
|------|--------------------------|
| 1 | 17 |
| 2 | 21 |
| 3 | 19 |
| 4 | 23 |
| 5 | 18 |
| 6 | 16 |
| 7 | 20 |
| 8 | 18 |
| 9 | 22 |
| 10 | 20 |
| 11 | 15 |
| 12 | 22 |

The term *moving* is used because every time a new observation becomes available for the time series, it replaces the oldest observation in equation (18.1) and a new average is computed. As a result, the average will change, or move, as new observations become available.

To illustrate the moving averages method, consider the 12 weeks of data in Table 18.1 and Figure 18.5. These data show the number of gallons of gasoline sold by a gasoline distributor in Bennington, Vermont, over the past 12 weeks. Figure 18.5 indicates that, although random variability is present, the time series appears to be stable over time. Hence, the smoothing methods of this section are applicable.

To use moving averages to forecast gasoline sales, we must first select the number of data values to be included in the moving average. As an example, let us compute forecasts using a three-week moving average. The moving average calculation for the first three weeks of the gasoline sales time series is

$$\text{Moving average (weeks 1–3)} = \frac{17 + 21 + 19}{3} = 19$$

We then use this moving average as the forecast for week 4. Because the actual value observed in week 4 is 23, the forecast error in week 4 is $23 - 19 = 4$. In general, the error associated with any forecast is the difference between the observed value of the time series and the forecast.

The calculation for the second three-week moving average is

$$\text{Moving average (weeks 2–4)} = \frac{21 + 19 + 23}{3} = 21$$

**FIGURE 18.5   GASOLINE SALES TIME SERIES**

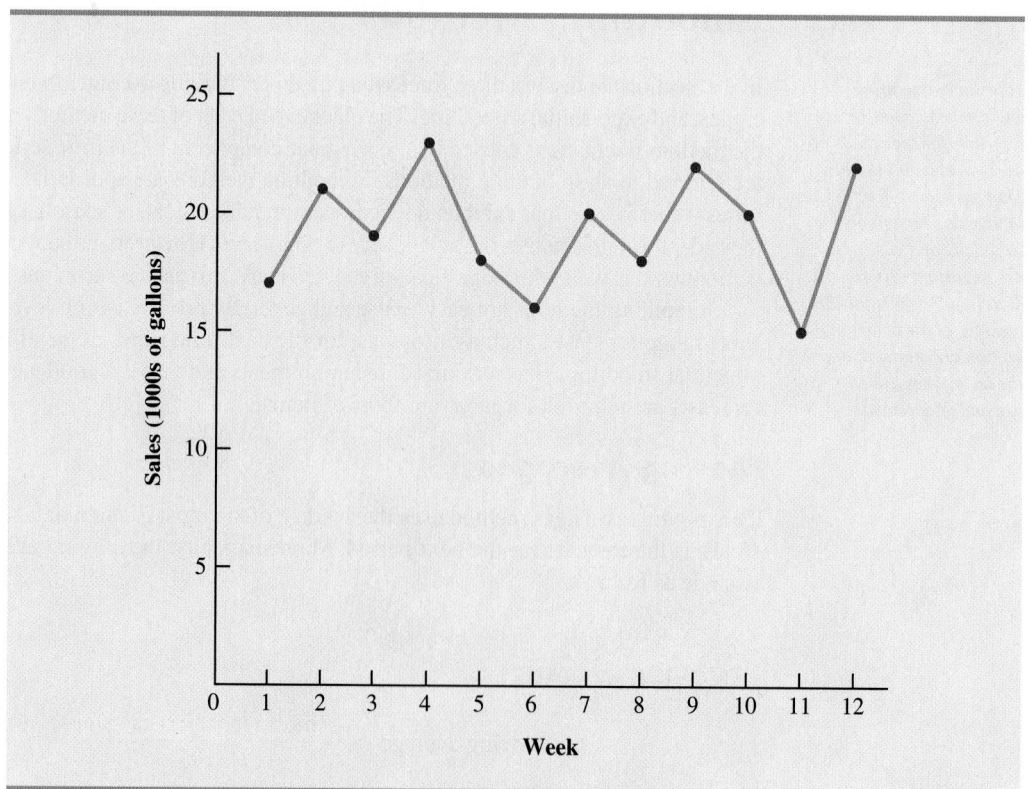

Hence, the forecast for week 5 is 21. The error associated with this forecast is $18 - 21 = -3$. Thus, the forecast error may be positive or negative depending on whether the forecast is too low or too high. A complete summary of the three-week moving average calculations for the gasoline sales time series is provided in Table 18.2 and Figure 18.6.

*Forecast accuracy is not the only consideration. Sometimes the most accurate method requires data on related time series that are difficult or costly to obtain. Trade-offs are often made between cost and forecast accuracy.*

**Forecast Accuracy** An important consideration in selecting a forecasting method is the accuracy of the forecast. Clearly, we want forecast errors to be small. The last two columns of Table 18.2, which contain the forecast errors and the squared forecast errors, can be used to develop a measure of forecast accuracy.

For the gasoline sales time series, we can use the last column of Table 18.2 to compute the average of the sum of the squared errors. Doing so we obtain

$$\text{Average of the sum of squared errors} = \frac{92}{9} = 10.22$$

This average of the sum of squared errors is commonly referred to as the **mean squared error (MSE)**. The MSE is an often-used measure of the accuracy of a forecasting method and is the one we use in this chapter.

As we indicated previously, to use the moving averages method, we must first select the number of data values to be included in the moving average. Not surprisingly, for a particular time series, moving averages of different lengths will differ in their ability to forecast the time series accurately. One possible approach to choosing the number of values to be included in the moving average is to use trial and error to identify the length that minimizes the MSE. Then, if we are willing to assume that the length that is best for the past will also be best for the future, we would forecast the next value in the time series by using the number of data values that minimized the MSE for the historical time series. Exercise 2 at the end of the section will ask you to consider four-week and five-week moving averages for the gasoline sales data. A comparison of the MSEs will indicate the number of weeks of data you may want to include in the moving average calculation.

## Weighted Moving Averages

In the moving averages method, each observation in the moving average calculation receives the same weight. One variation, known as **weighted moving averages**, involves selecting a different weight for each data value and then computing a weighted average of the most recent $n$ values as

**TABLE 18.2    SUMMARY OF THREE-WEEK MOVING AVERAGE CALCULATIONS**

| Week | Time Series Value | Moving Average Forecast | Forecast Error | Squared Forecast Error |
|------|------------------|------------------------|----------------|------------------------|
| 1 | 17 | | | |
| 2 | 21 | | | |
| 3 | 19 | | | |
| 4 | 23 | 19 | 4 | 16 |
| 5 | 18 | 21 | −3 | 9 |
| 6 | 16 | 20 | −4 | 16 |
| 7 | 20 | 19 | 1 | 1 |
| 8 | 18 | 18 | 0 | 0 |
| 9 | 22 | 18 | 4 | 16 |
| 10 | 20 | 20 | 0 | 0 |
| 11 | 15 | 20 | −5 | 25 |
| 12 | 22 | 19 | 3 | 9 |
| | | Totals | 0 | 92 |

FIGURE 18.6    GASOLINE SALES TIME SERIES AND THREE-WEEK MOVING
AVERAGE FORECASTS

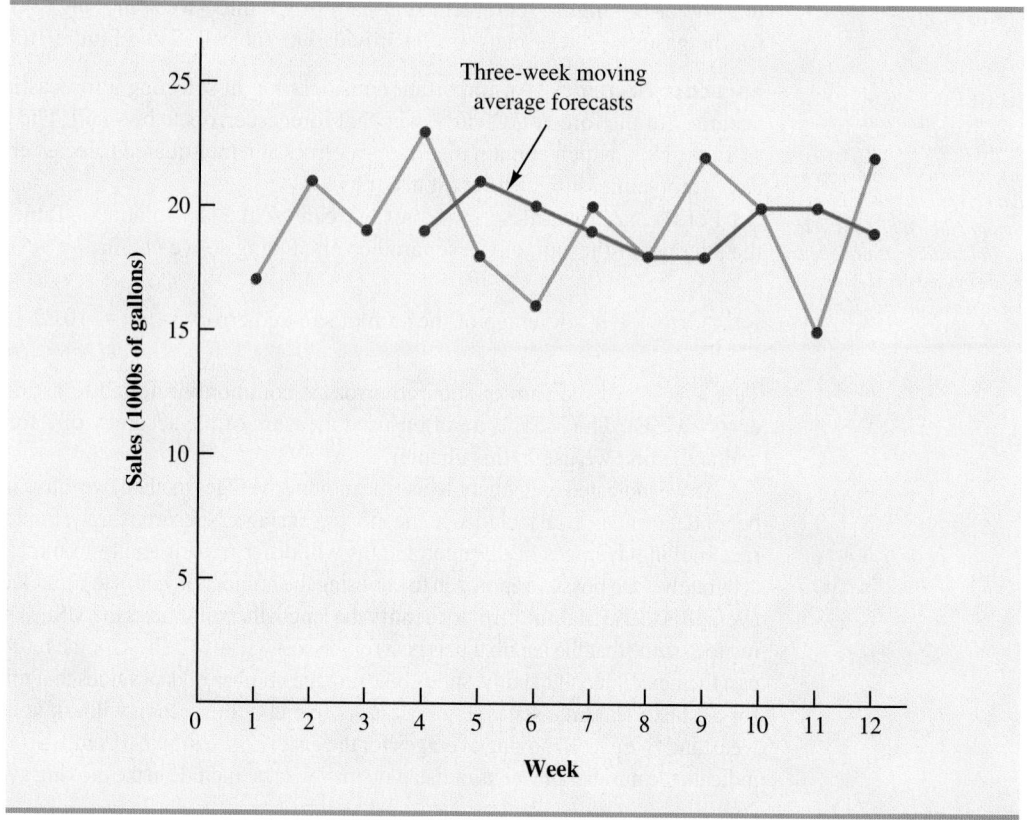

the forecast. In most cases, the most recent observation receives the most weight, and the weight decreases for older data values. For example, we can use the gasoline sales time series to illustrate the computation of a weighted three-week moving average, with the most recent observation receiving a weight three times as great as that given the oldest observation, and the next oldest observation receiving a weight twice as great as the oldest. For week 4 the computation is:

$$\text{Forecast for week 4} = \tfrac{1}{6}(17) + \tfrac{2}{6}(21) + \tfrac{3}{6}(19) = 19.33$$

Note that for the weighted moving average the sum of the weights is equal to 1. Actually the sum of the weights for the simple moving average also equalled 1: Each weight was 1/3. However, recall that the simple or unweighted moving average provided a forecast of 19.

**Forecast Accuracy**  To use the weighted moving averages method we must first select the number of data values to be included in the weighted moving average and then choose weights for each of the data values. In general, if we believe that the recent past is a better predictor of the future than the distant past, larger weights should be given to the more recent observations. However, when the time series is highly variable, selecting approximately equal weights for the data values may be best. Note that the only requirement in selecting the weights is that their sum must equal 1. To determine whether one particular combination of number of data values and weights provides a more accurate forecast than another combination, we will continue to use the MSE criterion as the measure of forecast accuracy. That is, if we assume that the combination that is best for the past will also be best for the future, we would use the combination of number of data values and weights that minimized MSE for the historical time series to forecast the next value in the time series.

## Exponential Smoothing

*Exponential smoothing is simple and has few data requirements, which makes it an inexpensive approach for firms that make many forecasts each period.*

**Exponential smoothing** uses a weighted average of past time series values as the forecast; it is a special case of the weighted moving averages method in which we select only one weight—the weight for the most recent observation. The weights for the other data values are computed automatically and become smaller as the observations move farther into the past. The basic exponential smoothing model follows.

EXPONENTIAL SMOOTHING MODEL

$$F_{t+1} = \alpha Y_t + (1 - \alpha)F_t \qquad (18.2)$$

where

$$F_{t+1} = \text{forecast of the time series for period } t + 1$$
$$Y_t = \text{actual value of the time series in period } t$$
$$F_t = \text{forecast of the time series for period } t$$
$$\alpha = \text{smoothing constant } (0 \le \alpha \le 1)$$

Equation (18.2) shows that the forecast for period $t + 1$ is a weighted average of the actual value in period $t$ and the forecast for period $t$; note in particular that the weight given to the actual value in period $t$ is $\alpha$ and that the weight given to the forecast in period $t$ is $1 - \alpha$. We can demonstrate that the exponential smoothing forecast for any period is also a weighted average of *all the previous actual values* for the time series with a time series consisting of three periods of data: $Y_1$, $Y_2$, and $Y_3$. To start the calculations, we let $F_1$ equal the actual value of the time series in period 1; that is, $F_1 = Y_1$. Hence, the forecast for period 2 is

$$
\begin{aligned}
F_2 &= \alpha Y_1 + (1 - \alpha)F_1 \\
&= \alpha Y_1 + (1 - \alpha)Y_1 \\
&= Y_1
\end{aligned}
$$

Thus, the exponential smoothing forecast for period 2 is equal to the actual value of the time series in period 1.

The forecast for period 3 is

$$F_3 = \alpha Y_2 + (1 - \alpha)F_2 = \alpha Y_2 + (1 - \alpha)Y_1$$

Finally, substituting this expression for $F_3$ in the expression for $F_4$, we obtain

$$
\begin{aligned}
F_4 &= \alpha Y_3 + (1 - \alpha)F_3 \\
&= \alpha Y_3 + (1 - \alpha)[\alpha Y_2 + (1 - \alpha)Y_1] \\
&= \alpha Y_3 + \alpha(1 - \alpha)Y_2 + (1 - \alpha)^2 Y_1
\end{aligned}
$$

*The term exponential smoothing comes from the exponential nature of the weighting scheme for the historical values.*

Hence, $F_4$ is a weighted average of the first three time series values. The sum of the coefficients, or weights, for $Y_1$, $Y_2$, and $Y_3$ equals one. A similar argument can be made to show that, in general, any forecast $F_{t+1}$ is a weighted average of all the previous time series values.

Despite the fact that exponential smoothing provides a forecast that is a weighted average of all past observations, all past data do not need to be saved to compute the forecast for the next period. In fact, once the **smoothing constant** $\alpha$ is selected, only two pieces of information are needed to compute the forecast. Equation (18.2) shows that with a given $\alpha$ we can compute the forecast for period $t + 1$ simply by knowing the actual and forecast time series values for period $t$—that is, $Y_t$ and $F_t$.

To illustrate the exponential smoothing approach to forecasting, consider the gasoline sales time series in Table 18.1 and Figure 18.5. As indicated, the exponential smoothing forecast for period 2 is equal to the actual value of the time series in period 1. Thus, with $Y_1 = 17$, we will set $F_2 = 17$ to start the exponential smoothing computations. Referring to the time series data in Table 18.1, we find an actual time series value in period 2 of $Y_2 = 21$. Thus, period 2 has a forecast error of $21 - 17 = 4$.

Continuing with the exponential smoothing computations using a smoothing constant of $\alpha = .2$, we obtain the following forecast for period 3.

$$F_3 = .2Y_2 + .8F_2 = .2(21) + .8(17) = 17.8$$

Once the actual time series value in period 3, $Y_3 = 19$, is known, we can generate a forecast for period 4 as follows.

$$F_4 = .2Y_3 + .8F_3 = .2(19) + .8(17.8) = 18.04$$

By continuing the exponential smoothing calculations, we can determine the weekly forecast values and the corresponding weekly forecast errors, as shown in Table 18.3. Note that we have not shown an exponential smoothing forecast or the forecast error for period 1 because no forecast was made. For week 12, we have $Y_{12} = 22$ and $F_{12} = 18.48$. Can we use this information to generate a forecast for week 13 before the actual value of week 13 becomes known? Using the exponential smoothing model, we have

$$F_{13} = .2Y_{12} + .8F_{12} = .2(22) + .8(18.48) = 19.18$$

Thus, the exponential smoothing forecast of the amount sold in week 13 is 19.18, or 19,180 gallons of gasoline. With this forecast, the firm can make plans and decisions accordingly. The accuracy of the forecast will not be known until the end of week 13.

Figure 18.7 is the plot of the actual and forecast time series values. Note in particular how the forecasts "smooth out" the irregular fluctuations in the time series.

**Forecast Accuracy**   In the preceding exponential smoothing calculations, we used a smoothing constant of $\alpha = .2$. Although any value of $\alpha$ between 0 and 1 is acceptable, some

TABLE 18.3   SUMMARY OF THE EXPONENTIAL SMOOTHING FORECASTS AND FORECAST ERRORS FOR GASOLINE SALES WITH SMOOTHING CONSTANT $\alpha = .2$

| Week $(t)$ | Time Series Value $(Y_t)$ | Exponential Smoothing Forecast $(F_t)$ | Forecast Error $(Y_t - F_t)$ |
|---|---|---|---|
| 1 | 17 | | |
| 2 | 21 | 17.00 | 4.00 |
| 3 | 19 | 17.80 | 1.20 |
| 4 | 23 | 18.04 | 4.96 |
| 5 | 18 | 19.03 | −1.03 |
| 6 | 16 | 18.83 | −2.83 |
| 7 | 20 | 18.26 | 1.74 |
| 8 | 18 | 18.61 | −.61 |
| 9 | 22 | 18.49 | 3.51 |
| 10 | 20 | 19.19 | .81 |
| 11 | 15 | 19.35 | −4.35 |
| 12 | 22 | 18.48 | 3.52 |

FIGURE 18.7    ACTUAL AND FORECAST GASOLINE SALES TIME SERIES
WITH SMOOTHING CONSTANT $\alpha = .2$

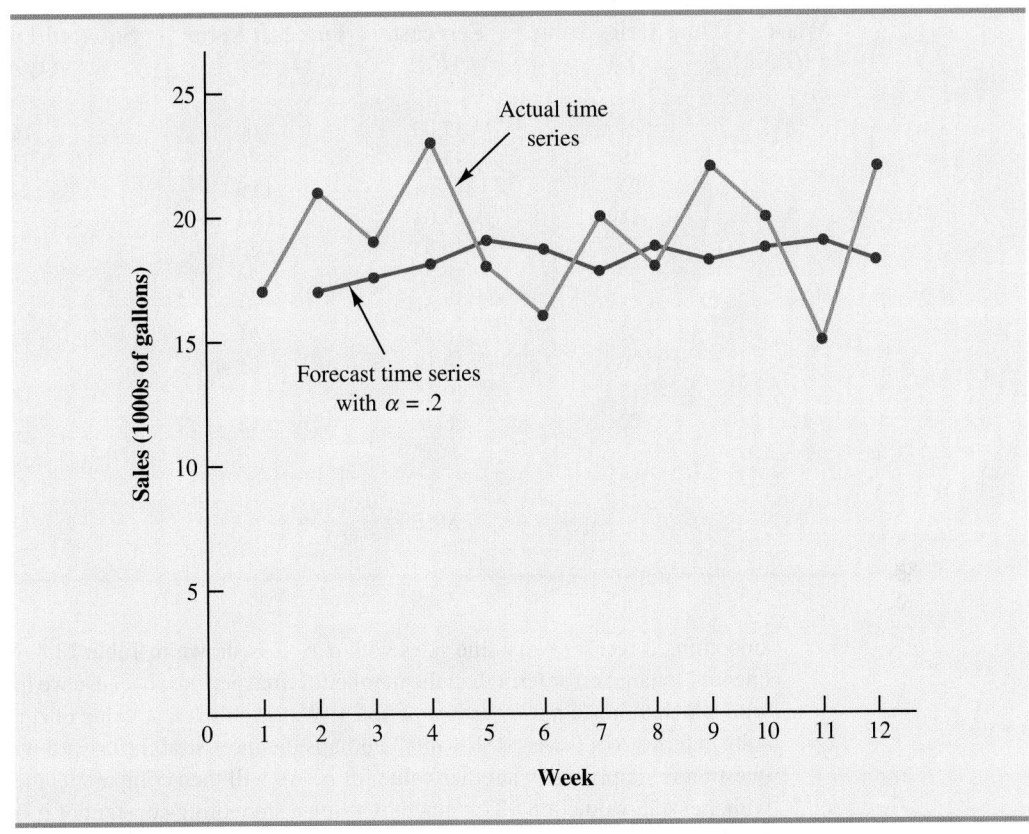

values will yield better forecasts than others. Insight into choosing a good value for $\alpha$ can be obtained by rewriting the basic exponential smoothing model as follows.

$$F_{t+1} = \alpha Y_t + (1 - \alpha)F_t$$
$$F_{t+1} = \alpha Y_t + F_t - \alpha F_t$$
$$F_{t+1} = F_t + \alpha(Y_t - F_t) \tag{18.3}$$

Forecast
in period $t$

Forecast error
in period $t$

Thus, the new forecast $F_{t+1}$ is equal to the previous forecast $F_t$ plus an adjustment, which is $\alpha$ times the most recent forecast error, $Y_t - F_t$. That is, the forecast in period $t + 1$ is obtained by adjusting the forecast in period $t$ by a fraction of the forecast error. If the time series contains substantial random variability, a small value of the smoothing constant is preferred. The reason for this choice is that, because much of the forecast error is due to random variability, we do not want to overreact and adjust the forecasts too quickly. For a time series with relatively little random variability, larger values of the smoothing constant provide the advantage of quickly adjusting the forecasts when forecasting errors occur and thus allowing the forecasts to react faster to changing conditions.

The criterion we will use to determine a desirable value for the smoothing constant $\alpha$ is the same as the criterion we proposed for determining the number of periods of data to include in the moving averages calculation. That is, we choose the value of $\alpha$ that minimizes the mean squared error (MSE). A summary of the MSE calculations for the exponential

TABLE 18.4    MSE COMPUTATIONS FOR FORECASTING GASOLINE SALES WITH $\alpha = .2$

| Week (t) | Time Series Value $(Y_t)$ | Forecast $(F_t)$ | Forecast Error $(Y_t - F_t)$ | Squared Forecast Error $(Y_t - F_t)^2$ |
|---|---|---|---|---|
| 1 | 17 | | | |
| 2 | 21 | 17.00 | 4.00 | 16.00 |
| 3 | 19 | 17.80 | 1.20 | 1.44 |
| 4 | 23 | 18.04 | 4.96 | 24.60 |
| 5 | 18 | 19.03 | −1.03 | 1.06 |
| 6 | 16 | 18.83 | −2.83 | 8.01 |
| 7 | 20 | 18.26 | 1.74 | 3.03 |
| 8 | 18 | 18.61 | −.61 | .37 |
| 9 | 22 | 18.49 | 3.51 | 12.32 |
| 10 | 20 | 19.19 | .81 | .66 |
| 11 | 15 | 19.35 | −4.35 | 18.92 |
| 12 | 22 | 18.48 | 3.52 | 12.39 |
| | | | Total | 98.80 |

$$\text{MSE} = \frac{98.80}{11} = 8.98$$

smoothing forecast of gasoline sales with $\alpha = .2$ is shown in Table 18.4. Note that there is one less squared error term than the number of time periods, because we had no past values with which to make a forecast for period 1. Would a different value of $\alpha$ provide better results in terms of a lower MSE value? Perhaps the most straightforward way to answer this question is simply to try another value for $\alpha$. We will then compare its mean squared error with the MSE value of 8.98 obtained by using a smoothing constant of $\alpha = .2$.

The exponential smoothing results with $\alpha = .3$ are shown in Table 18.5. With MSE = 9.35, we see that for the current data set, a smoothing constant of $\alpha = .3$ results in less fore-

TABLE 18.5    MSE COMPUTATIONS FOR FORECASTING GASOLINE SALES WITH $\alpha = .3$

| Week (t) | Time Series Value $(Y_t)$ | Forecast $(F_t)$ | Forecast Error $(Y_t - F_t)$ | Squared Forecast Error $(Y_t - F_t)^2$ |
|---|---|---|---|---|
| 1 | 17 | | | |
| 2 | 21 | 17.00 | 4.00 | 16.00 |
| 3 | 19 | 18.20 | .80 | .64 |
| 4 | 23 | 18.44 | 4.56 | 20.79 |
| 5 | 18 | 19.81 | −1.81 | 3.28 |
| 6 | 16 | 19.27 | −3.27 | 10.69 |
| 7 | 20 | 18.29 | 1.71 | 2.92 |
| 8 | 18 | 18.80 | −.80 | .64 |
| 9 | 22 | 18.56 | 3.44 | 11.83 |
| 10 | 20 | 19.59 | .41 | .17 |
| 11 | 15 | 19.71 | −4.71 | 22.18 |
| 12 | 22 | 18.30 | 3.70 | 13.69 |
| | | | Total | 102.83 |

$$\text{MSE} = \frac{102.83}{11} = 9.35$$

cast accuracy than a smoothing constant of $\alpha = .2$. Thus, we would be inclined to prefer the original smoothing constant of $\alpha = .2$. Using a trial-and-error calculation with other values of $\alpha$, we can find a "good" value for the smoothing constant. This value can be used in the exponential smoothing model to provide forecasts for the future. At a later date, after new time series observations are obtained, we analyze the newly collected time series data to determine whether the smoothing constant should be revised to provide better forecasting results.

## NOTES AND COMMENTS

1. Another measure of forecast accuracy is the *mean absolute deviation* (MAD). This measure is simply the average of the absolute values of all the forecast errors. Using the errors given in Table 18.2, we obtain

$$\text{MAD} = \frac{4+3+4+1+0+4+0+5+3}{9} = 2.67$$

One major difference between MSE and MAD is that the MSE measure is influenced much more by large forecast errors than by small errors (because for the MSE measure the errors are squared). The selection of the best measure of forecasting accuracy is not a simple matter. Indeed, forecasting experts often disagree as to which measure should be used. We use the MSE measure in this chapter.

2. Spreadsheet packages are an effective aid in choosing a good value of $\alpha$ for exponential smoothing and selecting weights for the weighted moving averages method. With the time series data and the forecasting formulas in the spreadsheets, you can experiment with different values of $\alpha$ (or moving average weights) and choose the value(s) of $\alpha$ providing the smallest MSE or MAD.

## Exercises

### Methods

1. Consider the following time series data.

| Week | 1 | 2 | 3 | 4 | 5 | 6 |
|------|---|----|----|----|----|---|
| Value | 8 | 13 | 15 | 17 | 16 | 9 |

a. Develop a three-week moving average for this time series. What is the forecast for week 7?
b. Compute the MSE for the three-week moving average.
c. Use $\alpha = .2$ to compute the exponential smoothing values for the time series. What is the forecast for week 7?
d. Compare the three-week moving average forecast with the exponential smoothing forecast using $\alpha = .2$. Which appears to provide the better forecast?
e. Use a smoothing constant of .4 to compute the exponential smoothing values. Does a smoothing constant of .2 or .4 appear to provide the better forecast? Explain.

2. Refer to the gasoline sales time series data in Table 18.1.
a. Compute four-week and five-week moving averages for the time series.
b. Compute the MSE for the four-week and five-week moving average forecasts.
c. What appears to be the best number of weeks of past data to use in the moving average computation? Remember that the MSE for the three-week moving average is 10.22.

3. Refer again to the gasoline sales time series data in Table 18.1.
a. Using a weight of 1/2 for the most recent observation, 1/3 for the second most recent, and 1/6 for third most recent, compute a three-week weighted moving average for the time series.

b.  Compute the MSE for the weighted moving average in part (a). Do you prefer this weighted moving average to the unweighted moving average? Remember that the MSE for the unweighted moving average is 10.22.

c.  Suppose you are allowed to choose any weights as long as they sum to one. Could you always find a set of weights that would make the MSE smaller for a weighted moving average than for an unweighted moving average? Why or why not?

4.  With the gasoline time series data from Table 18.1, show the exponential smoothing forecasts using $\alpha = .1$. Applying the MSE criterion, would you prefer a smoothing constant of $\alpha = .1$ or $\alpha = .2$ for the gasoline sales time series?

5.  With a smoothing constant of $\alpha = .2$, equation (18.2) shows that the forecast for week 13 of the gasoline sales data from Table 18.1 is given by $F_{13} = .2Y_{12} + .8F_{12}$. However, the forecast for week 12 is given by $F_{12} = .2Y_{11} + .8F_{11}$. Thus, we could combine these two results to show that the forecast for week 13 can be written

$$F_{13} = .2Y_{12} + .8(.2Y_{11} + .8F_{11}) = .2Y_{12} + .16Y_{11} + .64F_{11}$$

a.  Making use of the fact that $F_{11} = .2Y_{10} = .8F_{10}$ (and similarly for $F_{10}$ and $F_9$), continue to expand the expression for $F_{13}$ until it is written in terms of the past data values $Y_{12}, Y_{11}, Y_{10}, Y_9, Y_8$, and the forecast for period 8.

b.  Refer to the coefficients or weights for the past values $Y_{12}, Y_{11}, Y_{10}, Y_9, Y_8$; what observation can you make about how exponential smoothing weights past data values in arriving at new forecasts? Compare this weighting pattern with the weighting pattern of the moving averages method.

## Applications

6.  For the Hawkins Company, the monthly percentages of all shipments received on time over the past 12 months are 80, 82, 84, 83, 83, 84, 85, 84, 82, 83, 84, and 83.

a.  Compare a three-month moving average forecast with an exponential smoothing forecast for $\alpha = .2$. Which provides the better forecasts?

b.  What is the forecast for next month?

7.  Corporate triple A bond interest rates for 12 consecutive months follow.

9.5   9.3   9.4   9.6   9.8   9.7   9.8   10.5   9.9   9.7   9.6   9.6

a.  Develop three-month and four-month moving averages for this time series. Does the three-month or four-month moving average provide the better forecasts? Explain.

b.  What is the moving average forecast for the next month?

8.  The values of Alabama building contracts (in millions of dollars) for a 12-month period follow.

240   350   230   260   280   320   220   310   240   310   240   230

a.  Compare a three-month moving averages forecast with an exponential smoothing forecast. Use $\alpha = .2$. Which provides the better forecasts?

b.  What is the forecast for the next month?

9.  The following time series shows the sales of a particular product over the past 12 months.

| Month | Sales | Month | Sales |
|---|---|---|---|
| 1 | 105 | 7 | 145 |
| 2 | 135 | 8 | 140 |
| 3 | 120 | 9 | 100 |
| 4 | 105 | 10 | 80 |
| 5 | 90 | 11 | 100 |
| 6 | 120 | 12 | 110 |

a.  Use $\alpha = .3$ to compute the exponential smoothing values for the time series.
b.  Use a smoothing constant of .5 to compute the exponential smoothing values. Does a smoothing constant of .3 or .5 appear to provide the better forecasts?

10. Ten weeks of data on the Commodity Futures Index are 7.35, 7.40, 7.55, 7.56, 7.60, 7.52, 7.52, 7.70, 7.62, and 7.55.
a.  Compute the exponential smoothing values for $\alpha = .2$.
b.  Compute the exponential smoothing values for $\alpha = .3$.
c.  Which exponential smoothing model provides the better forecasts? Forecast week 11.

11. The following data represent 15 quarters of manufacturing capacity utilization (in percentages).

| Quarter/Year | Utilization (%) | Quarter/Year | Utilization (%) |
|---|---|---|---|
| 1/2000 | 82.5 | 1/2002 | 78.8 |
| 2/2000 | 81.3 | 2/2002 | 78.7 |
| 3/2000 | 81.3 | 3/2002 | 78.4 |
| 4/2000 | 79.0 | 4/2002 | 80.0 |
| 1/2001 | 76.6 | 1/2003 | 80.7 |
| 2/2001 | 78.0 | 2/2003 | 80.7 |
| 3/2001 | 78.4 | 3/2003 | 80.8 |
| 4/2001 | 78.0 | | |

a.  Compute three- and four-quarter moving averages for this time series. Which moving average provides the better forecast for the fourth quarter of 2003?
b.  Use smoothing constants of $\alpha = .4$ and $\alpha = .5$ to develop forecasts for the fourth quarter of 2003. Which smoothing constant provides the better forecast?
c.  On the basis of the analyses in parts (a) and (b), which method—moving averages or exponential smoothing—provides the better forecast? Explain.

# 18.3   Trend Projection

In this section we show how to forecast a time series that has a long-term linear trend. The type of time series for which the trend projection method is applicable shows a consistent increase or decrease over time; because it is not stable, the smoothing methods described in the preceding section are not applicable.

Consider the time series for bicycle sales of a particular manufacturer over the past 10 years, as shown in Table 18.6 and Figure 18.8. Note that 21,600 bicycles were sold in year 1, 22,900 were sold in year 2, and so on. In year 10, the most recent year, 31,400 bicycles were sold. Although Figure 18.8 shows some up and down movement over the past 10 years, the time series seems to have an overall increasing or upward trend.

We do not want the trend component of a time series to follow each and every up and down movement. Rather, the trend component should reflect the gradual shifting—in this case, growth—of the time series values. After we view the time series data in Table 18.6 and the graph in Figure 18.8, we might agree that a linear trend as shown in Figure 18.9 provides a reasonable description of the long-run movement in the series.

We use the bicycle sales data to illustrate the calculations involved in applying regression analysis to identify a linear trend. Recall that in the discussion of simple linear regression in Chapter 14, we described how the least squares method is used to find the best straight-line relationship between two variables. We will use that same methodology to develop the trend line for the bicycle sales time series. Specifically, we will be using regression analysis to estimate the relationship between time and sales volume.

**TABLE 18.6**

**BICYCLE SALES TIME SERIES**

| Year $(t)$ | Sales (1000s) $(Y_t)$ |
|---|---|
| 1 | 21.6 |
| 2 | 22.9 |
| 3 | 25.5 |
| 4 | 21.9 |
| 5 | 23.9 |
| 6 | 27.5 |
| 7 | 31.5 |
| 8 | 29.7 |
| 9 | 28.6 |
| 10 | 31.4 |

FIGURE 18.8    BICYCLE SALES TIME SERIES

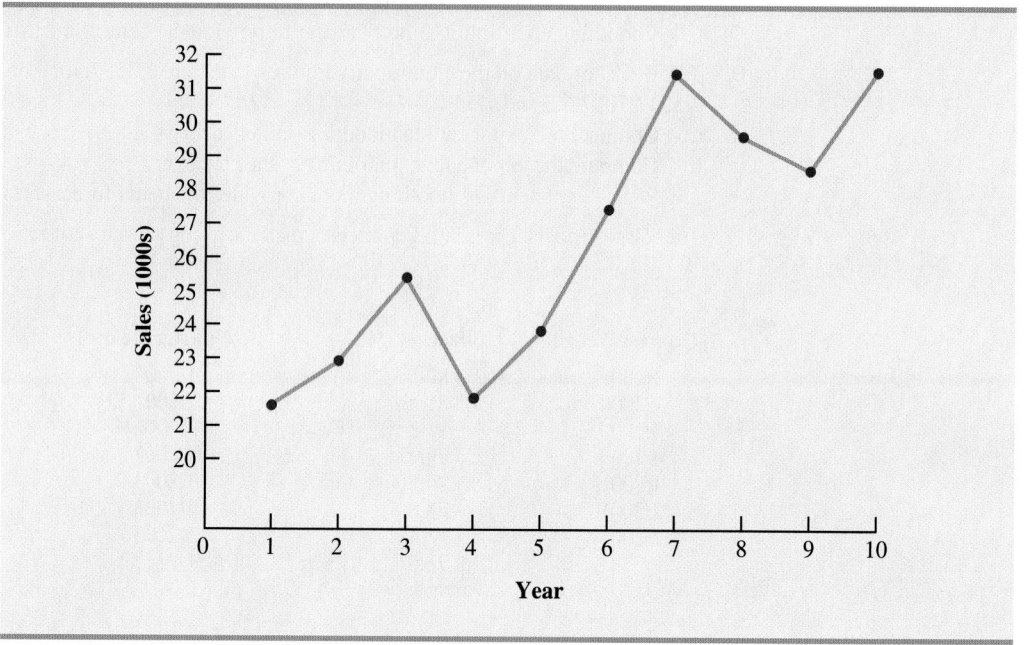

FIGURE 18.9    TREND REPRESENTED BY A LINEAR FUNCTION FOR BICYCLE SALES

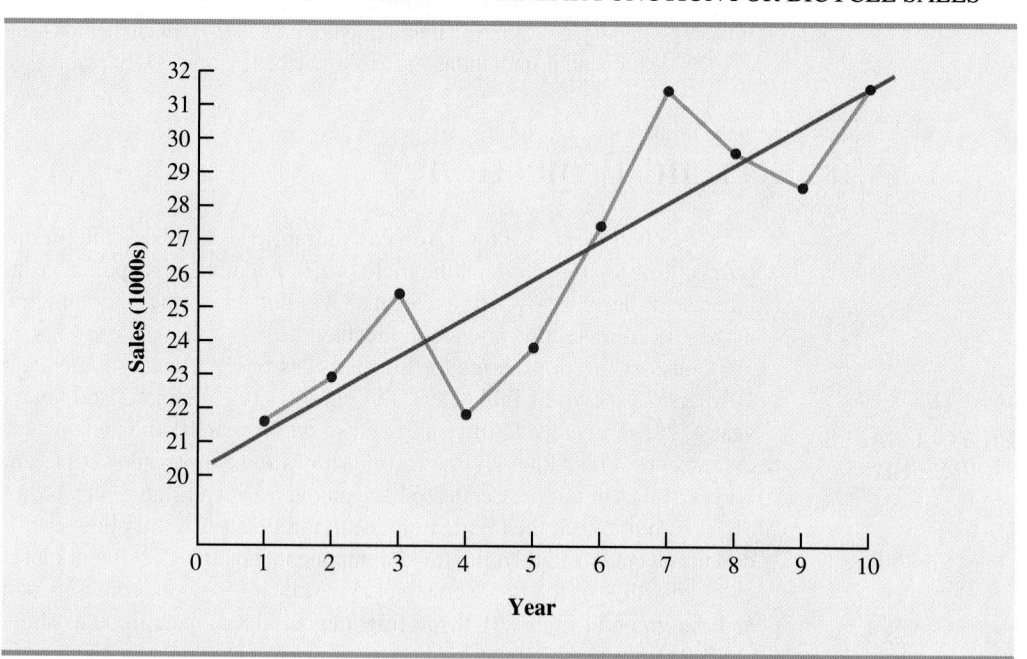

In Chapter 14 the estimated regression equation describing a straight-line relationship between an independent variable $x$ and a dependent variable $y$ was written

$$\hat{y} = b_0 + b_1 x \tag{18.4}$$

To emphasize the fact that, in forecasting, the independent variable is time, we will use $t$ in equation (18.4) instead of $x$; in addition, we will use $T_t$ in place of $\hat{y}$. Thus, for a linear trend, the estimated sales volume expressed as a function of time can be written as follows.

---

EQUATION FOR LINEAR TREND

$$T_t = b_0 + b_1 t \tag{18.5}$$

where

$T_t$ = trend value of the time series in period $t$

$b_0$ = intercept of the trend line

$b_1$ = slope of the trend line

$t$ = time

---

In equation (18.5), we will let $t = 1$ for the time of the first observation on the time series data, $t = 2$ for the time of the second observation, and so on. Note that for the time series on bicycle sales, $t = 1$ corresponds to the oldest time series value and $t = 10$ corresponds to the most recent year's data. Formulas for computing the estimated regression coefficients ($b_1$ and $b_0$) in equation (18.5) follow.

---

COMPUTING THE SLOPE ($b_1$) AND INTERCEPT ($b_0$)

$$b_1 = \frac{\Sigma t Y_t - (\Sigma t \Sigma Y_t)/n}{\Sigma t^2 - (\Sigma t)^2/n} \tag{18.6}$$

$$b_0 = \bar{Y} - b_1 \bar{t} \tag{18.7}$$

where

$Y_t$ = value of the time series in period $t$

$n$ = number of periods

$\bar{Y}$ = average value of the time series; that is, $\bar{Y} = \Sigma Y_t/n$

$\bar{t}$ = average value of $t$; that is, $\bar{t} = \Sigma t/n$

---

Using equations (18.6) and (18.7) and the bicycle sales data of Table 18.6, we can compute $b_0$ and $b_1$ as follows:

| $t$ | $Y_t$ | $tY_t$ | $t^2$ |
|---|---|---|---|
| 1 | 21.6 | 21.6 | 1 |
| 2 | 22.9 | 45.8 | 4 |
| 3 | 25.5 | 76.5 | 9 |
| 4 | 21.9 | 87.6 | 16 |
| 5 | 23.9 | 119.5 | 25 |
| 6 | 27.5 | 165.0 | 36 |

*(continued)*

| $t$ | $Y_t$ | $tY_t$ | $t^2$ |
|---|---|---|---|
| 7 | 31.5 | 220.5 | 49 |
| 8 | 29.7 | 237.6 | 64 |
| 9 | 28.6 | 257.4 | 81 |
| 10 | 31.4 | 314.0 | 100 |
| Totals 55 | 264.5 | 1545.5 | 385 |

$$\bar{t} = \frac{55}{10} = 5.5$$

$$\bar{Y} = \frac{264.5}{10} = 26.45$$

$$b_1 = \frac{1545.5 - (55)(264.5)/10}{385 - (55)^2/10} = 1.10$$

$$b_0 = 26.45 - 1.10(5.5) = 20.4$$

Therefore,

$$T_t = 20.4 + 1.1t \qquad (18.8)$$

is the expression for the linear trend component for the bicycle sales time series.

The slope of 1.1 indicates that over the past 10 years the firm experienced average growth in sales of about 1100 units per year. If we assume that the past 10-year trend in sales is a good indicator of the future, equation (18.8) can be used to project the trend component of the time series. For example, substituting $t = 11$ into equation (18.8) yields next year's trend projection, $T_{11}$.

*Before the trend equation is used to develop a forecast, a statistical test of significance (see Chapter 14) should be conducted. In practice, such a test would be a routine part of fitting the trend line.*

$$T_{11} = 20.4 + 1.1(11) = 32.5$$

Thus, using the trend component only, we would forecast sales of 32,500 bicycles next year.

The use of a linear function to model the trend is common. However, as we discussed previously, sometimes time series have a curvilinear, or nonlinear, trend similar to those in Figure 18.10. In Chapter 16 we discussed how regression analysis can be used to model curvilinear relationships of the type shown in panel A of Figure 18.10. More advanced texts discuss in detail how to develop regression models for more complex relationships, such as the one shown in panel B of Figure 18.10.

**FIGURE 18.10    SOME POSSIBLE FORMS OF NONLINEAR TREND PATTERNS**

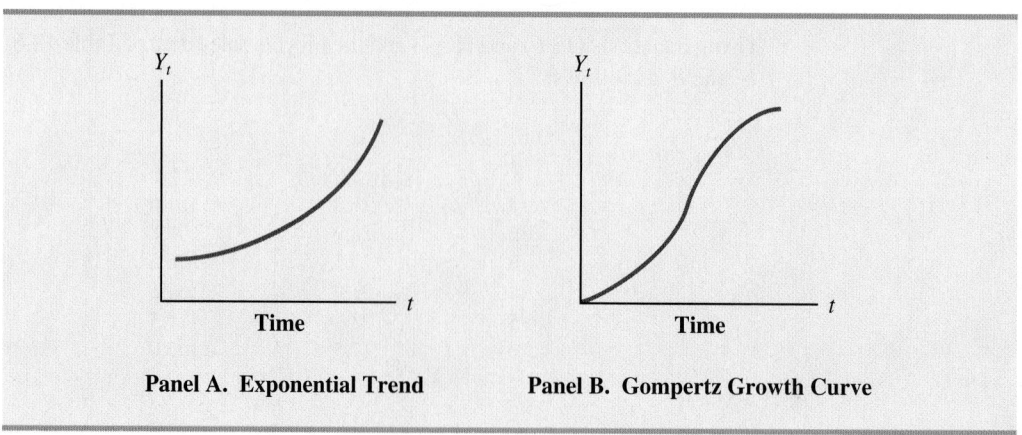

Panel A.  Exponential Trend          Panel B.  Gompertz Growth Curve

## Exercises

### Methods

12. Consider the following time series.

| $t$ | 1 | 2 | 3 | 4 | 5 |
|-----|---|---|---|---|---|
| $Y_t$ | 6 | 11 | 9 | 14 | 15 |

Develop an equation for the linear trend component of this time series. What is the forecast for $t = 6$?

13. Consider the following time series.

| $t$ | 1 | 2 | 3 | 4 | 5 | 6 |
|-----|---|---|---|---|---|---|
| $Y_t$ | 205 | 202 | 195 | 190 | 191 | 188 |

Develop an equation for the linear trend component for this time series. What is the forecast for $t = 7$?

### Applications

14. The enrollment data (in thousands) for a state college over the past six years are shown.

| Year | 1 | 2 | 3 | 4 | 5 | 6 |
|------|---|---|---|---|---|---|
| Enrollment | 20.5 | 20.2 | 19.5 | 19.0 | 19.1 | 18.8 |

Develop the equation for the linear trend component of this time series. Comment on what is happening to enrollment at this institution.

15. The following table gives average attendance figures for home football games at a major university for the past seven years. Develop the equation for the linear trend component of this time series.

| Year | Attendance |
|------|------------|
| 1 | 28,000 |
| 2 | 30,000 |
| 3 | 31,500 |
| 4 | 30,400 |
| 5 | 30,500 |
| 6 | 32,200 |
| 7 | 30,800 |

16. Automobile sales at B.J. Scott Motors, Inc., provided the following 10-year time series.

| Year | Sales | Year | Sales |
|------|-------|------|-------|
| 1 | 400 | 6 | 260 |
| 2 | 390 | 7 | 300 |
| 3 | 320 | 8 | 320 |
| 4 | 340 | 9 | 340 |
| 5 | 270 | 10 | 370 |

Plot the time series and comment on the appropriateness of a linear trend. What type of functional form do you believe would be most appropriate for the trend pattern of this time series?

17. The president of a small manufacturing firm is concerned about the continual increase in manufacturing costs over the past several years. The following figures provide a time series of the cost per unit for the firm's leading product over the past eight years.

| Year | Cost/Unit ($) | Year | Cost/Unit ($) |
|------|---------------|------|---------------|
| 1 | 20.00 | 5 | 26.60 |
| 2 | 24.50 | 6 | 30.00 |
| 3 | 28.20 | 7 | 31.00 |
| 4 | 27.50 | 8 | 36.00 |

a. Show a graph of this time series. Does a linear trend appear to be present?
b. Develop the equation for the linear trend component of the time series. What is the average cost increase that the firm has been realizing per year?

18. Earnings per share for the Walgreen Company for a 10-year period follow.

.64   .73   .94   1.14   1.33   1.53   1.67   1.68   2.10   2.50

a. Use a linear trend projection to forecast this time series for the coming year.
b. What does this time series analysis tell you about the Walgreen Company? Do the historical data indicate that the Walgreen Company is a good investment?

19. TV ratings provided by Nielsen Media Research show the percent of TV-owning households tuned in to a particular program. The following data show the rating for the top-rated TV show of each season, from 1950–1951 to 2000–2001 (*The New York Times Almanac*, 2002).

| Season | Rating | Season | Rating |
|--------|--------|--------|--------|
| 1987–1988 | 27.8 | 1994–1995 | 20.5 |
| 1988–1989 | 25.5 | 1995–1996 | 22.0 |
| 1989–1990 | 23.4 | 1996–1997 | 21.2 |
| 1990–1991 | 21.6 | 1997–1998 | 22.0 |
| 1991–1992 | 21.7 | 1998–1999 | 17.8 |
| 1992–1993 | 21.6 | 1999–2000 | 16.6 |
| 1993–1994 | 21.9 | 2000–2001 | 17.4 |

a. Graph this time series. Does a linear trend appear to be present?
b. Develop a linear trend equation for this time series.
c. Use the trend equation to estimate the rating for the 2001–2002 season.

20. Gross revenue data (in millions of dollars) for Regional Airlines for a 10-year period follow.

| Year | Revenue | Year | Revenue |
|------|---------|------|---------|
| 1 | 2428 | 6 | 4264 |
| 2 | 2951 | 7 | 4738 |
| 3 | 3533 | 8 | 4460 |
| 4 | 3618 | 9 | 5318 |
| 5 | 3616 | 10 | 6915 |

a. Develop a linear trend equation for this time series. Comment on what the equation tells about the gross revenue for Regional Airlines for the 10-year period.
b. Provide the forecasts for gross revenue for years 11 and 12.

21.  The Federal Election Commission maintains data showing the voting age population, the number of registered voters, and the turnout for federal elections. The following table shows the national voter turnout in presidential elections as a percentage of the voting age population from 1964 to 2000 (http://www.fec.gov).

| Year | Percent Voting |
|------|----------------|
| 1964 | 61.92 |
| 1968 | 60.84 |
| 1972 | 55.21 |
| 1976 | 53.55 |
| 1980 | 52.56 |
| 1984 | 53.11 |
| 1988 | 50.11 |
| 1992 | 55.09 |
| 1996 | 49.08 |
| 2000 | 51.30 |

a.  Graph this time series. Does a linear trend appear to be present?
b.  Develop the equation for the linear trend component for the time series. What is the average decrease in the percent voting per presidential election?
c.  Use the trend equation to forecast the percent voting in 2004.

# 18.4  Trend and Seasonal Components

We showed how to forecast a time series that has a trend component. In this section we extend the discussion by showing how to forecast a time series that has both trend and seasonal components.

Many situations in business and economics involve period-to-period comparisons. We might be interested to learn that unemployment is up 2% compared to last month, steel production is up 5% over last month, or that the production of electric power is down 3% from the previous month. Care must be exercised in using such information, however, because whenever a seasonal influence is present, such comparisons may be misleading. For instance, the fact that electric power consumption is down 3% from August to September might be only the seasonal effect associated with a decrease in the use of air conditioning and not because of a long-term decline in the use of electric power. Indeed, after adjusting for the seasonal effect, we might even find that the use of electric power increased.

Removing the seasonal effect from a time series is known as deseasonalizing the time series. After we do so, period-to-period comparisons are more meaningful and can help identify whether a trend exists. The approach we take in this section is appropriate in situations when only seasonal effects are present or in situations when both seasonal and trend components are present. The first step is to compute seasonal indexes and use them to deseasonalize the data. Then, if a trend is apparent in the deseasonalized data, we use regression analysis on the deseasonalized data to estimate the trend component.

## Multiplicative Model

In addition to a trend component ($T$) and a seasonal component ($S$), we will assume that the time series involves an irregular component ($I$). The irregular component accounts for any random effects in the time series that cannot be explained by the trend and seasonal components. Using $T_t$, $S_t$, and $I_t$ to identify the trend, seasonal, and irregular components at time $t$, we will assume that the time series value, denoted $Y_t$, can be described by the following **multiplicative time series model**.

$$Y_t = T_t \times S_t \times I_t \tag{18.9}$$

In this model, $T_t$ is the trend measured in units of the item being forecast. However, the $S_t$ and $I_t$ components are measured in relative terms, with values above 1.00 indicating effects above the trend and values below 1.00 indicating effects below the trend.

We will illustrate the use of the multiplicative model with trend, seasonal, and irregular components by working with the quarterly data in Table 18.7 and Figure 18.11. These data show television set sales (in thousands of units) for a particular manufacturer over the past four years. We begin by showing how to identify the seasonal component of the time series.

## Calculating the Seasonal Indexes

Figure 18.11 indicates that sales are lowest in the second quarter of each year and increase in quarters 3 and 4. Thus, we conclude that a seasonal pattern exists for television set sales. The computational procedure used to identify each quarter's seasonal influence begins by computing a moving average to separate the combined seasonal and irregular components, $S_t$ and $I_t$, from the trend component $T_t$.

To do so, we use one year of data in each calculation. Because we are working with a quarterly series, we will use four data values in each moving average. The moving average calculation for the first four quarters of the television set sales data is

$$\text{First moving average} = \frac{4.8 + 4.1 + 6.0 + 6.5}{4} = \frac{21.4}{4} = 5.35$$

Note that the moving average calculation for the first four quarters yields the average quarterly sales over year 1 of the time series. Continuing the moving average calculations, we

**TABLE 18.7**

QUARTERLY DATA
FOR TELEVISION
SET SALES

| Year | Quarter | Sales (1000s) |
|------|---------|---------------|
| 1    | 1       | 4.8           |
|      | 2       | 4.1           |
|      | 3       | 6.0           |
|      | 4       | 6.5           |
| 2    | 1       | 5.8           |
|      | 2       | 5.2           |
|      | 3       | 6.8           |
|      | 4       | 7.4           |
| 3    | 1       | 6.0           |
|      | 2       | 5.6           |
|      | 3       | 7.5           |
|      | 4       | 7.8           |
| 4    | 1       | 6.3           |
|      | 2       | 5.9           |
|      | 3       | 8.0           |
|      | 4       | 8.4           |

**FIGURE 18.11**   QUARTERLY TELEVISION SET SALES TIME SERIES

next add the 5.8 value for the first quarter of year 2 and drop the 4.8 for the first quarter of year 1. Thus, the second moving average is

$$\text{Second moving average} = \frac{4.1 + 6.0 + 6.5 + 5.8}{4} = \frac{22.4}{4} = 5.60$$

Similarly, the third moving average calculation is $(6.0 + 6.5 + 5.8 + 5.2)/4 = 5.875$.

Before we proceed with the moving average calculations for the entire time series, we return to the first moving average calculation, which resulted in a value of 5.35. The 5.35 value represents an average quarterly sales volume (across all seasons) for year 1. As we look back at the calculation of the 5.35 value, associating 5.35 with the "middle" quarter of the moving average group makes sense. Note, however, that we encounter some difficulty in identifying the middle quarter; with four quarters in the moving average there is no middle quarter. The 5.35 value corresponds to the last half of quarter 2 and the first half of quarter 3. Similarly, if we go to the next moving average value of 5.60, the middle corresponds to the last half of quarter 3 and the first half of quarter 4.

Recall that the reason for computing moving averages is to isolate the combined seasonal and irregular components. However, the moving average values we computed do not correspond directly to the original quarters of the time series. We can resolve this difficulty by using the midpoints between successive moving average values. For example, if 5.35 corresponds to the first half of quarter 3 and 5.60 corresponds to the last half of quarter 3, we can use $(5.35 + 5.60)/2 = 5.475$ as the moving average value for quarter 3. Similarly, we associate a moving average value of $(5.60 + 5.875)/2 = 5.738$ with quarter 4. The result is a *centered moving average*. Table 18.8 shows a complete summary of the moving average calculations for the television set sales data.

If the number of data points in a moving average calculation is an odd number, the middle point will correspond to one of the periods in the time series. In such cases, we would not have to center the moving average values to correspond to a particular time period as we have done in the calculations in Table 18.8.

What do the centered moving averages in Table 18.8 tell us about this time series? Figure 18.12 is a plot of the actual time series values and the centered moving average values. Note particularly how the centered moving average values tend to "smooth out" both the seasonal and irregular fluctuations in the time series. The moving average values computed for four quarters of data do not include the fluctuations due to seasonal influences because the seasonal effect has been averaged out. Each point in the centered moving average represents the value of the time series as though there were no seasonal or irregular influence.

By dividing each time series observation by the corresponding centered moving average, we can identify the seasonal irregular effect in the time series. For example, the third quarter of year 1 shows $6.0/5.475 = 1.096$ as the combined seasonal irregular value. Table 18.9 summarizes the seasonal irregular values for the entire time series.

Consider the third quarter. The results from years 1, 2, and 3 show third-quarter values of 1.096, 1.075, and 1.109, respectively. Thus, in all cases, the seasonal irregular value appears to have an above-average influence in the third quarter. With the year-to-year fluctuations in the seasonal irregular value attributable primarily to the irregular component, we can average the computed values to eliminate the irregular influence and obtain an estimate of the third-quarter seasonal influence.

$$\text{Seasonal effect of third quarter} = \frac{1.096 + 1.075 + 1.109}{3} = 1.09$$

We refer to 1.09 as the *seasonal index* for the third quarter. In Table 18.10 we summarize the calculations involved in computing the seasonal indexes for the television set sales time

**TABLE 18.8    CENTERED MOVING AVERAGE CALCULATIONS FOR THE TELEVISION SET SALES TIME SERIES**

| Year | Quarter | Sales (1000s) | Four-Quarter Moving Average | Centered Moving Average |
|------|---------|---------------|------------------------------|--------------------------|
| 1    | 1       | 4.8           |                              |                          |
|      | 2       | 4.1           |                              |                          |
|      |         |               | 5.350                        |                          |
|      | 3       | 6.0           |                              | 5.475                    |
|      |         |               | 5.600                        |                          |
|      | 4       | 6.5           |                              | 5.738                    |
|      |         |               | 5.875                        |                          |
| 2    | 1       | 5.8           |                              | 5.975                    |
|      |         |               | 6.075                        |                          |
|      | 2       | 5.2           |                              | 6.188                    |
|      |         |               | 6.300                        |                          |
|      | 3       | 6.8           |                              | 6.325                    |
|      |         |               | 6.350                        |                          |
|      | 4       | 7.4           |                              | 6.400                    |
|      |         |               | 6.450                        |                          |
| 3    | 1       | 6.0           |                              | 6.538                    |
|      |         |               | 6.625                        |                          |
|      | 2       | 5.6           |                              | 6.675                    |
|      |         |               | 6.725                        |                          |
|      | 3       | 7.5           |                              | 6.763                    |
|      |         |               | 6.800                        |                          |
|      | 4       | 7.8           |                              | 6.838                    |
|      |         |               | 6.875                        |                          |
| 4    | 1       | 6.3           |                              | 6.938                    |
|      |         |               | 7.000                        |                          |
|      | 2       | 5.9           |                              | 7.075                    |
|      |         |               | 7.150                        |                          |
|      | 3       | 8.0           |                              |                          |
|      | 4       | 8.4           |                              |                          |

series. Thus, the seasonal indexes for the four quarters are: quarter 1, .93; quarter 2, .84; quarter 3, 1.09; and quarter 4, 1.14.

Interpretation of the values in Table 18.10 provides some observations about the seasonal component in television set sales. The best sales quarter is the fourth quarter, with sales averaging 14% above the average quarterly value. The worst, or slowest, sales quarter is the second quarter; its seasonal index of .84 shows that the sales average is 16% below the average quarterly sales. The seasonal component corresponds clearly to the intuitive expectation that television viewing interest and thus television purchase patterns tend to peak in the fourth quarter because of the coming winter season and reduction in outdoor activities. The low second-quarter sales reflect the reduced interest in television viewing due to the spring and presummer activities of potential customers.

One final adjustment is sometimes necessary in obtaining the seasonal indexes. The multiplicative model requires that the average seasonal index equal 1.00, so the sum of the four seasonal indexes in Table 18.10 must equal 4.00. In other words the seasonal effects must even out over the year. The average of the seasonal indexes in our example is equal to

FIGURE 18.12   QUARTERLY TELEVISION SET SALES TIME SERIES AND CENTERED
MOVING AVERAGE

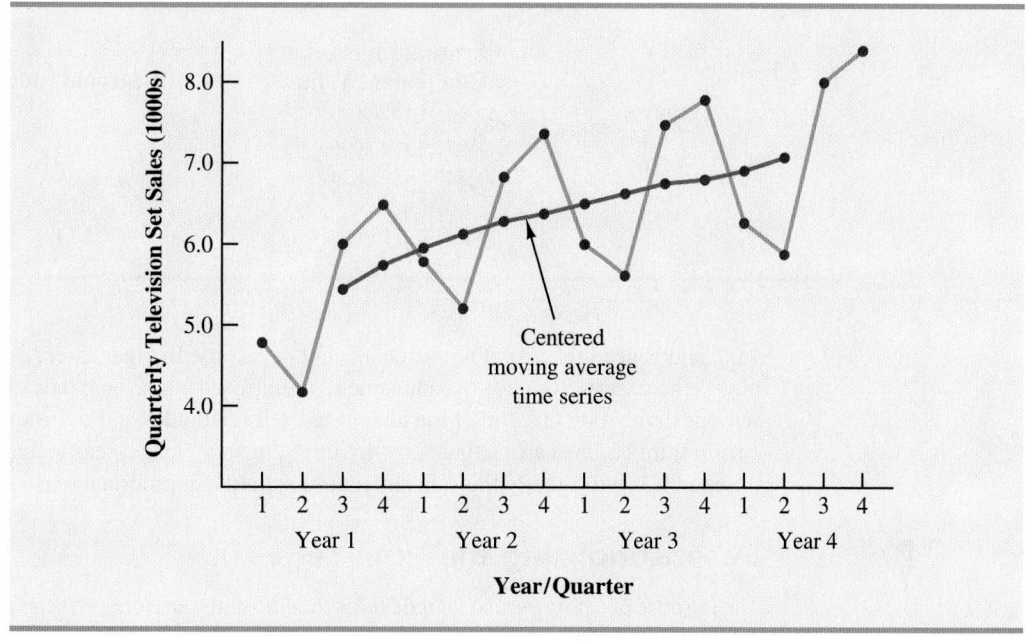

TABLE 18.9   SEASONAL IRREGULAR VALUES FOR THE TELEVISION SET SALES
TIME SERIES

| Year | Quarter | Sales (1000s) | Centered Moving Average | Seasonal Irregular Value |
|------|---------|---------------|-------------------------|--------------------------|
| 1 | 1 | 4.8 | | |
|   | 2 | 4.1 | | |
|   | 3 | 6.0 | 5.475 | 1.096 |
|   | 4 | 6.5 | 5.738 | 1.133 |
| 2 | 1 | 5.8 | 5.975 | .971 |
|   | 2 | 5.2 | 6.188 | .840 |
|   | 3 | 6.8 | 6.325 | 1.075 |
|   | 4 | 7.4 | 6.400 | 1.156 |
| 3 | 1 | 6.0 | 6.538 | .918 |
|   | 2 | 5.6 | 6.675 | .839 |
|   | 3 | 7.5 | 6.763 | 1.109 |
|   | 4 | 7.8 | 6.838 | 1.141 |
| 4 | 1 | 6.3 | 6.938 | .908 |
|   | 2 | 5.9 | 7.075 | .834 |
|   | 3 | 8.0 | | |
|   | 4 | 8.4 | | |

TABLE 18.10     SEASONAL INDEX CALCULATIONS FOR THE TELEVISION SET SALES
TIME SERIES

| Quarter | Seasonal Irregular Component Values $(S_t I_t)$ | Seasonal Index $(S_t)$ |
|---|---|---|
| 1 | .971, .918, .908 | .93 |
| 2 | .840, .839, .834 | .84 |
| 3 | 1.096, 1.075, 1.109 | 1.09 |
| 4 | 1.133, 1.156, 1.141 | 1.14 |

1.00, and hence this type of adjustment is not necessary. In other cases, a slight adjustment may be necessary. To make the adjustment, multiply each seasonal index by the number of seasons divided by the sum of the unadjusted seasonal indexes. For instance, for quarterly data multiply each seasonal index by 4/(sum of the unadjusted seasonal indexes). Some of the exercises will require this adjustment to obtain the appropriate seasonal indexes.

## Deseasonalizing the Time Series

*With deseasonalized data, comparing sales in successive periods makes sense. With data that have not been deseasonalized, relevant comparisons can often be made between sales in the current period and sales in the same period one year ago.*

The purpose of finding seasonal indexes is to remove the seasonal effects from a time series. This process is referred to as *deseasonalizing* the time series. Economic time series adjusted for seasonal variations (**deseasonalized time series**) are often reported in publications such as the *Survey of Current Business, The Wall Street Journal,* and *Business Week.* Using the notation of the multiplicative model, we have

$$Y_t = T_t \times S_t \times I_t$$

By dividing each time series observation by the corresponding seasonal index, we remove the effect of season from the time series. The deseasonalized time series for television set sales is summarized in Table 18.11. A graph of the deseasonalized television set sales time series is shown in Figure 18.13.

## Using the Deseasonalized Time Series to Identify Trend

Although the graph in Figure 18.13 shows some random up and down movement over the past 16 quarters, the time series seems to have an upward linear trend. To identify this trend, we will use the same procedure as in the preceding section; in this case, the data are quarterly deseasonalized sales values. Thus, for a linear trend, the estimated sales volume expressed as a function of time is

$$T_t = b_0 + b_1 t$$

where

$T_t$ = trend value for television set sales in period $t$

$b_0$ = intercept of the trend line

$b_1$ = slope of the trend line

As before, $t = 1$ corresponds to the time of the first observation for the time series, $t = 2$ corresponds to the time of the second observation, and so on. Thus, for the deseasonalized

TABLE 18.11    DESEASONALIZED VALUES FOR THE TELEVISION SET SALES TIME SERIES

| Year | Quarter | Sales (1000s) $(Y_t)$ | Seasonal Index $(S_t)$ | Deseasonalized Sales $(Y_t/S_t = T_t I_t)$ |
|---|---|---|---|---|
| 1 | 1 | 4.8 | .93 | 5.16 |
|   | 2 | 4.1 | .84 | 4.88 |
|   | 3 | 6.0 | 1.09 | 5.50 |
|   | 4 | 6.5 | 1.14 | 5.70 |
| 2 | 1 | 5.8 | .93 | 6.24 |
|   | 2 | 5.2 | .84 | 6.19 |
|   | 3 | 6.8 | 1.09 | 6.24 |
|   | 4 | 7.4 | 1.14 | 6.49 |
| 3 | 1 | 6.0 | .93 | 6.45 |
|   | 2 | 5.6 | .84 | 6.67 |
|   | 3 | 7.5 | 1.09 | 6.88 |
|   | 4 | 7.8 | 1.14 | 6.84 |
| 4 | 1 | 6.3 | .93 | 6.77 |
|   | 2 | 5.9 | .84 | 7.02 |
|   | 3 | 8.0 | 1.09 | 7.34 |
|   | 4 | 8.4 | 1.14 | 7.37 |

television set sales time series, $t = 1$ corresponds to the first deseasonalized quarterly sales value and $t = 16$ corresponds to the most recent deseasonalized quarterly sales value. The formulas for computing the value of $b_0$ and the value of $b_1$ follow.

$$b_1 = \frac{\Sigma t Y_t - (\Sigma t \Sigma Y_t)/n}{\Sigma t^2 - (\Sigma t)^2/n}$$

$$b_0 = \bar{Y} - b_1 \bar{t}$$

FIGURE 18.13    DESEASONALIZED TELEVISION SET SALES TIME SERIES

Note, however, that $Y_t$ now refers to the deseasonalized time series value at time $t$ and not to the actual value of the time series. Using the given relationships for $b_0$ and $b_1$ and the deseasonalized sales data of Table 18.11, we have the following calculations.

| $t$ | $Y_t$ (Deseasonalized) | $tY_t$ | $t^2$ |
|---|---|---|---|
| 1 | 5.16 | 5.16 | 1 |
| 2 | 4.88 | 9.76 | 4 |
| 3 | 5.50 | 16.50 | 9 |
| 4 | 5.70 | 22.80 | 16 |
| 5 | 6.24 | 31.20 | 25 |
| 6 | 6.19 | 37.14 | 36 |
| 7 | 6.24 | 43.68 | 49 |
| 8 | 6.49 | 51.92 | 64 |
| 9 | 6.45 | 58.05 | 81 |
| 10 | 6.67 | 66.70 | 100 |
| 11 | 6.88 | 75.68 | 121 |
| 12 | 6.84 | 82.08 | 144 |
| 13 | 6.77 | 88.01 | 169 |
| 14 | 7.02 | 98.28 | 196 |
| 15 | 7.34 | 110.10 | 225 |
| 16 | 7.37 | 117.92 | 256 |
| Totals  136 | 101.74 | 914.98 | 1496 |

where

$$\bar{t} = \frac{136}{16} = 8.5$$

$$\bar{Y} = \frac{101.74}{16} = 6.359$$

$$b_1 = \frac{914.98 - (136)(101.74)/16}{1496 - (136)^2/16} = 0.148$$

$$b_0 = 6.359 - 0.148(8.5) = 5.101$$

Therefore,

$$T_t = 5.101 + 0.148t$$

is the expression for the linear trend component of the time series.

The slope of 0.148 indicates that over the past 16 quarters, the firm averaged deseasonalized growth in sales of about 148 sets per quarter. If we assume that the past 16-quarter trend in sales data is a reasonably good indicator of the future, this equation can be used to project the trend component of the time series for future quarters. For example, substituting $t = 17$ into the equation yields next quarter's trend projection, $T_{17}$.

$$T_{17} = 5.101 + 0.148(17) = 7.617$$

**TABLE 18.12    QUARTERLY FORECASTS FOR THE TELEVISION SET SALES TIME SERIES**

| Year | Quarter | Trend Forecast | Seasonal Index (see Table 18.11) | Quarterly Forecast |
|------|---------|----------------|----------------------------------|--------------------|
| 5 | 1 | 7617 | .93 | (7617)(.93)  = 7084 |
|   | 2 | 7765 | .84 | (7765)(.84)  = 6523 |
|   | 3 | 7913 | 1.09 | (7913)(1.09) = 8625 |
|   | 4 | 8061 | 1.14 | (8061)(1.14) = 9190 |

Thus, the trend component yields a sales forecast of 7617 television sets for the next quarter. Similarly, the trend component produces sales forecasts of 7765, 7913, and 8061 television sets in quarters 18, 19, and 20, respectively.

## Seasonal Adjustments

The final step in developing the forecast when both trend and seasonal components are present is to use the seasonal index to adjust the trend projection. Returning to the television set sales example, we have a trend projection for the next four quarters. Now we must adjust the forecast for the seasonal effect. The seasonal index for the first quarter of year 5 ($t = 17$) is 0.93, so we obtain the quarterly forecast by multiplying the forecast based on trend ($T_{17} = 7617$) by the seasonal index (0.93). Thus, the forecast for the next quarter is 7617(0.93) = 7084. Table 18.12 gives the quarterly forecast for quarters 17 through 20. The high-volume fourth quarter has a 9190-unit forecast, and the low-volume second quarter has a 6523-unit forecast.

## Models Based on Monthly Data

In the preceding television set sales example, we used quarterly data to illustrate the computation of seasonal indexes. However, many businesses use monthly rather than quarterly forecasts. In such cases, the procedures introduced in this section can be applied with minor modifications. First, a 12-month moving average replaces the four-quarter moving average; second, 12 monthly seasonal indexes, rather than four quarterly seasonal indexes, must be computed. Other than these changes, the computational and forecasting procedures are identical.

## Cyclical Component

Mathematically, the multiplicative model of equation (18.9) can be expanded to include a cyclical component.

$$Y_t = T_t \times C_t \times S_t \times I_t \tag{18.10}$$

The cyclical component, like the seasonal component, is expressed as a percentage of trend. As mentioned in Section 18.1, this component is attributable to multiyear cycles in the time series. It is analogous to the seasonal component, but over a longer period of time. However, because of the length of time involved, obtaining enough relevant data to estimate the cyclical component is often difficult. Another difficulty is that cycles usually vary in length. We leave further discussion of the cyclical component to texts on forecasting methods.

## Exercises

### Methods

22. Consider the following time series data.

| | Year | | |
|---|---|---|---|
| Quarter | 1 | 2 | 3 |
| 1 | 4 | 6 | 7 |
| 2 | 2 | 3 | 6 |
| 3 | 3 | 5 | 6 |
| 4 | 5 | 7 | 8 |

    a. Show the four-quarter and centered moving average values for this time series.
    b. Compute seasonal indexes for the four quarters.

### Applications

23. The quarterly sales data (number of copies sold) for a college textbook over the past three years follow.

| Quarter | Year 1 | Year 2 | Year 3 |
|---|---|---|---|
| 1 | 1690 | 1800 | 1850 |
| 2 | 940 | 900 | 1100 |
| 3 | 2625 | 2900 | 2930 |
| 4 | 2500 | 2360 | 2615 |

    a. Show the four-quarter and centered moving average values for this time series.
    b. Compute seasonal indexes for the four quarters.
    c. When does the textbook publisher have the largest seasonal index? Does this result appear reasonable? Explain.

24. Identify the monthly seasonal indexes for the three years of expenses for a six-unit apartment house in southern Florida as given here. Use a 12-month moving average calculation.

| | Expenses | | |
|---|---|---|---|
| | Year 1 | Year 2 | Year 3 |
| January | 170 | 180 | 195 |
| February | 180 | 205 | 210 |
| March | 205 | 215 | 230 |
| April | 230 | 245 | 280 |
| May | 240 | 265 | 290 |
| June | 315 | 330 | 390 |
| July | 360 | 400 | 420 |
| August | 290 | 335 | 330 |
| September | 240 | 260 | 290 |
| October | 240 | 270 | 295 |
| November | 230 | 255 | 280 |
| December | 195 | 220 | 250 |

25. Air pollution control specialists in southern California monitor the amount of ozone, carbon dioxide, and nitrogen dioxide in the air on an hourly basis. The hourly time series data exhibit seasonality, with the levels of pollutants showing patterns over the hours in the day. On July 15, 16, and 17, the following levels of nitrogen dioxide were observed in the downtown area for the 12 hours from 6:00 A.M. to 6:00 P.M.

| **July 15:** | 25 | 28 | 35 | 50 | 60 | 60 | 40 | 35 | 30 | 25 | 25 | 20 |
| **July 16:** | 28 | 30 | 35 | 48 | 60 | 65 | 50 | 40 | 35 | 25 | 20 | 20 |
| **July 17:** | 35 | 42 | 45 | 70 | 72 | 75 | 60 | 45 | 40 | 25 | 25 | 25 |

   a. Identify the hourly seasonal indexes for the 12 readings each day.
   b. With the seasonal indexes from part (a), the data were deseasonalized; the trend equation developed for the deseasonalized data was $T_t = 32.983 + .3922t$. Using the trend component only, develop forecasts for the 12 hours for July 18.
   c. Use the seasonal indexes from part (a) to adjust the trend forecasts developed in part (b).

26. Electric power consumption is measured in kilowatt-hours (kWh). The local utility company offers an interrupt program whereby commercial customers that participate receive favorable rates but must agree to cut back consumption if the utility requests them to do so. Timko Products cut back consumption at 12:00 noon Thursday. To assess the savings, the utility must estimate Timko's usage without the interrupt. The period of interrupted service was from noon to 8:00 P.M. Data on electric power consumption for the previous 72 hours are available.

| Time Period | Monday | Tuesday | Wednesday | Thursday |
|---|---|---|---|---|
| 12–4 A.M. | — | 19,281 | 31,209 | 27,330 |
| 4–8 A.M. | — | 33,195 | 37,014 | 32,715 |
| 8–12 noon | — | 99,516 | 119,968 | 152,465 |
| 12–4 P.M. | 124,299 | 123,666 | 156,033 | |
| 4–8 P.M. | 113,545 | 111,717 | 128,889 | |
| 8–12 midnight | 41,300 | 48,112 | 73,923 | |

   a. Is there a seasonal effect over the 24-hour period? Compute seasonal indexes for the six 4-hour periods.
   b. Use trend adjusted for seasonal indexes to estimate Timko's normal usage over the period of interrupted service.

# Regression Analysis

In the discussion of regression analysis in Chapters 14, 15, and 16, we showed how one or more independent variables could be used to predict the value of a single dependent variable. Looking at regression analysis as a forecasting tool, we can view the time series value that we want to forecast as the dependent variable. Hence, if we can identify a good set of related independent, or predictor, variables we may be able to develop an estimated regression equation for predicting or forecasting the time series.

The approach we used in Section 18.3 to fit a linear trend line to the bicycle sales time series is a special case of regression analysis. In that example, two variables—bicycle sales and time—were shown to be linearly related.* The inherent complexity of most real-world problems necessitates the consideration of more than one variable to predict the variable of

---

*In a purely technical sense, the number of bicycles sold is not viewed as being related to time; instead, time is used as a surrogate for variables to which the number of bicycles sold is actually related but which are either unknown or too difficult or too costly to measure.

interest. The statistical technique known as multiple regression analysis can be used in such situations.

Recall that to develop an estimated multiple regression equation, we need a sample of observations for the dependent variable and all independent variables. In time series analysis the $n$ periods of time series data provide a sample of $n$ observations on each variable that can be used in the analysis. For a function involving $k$ independent variables, we use the following notation.

$$Y_t = \text{value of the time series in period } t$$
$$x_{1t} = \text{value of independent variable 1 in period } t$$
$$x_{2t} = \text{value of independent variable 2 in period } t$$
$$.$$
$$.$$
$$.$$
$$x_{kt} = \text{value of independent variable } k \text{ in period } t$$

The $n$ periods of data necessary to develop the estimated regression equation would appear as shown in the following table.

| Period | Time Series $(Y_t)$ | Value of Independent Variables | | | | | | |
|--------|---------------------|----------|----------|----------|---|---|---|----------|
| | | $x_{1t}$ | $x_{2t}$ | $x_{3t}$ | . | . | . | $x_{kt}$ |
| 1 | $Y_1$ | $x_{11}$ | $x_{21}$ | $x_{31}$ | . | . | . | $x_{k1}$ |
| 2 | $Y_2$ | $x_{12}$ | $x_{22}$ | $x_{32}$ | . | . | . | $x_{k2}$ |
| . | . | . | . | . | . | . | . | . |
| . | . | . | . | . | . | . | . | . |
| . | . | . | . | . | . | . | . | . |
| $n$ | $Y_n$ | $x_{1n}$ | $x_{2n}$ | $x_{3n}$ | . | . | . | $x_{kn}$ |

As you might imagine, several choices are possible for the independent variables in a forecasting model. One possible choice for an independent variable is simply time. It was the choice made in Section 18.3 when we estimated the trend of the time series using a linear function of the independent variable time. Letting $x_{1t} = t$, we obtain an estimated regression equation of the form

$$\hat{Y}_t = b_0 + b_1 t$$

where $\hat{Y}_t$ is the estimate of the time series value $Y_t$ and where $b_0$ and $b_1$ are the estimated regression coefficients. In a more complex model, additional terms could be added corresponding to time raised to other powers. For example, if $x_{2t} = t^2$ and $x_{3t} = t^3$, the estimated regression equation would become

$$\hat{Y}_t = b_0 + b_1 x_{1t} + b_2 x_{2t} + b_3 x_{3t}$$
$$= b_0 + b_1 t + b_2 t^2 + b_3 t^3$$

Note that this model provides a forecast of a time series with curvilinear characteristics over time.

Other regression-based forecasting models have a mixture of economic and demographic independent variables. For example, in forecasting sales of refrigerators, we might select the following independent variables.

$$x_{1t} = \text{price in period } t$$
$$x_{2t} = \text{total industry sales in period } t - 1$$
$$x_{3t} = \text{number of building permits for new houses in period } t - 1$$
$$x_{4t} = \text{population forecast for period } t$$
$$x_{5t} = \text{advertising budget for period } t$$

According to the usual multiple regression procedure, an estimated regression equation with five independent variables would be used to develop forecasts.

*Spyros Makridakis, a noted forecasting expert, conducted research showing that simple techniques usually outperform more complex procedures for short-term forecasting. Using a more sophisticated and expensive procedure will not guarantee better forecasts.*

Whether a regression approach provides a good forecast depends largely on how well we are able to identify and obtain data for independent variables that are closely related to the time series. Generally, during the development of an estimated regression equation, we will want to consider many possible sets of independent variables. Thus, part of the regression analysis procedure should be the selection of the set of independent variables that provides the best forecasting model.

In the chapter introduction we stated that the **causal forecasting models** use other time series related to the one being forecast in an effort to explain the cause of a time series' behavior. Regression analysis is the tool most often used in developing such causal models. The related time series become the independent variables, and the time series being forecast is the dependent variable.

In another type of regression-based forecasting model, the independent variables are all previous values of the same time series. For example, if the time series values are denoted $Y_1, Y_2, \ldots, Y_n$, then with a dependent variable $Y_t$, we might try to find an estimated regression equation relating $Y_t$ to the most recent times series values $Y_{t-1}, Y_{t-2}$, and so on. With the three most recent periods as independent variables, the estimated regression equation would be

$$\hat{Y}_t = b_0 + b_1 Y_{t-1} + b_2 Y_{t-2} + b_3 Y_{t-3}$$

Regression models in which the independent variables are previous values of the time series are referred to as **autoregressive models**.

Finally, another regression-based forecasting approach incorporates a mixture of the independent variables previously discussed. For example, we might select a combination of time variables, some economic/demographic variables, and some previous values of the time series variable itself.

# 18.6 Qualitative Approaches

*If historical data are not available, managers must use a qualitative technique to develop forecasts. But the cost of using qualitative techniques can be high because of the time commitment required from the people involved.*

In the preceding sections we discussed several types of quantitative forecasting methods. Most of those techniques require historical data on the variable of interest, so they cannot be applied when historical data are not available. Furthermore, even when such data are available, a significant change in environmental conditions affecting the time series may make the use of past data questionable in predicting future values of the time series. For example, a government-imposed gasoline rationing program would raise questions about the validity of a gasoline sales forecast based on historical data. Qualitative forecasting techniques afford an alternative in these and other cases.

## Delphi Method

One of the most commonly used qualitative forecasting techniques is the **Delphi method**, originally developed by a research group at the Rand Corporation. It is an attempt to develop forecasts through "group consensus." In its usual application, the members of a panel of experts—all of whom are physically separated from and unknown to each other—are asked to respond to a series of questionnaires. The responses from the first questionnaire are tabulated and used to prepare a second questionnaire that contains information and opinions of the entire group. Each respondent is then asked to reconsider and possibly revise his or her previous response in light of the group information provided. This process continues until the coordinator feels that some degree of consensus has been reached. The goal of the Delphi method is not to produce a single answer as output, but instead to produce a relatively narrow spread of opinions within which the majority of experts concur.

## Expert Judgment

*Empirical evidence and theoretical arguments suggest that between 5 and 20 experts should be used in judgmental forecasting. However, in situations involving exponential growth, judgmental forecasts may be inappropriate.*

Qualitative forecasts often are based on the judgment of a single expert or represent the consensus of a group of experts. For example, each year a group of experts at Merrill Lynch gather to forecast the level of the Dow Jones Industrial Average and the prime rate for the next year. In doing so, the experts individually consider information that they believe will influence the stock market and interest rates; then they combine their conclusions into a forecast. No formal model is used, and no two experts are likely to consider the same information in the same way.

Expert judgment is a forecasting method that is commonly recommended when conditions in the past are not likely to hold in the future. Even though no formal quantitative model is used, expert judgment has provided good forecasts in many situations.

## Scenario Writing

The qualitative procedure known as **scenario writing** consists of developing a conceptual scenario of the future based on a well-defined set of assumptions. Different sets of assumptions lead to different scenarios. The job of the decision maker is to decide how likely each scenario is and then to make decisions accordingly.

## Intuitive Approaches

*Subjective* or *intuitive qualitative* approaches are based on the ability of the human mind to process a variety of information that, in most cases, is difficult to quantify. These techniques are often used in group work, wherein a committee or panel seeks to develop new ideas or solve complex problems through a series of "brainstorming sessions." In such sessions, individuals are freed from the usual group restrictions of peer pressure and criticism because they can present any idea or opinion without regard to its relevancy and, even more important, without fear of criticism.

## Summary

This chapter provided an introduction to the basic methods of time series analysis and forecasting. First, we showed that to explain the behavior of a time series, it is often helpful to think of the time series as consisting of four separate components: trend, cyclical, seasonal, and irregular. By isolating these components and measuring their apparent effect, one can forecast future values of the time series.

We discussed how smoothing methods can be used to forecast a time series that exhibits no significant trend, seasonal, or cyclical effect. The moving averages approach consists of computing an average of past data values and then using that average as the forecast for the next period. In the exponential smoothing method, a weighted average of past time series values is used to compute a forecast.

For time series that have only a long-term trend, we showed how regression analysis could be used to make trend projections. For time series in which both trend and seasonal influences are significant, we showed how to isolate the effects of the two factors and prepare better forecasts. Finally, regression analysis was described as a procedure for developing causal forecasting models. A causal forecasting model is one that relates the time series value (dependent variable) to other independent variables that are believed to explain (cause) the time series behavior.

Qualitative forecasting methods were discussed as approaches that could be used when little or no historical data are available. These methods are also considered most appropriate when the past pattern of the time series is not expected to continue into the future.

## Glossary

**Time series** A set of observations on a variable measured at successive points in time or over successive periods of time.

**Forecast** A prediction of future values of a time series.

**Trend** The long-run shift or movement in the time series observable over several periods of time.

**Cyclical component** The component of the time series that results in periodic above-trend and below-trend behavior of the time series lasting more than one year.

**Seasonal component** The component of the time series that shows a periodic pattern over one year or less.

**Irregular component** The component of the time series that reflects the random variation of the time series values beyond what can be explained by the trend, cyclical, and seasonal components.

**Moving averages** A method of forecasting or smoothing a time series that uses the average of the most recent $n$ data values in the time series as the forecast for the next period.

**Mean squared error (MSE)** A measure of the accuracy of a forecasting method. This measure is the average of the sum of the squared differences between the forecast values and the actual time series values.

**Weighted moving averages** A method of forecasting or smoothing a time series by computing a weighted average of past data values. The sum of the weights must equal one.

**Exponential smoothing** A forecasting technique that uses a weighted average of past time series values as the forecast.

**Smoothing constant** A parameter of the exponential smoothing model that provides the weight given to the most recent time series value in the calculation of the forecast value.

**Multiplicative time series model** A model whereby the separate components of the time series are multiplied together to identify the actual time series value. When the four components of trend, cyclical, seasonal, and irregular are assumed present, we obtain $Y_t = T_t \times C_t \times S_t \times I_t$. When the cyclical component is not modeled, we obtain $Y_t = T_t \times S_t \times I_t$.

**Deseasonalized time series** A time series from which the effect of season has been removed by dividing each original time series observation by the corresponding seasonal index.

**Causal forecasting methods** Forecasting methods that relate a time series to other variables that are believed to explain or cause its behavior.

**Autoregressive model** A time series model whereby a regression relationship based on past time series values is used to predict the future time series values.

**Delphi method** A qualitative forecasting method that obtains forecasts through group consensus.

**Scenario writing** A qualitative forecasting method that consists of developing a conceptual scenario of the future based on a well-defined set of assumptions.

## Key Formulas

**Moving Average**

$$\text{Moving average} = \frac{\Sigma(\text{most recent } n \text{ data values})}{n} \qquad (18.1)$$

**Exponential Smoothing Model**

$$F_{t+1} = \alpha Y_t + (1 - \alpha)F_t \qquad (18.2)$$

**Equation for Linear Trend**

$$T_t = b_0 + b_1 t \qquad (18.5)$$

**Multiplicative Time Series Model with Trend, Seasonal, and Irregular Components**

$$Y_t = T_t \times S_t \times I_t \qquad (18.9)$$

**Multiplicative Time Series Model with Trend, Cyclical, Seasonal, and Irregular Components**

$$Y_t = T_t \times C_t \times S_t \times I_t \qquad (18.10)$$

## Supplementary Exercises

27. Moving averages often are used to identify movements in stock prices. Daily closing prices (in dollars per share) for SanDisk for August 16, 2002, through September 3, 2002, follow (http://www.finance.yahoo.com).

| Day | Price ($) | Day | Price ($) |
|---|---|---|---|
| August 16 | 14.45 | August 26 | 16.45 |
| August 19 | 15.75 | August 27 | 15.60 |
| August 20 | 16.45 | August 28 | 15.09 |
| August 21 | 17.40 | August 29 | 16.42 |
| August 22 | 17.32 | August 30 | 16.21 |
| August 23 | 15.96 | September 3 | 15.22 |

   a. Use a five-month moving average to smooth the time series. Forecast the closing price for September 4, 2002.
   b. Use a four-month weighted moving average to smooth the time series. Use a weight of .4 for the most recent period, .3 for the next period back, .2 for the third period back, and .1 for the fourth period back. Forecast the closing price for September 4, 2002.
   c. Use exponential smoothing with a smoothing constant of $\alpha = .7$ to smooth the time series. Forecast the closing price for September 4, 2002.
   d. Which of the three methods do you prefer? Why?

28. For the 2001–2002 National Basketball Association season, Philadelphia 76ers Allen Iverson was the scoring leader with an average of 31.4 points per game. The following data show the average number of points per game for the scoring leader from the 1991–1992 season to the 2001–2002 season (*The World Almanac 2002;* http://www.nba.com).

| Season | Average | Season | Average |
|--------|---------|--------|---------|
| 1991–1992 | 30.1 | 1997–1998 | 28.7 |
| 1992–1993 | 32.6 | 1998–1999 | 26.8 |
| 1993–1994 | 29.8 | 1999–2000 | 29.7 |
| 1994–1995 | 29.3 | 2000–2001 | 31.1 |
| 1995–1996 | 30.4 | 2001–2002 | 31.4 |
| 1996–1997 | 29.6 | | |

   a. Use exponential smoothing to forecast this time series. Consider smoothing constants of $\alpha = .1$ and .2. What value of the smoothing constant provides the best forecast?
   b. What is the forecast of the leading scoring average for the 2002–2003 season?

29. The percentage of individual investors' portfolios committed to stock depends on the state of the economy. As of April 1997, a typical portfolio consisted of cash (19%), stocks (30%), stock funds (37%), bonds (8%), and bond funds (6%) (*AAII Journal,* June 1997). The following table reports the percentage of stocks in a typical portfolio in nine quarters from 1995 to 1997.

| Quarter | Stock % |
|---------|---------|
| 1st—1995 | 29.8 |
| 2nd—1995 | 31.0 |
| 3rd—1995 | 29.9 |
| 4th—1995 | 30.1 |
| 1st—1996 | 32.2 |
| 2nd—1996 | 31.5 |
| 3rd—1996 | 32.0 |
| 4th—1996 | 31.9 |
| 1st—1997 | 30.0 |

   a. Use exponential smoothing to forecast this time series. Consider smoothing constants of $\alpha = .2, .3,$ and .4. What value of the smoothing constant provides the best forecast?
   b. What is the forecast of the percentage of assets committed to stocks for the second quarter of 1997?

30. A chain of grocery stores noted the weekly demand (in cases) reported in the following table for a particular brand of automatic dishwasher detergent. Use exponential smoothing with $\alpha = .2$ to develop a forecast for week 11.

| Week | Demand | Week | Demand |
|------|--------|------|--------|
| 1 | 22 | 6 | 24 |
| 2 | 18 | 7 | 20 |
| 3 | 23 | 8 | 19 |
| 4 | 21 | 9 | 18 |
| 5 | 17 | 10 | 21 |

31. United Dairies, Inc., supplies milk to several independent grocers throughout Dade County, Florida. Managers at United Dairies want to develop a forecast of the number of half-gallons of milk sold per week. Sales data for the past 12 weeks follow.

| Week | Sales | Week | Sales |
|------|-------|------|-------|
| 1 | 2750 | 7 | 3300 |
| 2 | 3100 | 8 | 3100 |
| 3 | 3250 | 9 | 2950 |
| 4 | 2800 | 10 | 3000 |
| 5 | 2900 | 11 | 3200 |
| 6 | 3050 | 12 | 3150 |

Use exponential smoothing with $\alpha = .4$ to develop a forecast of demand for week 13.

32. The Garden Avenue Seven sells tapes of its musical performances. The following table reports sales (in units) for the past 18 months. The group's manager wants an accurate method for forecasting future sales.

| Month | Sales | Month | Sales | Month | Sales |
|-------|-------|-------|-------|-------|-------|
| 1 | 293 | 7 | 381 | 13 | 549 |
| 2 | 283 | 8 | 431 | 14 | 544 |
| 3 | 322 | 9 | 424 | 15 | 601 |
| 4 | 355 | 10 | 433 | 16 | 587 |
| 5 | 346 | 11 | 470 | 17 | 644 |
| 6 | 379 | 12 | 481 | 18 | 660 |

   a. Use exponential smoothing with $\alpha = .3, .4,$ and $.5$. Which value of $\alpha$ provides the best forecasts?

   b. Use trend projection to provide a forecast. What is the value of MSE?

   c. Which method of forecasting would you recommend to the manager? Why?

33. The Mayfair Department Store in Davenport, Iowa, is trying to determine the amount of sales lost while it was shut down during July and August because of damage caused by the Mississippi River flood. Sales data for January through June follow.

| Month | Sales ($1000s) | Month | Sales ($1000s) |
|-------|----------------|-------|----------------|
| January | 185.72 | April | 210.36 |
| February | 167.84 | May | 255.57 |
| March | 205.11 | June | 261.19 |

   a. Use exponential smoothing, with $\alpha = .4$, to develop a forecast for July and August. (*Hint:* Use the forecast for July as the actual sales in July in developing the August forecast.) Comment on the use of exponential smoothing for forecasts more than one period into the future.

   b. Use trend projection to forecast sales for July and August.

   c. Mayfair's insurance company proposed a settlement based on lost sales of $240,000 in July and August. Is this amount fair? If not, what amount would you recommend as a counteroffer?

34. Canton Supplies, Inc., is a service firm that employs approximately 100 individuals. Managers of Canton Supplies are concerned about meeting monthly cash obligations and want to develop a forecast of monthly cash requirements. Because of a recent change in operat-

ing policy, only the past seven months of data are considered to be relevant. With the following historical data, use trend projection to develop a forecast of cash requirements for each of the next two months.

| Month | 1 | 2 | 3 | 4 | 5 | 6 | 7 |
|---|---|---|---|---|---|---|---|
| **Cash Required ($1000s)** | 205 | 212 | 218 | 224 | 230 | 240 | 246 |

35. The following data report the number of U.S. cellular telephone subscribers (in millions) by year from 1994 to 2000 (*The World Almanac and Book of Facts*, 2002).

| Year | Number | Year | Number |
|---|---|---|---|
| 1994 | 24 | 1998 | 69 |
| 1995 | 34 | 1999 | 86 |
| 1996 | 44 | 2000 | 109 |
| 1997 | 55 | | |

   a. Develop a linear trend equation for this time series. Comment on what the equation tells about the number of cellular telephone subscribers for the seven-year period.
   b. Provide forecasts of the number of cellular telephone subscribers for 2001 and 2002.

36. The Costello Music Company has been in business for five years. During that time, sales of electric organs increased from 12 units in the first year to 76 units in the most recent year. Fred Costello, the firm's owner, wants to develop a forecast of organ sales for the coming year. The historical data follow.

| Year | 1 | 2 | 3 | 4 | 5 |
|---|---|---|---|---|---|
| **Sales** | 12 | 28 | 34 | 50 | 76 |

   a. Show a graph of this time series. Does a linear trend appear to be present?
   b. Develop the equation for the linear trend component for the time series. What is the average increase in sales that the firm has been realizing per year?

37. Hudson Marine has been an authorized dealer for C&D marine radios for the past seven years. The following table reports the number of radios sold each year.

| Year | 1 | 2 | 3 | 4 | 5 | 6 | 7 |
|---|---|---|---|---|---|---|---|
| **Number Sold** | 35 | 50 | 75 | 90 | 105 | 110 | 130 |

   a. Show a graph of this time series. Does a linear trend appear to be present?
   b. Develop the equation for the linear trend component of the time series.
   c. Use the linear trend developed in part (b) to develop a forecast for annual sales in year 8.

38. The League of American Theatres and Producers, Inc., collects a variety of statistics for Broadway plays, such as the gross revenue, the length of play run, and the number of new productions. The following data show the season attendance (in millions) for Broadway shows from 1990 to 2001 (*The World Almanac*, 2002).

| Season | Attendance (millions) | Season | Attendance (millions) |
|---|---|---|---|
| 1990–1991 | 7.3 | 1996–1997 | 10.6 |
| 1991–1992 | 7.4 | 1997–1998 | 11.5 |
| 1992–1993 | 7.9 | 1998–1999 | 11.7 |
| 1993–1994 | 8.1 | 1999–2000 | 11.4 |
| 1994–1995 | 9.0 | 2000–2001 | 11.9 |
| 1995–1996 | 9.5 | | |

a. Plot the time series and comment on the appropriateness of a linear trend.
b. Develop the equation for the linear trend component for this time series.
c. What is the average increase in attendance per season?
d. Use the trend equation to forecast attendance for the 2001–2002 season.

39. Over the past 25 years the United States Golf Association (USGA) tested thousands of golf balls for conformance with the overall distance standard. The following table gives the number of golf balls tested by the USGA by year from 1992 to 2002 (*Golf Journal*, October 2002).

| Year | Number | Year | Number |
|------|--------|------|--------|
| 1992 | 465 | 1997 | 919 |
| 1993 | 602 | 1998 | 916 |
| 1994 | 646 | 1999 | 861 |
| 1995 | 755 | 2000 | 834 |
| 1996 | 807 | 2001 | 821 |

Plot the time series and comment on the appropriateness of a linear trend. What type of functional form do you believe would be most appropriate for the trend pattern of this time series?

40. Refer to the Hudson Marine problem in exercise 37. Suppose the quarterly sales values for the seven years of historical data are as follow.

| Year | Quarter 1 | Quarter 2 | Quarter 3 | Quarter 4 | Total Yearly Sales |
|------|-----------|-----------|-----------|-----------|--------------------|
| 1 | 6 | 15 | 10 | 4 | 35 |
| 2 | 10 | 18 | 15 | 7 | 50 |
| 3 | 14 | 26 | 23 | 12 | 75 |
| 4 | 19 | 28 | 25 | 18 | 90 |
| 5 | 22 | 34 | 28 | 21 | 105 |
| 6 | 24 | 36 | 30 | 20 | 110 |
| 7 | 28 | 40 | 35 | 27 | 130 |

a. Show the four-quarter moving average values for this time series. Plot both the original time series and the moving average series on the same graph.
b. Compute the seasonal indexes for the four quarters.
c. When does Hudson Marine experience the largest seasonal effect? Does this result seem reasonable? Explain.

41. Consider the Costello Music Company problem in exercise 36. The quarterly sales data follow.

| Year | Quarter 1 | Quarter 2 | Quarter 3 | Quarter 4 | Total Yearly Sales |
|------|-----------|-----------|-----------|-----------|--------------------|
| 1 | 4 | 2 | 1 | 5 | 12 |
| 2 | 6 | 4 | 4 | 14 | 28 |
| 3 | 10 | 3 | 5 | 16 | 34 |
| 4 | 12 | 9 | 7 | 22 | 50 |
| 5 | 18 | 10 | 13 | 35 | 76 |

a. Compute the seasonal indexes for the four quarters.
b. When does Costello Music experience the largest seasonal effect? Does this result appear reasonable? Explain.

42. Refer to the Hudson Marine data in exercise 40.
    a. Deseasonalize the data and use the deseasonalized time series to identify the trend.
    b. Use the results of part (a) to develop a quarterly forecast for next year based on trend.
    c. Use the seasonal indexes developed in exercise 40 to adjust the forecasts developed in part (b) to account for the effect of season.

43. Consider the Costello Music Company time series in exercise 41.
    a. Deseasonalize the data and use the deseasonalized time series to identify the trend.
    b. Use the results of part (a) to develop a quarterly forecast for next year based on trend.
    c. Use the seasonal indexes developed in exercise 41 to adjust the forecasts developed in part (b) to account for the effect of season.

## Case Problem 1    Forecasting Food and Beverage Sales

The Vintage Restaurant, on Captiva Island near Fort Myers, Florida, is owned and operated by Karen Payne. The restaurant just completed its third year of operation. During that time, Karen sought to establish a reputation for the restaurant as a high-quality dining establishment that specializes in fresh seafood. Through the efforts of Karen and her staff, her restaurant has become one of the best and fastest-growing restaurants on the island.

Karen believes that to plan for the growth of the restaurant in the future, she needs to develop a system that will enable her to forecast food and beverage sales by month for up to one year in advance. Karen compiled the following data (in thousands of dollars) on total food and beverage sales for the three years of operation.

| Month | First Year | Second Year | Third Year |
|---|---|---|---|
| January | 242 | 263 | 282 |
| February | 235 | 238 | 255 |
| March | 232 | 247 | 265 |
| April | 178 | 193 | 205 |
| May | 184 | 193 | 210 |
| June | 140 | 149 | 160 |
| July | 145 | 157 | 166 |
| August | 152 | 161 | 174 |
| September | 110 | 122 | 126 |
| October | 130 | 130 | 148 |
| November | 152 | 167 | 173 |
| December | 206 | 230 | 235 |

## Managerial Report

Perform an analysis of the sales data for the Vintage Restaurant. Prepare a report for Karen that summarizes your findings, forecasts, and recommendations. Include the following:

1. A graph of the time series.
2. An analysis of the seasonality of the data. Indicate the seasonal indexes for each month, and comment on the high and low seasonal sales months. Do the seasonal indexes make intuitive sense? Discuss.
3. A forecast of sales for January through December of the fourth year.
4. Recommendations as to when the system that you develop should be updated to account for new sales data.
5. Any detailed calculations of your analysis in the appendix of your report.

Assume that January sales for the fourth year turn out to be $295,000. What was your forecast error? If this error is large, Karen may be puzzled about the difference between your forecast and the actual sales value. What can you do to resolve her uncertainty in the forecasting procedure?

## Case Problem 2    Forecasting Lost Sales

The Carlson Department Store suffered heavy damage when a hurricane struck on August 31, 2003. The store was closed for four months (September 2003 through December 2003), and Carlson is now involved in a dispute with its insurance company about the amount of lost sales during the time the store was closed. Two key issues must be resolved: (1) the amount of sales Carlson would have made if the hurricane had not struck and (2) whether Carlson is entitled to any compensation for excess sales due to increased business activity after the storm. More than $8 billion in federal disaster relief and insurance money came into the county, resulting in increased sales at department stores and numerous other businesses.

Table 18.13 gives Carlson's sales data for the 48 months preceding the storm. Table 18.14 reports total sales for the 48 months preceding the storm for all department stores in the county, as well as the total sales in the county for the four months the Carlson Department Store was closed. Carlson's managers asked you to analyze these data and develop estimates of the lost sales at the Carlson Department Store for the months of September through December 2003. They also asked you to determine whether a case can be made for excess storm-related sales during the same period. If such a case can be made, Carlson is entitled to compensation for excess sales it would have earned in addition to ordinary sales.

### Managerial Report

Prepare a report for the managers of the Carlson Department Store that summarizes your findings, forecasts, and recommendations. Include the following:

1. An estimate of sales had there been no hurricane.
2. An estimate of countywide department store sales had there been no hurricane.
3. An estimate of lost sales for the Carlson Department Store for September through December 2003.

TABLE 18.13    SALES FOR CARLSON DEPARTMENT STORE, SEPTEMBER 1999 THROUGH AUGUST 2003 ($ MILLIONS)

| Month | 1999 | 2000 | 2001 | 2002 | 2003 |
|---|---|---|---|---|---|
| January | | 1.45 | 2.31 | 2.31 | 2.56 |
| February | | 1.80 | 1.89 | 1.99 | 2.28 |
| March | | 2.03 | 2.02 | 2.42 | 2.69 |
| April | | 1.99 | 2.23 | 2.45 | 2.48 |
| May | | 2.32 | 2.39 | 2.57 | 2.73 |
| June | | 2.20 | 2.14 | 2.42 | 2.37 |
| July | | 2.13 | 2.27 | 2.40 | 2.31 |
| August | | 2.43 | 2.21 | 2.50 | 2.23 |
| September | 1.71 | 1.90 | 1.89 | 2.09 | |
| October | 1.90 | 2.13 | 2.29 | 2.54 | |
| November | 2.74 | 2.56 | 2.83 | 2.97 | |
| December | 4.20 | 4.16 | 4.04 | 4.35 | |

**TABLE 18.14**    DEPARTMENT STORE SALES FOR THE COUNTY, SEPTEMBER 1999
THROUGH DECEMBER 2003 ($ MILLIONS)

| Month | 1999 | 2000 | 2001 | 2002 | 2003 |
|---|---|---|---|---|---|
| January | | 46.8 | 46.8 | 43.8 | 48.0 |
| February | | 48.0 | 48.6 | 45.6 | 51.6 |
| March | | 60.0 | 59.4 | 57.6 | 57.6 |
| April | | 57.6 | 58.2 | 53.4 | 58.2 |
| May | | 61.8 | 60.6 | 56.4 | 60.0 |
| June | | 58.2 | 55.2 | 52.8 | 57.0 |
| July | | 56.4 | 51.0 | 54.0 | 57.6 |
| August | | 63.0 | 58.8 | 60.6 | 61.8 |
| September | 55.8 | 57.6 | 49.8 | 47.4 | 69.0 |
| October | 56.4 | 53.4 | 54.6 | 54.6 | 75.0 |
| November | 71.4 | 71.4 | 65.4 | 67.8 | 85.2 |
| December | 117.6 | 114.0 | 102.0 | 100.2 | 121.8 |

In addition, use the countywide actual department stores sales for September through
December 2003 and the estimate in part (2) to make a case for or against excess storm-
related sales.

## Appendix 18.1    Forecasting with Minitab

In this appendix we show how Minitab can be used to develop forecasts using three forecasting methods: moving averages, exponential smoothing, and trend projection.

### Moving Averages

**CD** file

Gasoline

To show how Minitab can be used to develop forecasts using the moving averages method,
we will develop a forecast for the gasoline sales time series in Table 18.1 and Figure 18.5.
The sales data for the 12 weeks are entered into column 2 of the worksheet. The following
steps can be used to produce a three-week moving average forecast for week 13.

**Step 1.** Select the **Stat** menu
**Step 2.** Choose **Time Series**
**Step 3.** Choose **Moving Average**
**Step 4.** When the **Moving Average** dialog box appears:
      Enter C2 in the **Variable** box
      Enter 3 in the **MA length** box
      Select **Generate forecasts**
      Enter 1 in the **Number of forecasts** box
      Enter 12 in the **Starting from origin** box
      Click **OK**

The three-week moving average forecast for week 13 is shown in the session window. The
mean square error of 10.22 is labeled as MSD in the Minitab output. Many other output options are available, including a summary table similar to Table 18.2 and graphical output
similar to Figure 18.6.

## Exponential Smoothing

**Gasoline**

To show how Minitab can be used to develop an exponential smoothing forecast, we will again develop a forecast of sales in week 13 for the gasoline sales time series in Table 18.1 and Figure 18.5. The sales data for the 12 weeks are entered into column 2 of the worksheet. The following steps can be used to produce a forecast for week 13 using a smoothing constant of $\alpha = .2$.

> **Step 1.** Select the **Stat** menu
> **Step 2.** Choose **Time Series**
> **Step 3.** Choose **Single Exp Smoothing**
> **Step 4.** When the Single Exponential Smoothing dialog box appears:
>> Enter C2 in the **Variable** box
>> Select the **Use** option for the Weight to Use in Smoothing
>> Enter 0.2 in the Use box
>> Select **Generate forecasts**
>> Enter 1 in the **Number of forecasts** box
>> Enter 12 in the **Starting from origin** box
>> Select **Options**
> **Step 5.** When the Single Exponential Smoothing—Options dialog box appears:
>> Enter 1 in the **Use average of first** box
>> Click **OK**
> **Step 6.** When the Single Exponential Smoothing dialog box appears:
>> Click **OK**

The exponential smoothing forecast for week 13 is shown in the session window. The mean square error is labeled as MSD in the Minitab output.* Many other output options are available, including a summary table similar to Table 18.3 and graphical output similar to Figure 18.7.

## Trend Projection

**Bicycle**

To show how Minitab can be used for trend projection, we develop a forecast for the bicycle sales time series in Table 18.6 and Figure 18.8. The year numbers are entered into column C1 and the sales data are entered into column C2 of the worksheet. The following steps can be used to produce a forecast for week 13 using trend projection.

> **Step 1.** Select the **Stat** menu
> **Step 2.** Choose **Time Series**
> **Step 3.** Choose **Trend Analysis**
> **Step 4.** When the Trend Analysis dialog box appears:
>> Enter C2 in the **Variable** box
>> Choose **Linear** for the Model Type
>> Select **Generate forecasts**
>> Enter 1 in the **Number of forecasts** box
>> Enter 10 in the **Starting from origin** box
>> Click **OK**

The equation for linear trend and the forecast for the next period are shown in the session window.

---

*The value of MSD computed by Minitab is not the same as the value of MSE that appears in Table 18.4. Minitab uses a forecast of 17 for week 1 and computes MSD using all 12 time periods of data. In Section 18.2 we compute MSE using only the data for weeks 2 through 12, because we had no past values with which to make a forecast for period 1.

# Appendix 18.2   Forecasting with Excel

In this appendix we show how Excel can be used to develop forecasts using three forecasting methods: moving averages, exponential smoothing, and trend projection.

## Moving Averages

**Gasoline**

To show how Excel can be used to develop forecasts using the moving averages method, we will develop a forecast for the gasoline sales time series in Table 18.1 and Figure 18.5. The sales data for the 12 weeks are entered into worksheet rows 2 through 13 of column B. The following steps can be used to produce a three-week moving average.

> **Step 1.** Select the **Tools** menu
> **Step 2.** Choose **Data Analysis**
> **Step 3.** Choose **Moving Average** from the list of Analysis Tools
>      Click **OK**
> **Step 4.** When the Moving Average dialog box appears:
>      Enter B2:B13 in the **Input Range** box
>      Enter 3 in the **Interval** box
>      Enter C2 in the **Output Range** box
>      Click **OK**

The three-week moving average forecasts will appear in column B of the worksheet. Forecasts for periods of other length can be computed easily by entering a different value in the **Interval** box.

## Exponential Smoothing

**Gasoline**

To show how Excel can be used for exponential smoothing, we again develop a forecast for the gasoline sales time series in Table 18.1 and Figure 18.5. The sales data for the 12 weeks are entered into worksheet rows 2 through 13 of column B. The following steps can be used to produce a forecast using a smoothing constant of $\alpha = .2$.

> **Step 1.** Select the **Tools** menu
> **Step 2.** Choose **Data Analysis**
> **Step 3.** Choose **Exponential Smoothing** from the list of Analysis Tools
>      Click **OK**
> **Step 4.** When the Exponential Smoothing dialog box appears:
>      Enter B2:B13 in the **Input Range** box
>      Enter .8 in the **Damping factor** box
>      Enter C2 in the **Output Range** box
>      Click **OK**

The exponential smoothing forecasts will appear in column B of the worksheet. Note that the value we entered in the Damping factor box is $1 - \alpha$; forecasts for other smoothing constants can be computed easily by entering a different value for $1 - \alpha$ in the Damping factor box.

## Trend Projection

**Bicycle**

To show how Excel can be used for trend projection, we develop a forecast for the bicycle sales time series in Table 18.6 and Figure 18.8. The data, with appropriate labels in row 1, are entered into worksheet rows 1 through 11 of columns A and B. The following steps can be used to produce a forecast for year 11 by trend projection.

**Step 1.** Select an empty cell in the worksheet

**Step 2.** Select the **Insert** menu

**Step 3.** Choose **Function**

**Step 4.** When the Insert Function dialog box appears:

     Choose **Statistical** in the Or select a category box

     Choose **Forecast** in the Select a function box

     Click **OK**

**Step 5.** When the Forecast Function Arguments dialog box appears:

     Enter 11 in the **x** box

     Enter B2:B11 in the **Known y's** box

     Enter A2:A11 in the **Known x's** box

     Click **OK**

The forecast for year 11, in this case 32.5, will appear in the cell selected in step 1.

# Nonparametric Methods

**CONTENTS**

## WEST SHELL REALTORS*
*CINCINNATI, OHIO*

West Shell Realtors was founded in 1958 with one office and a sales staff of three people. In 1964, the company began a long-term expansion program, with new offices added almost yearly. Over the years, West Shell grew to become one of the largest realtors in Greater Cincinnati, with offices in southwest Ohio, southeast Indiana, and northern Kentucky.

Statistical analysis helps real estate firms such as West Shell monitor sales performance. Monthly reports are generated for each of West Shell's offices as well as for the total company. Statistical summaries of total sales dollars, number of units sold, and median selling price per unit are essential in keeping both office managers and the company's top managers informed of progress and trouble spots in the organization.

In addition to monthly summaries of ongoing operations, the company uses statistical considerations to guide corporate plans and strategies. West Shell has implemented a strategy of planned expansion. Each time an expansion plan calls for the establishment of a new sales office, the company must address the question of office location. Selling prices of homes, turnover rates, and forecast sales volumes are the types of data used in evaluating and comparing alternative locations.

In one instance, West Shell identified two suburbs, Clifton and Roselawn, as prime candidates for a new office. A variety of factors were considered in comparing the two areas, including selling prices of homes. West Shell employed nonparametric

West Shell uses statistical analysis of home sales to remain competitive. © Courtesy of Coldwell Banker West Shell.

statistical methods to help identify any differences in sales patterns for the two areas.

Samples of 25 sales in the Clifton area and 18 sales in the Roselawn area were taken, and the Mann-Whitney-Wilcoxon rank-sum test was chosen as an appropriate statistical test of the difference in the pattern of selling prices. At the .05 level of significance, the Mann-Whitney-Wilcoxon test did not allow rejection of the null hypothesis that the two populations of selling prices were identical. Thus, West Shell was able to focus on criteria other than selling prices of homes in the site selection process.

In this chapter we will show how nonparametric statistical tests such as the Mann-Whitney-Wilcoxon test are applied. We will also discuss the proper interpretation of such tests.

---

*The authors are indebted to Rodney Fightmaster of West Shell Realtors for providing this Statistics in Practice.

The statistical methods presented thus far in the text are generally known as *parametric methods.* In this chapter we introduce several **nonparametric methods.** Such methods are often applicable in situations where the parametric methods of the preceding chapters are not. Nonparametric methods typically require less restrictive assumptions about the level of data measurement and fewer assumptions about the form of the probability distributions generating the sample data.

One consideration in determining whether a parametric or a nonparametric method is appropriate is the scale of measurement used to generate the data. All data are generated by one of four scales of measurement: nominal, ordinal, interval, and ratio. Hence, all statistical analyses are conducted with either nominal, ordinal, interval, or ratio data.

Let us define and provide examples of the four scales of measurement.

1. *Nominal scale.* The scale of measurement is nominal if the data are labels or categories used to define an attribute of an element. Nominal data may be numeric or nonnumeric.
   **Examples.** The exchange where a stock is listed (NYSE, NASDAQ, or AMEX) is nonnumeric nominal data. An individual's social security number is numeric nominal data.

**2.** *Ordinal scale.* The scale of measurement is ordinal if the data can be used to rank, or order, the observations. Ordinal data may be numeric or nonnumeric.

> **Examples.** The measures small, medium, and large for the size of an item are nonnumeric ordinal data. The class ranks of individuals measured as 1, 2, 3, . . . are numeric ordinal data.

**3.** *Interval scale.* The scale of measurement is interval if the data have the properties of ordinal data and the interval between observations is expressed in terms of a fixed unit of measure. Interval data must be numeric.

> **Examples.** Measures of temperature are interval data. Suppose it is 70 degrees in one location and 40 degrees in another. We can rank the locations with respect to warmth: the first location is warmer than the second. The fixed unit of measure, a degree, enables us to say how much warmer it is at the first location: 30 degrees.

**4.** *Ratio scale.* The scale of measurement is ratio if the data have the properties of interval data and the ratio of measures is meaningful. Ratio data must be numeric.

> **Examples.** Variables such as distance, height, weight, and time are measured on a ratio scale. Temperature measures are not ratio data because there is no inherently defined zero point. For instance, the freezing point of water is 32 degrees on a Fahrenheit scale and zero degrees on a Celsius scale. Ratios are not meaningful with temperature data. For instance, it makes no sense to say that 80 degrees is twice as warm as 40 degrees.

*In Chapter 1 we pointed out that nominal and ordinal scales provide qualitative data. Interval and ratio scales provide quantitative data.*

*If the level of data measurement is nominal or ordinal, computations of means, variances, and standard deviations are not meaningful. Thus, with these kinds of data, many of the statistical procedures discussed previously cannot be employed.*

Most of the statistical methods referred to as parametric require the use of interval- or ratio-scaled data. With these levels of measurement, arithmetic operations are meaningful, and means, variances, standard deviations, and so on can be computed, interpreted, and used in the analysis. With nominal or ordinal data, it is inappropriate to compute means, variances, and standard deviations; hence, parametric methods normally cannot be used. Nonparametric methods are often the only way to analyze such data and draw statistical conclusions.

In general, for a statistical method to be classified as nonparametric, it must satisfy at least one of the following conditions.*

**1.** The method can be used with nominal data.
**2.** The method can be used with ordinal data.
**3.** The method can be used with interval or ratio data when no assumption can be made about the population probability distribution.

If the level of data measurement is interval or ratio and if the necessary probability distribution assumptions for the population are appropriate, parametric methods provide more powerful or more discerning statistical procedures. In many cases where a nonparametric method as well as a parametric method can be applied, the nonparametric method is almost as good or almost as powerful as the parametric method. In cases where the data are nominal or ordinal or in cases where the assumptions required by parametric methods are inappropriate, only nonparametric methods are available. Because of the less restrictive data measurement requirements and the fewer assumptions needed about the population distribution, nonparametric methods are regarded as more generally applicable than parametric methods. The sign test, the Wilcoxon signed-rank test, the Mann-Whitney-Wilcoxon test, the Kruskal-Wallis test, and the Spearman rank correlation are the nonparametric methods presented in this chapter.

---

*See W. J. Conover, *Practical Nonparametric Statistics,* 3rd ed. (John Wiley & Sons, 1998).

##  19.1 Sign Test

A common market-research application of the **sign test** involves using a sample of $n$ potential customers to identify a preference for one of two brands of a product such as coffee, soft drinks, or detergents. The $n$ expressions of preference are nominal data because the consumer simply names, or labels, a preference. Given these data, our objective is to determine whether a difference in preference exists between the two items being compared. As we will see, the sign test is a nonparametric statistical procedure for answering this question.

### Small-Sample Case

The small-sample case for the sign test should be used whenever $n \leq 20$. Let us illustrate the use of the sign test for the small-sample case by considering a study conducted for Sun Coast Farms; Sun Coast produces an orange juice product marketed under the name Citrus Valley. A competitor of Sun Coast Farms produces an orange juice product known as Tropical Orange. In a study of consumer preferences for the two brands, 12 individuals were given unmarked samples of each product. The brand each individual tasted first was selected randomly. After tasting the two products, the individuals were asked to state a preference for one of the two brands. The purpose of the study is to determine whether consumers prefer one product over the other. Letting $p$ indicate the proportion of the population of consumers favoring Citrus Valley, we want to test the following hypotheses.

$$H_0: p = .50$$
$$H_a: p \neq .50$$

If $H_0$ cannot be rejected, we will have no evidence indicating a difference in preference for the two brands of orange juice. However, if $H_0$ can be rejected, we can conclude that the consumer preferences are different for the two brands. In that case, the brand selected by the greater number of consumers can be considered the more preferred brand.

In the following discussion we will show how the small-sample version of the sign test can be used to test the hypothesis and draw a conclusion about consumer preference. To record the preference data for the 12 individuals participating in the study, we use a plus sign if the individual expresses a preference for Citrus Valley and a minus sign if the individual expresses a preference for Tropical Orange. Because the data are recorded in terms of plus or minus signs, this nonparametric test is called the sign test.

The number of plus signs is the test statistic. Under the assumption that $H_0$ is true ($p = .50$), its sampling distribution is a binomial distribution with $p = .50$. With a sample size of $n = 12$, Table 5 in Appendix B shows the probabilities for the binomial distribution with $p = .50$ as displayed in Table 19.1. Figure 19.1 is a graphical representation of this binomial sampling distribution. It shows the probability of the number of plus signs under the assumption that $H_0$ is true. Let us proceed with the test to determine whether there is a difference in consumer preference for the two brands of orange juice. We will use a .05 level of significance.

The preference data obtained are shown in Table 19.2. The two plus signs indicate two consumers preferred Citrus Valley. We can now use the binomial probabilities to determine the $p$-value for the test. With a two-tailed test, the $p$-value is found by doubling the probability in the tail of the binomial sampling distribution. For Sun Coast Farms, the number of plus signs (2) is in the lower tail of the distribution. So the probability in the tail is the probability of 2, 1, and 0 plus signs. Adding these probabilities, we obtain $.0161 + .0029 + .0002 = .0192$. Doubling this value, we obtain the $p$-value $= 2(.0192) = .0384$. With $p$-value $\leq \alpha = .05$, we reject $H_0$. The taste test provides evidence that consumer preference differs signifi-

---

**TABLE 19.1**

**BINOMIAL PROBABILITIES WITH $n = 12$, $p = .50$**

| Number of Plus Signs | Probability |
|---|---|
| 0 | .0002 |
| 1 | .0029 |
| 2 | .0161 |
| 3 | .0537 |
| 4 | .1208 |
| 5 | .1934 |
| 6 | .2256 |
| 7 | .1934 |
| 8 | .1208 |
| 9 | .0537 |
| 10 | .0161 |
| 11 | .0029 |
| 12 | .0002 |

*Exact binomial probabilities are readily available when the sample size is less than or equal to 20. See Table 5 of Appendix B.*

FIGURE 19.1   BINOMIAL SAMPLING DISTRIBUTION FOR THE NUMBER OF PLUS SIGNS
WHEN $n = 12$ AND $p = .50$

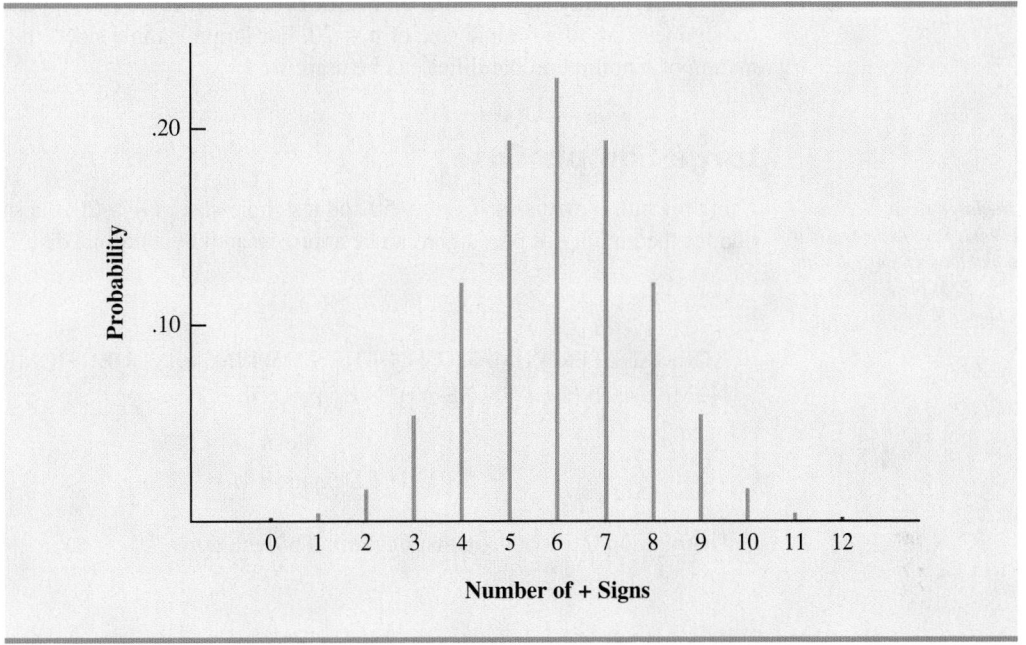

cantly for the two brands of orange juice. We would advise Sun Coast Farms that consumers
prefer Tropical Orange.

The Sun Coast Farms hypothesis test was a two-tailed test. As a result, the $p$-value was
found by doubling the probability in the tail of the binomial distribution. One-tailed sign
tests are also possible. If the test is a lower tail test, the $p$-value is the probability that the
number of plus signs is less than or equal to the observed number. If the test is an upper tail
test, the $p$-value is the probability that the number of plus signs is greater than or equal to
the observed number.

In the Sun Coast Farms taste test, all 12 individuals were able to state a preference for
one of the two brands of orange juice. In other applications of the sign test, one or more

TABLE 19.2   PREFERENCE DATA FOR THE SUN COAST FARMS TASTE TEST

| Individual | Brand Preference | Recorded Data |
|:---:|:---:|:---:|
| 1 | Tropical Orange | − |
| 2 | Tropical Orange | − |
| 3 | Citrus Valley | + |
| 4 | Tropical Orange | − |
| 5 | Tropical Orange | − |
| 6 | Tropical Orange | − |
| 7 | Tropical Orange | − |
| 8 | Tropical Orange | − |
| 9 | Citrus Valley | + |
| 10 | Tropical Orange | − |
| 11 | Tropical Orange | − |
| 12 | Tropical Orange | − |

individuals in the sample may not be able to state a preference. If a preference cannot be indicated, the response is discarded from the sample and the sign test is based on a smaller sample size. Finally, the binomial probabilities shown in Table 5 of Appendix B can be used for sign tests up to a sample size of $n = 20$. For larger sample sizes, the normal approximation of binomial probabilities can be used.

## Large-Sample Case

*The large-sample sign test is equivalent to the test of a population proportion with $p = .50$ as presented in Chapter 9.*

Using the null hypothesis $H_0$: $p = .50$ and a sample size of $n > 20$, the sampling distribution for the number of plus signs can be approximated by a normal distribution.

> NORMAL APPROXIMATION OF THE SAMPLING DISTRIBUTION OF THE NUMBER OF PLUS SIGNS WHEN $H_0$: $p = .50$
>
> $$\text{Mean: } \mu = .50n \qquad (19.1)$$
> $$\text{Standard Deviation: } \sigma = \sqrt{.25n} \qquad (19.2)$$
>
> Distribution form: approximately normal provided $n > 20$.

Let us consider an application of the sign test to political polling. A poll taken during a recent presidential election campaign asked 200 registered voters to rate the Democratic and Republican candidates in terms of best overall foreign policy. Results of the poll showed 72 rated the Democratic candidate higher, 103 rated the Republican candidate higher, and 25 indicated no difference between the candidates. Does the poll indicate a significant difference between the two candidates in terms of public opinion about their foreign policies?

*Ties are handled by dropping the items from the analysis.*

Using the sign test, we see that $n = 200 - 25 = 175$ individuals were able to indicate the candidate they believed had the best overall foreign policy. Using equations (19.1) and (19.2), we find that the sampling distribution of the number of plus signs has the following properties.

$$\mu = .50n = .50(175) = 87.5$$
$$\sigma = \sqrt{.25n} = \sqrt{.25(175)} = 6.6$$

In addition, with $n = 175$ we can assume that the sampling distribution is approximately normal. This distribution is shown in Figure 19.2.

Let us proceed with the sign test and use a .05 level of significance to draw a conclusion. Based on the number of times the Democratic candidate received the higher foreign policy rating as the number of plus signs ($x = 72$), we can calculate the following value for the test statistic.

$$z = \frac{x - \mu}{\sigma} = \frac{72 - 87.5}{6.6} = -2.35$$

*If the analysis used the number of times the Republican candidate was rated higher, $z = 2.35$ would lead us to the same conclusion.*

The standard normal distribution table shows that the area in the tail to the left of $z = -2.35$ is $(.5000 - .4906) = .0094$. With a two-tailed test, the $p$-value $= 2(.0094) = .0188$. With $p$-value $\leq \alpha = .05$, we reject $H_0$. The study indicates that the candidates are perceived to differ in terms of public opinion about their foreign policy.

FIGURE 19.2  PROBABILITY DISTRIBUTION OF THE NUMBER OF PLUS SIGNS
FOR A SIGN TEST WITH $n = 175$

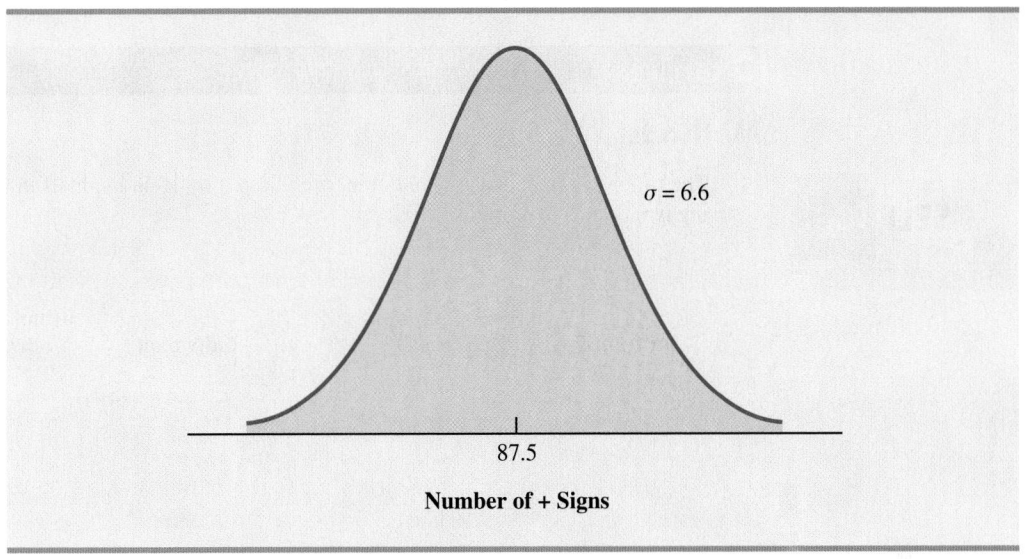

## Hypothesis Test About a Median

In Chapter 9 we described how hypothesis tests can be used to make an inference about a population mean. We now show how the sign test can be used to conduct hypothesis tests about a population median. Recall that the median splits a population in such a way that 50% of the values are at the median or above and 50% are at the median or below. We can apply the sign test by using a plus sign whenever the data in the sample are above the hypothesized value of the median and a minus sign whenever the data in the sample are below the hypothesized value of the median. Any data exactly equal to the hypothesized value of the median should be discarded. The computations for the sign test are done in exactly the same way as before.

For example, the following hypothesis test is being conducted about the median price of new homes in St. Louis, Missouri.

$$H_0\text{: Median} = \$130,000$$
$$H_a\text{: Median} \neq \$130,000$$

In a sample of 62 new homes, 34 have prices above $130,000, 26 have prices below $130,000, and two have prices of exactly $130,000.

Using equations (19.1) and (19.2) for the $n = 60$ homes with prices different from $130,000, we obtain

$$\mu = .50n = .50(60) = 30$$
$$\sigma = \sqrt{.25n} = \sqrt{.25(60)} = 3.87$$

With $x = 34$ as the number of plus signs, the test statistic becomes

$$z = \frac{x - \mu}{\sigma} = \frac{34 - 30}{3.87} = 1.03$$

Using the standard normal distribution table and $z = 1.03$, we find the two-tailed $p$-value $= 2(.5000 - .3485) = .303$. With $p$-value $> .05$, we cannot reject $H_0$. Based on the sample data, we are unable to reject the null hypothesis that the median selling price of a new in St. Louis is $130,000.

## Exercises

### Methods

1. The following table lists the preferences indicated by 10 individuals in taste tests involving two brands of a product.

| Individual | Brand A Versus Brand B | Individual | Brand A Versus Brand B |
|:---:|:---:|:---:|:---:|
| 1 | + | 6 | + |
| 2 | + | 7 | − |
| 3 | + | 8 | + |
| 4 | − | 9 | − |
| 5 | + | 10 | + |

With $\alpha = .05$, test for a significant difference in the preferences for the two brands. A plus indicates a preference for brand A over brand B.

2. The following hypothesis test is to be conducted.

$$H_0: \text{Median} \leq 150$$
$$H_a: \text{Median} > 150$$

A sample of size 30 yields 22 cases in which a value greater than 150 is obtained, three cases in which a value of exactly 150 is obtained, and five cases in which a value less than 150 is obtained. Use $\alpha = .01$ and conduct the hypothesis test.

### Applications

3. Are stock splits beneficial to stockholders? SNL Securities studied stock splits in the banking industry over an 18-month period and found that stock splits tended to increase the value of an individual's stock holding. Assume that of a sample of 20 recent stock splits, 14 led to an increase in value, four led to a decrease in value, and two resulted in no change. Suppose a sign test is to be used to determine whether stock splits continue to be beneficial for holders of bank stocks.
   a. What are the null and alternative hypotheses?
   b. With $\alpha = .05$, what is your conclusion?

4. A poll asked 1253 adults a series of questions about the state of the economy and their children's future. One question was, "Do you expect your children to have a better life than you have had, a worse life, or a life about as good as yours?" The responses were 34% better, 29% worse, 33% about the same, and 4% not sure. Use the sign test and a .05 level of significance to determine whether more adults feel their children will have a better future than feel their children will have a worse future. What is your conclusion?

5. Nielsen Media Research identified *ER* and *Seinfeld* as the top-rated network television shows for 1996–1997. Assume that in a local television preference poll, 410 individuals were asked to indicate their favorite network television show: 185 selected *ER*, 165 selected *Seinfeld*, and 60 selected another television show. Use a .05 level of significance to test the hypothesis that *ER* and *Seinfeld* have the same level of preference. What is your conclusion?

6.  In 1996, competition in the consumer PC market was led by Packard Bell and Compaq (*USA Today,* July 21, 1997). A sample of 500 purchases showed 202 Packard Bell computers, 158 Compaq computers, and 140 other computers including IBM, Apple, and NEC. Use a .05 level of significance to test the hypothesis that Packard Bell and Compaq have the same share of the consumer PC market. What is your conclusion?

7.  The median annual income of subscribers to *Barron's* magazine is $131,000 (barrons-mag.com, July 28, 2000). Assume a sample of 300 subscribers to *The Wall Street Journal* found 165 subscribers with an income over $131,000 and 135 subscribers with an income under $131,000. Can you conclude that there is any difference between the median incomes of the two subscriber groups? At $\alpha = .05$, what is your conclusion?

8.  In a sample of 150 college basketball games, the home team won 98 games. Test to see whether the data support the claim of a home-team advantage in college basketball. Use a .05 level of significance. What is your conclusion?

9.  The median number of part-time employees at fast-food restaurants in a particular city was known to be 15 last year. City officials think the use of part-time employees may be increasing. A sample of nine fast-food restaurants showed that more than 15 part-time employees worked at seven of the restaurants, one restaurant had exactly 15 part-time employees, and one had fewer than 15 part-time employees. Test at $\alpha = .05$ to see whether the median number of part-time employees increased.

10.  According to a national survey, the median annual income adults say would make their dreams come true is $152,000. Suppose that of a sample of 225 individuals in Ohio, 122 individuals report that the amount of income needed to make their dreams come true is less than $152,000, and 103 report that the amount needed is more than $152,000. Test the null hypothesis that the median amount of annual income needed to make dreams come true in Ohio is $152,000. Use $\alpha = .05$. What is your conclusion?

11.  The U.S. Bureau of Labor Statistics reported the 1996 median weekly earnings for women in administrative and managerial positions to be $585. A sample of administrative and managerial working women in the Chicago area provided the following data. Use the sample data to test $H_0$: median $\leq 585$, $H_a$: median $> 585$ for the population of administrative and managerial working women in Chicago. Use a .05 level of significance. What is your conclusion?

**Chicago**

| | | | | |
|---|---|---|---|---|
| 622 | 516 | 631 | 498 | 715 |
| 571 | 494 | 525 | 664 | 721 |
| 657 | 692 | 551 | 580 | 649 |
| 706 | 597 | 518 | 725 | 635 |
| 548 | 604 | 671 | 607 | 487 |
| 583 | 702 | 622 | 714 | 693 |
| 600 | 721 | 662 | 633 | 681 |
| 624 | 551 | 632 | 544 | 485 |
| 655 | 721 | 669 | 677 | 609 |
| 656 | 562 | 721 | 489 | 582 |

# 19.2   Wilcoxon Signed–Rank Test

The **Wilcoxon signed-rank test** is the nonparametric alternative to the parametric matched-sample test presented in Chapter 10. In the matched-sample situation, each experimental unit generates two paired or matched observations, one from population 1 and one from population 2. The differences between the matched observations provide insight about the differences between the two populations.

A manufacturing firm is attempting to determine whether two production methods differ in task completion time. A sample of 11 workers was selected, and each worker completed a production task using each of the production methods. The production method that each worker used first was selected randomly. Thus, each worker in the sample provided a pair of observations, as shown in Table 19.3. A positive difference in task completion times indicates that method 1 required more time, and a negative difference in times indicates that method 2 required more time. Do the data indicate that the methods are significantly different in terms of task completion times?

In effect, we have two populations of task completion times, one population associated with each method. The following hypotheses will be tested.

$H_0$: The populations are identical

$H_a$: The populations are not identical

If $H_0$ cannot be rejected, we will not have evidence to conclude that the task completion times differ for the two methods. However, if $H_0$ can be rejected, we will conclude that the two methods differ in task completion time.

The first step of the Wilcoxon signed-rank test requires a ranking of the *absolute value* of the differences between the two methods. We discard any differences of zero and then rank the remaining absolute differences from lowest to highest. Tied differences are assigned the average ranking of their positions in the combined data set. The ranking of the absolute values of differences is shown in the fourth column of Table 19.4. Note that the difference of zero for worker 8 is discarded from the rankings; then the smallest absolute difference of .1 is assigned the rank of 1. This ranking of absolute differences continues with the largest absolute difference of .9 assigned the rank of 10. The tied absolute differences for workers 3 and 5 are assigned the average rank of 3.5 and the tied absolute differences for workers 4 and 10 are assigned the average rank of 5.5.

Once the ranks of the absolute differences have been determined, the ranks are given the sign of the original difference in the data. For example, the .1 difference for worker 7, which was assigned the rank of 1, is given the value of $+1$ because the observed difference between the two methods was positive. The .2 difference, which was assigned the rank of 2, is given the value of $-2$ because the observed difference between the two methods was negative for worker 2. The complete list of signed ranks, as well as their sum, is shown in the last column of Table 19.4.

Let us return to the original hypothesis of identical population task completion times for the two methods. If the populations representing task completion times for each of the two methods are identical, we would expect the positive ranks and the negative ranks to cancel

TABLE 19.3    PRODUCTION TASK COMPLETION TIMES (MINUTES)

| Worker | Method 1 | Method 2 | Difference |
|--------|----------|----------|------------|
| 1 | 10.2 | 9.5 | .7 |
| 2 | 9.6 | 9.8 | −.2 |
| 3 | 9.2 | 8.8 | .4 |
| 4 | 10.6 | 10.1 | .5 |
| 5 | 9.9 | 10.3 | −.4 |
| 6 | 10.2 | 9.3 | .9 |
| 7 | 10.6 | 10.5 | .1 |
| 8 | 10.0 | 10.0 | .0 |
| 9 | 11.2 | 10.6 | .6 |
| 10 | 10.7 | 10.2 | .5 |
| 11 | 10.6 | 9.8 | .8 |

TABLE 19.4  RANKING OF ABSOLUTE DIFFERENCES FOR THE PRODUCTION TASK
COMPLETION TIME EXAMPLE

| Worker | Difference | Absolute Value of Difference | Rank | Signed Rank |
|--------|-----------|------------------------------|------|-------------|
| 1 | .7 | .7 | 8 | + 8 |
| 2 | −.2 | .2 | 2 | + 2 |
| 3 | .4 | .4 | 3.5 | + 3.5 |
| 4 | .5 | .5 | 5.5 | + 5.5 |
| 5 | −.4 | .4 | 3.5 | − 3.5 |
| 6 | .9 | .9 | 10 | +10 |
| 7 | .1 | .1 | 1 | + 1 |
| 8 | .0 | .0 | — | — |
| 9 | .6 | .6 | 7 | + 7 |
| 10 | .5 | .5 | 5.5 | + 5.5 |
| 11 | .8 | .8 | 9 | + 9 |
| | | | Sum of Signed Ranks | +44.0 |

each other, so that the sum of the signed rank values would be approximately zero. Thus, the test for significance under the Wilcoxon signed-rank test involves determining whether the computed sum of signed ranks (+44 in our example) is significantly different from zero.

Let $T$ denote the sum of the signed-rank values in a Wilcoxon signed-rank test. It can be shown that if the two populations are identical and the number of matched pairs of data is 10 or more, the sampling distribution of $T$ can be approximated by a normal distribution as follows.

SAMPLING DISTRIBUTION OF $T$ FOR IDENTICAL POPULATIONS

$$\text{Mean: } \mu_T = 0 \tag{19.3}$$

$$\text{Standard deviation: } \sigma_T = \sqrt{\frac{n(n + 1)(2n + 1)}{6}} \tag{19.4}$$

Distribution form: approximately normal provided $n \geq 10$.

For the example, we have $n = 10$ after discarding the observation with the difference of zero (worker 8). Thus, using equation (19.4), we have

$$\sigma_T = \sqrt{\frac{10(11)(21)}{6}} = 19.62$$

Figure 19.3 is the sampling distribution of $T$ under the assumption of identical populations.

Let us proceed with the Wilcoxon signed-rank test and use a .05 level of significance to draw a conclusion. With the sum of the signed-rank values $T = 44$, we calculate the following value for the test statistic.

$$z = \frac{T - \mu_T}{\sigma_T} = \frac{44 - 0}{19.62} = 2.24$$

Using the standard normal distribution table and $z = 2.24$, we find the two-tailed $p$-value = $2(.5000 - .4875) = .025$. With $p$-value $\leq \alpha = .05$, we reject $H_0$ and conclude that the

FIGURE 19.3   SAMPLING DISTRIBUTION OF THE WILCOXON *T* FOR THE PRODUCTION
TASK COMPLETION TIME EXAMPLE

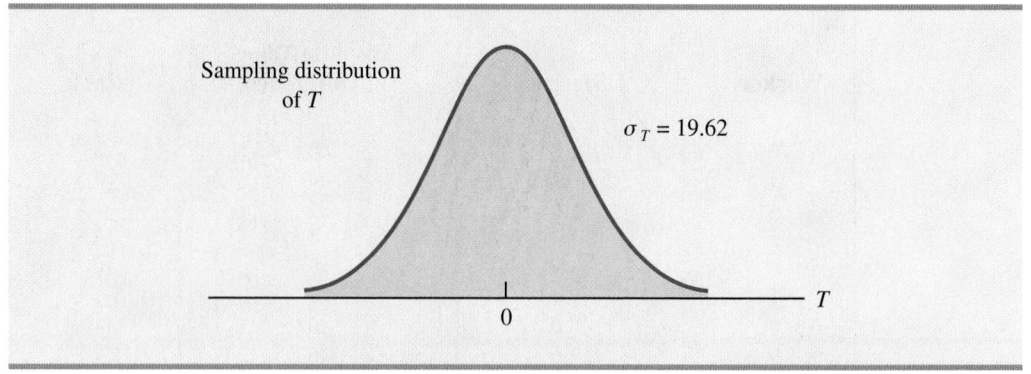

Sampling distribution
of *T*

$\sigma_T = 19.62$

0

*T*

two populations are not identical and that the methods differ in task completion time.
Method 2's shorter completion times for 8 of the workers lead us to conclude that method 2
is the preferred production method.

## Exercises

### Applications

12.  Two fuel additives are tested to determine their effect on miles per gallon for passenger cars.
     Test results for 12 cars follow; each car was tested with both fuel additives. Use $\alpha = .05$ and
     the Wilcoxon signed-rank test to see whether there is a significant difference in the additives.

| | Additive | | | Additive | |
| Car | 1 | 2 | Car | 1 | 2 |
|---|---|---|---|---|---|
| 1 | 20.12 | 18.05 | 7 | 16.16 | 17.20 |
| 2 | 23.56 | 21.77 | 8 | 18.55 | 14.98 |
| 3 | 22.03 | 22.57 | 9 | 21.87 | 20.03 |
| 4 | 19.15 | 17.06 | 10 | 24.23 | 21.15 |
| 5 | 21.23 | 21.22 | 11 | 23.21 | 22.78 |
| 6 | 24.77 | 23.80 | 12 | 25.02 | 23.70 |

13.  A sample of 10 men was used in a study to test the effects of a relaxant on the time required
     to fall asleep for male adults. Data for 10 subjects showing the number of minutes required
     to fall asleep with and without the relaxant follow. Use a .05 level of significance to deter-
     mine whether the relaxant reduces the time required to fall asleep. What is your conclusion?

| Subject | Without Relaxant | With Relaxant | Subject | Without Relaxant | With Relaxant |
|---|---|---|---|---|---|
| 1 | 15 | 10 | 6 | 7 | 5 |
| 2 | 12 | 10 | 7 | 8 | 10 |
| 3 | 22 | 12 | 8 | 10 | 7 |
| 4 | 8 | 11 | 9 | 14 | 11 |
| 5 | 10 | 9 | 10 | 9 | 6 |

14. Rental car gasoline prices per gallon were sampled at 10 major airports. Data for Avis and Budget car rental companies follow (*USA Today,* April 4, 2000).

| Airport | Avis | Budget |
|---------|------|--------|
| Boston Logan | 1.58 | 1.39 |
| Chicago O'Hare | 1.60 | 1.55 |
| Chicago Midway | 1.53 | 1.55 |
| Denver | 1.55 | 1.51 |
| Fort Lauderdale | 1.57 | 1.58 |
| Los Angeles | 1.80 | 1.74 |
| Miami | 1.62 | 1.60 |
| New York (JFK) | 1.69 | 1.60 |
| Orange County, CA | 1.75 | 1.59 |
| Washington (Dulles) | 1.55 | 1.54 |

Use $\alpha = .05$ to test the hypothesis that there is no difference between the two populations. What is your conclusion?

15. A test was conducted of two overnight mail delivery services. Two samples of identical deliveries were set up so that both delivery services were notified of the need for a delivery at the same time. The hours required to make each delivery follow. Do the data shown suggest a difference in the delivery times for the two services? Use a .05 level of significance for the test.

| Delivery | Service 1 | Service 2 |
|----------|-----------|-----------|
| 1 | 24.5 | 28.0 |
| 2 | 26.0 | 25.5 |
| 3 | 28.0 | 32.0 |
| 4 | 21.0 | 20.0 |
| 5 | 18.0 | 19.5 |
| 6 | 36.0 | 28.0 |
| 7 | 25.0 | 29.0 |
| 8 | 21.0 | 22.0 |
| 9 | 24.0 | 23.5 |
| 10 | 26.0 | 29.5 |
| 11 | 31.0 | 30.0 |

16. The 1997 price/earnings ratios for a sample of 12 stocks are shown in the following list (*Barron's,* December 8, 1997). Assume that a financial analyst provided the estimated price/earnings ratio for 1998. Using a .05 level of significance, what is your conclusion about the differences between the price/earnings ratios for 1997 and 1998?

| Stock | 1997 P/E Ratio | 1998 P/E Ratio (Est.) |
|-------|----------------|------------------------|
| Coca-Cola | 40 | 32 |
| Du Pont | 24 | 22 |
| Eastman Kodak | 21 | 23 |
| General Electric | 30 | 23 |
| General Mills | 25 | 19 |
| IBM | 19 | 19 |
| McDonald's | 20 | 17 |
| Merck | 29 | 19 |
| Motorola | 35 | 20 |
| Philip Morris | 17 | 18 |
| Walt Disney | 33 | 27 |
| Xerox | 20 | 16 |

17. Ten test-market cities were selected as part of a market research study designed to evaluate the effectiveness of a particular advertising campaign. The sales dollars for each city were recorded for the week prior to the promotional program. Then the campaign was conducted for two weeks and new sales data were collected for the week immediately after the campaign. The two sets of sales data (in thousands of dollars) follow.

| City | Precampaign Sales | Postcampaign Sales |
|---|---|---|
| Kansas City | 130 | 160 |
| Dayton | 100 | 105 |
| Cincinnati | 120 | 140 |
| Columbus | 95 | 90 |
| Cleveland | 140 | 130 |
| Indianapolis | 80 | 82 |
| Louisville | 65 | 55 |
| St. Louis | 90 | 105 |
| Pittsburgh | 140 | 152 |
| Peoria | 125 | 140 |

Use $\alpha = .05$. What conclusion would you draw about the value of the advertising program?

#  **19.3** Mann-Whitney-Wilcoxon Test

In this section we present another nonparametric method that can be used to determine whether a difference exists between two populations. This test, unlike the signed-rank test, is not based on a matched sample. Two independent samples, one from each population, are used. The test was developed jointly by Mann, Whitney, and Wilcoxon. It is sometimes called the *Mann-Whitney test* and sometimes the *Wilcoxon rank-sum test*. Both the Mann-Whitney and Wilcoxon versions of this test are equivalent; we refer to it as the **Mann-Whitney-Wilcoxon (MWW) test**.

The nonparametric MWW test does not require interval data or the assumption that the populations are normally distributed. The only requirement of the MWW test is that the measurement scale for the data is at least ordinal. Then, instead of testing for the difference between the means of the two populations, the MWW test determines whether the two populations are identical. The hypotheses for the MWW test are as follows.

$H_0$: The two populations are identical

$H_a$: The two populations are not identical

We demonstrate how the MWW test can be applied by first showing an application for the small-sample case.

## Small-Sample Case

The small-sample case for the MWW test should be used whenever the sample sizes for both populations are less than or equal to 10. We illustrate the use of the MWW test for the small-sample case by considering the academic potential of students attending Johnston High School. The majority of students attending Johnston High School previously attended either Garfield Junior High School or Mulberry Junior High School. The question raised by school administrators was whether the population of students who had attended Garfield was identical to the population of students who had attended Mulberry in terms of academic potential. The following hypotheses were considered.

$H_0$: The two populations are identical in terms of academic potential

$H_a$: The two populations are not identical in terms of academic potential

TABLE 19.5   HIGH SCHOOL CLASS STANDING DATA

| Garfield Students | | Mulberry Students | |
|---|---|---|---|
| **Student** | **Class Standing** | **Student** | **Class Standing** |
| Fields | 8 | Hart | 70 |
| Clark | 52 | Phipps | 202 |
| Jones | 112 | Kirkwood | 144 |
| Tibbs | 21 | Abbott | 175 |
| | | Guest | 146 |

Using high school records, Johnston High School administrators selected a random sample of four high school students who attended Garfield Junior High and another random sample of five students who attended Mulberry Junior High. The current high school class standing was recorded for each of the nine students used in the study. The ordinal class standings for the nine students are listed in Table 19.5.

The first step in the MWW procedure is to rank the *combined* data from the two samples from low to high. The lowest value (class standing 8) receives a rank of 1 and the highest value (class standing 202) receives a rank of 9. The ranking of the nine students is given in Table 19.6.

The next step is to sum the ranks for each sample separately. This calculation is shown in Table 19.7. The MWW procedure can use the sum of the ranks for either sample. In the following discussion, we use the sum of the ranks for the sample of four students from Garfield. We denote this sum by the symbol $T$. Thus, for our example, $T = 11$.

Let us consider the properties of the sum of the ranks for the Garfield sample. With four students in the sample, Garfield could have the top four students in the study. If this were the case, $T = 1 + 2 + 3 + 4 = 10$ would be the smallest value possible for the rank sum $T$. Conversely, Garfield could have the bottom four students, in which case $T = 6 + 7 + 8 + 9 = 30$ would be the largest value possible for $T$. Hence, $T$ for the Garfield sample must take a value between 10 and 30.

Note that values of $T$ near 10 imply that Garfield has the significantly better, or higher ranking, students, whereas values of $T$ near 30 imply that Garfield has the significantly weaker, or lower ranking, students. Thus, if the two populations of students were identical in terms of academic potential, we would expect the value of $T$ to be near the average of the two values, or $(10 + 30)/2 = 20$.

Critical values of the MWW $T$ statistic are provided in Table 9 of Appendix B for cases in which both sample sizes are less than or equal to 10. In that table, $n_1$ refers to the sample size corresponding to the sample whose rank sum is being used in the test. The value of $T_L$ is read directly from the table and the value of $T_U$ is computed from equation (19.5).

$$T_U = n_1(n_1 + n_2 + 1) - T_L \qquad \text{(19.5)}$$

TABLE 19.6   RANKING OF HIGH SCHOOL STUDENTS

| Student | Class Standing | Combined Sample Rank | Student | Class Standing | Combined Sample Rank |
|---|---|---|---|---|---|
| Fields | 8 | 1 | Kirkwood | 144 | 6 |
| Tibbs | 21 | 2 | Guest | 146 | 7 |
| Clark | 52 | 3 | Abbott | 175 | 8 |
| Hart | 70 | 4 | Phipps | 202 | 9 |
| Jones | 112 | 5 | | | |

**TABLE 19.7** RANK SUMS FOR HIGH SCHOOL STUDENTS FROM EACH JUNIOR HIGH SCHOOL

| | Garfield Students | | | Mulberry Students | |
|---|---|---|---|---|---|
| Student | Class Standing | Sample Rank | Student | Class Standing | Sample Rank |
| Fields | 8 | 1 | Hart | 70 | 4 |
| Clark | 52 | 3 | Phipps | 202 | 9 |
| Jones | 112 | 5 | Kirkwood | 144 | 6 |
| Tibbs | 21 | 2 | Abbott | 175 | 8 |
| | | | Guest | 146 | 7 |
| Sum of Ranks | | 11 | | | 34 |

Neither the value of $T_L$ nor the value of $T_U$ is in the rejection region. The null hypothesis of identical populations should be rejected only if $T$ is strictly less than $T_L$ or strictly greater than $T_U$.

For example, using Table 9 of Appendix B with a .05 level of significance, we see that the lower tail critical value for the MWW statistic with $n_1 = 4$ (Garfield) and $n_2 = 5$ (Mulberry) is $T_L = 12$. The upper tail critical value for the MWW statistic computed by using equation (19.5) is

$$T_U = 4(4 + 5 + 1) - 12 = 28$$

Thus, the MWW decision rule indicates that the null hypothesis of identical populations can be rejected if the sum of the ranks for the first sample (Garfield) is less than 12 or greater than 28. The rejection rule can be written as

$$\text{Reject } H_0 \text{ if } T < 12 \text{ or if } T > 28$$

*If we conducted the test with the rank sum of the Mulberry students, we would have $n_1 = 5$, $n_2 = 4$, $T_L = 17$, $T_U = 33$, and $T = 34$. With $T > T_U$, we would reach the same conclusion to reject $H_0$.*

Referring to Table 19.7, we see that $T = 11$. Hence, the null hypothesis $H_0$ is rejected, and we can conclude that the population of students at Garfield differs from the population of students at Mulberry in terms of academic potential. The higher class ranking obtained by the sample of Garfield students suggests that Garfield students are better prepared for high school than the Mulberry students.

## Large-Sample Case

When both sample sizes are greater than or equal to 10, a normal approximation of the distribution of $T$ can be used to conduct the analysis for the MWW test. We illustrate the large-sample case by considering a situation at Third National Bank.

Third National Bank has two branch offices. Data collected from two independent simple random samples, one from each branch, are given in Table 19.8. Do the data indicate whether the populations of checking account balances at the two branch banks are identical?

The first step in the MWW test is to rank the *combined* data from the lowest to the highest values. Using the combined set of 22 observations in Table 19.8, we find the lowest data value of $750$ (sixth item of sample 2) and assign to it a rank of 1. Continuing the ranking gives us the following list.

| Balance ($) | Item | Assigned Rank |
|---|---|---|
| 750 | 6th of sample 2 | 1 |
| 800 | 5th of sample 2 | 2 |
| 805 | 7th of sample 1 | 3 |

| Balance ($) | Item | Assigned Rank |
|:---:|:---:|:---:|
| 850 | 2nd of sample 2 | 4 |
| . | . | . |
| . | . | . |
| . | . | . |
| 1195 | 4th of sample 1 | 21 |
| 1200 | 3rd of sample 1 | 22 |

In ranking the combined data, we may find that two or more data values are the same. In that case, the tied values are given the *average* ranking of their positions in the combined data set. For example, the balance of $945 (eighth item of sample 1) will be assigned the rank of 11. However, the next two values in the data set are tied with values of $950 (see the sixth item of sample 1 and the fourth item of sample 2). Because these two values will be considered for assigned ranks of 12 and 13, they are both assigned the rank of 12.5. At the next highest data value of $955, we continue the ranking process by assigning $955 the rank of 14. Table 19.9 is the entire data set with the assigned rank of each observation.

The next step in the MWW test is to sum the ranks for each sample. The sums are given in Table 19.9. The test procedure can be based on the sum of the ranks for either sample. We use the sum of the ranks for the sample from branch 1. Thus, for this example, $T = 169.5$.

Given that the sample sizes are $n_1 = 12$ and $n_2 = 10$, we can use the normal approximation to the sampling distribution of the rank sum $T$. The appropriate sampling distribution is given by the following expressions.

---

**SAMPLING DISTRIBUTION OF $T$ FOR IDENTICAL POPULATIONS**

$$\text{Mean: } \mu_T = \tfrac{1}{2} n_1(n_1 + n_2 + 1) \tag{19.6}$$

$$\text{Standard Deviation: } \sigma_T = \sqrt{\tfrac{1}{12} n_1 n_2 (n_1 + n_2 + 1)} \tag{19.7}$$

Distribution form: approximately normal provided $n_1 \geq 10$ and $n_2 \geq 10$.

---

**TABLE 19.8   ACCOUNT BALANCES FOR TWO BRANCHES OF THIRD NATIONAL BANK**

| Branch 1 | | Branch 2 | |
|:---:|:---:|:---:|:---:|
| Account | Balance ($) | Account | Balance ($) |
| 1 | 1095 | 1 | 885 |
| 2 | 955 | 2 | 850 |
| 3 | 1200 | 3 | 915 |
| 4 | 1195 | 4 | 950 |
| 5 | 925 | 5 | 800 |
| 6 | 950 | 6 | 750 |
| 7 | 805 | 7 | 865 |
| 8 | 945 | 8 | 1000 |
| 9 | 875 | 9 | 1050 |
| 10 | 1055 | 10 | 935 |
| 11 | 1025 | | |
| 12 | 975 | | |

TABLE 19.9   COMBINED RANKING OF THE DATA IN THE TWO SAMPLES FROM THIRD NATIONAL BANK

| | Branch 1 | | | Branch 2 | |
| Account | Balance ($) | Rank | Account | Balance ($) | Rank |
|---|---|---|---|---|---|
| 1 | 1095 | 20 | 1 | 885 | 7 |
| 2 | 955 | 14 | 2 | 850 | 4 |
| 3 | 1200 | 22 | 3 | 915 | 8 |
| 4 | 1195 | 21 | 4 | 950 | 12.5 |
| 5 | 925 | 9 | 5 | 800 | 2 |
| 6 | 950 | 12.5 | 6 | 750 | 1 |
| 7 | 805 | 3 | 7 | 865 | 5 |
| 8 | 945 | 11 | 8 | 1000 | 16 |
| 9 | 875 | 6 | 9 | 1050 | 18 |
| 10 | 1055 | 19 | 10 | 935 | 10 |
| 11 | 1025 | 17 | | Sum of Ranks | 83.5 |
| 12 | 975 | 15 | | | |
| | Sum of Ranks | 169.5 | | | |

For branch 1, we have

$$\mu_T = \tfrac{1}{2} 12(12 + 10 + 1) = 138$$
$$\sigma_T = \sqrt{\tfrac{1}{12} 12(10)(12 + 10 + 1)} = 15.17$$

Figure 19.4 is the sampling distribution of $T$. Let us proceed with the MWW test and use a .05 level of significance to draw a conclusion. With the sum of the ranks for branch 1 $T = 169.5$, we calculate the following value for the test statistic.

$$z = \frac{T - \mu_T}{\sigma_T} = \frac{169.5 - 138}{15.17} = 2.08$$

FIGURE 19.4   SAMPLING DISTRIBUTION OF $T$ FOR THE THIRD NATIONAL BANK EXAMPLE

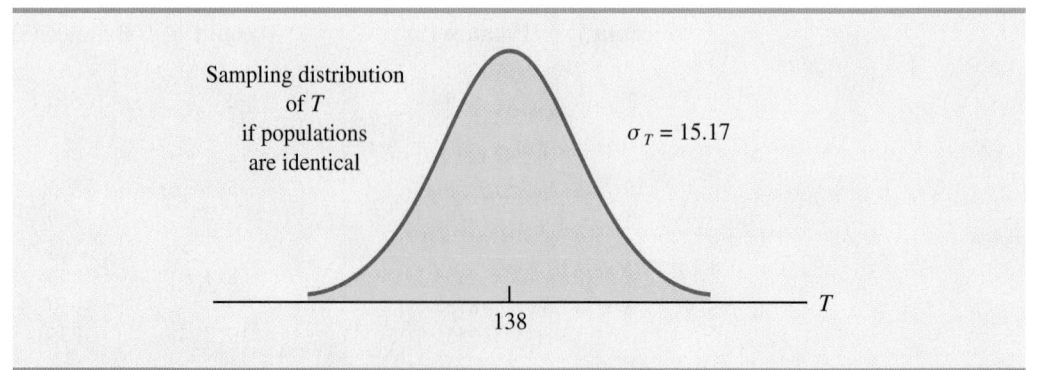

Sampling distribution of $T$ if populations are identical

$\sigma_T = 15.17$

138

$T$

Using the standard normal distribution table and $z = 2.08$, we find the two-tailed $p$-value $= 2(.5000 - .4812) = .0376$. With $p$-value $\leq \alpha = .05$, we reject $H_0$ and conclude the two populations are not identical; that is, the populations of account balances at the branch banks are not the same.

In summary, the Mann-Whitney-Wilcoxon rank-sum test consists of the following steps to determine whether two independent random samples are selected from identical populations.

1. Rank the combined sample observations from lowest to highest, with tied values being assigned the average of the tied rankings.
2. Compute $T$, the sum of the ranks for the first sample.
3. In the large-sample case, make the test for significant differences between the two populations by using the observed value of $T$ and comparing it to the sampling distribution of $T$ for identical populations using equations (19.6) and (19.7). The value of the standardized test statistic $z$ and the $p$-value provide the basis for deciding whether to reject $H_0$. In the small-sample case, use Table 9 in Appendix B to find the critical values for the test.

## NOTES AND COMMENTS

The nonparametric test discussed in this section is used to determine whether two populations are identical. The parametric statistical tests described in Chapter 10 test the equality of two population means. When we reject the hypothesis that the means are equal, we conclude that the populations differ in their means. When we reject the hypothesis that the populations are identical by using the MWW test, we cannot state how they differ. The populations could have different means, different medians, different variances, or different forms. Nonetheless, if we believe that the populations are the same in every aspect but the means, a rejection of $H_0$ by the nonparametric method implies that the means differ.

## Exercises

## Applications

18. Two fuel additives are being tested to determine their effect on gas mileage. Seven cars were tested with additive 1 and nine cars were tested with additive 2. The following data show the miles per gallon obtained with the two additives. Use $\alpha = .05$ and the MWW test to see whether there is a significant difference in gasoline mileage for the two additives.

| Additive 1 | Additive 2 |
|------------|------------|
| 17.3 | 18.7 |
| 18.4 | 17.8 |
| 19.1 | 21.3 |
| 16.7 | 21.0 |
| 18.2 | 22.1 |
| 18.6 | 18.7 |
| 17.5 | 19.8 |
| | 20.7 |
| | 20.2 |

19. Samples of starting annual salaries for individuals entering the public accounting and financial planning professions follow (*Fortune*, June 26, 1995). Annual salaries are shown in thousands of dollars.

| Public Accountant | Financial Planner | Public Accountant | Financial Planner |
|---|---|---|---|
| 25.2 | 24.0 | 30.0 | 28.6 |
| 33.8 | 24.2 | 25.9 | 24.7 |
| 31.3 | 28.1 | 34.5 | 28.9 |
| 33.2 | 30.9 | 31.7 | 26.8 |
| 29.2 | 26.9 | 26.9 | 23.9 |

a. Use a .05 level of significance and test the hypothesis that there is no difference between the starting annual salaries of public accountants and financial planners. What is your conclusion?
b. What are the sample mean annual salaries for the two professions?

20. The gap between the earnings of men and women with equal education is narrowing but has not closed (*USA Today*, September 15, 2000). Sample data for seven men and seven women with bachelor's degrees are as follows. Data are shown in thousands of dollars.

| Men | 30.6 | 75.5 | 45.2 | 62.2 | 38.2 | 49.9 | 55.3 |
|---|---|---|---|---|---|---|---|
| **Women** | 44.5 | 35.4 | 27.9 | 40.5 | 25.8 | 47.5 | 24.8 |

a. What is the median salary for men? For women?
b. Use $\alpha = .05$ and conduct the hypothesis test for equal populations. What is your conclusion?

21. Mileage performance tests were conducted for two models of automobiles. Twelve automobiles of each model were selected randomly and a miles-per-gallon rating for each model was developed on the basis of 1000 miles of highway driving. The data follow.

| Model 1 | | Model 2 | |
|---|---|---|---|
| **Automobile** | **Miles per Gallon** | **Automobile** | **Miles per Gallon** |
| 1 | 20.6 | 1 | 21.3 |
| 2 | 19.9 | 2 | 17.6 |
| 3 | 18.6 | 3 | 17.4 |
| 4 | 18.9 | 4 | 18.5 |
| 5 | 18.8 | 5 | 19.7 |
| 6 | 20.2 | 6 | 21.1 |
| 7 | 21.0 | 7 | 17.3 |
| 8 | 20.5 | 8 | 18.8 |
| 9 | 19.8 | 9 | 17.8 |
| 10 | 19.8 | 10 | 16.9 |
| 11 | 19.2 | 11 | 18.0 |
| 12 | 20.5 | 12 | 20.1 |

Use $\alpha = .10$ and test for a significant difference in the populations of miles-per-gallon ratings for the two models.

22. *Business Week* annually publishes statistics on the world's 1000 largest companies. A company's price/earnings (P/E) ratio is the company's current stock price divided by the latest 12 months' earnings per share. Listed in Table 19.10 are the P/E ratios for a sample of 10 Japanese and 12 U.S. companies. Is the difference in P/E ratios between the two countries significant? Use the MWW test and $\alpha = .01$ to support your conclusion.

**TABLE 19.10    P/E RATIOS FOR JAPANESE AND U.S. COMPANIES**

| Japan | | United States | |
|---|---|---|---|
| **Company** | **P/E Ratio** | **Company** | **P/E Ratio** |
| Sumitomo Corp. | 153 | Gannet | 19 |
| Kinden | 21 | Motorola | 24 |
| Heiwa | 18 | Schlumberger | 24 |
| NCR Japan | 125 | Oracle Systems | 43 |
| Suzuki Motor | 31 | Gap | 22 |
| Fuji Bank | 213 | Winn-Dixie | 14 |
| Sumitomo Chemical | 64 | Ingersoll-Rand | 21 |
| Seibu Railway | 666 | American Electric Power | 14 |
| Shiseido | 33 | Hercules | 21 |
| Toho Gas | 68 | Times Mirror | 38 |
| | | WellPoint Health | 15 |
| | | Northern States Power | 14 |

23. Police records show the following numbers of daily crime reports for a sample of days during the winter months and a sample of days during the summer months. Use a .05 level of significance to determine whether there is a significant difference between the winter and summer months in terms of the number of crime reports.

| Winter | Summer |
|---|---|
| 18 | 28 |
| 20 | 18 |
| 15 | 24 |
| 16 | 32 |
| 21 | 18 |
| 20 | 29 |
| 12 | 23 |
| 16 | 38 |
| 19 | 28 |
| 20 | 18 |

24. A certain brand of microwave oven was priced at 10 stores in Dallas and 13 stores in San Antonio. The data follow. Use a .05 level of significance and test whether prices for the microwave oven are the same in the two cities.

| Dallas | San Antonio |
|---|---|
| 445 | 460 |
| 489 | 451 |
| 405 | 435 |
| 485 | 479 |
| 439 | 475 |
| 449 | 445 |
| 436 | 429 |
| 420 | 434 |
| 430 | 410 |
| 405 | 422 |
| | 425 |
| | 459 |
| | 430 |

25. The National Association of Home Builders provided data on the cost of the most popular home remodeling projects. Use the Mann-Whitney-Wilcoxon test to see whether it can be concluded that the cost of kitchen remodeling differs from the cost of master bedroom remodeling. Use a .05 level of significance.

| Kitchen | Master Bedroom |
|---------|----------------|
| 25,200 | 18,000 |
| 17,400 | 22,900 |
| 22,800 | 26,400 |
| 21,900 | 24,800 |
| 19,700 | 26,900 |
| 23,000 | 17,800 |
| 19,700 | 24,600 |
| 16,900 | 21,000 |
| 21,800 | |
| 23,600 | |

# 19.4 Kruskal-Wallis Test

The MWW test in Section 19.3 can be used to test whether two populations are identical. Kruskal and Wallis extended the test to the case of three or more populations. The hypotheses for the **Kruskal-Wallis test** with $k \geq 3$ populations can be written as follows.

$$H_0: \text{All populations are identical}$$
$$H_a: \text{Not all populations are identical}$$

The Kruskal-Wallis test is based on the analysis of independent random samples from each of the $k$ populations.

In Chapter 13 we showed that analysis of variance (ANOVA) can be used to test for the equality of means among three or more populations. The ANOVA procedure requires interval or ratio data and the assumption that the $k$ populations are normally distributed.

The nonparametric Kruskal-Wallis test can be used with ordinal data as well as with interval or ratio data. In addition, the Kruskal-Wallis test does not require the assumption of normally distributed populations. Hence, whenever the data from $k \geq 3$ populations are ordinal, or whenever the assumption of normally distributed populations is questionable, the Kruskal-Wallis test provides an alternate statistical procedure for testing whether the populations are identical. We demonstrate the Kruskal-Wallis test by using it in an employee selection application.

*This test is an alternative to ANOVA in Chapter 13, which focused on the equality of the means of k populations.*

Williams Manufacturing Company hires employees for its management staff from three local colleges. Recently, the company's personnel department began collecting and reviewing annual performance ratings in an attempt to determine whether there are differences in performance among the managers hired from these colleges. Performance rating data are available from independent samples of seven employees from college A, six employees from college B, and seven employees from college C. These data are summarized in Table 19.11; the overall performance rating of each manager is given on a 0–100 scale, with 100 being the highest possible performance rating.

Suppose we want to test whether the three populations are identical in terms of performance evaluations. We will use a .05 level of significance. The Kruskal-Wallis test statistic, which is based on the sum of ranks for each of the samples, can be computed as follows.

**TABLE 19.11**

PERFORMANCE EVALUATION RATINGS FOR 20 WILLIAMS EMPLOYEES

| College A | College B | College C |
|-----------|-----------|-----------|
| 25 | 60 | 50 |
| 70 | 20 | 70 |
| 60 | 30 | 60 |
| 85 | 15 | 80 |
| 95 | 40 | 90 |
| 90 | 35 | 70 |
| 80 | | 75 |

KRUSKAL-WALLIS TEST STATISTIC

$$W = \left[ \frac{12}{n_T(n_T + 1)} \sum_{i=1}^{k} \frac{R_i^2}{n_i} \right] - 3(n_T + 1) \qquad (19.8)$$

where

$$k = \text{the number of populations}$$
$$n_i = \text{the number of items in sample } i$$
$$n_T = \Sigma n_i = \text{total number of items in all samples}$$
$$R_i = \text{sum of the ranks for sample } i$$

Kruskal and Wallis were able to show that, under the null hypothesis in which the populations are identical, the sampling distribution of $W$ can be approximated by a chi-square distribution with $k - 1$ degrees of freedom. This approximation is generally acceptable if each of the sample sizes is greater than or equal to five. The null hypothesis of identical populations will be rejected if the test statistic is large. As a result, the procedure uses an upper tail test.

*The Kruskal-Wallis test uses only the ordinal rank of the data.*

To compute the $W$ statistic for our example, we must first rank all 20 data items. The lowest data value of 15 from the college B sample receives a rank of 1, whereas the highest data value of 95 from the college A sample receives a rank of 20. The data values, their associated ranks, and the sum of the ranks for the three samples are given in Table 19.12. Note that we assign the average rank to tied items;* for example, the data values of 60, 70, 80, and 90 had ties.

The sample sizes are

$$n_1 = 7 \qquad n_2 = 6 \qquad n_3 = 7$$

and

$$n_T = \Sigma n_i = 7 + 6 + 7 = 20$$

We compute the $W$ statistic by using equation (19.8).

$$W = \frac{12}{20(21)} \left[ \frac{(95)^2}{7} + \frac{(27)^2}{6} + \frac{(88)^2}{7} \right] - 3(20 + 1) = 8.92$$

*The computer procedures in Appendixes 11.1 and 11.2 show how Minitab and Excel can be used to compute the p-value.*

We can now use the chi-square distribution table (Table 3 of Appendix B) to determine the $p$-value for the test. Using $k - 1 = 3 - 1 = 2$ degrees of freedom, we find $\chi^2 = 7.378$ has an area of .025 in the upper tail of the distribution and $\chi^2 = 9.21$ has an area of .01 in the upper tail distribution. With $W = 8.92$ between 7.378 and 9.21, we can conclude that the area in the upper tail of the distribution is between .025 and .01. Because it is an upper tail test, we can conclude that the $p$-value is between .025 and .01. Minitab or Excel will show $p$-value $= .0116$. Because $p$-value $\leq \alpha = .05$, we reject $H_0$ and conclude that the three populations are not identical. Manager performance differs significantly depending

---

*If numerous tied ranks are observed, equation (19.8) must be modified; the modified formula is given in *Practical Nonparametric Statistics* by W. J. Conover.

**TABLE 19.12    COMBINED RANKINGS FOR THE 20 WILLIAMS EMPLOYEES**

| College A | Rank | College B | Rank | College C | Rank |
|-----------|------|-----------|------|-----------|------|
| 25 | 3 | 60 | 9 | 50 | 7 |
| 70 | 12 | 20 | 2 | 70 | 12 |
| 60 | 9 | 30 | 4 | 60 | 9 |
| 85 | 17 | 15 | 1 | 80 | 15.5 |
| 95 | 20 | 40 | 6 | 90 | 18.5 |
| 90 | 18.5 | 35 | 5 | 70 | 12 |
| 80 | 15.5 | | | 75 | 14 |
| Sum of Ranks | 95 | | 27 | | 88 |

on the college attended. Furthermore, because the performance ratings are lowest for college B, it would be reasonable for the company to either cut back recruiting from college B or at least evaluate its graduates more thoroughly.

## NOTES AND COMMENTS

The Kruskal-Wallis procedure illustrated in the example began with the collection of interval-scaled data showing employee performance evaluation ratings. The procedure also would work if the data were the ordinal rankings of the 20 employees. In that case, the Kruskal-Wallis test could be applied directly to the original data; the step of constructing the rank orderings from the performance evaluation ratings would be omitted.

## Exercises

## Methods

26.   Three products received the following performance ratings by a panel of 15 consumers.

| | Product | |
|---|---|---|
| **A** | **B** | **C** |
| 50 | 80 | 60 |
| 62 | 95 | 45 |
| 75 | 98 | 30 |
| 48 | 87 | 58 |
| 65 | 90 | 57 |

Use the Kruskal-Wallis test and $\alpha = .05$ to determine whether there is a significant difference in the performance ratings for the products.

27.   Three admission test preparation programs are being evaluated. The scores obtained by a sample of 20 people who used the test preparation programs provided the following data. Use the Kruskal-Wallis test to determine whether there is a significant difference among the three test preparation programs. Use $\alpha = .01$.

|         | Program |         |
|---------|---------|---------|
| **A**   | **B**   | **C**   |
| 540     | 450     | 600     |
| 400     | 540     | 630     |
| 490     | 400     | 580     |
| 530     | 410     | 490     |
| 490     | 480     | 590     |
| 610     | 370     | 620     |
|         | 550     | 570     |

## Applications

28. Forty-minute workouts of one of the following activities three days a week will lead to a loss of weight. The following sample data show the number of calories burned during 40-minute workouts for three different activities. Do these data indicate differences in the amount of calories burned for the three activities? Use a .05 level of significance. What is your conclusion?

| **Swimming** | **Tennis** | **Cycling** |
|--------------|------------|-------------|
| 408          | 415        | 385         |
| 380          | 485        | 250         |
| 425          | 450        | 295         |
| 400          | 420        | 402         |
| 427          | 530        | 268         |

29. The miles-per-gallon data obtained from tests on three different automobiles are reported as follows. Use the Kruskal-Wallis test with $\alpha = .05$ to determine whether there is a significant difference in the gasoline mileage for the three automobiles.

|       | Automobile |       |
|-------|------------|-------|
| **A** | **B**      | **C** |
| 19    | 19         | 24    |
| 21    | 20         | 26    |
| 20    | 22         | 23    |
| 19    | 21         | 25    |
| 21    | 23         | 27    |

30. A large corporation sends many of its first-level managers to an off-site supervisory skills course. Four different management development centers offer this course, and the corporation wants to determine whether they differ in the quality of training provided. A sample of 20 employees who attended these programs is chosen and the employees ranked in terms of supervisory skills. The results follow.

| **Course** | **Supervisory Skills Rank** |    |    |    |    |
|------------|-----|-----|-----|-----|-----|
| 1          | 3   | 14  | 10  | 12  | 13  |
| 2          | 2   | 7   | 1   | 5   | 11  |
| 3          | 19  | 16  | 9   | 18  | 17  |
| 4          | 20  | 4   | 15  | 6   | 8   |

Note that the top-ranked supervisor attended course 2 and the lowest-ranked supervisor attended course 4. Use $\alpha = .05$ and test to see whether there is a significant difference in the training provided by the four programs.

31. The better-selling candies are high in calories. Assume that the following data show the calorie content from samples of M&Ms, Kit Kat, and Milky Way II. Test for significant differences in the calorie content of these three candies. At a .05 level of significance, what is your conclusion?

| M&Ms | Kit Kat | Milky Way II |
|------|---------|--------------|
| 230 | 225 | 200 |
| 210 | 205 | 208 |
| 240 | 245 | 202 |
| 250 | 235 | 190 |
| 230 | 220 | 180 |

# Rank Correlation

*The Spearman rank-correlation coefficient is equal to the Pearson correlation coefficient applied to ordinal or rank data.*

The correlation coefficient is a measure of the linear association between two variables for which interval or ratio data are available. In this section, we consider measures of association between two variables when only ordinal data are available. The **Spearman rank-correlation coefficient** $r_s$ has been developed for this purpose.

SPEARMAN RANK-CORRELATION COEFFICIENT

$$r_s = 1 - \frac{6\Sigma d_i^2}{n(n^2 - 1)} \qquad (19.9)$$

where

$n$ = the number of items or individuals being ranked
$x_i$ = the rank of item $i$ with respect to one variable
$y_i$ = the rank of item $i$ with respect to a second variable
$d_i = x_i - y_i$

Let us illustrate the use of the Spearman rank-correlation coefficient with an example. A company wants to determine whether individuals who were expected at the time of employment to be better salespersons actually turn out to have better sales records. To investigate this question, the vice president in charge of personnel carefully reviewed the original job interview summaries, academic records, and letters of recommendation for 10 current members of the firm's salesforce. After the review, the vice president ranked the 10 individuals in terms of their potential for success, basing the assessment solely on the information available at the time of employment. Then a list was obtained of the number of units sold by each salesperson over the first two years. On the basis of actual sales performance, a second ranking of the 10 salespersons was carried out. Table 19.13 gives the relevant data

**TABLE 19.13   SALES POTENTIAL AND ACTUAL TWO-YEAR SALES DATA FOR 10 SALESPEOPLE**

| Salesperson | Ranking of Potential | Two-Year Sales (units) | Ranking According to Two-Year Sales |
|---|---|---|---|
| A | 2 | 400 | 1 |
| B | 4 | 360 | 3 |
| C | 7 | 300 | 5 |
| D | 1 | 295 | 6 |
| E | 6 | 280 | 7 |
| F | 3 | 350 | 4 |
| G | 10 | 200 | 10 |
| H | 9 | 260 | 8 |
| I | 8 | 220 | 9 |
| J | 5 | 385 | 2 |

and the two rankings. The statistical question is whether there is agreement between the ranking of potential at the time of employment and the ranking based on the actual sales performance over the first two years.

Let us compute the Spearman rank-correlation coefficient for the data in Table 19.13. The computations are summarized in Table 19.14. We see that the rank-correlation coefficient is a positive .73. The Spearman rank-correlation coefficient ranges from $-1.0$ to $+1.0$ and its interpretation is similar to that of the sample correlation coefficient in that positive values near 1.0 indicate a strong association between the rankings; as one rank increases, the other rank increases. Rank correlations near $-1.0$ indicate a strong negative association between the rankings; as one rank increases, the other rank decreases. The value $r_s = .73$ indicates a positive correlation between potential and actual performance. Individuals ranked high on potential tend to rank high on performance.

**TABLE 19.14   COMPUTATION OF THE SPEARMAN RANK-CORRELATION COEFFICIENT FOR SALES POTENTIAL AND SALES PERFORMANCE**

| Salesperson | $x_i$ = Ranking of Potential | $y_i$ = Ranking of Sales Performance | $d_i = x_i - y_i$ | $d_i^2$ |
|---|---|---|---|---|
| A | 2 | 1 | 1 | 1 |
| B | 4 | 3 | 1 | 1 |
| C | 7 | 5 | 2 | 4 |
| D | 1 | 6 | $-5$ | 25 |
| E | 6 | 7 | $-1$ | 1 |
| F | 3 | 4 | $-1$ | 1 |
| G | 10 | 10 | 0 | 0 |
| H | 9 | 8 | 1 | 1 |
| I | 8 | 9 | $-1$ | 1 |
| J | 5 | 2 | 3 | 9 |
| | | | | $\Sigma d_i^2 = 44$ |

$$r_s = 1 - \frac{6\Sigma d_i^2}{n(n^2 - 1)} = 1 - \frac{6(44)}{10(100 - 1)} = .73$$

## Test for Significant Rank Correlation

At this point, we have seen how sample results can be used to compute the sample rank-correlation coefficient. As with many other statistical procedures, we may want to use the sample results to make an inference about the population rank correlation $\rho_s$. To make an inference about the population rank correlation, we must test the following hypotheses.

$$H_0: \rho_s = 0$$
$$H_a: \rho_s \neq 0$$

Under the null hypothesis of no rank correlation ($\rho_s = 0$), the rankings are independent, and the sampling distribution of $r_s$ is as follows.

---

SAMPLING DISTRIBUTION OF $r_s$

$$\text{Mean: } \mu_{r_s} = 0 \qquad\qquad (19.10)$$

$$\text{Standard Deviation: } \sigma_{r_s} = \sqrt{\frac{1}{n-1}}$$

Distribution form: approximately normal provided $n \geq 10$.

---

The sample rank-correlation coefficient for sales potential and sales performance is $r_s = .73$. With this value, we can test for a significant rank correlation. From equation (19.10) we have $\mu_{r_s} = 0$ and from (19.11) we have $\sigma_{r_s} = \sqrt{1/(10-1)} = .33$. Using the test statistic, we have

$$z = \frac{r_s - \mu_{r_s}}{\sigma_{r_s}} = \frac{.73 - 0}{.33} = 2.20$$

Using the standard normal distribution table and $z = 2.20$, we find the $p$-value $= 2(.5000 - .4861) = .0278$. With a .05 level of significance, $p$-value $\leq \alpha = .05$ leads to the rejection of the hypothesis that the rank correlation is zero. Thus, we can conclude that there is a significant rank correlation between sales potential and sales performance.

---

## Exercises

## Methods

32. Consider the following set of rankings for a sample of 10 elements.

| Element | $x_i$ | $y_i$ | Element | $x_i$ | $y_i$ |
|---------|-------|-------|---------|-------|-------|
| 1 | 10 | 8 | 6 | 2 | 7 |
| 2 | 6 | 4 | 7 | 8 | 6 |
| 3 | 7 | 10 | 8 | 5 | 3 |
| 4 | 3 | 2 | 9 | 1 | 1 |
| 5 | 4 | 5 | 10 | 9 | 9 |

a. Compute the Spearman rank-correlation coefficient for the data.
b. Use $\alpha = .05$ and test for significant rank correlation. What is your conclusion?

33.   Consider the following two sets of rankings for six items.

| | Case One | | | Case Two | |
|---|---|---|---|---|---|
| **Item** | **First Ranking** | **Second Ranking** | **Item** | **First Ranking** | **Second Ranking** |
| A | 1 | 1 | A | 1 | 6 |
| B | 2 | 2 | B | 2 | 5 |
| C | 3 | 3 | C | 3 | 4 |
| D | 4 | 4 | D | 4 | 3 |
| E | 5 | 5 | E | 5 | 2 |
| F | 6 | 6 | F | 6 | 1 |

Note that in the first case the rankings are identical, whereas in the second case the rankings are exactly opposite. What value should you expect for the Spearman rank-correlation coefficient for each of these cases? Explain. Calculate the rank-correlation coefficient for each case.

## Applications

34.   For a sample of 11 states, the following table gives the ranks on pupil-teacher ratio (1 = lowest, 11 = highest) and expenditure per pupil (1 = highest, 11 = lowest).

| | Rank | | | Rank | |
|---|---|---|---|---|---|
| **State** | **Pupil-Teacher Ratio** | **Expenditure per Pupil** | **State** | **Pupil-Teacher Ratio** | **Expenditure per Pupil** |
| Arizona | 10 | 9 | Massachusetts | 1 | 1 |
| Colorado | 8 | 5 | Nebraska | 2 | 7 |
| Florida | 6 | 4 | North Dakota | 7 | 8 |
| Idaho | 11 | 2 | South Dakota | 5 | 10 |
| Iowa | 4 | 6 | Washington | 9 | 3 |
| Louisiana | 3 | 11 | | | |

At the $\alpha = .05$ level, does there appear to be a relationship between expenditure per pupil and pupil-teacher ratio?

35.   A national study by Harris Interactive, Inc., evaluated the top Internet companies and their reputations (*The Wall Street Journal,* November 18, 1999). The following two lists show how 10 Internet companies ranked in terms of reputation and percentage of respondents who said they would purchase the company's stock. A positive rank correlation is anticipated because it seems reasonable to expect that a company with a higher reputation would be a more desirable purchase.

| | **Reputation** | **Probable Purchase** |
|---|---|---|
| Microsoft | 1 | 3 |
| Intel | 2 | 4 |
| Dell | 3 | 1 |
| Lucent | 4 | 2 |
| Texas Instruments | 5 | 9 |
| Cisco Systems | 6 | 5 |
| Hewlett-Packard | 7 | 10 |
| IBM | 8 | 6 |
| Motorola | 9 | 7 |
| Yahoo | 10 | 8 |

a.  Compute the rank correlation between reputation and probable purchase.
b.  Test for a significant positive rank correlation. What is the $p$-value?
c.  At $\alpha = .05$, what is your conclusion?

36. The 1996 rankings of a sample of professional golfers in both driving distance and putting follows (*Golf Digest,* January 1997). What is the rank correlation between driving distance and putting? Use a .10 level of significance.

| Professional Golfer | Driving Distance | Putting |
|---|---|---|
| Fred Couples | 1 | 5 |
| David Duval | 5 | 6 |
| Ernie Els | 4 | 10 |
| Nick Faldo | 9 | 2 |
| Tom Lehman | 6 | 7 |
| Justin Leonard | 10 | 3 |
| Davis Love III | 2 | 8 |
| Phil Mickelson | 3 | 9 |
| Greg Norman | 7 | 4 |
| Mark O'Meara | 8 | 1 |

37. A student organization surveyed both recent graduates and current students to obtain information on the quality of teaching at a particular university. An analysis of the responses provided the following teaching-ability rankings. Do the rankings given by the current students agree with the rankings given by the recent graduates? Use $\alpha = .10$ and test for a significant rank correlation.

| Professor | Ranking by Current Students | Ranking by Recent Graduates |
|---|---|---|
| 1 | 4 | 6 |
| 2 | 6 | 8 |
| 3 | 8 | 5 |
| 4 | 3 | 1 |
| 5 | 1 | 2 |
| 6 | 2 | 3 |
| 7 | 5 | 7 |
| 8 | 10 | 9 |
| 9 | 7 | 4 |
| 10 | 9 | 10 |

## Summary

In this chapter we presented several statistical procedures that are classified as nonparametric methods. Because nonparametric methods can be applied to nominal and ordinal data as well as interval and ratio data and do not require population distribution assumptions, they expand the class of problems that can be subjected to statistical analysis.

The sign test is a nonparametric procedure for identifying differences between two populations when the only data available are nominal data. In the small-sample case, the binominal probability distribution can be used to determine the critical values for the sign test;

in the large-sample case, a normal approximation can be used. The Wilcoxon signed-rank test is a procedure for analyzing matched-sample data whenever interval- or ratio-scaled data are available for each matched pair. No assumptions are made about the population distribution. The Wilcoxon procedure tests the hypothesis that the two populations being considered are identical.

The Mann-Whitney-Wilcoxon test is a nonparametric method for testing for a difference between two populations based on two independent random samples. Tables were presented for the small-sample case, and a normal approximation was provided for the large-sample case. The Kruskal-Wallis test extends the Mann-Whitney-Wilcoxon test to the case of three or more populations. The Kruskal-Wallis test is the nonparametric analog of the parametric ANOVA test for differences among population means.

In the last section of this chapter we introduced the Spearman rank-correlation coefficient as a measure of association for two ordinal or rank-ordered sets of items.

## Glossary

**Nonparametric methods** Statistical methods that require few, if any, assumptions about the population probability distributions and the level of measurement. These methods can be applied when nominal or ordinal data are available.

**Sign test** A nonparametric statistical test for identifying differences between two populations based on the analysis of nominal data.

**Wilcoxon signed-rank test** A nonparametric statistical test for identifying differences between two populations based on the analysis of two matched or paired samples.

**Mann-Whitney-Wilcoxon (MWW) test** A nonparametric statistical test for identifying differences between two populations based on the analysis of two independent samples.

**Kruskal-Wallis test** A nonparametric test for identifying differences among three or more populations.

**Spearman rank-correlation coefficient** A correlation measure based on rank-ordered data for two variables.

## Key Formulas

### Sign Test (Large-Sample Case)

$$\text{Mean: } \mu = .50n \tag{19.1}$$

$$\text{Standard Deviation: } \sigma = \sqrt{.25n} \tag{19.2}$$

### Wilcoxon Signed-Rank Test

$$\text{Mean: } \mu_T = 0 \tag{19.3}$$

$$\text{Standard Deviation: } \sigma_T = \sqrt{\frac{n(n+1)(2n+1)}{6}} \tag{19.4}$$

### Mann-Whitney-Wilcoxon Test (Large-Sample)

$$\text{Mean: } \mu_T = \tfrac{1}{2} n_1(n_1 + n_2 + 1) \tag{19.6}$$

$$\text{Standard Deviation: } \sigma_T = \sqrt{\tfrac{1}{12} n_1 n_2(n_1 + n_2 + 1)} \tag{19.7}$$

Kruskal-Wallis Test Statistic

$$W = \left[ \frac{12}{n_T(n_T + 1)} \sum_{i=1}^{k} \frac{R_i^2}{n_i} \right] - 3(n_T + 1) \tag{19.8}$$

Spearman Rank-Correlation Coefficient

$$r_s = 1 - \frac{6\Sigma d_i^2}{n(n^2 - 1)} \tag{19.9}$$

## Supplementary Exercises

38. The American Opinion Survey (*The Wall Street Journal,* March 4, 1997) asked the following question: Do you favor or oppose providing tax-funded vouchers or tax deductions to parents who send their children to private schools? Of the 2010 individuals surveyed, 905 favored the support, 1045 opposed the support, and 60 offered no opinion. Do the data indicate a significant difference in the preferences for the support for parents who send their children to private schools? Use a .05 level of significance.

39. The national median sales price of existing one-family homes is $118,000 (*The Wall Street Journal Almanac,* 1998). Assume that the following data were obtained for sales of existing one-family homes in Houston and Boston.

| | Greater than $118,000 | Equal to $118,000 | Less than $118,000 |
|---|---|---|---|
| Houston | 11 | 2 | 32 |
| Boston | 27 | 1 | 13 |

a. Is the median resale price in Houston lower than the national median of $118,000? Use a statistical test with $\alpha = .05$ to support your conclusion.
b. Is the median resale price in Boston higher than the national median of $118,000? Use a statistical test with $\alpha = .05$ to support your conclusion.

40. Twelve homemakers were asked to estimate the retail selling price of two models of refrigerators. Their estimates of selling price are shown in the following table. Use these data and test at the .05 level of significance to determine whether there is a difference between the two models in terms of homemakers' perceptions of selling price.

| Homemaker | Model 1 | Model 2 | Homemaker | Model 1 | Model 2 |
|---|---|---|---|---|---|
| 1 | $650 | $900 | 7 | $700 | $ 890 |
| 2 | 760 | 720 | 8 | 690 | 920 |
| 3 | 740 | 690 | 9 | 900 | 1000 |
| 4 | 700 | 850 | 10 | 500 | 690 |
| 5 | 590 | 920 | 11 | 610 | 700 |
| 6 | 620 | 800 | 12 | 720 | 700 |

41. A study was designed to evaluate the weight-gain potential of a new poultry feed. A sample of 12 chickens was used in a six-week study. The weight of each chicken was recorded before and after the six-week test period. The differences between the before and after weights of the 12 chickens are 1.5, 1.2, −.2, .0, .5, .7, .8, 1.0, .0, .6, .2, −.01. A negative value indicates a weight loss during the test period, whereas .0 indicates no weight change

over the period. Use a .05 level of significance to determine whether the new feed appears to provide a weight gain for the chickens.

42. The following data are product weights for items produced on two production lines. Test for a difference between the product weights for the two lines. Use $\alpha = .10$.

| Production Line 1 | Production Line 2 |
|:---:|:---:|
| 13.6 | 13.7 |
| 13.8 | 14.1 |
| 14.0 | 14.2 |
| 13.9 | 14.0 |
| 13.4 | 14.6 |
| 13.2 | 13.5 |
| 13.3 | 14.4 |
| 13.6 | 14.8 |
| 12.9 | 14.5 |
| 14.4 | 14.3 |
|  | 15.0 |
|  | 14.9 |

43. A client wants to determine whether there is a significant difference in the time required to complete a program evaluation with the three different methods that are in common use. The times (in hours) required for each of 18 evaluators to conduct a program evaluation follow.

| Method 1 | Method 2 | Method 3 |
|:---:|:---:|:---:|
| 68 | 62 | 58 |
| 74 | 73 | 67 |
| 65 | 75 | 69 |
| 76 | 68 | 57 |
| 77 | 72 | 59 |
| 72 | 70 | 62 |

Use $\alpha = .05$ and test to see whether there is a significant difference in the time required by the three methods.

44. A sample of 20 engineers employed with a company for three years has been rank-ordered with respect to managerial potential. Some of the engineers attended the company's management-development course, others attended an off-site management-development program at a local university, and the remainder did not attended any program. Use the following rankings and $\alpha = .025$ to test for a significant difference in the managerial potential of the three groups.

| No Program | Company Program | Off-Site Program |
|:---:|:---:|:---:|
| 16 | 12 | 7 |
| 9 | 20 | 1 |
| 10 | 17 | 4 |
| 15 | 19 | 2 |
| 11 | 6 | 3 |
| 13 | 18 | 8 |
|  | 14 | 5 |

45. Course-evaluation ratings for four instructors follow. Use $\alpha = .05$ and the Kruskal-Wallis procedure to test for a significant difference in teaching abilities.

| Instructor | Course-Evaluation Rating | | | | | | | | |
|---|---|---|---|---|---|---|---|---|---|
| Black | 88 | 80 | 79 | 68 | 96 | 69 | | | |
| Jennings | 87 | 78 | 82 | 85 | 99 | 99 | 85 | 94 | |
| Swanson | 88 | 76 | 68 | 82 | 85 | 82 | 84 | 83 | 81 |
| Wilson | 80 | 85 | 56 | 71 | 89 | 87 | | | |

46. A sample of 15 students received the following rankings on midterm and final examinations in a statistics course.

| Rank | | Rank | | Rank | |
|---|---|---|---|---|---|
| Midterm | Final | Midterm | Final | Midterm | Final |
| 1 | 4 | 6 | 2 | 11 | 14 |
| 2 | 7 | 7 | 5 | 12 | 15 |
| 3 | 1 | 8 | 12 | 13 | 11 |
| 4 | 3 | 9 | 6 | 14 | 10 |
| 5 | 8 | 10 | 9 | 15 | 13 |

Compute the Spearman rank-correlation coefficient for the data and test for a significant correlation with $\alpha = .10$.

# CHAPTER 20

# Statistical Methods for Quality Control

## DOW CHEMICAL U.S.A.*
### *FREEPORT, TEXAS*

Dow Chemical U.S.A., Texas Operations, began in 1940 when The Dow Chemical Company purchased 800 acres of Texas land on the Gulf Coast to build a magnesium production facility. That original site has expanded to cover more than 5000 acres and holds one of the largest petrochemical complexes in the world. Among the products from Texas Operations are magnesium, styrene, plastics, adhesives, solvent, glycol, and chlorine. Some products are made solely for use in other processes, but many end up as essential ingredients in products such as pharmaceuticals, toothpastes, dog food, water hoses, ice chests, milk cartons, garbage bags, shampoos, and furniture.

Dow's Texas Operations produce more than 30% of the world's magnesium, an extremely lightweight metal used in products ranging from tennis racquets to suitcases to "mag" wheels. The Magnesium Department was the first group in Texas Operations to train its technical people and managers in the use of statistical quality control. Some of the earliest successful applications of statistical quality control were in chemical processing.

In one application involving the operation of a drier, samples of the output were taken at periodic intervals; the average value for each sample was computed and recorded on a chart called an $\bar{x}$ chart. Such a chart enabled Dow analysts to monitor trends in the output that might indicate the process was not operating correctly. In one instance, analysts began to observe values for the sample mean that were not indicative of a process

Statistical quality control has enabled Dow Chemical U.S.A. to improve its processing methods and output. © Dan Guravich/Corbis.

operating within its design limits. On further examination of the control chart and the operation itself, the analysts found that the variation could be traced to problems involving one operator. The $\bar{x}$ chart recorded after retraining the operator showed a significant improvement in the process quality.

Dow Chemical achieves quality improvements everywhere it applies statistical quality control. Documented savings of several hundred thousand dollars per year are realized, and new applications are continually being discovered.

In this chapter we will show how an $\bar{x}$ chart such as the one used by Dow Chemical can be developed. Such charts are a part of statistical quality control known as statistical process control. We will also discuss methods of quality control for situations in which a decision to accept or reject a group of items is based on a sample.

---

*The authors are indebted to Clifford B. Wilson, Magnesium Technical Manager, The Dow Chemical Company, for providing this Statistics in Practice.

The American Society for Quality (ASQ) defines *quality* as "the totality of features and characteristics of a product or service that bears on its ability to satisfy given needs." In other words, quality measures how well a product or service meets customer needs. Organizations recognize that to be competitive in today's global economy, they must strive for high levels of quality. As a result, an increased emphasis falls on methods for monitoring and maintaining quality.

*Quality assurance* refers to the entire system of policies, procedures, and guidelines established by an organization to achieve and maintain quality. Quality assurance consists of two principal functions: quality engineering and quality control. The objective of *quality engineering* is to include quality in the design of products and processes and to identify potential quality problems prior to production. **Quality control** consists of making a series of inspections and measurements to determine whether quality standards are being met. If quality standards are not being met, corrective and/or preventive action can be taken to achieve and maintain conformance. As we will show in this chapter, statistical techniques are extremely useful in quality control.

Traditional manufacturing approaches to quality control have been found to be less than satisfactory and are being replaced by improved managerial tools and techniques. Ironically, it was two U.S. consultants, Dr. W. Edwards Deming and Dr. Joseph Juran, who helped educate the Japanese in quality management.

*After World War II, Dr. W. Edwards Deming became a consultant to Japanese industry; he is credited with being the person who convinced top managers in Japan to use the methods of statistical quality control.*

Although quality is everybody's job, Deming stressed that quality must be led by managers. He developed a list of 14 points that he believed are the key responsibilities of managers. For instance, Deming stated that managers must cease dependence on mass inspection; must end the practice of awarding business solely on the basis of price; must seek continual improvement in all production processes and services; must foster a team-oriented environment; and must eliminate numerical goals, slogans, and work standards that prescribe numerical quotas. Perhaps most important, managers must create a work environment in which a commitment to quality and productivity is maintained at all times.

In 1987, the U.S. Congress enacted Public Law 107, the Malcolm Baldrige National Quality Improvement Act. The Baldrige Award is given annually to U.S. firms that excel in quality. This award, along with the perspectives of individuals like Dr. Deming and Dr. Juran, helped top managers recognize that improving service quality and product quality is the most critical challenge facing their companies. Winners of the Malcolm Baldrige Award include Motorola, IBM, Xerox, and FedEx. In this chapter we present two statistical methods used in quality control. The first method, *statistical process control,* uses graphical displays known as *control charts* to monitor a production process; the goal is to determine whether the process can be continued or whether it should be adjusted to achieve a desired quality level. The second method, *acceptance sampling,* is used in situations where a decision to accept or reject a group of items must be based on the quality found in a sample.

## 20.1    Statistical Process Control

In this section we consider quality control procedures for a production process whereby goods are manufactured continuously. On the basis of sampling and inspection of production output, a decision will be made to either continue the production process or adjust it to bring the items or goods being produced up to acceptable quality standards.

*Continuous improvement is one of the most important concepts of the total quality management movement. The most important use of a control chart is in improving the process.*

Despite high standards of quality in manufacturing and production operations, machine tools will invariably wear out, vibrations will throw machine settings out of adjustment, purchased materials will be defective, and human operators will make mistakes. Any or all of these factors can result in poor quality output. Fortunately, procedures are available for monitoring production output so that poor quality can be detected early and the production process can be adjusted or corrected.

If the variation in the quality of the production output is due to **assignable causes** such as tools wearing out, incorrect machine settings, poor quality raw materials, or operator error, the process should be adjusted or corrected as soon as possible. Alternatively, if the variation is due to what are called **common causes**—that is, randomly occurring variations in materials, temperature, humidity, and so on, which the manufacturer cannot possibly control—the process does not need to be adjusted. The main objective of statistical process control is to determine whether variations in output are due to assignable causes or common causes.

Whenever assignable causes are detected, we conclude that the process is *out of control.* In that case, corrective action will be taken to bring the process back to an acceptable level of quality. However, if the variation in the output of a production process is due only to common causes, we conclude that the process is *in statistical control,* or simply *in control;* in such cases, no changes or adjustments are necessary.

*Control charts provide an ongoing test of the hypothesis that the process is in control.*

The statistical procedures for process control are based on the hypothesis testing methodology presented in Chapter 9. The null hypothesis $H_0$ is formulated in terms of the production process being in control. The alternative hypothesis $H_a$ is formulated in terms of the production process being out of control. Table 20.1 shows that correct decisions to continue an in-control process and adjust an out-of-control process are possible. However, as with other hypothesis testing procedures, both a Type I error (adjusting an in-control process) and a Type II error (allowing an out-of-control process to continue) are also possible.

## Control Charts

*Control charts that are based on data that can be measured on a continuous scale are called variables control charts. The $\bar{x}$ chart is a variables control chart.*

A **control chart** provides a basis for deciding whether the variation in the output is due to common causes (in control) or assignable causes (out of control). Whenever an out-of-control situation is detected, adjustments or other corrective action will be taken to bring the process back into control.

Control charts can be classified by the type of data they contain. An $\bar{x}$ **chart** is used if the quality of the output of the process is measured in terms of a variable such as length, weight, temperature, and so on. In that case, the decision to continue or to adjust the production process will be based on the mean value found in a sample of the output. To introduce some of the concepts common to all control charts, let us consider some specific features of an $\bar{x}$ chart.

Figure 20.1 shows the general structure of an $\bar{x}$ chart. The center line of the chart corresponds to the mean of the process when the process is *in control*. The vertical line identifies the scale of measurement for the variable of interest. Each time a sample is taken from the production process, a value of the sample mean $\bar{x}$ is computed and a data point showing the value of $\bar{x}$ is plotted on the control chart.

The two lines labeled UCL and LCL are important in determining whether the process is in control or out of control. The lines are called the *upper control limit* and the *lower control limit,* respectively. They are chosen so that when the process is in control, there will be a high probability that the value of $\bar{x}$ will be between the two control limits. Values outside the control limits provide strong statistical evidence that the process is out of control and corrective action should be taken.

Over time, more and more data points will be added to the control chart. The order of the data points will be from left to right as the process is sampled. In essence, every time a point is plotted on the control chart, we are carrying out a hypothesis test to determine whether the process is in control.

In addition to the $\bar{x}$ chart, other control charts can be used to monitor the range of the measurements in the sample (**R chart**), the proportion defective in the sample (**p chart**), and the number of defective items in the sample (**np chart**). In each case, the control chart has an LCL, a center line, and a UCL similar to the $\bar{x}$ chart in Figure 20.1. The major difference

**TABLE 20.1     THE OUTCOMES OF STATISTICAL PROCESS CONTROL**

| | | State of Production Process | |
| --- | --- | --- | --- |
| | | $H_0$ True<br>Process in Control | $H_0$ False<br>Process Out of Control |
| Decision | **Continue Process** | Correct decision | Type II error<br>(allowing an out-of-control<br>process to continue) |
| | **Adjust Process** | Type I error<br>(adjusting an in-control process) | Correct decision |

FIGURE 20.1   $\bar{x}$ CHART STRUCTURE

among the charts is what the vertical axis measures; for instance, in a $p$ chart the measurement scale denotes the proportion of defective items in the sample instead of the sample mean. In the following discussion, we will illustrate the construction and use of the $\bar{x}$ chart, $R$ chart, $p$ chart, and $np$ chart.

## $\bar{x}$ Chart: Process Mean and Standard Deviation Known

To illustrate the construction of an $\bar{x}$ chart, let us consider the situation at KJW Packaging. This company operates a production line where cartons of cereal are filled. Suppose KJW knows that when the process is operating correctly—and hence the system is in control— the mean filling weight is $\mu = 16.05$ ounces, and the process standard deviation is $\sigma = .10$ ounces. In addition, assume the filling weights are normally distributed. This distribution is shown in Figure 20.2.

FIGURE 20.2   NORMAL DISTRIBUTION OF CEREAL CARTON FILLING WEIGHTS

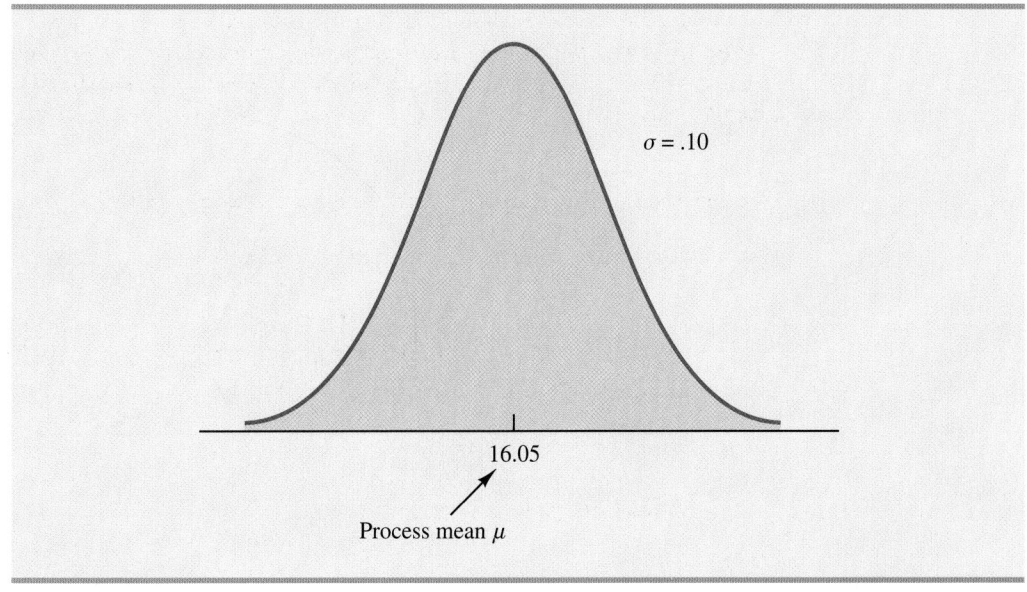

The sampling distribution of $\bar{x}$, as presented in Chapter 7, can be used to determine the variation that can be expected in $\bar{x}$ values for a process that is in control. Let us first briefly review the properties of the sampling distribution of $\bar{x}$. First, recall that the expected value or mean of $\bar{x}$ is equal to $\mu$, the mean filling weight when the production line is in control. For samples of size $n$, the equation for the standard deviation of $\bar{x}$, called the standard error of the mean, is

$$\sigma_{\bar{x}} = \frac{\sigma}{\sqrt{n}} \qquad\qquad (20.1)$$

In addition, because the filling weights are normally distributed, the sampling distribution of $\bar{x}$ is normally distributed for any sample size. Thus, the sampling distribution of $\bar{x}$ is a normal distribution with mean $\mu$ and standard deviation $\sigma_{\bar{x}}$. This distribution is shown in Figure 20.3.

The sampling distribution of $\bar{x}$ is used to determine what values of $\bar{x}$ are reasonable if the process is in control. The general practice in quality control is to define as reasonable any value of $\bar{x}$ that is within 3 standard deviations, or standard errors, above or below the mean value. Recall from the study of the normal probability distribution that approximately 99.7% of the values of a normally distributed random variable are within $\pm 3$ standard deviations of its mean value. Thus, if a value of $\bar{x}$ is within the interval $\mu - 3\sigma_{\bar{x}}$ to $\mu + 3\sigma_{\bar{x}}$, we will assume that the process is in control. In summary, then, the control limits for an $\bar{x}$ chart are as follows.

---

**CONTROL LIMITS FOR AN $\bar{x}$ CHART: PROCESS MEAN AND STANDARD DEVIATION KNOWN**

$$\text{UCL} = \mu + 3\sigma_{\bar{x}} \qquad\qquad (20.2)$$
$$\text{LCL} = \mu - 3\sigma_{\bar{x}} \qquad\qquad (20.3)$$

---

Reconsider the KJW Packaging example with the process distribution of filling weights shown in Figure 20.2 and the sampling distribution of $\bar{x}$ shown in Figure 20.3. Assume that

**FIGURE 20.3    SAMPLING DISTRIBUTION OF $\bar{x}$ FOR A SAMPLE OF $n$ FILLING WEIGHTS**

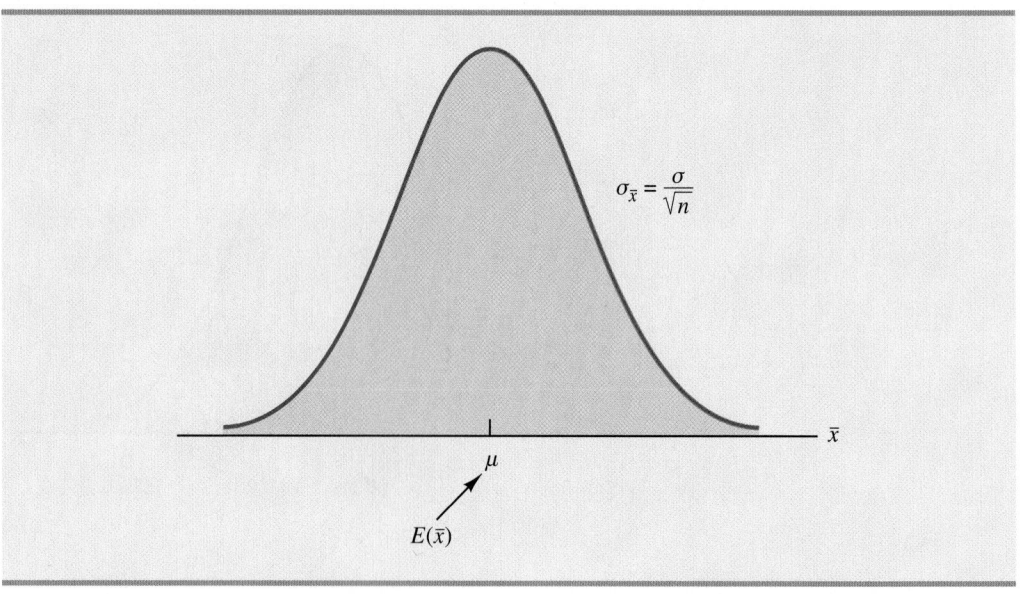

a quality control inspector periodically samples six cartons and uses the sample mean filling weight to determine whether the process is in control or out of control. Using equation (20.1), we find that the standard error of the mean is $\sigma_{\bar{x}} = \sigma/\sqrt{n} = .10/\sqrt{6} = .04$. Thus, with the process mean at 16.05, the control limits are UCL = 16.05 + 3(.04) = 16.17 and LCL = 16.05 − 3(.04) = 15.93. Figure 20.4 is the control chart with the results of 10 samples taken over a 10-hour period. For ease of reading, the sample numbers 1 through 10 are listed below the chart.

Note that the mean for the fifth sample in Figure 20.4 shows that the process is out of control. The fifth sample mean is below the LCL indicating that assignable causes of output variation are present and that underfilling is occurring. As a result, corrective action was taken at this point to bring the process back into control. The fact that the remaining points on the $\bar{x}$ chart are within the upper and lower control limits indicates that the corrective action was successful.

## $\bar{x}$ Chart: Process Mean and Standard Deviation Unknown

In the KJW Packaging example, we showed how an $\bar{x}$ chart can be developed when the mean and standard deviation of the process are known. In most situations, the process mean and standard deviation must be estimated by using samples that are selected from the process when it is in control. For instance, KJW might select a random sample of five boxes each morning and five boxes each afternoon for 10 days of in-control operation. For each subgroup, or sample, the mean and standard deviation of the sample are computed. The overall averages of both the sample means and the sample standard deviations are used to construct control charts for both the process mean and the process standard deviation.

*It is important to maintain control over both the mean and the variability of a process.*

In practice, it is more common to monitor the variability of the process by using the range instead of the standard deviation because the range is easier to compute. The range can be used to provide good estimates of the process standard deviation; thus it can be used to construct upper and lower control limits for the $\bar{x}$ chart with little computational effort. To illustrate, let us consider the problem facing Jensen Computer Supplies, Inc.

Jensen Computer Supplies (JCS) manufactures 3.5-inch-diameter computer disks; they just finished adjusting their production process so that it is operating in control. Suppose random samples of five disks could be taken during the first hour of operation, during the second

**FIGURE 20.4    THE $\bar{x}$ CHART FOR THE CEREAL CARTON FILLING PROCESS**

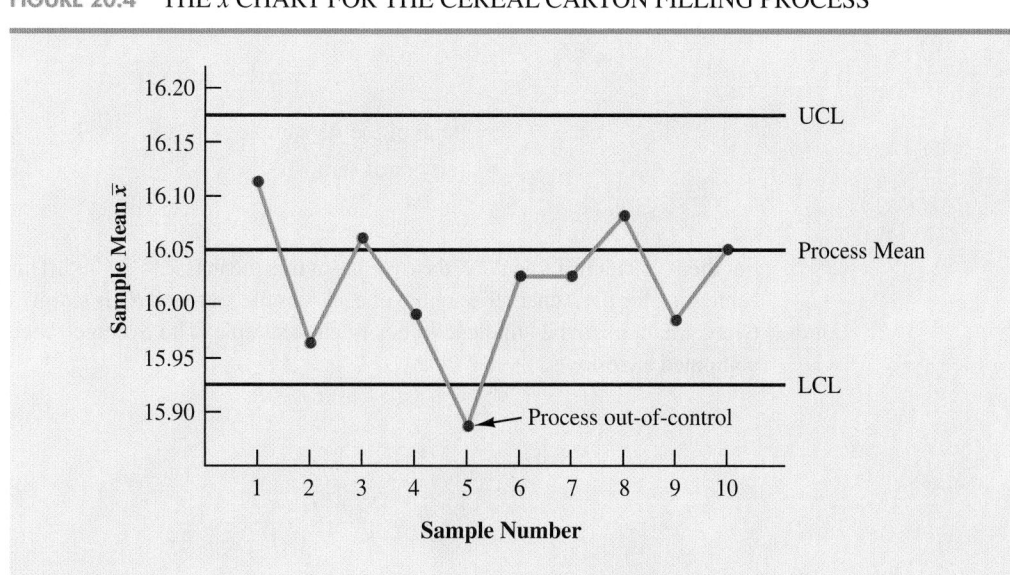

**TABLE 20.2   DATA FOR THE JENSEN COMPUTER SUPPLIES PROBLEM**

| Sample Number | Observations | | | | | Sample Mean $\bar{x}_j$ | Sample Range $R_j$ |
|---|---|---|---|---|---|---|---|
| 1 | 3.5056 | 3.5086 | 3.5144 | 3.5009 | 3.5030 | 3.5065 | .0135 |
| 2 | 3.4882 | 3.5085 | 3.4884 | 3.5250 | 3.5031 | 3.5026 | .0368 |
| 3 | 3.4897 | 3.4898 | 3.4995 | 3.5130 | 3.4969 | 3.4978 | .0233 |
| 4 | 3.5153 | 3.5120 | 3.4989 | 3.4900 | 3.4837 | 3.5000 | .0316 |
| 5 | 3.5059 | 3.5113 | 3.5011 | 3.4773 | 3.4801 | 3.4951 | .0340 |
| 6 | 3.4977 | 3.4961 | 3.5050 | 3.5014 | 3.5060 | 3.5012 | .0099 |
| 7 | 3.4910 | 3.4913 | 3.4976 | 3.4831 | 3.5044 | 3.4935 | .0213 |
| 8 | 3.4991 | 3.4853 | 3.4830 | 3.5083 | 3.5094 | 3.4970 | .0264 |
| 9 | 3.5099 | 3.5162 | 3.5228 | 3.4958 | 3.5004 | 3.5090 | .0270 |
| 10 | 3.4880 | 3.5015 | 3.5094 | 3.5102 | 3.5146 | 3.5047 | .0266 |
| 11 | 3.4881 | 3.4887 | 3.5141 | 3.5175 | 3.4863 | 3.4989 | .0312 |
| 12 | 3.5043 | 3.4867 | 3.4946 | 3.5018 | 3.4784 | 3.4932 | .0259 |
| 13 | 3.5043 | 3.4769 | 3.4944 | 3.5014 | 3.4904 | 3.4935 | .0274 |
| 14 | 3.5004 | 3.5030 | 3.5082 | 3.5045 | 3.5234 | 3.5079 | .0230 |
| 15 | 3.4846 | 3.4938 | 3.5065 | 3.5089 | 3.5011 | 3.4990 | .0243 |
| 16 | 3.5145 | 3.4832 | 3.5188 | 3.4935 | 3.4989 | 3.5018 | .0356 |
| 17 | 3.5004 | 3.5042 | 3.4954 | 3.5020 | 3.4889 | 3.4982 | .0153 |
| 18 | 3.4959 | 3.4823 | 3.4964 | 3.5082 | 3.4871 | 3.4940 | .0259 |
| 19 | 3.4878 | 3.4864 | 3.4960 | 3.5070 | 3.4984 | 3.4951 | .0206 |
| 20 | 3.4969 | 3.5144 | 3.5053 | 3.4985 | 3.4885 | 3.5007 | .0259 |

**Jensen**

hour of operation, and so on, until 20 samples have been selected. Table 20.2 provides the diameter of each disk sampled as well as the mean $\bar{x}_j$ and range $R_j$ for each of the samples.

The estimate of the process mean $\mu$ is given by the overall sample mean.

---

OVERALL SAMPLE MEAN

$$\bar{\bar{x}} = \frac{\bar{x}_1 + \bar{x}_2 + \cdots + \bar{x}_k}{k} \tag{20.4}$$

where

$\bar{x}_j$ = mean of the $j$th sample $j = 1, 2, \ldots, k$

$k$ = number of samples

---

For the JCS data in Table 20.2, the overall sample mean is $\bar{\bar{x}} = 3.4995$. This value will be the center line for the $\bar{x}$ chart. The range of each sample, denoted $R_j$, is simply the difference between the largest and smallest values in each sample. The average range for $k$ samples is computed as follows.

---

AVERAGE RANGE

$$\bar{R} = \frac{R_1 + R_2 + \cdots + R_k}{k} \tag{20.5}$$

where

$$R_j = \text{range of the } j\text{th sample}, j = 1, 2, \ldots, k$$
$$k = \text{number of samples}$$

For the JCS data in Table 20.2, the average range is $\bar{R} = .0253$.

In the preceding section we showed that the upper and lower control limits for the $\bar{x}$ chart are

$$\bar{x} \pm 3 \frac{\sigma}{\sqrt{n}} \tag{20.6}$$

*The overall sample mean $\bar{\bar{x}}$ is used to estimate $\mu$ and the sample ranges are used to develop an estimate of $\sigma$.*

Hence, to construct the control limits for the $\bar{x}$ chart, we need to estimate $\mu$ and $\sigma$, the mean and standard deviation of the process. An estimate of $\mu$ is given by $\bar{\bar{x}}$. An estimate of $\sigma$ can be developed by using the range data.

It can be shown that an estimator of the process standard deviation $\sigma$ is the average range divided by $d_2$, a constant that depends on the sample size $n$. That is,

$$\text{Estimator of } \sigma = \frac{\bar{R}}{d_2} \tag{20.7}$$

The *American Society for Testing and Materials Manual on Presentation of Data and Control Chart Analysis* provides values for $d_2$ as shown in Table 20.3. For instance, when $n = 5$, $d_2 = 2.326$, and the estimate of $\sigma$ is the average range divided by 2.326. If we substitute $\bar{R}/d_2$ for $\sigma$ in expression (20.6), we can write the control limits for the $\bar{x}$ chart as

$$\bar{\bar{x}} \pm 3 \frac{\bar{R}/d_2}{\sqrt{n}} = \bar{\bar{x}} \pm \frac{3}{d_2\sqrt{n}} \bar{R} = \bar{\bar{x}} \pm A_2\bar{R} \tag{20.8}$$

Note that $A_2 = 3/(d_2\sqrt{n})$ is a constant that depends only on the sample size. Values for $A_2$ are provided in Table 20.3. For $n = 5$, $A_2 = .577$; thus, the control limits for the $\bar{x}$ chart are

$$3.4995 \pm (.577)(.0253) = 3.4995 \pm .0146$$

Hence, UCL = 3.514 and LCL = 3.485.

Figure 20.5 shows the $\bar{x}$ chart for the Jensen Computer Supplies problem. We used the data in Table 20.2 and Minitab's control chart routine to construct the chart. The center line is shown at the overall sample mean $\bar{\bar{x}} = 3.499$. The upper control limit (UCL) is 3.514 and the lower control (LCL) is 3.485. The $\bar{x}$ chart shows the 20 sample means plotted over time. Because all 20 sample means are within the control limits, the indication is that the mean of the Jensen manufacturing process is in control. This chart can now be used to monitor the process mean on an ongoing basis.

## $R$ Chart

Let us now consider a range chart ($R$ chart) that can be used to control the variability of a process. To develop the $R$ chart, we need to think of the range of a sample as a random variable with its own mean and standard deviation. The average range $\bar{R}$ provides an estimate

**TABLE 20.3**   FACTORS FOR $\bar{x}$ AND $R$ CONTROL CHARTS

| Observations in Sample, $n$ | $d_2$ | $A_2$ | $d_3$ | $D_3$ | $D_4$ |
|---|---|---|---|---|---|
| 2 | 1.128 | 1.880 | 0.853 | 0 | 3.267 |
| 3 | 1.693 | 1.023 | 0.888 | 0 | 2.574 |
| 4 | 2.059 | 0.729 | 0.880 | 0 | 2.282 |
| 5 | 2.326 | 0.577 | 0.864 | 0 | 2.114 |
| 6 | 2.534 | 0.483 | 0.848 | 0 | 2.004 |
| 7 | 2.704 | 0.419 | 0.833 | 0.076 | 1.924 |
| 8 | 2.847 | 0.373 | 0.820 | 0.136 | 1.864 |
| 9 | 2.970 | 0.337 | 0.808 | 0.184 | 1.816 |
| 10 | 3.078 | 0.308 | 0.797 | 0.223 | 1.777 |
| 11 | 3.173 | 0.285 | 0.787 | 0.256 | 1.744 |
| 12 | 3.258 | 0.266 | 0.778 | 0.283 | 1.717 |
| 13 | 3.336 | 0.249 | 0.770 | 0.307 | 1.693 |
| 14 | 3.407 | 0.235 | 0.763 | 0.328 | 1.672 |
| 15 | 3.472 | 0.223 | 0.756 | 0.347 | 1.653 |
| 16 | 3.532 | 0.212 | 0.750 | 0.363 | 1.637 |
| 17 | 3.588 | 0.203 | 0.744 | 0.378 | 1.622 |
| 18 | 3.640 | 0.194 | 0.739 | 0.391 | 1.608 |
| 19 | 3.689 | 0.187 | 0.734 | 0.403 | 1.597 |
| 20 | 3.735 | 0.180 | 0.729 | 0.415 | 1.585 |
| 21 | 3.778 | 0.173 | 0.724 | 0.425 | 1.575 |
| 22 | 3.819 | 0.167 | 0.720 | 0.434 | 1.566 |
| 23 | 3.858 | 0.162 | 0.716 | 0.443 | 1.557 |
| 24 | 3.895 | 0.157 | 0.712 | 0.451 | 1.548 |
| 25 | 3.931 | 0.153 | 0.708 | 0.459 | 1.541 |

*Source:* Adapted from Table 27 of ASTM STP 15D, *ASTM Manual on Presentation of Data and Control Chart Analysis.* Copyright 1976 American Society for Testing and Materials, Philadelphia, PA. Reprinted with permission.

**FIGURE 20.5**   $\bar{x}$ CHART FOR THE JENSEN COMPUTER SUPPLIES PROBLEM of the mean of this random variable. Moreover, it can be shown that an estimate of the standard deviation of the range is

$$\hat{\sigma}_R = d_3 \frac{\bar{R}}{d_2} \tag{20.9}$$

where $d_2$ and $d_3$ are constants that depend on the sample size; values of $d_2$ and $d_3$ are also provided in Table 20.3. Thus, the UCL for the $R$ chart is given by

$$\bar{R} + 3\hat{\sigma}_R = \bar{R}\left(1 + 3\frac{d_3}{d_2}\right) \tag{20.10}$$

and the LCL is

$$\bar{R} - 3\hat{\sigma}_R = \bar{R}\left(1 - 3\frac{d_3}{d_2}\right) \tag{20.11}$$

If we let

$$D_4 = 1 + 3\frac{d_3}{d_2} \tag{20.12}$$

$$D_3 = 1 - 3\frac{d_3}{d_2} \tag{20.13}$$

we can write the control limits for the $R$ chart as

$$\text{UCL} = \bar{R}D_4 \tag{20.14}$$

$$\text{LCL} = \bar{R}D_3 \tag{20.15}$$

Values for $D_3$ and $D_4$ are also provided in Table 20.3. Note that for $n = 5$, $D_3 = 0$, and $D_4 = 2.115$. Thus, with $\bar{R} = .0253$, the control limits are

$$\text{UCL} = .0253(2.115) = .0535$$
$$\text{LCL} = .0253(0) = 0$$

*If the R chart indicates that the process is out of control, the $\bar{x}$ chart should not be interpreted until the R chart indicates the process variability is in control.*

Figure 20.6 shows the $R$ chart for the Jensen Computer Supplies problem. We used the data in Table 20.2 and Minitab's control chart routine to construct the chart. The center line is shown at the overall mean of the 20 sample ranges, $\bar{R} = .02527$. The UCL is .05344 and the LCL is 0.0. The $R$ chart shows the 20 sample ranges plotted over time. Because all 20 sample ranges are within the control limits, we confirm that the process was in control during the sampling period.

## p Chart

*Control charts that are based on data indicating the presence of a defect or a number of defects are called attributes control charts. A p chart is an attributes control chart.*

Let us consider the case in which the output quality is measured by either nondefective or defective items. The decision to continue or to adjust the production process will be based on $\bar{p}$, the proportion of defective items found in a sample. The control chart used for proportion-defective data is called a $p$ chart.

To illustrate the construction of a $p$ chart, consider the use of automated mail-sorting machines in a post office. These automated machines scan the zip codes on letters and divert each letter to its proper carrier route. Even when a machine is operating properly, some

**FIGURE 20.6**    *R* CHART FOR THE JENSEN COMPUTER SUPPLIES PROBLEM

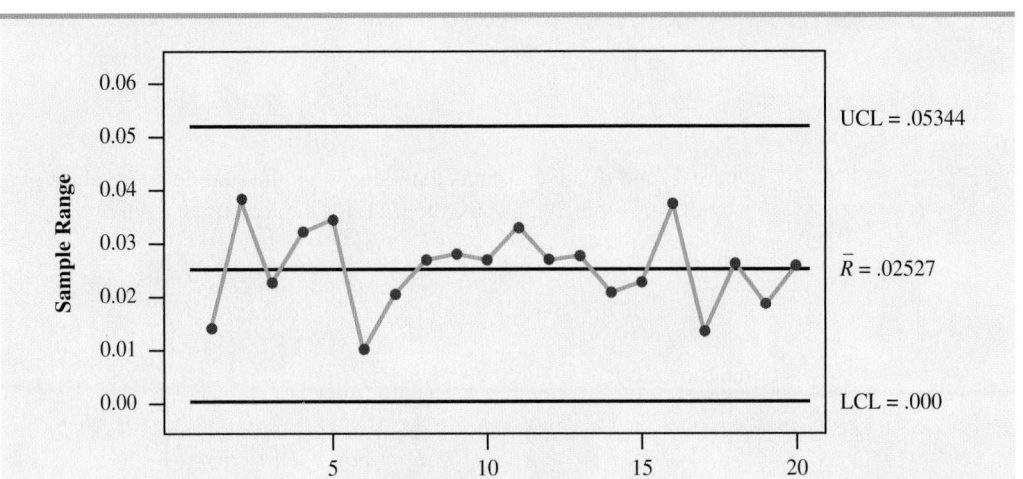

letters are diverted to incorrect routes. Assume that when a machine is operating correctly, or in a state of control, 3% of the letters are incorrectly diverted. Thus $p$, the proportion of letters incorrectly diverted when the process is in control, is .03.

The sampling distribution of $\bar{p}$, as presented in Chapter 7, can be used to determine the variation that can be expected in $\bar{p}$ values for a process that is in control. Recall that the expected value or mean of $\bar{p}$ is $p$, the proportion defective when the process is in control. With samples of size $n$, the formula for the standard deviation of $\bar{p}$, called the standard error of the proportion, is

$$\sigma_{\bar{p}} = \sqrt{\frac{p(1-p)}{n}} \tag{20.16}$$

We also learned in Chapter 7 that the sampling distribution of $\bar{p}$ can be approximated by a normal distribution whenever the sample size is large. With $\bar{p}$, the sample size can be considered large whenever the following two conditions are satisfied.

$$np \geq 5$$
$$n(1-p) \geq 5$$

In summary, whenever the sample size is large, the sampling distribution of $\bar{p}$ can be approximated by a normal distribution with mean $p$ and standard deviation $\sigma_{\bar{p}}$. This distribution is shown in Figure 20.7.

To establish control limits for a $p$ chart, we follow the same procedure we used to establish control limits for an $\bar{x}$ chart. That is, the limits for the control chart are set at 3 standard deviations, or standard errors, above and below the proportion defective when the process is in control. Thus, we have the following control limits.

**CONTROL LIMITS FOR A $p$ CHART**

$$\text{UCL} = p + 3\sigma_{\bar{p}} \tag{20.17}$$
$$\text{LCL} = p - 3\sigma_{\bar{p}} \tag{20.18}$$

FIGURE 20.7    SAMPLING DISTRIBUTION OF $\bar{p}$

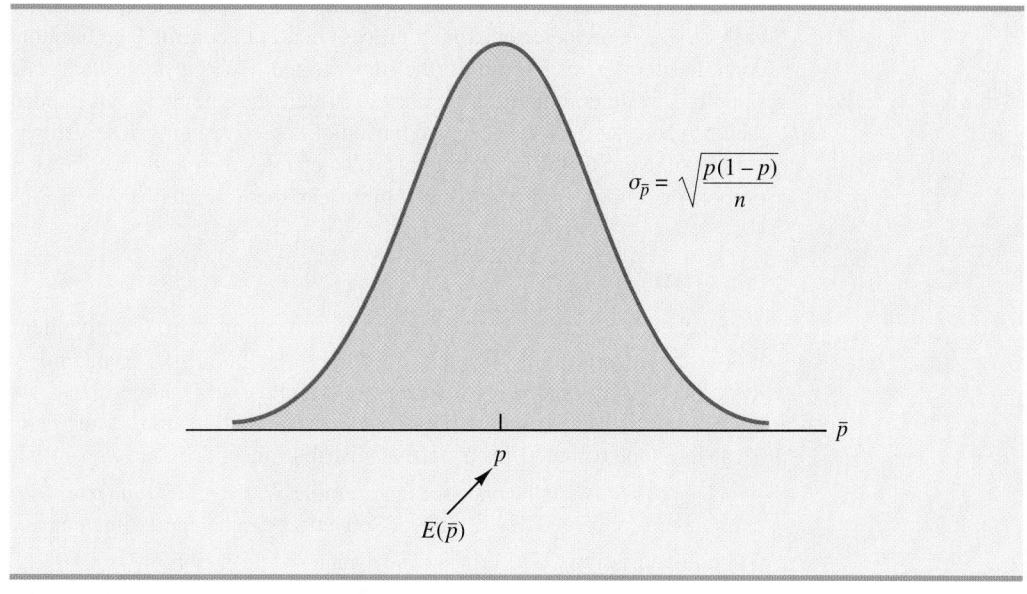

With $p = .03$ and samples of size $n = 200$, equation (20.16) shows that the standard error is

$$\sigma_{\bar{p}} = \sqrt{\frac{.03(1 - .03)}{200}} = .0121$$

Hence, the control limits are UCL $= .03 + 3(.0121) = .0663$, and LCL $= .03 - 3(.0121) = -.0063$. Whenever equation (20.18) provides a negative value for LCL, LCL is set equal to zero in the control chart.

Figure 20.8 is the control chart for the mail-sorting process. The points plotted show the sample proportion defective found in samples of letters taken from the process. All points are within the control limits, providing no evidence to conclude that the sorting process is out of control. In fact, the $p$ chart indicates that the process is in control and should continue to operate.

FIGURE 20.8    $p$ CHART FOR THE PROPORTION DEFECTIVE IN A MAIL-SORTING PROCESS

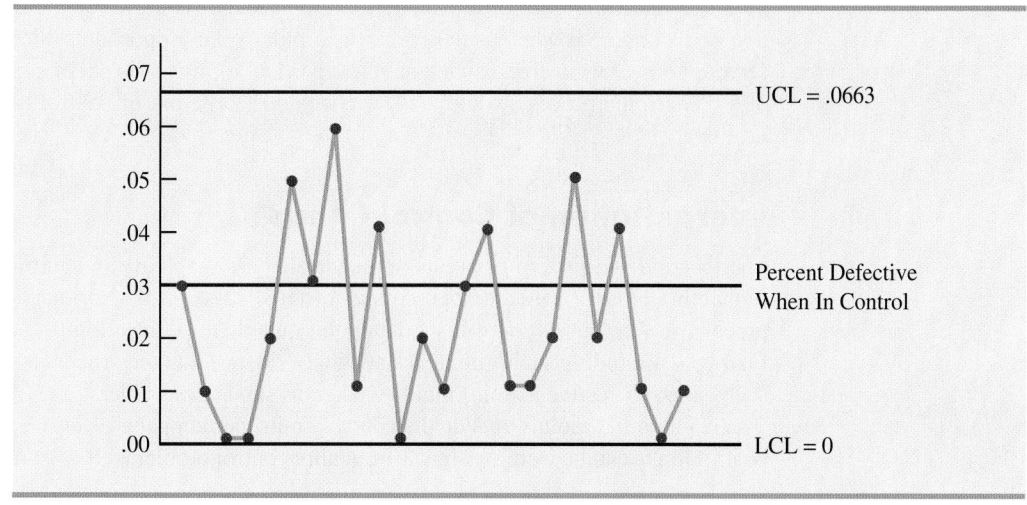

If the proportion of defective items for a process that is in control is not known, that value is first estimated by using sample data. Suppose, for example, that $k$ different samples, each of size $n$, are selected from a process that is in control. The fraction or proportion of defective items in each sample is then determined. Treating all the data collected as one large sample, we can compute the proportion of defective items for all the data; that value can then be used to estimate $p$, the proportion of defective items observed when the process is in control. Note that this estimate of $p$ also enables us to estimate the standard error of the proportion; upper and lower control limits can then be established.

## $np$ **Chart**

An $np$ chart is a control chart developed for the number of defective items in a sample. In this case, $n$ is the sample size and $p$ is the probability of observing a defective item when the process is in control. Whenever the sample size is large, that is when $np \geq 5$ and $n(1 - p) \geq 5$, the distribution of the number of defective items observed in a sample of size $n$ can be approximated by a normal distribution with mean $np$ and standard deviation $\sqrt{np(1 - p)}$. Thus, for the mail-sorting example, with $n = 200$ and $p = .03$, the number of defective items observed in a sample of 200 letters can be approximated by a normal distribution with a mean of $200(.03) = 6$ and a standard deviation of $\sqrt{200(.03)(.97)} = 2.4125$.

The control limits for an $np$ chart are set at 3 standard deviations above and below the expected number of defective items observed when the process is in control. Thus, we have the following control limits.

CONTROL LIMITS FOR AN $np$ CHART

$$\text{UCL} = np + 3\sqrt{np(1 - p)} \qquad (20.19)$$
$$\text{LCL} = np - 3\sqrt{np(1 - p)} \qquad (20.20)$$

For the mail-sorting process example, with $p = .03$ and $n = 200$, the control limits are UCL = $6 + 3(2.4125) = 13.2375$, and LCL = $6 - 3(2.4125) = -1.2375$. When LCL is negative, LCL is set equal to zero in the control chart. Hence, if the number of letters diverted to incorrect routes is greater than 13, the process is concluded to be out of control.

The information provided by an $np$ chart is equivalent to the information provided by the $p$ chart; the only difference is that the $np$ chart is a plot of the number of defective items observed whereas the $p$ chart is a plot of the proportion of defective items observed. Thus, if we were to conclude that a particular process is out of control on the basis of a $p$ chart, the process would also be concluded to be out of control on the basis of an $np$ chart.

## **Interpretation of Control Charts**

The location and pattern of points in a control chart enable us to determine, with a small probability of error, whether a process is in statistical control. A primary indication that a process may be out of control is a data point outside the control limits, such as point 5 in Figure 20.4. Finding such a point is statistical evidence that the process is out of control; in such cases, corrective action should be taken as soon as possible.

In addition to points outside the control limits, certain patterns of the points within the control limits can be warning signals of quality control problems. For example, assume that all the data points are within the control limits but that a large number of points are on one side of the center line. This pattern may indicate that an equipment problem, a change in materials, or some other assignable cause of a shift in quality has occurred. Careful investigation of the production process should be undertaken to determine whether quality has changed.

*Even if all points are within the upper and lower control limits, a process may not be in control. Trends in the sample data points or unusually long runs above or below the center line may also indicate out-of-control conditions.*

Another pattern to watch for in control charts is a gradual shift, or trend, over time. For example, as tools wear out, the dimensions of machined parts will gradually deviate from their designed levels. Gradual changes in temperature or humidity, general equipment deterioration, dirt buildup, or operator fatigue may also result in a trend pattern in control charts. Six or seven points in a row that indicate either an increasing or decreasing trend should be cause for concern, even if the data points are all within the control limits. When such a pattern occurs, the process should be reviewed for possible changes or shifts in quality. Corrective action to bring the process back into control may be necessary.

## NOTES AND COMMENTS

**1.** Because the control limits for the $\bar{x}$ chart depend on the value of the average range, these limits will not have much meaning unless the process variability is in control. In practice, the $R$ chart is usually constructed before the $\bar{x}$ chart; if the $R$ chart indicates that the process variability is in control, then the $\bar{x}$ chart is constructed. Minitab's Xbar-R option provides the $\bar{x}$ chart and the

$R$ chart simultaneously. The steps of this procedure are described in Appendix 20.1.

**2.** An *np* chart is used to monitor a process in terms of the number of defects. The Motorola Six Sigma Quality Level sets a goal of producing no more than 3.4 defects per million operations (*American Production and Inventory Control,* July 1991); this goal implies $p = .0000034$.

## Exercises

### Methods

1. A process that is in control has a mean of $\mu = 12.5$ and a standard deviation of $\sigma = .8$.
   a. Construct an chart if samples of size 4 are to be used.
   b. Repeat part (a) for samples of size 8 and 16.
   c. What happens to the limits of the control chart as the sample size is increased? Discuss why this is reasonable.

2. Twenty-five samples, each of size 5, were selected from a process that was in control. The sum of all the data collected was 677.5 pounds.
   a. What is an estimate of the process mean (in terms of pounds per unit) when the process is in control?
   b. Develop the control chart for this process if samples of size 5 will be used. Assume that the process standard deviation is .5 when the process is in control, and that the mean of the process is the estimate developed in part (a).

3. Twenty-five samples of 100 items each were inspected when a process was considered to be operating satisfactorily. In the 25 samples, a total of 135 items were found to be defective.
   a. What is an estimate of the proportion defective when the process is in control?
   b. What is the standard error of the proportion if samples of size 100 will be used for statistical process control?
   c. Compute the upper and lower control limits for the control chart.

 **SELF** test

4. A process sampled 20 times with a sample of size 8 resulted in $\bar{\bar{x}} = 28.5$ and $\bar{R} = 1.6$. Compute the upper and lower control limits for the $\bar{x}$ and R charts for this process.

## Applications

5. Temperature is used to measure the output of a production process. When the process is in control, the mean of the process is $\mu = 128.5$ and the standard deviation is $\sigma = .4$.
   a. Construct an $\bar{x}$ chart if samples of size 6 are to be used.
   b. Is the process in control for a sample providing the following data?

   | 128.8 | 128.2 | 129.1 | 128.7 | 128.4 | 129.2 |
   |-------|-------|-------|-------|-------|-------|

   c. Is the process in control for a sample providing the following data?

   | 129.3 | 128.7 | 128.6 | 129.2 | 129.5 | 129.0 |
   |-------|-------|-------|-------|-------|-------|

6. A quality control process monitors the weight per carton of laundry detergent. Control limits are set at UCL = 20.12 ounces and LCL = 19.90 ounces. Samples of size 5 are used for the sampling and inspection process. What are the process mean and process standard deviation for the manufacturing operation?

7. The Goodman Tire and Rubber Company periodically tests its tires for tread wear under simulated road conditions. To study and control the manufacturing process, 20 samples, each containing three radial tires, were chosen from different shifts over several days of operation, with the following results. Assuming that these data were collected when the manufacturing process was believed to be operating in control, develop the $R$ and $\bar{x}$ charts.

**Tires**

| Sample | Tread Wear* | | |
|--------|------|------|------|
| 1 | 31 | 42 | 28 |
| 2 | 26 | 18 | 35 |
| 3 | 25 | 30 | 34 |
| 4 | 17 | 25 | 21 |
| 5 | 38 | 29 | 35 |
| 6 | 41 | 42 | 36 |
| 7 | 21 | 17 | 29 |
| 8 | 32 | 26 | 28 |
| 9 | 41 | 34 | 33 |
| 10 | 29 | 17 | 30 |
| 11 | 26 | 31 | 40 |
| 12 | 23 | 19 | 25 |
| 13 | 17 | 24 | 32 |
| 14 | 43 | 35 | 17 |
| 15 | 18 | 25 | 29 |
| 16 | 30 | 42 | 31 |
| 17 | 28 | 36 | 32 |
| 18 | 40 | 29 | 31 |
| 19 | 18 | 29 | 28 |
| 20 | 22 | 34 | 26 |

*Hundredths of an inch

8. Over several weeks of normal, or in-control, operation, 20 samples of 150 packages each of synthetic-gut tennis strings were tested for breaking strength. A total of 141 packages of the 3000 tested failed to conform to the manufacturer's specifications.
   a. What is an estimate of the process proportion defective when the system is in control?
   b. Compute the upper and lower control limits for a $p$ chart.
   c. With the results of part (b), what conclusion should be made about the process if tests on a new sample of 150 packages find 12 defective? Do there appear to be assignable causes in this situation?
   d. Compute the upper and lower control limits for an $np$ chart.

e.  Answer part (c) using the results of part (d).

f.  Which control chart would be preferred in this situation? Explain.

9.  An automotive industry supplier produces pistons for several models of automobiles. Twenty samples, each consisting of 200 pistons, were selected when the process was known to be operating correctly. The numbers of defective pistons found in the samples follow.

| 8  | 10 | 6  | 4 | 5 | 7 | 8 | 12 | 8 | 15 |
|----|----|----|---|---|---|---|----|---|----|
| 14 | 10 | 10 | 7 | 5 | 8 | 6 | 10 | 4 | 8  |

a.  What is an estimate of the proportion defective for the piston manufacturing process when it is in control?

b.  Construct a $p$ chart for the manufacturing process, assuming each sample has 200 pistons.

c.  With the results of part (b), what conclusion should be made if a sample of 200 has 20 defective pistons?

d.  Compute the upper and lower control limits for an $np$ chart.

e.  Answer part (c) using the results of part (d).

 **20.2**  # Acceptance Sampling

In acceptance sampling, the items of interest can be incoming shipments of raw materials or purchased parts as well as finished goods from final assembly. Suppose we want to decide whether to accept or reject a group of items on the basis of specified quality characteristics. In quality control terminology, the group of items is a **lot**, and **acceptance sampling** is a statistical method that enables us to base the accept-reject decision on the inspection of a sample of items from the lot.

The general steps of acceptance sampling are shown in Figure 20.9. After a lot is received, a sample of items is selected for inspection. The results of the inspection are compared to specified quality characteristics. If the quality characteristics are satisfied, the lot is accepted and sent to production or shipped to customers. If the lot is rejected, managers must decide on its disposition. In some cases, the decision may be to keep the lot and remove the unacceptable or nonconforming items. In other cases, the lot may be returned to the supplier at the supplier's expense; the extra work and cost placed on the supplier can motivate the supplier to provide high-quality lots. Finally, if the rejected lot consists of finished goods, the goods must be scrapped or reworked to meet acceptable quality standards.

*Acceptance sampling has the following advantages over 100% inspection:*

*1. Usually less expensive*

*2. Less product damage due to less handling and testing*

*3. Fewer inspectors required*

*4. The only approach possible if destructive testing must be used*

The statistical procedure of acceptance sampling is based on the hypothesis testing methodology presented in Chapter 9. The null and alternative hypotheses are stated as follows.

$$H_0: \text{Good-quality lot}$$
$$H_a: \text{Poor-quality lot}$$

Table 20.4 shows the results of the hypothesis testing procedure. Note that correct decisions correspond to accepting a good-quality lot and rejecting a poor-quality lot. However, as with other hypothesis testing procedures, we need to be aware of the possibilities of making a Type I error (rejecting a good-quality lot) or a Type II error (accepting a poor-quality lot).

The probability of a Type I error creates a risk for the producer of the lot and is known as the **producer's risk**. For example, a producer's risk of .05 indicates a 5% chance that a good-quality lot will be erroneously rejected. The probability of a Type II error, on the other hand, creates a risk for the consumer of the lot and is known as the **consumer's risk**. For example, a consumer's risk of .10 means a 10% chance that a poor-quality lot will be erroneously accepted and thus used in production or shipped to the customer. Specific values for the producer's risk and the consumer's risk can be controlled by the person designing the acceptance sampling procedure. To illustrate how to assign risk values, let us consider the problem faced by KALI, Inc.

FIGURE 20.9    ACCEPTANCE SAMPLING PROCEDURE

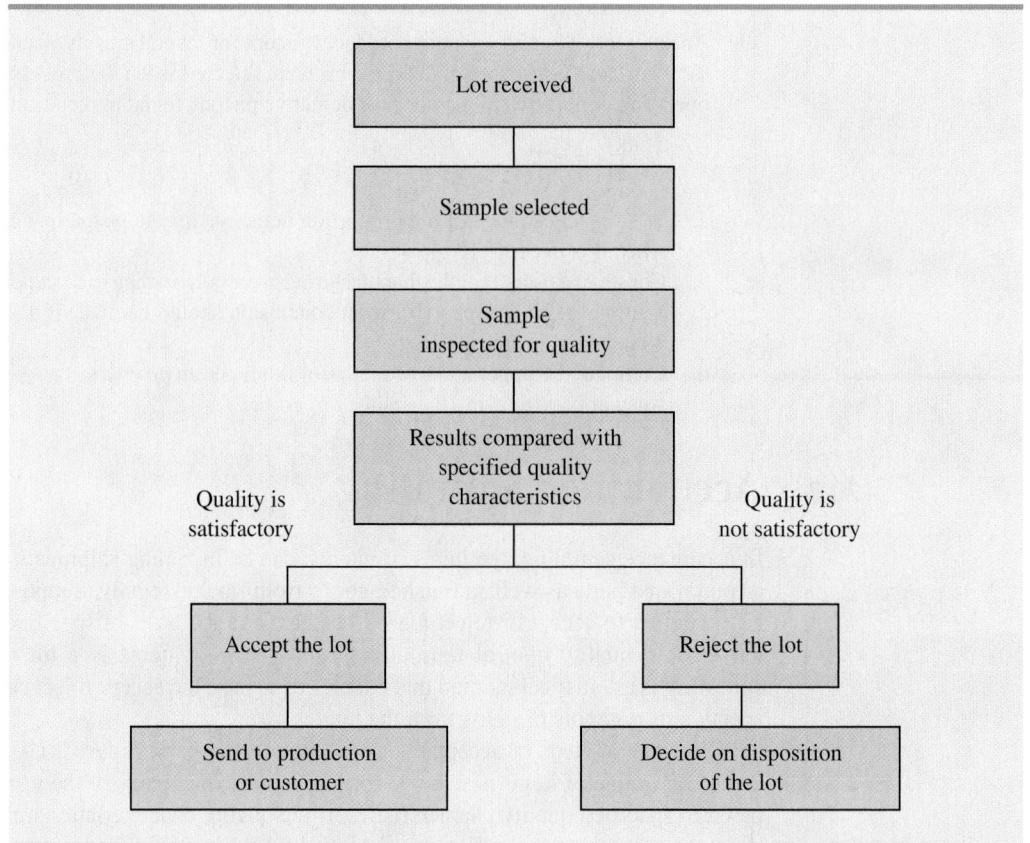

## KALI, Inc.: An Example of Acceptance Sampling

KALI, Inc., manufactures home appliances that are marketed under a variety of trade names. However, KALI does not manufacture every component used in its products. Several components are purchased directly from suppliers. For example, one of the components that KALI purchases for use in home air conditioners is an overload protector, a device that turns off the compressor if it overheats. The compressor can be seriously damaged if the overload protector does not function properly, and therefore KALI is concerned about the quality of the overload protectors. One way to ensure quality would be to test every component re-

TABLE 20.4    THE OUTCOMES OF ACCEPTANCE SAMPLING

| | | State of the Lot | |
| --- | --- | --- | --- |
| | | $H_0$ True Good-Quality Lot | $H_0$ False Poor-Quality Lot |
| Decision | **Accept the Lot** | Correct decision | Type II error (accepting a poor-quality lot) |
| | **Reject the Lot** | Type I error (rejecting a good-quality lot) | Correct decision |

ceived through an approach known as 100% inspection. However, to determine proper functioning of an overload protector, the device must be subjected to time-consuming and expensive tests, and KALI cannot justify testing every overload protector it receives.

Instead, KALI uses an acceptance sampling plan to monitor the quality of the overload protectors. The acceptance sampling plan requires that KALI's quality control inspectors select and test a sample of overload protectors from each shipment. If very few defective units are found in the sample, the lot is probably of good quality and should be accepted. However, if a large number of defective units are found in the sample, the lot is probably of poor quality and should be rejected.

An acceptance sampling plan consists of a sample size $n$ and an acceptance criterion $c$. The **acceptance criterion** is the maximum number of defective items that can be found in the sample and still indicate an acceptable lot. For example, for the KALI problem let us assume that a sample of 15 items will be selected from each incoming shipment or lot. Furthermore, assume that the manager of quality control states that the lot can be accepted only if no defective items are found. In this case, the acceptance sampling plan established by the quality control manager is $n = 15$ and $c = 0$.

This acceptance sampling plan is easy for the quality control inspector to implement. The inspector simply selects a sample of 15 items, performs the tests, and reaches a conclusion based on the following decision rule.

- *Accept the lot* if zero defective items are found.
- *Reject the lot* if one or more defective items are found.

Before implementing this acceptance sampling plan, the quality control manager wants to evaluate the risks or errors possible under the plan. The plan will be implemented only if both the producer's risk (Type I error) and the consumer's risk (Type II error) are controlled at reasonable levels.

## Computing the Probability of Accepting a Lot

The key to analyzing both the producer's risk and the consumer's risk is a "what-if" type of analysis. That is, we will assume that a lot has some known percentage of defective items and compute the probability of accepting the lot for a given sampling plan. By varying the assumed percentage of defective items, we can examine the effect of the sampling plan on both types of risks.

Let us begin by assuming that a large shipment of overload protectors has been received and that 5% of the overload protectors in the shipment are defective. For a shipment or lot with 5% of the items defective, what is the probability that the $n = 15$, $c = 0$ sampling plan will lead us to accept the lot? Because each overload protector tested will be either defective or nondefective and because the lot size is large, the number of defective items in a sample of 15 has a *binomial distribution*. The binomial probability function, which was presented in Chapter 5, follows.

BINOMIAL PROBABILITY FUNCTION FOR ACCEPTANCE SAMPLING

$$f(x) = \frac{n!}{x!(n-x)!} p^x (1-p)^{(n-x)} \tag{20.21}$$

where

$n$ = the sample size
$p$ = the proportion of defective items in the lot
$x$ = the number of defective items in the sample
$f(x)$ = the probability of $x$ defective items in the sample

For the KALI acceptance sampling plan, $n = 15$; thus, for a lot with 5% defective ($p = .05$), we have

$$f(x) = \frac{15!}{x!(15 - x)!} (.05)^x (1 - .05)^{(15-x)} \qquad \textbf{(20.22)}$$

Using equation (20.22), $f(0)$ will provide the probability that zero overload protectors will be defective and the lot will be accepted. In using equation (20.22), recall that $0! = 1$. Thus, the probability computation for $f(0)$ is

$$f(0) = \frac{15!}{0!(15 - 0)!} (.05)^0 (1 - .05)^{(15-0)}$$

$$= \frac{15!}{0!(15)!} (.05)^0 (.95)^{15} = (.95)^{15} = .4633$$

We now know that the $n = 15$, $c = 0$ sampling plan has a .4633 probability of accepting a lot with 5% defective items. Hence, there must be a corresponding $1 - .4633 = .5367$ probability of rejecting a lot with 5% defective items.

Tables of binomial probabilities (see Table 5, Appendix B) can help reduce the computational effort in determining the probabilities of accepting lots. Selected binomial probabilities for $n = 15$ and $n = 20$ are listed in Table 20.5. Using this table, we can determine that if the lot contains 10% defective items, there is a .2059 probability that the $n = 15$, $c = 0$ sampling plan will indicate an acceptable lot. The probability that the $n = 15$, $c = 0$

**TABLE 20.5   SELECTED BINOMIAL PROBABILITIES FOR SAMPLES OF SIZE 15 AND 20**

| $n$ | $x$ | .01 | .02 | .03 | .04 | .05 | .10 | .15 | .20 | .25 |
|---|---|---|---|---|---|---|---|---|---|---|
| 15 | 0 | .8601 | .7386 | .6333 | .5421 | .4633 | .2059 | .0874 | .0352 | .0134 |
|  | 1 | .1303 | .2261 | .2938 | .3388 | .3658 | .3432 | .2312 | .1319 | .0668 |
|  | 2 | .0092 | .0323 | .0636 | .0988 | .1348 | .2669 | .2856 | .2309 | .1559 |
|  | 3 | .0004 | .0029 | .0085 | .0178 | .0307 | .1285 | .2184 | .2501 | .2252 |
|  | 4 | .0000 | .0002 | .0008 | .0022 | .0049 | .0428 | .1156 | .1876 | .2252 |
|  | 5 | .0000 | .0000 | .0001 | .0002 | .0006 | .0105 | .0449 | .1032 | .1651 |
|  | 6 | .0000 | .0000 | .0000 | .0000 | .0000 | .0019 | .0132 | .0430 | .0917 |
|  | 7 | .0000 | .0000 | .0000 | .0000 | .0000 | .0003 | .0030 | .0138 | .0393 |
|  | 8 | .0000 | .0000 | .0000 | .0000 | .0000 | .0000 | .0005 | .0035 | .0131 |
|  | 9 | .0000 | .0000 | .0000 | .0000 | .0000 | .0000 | .0001 | .0007 | .0034 |
|  | 10 | .0000 | .0000 | .0000 | .0000 | .0000 | .0000 | .0000 | .0001 | .0007 |
| 20 | 0 | .8179 | .6676 | .5438 | .4420 | .3585 | .1216 | .0388 | .0115 | .0032 |
|  | 1 | .1652 | .2725 | .3364 | .3683 | .3774 | .2702 | .1368 | .0576 | .0211 |
|  | 2 | .0159 | .0528 | .0988 | .1458 | .1887 | .2852 | .2293 | .1369 | .0669 |
|  | 3 | .0010 | .0065 | .0183 | .0364 | .0596 | .1901 | .2428 | .2054 | .1339 |
|  | 4 | .0000 | .0006 | .0024 | .0065 | .0133 | .0898 | .1821 | .2182 | .1897 |
|  | 5 | .0000 | .0000 | .0002 | .0009 | .0022 | .0319 | .1028 | .1746 | .2023 |
|  | 6 | .0000 | .0000 | .0000 | .0001 | .0003 | .0089 | .0454 | .1091 | .1686 |
|  | 7 | .0000 | .0000 | .0000 | .0000 | .0000 | .0020 | .0160 | .0545 | .1124 |
|  | 8 | .0000 | .0000 | .0000 | .0000 | .0000 | .0004 | .0046 | .0222 | .0609 |
|  | 9 | .0000 | .0000 | .0000 | .0000 | .0000 | .0001 | .0011 | .0074 | .0271 |
|  | 10 | .0000 | .0000 | .0000 | .0000 | .0000 | .0000 | .0002 | .0020 | .0099 |
|  | 11 | .0000 | .0000 | .0000 | .0000 | .0000 | .0000 | .0000 | .0005 | .0030 |
|  | 12 | .0000 | .0000 | .0000 | .0000 | .0000 | .0000 | .0000 | .0001 | .0008 |

The column group header "$p$" spans columns .01 through .25.

TABLE 20.6    PROBABILITY OF ACCEPTING THE LOT FOR THE KALI PROBLEM WITH
$n = 15$ AND $c = 0$

| Percent Defective in the Lot | Probability of Accepting the Lot |
|:---:|:---:|
| 1 | .8601 |
| 2 | .7386 |
| 3 | .6333 |
| 4 | .5421 |
| 5 | .4633 |
| 10 | .2059 |
| 15 | .0874 |
| 20 | .0352 |
| 25 | .0134 |

sampling plan will lead to the acceptance of lots with 1%, 2%, 3%, . . . defective items is summarized in Table 20.6.

Using the probabilities in Table 20.6, a graph of the probability of accepting the lot versus the percent defective in the lot can be drawn as shown in Figure 20.10. This graph, or curve, is called the **operating characteristic (OC) curve** for the $n = 15, c = 0$ acceptance sampling plan.

Perhaps we should consider other sampling plans, ones with different sample sizes $n$ or different acceptance criteria $c$. First consider the case in which the sample size remains $n = 15$ but the acceptance criterion increases from $c = 0$ to $c = 1$. That is, we will now accept the lot if zero or one defective component is found in the sample. For a lot with 5% defective items ($p = .05$), Table 20.5 shows that with $n = 15$ and $p = .05$, $f(0) = .4633$

FIGURE 20.10    OPERATING CHARACTERISTIC CURVE FOR THE $n = 15, c = 0$
ACCEPTANCE SAMPLING PLAN

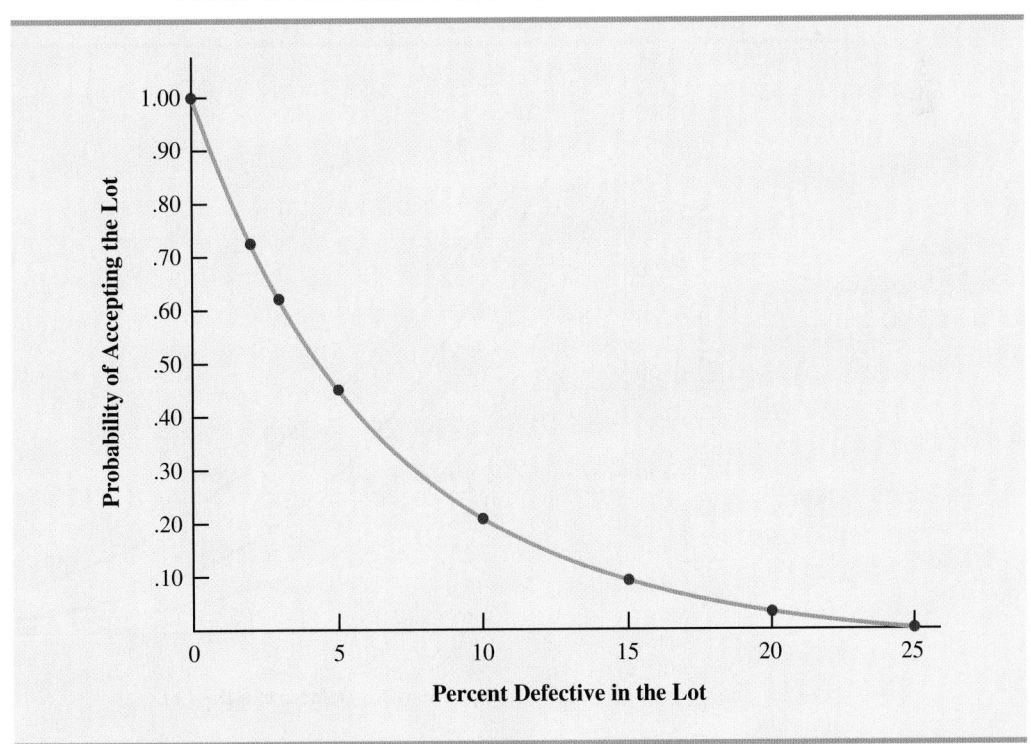

and $f(1) = .3658$. Thus, there is a $.4633 + .3658 = .8291$ probability that the $n = 15, c = 1$ plan will lead to the acceptance of a lot with 5% defective items.

Continuing these calculations we obtain Figure 20.11, which shows the operating characteristic curves for four alternative acceptance sampling plans for the KALI problem. Samples of size 15 and 20 are considered. Note that regardless of the proportion defective in the lot, the $n = 15, c = 1$ sampling plan provides the highest probabilities of accepting the lot. The $n = 20, c = 0$ sampling plan provides the lowest probabilities of accepting the lot; however, that plan also provides the highest probabilities of rejecting the lot.

## Selecting an Acceptance Sampling Plan

Now that we know how to use the binomial distribution to compute the probability of accepting a lot with a given proportion defective, we are ready to select the values of $n$ and $c$ that determine the desired acceptance sampling plan for the application being studied. To develop this plan, managers must specify two values for the fraction defective in the lot. One value, denoted $p_0$, will be used to control for the producer's risk, and the other value, denoted $p_1$, will be used to control for the consumer's risk.

We will use the following notation.

$\alpha$ = the producer's risk; the probability of rejecting a lot with $p_0$ defective items
$\beta$ = the consumer's risk; the probability of accepting a lot with $p_1$ defective items

Suppose that for the KALI problem, the managers specify that $p_0 = .03$ and $p_1 = .15$. From the OC curve for $n = 15, c = 0$ in Figure 20.12, we see that $p_0 = .03$ provides a producer's risk of approximately $1 - .63 = .37$, and $p_1 = .15$ provides a consumer's risk of approximately .09. Thus, if the managers are willing to tolerate both a .37 probability of rejecting a lot with 3%

**FIGURE 20.11**   OPERATING CHARACTERISTIC CURVES FOR FOUR ACCEPTANCE SAMPLING PLANS

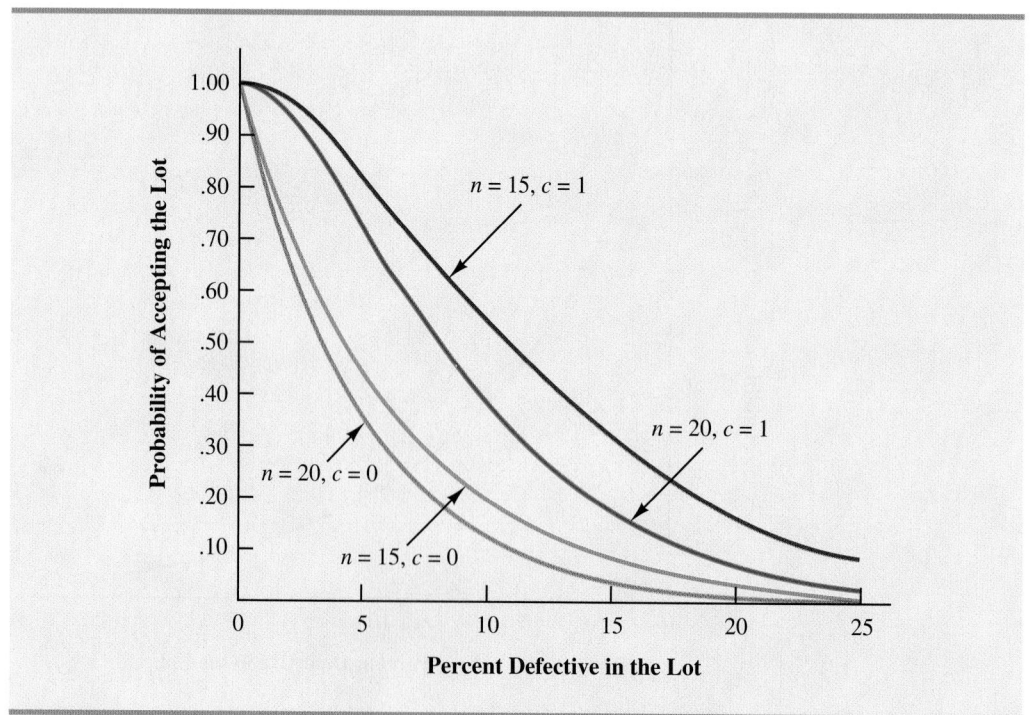

**FIGURE 20.12**   OPERATING CHARACTERISTIC CURVE FOR $n = 15$, $c = 0$ WITH $p_0 = .03$ AND $p_1 = .15$

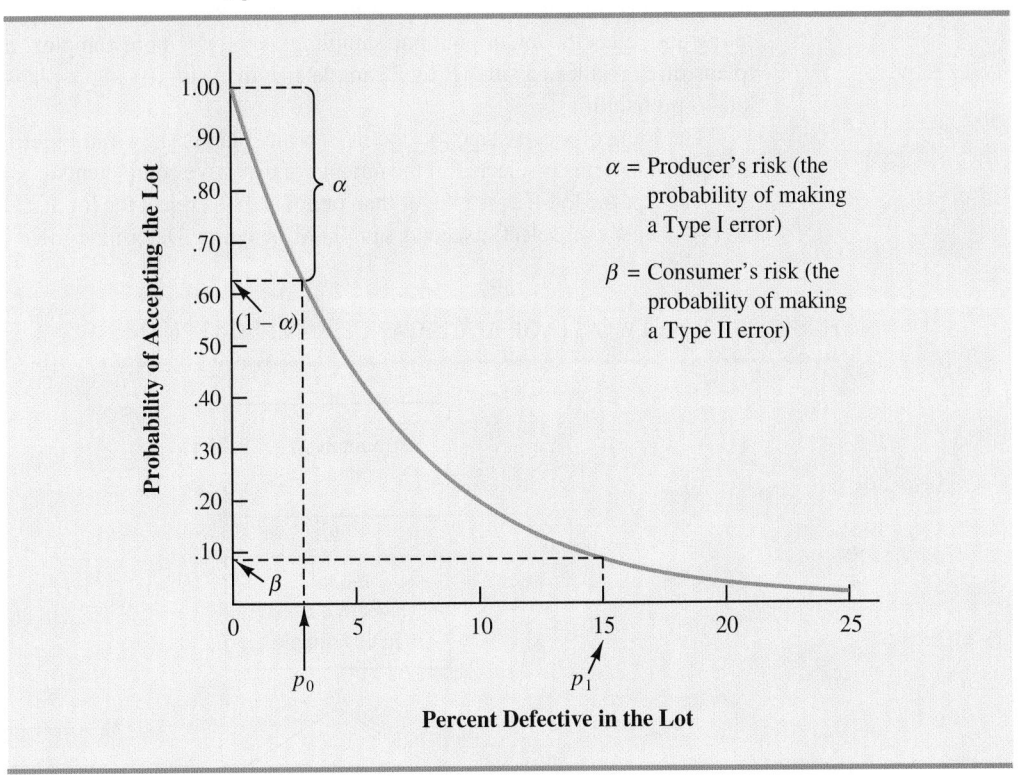

defective items (producer's risk) and a .09 probability of accepting a lot with 15% defective items (consumer's risk), the $n = 15$, $c = 0$ acceptance sampling plan would be acceptable.

Suppose, however, that the managers request a producer's risk of $\alpha = .10$ and a consumer's risk of $\beta = .20$. We see that now the $n = 15$, $c = 0$ sampling plan has a better-than-desired consumer's risk but an unacceptably large producer's risk. The fact that $\alpha = .37$ indicates that 37% of the lots will be erroneously rejected when only 3% of the items in them are defective. The producer's risk is too high, and a different acceptance sampling plan should be considered.

Using $p_0 = .03$, $\alpha = .10$, $p_1 = .15$, and $\beta = .20$, Figure 20.11 shows that the acceptance sampling plan with $n = 20$ and $c = 1$ comes closest to meeting both the producer's and the consumer's risk requirements. Exercise 13 at the end of this section will ask you to compute the producer's risk and the consumer's risk for the $n = 20$, $c = 1$ sampling plan.

As shown in this section, several computations and several operating characteristic curves may need to be considered to determine the sampling plan with the desired producer's and consumer's risk. Fortunately, tables of sampling plans are published. For example, the American Military Standard Table, MIL-STD-105D, provides information helpful in designing acceptance sampling plans. More advanced texts on quality control, such as those listed in the bibliography, describe the use of such tables. The advanced texts also discuss the role of sampling costs in determining the optimal sampling plan.

## Multiple Sampling Plans

The acceptance sampling procedure we presented for the KALI problem is a *single-sample* plan. It is called a single-sample plan because only one sample or sampling stage is used. After the number of defective components in the sample is determined, a decision must be made to accept or reject the lot. An alternative to the single-sample plan is a **multiple sampling plan**, in which two or more stages of sampling are used. At each stage a decision is made among three possibilities: stop sampling and accept the lot, stop sampling and reject the lot, or continue sampling. Although more complex, multiple sampling plans often result in a smaller total sample size than single-sample plans with the same $\alpha$ and $\beta$ probabilities.

The logic of a two-stage, or double-sample, plan is shown in Figure 20.13. Initially a sample of $n_1$ items is selected. If the number of defective components $x_1$ is less than or equal to $c_1$, accept the lot. If $x_1$ is greater than or equal to $c_2$, reject the lot. If $x_1$ is between $c_1$ and $c_2$ $(c_1 < x_1 < c_2)$, select a second sample of $n_2$ items. Determine the combined, or total,

**FIGURE 20.13   A TWO-STAGE ACCEPTANCE SAMPLING PLAN**

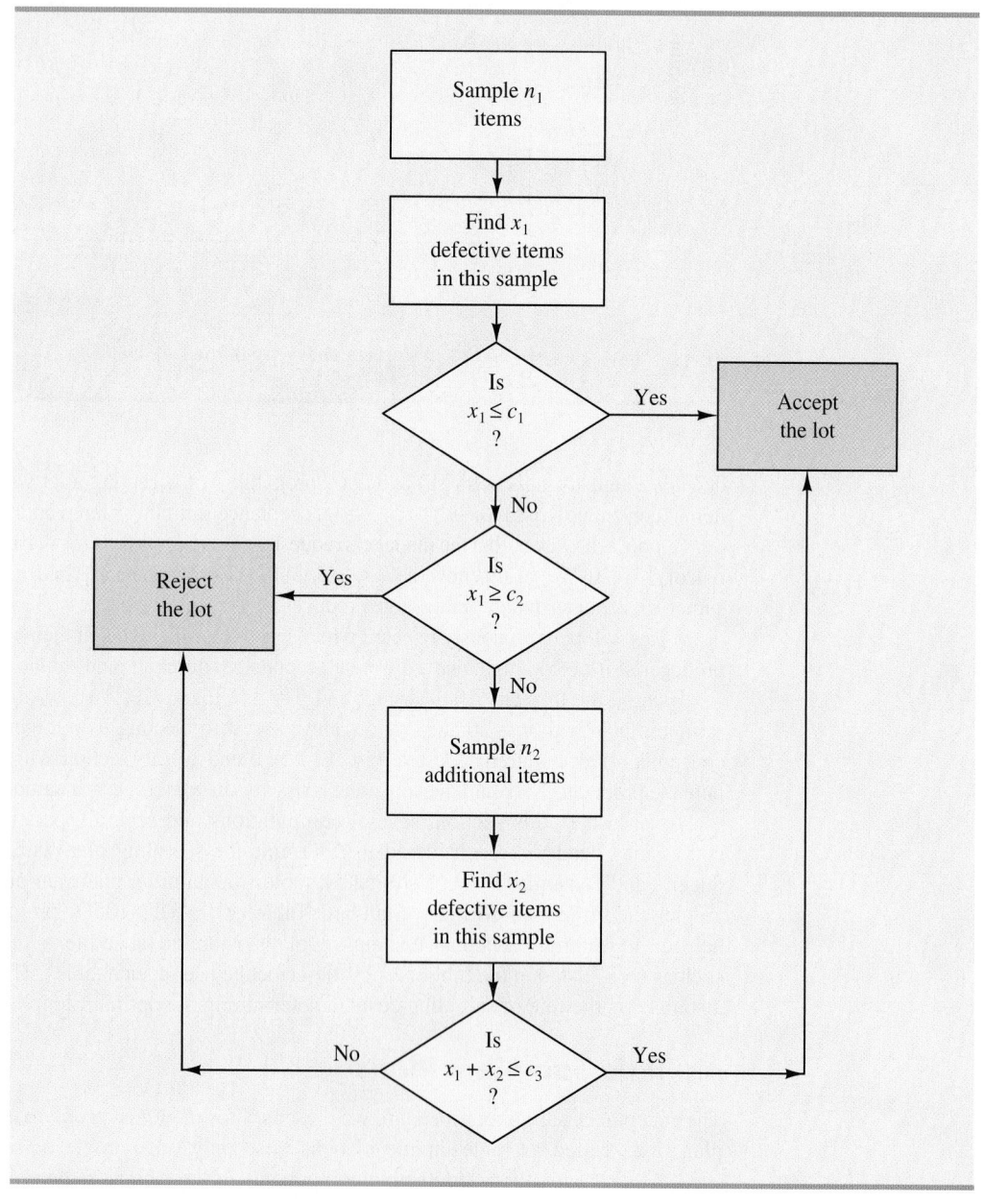

number of defective components from the first sample ($x_1$) and the second sample ($x_2$). If $x_1 + x_2 \leq c_3$, accept the lot; otherwise reject the lot. The development of the double-sample plan is more difficult because the sample sizes $n_1$ and $n_2$ and the acceptance numbers $c_1$, $c_2$, and $c_3$ must meet both the producer's and consumer's risks desired.

## NOTES AND COMMENTS

1. The use of the binomial distribution for acceptance sampling is based on the assumption of large lots. If the lot size is small, the hypergeometric distribution is appropriate. Experts in the field of quality control indicate that the Poisson distribution provides a good approximation for acceptance sampling when the sample size is at least 16, the lot size is at least 10 times the sample size, and $p$ is less than .1. For larger sample sizes, the normal approximation to the binomial distribution can be used.

2. In the MIL-ST-105D sampling tables, $p_0$ is called the acceptable quality level (AQL). In some sampling tables, $p_1$ is called the lot tolerance percent defective (LTPD) or the rejectable quality level (RQL). Many of the published sampling plans also use quality indexes such as the indifference quality level (IQL) and the average outgoing quality limit (AOQL). The more advanced texts listed in the bibliography provide a complete discussion of these other indexes.

3. In this section we provided an introduction to *attributes sampling plans*. In these plans each item sampled is classified as nondefective or defective. In *variables sampling plans,* a sample is taken and a measurement of the quality characteristic is taken. For example, for gold jewelry a measurement of quality may be the amount of gold it contains. A simple statistic such as the average amount of gold in the sample jewelry is computed and compared with an allowable value to determine whether to accept or reject the lot.

## Exercises

### Methods

10. For an acceptance sampling plan with $n = 25$ and $c = 0$, find the probability of accepting a lot that has a defect rate of 2%. What is the probability of accepting the lot if the defect rate is 6%?

11. Consider an acceptance sampling plan with $n = 20$ and $c = 0$. Compute the producer's risk for each of the following cases.
    a.   The lot has a defect rate of 2%.
    b.   The lot has a defect rate of 6%.

12. Repeat exercise 11 for the acceptance sampling plan with $n = 20$ and $c = 1$. What happens to the producer's risk as the acceptance number $c$ is increased? Explain.

### Applications

13. Refer to the KALI problem presented in this section. The quality control manager requested a producer's risk of .10 when $p_0$ was .03 and a consumer's risk of .20 when $p_1$ was .15. Consider the acceptance sampling plan based on a sample size of 20 and an acceptance number of 1. Answer the following questions.
    a.   What is the producer's risk for the $n = 20$, $c = 1$ sampling plan?
    b.   What is the consumer's risk for the $n = 20$, $c = 1$ sampling plan?
    c.   Does the $n = 20$, $c = 1$ sampling plan satisfy the risks requested by the quality control manager? Discuss.

14. To inspect incoming shipments of raw materials, a manufacturer is considering samples of sizes 10, 15, and 20. Use the binomial probabilities from Table 5 of Appendix B to select a sampling plan that provides a producer's risk of $\alpha = .03$ when $p_0$ is .05 and a consumer's risk of $\beta = .12$ when $p_1$ is .30.

15. A domestic manufacturer of watches purchases quartz crystals from a Swiss firm. The crystals are shipped in lots of 1000. The acceptance sampling procedure uses 20 randomly selected crystals.

a. Construct operating characteristic curves for acceptance numbers of 0, 1, and 2.

b. If $p_0$ is .01 and $p_1 = .08$, what are the producer's and consumer's risks for each sampling plan in part (a)?

## Summary

In this chapter we discussed how statistical methods can be used to assist in the control of quality. We first presented the $\bar{x}$, $R$, $p$, and $np$ control charts as graphical aids in monitoring process quality. Control limits are established for each chart; samples are selected periodically, and the data points plotted on the control chart. Data points outside the control limits indicate that the process is out of control and that corrective action should be taken. Patterns of data points within the control limits can also indicate potential quality control problems and suggest that corrective action may be warranted.

We also considered the technique known as acceptance sampling. With this procedure, a sample is selected and inspected. The number of defective items in the sample provides the basis for accepting or rejecting the lot. The sample size and the acceptance criterion can be adjusted to control both the producer's risk (Type I error) and the consumer's risk (Type II error).

## Glossary

**Quality control** A series of inspections and measurements that determine whether quality standards are being met.

**Assignable causes** Variations in process outputs that are due to factors such as machine tools wearing out, incorrect machine settings, poor-quality raw materials, operator error, and so on. Corrective action should be taken when assignable causes of output variation are detected.

**Common causes** Normal or natural variations in process outputs that are due purely to chance. No corrective action is necessary when output variations are due to common causes.

**Control chart** A graphical tool used to help determine whether a process is in control or out of control.

**$\bar{x}$ chart** A control chart used when the quality of the output of a process is measured in terms of the mean value of a variable such as a length, weight, temperature, and so on.

**$R$ chart** A control chart used when the quality of the output of a process is measured in terms of the range of a variable.

**$p$ chart** A control chart used when the quality of the output of a process is measured in terms of the proportion defective.

**$np$ chart** A control chart used to monitor the quality of the output of a process in terms of the number of defective items.

**Lot** A group of items such as incoming shipments of raw materials or purchased parts as well as finished goods from final assembly.

**Acceptance sampling** A statistical method in which the number of defective items found in a sample is used to determine whether a lot should be accepted or rejected.

**Producer's risk** The risk of rejecting a good-quality lot; a Type I error.

**Consumer's risk** The risk of accepting a poor-quality lot; a Type II error.

**Acceptance criterion** The maximum number of defective items that can be found in the sample and still indicate an acceptable lot.

**Operating characteristic curve** A graph showing the probability of accepting the lot as a function of the percentage defective in the lot. This curve can be used to help determine whether a particular acceptance sampling plan meets both the producer's and the consumer's risk requirements.

**Multiple sampling plan** A form of acceptance sampling in which more than one sample or stage is used. On the basis of the number of defective items found in a sample, a decision will be made to accept the lot, reject the lot, or continue sampling.

## Key Formulas

**Standard Error of the Mean**

$$\sigma_{\bar{x}} = \frac{\sigma}{\sqrt{n}} \tag{20.1}$$

**Control Limits for an $\bar{x}$ Chart: Process Mean and Standard Deviation Known**

$$\text{UCL} = \mu + 3\sigma_{\bar{x}} \tag{20.2}$$
$$\text{LCL} = \mu - 3\sigma_{\bar{x}} \tag{20.3}$$

**Overall Sample Mean**

$$\bar{\bar{x}} = \frac{\bar{x}_1 + \bar{x}_2 + \cdots + \bar{x}_k}{k} \tag{20.4}$$

**Average Range**

$$\bar{R} = \frac{R_1 + R_2 + \cdots + R_k}{k} \tag{20.5}$$

**Control Limits for an $\bar{x}$ Chart: Process Mean and Standard Deviation Unknown**

$$\bar{\bar{x}} \pm A_2\bar{R} \tag{20.8}$$

**Control Limits for an $R$ Chart**

$$\text{UCL} = \bar{R}D_4 \tag{20.14}$$
$$\text{LCL} = \bar{R}D_3 \tag{20.15}$$

**Standard Error of the Proportion**

$$\sigma_{\bar{p}} = \sqrt{\frac{p(1-p)}{n}} \tag{20.16}$$

**Control Limits for a $p$ Chart**

$$\text{UCL} = p + 3\sigma_{\bar{p}} \tag{20.17}$$
$$\text{LCL} = p - 3\sigma_{\bar{p}} \tag{20.18}$$

**Control Limits for an $np$ Chart**

$$\text{UCL} = np + 3\sqrt{np(1-p)} \tag{20.19}$$
$$\text{LCL} = np - 3\sqrt{np(1-p)} \tag{20.20}$$

Binomial Probability Function for Acceptance Sampling

$$f(x) = \frac{n!}{x!(n-x)!} p^x (1-p)^{(n-x)} \qquad (20.21)$$

## Supplementary Exercises

16. Samples of size 5 provided the following 20 sample means for a production process that is believed to be in control.

| | | |
|---|---|---|
| 95.72 | 95.24 | 95.18 |
| 95.44 | 95.46 | 95.32 |
| 95.40 | 95.44 | 95.08 |
| 95.50 | 95.80 | 95.22 |
| 95.56 | 95.22 | 95.04 |
| 95.72 | 94.82 | 95.46 |
| 95.60 | 95.78 | |

a. Based on these data, what is an estimate of the mean when the process is in control?
b. Assume that the process standard deviation is $\sigma = .50$ and develop a control chart for this production process. Assume that the mean of the process is the estimate developed in part (a).
c. Do any of the 20 sample means indicate that the process was out of control?

17. Product filling weights are normally distributed with a mean of 350 grams and a standard deviation of 15 grams.
a. Develop the control limits for samples of size 10, 20, and 30.
b. What happens to the control limits as the sample size is increased?
c. What happens when a Type I error is made?
d. What happens when a Type II error is made?
e. What is the probability of a Type I error for samples of size 10, 20, and 30?
f. What is the advantage of increasing the sample size for control chart purposes? What error probability is reduced as the sample size is increased?

18. Twenty-five samples of size 5 resulted in $\bar{\bar{x}} = 5.42$ and $\bar{R} = 2.0$. Compute control limits for the $\bar{x}$ and $R$ charts, and estimate the standard deviation of the process.

19. The following are quality control data for a manufacturing process at Kensport Chemical Company. The data show the temperature in degrees centigrade at five points in time during a manufacturing cycle. The company is interested in using control charts to monitor the temperature of its manufacturing process. Construct the $\bar{x}$ chart and $R$ chart. What conclusions can be made about the quality of the process?

| Sample | $\bar{x}$ | $R$ | Sample | $\bar{x}$ | $R$ |
|---|---|---|---|---|---|
| 1 | 95.72 | 1.0 | 11 | 95.80 | .6 |
| 2 | 95.24 | .9 | 12 | 95.22 | .2 |
| 3 | 95.18 | .8 | 13 | 95.56 | 1.3 |
| 4 | 95.44 | .4 | 14 | 95.22 | .5 |
| 5 | 95.46 | .5 | 15 | 95.04 | .8 |
| 6 | 95.32 | 1.1 | 16 | 95.72 | 1.1 |
| 7 | 95.40 | .9 | 17 | 94.82 | .6 |
| 8 | 95.44 | .3 | 18 | 95.46 | .5 |
| 9 | 95.08 | .2 | 19 | 95.60 | .4 |
| 10 | 95.50 | .6 | 20 | 95.74 | .6 |

20.  The following were collected for the Master Blend Coffee production process. The data show the filling weights based on samples of 3-pound cans of coffee. Use these data to construct the $\bar{x}$ and $R$ chart. What conclusions can be made about the quality of the production process?

**Coffee**

|        | Observations | | | | |
|--------|------|------|------|------|------|
| Sample | 1 | 2 | 3 | 4 | 5 |
| 1      | 3.05 | 3.08 | 3.07 | 3.11 | 3.11 |
| 2      | 3.13 | 3.07 | 3.05 | 3.10 | 3.10 |
| 3      | 3.06 | 3.04 | 3.12 | 3.11 | 3.10 |
| 4      | 3.09 | 3.08 | 3.09 | 3.09 | 3.07 |
| 5      | 3.10 | 3.06 | 3.06 | 3.07 | 3.08 |
| 6      | 3.08 | 3.10 | 3.13 | 3.03 | 3.06 |
| 7      | 3.06 | 3.06 | 3.08 | 3.10 | 3.08 |
| 8      | 3.11 | 3.08 | 3.07 | 3.07 | 3.07 |
| 9      | 3.09 | 3.09 | 3.08 | 3.07 | 3.09 |
| 10     | 3.06 | 3.11 | 3.07 | 3.09 | 3.07 |

21.  Consider the following situations. Comment on whether the situation might cause concern about the quality of the process.
   a.  A $p$ chart has LCL = 0 and UCL = .068. When the process is in control, the proportion defective is .033. Plot the following seven sample results: .035, .062, .055, .049, .058, .066, and .055. Discuss.
   b.  An $\bar{x}$ chart has LCL = 22.2 and UCL = 24.5. The mean is $\mu = 23.35$ when the process is in control. Plot the following seven sample results: 22.4, 22.6, 22.65, 23.2, 23.4, 23.85, and 24.1. Discuss.

22.  Managers of 1200 different retail outlets make twice-a-month restocking orders from a central warehouse. Past experience shows that 4% of the orders result in one or more errors such as wrong item shipped, wrong quantity shipped, and item requested but not shipped. Random samples of 200 orders are selected monthly and checked for accuracy.
   a.  Construct a control chart for this situation.
   b.  Six months of data show the following numbers of orders with one or more errors: 10, 15, 6, 13, 8, and 17. Plot the data on the control chart. What does your plot indicate about the order process?

23.  An $n = 10$, $c = 2$ acceptance sampling plan is being considered; assume that $p_0 = .05$ and $p_1 = .20$.
   a.  Compute both producer's and consumer's risk for this acceptance sampling plan.
   b.  Would the producer, the consumer, or both be unhappy with the proposed sampling plan?
   c.  What change in the sampling plan, if any, would you recommend?

24.  An acceptance sampling plan with $n = 15$ and $c = 1$ has been designed with a producer's risk of .075.
   a.  Was the value of $p_0$ .01, .02, .03, .04, or .05? What does this value mean?
   b.  What is the consumer's risk associated with this plan if $p_1$ is .25?

25.  A manufacturer produces lots of a canned food product. Let $p$ denote the proportion of the lots that do not meet the product quality specifications. An $n = 25$, $c = 0$ acceptance sampling plan will be used.
   a.  Compute points on the operating characteristic curve when $p = .01, .03, .10,$ and $.20$.
   b.  Plot the operating characteristic curve.
   c.  What is the probability that the acceptance sampling plan will reject a lot containing .01 defective?

26. Sometimes an acceptance sampling plan will be based on a large sample. In this case, the normal approximation to the binomial distribution can be used to compute the producer's and the consumer's risk associated with the plan. Referring to Chapter 6, we know that the normal distribution used to approximate binomial probabilities has a mean of $np$ and a standard deviation of $\sqrt{np(1-p)}$. Assume that an acceptance sampling plan is $n = 250$, $c = 10$.

   a. What is the producer's risk if $p_0$ is .02? As discussed in Chapter 6, a continuity correction factor should be used in this case. Thus, the probability of acceptance is based on the normal probability of the random variable being less than or equal to 10.5.

   b. What is the consumer's risk if $p_1$ is .08?

   c. What is an advantage of a large sample size for acceptance sampling? What is a disadvantage?

## Appendix 20.1  Control Charts with Minitab

**CD** file

Jensen

In this appendix we describe the steps required to generate Minitab control charts using the Jensen sample data shown in Table 20.2. The sample number appears in column C1. The first observation is in column C2, the second observation is in column C3, and so on. The following steps describe how to use Minitab to produce both the $\bar{x}$ chart and $R$ chart simultaneously.

**Step 1.** Select the **Stat** menu
**Step 2.** Choose **Control Charts**
**Step 3.** Choose **Variables Charts for Subgroups**
**Step 4.** Choose **Xbar-R**
**Step 5.** When the Xbar-R Chart dialog box appears:
   Select **Subgroups across rows of**
   Enter C2-C6 in the **Subgroups across rows of** box
   Select **Xbar-R Options**
**Step 6.** When the Tests dialog box appears:
   Select the **Tests** tab
   Choose **One point > 3.0 standard deviations from center line***
   Click **OK**
**Step 7.** When the Xbar-R Chart dialog box appears
   Click **OK**

The $\bar{x}$ chart and the $R$ chart will be shown together on the Minitab output. The choices available under step 3 of the preceding Minitab procedure provide access to a variety of control chart options. For example, the $\bar{x}$ and the $R$ chart can be selected separately. Additional options include the $p$ chart, the $np$ chart, and others.

---

*Minitab provides several additional tests for detecting special causes of variation and out-of-control conditions. The user may select several of these tests simultaneously.

# Decision Analysis

**CONTENTS**

## OHIO EDISON COMPANY*
*AKRON, OHIO*

Ohio Edison Company is an operating company of FirstEnergy Corporation. Ohio Edison and its subsidiary, Pennsylvania Power Company, provide electrical service to more than 1 million customers in central and northeastern Ohio and western Pennsylvania. Most of the electricity is generated by coal-fired power plants. Because of evolving pollution-control requirements, Ohio Edison embarked on a program to replace the existing pollution-control equipment at most of its generating plants.

To meet new emission limits for sulfur dioxide at one of its largest power plants, Ohio Edison decided to burn low-sulfur coal in four of the smaller units at the plant and to install fabric filters on those units to control particulate emissions. Fabric filters use thousands of fabric bags to filter out particles and function in much the same way as a household vacuum cleaner.

It was considered likely, although not certain, that the three larger units at the plant would burn medium- to high-sulfur coal. Preliminary studies narrowed the particulate equipment choice for these larger units to fabric filters and electrostatic precipitators (which remove particles suspended in the flue gas by passing it through a strong electrical field). Among the uncertainties that would affect the final choice were the way some air quality laws and regulations might be interpreted, potential future changes in air quality laws and regulations, and fluctuations in construction costs.

Because of the complexity of the problem, the high degree of uncertainty associated with factors affecting the decision, and the cost impact on Ohio Edison, decision analysis was used in the selection process. A graphical description of the problem, referred to as a decision tree, was developed. The measure used to evaluate the outcomes depicted on the decision tree was the annual revenue requirements for the three large units over their remaining lifetime. Revenue requirements were the monies that would have to be collected from the utility customers to recover costs resulting from the installation of the new pollution-control

Some utility companies generate electric power by using modern hydroelectric plants. © PhotoDisc/Getty Images.

equipment. An analysis of the decision tree led to the following conclusions.

- The expected value of annual revenue requirements for the electrostatic precipitators was approximately $1 million less than that for the fabric filters.
- The fabric filters had a higher probability of high revenue requirements than the electrostatic precipitators.
- The electrostatic precipitators had nearly a .8 probability of having lower annual revenue requirements.

These results led Ohio Edison to select the electrostatic precipitators for the generating units in question. Had the decision analysis not been performed, the particulate-control decision might have been based chiefly on capital cost, a decision measure that favored the fabric filter equipment. It was felt that the use of decision analysis identified the option with both lower expected revenue requirements and lower risk.

In this chapter we will introduce the methodology of decision analysis that Ohio Edison used. The focus will be on showing how decision analysis can identify the best decision alternative given an uncertain or risk-filled pattern of future events.

*The authors are indebted to Thomas J. Madden and M. S. Hyrnick of Ohio Edison Company for providing this Statistics in Practice.

Decision analysis can be used to develop an optimal decision strategy when a decision maker is faced with several decision alternatives and an uncertain or risk-filled pattern of future events. We begin the study of decision analysis by considering decision problems that involve reasonably few decision alternatives and reasonably few future events. Payoff tables are introduced to provide a structure for decision problems. We then introduce decision trees to show the sequential nature of the problems. Decision trees are used to analyze more complex problems and to identify an optimal sequence of decisions, referred to as an optimal decision strategy. In the last section, we show how Bayes' theorem, presented in Chapter 4, can be used to compute branch probabilities for decision trees. The Excel decision analysis add-in TreePlan and instructions for using TreePlan are provided on the ASW Web site, http://asw.swlearning.com.

*An example of the decision analysis software Treeplan is provided in Appendix 21.1.*

## 21.1  Problem Formulation

The first step in the decision analysis process is problem formulation. We begin with a verbal statement of the problem. We then identify the decision alternatives, the uncertain future events, referred to as **chance events**, and the **consequences** associated with each decision alternative and each chance event outcome. Let us begin by considering a construction project of the Pittsburgh Development Corporation.

Pittsburgh Development Corporation (PDC) purchased land that will be the site of a new luxury condominium complex. The location provides a spectacular view of downtown Pittsburgh and the Golden Triangle where the Allegheny and Monongahela rivers meet to form the Ohio River. PDC plans to price the individual condominium units between $300,000 and $1,400,000.

PDC commissioned preliminary architectural drawings for three different-sized projects: one with 30 condominiums, one with 60 condominiums, and one with 90 condominiums. The financial success of the project depends upon the size of the condominium complex and the chance event concerning the demand for the condominiums. The statement of the PDC decision problem is to select the size of the new luxury condominium project that will lead to the largest profit given the uncertainty concerning the demand for the condominiums.

Given the statement of the problem, it is clear that the decision is to select the best size for the condominium complex. PDC has the following three decision alternatives:

$$d_1 = \text{a small complex with 30 condominiums}$$
$$d_2 = \text{a medium complex with 60 condominiums}$$
$$d_3 = \text{a large complex with 90 condominiums}$$

A factor in selecting the best decision alternative is the uncertainty associated with the chance event concerning the demand for the condominiums. When asked about the possible demand for the condominiums, PDC's president acknowledged a wide range of possibilities, but decided that it would be adequate to consider two possible chance event outcomes: a strong demand and a weak demand.

In decision analysis, the possible outcomes for a chance event are referred to as the **states of nature**. The states of nature are defined so that one and only one of the possible states of nature will occur. For the PDC problem, the chance event concerning the demand for the condominiums has two states of nature:

$$s_1 = \text{strong demand for the condominiums}$$
$$s_2 = \text{weak demand for the condominiums}$$

Management must first select a decision alternative (complex size), then a state of nature follows (demand for the condominiums), and finally a consequence will occur. In this case, the consequence is PDC's profit.

## Payoff Tables

Given the three decision alternatives and the two states of nature, which complex size should PDC choose? To answer this question, PDC will need to know the consequence associated with each decision alternative and each state of nature. In decision analysis, we refer to the consequence resulting from a specific combination of a decision alternative and a state of nature as a **payoff**. A table showing payoffs for all combinations of decision alternatives and states of nature is a **payoff table**.

*Payoffs can be expressed in terms of profit, cost, time, distance, or any other measure appropriate for the decision problem being analyzed.*

Because PDC wants to select the complex size that provides the largest profit, profit is used as the consequence. The payoff table with profits expressed in millions of dollars is shown in Table 21.1. Note, for example, that if a medium complex is built and demand turns out to be strong, a profit of $14 million will be realized. We will use the notation $V_{ij}$ to denote the payoff associated with decision alternative $i$ and state of nature $j$. Using Table 21.1, $V_{31} = 20$ indicates a payoff of $20 million occurs if the decision is to build a large complex ($d_3$) and the strong demand state of nature ($s_1$) occurs. Similarly, $V_{32} = -9$ indicates a loss of $9 million if the decision is to build a large complex ($d_3$) and the weak demand state of nature ($s_2$) occurs.

## Decision Trees

A **decision tree** graphically shows the sequential nature of the decision-making process. Figure 21.1 presents a decision tree for the PDC problem, demonstrating the natural or logical progression that will occur over time. First, PDC must make a decision regarding the size of the condominium complex ($d_1$, $d_2$, or $d_3$). Then, after the decision is implemented, either state of nature $s_1$ or $s_2$ will occur. The number at each end point of the tree indicates the payoff associated with a particular sequence. For example the topmost payoff of 8 indicates that an $8 million profit is anticipated if PDC constructs a small condominium complex ($d_1$) and demand turns out to be strong ($s_1$). The next payoff of 7 indicates an anticipated profit of $7 million if PDC constructs a small condominium complex ($d_1$) and demand turns out to be weak ($s_2$). Thus, the decision tree shows graphically the sequences of decision alternatives and states of nature that provide the six possible payoffs.

The decision tree in Figure 21.1 has four **nodes**, numbered 1–4, that represent the decisions and chance events. Squares are used to depict **decision nodes** and circles are used to depict **chance nodes**. Thus, node 1 is a decision node, and nodes 2, 3, and 4 are chance nodes. The **branches** leaving the decision node correspond to the decision alternatives. The branches leaving each chance node correspond to the states of nature. The payoffs are shown at the end of the states-of-nature branches. We now turn to the question: How can the deci-

**TABLE 21.1**    PAYOFF TABLE FOR THE PDC CONDOMINIUM PROJECT
(PAYOFFS IN $ MILLIONS)

| Decision Alternative | State of Nature | |
| --- | --- | --- |
| | Strong Demand $s_1$ | Weak Demand $s_2$ |
| Small complex, $d_1$ | 8 | 7 |
| Medium complex, $d_2$ | 14 | 5 |
| Large complex, $d_3$ | 20 | -9 |

FIGURE 21.1    DECISION TREE FOR THE PDC CONDOMINIUM PROJECT
(PAYOFFS IN $ MILLIONS)

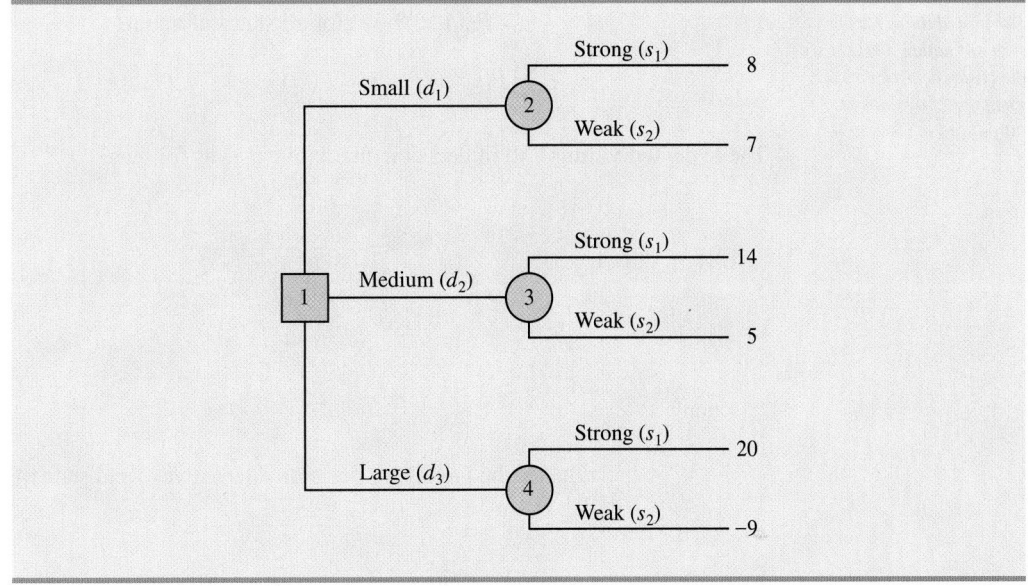

sion maker use the information in the payoff table or the decision tree to select the best decision alternative?

---

**NOTES AND COMMENTS**

1. Experts in problem solving agree that the first step in solving a complex problem is to decompose it into a series of smaller subproblems. Decision trees provide a useful way to show how a problem can be decomposed and the sequential nature of the decision process.

2. People often view the same problem from different perspectives. Thus, the discussion regarding the development of a decision tree may provide additional insight about the problem.

---

 # Decision Making with Probabilities

Once we define the decision alternatives and the states of nature for the chance events, we can focus on determining probabilities for the states of nature. The classical method, the relative frequency method, or the subjective method of assigning probabilities discussed in Chapter 4 may be used to identify these probabilities. After determining the appropriate probabilities, we show how to use the **expected value approach** to identify the best, or recommended, decision alternative for the problem.

## Expected Value Approach

We begin by defining the expected value of a decision alternative. Let

$$N = \text{the number of states of nature}$$
$$P(s_j) = \text{the probability of state of nature } s_j$$

Because one and only one of the $N$ states of nature can occur, the probabilities must satisfy two conditions:

*The probabilities for the states of nature must satisfy the basic requirements for assigning probabilities introduced in Chapter 4.*

$$P(s_j) \geq 0 \qquad \text{for all states of nature} \tag{21.1}$$

$$\sum_{j=1}^{N} P(s_j) = P(s_1) + P(s_2) + \cdots + P(s_N) = 1 \tag{21.2}$$

The **expected value (EV)** of decision alternative $d_i$ is as follows.

---

EXPECTED VALUE

$$EV(d_i) = \sum_{j=1}^{N} P(s_j)V_{ij} \tag{21.3}$$

where

$V_{ij}$ = the value of the payoff for decision alternative $d_i$ and state of nature $s_j$.

---

In words, the expected value of a decision alternative is the sum of weighted payoffs for the decision alternative. The weight for a payoff is the probability of the associated state of nature and therefore the probability that the payoff will occur. Let us return to the PDC problem to see how the expected value approach can be applied.

PDC is optimistic about the potential for the luxury high-rise condominium complex. Suppose that this optimism leads to an initial subjective probability assessment of .8 that demand will be strong $(s_1)$ and a corresponding probability of .2 that demand will be weak $(s_2)$. Thus, $P(s_1) = .8$ and $P(s_2) = .2$. Using the payoff values in Table 21.1 and equation (21.3), we compute the expected value for each of the three decision alternatives as follows:

$$EV(d_1) = .8(8) \ + .2(7) \ \ = \ \ 7.8$$
$$EV(d_2) = .8(14) + .2(5) \ \ = \ 12.2$$
$$EV(d_3) = .8(20) + .2(-9) = 14.2$$

Thus, using the expected value approach, we find that the large condominium complex, with an expected value of \$14.2 million, is the recommended decision.

The calculations required to identify the decision alternative with the best expected value can be conveniently carried out on a decision tree. Figure 21.2 shows the decision tree for the PDC problem with state-of-nature branch probabilities. Working backward through the decision tree, we first compute the expected value at each chance node; that is, at each chance node, we weight each possible payoff by its probability of occurrence. By doing so, we obtain the expected values for nodes 2, 3, and 4, as shown in Figure 21.3.

Because the decision maker controls the branch leaving decision node 1 and because we are trying to maximize the expected profit, the best decision alternative at node 1 is $d_3$. Thus, the decision tree analysis leads to a recommendation of $d_3$ with an expected value of \$14.2 million. Note that this recommendation is also obtained with the expected value approach in conjunction with the payoff table.

*Computer software packages are available to help in constructing more complex decision trees.*

Other decision problems may be substantially more complex than the PDC problem, but if a reasonable number of decision alternatives and states of nature are present, you can use the decision tree approach outlined here. First, draw a decision tree consisting of decision nodes, chance nodes, and branches that describe the sequential nature of the problem. If you use the expected value approach, the next step is to determine the probabilities for

FIGURE 21.2    PDC DECISION TREE WITH STATE-OF-NATURE BRANCH PROBABILITIES

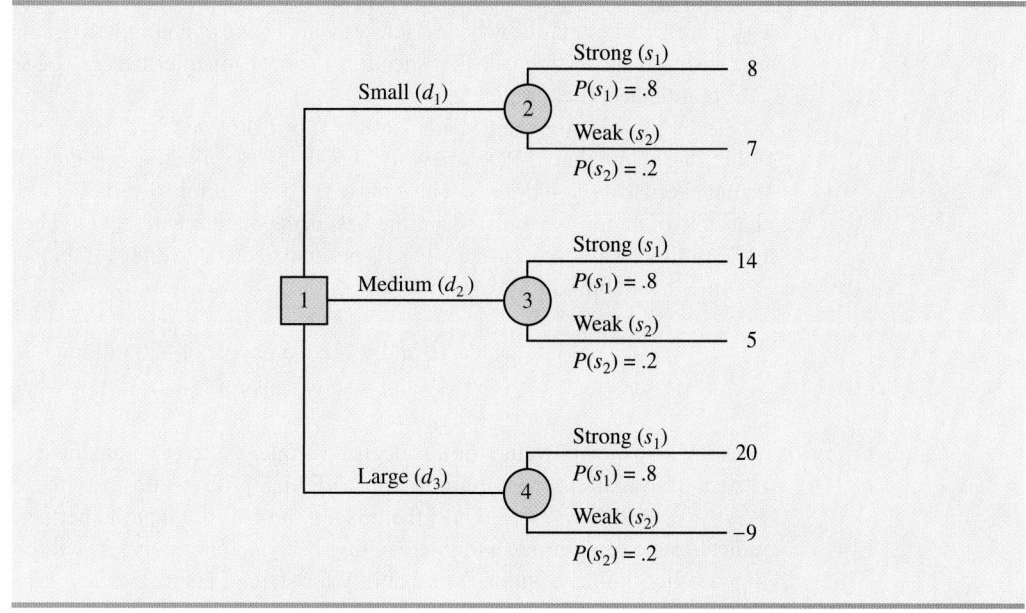

each of the states of nature and compute the expected value at each chance node. Then select the decision branch leading to the chance node with the best expected value. The decision alternative associated with this branch is the recommended decision.

## Expected Value of Perfect Information

Suppose that PDC has the opportunity to conduct a market research study that would help evaluate buyer interest in the condominium project and provide information that management could use to improve the probability assessments for the states of nature. To determine the potential value of this information, we begin by supposing that the study could provide *perfect information* regarding the states of nature; that is, we assume for the moment that

FIGURE 21.3    APPLYING THE EXPECTED VALUE APPROACH USING DECISION TREES

PDC could determine with certainty, prior to making a decision, which state of nature is going to occur. To make use of this perfect information, we will develop a decision strategy that PDC should follow once it knows which state of nature will occur. A decision strategy is simply a decision rule that specifies the decision alternative to be selected after new information becomes available.

To help determine the decision strategy for PDC, we reproduce PDC's payoff table in Table 21.2. Note that, if PDC knew for sure that state of nature $s_1$ would occur, the best decision alternative would be $d_3$, with a payoff of $20 million. Similarly, if PDC knew for sure that state of nature $s_2$ would occur, the best decision alternative would be $d_1$, with a payoff of $7 million. Thus, we can state PDC's optimal decision strategy if the perfect information becomes available as follows:

If $s_1$, select $d_3$ and receive a payoff of $20 million.

If $s_2$, select $d_1$ and receive a payoff of $7 million.

What is the expected value for this decision strategy? To compute the expected value with perfect information, we return to the original probabilities for the states of nature: $P(s_1) = .8$, and $P(s_2) = .2$. Thus, there is a .8 probability that the perfect information will indicate state of nature $s_1$ and the resulting decision alternative $d_3$ will provide a $20 million profit. Similarly, with a .2 probability for state of nature $s_2$, the optimal decision alternative $d_1$ will provide a $7 million profit. Thus, using equation (21.3), the expected value of the decision strategy based on perfect information is

$$.8(20) + .2(7) = 17.4$$

We refer to the expected value of $17.4 million as the *expected value with perfect information* (EVwPI).

Earlier in this section we showed that the recommended decision using the expected value approach is decision alternative $d_3$, with an expected value of $14.2 million. Because this decision recommendation and expected value computation were made without the benefit of perfect information, $14.2 million is referred to as the *expected value without perfect information* (EVwoPI).

*It would be worth $3.2 million for PDC to learn the level of market acceptance before selecting a decision alternative.*

The expected value with perfect information is $17.4 million, and the expected value without perfect information is $14.2; therefore, the expected value of the perfect information (EVPI) is $17.4 − $14.2 = $3.2 million. In other words, $3.2 million represents the additional expected value that can be obtained if perfect information were available about the states of nature. Generally speaking, a market research study will not provide "perfect" information; however, if the market research study is a good one, the information gathered might be worth a sizable portion of the $3.2 million. Given the EVPI of $3.2 million, PDC might seriously consider a market survey as a way to obtain more information about the states of nature.

**TABLE 21.2**   PAYOFF TABLE FOR THE PDC CONDOMINIUM PROJECT ($ MILLIONS)

| | State of Nature | |
|---|---|---|
| Decision Alternative | Strong Demand $s_1$ | Weak Demand $s_2$ |
| Small complex, $d_1$ | 8 | 7 |
| Medium complex, $d_2$ | 14 | 5 |
| Large complex, $d_3$ | 20 | −9 |

In general, the **expected value of perfect information** is computed as follows:

EXPECTED VALUE OF PERFECT INFORMATION

$$EVPI = |EVwPI - EVwoPI| \qquad (21.4)$$

where

$EVPI$ = expected value of perfect information
$EVwPI$ = expected value *with* perfect information about the states of nature
$EVwoPI$ = expected value *without* perfect information about the states of nature

Note the role of the absolute value in equation (21.4). For minimization problems, information helps reduce or lower cost, thus the expected value with perfect information is less than or equal to the expected value without perfect information. In this case, EVPI is the magnitude of the difference between EVwPI and EVwoPI, or the absolute value of the difference as shown in equation (21.4).

## Exercises

## Methods

1. The following payoff table shows profit for a decision analysis problem with two decision alternatives and three states of nature.

|  | | States of Nature | |
| --- | :---: | :---: | :---: |
| Decision Alternative | $s_1$ | $s_2$ | $s_3$ |
| $d_1$ | 250 | 100 | 25 |
| $d_2$ | 100 | 100 | 75 |

   a. Construct a decision tree for this problem.
   b. Suppose that the decision maker obtains the probabilities $P(s_1) = .65$, $P(s_2) = .15$, and $P(s_3) = .20$. Use the expected value approach to determine the optimal decision.

2. A decision maker faced with four decision alternatives and four states of nature develops the following profit payoff table.

|  | | States of Nature | | |
| --- | :---: | :---: | :---: | :---: |
| Decision Alternative | $s_1$ | $s_2$ | $s_3$ | $s_4$ |
| $d_1$ | 14 | 9 | 10 | 5 |
| $d_2$ | 11 | 10 | 8 | 7 |
| $d_3$ | 9 | 10 | 10 | 11 |
| $d_4$ | 8 | 10 | 11 | 13 |

   The decision maker obtains information that enables the following probabilities assessments: $P(s_1) = .5$, $P(s_2) = .2$, $P(s_3) = .2$, and $P(s_1) = .1$.
   a. Use the expected value approach to determine the optimal solution.
   b. Now assume that the entries in the payoff table are costs. Use the expected value approach to determine the optimal decision.

## Applications

3. Hudson Corporation is considering three options for managing its data processing operation: continue with its own staff, hire an outside vendor to do the managing (referred to as *outsourcing*), or use a combination of its own staff and an outside vendor. The cost of the operation depends on future demand. The annual cost of each option (in thousands of dollars) depends on demand as follows.

| Staffing Options | Demand | | |
| --- | --- | --- | --- |
| | High | Medium | Low |
| Own staff | 650 | 650 | 600 |
| Outside vendor | 900 | 600 | 300 |
| Combination | 800 | 650 | 500 |

   a.  If the demand probabilities are .2, .5, and .3, which decision alternative will minimize the expected cost of the data processing operation? What is the expected annual cost associated with your recommendation?
   b.  What is the expected value of perfect information?

4. Myrtle Air Express decided to offer direct service from Cleveland to Myrtle Beach. Management must decide between a full price service using the company's new fleet of jet aircraft and a discount service using smaller capacity commuter planes. It is clear that the best choice depends on the market reaction to the service Myrtle Air offers. Management developed estimates of the contribution to profit for each type of service based upon two possible levels of demand for service to Myrtle Beach: strong and weak. The following table shows the estimated quarterly profits (in thousands of dollars).

| Service | Demand for Service | |
| --- | --- | --- |
| | Strong | Weak |
| Full Price | $960 | −$490 |
| Discount | $670 | $320 |

   a.  What is the decision to be made, what is the chance event, and what is the consequence for this problem? How many decision alternatives are there? How many outcomes are there for the chance event?
   b.  Suppose that management of Myrtle Air Express believes that the probability of strong demand is .7 and the probability of weak demand is .3. Use the expected value approach to determine an optimal decision.
   c.  Suppose that the probability of strong demand is .8 and the probability of weak demand is .2. What is the optimal decision using the expected value approach?

5. The distance from Potsdam to larger markets and limited air service have hindered the town in attracting new industry. Air Express, a major overnight delivery service is considering establishing a regional distribution center in Potsdam. But Air Express will not establish the center unless the length of the runway at the local airport is increased. Another candidate for new development is Diagnostic Research, Inc. (DRI), a leading producer of medical testing equipment. DRI is considering building a new manufacturing plant. Increasing the length of the runway is not a requirement for DRI, but the planning commission feels that doing so will help convince DRI to locate their new plant in Potsdam.

Assuming that the town lengthens the runway, the Potsdam planning commission believes that the probabilities shown in the following table are applicable.

|                      | DRI Plant | No DRI Plant |
|----------------------|-----------|--------------|
| **Air Express Center**    | .30       | .10          |
| **No Air Express Center** | .40       | .20          |

For instance, the probability that Air Express will establish a distribution center and DRI will build a plant is .30.

The estimated annual revenue to the town, after deducting the cost of lengthening the runway, is as follows:

|                      | DRI Plant  | No DRI Plant |
|----------------------|------------|--------------|
| **Air Express Center**    | $600,000   | $150,000     |
| **No Air Express Center** | $250,000   | −$200,000    |

If the runway expansion project is not conducted, the planning commission assesses the probability DRI will locate their new plant in Potsdam at .6; in this case, the estimated annual revenue to the town will be $450,000. If the runway expansion project is not conducted and DRI does not locate in Potsdam, the annual revenue will be $0 since no cost will have been incurred and no revenues will be forthcoming.

a.   What is the decision to be made, what is the chance event, and what is the consequence?
b.   Compute the expected annual revenue associated with the decision alternative to lengthen the runway.
c.   Compute the expected annual revenue associated with the decision alternative to not lengthen the runway.
d.   Should the town elect to lengthen the runway? Explain.
e.   Suppose that the probabilities associated with lengthening the runway were as follows:

|                      | DRI Plant | No DRI Plant |
|----------------------|-----------|--------------|
| **Air Express Center**    | .40       | .10          |
| **No Air Express Center** | .30       | .20          |

What effect, if any, would this change in the probabilities have on the recommended decision?

6.   Seneca Hill Winery recently purchased land for the purpose of establishing a new vineyard. Management is considering two varieties of white grapes for the new vineyard: Chardonnay and Riesling. The Chardonnay grapes would be used to produce a dry Chardonnay wine, and the Riesling grapes would be used to produce a semi-dry Riesling wine. It takes approximately four years from the time of planting before new grapes can be harvested. This length of time creates a great deal of uncertainty concerning future demand and makes the decision concerning the type of grapes to plant difficult. Three possibilities are being considered: Chardonnay grapes only; Riesling grapes only; and both Chardonnay and Riesling grapes. Seneca management decided that for planning purposes it would be adequate to consider only two demand possibilities for each type of

wine: strong or weak. With two possibilities for each type of wine it was necessary to assess four probabilities. With the help of some forecasts in industry publications management made the following probability assessments.

| | Riesling Demand | |
|---|---|---|
| Chardonnay Demand | Weak | Strong |
| Weak | .05 | .50 |
| Strong | .25 | .20 |

Revenue projections show an annual contribution to profit of $20,000 if Seneca Hill only plants Chardonnay grapes and demand is weak for Chardonnay wine, and $70,000 if they only plant Chardonnay grapes and demand is strong for Chardonnay wine. If they only plant Riesling grapes, the annual profit projection is $25,000 if demand is weak for Riesling grapes and $45,000 if demand is strong for Riesling grapes. If Seneca plants both types of grapes, the annual profit projections are shown in the following table.

| | Riesling Demand | |
|---|---|---|
| Chardonnay Demand | Weak | Strong |
| Weak | $22,000 | $40,000 |
| Strong | $26,000 | $60,000 |

a. What is the decision to be made, what is the chance event, and what is the consequence? Identify the alternatives for the decisions and the possible outcomes for the chance events.
b. Develop a decision tree.
c. Use the expected value approach to recommend which alternative Seneca Hill Winery should follow in order to maximize expected annual profit.
d. Suppose management is concerned about the probability assessments when demand for Chardonnay wine is strong. Some believe it is likely for Riesling demand to also be strong in this case. Suppose the probability of strong demand for Chardonnay and weak demand for Riesling is .05 and that the probability of strong demand for Chardonnay and strong demand for Riesling is .40. How does this change the recommended decision? Assume that the probabilities when Chardonnay demand is weak are still .05 and .50.
e. Other members of the management team expect the Chardonnay market to become saturated at some point in the future causing a fall in prices. Suppose that the annual profit projections fall to $50,000 when demand for Chardonnay is strong and Chardonnay grapes only are planted. Using the original probability assessments, determine how this change would affect the optimal decision.

7. The Lake Placid Town Council has decided to build a new community center to be used for conventions, concerts, and other public events, but considerable controversy surrounds the appropriate size. Many influential citizens want a large center that would be a showcase for the area, but the mayor feels that if demand does not support such a center, the community will lose a large amount of money. To provide structure for the decision process, the council narrowed the building alternatives to three sizes: small, medium, and large. Everybody agreed that the critical factor in choosing the best size is the number of people who will want to use the new facility. A regional planning consultant provided demand estimates under three scenarios: worst case, base case, and best case. The worst-case scenario corresponds to a situation in which tourism drops significantly; the base-case scenario corresponds to a situation in which Lake Placid continues to attract visitors at cur-

rent levels; and the best-case scenario corresponds to a significant increase in tourism. The consultant has provided probability assessments of .10, .60, and .30 for the worst-case, base-case, and best-case scenarios, respectively.

The town council suggested using net cash flow over a five-year planning horizon as the criterion for deciding on the best size. A consultant developed the following projections of net cash flow (in thousands of dollars) for a five-year planning horizon. All costs, including the consultant's fee, are included.

| | Demand Scenario | | |
| --- | --- | --- | --- |
| Center Size | Worst Case | Base Case | Best Case |
| Small | 400 | 500 | 660 |
| Medium | −250 | 650 | 800 |
| Large | −400 | 580 | 990 |

a.  What decision should Lake Placid make using the expected value approach?
b.  Compute the expected value of perfect information. Do you think it would be worth trying to obtain additional information concerning which scenario is likely to occur?
c.  Suppose the probability of the worst-case scenario increases to .2, the probability of the base-case scenario decreases to .5, and the probability of the best-case scenario remains at .3. What effect, if any, would these changes have on the decision recommendation?
d.  The consultant suggested that an expenditure of $150,000 on a promotional campaign over the planning horizon will effectively reduce the probability of the worst-case scenario to zero. If the campaign can be expected to also increase the probability of the best-case scenario to .4, is it a good investment?

#  Decision Analysis with Sample Information

In applying the expected value approach, we showed how probability information about the states of nature affects the expected value calculations and thus the decision recommendation. Frequently, decision makers have preliminary or **prior probability** assessments for the states of nature that are the best probability values available at that time. However, to make the best possible decision, the decision maker may want to seek additional information about the states of nature. This new information can be used to revise or update the prior probabilities so that the final decision is based on more accurate probabilities for the states of nature. Most often, additional information is obtained through experiments designed to provide **sample information** about the states of nature. Raw material sampling, product testing, and market research studies are examples of experiments (or studies) that may enable management to revise or update the state-of-nature probabilities. These revised probabilities are called **posterior probabilities**.

Let us return to the PDC problem and assume that management is considering a six-month market research study designed to learn more about potential market acceptance of the PDC condominium project. Management anticipates that the market research study will provide one of the following two results:

1.  **Favorable report:** A significant number of the individuals contacted express interest in purchasing a PDC condominium.
2.  **Unfavorable report:** Very few of the individuals contacted express interest in purchasing a PDC condominium.

## Decision Tree

The decision tree for the PDC problem with sample information shows the logical sequence for the decisions and the chance events in Figure 21.4. First, PDC's management must decide whether the market research should be conducted. If it is conducted, PDC's management must be prepared to make a decision about the size of the condominium project if the market research report is favorable and, possibly, a different decision about the size of the condominium project if the market research report is unfavorable.

**FIGURE 21.4    THE PDC DECISION TREE INCLUDING THE MARKET RESEARCH STUDY**

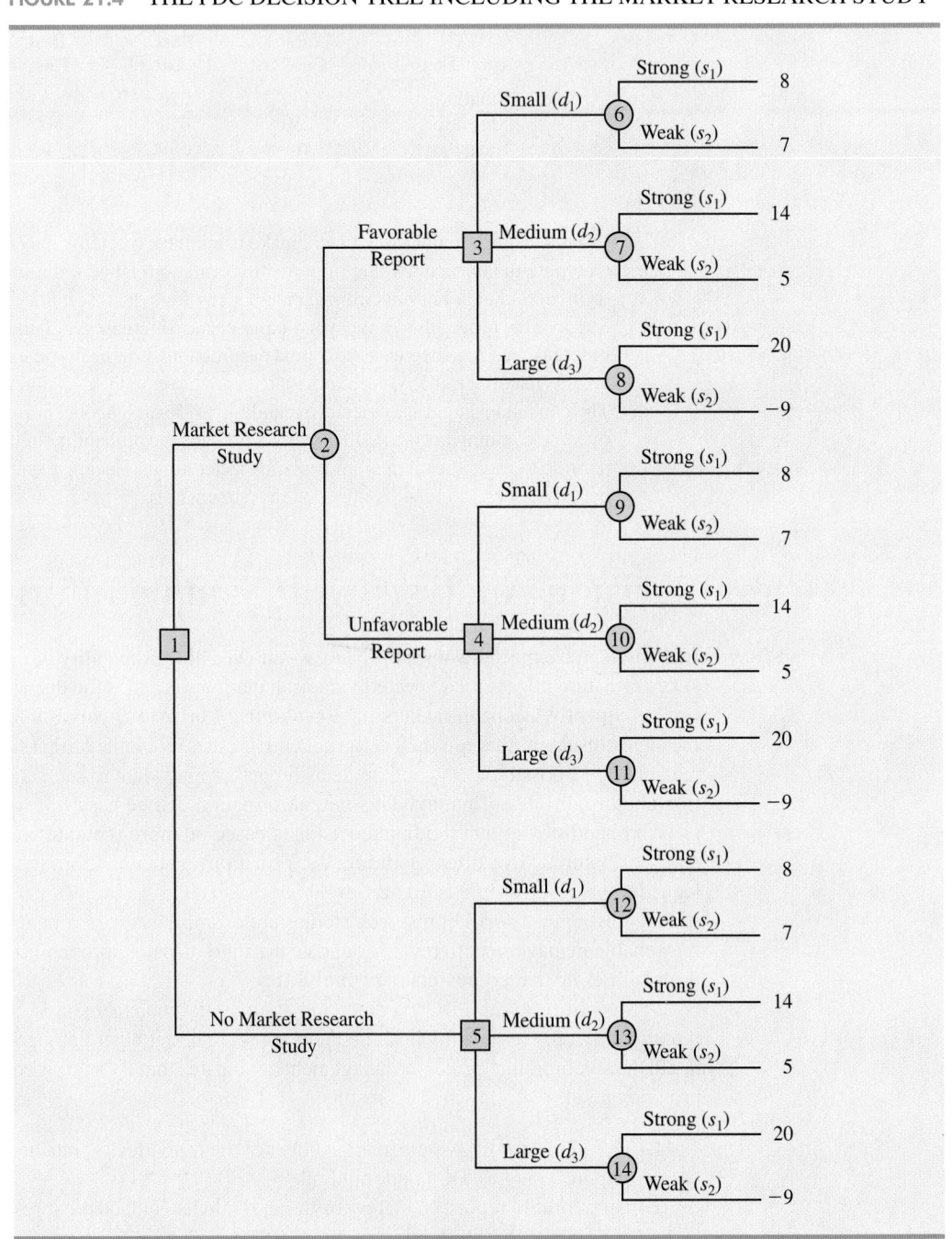

In Figure 21.4, the squares are decision nodes and the circles are chance nodes. At each decision node, the branch of the tree that is taken is based on the decision made. At each chance node, the branch of the tree that is taken is based on probability or chance. For example, decision node 1 shows that PDC must first make the decision whether to conduct the market research study. If the market research study is undertaken, chance node 2 indicates that both the favorable report branch and the unfavorable report branch are not under PDC's control and will be determined by chance. Node 3 is a decision node, indicating that PDC must make the decision to construct the small, medium, or large complex if the market research report is favorable. Node 4 is a decision node showing that PDC must make the decision to construct the small, medium, or large complex if the market research report is unfavorable. Node 5 is a decision node indicating that PDC must make the decision to construct the small, medium, or large complex if the market research is not undertaken. Nodes 6 to 14 are chance nodes indicating that the strong demand or weak demand state-of-nature branches will be determined by chance.

*We explain in Section 21.4 how these probabilities can be developed.*

Analysis of the decision tree and the choice of an optimal strategy requires that we know the branch probabilities corresponding to all chance nodes. PDC developed the following branch probabilities.

If the market research study is undertaken

$$P(\text{Favorable report}) = P(F) = .77$$
$$P(\text{Unfavorable report}) = P(U) = .23$$

If the market research report is favorable

$$P(\text{Strong demand given a favorable report}) = P(s_1|F) = .94$$
$$P(\text{Weak demand given a favorable report}) = P(s_2|F) = .06$$

If the market research report is unfavorable

$$P(\text{Strong demand given an unfavorable report}) = P(s_1|U) = .35$$
$$P(\text{Weak demand given an unfavorable report}) = P(s_2|U) = .65$$

If the market research report is not undertaken the prior probabilities are applicable.

$$P(\text{Strong demand}) = P(s_1) = .80$$
$$P(\text{Weak demand}) = P(s_2) = .20$$

The branch probabilities are shown on the decision tree in Figure 21.5.

## Decision Strategy

A **decision strategy** is a sequence of decisions and chance outcomes where the decisions chosen depend on the yet to be determined outcomes of chance events. The approach used to determine the optimal decision strategy is based on a backward pass through the decision tree using the following steps:

1. At chance nodes, compute the expected value by multiplying the payoff at the end of each branch by the corresponding branch probability.
2. At decision nodes, select the decision branch that leads to the best expected value. This expected value becomes the expected value at the decision node.

**FIGURE 21.5** THE PDC DECISION TREE WITH BRANCH PROBABILITIES

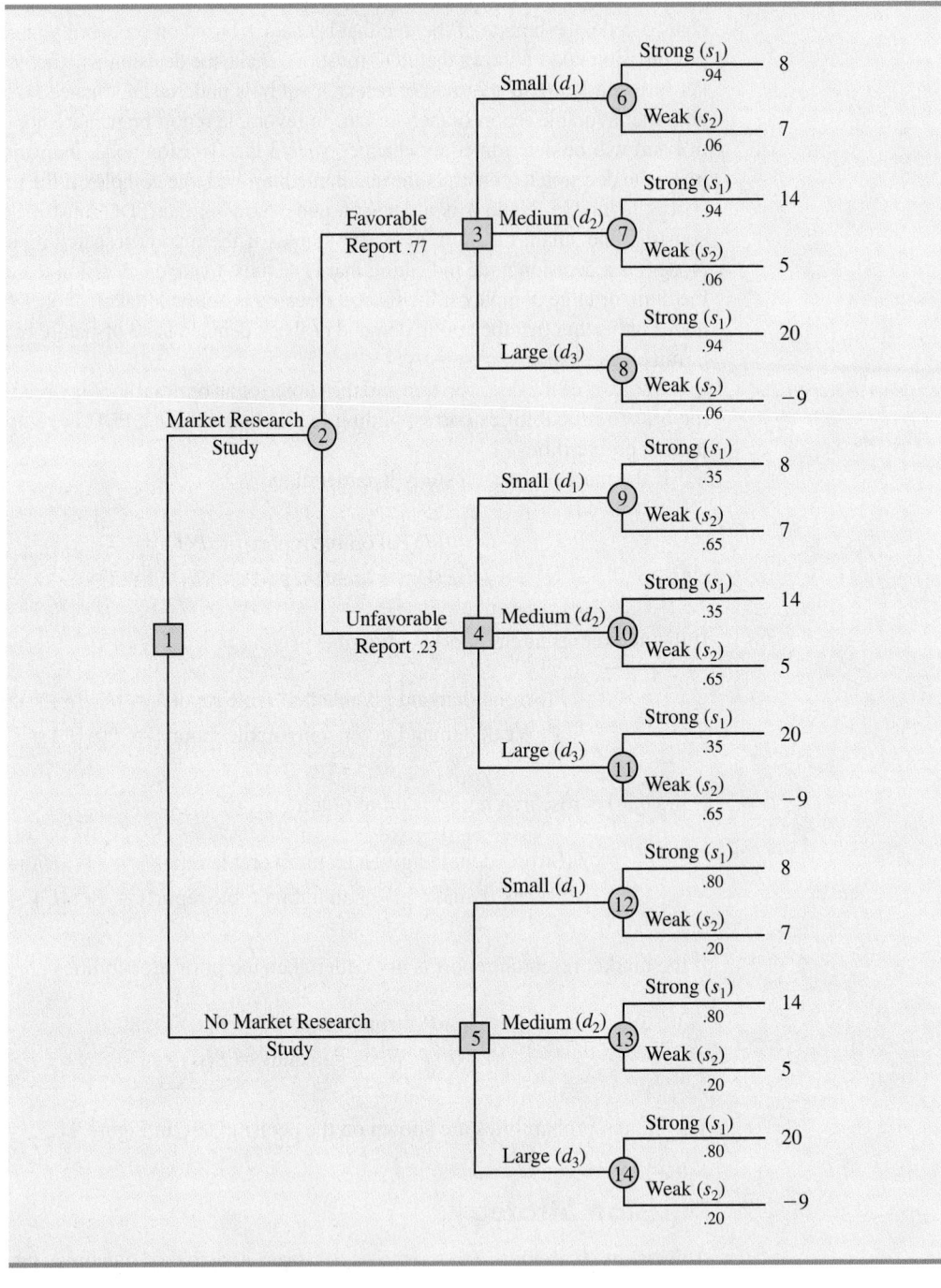

Starting the backward pass calculations by computing the expected values at chance nodes 6 to 14 provides the following results.

$$
\begin{aligned}
EV(\text{Node } 6) &= .94(8) &+ .06(7) &= 7.94 \\
EV(\text{Node } 7) &= .94(14) &+ .06(5) &= 13.46 \\
EV(\text{Node } 8) &= .94(20) &+ .06(-9) &= 18.26 \\
EV(\text{Node } 9) &= .35(8) &+ .65(7) &= 7.35 \\
EV(\text{Node } 10) &= .35(14) &+ .65(5) &= 8.15 \\
EV(\text{Node } 11) &= .35(20) &+ .65(-9) &= 1.15 \\
EV(\text{Node } 12) &= .80(8) &+ .20(7) &= 7.80 \\
EV(\text{Node } 13) &= .80(14) &+ .20(5) &= 12.20 \\
EV(\text{Node } 14) &= .80(20) &+ .20(-9) &= 14.20
\end{aligned}
$$

Figure 21.6 shows the reduced decision tree after computing expected values at these chance nodes.

Next move to decision nodes 3, 4, and 5. For each of these nodes, we select the decision alternative branch that leads to the best expected value. For example, at node 3 we have the choice of the small complex branch with EV(Node 6) = 7.94, the medium complex branch with EV(Node 7) = 13.46, and the large complex branch with EV(Node 8) = 18.26. Thus, we select the large complex decision alternative branch and the expected value at node 3 becomes EV(Node 3) = 18.26.

For node 4, we select the best expected value from nodes 9, 10, and 11. The best decision alternative is the medium complex branch that provides EV(Node 4) = 8.15. For node 5, we select the best expected value from nodes 12, 13, and 14. The best decision alternative is the large complex branch that provides EV(Node 5) = 14.20. Figure 21.7 shows the reduced decision tree after choosing the best decisions at nodes 3, 4, and 5.

The expected value at chance node 2 can now be computed as follows:

$$
\begin{aligned}
EV(\text{Node } 2) &= .77EV(\text{Node } 3) + .23EV(\text{Node } 4) \\
&= .77(18.26) + .23(8.15) = 15.93
\end{aligned}
$$

This calculation reduces the decision tree to one involving only the two decision branches from node 1 (see Figure 21.8).

Finally, the decision can be made at decision node 1 by selecting the best expected values from nodes 2 and 5. This action leads to the decision alternative to conduct the market research study, which provides an overall expected value of 15.93.

The optimal decision for PDC is to conduct the market research study and then carry out the following decision strategy:

If the market research is favorable, construct the large condominium complex.

If the market research is unfavorable, construct the medium condominium complex.

The analysis of the PDC decision tree illustrates the methods that can be used to analyze more complex sequential decision problems. First, draw a decision tree consisting of decision and chance nodes and branches that describe the sequential nature of the problem. Determine the probabilities for all chance outcomes. Then, by working backward through the tree, compute expected values at all chance nodes and select the best decision branch at all decision nodes. The sequence of optimal decision branches determines the optimal decision strategy for the problem.

FIGURE 21.6 PDC DECISION TREE AFTER COMPUTING EXPECTED VALUES AT CHANCE NODES 6 TO 14

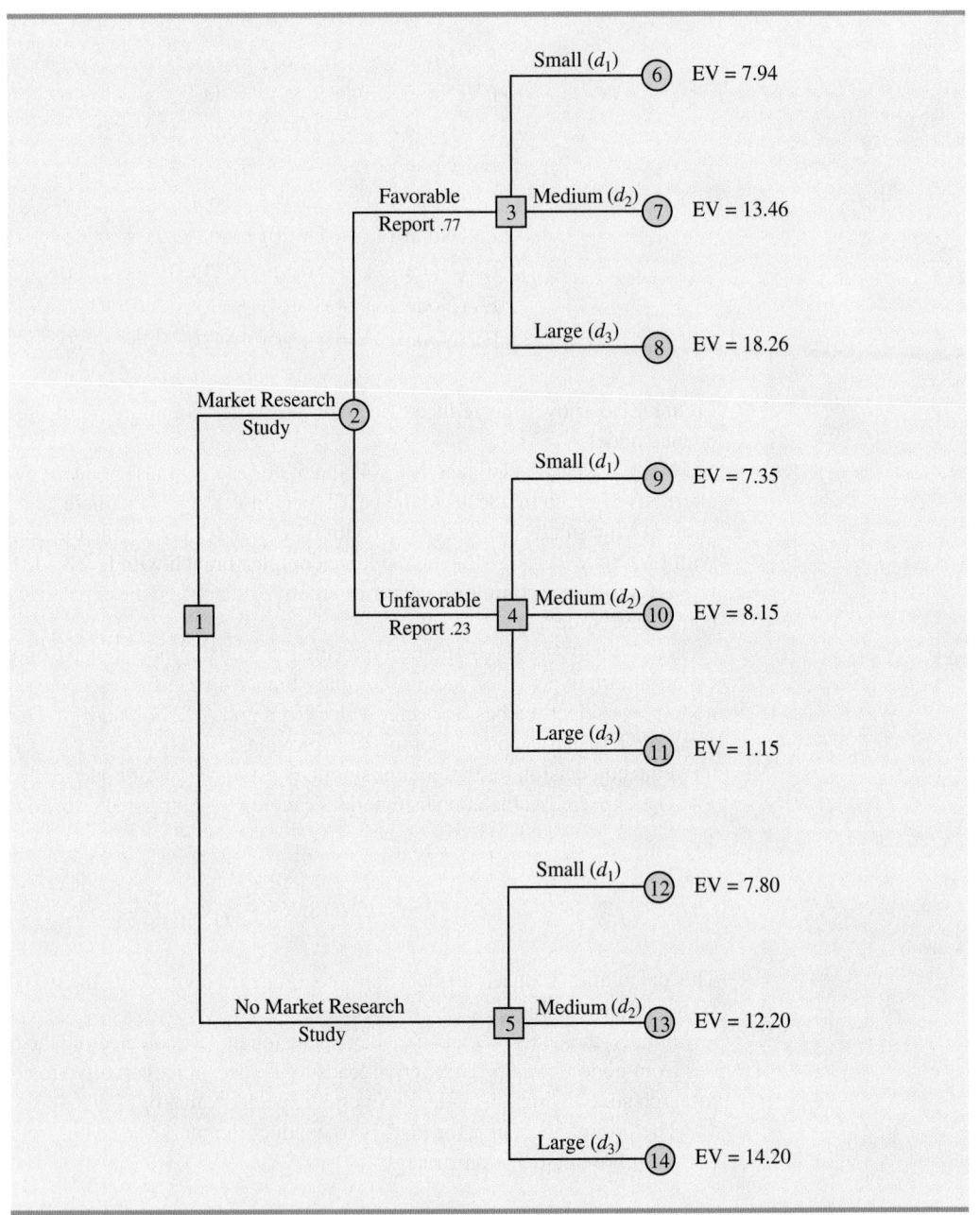

## Expected Value of Sample Information

*The EVSI = $1.73 million suggests PDC should be willing to pay up to $1.73 million to conduct the market research study.*

In the PDC problem, the market research study is the sample information used to determine the optimal decision strategy. The expected value associated with the market research study is $15.93. In Section 21.3 we showed that the best expected value if the market research study is *not* undertaken is $14.20. Thus, we can conclude that the difference, $15.93 − $14.20 = $1.73, is the **expected value of sample information (EVSI)**. In other words,

FIGURE 21.7    PDC DECISION TREE AFTER CHOOSING BEST DECISIONS AT NODES 3, 4,
AND 5

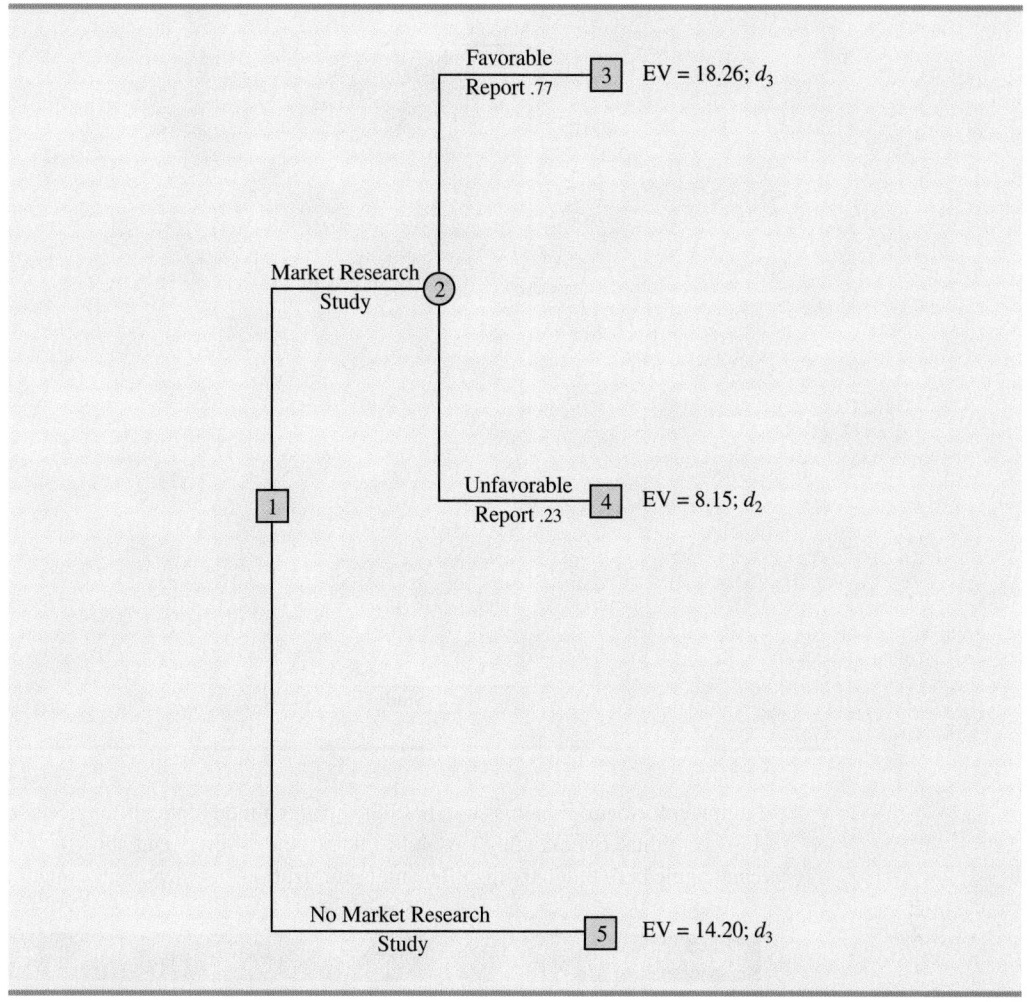

conducting the market research study adds $1.73 million to the PDC expected value. In general, the expected value of sample information is as follows:

EXPECTED VALUE OF SAMPLE INFORMATION

$$\text{EVSI} = \left| \text{EVwSI} - \text{EVwoSI} \right| \tag{21.5}$$

where

    EVSI = expected value of sample information

  EVwSI = expected value *with* sample information about the states of nature

EVwoSI = expected value *without* sample information about the states of nature

Note the role of the absolute value in equation (21.5). For minimization problems the expected value with sample information is always less than or equal to the expected value without

FIGURE 21.8    PDC DECISION TREE REDUCED TO TWO DECISION BRANCHES

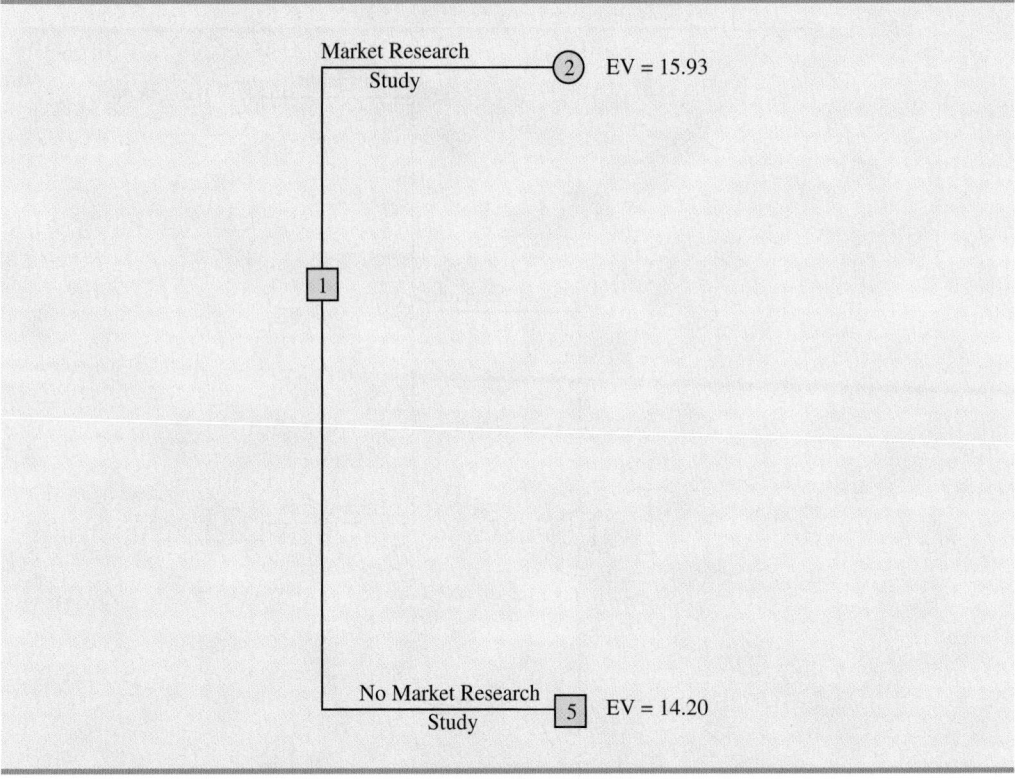

sample information. In this case, EVSI is the magnitude of the difference between EVwSI and EVwoSI; thus, by taking the absolute value of the difference as shown in equation (21.5), we can handle both the maximization and minimization cases with one equation.

## Exercises

### Methods

8.  Consider a variation of the PDC decision tree shown in Figure 21.5. The company must first decide whether to undertake the market research study. If the market research study is conducted, the outcome will either be favorable ($F$) or unfavorable ($U$). Assume there are only two decision alternatives $d_1$ and $d_2$ and two states of nature $s_1$ and $s_2$. The payoff table showing profit is as follows:

|  | State of Nature | |
| Decision Alternative | $s_1$ | $s_2$ |
| --- | --- | --- |
| $d_1$ | 100 | 300 |
| $d_2$ | 400 | 200 |

a.  Show the decision tree.
b.  Use the following probabilities. What is the optimal decision strategy?

$$P(F) = .56 \qquad P(s_1 \mid F) = .57 \qquad P(s_1 \mid U) = .18 \qquad P(s_1) = .40$$
$$P(U) = .44 \qquad P(s_2 \mid F) = .43 \qquad P(s_2 \mid U) = .82 \qquad P(s_2) = .60$$

## Applications

9.   A real estate investor has the opportunity to purchase land currently zoned residential. If the county board approves a request to rezone the property as commercial within the next year, the investor will be able to lease the land to a large discount firm that wants to open a new store on the property. However, if the zoning change is not approved, the investor will have to sell the property at a loss. Profits (in thousands of dollars) are shown in the following payoff table.

|                               | State of Nature | |
| ----------------------------- | :-------------: | :-------------: |
|                               | **Rezoning Approved** | **Rezoning Not Approved** |
| **Decision Alternative**      | $s_1$           | $s_2$           |
| **Purchase, $d_1$**           | 600             | −200            |
| **Do not purchase, $d_2$**    | 0               | 0               |

   a.   If the probability that the rezoning will be approved is .5, what decision is recommended? What is the expected profit?
   b.   The investor can purchase an option to buy the land. Under the option, the investor maintains the rights to purchase the land anytime during the next three months while learning more about possible resistance to the rezoning proposal from area residents. Probabilities are as follows.

   $$\text{Let} \quad H = \text{high resistance to rezoning}$$
   $$L = \text{low resistance to rezoning}$$

   $$P(H) = .55 \quad P(s_1 \mid H) = .18 \quad P(s_2 \mid H) = .82$$
   $$P(L) = .45 \quad P(s_1 \mid L) = .89 \quad P(s_2 \mid L) = .11$$

   What is the optimal decision strategy if the investor uses the option period to learn more about the resistance from area residents before making the purchase decision?
   c.   If the option will cost the investor an additional $10,000, should the investor purchase the option? Why or why not? What is the maximum that the investor should be willing to pay for the option?

10.  Dante Development Corporation is considering bidding on a contract for a new office building complex. Figure 21.9 shows the decision tree prepared by one of Dante's analysts. At node 1, the company must decide whether to bid on the contract. The cost of preparing the bid is $200,000. The upper branch from node 2 shows that the company has a .8 probability of winning the contract if it submits a bid. If the company wins the bid, it will have to pay $2,000,000 to become a partner in the project. Node 3 shows that the company will then consider doing a market research study to forecast demand for the office units prior to beginning construction. The cost of this study is $150,000. Node 4 is a chance node showing the possible outcomes of the market research study.
      Nodes 5, 6, and 7 are similar in that they are the decision nodes for Dante to either build the office complex or sell the rights in the project to another developer. The decision to build the complex will result in an income of $5,000,000 if demand is high and $3,000,000 if demand is moderate. If Dante chooses to sell its rights in the project to another developer, income from the sale is estimated to be $3,500,000. The probabilities shown at nodes 4, 8, and 9 are based on the projected outcomes of the market research study.
   a.   Verify Dante's profit projections shown at the ending branches of the decision tree by calculating the payoffs of $2,650,000 and $650,000 for first two outcomes.
   b.   What is the optimal decision strategy for Dante, and what is the expected profit for this project?
   c.   What would the cost of the market research study have to be before Dante would change its decision about conducting the study?

**FIGURE 21.9   DECISION TREE FOR THE DANTE DEVELOPMENT CORPORATION**

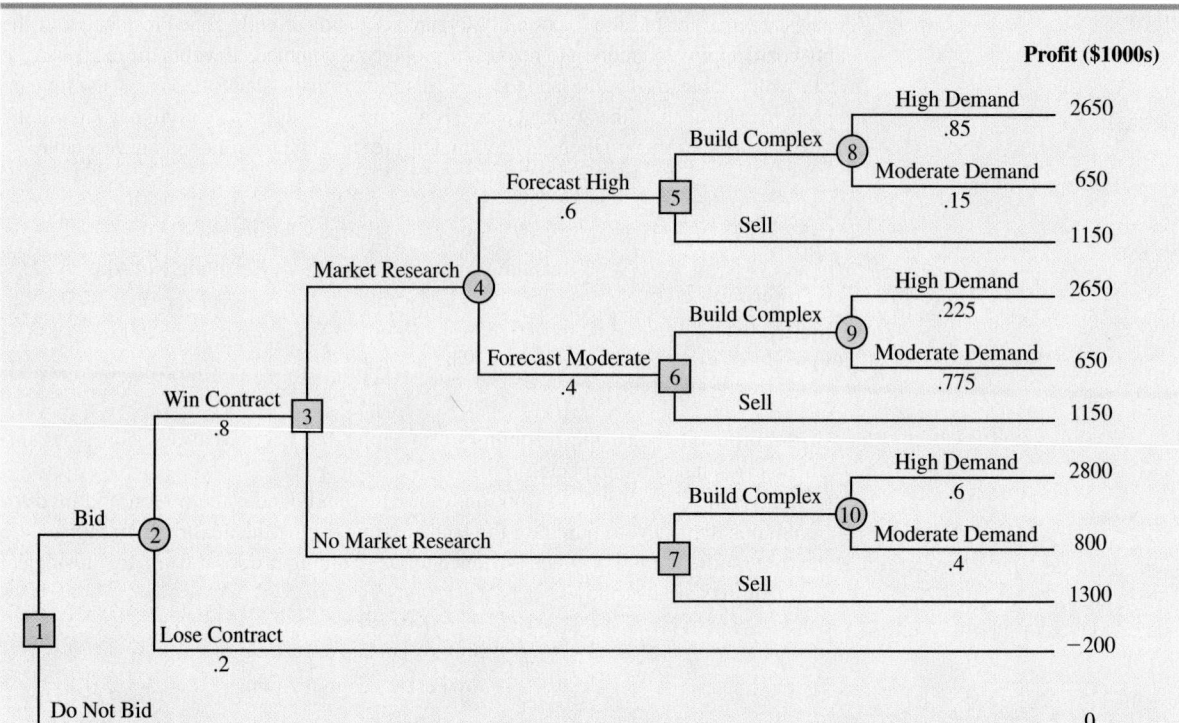

11.  Hale's TV Productions is considering producing a pilot for a comedy series in the hope of selling it to a major television network. The network may decide to reject the series, but it may also decide to purchase the rights to the series for either one or two years. At this point in time, Hale may either produce the pilot and wait for the network's decision or transfer the rights for the pilot and series to a competitor for $100,000. Hale's decision alternatives and profits (in thousands of dollars) are as follows:

| Decision Alternative | State of Nature | | |
|---|---|---|---|
| | Reject, $s_1$ | 1 Year, $s_2$ | 2 Years, $s_3$ |
| Produce pilot, $d_1$ | −100 | 50 | 150 |
| Sell to competitor, $d_2$ | 100 | 100 | 100 |

The probabilities for the states of nature are $P(s_1) = .2$, $P(s_2) = .3$, and $P(s_3) = .5$. For a consulting fee of $5000, an agency will review the plans for the comedy series and indicate the overall chances of a favorable network reaction to the series. Assume that the agency review will result in a favorable $(F)$ or an unfavorable $(U)$ review and that the following probabilities are relevant.

$$P(F) = .69 \quad P(s_1 \mid F) = .09 \quad P(s_1 \mid U) = .45$$
$$P(U) = .31 \quad P(s_2 \mid F) = .26 \quad P(s_2 \mid U) = .39$$
$$P(s_3 \mid F) = .65 \quad P(s_3 \mid U) = .16$$

a.  Construct a decision tree for this problem.
b.  What is the recommended decision if the agency opinion is not used? What is the expected value?

    c.    What is the expected value of perfect information?

    d.    What is Hale's optimal decision strategy assuming the agency's information is used?

    e.    What is the expected value of the agency's information?

    f.    Is the agency's information worth the $5000 fee? What is the maximum that Hale should be willing to pay for the information?

    g.    What is the recommended decision?

12.    Martin's Service Station is considering entering the snowplowing business for the coming winter season. Martin can purchase either a snowplow blade attachment for the station's pick-up truck or a new heavy-duty snowplow truck. After analyzing the situation, Martin believes that either alternative would be a profitable investment if the snowfall is heavy. Smaller profits would result if the snowfall is moderate, and losses would result if the snowfall is light. The following profits/losses apply.

|  | State of Nature | | |
|---|---|---|---|
| Decision Alternatives | Heavy, $s_1$ | Moderate, $s_2$ | Light, $s_3$ |
| Blade attachment, $d_1$ | 3500 | 1000 | −1500 |
| New snowplow, $d_2$ | 7000 | 2000 | −9000 |

The probabilities for the states of nature are $P(s_1) = .4$, $P(s_2) = .3$, and $P(s_3) = .3$. Suppose that Martin decides to wait until September before making a final decision. Assessments of the probabilities associated with a normal $(N)$ or unseasonably cold $(U)$ September are as follows:

$$P(N) = .8 \qquad P(s_1 \mid N) = .35 \qquad P(s_1 \mid U) = .62$$
$$P(U) = .2 \qquad P(s_2 \mid N) = .30 \qquad P(s_2 \mid U) = .31$$
$$\qquad\qquad P(s_3 \mid N) = .35 \qquad P(s_3 \mid U) = .07$$

    a.    Construct a decision tree for this problem.

    b.    What is the recommended decision if Martin does not wait until September? What is the expected value?

    c.    What is the expected value of perfect information?

    d.    What is Martin's optimal decision strategy if the decision is not made until the September weather is determined? What is the expected value of this decision strategy?

13.    Lawson's Department Store faces a buying decision for a seasonal product for which demand can be high, medium, or low. The purchaser for Lawson's can order 1, 2, or 3 lots of the product before the season begins but cannot reorder later. Profit projections (in thousands of dollars) are shown.

|  | State of Nature | | |
|---|---|---|---|
|  | High Demand | Medium Demand | Low Demand |
| Decision Alternative | $s_1$ | $s_2$ | $s_3$ |
| Order 1 lot, $d_1$ | 60 | 60 | 50 |
| Order 2 lots, $d_2$ | 80 | 80 | 30 |
| Order 3 lots, $d_3$ | 100 | 70 | 10 |

    a.    If the prior probabilities for the three states of nature are .3, .3, and .4, respectively, what is the recommended order quantity?

    b.    At each preseason sales meeting, the vice president of sales provides a personal opinion regarding potential demand for this product. Because of the vice president's enthusiasm and optimistic nature, the predictions of market conditions have always been either "excellent" ($E$) or "very good" ($V$). Probabilities are as follows. What is the optimal decision strategy?

$$P(E) = .7 \quad P(s_1 \mid E) = .34 \quad P(s_1 \mid V) = .20$$
$$P(V) = .3 \quad P(s_2 \mid E) = .32 \quad P(s_2 \mid V) = .26$$
$$P(s_3 \mid E) = .34 \quad P(s_3 \mid V) = .54$$

c.  Compute EVPI and EVSI. Discuss whether the firm should consider a consulting expert who could provide independent forecasts of market conditions for the product.

#  Computing Branch Probabilities Using Bayes' Theorem

In Section 21.3 the branch probabilities for the PDC decision tree chance nodes were specified in the problem description. No computations were required to determine these probabilities. In this section we show how **Bayes' theorem**, a topic covered in Chapter 4, can be used to compute branch probabilities for decision trees.

The PDC decision tree is shown again in Figure 21.10. Let

$$F = \text{Favorable market research report}$$
$$U = \text{Unfavorable market research report}$$
$$s_1 = \text{Strong demand (state of nature 1)}$$
$$s_2 = \text{Weak demand (state of nature 2)}$$

At chance node 2, we need to know the branch probabilities $P(F)$ and $P(U)$. At chance nodes 6, 7, and 8, we need to know the branch probabilities $P(s_1 \mid F)$, the probability of state of nature 1 given a favorable market research report, and $P(s_2 \mid F)$, the probability of state of nature 2 given a favorable market research report. $P(s_1 \mid F)$ and $P(s_2 \mid F)$ are referred to as *posterior probabilities* because they are conditional probabilities based on the outcome of the sample information. At chance nodes 9, 10, and 11, we need to know the branch probabilities $P(s_1 \mid U)$ and $P(s_2 \mid U)$; note that these are also posterior probabilities, denoting the probabilities of the two states of nature *given* that the market research report is unfavorable. Finally at chance nodes 12, 13, and 14, we need the probabilities for the states of nature, $P(s_1)$ and $P(s_2)$, if the market research study is not undertaken.

In making the probability computations, we need to know PDC's assessment of the probabilities for the two states of nature, $P(s_1)$ and $P(s_2)$, which are the prior probabilities as discussed earlier. In addition, we must know the **conditional probability** of the market research outcomes (the sample information) *given* each state of nature. For example, we need to know the conditional probability of a favorable market research report given that strong demand exists for the PDC project; note that this conditional probability of $F$ given state of nature $s_1$ is written $P(F \mid s_1)$. To carry out the probability calculations, we will need conditional probabilities for all sample outcomes given all states of nature, that is, $P(F \mid s_1)$, $P(F \mid s_2)$, $P(U \mid s_1)$, and $P(U \mid s_2)$. In the PDC problem, we assume that the following assessments are available for these conditional probabilities.

|  | Market Research | |
|---|---|---|
| State of Nature | Favorable, $F$ | Unfavorable, $U$ |
| Strong demand, $s_1$ | $P(F \mid s_1) = .90$ | $P(U \mid s_1) = .10$ |
| Weak demand, $s_2$ | $P(F \mid s_2) = .25$ | $P(U \mid s_2) = .75$ |

**FIGURE 21.10    THE PDC DECISION TREE**

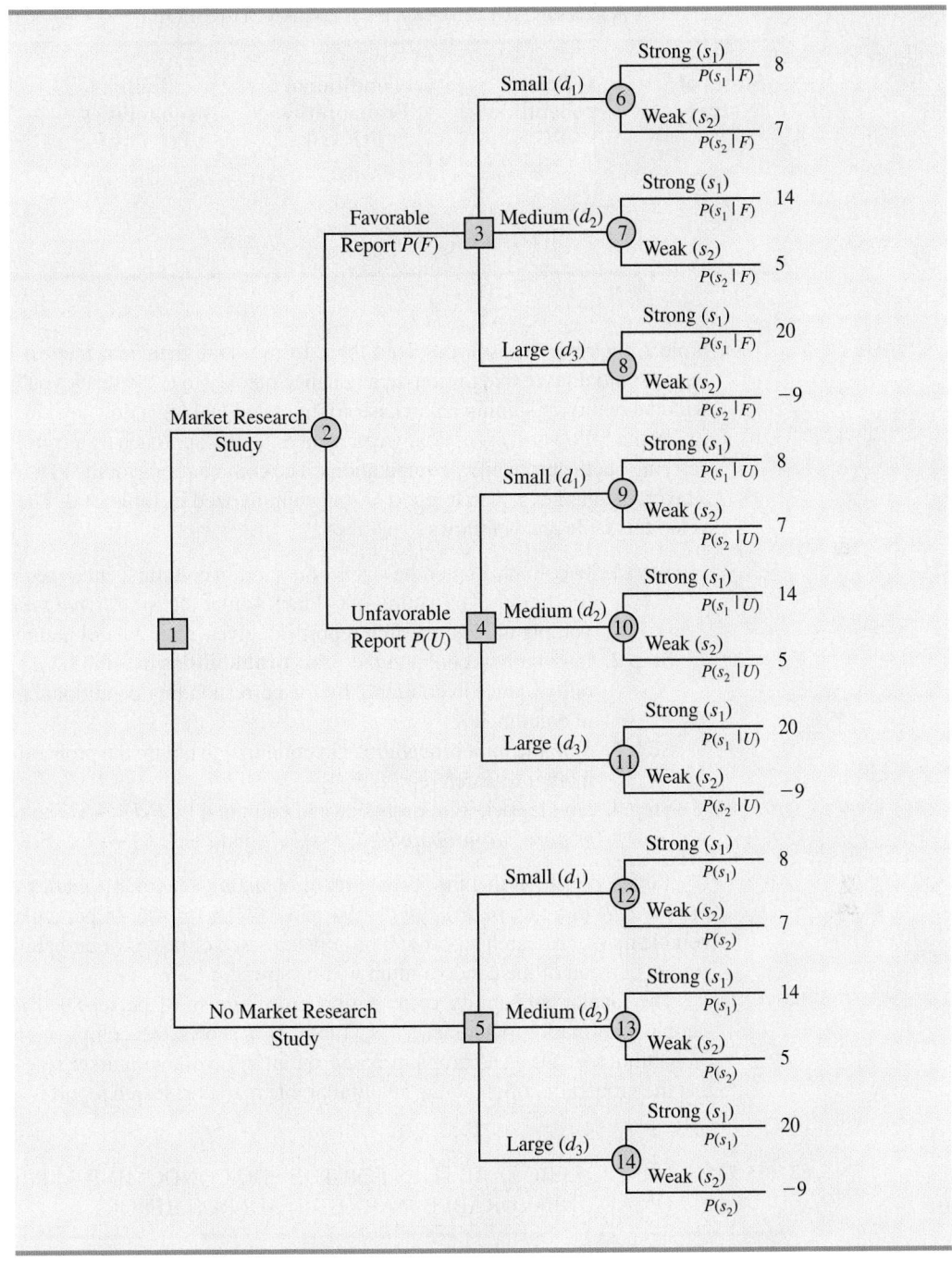

Note that the preceding probability assessments provide a reasonable degree of confidence in the market research study. If the true state of nature is $s_1$, the probability of a favorable market research report is .90, and the probability of an unfavorable market research report is .10. If the true state of nature is $s_2$, the probability of a favorable market research report is .25, and the probability of an unfavorable market research report is .75. The reason for a .25 probability of a potentially misleading favorable market research report for state of nature $s_2$ is that when some potential buyers first hear about the new condominium

TABLE 21.3   BRANCH PROBABILITIES FOR THE PDC CONDOMINIUM PROJECT BASED ON A FAVORABLE MARKET RESEARCH REPORT

| States of Nature $s_j$ | Prior Probabilities $P(s_j)$ | Conditional Probabilities $P(F \mid s_j)$ | Joint Probabilities $P(F \cap s_j)$ | Posterior Probabilities $P(s_j \mid F)$ |
|---|---|---|---|---|
| $s_1$ | .8 | .90 | .72 | .94 |
| $s_2$ | .2 | .25 | .05 | .06 |
| | 1.0 | | $P(F) = .77$ | 1.00 |

project, their enthusiasm may lead them to overstate their real interest in it. A potential buyer's initial favorable response can change quickly to a "no thank you" when later faced with the reality of signing a purchase contract and making a down payment.

In the following discussion, we present a tabular approach as a convenient method for carrying out the probability computations. The computations for the PDC problem based on a favorable market research report ($F$) are summarized in Table 21.3. The steps used to develop this table are as follows.

**Step 1.** In column 1 enter the states of nature. In column 2 enter the *prior probabilities* for the states of nature. In column 3 enter the *conditional probabilities* of a favorable market research report ($F$) given each state of nature.

**Step 2.** In column 4 compute the **joint probabilities** by multiplying the prior probability values in column 2 by the corresponding conditional probability values in column 3.

**Step 3.** Sum the joint probabilities in column 4 to obtain the probability of a favorable market research report, $P(F)$.

**Step 4.** Divide each joint probability in column 4 by $P(F) = .77$ to obtain the revised or *posterior probabilities*, $P(s_1 \mid F)$ and $P(s_2 \mid F)$.

Table 21.3 shows that the probability of obtaining a favorable market research report is $P(F) = .77$. In addition, $P(s_1 \mid F) = .94$ and $P(s_2 \mid F) = .06$. In particular, note that a favorable market research report will prompt a revised or posterior probability of .94 that the market demand of the condominium will be strong, $s_1$.

The tabular probability computation procedure must be repeated for each possible sample information outcome. Thus, Table 21.4 shows the computations of the branch probabilities of the PDC problem based on an unfavorable market research report. Note that the probability of obtaining an unfavorable market research report is $P(U) = .23$. If an

TABLE 21.4   BRANCH PROBABILITIES FOR THE PDC CONDOMINIUM PROJECT BASED ON AN UNFAVORABLE MARKET RESEARCH REPORT

| States of Nature $s_j$ | Prior Probabilities $P(s_j)$ | Conditional Probabilities $P(U \mid s_j)$ | Joint Probabilities $P(U \cap s_j)$ | Posterior Probabilities $P(s_j \mid U)$ |
|---|---|---|---|---|
| $s_1$ | .8 | .10 | .08 | .35 |
| $s_2$ | .2 | .75 | .15 | .65 |
| | 1.0 | | $P(U) = .23$ | 1.00 |

unfavorable report is obtained, the posterior probability of a strong market demand, $s_1$, is .35 and of a weak market demand, $s_2$, is .65. The branch probabilities from Tables 21.3 and 21.4 were shown on the PDC decision tree in Figure 21.5.

*Exercise 14 asks you to compute posterior probabilities.*

The discussion in this section shows an underlying relationship between the probabilities on the various branches in a decision tree. To assume different prior probabilities, $P(s_1)$ and $P(s_2)$, without determining how these changes would alter $P(F)$ and $P(U)$, as well as the posterior probabilities $P(s_1 \mid F)$, $P(s_2 \mid F)$, $P(s_1 \mid U)$, and $P(s_2 \mid U)$, would be inappropriate.

## Exercises

### Methods

14. Suppose that you are given a decision situation with three possible states of nature: $s_1$, $s_2$, and $s_3$. The prior probabilities are $P(s_1) = .2$, $P(s_2) = .5$, and $P(s_3) = .3$. With sample information $I$, $P(I \mid s_1) = .1$, $P(I \mid s_2) = .05$, and $P(I \mid s_3) = .2$. Compute the revised or posterior probabilities: $P(s_1 \mid I)$, $P(s_2 \mid I)$, and $P(s_3 \mid I)$.

15. In the following profit payoff table for a decision problem with two states of nature and three decision alternatives, the prior probabilities for $s_1$ and $s_2$ are $P(s_1) = .8$ and $P(s_2) = .2$.

|                      | State of Nature | |
| -------------------- | ----- | ----- |
| Decision Alternative | $s_1$ | $s_2$ |
| $d_1$                | 15    | 10    |
| $d_2$                | 10    | 12    |
| $d_3$                | 8     | 20    |

a. What is the optimal decision?
b. Find the EVPI.
c. Suppose that sample information $I$ is obtained, with $P(I \mid s_1) = .20$ and $P(I \mid s_2) = .75$. Find the posterior probabilities $P(s_1 \mid I)$ and $P(s_2 \mid I)$. Recommend a decision alternative based on these probabilities.

### Applications

16. To save on expenses, Rona and Jerry agreed to form a carpool for traveling to and from work. Rona preferred to use the somewhat longer but more consistent Queen City Avenue. Although Jerry preferred the quicker expressway, he agreed with Rona that they should take Queen City Avenue if the expressway had a traffic jam. The following payoff table provides the one-way time estimate in minutes for traveling to and from work.

|                            | State of Nature | |
| -------------------------- | --------------- | --------------- |
|                            | Expressway Open | Expressway Jammed |
| Decision Alternative       | $s_1$           | $s_2$           |
| Queen City Avenue, $d_1$   | 30              | 30              |
| Expressway, $d_2$          | 25              | 45              |

Based on their experience with traffic problems, Rona and Jerry agreed on a .15 probability that the expressway would be jammed.

In addition, they agreed that weather seemed to affect the traffic conditions on the expressway. Let

$$C = \text{clear}$$
$$O = \text{overcast}$$
$$R = \text{rain}$$

The following conditional probabilities apply.

$$P(C \mid s_1) = .8 \qquad P(O \mid s_1) = .2 \qquad P(R \mid s_1) = .0$$
$$P(C \mid s_2) = .1 \qquad P(O \mid s_2) = .3 \qquad P(R \mid s_2) = .6$$

a.  Use Bayes' theorem for probability revision to compute the probability of each weather condition and the conditional probability of the expressway open $s_1$ or jammed $s_2$ given each weather condition.
b.  Show the decision tree for this problem.
c.  What is the optimal decision strategy, and what is the expected travel time?

17. The Gorman Manufacturing Company must decide whether to manufacture a component part at its Milan, Michigan plant or purchase the component part from a supplier. The resulting profit is dependent upon the demand for the product. The following payoff table shows the projected profit (in thousands of dollars).

|  | State of Nature | | |
| --- | --- | --- | --- |
| Decision Alternative | Low Demand $s_1$ | Medium Demand $s_2$ | High Demand $s_3$ |
| Manufacture, $d_1$ | −20 | 40 | 100 |
| Purchase, $d_2$ | 10 | 45 | 70 |

The state-of-nature probabilities are $P(s_1) = .35$, $P(s_2) = .35$, and $P(s_3) = .30$.
a.  Use a decision tree to recommend a decision.
b.  Use EVPI to determine whether Gorman should attempt to obtain a better estimate of demand.
c.  A test market study of the potential demand for the product is expected to report either a favorable $(F)$ or unfavorable $(U)$ condition. The relevant conditional probabilities are as follows:

$$P(F \mid s_1) = .10 \qquad P(U \mid s_1) = .90$$
$$P(F \mid s_2) = .40 \qquad P(U \mid s_2) = .60$$
$$P(F \mid s_3) = .60 \qquad P(U \mid s_3) = .40$$

What is the probability that the market research report will be favorable?
d.  What is Gorman's optimal decision strategy?
e.  What is the expected value of the market research information?

## Summary

Decision analysis can be used to determine a recommended decision alternative or an optimal decision strategy when a decision maker is faced with an uncertain and risk-filled pattern of future events. The goal of decision analysis is to identify the best decision alternative or the optimal decision strategy given information about the uncertain events and the possible consequences or payoffs. The uncertain future events are called chance events and the outcomes of the chance events are called states of nature.

We showed how payoff tables and decision trees could be used to structure a decision problem and describe the relationships among the decisions, the chance events, and the consequences. With probability assessments provided for the states of nature, the expected value approach was used to identify the recommended decision alternative or decision strategy.

In cases where sample information about the chance events is available, a sequence of decisions can be made. First we decide whether to obtain the sample information. If the answer to this decision is yes, an optimal decision strategy based on the specific sample information must be developed. In this situation, decision trees and the expected value approach can be used to determine the optimal decision strategy.

*The Excel add-in TreePlan is available on the CD that accompanies this text.*

The Excel add-in TreePlan can be used to set up the decision trees and solve the decision problems presented in this chapter. The TreePlan software and a manual for using TreePlan are on the ASW Web site. An example showing how to use TreePlan for the PDC problem in Section 21.1 is provided in the end-of-chapter appendix.

## Glossary

**Chance event** An uncertain future event affecting the consequence, or payoff, associated with a decision.

**Consequence** The result obtained when a decision alternative is chosen and a chance event occurs. A measure of the consequence is often called a payoff.

**States of nature** The possible outcomes for chance events that affect the payoff associated with a decision alternative.

**Payoff** A measure of the consequence of a decision such as profit, cost, or time. Each combination of a decision alternative and a state of nature has an associated payoff (consequence).

**Payoff table** A tabular representation of the payoffs for a decision problem.

**Decision tree** A graphical representation of the decision problem that shows the sequential nature of the decision-making process.

**Node** An intersection or junction point of an influence diagram or a decision tree.

**Decision nodes** Nodes indicating points where a decision is made.

**Chance nodes** Nodes indicating points where an uncertain event will occur.

**Branch** Lines showing the alternatives from decision nodes and the outcomes from chance nodes.

**Expected value approach** An approach to choosing a decision alternative that is based on the expected value of each decision alternative. The recommended decision alternative is the one that provides the best expected value.

**Expected value (EV)** For a chance node, it is the weighted average of the payoffs. The weights are the state-of-nature probabilities.

**Expected value of perfect information (EVPI)** The expected value of information that would tell the decision maker exactly which state of nature is going to occur (i.e., perfect information).

**Prior probabilities** The probabilities of the states of nature prior to obtaining sample information.

**Sample information** New information obtained through research or experimentation that enables an updating or revision of the state-of-nature probabilities.

**Posterior (revised) probabilities** The probabilities of the states of nature after revising the prior probabilities based on sample information.

**Decision strategy** A strategy involving a sequence of decisions and chance outcomes to provide the optimal solution to a decision problem.

**Expected value of sample information (EVSI)** The difference between the expected value of an optimal strategy based on sample information and the "best" expected value without any sample information.

**Bayes' theorem** A theorem that enables the use of sample information to revise prior probabilities.

**Conditional probabilities** The probability of one event given the known outcome of a (possibly) related event.

**Joint probabilities** The probabilities of both sample information and a particular state of nature occurring simultaneously.

## Key Formulas

**Expected Value**

$$EV(d_i) = \sum_{j=1}^{N} P(s_j)V_{ij} \tag{21.3}$$

**Expected Value of Perfect Information**

$$EVPI = |EVwPI - EVwoPI| \tag{21.4}$$

**Expected Value of Sample Information**

$$EVSI = |EVwSI - EVwoSI| \tag{21.5}$$

## Case Problem  Lawsuit Defense Strategy

John Campbell, an employee of Manhattan Construction Company, claims to have injured his back as a result of a fall while repairing the roof at one of the Eastview apartment buildings. In a lawsuit asking for damages of $1,500,000, filed against Doug Reynolds, the owner of Eastview Apartments, John claims that the roof had rotten sections and that his fall could have been prevented if Mr. Reynolds had told Manhattan Construction about the problem. Mr. Reynolds notified his insurance company, Allied Insurance, of the lawsuit. Allied must defend Mr. Reynolds and decide what action to take regarding the lawsuit.

Following some depositions and a series of discussions between both sides, John Campbell offered to accept a settlement of $750,000. Thus, one option is for Allied to pay John $750,000 to settle the claim. Allied is also considering making John a counteroffer of $400,000 in the hope that he will accept a lesser amount to avoid the time and cost of going to trial. Allied's preliminary investigation shows that John has a strong case; Allied is concerned that John may reject their counteroffer and request a jury trial. Allied's lawyers spent some time exploring John's likely reaction if they make a counteroffer of $400,000.

The lawyers concluded that it is adequate to consider three possible outcomes to represent John's possible reaction to a counteroffer of $400,000: (1) John will accept the counteroffer and the case will be closed; (2) John will reject the counteroffer and elect to have a jury decide the settlement amount; or (3) John will make a counteroffer to Allied of $600,000. If John does make a counteroffer, Allied has decided that they will not make additional counteroffers. They will either accept John's counteroffer of $600,000 or go to trial.

If the case goes to a jury trial, Allied considers three outcomes possible: (1) the jury rejects John's claim and Allied will not be required to pay any damages; (2) the jury finds in favor of John and awards him $750,000 in damages; or (3) the jury concludes that John has a strong case and awards him the full amount of $1,500,000.

Key considerations as Allied develops its strategy for disposing of the case are the probabilities associated with John's response to an Allied counteroffer of $400,000, and the probabilities associated with the three possible trial outcomes. Allied's lawyers believe the probability that John will accept a counteroffer of $400,000 is .10, the probability that John will reject a counteroffer of $400,000 is .40, and the probability that John will, himself, make a counteroffer to Allied of $600,000 is .50. If the case goes to court, they believe that the probability the jury will award John damages of $1,500,000 is .30, the probability that the jury will award John damages of $750,000 is .50, and the probability that the jury will award John nothing is .20.

## Managerial Report

Perform an analysis of the problem facing Allied Insurance and prepare a report that summarizes your findings and recommendations. Be sure to include the following items:

1. A decision tree
2. A recommendation regarding whether Allied should accept John's initial offer to settle the claim for $750,000
3. A decision strategy that Allied should follow if they decide to make John a counteroffer of $400,000
4. A risk profile for your recommended strategy

## Appendix 21.1   Solving the PDC Problem with TreePlan

TreePlan* is an Excel add-in that can be used to develop decision trees for decision analysis problems. The software package is provided on the ASW Web site. A manual containing additional information on starting and using TreePlan is also included. In the following example, we show how to use TreePlan to build a decision tree and solve the PDC problem presented in Section 21.1. The decision tree for the PDC problem is shown in Figure 21.11.

### Getting Started: An Initial Decision Tree

We begin by assuming that TreePlan has been installed and an Excel workbook is open. To build a TreePlan version of the PDC decision tree proceed as follows:

**Step 1.** Select cell A1
**Step 2.** Select the **Tools** menu and choose **Decision Tree**
**Step 3.** When the TreePlan New dialog box appears:
          Click **New Tree**

---

*TreePlan was developed by Professor Michael R. Middleton at the University of San Francisco and modified for use by Professor James E. Smith at Duke University. The TreePlan Web site is located at http://www.treeplan.com.

FIGURE 21.11   PDC DECISION TREE

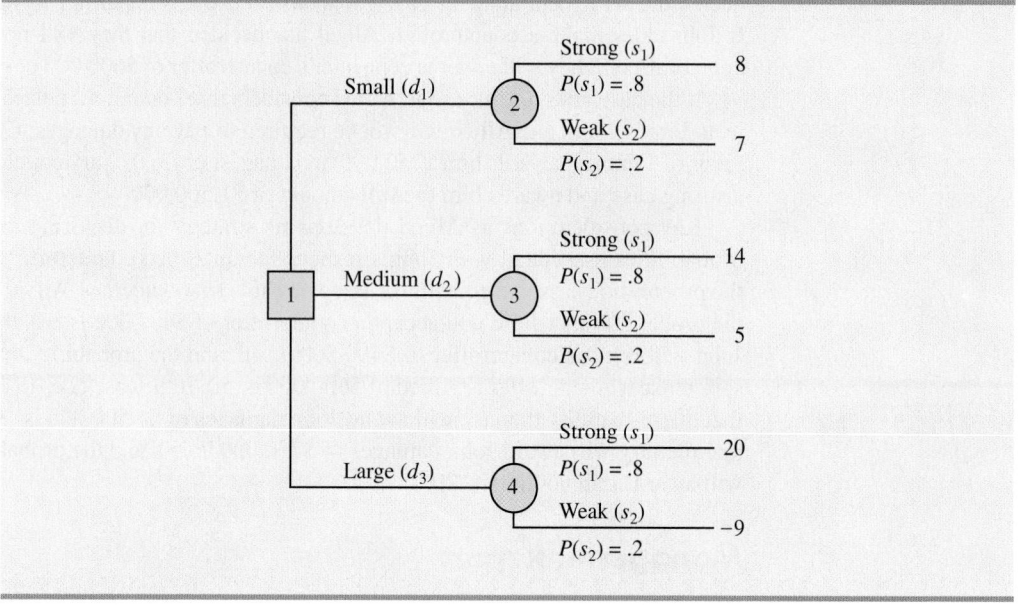

A decision tree with one decision node and two branches appears as follows:

|   | A | B | C | D | E | F | G |
|---|---|---|---|---|---|---|---|
| 1 |   |   |   |   |   |   |   |
| 2 |   |   |   | Decision 1 |   |   |   |
| 3 |   |   |   |   |   |   | 0 |
| 4 |   |   |   | 0 | 0 |   |   |
| 5 |   |   | 1 |   |   |   |   |
| 6 |   | 0 |   |   |   |   |   |
| 7 |   |   |   | Decision 2 |   |   |   |
| 8 |   |   |   |   |   |   | 0 |
| 9 |   |   |   | 0 | 0 |   |   |

## Adding a Branch

The PDC problem includes three decision alternatives (small, medium, and large condominium complexes), so we must add another decision branch to the tree.

> **Step 1.** Select cell B5
> **Step 2.** Select the **Tools** menu and choose **Decision Tree**
> **Step 3.** When the TreePlan Decision dialog box appears:
>     Select **Add branch**
>     Click **OK**

A revised tree with three decision branches now appears in the Excel worksheet.

## Naming the Decision Alternatives

The decision alternatives can be named by selecting the cells containing the labels Decision 1, Decision 2, and Decision 3, and then entering the corresponding PDC names Small, Medium, and Large. After naming the alternatives, the PDC tree with three decision branches appears as follows:

| | A | B | C | D | E | F | G |
|---|---|---|---|---|---|---|---|
| 1 | | | | | | | |
| 2 | | | | Small | | | |
| 3 | | | | | | | 0 |
| 4 | | | | 0 | 0 | | |
| 5 | | | | | | | |
| 6 | | | | | | | |
| 7 | | | | Medium | | | |
| 8 | | 1 | | | | | 0 |
| 9 | | 0 | | 0 | 0 | | |
| 10 | | | | | | | |
| 11 | | | | | | | |
| 12 | | | | Large | | | |
| 13 | | | | | | | 0 |
| 14 | | | | 0 | 0 | | |

## Adding Chance Nodes

The chance event for the PDC problem is the demand for the condominiums, which may be either strong or weak. Thus, a chance node with two branches must be added at the end of each decision alternative branch.

**Step 1.** Select cell F3

**Step 2.** Select the **Tools** menu and choose **Decision Tree**

**Step 3.** When the TreePlan Terminal dialog box appears:

Select **Change to event node**

Select **Two** in the **Branches** section

Click **OK**

The tree now appears as follows:

| | A | B | C | D | E | F | G | H | I | J | K |
|---|---|---|---|---|---|---|---|---|---|---|---|
| 1 | | | | | | | | 0.5 | | | |
| 2 | | | | | | | | Event 4 | | | |
| 3 | | | | | | | | | | | 0 |
| 4 | | | | Small | | | | 0 | 0 | | |
| 5 | | | | | | | | | | | |
| 6 | | | | | 0 | 0 | | 0.5 | | | |
| 7 | | | | | | | | Event 5 | | | |
| 8 | | | | | | | | | | | 0 |
| 9 | | | | | | | | 0 | 0 | | |
| 10 | | | | | | | | | | | |
| 11 | | 1 | | | | | | | | | |
| 12 | | 0 | | Medium | | | | | | | |
| 13 | | | | | | | | | | | 0 |
| 14 | | | | | 0 | 0 | | | | | |
| 15 | | | | | | | | | | | |
| 16 | | | | | | | | | | | |
| 17 | | | | Large | | | | | | | |
| 18 | | | | | | | | | | | 0 |
| 19 | | | | | 0 | 0 | | | | | |

We next select the cells containing Event 4 and Event 5 and rename them Strong and Weak to provide the proper names for the PDC states of nature. After doing so we can copy the subtree for the chance node in cell F5 to the other two decision branches to complete the structure of the PDC decision tree.

**Step 1.** Select cell F5
**Step 2.** Select the **Tools** menu and choose **Decision Tree**
**Step 3.** When the TreePlan event dialog box appears:
Select **Copy subtree**
Click **OK**
**Step 4.** Select cell F13
**Step 5.** Select the **Tools** menu and choose **Decision Tree**
**Step 6.** When the TreePlan Terminal dialog box appears
Select **Paste subtree**
Click **OK**

This copy/paste procedure places a chance node at the end of the Medium decision branch. Repeating the same copy/paste procedure for the Large decision branch completes the structure of the PDC decision tree as shown in Figure 21.12.

**FIGURE 21.12   THE PDC DECISION TREE DEVELOPED BY TREEPLAN**

## Inserting Probabilities and Payoffs

TreePlan provides the capability of inserting probabilities and payoffs into the decision tree. In Figure 21.12, we see that TreePlan automatically assigned an equal probability .5 to each of the states of nature. For PDC, the probability of strong demand is .8 and the probability of weak demand is .2. We can select cells H1, H6, H11, H16, H21, and H26 and insert the appropriate probabilities. The payoffs for the chance outcomes are inserted in cells H4, H9, H14, H19, H24, and H29. After inserting the PDC probabilities and payoffs, the PDC decision tree appears as shown in Figure 21.13.

Note that the payoffs also appear in the right-hand margin of the decision tree. The payoffs in the right margin are computed by a formula that adds the payoffs on all of the branches leading to the associated terminal node. For the PDC problem, no payoffs are associated with the decision alternative branches so we leave the default values of zero in cells D6, D16, and D26. The PDC decision tree is now complete.

## Interpreting the Result

When probabilities and payoffs are inserted, TreePlan automatically makes the backward pass computations necessary to compute expected values and determine the optimal solution. Optimal decisions are identified by the number in the corresponding decision node. In

**FIGURE 21.13    THE PDC DECISION TREE WITH BRANCH PROBABILITIES AND PAYOFFS**

the PDC decision tree in Figure 21.13, cell B15 contains the decision node. Note that a 3 appears in this node, which tells us that decision alternative branch 3 provides the optimal decision. Thus, decision analysis recommends PDC construct the Large condominium complex. The expected value of this decision appears at the beginning of the tree in cell A16. Thus, we see the optimal expected value is $14.2 million. The expected values of the other decision alternatives are displayed at the end of the corresponding decision branch. Thus, referring to cells E6 and E16, we see that the expected value of the Small complex is $7.8 million and the expected value of the Medium complex is $12.2 million.

## Other Options

TreePlan defaults to a maximization objective. If you would like a minimization objective, follow these steps:

**Step 1.** Select the **Tools** menu and choose **Decision Tree**
**Step 2.** Select **Options**
**Step 3.** Choose **Minimize (costs)**
            Click **OK**

In using a TreePlan decision tree, we can modify probabilities and payoffs and quickly observe the impact of the changes on the optimal solution. Using this "what if" type of sensitivity analysis, we can identify changes in probabilities and payoffs that would change the optimal decision. Also, because TreePlan is an Excel add-in, most of Excel's capabilities are available. For instance, we could use boldface to highlight the name of the optimal decision alternative on the final decision tree solution. A variety of other options provided by TreePlan are contained in the TreePlan manual. Computer software packages such as TreePlan make it easier to do a thorough analysis of a decision problem.

# APPENDICES

## General

Bowerman, B. L., and R. T. O'Connell. *Applied Statistics: Improving Business Processes.* Irwin, 1996.

Freedman, D., R. Pisani, and R. Purves. *Statistics*, 3rd ed. W. W. Norton, 1997.

Hogg, R. V., and A. T. Craig. *Introduction to Mathematical Statistics*, 5th ed. Prentice Hall, 1994.

Hogg, R. V., and E. A. Tanis. *Probability and Statistical Inference*, 6th ed. Prentice Hall, 2001.

Joiner, B. L., and B. F. Ryan. *Minitab Handbook.* Brooks/Cole, 2000.

Miller, I., and M. Miller. *John E. Freund's Mathematical Statistics.* Prentice Hall, 1998.

Moore, D. S., and G. P. McCabe. *Introduction to the Practice of Statistics*, 4th ed. Freeman, 2003.

Roberts, H. *Data Analysis for Managers with Minitab.* Scientific Press, 1991.

Tanur, J. M. *Statistics: A Guide to the Unknown,* 4th ed. Brooks/Cole, 2002.

Tukey, J. W. *Exploratory Data Analysis.* Addison-Wesley, 1977.

## Experimental Design

Cochran, W. G., and G. M. Cox. *Experimental Designs,* 2d ed. Wiley, 1992.

Hicks, C. R., and K. V. Turner. *Fundamental Concepts in the Design of Experiments,* 5th ed. Oxford University Press, 1999.

Montgomery, D. C. *Design and Analysis of Experiments,* 5th ed. Wiley, 2000.

Winer, B. J., K. M. Michels, and D. R. Brown. *Statistical Principles in Experimental Design,* 3rd ed. McGraw-Hill, 1991.

Wu, C. F. Jeff, and M. Hamada. *Experiments: Planning, Analysis, and Parameter Optimization.* Wiley, 2000.

## Forecasting

Bowerman, B. L., and R. T. O'Connell. *Forecasting and Time Series: An Applied Approach,* 3rd ed. Brooks/Cole, 2000.

Box, G. E. P., G. C. Reinsel, and G. Jenkins. *Time Series Analysis: Forecasting and Control,* 3rd ed. Prentice Hall, 1994.

Makridakis, S., S. C. Wheelwright, and R. J. Hyndman. *Forecasting: Methods and Applications,* 3rd ed. Wiley, 1997.

## Index Numbers

U.S. Department of Commerce. *Survey of Current Business.*

U.S. Department of Labor, Bureau of Labor Statistics. *CPI Detailed Report.*

U.S. Department of Labor. *Producer Price Indexes.*

## Nonparametric Methods

Conover, W. J. *Practical Nonparametric Statistics,* 3rd ed. Wiley, 1998.

Gibbons, J. D., and S. Chakraborti. *Nonparametric Statistical Inference,* 3rd ed. Marcel Dekker, 1992.

Siegel, S., and N. J. Castellan. *Nonparametric Statistics for the Behavioral Sciences,* 2d ed. McGraw-Hill, 1990.

Sprent, P. *Applied Non-Parametric Statistical Methods.* CRC, 1993.

## Probability

Hogg, R. V., and E. A. Tanis. *Probability and Statistical Inference,* 6th ed. Prentice Hall, 2001.

Ross, S. M. *Introduction to Probability Models,* 7th ed. Academic Press, 2000.

Wackerly, D. D., W. Mendenhall, and R. L. Scheaffer. *Mathematical Statistics with Applications,* 6th ed. Duxbury Press, 2002.

## Quality Control

Deming, W. E. *Quality, Productivity, and Competitive Position.* MIT, 1982.

Evans, J. R., and W. M. Lindsay. *The Management and Control of Quality,* 5th ed. South-Western, 2001.

Gryna, F. M., and I. M. Juran. *Quality Planning and Analysis: From Product Development Through Use,* 3rd ed. McGraw-Hill, 1993.

Ishikawa, K. *Introduction to Quality Control.* Kluwer Academic, 1991.

Montgomery, D. C. *Introduction to Statistical Quality Control,* 4th ed. Wiley, 2000.

## Regression Analysis

Belsley, D. A. *Conditioning Diagnostics: Collinearity and Weak Data in Regression.* Wiley, 1991.

Chatterjee, S., and B. Price. *Regression Analysis by Example,* 3rd ed. Wiley, 1999.

Draper, N. R., and H. Smith. *Applied Regression Analysis,* 3rd ed. Wiley, 1998.

Graybill, F. A., and H. Iyer. *Regression Analysis: Concepts and Applications.* Duxbury Press, 1994.

Hosmer, D. W., and S. Lemeshow. *Applied Logistic Regression,* 2nd ed. Wiley, 2000.

Kleinbaum, D. G., L. L. Kupper, and K. E. Muller. *Applied Regression Analysis and Other Multivariate Methods,* 3rd ed. Duxbury Press, 1997.

Kutner, M. H., C. J. Nachtschiem, W. Wasserman, and J. Neter. *Applied Linear Statistical Models,* 4th ed. Irwin, 1996.

Mendenhall, M., and T. Sincich. *A Second Course in Statistics: Regression Analysis,* 5th ed. Prentice Hall, 1996.

Myers, R. H. *Classical and Modern Regression with Applications,* 2d ed. PWS, 1990.

## Decision Analysis

Chernoff, H., and L. E. Moses. *Elementary Decision Theory.* Dover, 1987.

Clemen, R. T., and T. Reilly. *Making Hard Decisions with Decision Tools.* Duxbury Press, 2001.

Goodwin, P., and G. Wright. *Decision Analysis for Management Judgment.* 2nd ed. Wiley, 1999.

Pratt, J. W., H. Raiffa, and R. Schlaifer. *Introduction to Statistical Decision Theory.* MIT Press, 1995.

Raiffa, H. *Decision Analysis.* McGraw-Hill, 1997.

## Sampling

Cochran, W. G. *Sampling Techniques,* 3rd ed. Wiley, 1977.

Deming, W. E. *Some Theory of Sampling.* Dover, 1984.

Hansen, M. H., W. N. Hurwitz, W. G. Madow, and M. N. Hanson. *Sample Survey Methods and Theory.* Wiley, 1993.

Kish, L. *Survey Sampling.* Wiley, 1995.

Levy, P. S., and S. Lemeshow. *Sampling of Populations: Methods and Applications,* 3rd ed. Wiley, 1999.

Scheaffer, R. L., W. Mendenhall, and L. Ott. *Elementary Survey Sampling,* 5th ed. Duxbury Press, 1996.

# Appendix B: Tables

**TABLE 1** STANDARD NORMAL DISTRIBUTION

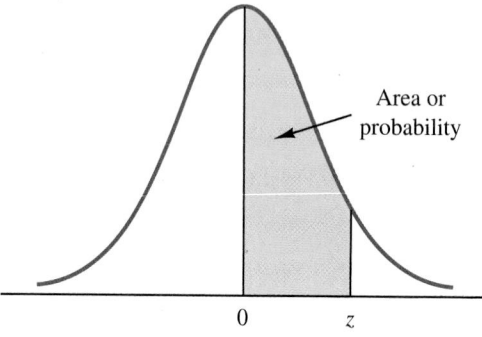

Area or probability

Entries in the table give the area under the curve between the mean and $z$ standard deviations above the mean. For example, for $z = 1.25$ the area under the curve between the mean and $z$ is .3944.

| z | .00 | .01 | .02 | .03 | .04 | .05 | .06 | .07 | .08 | .09 |
|---|-----|-----|-----|-----|-----|-----|-----|-----|-----|-----|
| .0 | .0000 | .0040 | .0080 | .0120 | .0160 | .0199 | .0239 | .0279 | .0319 | .0359 |
| .1 | .0398 | .0438 | .0478 | .0517 | .0557 | .0596 | .0636 | .0675 | .0714 | .0753 |
| .2 | .0793 | .0832 | .0871 | .0910 | .0948 | .0987 | .1026 | .1064 | .1103 | .1141 |
| .3 | .1179 | .1217 | .1255 | .1293 | .1331 | .1368 | .1406 | .1443 | .1480 | .1517 |
| .4 | .1554 | .1591 | .1628 | .1664 | .1700 | .1736 | .1772 | .1808 | .1844 | .1879 |
| .5 | .1915 | .1950 | .1985 | .2019 | .2054 | .2088 | .2123 | .2157 | .2190 | .2224 |
| .6 | .2257 | .2291 | .2324 | .2357 | .2389 | .2422 | .2454 | .2486 | .2517 | .2549 |
| .7 | .2580 | .2611 | .2642 | .2673 | .2704 | .2734 | .2764 | .2794 | .2823 | .2852 |
| .8 | .2881 | .2910 | .2939 | .2967 | .2995 | .3023 | .3051 | .3078 | .3106 | .3133 |
| .9 | .3159 | .3186 | .3212 | .3238 | .3264 | .3289 | .3315 | .3340 | .3365 | .3389 |
| 1.0 | .3413 | .3438 | .3461 | .3485 | .3508 | .3531 | .3554 | .3577 | .3599 | .3621 |
| 1.1 | .3643 | .3665 | .3686 | .3708 | .3729 | .3749 | .3770 | .3790 | .3810 | .3830 |
| 1.2 | .3849 | .3869 | .3888 | .3907 | .3925 | .3944 | .3962 | .3980 | .3997 | .4015 |
| 1.3 | .4032 | .4049 | .4066 | .4082 | .4099 | .4115 | .4131 | .4147 | .4162 | .4177 |
| 1.4 | .4192 | .4207 | .4222 | .4236 | .4251 | .4265 | .4279 | .4292 | .4306 | .4319 |
| 1.5 | .4332 | .4345 | .4357 | .4370 | .4382 | .4394 | .4406 | .4418 | .4429 | .4441 |
| 1.6 | .4452 | .4463 | .4474 | .4484 | .4495 | .4505 | .4515 | .4525 | .4535 | .4545 |
| 1.7 | .4554 | .4564 | .4573 | .4582 | .4591 | .4599 | .4608 | .4616 | .4625 | .4633 |
| 1.8 | .4641 | .4649 | .4656 | .4664 | .4671 | .4678 | .4686 | .4693 | .4699 | .4706 |
| 1.9 | .4713 | .4719 | .4726 | .4732 | .4738 | .4744 | .4750 | .4756 | .4761 | .4767 |
| 2.0 | .4772 | .4778 | .4783 | .4788 | .4793 | .4798 | .4803 | .4808 | .4812 | .4817 |
| 2.1 | .4821 | .4826 | .4830 | .4834 | .4838 | .4842 | .4846 | .4850 | .4854 | .4857 |
| 2.2 | .4861 | .4864 | .4868 | .4871 | .4875 | .4878 | .4881 | .4884 | .4887 | .4890 |
| 2.3 | .4893 | .4896 | .4898 | .4901 | .4904 | .4906 | .4909 | .4911 | .4913 | .4916 |
| 2.4 | .4918 | .4920 | .4922 | .4925 | .4927 | .4929 | .4931 | .4932 | .4934 | .4936 |
| 2.5 | .4938 | .4940 | .4941 | .4943 | .4945 | .4946 | .4948 | .4949 | .4951 | .4952 |
| 2.6 | .4953 | .4955 | .4956 | .4957 | .4959 | .4960 | .4961 | .4962 | .4963 | .4964 |
| 2.7 | .4965 | .4966 | .4967 | .4968 | .4969 | .4970 | .4971 | .4972 | .4973 | .4974 |
| 2.8 | .4974 | .4975 | .4976 | .4977 | .4977 | .4978 | .4979 | .4979 | .4980 | .4981 |
| 2.9 | .4981 | .4982 | .4982 | .4983 | .4984 | .4984 | .4985 | .4985 | .4986 | .4986 |
| 3.0 | .4987 | .4987 | .4987 | .4988 | .4988 | .4989 | .4989 | .4989 | .4990 | .4990 |

## TABLE 2    *t* DISTRIBUTION

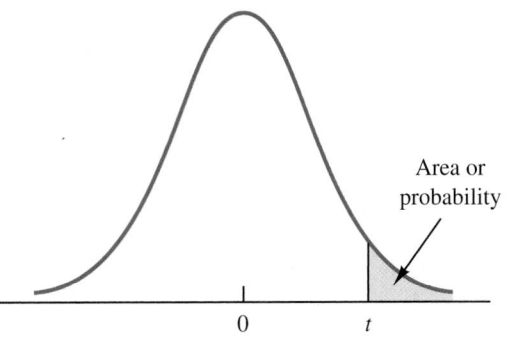

Area or probability

Entries in the table give *t* values for an area or probability in the upper tail of the *t* distribution. For example, with 10 degrees of freedom and a .05 area in the upper tail, $t_{.05} = 1.812$.

| Degrees of Freedom | Area in Upper Tail | | | | | |
|---|---|---|---|---|---|---|
| | .20 | .10 | .05 | .025 | .01 | .005 |
| 1 | 1.376 | 3.078 | 6.314 | 12.706 | 31.821 | 63.656 |
| 2 | 1.061 | 1.886 | 2.920 | 4.303 | 6.965 | 9.925 |
| 3 | .978 | 1.638 | 2.353 | 3.182 | 4.541 | 5.841 |
| 4 | .941 | 1.533 | 2.132 | 2.776 | 3.747 | 4.604 |
| 5 | .920 | 1.476 | 2.015 | 2.571 | 3.365 | 4.032 |
| 6 | .906 | 1.440 | 1.943 | 2.447 | 3.143 | 3.707 |
| 7 | .896 | 1.415 | 1.895 | 2.365 | 2.998 | 3.499 |
| 8 | .889 | 1.397 | 1.860 | 2.306 | 2.896 | 3.355 |
| 9 | .883 | 1.383 | 1.833 | 2.262 | 2.821 | 3.250 |
| 10 | .879 | 1.372 | 1.812 | 2.228 | 2.764 | 3.169 |
| 11 | .876 | 1.363 | 1.796 | 2.201 | 2.718 | 3.106 |
| 12 | .873 | 1.356 | 1.782 | 2.179 | 2.681 | 3.055 |
| 13 | .870 | 1.350 | 1.771 | 2.160 | 2.650 | 3.012 |
| 14 | .868 | 1.345 | 1.761 | 2.145 | 2.624 | 2.977 |
| 15 | .866 | 1.341 | 1.753 | 2.131 | 2.602 | 2.947 |
| 16 | .865 | 1.337 | 1.746 | 2.120 | 2.583 | 2.921 |
| 17 | .863 | 1.333 | 1.740 | 2.110 | 2.567 | 2.898 |
| 18 | .862 | 1.330 | 1.734 | 2.101 | 2.552 | 2.878 |
| 19 | .861 | 1.328 | 1.729 | 2.093 | 2.539 | 2.861 |
| 20 | .860 | 1.325 | 1.725 | 2.086 | 2.528 | 2.845 |
| 21 | .859 | 1.323 | 1.721 | 2.080 | 2.518 | 2.831 |
| 22 | .858 | 1.321 | 1.717 | 2.074 | 2.508 | 2.819 |
| 23 | .858 | 1.319 | 1.714 | 2.069 | 2.500 | 2.807 |
| 24 | .857 | 1.318 | 1.711 | 2.064 | 2.492 | 2.797 |
| 25 | .856 | 1.316 | 1.708 | 2.060 | 2.485 | 2.787 |
| 26 | .856 | 1.315 | 1.706 | 2.056 | 2.479 | 2.779 |
| 27 | .855 | 1.314 | 1.703 | 2.052 | 2.473 | 2.771 |
| 28 | .855 | 1.313 | 1.701 | 2.048 | 2.467 | 2.763 |
| 29 | .854 | 1.311 | 1.699 | 2.045 | 2.462 | 2.756 |
| 30 | .854 | 1.310 | 1.697 | 2.042 | 2.457 | 2.750 |
| 31 | .853 | 1.309 | 1.696 | 2.040 | 2.453 | 2.744 |
| 32 | .853 | 1.309 | 1.694 | 2.037 | 2.449 | 2.738 |
| 33 | .853 | 1.308 | 1.692 | 2.035 | 2.445 | 2.733 |
| 34 | .852 | 1.307 | 1.691 | 2.032 | 2.441 | 2.728 |

**TABLE 2**    *t* DISTRIBUTION (*Continued*)

| Degrees of Freedom | Area in Upper Tail | | | | | |
|---|---|---|---|---|---|---|
| | .20 | .10 | .05 | .025 | .01 | .005 |
| 35 | .852 | 1.306 | 1.690 | 2.030 | 2.438 | 2.724 |
| 36 | .852 | 1.306 | 1.688 | 2.028 | 2.434 | 2.719 |
| 37 | .851 | 1.305 | 1.687 | 2.026 | 2.431 | 2.715 |
| 38 | .851 | 1.304 | 1.686 | 2.024 | 2.429 | 2.712 |
| 39 | .851 | 1.304 | 1.685 | 2.023 | 2.426 | 2.708 |
| 40 | .851 | 1.303 | 1.684 | 2.021 | 2.423 | 2.704 |
| 41 | .850 | 1.303 | 1.683 | 2.020 | 2.421 | 2.701 |
| 42 | .850 | 1.302 | 1.682 | 2.018 | 2.418 | 2.698 |
| 43 | .850 | 1.302 | 1.681 | 2.017 | 2.416 | 2.695 |
| 44 | .850 | 1.301 | 1.680 | 2.015 | 2.414 | 2.692 |
| 45 | .850 | 1.301 | 1.679 | 2.014 | 2.412 | 2.690 |
| 46 | .850 | 1.300 | 1.679 | 2.013 | 2.410 | 2.687 |
| 47 | .849 | 1.300 | 1.678 | 2.012 | 2.408 | 2.685 |
| 48 | .849 | 1.299 | 1.677 | 2.011 | 2.407 | 2.682 |
| 49 | .849 | 1.299 | 1.677 | 2.010 | 2.405 | 2.680 |
| 50 | .849 | 1.299 | 1.676 | 2.009 | 2.403 | 2.678 |
| 51 | .849 | 1.298 | 1.675 | 2.008 | 2.402 | 2.676 |
| 52 | .849 | 1.298 | 1.675 | 2.007 | 2.400 | 2.674 |
| 53 | .848 | 1.298 | 1.674 | 2.006 | 2.399 | 2.672 |
| 54 | .848 | 1.297 | 1.674 | 2.005 | 2.397 | 2.670 |
| 55 | .848 | 1.297 | 1.673 | 2.004 | 2.396 | 2.668 |
| 56 | .848 | 1.297 | 1.673 | 2.003 | 2.395 | 2.667 |
| 57 | .848 | 1.297 | 1.672 | 2.002 | 2.394 | 2.665 |
| 58 | .848 | 1.296 | 1.672 | 2.002 | 2.392 | 2.663 |
| 59 | .848 | 1.296 | 1.671 | 2.001 | 2.391 | 2.662 |
| 60 | .848 | 1.296 | 1.671 | 2.000 | 2.390 | 2.660 |
| 61 | .848 | 1.296 | 1.670 | 2.000 | 2.389 | 2.659 |
| 62 | .847 | 1.295 | 1.670 | 1.999 | 2.388 | 2.657 |
| 63 | .847 | 1.295 | 1.669 | 1.998 | 2.387 | 2.656 |
| 64 | .847 | 1.295 | 1.669 | 1.998 | 2.386 | 2.655 |
| 65 | .847 | 1.295 | 1.669 | 1.997 | 2.385 | 2.654 |
| 66 | .847 | 1.295 | 1.668 | 1.997 | 2.384 | 2.652 |
| 67 | .847 | 1.294 | 1.668 | 1.996 | 2.383 | 2.651 |
| 68 | .847 | 1.294 | 1.668 | 1.995 | 2.382 | 2.650 |
| 69 | .847 | 1.294 | 1.667 | 1.995 | 2.382 | 2.649 |
| 70 | .847 | 1.294 | 1.667 | 1.994 | 2.381 | 2.648 |
| 71 | .847 | 1.294 | 1.667 | 1.994 | 2.380 | 2.647 |
| 72 | .847 | 1.293 | 1.666 | 1.993 | 2.379 | 2.646 |
| 73 | .847 | 1.293 | 1.666 | 1.993 | 2.379 | 2.645 |
| 74 | .847 | 1.293 | 1.666 | 1.993 | 2.378 | 2.644 |
| 75 | .846 | 1.293 | 1.665 | 1.992 | 2.377 | 2.643 |
| 76 | .846 | 1.293 | 1.665 | 1.992 | 2.376 | 2.642 |
| 77 | .846 | 1.293 | 1.665 | 1.991 | 2.376 | 2.641 |
| 78 | .846 | 1.292 | 1.665 | 1.991 | 2.375 | 2.640 |
| 79 | .846 | 1.292 | 1.664 | 1.990 | 2.374 | 2.639 |

**TABLE 2**   *t* DISTRIBUTION (*Continued*)

| Degrees of Freedom | Area in Upper Tail | | | | | |
|---|---|---|---|---|---|---|
| | **.20** | **.10** | **.05** | **.025** | **.01** | **.005** |
| 80 | .846 | 1.292 | 1.664 | 1.990 | 2.374 | 2.639 |
| 81 | .846 | 1.292 | 1.664 | 1.990 | 2.373 | 2.638 |
| 82 | .846 | 1.292 | 1.664 | 1.989 | 2.373 | 2.637 |
| 83 | .846 | 1.292 | 1.663 | 1.989 | 2.372 | 2.636 |
| 84 | .846 | 1.292 | 1.663 | 1.989 | 2.372 | 2.636 |
| 85 | .846 | 1.292 | 1.663 | 1.988 | 2.371 | 2.635 |
| 86 | .846 | 1.291 | 1.663 | 1.988 | 2.370 | 2.634 |
| 87 | .846 | 1.291 | 1.663 | 1.988 | 2.370 | 2.634 |
| 88 | .846 | 1.291 | 1.662 | 1.987 | 2.369 | 2.633 |
| 89 | .846 | 1.291 | 1.662 | 1.987 | 2.369 | 2.632 |
| 90 | .846 | 1.291 | 1.662 | 1.987 | 2.368 | 2.632 |
| 91 | .846 | 1.291 | 1.662 | 1.986 | 2.368 | 2.631 |
| 92 | .846 | 1.291 | 1.662 | 1.986 | 2.368 | 2.630 |
| 93 | .846 | 1.291 | 1.661 | 1.986 | 2.367 | 2.630 |
| 94 | .845 | 1.291 | 1.661 | 1.986 | 2.367 | 2.629 |
| 95 | .845 | 1.291 | 1.661 | 1.985 | 2.366 | 2.629 |
| 96 | .845 | 1.290 | 1.661 | 1.985 | 2.366 | 2.628 |
| 97 | .845 | 1.290 | 1.661 | 1.985 | 2.365 | 2.627 |
| 98 | .845 | 1.290 | 1.661 | 1.984 | 2.365 | 2.627 |
| 99 | .845 | 1.290 | 1.660 | 1.984 | 2.364 | 2.626 |
| 100 | .845 | 1.290 | 1.660 | 1.984 | 2.364 | 2.626 |
| ∞ | .842 | 1.282 | 1.645 | 1.960 | 2.326 | 2.576 |

**TABLE 3   CHI-SQUARE DISTRIBUTION**

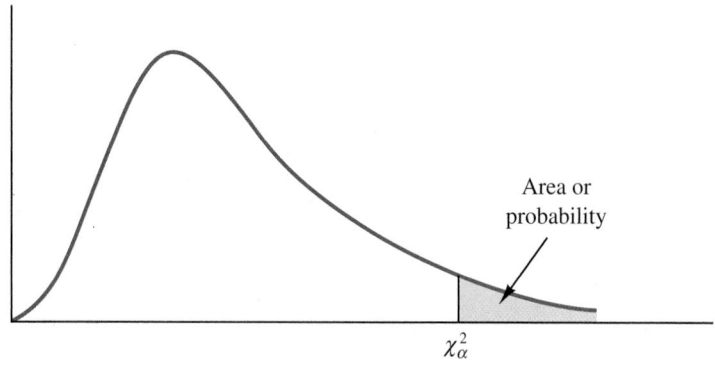

Entries in the table give $\chi^2$ values, where $\alpha$ is the area or probability in the upper tail of the chi-square distribution. For example, with 10 degrees of freedom and a .01 area in the upper tail, $\chi^2_{.01} = 23.209$.

| Degrees of Freedom | Area in Upper Tail | | | | | | | | | |
|---|---|---|---|---|---|---|---|---|---|---|
| | .995 | .99 | .975 | .95 | .90 | .10 | .05 | .025 | .01 | .005 |
| 1 | .000 | .000 | .001 | .004 | .016 | 2.706 | 3.841 | 5.024 | 6.635 | 7.879 |
| 2 | .010 | .020 | .051 | .103 | .211 | 4.605 | 5.991 | 7.378 | 9.210 | 10.597 |
| 3 | .072 | .115 | .216 | .352 | .584 | 6.251 | 7.815 | 9.348 | 11.345 | 12.838 |
| 4 | .207 | .297 | .484 | .711 | 1.064 | 7.779 | 9.488 | 11.143 | 13.277 | 14.860 |
| 5 | .412 | .554 | .831 | 1.145 | 1.610 | 9.236 | 11.070 | 12.832 | 15.086 | 16.750 |
| 6 | .676 | .872 | 1.237 | 1.635 | 2.204 | 10.645 | 12.592 | 14.449 | 16.812 | 18.548 |
| 7 | .989 | 1.239 | 1.690 | 2.167 | 2.833 | 12.017 | 14.067 | 16.013 | 18.475 | 20.278 |
| 8 | 1.344 | 1.647 | 2.180 | 2.733 | 3.490 | 13.362 | 15.507 | 17.535 | 20.090 | 21.955 |
| 9 | 1.735 | 2.088 | 2.700 | 3.325 | 4.168 | 14.684 | 16.919 | 19.023 | 21.666 | 23.589 |
| 10 | 2.156 | 2.558 | 3.247 | 3.940 | 4.865 | 15.987 | 18.307 | 20.483 | 23.209 | 25.188 |
| 11 | 2.603 | 3.053 | 3.816 | 4.575 | 5.578 | 17.275 | 19.675 | 21.920 | 24.725 | 26.757 |
| 12 | 3.074 | 3.571 | 4.404 | 5.226 | 6.304 | 18.549 | 21.026 | 23.337 | 26.217 | 28.300 |
| 13 | 3.565 | 4.107 | 5.009 | 5.892 | 7.041 | 19.812 | 22.362 | 24.736 | 27.688 | 29.819 |
| 14 | 4.075 | 4.660 | 5.629 | 6.571 | 7.790 | 21.064 | 23.685 | 26.119 | 29.141 | 31.319 |
| 15 | 4.601 | 5.229 | 6.262 | 7.261 | 8.547 | 22.307 | 24.996 | 27.488 | 30.578 | 32.801 |
| 16 | 5.142 | 5.812 | 6.908 | 7.962 | 9.312 | 23.542 | 26.296 | 28.845 | 32.000 | 34.267 |
| 17 | 5.697 | 6.408 | 7.564 | 8.672 | 10.085 | 24.769 | 27.587 | 30.191 | 33.409 | 35.718 |
| 18 | 6.265 | 7.015 | 8.231 | 9.390 | 10.865 | 25.989 | 28.869 | 31.526 | 34.805 | 37.156 |
| 19 | 6.844 | 7.633 | 8.907 | 10.117 | 11.651 | 27.204 | 30.144 | 32.852 | 36.191 | 38.582 |
| 20 | 7.434 | 8.260 | 9.591 | 10.851 | 12.443 | 28.412 | 31.410 | 34.170 | 37.566 | 39.997 |
| 21 | 8.034 | 8.897 | 10.283 | 11.591 | 13.240 | 29.615 | 32.671 | 35.479 | 38.932 | 41.401 |
| 22 | 8.643 | 9.542 | 10.982 | 12.338 | 14.041 | 30.813 | 33.924 | 36.781 | 40.289 | 42.796 |
| 23 | 9.260 | 10.196 | 11.689 | 13.091 | 14.848 | 32.007 | 35.172 | 38.076 | 41.638 | 44.181 |
| 24 | 9.886 | 10.856 | 12.401 | 13.848 | 15.659 | 33.196 | 36.415 | 39.364 | 42.980 | 45.558 |
| 25 | 10.520 | 11.524 | 13.120 | 14.611 | 16.473 | 34.382 | 37.652 | 40.646 | 44.314 | 46.928 |
| 26 | 11.160 | 12.198 | 13.844 | 15.379 | 17.292 | 35.563 | 38.885 | 41.923 | 45.642 | 48.290 |
| 27 | 11.808 | 12.878 | 14.573 | 16.151 | 18.114 | 36.741 | 40.113 | 43.195 | 46.963 | 49.645 |
| 28 | 12.461 | 13.565 | 15.308 | 16.928 | 18.939 | 37.916 | 41.337 | 44.461 | 48.278 | 50.994 |
| 29 | 13.121 | 14.256 | 16.047 | 17.708 | 19.768 | 39.087 | 42.557 | 45.722 | 49.588 | 52.335 |

**TABLE 3**    CHI-SQUARE DISTRIBUTION (*Continued*)

| Degrees of Freedom | Area in Upper Tail | | | | | | | | | |
|---|---|---|---|---|---|---|---|---|---|---|
| | .995 | .99 | .975 | .95 | .90 | .10 | .05 | .025 | .01 | .005 |
| 30 | 13.787 | 14.953 | 16.791 | 18.493 | 20.599 | 40.256 | 43.773 | 46.979 | 50.892 | 53.672 |
| 35 | 17.192 | 18.509 | 20.569 | 22.465 | 24.797 | 46.059 | 49.802 | 53.203 | 57.342 | 60.275 |
| 40 | 20.707 | 22.164 | 24.433 | 26.509 | 29.051 | 51.805 | 55.758 | 59.342 | 63.691 | 66.766 |
| 45 | 24.311 | 25.901 | 28.366 | 30.612 | 33.350 | 57.505 | 61.656 | 65.410 | 69.957 | 73.166 |
| 50 | 27.991 | 29.707 | 32.357 | 34.764 | 37.689 | 63.167 | 67.505 | 71.420 | 76.154 | 79.490 |
| 55 | 31.735 | 33.571 | 36.398 | 38.958 | 42.060 | 68.796 | 73.311 | 77.380 | 82.292 | 85.749 |
| 60 | 35.534 | 37.485 | 40.482 | 43.188 | 46.459 | 74.397 | 79.082 | 83.298 | 88.379 | 91.952 |
| 65 | 39.383 | 41.444 | 44.603 | 47.450 | 50.883 | 79.973 | 84.821 | 89.177 | 94.422 | 98.105 |
| 70 | 43.275 | 45.442 | 48.758 | 51.739 | 55.329 | 85.527 | 90.531 | 95.023 | 100.425 | 104.215 |
| 75 | 47.206 | 49.475 | 52.942 | 56.054 | 59.795 | 91.061 | 96.217 | 100.839 | 106.393 | 110.285 |
| 80 | 51.172 | 53.540 | 57.153 | 60.391 | 64.278 | 96.578 | 101.879 | 106.629 | 112.329 | 116.321 |
| 85 | 55.170 | 57.634 | 61.389 | 64.749 | 68.777 | 102.079 | 107.522 | 112.393 | 118.236 | 122.324 |
| 90 | 59.196 | 61.754 | 65.647 | 69.126 | 73.291 | 107.565 | 113.145 | 118.136 | 124.116 | 128.299 |
| 95 | 63.250 | 65.898 | 69.925 | 73.520 | 77.818 | 113.038 | 118.752 | 123.858 | 129.973 | 134.247 |
| 100 | 67.328 | 70.065 | 74.222 | 77.929 | 82.358 | 118.498 | 124.342 | 129.561 | 135.807 | 140.170 |

**TABLE 4   F DISTRIBUTION**

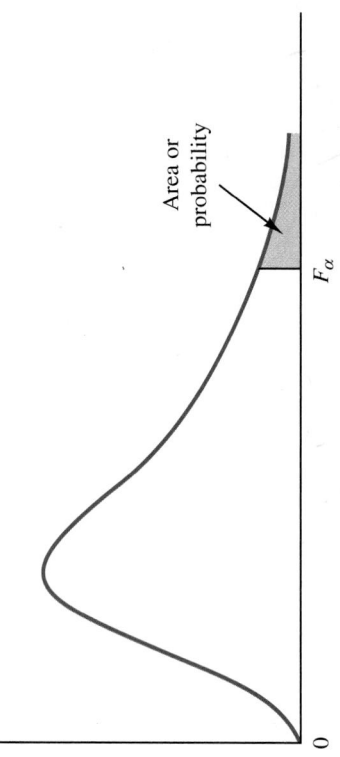

Area or probability

$F_\alpha$

Entries in the table give $F_\alpha$ values, where $\alpha$ is the area or probability in the upper tail of the $F$ distribution. For example, with 4 numerator degrees of freedom, 8 denominator degrees of freedom, and a .05 area in the upper tail, $F_{.05} = 3.84$.

| Denominator Degrees of Freedom | Area in Upper Tail | Numerator Degrees of Freedom | | | | | | | | | | | | | | | | | |
|---|---|---|---|---|---|---|---|---|---|---|---|---|---|---|---|---|---|---|---|
| | | 1 | 2 | 3 | 4 | 5 | 6 | 7 | 8 | 9 | 10 | 15 | 20 | 25 | 30 | 40 | 60 | 100 | 1000 |
| 1 | .10 | 39.86 | 49.50 | 53.59 | 55.83 | 57.24 | 58.20 | 58.91 | 59.44 | 59.86 | 60.19 | 61.22 | 61.74 | 62.05 | 62.26 | 62.53 | 62.79 | 63.01 | 63.30 |
| | .05 | 161.45 | 199.50 | 215.71 | 224.58 | 230.16 | 233.99 | 236.77 | 238.88 | 240.54 | 244.88 | 245.95 | 248.02 | 249.26 | 250.10 | 251.14 | 252.20 | 253.04 | 254.19 |
| | .025 | 647.79 | 799.48 | 864.15 | 899.60 | 921.83 | 937.11 | 948.20 | 956.64 | 963.28 | 968.63 | 984.87 | 993.08 | 998.09 | 1001.40 | 1005.60 | 1009.79 | 1013.16 | 1017.76 |
| | .01 | 4052.18 | 4999.34 | 5403.53 | 5624.26 | 5763.96 | 5858.95 | 5928.33 | 5980.95 | 6022.40 | 6055.93 | 6156.97 | 6208.66 | 6239.86 | 6260.35 | 6286.43 | 6312.97 | 6333.92 | 6362.80 |
| 2 | .10 | 8.53 | 9.00 | 9.16 | 9.24 | 9.29 | 9.33 | 9.35 | 9.37 | 9.38 | 9.39 | 9.42 | 9.44 | 9.45 | 9.46 | 9.47 | 9.47 | 9.48 | 9.49 |
| | .05 | 18.51 | 19.00 | 19.16 | 19.25 | 19.30 | 19.33 | 19.35 | 19.37 | 19.38 | 19.40 | 19.43 | 19.45 | 19.46 | 19.46 | 19.47 | 19.48 | 19.49 | 19.49 |
| | .025 | 38.51 | 39.00 | 39.17 | 39.25 | 39.30 | 39.33 | 39.36 | 39.37 | 39.39 | 39.40 | 39.43 | 39.45 | 39.46 | 39.46 | 39.48 | 39.48 | 39.49 | 39.50 |
| | .01 | 98.50 | 99.00 | 99.16 | 99.25 | 99.30 | 99.33 | 99.36 | 99.38 | 99.39 | 99.40 | 99.43 | 99.45 | 99.46 | 99.47 | 99.48 | 99.48 | 99.49 | 99.50 |
| 3 | .10 | 5.54 | 5.46 | 5.39 | 5.34 | 5.31 | 5.28 | 5.27 | 5.25 | 5.24 | 5.23 | 5.20 | 5.18 | 5.17 | 5.17 | 5.16 | 5.15 | 5.14 | 5.13 |
| | .05 | 10.13 | 9.55 | 9.28 | 9.12 | 9.01 | 8.94 | 8.89 | 8.85 | 8.81 | 8.79 | 8.70 | 8.66 | 8.63 | 8.62 | 8.59 | 8.57 | 8.55 | 8.53 |
| | .025 | 17.44 | 16.04 | 15.44 | 15.10 | 14.88 | 14.73 | 14.62 | 14.54 | 14.47 | 14.42 | 14.25 | 14.17 | 14.12 | 14.08 | 14.04 | 13.99 | 13.96 | 13.91 |
| | .01 | 34.12 | 30.82 | 29.46 | 28.71 | 28.24 | 27.91 | 27.67 | 27.49 | 27.34 | 27.23 | 26.87 | 26.69 | 26.58 | 26.50 | 26.41 | 26.32 | 26.24 | 26.14 |
| 4 | .10 | 4.54 | 4.32 | 4.19 | 4.11 | 4.05 | 4.01 | 3.98 | 3.95 | 3.94 | 3.92 | 3.87 | 3.84 | 3.83 | 3.82 | 3.80 | 3.79 | 3.78 | 3.76 |
| | .05 | 7.71 | 6.94 | 6.59 | 6.39 | 6.26 | 6.16 | 6.09 | 6.04 | 6.00 | 5.96 | 5.86 | 5.80 | 5.77 | 5.75 | 5.72 | 5.69 | 5.66 | 5.63 |
| | .025 | 12.22 | 10.65 | 9.98 | 9.60 | 9.36 | 9.20 | 9.07 | 8.98 | 8.90 | 8.84 | 8.66 | 8.56 | 8.50 | 8.46 | 8.41 | 8.36 | 8.32 | 8.26 |
| | .01 | 21.20 | 18.00 | 16.69 | 15.98 | 15.52 | 15.21 | 14.98 | 14.80 | 14.66 | 14.55 | 14.20 | 14.02 | 13.91 | 13.84 | 13.75 | 13.65 | 13.58 | 13.47 |
| 5 | .10 | 4.06 | 3.78 | 3.62 | 3.52 | 3.45 | 3.40 | 3.37 | 3.34 | 3.32 | 3.30 | 3.324 | 3.21 | 3.19 | 3.17 | 3.16 | 3.14 | 3.13 | 3.11 |
| | .05 | 6.61. | 5.79 | 5.41 | 5.19 | 5.05 | 4.95 | 4.88 | 4.82 | 4.77 | 4.74 | 4.62 | 4.56 | 4.52 | 4.50 | 4.46 | 4.43 | 4.41 | 4.37 |
| | .025 | 10.01 | 8.43 | 7.76 | 7.39 | 7.15 | 6.98 | 6.85 | 6.76 | 6.68 | 6.62 | 6.43 | 6.33 | 6.27 | 6.23 | 6.18 | 6.12 | 6.08 | 6.02 |
| | .01 | 16.26 | 13.27 | 12.06 | 11.39 | 10.97 | 10.67 | 10.46 | 10.29 | 10.16 | 10.05 | 9.72 | 9.55 | 9.45 | 9.38 | 9.29 | 9.20 | 9.13 | 9.03 |

Numerator Degrees of Freedom

| Denominator Degrees of Freedom | Area in Upper Tail | 1 | 2 | 3 | 4 | 5 | 6 | 7 | 8 | 9 | 10 | 15 | 20 | 25 | 30 | 40 | 60 | 100 | 1000 |
|---|---|---|---|---|---|---|---|---|---|---|---|---|---|---|---|---|---|---|---|
| 6 | .10 | 3.78 | 3.46 | 3.29 | 3.18 | 3.11 | 3.05 | 3.01 | 2.98 | 2.96 | 2.94 | 2.87 | 2.84 | 2.81 | 2.80 | 2.78 | 2.76 | 2.75 | 2.72 |
|  | .05 | 5.99 | 5.14 | 4.76 | 4.53 | 4.39 | 4.28 | 4.21 | 4.15 | 4.10 | 4.06 | 3.94 | 3.87 | 3.83 | 3.81 | 3.77 | 3.74 | 3.71 | 3.67 |
|  | .025 | 8.81 | 7.26 | 6.60 | 6.23 | 5.99 | 5.82 | 5.70 | 5.60 | 5.52 | 5.46 | 5.27 | 5.17 | 5.11 | 5.07 | 5.01 | 4.96 | 4.92 | 4.86 |
|  | .01 | 13.75 | 10.92 | 9.78 | 9.15 | 8.75 | 8.47 | 8.26 | 8.10 | 7.98 | 7.87 | 7.56 | 7.40 | 7.30 | 7.23 | 7.14 | 7.06 | 6.99 | 6.89 |
| 7 | .10 | 3.59 | 3.26 | 3.07 | 2.96 | 2.88 | 2.83 | 2.78 | 2.75 | 2.72 | 2.70 | 2.63 | 2.59 | 2.57 | 2.56 | 2.54 | 2.51 | 2.50 | 2.47 |
|  | .05 | 5.59 | 4.74 | 4.35 | 4.12 | 3.97 | 3.87 | 3.79 | 3.73 | 3.68 | 3.64 | 3.51 | 3.44 | 3.40 | 3.38 | 3.34 | 3.30 | 3.27 | 3.23 |
|  | .025 | 8.07 | 6.54 | 5.89 | 5.52 | 5.29 | 5.12 | 4.99 | 4.90 | 4.82 | 4.76 | 4.57 | 4.47 | 4.40 | 4.36 | 4.31 | 4.25 | 4.21 | 4.15 |
|  | .01 | 12.25 | 9.55 | 8.45 | 7.85 | 7.46 | 7.19 | 6.99 | 6.84 | 6.72 | 6.62 | 6.31 | 6.16 | 6.06 | 5.99 | 5.91 | 5.82 | 5.75 | 5.66 |
| 8 | .10 | 3.46 | 3.11 | 2.92 | 2.81 | 2.73 | 2.67 | 2.62 | 2.59 | 2.56 | 2.54 | 2.46 | 2.42 | 2.40 | 2.38 | 2.36 | 2.34 | 2.32 | 2.30 |
|  | .05 | 5.32 | 4.46 | 4.07 | 3.84 | 3.69 | 3.58 | 3.50 | 3.44 | 3.39 | 3.35 | 3.22 | 3.15 | 3.11 | 3.08 | 3.04 | 3.01 | 2.97 | 2.93 |
|  | .025 | 7.57 | 6.06 | 5.42 | 5.05 | 4.82 | 4.65 | 4.53 | 4.43 | 4.36 | 4.30 | 4.10 | 4.00 | 3.94 | 3.89 | 3.84 | 3.78 | 3.74 | 3.68 |
|  | .01 | 11.26 | 8.65 | 7.59 | 7.01 | 6.63 | 6.37 | 6.18 | 6.03 | 5.91 | 5.81 | 5.52 | 5.36 | 5.26 | 5.20 | 5.12 | 5.03 | 4.96 | 4.87 |
| 9 | .10 | 3.36 | 3.01 | 2.81 | 2.69 | 2.61 | 2.55 | 2.51 | 2.47 | 2.44 | 2.42 | 2.34 | 2.30 | 2.27 | 2.25 | 2.23 | 2.21 | 2.19 | 2.16 |
|  | .05 | 5.12 | 4.26 | 3.86 | 3.63 | 3.48 | 3.37 | 3.29 | 3.23 | 3.18 | 3.14 | 3.01 | 2.94 | 2.89 | 2.86 | 2.83 | 2.79 | 2.76 | 2.71 |
|  | .025 | 7.21 | 5.71 | 5.08 | 4.72 | 4.48 | 4.32 | 4.20 | 4.10 | 4.03 | 3.96 | 3.77 | 3.67 | 3.60 | 3.56 | 3.51 | 3.45 | 3.40 | 3.34 |
|  | .01 | 10.56 | 8.02 | 6.99 | 6.42 | 6.06 | 5.80 | 5.61 | 5.47 | 5.35 | 5.26 | 4.96 | 4.81 | 4.71 | 4.65 | 4.57 | 4.48 | 4.41 | 4.32 |
| 10 | .10 | 3.29 | 2.92 | 2.73 | 2.61 | 2.52 | 2.46 | 2.41 | 2.38 | 2.35 | 2.32 | 2.24 | 2.20 | 2.17 | 2.16 | 2.13 | 2.11 | 2.09 | 2.06 |
|  | .05 | 4.96 | 4.10 | 3.71 | 3.48 | 3.33 | 3.22 | 3.14 | 3.07 | 3.02 | 2.98 | 2.85 | 2.77 | 2.73 | 2.70 | 2.66 | 2.62 | 2.59 | 2.54 |
|  | .025 | 6.94 | 5.46 | 4.83 | 4.47 | 4.24 | 4.07 | 3.95 | 3.85 | 3.78 | 3.72 | 3.52 | 3.42 | 3.35 | 3.31 | 3.26 | 3.20 | 3.15 | 3.09 |
|  | .01 | 10.04 | 7.56 | 6.55 | 5.99 | 5.64 | 5.39 | 5.20 | 5.06 | 4.94 | 4.85 | 4.56 | 4.41 | 4.31 | 4.25 | 4.17 | 4.08 | 4.01 | 3.92 |
| 11 | .10 | 3.23 | 2.86 | 2.66 | 2.54 | 2.45 | 2.39 | 2.34 | 2.30 | 2.27 | 2.25 | 2.17 | 2.12 | 2.10 | 2.08 | 2.05 | 2.03 | 2.01 | 1.98 |
|  | .05 | 4.84 | 3.98 | 3.59 | 3.36 | 3.20 | 3.09 | 3.01 | 2.95 | 2.90 | 2.85 | 2.72 | 2.65 | 2.60 | 2.57 | 2.53 | 2.49 | 2.46 | 2.41 |
|  | .025 | 6.72 | 5.26 | 4.63 | 4.28 | 4.04 | 3.88 | 3.76 | 3.66 | 3.59 | 3.53 | 3.33 | 3.23 | 3.16 | 3.12 | 3.06 | 3.00 | 2.96 | 2.89 |
|  | .01 | 9.65 | 7.21 | 6.22 | 5.67 | 5.32 | 5.07 | 4.89 | 4.74 | 4.63 | 4.54 | 4.25 | 4.10 | 4.01 | 3.94 | 3.86 | 3.78 | 3.71 | 3.61 |
| 12 | .10 | 3.18 | 2.81 | 2.61 | 2.48 | 2.39 | 2.33 | 2.28 | 2.24 | 2.21 | 2.19 | 2.10 | 2.06 | 2.03 | 2.01 | 1.99 | 1.96 | 1.94 | 1.91 |
|  | .05 | 4.75 | 3.89 | 3.49 | 3.26 | 3.11 | 3.00 | 2.91 | 2.85 | 2.80 | 2.75 | 2.62 | 2.54 | 2.50 | 2.47 | 2.43 | 2.38 | 2.35 | 2.30 |
|  | .025 | 6.55 | 5.10 | 4.47 | 4.12 | 3.89 | 3.73 | 3.61 | 3.51 | 3.44 | 3.37 | 3.18 | 3.07 | 3.01 | 2.96 | 2.91 | 2.85 | 2.80 | 2.73 |
|  | .01 | 9.33 | 6.93 | 5.95 | 5.41 | 5.06 | 4.82 | 4.64 | 4.50 | 4.39 | 4.30 | 4.01 | 3.86 | 3.76 | 3.70 | 3.62 | 3.54 | 3.47 | 3.37 |
| 13 | .10 | 3.14 | 2.76 | 2.56 | 2.43 | 2.35 | 2.28 | 2.23 | 2.20 | 2.16 | 2.14 | 2.05 | 2.01 | 1.98 | 1.96 | 1.93 | 1.90 | 1.88 | 1.85 |
|  | .05 | 4.67 | 3.81 | 3.41 | 3.18 | 3.03 | 2.92 | 2.83 | 2.77 | 2.71 | 2.67 | 2.53 | 2.46 | 2.41 | 2.38 | 2.34 | 2.30 | 2.26 | 2.21 |
|  | .025 | 6.41 | 4.97 | 4.35 | 4.00 | 3.77 | 3.60 | 3.48 | 3.39 | 3.31 | 3.25 | 3.05 | 2.95 | 2.88 | 2.84 | 2.78 | 2.72 | 2.67 | 2.60 |
|  | .01 | 9.07 | 6.70 | 5.74 | 5.21 | 4.86 | 4.62 | 4.44 | 4.30 | 4.19 | 4.10 | 3.82 | 3.66 | 3.57 | 3.51 | 3.43 | 3.34 | 3.27 | 3.18 |
| 14 | .10 | 3.10 | 2.73 | 2.52 | 2.39 | 2.31 | 2.24 | 2.19 | 2.15 | 2.12 | 2.10 | 2.01 | 1.96 | 1.93 | 1.91 | 1.89 | 1.86 | 1.83 | 1.80 |
|  | .05 | 4.60 | 3.74 | 3.34 | 3.11 | 2.96 | 2.85 | 2.76 | 2.70 | 2.65 | 2.60 | 2.46 | 2.39 | 2.34 | 2.31 | 2.27 | 2.22 | 2.19 | 2.14 |
|  | .025 | 6.30 | 4.86 | 4.24 | 3.89 | 3.66 | 3.50 | 3.38 | 3.29 | 3.21 | 3.15 | 2.95 | 2.84 | 2.78 | 2.73 | 2.67 | 2.61 | 2.56 | 2.50 |
|  | .01 | 8.86 | 6.51 | 5.56 | 5.04 | 4.69 | 4.46 | 4.28 | 4.14 | 4.03 | 3.94 | 3.66 | 3.51 | 3.41 | 3.35 | 3.27 | 3.18 | 3.11 | 3.02 |
| 15 | .10 | 3.07 | 2.70 | 2.49 | 2.36 | 2.27 | 2.21 | 2.16 | 2.12 | 2.09 | 2.06 | 1.97 | 1.92 | 1.89 | 1.87 | 1.85 | 1.82 | 1.79 | 1.76 |
|  | .05 | 4.54 | 3.68 | 3.29 | 3.06 | 2.90 | 2.79 | 2.71 | 2.64 | 2.59 | 2.54 | 2.40 | 2.33 | 2.28 | 2.25 | 2.20 | 2.16 | 2.12 | 2.07 |
|  | .025 | 6.20 | 4.77 | 4.15 | 3.80 | 3.58 | 3.41 | 3.29 | 3.20 | 3.12 | 3.06 | 2.86 | 2.76 | 2.69 | 2.64 | 2.59 | 2.52 | 2.47 | 2.40 |
|  | .01 | 8.68 | 6.36 | 5.42 | 4.89 | 4.56 | 4.32 | 4.14 | 4.00 | 3.89 | 3.80 | 3.52 | 3.37 | 3.28 | 3.21 | 3.13 | 3.05 | 2.98 | 2.88 |

**TABLE 4**  *F* DISTRIBUTION (*continued*)

| Denominator Degrees of Freedom | Area in Upper Tail | Numerator Degrees of Freedom | | | | | | | | | | | | | | | | | |
|---|---|---|---|---|---|---|---|---|---|---|---|---|---|---|---|---|---|---|---|
| | | 1 | 2 | 3 | 4 | 5 | 6 | 7 | 8 | 9 | 10 | 15 | 20 | 25 | 30 | 40 | 60 | 100 | 1000 |
| 16 | .10 | 3.05 | 2.67 | 2.46 | 2.33 | 2.24 | 2.18 | 2.13 | 2.09 | 2.06 | 2.03 | 1.94 | 1.89 | 1.86 | 1.84 | 1.81 | 1.78 | 1.76 | 1.72 |
| | .05 | 4.49 | 3.63 | 3.24 | 3.01 | 2.85 | 2.74 | 2.66 | 2.59 | 2.54 | 2.49 | 2.35 | 2.28 | 2.23 | 2.19 | 2.15 | 2.11 | 2.07 | 2.02 |
| | .025 | 6.12 | 4.69 | 4.08 | 3.73 | 3.50 | 3.34 | 3.22 | 3.12 | 3.05 | 2.99 | 2.79 | 2.68 | 2.61 | 2.57 | 2.51 | 2.45 | 2.40 | 2.32 |
| | .01 | 8.53 | 6.23 | 5.29 | 4.77 | 4.44 | 4.20 | 4.03 | 3.89 | 3.78 | 3.69 | 3.41 | 3.26 | 3.16 | 3.10 | 3.02 | 2.93 | 2.86 | 2.76 |
| 17 | .10 | 3.03 | 2.64 | 2.44 | 2.31 | 2.22 | 2.15 | 2.10 | 2.06 | 2.03 | 2.00 | 1.91 | 1.86 | 1.83 | 1.81 | 1.78 | 1.75 | 1.73 | 1.69 |
| | .05 | 4.45 | 3.59 | 3.20 | 2.96 | 2.81 | 2.70 | 2.61 | 2.55 | 2.49 | 2.45 | 2.31 | 2.23 | 2.18 | 2.15 | 2.10 | 2.06 | 2.02 | 1.97 |
| | .025 | 6.04 | 4.62 | 4.01 | 3.66 | 3.44 | 3.28 | 3.16 | 3.06 | 2.98 | 2.92 | 2.72 | 2.62 | 2.55 | 2.50 | 2.44 | 2.38 | 2.33 | 2.26 |
| | .01 | 8.40 | 6.11 | 5.19 | 4.67 | 4.34 | 4.10 | 3.93 | 3.79 | 3.68 | 3.59 | 3.31 | 3.16 | 3.07 | 3.00 | 2.92 | 2.83 | 2.76 | 2.66 |
| 18 | .10 | 3.01 | 2.62 | 2.42 | 2.29 | 2.20 | 2.13 | 2.08 | 2.04 | 2.00 | 1.98 | 1.89 | 1.84 | 1.80 | 1.78 | 1.75 | 1.72 | 1.70 | 1.66 |
| | .05 | 4.41 | 3.55 | 3.16 | 2.93 | 2.77 | 2.66 | 2.58 | 2.51 | 2.46 | 2.41 | 2.27 | 2.19 | 2.14 | 2.11 | 2.06 | 2.02 | 1.98 | 1.92 |
| | .025 | 5.98 | 4.56 | 3.95 | 3.61 | 3.38 | 3.22 | 3.10 | 3.01 | 2.93 | 2.87 | 2.67 | 2.56 | 2.49 | 2.44 | 2.38 | 2.32 | 2.27 | 2.20 |
| | .01 | 8.29 | 6.01 | 5.09 | 4.58 | 4.25 | 4.01 | 3.84 | 3.71 | 3.60 | 3.51 | 3.23 | 3.08 | 2.98 | 2.92 | 2.84 | 2.75 | 2.68 | 2.58 |
| 19 | .10 | 2.99 | 2.61 | 2.40 | 2.27 | 2.18 | 2.11 | 2.06 | 2.02 | 1.98 | 1.96 | 1.86 | 1.81 | 1.78 | 1.76 | 1.73 | 1.70 | 1.67 | 1.64 |
| | .05 | 4.38 | 3.52 | 3.13 | 2.90 | 2.74 | 2.63 | 2.54 | 2.48 | 2.42 | 2.38 | 2.23 | 2.16 | 2.11 | 2.07 | 2.03 | 1.98 | 1.94 | 1.88 |
| | .025 | 5.92 | 4.51 | 3.90 | 3.56 | 3.33 | 3.17 | 3.05 | 2.96 | 2.88 | 2.82 | 2.62 | 2.51 | 2.44 | 2.39 | 2.33 | 2.27 | 2.22 | 2.14 |
| | .01 | 8.18 | 5.93 | 5.01 | 4.50 | 4.17 | 3.94 | 3.77 | 3.63 | 3.52 | 3.43 | 3.15 | 3.00 | 2.91 | 2.84 | 2.76 | 2.67 | 2.60 | 2.50 |
| 20 | .10 | 2.97 | 2.59 | 2.38 | 2.25 | 2.16 | 2.09 | 2.04 | 2.00 | 1.96 | 1.94 | 1.84 | 1.79 | 1.76 | 1.74 | 1.71 | 1.68 | 1.65 | 1.61 |
| | .05 | 4.35 | 3.49 | 3.10 | 2.87 | 2.71 | 2.60 | 2.51 | 2.45 | 2.39 | 2.35 | 2.20 | 2.12 | 2.07 | 2.04 | 1.99 | 1.95 | 1.91 | 1.85 |
| | .025 | 5.87 | 4.46 | 3.86 | 3.51 | 3.29 | 3.13 | 3.01 | 2.91 | 2.84 | 2.77 | 2.57 | 2.46 | 2.40 | 2.35 | 2.29 | 2.22 | 2.17 | 2.09 |
| | .01 | 8.10 | 5.85 | 4.94 | 4.43 | 4.10 | 3.87 | 3.70 | 3.56 | 3.46 | 3.37 | 3.09 | 2.94 | 2.84 | 2.78 | 2.69 | 2.61 | 2.54 | 2.43 |
| 21 | .10 | 2.96 | 2.57 | 2.36 | 2.23 | 2.14 | 2.08 | 2.02 | 1.98 | 1.95 | 1.92 | 1.83 | 1.78 | 1.74 | 1.72 | 1.69 | 1.66 | 1.63 | 1.59 |
| | .05 | 4.32 | 3.47 | 3.07 | 2.84 | 2.68 | 2.57 | 2.49 | 2.42 | 2.37 | 2.32 | 2.18 | 2.10 | 2.05 | 2.01 | 1.96 | 1.92 | 1.88 | 1.82 |
| | .025 | 5.83 | 4.42 | 3.82 | 3.48 | 3.25 | 3.09 | 2.97 | 2.87 | 2.80 | 2.73 | 2.53 | 2.42 | 2.36 | 2.31 | 2.25 | 2.18 | 2.13 | 2.05 |
| | .01 | 8.02 | 5.78 | 4.87 | 4.37 | 4.04 | 3.81 | 3.64 | 3.51 | 3.40 | 3.31 | 3.03 | 2.88 | 2.79 | 2.72 | 2.64 | 2.55 | 2.48 | 2.37 |
| 22 | .10 | 2.95 | 2.56 | 2.35 | 2.22 | 2.13 | 2.06 | 2.01 | 1.97 | 1.93 | 1.90 | 1.81 | 1.76 | 1.73 | 1.70 | 1.67 | 1.64 | 1.61 | 1.57 |
| | .05 | 4.30 | 3.44 | 3.05 | 2.82 | 2.66 | 2.55 | 2.46 | 2.40 | 2.34 | 2.30 | 2.15 | 2.07 | 2.02 | 1.98 | 1.94 | 1.89 | 1.85 | 1.79 |
| | .025 | 5.79 | 4.38 | 3.78 | 3.44 | 3.22 | 3.05 | 2.93 | 2.84 | 2.76 | 2.70 | 2.50 | 2.39 | 2.32 | 2.27 | 2.21 | 2.14 | 2.09 | 2.01 |
| | .01 | 7.95 | 5.72 | 4.82 | 4.31 | 3.99 | 3.76 | 3.59 | 3.45 | 3.35 | 3.26 | 2.98 | 2.83 | 2.73 | 2.67 | 2.58 | 2.50 | 2.42 | 2.32 |
| 23 | .10 | 2.94 | 2.55 | 2.34 | 2.21 | 2.11 | 2.05 | 1.99 | 1.95 | 1.92 | 1.89 | 1.80 | 1.74 | 1.71 | 1.69 | 1.66 | 1.62 | 1.59 | 1.55 |
| | .05 | 4.28 | 3.42 | 3.03 | 2.80 | 2.64 | 2.53 | 2.44 | 2.37 | 2.32 | 2.27 | 2.13 | 2.05 | 2.00 | 1.96 | 1.91 | 1.86 | 1.82 | 1.76 |
| | .025 | 5.75 | 4.35 | 3.75 | 3.41 | 3.18 | 3.02 | 2.90 | 2.81 | 2.73 | 2.67 | 2.47 | 2.36 | 2.29 | 2.24 | 2.18 | 2.11 | 2.06 | 1.98 |
| | .01 | 7.88 | 5.66 | 4.76 | 4.26 | 3.94 | 3.71 | 3.54 | 3.41 | 3.30 | 3.21 | 2.93 | 2.78 | 2.69 | 2.62 | 2.54 | 2.45 | 2.37 | 2.27 |
| 24 | .10 | 2.93 | 2.54 | 2.33 | 2.19 | 2.10 | 2.04 | 1.98 | 1.94 | 1.91 | 1.88 | 1.78 | 1.73 | 1.70 | 1.67 | 1.64 | 1.61 | 1.58 | 1.54 |
| | .05 | 4.26 | 3.40 | 3.01 | 2.78 | 2.62 | 2.51 | 2.42 | 2.36 | 2.30 | 2.25 | 2.11 | 2.03 | 1.97 | 1.94 | 1.89 | 1.84 | 1.80 | 1.74 |
| | .025 | 5.72 | 4.32 | 3.72 | 3.38 | 3.15 | 2.99 | 2.87 | 2.78 | 2.70 | 2.64 | 2.44 | 2.33 | 2.26 | 2.21 | 2.15 | 2.08 | 2.02 | 1.94 |
| | .01 | 7.82 | 5.61 | 4.72 | 4.22 | 3.90 | 3.67 | 3.50 | 3.36 | 3.26 | 3.17 | 2.89 | 2.74 | 2.64 | 2.58 | 2.49 | 2.40 | 2.33 | 2.22 |

Numerator Degrees of Freedom

| Denominator Degrees of Freedom | Area in Upper Tail | 1 | 2 | 3 | 4 | 5 | 6 | 7 | 8 | 9 | 10 | 15 | 20 | 25 | 30 | 40 | 60 | 100 | 1000 |
|---|---|---|---|---|---|---|---|---|---|---|---|---|---|---|---|---|---|---|---|
| 25 | .10 | 2.92 | 2.53 | 2.32 | 2.18 | 2.09 | 2.02 | 1.97 | 1.93 | 1.89 | 1.87 | 1.77 | 1.72 | 1.68 | 1.66 | 1.63 | 1.59 | 1.56 | 1.52 |
|  | .05 | 4.24 | 3.39 | 2.99 | 2.76 | 2.60 | 2.49 | 2.40 | 2.34 | 2.28 | 2.24 | 2.09 | 2.01 | 1.96 | 1.92 | 1.87 | 1.82 | 1.78 | 1.72 |
|  | .025 | 5.69 | 4.29 | 3.69 | 3.35 | 3.13 | 2.97 | 2.85 | 2.75 | 2.68 | 2.61 | 2.41 | 2.30 | 2.23 | 2.18 | 2.12 | 2.05 | 2.00 | 1.91 |
|  | .01 | 7.77 | 5.57 | 4.68 | 4.18 | 3.85 | 3.63 | 3.46 | 3.32 | 3.22 | 3.13 | 2.85 | 2.70 | 2.60 | 2.54 | 2.45 | 2.36 | 2.29 | 2.18 |
| 26 | .10 | 2.91 | 2.52 | 2.31 | 2.17 | 2.08 | 2.01 | 1.96 | 1.92 | 1.88 | 1.86 | 1.76 | 1.71 | 1.67 | 1.65 | 1.61 | 1.58 | 1.55 | 1.51 |
|  | .05 | 4.23 | 3.37 | 2.98 | 2.74 | 2.59 | 2.47 | 2.39 | 2.32 | 2.27 | 2.22 | 2.07 | 1.99 | 1.94 | 1.90 | 1.85 | 1.80 | 1.76 | 1.70 |
|  | .025 | 5.66 | 4.27 | 3.67 | 3.33 | 3.10 | 2.94 | 2.82 | 2.73 | 2.65 | 2.59 | 2.39 | 2.28 | 2.21 | 2.16 | 2.09 | 2.03 | 1.97 | 1.89 |
|  | .01 | 7.72 | 5.53 | 4.64 | 4.14 | 3.82 | 3.59 | 3.42 | 3.29 | 3.18 | 3.09 | 2.81 | 2.66 | 2.57 | 2.50 | 2.42 | 2.33 | 2.25 | 2.14 |
| 27 | .10 | 2.90 | 2.51 | 2.30 | 2.17 | 2.07 | 2.00 | 1.95 | 1.91 | 1.87 | 1.85 | 1.75 | 1.70 | 1.66 | 1.64 | 1.60 | 1.57 | 1.54 | 1.50 |
|  | .05 | 4.21 | 3.35 | 2.96 | 2.73 | 2.57 | 2.46 | 2.37 | 2.31 | 2.25 | 2.20 | 2.06 | 1.97 | 1.92 | 1.88 | 1.84 | 1.79 | 1.74 | 1.68 |
|  | .025 | 5.63 | 4.24 | 3.65 | 3.31 | 3.08 | 2.92 | 2.80 | 2.71 | 2.63 | 2.57 | 2.36 | 2.25 | 2.18 | 2.13 | 2.07 | 2.00 | 1.94 | 1.86 |
|  | .01 | 7.68 | 5.49 | 4.60 | 4.11 | 3.78 | 3.56 | 3.39 | 3.26 | 3.15 | 3.06 | 2.78 | 2.63 | 2.54 | 2.47 | 2.38 | 2.29 | 2.22 | 2.11 |
| 28 | .10 | 2.89 | 2.50 | 2.29 | 2.16 | 2.06 | 2.00 | 1.94 | 1.90 | 1.87 | 1.84 | 1.74 | 1.69 | 1.65 | 1.63 | 1.59 | 1.56 | 1.53 | 1.48 |
|  | .05 | 4.20 | 3.34 | 2.95 | 2.71 | 2.56 | 2.45 | 2.36 | 2.29 | 2.24 | 2.19 | 2.04 | 1.96 | 1.91 | 1.87 | 1.82 | 1.77 | 1.73 | 1.66 |
|  | .025 | 5.61 | 4.22 | 3.63 | 3.29 | 3.06 | 2.90 | 2.78 | 2.69 | 2.61 | 2.55 | 2.34 | 2.23 | 2.16 | 2.11 | 2.05 | 1.98 | 1.92 | 1.84 |
|  | .01 | 7.64 | 5.45 | 4.57 | 4.07 | 3.75 | 3.53 | 3.36 | 3.23 | 3.12 | 3.03 | 2.75 | 2.60 | 2.51 | 2.44 | 2.35 | 2.26 | 2.19 | 2.08 |
| 29 | .10 | 2.89 | 2.50 | 2.28 | 2.15 | 2.06 | 1.99 | 1.93 | 1.89 | 1.86 | 1.83 | 1.73 | 1.68 | 1.64 | 1.62 | 1.58 | 1.55 | 1.52 | 1.47 |
|  | .05 | 4.18 | 3.33 | 2.93 | 2.70 | 2.55 | 2.43 | 2.35 | 2.28 | 2.22 | 2.18 | 2.03 | 1.94 | 1.89 | 1.85 | 1.81 | 1.75 | 1.71 | 1.65 |
|  | .025 | 5.59 | 4.20 | 3.61 | 3.27 | 3.04 | 2.88 | 2.76 | 2.67 | 2.59 | 2.53 | 2.32 | 2.21 | 2.14 | 2.09 | 2.03 | 1.96 | 1.90 | 1.82 |
|  | .01 | 7.60 | 5.42 | 4.54 | 4.04 | 3.73 | 3.50 | 3.33 | 3.20 | 3.09 | 3.00 | 2.73 | 2.57 | 2.48 | 2.41 | 2.33 | 2.23 | 2.16 | 2.05 |
| 30 | .10 | 2.88 | 2.49 | 2.28 | 2.14 | 2.05 | 1.98 | 1.93 | 1.88 | 1.85 | 1.82 | 1.72 | 1.67 | 1.63 | 1.61 | 1.57 | 1.54 | 1.51 | 1.46 |
|  | .05 | 4.17 | 3.32 | 2.92 | 2.69 | 2.53 | 2.42 | 2.33 | 2.27 | 2.21 | 2.16 | 2.01 | 1.93 | 1.88 | 1.84 | 1.79 | 1.74 | 1.70 | 1.63 |
|  | .025 | 5.57 | 4.18 | 3.59 | 3.25 | 3.03 | 2.87 | 2.75 | 2.65 | 2.57 | 2.51 | 2.31 | 2.20 | 2.12 | 2.07 | 2.01 | 1.94 | 1.88 | 1.80 |
|  | .01 | 7.56 | 5.39 | 4.51 | 4.02 | 3.70 | 3.47 | 3.30 | 3.17 | 3.07 | 2.98 | 2.70 | 2.55 | 2.45 | 2.39 | 2.30 | 2.21 | 2.13 | 2.02 |
| 40 | .10 | 2.84 | 2.44 | 2.23 | 2.09 | 2.00 | 1.93 | 1.87 | 1.83 | 1.79 | 1.76 | 1.66 | 1.61 | 1.57 | 1.54 | 1.51 | 1.47 | 1.43 | 1.38 |
|  | .05 | 4.08 | 3.23 | 2.84 | 2.61 | 2.45 | 2.34 | 2.25 | 2.18 | 2.12 | 2.08 | 1.92 | 1.84 | 1.78 | 1.74 | 1.69 | 1.64 | 1.59 | 1.52 |
|  | .025 | 5.42 | 4.05 | 3.46 | 3.13 | 2.90 | 2.74 | 2.62 | 2.53 | 2.45 | 2.39 | 2.18 | 2.07 | 1.99 | 1.94 | 1.88 | 1.80 | 1.74 | 1.65 |
|  | .01 | 7.31 | 5.18 | 4.31 | 3.83 | 3.51 | 3.29 | 3.12 | 2.99 | 2.89 | 2.80 | 2.52 | 2.37 | 2.27 | 2.20 | 2.11 | 2.02 | 1.94 | 1.82 |
| 60 | .10 | 2.79 | 2.39 | 2.18 | 2.04 | 1.95 | 1.87 | 1.82 | 1.77 | 1.74 | 1.71 | 1.60 | 1.54 | 1.50 | 1.48 | 1.44 | 1.40 | 1.36 | 1.30 |
|  | .05 | 4.00 | 3.15 | 2.76 | 2.53 | 2.37 | 2.25 | 2.17 | 2.10 | 2.04 | 1.99 | 1.84 | 1.75 | 1.69 | 1.65 | 1.59 | 1.53 | 1.48 | 1.40 |
|  | .025 | 5.29 | 3.93 | 3.34 | 3.01 | 2.79 | 2.63 | 2.51 | 2.41 | 2.33 | 2.27 | 2.06 | 1.94 | 1.87 | 1.82 | 1.74 | 1.67 | 1.60 | 1.49 |
|  | .01 | 7.08 | 4.98 | 4.13 | 3.65 | 3.34 | 3.12 | 2.95 | 2.82 | 2.72 | 2.63 | 2.35 | 2.20 | 2.10 | 2.03 | 1.94 | 1.84 | 1.75 | 1.62 |
| 100 | .10 | 2.76 | 2.36 | 2.14 | 2.00 | 1.91 | 1.83 | 1.78 | 1.73 | 1.69 | 1.66 | 1.56 | 1.49 | 1.45 | 1.42 | 1.38 | 1.34 | 1.29 | 1.22 |
|  | .05 | 3.94 | 3.09 | 2.70 | 2.46 | 2.31 | 2.19 | 2.10 | 2.03 | 1.97 | 1.93 | 1.77 | 1.68 | 1.62 | 1.57 | 1.52 | 1.45 | 1.39 | 1.30 |
|  | .025 | 5.18 | 3.83 | 3.25 | 2.92 | 2.70 | 2.54 | 2.42 | 2.32 | 2.24 | 2.18 | 1.97 | 1.85 | 1.77 | 1.71 | 1.64 | 1.56 | 1.48 | 1.36 |
|  | .01 | 6.90 | 4.82 | 3.98 | 3.51 | 3.21 | 2.99 | 2.82 | 2.69 | 2.59 | 2.50 | 2.22 | 2.07 | 1.97 | 1.89 | 1.80 | 1.69 | 1.60 | 1.45 |
| 1000 | .10 | 2.71 | 2.31 | 2.09 | 1.95 | 1.85 | 1.78 | 1.72 | 1.68 | 1.64 | 1.61 | 1.49 | 1.43 | 1.38 | 1.35 | 1.30 | 1.25 | 1.20 | 1.08 |
|  | .05 | 3.85 | 3.00 | 2.61 | 2.38 | 2.22 | 2.11 | 2.02 | 1.95 | 1.89 | 1.84 | 1.68 | 1.58 | 1.52 | 1.47 | 1.41 | 1.33 | 1.26 | 1.11 |
|  | .025 | 5.04 | 3.70 | 3.13 | 2.80 | 2.58 | 2.42 | 2.30 | 2.20 | 2.13 | 2.06 | 1.85 | 1.72 | 1.64 | 1.58 | 1.50 | 1.41 | 1.32 | 1.13 |
|  | .01 | 6.66 | 4.63 | 3.80 | 3.34 | 3.04 | 2.82 | 2.66 | 2.53 | 2.43 | 2.34 | 2.06 | 1.90 | 1.79 | 1.72 | 1.61 | 1.50 | 1.38 | 1.16 |

**TABLE 5** BINOMIAL PROBABILITIES

Entries in the table give the probability of $x$ successes in $n$ trials of a binomial experiment, where $p$ is the probability of a success on one trial. For example, with six trials and $p = .05$, the probability of two successes is .0305.

| | | | | | | $p$ | | | | |
|---|---|---|---|---|---|---|---|---|---|---|
| $n$ | $x$ | .01 | .02 | .03 | .04 | .05 | .06 | .07 | .08 | .09 |
| 2 | 0 | .9801 | .9604 | .9409 | .9216 | .9025 | .8836 | .8649 | .8464 | .8281 |
| | 1 | .0198 | .0392 | .0582 | .0768 | .0950 | .1128 | .1302 | .1472 | .1638 |
| | 2 | .0001 | .0004 | .0009 | .0016 | .0025 | .0036 | .0049 | .0064 | .0081 |
| 3 | 0 | .9703 | .9412 | .9127 | .8847 | .8574 | .8306 | .8044 | .7787 | .7536 |
| | 1 | .0294 | .0576 | .0847 | .1106 | .1354 | .1590 | .1816 | .2031 | .2236 |
| | 2 | .0003 | .0012 | .0026 | .0046 | .0071 | .0102 | .0137 | .0177 | .0221 |
| | 3 | .0000 | .0000 | .0000 | .0001 | .0001 | .0002 | .0003 | .0005 | .0007 |
| 4 | 0 | .9606 | .9224 | .8853 | .8493 | .8145 | .7807 | .7481 | .7164 | .6857 |
| | 1 | .0388 | .0753 | .1095 | .1416 | .1715 | .1993 | .2252 | .2492 | .2713 |
| | 2 | .0006 | .0023 | .0051 | .0088 | .0135 | .0191 | .0254 | .0325 | .0402 |
| | 3 | .0000 | .0000 | .0001 | .0002 | .0005 | .0008 | .0013 | .0019 | .0027 |
| | 4 | .0000 | .0000 | .0000 | .0000 | .0000 | .0000 | .0000 | .0000 | .0001 |
| 5 | 0 | .9510 | .9039 | .8587 | .8154 | .7738 | .7339 | .6957 | .6591 | .6240 |
| | 1 | .0480 | .0922 | .1328 | .1699 | .2036 | .2342 | .2618 | .2866 | .3086 |
| | 2 | .0010 | .0038 | .0082 | .0142 | .0214 | .0299 | .0394 | .0498 | .0610 |
| | 3 | .0000 | .0001 | .0003 | .0006 | .0011 | .0019 | .0030 | .0043 | .0060 |
| | 4 | .0000 | .0000 | .0000 | .0000 | .0000 | .0001 | .0001 | .0002 | .0003 |
| | 5 | .0000 | .0000 | .0000 | .0000 | .0000 | .0000 | .0000 | .0000 | .0000 |
| 6 | 0 | .9415 | .8858 | .8330 | .7828 | .7351 | .6899 | .6470 | .6064 | .5679 |
| | 1 | .0571 | .1085 | .1546 | .1957 | .2321 | .2642 | .2922 | .3164 | .3370 |
| | 2 | .0014 | .0055 | .0120 | .0204 | .0305 | .0422 | .0550 | .0688 | .0833 |
| | 3 | .0000 | .0002 | .0005 | .0011 | .0021 | .0036 | .0055 | .0080 | .0110 |
| | 4 | .0000 | .0000 | .0000 | .0000 | .0001 | .0002 | .0003 | .0005 | .0008 |
| | 5 | .0000 | .0000 | .0000 | .0000 | .0000 | .0000 | .0000 | .0000 | .0000 |
| | 6 | .0000 | .0000 | .0000 | .0000 | .0000 | .0000 | .0000 | .0000 | .0000 |
| 7 | 0 | .9321 | .8681 | .8080 | .7514 | .6983 | .6485 | .6017 | .5578 | .5168 |
| | 1 | .0659 | .1240 | .1749 | .2192 | .2573 | .2897 | .3170 | .3396 | .3578 |
| | 2 | .0020 | .0076 | .0162 | .0274 | .0406 | .0555 | .0716 | .0886 | .1061 |
| | 3 | .0000 | .0003 | .0008 | .0019 | .0036 | .0059 | .0090 | .0128 | .0175 |
| | 4 | .0000 | .0000 | .0000 | .0001 | .0002 | .0004 | .0007 | .0011 | .0017 |
| | 5 | .0000 | .0000 | .0000 | .0000 | .0000 | .0000 | .0000 | .0001 | .0001 |
| | 6 | .0000 | .0000 | .0000 | .0000 | .0000 | .0000 | .0000 | .0000 | .0000 |
| | 7 | .0000 | .0000 | .0000 | .0000 | .0000 | .0000 | .0000 | .0000 | .0000 |
| 8 | 0 | .9227 | .8508 | .7837 | .7214 | .6634 | .6096 | .5596 | .5132 | .4703 |
| | 1 | .0746 | .1389 | .1939 | .2405 | .2793 | .3113 | .3370 | .3570 | .3721 |
| | 2 | .0026 | .0099 | .0210 | .0351 | .0515 | .0695 | .0888 | .1087 | .1288 |
| | 3 | .0001 | .0004 | .0013 | .0029 | .0054 | .0089 | .0134 | .0189 | .0255 |
| | 4 | .0000 | .0000 | .0001 | .0002 | .0004 | .0007 | .0013 | .0021 | .0031 |
| | 5 | .0000 | .0000 | .0000 | .0000 | .0000 | .0000 | .0001 | .0001 | .0002 |
| | 6 | .0000 | .0000 | .0000 | .0000 | .0000 | .0000 | .0000 | .0000 | .0000 |
| | 7 | .0000 | .0000 | .0000 | .0000 | .0000 | .0000 | .0000 | .0000 | .0000 |
| | 8 | .0000 | .0000 | .0000 | .0000 | .0000 | .0000 | .0000 | .0000 | .0000 |

TABLE 5    BINOMIAL PROBABILITIES (*Continued*)

| n | x | .01 | .02 | .03 | .04 | .05 | .06 | .07 | .08 | .09 |
|---|---|-----|-----|-----|-----|-----|-----|-----|-----|-----|
| 9 | 0 | .9135 | .8337 | .7602 | .6925 | .6302 | .5730 | .5204 | .4722 | .4279 |
|   | 1 | .0830 | .1531 | .2116 | .2597 | .2985 | .3292 | .3525 | .3695 | .3809 |
|   | 2 | .0034 | .0125 | .0262 | .0433 | .0629 | .0840 | .1061 | .1285 | .1507 |
|   | 3 | .0001 | .0006 | .0019 | .0042 | .0077 | .0125 | .0186 | .0261 | .0348 |
|   | 4 | .0000 | .0000 | .0001 | .0003 | .0006 | .0012 | .0021 | .0034 | .0052 |
|   | 5 | .0000 | .0000 | .0000 | .0000 | .0000 | .0001 | .0002 | .0003 | .0005 |
|   | 6 | .0000 | .0000 | .0000 | .0000 | .0000 | .0000 | .0000 | .0000 | .0000 |
|   | 7 | .0000 | .0000 | .0000 | .0000 | .0000 | .0000 | .0000 | .0000 | .0000 |
|   | 8 | .0000 | .0000 | .0000 | .0000 | .0000 | .0000 | .0000 | .0000 | .0000 |
|   | 9 | .0000 | .0000 | .0000 | .0000 | .0000 | .0000 | .0000 | .0000 | .0000 |
| 10 | 0 | .9044 | .8171 | .7374 | .6648 | .5987 | .5386 | .4840 | .4344 | .3894 |
|   | 1 | .0914 | .1667 | .2281 | .2770 | .3151 | .3438 | .3643 | .3777 | .3851 |
|   | 2 | .0042 | .0153 | .0317 | .0519 | .0746 | .0988 | .1234 | .1478 | .1714 |
|   | 3 | .0001 | .0008 | .0026 | .0058 | .0105 | .0168 | .0248 | .0343 | .0452 |
|   | 4 | .0000 | .0000 | .0001 | .0004 | .0010 | .0019 | .0033 | .0052 | .0078 |
|   | 5 | .0000 | .0000 | .0000 | .0000 | .0001 | .0001 | .0003 | .0005 | .0009 |
|   | 6 | .0000 | .0000 | .0000 | .0000 | .0000 | .0000 | .0000 | .0000 | .0001 |
|   | 7 | .0000 | .0000 | .0000 | .0000 | .0000 | .0000 | .0000 | .0000 | .0000 |
|   | 8 | .0000 | .0000 | .0000 | .0000 | .0000 | .0000 | .0000 | .0000 | .0000 |
|   | 9 | .0000 | .0000 | .0000 | .0000 | .0000 | .0000 | .0000 | .0000 | .0000 |
|   | 10 | .0000 | .0000 | .0000 | .0000 | .0000 | .0000 | .0000 | .0000 | .0000 |
| 12 | 0 | .8864 | .7847 | .6938 | .6127 | .5404 | .4759 | .4186 | .3677 | .3225 |
|   | 1 | .1074 | .1922 | .2575 | .3064 | .3413 | .3645 | .3781 | .3837 | .3827 |
|   | 2 | .0060 | .0216 | .0438 | .0702 | .0988 | .1280 | .1565 | .1835 | .2082 |
|   | 3 | .0002 | .0015 | .0045 | .0098 | .0173 | .0272 | .0393 | .0532 | .0686 |
|   | 4 | .0000 | .0001 | .0003 | .0009 | .0021 | .0039 | .0067 | .0104 | .0153 |
|   | 5 | .0000 | .0000 | .0000 | .0001 | .0002 | .0004 | .0008 | .0014 | .0024 |
|   | 6 | .0000 | .0000 | .0000 | .0000 | .0000 | .0000 | .0001 | .0001 | .0003 |
|   | 7 | .0000 | .0000 | .0000 | .0000 | .0000 | .0000 | .0000 | .0000 | .0000 |
|   | 8 | .0000 | .0000 | .0000 | .0000 | .0000 | .0000 | .0000 | .0000 | .0000 |
|   | 9 | .0000 | .0000 | .0000 | .0000 | .0000 | .0000 | .0000 | .0000 | .0000 |
|   | 10 | .0000 | .0000 | .0000 | .0000 | .0000 | .0000 | .0000 | .0000 | .0000 |
|   | 11 | .0000 | .0000 | .0000 | .0000 | .0000 | .0000 | .0000 | .0000 | .0000 |
|   | 12 | .0000 | .0000 | .0000 | .0000 | .0000 | .0000 | .0000 | .0000 | .0000 |
| 15 | 0 | .8601 | .7386 | .6333 | .5421 | .4633 | .3953 | .3367 | .2863 | .2430 |
|   | 1 | .1303 | .2261 | .2938 | .3388 | .3658 | .3785 | .3801 | .3734 | .3605 |
|   | 2 | .0092 | .0323 | .0636 | .0988 | .1348 | .1691 | .2003 | .2273 | .2496 |
|   | 3 | .0004 | .0029 | .0085 | .0178 | .0307 | .0468 | .0653 | .0857 | .1070 |
|   | 4 | .0000 | .0002 | .0008 | .0022 | .0049 | .0090 | .0148 | .0223 | .0317 |
|   | 5 | .0000 | .0000 | .0001 | .0002 | .0006 | .0013 | .0024 | .0043 | .0069 |
|   | 6 | .0000 | .0000 | .0000 | .0000 | .0000 | .0001 | .0003 | .0006 | .0011 |
|   | 7 | .0000 | .0000 | .0000 | .0000 | .0000 | .0000 | .0000 | .0001 | .0001 |
|   | 8 | .0000 | .0000 | .0000 | .0000 | .0000 | .0000 | .0000 | .0000 | .0000 |
|   | 9 | .0000 | .0000 | .0000 | .0000 | .0000 | .0000 | .0000 | .0000 | .0000 |
|   | 10 | .0000 | .0000 | .0000 | .0000 | .0000 | .0000 | .0000 | .0000 | .0000 |
|   | 11 | .0000 | .0000 | .0000 | .0000 | .0000 | .0000 | .0000 | .0000 | .0000 |
|   | 12 | .0000 | .0000 | .0000 | .0000 | .0000 | .0000 | .0000 | .0000 | .0000 |
|   | 13 | .0000 | .0000 | .0000 | .0000 | .0000 | .0000 | .0000 | .0000 | .0000 |
|   | 14 | .0000 | .0000 | .0000 | .0000 | .0000 | .0000 | .0000 | .0000 | .0000 |
|   | 15 | .0000 | .0000 | .0000 | .0000 | .0000 | .0000 | .0000 | .0000 | .0000 |

**TABLE 5**   BINOMIAL PROBABILITIES (*Continued*)

| | | | | | | *p* | | | | |
|---|---|---|---|---|---|---|---|---|---|---|
| *n* | *x* | .01 | .02 | .03 | .04 | .05 | .06 | .07 | .08 | .09 |
| 18 | 0 | .8345 | .6951 | .5780 | .4796 | .3972 | .3283 | .2708 | .2229 | .1831 |
| | 1 | .1517 | .2554 | .3217 | .3597 | .3763 | .3772 | .3669 | .3489 | .3260 |
| | 2 | .0130 | .0443 | .0846 | .1274 | .1683 | .2047 | .2348 | .2579 | .2741 |
| | 3 | .0007 | .0048 | .0140 | .0283 | .0473 | .0697 | .0942 | .1196 | .1446 |
| | 4 | .0000 | .0004 | .0016 | .0044 | .0093 | .0167 | .0266 | .0390 | .0536 |
| | 5 | .0000 | .0000 | .0001 | .0005 | .0014 | .0030 | .0056 | .0095 | .0148 |
| | 6 | .0000 | .0000 | .0000 | .0000 | .0002 | .0004 | .0009 | .0018 | .0032 |
| | 7 | .0000 | .0000 | .0000 | .0000 | .0000 | .0000 | .0001 | .0003 | .0005 |
| | 8 | .0000 | .0000 | .0000 | .0000 | .0000 | .0000 | .0000 | .0000 | .0001 |
| | 9 | .0000 | .0000 | .0000 | .0000 | .0000 | .0000 | .0000 | .0000 | .0000 |
| | 10 | .0000 | .0000 | .0000 | .0000 | .0000 | .0000 | .0000 | .0000 | .0000 |
| | 11 | .0000 | .0000 | .0000 | .0000 | .0000 | .0000 | .0000 | .0000 | .0000 |
| | 12 | .0000 | .0000 | .0000 | .0000 | .0000 | .0000 | .0000 | .0000 | .0000 |
| | 13 | .0000 | .0000 | .0000 | .0000 | .0000 | .0000 | .0000 | .0000 | .0000 |
| | 14 | .0000 | .0000 | .0000 | .0000 | .0000 | .0000 | .0000 | .0000 | .0000 |
| | 15 | .0000 | .0000 | .0000 | .0000 | .0000 | .0000 | .0000 | .0000 | .0000 |
| | 16 | .0000 | .0000 | .0000 | .0000 | .0000 | .0000 | .0000 | .0000 | .0000 |
| | 17 | .0000 | .0000 | .0000 | .0000 | .0000 | .0000 | .0000 | .0000 | .0000 |
| | 18 | .0000 | .0000 | .0000 | .0000 | .0000 | .0000 | .0000 | .0000 | .0000 |
| 20 | 0 | .8179 | .6676 | .5438 | .4420 | .3585 | .2901 | .2342 | .1887 | .1516 |
| | 1 | .1652 | .2725 | .3364 | .3683 | .3774 | .3703 | .3526 | .3282 | .3000 |
| | 2 | .0159 | .0528 | .0988 | .1458 | .1887 | .2246 | .2521 | .2711 | .2818 |
| | 3 | .0010 | .0065 | .0183 | .0364 | .0596 | .0860 | .1139 | .1414 | .1672 |
| | 4 | .0000 | .0006 | .0024 | .0065 | .0133 | .0233 | .0364 | .0523 | .0703 |
| | 5 | .0000 | .0000 | .0002 | .0009 | .0022 | .0048 | .0088 | .0145 | .0222 |
| | 6 | .0000 | .0000 | .0000 | .0001 | .0003 | .0008 | .0017 | .0032 | .0055 |
| | 7 | .0000 | .0000 | .0000 | .0000 | .0000 | .0001 | .0002 | .0005 | .0011 |
| | 8 | .0000 | .0000 | .0000 | .0000 | .0000 | .0000 | .0000 | .0001 | .0002 |
| | 9 | .0000 | .0000 | .0000 | .0000 | .0000 | .0000 | .0000 | .0000 | .0000 |
| | 10 | .0000 | .0000 | .0000 | .0000 | .0000 | .0000 | .0000 | .0000 | .0000 |
| | 11 | .0000 | .0000 | .0000 | .0000 | .0000 | .0000 | .0000 | .0000 | .0000 |
| | 12 | .0000 | .0000 | .0000 | .0000 | .0000 | .0000 | .0000 | .0000 | .0000 |
| | 13 | .0000 | .0000 | .0000 | .0000 | .0000 | .0000 | .0000 | .0000 | .0000 |
| | 14 | .0000 | .0000 | .0000 | .0000 | .0000 | .0000 | .0000 | .0000 | .0000 |
| | 15 | .0000 | .0000 | .0000 | .0000 | .0000 | .0000 | .0000 | .0000 | .0000 |
| | 16 | .0000 | .0000 | .0000 | .0000 | .0000 | .0000 | .0000 | .0000 | .0000 |
| | 17 | .0000 | .0000 | .0000 | .0000 | .0000 | .0000 | .0000 | .0000 | .0000 |
| | 18 | .0000 | .0000 | .0000 | .0000 | .0000 | .0000 | .0000 | .0000 | .0000 |
| | 19 | .0000 | .0000 | .0000 | .0000 | .0000 | .0000 | .0000 | .0000 | .0000 |
| | 20 | .0000 | .0000 | .0000 | .0000 | .0000 | .0000 | .0000 | .0000 | .0000 |

**TABLE 5**    BINOMIAL PROBABILITIES (*Continued*)

| | | | | | | *p* | | | | |
|---|---|---|---|---|---|---|---|---|---|---|
| *n* | *x* | **.10** | **.15** | **.20** | **.25** | **.30** | **.35** | **.40** | **.45** | **.50** |
| 2 | 0 | .8100 | .7225 | .6400 | .5625 | .4900 | .4225 | .3600 | .3025 | .2500 |
| | 1 | .1800 | .2550 | .3200 | .3750 | .4200 | .4550 | .4800 | .4950 | .5000 |
| | 2 | .0100 | .0225 | .0400 | .0625 | .0900 | .1225 | .1600 | .2025 | .2500 |
| 3 | 0 | .7290 | .6141 | .5120 | .4219 | .3430 | .2746 | .2160 | .1664 | .1250 |
| | 1 | .2430 | .3251 | .3840 | .4219 | .4410 | .4436 | .4320 | .4084 | .3750 |
| | 2 | .0270 | .0574 | .0960 | .1406 | .1890 | .2389 | .2880 | .3341 | .3750 |
| | 3 | .0010 | .0034 | .0080 | .0156 | .0270 | .0429 | .0640 | .0911 | .1250 |
| 4 | 0 | .6561 | .5220 | .4096 | .3164 | .2401 | .1785 | .1296 | .0915 | .0625 |
| | 1 | .2916 | .3685 | .4096 | .4219 | .4116 | .3845 | .3456 | .2995 | .2500 |
| | 2 | .0486 | .0975 | .1536 | .2109 | .2646 | .3105 | .3456 | .3675 | .3750 |
| | 3 | .0036 | .0115 | .0256 | .0469 | .0756 | .1115 | .1536 | .2005 | .2500 |
| | 4 | .0001 | .0005 | .0016 | .0039 | .0081 | .0150 | .0256 | .0410 | .0625 |
| 5 | 0 | .5905 | .4437 | .3277 | .2373 | .1681 | .1160 | .0778 | .0503 | .0312 |
| | 1 | .3280 | .3915 | .4096 | .3955 | .3602 | .3124 | .2592 | .2059 | .1562 |
| | 2 | .0729 | .1382 | .2048 | .2637 | .3087 | .3364 | .3456 | .3369 | .3125 |
| | 3 | .0081 | .0244 | .0512 | .0879 | .1323 | .1811 | .2304 | .2757 | .3125 |
| | 4 | .0004 | .0022 | .0064 | .0146 | .0284 | .0488 | .0768 | .1128 | .1562 |
| | 5 | .0000 | .0001 | .0003 | .0010 | .0024 | .0053 | .0102 | .0185 | .0312 |
| 6 | 0 | .5314 | .3771 | .2621 | .1780 | .1176 | .0754 | .0467 | .0277 | .0156 |
| | 1 | .3543 | .3993 | .3932 | .3560 | .3025 | .2437 | .1866 | .1359 | .0938 |
| | 2 | .0984 | .1762 | .2458 | .2966 | .3241 | .3280 | .3110 | .2780 | .2344 |
| | 3 | .0146 | .0415 | .0819 | .1318 | .1852 | .2355 | .2765 | .3032 | .3125 |
| | 4 | .0012 | .0055 | .0154 | .0330 | .0595 | .0951 | .1382 | .1861 | .2344 |
| | 5 | .0001 | .0004 | .0015 | .0044 | .0102 | .0205 | .0369 | .0609 | .0938 |
| | 6 | .0000 | .0000 | .0001 | .0002 | .0007 | .0018 | .0041 | .0083 | .0156 |
| 7 | 0 | .4783 | .3206 | .2097 | .1335 | .0824 | .0490 | .0280 | .0152 | .0078 |
| | 1 | .3720 | .3960 | .3670 | .3115 | .2471 | .1848 | .1306 | .0872 | .0547 |
| | 2 | .1240 | .2097 | .2753 | .3115 | .3177 | .2985 | .2613 | .2140 | .1641 |
| | 3 | .0230 | .0617 | .1147 | .1730 | .2269 | .2679 | .2903 | .2918 | .2734 |
| | 4 | .0026 | .0109 | .0287 | .0577 | .0972 | .1442 | .1935 | .2388 | .2734 |
| | 5 | .0002 | .0012 | .0043 | .0115 | .0250 | .0466 | .0774 | .1172 | .1641 |
| | 6 | .0000 | .0001 | .0004 | .0013 | .0036 | .0084 | .0172 | .0320 | .0547 |
| | 7 | .0000 | .0000 | .0000 | .0001 | .0002 | .0006 | .0016 | .0037 | .0078 |
| 8 | 0 | .4305 | .2725 | .1678 | .1001 | .0576 | .0319 | .0168 | .0084 | .0039 |
| | 1 | .3826 | .3847 | .3355 | .2670 | .1977 | .1373 | .0896 | .0548 | .0312 |
| | 2 | .1488 | .2376 | .2936 | .3115 | .2965 | .2587 | .2090 | .1569 | .1094 |
| | 3 | .0331 | .0839 | .1468 | .2076 | .2541 | .2786 | .2787 | .2568 | .2188 |
| | 4 | .0046 | .0185 | .0459 | .0865 | .1361 | .1875 | .2322 | .2627 | .2734 |
| | 5 | .0004 | .0026 | .0092 | .0231 | .0467 | .0808 | .1239 | .1719 | .2188 |
| | 6 | .0000 | .0002 | .0011 | .0038 | .0100 | .0217 | .0413 | .0703 | .1094 |
| | 7 | .0000 | .0000 | .0001 | .0004 | .0012 | .0033 | .0079 | .0164 | .0313 |
| | 8 | .0000 | .0000 | .0000 | .0000 | .0001 | .0002 | .0007 | .0017 | .0039 |

**TABLE 5    BINOMIAL PROBABILITIES** (*Continued*)

| $n$ | $x$ | .10 | .15 | .20 | .25 | .30 | .35 | .40 | .45 | .50 |
|---|---|---|---|---|---|---|---|---|---|---|
| 9 | 0 | .3874 | .2316 | .1342 | .0751 | .0404 | .0207 | .0101 | .0046 | .0020 |
| | 1 | .3874 | .3679 | .3020 | .2253 | .1556 | .1004 | .0605 | .0339 | .0176 |
| | 2 | .1722 | .2597 | .3020 | .3003 | .2668 | .2162 | .1612 | .1110 | .0703 |
| | 3 | .0446 | .1069 | .1762 | .2336 | .2668 | .2716 | .2508 | .2119 | .1641 |
| | 4 | .0074 | .0283 | .0661 | .1168 | .1715 | .2194 | .2508 | .2600 | .2461 |
| | 5 | .0008 | .0050 | .0165 | .0389 | .0735 | .1181 | .1672 | .2128 | .2461 |
| | 6 | .0001 | .0006 | .0028 | .0087 | .0210 | .0424 | .0743 | .1160 | .1641 |
| | 7 | .0000 | .0000 | .0003 | .0012 | .0039 | .0098 | .0212 | .0407 | .0703 |
| | 8 | .0000 | .0000 | .0000 | .0001 | .0004 | .0013 | .0035 | .0083 | .0176 |
| | 9 | .0000 | .0000 | .0000 | .0000 | .0000 | .0001 | .0003 | .0008 | .0020 |
| 10 | 0 | .3487 | .1969 | .1074 | .0563 | .0282 | .0135 | .0060 | .0025 | .0010 |
| | 1 | .3874 | .3474 | .2684 | .1877 | .1211 | .0725 | .0403 | .0207 | .0098 |
| | 2 | .1937 | .2759 | .3020 | .2816 | .2335 | .1757 | .1209 | .0763 | .0439 |
| | 3 | .0574 | .1298 | .2013 | .2503 | .2668 | .2522 | .2150 | .1665 | .1172 |
| | 4 | .0112 | .0401 | .0881 | .1460 | .2001 | .2377 | .2508 | .2384 | .2051 |
| | 5 | .0015 | .0085 | .0264 | .0584 | .1029 | .1536 | .2007 | .2340 | .2461 |
| | 6 | .0001 | .0012 | .0055 | .0162 | .0368 | .0689 | .1115 | .1596 | .2051 |
| | 7 | .0000 | .0001 | .0008 | .0031 | .0090 | .0212 | .0425 | .0746 | .1172 |
| | 8 | .0000 | .0000 | .0001 | .0004 | .0014 | .0043 | .0106 | .0229 | .0439 |
| | 9 | .0000 | .0000 | .0000 | .0000 | .0001 | .0005 | .0016 | .0042 | .0098 |
| | 10 | .0000 | .0000 | .0000 | .0000 | .0000 | .0000 | .0001 | .0003 | .0010 |
| 12 | 0 | .2824 | .1422 | .0687 | .0317 | .0138 | .0057 | .0022 | .0008 | .0002 |
| | 1 | .3766 | .3012 | .2062 | .1267 | .0712 | .0368 | .0174 | .0075 | .0029 |
| | 2 | .2301 | .2924 | .2835 | .2323 | .1678 | .1088 | .0639 | .0339 | .0161 |
| | 3 | .0853 | .1720 | .2362 | .2581 | .2397 | .1954 | .1419 | .0923 | .0537 |
| | 4 | .0213 | .0683 | .1329 | .1936 | .2311 | .2367 | .2128 | .1700 | .1208 |
| | 5 | .0038 | .0193 | .0532 | .1032 | .1585 | .2039 | .2270 | .2225 | .1934 |
| | 6 | .0005 | .0040 | .0155 | .0401 | .0792 | .1281 | .1766 | .2124 | .2256 |
| | 7 | .0000 | .0006 | .0033 | .0115 | .0291 | .0591 | .1009 | .1489 | .1934 |
| | 8 | .0000 | .0001 | .0005 | .0024 | .0078 | .0199 | .0420 | .0762 | .1208 |
| | 9 | .0000 | .0000 | .0001 | .0004 | .0015 | .0048 | .0125 | .0277 | .0537 |
| | 10 | .0000 | .0000 | .0000 | .0000 | .0002 | .0008 | .0025 | .0068 | .0161 |
| | 11 | .0000 | .0000 | .0000 | .0000 | .0000 | .0001 | .0003 | .0010 | .0029 |
| | 12 | .0000 | .0000 | .0000 | .0000 | .0000 | .0000 | .0000 | .0001 | .0002 |
| 15 | 0 | .2059 | .0874 | .0352 | .0134 | .0047 | .0016 | .0005 | .0001 | .0000 |
| | 1 | .3432 | .2312 | .1319 | .0668 | .0305 | .0126 | .0047 | .0016 | .0005 |
| | 2 | .2669 | .2856 | .2309 | .1559 | .0916 | .0476 | .0219 | .0090 | .0032 |
| | 3 | .1285 | .2184 | .2501 | .2252 | .1700 | .1110 | .0634 | .0318 | .0139 |
| | 4 | .0428 | .1156 | .1876 | .2252 | .2186 | .1792 | .1268 | .0780 | .0417 |
| | 5 | .0105 | .0449 | .1032 | .1651 | .2061 | .2123 | .1859 | .1404 | .0916 |
| | 6 | .0019 | .0132 | .0430 | .0917 | .1472 | .1906 | .2066 | .1914 | .1527 |
| | 7 | .0003 | .0030 | .0138 | .0393 | .0811 | .1319 | .1771 | .2013 | .1964 |
| | 8 | .0000 | .0005 | .0035 | .0131 | .0348 | .0710 | .1181 | .1647 | .1964 |
| | 9 | .0000 | .0001 | .0007 | .0034 | .0116 | .0298 | .0612 | .1048 | .1527 |
| | 10 | .0000 | .0000 | .0001 | .0007 | .0030 | .0096 | .0245 | .0515 | .0916 |
| | 11 | .0000 | .0000 | .0000 | .0001 | .0006 | .0024 | .0074 | .0191 | .0417 |
| | 12 | .0000 | .0000 | .0000 | .0000 | .0001 | .0004 | .0016 | .0052 | .0139 |
| | 13 | .0000 | .0000 | .0000 | .0000 | .0000 | .0001 | .0003 | .0010 | .0032 |
| | 14 | .0000 | .0000 | .0000 | .0000 | .0000 | .0000 | .0000 | .0001 | .0005 |
| | 15 | .0000 | .0000 | .0000 | .0000 | .0000 | .0000 | .0000 | .0000 | .0000 |

**TABLE 5**   BINOMIAL PROBABILITIES (*Continued*)

| n | x | .10 | .15 | .20 | .25 | .30 | .35 | .40 | .45 | .50 |
|---|---|-----|-----|-----|-----|-----|-----|-----|-----|-----|
| 18 | 0 | .1501 | .0536 | .0180 | .0056 | .0016 | .0004 | .0001 | .0000 | .0000 |
|    | 1 | .3002 | .1704 | .0811 | .0338 | .0126 | .0042 | .0012 | .0003 | .0001 |
|    | 2 | .2835 | .2556 | .1723 | .0958 | .0458 | .0190 | .0069 | .0022 | .0006 |
|    | 3 | .1680 | .2406 | .2297 | .1704 | .1046 | .0547 | .0246 | .0095 | .0031 |
|    | 4 | .0700 | .1592 | .2153 | .2130 | .1681 | .1104 | .0614 | .0291 | .0117 |
|    | 5 | .0218 | .0787 | .1507 | .1988 | .2017 | .1664 | .1146 | .0666 | .0327 |
|    | 6 | .0052 | .0301 | .0816 | .1436 | .1873 | .1941 | .1655 | .1181 | .0708 |
|    | 7 | .0010 | .0091 | .0350 | .0820 | .1376 | .1792 | .1892 | .1657 | .1214 |
|    | 8 | .0002 | .0022 | .0120 | .0376 | .0811 | .1327 | .1734 | .1864 | .1669 |
|    | 9 | .0000 | .0004 | .0033 | .0139 | .0386 | .0794 | .1284 | .1694 | .1855 |
|    | 10 | .0000 | .0001 | .0008 | .0042 | .0149 | .0385 | .0771 | .1248 | .1669 |
|    | 11 | .0000 | .0000 | .0001 | .0010 | .0046 | .0151 | .0374 | .0742 | .1214 |
|    | 12 | .0000 | .0000 | .0000 | .0002 | .0012 | .0047 | .0145 | .0354 | .0708 |
|    | 13 | .0000 | .0000 | .0000 | .0000 | .0002 | .0012 | .0045 | .0134 | .0327 |
|    | 14 | .0000 | .0000 | .0000 | .0000 | .0000 | .0002 | .0011 | .0039 | .0117 |
|    | 15 | .0000 | .0000 | .0000 | .0000 | .0000 | .0000 | .0002 | .0009 | .0031 |
|    | 16 | .0000 | .0000 | .0000 | .0000 | .0000 | .0000 | .0000 | .0001 | .0006 |
|    | 17 | .0000 | .0000 | .0000 | .0000 | .0000 | .0000 | .0000 | .0000 | .0001 |
|    | 18 | .0000 | .0000 | .0000 | .0000 | .0000 | .0000 | .0000 | .0000 | .0000 |
| 20 | 0 | .1216 | .0388 | .0115 | .0032 | .0008 | .0002 | .0000 | .0000 | .0000 |
|    | 1 | .2702 | .1368 | .0576 | .0211 | .0068 | .0020 | .0005 | .0001 | .0000 |
|    | 2 | .2852 | .2293 | .1369 | .0669 | .0278 | .0100 | .0031 | .0008 | .0002 |
|    | 3 | .1901 | .2428 | .2054 | .1339 | .0716 | .0323 | .0123 | .0040 | .0011 |
|    | 4 | .0898 | .1821 | .2182 | .1897 | .1304 | .0738 | .0350 | .0139 | .0046 |
|    | 5 | .0319 | .1028 | .1746 | .2023 | .1789 | .1272 | .0746 | .0365 | .0148 |
|    | 6 | .0089 | .0454 | .1091 | .1686 | .1916 | .1712 | .1244 | .0746 | .0370 |
|    | 7 | .0020 | .0160 | .0545 | .1124 | .1643 | .1844 | .1659 | .1221 | .0739 |
|    | 8 | .0004 | .0046 | .0222 | .0609 | .1144 | .1614 | .1797 | .1623 | .1201 |
|    | 9 | .0001 | .0011 | .0074 | .0271 | .0654 | .1158 | .1597 | .1771 | .1602 |
|    | 10 | .0000 | .0002 | .0020 | .0099 | .0308 | .0686 | .1171 | .1593 | .1762 |
|    | 11 | .0000 | .0000 | .0005 | .0030 | .0120 | .0336 | .0710 | .1185 | .1602 |
|    | 12 | .0000 | .0000 | .0001 | .0008 | .0039 | .0136 | .0355 | .0727 | .1201 |
|    | 13 | .0000 | .0000 | .0000 | .0002 | .0010 | .0045 | .0146 | .0366 | .0739 |
|    | 14 | .0000 | .0000 | .0000 | .0000 | .0002 | .0012 | .0049 | .0150 | .0370 |
|    | 15 | .0000 | .0000 | .0000 | .0000 | .0000 | .0003 | .0013 | .0049 | .0148 |
|    | 16 | .0000 | .0000 | .0000 | .0000 | .0000 | .0000 | .0003 | .0013 | .0046 |
|    | 17 | .0000 | .0000 | .0000 | .0000 | .0000 | .0000 | .0000 | .0002 | .0011 |
|    | 18 | .0000 | .0000 | .0000 | .0000 | .0000 | .0000 | .0000 | .0000 | .0002 |
|    | 19 | .0000 | .0000 | .0000 | .0000 | .0000 | .0000 | .0000 | .0000 | .0000 |
|    | 20 | .0000 | .0000 | .0000 | .0000 | .0000 | .0000 | .0000 | .0000 | .0000 |

**TABLE 6 VALUES OF $e^{-\mu}$**

| $\mu$ | $e^{-\mu}$ | $\mu$ | $e^{-\mu}$ | $\mu$ | $e^{-\mu}$ |
|---|---|---|---|---|---|
| .00 | 1.0000 | 2.00 | .1353 | 4.00 | .0183 |
| .05 | .9512 | 2.05 | .1287 | 4.05 | .0174 |
| .10 | .9048 | 2.10 | .1225 | 4.10 | .0166 |
| .15 | .8607 | 2.15 | .1165 | 4.15 | .0158 |
| .20 | .8187 | 2.20 | .1108 | 4.20 | .0150 |
| .25 | .7788 | 2.25 | .1054 | 4.25 | .0143 |
| .30 | .7408 | 2.30 | .1003 | 4.30 | .0136 |
| .35 | .7047 | 2.35 | .0954 | 4.35 | .0129 |
| .40 | .6703 | 2.40 | .0907 | 4.40 | .0123 |
| .45 | .6376 | 2.45 | .0863 | 4.45 | .0117 |
| .50 | .6065 | 2.50 | .0821 | 4.50 | .0111 |
| .55 | .5769 | 2.55 | .0781 | 4.55 | .0106 |
| .60 | .5488 | 2.60 | .0743 | 4.60 | .0101 |
| .65 | .5220 | 2.65 | .0707 | 4.65 | .0096 |
| .70 | .4966 | 2.70 | .0672 | 4.70 | .0091 |
| .75 | .4724 | 2.75 | .0639 | 4.75 | .0087 |
| .80 | .4493 | 2.80 | .0608 | 4.80 | .0082 |
| .85 | .4274 | 2.85 | .0578 | 4.85 | .0078 |
| .90 | .4066 | 2.90 | .0550 | 4.90 | .0074 |
| .95 | .3867 | 2.95 | .0523 | 4.95 | .0071 |
| 1.00 | .3679 | 3.00 | .0498 | 5.00 | .0067 |
| 1.05 | .3499 | 3.05 | .0474 | 6.00 | .0025 |
| 1.10 | .3329 | 3.10 | .0450 | 7.00 | .0009 |
| 1.15 | .3166 | 3.15 | .0429 | 8.00 | .000335 |
| 1.20 | .3012 | 3.20 | .0408 | 9.00 | .000123 |
|  |  |  |  | 10.00 | .000045 |
| 1.25 | .2865 | 3.25 | .0388 |  |  |
| 1.30 | .2725 | 3.30 | .0369 |  |  |
| 1.35 | .2592 | 3.35 | .0351 |  |  |
| 1.40 | .2466 | 3.40 | .0334 |  |  |
| 1.45 | .2346 | 3.45 | .0317 |  |  |
| 1.50 | .2231 | 3.50 | .0302 |  |  |
| 1.55 | .2122 | 3.55 | .0287 |  |  |
| 1.60 | .2019 | 3.60 | .0273 |  |  |
| 1.65 | .1920 | 3.65 | .0260 |  |  |
| 1.70 | .1827 | 3.70 | .0247 |  |  |
| 1.75 | .1738 | 3.75 | .0235 |  |  |
| 1.80 | .1653 | 3.80 | .0224 |  |  |
| 1.85 | .1572 | 3.85 | .0213 |  |  |
| 1.90 | .1496 | 3.90 | .0202 |  |  |
| 1.95 | .1423 | 3.95 | .0193 |  |  |

## TABLE 7    POISSON PROBABILITIES

Entries in the table give the probability of $x$ occurrences for a Poisson process with a mean $\mu$. For example, when $\mu = 2.5$, the probability of four occurrences is .1336.

### $\mu$

| $x$ | 0.1 | 0.2 | 0.3 | 0.4 | 0.5 | 0.6 | 0.7 | 0.8 | 0.9 | 1.0 |
|---|---|---|---|---|---|---|---|---|---|---|
| 0 | .9048 | .8187 | .7408 | .6703 | .6065 | .5488 | .4966 | .4493 | .4066 | .3679 |
| 1 | .0905 | .1637 | .2222 | .2681 | .3033 | .3293 | .3476 | .3595 | .3659 | .3679 |
| 2 | .0045 | .0164 | .0333 | .0536 | .0758 | .0988 | .1217 | .1438 | .1647 | .1839 |
| 3 | .0002 | .0011 | .0033 | .0072 | .0126 | .0198 | .0284 | .0383 | .0494 | .0613 |
| 4 | .0000 | .0001 | .0002 | .0007 | .0016 | .0030 | .0050 | .0077 | .0111 | .0153 |
| 5 | .0000 | .0000 | .0000 | .0001 | .0002 | .0004 | .0007 | .0012 | .0020 | .0031 |
| 6 | .0000 | .0000 | .0000 | .0000 | .0000 | .0000 | .0001 | .0002 | .0003 | .0005 |
| 7 | .0000 | .0000 | .0000 | .0000 | .0000 | .0000 | .0000 | .0000 | .0000 | .0001 |

### $\mu$

| $x$ | 1.1 | 1.2 | 1.3 | 1.4 | 1.5 | 1.6 | 1.7 | 1.8 | 1.9 | 2.0 |
|---|---|---|---|---|---|---|---|---|---|---|
| 0 | .3329 | .3012 | .2725 | .2466 | .2231 | .2019 | .1827 | .1653 | .1496 | .1353 |
| 1 | .3662 | .3614 | .3543 | .3452 | .3347 | .3230 | .3106 | .2975 | .2842 | .2707 |
| 2 | .2014 | .2169 | .2303 | .2417 | .2510 | .2584 | .2640 | .2678 | .2700 | .2707 |
| 3 | .0738 | .0867 | .0998 | .1128 | .1255 | .1378 | .1496 | .1607 | .1710 | .1804 |
| 4 | .0203 | .0260 | .0324 | .0395 | .0471 | .0551 | .0636 | .0723 | .0812 | .0902 |
| 5 | .0045 | .0062 | .0084 | .0111 | .0141 | .0176 | .0216 | .0260 | .0309 | .0361 |
| 6 | .0008 | .0012 | .0018 | .0026 | .0035 | .0047 | .0061 | .0078 | .0098 | .0120 |
| 7 | .0001 | .0002 | .0003 | .0005 | .0008 | .0011 | .0015 | .0020 | .0027 | .0034 |
| 8 | .0000 | .0000 | .0001 | .0001 | .0001 | .0002 | .0003 | .0005 | .0006 | .0009 |
| 9 | .0000 | .0000 | .0000 | .0000 | .0000 | .0000 | .0001 | .0001 | .0001 | .0002 |

### $\mu$

| $x$ | 2.1 | 2.2 | 2.3 | 2.4 | 2.5 | 2.6 | 2.7 | 2.8 | 2.9 | 3.0 |
|---|---|---|---|---|---|---|---|---|---|---|
| 0 | .1225 | .1108 | .1003 | .0907 | .0821 | .0743 | .0672 | .0608 | .0550 | .0498 |
| 1 | .2572 | .2438 | .2306 | .2177 | .2052 | .1931 | .1815 | .1703 | .1596 | .1494 |
| 2 | .2700 | .2681 | .2652 | .2613 | .2565 | .2510 | .2450 | .2384 | .2314 | .2240 |
| 3 | .1890 | .1966 | .2033 | .2090 | .2138 | .2176 | .2205 | .2225 | .2237 | .2240 |
| 4 | .0992 | .1082 | .1169 | .1254 | .1336 | .1414 | .1488 | .1557 | .1622 | .1680 |
| 5 | .0417 | .0476 | .0538 | .0602 | .0668 | .0735 | .0804 | .0872 | .0940 | .1008 |
| 6 | .0146 | .0174 | .0206 | .0241 | .0278 | .0319 | .0362 | .0407 | .0455 | .0504 |
| 7 | .0044 | .0055 | .0068 | .0083 | .0099 | .0118 | .0139 | .0163 | .0188 | .0216 |
| 8 | .0011 | .0015 | .0019 | .0025 | .0031 | .0038 | .0047 | .0057 | .0068 | .0081 |
| 9 | .0003 | .0004 | .0005 | .0007 | .0009 | .0011 | .0014 | .0018 | .0022 | .0027 |
| 10 | .0001 | .0001 | .0001 | .0002 | .0002 | .0003 | .0004 | .0005 | .0006 | .0008 |
| 11 | .0000 | .0000 | .0000 | .0000 | .0000 | .0001 | .0001 | .0001 | .0002 | .0002 |
| 12 | .0000 | .0000 | .0000 | .0000 | .0000 | .0000 | .0000 | .0000 | .0000 | .0001 |

**TABLE 7 POISSON PROBABILITIES** (*Continued*)

| | $\mu$ | | | | | | | | | |
|---|---|---|---|---|---|---|---|---|---|---|
| x | 3.1 | 3.2 | 3.3 | 3.4 | 3.5 | 3.6 | 3.7 | 3.8 | 3.9 | 4.0 |
| 0 | .0450 | .0408 | .0369 | .0344 | .0302 | .0273 | .0247 | .0224 | .0202 | .0183 |
| 1 | .1397 | .1304 | .1217 | .1135 | .1057 | .0984 | .0915 | .0850 | .0789 | .0733 |
| 2 | .2165 | .2087 | .2008 | .1929 | .1850 | .1771 | .1692 | .1615 | .1539 | .1465 |
| 3 | .2237 | .2226 | .2209 | .2186 | .2158 | .2125 | .2087 | .2046 | .2001 | .1954 |
| 4 | .1734 | .1781 | .1823 | .1858 | .1888 | .1912 | .1931 | .1944 | .1951 | .1954 |
| 5 | .1075 | .1140 | .1203 | .1264 | .1322 | .1377 | .1429 | .1477 | .1522 | .1563 |
| 6 | .0555 | .0608 | .0662 | .0716 | .0771 | .0826 | .0881 | .0936 | .0989 | .1042 |
| 7 | .0246 | .0278 | .0312 | .0348 | .0385 | .0425 | .0466 | .0508 | .0551 | .0595 |
| 8 | .0095 | .0111 | .0129 | .0148 | .0169 | .0191 | .0215 | .0241 | .0269 | .0298 |
| 9 | .0033 | .0040 | .0047 | .0056 | .0066 | .0076 | .0089 | .0102 | .0116 | .0132 |
| 10 | .0010 | .0013 | .0016 | .0019 | .0023 | .0028 | .0033 | .0039 | .0045 | .0053 |
| 11 | .0003 | .0004 | .0005 | .0006 | .0007 | .0009 | .0011 | .0013 | .0016 | .0019 |
| 12 | .0001 | .0001 | .0001 | .0002 | .0002 | .0003 | .0003 | .0004 | .0005 | .0006 |
| 13 | .0000 | .0000 | .0000 | .0000 | .0001 | .0001 | .0001 | .0001 | .0002 | .0002 |
| 14 | .0000 | .0000 | .0000 | .0000 | .0000 | .0000 | .0000 | .0000 | .0000 | .0001 |

| | $\mu$ | | | | | | | | | |
|---|---|---|---|---|---|---|---|---|---|---|
| x | 4.1 | 4.2 | 4.3 | 4.4 | 4.5 | 4.6 | 4.7 | 4.8 | 4.9 | 5.0 |
| 0 | .0166 | .0150 | .0136 | .0123 | .0111 | .0101 | .0091 | .0082 | .0074 | .0067 |
| 1 | .0679 | .0630 | .0583 | .0540 | .0500 | .0462 | .0427 | .0395 | .0365 | .0337 |
| 2 | .1393 | .1323 | .1254 | .1188 | .1125 | .1063 | .1005 | .0948 | .0894 | .0842 |
| 3 | .1904 | .1852 | .1798 | .1743 | .1687 | .1631 | .1574 | .1517 | .1460 | .1404 |
| 4 | .1951 | .1944 | .1933 | .1917 | .1898 | .1875 | .1849 | .1820 | .1789 | .1755 |
| 5 | .1600 | .1633 | .1662 | .1687 | .1708 | .1725 | .1738 | .1747 | .1753 | .1755 |
| 6 | .1093 | .1143 | .1191 | .1237 | .1281 | .1323 | .1362 | .1398 | .1432 | .1462 |
| 7 | .0640 | .0686 | .0732 | .0778 | .0824 | .0869 | .0914 | .0959 | .1002 | .1044 |
| 8 | .0328 | .0360 | .0393 | .0428 | .0463 | .0500 | .0537 | .0575 | .0614 | .0653 |
| 9 | .0150 | .0168 | .0188 | .0209 | .0232 | .0255 | .0280 | .0307 | .0334 | .0363 |
| 10 | .0061 | .0071 | .0081 | .0092 | .0104 | .0118 | .0132 | .0147 | .0164 | .0181 |
| 11 | .0023 | .0027 | .0032 | .0037 | .0043 | .0049 | .0056 | .0064 | .0073 | .0082 |
| 12 | .0008 | .0009 | .0011 | .0014 | .0016 | .0019 | .0022 | .0026 | .0030 | .0034 |
| 13 | .0002 | .0003 | .0004 | .0005 | .0006 | .0007 | .0008 | .0009 | .0011 | .0013 |
| 14 | .0001 | .0001 | .0001 | .0001 | .0002 | .0002 | .0003 | .0003 | .0004 | .0005 |
| 15 | .0000 | .0000 | .0000 | .0000 | .0001 | .0001 | .0001 | .0001 | .0001 | .0002 |

| | $\mu$ | | | | | | | | | |
|---|---|---|---|---|---|---|---|---|---|---|
| x | 5.1 | 5.2 | 5.3 | 5.4 | 5.5 | 5.6 | 5.7 | 5.8 | 5.9 | 6.0 |
| 0 | .0061 | .0055 | .0050 | .0045 | .0041 | .0037 | .0033 | .0030 | .0027 | .0025 |
| 1 | .0311 | .0287 | .0265 | .0244 | .0225 | .0207 | .0191 | .0176 | .0162 | .0149 |
| 2 | .0793 | .0746 | .0701 | .0659 | .0618 | .0580 | .0544 | .0509 | .0477 | .0446 |
| 3 | .1348 | .1293 | .1239 | .1185 | .1133 | .1082 | .1033 | .0985 | .0938 | .0892 |
| 4 | .1719 | .1681 | .1641 | .1600 | .1558 | .1515 | .1472 | .1428 | .1383 | .1339 |

**TABLE 7   POISSON PROBABILITIES** (*Continued*)

| x | | | | | | | | | | |
|---|---|---|---|---|---|---|---|---|---|---|
| 5 | .1753 | .1748 | .1740 | .1728 | .1714 | .1697 | .1678 | .1656 | .1632 | .1606 |
| 6 | .1490 | .1515 | .1537 | .1555 | .1571 | .1587 | .1594 | .1601 | .1605 | .1606 |
| 7 | .1086 | .1125 | .1163 | .1200 | .1234 | .1267 | .1298 | .1326 | .1353 | .1377 |
| 8 | .0692 | .0731 | .0771 | .0810 | .0849 | .0887 | .0925 | .0962 | .0998 | .1033 |
| 9 | .0392 | .0423 | .0454 | .0486 | .0519 | .0552 | .0586 | .0620 | .0654 | .0688 |
| 10 | .0200 | .0220 | .0241 | .0262 | .0285 | .0309 | .0334 | .0359 | .0386 | .0413 |
| 11 | .0093 | .0104 | .0116 | .0129 | .0143 | .0157 | .0173 | .0190 | .0207 | .0225 |
| 12 | .0039 | .0045 | .0051 | .0058 | .0065 | .0073 | .0082 | .0092 | .0102 | .0113 |
| 13 | .0015 | .0018 | .0021 | .0024 | .0028 | .0032 | .0036 | .0041 | .0046 | .0052 |
| 14 | .0006 | .0007 | .0008 | .0009 | .0011 | .0013 | .0015 | .0017 | .0019 | .0022 |
| 15 | .0002 | .0002 | .0003 | .0003 | .0004 | .0005 | .0006 | .0007 | .0008 | .0009 |
| 16 | .0001 | .0001 | .0001 | .0001 | .0001 | .0002 | .0002 | .0002 | .0003 | .0003 |
| 17 | .0000 | .0000 | .0000 | .0000 | .0000 | .0001 | .0001 | .0001 | .0001 | .0001 |

$\mu$

| x | 6.1 | 6.2 | 6.3 | 6.4 | 6.5 | 6.6 | 6.7 | 6.8 | 6.9 | 7.0 |
|---|---|---|---|---|---|---|---|---|---|---|
| 0 | .0022 | .0020 | .0018 | .0017 | .0015 | .0014 | .0012 | .0011 | .0010 | .0009 |
| 1 | .0137 | .0126 | .0116 | .0106 | .0098 | .0090 | .0082 | .0076 | .0070 | .0064 |
| 2 | .0417 | .0390 | .0364 | .0340 | .0318 | .0296 | .0276 | .0258 | .0240 | .0223 |
| 3 | .0848 | .0806 | .0765 | .0726 | .0688 | .0652 | .0617 | .0584 | .0552 | .0521 |
| 4 | .1294 | .1249 | .1205 | .1162 | .1118 | .1076 | .1034 | .0992 | .0952 | .0912 |
| 5 | .1579 | .1549 | .1519 | .1487 | .1454 | .1420 | .1385 | .1349 | .1314 | .1277 |
| 6 | .1605 | .1601 | .1595 | .1586 | .1575 | .1562 | .1546 | .1529 | .1511 | .1490 |
| 7 | .1399 | .1418 | .1435 | .1450 | .1462 | .1472 | .1480 | .1486 | .1489 | .1490 |
| 8 | .1066 | .1099 | .1130 | .1160 | .1188 | .1215 | .1240 | .1263 | .1284 | .1304 |
| 9 | .0723 | .0757 | .0791 | .0825 | .0858 | .0891 | .0923 | .0954 | .0985 | .1014 |
| 10 | .0441 | .0469 | .0498 | .0528 | .0558 | .0588 | .0618 | .0649 | .0679 | .0710 |
| 11 | .0245 | .0265 | .0285 | .0307 | .0330 | .0353 | .0377 | .0401 | .0426 | .0452 |
| 12 | .0124 | .0137 | .0150 | .0164 | .0179 | .0194 | .0210 | .0227 | .0245 | .0264 |
| 13 | .0058 | .0065 | .0073 | .0081 | .0089 | .0098 | .0108 | .0119 | .0130 | .0142 |
| 14 | .0025 | .0029 | .0033 | .0037 | .0041 | .0046 | .0052 | .0058 | .0064 | .0071 |
| 15 | .0010 | .0012 | .0014 | .0016 | .0018 | .0020 | .0023 | .0026 | .0029 | .0033 |
| 16 | .0004 | .0005 | .0005 | .0006 | .0007 | .0008 | .0010 | .0011 | .0013 | .0014 |
| 17 | .0001 | .0002 | .0002 | .0002 | .0003 | .0003 | .0004 | .0004 | .0005 | .0006 |
| 18 | .0000 | .0001 | .0001 | .0001 | .0001 | .0001 | .0001 | .0002 | .0002 | .0002 |
| 19 | .0000 | .0000 | .0000 | .0000 | .0000 | .0000 | .0000 | .0001 | .0001 | .0001 |

$\mu$

| x | 7.1 | 7.2 | 7.3 | 7.4 | 7.5 | 7.6 | 7.7 | 7.8 | 7.9 | 8.0 |
|---|---|---|---|---|---|---|---|---|---|---|
| 0 | .0008 | .0007 | .0007 | .0006 | .0006 | .0005 | .0005 | .0004 | .0004 | .0003 |
| 1 | .0059 | .0054 | .0049 | .0045 | .0041 | .0038 | .0035 | .0032 | .0029 | .0027 |
| 2 | .0208 | .0194 | .0180 | .0167 | .0156 | .0145 | .0134 | .0125 | .0116 | .0107 |
| 3 | .0492 | .0464 | .0438 | .0413 | .0389 | .0366 | .0345 | .0324 | .0305 | .0286 |
| 4 | .0874 | .0836 | .0799 | .0764 | .0729 | .0696 | .0663 | .0632 | .0602 | .0573 |

TABLE 7  POISSON PROBABILITIES (*Continued*)

| | | | | | $\mu$ | | | | | |
|---|---|---|---|---|---|---|---|---|---|---|
| x | 7.1 | 7.2 | 7.3 | 7.4 | 7.5 | 7.6 | 7.7 | 7.8 | 7.9 | 8.0 |
| 5 | .1241 | .1204 | .1167 | .1130 | .1094 | .1057 | .1021 | .0986 | .0951 | .0916 |
| 6 | .1468 | .1445 | .1420 | .1394 | .1367 | .1339 | .1311 | .1282 | .1252 | .1221 |
| 7 | .1489 | .1486 | .1481 | .1474 | .1465 | .1454 | .1442 | .1428 | .1413 | .1396 |
| 8 | .1321 | .1337 | .1351 | .1363 | .1373 | .1382 | .1388 | .1392 | .1395 | .1396 |
| 9 | .1042 | .1070 | .1096 | .1121 | .1144 | .1167 | .1187 | .1207 | .1224 | .1241 |
| 10 | .0740 | .0770 | .0800 | .0829 | .0858 | .0887 | .0914 | .0941 | .0967 | .0993 |
| 11 | .0478 | .0504 | .0531 | .0558 | .0585 | .0613 | .0640 | .0667 | .0695 | .0722 |
| 12 | .0283 | .0303 | .0323 | .0344 | .0366 | .0388 | .0411 | .0434 | .0457 | .0481 |
| 13 | .0154 | .0168 | .0181 | .0196 | .0211 | .0227 | .0243 | .0260 | .0278 | .0296 |
| 14 | .0078 | .0086 | .0095 | .0104 | .0113 | .0123 | .0134 | .0145 | .0157 | .0169 |
| 15 | .0037 | .0041 | .0046 | .0051 | .0057 | .0062 | .0069 | .0075 | .0083 | .0090 |
| 16 | .0016 | .0019 | .0021 | .0024 | .0026 | .0030 | .0033 | .0037 | .0041 | .0045 |
| 17 | .0007 | .0008 | .0009 | .0010 | .0012 | .0013 | .0015 | .0017 | .0019 | .0021 |
| 18 | .0003 | .0003 | .0004 | .0004 | .0005 | .0006 | .0006 | .0007 | .0008 | .0009 |
| 19 | .0001 | .0001 | .0001 | .0002 | .0002 | .0002 | .0003 | .0003 | .0003 | .0004 |
| 20 | .0000 | .0000 | .0001 | .0001 | .0001 | .0001 | .0001 | .0001 | .0001 | .0002 |
| 21 | .0000 | .0000 | .0000 | .0000 | .0000 | .0000 | .0000 | .0000 | .0001 | .0001 |

| | | | | | $\mu$ | | | | | |
|---|---|---|---|---|---|---|---|---|---|---|
| x | 8.1 | 8.2 | 8.3 | 8.4 | 8.5 | 8.6 | 8.7 | 8.8 | 8.9 | 9.0 |
| 0 | .0003 | .0003 | .0002 | .0002 | .0002 | .0002 | .0002 | .0002 | .0001 | .0001 |
| 1 | .0025 | .0023 | .0021 | .0019 | .0017 | .0016 | .0014 | .0013 | .0012 | .0011 |
| 2 | .0100 | .0092 | .0086 | .0079 | .0074 | .0068 | .0063 | .0058 | .0054 | .0050 |
| 3 | .0269 | .0252 | .0237 | .0222 | .0208 | .0195 | .0183 | .0171 | .0160 | .0150 |
| 4 | .0544 | .0517 | .0491 | .0466 | .0443 | .0420 | .0398 | .0377 | .0357 | .0337 |
| 5 | .0882 | .0849 | .0816 | .0784 | .0752 | .0722 | .0692 | .0663 | .0635 | .0607 |
| 6 | .1191 | .1160 | .1128 | .1097 | .1066 | .1034 | .1003 | .0972 | .0941 | .0911 |
| 7 | .1378 | .1358 | .1338 | .1317 | .1294 | .1271 | .1247 | .1222 | .1197 | .1171 |
| 8 | .1395 | .1392 | .1388 | .1382 | .1375 | .1366 | .1356 | .1344 | .1332 | .1318 |
| 9 | .1256 | .1269 | .1280 | .1290 | .1299 | .1306 | .1311 | .1315 | .1317 | .1318 |
| 10 | .1017 | .1040 | .1063 | .1084 | .1104 | .1123 | .1140 | .1157 | .1172 | .1186 |
| 11 | .0749 | .0776 | .0802 | .0828 | .0853 | .0878 | .0902 | .0925 | .0948 | .0970 |
| 12 | .0505 | .0530 | .0555 | .0579 | .0604 | .0629 | .0654 | .0679 | .0703 | .0728 |
| 13 | .0315 | .0334 | .0354 | .0374 | .0395 | .0416 | .0438 | .0459 | .0481 | .0504 |
| 14 | .0182 | .0196 | .0210 | .0225 | .0240 | .0256 | .0272 | .0289 | .0306 | .0324 |
| 15 | .0098 | .0107 | .0116 | .0126 | .0136 | .0147 | .0158 | .0169 | .0182 | .1094 |
| 16 | .0050 | .0055 | .0060 | .0066 | .0072 | .0079 | .0086 | .0093 | .0101 | .0109 |
| 17 | .0024 | .0026 | .0029 | .0033 | .0036 | .0040 | .0044 | .0048 | .0053 | .0058 |
| 18 | .0011 | .0012 | .0014 | .0015 | .0017 | .0019 | .0021 | .0024 | .0026 | .0029 |
| 19 | .0005 | .0005 | .0006 | .0007 | .0008 | .0009 | .0010 | .0011 | .0012 | .0014 |
| 20 | .0002 | .0002 | .0002 | .0003 | .0003 | .0004 | .0004 | .0005 | .0005 | .0006 |
| 21 | .0001 | .0001 | .0001 | .0001 | .0001 | .0002 | .0002 | .0002 | .0002 | .0003 |
| 22 | .0000 | .0000 | .0000 | .0000 | .0001 | .0001 | .0001 | .0001 | .0001 | .0001 |

**TABLE 7**    POISSON PROBABILITIES (*Continued*)

| | | | | | $\mu$ | | | | | |
|---|---|---|---|---|---|---|---|---|---|---|
| $x$ | **9.1** | **9.2** | **9.3** | **9.4** | **9.5** | **9.6** | **9.7** | **9.8** | **9.9** | **10** |
| 0 | .0001 | .0001 | .0001 | .0001 | .0001 | .0001 | .0001 | .0001 | .0001 | .0000 |
| 1 | .0010 | .0009 | .0009 | .0008 | .0007 | .0007 | .0006 | .0005 | .0005 | .0005 |
| 2 | .0046 | .0043 | .0040 | .0037 | .0034 | .0031 | .0029 | .0027 | .0025 | .0023 |
| 3 | .0140 | .0131 | .0123 | .0115 | .0107 | .0100 | .0093 | .0087 | .0081 | .0076 |
| 4 | .0319 | .0302 | .0285 | .0269 | .0254 | .0240 | .0226 | .0213 | .0201 | .0189 |
| 5 | .0581 | .0555 | .0530 | .0506 | .0483 | .0460 | .0439 | .0418 | .0398 | .0378 |
| 6 | .0881 | .0851 | .0822 | .0793 | .0764 | .0736 | .0709 | .0682 | .0656 | .0631 |
| 7 | .1145 | .1118 | .1091 | .1064 | .1037 | .1010 | .0982 | .0955 | .0928 | .0901 |
| 8 | .1302 | .1286 | .1269 | .1251 | .1232 | .1212 | .1191 | .1170 | .1148 | .1126 |
| 9 | .1317 | .1315 | .1311 | .1306 | .1300 | .1293 | .1284 | .1274 | .1263 | .1251 |
| 10 | .1198 | .1210 | .1219 | .1228 | .1235 | .1241 | .1245 | .1249 | .1250 | .1251 |
| 11 | .0991 | .1012 | .1031 | .1049 | .1067 | .1083 | .1098 | .1112 | .1125 | .1137 |
| 12 | .0752 | .0776 | .0799 | .0822 | .0844 | .0866 | .0888 | .0908 | .0928 | .0948 |
| 13 | .0526 | .0549 | .0572 | .0594 | .0617 | .0640 | .0662 | .0685 | .0707 | .0729 |
| 14 | .0342 | .0361 | .0380 | .0399 | .0419 | .0439 | .0459 | .0479 | .0500 | .0521 |
| 15 | .0208 | .0221 | .0235 | .0250 | .0265 | .0281 | .0297 | .0313 | .0330 | .0347 |
| 16 | .0118 | .0127 | .0137 | .0147 | .0157 | .0168 | .0180 | .0192 | .0204 | .0217 |
| 17 | .0063 | .0069 | .0075 | .0081 | .0088 | .0095 | .0103 | .0111 | .0119 | .0128 |
| 18 | .0032 | .0035 | .0039 | .0042 | .0046 | .0051 | .0055 | .0060 | .0065 | .0071 |
| 19 | .0015 | .0017 | .0019 | .0021 | .0023 | .0026 | .0028 | .0031 | .0034 | .0037 |
| 20 | .0007 | .0008 | .0009 | .0010 | .0011 | .0012 | .0014 | .0015 | .0017 | .0019 |
| 21 | .0003 | .0003 | .0004 | .0004 | .0005 | .0006 | .0006 | .0007 | .0008 | .0009 |
| 22 | .0001 | .0001 | .0002 | .0002 | .0002 | .0002 | .0003 | .0003 | .0004 | .0004 |
| 23 | .0000 | .0001 | .0001 | .0001 | .0001 | .0001 | .0001 | .0001 | .0002 | .0002 |
| 24 | .0000 | .0000 | .0000 | .0000 | .0000 | .0000 | .0000 | .0001 | .0001 | .0001 |

| | | | | | $\mu$ | | | | | |
|---|---|---|---|---|---|---|---|---|---|---|
| $x$ | **11** | **12** | **13** | **14** | **15** | **16** | **17** | **18** | **19** | **20** |
| 0 | .0000 | .0000 | .0000 | .0000 | .0000 | .0000 | .0000 | .0000 | .0000 | .0000 |
| 1 | .0002 | .0001 | .0000 | .0000 | .0000 | .0000 | .0000 | .0000 | .0000 | .0000 |
| 2 | .0010 | .0004 | .0002 | .0001 | .0000 | .0000 | .0000 | .0000 | .0000 | .0000 |
| 3 | .0037 | .0018 | .0008 | .0004 | .0002 | .0001 | .0000 | .0000 | .0000 | .0000 |
| 4 | .0102 | .0053 | .0027 | .0013 | .0006 | .0003 | .0001 | .0001 | .0000 | .0000 |
| 5 | .0224 | .0127 | .0070 | .0037 | .0019 | .0010 | .0005 | .0002 | .0001 | .0001 |
| 6 | .0411 | .0255 | .0152 | .0087 | .0048 | .0026 | .0014 | .0007 | .0004 | .0002 |
| 7 | .0646 | .0437 | .0281 | .0174 | .0104 | .0060 | .0034 | .0018 | .0010 | .0005 |
| 8 | .0888 | .0655 | .0457 | .0304 | .0194 | .0120 | .0072 | .0042 | .0024 | .0013 |
| 9 | .1085 | .0874 | .0661 | .0473 | .0324 | .0213 | .0135 | .0083 | .0050 | .0029 |
| 10 | .1194 | .1048 | .0859 | .0663 | .0486 | .0341 | .0230 | .0150 | .0095 | .0058 |
| 11 | .1194 | .1144 | .1015 | .0844 | .0663 | .0496 | .0355 | .0245 | .0164 | .0106 |
| 12 | .1094 | .1144 | .1099 | .0984 | .0829 | .0661 | .0504 | .0368 | .0259 | .0176 |
| 13 | .0926 | .1056 | .1099 | .1060 | .0956 | .0814 | .0658 | .0509 | .0378 | .0271 |
| 14 | .0728 | .0905 | .1021 | .1060 | .1024 | .0930 | .0800 | .0655 | .0514 | .0387 |

**TABLE 7**    POISSON PROBABILITIES (*Continued*)

| x | 11 | 12 | 13 | 14 | 15 | 16 | 17 | 18 | 19 | 20 |
|---|----|----|----|----|----|----|----|----|----|----|
| 15 | .0534 | .0724 | .0885 | .0989 | .1024 | .0992 | .0906 | .0786 | .0650 | .0516 |
| 16 | .0367 | .0543 | .0719 | .0866 | .0960 | .0992 | .0963 | .0884 | .0772 | .0646 |
| 17 | .0237 | .0383 | .0550 | .0713 | .0847 | .0934 | .0963 | .0936 | .0863 | .0760 |
| 18 | .0145 | .0256 | .0397 | .0554 | .0706 | .0830 | .0909 | .0936 | .0911 | .0844 |
| 19 | .0084 | .0161 | .0272 | .0409 | .0557 | .0699 | .0814 | .0887 | .0911 | .0888 |
| 20 | .0046 | .0097 | .0177 | .0286 | .0418 | .0559 | .0692 | .0798 | .0866 | .0888 |
| 21 | .0024 | .0055 | .0109 | .0191 | .0299 | .0426 | .0560 | .0684 | .0783 | .0846 |
| 22 | .0012 | .0030 | .0065 | .0121 | .0204 | .0310 | .0433 | .0560 | .0676 | .0769 |
| 23 | .0006 | .0016 | .0037 | .0074 | .0133 | .0216 | .0320 | .0438 | .0559 | .0669 |
| 24 | .0003 | .0008 | .0020 | .0043 | .0083 | .0144 | .0226 | .0328 | .0442 | .0557 |
| 25 | .0001 | .0004 | .0010 | .0024 | .0050 | .0092 | .0154 | .0237 | .0336 | .0446 |
| 26 | .0000 | .0002 | .0005 | .0013 | .0029 | .0057 | .0101 | .0164 | .0246 | .0343 |
| 27 | .0000 | .0001 | .0002 | .0007 | .0016 | .0034 | .0063 | .0109 | .0173 | .0254 |
| 28 | .0000 | .0000 | .0001 | .0003 | .0009 | .0019 | .0038 | .0070 | .0117 | .0181 |
| 29 | .0000 | .0000 | .0001 | .0002 | .0004 | .0011 | .0023 | .0044 | .0077 | .0125 |
| 30 | .0000 | .0000 | .0000 | .0001 | .0002 | .0006 | .0013 | .0026 | .0049 | .0083 |
| 31 | .0000 | .0000 | .0000 | .0000 | .0001 | .0003 | .0007 | .0015 | .0030 | .0054 |
| 32 | .0000 | .0000 | .0000 | .0000 | .0001 | .0001 | .0004 | .0009 | .0018 | .0034 |
| 33 | .0000 | .0000 | .0000 | .0000 | .0000 | .0001 | .0002 | .0005 | .0010 | .0020 |
| 34 | .0000 | .0000 | .0000 | .0000 | .0000 | .0000 | .0001 | .0002 | .0006 | .0012 |
| 35 | .0000 | .0000 | .0000 | .0000 | .0000 | .0000 | .0000 | .0001 | .0003 | .0007 |
| 36 | .0000 | .0000 | .0000 | .0000 | .0000 | .0000 | .0000 | .0001 | .0002 | .0004 |
| 37 | .0000 | .0000 | .0000 | .0000 | .0000 | .0000 | .0000 | .0000 | .0001 | .0002 |
| 38 | .0000 | .0000 | .0000 | .0000 | .0000 | .0000 | .0000 | .0000 | .0000 | .0001 |
| 39 | .0000 | .0000 | .0000 | .0000 | .0000 | .0000 | .0000 | .0000 | .0000 | .0001 |

**TABLE 8    CRITICAL VALUES FOR THE DURBIN-WATSON TEST
FOR AUTOCORRELATION**

Entries in the table give the critical values for a one-tailed Durbin-Watson test for auto-correlation. For a two-tailed test, the level of significance is doubled.

**Significance Points of $d_L$ and $d_U$: $\alpha = .05$**
**Number of Independent Variables**

| k | 1 | | 2 | | 3 | | 4 | | 5 | |
|---|---|---|---|---|---|---|---|---|---|---|
| n | $d_L$ | $d_U$ | $d_L$ | $d_U$ | $d_L$ | $d_U$ | $d_L$ | $d_U$ | $d_L$ | $d_U$ |
| 15 | 1.08 | 1.36 | 0.95 | 1.54 | 0.82 | 1.75 | 0.69 | 1.97 | 0.56 | 2.21 |
| 16 | 1.10 | 1.37 | 0.98 | 1.54 | 0.86 | 1.73 | 0.74 | 1.93 | 0.62 | 2.15 |
| 17 | 1.13 | 1.38 | 1.02 | 1.54 | 0.90 | 1.71 | 0.78 | 1.90 | 0.67 | 2.10 |
| 18 | 1.16 | 1.39 | 1.05 | 1.53 | 0.93 | 1.69 | 0.82 | 1.87 | 0.71 | 2.06 |
| 19 | 1.18 | 1.40 | 1.08 | 1.53 | 0.97 | 1.68 | 0.86 | 1.85 | 0.75 | 2.02 |
| 20 | 1.20 | 1.41 | 1.10 | 1.54 | 1.00 | 1.68 | 0.90 | 1.83 | 0.79 | 1.99 |
| 21 | 1.22 | 1.42 | 1.13 | 1.54 | 1.03 | 1.67 | 0.93 | 1.81 | 0.83 | 1.96 |
| 22 | 1.24 | 1.43 | 1.15 | 1.54 | 1.05 | 1.66 | 0.96 | 1.80 | 0.86 | 1.94 |
| 23 | 1.26 | 1.44 | 1.17 | 1.54 | 1.08 | 1.66 | 0.99 | 1.79 | 0.90 | 1.92 |
| 24 | 1.27 | 1.45 | 1.19 | 1.55 | 1.10 | 1.66 | 1.01 | 1.78 | 0.93 | 1.90 |
| 25 | 1.29 | 1.45 | 1.21 | 1.55 | 1.12 | 1.66 | 1.04 | 1.77 | 0.95 | 1.89 |
| 26 | 1.30 | 1.46 | 1.22 | 1.55 | 1.14 | 1.65 | 1.06 | 1.76 | 0.98 | 1.88 |
| 27 | 1.32 | 1.47 | 1.24 | 1.56 | 1.16 | 1.65 | 1.08 | 1.76 | 1.01 | 1.86 |
| 28 | 1.33 | 1.48 | 1.26 | 1.56 | 1.18 | 1.65 | 1.10 | 1.75 | 1.03 | 1.85 |
| 29 | 1.34 | 1.48 | 1.27 | 1.56 | 1.20 | 1.65 | 1.12 | 1.74 | 1.05 | 1.84 |
| 30 | 1.35 | 1.49 | 1.28 | 1.57 | 1.21 | 1.65 | 1.14 | 1.74 | 1.07 | 1.83 |
| 31 | 1.36 | 1.50 | 1.30 | 1.57 | 1.23 | 1.65 | 1.16 | 1.74 | 1.09 | 1.83 |
| 32 | 1.37 | 1.50 | 1.31 | 1.57 | 1.24 | 1.65 | 1.18 | 1.73 | 1.11 | 1.82 |
| 33 | 1.38 | 1.51 | 1.32 | 1.58 | 1.26 | 1.65 | 1.19 | 1.73 | 1.13 | 1.81 |
| 34 | 1.39 | 1.51 | 1.33 | 1.58 | 1.27 | 1.65 | 1.21 | 1.73 | 1.15 | 1.81 |
| 35 | 1.40 | 1.52 | 1.34 | 1.58 | 1.28 | 1.65 | 1.22 | 1.73 | 1.16 | 1.80 |
| 36 | 1.41 | 1.52 | 1.35 | 1.59 | 1.29 | 1.65 | 1.24 | 1.73 | 1.18 | 1.80 |
| 37 | 1.42 | 1.53 | 1.36 | 1.59 | 1.31 | 1.66 | 1.25 | 1.72 | 1.19 | 1.80 |
| 38 | 1.43 | 1.54 | 1.37 | 1.59 | 1.32 | 1.66 | 1.26 | 1.72 | 1.21 | 1.79 |
| 39 | 1.43 | 1.54 | 1.38 | 1.60 | 1.33 | 1.66 | 1.27 | 1.72 | 1.22 | 1.79 |
| 40 | 1.44 | 1.54 | 1.39 | 1.60 | 1.34 | 1.66 | 1.29 | 1.72 | 1.23 | 1.79 |
| 45 | 1.48 | 1.57 | 1.43 | 1.62 | 1.38 | 1.67 | 1.34 | 1.72 | 1.29 | 1.78 |
| 50 | 1.50 | 1.59 | 1.46 | 1.63 | 1.42 | 1.67 | 1.38 | 1.72 | 1.34 | 1.77 |
| 55 | 1.53 | 1.60 | 1.49 | 1.64 | 1.45 | 1.68 | 1.41 | 1.72 | 1.38 | 1.77 |
| 60 | 1.55 | 1.62 | 1.51 | 1.65 | 1.48 | 1.69 | 1.44 | 1.73 | 1.41 | 1.77 |
| 65 | 1.57 | 1.63 | 1.54 | 1.66 | 1.50 | 1.70 | 1.47 | 1.73 | 1.44 | 1.77 |
| 70 | 1.58 | 1.64 | 1.55 | 1.67 | 1.52 | 1.70 | 1.49 | 1.74 | 1.46 | 1.77 |
| 75 | 1.60 | 1.65 | 1.57 | 1.68 | 1.54 | 1.71 | 1.51 | 1.74 | 1.49 | 1.77 |
| 80 | 1.61 | 1.66 | 1.59 | 1.69 | 1.56 | 1.72 | 1.53 | 1.74 | 1.51 | 1.77 |
| 85 | 1.62 | 1.67 | 1.60 | 1.70 | 1.57 | 1.72 | 1.55 | 1.75 | 1.52 | 1.77 |
| 90 | 1.63 | 1.68 | 1.61 | 1.70 | 1.59 | 1.73 | 1.57 | 1.75 | 1.54 | 1.78 |
| 95 | 1.64 | 1.69 | 1.62 | 1.71 | 1.60 | 1.73 | 1.58 | 1.75 | 1.56 | 1.78 |
| 100 | 1.65 | 1.69 | 1.63 | 1.72 | 1.61 | 1.74 | 1.59 | 1.76 | 1.57 | 1.78 |

**TABLE 8**   CRITICAL VALUES FOR THE DURBIN-WATSON TEST
FOR AUTOCORRELATION (*Continued*)

**Significance Points of $d_L$ and $d_U$: $\alpha = .025$**
**Number of Independent Variables**

| $k$ | 1 | | 2 | | 3 | | 4 | | 5 | |
|---|---|---|---|---|---|---|---|---|---|---|
| $n$ | $d_L$ | $d_U$ | $d_L$ | $d_U$ | $d_L$ | $d_U$ | $d_L$ | $d_U$ | $d_L$ | $d_U$ |
| 15 | 0.95 | 1.23 | 0.83 | 1.40 | 0.71 | 1.61 | 0.59 | 1.84 | 0.48 | 2.09 |
| 16 | 0.98 | 1.24 | 0.86 | 1.40 | 0.75 | 1.59 | 0.64 | 1.80 | 0.53 | 2.03 |
| 17 | 1.01 | 1.25 | 0.90 | 1.40 | 0.79 | 1.58 | 0.68 | 1.77 | 0.57 | 1.98 |
| 18 | 1.03 | 1.26 | 0.93 | 1.40 | 0.82 | 1.56 | 0.72 | 1.74 | 0.62 | 1.93 |
| 19 | 1.06 | 1.28 | 0.96 | 1.41 | 0.86 | 1.55 | 0.76 | 1.72 | 0.66 | 1.90 |
| 20 | 1.08 | 1.28 | 0.99 | 1.41 | 0.89 | 1.55 | 0.79 | 1.70 | 0.70 | 1.87 |
| 21 | 1.10 | 1.30 | 1.01 | 1.41 | 0.92 | 1.54 | 0.83 | 1.69 | 0.73 | 1.84 |
| 22 | 1.12 | 1.31 | 1.04 | 1.42 | 0.95 | 1.54 | 0.86 | 1.68 | 0.77 | 1.82 |
| 23 | 1.14 | 1.32 | 1.06 | 1.42 | 0.97 | 1.54 | 0.89 | 1.67 | 0.80 | 1.80 |
| 24 | 1.16 | 1.33 | 1.08 | 1.43 | 1.00 | 1.54 | 0.91 | 1.66 | 0.83 | 1.79 |
| 25 | 1.18 | 1.34 | 1.10 | 1.43 | 1.02 | 1.54 | 0.94 | 1.65 | 0.86 | 1.77 |
| 26 | 1.19 | 1.35 | 1.12 | 1.44 | 1.04 | 1.54 | 0.96 | 1.65 | 0.88 | 1.76 |
| 27 | 1.21 | 1.36 | 1.13 | 1.44 | 1.06 | 1.54 | 0.99 | 1.64 | 0.91 | 1.75 |
| 28 | 1.22 | 1.37 | 1.15 | 1.45 | 1.08 | 1.54 | 1.01 | 1.64 | 0.93 | 1.74 |
| 29 | 1.24 | 1.38 | 1.17 | 1.45 | 1.10 | 1.54 | 1.03 | 1.63 | 0.96 | 1.73 |
| 30 | 1.25 | 1.38 | 1.18 | 1.46 | 1.12 | 1.54 | 1.05 | 1.63 | 0.98 | 1.73 |
| 31 | 1.26 | 1.39 | 1.20 | 1.47 | 1.13 | 1.55 | 1.07 | 1.63 | 1.00 | 1.72 |
| 32 | 1.27 | 1.40 | 1.21 | 1.47 | 1.15 | 1.55 | 1.08 | 1.63 | 1.02 | 1.71 |
| 33 | 1.28 | 1.41 | 1.22 | 1.48 | 1.16 | 1.55 | 1.10 | 1.63 | 1.04 | 1.71 |
| 34 | 1.29 | 1.41 | 1.24 | 1.48 | 1.17 | 1.55 | 1.12 | 1.63 | 1.06 | 1.70 |
| 35 | 1.30 | 1.42 | 1.25 | 1.48 | 1.19 | 1.55 | 1.13 | 1.63 | 1.07 | 1.70 |
| 36 | 1.31 | 1.43 | 1.26 | 1.49 | 1.20 | 1.56 | 1.15 | 1.63 | 1.09 | 1.70 |
| 37 | 1.32 | 1.43 | 1.27 | 1.49 | 1.21 | 1.56 | 1.16 | 1.62 | 1.10 | 1.70 |
| 38 | 1.33 | 1.44 | 1.28 | 1.50 | 1.23 | 1.56 | 1.17 | 1.62 | 1.12 | 1.70 |
| 39 | 1.34 | 1.44 | 1.29 | 1.50 | 1.24 | 1.56 | 1.19 | 1.63 | 1.13 | 1.69 |
| 40 | 1.35 | 1.45 | 1.30 | 1.51 | 1.25 | 1.57 | 1.20 | 1.63 | 1.15 | 1.69 |
| 45 | 1.39 | 1.48 | 1.34 | 1.53 | 1.30 | 1.58 | 1.25 | 1.63 | 1.21 | 1.69 |
| 50 | 1.42 | 1.50 | 1.38 | 1.54 | 1.34 | 1.59 | 1.30 | 1.64 | 1.26 | 1.69 |
| 55 | 1.45 | 1.52 | 1.41 | 1.56 | 1.37 | 1.60 | 1.33 | 1.64 | 1.30 | 1.69 |
| 60 | 1.47 | 1.54 | 1.44 | 1.57 | 1.40 | 1.61 | 1.37 | 1.65 | 1.33 | 1.69 |
| 65 | 1.49 | 1.55 | 1.46 | 1.59 | 1.43 | 1.62 | 1.40 | 1.66 | 1.36 | 1.69 |
| 70 | 1.51 | 1.57 | 1.48 | 1.60 | 1.45 | 1.63 | 1.42 | 1.66 | 1.39 | 1.70 |
| 75 | 1.53 | 1.58 | 1.50 | 1.61 | 1.47 | 1.64 | 1.45 | 1.67 | 1.42 | 1.70 |
| 80 | 1.54 | 1.59 | 1.52 | 1.62 | 1.49 | 1.65 | 1.47 | 1.67 | 1.44 | 1.70 |
| 85 | 1.56 | 1.60 | 1.53 | 1.63 | 1.51 | 1.65 | 1.49 | 1.68 | 1.46 | 1.71 |
| 90 | 1.57 | 1.61 | 1.55 | 1.64 | 1.53 | 1.66 | 1.50 | 1.69 | 1.48 | 1.71 |
| 95 | 1.58 | 1.62 | 1.56 | 1.65 | 1.54 | 1.67 | 1.52 | 1.69 | 1.50 | 1.71 |
| 100 | 1.59 | 1.63 | 1.57 | 1.65 | 1.55 | 1.67 | 1.53 | 1.70 | 1.51 | 1.72 |

TABLE 8    CRITICAL VALUES FOR THE DURBIN-WATSON TEST FOR
AUTOCORRELATION (*Continued*)

**Significance Points of $d_L$ and $d_U$: $\alpha = .01$**
**Number of Independent Variables**

| | 1 | | 2 | | 3 | | 4 | | 5 | |
| $k$ | $d_L$ | $d_U$ | $d_L$ | $d_U$ | $d_L$ | $d_U$ | $d_L$ | $d_U$ | $d_L$ | $d_U$ |
| $n$ | | | | | | | | | | |
|---|---|---|---|---|---|---|---|---|---|---|
| 15 | 0.81 | 1.07 | 0.70 | 1.25 | 0.59 | 1.46 | 0.49 | 1.70 | 0.39 | 1.96 |
| 16 | 0.84 | 1.09 | 0.74 | 1.25 | 0.63 | 1.44 | 0.53 | 1.66 | 0.44 | 1.90 |
| 17 | 0.87 | 1.10 | 0.77 | 1.25 | 0.67 | 1.43 | 0.57 | 1.63 | 0.48 | 1.85 |
| 18 | 0.90 | 1.12 | 0.80 | 1.26 | 0.71 | 1.42 | 0.61 | 1.60 | 0.52 | 1.80 |
| 19 | 0.93 | 1.13 | 0.83 | 1.26 | 0.74 | 1.41 | 0.65 | 1.58 | 0.56 | 1.77 |
| 20 | 0.95 | 1.15 | 0.86 | 1.27 | 0.77 | 1.41 | 0.68 | 1.57 | 0.60 | 1.74 |
| 21 | 0.97 | 1.16 | 0.89 | 1.27 | 0.80 | 1.41 | 0.72 | 1.55 | 0.63 | 1.71 |
| 22 | 1.00 | 1.17 | 0.91 | 1.28 | 0.83 | 1.40 | 0.75 | 1.54 | 0.66 | 1.69 |
| 23 | 1.02 | 1.19 | 0.94 | 1.29 | 0.86 | 1.40 | 0.77 | 1.53 | 0.70 | 1.67 |
| 24 | 1.04 | 1.20 | 0.96 | 1.30 | 0.88 | 1.41 | 0.80 | 1.53 | 0.72 | 1.66 |
| 25 | 1.05 | 1.21 | 0.98 | 1.30 | 0.90 | 1.41 | 0.83 | 1.52 | 0.75 | 1.65 |
| 26 | 1.07 | 1.22 | 1.00 | 1.31 | 0.93 | 1.41 | 0.85 | 1.52 | 0.78 | 1.64 |
| 27 | 1.09 | 1.23 | 1.02 | 1.32 | 0.95 | 1.41 | 0.88 | 1.51 | 0.81 | 1.63 |
| 28 | 1.10 | 1.24 | 1.04 | 1.32 | 0.97 | 1.41 | 0.90 | 1.51 | 0.83 | 1.62 |
| 29 | 1.12 | 1.25 | 1.05 | 1.33 | 0.99 | 1.42 | 0.92 | 1.51 | 0.85 | 1.61 |
| 30 | 1.13 | 1.26 | 1.07 | 1.34 | 1.01 | 1.42 | 0.94 | 1.51 | 0.88 | 1.61 |
| 31 | 1.15 | 1.27 | 1.08 | 1.34 | 1.02 | 1.42 | 0.96 | 1.51 | 0.90 | 1.60 |
| 32 | 1.16 | 1.28 | 1.10 | 1.35 | 1.04 | 1.43 | 0.98 | 1.51 | 0.92 | 1.60 |
| 33 | 1.17 | 1.29 | 1.11 | 1.36 | 1.05 | 1.43 | 1.00 | 1.51 | 0.94 | 1.59 |
| 34 | 1.18 | 1.30 | 1.13 | 1.36 | 1.07 | 1.43 | 1.01 | 1.51 | 0.95 | 1.59 |
| 35 | 1.19 | 1.31 | 1.14 | 1.37 | 1.08 | 1.44 | 1.03 | 1.51 | 0.97 | 1.59 |
| 36 | 1.21 | 1.32 | 1.15 | 1.38 | 1.10 | 1.44 | 1.04 | 1.51 | 0.99 | 1.59 |
| 37 | 1.22 | 1.32 | 1.16 | 1.38 | 1.11 | 1.45 | 1.06 | 1.51 | 1.00 | 1.59 |
| 38 | 1.23 | 1.33 | 1.18 | 1.39 | 1.12 | 1.45 | 1.07 | 1.52 | 1.02 | 1.58 |
| 39 | 1.24 | 1.34 | 1.19 | 1.39 | 1.14 | 1.45 | 1.09 | 1.52 | 1.03 | 1.58 |
| 40 | 1.25 | 1.34 | 1.20 | 1.40 | 1.15 | 1.46 | 1.10 | 1.52 | 1.05 | 1.58 |
| 45 | 1.29 | 1.38 | 1.24 | 1.42 | 1.20 | 1.48 | 1.16 | 1.53 | 1.11 | 1.58 |
| 50 | 1.32 | 1.40 | 1.28 | 1.45 | 1.24 | 1.49 | 1.20 | 1.54 | 1.16 | 1.59 |
| 55 | 1.36 | 1.43 | 1.32 | 1.47 | 1.28 | 1.51 | 1.25 | 1.55 | 1.21 | 1.59 |
| 60 | 1.38 | 1.45 | 1.35 | 1.48 | 1.32 | 1.52 | 1.28 | 1.56 | 1.25 | 1.60 |
| 65 | 1.41 | 1.47 | 1.38 | 1.50 | 1.35 | 1.53 | 1.31 | 1.57 | 1.28 | 1.61 |
| 70 | 1.43 | 1.49 | 1.40 | 1.52 | 1.37 | 1.55 | 1.34 | 1.58 | 1.31 | 1.61 |
| 75 | 1.45 | 1.50 | 1.42 | 1.53 | 1.39 | 1.56 | 1.37 | 1.59 | 1.34 | 1.62 |
| 80 | 1.47 | 1.52 | 1.44 | 1.54 | 1.42 | 1.57 | 1.39 | 1.60 | 1.36 | 1.62 |
| 85 | 1.48 | 1.53 | 1.46 | 1.55 | 1.43 | 1.58 | 1.41 | 1.60 | 1.39 | 1.63 |
| 90 | 1.50 | 1.54 | 1.47 | 1.56 | 1.45 | 1.59 | 1.43 | 1.61 | 1.41 | 1.64 |
| 95 | 1.51 | 1.55 | 1.49 | 1.57 | 1.47 | 1.60 | 1.45 | 1.62 | 1.42 | 1.64 |
| 100 | 1.52 | 1.56 | 1.50 | 1.58 | 1.48 | 1.60 | 1.46 | 1.63 | 1.44 | 1.65 |

**TABLE 9    $T_L$ VALUES FOR THE MANN-WHITNEY-WILCOXON TEST**

Reject the hypothesis of identical populations if the sum of the ranks for the $n_1$ items is *less* than the value $T_L$ shown in the following table or if the sum of the ranks for the $n_1$ items is *greater* than the value $T_U$ where

$$T_U = n_1(n_1 + n_2 + 1) - T_L$$

**$\alpha = .10$**

| | | $n_2$ | | | | | | | | |
|---|---|---|---|---|---|---|---|---|---|---|
| | | 2 | 3 | 4 | 5 | 6 | 7 | 8 | 9 | 10 |
| | 2 | 3 | 3 | 3 | 4 | 4 | 4 | 5 | 5 | 5 |
| | 3 | 6 | 7 | 7 | 8 | 9 | 9 | 10 | 11 | 11 |
| | 4 | 10 | 11 | 12 | 13 | 14 | 15 | 16 | 17 | 18 |
| | 5 | 16 | 17 | 18 | 20 | 21 | 22 | 24 | 25 | 27 |
| $n_1$ | 6 | 22 | 24 | 25 | 27 | 29 | 30 | 32 | 34 | 36 |
| | 7 | 29 | 31 | 33 | 35 | 37 | 40 | 42 | 44 | 46 |
| | 8 | 38 | 40 | 42 | 45 | 47 | 50 | 52 | 55 | 57 |
| | 9 | 47 | 50 | 52 | 55 | 58 | 61 | 64 | 67 | 70 |
| | 10 | 57 | 60 | 63 | 67 | 70 | 73 | 76 | 80 | 83 |

**$\alpha = .05$**

| | | $n_2$ | | | | | | | | |
|---|---|---|---|---|---|---|---|---|---|---|
| | | 2 | 3 | 4 | 5 | 6 | 7 | 8 | 9 | 10 |
| | 2 | 3 | 3 | 3 | 3 | 3 | 3 | 4 | 4 | 4 |
| | 3 | 6 | 6 | 6 | 7 | 8 | 8 | 9 | 9 | 10 |
| | 4 | 10 | 10 | 11 | 12 | 13 | 14 | 15 | 15 | 16 |
| | 5 | 15 | 16 | 17 | 18 | 19 | 21 | 22 | 23 | 24 |
| $n_1$ | 6 | 21 | 23 | 24 | 25 | 27 | 28 | 30 | 32 | 33 |
| | 7 | 28 | 30 | 32 | 34 | 35 | 37 | 39 | 41 | 43 |
| | 8 | 37 | 39 | 41 | 43 | 45 | 47 | 50 | 52 | 54 |
| | 9 | 46 | 48 | 50 | 53 | 56 | 58 | 61 | 63 | 66 |
| | 10 | 56 | 59 | 61 | 64 | 67 | 70 | 73 | 76 | 79 |

**TABLE 10  CRITICAL VALUES OF THE STUDENTIZED RANGE DISTRIBUTION**

$\alpha = .05$

| Degrees of Freedom | Number of Populations | | | | | | | | | | | | | | | | | | |
|---|---|---|---|---|---|---|---|---|---|---|---|---|---|---|---|---|---|---|---|
| | 2 | 3 | 4 | 5 | 6 | 7 | 8 | 9 | 10 | 11 | 12 | 13 | 14 | 15 | 16 | 17 | 18 | 19 | 20 |
| 1 | 18.0 | 27.0 | 32.8 | 37.1 | 40.4 | 43.1 | 45.4 | 47.4 | 49.1 | 50.6 | 52.0 | 53.2 | 54.3 | 55.4 | 56.3 | 57.2 | 58.0 | 58.8 | 59.6 |
| 2 | 6.08 | 8.33 | 9.80 | 10.9 | 11.7 | 12.4 | 13.0 | 13.5 | 14.0 | 14.4 | 14.7 | 15.1 | 15.4 | 15.7 | 15.9 | 16.1 | 16.4 | 16.6 | 16.8 |
| 3 | 4.50 | 5.91 | 6.82 | 7.50 | 8.04 | 8.48 | 8.85 | 9.18 | 9.46 | 9.72 | 9.95 | 10.2 | 10.3 | 10.5 | 10.7 | 10.8 | 11.0 | 11.1 | 11.2 |
| 4 | 3.93 | 5.04 | 5.76 | 6.29 | 6.71 | 7.05 | 7.35 | 7.60 | 7.83 | 8.03 | 8.21 | 8.37 | 8.52 | 8.66 | 8.79 | 8.91 | 9.03 | 9.13 | 9.23 |
| 5 | 3.64 | 4.60 | 5.22 | 5.67 | 6.03 | 6.33 | 6.58 | 6.80 | 6.99 | 7.17 | 7.32 | 7.47 | 7.60 | 7.72 | 7.83 | 7.93 | 8.03 | 8.12 | 8.21 |
| 6 | 3.46 | 4.34 | 4.90 | 5.30 | 5.63 | 5.90 | 6.12 | 6.32 | 6.49 | 6.65 | 6.79 | 6.92 | 7.03 | 7.14 | 7.24 | 7.34 | 7.43 | 7.51 | 7.59 |
| 7 | 3.34 | 4.16 | 4.68 | 5.06 | 5.36 | 5.61 | 5.82 | 6.00 | 6.16 | 6.30 | 6.43 | 6.55 | 6.66 | 6.76 | 6.85 | 6.94 | 7.02 | 7.10 | 7.17 |
| 8 | 3.26 | 4.04 | 4.53 | 4.89 | 5.17 | 5.40 | 5.60 | 5.77 | 5.92 | 6.05 | 6.18 | 6.29 | 6.39 | 6.48 | 6.57 | 6.65 | 6.73 | 6.80 | 6.87 |
| 9 | 3.20 | 3.95 | 4.41 | 4.76 | 5.02 | 5.24 | 5.43 | 5.59 | 5.74 | 5.87 | 5.98 | 6.09 | 6.19 | 6.28 | 6.36 | 6.44 | 6.51 | 6.58 | 6.64 |
| 10 | 3.15 | 3.88 | 4.33 | 4.65 | 4.91 | 5.12 | 5.30 | 5.46 | 5.60 | 5.72 | 5.83 | 5.93 | 6.03 | 6.11 | 6.19 | 6.27 | 6.34 | 6.40 | 6.47 |
| 11 | 3.11 | 3.82 | 4.26 | 4.57 | 4.82 | 5.03 | 5.20 | 5.35 | 5.49 | 5.61 | 5.71 | 5.81 | 5.90 | 5.98 | 6.06 | 6.13 | 6.20 | 6.27 | 6.33 |
| 12 | 3.08 | 3.77 | 4.20 | 4.51 | 4.75 | 4.95 | 5.12 | 5.27 | 5.39 | 5.51 | 5.61 | 5.71 | 5.80 | 5.88 | 5.95 | 6.02 | 6.09 | 6.15 | 6.21 |
| 13 | 3.06 | 3.73 | 4.15 | 4.45 | 4.69 | 4.88 | 5.05 | 5.19 | 5.32 | 5.43 | 5.53 | 5.63 | 5.71 | 5.79 | 5.86 | 5.93 | 5.99 | 6.05 | 6.11 |
| 14 | 3.03 | 3.70 | 4.11 | 4.41 | 4.64 | 4.83 | 4.99 | 5.13 | 5.25 | 5.36 | 5.46 | 5.55 | 5.64 | 5.71 | 5.79 | 5.85 | 5.91 | 5.97 | 6.03 |
| 15 | 3.01 | 3.67 | 4.08 | 4.37 | 4.59 | 4.78 | 4.94 | 5.08 | 5.20 | 5.31 | 5.40 | 5.49 | 5.57 | 5.65 | 5.72 | 5.78 | 5.85 | 5.90 | 5.96 |
| 16 | 3.00 | 3.65 | 4.05 | 4.33 | 4.56 | 4.74 | 4.90 | 5.03 | 5.15 | 5.26 | 5.35 | 5.44 | 5.52 | 5.59 | 5.66 | 5.73 | 5.79 | 5.84 | 5.90 |
| 17 | 2.98 | 3.63 | 4.02 | 4.30 | 4.52 | 4.70 | 4.86 | 4.99 | 5.11 | 5.21 | 5.31 | 5.39 | 5.47 | 5.54 | 5.61 | 5.67 | 5.73 | 5.79 | 5.84 |
| 18 | 2.97 | 3.61 | 4.00 | 4.28 | 4.49 | 4.67 | 4.82 | 4.96 | 5.07 | 5.17 | 5.27 | 5.35 | 5.43 | 5.50 | 5.57 | 5.63 | 5.69 | 5.74 | 5.79 |
| 19 | 2.96 | 3.59 | 3.98 | 4.25 | 4.47 | 4.65 | 4.79 | 4.92 | 5.04 | 5.14 | 5.23 | 5.31 | 5.39 | 5.46 | 5.53 | 5.59 | 5.65 | 5.70 | 5.75 |
| 20 | 2.95 | 3.58 | 3.96 | 4.23 | 4.45 | 4.62 | 4.77 | 4.90 | 5.01 | 5.11 | 5.20 | 5.28 | 5.36 | 5.43 | 5.49 | 5.55 | 5.61 | 5.66 | 5.71 |
| 24 | 2.92 | 3.53 | 3.90 | 4.17 | 4.37 | 4.54 | 4.68 | 4.81 | 4.92 | 5.01 | 5.10 | 5.18 | 5.25 | 5.32 | 5.38 | 5.44 | 5.49 | 5.55 | 5.59 |
| 30 | 2.89 | 3.49 | 3.85 | 4.10 | 4.30 | 4.46 | 4.60 | 4.72 | 4.82 | 4.92 | 5.00 | 5.08 | 5.15 | 5.21 | 5.27 | 5.33 | 5.38 | 5.43 | 5.47 |
| 40 | 2.86 | 3.44 | 3.79 | 4.04 | 4.23 | 4.39 | 4.52 | 4.63 | 4.73 | 4.82 | 4.90 | 4.98 | 5.04 | 5.11 | 5.16 | 5.22 | 5.27 | 5.31 | 5.36 |
| 60 | 2.83 | 3.40 | 3.74 | 3.98 | 4.16 | 4.31 | 4.44 | 4.55 | 4.65 | 4.73 | 4.81 | 4.88 | 4.94 | 5.00 | 5.06 | 5.11 | 5.15 | 5.20 | 5.24 |
| 120 | 2.80 | 3.36 | 3.68 | 3.92 | 4.10 | 4.24 | 4.36 | 4.47 | 4.56 | 4.64 | 4.71 | 4.78 | 4.84 | 4.90 | 4.95 | 5.00 | 5.04 | 5.09 | 5.13 |
| $\infty$ | 2.77 | 3.31 | 3.63 | 3.86 | 4.03 | 4.17 | 4.29 | 4.39 | 4.47 | 4.55 | 4.62 | 4.68 | 4.74 | 4.80 | 4.85 | 4.89 | 4.93 | 4.97 | 5.01 |

TABLE 10   CRITICAL VALUES OF THE STUDENTIZED RANGE DISTRIBUTION (Continued)

$\alpha = .01$

| Degrees of Freedom | Number of Populations | | | | | | | | | | | | | | | | | | |
|---|---|---|---|---|---|---|---|---|---|---|---|---|---|---|---|---|---|---|---|
| | 2 | 3 | 4 | 5 | 6 | 7 | 8 | 9 | 10 | 11 | 12 | 13 | 14 | 15 | 16 | 17 | 18 | 19 | 20 |
| 1 | 90.0 | 135.0 | 164.0 | 186.0 | 202.0 | 216.0 | 227.0 | 237.0 | 246.0 | 253.0 | 260.0 | 266.0 | 272.0 | 277.0 | 282.0 | 286.0 | 290.0 | 294.0 | 298.0 |
| 2 | 14.0 | 19.0 | 22.3 | 24.7 | 26.6 | 28.2 | 29.5 | 30.7 | 31.7 | 32.6 | 33.4 | 34.1 | 34.8 | 35.4 | 36.0 | 36.5 | 37.0 | 37.5 | 37.9 |
| 3 | 8.26 | 10.6 | 12.2 | 13.3 | 14.2 | 15.0 | 15.6 | 16.2 | 16.7 | 17.1 | 17.5 | 17.9 | 18.2 | 18.5 | 18.8 | 19.1 | 19.3 | 19.5 | 19.8 |
| 4 | 6.51 | 8.12 | 9.17 | 9.96 | 10.6 | 11.1 | 11.5 | 11.9 | 12.3 | 12.6 | 12.8 | 13.1 | 13.3 | 13.5 | 13.7 | 13.9 | 14.1 | 14.2 | 14.4 |
| 5 | 5.70 | 6.97 | 7.80 | 8.42 | 8.91 | 9.32 | 9.67 | 9.97 | 10.2 | 10.5 | 10.7 | 10.9 | 11.1 | 11.2 | 11.4 | 11.6 | 11.7 | 11.8 | 11.9 |
| 6 | 5.24 | 6.33 | 7.03 | 7.56 | 7.97 | 8.32 | 8.61 | 8.87 | 9.10 | 9.30 | 9.49 | 9.65 | 9.81 | 9.95 | 10.1 | 10.2 | 10.3 | 10.4 | 10.5 |
| 7 | 4.95 | 5.92 | 6.54 | 7.01 | 7.37 | 7.68 | 7.94 | 8.17 | 8.37 | 8.55 | 8.71 | 8.86 | 9.00 | 9.12 | 9.24 | 9.35 | 9.46 | 9.55 | 9.65 |
| 8 | 4.74 | 5.63 | 6.20 | 6.63 | 6.96 | 7.24 | 7.47 | 7.68 | 7.87 | 8.03 | 8.18 | 8.31 | 8.44 | 8.55 | 8.66 | 8.76 | 8.85 | 8.94 | 9.03 |
| 9 | 4.60 | 5.43 | 5.96 | 6.35 | 6.66 | 6.91 | 7.13 | 7.32 | 7.49 | 7.65 | 7.78 | 7.91 | 8.03 | 8.13 | 8.23 | 8.32 | 8.41 | 8.49 | 8.57 |
| 10 | 4.48 | 5.27 | 5.77 | 6.14 | 6.43 | 6.67 | 6.87 | 7.05 | 7.21 | 7.36 | 7.48 | 7.60 | 7.71 | 7.81 | 7.91 | 7.99 | 8.07 | 8.15 | 8.22 |
| 11 | 4.39 | 5.14 | 5.62 | 5.97 | 6.25 | 6.48 | 6.67 | 6.84 | 6.99 | 7.13 | 7.25 | 7.36 | 7.46 | 7.56 | 7.65 | 7.73 | 7.81 | 7.88 | 7.95 |
| 12 | 4.32 | 5.04 | 5.50 | 5.84 | 6.10 | 6.32 | 6.51 | 6.67 | 6.81 | 6.94 | 7.06 | 7.17 | 7.26 | 7.36 | 7.44 | 7.52 | 7.59 | 7.66 | 7.73 |
| 13 | 4.26 | 4.96 | 5.40 | 5.73 | 5.98 | 6.19 | 6.37 | 6.53 | 6.67 | 6.79 | 6.90 | 7.01 | 7.10 | 7.19 | 7.27 | 7.34 | 7.42 | 7.48 | 7.55 |
| 14 | 4.21 | 4.89 | 5.32 | 5.63 | 5.88 | 6.08 | 6.26 | 6.41 | 6.54 | 6.66 | 6.77 | 6.87 | 6.96 | 7.05 | 7.12 | 7.20 | 7.27 | 7.33 | 7.39 |
| 15 | 4.17 | 4.83 | 5.25 | 5.56 | 5.80 | 5.99 | 6.16 | 6.31 | 6.44 | 6.55 | 6.66 | 6.76 | 6.84 | 6.93 | 7.00 | 7.07 | 7.14 | 7.20 | 7.26 |
| 16 | 4.13 | 4.78 | 5.19 | 5.49 | 5.72 | 5.92 | 6.08 | 6.22 | 6.35 | 6.46 | 6.56 | 6.66 | 6.74 | 6.82 | 6.90 | 6.97 | 7.03 | 7.09 | 7.15 |
| 17 | 4.10 | 4.74 | 5.14 | 5.43 | 5.66 | 5.85 | 6.01 | 6.15 | 6.27 | 6.38 | 6.48 | 6.57 | 6.66 | 6.73 | 6.80 | 6.87 | 6.94 | 7.00 | 7.05 |
| 18 | 4.07 | 4.70 | 5.09 | 5.38 | 5.60 | 5.79 | 5.94 | 6.08 | 6.20 | 6.31 | 6.41 | 6.50 | 6.58 | 6.65 | 6.72 | 6.79 | 6.85 | 6.91 | 6.96 |
| 19 | 4.05 | 4.67 | 5.05 | 5.33 | 5.55 | 5.73 | 5.89 | 6.02 | 6.14 | 6.25 | 6.34 | 6.43 | 6.51 | 6.58 | 6.65 | 6.72 | 6.78 | 6.84 | 6.89 |
| 20 | 4.02 | 4.64 | 5.02 | 5.29 | 5.51 | 5.69 | 5.84 | 5.97 | 6.09 | 6.19 | 6.29 | 6.37 | 6.45 | 6.52 | 6.59 | 6.65 | 6.71 | 6.76 | 6.82 |
| 24 | 3.96 | 4.54 | 4.91 | 5.17 | 5.37 | 5.54 | 5.69 | 5.81 | 5.92 | 6.02 | 6.11 | 6.19 | 6.26 | 6.33 | 6.39 | 6.45 | 6.51 | 6.56 | 6.61 |
| 30 | 3.89 | 4.45 | 4.80 | 5.05 | 5.24 | 5.40 | 5.54 | 5.65 | 5.76 | 5.85 | 5.93 | 6.01 | 6.08 | 6.14 | 6.20 | 6.26 | 6.31 | 6.36 | 6.41 |
| 40 | 3.82 | 4.37 | 4.70 | 4.93 | 5.11 | 5.27 | 5.39 | 5.50 | 5.60 | 5.69 | 5.77 | 5.84 | 5.90 | 5.96 | 6.02 | 6.07 | 6.12 | 6.17 | 6.21 |
| 60 | 3.76 | 4.28 | 4.60 | 4.82 | 4.99 | 5.13 | 5.25 | 5.36 | 5.45 | 5.53 | 5.60 | 5.67 | 5.73 | 5.79 | 5.84 | 5.89 | 5.93 | 5.98 | 6.02 |
| 120 | 3.70 | 4.20 | 4.50 | 4.71 | 4.87 | 5.01 | 5.12 | 5.21 | 5.30 | 5.38 | 5.44 | 5.51 | 5.56 | 5.61 | 5.66 | 5.71 | 5.75 | 5.79 | 5.83 |
| ∞ | 3.64 | 4.12 | 4.40 | 4.60 | 4.76 | 4.88 | 4.99 | 5.08 | 5.16 | 5.23 | 5.29 | 5.35 | 5.40 | 5.45 | 5.49 | 5.54 | 5.57 | 5.61 | 5.65 |

Reprinted by permission of Oxford University Press on behalf of The Biometrika Trustees from Biometrika Tables for Statisticians, E. S. Pearson and H. O. Hartley, Vol. 1, 3rd ed., 1966, pp. 176–177

# Appendix C:   Summation Notation

## Summations

*Definition*

$$\sum_{i=1}^{n} x_i = x_1 + x_2 + \cdots + x_n \tag{C.1}$$

Example for $x_1 = 5, x_2 = 8, x_3 = 14$:

$$\sum_{i=1}^{3} x_i = x_1 + x_2 + x_3$$
$$= 5 + 8 + 14$$
$$= 27$$

*Result 1*

For a constant $c$:

$$\sum_{i=1}^{n} c = \underbrace{(c + c + \cdots + c)}_{n \text{ times}} = nc \tag{C.2}$$

Example for $c = 5, n = 10$:

$$\sum_{i=1}^{10} 5 = 10(5) = 50$$

Example for $c = \bar{x}$:

$$\sum_{i=1}^{n} \bar{x} = n\bar{x}$$

*Result 2*

$$\sum_{i=1}^{n} cx_i = cx_1 + cx_2 + \cdots + cx_n$$
$$= c(x_1 + x_2 + \cdots + x_n) = c\sum_{i=1}^{n} x_i \tag{C.3}$$

Example for $x_1 = 5, x_2 = 8, x_3 = 14, c = 2$:

$$\sum_{i=1}^{3} 2x_i = 2\sum_{i=1}^{3} x_i = 2(27) = 54$$

*Result 3*

$$\sum_{i=1}^{n} (ax_i + by_i) = a\sum_{i=1}^{n} x_i + b\sum_{i=1}^{n} y_i \tag{C.4}$$

Example for $x_1 = 5$, $x_2 = 8$, $x_3 = 14$, $a = 2$, $y_1 = 7$, $y_2 = 3$, $y_3 = 8$, $b = 4$:

$$\sum_{i=1}^{3}(2x_i + 4y_i) = 2\sum_{i=1}^{3}x_i + 4\sum_{i=1}^{3}y_i$$
$$= 2(27) + 4(18)$$
$$= 54 + 72$$
$$= 126$$

## Double Summations

Consider the following data involving the variable $x_{ij}$, where $i$ is the subscript denoting the row position and $j$ is the subscript denoting the column position:

|  |  | Column | | |
|---|---|---|---|---|
|  |  | **1** | **2** | **3** |
| **Row** | **1** | $x_{11} = 10$ | $x_{12} = 8$ | $x_{13} = 6$ |
|  | **2** | $x_{21} = 7$ | $x_{22} = 4$ | $x_{23} = 12$ |

*Definition*

$$\sum_{i=1}^{n}\sum_{j=1}^{m}x_{ij} = (x_{11} + x_{12} + \cdots + x_{1m}) + (x_{21} + x_{22} + \cdots + x_{2m})$$
$$+ (x_{31} + x_{32} + \cdots + x_{3m}) + \cdots + (x_{n1} + x_{n2} + \cdots + x_{nm}) \quad \text{(C.5)}$$

Example:

$$\sum_{i=1}^{2}\sum_{j=1}^{3}x_{ij} = x_{11} + x_{12} + x_{13} + x_{21} + x_{22} + x_{23}$$
$$= 10 + 8 + 6 + 7 + 4 + 12$$
$$= 47$$

*Definition*

$$\sum_{i=1}^{n}x_{ij} = x_{1j} + x_{2j} + \cdots + x_{nj} \quad \text{(C.6)}$$

Example:

$$\sum_{i=1}^{2}x_{i2} = x_{12} + x_{22}$$
$$= 8 + 4$$
$$= 12$$

## Shorthand Notation

Sometimes when a summation is for all values of the subscript, we use the following shorthand notations:

$$\sum_{i=1}^{n}x_i = \sum x_i \quad \text{(C.7)}$$

$$\sum_{i=1}^{n}\sum_{j=1}^{m}x_{ij} = \sum\sum x_{ij} \quad \text{(C.8)}$$

$$\sum_{i=1}^{n}x_{ij} = \sum_{i}x_{ij} \quad \text{(C.9)}$$

## Chapter 1

**2. a.** 9
   **b.** 4
   **c.** Qualitative: country and room rate
      Quantitative: number of rooms and overall score
   **d.** Country is nominal; room rate is ordinal; number of rooms is ratio; overall score is interval

**3. a.** Average number of rooms = 808/9 = 89.78, or approximately 90 rooms
   **b.** Average overall score = 732.1/9 = 81.3
   **c.** 2 of 9 are located in England; approximately 22%
   **d.** 4 of 9 have a room rate of $$; approximately 44%

**4. a.** 10
   **b.** All brands of minisystems manufactured
   **c.** $314
   **d.** $314

**6.** Questions a, c, and d provide quantitative data
   Questions b and e provide qualitative data

**8. a.** 1005
   **b.** Qualitative
   **c.** Percentages
   **d.** Approximately 291

**10. a.** Quantitative; ratio
   **b.** Qualitative; nominal
   **c.** Qualitative; ordinal
   **d.** Qualitative; nominal
   **e.** Quantitative; ratio

**12. a.** All visitors to Hawaii
   **b.** Yes
   **c.** First and fourth questions provide quantitative data
      Second and third questions provide qualitative data

**13. a.** Quantitative
   **b.** Time series with 6 observations
   **c.** Earnings for Volkswagen
   **d.** An increase would be expected in 2003, but it appears that the rate of increase is slowing

**14. a.** Qualitative

**16. a.** Product taste tests and test marketing
   **b.** Specially designed statistical studies

**18. a.** 40%
   **b.** Qualitative

**20. a.** 43% of managers were bullish or very bullish, and 21% of managers expected health care to be the leading industry over the next 12 months

   **b.** The average 12-month return estimate is 11.2% for the population of investment managers.
   **c.** The sample average of 2.5 years is an estimate of how long the population of investment managers think it will take to resume sustainable growth.

**22. a.** All adult viewers reached by the station
   **b.** Viewers contacted in the telephone survey
   **c.** Too difficult and costly to reach the entire population

**24. a.** Correct
   **b.** Incorrect
   **c.** Correct
   **d.** Incorrect
   **e.** Incorrect

## Chapter 2

**2. a.** .20
   **b.** 40
   **c/d.**

| Class | Frequency | Percent Frequency |
|-------|-----------|-------------------|
| A | 44 | 22 |
| B | 36 | 18 |
| C | 80 | 40 |
| D | 40 | 20 |
| Total | 200 | 100 |

**3. a.** 360° × 58/120 = 174°
   **b.** 360° × 42/120 = 126°
   **c.**

   **d.**

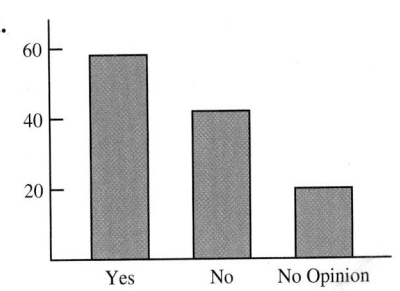

**4. a.** Qualitative

**b.**

| TV Show | Frequency | Percent Frequency |
|---|---|---|
| Millionaire | 24 | 48 |
| Frasier | 15 | 30 |
| Chicago Hope | 7 | 14 |
| Charmed | 4 | 8 |
| Total | 50 | 100 |

**d.** Millionaire has the largest market share; Frasier is second

**6. a.**

| Book | Frequency | Percent Frequency |
|---|---|---|
| 7 Habits | 10 | 16.66 |
| Millionaire | 16 | 26.67 |
| Motley | 9 | 15.00 |
| Dad | 13 | 21.67 |
| WSJ Guide | 6 | 10.00 |
| Other | 6 | 10.00 |
| Total | 60 | 100.00 |

**b.** First 5: *Millionaire, Dad, 7 Habits, Motley, WSJ Guide*
**c.** 48.33%

**7.**

| Rating | Frequency | Relative Frequency |
|---|---|---|
| Outstanding | 19 | .38 |
| Very good | 13 | .26 |
| Good | 10 | .20 |
| Average | 6 | .12 |
| Poor | 2 | .04 |

Management should be pleased with these results: 64% of the ratings are very good to outstanding, and 84% of the ratings are good or better; comparing these ratings to previous results will show whether the restaurant is making improvements in its customers' ratings of food quality

**8. a.**

| Position | Frequency | Relative Frequency |
|---|---|---|
| P | 17 | .309 |
| H | 4 | .073 |
| 1 | 5 | .091 |
| 2 | 4 | .073 |
| 3 | 2 | .036 |
| S | 5 | .091 |
| L | 6 | .109 |
| C | 5 | .091 |
| R | 7 | .127 |
| Totals | 55 | 1.000 |

**b.** Pitcher
**c.** 3rd base

**d.** Right field
**e.** Infielders 16 to outfielders 18

**10. a.** The data are ordinal; they simply provide quality classifications.

**b.**

| Response | Frequency | Relative Frequency |
|---|---|---|
| 3 | 2 | .03 |
| 4 | 4 | .07 |
| 5 | 12 | .20 |
| 6 | 24 | .40 |
| 7 | 18 | .30 |
| Totals | 60 | 1.00 |

**12.**

| Class | Cumulative Frequency | Cumulative Relative Frequency |
|---|---|---|
| ≤19 | 10 | .20 |
| ≤29 | 24 | .48 |
| ≤39 | 41 | .82 |
| ≤49 | 48 | .96 |
| ≤59 | 50 | 1.00 |

**14. b/c.**

| Class | Frequency | Percent Frequency |
|---|---|---|
| 6.0–7.9 | 4 | 20 |
| 8.0–9.9 | 2 | 10 |
| 10.0–11.9 | 8 | 40 |
| 12.0–13.9 | 3 | 15 |
| 14.0–15.9 | 3 | 15 |
| Totals | 20 | 100 |

**15. a/b.**

| Waiting Time | Frequency | Relative Frequency |
|---|---|---|
| 0–4 | 4 | .20 |
| 5–9 | 8 | .40 |
| 10–14 | 5 | .25 |
| 15–19 | 2 | .10 |
| 20–24 | 1 | .05 |
| Totals | 20 | 1.00 |

**c/d.**

| Waiting Time | Cumulative Frequency | Cumulative Relative Frequency |
|---|---|---|
| ≤4 | 4 | .20 |
| ≤9 | 12 | .60 |
| ≤14 | 17 | .85 |
| ≤19 | 19 | .95 |
| ≤24 | 20 | 1.00 |

**e.** 12/20 = .60

**16. a.** Adjusted Gross Income

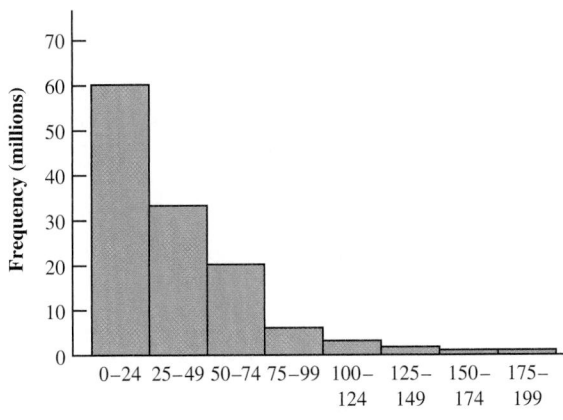

Income ($1000s)

Histogram is skewed to the right.

**b.** Exam Scores

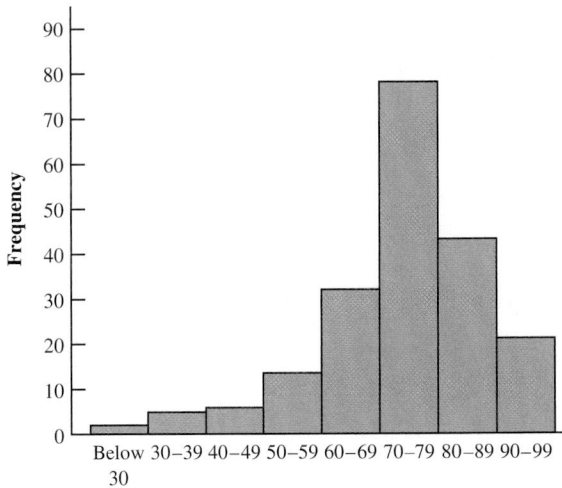

Score

Histogram is skewed to the left

**c.**

Data

Histogram skewed slightly to the left, but roughly symmetric

**18. a.** Lowest salary: $93,000
Highest salary: $178,000

**b.**

| Salary ($1000s) | Frequency | Relative Frequency | Percent Frequency |
|---|---|---|---|
| 91–105 | 4 | 0.08 | 8 |
| 106–120 | 5 | 0.10 | 10 |
| 121–135 | 11 | 0.22 | 22 |
| 136–150 | 18 | 0.36 | 36 |
| 151–165 | 9 | 0.18 | 18 |
| 166–180 | 3 | 0.06 | 6 |
| Total | 50 | 1.00 | 100 |

**c.** 20/50

**d.** 24%

**20. a.** 48.9%
**b.** 51.1%
**c.** 43.4%
**d.** 97.075 million
**e.** 46.6125 million

**22.**
```
5 | 7  8
6 | 4  5  8
7 | 0  2  2  5  5  6  8
8 | 0  2  3  5
```

**23.** Leaf unit = .1
```
 6 | 3
 7 | 5  5  7
 8 | 1  3  4  8
 9 | 3  6
10 | 0  4  5
11 | 3
```

**24.** Leaf Unit = 10
```
11 | 6
12 | 0  2
13 | 0  6  7
14 | 2  2  7
15 | 5
16 | 0  2  8
17 | 0  2  3
```

**25.**
```
 9 | 8  9
10 | 2  4  6  6
11 | 4  5  7  8  8  9
12 | 2  4  5  7
13 | 1  2
14 | 4
15 | 1
```

**26. a.**

| 1 | 0 3 7 7 |
|---|---|
| 2 | 4 5 5 |
| 3 | 0 0 5 5 9 |
| 4 | 0 0 0 5 5 8 |
| 5 | 0 0 0 4 5 5 |

**b.**

| 0 | 5 7 |
|---|---|
| 1 | 0 1 1 3 4 |
| 1 | 5 5 5 8 |
| 2 | 0 0 0 0 0 0 |
| 2 | 5 5 |
| 3 | 0 0 0 |
| 3 | 6 |
| 4 | |
| 4 | |
| 5 | |
| 5 | |
| 6 | 3 |

**28. a.**

| 0 | 5 8 |
|---|---|
| 1 | 1 1 3 3 4 4 |
| 1 | 5 6 7 8 9 9 |
| 2 | 2 3 3 3 5 5 |
| 2 | 6 8 |
| 3 | |
| 3 | 6 7 7 9 |
| 4 | 0 |
| 4 | 7 8 |
| 5 | |
| 5 | |
| 6 | 0 |

**b.**

| 2000 P/E Forecast | Frequency | Relative Frequency |
|---|---|---|
| 5–9 | 2 | 6.7 |
| 10–14 | 6 | 20.0 |
| 15–19 | 6 | 20.0 |
| 20–24 | 6 | 20.0 |
| 25–29 | 2 | 6.7 |
| 30–34 | 0 | 0.0 |
| 35–39 | 4 | 13.3 |
| 40–44 | 1 | 3.3 |
| 45–49 | 2 | 6.7 |
| 50–54 | 0 | 0.0 |
| 55–59 | 0 | 0.0 |
| 60–64 | 1 | 3.3 |
| Total | 30 | 100.0 |

**29. a.**

| | | y | | |
|---|---|---|---|---|
| | | 1 | 2 | Total |
| | A | 5 | 0 | 5 |
| $x$ | B | 11 | 2 | 13 |
| | C | 2 | 10 | 12 |
| | Total | 18 | 12 | 30 |

**b.**

| | | y | | |
|---|---|---|---|---|
| | | 1 | 2 | Total |
| | A | 100.0 | 0.0 | 100.0 |
| $x$ | B | 84.6 | 15.4 | 100.0 |
| | C | 16.7 | 83.3 | 100.0 |

**c.**

| | | y | |
|---|---|---|---|
| | | 1 | 2 |
| | A | 27.8 | 0.0 |
| $x$ | B | 61.1 | 16.7 |
| | C | 11.1 | 83.3 |
| | Total | 100.0 | 100.0 |

**d.** A values are always in $y = 1$
B values are most often in $y = 1$
C values are most often in $y = 2$

**30. a.**

**b.** A negative relationship between $x$ and $y$; $y$ decreases as $x$ increases

**32. a.**

| Education Level | Household Income ($1000s) | | | | | |
|---|---|---|---|---|---|---|
| | Under 24.9 | 25.0–49.9 | 50.0–74.9 | 75.0–99.9 | 100 or more | Total |
| Not H.S. Graduate | 32.70 | 14.82 | 8.27 | 5.02 | 2.53 | 15.86 |
| H.S. Graduate | 35.74 | 35.56 | 31.48 | 25.39 | 14.47 | 30.78 |
| Some College | 21.17 | 29.77 | 30.25 | 29.82 | 22.26 | 26.37 |
| Bachelor's Degree | 7.53 | 14.43 | 20.56 | 25.03 | 33.88 | 17.52 |
| Beyond Bach. Deb. | 2.86 | 5.42 | 9.44 | 14.74 | 26.86 | 9.48 |
| Total | 100.00 | 100.00 | 100.00 | 100.00 | 100.00 | 100.00 |

15.86% of the heads of households did not graduate from high school

**b.** 26.86%, 39.72%

**34. a.**

| Sales/ Margins/ ROE | EPS Rating | | | | | |
|---|---|---|---|---|---|---|
| | 0–19 | 20–39 | 40–59 | 60–79 | 80–100 | Total |
| A | | | | 1 | 8 | 9 |
| B | | 1 | 4 | 5 | 2 | 12 |
| C | 1 | | 1 | 2 | 3 | 7 |
| D | 3 | 1 | | 1 | | 5 |
| E | | 2 | 1 | | | 3 |
| Total | 4 | 4 | 6 | 9 | 13 | 36 |

**b.**

| Sales/ Margins/ ROE | EPS Rating | | | | | |
|---|---|---|---|---|---|---|
| | 0–19 | 20–39 | 40–59 | 60–79 | 80–100 | Total |
| A | | | | 11.11 | 88.89 | 100 |
| B | | 8.33 | 33.33 | 41.67 | 16.67 | 100 |
| C | 14.29 | | 14.29 | 28.57 | 42.86 | 100 |
| D | 60.00 | 20.00 | | 20.00 | | 100 |
| E | | 66.67 | 33.33 | | | 100 |

Higher EPS ratings seem to be associated with higher ratings on Sales/Margins/ROE

**36. b.** No apparent relationship

**38. a.**

| Vehicle | Frequency | Percent Frequency |
|---|---|---|
| F-Series | 17 | 34 |
| Silverado | 12 | 24 |
| Taurus | 8 | 16 |
| Camry | 7 | 14 |
| Accord | 6 | 12 |
| | 50 | 100 |

**b.** Ford F-Series Pickup and Chevrolet Silverado

**40. a.**

| Response | Frequency | Percent Frequency |
|---|---|---|
| Accuracy | 16 | 16 |
| Approach shots | 3 | 3 |
| Mental approach | 17 | 17 |
| Power | 8 | 8 |
| Practice | 15 | 15 |
| Putting | 10 | 10 |
| Short game | 24 | 24 |
| Strategic decisions | 7 | 7 |
| Total | 100 | 100 |

**b.** Poor short game, poor mental approach, lack of accuracy, and limited practice

**42. a/b.**

| Closing Price | Freq. | Rel. Freq. | Cum. Freq. | Cum. Rel. Freq. |
|---|---|---|---|---|
| 0–9.99 | 9 | .225 | 9 | .225 |
| 10–19.99 | 10 | .250 | 19 | .475 |
| 20–29.99 | 5 | .125 | 24 | .600 |
| 30–39.99 | 11 | .275 | 35 | .875 |
| 40–49.99 | 2 | .050 | 37 | .925 |
| 50–59.99 | 2 | .050 | 39 | .975 |
| 60–69.99 | 0 | .000 | 39 | .975 |
| 70–79.99 | 1 | .025 | 40 | 1.000 |
| Totals | 40 | 1.000 | | |

**44.**

| Income ($) | Frequency | Relative Frequency |
|---|---|---|
| 18,000–21,999 | 13 | 0.255 |
| 22,000–25,999 | 20 | 0.392 |
| 26,000–29,999 | 12 | 0.235 |
| 30,000–33,999 | 4 | 0.078 |
| 34,000–37,999 | 2 | 0.039 |
| Total | 51 | 1.000 |

**46. a. High Temperature**

```
3 |
4 |
5 | 7
6 | 1  4  4  4  4  6  8
7 | 3  5  7  9
8 | 0  1  1  4  6
9 | 0  2  3
```

**b. Low Temperature**

```
3 | 9
4 | 3  6  8
5 | 0  0  0  2  4  4  5  5  7  9
6 | 1  8
7 | 2  4  5  5
8 |
9 |
```

**c.** The range of low temperatures is below the range of high temperatures

**d.** 8 cities

**e.**

|  | Frequency | |
|---|---|---|
| Temperature | High Temp. | Low Temp. |
| 30–39 | 0 | 1 |
| 40–49 | 0 | 3 |
| 50–59 | 1 | 10 |
| 60–69 | 7 | 2 |
| 70–79 | 4 | 4 |
| 80–89 | 5 | 0 |
| 90–99 | 3 | 0 |
| Total | 20 | 20 |

**48. a.**

|  | Satisfaction Score | | | | | | |
|---|---|---|---|---|---|---|---|
| Occupation | 30–39 | 40–49 | 50–59 | 60–69 | 70–79 | 80–89 | Total |
| Cabinetmaker |  |  | 2 | 4 | 3 | 1 | 10 |
| Lawyer | 1 | 5 | 2 | 1 | 1 |  | 10 |
| Physical Therapist |  |  | 5 | 2 | 1 | 2 | 10 |
| Systems Analyst |  | 2 | 1 | 4 | 3 |  | 10 |
| Total | 1 | 7 | 10 | 11 | 8 | 3 | 40 |

**b.**

|  | Satisfaction Score | | | | | | |
|---|---|---|---|---|---|---|---|
| Occupation | 30–39 | 40–49 | 50–59 | 60–69 | 70–79 | 80–89 | Total |
| Cabinetmaker |  |  | 20 | 40 | 30 | 10 | 100 |
| Lawyer | 10 | 50 | 20 | 10 | 10 |  | 100 |
| Physical Therapist |  |  | 50 | 20 | 10 | 20 | 100 |
| Systems Analyst |  | 20 | 10 | 40 | 30 |  | 100 |

**c.** Cabinetmakers seem to have the highest job satisfaction scores; lawyers seem to have the lowest

**50. a.** Row totals: 247; 54; 82; 121
Column totals: 149; 317; 17; 7; 14

**b.**

| Year | Freq. | Fuel | Freq. |
|---|---|---|---|
| 1973 or before | 247 | Elect. | 149 |
| 1974–79 | 54 | Nat. Gas | 317 |
| 1980–86 | 82 | Oil | 17 |
| 1987–91 | 121 | Propane | 7 |
| Total | 504 | Other | 14 |
|  |  | Total | 504 |

**c.** Crosstabulation of column percentages

| Year Constructed | Fuel Type | | | | |
|---|---|---|---|---|---|
|  | Elect. | Nat. Gas | Oil | Propane | Other |
| 1973 or before | 26.9 | 57.7 | 70.5 | 71.4 | 50.0 |
| 1974–1979 | 16.1 | 8.2 | 11.8 | 28.6 | 0.0 |
| 1980–1986 | 24.8 | 12.0 | 5.9 | 0.0 | 42.9 |
| 1987–1991 | 32.2 | 22.1 | 11.8 | 0.0 | 7.1 |
| Total | 100.0 | 100.0 | 100.0 | 100.0 | 100.0 |

**d.** Crosstabulation of row percentages.

| Year Constructed | Fuel Type | | | | | |
|---|---|---|---|---|---|---|
|  | Elect. | Nat. Gas | Oil | Propane | Other | Total |
| 1973 or before | 16.2 | 74.1 | 4.9 | 2.0 | 2.8 | 100.0 |
| 1974–1979 | 44.5 | 48.1 | 3.7 | 3.7 | 0.0 | 100.0 |
| 1980–1986 | 45.1 | 46.4 | 1.2 | 0.0 | 7.3 | 100.0 |
| 1987–1991 | 39.7 | 57.8 | 1.7 | 0.0 | 0.8 | 100.0 |

**52. a.** Crosstabulation of market value and profit

| Market Value ($1000s) | Profit ($1000s) | | | | |
|---|---|---|---|---|---|
|  | 0–300 | 300–600 | 600–900 | 900–1200 | Total |
| 0–8000 | 23 | 4 |  |  | 27 |
| 8000–16,000 | 4 | 4 | 2 | 2 | 12 |
| 16,000–24,000 |  | 2 | 1 | 1 | 4 |
| 24,000–32,000 |  | 1 | 2 | 1 | 4 |
| 32,000–40,000 |  | 2 | 1 |  | 3 |
| Total | 27 | 13 | 6 | 4 | 50 |

**b.** Crosstabulation of row percentages

| Market Value ($1000s) | Profit ($1000s) | | | | |
|---|---|---|---|---|---|
|  | 0–300 | 300–600 | 600–900 | 900–1200 | Total |
| 0–8000 | 85.19 | 14.81 | 0.00 | 0.00 | 100 |
| 8000–16,000 | 33.33 | 33.33 | 16.67 | 16.67 | 100 |
| 16,000–24,000 | 0.00 | 50.00 | 25.00 | 25.00 | 100 |
| 24,000–32,000 | 0.00 | 25.00 | 50.00 | 25.00 | 100 |
| 32,000–40,000 | 0.00 | 66.67 | 33.33 | 0.00 | 100 |

**c.** A positive relationship is indicated between profit and market value; as profit goes up, market value goes up

**54. b.** A positive relationship is demonstrated between market value and stockholders' equity

# Chapter 3

**2.** 16, 16.5

**3.** Arrange data in order: 15, 20, 25, 25, 27, 28, 30, 34
$i = \dfrac{20}{100}(8) = 1.6$; round up to position 2

20th percentile = 20

$i = \dfrac{25}{100}(8) = 2$; use positions 2 and 3

25th percentile $= \dfrac{20 + 25}{2} = 22.5$

$i = \dfrac{65}{100}(8) = 5.2$; round up to position 6

65th percentile = 28

$i = \dfrac{75}{100}(8) = 6$; use positions 6 and 7

75th percentile $= \dfrac{28 + 30}{2} = 29$

**4.** 59.727, 57, 53

**6. a.** 36.32; 39.48; multimodal
   **b.** 20.46, 19.85, bimodal (19.95, 29.95)
   **c.** Broker-assisted trade
   **d.** More related to broker-assisted vs. online

**8. a.** $\bar{x} = \dfrac{\Sigma x_i}{n} = \dfrac{695}{20} = 34.75$

   Mode = 25 (appears three times)

   **b.** Data in order: 18, 20, 25, 25, 25, 26, 27, 27, 28, 33, 36, 37, 40, 40, 42, 45, 46, 48, 53, 54

   Median (10th and 11th positions)

   $\dfrac{33 + 36}{2} = 34.5$

   At home workers are slightly younger

   **c.** $i = \dfrac{25}{100}(20) = 5$; use positions 5 and 6

   $Q_1 = \dfrac{25 + 26}{2} = 25.5$

   $i = \dfrac{75}{100}(20) = 15$; use positions 15 and 16

   $Q_3 = \dfrac{42 + 45}{2} = 43.5$

   **d.** $i = \dfrac{32}{100}(20) = 6.4$; round up to position 7

   32nd percentile = 27
   At least 32% of the people are 27 or younger

**10. a.** 48.33, 49; do not report a mode
    **b.** 45, 55

**12. a.** \$639
    **b.** 98.8 pictures
    **c.** 110.2 minutes

**14.** 16, 4

**15.** Range = 34 − 15 = 19
    Arrange data in order: 15, 20, 25, 25, 27, 28, 30, 34

    $i = \dfrac{25}{100}(8) = 2$; $Q_1 = \dfrac{20 + 25}{2} = 22.5$

    $i = \dfrac{75}{100}(8) = 6$; $Q_3 = \dfrac{28 + 30}{2} = 29$

IQR $= Q_3 - Q_1 = 29 - 22.5 = 6.5$

$\bar{x} = \dfrac{\Sigma x_i}{n} = \dfrac{204}{8} = 25.5$

| $x_i$ | $(x_i - \bar{x})$ | $(x_i - \bar{x})^2$ |
|---|---|---|
| 27 | 1.5 | 2.25 |
| 25 | −.5 | .25 |
| 20 | −5.5 | 30.25 |
| 15 | −10.5 | 110.25 |
| 30 | 4.5 | 20.25 |
| 34 | 8.5 | 72.25 |
| 28 | 2.5 | 6.25 |
| 25 | −.5 | .25 |
|  |  | 242.00 |

$s^2 = \dfrac{\Sigma(x_i - \bar{x})^2}{n - 1} = \dfrac{242}{8 - 1} = 34.57$

$s = \sqrt{34.57} = 5.88$

**16. a.** Range = 190 − 168 = 22

   **b.** $\bar{x} = \dfrac{\Sigma x_i}{n} = \dfrac{1068}{6} = 178$

   $s^2 = \dfrac{\Sigma(x_i - \bar{x})^2}{n - 1}$

   $= \dfrac{4^2 + (-10)^2 + 6^2 + 12^2 + (-8)^2 + (-4)^2}{6 - 1}$

   $= \dfrac{376}{5} = 75.2$

   **c.** $s = \sqrt{75.2} = 8.67$

   **d.** $\dfrac{s}{\bar{x}}(100) = \dfrac{8.67}{178}(100\%) = 4.87\%$

**18. a.** Mainland: 115.13; 111.56
       Asia: 36.62; 36.695
    **b.** Mainland: 86.24; 26.82; 23.30%
       Asia: 42.97; 11.40; 31.13%
    **c.** Greater mean and standard deviation for Mainland

**20.** *Dawson:* range = 2, s = .67
       *Clark:* range = 8, s = 2.58

**22. a.** 45.05, 23.98; 57.50, 11.475
    **b.** 190.67, 13.81; 140.63, 11.86
    **c.** 38.02%; 57.97%
    **d.** Greater for broker-assisted trades

**24.** *Quarter-milers:* s = .0564, Coef. of Var. = 5.8%
       *Milers:* s = .1295, Coef. of Var. = 2.9%

**26.** .20, 1.50, 0, −.50, −2.20

**27.** Chebyshev's theorem: *at least* $(1 - 1/z^2)$

   **a.** $z = \dfrac{40 - 30}{5} = 2$; $1 - \dfrac{1}{(2)^2} = .75$

   **b.** $z = \dfrac{45 - 30}{5} = 3$; $1 - \dfrac{1}{(3)^2} = .89$

**c.** $z = \dfrac{38 - 30}{5} = 1.6; \ 1 - \dfrac{1}{(1.6)^2} = .61$

**d.** $z = \dfrac{42 - 30}{5} = 2.4; \ 1 - \dfrac{1}{(2.4)^2} = .83$

**e.** $z = \dfrac{48 - 30}{5} = 3.6; \ 1 - \dfrac{1}{(3.6)^2} = .92$

**28. a.** 95%
   **b.** Almost all
   **c.** 68%

**30. a.** 34%
   **b.** 81.5%
   **c.** 16%

**32. a.** −.95
   **b.** 3.90
   **c.** Labor cost in part (b) is an outlier

**34. a.** 100; 13.88 or approximately 14
   **b.** 16%
   **c.** 11.1 and 10.77; no outliers

**36.** 15, 22.5, 26, 29, 34

**38.** Arrange data in order: 5, 6, 8, 10, 10, 12, 15, 16, 18

$i = \dfrac{25}{100}(9) = 2.25$; round up to position 3

$Q_1 = 8$

Median (5th position) = 10

$i = \dfrac{75}{100}(9) = 6.75$; round up to position 7

$Q_3 = 15$

5-number summary: 5, 8, 10, 15, 18

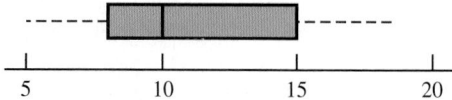

**40. a.** 5, 9.6, 14.5, 19.2, 52.7
   **b.** Limits: −4.8, 33.6
   **c.** 41.6 is an outlier
       52.7 is an outlier

**41. a.** Arrange data in order low to high

$i = \dfrac{25}{100}(21) = 5.25$; round up to 6th position

$Q_1 = 1872$

Median (11th position) = 4019

$i = \dfrac{75}{100}(21) = 15.75$; round up to 16th position

$Q_3 = 8305$

5-number summary: 608, 1872, 4019, 8305, 14138
   **b.** IQR $= Q_3 - Q_1 = 8305 - 1872 = 6433$
     Lower limit: $1872 - 1.5(6433) = -7777$
     Upper limit: $8305 + 1.5(6433) = 17{,}955$
   **c.** No; data are within limits

**d.** $41{,}138 > 27{,}604$; $41{,}138$ would be an outlier; data value would be reviewed and corrected

**e.**

**42. a.** 105.7933, 52.7
   **b.** 15.7, 78.3
   **c.** Silicon Graphics, Toys R Us
   **d.** 26.73; much greater

**44. a.** 37.48, 23.67
   **b.** 7.91, 51.92
   **c.** Limits: −58.11, 117.94
     Russia and Turkey are outliers

**45. b.** There appears to be a negative linear relationship between $x$ and $y$
   **c.**

| $x_i$ | $y_i$ | $x_i - \bar{x}$ | $y_i - \bar{y}$ | $(x_i - \bar{x})(y_i - \bar{y})$ |
|---|---|---|---|---|
| 4 | 50 | −4 | 4 | −16 |
| 6 | 50 | −2 | 4 | −8 |
| 11 | 40 | 3 | −6 | −18 |
| 3 | 60 | −5 | 14 | −70 |
| 16 | 30 | 8 | −16 | −128 |
| 40 | 230 | 0 | 0 | −240 |

$\bar{x} = 8; \ \bar{y} = 46$

$s_{xy} = \dfrac{\Sigma(x_i - \bar{x})(y_i - \bar{y})}{n - 1} = \dfrac{-240}{4} = -60$

The sample covariance indicates a negative linear association between $x$ and $y$

**d.** $r_{xy} = \dfrac{s_{xy}}{s_x s_y} = \dfrac{-60}{(5.43)(11.40)} = -.969$

The sample correlation coefficient of −.969 is indicative of a strong negative linear relationship

**46. b.** There appears to be a positive linear relationship between $x$ and $y$
   **c.** $s_{xy} = 26.5$
   **d.** $r_{xy} = .693$

**48.** −.91; negative relationship

**50. a.** .92
   **b.** Strong positive linear relationship

**52. a.** 3.69
   **b.** 3.175

**53. a.**

| $f_i$ | $M_i$ | $f_i M_i$ |
|---|---|---|
| 4 | 5 | 20 |
| 7 | 10 | 70 |
| 9 | 15 | 135 |
| 5 | 20 | 100 |
| 25 | | 325 |

$\bar{x} = \dfrac{\Sigma f_i M_i}{n} = \dfrac{325}{25} = 13$

**b.**

| $f_i$ | $M_i$ | $(M_i - \bar{x})$ | $(M_i - \bar{x})^2$ | $f_i(M_i - \bar{x})^2$ |
|---|---|---|---|---|
| 4 | 5 | $-8$ | 64 | 256 |
| 7 | 10 | $-3$ | 9 | 63 |
| 9 | 15 | 2 | 4 | 36 |
| 5 | 20 | 7 | 49 | 245 |
| 25 | | | | 600 |

$$s^2 = \frac{\Sigma f_i(M_i - \bar{x})^2}{n-1} = \frac{600}{25-1} = 25$$

$$s = \sqrt{25} = 5$$

**54. a.**

| Grade $x_i$ | Weight $w_i$ |
|---|---|
| 4 (A) | 9 |
| 3 (B) | 15 |
| 2 (C) | 33 |
| 1 (D) | 3 |
| 0 (F) | 0 |
| | 60 credit hours |

$$\bar{x} = \frac{\Sigma w_i x_i}{\Sigma w_i} = \frac{9(4) + 15(3) + 33(2) + 3(1)}{9 + 15 + 33 + 3}$$

$$= \frac{150}{60} = 2.5$$

**b.** Yes

**56.** 10.74, 25.63, 5.06; Estimate = 1288.8

**58. a.** 138.52, 129, 0
**b.** No, much more
**c.** 95, 169
**d.** 467, 74
**e.** 9271.01, 96.29
**f.** Significantly skewed to right
**g.** Yes, the $467 value

**60. a.** 18.57, 16.5
**b.** 53.49, 7.31
**c.** Quantex
**d.** 1.15
**e.** $-.90$
**f.** No

**62. a.** $\bar{x} = 83.135\ s = 16.173$
**b.** $50,789 to $115,481
**c.** Same range as in part (b); higher probability
**d.** Danbury, CT, is an outlier

**64. a.** 502.67; positive linear relationship
**b.** .933

**66. b.** .9856, strong positive relationship

**68. a.** 817
**b.** 833

**70. a.** 60.68
**b.** $s^2 = 31.23$; $s = 5.59$

# Chapter 4

**2.** $\binom{6}{3} = \frac{6!}{3!3!} = \frac{6 \cdot 5 \cdot 4 \cdot 3 \cdot 2 \cdot 1}{(3 \cdot 2 \cdot 1)(3 \cdot 2 \cdot 1)} = 20$

| | | | |
|---|---|---|---|
| ABC | ACE | BCD | BEF |
| ABD | ACF | BCE | CDE |
| ABE | ADE | BCF | CDF |
| ABF | ADF | BDE | CEF |
| ACD | AEF | BDF | DEF |

**4. b.** (H,H,H), (H,H,T), (H,T,H), (H,T,T),
(T,H,H), (T,H,T), (T,T,H), (T,T,T)
**c.** $\frac{1}{8}$

**6.** $P(E_1) = .40$, $P(E_2) = .26$, $P(E_3) = .34$
The relative frequency method was used

**8. a.** 4: Commission Positive—Council Approves
Commission Positive—Council Disapproves
Commission Negative—Council Approves
Commission Negative—Council Disapproves

**9.** $\binom{50}{4} = \frac{50!}{4!46!} = \frac{50 \cdot 49 \cdot 48 \cdot 47}{4 \cdot 3 \cdot 2 \cdot 1} = 230,300$

**10. a.** Use the relative frequency approach
$P(\text{California}) = 1,434/2,374 = .60$
**b.** Number not from four states
$= 2,374 - 1,434 - 390 - 217 - 112$
$= 221$
$P(\text{Not from 4 states}) = 221/2,374 = .09$
**c.** $P(\text{Not in early stages}) = 1 - .22 = .78$
**d.** Estimate of number of Massachusetts' companies in early stage of development $= (.22)390 \approx 86$
**e.** If we assume the size of the awards did not differ by state, we can multiply the probability an award went to Colorado by the total venture funds disbursed to get an estimate

Estimate of Colorado funds $= (112/2374)(\$32.4)$
$= \$1.53$ billion

Authors' Note: The actual amount going to Colorado was $1.74 billion

**12. a.** 2,869,685
**b.** 1/2,869,685
**c.** 1/120,526,770

**14. a.** $\frac{1}{4}$
**b.** $\frac{1}{2}$
**c.** $\frac{3}{4}$

**15. a.** $S = $ (ace of clubs, ace of diamonds, ace of hearts, ace of spades)
**b.** $S = $ (2 of clubs, 3 of clubs, . . . , 10 of clubs, J of clubs, Q of clubs, K of clubs, A of clubs)
**c.** There are 12; jack, queen, or king in each of the four suits
**d.** For (a): 4/52 = 1/13 = .08
For (b): 13/52 = 1/4 = .25
For (c): 12/52 = .23

**16. a.** 36
　**c.** $\frac{1}{6}$
　**d.** $\frac{5}{18}$
　**e.** No; $P(\text{odd}) = P(\text{even}) = \frac{1}{2}$
　**f.** Classical

**17. a.** (4, 6), (4, 7), (4, 8)
　**b.** $.05 + .10 + .15 = .30$
　**c.** (2, 8), (3, 8), (4, 8)
　**d.** $.05 + .05 + .15 = .25$
　**e.** .15

**18. a.** $P(0) = .05$
　**b.** $P(4 \text{ or } 5) = .20$
　**c.** $P(0, 1, \text{ or } 2) = .55$

**20. a.** .112
　**b.** .086
　**c.** .49

**22. a.** .40, .40, .60
　**b.** .80, yes
　**c.** $A^c = (E_3, E_4, E_5); C^c = (E_1, E_4);$
　　$P(A^c) = .60; P(C^c) = .40$
　**d.** $(E_1, E_2, E_5); .60$
　**e.** .80

**23. a.** $P(A) = P(E_1) + P(E_4) + P(E_6)$
　　　$= .05 + .25 + .10 = .40$
　　$P(B) = P(E_2) + P(E_4) + P(E_7)$
　　　$= .20 + .25 + .05 = .50$
　　$P(C) = P(E_2) + P(E_3) + P(E_5) + P(E_7)$
　　　$= .20 + .20 + .15 + .05 = .60$
　**b.** $A \cup B = \{E_1, E_2, E_4, E_6, E_7\};$
　　$P(A \cup B) = P(E_1) + P(E_2) + P(E_4) + P(E_6) + P(E_7)$
　　　$= .05 + .20 + .25 + .10 + .05$
　　　$= .65$
　**c.** $A \cap B = \{E_4\}; P(A \cap B) = P(E_4) = .25$
　**d.** Yes, they are mutually exclusive
　**e.** $B^c = \{E_1, E_3, E_5, E_6\};$
　　$P(B^c) = P(E_1) + P(E_3) + P(E_5) + P(E_6)$
　　　$= .05 + .20 + .15 + .10$
　　　$= .50$

**24. a.** .05
　**b.** .70

**26. a.** .30, .23
　**b.** .17
　**c.** .64

**28.** Let $B$ = rented a car for business reasons
　　　$P$ = rented a car for personal reasons
　**a.** $P(B \cup P) = P(B) + P(P) - P(B \cap P)$
　　　$= .540 + .458 - .300$
　　　$= .698$
　**b.** $P(\text{Neither}) = 1 - .698 = .302$

**30. a.** $P(A \mid B) = \dfrac{P(A \cap B)}{P(B)} = \dfrac{.40}{.60} = .6667$
　**b.** $P(B \mid A) = \dfrac{P(A \cap B)}{P(A)} = \dfrac{.40}{.50} = .80$
　**c.** No, because $P(A \mid B) \neq P(A)$

**32. a.**

|  | Single | Married | Total |
|---|---|---|---|
| **Under 30** | .55 | .10 | .65 |
| **30 or Over** | .20 | .15 | .35 |
| **Total** | .75 | .25 | 1.0 |

　**b.** Higher probability of under 30
　**c.** Higher probability of single
　**d.** .55
　**e.** .8462
　**f.** No

**33. a.**

Reason for Applying

|  | Quality | Cost/ Convenience | Other | Total |
|---|---|---|---|---|
| **Full-time** | .218 | .204 | .039 | .461 |
| **Part-time** | .208 | .307 | .024 | .539 |
| **Total** | .426 | .511 | .063 | 1.000 |

　**b.** A student is most likely to cite cost or convenience as the first reason (probability = .511); school quality is the reason cited by the second largest number of students (probability = .426)
　**c.** $P(\text{quality} \mid \text{full-time}) = .218/.461 = .473$
　**d.** $P(\text{quality} \mid \text{part-time}) = .208/.539 = .386$
　**e.** For independence, we must have $P(A)P(B) = P(A \cap B)$; from the table

　　$P(A \cap B) = .218, P(A) = .461, P(B) = .426$
　　$P(A)P(B) = (.461)(.426) = .196$

　　Because $P(A)P(B) \neq P(A \cap B)$, the events are not independent

**34. a.** .44
　**b.** .15
　**c.** .0225
　**d.** .0025
　**e.** .136
　**f.** .106

**36. b.** .075
　**c.** .20
　**d.** .25
　**e.** .15
　**f.** .60
　**g.** .275

**38. a.** .0209

**b.** .0141, .027

**c.** No

**d.** .0202, .0458

**e.** Yes

**39. a.** Yes, because $P(A_1 \cap A_2) = 0$

**b.** $P(A_1 \cap B) = P(A_1)P(B \mid A_1) = .40(.20) = .08$
$P(A_2 \cap B) = P(A_2)P(B \mid A_2) = .60(.05) = .03$

**c.** $P(B) = P(A_1 \cap B) + P(A_2 \cap B) = .08 + .03 = .11$

**d.** $P(A_1 \mid B) = \dfrac{.08}{.11} = .7273$

$P(A_2 \mid B) = \dfrac{.03}{.11} = .2727$

**40. a.** .10, .20, .09

**b.** .51

**c.** .26, .51, .23

**42.** $M =$ missed payment
$D_1 =$ customer defaults
$D_2 =$ customer does not default
$P(D_1) = .05, P(D_2) = .95, P(M \mid D_2) = .2, P(M \mid D_1) = 1$

**a.** $P(D_1 \mid M) = \dfrac{P(D_1)P(M \mid D_1)}{P(D_1)P(M \mid D_1) + P(D_2)P(M \mid D_2)}$

$= \dfrac{(.05)(1)}{(.05)(1) + (.95)(.2)}$

$= \dfrac{.05}{.24} = .21$

**b.** Yes, the probability of default is greater than .20

**44.** .6754

**46. a.** .68

**b.** 52

**c.** 10

**48. a.** 315

**b.** .29

**c.** No

**d.** Republicans

**50. a.** .76

**b.** .24

**52. b.** .2022

**c.** .4618

**d.** .4005

**54. a.** .49

**b.** .44

**c.** .54

**d.** No

**e.** Yes

**56. a.** .25

**b.** .125

**c.** .0125

**d.** .10

**e.** No

**58.** 3.44%

**60. a.** .40

**b.** .67

## Chapter 5

**1. a.** Head, Head $(H, H)$
Head, Tail $(H, T)$
Tail, Head $(T, H)$
Tail, Tail $(T, T)$

**b.** $x =$ number of heads on two coin tosses

**c.**

| Outcome | Values of $x$ |
|---------|---------------|
| $(H, H)$ | 2 |
| $(H, T)$ | 1 |
| $(T, H)$ | 1 |
| $(T, T)$ | 0 |

**d.** Discrete; it may assume 3 values: 0, 1, and 2

**2. a.** $x =$ time in minutes to assemble product

**b.** Any positive value: $x > 0$

**c.** Continuous

**3.** Let $Y =$ position is offered
$N =$ position is not offered

**a.** $S = \{(Y, Y, Y), (Y, Y, N), (Y, N, Y), (Y, N, N), (N, Y, Y),$
$(N, Y, N), (N, N, Y), (N, N, N)\}$

**b.** Let $N =$ number of offers made; $N$ is a discrete random variable

**c.**

| Experimental Outcome | $(Y, Y, Y)$ | $(Y, Y, N)$ | $(Y, N, Y)$ | $(Y, N, N)$ | $(N, Y, Y)$ | $(N, Y, N)$ | $(N, N, Y)$ | $(N, N, N)$ |
|---|---|---|---|---|---|---|---|---|
| Value of $N$ | 3 | 2 | 2 | 1 | 2 | 1 | 1 | 0 |

**4.** $x = 0, 1, 2, \ldots, 12$

**6. a.** $0, 1, 2, \ldots, 20$; discrete

**b.** $0, 1, 2, \ldots$; discrete

**c.** $0, 1, 2, \ldots, 50$; discrete

**d.** $0 \le x \le 8$; continuous

**e.** $x > 0$; continuous

**7. a.** $f(x) \ge 0$ for all values of $x$
$\Sigma f(x) = 1$; therefore, it is a valid probability distribution

**b.** Probability $x = 30$ is $f(30) = .25$

**c.** Probability $x \le 25$ is $f(20) + f(25) = .20 + .15 = .35$

**d.** Probability $x > 30$ is $f(35) = .40$

**8. a.**

| $x$ | $f(x)$ | |
|-----|--------|------|
| 1 | $3/20 =$ | .15 |
| 2 | $5/20 =$ | .25 |
| 3 | $8/20 =$ | .40 |
| 4 | $4/20 =$ | .20 |
| | Total | 1.00 |

**b.**

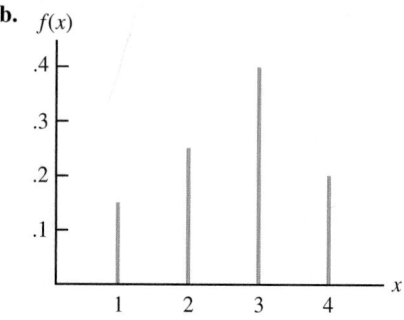

$f(x)$

**c.** $f(x) \geq 0$ for $x = 1, 2, 3, 4$
$\Sigma f(x) = 1$

**10. a.**

| $x$ | 1 | 2 | 3 | 4 | 5 |
|---|---|---|---|---|---|
| $f(x)$ | .05 | .09 | .03 | .42 | .41 |

**b.**

| $x$ | 1 | 2 | 3 | 4 | 5 |
|---|---|---|---|---|---|
| $f(x)$ | .04 | .10 | .12 | .46 | .28 |

**c.** .83
**d.** .28
**e.** Senior executives more satisfied

**12. a.** Yes
**b.** .65

**14. a.** .05
**b.** .70
**c.** .40

**16. a.**

| $y$ | $f(y)$ | $yf(y)$ |
|---|---|---|
| 2 | .20 | .40 |
| 4 | .30 | 1.20 |
| 7 | .40 | 2.80 |
| 8 | .10 | .80 |
| Totals | 1.00 | 5.20 |

$E(y) = \mu = 5.20$

**b.**

| $y$ | $y - \mu$ | $(y - \mu)^2$ | $f(y)$ | $(y - \mu)^2 f(y)$ |
|---|---|---|---|---|
| 2 | -3.20 | 10.24 | .20 | 2.048 |
| 4 | -1.20 | 1.44 | .30 | .432 |
| 7 | 1.80 | 3.24 | .40 | 1.296 |
| 8 | 2.80 | 7.84 | .10 | .784 |
| | | | Total | 4.560 |

$Var(y) = 4.56$

$\sigma = \sqrt{4.56} = 2.14$

**18. a/b.**

| $x$ | $f(x)$ | $xf(x)$ | $x - \mu$ | $(x - \mu)^2$ | $(x - \mu)^2 f(x)$ |
|---|---|---|---|---|---|
| 0 | 0.04 | 0.00 | -1.84 | 3.39 | 0.12 |
| 1 | 0.34 | 0.34 | -0.84 | 0.71 | 0.24 |
| 2 | 0.41 | 0.82 | 0.16 | 0.02 | 0.01 |
| 3 | 0.18 | 0.53 | 1.16 | 1.34 | 0.24 |
| 4 | 0.04 | 0.15 | 2.16 | 4.66 | 0.17 |
| Total | 1.00 | 1.84 | | | 0.79 |
| | | ↑ | | | ↑ |
| | | $E(x)$ | | | $Var(x)$ |

**c/d.**

| $y$ | $f(y)$ | $yf(y)$ | $y - \mu$ | $(y - \mu)^2$ | $y - \mu)^2 f(y)$ |
|---|---|---|---|---|---|
| 0 | 0.00 | 0.00 | -2.93 | 8.58 | 0.01 |
| 1 | 0.03 | 0.03 | -1.93 | 3.72 | 0.12 |
| 2 | 0.23 | 0.45 | -0.93 | 0.86 | 0.20 |
| 3 | 0.52 | 1.55 | 0.07 | 0.01 | 0.00 |
| 4 | 0.22 | 0.90 | 1.07 | 1.15 | 0.26 |
| Total | 1.00 | 2.93 | | | 0.59 |
| | | ↑ | | | ↑ |
| | | $E(y)$ | | | $Var(y)$ |

**e.** The number of bedrooms in owner-occupied houses is greater than in renter-occupied houses; the expected number of bedrooms is $1.09 = 2.93 - 1.84$ greater and the variability in the number of bedrooms is less for the owner-occupied houses

**20. a.** 166
**b.** -94; concern is to protect against the expense of a big accident

**22. a.** 445
**b.** 1250 loss

**24. a.** Medium: 145; large: 140
**b.** Medium: 2725; large: 12,400

**25. a.**

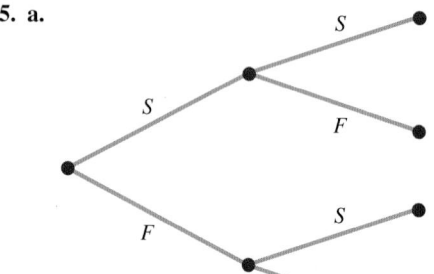

**b.** $f(1) = \binom{2}{1}(.4)^1(.6)^1 = \dfrac{2!}{1!1!}(.4)(.6) = .48$

**c.** $f(0) = \binom{2}{0}(.4)^0(.6)^2 = \dfrac{2!}{0!2!}(1)(.36) = .36$

**d.** $f(2) = \binom{2}{2}(.4)^2(.6)^0 = \dfrac{2!}{2!0!}(.16)(.1) = .16$

**e.** $P(x \geq 1) = f(1) + f(2) = .48 + .16 = .64$

**f.**  $E(x) = np = 2(.4) = .8$
$\text{Var}(x) = np(1 - p) = 2(.4)(.6) = .48$
$\sigma = \sqrt{.48} = .6928$

**26. a.** $f(0) = .3487$

  **b.** $f(2) = .1937$

  **c.** $.9298$

  **d.** $.6513$

  **e.** $1$

  **f.** $\sigma^2 = .9000, \sigma = .9487$

**28. a.** $.3292$

  **b.** $.6422$

  **c.** $.0182$

**30. a.** Probability of a defective part being produced must be .03 for each part selected; parts must be selected independently

  **b.** Let $D$ = defective
   $G$ = not defective

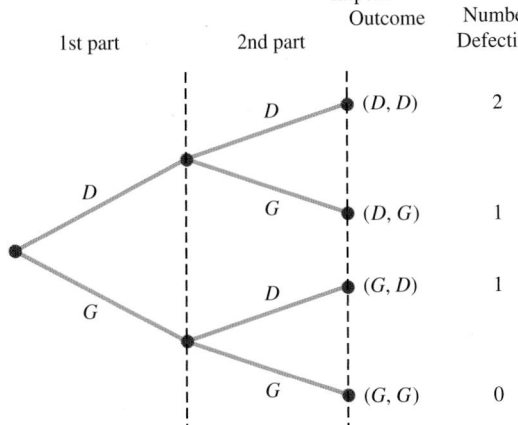

| 1st part | 2nd part | Experimental Outcome | Number Defective |
|---|---|---|---|

(see tree diagram)
$D$ — $D$ → $(D, D)$    2
$D$ — $G$ → $(D, G)$    1
$G$ — $D$ → $(G, D)$    1
$G$ — $G$ → $(G, G)$    0

  **c.** Two outcomes result in exactly one defect

  **d.** $P(\text{no defects}) = (.97)(.97) = .9409$
$P(1 \text{ defect}) = 2(.03)(.97) = .0582$
$P(2 \text{ defects}) = (.03)(.03) = .0009$

**32. a.** $.90$

  **b.** $.99$

  **c.** $.999$

  **d.** Yes

**34. a.** $.0634$

  **b.** $.0634$

  **c.** $.9729$

**38. a.** $f(x) = \dfrac{3^x e^{-3}}{x!}$

  **b.** $.2241$

  **c.** $.1494$

  **d.** $.8008$

**39. a.** $f(x) = \dfrac{2^x e^{-2}}{x!}$

  **b.** $\mu = 6$ for 3 time periods

  **c.** $f(x) = \dfrac{6^x e^{-6}}{x!}$

  **d.** $f(2) = \dfrac{2^2 e^{-2}}{2!} = \dfrac{4(.1353)}{2} = .2706$

  **e.** $f(6) = \dfrac{6^6 e^{-6}}{6!} = .1606$

  **f.** $f(5) = \dfrac{4^5 e^{-4}}{5!} = .1563$

**40. a.**   $\mu = 48(5/60) = 4$
$f(3) = \dfrac{4^3 e^{-4}}{3!} = \dfrac{(64)(.0183)}{6} = .1952$

  **b.**   $\mu = 48(15/60) = 12$
$f(10) = \dfrac{12^{10} e^{-12}}{10!} = .1048$

  **c.**   $\mu = 48(5/60) = 4$; one can expect four callers to be waiting after 5 minutes
$f(0) = \dfrac{4^0 e^{-4}}{0!} = .0183$; the probability none will be waiting after 5 minutes is .0183

  **d.**   $\mu = 48(3/60) = 2.4$
$f(0) = \dfrac{2.4^0 e^{-2.4}}{0!} = .0907$; the probability of no interruptions in 3 minutes is .0907

**42. a.** $f(0) = \dfrac{7^0 e^{-7}}{0!} = e^{-7} = .0009$

  **b.** probability $= 1 - [f(0) + f(1)]$
$f(1) = \dfrac{7^1 e^{-7}}{1!} = 7e^{-7} = .0064$
probability $= 1 - [.0009 + .0064] = .9927$

  **c.** $\mu = 3.5$
$f(0) = \dfrac{3.5^0 e^{-3.5}}{0!} = e^{-3.5} = .0302$
probability $= 1 - f(0) = 1 - .0302 = .9698$

  **d.**
probability $= 1 - [f(0) + f(1) + f(2) + f(3) + f(4)]$
$= 1 - [.0009 + .0064 + .0223 + .0521 + .0912]$
$= .8271$

**44. a.** $\mu = 1.25$

  **b.** $.2865$

  **c.** $.3581$

  **d.** $.3554$

**46. a.** $f(1) = \dfrac{\binom{3}{1}\binom{10-3}{4-1}}{\binom{10}{4}} = \dfrac{\left(\frac{3!}{1!2!}\right)\left(\frac{7!}{3!4!}\right)}{\frac{10!}{4!6!}}$

$= \dfrac{(3)(35)}{210} = .50$

**b.** $f(2) = \dfrac{\binom{3}{2}\binom{10-3}{2-2}}{\binom{10}{2}} = \dfrac{(3)(1)}{45} = .067$

**c.** $f(0) = \dfrac{\binom{3}{0}\binom{10-3}{2-0}}{\binom{10}{2}} = \dfrac{(1)(21)}{45} = .4667$

**d.** $f(2) = \dfrac{\binom{3}{2}\binom{10-3}{4-2}}{\binom{10}{4}} = \dfrac{(3)(21)}{210} = .30$

**48. a.** .50

  **b.** .3333

**50.** $N = 60, n = 10$

  **a.** $r = 20, x = 0$

$f(0) = \dfrac{\binom{20}{0}\binom{40}{10}}{\binom{60}{10}} = \dfrac{(1)\left(\frac{40!}{10!30!}\right)}{\frac{60!}{10!50!}}$

$= \left(\dfrac{40!}{10!30!}\right)\left(\dfrac{10!50!}{60!}\right)$

$= \dfrac{40\cdot39\cdot38\cdot37\cdot36\cdot35\cdot34\cdot33\cdot32\cdot31}{60\cdot59\cdot58\cdot57\cdot56\cdot55\cdot54\cdot53\cdot52\cdot51}$

$\approx .01$

  **b.** $r = 20, x = 1$

$f(1) = \dfrac{\binom{20}{1}\binom{40}{9}}{\binom{60}{10}} = 20\left(\dfrac{40!}{9!31!}\right)\left(\dfrac{10!50!}{60!}\right)$

$\approx .07$

  **c.** $1 - f(0) - f(1) = 1 - .08 = .92$

  **d.** Same as the probability one will be from Hawaii; in part (b) it was equal to approximately .07

**52. a.** .5333

  **b.** .6667

  **c.** .7778

  **d.** $n = 7$

**54. a.**

| $x$ | 1 | 2 | 3 | 4 | 5 |
|-----|-----|-----|-----|-----|-----|
| $f(x)$ | .24 | .21 | .10 | .21 | .24 |

  **b.** 3.00, 2.34

  **c.** Bonds: $E(x) = 1.36$, $\text{Var}(x) = .23$

   Stocks: $E(x) = 4$, $\text{Var}(x) = 1$

**56. a.** .0364

  **b.** .4420

**c.** 48

**d.** 6.7882

**58. a.** .9510

  **b.** .0480

  **c.** .0490

**60. a.** 328

  **b.** 13.91

  **c.** 13.91

**62.** .1912

**64. a.** .2240

  **b.** .5767

**66. a.** .4667

  **b.** .4667

  **c.** .0667

# Chapter 6

**1. a.**

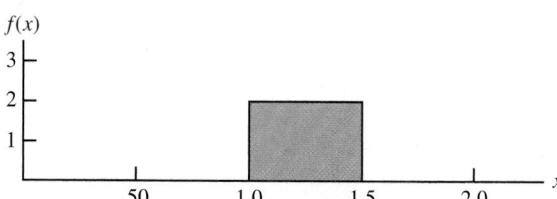

  **b.** $P(x = 1.25) = 0$; the probability of any single point is zero because the area under the curve above any single point is zero

  **c.** $P(1.0 \le x \le 1.25) = 2(.25) = .50$

  **d.** $P(1.20 < x < 1.5) = 2(.30) = .60$

**2. b.** .50

  **c.** .60

  **d.** 15

  **e.** 8.33

**4. a.**

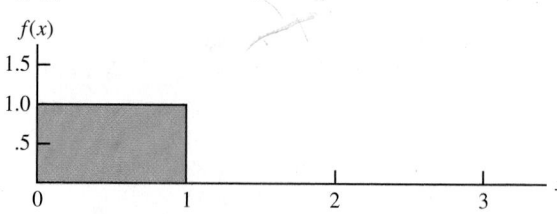

  **b.** $P(.25 < x < .75) = 1(.50) = .50$

  **c.** $P(x \le .30) = 1(.30) = .30$

  **d.** $P(x > .60) = 1(.40) = .40$

**6. a.** .40

  **b.** .64

  **c.** .68

**10. a.** .3413

  **b.** .4332

  **c.** .4772

  **d.** .4938

**12. a.** .2967
 **b.** .4418
 **c.** .3300
 **d.** .5910
 **e.** .8849
 **f.** .2389

**13. a.** $.6879 - .0239 = .6640$
 **b.** $.8888 - .6985 = .1903$
 **c.** $.9599 - .8508 = .1091$

**14. a.** $z = 1.96$
 **b.** $z = .61$
 **c.** $z = 1.12$
 **d.** $z = .44$

**15. a.** Look in the table for an area of $.5000 - .2119 = .2881$; $z = .80$ cuts off an area of .2119 in the upper tail. Thus, for an area of .2119 in the lower tail, $z = -.80$
 **b.** Look in the table for an area of $.9030/2 = .4515$; $z = 1.66$
 **c.** Look in the table for an area of $.2052/2 = .1026$; $z = .26$
 **d.** Look in the table for an area of $.4948$; $z = 2.56$
 **e.** Look in the table for an area of $.1915$; because the value we are seeking is below the mean, the $z$ value must be negative; thus, $z = -.50$

**16. a.** $z = 2.33$
 **b.** $z = 1.96$
 **c.** $z = 1.645$
 **d.** $z = 1.28$

**18.** $\mu = 30$ and $\sigma = 8.2$

 **a.** At $x = 40$, $z = \dfrac{40 - 30}{8.2} = 1.22$

 $P(z \le 1.22) = .5000 + .3888 = .8888$
 $P(x \ge 40) = 1.000 - .8888 = .1112$

 **b.** At $x = 20$, $z = \dfrac{20 - 30}{8.2} = -1.22$

 $P(z > -1.22) = .5000 + .3888 = .8888$
 $P(x \le 20) = 1.0000 - .8888 = .1112$

 **c.** A $z$-value of 1.28 cuts off an area of approximately 10% in the upper tail
 $x = 30 + 8.2(1.28)$
 $\quad = 40.50$
 A stock price of $40.50 or higher will put a company in the top 10%

**20. a.** .0885
 **b.** 12.51%
 **c.** 93.8 hours or more

**22. a.** .4194
 **b.** $517.44 or more
 **c.** .0166

**24. a.** 902.75, 114.185
 **b.** .1841
 **c.** .1977
 **d.** 1,091 million

**26. a.** $\mu = np = 100(.20) = 20$
 $\sigma^2 = np(1 - p) = 100(.20)(.80) = 16$
 $\sigma = \sqrt{16} = 4$

 **b.** Yes, because $np = 20$ and $n(1 - p) = 80$
 **c.** $P(23.5 \le x \le 24.5)$

 $z = \dfrac{24.5 - 20}{4} = +1.13 \qquad \text{Area} = .3708$

 $z = \dfrac{23.5 - 20}{4} = +.88 \qquad \text{Area} = .3106$

 $P(23.5 \le x \le 24.5) = .3708 - .3106 = .0602$
 **d.** $P(17.5 \le x \le 22.5)$

 $z = \dfrac{17.5 - 20}{4} = -.63 \qquad \text{Area} = .2357$

 $z = \dfrac{22.5 - 20}{4} = +.63 \qquad \text{Area} = .2357$

 $P(17.5 \le x \le 22.5) = .2357 + .2357 = .4714$
 **e.** $P(x \le 15.5)$

 $z = \dfrac{15.5 - 20}{4} = -1.13 \qquad \text{Area} = .3708$

 $P(x \le 15.5) = .5000 - .3708 = .1292$

**28. a.** .1867
 **b.** 125
 **c.** It's a toss up

**30. a.** 328
 **b.** .0239
 **c.** .9394

**32. a.** .5276
 **b.** .3935
 **c.** .4724
 **d.** .1341

**33. a.** $P(x \le x_0) = 1 - e^{-x_0/3}$
 **b.** $P(x \le 2) = 1 - e^{-2/3} = 1 - .5134 = .4866$
 **c.** $P(x \ge 3) = 1 - P(x \le 3) = 1 - (1 - e^{-3/3})$
 $\qquad = e^{-1} = .3679$
 **d.** $P(x \le 5) = 1 - e^{-5/3} = 1 - .1889 = .8111$
 **e.** $P(2 \le x \le 5) = P(x \le 5) - P(x \le 2)$
 $\qquad\qquad = .8111 - .4866 = .3245$

**34. a.** .3935
 **b.** .2231
 **c.** .3834

**35. a.**

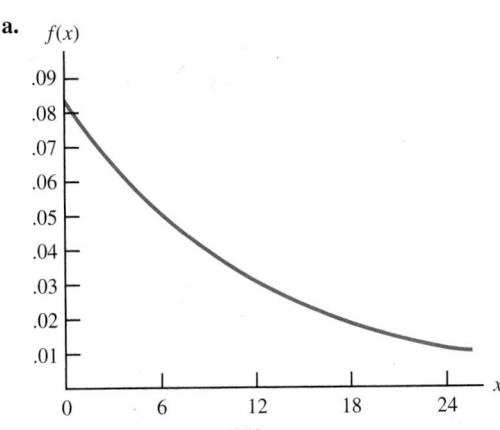

**b.** $P(x \le 12) = 1 - e^{-12/12} = 1 - .3679 = .6321$

**c.** $P(x \leq 6) = 1 - e^{-6/12} = 1 - .6065 = .3935$

**d.** $P(x \geq 30) = 1 - P(x < 30)$
$$= 1 - (1 - e^{-30/12})$$
$$= .0821$$

**36. a.** 50 hours
   **b.** .3935
   **c.** .1353

**38. a.** $f(x) = 30e^{-30x}$
   **b.** .0821
   **c.** .7135

**40. a.** $63,000
   **b.** $43,800 or less
   **c.** 12.92%
   **d.** $87,675

**42. a.** 3229
   **b.** .2244
   **c.** $12,382 or more

**44. a.** .0228
   **b.** $50

**46. a.** 38.3%
   **b.** 3.59% better, 96.41% worse
   **c.** 38.21%

**48.** $\mu = 19.23$ ounces

**50. a.** Lose $240
   **b.** .1788
   **c.** .3557
   **d.** .0594

**52. a.** $\frac{1}{7}$ minute
   **b.** $7e^{-7x}$
   **c.** .0009
   **d.** .2466

**54. a.** 2 minutes
   **b.** .2212
   **c.** .3935
   **d.** .0821

## Chapter 7

**1. a.** AB, AC, AD, AE, BC, BD, BE, CD, CE, DE
   **b.** With 10 samples, each has a $\frac{1}{10}$ probability
   **c.** E and C because 8 and 0 do not apply; 5 identifies E; 7 does not apply; 5 is skipped because E is already in the sample; 3 identifies C; 2 is not needed because the sample of size 2 is complete

**2.** 22, 147, 229, 289

**3.** 459, 147, 385, 113, 340, 401, 215, 2, 33, 348

**4. a.** Nasdaq 100, Oracle, Microsoft, Lucent, Applied Materials
   **b.** 252

**6.** 2782, 493, 825, 1807, 289

**8.** Maryland, Iowa, Florida State, Virginia, Pittsburgh, Oklahoma

**10.** Finite, infinite, infinite, infinite, finite

**11. a.** $\bar{x} = \dfrac{\Sigma x_i}{n} = \dfrac{54}{6} = 9$

   **b.** $s = \sqrt{\dfrac{\Sigma(x_i - \bar{x})^2}{n-1}}$

$\Sigma(x_i - \bar{x})^2 = (-4)^2 + (-1)^2 + 1^2 + (-2)^2 + 1^2 + 5^2$
$$= 48$$

$$s = \sqrt{\dfrac{48}{6-1}} = 3.1$$

**12. a.** .50
   **b.** .3667

**13. a.** $\bar{x} = \dfrac{\Sigma x_i}{n} = \dfrac{465}{5} = 93$

   **b.**

| $x_i$ | $(x_i - \bar{x})$ | $(x_i - \bar{x})^2$ |
|---|---|---|
| 94 | +1 | 1 |
| 100 | +7 | 49 |
| 85 | −8 | 64 |
| 94 | +1 | 1 |
| 92 | −1 | 1 |
| Totals 465 | 0 | 116 |

$$s = \sqrt{\dfrac{\Sigma(x_i - \bar{x})^2}{n-1}} = \sqrt{\dfrac{116}{4}} = 5.39$$

**14. a.** .19
   **b.** .32
   **c.** .79

**16.** .80

**18. a.** 200
   **b.** 5
   **c.** Normal with $E(\bar{x}) = 200$ and $\sigma_{\bar{x}} = 5$
   **d.** The probability distribution of $\bar{x}$

**19. a.** The sampling distribution is normal with:
$$E(\bar{x}) = \mu = 200$$
$$\sigma_{\bar{x}} = \dfrac{\sigma}{\sqrt{n}} = \dfrac{50}{\sqrt{100}} = 5$$
For $+5$, $(\bar{x} - \mu) = 5$,
$$z = \dfrac{\bar{x} - \mu}{\sigma_{\bar{x}}} = \dfrac{5}{5} = 1$$
Area $= 2(.3413) = .6826$

   **b.** For $\pm 10$, $(\bar{x} - \mu) = 10$,
$$z = \dfrac{\bar{x} - \mu}{\sigma_{\bar{x}}} = \dfrac{10}{5} = 2$$
Area $= 2(.4772) = .9544$

**20.** 3.54, 2.50, 2.04, 1.77
$\sigma_{\bar{x}}$ decreases as $n$ increases

**22. a.** Normal with $E(\bar{x}) = 51,800$ and $\sigma_{\bar{x}} = 516.40$

  **b.** $\sigma_{\bar{x}}$ decreases to 365.15

  **c.** $\sigma_{\bar{x}}$ decreases as $n$ increases

**23. a.**

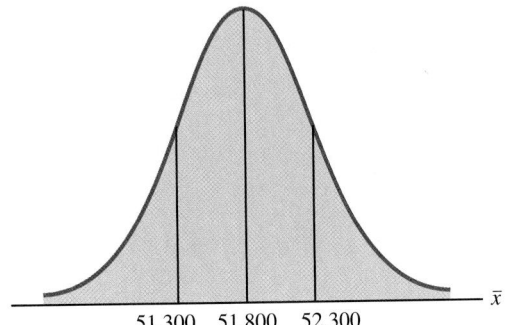

$$\sigma_{\bar{x}} = \frac{\sigma}{\sqrt{n}} = \frac{4000}{\sqrt{60}} = 516.40$$

$$z = \frac{52,300 - 51,800}{516.40} = +.97$$

Area = 2(.3340) = .6680

  **b.** $\sigma_{\bar{x}} = \dfrac{\sigma}{\sqrt{n}} = \dfrac{4000}{\sqrt{120}} = 365.15$

$$z = \frac{52,300 - 51,800}{365.15} = +1.37$$

Area = 2(.4147) = .8294

**24. a.** Normal with $E(\bar{x}) = 4260$ and $\sigma_{\bar{x}} = 127.28$

  **b.** .95

  **c.** .5704

**26. a.** .5034, .6212, .7888, .9232, .9876

  **b.** Higher probability within ±250

**28. a.** Normal with $E(\bar{x}) = 687$ and $\sigma_{\bar{x}} = 34.29$

  **b.** .9964

  **c.** .5346

  **d.** Increase the sample size

**30. a.** $n/N = .01$; no

  **b.** 1.29, 1.30; little difference

  **c.** .8764

**32. a.** $E(\bar{p}) = .40$

$$\sigma_{\bar{p}} = \sqrt{\frac{p(1-p)}{n}} = \sqrt{\frac{(.40)(.60)}{200}} = .0346$$

$$z = \frac{\bar{p} - p}{\sigma_{\bar{p}}} = \frac{.03}{.0346} = .87$$

Area = 2(.3078) = .6156

  **b.** $z = \dfrac{\bar{p} - p}{\sigma_{\bar{p}}} = \dfrac{.05}{.0346} = 1.44$

Area = 2(.4251) = .8502

**34. a.** .6156

  **b.** .7814

  **c.** .9488

  **d.** .9942

  **e.** Higher probability with larger $n$

**35. a.**

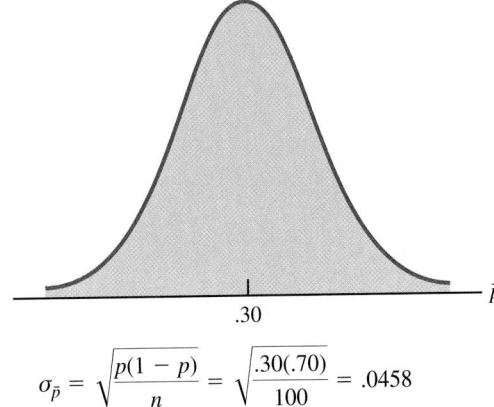

$$\sigma_{\bar{p}} = \sqrt{\frac{p(1-p)}{n}} = \sqrt{\frac{.30(.70)}{100}} = .0458$$

The normal distribution is appropriate because $np = 100(.30) = 30$ and $n(1-p) = 100(.70) = 70$ are both greater than 5

  **b.** $P(.20 \le \bar{p} \le .40) = ?$

$$z = \frac{.40 - .30}{.0458} = 2.18$$

Area = 2(.4854) = .9708

  **c.** $P(.25 \le \bar{p} \le .35) = ?$

$$z = \frac{.35 - .30}{.0458} = 1.09$$

Area = 2(.3621) = .7242

**36. a.** Normal with $E(\bar{p}) = .56$ and $\sigma_{\bar{p}} = .0287$

  **b.** .7062

  **c.** .8612, .9438

**38. a.** Normal with $E(\bar{p}) = .25$ and $\sigma_{\bar{p}} = .0306$

  **b.** .6730

  **c.** .8968

**40. a.** Normal with $E(\bar{p}) = .76$ and $\sigma_{\bar{p}} = .0214$

  **b.** .8384

  **c.** .9452

**42.** 112, 145, 73, 324, 293, 875, 318, 618

**44. a.** Normal with $E(\bar{x}) = 31.5$ and $\sigma_{\bar{x}} = 1.70$

  **b.** .4448

  **c.** .9232

**46. a.** 707

  **b.** .50

  **c.** .8414

  **d.** .9544

**48. a.** 625

  **b.** .7888

**50. a.** Normal with $E(\bar{p}) = .305$ and $\sigma_{\bar{p}} = .0326$

  **b.** .7814

  **c.** .4582

**52. a.** .9606

  **b.** .0495

**54. a.** 48

  **b.** Normal, $E(\bar{p}) = .25$, $\sigma_{\bar{p}} = .0625$

  **c.** .2119

## Chapter 8

**2.** Use $\bar{x} \pm z_{\alpha/2}(\sigma/\sqrt{n})$

  **a.** $32 \pm 1.645\,(6/\sqrt{50})$

    $32 \pm 1.4$; 30.6 to 33.4

  **b.** $32 \pm 1.96(6/\sqrt{50})$

    $32 \pm 1.66$; 30.34 to 33.66

  **c.** $32 \pm 2.576(6/\sqrt{50})$

    $32 \pm 2.19$; 29.81 to 34.19

**4.** 54

**5. a.** $1.96\sigma/\sqrt{n} = 1.96(5/\sqrt{49}) = 1.40$

  **b.** $24.80 \pm 1.40$; 23.40 to 26.20

**6.** 8.1 to 8.9

**8. a.** Population is at least approximately normal

  **b.** 3.1

  **c.** 4.1

**10. a.** 11,769 to 12,231

  **b.** 11,725 to 12,275

  **c.** 11,638 to 12,362

  **d.** Width increases to be more confident

**12. a.** 2.179

  **b.** $-1.676$

  **c.** 2.457

  **d.** $-1.708$ and 1.708

  **e.** $-2.014$ and 2.014

**13. a.** $\bar{x} = \dfrac{\Sigma x_i}{n} = \dfrac{80}{8} = 10$

  **b.** $s = \sqrt{\dfrac{\Sigma(x_i - \bar{x})^2}{n-1}} = \sqrt{\dfrac{84}{7}} = 3.46$

  **c.** $t_{.025}\left(\dfrac{s}{\sqrt{n}}\right) = 2.365\left(\dfrac{3.46}{\sqrt{8}}\right) = 2.9$

  **d.** $\bar{x} \pm t_{.025}\left(\dfrac{s}{\sqrt{n}}\right)$

    $10 \pm 2.9$ (7.1 to 12.9)

**14. a.** 21.5 to 23.5

  **b.** 21.3 to 23.7

  **c.** 20.9 to 24.1

  **d.** A larger margin of error and a wider interval

**15.** $\bar{x} \pm t_{\alpha/2}(s/\sqrt{n})$

  90% confidence: $df = 64$ and $t_{.05} = 1.669$

  $19.5 \pm 1.669\left(\dfrac{5.2}{\sqrt{65}}\right)$

  $19.5 \pm 1.08$ (18.42 to 20.58)

  95% confidence: $df = 64$ and $t_{.025} = 1.998$

  $19.5 \pm 1.998\left(\dfrac{5.2}{\sqrt{65}}\right)$

  $19.5 \pm 1.29$ (18.21 to 20.79)

**16. a.** 1.69

  **b.** 47.31 to 50.69

  **c.** Fewer hours and higher cost for United

**18. a.** 3.8

  **b.** .84

  **c.** 2.96 to 4.64

  **d.** Larger $n$ next time

**20.** 6.28 to 6.78

**22. a.** 6.86

  **b.** 6.54 to 7.18

**24. a.** Planning value of $\sigma = \dfrac{\text{Range}}{4} = \dfrac{36}{4} = 9$

  **b.** $n = \dfrac{z_{.025}^2\sigma^2}{E^2} = \dfrac{(1.96)^2(9)^2}{(3)^2} = 34.57$; use $n = 35$

  **c.** $n = \dfrac{(1.96)^2(9)^2}{(2)^2} = 77.79$; use $n = 78$

**25. a.** Use $n = \dfrac{z_{\alpha/2}^2\sigma^2}{E^2}$

    $n = \dfrac{(1.96)^2(6.82)^2}{(1.5)^2} = 79.41$; use $n = 80$

  **b.** $n = \dfrac{(1.645)^2(6.82)^2}{(2)^2} = 31.47$; use $n = 32$

**26. a.** 340

  **b.** 1358

  **c.** 8487

**28. a.** 343

  **b.** 487

  **c.** 840

  **d.** $n$ gets larger; No to 99% confidence

**30.** 81

**31. a.** $\bar{p} = \dfrac{100}{400} = .25$

  **b.** $\sqrt{\dfrac{\bar{p}(1-\bar{p})}{n}} = \sqrt{\dfrac{.25(.75)}{400}} = .0217$

  **c.** $\bar{p} \pm z_{.025}\sqrt{\dfrac{\bar{p}(1-\bar{p})}{n}}$

    $.25 \pm 1.96(.0217)$

    $.25 \pm .0424$; .2076 to .2924

**32. a.** .6733 to .7267

  **b.** .6682 to .7318

**34.** 1068

**35. a.** $\bar{p} = \dfrac{281}{611} = .4599$ (46%)

  **b.** $z_{.05}\sqrt{\dfrac{\bar{p}(1-\bar{p})}{n}} = 1.645\sqrt{\dfrac{4599(1-.4599)}{611}} = .0332$

  **c.** $\bar{p} \pm .0332$

    $.4599 \pm .0332$ (.4267 to .4931)

**36. a.** .4393

  **b.** .3870 to .4916

**38. a.** .0430

  **b.** .2170 to .3030

  **c.** 822

**39. a.** $n = \dfrac{1.96^2 p^*(1 - p^*)}{E^2}$

$n = \dfrac{1.96^2(.33)(.67)}{(.03)^2} = 943.75$; use $n = 944$

**b.** $n = \dfrac{2.576^2(.33)(.67)}{(.03)^2} = 1630.19$; use $n = 1631$

**40.** .0267, (.8333 to .8867)

**42. a.** .0442
**b.** 601, 1068, 2401, 9604

**44. a.** 2009
**b.** 47,991 to 52,009

**46. a.** 998
**b.** $24,479 to $26,455
**c.** $93.5 million
**d.** Yes; $21.4 (30%) over *Lost World*

**48. a.** 14 minutes
**b.** 13.38 to 14.62
**c.** 32 per day
**d.** staff reduction

**50.** 37

**52.** 176

**54. a.** .5420
**b.** .0508
**c.** .4912 to .5928

**56. a.** .68
**b.** .6391 to .7209

**58. a.** 1267
**b.** 1509

**60. a.** .3101
**b.** .2898 to .3304
**c.** 8219; No, this sample size is unnecessarily large

## Chapter 9

**2. a.** $H_0: \mu \leq 14$
$H_a: \mu > 14$
**b.** No evidence that the new plan increases sales
**c.** The research hypothesis $\mu > 14$ is supported; the new plan increases sales

**4. a.** $H_0: \mu \geq 220$
$H_a: \mu < 220$

**5. a.** Rejecting $H_0: \mu \leq 8.6$ when it is true
**b.** Accepting $H_0: \mu \leq 8.6$ when it is false

**6. a.** $H_0: \mu \leq 1$
$H_a: \mu > 1$
**b.** Claiming $\mu > 1$ when it is not true
**c.** Claiming $\mu \leq 1$ when it is not true

**8. a.** $H_0: \mu \geq 220$
$H_a: \mu < 220$
**b.** Claiming $\mu < 220$ when it is not true
**c.** Claiming $\mu \geq 220$ when it is not true

**10. a.** $z = \dfrac{\bar{x} - \mu_0}{\sigma/\sqrt{n}} = \dfrac{26.4 - 25}{6/\sqrt{40}} = 1.48$
**b.** Area = .4306
$p$-value = .5000 − .4306 = .0694
**c.** $p$-value > .01, do not reject $H_0$
**d.** Reject $H_0$ if $z \geq 2.33$
1.48 < 2.33, do not reject $H_0$

**11. a.** $z = \dfrac{\bar{x} - \mu_0}{\sigma/\sqrt{n}} = \dfrac{14.15 - 15}{3/\sqrt{50}} = -2.00$
**b.** Area = .4772
$p$-value = 2(.5000 − .4772) = .0456
**c.** $p$-value ≤ .05, reject $H_0$
**d.** Reject $H_0$ if $z \leq -1.96$ or $z \geq 1.96$
$-2.00 \leq -1.96$, reject $H_0$

**12. a.** .1056; do not reject $H_0$
**b.** .0062; reject $H_0$
**c.** ≈ 0; reject $H_0$
**d.** .7967; do not reject $H_0$

**14. a.** .3844; do not reject $H_0$
**b.** .0074; reject $H_0$
**c.** .0836; do not reject $H_0$

**15. a.** $H_0: \mu \geq 1056$
$H_a: \mu < 1056$
**b.** $z = \dfrac{\bar{x} - \mu_0}{\sigma/\sqrt{n}} = \dfrac{910 - 1056}{1600/\sqrt{400}} = -1.83$
$p$-value = .5000 − .4664 = .0336
**c.** $p$-value ≤ .05, reject $H_0$. The mean refund of "last-minute" filers is less than $1056
**d.** Reject $H_0$ if $z \leq -1.645$
$-1.83 \leq -1.645$, reject $H_0$

**16. a.** $H_0: \mu \leq 895$
$H_a: \mu > 895$
**b.** .1170
**c.** Do not reject $H_0$
**d.** Withhold judgment; collect more data

**18. a.** $H_0: \mu = 26,133$
$H_a: \mu \neq 26,133$
**b.** .0366
**c.** Reject $H_0$

**20. a.** $H_0: \mu \geq 181,900$
$H_a: \mu < 181,900$
**b.** −2.93
**c.** .0017
**d.** Reject $H_0$

**22. a.** $H_0: \mu = 8$
$H_a: \mu \neq 8$
**b.** .1706
**c.** Do not reject $H_0$
**d.** 7.83 to 8.97; Yes

**24. a.** $t = \dfrac{\bar{x} - \mu_0}{s/\sqrt{n}} = \dfrac{17 - 18}{4.5/\sqrt{48}} = -1.54$
**b.** Degrees of freedom = $n - 1 = 47$
Area in lower tail is between .05 and .10
$p$-value (two-tail) is between .10 and .20

  **c.** $p$-value $> .05$; do not reject $H_0$
  **d.** With $df = 47$, $t_{.025} = 2.012$
     Reject $H_0$ if $t \le -2.012$ or $t \ge 2.012$
     $t = -1.54$; do not reject $H_0$

**26. a.** Between .02 and .05; reject $H_0$
  **b.** Between .01 and .02; reject $H_0$
  **c.** Between .10 and .20; do not reject $H_0$

**27. a.** $H_0: \mu \ge 238$
     $H_a: \mu < 238$
  **b.** $t = \dfrac{\bar{x} - \mu_0}{s/\sqrt{n}} = \dfrac{231 - 238}{80/\sqrt{100}} = -.88$
     Degrees of freedom $= n - 1 = 99$
     $p$-value is between .10 and .20
  **c.** $p$-value $> .05$; do not reject $H_0$
     Cannot conclude mean weekly benefit in Virginia is less
     than the national mean
  **d.** $df = 99$     $t_{.05} = -1.66$
     Reject $H_0$ if $t \le -1.66$
     $-.88 > -1.66$; do not reject $H_0$

**28. a.** $H_0: \mu \le 3530$
     $H_a: \mu > 3530$
  **b.** Between .005 and .01
  **c.** Reject $H_0$

**30. a.** $H_0: \mu = 600$
     $H_a: \mu \ne 600$
  **b.** Between .20 and .40
  **c.** Do not reject $H_0$
  **d.** A larger sample size

**32. a.** $H_0: \mu = 10{,}192$
     $H_a: \mu \ne 10{,}192$
  **b.** Between .02 and .05
  **c.** Reject $H_0$

**34. a.** $H_0: \mu = 2$
     $H_a: \mu \ne 2$
  **b.** 2.2
  **c.** .52
  **d.** Between .20 and .40
  **e.** Do not reject $H_0$

**36. a.** $z = \dfrac{\bar{p} - p_0}{\sqrt{\dfrac{p_0(1 - p_0)}{n}}} = \dfrac{.68 - .75}{\sqrt{\dfrac{.75(1 - .75)}{300}}} = -2.80$
     $p$-value $= .5000 - .4974 = .0026$
     $p$-value $\le .05$; reject $H_0$
  **b.** $z = \dfrac{.72 - .75}{\sqrt{\dfrac{.75(1 - .75)}{300}}} = -1.20$
     $p$-value $= .5000 - .3849 = .1151$
     $p$-value $> .05$; do not reject $H_0$

  **c.** $z = \dfrac{.70 - .75}{\sqrt{\dfrac{.75(1 - .75)}{300}}} = -2.00$
     $p$-value $= .5000 - .4772 = .0228$
     $p$-value $\le .05$; reject $H_0$
  **d.** $z = \dfrac{.77 - .75}{\sqrt{\dfrac{.75(1 - .75)}{300}}} = .80$
     $p$-value $= .5000 + .2881 = .7881$
     $p$-value $> .05$; do not reject $H_0$

**38. a.** $H_0: p = .64$
     $H_a: p \ne .64$
  **b.** $\bar{p} = 52/100 = .52$
     $z = \dfrac{\bar{p} - p_0}{\sqrt{\dfrac{p_0(1 - p_0)}{n}}} = \dfrac{.52 - .64}{\sqrt{\dfrac{.64(1 - .64)}{100}}} = -2.50$
     Area $= .4938$
     $p$-value $= 2(.5000 - .4938) = .0124$
  **c.** $p$-value $\le .05$; reject $H_0$
     Proportion differs from the reported .64
  **d.** Yes, because $\bar{p} = .52$ indicates that fewer believe the
     supermarket brand is as good as the name brand

**40. a.** .2702
  **b.** $H_0: p \le .22$
     $H_a: p > .22$
     $p$-value $\approx 0$; reject $H_0$
  **c.** Helps evaluate the effectiveness of commercials

**42.** $H_0: p \le .24$
     $H_a: p > .24$
     $p$-value $= .0023$; reject $H_0$

**44. a.** $H_0: p \le .50$
     $H_a: p > .50$
  **b.** $p$-value $\approx 0$
  **c.** Reject $H_0$
  **d.** Yes

**46.**

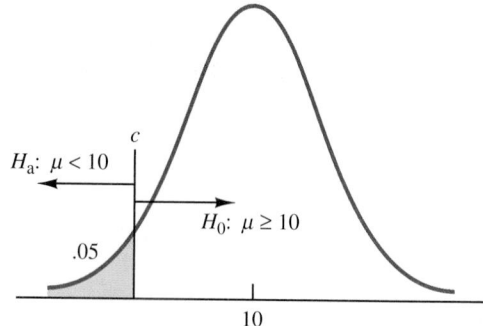

$c = 10 - 1.645(5/\sqrt{120}) = 9.25$
Reject $H_0$ if $\bar{x} < 9.25$

  **a.** When $\mu = 9$,
$$z = \dfrac{9.25 - 9}{5/\sqrt{120}} = .55$$
$$P(H_0) = (.5000 - .2088) = .2912$$

**b.** Type II error

**c.** When $\mu = 8$,

$$z = \frac{9.25 - 8}{5/\sqrt{120}} = 2.74$$

$$\beta = (.5000 - .4969) = .0031$$

**48. a.** Concluding $\mu \le 15$ when it is not true

**b.** .2676

**c.** .0179

**49. a.** $H_0: \mu \ge 25$

$H_a: \mu < 25$

Reject $H_0$ if $z < -2.05$

$$z = \frac{\bar{x} - \mu_0}{\sigma/\sqrt{n}} = \frac{\bar{x} - 25}{3/\sqrt{30}} = -2.05$$

Solve for $\bar{x} = 23.88$

Decision Rule: Accept $H_0$ if $\bar{x} > 23.88$

Reject $H_0$ if $\bar{x} \le 23.88$

**b.** For $\mu = 23$,

$$z = \frac{23.88 - 23}{3/\sqrt{30}} = 1.61$$

$$\beta = .5000 - .4463 = .0537$$

**c.** For $\mu = 24$,

$$z = \frac{23.88 - 24}{3/\sqrt{30}} = -.22$$

$$\beta = .5000 - .0871 = .5871$$

**d.** The Type II error cannot be made in this case; note that when $\mu = 25.5$, $H_0$ is true; the Type II error can only be made when $H_0$ is false

**50. a.** Concluding $\mu = 28$ when it is not true

**b.** .0853, .6179, .6179, .0853

**c.** .9147

**52.** .1151, .0015

Increasing $n$ reduces $\beta$

**54.** $n = \dfrac{(z_\alpha + z_\beta)^2 \sigma^2}{(\mu_0 - \mu_a)^2} = \dfrac{(1.645 + 1.28)^2 (5)^2}{(10 - 9)^2} = 214$

**56.** 109

**57.** At $\mu_0 = 400$, $\alpha = .02$; $z_{.02} = 2.05$

At $\mu_a = 385$, $\beta = .10$; $z_{.10} = 1.28$

With $\sigma = 30$,

$$n = \frac{(z_\alpha + z_\beta)^2 \sigma^2}{(\mu_0 - \mu_a)^2} = \frac{(2.05 + 1.28)^2 (30)^2}{(400 - 385)^2} = 44.4 \text{ or } 45$$

**58.** 324

**60. a.** $H_0: \mu = 16$

$H_a: \mu \ne 16$

**b.** .0286; reject $H_0$

Readjust line

**c.** .2186; do not reject $H_0$

Continue operation

**d.** $z = 2.19$; reject $H_0$

$z = -1.23$; do not reject $H_0$

Yes, same conclusion

**62. a.** $H_0: \mu \le 45,250$

$H_a: \mu > 45,250$

**b.** .0034

**c.** Reject $H_0$

**64.** $t = -.93$

$p$-value between .20 and .40

Do not reject $H_0$

**66.** $t = 2.26$

$p$-value between .01 and .025

Reject $H_0$

**68. a.** $H_0: p \le .50$

$H_a: p > .50$

**b.** .64

**c.** .0026; reject $H_0$

**70. a.** $H_0: p \le .50$

$H_a: p > .50$

**b.** .6381

**c.** .0023; reject $H_0$

**72.** $H_0: p \ge .90$

$H_a: p < .90$

$p$-value = .0808

Do not reject $H_0$

**74. a.** $H_0: \mu \le 72$

$H_a: \mu > 72$

**b.** .2912

**c.** .7939

**d.** 0, because $H_0$ is true

**76. a.** 45

**b.** .0192, .2358, .7291, .7291, .2358, .0192

## Chapter 10

**1. a.** $\bar{x}_1 - \bar{x}_2 = 13.6 - 11.6 = 2$

**b.** $z_{\alpha/2} = z_{.05} = 1.645$

$$\bar{x}_1 - \bar{x}_2 \pm 1.645 \sqrt{\frac{\sigma_1^2}{n_1} + \frac{\sigma_2^2}{n_2}}$$

$$2 \pm 1.645 \sqrt{\frac{(2.2)^2}{50} + \frac{(3)^2}{35}}$$

$2 \pm .98 \quad (1.02 \text{ to } 2.98)$

**c.** $z_{\alpha/2} = z_{.05} = 1.96$

$$2 \pm 1.96 \sqrt{\frac{(2.2)^2}{50} + \frac{(3)^2}{35}}$$

$2 \pm 1.17 \quad (.83 \text{ to } 3.17)$

**2. a.** $z = \dfrac{(\bar{x}_1 - \bar{x}_2) - D_0}{\sqrt{\dfrac{\sigma_1^2}{n_1} + \dfrac{\sigma_2^2}{n_2}}} = \dfrac{(25.2 - 22.8) - 0}{\sqrt{\dfrac{(5.2)^2}{40} + \dfrac{(6)^2}{50}}} = 2.03$

**b.** $p$-value = .5000 - .4788 = .0212

**c.** $p$-value $\le .05$; reject $H_0$

**4. a.** .32

**b.** .04

**c.** .28 to .36

**6.** $p$-value = .015

Reject $H_0$; an increase

**7. a.** $H_0: \mu_1 - \mu_2 = 0$

$H_a: \mu_1 - \mu_2 \neq 0$

**b.** $z = \dfrac{(\bar{x}_1 - \bar{x}_2) - D_0}{\sqrt{\dfrac{\sigma_1^2}{n_1} + \dfrac{\sigma_2^2}{n_2}}} = \dfrac{(40 - 35) - 0}{\sqrt{\dfrac{9^2}{36} + \dfrac{10^2}{49}}} = 2.41$

**c.** $p\text{-value} = 2(.5000 - .4920) = .0160$

**d.** $p\text{-value} \leq .05$; reject $H_0$

Conclude a difference between the population mean ages at the two stores

**8. a.** 1.08

**b.** .2802

**c.** Do not reject $H_0$; cannot conclude a difference exists

**9. a.** $\bar{x}_1 - \bar{x}_2 = 22.5 - 20.1 = 2.4$

**b.** $df = \dfrac{\left(\dfrac{s_1^2}{n_1} + \dfrac{s_2^2}{n_2}\right)^2}{\dfrac{1}{n_1 - 1}\left(\dfrac{s_1^2}{n_1}\right)^2 + \dfrac{1}{n_2 - 1}\left(\dfrac{s_2^2}{n_2}\right)^2}$

$= \dfrac{\left(\dfrac{2.5^2}{20} + \dfrac{4.8^2}{30}\right)^2}{\dfrac{1}{19}\left(\dfrac{2.5^2}{20}\right)^2 + \dfrac{1}{29}\left(\dfrac{4.8^2}{30}\right)^2} = 45.8$

**c.** $df = 45, t_{.025} = 2.014$

$t_{.025}\sqrt{\dfrac{s_1^2}{n_1} + \dfrac{s_2^2}{n_2}} = 2.014\sqrt{\dfrac{2.5^2}{20} + \dfrac{4.8^2}{30}} = 2.1$

**d.** $2.4 \pm 2.1$ (.3 to 4.5)

**10. a.** $t = \dfrac{(\bar{x}_1 - \bar{x}_2) - 0}{\sqrt{\dfrac{s_1^2}{n_1} + \dfrac{s_2^2}{n_2}}} = \dfrac{(13.6 - 10.1) - 0}{\sqrt{\dfrac{5.2^2}{35} + \dfrac{8.5^2}{40}}} = 2.18$

**b.** $df = \dfrac{\left(\dfrac{s_1^2}{n_1} + \dfrac{s_2^2}{n_2}\right)^2}{\dfrac{1}{n_1 - 1}\left(\dfrac{s_1^2}{n_1}\right)^2 + \dfrac{1}{n_2 - 1}\left(\dfrac{s_2^2}{n_2}\right)^2}$

$= \dfrac{\left(\dfrac{5.2^2}{35} + \dfrac{8.5^2}{40}\right)^2}{\dfrac{1}{34}\left(\dfrac{5.2^2}{35}\right)^2 + \dfrac{1}{39}\left(\dfrac{8.5^2}{40}\right)^2} = 65.7$

Use $df = 65$

**c.** $df = 65$, area in tail is between .01 and .025 two-tail $p$-value is between .02 and .05.

**d.** $p\text{-value} \leq .05$; reject $H_0$

**12. a.** $\bar{x}_1 - \bar{x}_2 = 22.5 - 18.6 = 3.9$ miles

**b.** $df = \dfrac{\left(\dfrac{s_1^2}{n_1} + \dfrac{s_2^2}{n_2}\right)^2}{\dfrac{1}{n_1 - 1}\left(\dfrac{s_1^2}{n_1}\right)^2 + \dfrac{1}{n_2 - 1}\left(\dfrac{s_2^2}{n_2}\right)^2}$

$= \dfrac{\left(\dfrac{8.4^2}{50} + \dfrac{7.4^2}{40}\right)^2}{\dfrac{1}{49}\left(\dfrac{8.4^2}{50}\right)^2 + \dfrac{1}{39}\left(\dfrac{7.4^2}{40}\right)^2} = 87.1$

Use $df = 87, t_{.025} = 1.988$

$3.9 \pm 1.988\sqrt{\dfrac{8.4^2}{50} + \dfrac{7.4^2}{40}}$

$3.9 \pm 3.3$ (.6 to 7.2)

**14. a.** $-1.6$; kitchens less

**b.** $-4.3$ to 1.1

**16. a.** $H_0: \mu_1 - \mu_2 = 0$

$H_a: \mu_1 - \mu_2 \neq 0$

**b.** 2.18

**c.** Between .02 and .05

**d.** Reject $H_0$; mean ages differ

**18. a.** $H_0: \mu_1 - \mu_2 = 0$

$H_a: \mu_1 - \mu_2 \neq 0$

**b.** 1.53

**c.** Between .10 and .20

**d.** Do not reject $H_0$

**20. a.** $H_0: \mu_1 - \mu_2 \geq 120$

$H_a: \mu_1 - \mu_2 < 120$

**b.** $-2.10$

Between .01 and .025

**c.** 32 to 118

**d.** Larger sample size

**21. a.** 1, 2, 0, 0, 2

**b.** $\bar{d} = \Sigma d_i/n = 5/5 = 1$

**c.** $s_d = \sqrt{\dfrac{\Sigma(d_i - \bar{d})^2}{n - 1}} = \sqrt{\dfrac{4}{5 - 1}} = 1$

**d.** $t = \dfrac{\bar{d} - \mu}{s_d/\sqrt{n}} = \dfrac{1 - 0}{1/\sqrt{5}} = 2.24$

$df = n - 1 = 4$

$p$-value is between .025 and .05

$p\text{-value} \leq .05$; reject $H_0$

**22. a.** 3, $-1$, 3, 5, 3, 0, 1

**b.** 2

**c.** 2.08

**d.** 2

**e.** .07 to 3.93

**23.** $H_0: \mu_d \leq 0$

$H_a: \mu_d > 0$

$\bar{d} = .625$

$s_d = 1.30$

$t = \dfrac{\bar{d} - \mu_d}{s_d/\sqrt{n}} = \dfrac{.625 - 0}{1.30/\sqrt{8}} = 1.36$

$df = n - 1 = 7$

$p$-value is between .10 and .20

$p\text{-value} > .05$; do not reject $H_0$

**24.** .16 to .35

**26.** $t = 1.63$

$p$-value between .10 and .20

Do not reject $H_0$

**28. a.** $t = -.60$

$p$-value greater than .40

Do not reject $H_0$

**b.** $-.103$

**c.** .39; larger sample size

**30. a.** .12

**b.** .0586 to .1814

**c.** .0469 to .1931

**31. a.** $\bar{p} = \dfrac{n_1\bar{p}_1 + n_2\bar{p}_2}{n_1 + n_2} = \dfrac{200(.22) + 300(.16)}{200 + 300} = .1840$

$$z = \dfrac{\bar{p}_1 - \bar{p}_2}{\sqrt{\bar{p}(1 - \bar{p})\left(\dfrac{1}{n_1} + \dfrac{1}{n_2}\right)}}$$

$$= \dfrac{.22 - .16}{\sqrt{.1840(1 - .1840)\left(\dfrac{1}{200} + \dfrac{1}{300}\right)}} = 1.70$$

$p$-value $= .5000 - .4554 = .0446$

**b.** $p$-value $\le .05$; reject $H_0$

**32.** $\bar{p}_1 = 220/400 = .55 \qquad \bar{p}_2 = 192/400 = .48$

$$\bar{p}_1 - \bar{p}_2 \pm z_{.025}\sqrt{\dfrac{\bar{p}_1(1 - \bar{p}_1)}{n_1} + \dfrac{\bar{p}_2(1 - \bar{p}_2)}{n_2}}$$

$$.55 - .48 \pm 1.96\sqrt{\dfrac{.55(1 - .55)}{400} + \dfrac{.48(1 - .48)}{400}}$$

$.07 \pm .0691 \qquad (.0009 \text{ to } .1391)$

7% more executives are predicting an increase in full-time jobs; the confidence interval shows the difference may be from 0% to 14%

**34. a.** .2206 (22%)

**b.** .1788 to .2624

**36. a.** .803

**b.** .849

**c.** $H_0: p_1 - p_2 \ge 0$

$H_a: p_1 - p_2 < 0$

**d.** $p$-value $= .0104$

Reject $H_0$

**38.** $p$-value $= .0055$

Reject $H_0$

**40.** $8,934 to $11,066

**42. a.** $H_0: \mu_1 - \mu_2 \le 0$

$H_a: \mu_1 - \mu_2 > 0$

**b.** $t = .60, df = 57$

$p$-value greater than .20

Do not reject $H_0$

**44. a.** $t = 4.99, p$-value $< .005$

Reject $H_0$

**b.** 13.4 to 30.6

**46. a.** $H_0: p_1 - p_2 \le 0$

$H_a: p_1 - p_2 > 0$

**b.** $z = 4.70, p$-value $\approx 0$

**c.** Reject $H_0$

**48.** $z = 2.37, p$-value $= .0178$

Reject $H_0$

# Chapter 11

**2.** $s^2 = 25$

**a.** With 19 degrees of freedom, $\chi^2_{.05} = 30.144$ and $\chi^2_{.95} = 10.117$

$$\dfrac{19(25)}{30.144} \le \sigma^2 \le \dfrac{19(25)}{10.117}$$

$$15.76 \le \sigma^2 \le 46.95$$

**b.** With 19 degrees of freedom, $\chi^2_{.025} = 32.852$ and $\chi^2_{.975} = 8.907$

$$\dfrac{19(25)}{32.852} \le \sigma^2 \le \dfrac{19(25)}{8.907}$$

$$14.46 \le \sigma^2 \le 53.33$$

**c.** $3.8 \le \sigma \le 7.3$

**4. a.** .22 to .71

**b.** .47 to .84

**6. a.** 13.3

**b.** 8.0 to 38.2

**8. a.** .00845

**b.** .092

**c.** .0042 to .0244

.065 to .156

**9.** $H_0: \sigma^2 \le .0004$

$H_a: \sigma^2 > .0004$

$$\chi^2 = \dfrac{(n - 1)s^2}{\sigma_0^2} = \dfrac{(30 - 1)(.0005)}{.0004} = 36.25$$

From table with 29 degrees of freedom, $p$-value greater than .10

$p$-value $> .05$; do not reject $H_0$

The product specification does not appear to be violated

**10.** $\chi^2 = 46.53$

$p$-value between .01 and .025

Reject $H_0$

**12. a.** .8106

**b.** $\chi^2 = 9.49$

$p$-value greater than .20

Do not reject $H_0$

**14. a.** $F = 2.4$

$p$-value between .025 and .05

Reject $H_0$

**b.** $F_{.05} = 2.2$; reject $H_0$

**15. a.** Larger sample variance is $s_1^2$

$$F = \dfrac{s_1^2}{s_2^2} = \dfrac{8.2}{4} = 2.05$$

Degrees of freedom: 20, 25

From table, area in tail is between .025 and .05

$p$-value for two-tailed test is between .05 and .10

$p$-value $> .05$; do not reject $H_0$

**b.** For a two-tailed test

$F_{\alpha/2} = F_{.025} = 2.30$

Reject $H_0$ if $F \ge 2.30$

$2.05 < 2.30$; do not reject $H_0$

**16.** $F = 2.63$

$p$-value less than .01

Reject $H_0$

**17. a.** Population 1 is 4-year-old automobiles

$H_0: \sigma_1^2 \leq \sigma_2^2$

$H_a: \sigma_1^2 > \sigma_2^2$

**b.** $F = \dfrac{s_1^2}{s_2^2} = \dfrac{170^2}{100^2} = 2.89$

Degrees of freedom: 25, 24

From tables, $p$-value is less than .01

$p$-value $\leq .01$; reject $H_0$

Conclude that 4-year-old automobiles have a larger variance in annual repair costs compared to 2-year-old automobiles, which is expected because older automobiles are more likely to have more expensive repairs that lead to greater variance in the annual repair costs

**18.** $F = 3.54$

$p$-value between .10 and .20

Do not reject $H_0$

**20.** $F = 5.29$

$p$-value $\approx 0$

Reject $H_0$

**22. a.** $F = 4$

$p$-value less than .01

Reject $H_0$

**24.** 10.72 to 24.68

**26. a.** $\chi^2 = 27.44$

$p$-value between .01 and .025

Reject $H_0$

**b.** .00012 to .00042

**28.** $\chi^2 = 31.50$

$p$-value between .05 and .10

Reject $H_0$

**30. a.** $n = 15$

**b.** 6.25 to 11.13

**32.** $F = 1.39$

Do not reject $H_0$

**34.** $F = 2.08$

$p$-value between .05 and .10

Reject $H_0$

## Chapter 12

**1.** Expected frequencies: $e_1 = 200(.40) = 80$

$e_2 = 200(.40) = 80$

$e_3 = 200(.20) = 40$

Actual frequencies: $f_1 = 60, f_2 = 120, f_3 = 20$

$\chi^2 = \dfrac{(60 - 80)^2}{80} + \dfrac{(120 - 80)^2}{80} + \dfrac{(20 - 40)^2}{40}$

$= \dfrac{400}{80} + \dfrac{1600}{80} + \dfrac{400}{40}$

$= 5 + 20 + 10 = 35$

Degrees of freedom: $k - 1 = 2$

$\chi^2 = 35$ shows $p$-value $\approx 0$

$p$-value $\leq .01$; reject $H_0$

**b.** Reject $H_0$ if $\chi^2 \geq 9.210$

$\chi^2 = 35$; reject $H_0$

**2.** $\chi^2 = 15.33, df = 3$

$p$-value less than .005

Reject $H_0$

**3.** $H_0: p_{ABC} = .29, p_{CBS} = .28, p_{NBC} = .25, p_{IND} = .18$

$H_a:$ The proportions are not

$p_{ABC} = .29, p_{CBS} = .28, p_{NBC} = .25, p_{IND} = .18$

Expected frequencies: $300(.29) = 87, 300(.28) = 84$

$300(.25) = 75, 300(.18) = 54$

$e_1 = 87, e_2 = 84, e_3 = 75, e_4 = 54$

Actual frequencies: $f_1 = 95, f_2 = 70, f_3 = 89, f_4 = 46$

$\chi^2 = \dfrac{(95 - 87)^2}{87} + \dfrac{(70 - 84)^2}{84} + \dfrac{(89 - 75)^2}{75}$

$+ \dfrac{(46 - 54)^2}{54} = 6.87$

Degrees of freedom: $k - 1 = 3$

$\chi^2 = 6.87$, $p$-value between .05 and .10

Do not reject $H_0$

**4.** $\chi^2 = 29.51, df = 5$

$p$-value $\approx 0$

Reject $H_0$

**6.** $\chi^2 = 10.69, df = 5$

$p$-value between .05 and .10

Reject $H_0$

**8.** $\chi^2 = 16.31, df = 3$

$p$-value less than .005

Reject $H_0$

**9.** $H_0:$ The column variable is independent of the row variable

$H_a:$ The column variable is not independent of the row variable

Expected frequencies:

|   | A | B | C |
|---|---|---|---|
| P | 28.5 | 39.9 | 45.6 |
| Q | 21.5 | 30.1 | 34.4 |

$\chi^2 = \dfrac{(20 - 28.5)^2}{28.5} + \dfrac{(44 - 39.9)^2}{39.9} + \dfrac{(50 - 46.5)^2}{45.6}$

$+ \dfrac{(30 - 21.5)^2}{21.5} + \dfrac{(26 - 30.1)^2}{30.1} + \dfrac{(30 - 34.4)^2}{34.4}$

$= 7.86$

Degrees of freedom: $(2 - 1)(3 - 1) = 2$

$\chi^2 = 7.86$, $p$-value between .01 and .025

Reject $H_0$

**10.** $\chi^2 = 19.77, df = 4$

$p$-value less than .005

Reject $H_0$

**11.** $H_0$: Type of ticket purchased is independent of the type of flight

$H_a$: Type of ticket purchased is not independent of the type of flight

Expected frequencies:

$e_{11} = 35.59$  $\qquad$ $e_{12} = 15.41$
$e_{21} = 150.73$ $\qquad$ $e_{22} = 65.27$
$e_{31} = 455.68$ $\qquad$ $e_{32} = 197.32$

| Ticket | Flight | Observed Frequency ($f_i$) | Expected Frequency ($e_i$) | $(f_i - e_i)^2/e_i$ |
|--------|--------|--------|--------|--------|
| First | Domestic | 29 | 35.59 | 1.22 |
| First | International | 22 | 15.41 | 2.82 |
| Business | Domestic | 95 | 150.73 | 20.61 |
| Business | International | 121 | 65.27 | 47.59 |
| Full-fare | Domestic | 518 | 455.68 | 8.52 |
| Full-fare | International | 135 | 197.32 | 19.68 |
| Totals | | 920 | | $\chi^2 = 100.43$ |

Degrees of freedom: $(3 - 1)(2 - 1) = 2$
$\chi^2 = 100.43$, $p$-value $\approx 0$
Reject $H_0$

**12. a.** $\chi^2 = 7.36$, $df = 2$
  $p$-value between .025 and .05
  Reject $H_0$
 **b.** Domestic 47.2%

**14.** $\chi^2 = 13.43$, $df = 5$
  $p$-value between .01 and .025
  Reject $H_0$

**16. a.** $\chi^2 = 7.85$, $df = 3$
  $p$-value between .025 and .05
  Reject $H_0$
 **b.** Pharmaceutical, 98.6%

**18.** $\chi^2 = 13.42$, $df = 4$
  $p$-value between .005 and .01
  Reject $H_0$

**20.** First estimate $\mu$ from the sample data (sample size $= 120$)

$$\mu = \frac{0(39) + 1(30) + 2(30) + 3(18) + 4(3)}{120}$$

$$= \frac{156}{120} = 1.3$$

Therefore, we use Poisson probabilities with $\mu = 1.3$ to compute expected frequencies

| $x$ | Observed Frequency | Poisson Probability | Expected Frequency | Difference $(f_i - e_i)$ |
|-----|--------|--------|--------|--------|
| 0 | 39 | .2725 | 32.70 | 6.30 |
| 1 | 30 | .3543 | 42.51 | -12.51 |
| 2 | 30 | .2303 | 27.63 | 2.37 |
| 3 | 18 | .0998 | 11.98 | 6.02 |
| 4 or more | 3 | .0431 | 5.16 | -2.17 |

$$\chi^2 = \frac{(6.30)^2}{32.70} + \frac{(-12.51)^2}{42.51} + \frac{(2.37)^2}{27.63} + \frac{(6.02)^2}{11.98}$$
$$+ \frac{(-2.17)^2}{5.16} = 9.04$$

Degrees of freedom: $5 - 1 - 1 = 3$
$\chi^2 = 9.04$, $p$-value between .025 and .05
Reject $H_0$; not a Poisson distribution

**21.** With $n = 30$ we will use six classes with .1667 of the probability associated with each class

$$\bar{x} = 22.8, s = 6.27$$

The $z$ values that create 6 intervals, each with probability .1667 are $-.98, -.43, 0, .43, .98$

| $z$ | Cutoff Value of $x$ |
|-----|--------|
| $-.98$ | $22.8 - .98(6.27) = 16.66$ |
| $-.43$ | $22.8 - .43(6.27) = 20.11$ |
| $0$ | $22.8 + .00(6.27) = 22.80$ |
| $.43$ | $22.8 + .43(6.27) = 25.49$ |
| $.98$ | $22.8 + .98(6.27) = 28.94$ |

| Interval | Observed Frequency | Expected Frequency | Difference |
|----------|--------|--------|--------|
| less than 16.66 | 3 | 5 | -2 |
| 16.66–20.11 | 7 | 5 | 2 |
| 20.11–22.80 | 5 | 5 | 0 |
| 22.80–25.49 | 7 | 5 | 2 |
| 25.49–28.94 | 3 | 5 | -2 |
| 28.94 and up | 5 | 5 | 0 |

$$\chi^2 = \frac{(-2)^2}{5} + \frac{(2)^2}{5} + \frac{(0)^2}{5} + \frac{(2)^2}{5} + \frac{(-2)^2}{5} + \frac{(0)^2}{5}$$
$$= \frac{16}{5} = 3.20$$

Degrees of freedom: $6 - 2 - 1 = 3$
$\chi^2 = 3.20$, $p$-value greater than .10
Do not reject $H_0$
Assumption of a normal distribution is not rejected

**22.** $\chi^2 = 4.30$, $df = 2$
  $p$-value greater than .10
  Do not reject $H_0$

**24.** $\chi^2 = 2.8$, $df = 3$
  $p$-value greater than .10
  Do not reject $H_0$

**26.** $\chi^2 = 8.04$, $df = 3$
  $p$-value between .025 and .05
  Reject $H_0$

**28.** $\chi^2 = 31.43$, $df = 3$
  $p$-value $\approx 0$
  Reject $H_0$

**30.** $\chi^2 = 42.53$, $df = 4$
$p$-value $\approx 0$
Reject $H_0$

**32.** $\chi^2 = 23.37$, $df = 3$
$p$-value $\approx 0$
Reject $H_0$

**34. a.** $\chi^2 = 12.86$, $df = 2$
$p$-value less than .005
Reject $H_0$
**b.** 66.9, 30.3, 2.9
54.0, 42.0, 4.0

**36.** $\chi^2 = 6.17$, $df = 6$
$p$-value greater than .10
Do not reject $H_0$

**38.** $\chi^2 = 7.75$, $df = 3$
$p$-value between .05 and .10
Do not reject $H_0$

# Chapter 13

**1. a.** $\bar{\bar{x}} = (30 + 45 + 36)/3 = 37$

$$\text{SSTR} = \sum_{j=1}^{k} n_j(\bar{x}_j - \bar{\bar{x}})^2$$

$$= 5(30 - 37)^2 + 5(45 - 37)^2 + 5(36 - 37)^2$$

$$= 570$$

$$\text{MSTR} = \frac{\text{SSTR}}{k - 1} = \frac{570}{2} = 285$$

**b.** $\text{SSE} = \sum_{j=1}^{k} (n_j - 1)s_j^2$

$$= 4(6) + 4(4) + 4(6.5) = 66$$

$$\text{MSE} = \frac{\text{SSE}}{n_T - k} = \frac{66}{15 - 3} = 5.5$$

**c.** $F = \dfrac{\text{MSTR}}{\text{MSE}} = \dfrac{285}{5.5} = 51.82$

From the $F$ table (2 degrees of freedom numerator and 12 denominator), $p$-value is less than .01

Because $p$-value $\leq \alpha = 0.5$, we reject the null hypothesis that the means of the three populations are equal

**d.**

| Source of Variation | Sum of Squares | Degrees of Freedom | Mean Square | F |
|---|---|---|---|---|
| Treatments | 570 | 2 | 285 | 51.82 |
| Error | 66 | 12 | 5.5 | |
| Total | 636 | 14 | | |

**2. a.** MSTR = 268
**b.** MSE = 92
**c.** Cannot reject $H_0$ because $p$-value is greater than .10

**d.**

| Source of Variation | Sum of Squares | Degrees of Freedom | Mean Square | F |
|---|---|---|---|---|
| Treatments | 536 | 2 | 268 | 2.91 |
| Error | 828 | 9 | 92 | |
| Total | 1364 | 11 | | |

**4. b.** Reject $H_0$ because $p$-value is less than .01

**6.**

| | Mfg 1 | Mfg 2 | Mfg 3 |
|---|---|---|---|
| Sample mean | 23 | 28 | 21 |
| Sample variance | 6.67 | 4.67 | 3.33 |

$$\bar{\bar{x}} = (23 + 28 + 21)/3 = 24$$

$$\text{SSTR} = \sum_{j=1}^{k} n_j(\bar{x}_j - \bar{\bar{x}})^2$$

$$= 4(23 - 24)^2 + 4(28 - 24)^2$$
$$+ 4(21 - 24)^2 = 104$$

$$\text{MSTR} = \frac{\text{SSTR}}{k - 1} = \frac{104}{2} = 52$$

$$\text{SSE} = \sum_{j=1}^{k} (n_j - 1)s_j^2$$

$$= 3(6.67) + 3(4.67) + 3(3.33) = 44.01$$

$$\text{MSE} = \frac{\text{SSE}}{n_T - k} = \frac{44.01}{12 - 3} = 4.89$$

$$F = \frac{\text{MSTR}}{\text{MSE}} = \frac{52}{4.89} = 10.63$$

From the $F$ table (2 degrees of freedom numerator and 9 denominator), $p$-value is less than .01

Actual $p$-value = .0043

Because $p$-value $\leq \alpha = .05$, we reject the null hypothesis that the mean time needed to mix a batch of material is the same for each manufacturer

**8.** Significant; $p$-value is less than .01

**10.** Significant; $p$-value = .042

**11. a.** $\text{LSD} = t_{\alpha/2}\sqrt{\text{MSE}\left(\dfrac{1}{n_i} + \dfrac{1}{n_j}\right)}$

$$= t_{.025}\sqrt{5.5\left(\frac{1}{5} + \frac{1}{5}\right)}$$

$$= 2.179\sqrt{2.2} = 3.23$$

$|\bar{x}_1 - \bar{x}_2| = |30 - 45| = 15 > \text{LSD}$; significant
$|\bar{x}_1 - \bar{x}_3| = |30 - 36| = 6 > \text{LSD}$; significant
$|\bar{x}_2 - \bar{x}_3| = |45 - 36| = 9 > \text{LSD}$; significant

**b.** $\bar{x}_1 - \bar{x}_2 \pm t_{\alpha/2}\sqrt{\text{MSE}\left(\dfrac{1}{n_1} + \dfrac{1}{n_2}\right)}$

$$(30 - 45) \pm 2.179\sqrt{5.5\left(\frac{1}{5} + \frac{1}{5}\right)}$$

$$-15 \pm 3.23 = -18.23 \text{ to } -11.77$$

**12. a.** Significant; $p$-value is between .01 and .025

    **b.** LSD = 15.34

        1 and 2; significant

        1 and 3; not significant

        2 and 3; significant

**13.** $\text{LSD} = t_{\alpha/2}\sqrt{\text{MSE}\left(\dfrac{1}{n_1} + \dfrac{1}{n_3}\right)}$

$$= t_{.025}\sqrt{4.89\left(\frac{1}{4} + \frac{1}{4}\right)}$$

$$= 2.262\sqrt{2.45} = 3.54$$

Because $|\bar{x}_1 - \bar{x}_3| = |23 - 21| = 2 < 3.54$, there does not appear to be any significant difference between the means of populations 1 and 3

**14.** $\bar{x}_1 - \bar{x}_2 \pm \text{LSD}$

    $23 - 28 \pm 3.54$

        $-5 \pm 3.54 = -8.54 \text{ to } -1.46$

**16. a.** Significant; $p$-value is less than .01

    **b.** Significant; $2.3 > \text{LSD} = 1.19$

**18.** LSD = 5.74

    Small and medium: not significant

    Small and large: significant

    Medium and large: not significant

**19. a.** $\bar{\bar{x}} = (156 + 142 + 134)/3 = 144$

$$\text{SSTR} = \sum_{j=1}^{k} n_j(\bar{x}_j - \bar{\bar{x}})^2$$

$$= 6(156 - 144)^2 + 6(142 - 144)^2 + 6(134 - 144)^2$$

$$= 1488$$

    **b.** $\text{MSTR} = \dfrac{\text{SSTR}}{k - 1} = \dfrac{1488}{2} = 744$

    **c.** $s_1^2 = 164.4, \quad s_2^2 = 131.2, \quad s_3^2 = 110.4$

$$\text{SSE} = \sum_{j=1}^{k} (n_j - 1)s_j^2$$

$$= 5(164.4) + 5(131.2) + 5(110.4)$$

$$= 2030$$

    **d.** $\text{MSE} = \dfrac{\text{SSE}}{n_T - k} = \dfrac{2030}{18 - 3} = 135.3$

    **e.** $F = \dfrac{\text{MSTR}}{\text{MSE}} = \dfrac{744}{135.3} = 5.50$

    From the $F$ table (2 degrees of freedom numerator and 15 denominator), $p$-value is between .01 and .025

    Actual $p$-value = .0162

    Because $p$-value $\leq \alpha = .05$, we reject the hypothesis that the means for the three treatments are equal

**20. a.**

| Source of Variation | Sum of Squares | Degrees of Freedom | Mean Square | F |
|---|---|---|---|---|
| Treatments | 1488 | 2 | 744 | 5.50 |
| Error | 2030 | 15 | 135.3 | |
| Total | 3518 | 17 | | |

    **b.** Significant difference between A and C

**22. a.** $H_0: \mu_1 = \mu_2 = \mu_3 = \mu_4 = \mu_5$

        $H_a$: Not all the population means are equal

    **b.** Reject $H_0$; $p$-value is less than .01

**24.** Significant; $p$-value is less than .01

**26. b.** Significant; $p$-value is less than .01

**28.** Not significant; $p$-value is greater than .10

**30.** Not significant; $p$-value is between .05 and .10

**32.** Means are all different (LSD = 2.53)

**34. *Treatment Means***

    $\bar{x}_{.1} = 13.6, \quad \bar{x}_{.2} = 11.0, \quad \bar{x}_{.3} = 10.6$

    ***Block Means***

    $\bar{x}_{1.} = 9, \quad \bar{x}_{2.} = 7.67, \quad \bar{x}_{3.} = 15.67, \quad \bar{x}_{4.} = 18.67, \quad \bar{x}_{5.} = 7.67$

    ***Overall Mean***

    $\bar{\bar{x}} = 176/15 = 11.73$

    *Step 1*

$$\text{SST} = \sum_{i}\sum_{j}(x_{ij} - \bar{\bar{x}})^2$$

$$= (10 - 11.73)^2 + (9 - 11.73)^2 + \cdots + (8 - 11.73)^2$$

$$= 354.93$$

    *Step 2*

$$\text{SSTR} = b\sum_{j}(\bar{x}_{.j} - \bar{\bar{x}})^2$$

$$= 5[(13.6 - 11.73)^2 + (11.0 - 11.73)^2 + (10.6 - 11.73)^2] = 26.53$$

    *Step 3*

$$\text{SSBL} = k\sum_{j}(\bar{x}_{i.} - \bar{\bar{x}})^2$$

$$= 3[(9 - 11.73)^2 + (7.67 - 11.73)^2 + (15.67 - 11.73)^2 + (18.67 - 11.73)^2 + (7.67 - 11.73)^2] = 312.32$$

    *Step 4*

$$\text{SSE} = \text{SST} - \text{SSTR} - \text{SSBL}$$

$$= 354.93 - 26.53 - 312.32 = 16.08$$

| Source of Variation | Sum of Squares | Degrees of Freedom | Mean Square | F |
|---|---|---|---|---|
| Treatments | 26.53 | 2 | 13.27 | 6.60 |
| Blocks | 312.32 | 4 | 78.08 | |
| Error | 16.08 | 8 | 2.01 | |
| Total | 354.93 | 14 | | |

From the $F$ table (2 numerator degrees of freedom and 8 denominator), $p$-value is between .01 and .025

Actual $p$-value = .0203

Because $p$-value $\leq \alpha = .05$, we reject the null hypothesis that the means of the three treatments are equal

**36.** Significant; $p$-value is less than .01

**38.** Significant; $p$-value is less than .01

**40.** Significant; $p$-value = .000

**41.** See Table D13.41

*Step 1*

$$SST = \sum_i \sum_j \sum_k (x_{ijk} - \bar{\bar{x}})^2$$
$$= (135 - 111)^2 + (165 - 111)^2 + \cdots$$
$$+ (136 - 111)^2 = 9028$$

*Step 2*

$$SSA = br \sum_i (\bar{x}_{i\cdot} - \bar{\bar{x}})^2$$
$$= 3(2)[(104 - 111)^2 + (118 - 111)^2] = 588$$

*Step 3*

$$SSB = ar \sum_j (\bar{x}_{\cdot j} - \bar{\bar{x}})^2$$
$$= 2(2)[(130 - 111)^2 + (97 - 111)^2 + (106 - 111)^2]$$
$$= 2328$$

*Step 4*

$$SSAB = r \sum_i \sum_j (\bar{x}_{ij} - \bar{x}_{i\cdot} - \bar{x}_{\cdot j} + \bar{\bar{x}})^2$$
$$= 2[(150 - 104 - 130 + 111)^2$$
$$+ (78 - 104 - 97 + 111)^2 + \cdots$$
$$+ (128 - 118 - 106 + 111)^2] = 4392$$

*Step 5*

$$SSE = SST - SSA - SSB - SSAB$$
$$= 9028 - 588 - 2328 - 4392 = 1720$$

| Source of Variation | Sum of Squares | Degrees of Freedom | Mean Square | $F$ |
|---|---|---|---|---|
| Factor A | 588 | 1 | 588 | 2.05 |
| Factor B | 2328 | 2 | 1164 | 4.06 |
| Interaction | 4392 | 2 | 2196 | 7.66 |
| Error | 1720 | 6 | 286.67 | |
| Total | 9028 | 11 | | |

Factor A: $F = 2.05$

From the $F$ table (1 degree of freedom numerator and 6 denominator), $p$-value is greater than .10

Actual $p$-value = .2022

Because $p$-value $> \alpha = .05$, factor A is not significant

Factor B: $F = 4.06$

From the $F$ table (2 degrees of freedom numerator and 6 denominator), $p$-value is between .05 and .10

Actual $p$-value = .0767

Because $p$-value $> \alpha = .05$, factor B is not significant

Interaction: $F = 7.66$

From the $F$ table (2 degrees of freedom numerator and 6 denominator), $p$-value is between .01 and .025

Actual $p$-value = .0223

Because $p$-value $\leq \alpha = .05$, interaction is significant

**42.** Factor A is significant; $p$-value = .025
Factor B is significant; $p$-value is between .01 and .025
Interaction is significant; $p$-value is less than .01

**44.** No significant effect due to the loading and unloading method, the type of ride, or interaction; $p$-value is greater than .10 for each test

**46.** Factor A is not significant
Factor B is significant
Interaction is significant

**48.** Significant; $p$-value = .000

**50.** Significant; $p$-value is less than .01

**52.** Significant; $p$-value = .000

**54.** Significant; $p$-value is between .01 and .025

**56.** Not significant; $p$-value is greater than .10

**58.** Significant; $p$-value is between .025 and .05

**60. a.** Significant; $p$-value is between .01 and .025

**62.** Significant; $p$-value = .000

**64.** Type of machine is significant; type of loading system and interaction are not significant

**TABLE D13.41**

| | | Factor B | | | Factor A Means |
|---|---|---|---|---|---|
| | | Level 1 | Level 2 | Level 3 | |
| Factor A | Level 1 | $\bar{x}_{11} = 150$ | $\bar{x}_{12} = 78$ | $\bar{x}_{13} = 84$ | $\bar{x}_{1\cdot} = 104$ |
| | Level 2 | $\bar{x}_{21} = 110$ | $\bar{x}_{22} = 116$ | $\bar{x}_{23} = 128$ | $\bar{x}_{2\cdot} = 118$ |
| Factor B Means | | $\bar{x}_{\cdot 1} = 130$ | $\bar{x}_{\cdot 2} = 97$ | $\bar{x}_{\cdot 3} = 106$ | $\bar{\bar{x}} = 111$ |

# Chapter 14

**1. a.**

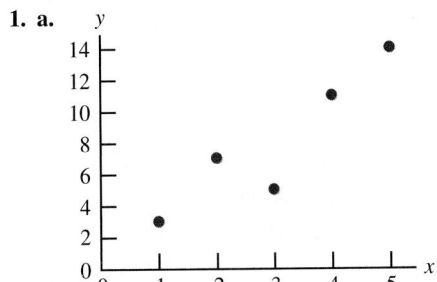

**b.** There appears to be a linear relationship between $x$ and $y$

**c.** Many different straight lines can be drawn to provide a linear approximation of the relationship between $x$ and $y$; in part (d) we will determine the equation of a straight line that "best" represents the relationship according to the least squares criterion

**d.** Summations needed to compute the slope and $y$-intercept:

$\Sigma x_i = 15, \quad \Sigma y_i = 40, \quad \Sigma(x_i - \bar{x})(y_i - \bar{y}) = 26,$
$\Sigma(x_i - \bar{x})^2 = 10$

$b_1 = \dfrac{\Sigma(x_i - \bar{x})(y_i - \bar{y})}{\Sigma(x_i - \bar{x})^2} = \dfrac{26}{10} = 2.6$

$b_0 = \bar{y} - b_1\bar{x} = 8 - (2.6)(3) = 0.2$
$\hat{y} = 0.2 - 2.6x$

**e.** $\hat{y} = .2 + 2.6x = .2 + 2.6(4) = 10.6$

**2. b.** There appears to be a linear relationship between $x$ and $y$
   **d.** $\hat{y} = 30.33 - 1.88x$
   **e.** 19.05

**4. a.**

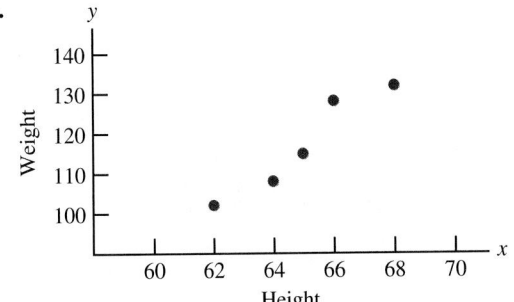

**b.** It indicates there may be a linear relationship between height and weight

**c.** Many different straight lines can be drawn to provide a linear approximation of the relationship between height and weight; in part (d) we will determine the equation of a straight line that "best" represents the relationship according to the least squares criterion

**d.** Summations needed to compute the slope and $y$-intercept:

$\Sigma x_i = 325, \quad \Sigma y_i = 585, \quad \Sigma(x_i - \bar{x})(y_i - \bar{y}) = 110,$
$\Sigma(x_i - \bar{x})^2 = 20$

$b_1 = \dfrac{\Sigma(x_i - \bar{x})(y_i - \bar{y})}{\Sigma(x_i - \bar{x})^2} = \dfrac{110}{20} = 5.5$

$b_0 = \bar{y} - b_1\bar{x} = 117 - (5.5)(65) = -240.5$
$\hat{y} = -240.5 + 5.5x$

**e.** $\hat{y} = -240.5 + 5.5(63) = 106$
The estimate of weight is 106 pounds

**6. c.** $\hat{y} = -10.16 + .18x$
   **e.** 11.95 or approximately \$12,000

**8. c.** $\hat{y} = 490.21 + 204.24x$
   **d.** 1307

**10. b.** $\hat{y} = 51.82 + .145x$
   **c.** 84.4

**12. c.** $\hat{y} = 1293 + .3165x$
   **d.** 25,031

**14. b.** $\hat{y} = 28.30 - .0415x$
   **c.** 26.2

**15. a.** $\hat{y}_i = .2 + 2.6x_i$ and $\bar{y} = 8$

| $x_i$ | $y_i$ | $\hat{y}_i$ | $y_i - \hat{y}_i$ | $(y_i - \hat{y}_i)^2$ | $y_i - \bar{y}$ | $(y_i - \bar{y})^2$ |
|---|---|---|---|---|---|---|
| 1 | 3 | 2.8 | .2 | .04 | −5 | 25 |
| 2 | 7 | 5.4 | 1.6 | 2.56 | −1 | 1 |
| 3 | 5 | 8.0 | −3.0 | 9.00 | −3 | 9 |
| 4 | 11 | 10.6 | .4 | .16 | 3 | 9 |
| 5 | 14 | 13.2 | .8 | .64 | 6 | 36 |
| | | | | SSE = 12.40 | | SST = 80 |

SSR = SST − SSE = 80 − 12.4 = 67.6

**b.** $r^2 = \dfrac{\text{SSR}}{\text{SST}} = \dfrac{67.6}{80} = .845$

The least squares line provided a good fit; 84.5% of the variability in $y$ has been explained by the least squares line

**c.** $r = \sqrt{.845} = +.9192$

**16. a.** SSE = 6.3325, SST = 114.80, SSR = 108.47
   **b.** $r^2 = .945$
   **c.** $r = -.9721$

**18. a.** The estimated regression equation and the mean for the dependent variable:

$\hat{y} = 1790.5 + 581.1x, \quad \bar{y} = 3650$

The sum of squares due to error and the total sum of squares:

$\text{SSE} = \Sigma(y_i - \hat{y}_i)^2 = 85,135.14$
$\text{SST} = \Sigma(y_i - \bar{y})^2 = 335,000$
Thus, SSR = SST − SSE
$= 335,000 - 85,135.14 = 249,864.86$

**b.** $r^2 = \dfrac{\text{SSR}}{\text{SST}} = \dfrac{249,864.86}{335,000} = .746$

The least squares line accounted for 74.6% of the total sum of squares

**c.** $r = \sqrt{.746} = +.8637$

**20. a.** $\hat{y} = -48.11 + 2.3325x$
  **b.** $r^2 = .82$
  **c.** $173,500

**22. a.** $\hat{y} = -745.80 + 117.917x$
  **b.** $r^2 = .7071$
  **c.** $r = +.84$

**23. a.** $s^2 = \text{MSE} = \dfrac{\text{SSE}}{n-2} = \dfrac{12.4}{3} = 4.133$

  **b.** $s = \sqrt{\text{MSE}} = \sqrt{4.133} = 2.033$

  **c.** $\Sigma(x_i - \bar{x})^2 = 10$

$$s_{b_1} = \frac{s}{\sqrt{\Sigma(x_i - \bar{x})^2}} = \frac{2.033}{\sqrt{10}} = .643$$

  **d.** $t = \dfrac{b_1 - \beta_1}{s_{b_1}} = \dfrac{2.6 - 0}{.643} = 4.04$

  From the $t$ table (3 degrees of freedom), area in tail is between .01 and .025

  $p$-value is between .02 and .05

  Actual $p$-value = .0272

  Because $p$-value $\leq \alpha$, we reject $H_0$: $\beta_1 = 0$

  **e.** $\text{MSR} = \dfrac{\text{SSR}}{1} = 67.6$

$$F = \frac{\text{MSR}}{\text{MSE}} = \frac{67.6}{4.133} = 16.36$$

  From the $F$ table (1 degree of freedom numerator and 3 denominator), $p$-value is between .025 and .05

  Actual $p$-value = .0272

  Because $p$-value $\leq \alpha$, we reject $H_0$: $\beta_1 = 0$

| Source of Variation | Sum of Squares | Degrees of Freedom | Mean Square | F |
|---|---|---|---|---|
| Regression | 67.6 | 1 | 67.6 | 16.36 |
| Error | 12.4 | 3 | 4.133 | |
| Total | 80 | 4 | | |

**24. a.** 2.11
  **b.** 1.453
  **c.** .262
  **d.** Significant; $p$-value is less than .01
  **e.** Significant; $p$-value is less than .01

**26. a.** $s^2 = \text{MSE} = \dfrac{\text{SSE}}{n-2} = \dfrac{85,135.14}{4} = 21,283.79$

$$s = \sqrt{\text{MSE}} = \sqrt{21,283.79} = 145.89$$

$$\Sigma(x_i - \bar{x})^2 = .74$$

$$s_{b_1} = \frac{s}{\sqrt{\Sigma(x_i - \bar{x})^2}} = \frac{145.89}{\sqrt{.74}} = 169.59$$

$$t = \frac{b_1 - \beta_1}{s_{b_1}} = \frac{581.08 - 0}{169.59} = 3.43$$

From the $t$ table (4 degrees of freedom), area in tail is between .01 and .025

$p$-value is between .02 and .05

Actual $p$-value = .0266

Because $p$-value $\leq \alpha$, we reject $H_0$: $\beta_1 = 0$

  **b.** $\text{MSR} = \dfrac{\text{SSR}}{1} = \dfrac{249,864.86}{1} = 249,864.86$

$$F = \frac{\text{MSR}}{\text{MSE}} = \frac{249,864.86}{21,283.79} = 11.74$$

From the $F$ table (1 degree of freedom numerator and 4 denominator), $p$-value is between .025 and .05

Actual $p$-value = .0266

Because $p$-value $\leq \alpha$, we reject $H_0$: $\beta_1 = 0$

  **c.**

| Source of Variation | Sum of Squares | Degrees of Freedom | Mean Square | F |
|---|---|---|---|---|
| Regression | 29,864.86 | 1 | 29,864.86 | 11.74 |
| Error | 85,135.14 | 4 | 21,283.79 | |
| Total | 335,000 | 5 | | |

**28.** They are related; $p$-value is less than .01

**30.** Significant; $p$-value is less than .01

**32. a.** $s = 2.033$

$$\bar{x} = 3, \Sigma(x_i - \bar{x})^2 = 10$$

$$s_{\hat{y}_p} = s\sqrt{\frac{1}{n} + \frac{(x_p - \bar{x})^2}{\Sigma(x_i - \bar{x})^2}}$$

$$= 2.033\sqrt{\frac{1}{5} + \frac{(4-3)^2}{10}} = 1.11$$

  **b.** $\hat{y} = .2 + 2.6x = .2 + 2.6(4) = 10.6$

$$\hat{y}_p \pm t_{\alpha/2}s_{\hat{y}_p}$$

$$10.6 \pm 3.182(1.11)$$

$$10.6 \pm 3.53, \text{ or } 7.07 \text{ to } 14.13$$

  **c.** $s_{\text{ind}} = s\sqrt{1 + \dfrac{1}{n} + \dfrac{(x_p - \bar{x})^2}{\Sigma(x_i - \bar{x})^2}}$

$$= 2.033\sqrt{1 + \frac{1}{5} + \frac{(4-3)^2}{10}} = 2.32$$

  **d.** $\hat{y}_p \pm t_{\alpha/2}s_{\text{ind}}$

$$10.6 \pm 3.182(2.32)$$

$$10.6 \pm 7.38, \text{ or } 3.22 \text{ to } 17.98$$

**34.** Confidence interval: $-.4$ to 4.98
  Prediction interval: $-2.27$ to 7.31

**35. a.** $s = 145.89, \bar{x} = 3.2, \Sigma(x_i - \bar{x})^2 = .74$

$$\hat{y} = 1790.5 + 581.1x = 1790.5 + 581.1(3)$$

$$= 3533.8$$

$$s_{\hat{y}_p} = s\sqrt{\frac{1}{n} + \frac{(x_p - \bar{x})^2}{\Sigma(x_i - \bar{x})^2}}$$

$$= 145.89\sqrt{\frac{1}{6} + \frac{(3 - 3.2)^2}{.74}} = 68.54$$

$\hat{y}_p \pm t_{\alpha/2}s_{\hat{y}_p}$

$3533.8 \pm 2.776(68.54)$

$3533.8 \pm 190.27$, or $3343.53 to $3724.07

**b.** $s_{ind} = s\sqrt{1 + \dfrac{1}{n} + \dfrac{(x_p - \bar{x})^2}{\Sigma(x_i - \bar{x})^2}}$

$= 145.89\sqrt{1 + \dfrac{1}{6} + \dfrac{(3 - 3.2)^2}{.74}} = 161.19$

$\hat{y}_p \pm t_{\alpha/2}s_{ind}$

$3533.8 \pm 2.776(161.19)$

$3533.8 \pm 447.46$, or $3086.34 to $3981.26

**36. a.** 80.86

**b.** 78.58 to 83.14

**c.** 72.92 to 88.80

**38. a.** $5046.67

**b.** $3815.10 to $6278.24

**c.** Not out of line

**40. a.** 9

**b.** $\hat{y} = 20.0 + 7.21x$

**c.** 1.3626

**d.** SSE = SST − SSR = 51,984.1 − 41,587.3 = 10,396.8

MSE = 10,396.8/7 = 1485.3

$F = \dfrac{\text{MSR}}{\text{MSE}} = \dfrac{41,587.3}{1485.3} = 28.0$

From the $F$ table (1 degree of freedom numerator and 7 denominator), $p$-value is less than .01

Actual $p$-value = .0011

Because $p$-value $\leq \alpha = .05$, we reject $H_0: \beta_1 = 0$

**e.** $\hat{y} = 20.0 + 7.21(50) = 380.5$, or $380,500

**42. a.** $\hat{y} = 80.0 + 50.0x$

**b.** 30

**c.** Significant; $p$-value is less than .01

**d.** $680,000

**44. b.** Yes

**c.** $\hat{y} = 37.1 - .779x$

**d.** Significant; $p$-value = 0.003

**e.** $r^2 = .434$; not a good fit

**f.** $12.27 to $22.90

**g.** $17.47 to $39.05

**45. a.** $\Sigma x_i = 70$,   $\Sigma y_i = 76$,   $\Sigma(x_i - \bar{x})(y_i - \bar{y}) = 200$,
$\Sigma(x_i - \bar{x})^2 = 126$

$b_1 = \dfrac{\Sigma(x_i - \bar{x})(y_i - \bar{y})}{\Sigma(x_i - \bar{x})^2} = \dfrac{200}{126} = 1.5873$

$b_0 = \bar{y} - b_1\bar{x} = 15.2 - (1.5873)(14) = -7.0222$

$\hat{y} = -7.02 + 1.59x$

**b.**

| $x_i$ | $y_i$ | $\hat{y}_i$ | $y_i - \hat{y}_i$ |
|---|---|---|---|
| 6 | 6 | 2.52 | 3.48 |
| 11 | 8 | 10.47 | −2.47 |
| 15 | 12 | 16.83 | −4.83 |
| 18 | 20 | 21.60 | −1.60 |
| 20 | 30 | 24.78 | 5.22 |

**c.**  $y - \hat{y}$

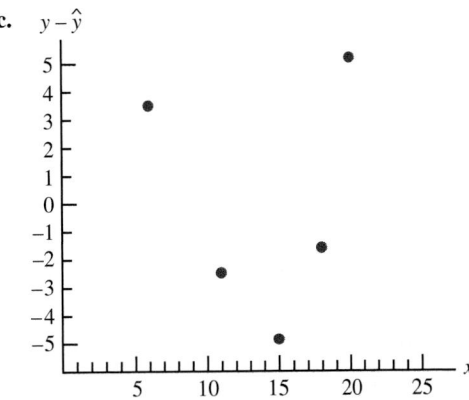

With only five observations, it is difficult to determine whether the assumptions are satisfied; however, the plot does suggest curvature in the residuals, which would indicate that the error term assumptions are not satisfied; the scatter diagram for these data also indicates that the underlying relationship between $x$ and $y$ may be curvilinear

**d.** $s^2 = 23.78$

$h_i = \dfrac{1}{n} + \dfrac{(x_i - \bar{x})^2}{\Sigma(x_i - \bar{x})^2}$

$= \dfrac{1}{5} + \dfrac{(x_i - 14)^2}{126}$

| $x_i$ | $h_i$ | $s_{y_i - \hat{y}_i}$ | $y_i - \hat{y}_i$ | Standardized Residuals |
|---|---|---|---|---|
| 6 | .7079 | 2.64 | 3.48 | 1.32 |
| 11 | .2714 | 4.16 | −2.47 | −.59 |
| 15 | .2079 | 4.34 | −4.83 | −1.11 |
| 18 | .3270 | 4.00 | −1.60 | −.40 |
| 20 | .4857 | 3.50 | 5.22 | 1.49 |

**e.** The plot of the standardized residuals against $\hat{y}$ has the same shape as the original residual plot; as stated in part (c), the curvature observed indicates that the assumptions regarding the error term may not be satisfied

**46. a.** $\hat{y} = 2.32 + .64x$

**b.** No; the variance does not appear to be the same for all values of $x$

**47. a.** Let $x$ = advertising expenditures and $y$ = revenue

$\hat{y} = 29.4 + 1.55x$

**b.** SST = 1002, SSE = 310.28, SSR = 691.72

$\text{MSR} = \dfrac{\text{SSR}}{1} = 691.72$

$\text{MSE} = \dfrac{\text{SSE}}{n - 2} = \dfrac{310.28}{5} = 62.0554$

$F = \dfrac{\text{MSR}}{\text{MSE}} = \dfrac{691.72}{62.0554} = 11.15$

From the $F$ table (1 degree of freedom numerator and 5 denominator), $p$-value is between .01 and .025

Actual $p$-value = .0206

Because $p$-value $\leq \alpha$ = .05, we conclude that the two variables are related

**c.**

| $x_i$ | $y_i$ | $\hat{y}_i = 29.40 + 1.55x_i$ | $y_i - \hat{y}_i$ |
|-------|-------|-------------------------------|-------------------|
| 1 | 19 | 30.95 | −11.95 |
| 2 | 32 | 32.50 | −.50 |
| 4 | 44 | 35.60 | 8.40 |
| 6 | 40 | 38.70 | 1.30 |
| 10 | 52 | 44.90 | 7.10 |
| 14 | 53 | 51.10 | 1.90 |
| 20 | 54 | 60.40 | −6.40 |

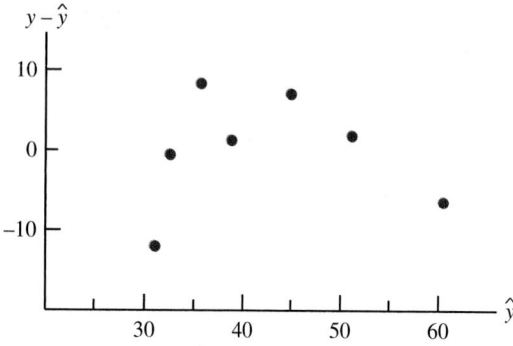

**d.** The residual plot leads us to question the assumption of a linear relationship between $x$ and $y$; even though the relationship is significant at the $\alpha$ = .05 level, it would be extremely dangerous to extrapolate beyond the range of the data

**48. b.** Yes

**50. a.** Using Minitab, we obtained the estimated regression equation $\hat{y}$ = 66.1 + .402$x$; a portion of the Minitab output is shown in Figure D14.50; the fitted values and standardized residuals are shown:

| $x_i$ | $y_i$ | $\hat{y}_i$ | Standardized Residuals |
|-------|-------|-------------|------------------------|
| 135 | 145 | 120.41 | 2.11 |
| 110 | 100 | 110.35 | −1.08 |
| 130 | 120 | 118.40 | .14 |
| 145 | 120 | 124.43 | −.38 |
| 175 | 130 | 136.50 | −.78 |
| 160 | 130 | 130.47 | −.04 |
| 120 | 110 | 114.38 | −.41 |

**b.**

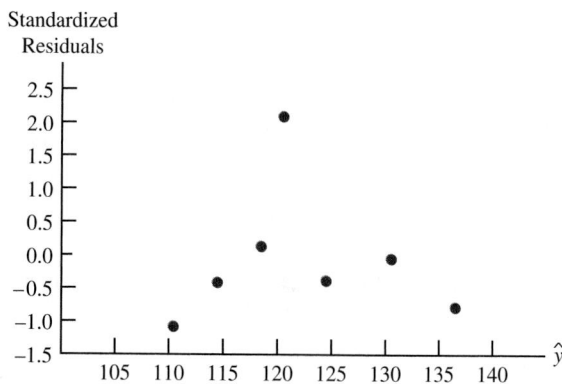

The standardized residual plot indicates that the observation $x$ = 135, $y$ = 145 may be an outlier; note that this observation has a standardized residual of 2.11

**FIGURE D14.50**

```
The regression equation is
Y = 66.1 + 0.402 X

Predictor      Coef     SE Coef      T        p
Constant      66.10       32.06    2.06    0.094
X            0.4023      0.2276    1.77    0.137

S = 12.62     R-sq = 38.5%     R-sq(adj) = 26.1%

Analysis of Variance

SOURCE           DF        SS       MS      F        p
Regression        1     497.2    497.2   3.12    0.137
Residual Error    5     795.7    159.1
Total             6    1292.9

Unusual Observations
Obs     X          Y        Fit    SE Fit    Residual    St Resid
  1    135    145.00     120.42      4.87       24.58       2.11R
```

**c.** The scatter diagram is shown:

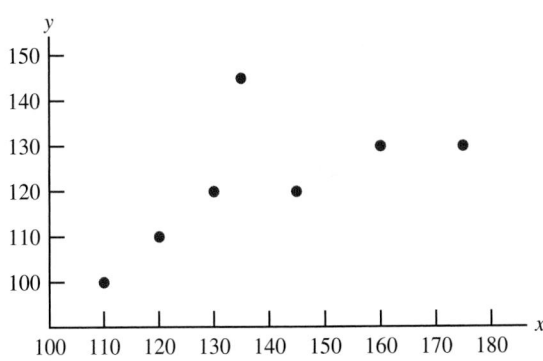

The scatter diagram also indicates that the observation $x = 135$, $y = 145$ may be an outlier; the implication is that for simple linear regression outliers can be identified by looking at the scatter diagram

**52. a.** A portion of the Minitab output is shown in Figure D14.52
   **b.** Minitab identifies observation 1 as having a large standardized residual; thus, we would consider observation 1 to be an outlier

**54. a.** $\hat{y} = 707 + .00482x$
   **b.** Observation 6 is an influential observation

**58. a.** $\hat{y} = 9.26 + .711x$
   **b.** Significant; $p$-value $= .001$
   **c.** $r^2 = .744$; good fit
   **d.** $13.53

**60. a.** Market beta $= .95$
   **b.** Significant; $p$-value $= .029$

**c.** $r^2 = .470$; not a good fit
**d.** Texas Instruments has a higher risk

**62. a.** $\hat{y} = 10.5 + .953x$
   **b.** Significant relationship; $p$-value $= .000$
   **c.** $2874 to $4952
   **d.** Yes

**64. a.** Negative linear relationship
   **b.** $\hat{y} = 8.10 - .344x$
   **c.** Significant; $p$-value $= .002$
   **d.** $r^2 = .711$; reasonably good fit
   **e.** 5.2 to 7.6 days

**66. a.** $\hat{y} = 5.85 + .830x$
   **b.** Significant; $p$-value $= .000$
   **c.** 84.65 points
   **d.** 65.35 to 103.96

## Chapter 15

**2. a.** The estimated regression equation is
   $\hat{y} = 45.06 + 1.94x_1$
   An estimate of $y$ when $x_1 = 45$ is
   $\hat{y} = 45.06 + 1.94(45) = 132.36$
   **b.** The estimated regression equation is
   $\hat{y} = 85.22 + 4.32x_2$
   An estimate of $y$ when $x_2 = 15$ is
   $\hat{y} = 85.22 + 4.32(15) = 150.02$
   **c.** The estimated regression equation is
   $\hat{y} = -18.37 + 2.01x_1 + 4.74x_2$
   An estimate of $y$ when $x_1 = 45$ and $x_2 = 15$ is
   $\hat{y} = -18.37 + 2.01(45) + 4.74(15) = 143.18$

**FIGURE D14.52**

```
The regression equation is
Shipment = 4.09 + 0.196 Media$


Predictor        Coef     SE Coef       T        p
Constant        4.089       2.168    1.89    0.096
Media$        0.19552     0.03635    5.38    0.000


S = 5.044      R-Sq = 78.3%      R-Sq(adj) = 75.6%


Analysis of Variance
Source              DF          SS         MS        F        p
Regression           1      735.84     735.84    28.93    0.000
Residual Error       8      203.51      25.44
Total                9      939.35


Unusual Observations
Obs     Media$     Shipment      Fit     SE Fit     Residual     St Resid
  1        120        36.30    27.55       3.30         8.75        2.30R


R denotes an observation with a large standardized residual
```

**4. a.** $255,000

**5. a.** The Minitab output is shown in Figure D15.5a
  **b.** The Minitab output is shown in Figure D15.5b
  **c.** It is 1.60 in part (a) and 2.29 in part (b); in part (a) the coefficient is an estimate of the change in revenue due to a one-unit change in television advertising expenditures; in part (b) it represents an estimate of the change in revenue due to a one-unit change in television advertising expenditures when the amount of newspaper advertising is held constant
  **d.** Revenue = 83.2 + 2.29(3.5) + 1.30(1.8) = 93.56 or $93,560

**6. a.** Speed = 49.8 + .015 Weight
  **b.** Speed = 80.5 − .00312 Weight + .105 Horsepwr
  **c.** 102.5

**8. a.** Return = 247 − 32.8 Safety + 34.6 ExpRatio
  **b.** 70.2

**10. a.** Revenue = 33.3 + 7.98 Cars
  **b.** Increase of 1000 cars will increase revenue by $7.98 million
  **c.** Revenue = 106 + 8.94 Cars − .191 Location

**12. a.** $R^2 = \dfrac{\text{SSR}}{\text{SST}} = \dfrac{14{,}052.2}{15{,}182.9} = .926$

  **b.** $R_a^2 = 1 - (1 - R^2)\dfrac{n-1}{n-p-1}$

  $= 1 - (1 - .926)\dfrac{10-1}{10-2-1} = .905$

  **c.** Yes; after adjusting for the number of independent variables in the model, we see that 90.5% of the variability in $y$ has been accounted for

---

**FIGURE D15.5a**

```
The regression equation is
Revenue = 88.6 + 1.60 TVAdv

Predictor      Coef      SE Coef        T         p
Constant     88.638        1.582    56.02     0.000
TVAdv         1.6039       0.4778     3.36     0.015

S = 1.215      R-sq = 65.3%      R-sq(adj) = 59.5%

Analysis of Variance

SOURCE            DF         SS        MS        F        p
Regression         1     16.640    16.640    11.27    0.015
Residual Error     6      8.860     1.477
Total              7     25.500
```

**FIGURE D15.5b**

```
The regression equation is
Revenue = 83.2 + 2.29 TVAdv + 1.30 NewsAdv

Predictor      Coef      SE Coef        T         p
Constant     83.230        1.574    52.88     0.000
TVAdv         2.2902       0.3041     7.53     0.001
NewsAdv       1.3010       0.3207     4.06     0.010

S = 0.6426     R-sq = 91.9%      R-sq(adj) = 88.7%

Analysis of Variance

SOURCE            DF         SS        MS        F        p
Regression         2     23.435    11.718    28.38    0.002
Residual Error     5      2.065     0.413
Total              7     25.500
```

**14. a.** .75

  **b.** .68

**15. a.** $R^2 = \dfrac{\text{SSR}}{\text{SST}} = \dfrac{23.435}{25.5} = .919$

$R_a^2 = 1 - (1 - R^2)\dfrac{n-1}{n-p-1}$

$= 1 - (1 - .919)\dfrac{8-1}{8-2-1} = .887$

  **b.** Multiple regression analysis is preferred because both $R^2$ and $R_a^2$ show an increased percentage of the variability of $y$ explained when both independent variables are used

**16. a.** No, $R^2 = .311$

  **b.** Better fit with multiple regression

**18. a.** $R^2 = .942$, $R_a^2 = .932$

  **b.** The fit is very good

**19. a.** $\text{MSR} = \dfrac{\text{SSR}}{p} = \dfrac{6216.375}{2} = 3108.188$

$\text{MSE} = \dfrac{\text{SSE}}{n-p-1} = \dfrac{507.75}{10-2-1} = 72.536$

  **b.** $F = \dfrac{\text{MSR}}{\text{MSE}} = \dfrac{3108.188}{72.536} = 42.85$

From the $F$ table (2 degrees of freedom numerator and 7 denominator), $p$-value is less than .01

Because $p$-value $\leq \alpha$, the overall model is significant

  **c.** $t = \dfrac{b_1}{s_{b_1}} = \dfrac{.5906}{.0813} = 7.26$

$p$-value is less than .01

Because $p$-value $\leq \alpha$, $\beta_1$ is significant

  **d.** $t = \dfrac{b_2}{s_{b_2}} = \dfrac{.4980}{.0567} = 8.78$

$p$-value is less than .01

Because $p$-value $\leq \alpha$, $\beta_2$ is significant

**20. a.** Significant; $p$-value $= .000$

  **b.** Significant; $p$-value $= .000$

  **c.** Significant; $p$-value $= .002$

**22. a.** SSE $= 4000$, $s^2 = 571.43$,

  MSR $= 6000$

  **b.** Significant; $p$-value is less than .01

**23. a.** $F = 28.38$

  $p$-value $= .002$

  Because $p$-value $\leq \alpha$, there is a significant relationship

  **b.** $t = 7.53$

  $p$-value $= .001$

  Because $p$-value $\leq \alpha$, $\beta_1$ is significant and $x_1$ should not be dropped from the model

  **c.** $t = 4.06$

  $p$-value $= .010$

  Because $p$-value $\leq \alpha$, $\beta_2$ is significant and $x_2$ should not be dropped from the model

**24. a.** Reject $H_0$: $\beta_1 = \beta_2 = 0$; $p$-value $= .000$

  **b.** Weight: Cannot reject $H_0$: $\beta_1 = 0$; $p$-value $= .386$

  Horsepwr: Reject $H_0$: $\beta_2 = 0$; $p$-value $= .000$

**26. a.** Significant; $p$-value $= .000$

  **b.** Significant; $p$-value $= .000$

  **c.** Not significant; $p$-value $= .087$

**28. a.** Using Minitab, the 95% confidence interval is 132.16 to 154.15

  **b.** Using Minitab, the 95% prediction interval is 111.15 at 175.17

**29. a.** See Minitab output in Figure D15.5b.

  $\hat{y} = 83.230 + 2.2902(3.5) + 1.3010(1.8) = 93.588$ or $\$93,588$

  **b.** Minitab results: 92.840 to 94.335, or $\$92,840$ to $\$94,335$

  **c.** Minitab results: 91.774 to 95.401, or $\$91,774$ to $\$95,401$

**30. a.** Speed $= 72.6 + .0968$ Horsepwr; estimate of speed is 101.29

  **b.** 99.490 to 103.089

  **c.** 94.596 to 107.984

**32. a.** $E(y) = \beta_0 + \beta_1 x_1 + \beta_2 x_2$

  where $x_2 = \begin{cases} 0 \text{ if level 1} \\ 1 \text{ if level 2} \end{cases}$

  **b.** $E(y) = \beta_0 + \beta_1 x_1 + \beta_2(0) = \beta_0 + \beta_1 x_1$

  **c.** $E(y) = \beta_0 + \beta_1 x_1 + \beta_2(1) = \beta_0 + \beta_1 x_1 + \beta_2$

  **d.** $\beta_2 = E(y \mid \text{level 2}) - E(y \mid \text{level 1})$

  $\beta_1$ is the change in $E(y)$ for a 1-unit change in $x_1$ holding $x_2$ constant

**34. a.** $\$15,300$, because $b_3 = 15.3$

  **b.** $\hat{y} = 10.1 - 4.2(2) + 6.8(8) + 15.3(0) = 56.1$

  Sales prediction: $\$56,100$

  **c.** $\hat{y} = 10.1 - 4.2(1) + 6.8(3) + 15.3(1) = 41.6$

  Sales prediction: $\$41,600$

**36. a.** $\hat{y} = 1.86 + 0.291$ Months $+ 1.10$ Type $- 0.609$ Person

  **b.** Significant; $p$-value $= .002$

  **c.** Person is not significant; $p$-value $= .167$

**38. a.** $\hat{y} = -91.8 + 1.08$ Age $+ .252$ Pressure $+ 8.74$ Smoker

  **b.** Significant; $p$-value $= .01$

  **c.** 95% prediction interval is 21.35 to 47.18 or a probability of .2135 to .4718; quit smoking and begin some type of treatment to reduce his blood pressure

**39. a.** The Minitab output is shown in Figure D15.39
   **b.** Minitab provides the following values:

| $x_i$ | $y_i$ | $\hat{y}_i$ | Standardized Residual |
|---|---|---|---|
| 1 | 3 | 2.8 | .16 |
| 2 | 7 | 5.4 | .94 |
| 3 | 5 | 8.0 | −1.65 |
| 4 | 11 | 10.6 | .24 |
| 5 | 14 | 13.2 | .62 |

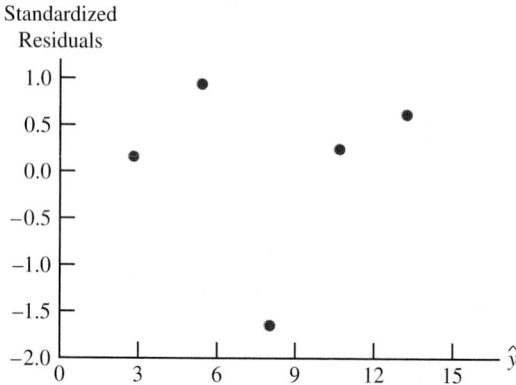

Standardized Residuals

The point (3,5) does not appear to follow the trend of the remaining data; however, the value of the standardized residual for this point, −1.65, is not large enough for us to conclude that (3,5) is an outlier

   **c.** Minitab provides the following values:

| $x_i$ | $y_i$ | Studentized Deleted Residual |
|---|---|---|
| 1 | 3 | .13 |
| 2 | 7 | .91 |
| 3 | 5 | −4.42 |
| 4 | 11 | .19 |
| 5 | 14 | .54 |

$t_{.025} = 4.303$ $(n − p − 2 = 5 − 1 − 2 = 2$ degrees of freedom)

Because the studentized deleted residual for (3,5) is $−4.42 < −4.303$, we conclude that the 3rd observation is an outlier

**40. a.** $\hat{y} = −53.3 + 3.11x$
   **b.** −1.40, −.15, 1.36, .47, −1.39; no
   **c.** .38, .28, .22, .20, .98; no
   **d.** .60, .00, .26, .03, 11.09; yes, the fifth observation

**41. a.** The Minitab output appears in Figure D15.5b; the estimated regression equation is

   Revenue = 83.2 + 2.29 TVAdv + 1.30 NewsAdv

   **b.** Minitab provides the following values:

| $\hat{y}_i$ | Standardized Residual | $\hat{y}_i$ | Standardized Residual |
|---|---|---|---|
| 96.63 | −1.62 | 94.39 | 1.10 |
| 90.41 | −1.08 | 94.24 | −.40 |
| 94.34 | 1.22 | 94.42 | −1.12 |
| 92.21 | −.37 | 93.35 | 1.08 |

Standardized Residuals

---

**FIGURE D15.39**

```
The regression equation is
Y = 0.20 + 2.60 X

Predictor      Coef     SE Coef       T         p
Constant      0.200       2.132    0.09     0.931
X            2.6000       0.6429    4.04     0.027

S = 2.033      R-sq = 84.5%      R-sq(adj) = 79.3%

Analysis of Variance
SOURCE              DF        SS         MS       F        p
Regression           1    67.600     67.600   16.35    0.027
Residual Error       3    12.400      4.133
Total                4    80.000
```

With relatively few observations, it is difficult to determine whether any of the assumptions regarding $\epsilon$ have been violated; for instance, an argument could be made that there does not appear to be any pattern in the plot; alternatively, an argument could be made that there is a curvilinear pattern in the plot

c. The values of the standardized residuals are greater than $-2$ and less than $+2$; thus, using this test, there are no outliers

As a further check for outliers, we used Minitab to compute the following studentized deleted residuals:

| Observation | Studentized Deleted Residual | Observation | Studentized Deleted Residual |
|---|---|---|---|
| 1 | −2.11 | 5 | 1.13 |
| 2 | −1.10 | 6 | −.36 |
| 3 | 1.31 | 7 | −1.16 |
| 4 | −.33 | 8 | 1.10 |

$t_{.025} = 2.776$ ($n - p - 2 = 8 - 2 - 2 = 4$ degrees of freedom)

Because none of the studentized deleted residuals are less than $-2.776$ or greater than $2.776$, we conclude that there are no outliers in the data

d. Minitab provides the following values:

| Observation | $h_i$ | $D_i$ |
|---|---|---|
| 1 | .63 | 1.52 |
| 2 | .65 | .70 |
| 3 | .30 | .22 |
| 4 | .23 | .01 |
| 5 | .26 | .14 |
| 6 | .14 | .01 |
| 7 | .66 | .81 |
| 8 | .13 | .06 |

The critical leverage value is

$$\frac{3(p + 1)}{n} = \frac{3(2 + 1)}{8} = 1.125$$

Because none of the values exceed 1.125, we conclude that there are no influential observations; however, using Cook's distance measure, we see that $D_1 > 1$ (rule of thumb critical value); thus, we conclude that the first observation is influential

Final conclusion: observation 1 is an influential observation

**42. b.** Unusual trend
  **c.** No outliers
  **d.** Observation 2 is an influential observation

**44. a.** $E(y) = \dfrac{e^{\beta_0 + \beta_1 x}}{1 + e^{\beta_0 + \beta_1 x}}$
  **b.** Estimate of the probability that a customer who does not have a Simmons credit card will make a purchase
  **c.** $\hat{g}(x) = -0.9445 + 1.0245 x$

**d.** .28 for customers that do not have a Simmons credit card
    .52 for customers that have a Simmons credit card
  **e.** Estimated odds ratio $= 2.79$

**46. a.** $E(y) = \dfrac{e^{\beta_0 + \beta_1 x}}{1 + e^{\beta_0 + \beta_1 x}}$
  **b.** $E(y) = \dfrac{e^{-2.6355 + 0.22018x}}{1 + e^{-2.6355 + 0.22018x}}$
  **c.** Significant; $p$-value $= .0002$
  **d.** .39
  **e.** \$1200
  **f.** Estimated odds ratio $= 1.25$

**48. a.** $E(y) = \dfrac{e^{\beta_0 + \beta_1 x}}{1 + e^{\beta_0 + \beta_1 x}}$
  **b.** $\hat{g}(x) = -2.805 + 1.1492x$
  **c.** .86
  **d.** Estimated odds ratio $= 3.16$

**50. b.** 67.39

**52. a.** $\hat{y} = -1.41 + .0235x_1 + .00486x_2$
  **b.** Significant
  **c.** $R^2 = .937$; $R_a^2 = 9.19$; good fit
  **d.** Both significant

**54. a.** Score $= 50.6 + 1.56$ RecRes
  **b.** $r^2 = .431$; not a good fit
  **c.** Score $= 33.5 + 1.90$ RecRes $+ 2.61$ Afford
    Significant
    $R_2^2 = .784$; much better fit

**56. a.** CityMPG $= 24.1 - 2.10$ Displace
    Significant; $p$-value $= .000$
  **b.** CityMPG $= 26.4 - 2.44$ Displace $- 1.20$ Drive4
  **c.** Significant; $p$-value $= .016$
  **d.** CityMPG $= 33.3 - 4.15$ Displace $- 1.24$ Drive4 $+ 2.16$ EightCyl
  **e.** Significant overall and individually

# Chapter 16

**1. a.** The Minitab output is shown in Figure D16.1a
  **b.** Because the $p$-value corresponding to $F = 6.85$ is $.059 > \alpha = .05$, the relationship is not significant
  **c.**

The scatter diagram suggests that a curvilinear relationship may be appropriate
  **d.** The Minitab output is shown in Figure D16.1d

## FIGURE D16.1a

```
The regression equation is
Y = - 6.8 + 1.23 X
```

| Predictor | Coef | SE Coef | T | p |
|-----------|------|---------|---|---|
| Constant | -6.77 | 14.17 | -0.48 | 0.658 |
| X | 1.2296 | 0.4697 | 2.62 | 0.059 |

```
S = 7.269     R-sq = 63.1%      R-sq(adj) = 53.9%
```

Analysis of Variance

| SOURCE | DF | SS | MS | F | p |
|--------|----|----|----|---|---|
| Regression | 1 | 362.13 | 362.13 | 6.85 | 0.059 |
| Residual Error | 4 | 211.37 | 52.84 | | |
| Total | 5 | 573.50 | | | |

## FIGURE D16.1d

```
The regression equation is
Y = - 169 + 12.2 X - 0.177 XSQ
```

| Predictor | Coef | SE Coef | T | p |
|-----------|------|---------|---|---|
| Constant | -168.88 | 39.79 | -4.74 | 0.024 |
| X | 12.187 | 2.663 | 4.58 | 0.020 |
| XSQ | -0.17704 | 0.04290 | -4.13 | 0.026 |

```
S = 3.248     R-sq = 94.5%      R-sq(adj) = 90.8%
```

Analysis of Variance

| SOURCE | DF | SS | MS | F | p |
|--------|----|----|----|---|---|
| Regression | 2 | 541.85 | 270.92 | 25.68 | 0.013 |
| Residual Error | 3 | 31.65 | 10.55 | | |
| Total | 5 | 573.50 | | | |

**e.** Because the $p$-value corresponding to $F = 25.68$ is $.013 < \alpha = .05$, the relationship is significant

**f.** $\hat{y} = -168.88 + 12.187(25) - .17704(25)^2 = 25.145$

**2. a.** $\hat{y} = 9.32 + .424x$; $p$-value $= .117$ indicates a weak relationship between $x$ and $y$

**b.** $\hat{y} = -8.10 + 2.41x - .0480x^2$
$R_a^2 = .932$; a good fit

**c.** 20.965

**4. a.** $\hat{y} = 943 + 8.71x$

**b.** Significant; $p$-value $= .005 < \alpha = .01$

**5. a.** The Minitab output is shown in Figure D16.5a

**b.** Because the $p$-value corresponding to $F = 73.15$ is $.003 < \alpha = .01$, the relationship is significant; we would reject $H_0$: $\beta_1 = \beta_2 = 0$

**c.** See Figure D16.5c

**6. b.** No, the relationship appears to be curvilinear

**c.** Several possible models; e.g.,
$\hat{y} = 2.90 - .185x + .00351x^2$

**8. a.** It appears that a simple linear regression model is not appropriate

**b.** 2005% $= 17.1 + 3.15$ 1999% $- .0445$ 1999%Sq

**c.** Log2000% $= 1.17 + .449$ Log1999%

**d.** Part (b); higher percentage of variability is explained

**10. a.** Significant; $F = 49.52 > 4.24$

**b.** Significant; $F = 48.3 > 3.42$

**11. a.** SSE $= 1805 - 1760 = 45$

$$F = \frac{\text{MSR}}{\text{MSE}} = \left(\frac{1760/4}{45/25}\right) = 244.44$$

**FIGURE D16.5a**

```
The regression equation is
Y = 433 + 37.4 X -0.383 XSQ

Predictor        Coef      SE Coef        T          p
Constant        432.6       141.2       3.06      0.055
X              37.429       7.807       4.79      0.017
XSQ           -0.3829      0.1036      -3.70      0.034

S = 15.83      R-sq = 98.0%     R-sq(adj) = 96.7%

Analysis of Variance

SOURCE              DF        SS         MS         F         p
Regression           2     36643      18322      73.15     0.003
Residual Error       3       751        250
Total                5     37395
```

**FIGURE D16.5c**

```
    Fit     Stdev.Fit              95% C.I.                 95% P.I.
 1302.01       9.93       (1270.41, 1333.61)       (1242.55, 1361.47)
```

$F_{.05} = 2.76$ (4 degrees of freedom numerator and 25 denominator)

Because $244.44 > 2.76$ we reject $H_0$; the relationship is significant

**b.** $SSE(x_1, x_2, x_3, x_4) = 45$

**c.** $SSE(x_2, x_3) = 1805 - 1705 = 100$

**d.** $F = \dfrac{(100 - 45)/2}{1.8} = 15.28 \qquad F_{.05} = 3.39$

Because $F = 15.28 > 3.39$, $x_1$ and $x_2$ are significant

**12. a.** The Minitab output is shown in Figure D16.12a

**b.** The Minitab output is shown in Figure D16.12b

**c.** $F = \dfrac{[SSE(\text{reduced}) - SSE(\text{full})]/(\text{\# extra terms})}{MSE(\text{full})}$

$= \dfrac{(23{,}157 - 14{,}317)/2}{1432} = 3.09$

$F_{.05} = 4.10$ (2 degrees of freedom numerator and 10 denominator)

Because $F = 3.09 < F_{.05} = 4.10$, the addition of the two independent variables is not significant

Note: Suppose that we consider adding only the number of interceptions made by the opponents; the corresponding Minitab output is shown in Figure D16.12c; in this case,

$F = \dfrac{(23{,}157 - 14{,}335)/1}{1303} = 6.77$

$F_{.05} = 4.84$ (1 degree of freedom numerator and 11 denominator)

Because $F = 6.77 > F_{.05} = 4.84$, the addition of the number of interceptions made by the opponents is significant

**14. a.** $\hat{y} = -111 + 1.32 \text{ Age} + .296 \text{ Pressure}$

**b.** $\hat{y} = -123 + 1.51 \text{ Age} + .448 \text{ Pressure} + 8.87 \text{ Smoker} - .00276 \text{ AgePress}$

**c.** Significant

**16. a.** The Minitab output is shown in Figure D16.16a

**b.** Stepwise procedure (see Figure D16.16b)

**c.** Backward elimination procedure (see Figure D16.16c)

**d.** Best subsets regression (see Figure D16.16d)

**18. a.** ScoreAvg $= 81.4 - .147$ Green%

**b.** ScoreAvg $= 58.2 - .00996$ Distance $- .152$ Green% $+ .869$ Putts

**c.** Yes

**d.** 72.65

**20.** $\hat{y} = -91.8 + 1.08 \text{ Age} + .252 \text{ Pressure} + 8.74 \text{ Smoker}$

**21. a.** The Minitab output is shown in Figure D16.21a

**b.** The Durbin-Watson statistic (obtained from Minitab) is $d = 1.96$. At $\alpha = .05$, $d_L = 1.10$, and $d_U = 1.37$; because $d > d_U$, there is no significant positive autocorrelation

**22.** $d = 1.60$; test is inconclusive

## FIGURE D16.12a

```
The regression equation is
Points = 170 + 6.61 TeamInt

Predictor     Coef    SE Coef     T       p
Constant    170.13     44.02    3.86    0.002
TeamInt      6.613      2.258   2.93    0.013

S = 43.93    R-sq = 41.7%    R-sq(adj) = 36.8%

Analysis of Variance

SOURCE          DF      SS       MS      F       p
Regression       1    16546    16546   8.57    0.013
Residual Error  12    23157     1930
Total           13    39703

Unusual Observations
Obs   TeamInt   Points    Fit   Stdev.Fit   Residual   St.Resid
 13      33.0    340.0   388.4      34.2       -48.4      -1.75 X

X denotes an observation whose X value gives it large influence.
```

## FIGURE D16.12b

```
The regression equation is
Points = 280 + 5.18 TeamInt - 0.0037 Rushing - 3.92 OpponInt

Predictor      Coef     SE Coef      T        p
Constant     280.34      81.42     3.44     0.006
TeamInt        5.176      2.073     2.50     0.032
Rushing       -0.00373    0.03336  -0.11     0.913
OpponInt      -3.918      1.651    -2.37     0.039

S = 37.84     R-sq = 63.9%     R-sq(adj) = 53.1%

Analysis of Variance

SOURCE          DF       SS       MS      F       p
Regression       3     25386     8462    5.91    0.014
Residual Error  10     14317     1432
Total           13     39703

SOURCE       DF     SEQ SS
Regression    1      16546
Error         1        776
Total         1       8064
```

## FIGURE D16.12c

```
The regression equation is
Points = 274 + 5.23 TeamInt - 3.96 OpponInt

Predictor       Coef     SE Coef         T        p
Constant      273.77       53.81      5.09    0.000
TeamInt        5.227       1.931      2.71    0.020
OpponInt      -3.965       1.524     -2.60    0.025


S = 36.10     R-sq = 63.9%     R-sq(adj) = 57.3%

Analysis of Variance

SOURCE             DF        SS        MS       F        p
Regression          2     25386     12684    9.73    0.004
Residual Error     11     14335      1303
Total              13     39703


SOURCE       DF    SEQ SS
TeamInt       1     16546
OpponInt      1      8822
```

## FIGURE D16.16a

```
The regression equation is
%College = -26.6 + 0.0970 SATScore

Predictor       Coef     SE Coef         T        p
Constant      -26.61       37.22     -0.72    0.485
SATScore     0.09703     0.03734      2.60    0.019


S = 12.83     R-sq = 29.7%     R-sq(adj) = 25.3%

Analysis of Variance

SOURCE             DF        SS        MS       F        p
Regression          1    1110.8    1110.8    6.75    0.019
Residual Error     16    2632.3     164.5
Total              17    3743.1
```

## FIGURE D16.16b

```
STEP               1         2
CONSTANT      -26.61    -26.93


SATScore       0.097     0.084
t-RATIO         2.60      2.46


%TakeSAT                 0.204
t-RATIO                   2.21


s               12.8      11.5
R-sq           29.68     46.93
```

**FIGURE D16.16c**

| STEP | 1 | 2 | 3 | 4 |
|---|---|---|---|---|
| CONSTANT | 33.71 | 17.46 | -32.47 | -26.93 |
| | | | | |
| Size | -1.56 | -1.39 | | |
| t-RATIO | -1.43 | -1.42 | | |
| | | | | |
| Spending | -0.0024 | -0.0026 | -0.0019 | |
| t-RATIO | -1.47 | -1.75 | -1.31 | |
| | | | | |
| Salary | -0.00026 | | | |
| t-RATIO | -0.40 | | | |
| | | | | |
| SATScore | 0.077 | 0.081 | 0.095 | 0.084 |
| t-RATIO | 2.06 | 2.36 | 2.77 | 2.46 |
| | | | | |
| %TakeSAT | 0.285 | 0.274 | 0.291 | 0.204 |
| t-RATIO | 2.47 | 2.53 | 2.60 | 2.21 |
| | | | | |
| S | 11.2 | 10.9 | 11.2 | 11.5 |
| R-sq | 59.65 | 59.10 | 52.71 | 46.93 |

**FIGURE D16.16d**

| | | | | S | S | % | | |
| | | | | p | A | T | | |
| | | | | e | S | T | a | |
| | | | | n | a | S | k | |
| | | | S | d | l | c | e | |
| | | | i | i | a | o | S | |
| | | Adj. | | z | n | r | r | A |
| Vars | R-sq | R-sq | S | e | g | y | e | T |
|---|---|---|---|---|---|---|---|---|
| 1 | 29.7 | 25.3 | 12.826 | | X | | | |
| 1 | 25.5 | 20.8 | 13.203 | | | X | | |
| 2 | 46.9 | 39.9 | 11.508 | | | X | X | |
| 2 | 38.2 | 30.0 | 12.417 | X | | X | | |
| 3 | 52.7 | 42.6 | 11.244 | X | | X | X | |
| 3 | 49.5 | 38.7 | 11.618 | X | | | X | X |
| 4 | 59.1 | 46.5 | 10.852 | X | X | | X | X |
| 4 | 52.8 | 38.3 | 11.660 | | X | X | X | X |
| 5 | 59.6 | 42.8 | 11.219 | X | X | X | X | X |

**23.**

| $x_1$ | $x_2$ | $x_3$ | Treatment |
|---|---|---|---|
| 0 | 0 | 0 | A |
| 1 | 0 | 0 | B |
| 0 | 1 | 0 | C |
| 0 | 0 | 1 | D |

$$E(y) = \beta_0 + \beta_1 x_1 + \beta_2 x_2 + \beta_3 x_3$$

**24.**

| $x_1$ | $x_2$ | Treatment |
|---|---|---|
| 0 | 0 | 1 |
| 1 | 0 | 2 |
| 0 | 1 | 3 |

$x_3 = 0$ if block 1; $x_3 = 1$ if block 2
$$E(y) = \beta_0 + \beta_1 x_1 + \beta_2 x_2 + \beta_3 x_3$$

**FIGURE D16.21a**

```
The regression equation is
P/E = 10.1 + 0.656 %Profit
```

| Predictor | Coef | SE Coef | T | p |
|-----------|------|---------|---|---|
| Constant | 10.052 | 3.736 | 2.69 | 0.018 |
| %Profit | 0.6562 | 0.2193 | 2.99 | 0.010 |

```
S = 5.648      R-sq = 39.0%     R-sq(adj) = 34.7%
```

Analysis of Variance

| SOURCE | DF | SS | MS | F | p |
|--------|----|----|-----|---|---|
| Regression | 1 | 285.64 | 285.64 | 8.95 | 0.010 |
| Residual Error | 14 | 446.64 | 31.90 | | |
| Total | 15 | 732.28 | | | |

**26. a.**

| $D_1$ | $D_2$ | Manufacturer |
|-------|-------|--------------|
| 0 | 0 | 1 |
| 1 | 0 | 2 |
| 0 | 1 | 3 |

$$E(y) = \beta_0 + \beta_1 D_1 + \beta_2 D_2$$

**b.** See Figure D16.26b

**c.** $H_0: \beta_1 = \beta_2 = 0$

**d.** Because the $p$-value is .004 $< \alpha = .05$, the mean time to mix a batch of material is not the same for each manufacturer

**28.** Significant difference between the two analyzers

**30. a.** Let ExS denote the interaction between expense ratio and safety rating

Perform% = 23.3 + 222 Expense% − 28.9 ExS

**b.** R-Sq (adj) = 65.3%; not bad

**c.** 25.8 or approximately 26%

**32. a.** AUDELAY = 63.0 + 11.1 INDUS; no significant positive autocorrelation

**34.** Significant differences between comfort levels for the three types of browsers

**36.** Significant; $p$-value = .004

**FIGURE D16.26b**

```
The regression equation is
Time = 23.0 + 5.00 D1 - 2.00 D2
```

| Predictor | Coef | SE Coef | T | p |
|-----------|------|---------|---|---|
| Constant | 23.000 | 1.106 | 20.80 | 0.000 |
| D1 | 5.000 | 1.563 | 3.20 | 0.011 |
| D2 | -2.000 | 1.563 | -1.28 | 0.233 |

```
S = 2.211      R-sq = 70.3%     R-sq(adj) = 63.7%
```

Analysis of Variance

| SOURCE | DF | SS | MS | F | p |
|--------|----|----|-----|---|---|
| Regression | 2 | 104.000 | 52.000 | 10.64 | 0.004 |
| Residual Error | 9 | 44.000 | 4.889 | | |
| Total | 11 | 148.000 | | | |

# Chapter 17

**1. a.**

| Item | Price Relative |
|------|----------------|
| A | $103 = (7.75/7.50)(100)$ |
| B | $238 = (1500/630)(100)$ |

**b.** $I_{2003} = \dfrac{7.75 + 1500.00}{7.50 + 630.00}(100) = \dfrac{1507.75}{637.50}(100) = 237$

**c.** $I_{2003} = \dfrac{7.75(1500) + 1500.00(2)}{7.50(1500) + 630.00(2)}(100)$

$= \dfrac{14,625.00}{12,510.00}(100) = 117$

**d.** $I_{2003} = \dfrac{7.75(1800) + 1500.00(1)}{7.50(1800) + 630.00(1)}(100)$

$= \dfrac{15,450.00}{14,130.00}(100) = 109$

**2. a.** 32%
   **b.** $8.14

**3. a.** Price relatives for A $= (6.00/5.45)100 = 110$
   B $= (5.95/5.60)100 = 106$
   C $= (6.20/5.50)100 = 113$

**b.** $I_{2003} = \dfrac{6.00 + 5.95 + 6.20}{5.45 + 5.60 + 5.50}(100) = 110$

**c.** $I_{2003} = \dfrac{6.00(150) + 5.95(200) + 6.20(120)}{5.45(150) + 5.60(200) + 5.50(120)}(100)$

$= 109$

9% increase over the two-year period

**4.** $I_{2003} = 105$

**6.**

| Item | Price Relative | Base Period Price | Usage | Weight | Weighted Price Relative |
|------|------|------|------|------|------|
| A | 150 | 22.00 | 20 | 440 | 66,000 |
| B | 90 | 5.00 | 50 | 250 | 22,500 |
| C | 120 | 14.00 | 40 | 560 | 67,200 |
| | | | Totals | 1250 | 155,700 |

$I = \dfrac{155,700}{1250} = 125$

**7. a.** Price relatives for A $= (3.95/2.50)100 = 158$
   B $= (9.90/8.75)100 = 113$
   C $= (.95/.99)100 = 96$

**b.**

| Item | Price Relative | Base Price | Quantity | Weight $P_{i0}Q_i$ | Weighted Price Relative |
|------|------|------|------|------|------|
| A | 158 | 2.50 | 25 | 62.5 | 9,875 |
| B | 113 | 8.75 | 15 | 131.3 | 14,837 |
| C | 96 | .99 | 60 | 59.4 | 5,702 |
| | | | Totals | 253.2 | 30,414 |

$I = \dfrac{30,414}{253.2} = 120$

Cost of raw materials is up 20% for the chemical

**8.** $I = 105$; portfolio is up 5%

**10. a.** Deflated 1980 wages: $\dfrac{\$7.27}{82.4}(100) = \$8.82$

Deflated 2000 wages: $\dfrac{\$14.36}{172.2}(100) = \$8.34$

**b.** $\dfrac{14.36}{7.27}(100) = 197.5$; the percentange increase in actual wages is 97.5%

**c.** $\dfrac{8.34}{8.82}(100) = 94.6$; the change in real wages is a decrease of 5.4%

**12. a.** 2420, 2449, 2242
Manufacturing shipments decreased slightly in constant dollars

**b.** 3032, 3057, 2822
**c.** PPI

**14.** $I = \dfrac{300(18.00) + 400(4.90) + 850(15.00)}{350(18.00) + 220(4.90) + 730(15.00)}(100)$

$= \dfrac{20,110}{18,328}(100) = 110$

**15.** $I = \dfrac{95(1200) + 75(1800) + 50(2000) + 70(1500)}{120(1200) + 86(1800) + 35(2000) + 60(1500)}(100)$

$= 99$

Quantities are down slightly

**16.** $I = 83$

**18. a.** 151, 197, 143, 178
   **b.** $I = 170$

**20.** $I_{Jan} = 73.5$, $I_{Mar} = 70.1$

**22.** $I = 86.2$

**24.** $36,082; $32,528; $27,913; $34,387; $40,551; $42,651; $46,458

**26.** $I = 143$; quantity is up 43%

# Chapter 18

**1. a.**

| Week | Time Series Value | Forecast | Forecast Error | Squared Forecast Error |
|------|-------------------|----------|----------------|------------------------|
| 1 | 8 | | | |
| 2 | 13 | | | |
| 3 | 15 | | | |
| 4 | 17 | 12 | 5 | 25 |
| 5 | 16 | 15 | 1 | 1 |
| 6 | 9 | 16 | −7 | 49 |
| | | | Total | 75 |

Forecast for week 7 is $(17 + 16 + 9)/3 = 14$

**b.** MSE $= 75/3 = 25$

**c.**

| Week (t) | Time Series Value ($Y_t$) | Forecast $F_t$ | Forecast Error $Y_t - F_t$ | Squared Error $(Y_t - F_t)^2$ |
|------|-------------------|----------|----------------|------------------------|
| 1 | 8 | | | |
| 2 | 13 | 8.00 | 5.00 | 25.00 |
| 3 | 15 | 9.00 | 6.00 | 36.00 |
| 4 | 17 | 10.20 | 6.80 | 46.24 |
| 5 | 16 | 11.56 | 4.44 | 19.71 |
| 6 | 9 | 12.45 | −3.45 | 11.90 |
| Total | | | | 138.85 |

Forecast for week 7 is $.2(9) + .8(12.45) = 11.76$

**d.** For the $\alpha = .2$ exponential smoothing forecast

$$MSE = \frac{138.85}{5} = 27.77$$

Because the three-week moving average has a smaller MSE, it appears to provide the better forecasts

**e.**

| Week (t) | Time Series Value ($Y_t$) | Forecast $F_t$ | Forecast Error $Y_t - F_t$ | Squared Error $(Y_t - F_t)^2$ |
|------|-------------------|----------|----------------|------------------------|
| 1 | 8 | | | |
| 2 | 13 | 8.0 | 5.0 | 25.00 |
| 3 | 15 | 10.0 | 5.0 | 25.00 |
| 4 | 17 | 12.0 | 5.0 | 25.00 |
| 5 | 16 | 14.0 | 2.0 | 4.00 |
| 6 | 9 | 14.8 | −5.8 | 33.64 |
| | | | Total | 112.64 |

$$MSE = \frac{112.64}{5} = 22.53$$

A smoothing constant of .4 appears to provide the better forecasts; for week 7 the forecast using $\alpha = .4$ is $.4(9) + .6(14.8) = 12.48$

**2. a.**

| Week | Four-Week | Five-Week |
|------|-----------|-----------|
| 10 | 19.00 | 18.80 |
| 11 | 20.00 | 19.20 |
| 12 | 18.75 | 19.00 |

**b.** 9.65, 7.41

**c.** Five weeks

**4.** Weeks 10, 11, and 12: 18.48, 18.63, 18.27
MSE $= 9.25$; $\alpha = .2$ is better

**6. a.** MSE (three-month) $= 1.24$
MSE $(\alpha = .2) = 3.55$
Use three-month moving averages

**b.** 83.3

**8. a.**

| Month | Time Series Value | Three-Month Moving Average Forecast | (Error)² | $\alpha = .2$ Forecast | (Error)² |
|-------|-------------------|------------------------|----------|------------------------|----------|
| 1 | 240 | | | | |
| 2 | 350 | | | 240.00 | 12,100.00 |
| 3 | 230 | | | 262.00 | 1,024.00 |
| 4 | 260 | 273.33 | 177.69 | 255.60 | 19.36 |
| 5 | 280 | 280.00 | 0.00 | 256.48 | 553.19 |
| 6 | 320 | 256.67 | 4,010.69 | 261.18 | 3,459.79 |
| 7 | 220 | 286.67 | 4,444.89 | 272.95 | 2,803.70 |
| 8 | 310 | 273.33 | 1,344.69 | 262.36 | 2,269.57 |
| 9 | 240 | 283.33 | 1,877.49 | 271.89 | 1,016.97 |
| 10 | 310 | 256.67 | 2,844.09 | 265.51 | 1,979.36 |
| 11 | 240 | 286.67 | 2,178.09 | 274.41 | 1,184.05 |
| 12 | 230 | 263.33 | 1,110.89 | 267.53 | 1,408.50 |
| Totals | | | 17,988.52 | | 27,818.49 |

MSE (three-month) $= 17,988.52/9 = 1998.72$

MSE $(\alpha = .2) = 27,818.49/11 = 2528.95$

Based on the preceding MSE values, the three-month moving average appears better; however, exponential smoothing was penalized by including month 2, which was difficult for any method to forecast. Using only the errors for months 4–12, the MSE for exponential smoothing is revised to

MSE$(\alpha = .2) = 14,694.49/9 = 1632.72$

Thus, exponential smoothing was better considering months 4–12

**b.** Using exponential smoothing,

$$F_{13} = \alpha Y_{12} + (1 - \alpha)F_{12}$$
$$= .20(230) + .80(267.53) = 260$$

**10. c.** Use $\alpha = .3$; $F_{11} = 7.57$

**12.** $\Sigma t = 15$, $\Sigma t^2 = 55$, $\Sigma Y_t = 55$, $\Sigma tY_t = 186$

$$b_1 = \frac{\Sigma tY_t - (\Sigma t\,\Sigma Y_t)/n}{\Sigma t^2 - (\Sigma t)^2/n}$$

$$= \frac{186 - (15)(55)/5}{55 - (15)^2/5} = 2.1$$

$$b_0 = \bar{Y} - b_1\bar{t} = 11 - 2.1(3) = 4.7$$

$$T_t = 4.7 + 2.1t$$

$$T_6 = 4.7 + 2.1(6) = 17.3$$

**14.** $\Sigma t = 21$, $\Sigma t^2 = 91$, $\Sigma Y_t = 117.1$, $\Sigma tY_t = 403.7$

$$b_1 = \frac{\Sigma tY_t - (\Sigma t\,\Sigma Y_t)/n}{\Sigma t^2 - (\Sigma t)^2/n}$$

$$= \frac{403.7 - (21)(117.1)/6}{91 - (21)^2/6} = -.3514$$

$$b_0 = \bar{Y} - b_1\bar{t} = 19.5167 - (-.3514)(3.5) = 20.7466$$

$$T_t = 20.7466 - .3514t$$

Enrollment appears to be decreasing by about 351 students per year

**16.** Consider a nonlinear trend

**18. a.** $T_t = .365 + .193t$; $2.49

   **b.** EPS increasing by an average of $.193 per year

**20. a.** $T_t = 1997.6 + 397.545t$

   **b.** $T_{11} = 6371$, $T_{12} = 6768$

**22. a.**

| Year | Quarter | $Y_t$ | Four-Quarter Moving Average | Centered Moving Average |
|---|---|---|---|---|
| 1 | 1 | 4 | | |
| | 2 | 2 | | |
| | | | 3.50 | |
| | 3 | 3 | | 3.750 |
| | | | 4.00 | |
| | 4 | 5 | | 4.125 |
| | | | 4.25 | |
| 2 | 1 | 6 | | 4.500 |
| | | | 4.75 | |
| | 2 | 3 | | 5.000 |
| | | | 5.25 | |
| | 3 | 5 | | 5.375 |
| | | | 5.50 | |
| | 4 | 7 | | 5.875 |
| | | | 6.25 | |
| 3 | 1 | 7 | | 6.375 |
| | | | 6.50 | |
| | 2 | 6 | | 6.625 |
| | | | 6.75 | |
| | 3 | 6 | | |
| | 4 | 8 | | |

**b.**

| Year | Quarter | $Y_t$ | Centered Moving Average | Seasonal–Irregular Component |
|---|---|---|---|---|
| 1 | 1 | 4 | | |
| | 2 | 2 | | |
| | 3 | 3 | 3.750 | .8000 |
| | 4 | 5 | 4.125 | 1.2121 |
| 2 | 1 | 6 | 4.500 | 1.3333 |
| | 2 | 3 | 5.000 | .6000 |
| | 3 | 5 | 5.375 | .9302 |
| | 4 | 7 | 5.875 | 1.1915 |
| 3 | 1 | 7 | 6.375 | 1.0980 |
| | 2 | 6 | 6.625 | .9057 |
| | 3 | 6 | | |
| | 4 | 8 | | |

| Quarter | Seasonal–Irregular Component Values | Seasonal Index |
|---|---|---|
| 1 | 1.3333, 1.0980 | 1.2157 |
| 2 | .6000, .9057 | .7529 |
| 3 | .8000, .9302 | .8651 |
| 4 | 1.2121, 1.1915 | 1.2018 |
| | Total | 4.0355 |

$$\text{Adjustment for seasonal index} = \frac{4}{4.0355} = .9912$$

| Quarter | Adjusted Seasonal Index |
|---|---|
| 1 | 1.2050 |
| 2 | .7463 |
| 3 | .8575 |
| 4 | 1.1912 |

**24.** Adjusted seasonal indexes: 0.707, 0.777, 0.827, 0.966, 1.016, 1.305, 1.494, 1.225, 0.976, 0.986, 0.936, 0.787
Note: adjustment = 0.996

**26. a.** Yes

   **b.** $12 - 4$: 166,761.13

      $4 - 8$: 146,052.99

**28. a.** .1 is better

   **b.** 29.99

**30.** 20.26

**32. a.** $\alpha = .5$

   **b.** $T_t = 244.778 + 22.088t$

   **c.** Trend projection; smaller MSE

**34.** $T_8 = 252.28$, $T_9 = 259.10$

**36. a.** Yes

   **b.** $T_t = -5 + 15t$

**38. a.** Linear trend appears to be appropriate
  **b.** $T_t = 6.4564 + .5345t$
  **c.** .5345 million
  **d.** 12.87 million

**40. b.** Adjusted seasonal indexes: 0.899, 1.362, 1.118, 0.621
     Note: adjustment = 1.0101
  **c.** Quarter 2; seems reasonable

**42. a.** $T_t = 6.329 + 1.055t$
  **b.** 36.92, 37.98, 39.03, 40.09
  **c.** 33.23, 51.65, 43.71, 24.86

# Chapter 19

**1.** Binomial probabilities for $n = 10, p = .50$

| $x$ | Probability | $x$ | Probability |
|---|---|---|---|
| 0 | .0010 | 6 | .2051 |
| 1 | .0098 | 7 | .1172 |
| 2 | .0439 | 8 | .0439 |
| 3 | .1172 | 9 | .0098 |
| 4 | .2051 | 10 | .0010 |
| 5 | .2461 | | |

Number of plus signs = 7
$$P(x \geq 7) = P(7) + P(8) + P(9) + P(10)$$
$$= .1172 + .0439 + .0098 + .0010$$
$$= .1719$$

$p$-value = 2(.1719) = .3438

$p$-value > .05; do not reject $H_0$

No indication difference exists

**2.** $n = 27$ cases in which a value different from 150 is obtained

Use normal approximation with $\mu = np = .5(27) = 13.5$ and $\sigma = \sqrt{.25n} = \sqrt{.25(27)} = 2.6$

Use $x = 22$ as the number of plus signs and obtain the following test statistic:

$$z = \frac{x - \mu}{\sigma} = \frac{22 - 13.5}{2.6} = 3.27$$

Largest table value $z = 3.09$

Area in tail = .5000 − .4990 = .001

For $z = 3.27$, $p$-value less than .001

$p$-value $\leq .01$; reject $H_0$ and conclude median > 150

**4.** We need to determine the number of "better" responses and the number of "worse" responses; the sum of the two is the sample size used for the study
$$n = .34(1253) + .29(1253) = 789.4$$

Use the large-sample test and the normal distribution; the value of $n = 789.4$ need not be integer.

Use $\mu = .5n = .5(789.4) = 394.7$
$\sigma = \sqrt{.25n} = \sqrt{.25(789.4)} = 14.05$

Let $p$ = proportion of adults who feel children will have a better future

$H_0: p \leq .50$
$H_a: p > .50$
$$x = .34(1253) = 426.0$$
$$z = \frac{x - \mu}{\sigma} = \frac{426.0 - 394.7}{14.05} = 2.23$$

$p$-value = .5000 − .4871 = .0129

Reject $H_0$ and conclude that more adults feel their children will have a better future

**6.** $z = 2.32$
$p$-value = .0204
Reject $H_0$

**8.** $z = 3.76$
$p$-value $\approx 0$
Reject $H_0$

**10.** $z = 1.27$
$p$-value = .2040
Do not reject $H_0$

**12.** $H_0$: The populations are identical
     $H_a$: The populations are not identical

| Additive | | | Absolute | | Signed |
|---|---|---|---|---|---|
| 1 | 2 | Difference | Value | Rank | Rank |
| 20.12 | 18.05 | 2.07 | 2.07 | 9 | +9 |
| 23.56 | 21.77 | 1.79 | 1.79 | 7 | +7 |
| 22.03 | 22.57 | −.54 | .54 | 3 | −3 |
| 19.15 | 17.06 | 2.09 | 2.09 | 10 | +10 |
| 21.23 | 21.22 | .01 | .01 | 1 | +1 |
| 24.77 | 23.80 | .97 | .97 | 4 | +4 |
| 16.16 | 17.20 | −1.04 | 1.04 | 5 | −5 |
| 18.55 | 14.98 | 3.57 | 3.57 | 12 | +12 |
| 21.87 | 20.03 | 1.84 | 1.84 | 8 | +8 |
| 24.23 | 21.15 | 3.08 | 3.08 | 11 | +11 |
| 23.21 | 22.78 | .43 | .43 | 2 | +2 |
| 25.02 | 23.70 | 1.32 | 1.32 | 6 | +6 |
| | | | | | $T = 62$ |

$\mu_T = 0$

$$\sigma_T = \sqrt{\frac{n(n + 1)(2n + 1)}{6}} = \sqrt{\frac{12(13)(25)}{6}} = 25.5$$

$$z = \frac{T - \mu_T}{\sigma_T} = \frac{62 - 0}{25.5} = 2.43$$

$p$-value = 2(.5000 − .4925) = .0150

Reject $H_0$ and conclude that there is a significant difference between the additives

**13.**

| Without Relaxant | With Relaxant | Difference | Rank of Absolute Difference | Signed Rank |
|---|---|---|---|---|
| 15 | 10 | 5 | 9 | +9 |
| 12 | 10 | 2 | 3 | +3 |
| 22 | 12 | 10 | 10 | +10 |
| 8 | 11 | −3 | 6.5 | −6.5 |
| 10 | 9 | 1 | 1 | +1 |
| 7 | 5 | 2 | 3 | +3 |
| 8 | 10 | −2 | 3 | −3 |
| 10 | 7 | 3 | 6.5 | +6.5 |
| 14 | 11 | 3 | 6.5 | +6.5 |
| 9 | 6 | 3 | 6.5 | +6.5 |
| | | | | $T = 36$ |

$\mu_T = 0$

$$\sigma_T = \sqrt{\frac{n(n+1)(2n+1)}{6}} = \sqrt{\frac{10(11)(21)}{6}} = 19.62$$

$$z = \frac{T - \mu_T}{\sigma_T} = \frac{36}{19.62} = 1.83$$

$p$-value $= .5000 - .4664 = .0336$

Reject $H_0$ and conclude there is a significant difference in favor of the relaxant

**14.** $z = 2.29$
$p$-value $= .0220$
Reject $H_0$

**16.** $z = 2.62$
$p$-value $= .0088$
Reject $H_0$

**18.** Rank the combined samples and find rank sum for each sample; this is a small-sample test because $n_1 = 7$ and $n_2 = 9$

| Additive 1 | | Additive 2 | |
|---|---|---|---|
| **MPG** | **Rank** | **MPG** | **Rank** |
| 17.3 | 2 | 18.7 | 8.5 |
| 18.4 | 6 | 17.8 | 4 |
| 19.1 | 10 | 21.3 | 15 |
| 16.7 | 1 | 21.0 | 14 |
| 18.2 | 5 | 22.1 | 16 |
| 18.6 | 7 | 18.7 | 8.5 |
| 17.5 | 3 | 19.8 | 11 |
| | 34 | 20.7 | 13 |
| | | 20.2 | 12 |
| | | | 102 |

$T = 34$
With $\alpha = .05$, $n_1 = 7$, and $n_2 = 9$
$T_L = 41$ and $T_U = 7(7 + 9 + 1) - 41 = 78$
Because $T = 34 < 41$, reject $H_0$ and conclude that there is a significant difference in gasoline mileage

**19. a.**

| Public Accountant | Rank | Financial Planner | Rank |
|---|---|---|---|
| 25.2 | 5 | 24.0 | 2 |
| 33.8 | 19 | 24.2 | 3 |
| 31.3 | 16 | 28.1 | 10 |
| 33.2 | 18 | 30.9 | 15 |
| 29.2 | 13 | 26.9 | 8.5 |
| 30.0 | 14 | 28.6 | 11 |
| 25.9 | 6 | 24.7 | 4 |
| 34.5 | 20 | 28.9 | 12 |
| 31.7 | 17 | 26.8 | 7 |
| 26.9 | 8.5 | 23.9 | 1 |
| | 136.5 | | 73.5 |

$$\mu_T = \frac{1}{2} n_1(n_1 + n_2 + 1) = \frac{1}{2}(10)(10 + 10 + 1) = 105$$

$$\sigma_T = \sqrt{\frac{1}{12} n_1 n_2 (n_1 + n_2 + 1)} = \sqrt{\frac{1}{12}(10)(10)(10 + 10 + 1)}$$

$= 13.23$

$T = 136.5$

$$z = \frac{136.5 - 105}{13.23} = 2.38$$

$p$-value $= 2(.5000 - .4913) = .0174$

Reject $H_0$ and conclude that salaries differ significantly for the two professions

**b.** Public Accountant    $30,200
Financial Planner    $26,700

**20. a.** Men 49.9, Women 35.4
**b.** $T = 36$, $T_L = 37$
Reject $H_0$

**22.** $z = 2.77$
$p$-value $= .0056$
Reject $H_0$

**24.** $z = -.25$
$p$-value $= .8026$
Do not reject $H_0$

**26.** Rankings:

| Product A | Product B | Product C |
|---|---|---|
| 4 | 11 | 7 |
| 8 | 14 | 2 |
| 10 | 15 | 1 |
| 3 | 12 | 6 |
| 9 | 13 | 5 |
| 34 | 65 | 21 |

$$W = \frac{12}{(15)(16)} \left[ \frac{(34)^2}{5} + \frac{(65)^2}{5} + \frac{(21)^5}{5} \right] - 3(15 + 1)$$

$= 58.22 - 48 = 10.22$    $(df = 2)$

$p$-value between .005 and .01

Reject $H_0$ and conclude the ratings for the products differ

**28.** Rankings:

| Swimming | Tennis | Cycling |
|:---:|:---:|:---:|
| 8 | 9 | 5 |
| 4 | 14 | 1 |
| 11 | 13 | 3 |
| 6 | 10 | 7 |
| 12 | 15 | 2 |
| 41 | 61 | 18 |

$$W = \frac{12}{15(15+1)}\left[\frac{41^2}{5} + \frac{61^2}{5} + \frac{18^2}{5}\right] - 3(15+1)$$

$$= 9.26 \quad (df = 2)$$

$p$-value between .005 and .01

Reject $H_0$ and conclude that activities differ

**30.** $W = 8.03$; $df = 3$

$p$-value between .025 and .05

Reject $H_0$

**32. a.** $\Sigma d_i^2 = 52$

$$r_s = 1 - \frac{6\Sigma d_i^2}{n(n^2-1)} = 1 - \frac{6(52)}{10(99)} = .68$$

**b.** $\sigma_{r_s} = \sqrt{\frac{1}{n-1}} = \sqrt{\frac{1}{9}} = .33$

$$z = \frac{r_s - 0}{\sigma_{r_s}} = \frac{.68}{.33} = 2.05$$

$p$-value = 2(.5000 − .4798) = .0404

Reject $H_0$ and conclude that significant rank correlation exists

**34.** $\Sigma d_i^2 = 250$

$$r_s = 1 - \frac{6\Sigma d_i^2}{n(n^2-1)} = 1 - \frac{6(250)}{11(120)} = -.136$$

$$\sigma_{r_s} = \sqrt{\frac{1}{n-1}} = \sqrt{\frac{1}{10}} = .32$$

$$z = \frac{r_s - 0}{\sigma_{r_s}} = \frac{-.136}{.32} = -.43$$

$p$-value = 2(.5000 − .1664) = .6672

Do not reject $H_0$; we cannot conclude that there is a significant relationship between the rankings

**36.** $r_s = -.71$, $z = -2.13$

$p$-value = .0332

Reject $H_0$

**38.** $z = -3.17$

$p$-value less than .02

Reject $H_0$

**40.** $z = -2.59$

$p$-value = .0096

Reject $H_0$

**42.** $z = -2.97$

$p$-value = .003

Reject $H_0$

**44.** $W = 12.61$; $df = 2$

$p$-value between .01 and .025

Reject $H_0$

**46.** $r_s = .76$, $z = 2.83$

$p$-value = .0046

Reject $H_0$

# Chapter 20

**2. a.** 5.42

**b.** UCL = 6.09, LCL = 4.75

**4.** *R chart:*

UCL = $\bar{R}D_4 = 1.6(1.864) = 2.98$

LCL = $\bar{R}D_3 = 1.6(.136) = .22$

$\bar{x}$ chart:

UCL = $\bar{\bar{x}} + A_2\bar{R} = 28.5 + .373(1.6) = 29.10$

LCL = $\bar{\bar{x}} - A_2\bar{R} = 28.5 - .373(1.6) = 27.90$

**6.** 20.01, .082

**8. a.** .0470

**b.** UCL = .0989, LCL = −0.0049 (use LCL = 0)

**c.** $\bar{p} = .08$; in control

**d.** UCL = 14.826, LCL = −0.726

Process is out of control if more than 14 defective

**e.** In control with 12 defective

**f.** $np$ chart

**10.** $f(x) = \dfrac{n!}{x!(n-x)!}p^x(1-p)^{n-x}$

When $p = .02$, the probability of accepting the lot is

$$f(0) = \frac{25!}{0!(25-0)!}(.02)^0(1-.02)^{25} = .6035$$

When $p = .06$, the probability of accepting the lot is

$$f(0) = \frac{25!}{0!(25-0)!}(.06)^0(1-.06)^{25} = .2129$$

**12.** $p_0 = .02$; producer's risk = .0599

$p_0 = .06$; producer's risk = .3396

Producer's risk decreases as the acceptance number $c$ is increased

**14.** $n = 20$, $c = 3$

**16. a.** 95.4

**b.** UCL = 96.07, LCL = 94.73

**c.** No

**18.**

| | R Chart | x̄ Chart |
|---|---|---|
| UCL | 4.23 | 6.57 |
| LCL | 0 | 4.27 |

Estimate of standard deviation = .86

**20.**

| | R Chart | x̄ Chart |
|---|---|---|
| UCL | .1121 | 3.112 |
| LCL | 0 | 3.051 |

**22. a.** UCL = .0817, LCL = −.0017 (use LCL = 0)

**24. a.** .03
**b.** $\beta = .0802$

**26. a.** Producer's risk = .0064
**b.** Consumer's risk = .0136
**c.** *Advantage:* excellent control
  *Disadvantage:* cost of taking a larger sample

## Chapter 21

**1. a.**

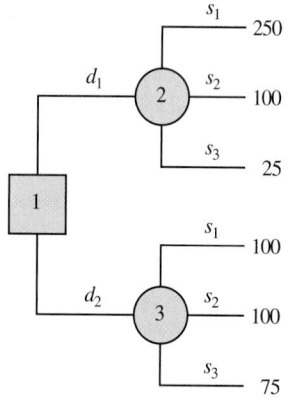

**b.** $EV(d_1) = .65(250) + .15(100) + .20(25) = 182.5$
$EV(d_2) = .65(100) + .15(100) + .20(75) = 95$
The optimal decision is $d_1$

**2. a.** $d_1$; $EV(d_1) = 11.3$
**b.** $d_4$; $EV(d_4) = 9.5$

**3. a.** EV(own staff) = .2(650) + .5(650) + .3(600)
  = 635
EV(outside vendor) = .2(900) + .5(600)
  + .3(300) = 570
EV(combination) = .2(800) + .5(650) + .3(500)
  = 635
Optimal decision: hire an outside vendor with an expected cost of $570,000

**b.** EVwPI + .2(650) = .5(600) + .3(300)
  = 520
EVPI = |520 − 570| = 50, or $50,000

**4. b.** Discount; EV = 565
**c.** Full Price; EV = 670

**6. c.** Chardonnay only; EV = 42.5
**d.** Both grapes; EV = 46.4
**e.** Both grapes; EV = 39.6

**8. a.**

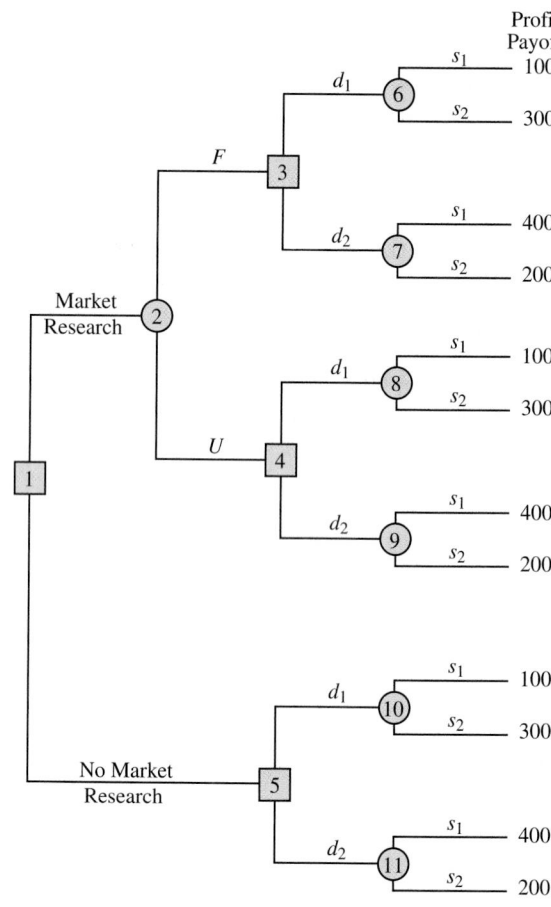

**b.** EV (node 6) = .57(100) + .43(300) = 186
EV (node 7) = .57(400) + .43(200) = 314
EV (node 8) = .18(100) + .82(300) = 264
EV (node 9) = .18(400) + .82(200) = 236
EV (node 10) = .40(100) + .60(300) = 220
EV (node 11) = .40(400) + .60(200) = 280

EV (node 3) = Max(186,314) = 314   $d_2$
EV (node 4) = Max(264,236) = 264   $d_1$
EV (node 5) = Max(220,280) = 280   $d_2$

EV (node 2) = .56(314) + .44(264) = 292
EV (node 1) = Max(292,280) = 292

∴ Market Research
   If Favorable, decision $d_2$
   If Unfavorable, decision $d_1$

**10. a.** $5000 - 200 - 2000 - 150 = 2650$
      $3000 - 200 - 2000 - 150 = 650$

**b.** Expected values at nodes

   8: 2350     5: 2350     9: 1100
   6: 1150     10: 2000    7: 2000
   4: 1870     3: 2000     2: 1560
   1: 1560

**c.** Cost would have to decrease by at least \$130,000

**12. b.** $d_1$, 1250
   **c.** 1700
   **d.** If $N$, $d_1$
      If $U$, $d_2$; 1666

**14.**

| State of Nature | $P(s_j)$ | $P(I\|s_j)$ | $P(I \cap s_j)$ | $P(s_j\|I)$ |
|---|---|---|---|---|
| $s_1$ | .2 | .10 | .020 | .1905 |
| $s_2$ | .5 | .05 | .025 | .2381 |
| $s_3$ | .3 | .20 | .060 | .5714 |
|  | 1.0 |  | $P(I) = .105$ | 1.0000 |

**16. a.** .695, .215, .090
      .98, .02
      .79, .21
      .00, 1.00

**c.** If $C$, Expressway
      If $O$, Expressway
      If $R$, Queen City
      26.6 minutes

# Index

*Note:* Chapter 22 can be found on the CD-ROM included with this book. Index entries found in this chapter are denoted by chapter number 22, hyphen, and page number.